NETWORK ANALYSIS

[INCLUDING TRANSMISSION LINES]

GYANENDRA K. MITHAL

M.E., F.I.E.T.E. (India) ; F.I.E. (India)

Former Professor and Head

Department of Electronics and Telecom. Engg.

Government Engineering College, Jabalpur

RAVI MITHAL

B.E. (Electronics) Jabalpur,

M.Tech. (Computers), Roorkee

Ph.D., I.I.T. Delhi

KHANNA PUBLISHERS®

Investing in Learning®

Operational Office :

4575/15, Onkar House, Opp. Happy School,

Ground Floor, Daryaganj, New Delhi 110 002

Phones : 011-45033819 • *Mob.* 09811541460

email : contactus@khannapublishers.in

Published by :
Romesh Chander Khanna & Vineet Khanna
for **KHANNA PUBLISHERS**
2-B, Nath Market, Nai Sarak
Delhi- 110 006 (India)

Website : www.khannapublishers.in

Hologram & Description

To all readers of our books, to prevent yourself from being defrauded by piraters, please make sure that there is an Hologram on the cover of our books with the below specifications. If you find any book without Hologram and Description, please mail us at **contactus@khannapublishers.in**

Thanking you

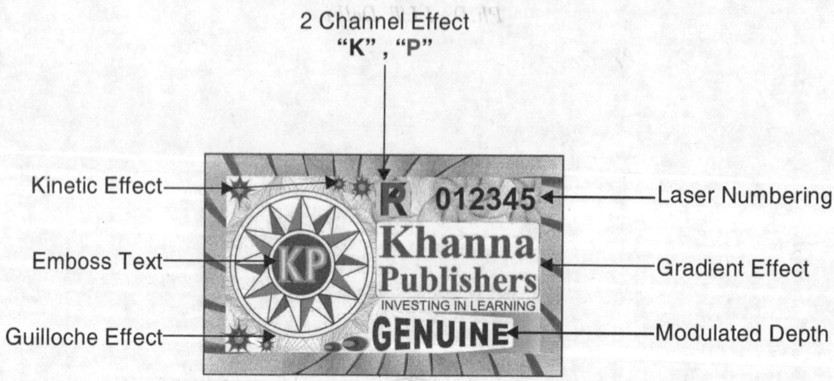

ISBN No. 978-81-7409-070-6

First Edition : 1988
Fifteenth Edition : 2022
First Reprint : 2026

***Price : Rs.* 729.00**

Preface

Network Analysis forms an important and essential course for Engineering Degree students offering either Electrical Engineering or Electronics and Telecommunication Engineering. The subject is also included in the Section B of Associate Membership Examinations of various professional institutions such as the Institution of Engineers (India), Institution of Electronics and Telecommunication Engineers (India) etc. This book is intended primarily to meet the needs of these students. It will also be of considerable use to practicing engineers in the field of Electrical Engineering and Electronics.

A large number of books on the subject are, no doubt, available. But the nature of treatment and the coverage vary widely. Some of the books adopt the classical approach exclusively while the others make exclusive use of Laplace Transforms and Pole and Zero technique, ignoring the classical method absolutely. This text smoothly blends the two techniques. It begins with the use of classical methods but switches over to liberal use of Laplace Transforms and Pole and Zero technique. The book deals with the subject quite comprehensively. Further a large number of solved example and exercises have been included to assist the students in attaining complete grasp of the subject.

The text begins with the study of network elements and various conventions. This is followed by topological description of networks and formulation of Kirchhoffs law, equilibrium equations on loop basis and node basis. Then comes steady state and transient analysis of simple networks involving first order and second order linear differential equations. Subsequently Laplace transformation is used in analysis which unifies the natural behaviour of the network with the characteristics of the excitation. Poles and zeros of the transforms are latter on used to give the network response. At this stage, the sinusoidal steady state analysis is taken up followed by frequency response plots including Bode plots, average power, insertion loss and other topics. Finally the study of transmission lines is taken up.

The author feels grateful to Shri Romesh Chander Khanna, proprietor of M/s Khanna Publishers, for providing the best possible assistance in the publication of this book.

The author will be glad to receive comments and suggestions for the improvement of the book.

G.K. MITHAL
RAVI MITHAL

Contents

Chapter *Page*

1

Network Elements

1.1. Introduction

Various laws of nature are explained by theories, put forth from time to time by scientists. Such theories are based on observed facts and are able to explain most of the observations. Each theory is in fact nothing but imaginary picture or a "conceptual scheme". Any conceptual scheme which is in a position to explain most of the existing phenomena or observations, is considered true until superceded by a more powerful conceptual scheme. Thus the well known atomic theory is nothing but a well accepted conceptual scheme protraying an atom as consisting of a central nucleus with electrons moving in orbits around it. This conceptual scheme explains most of the observed phenomena and is, therefore, considered true. Similarly we have the conceptual schemes of conservation of energy and conservation of charge.

One of the most celebrated conceptual schemes is the Maxwell equations which explain all electric and magnetic phenomena in terms of fields resulting from charge and current. Results deducted from Maxwell's equations have agreed with the observations for over a century. It should then be expected that this conceptual scheme should be exclusively used for describing every electric and magnetic phenomenon. But we find that although Maxwell's equations are most fundamental in nature, and have stood the test of time, they fail to provide description and computation of various electric and magnetic phenomena in a simple and lucid manner. Accordingly we embark upon another conceptual scheme which permits simplicity of description and computation of various electric and magnetic phenomena, namely the concept of electric circuit. This concept of electric circuit has great practical utility. Thus in most of the cases, we are not so much interested in electric and magnetic fields in an electric device as in voltages and currents. This scheme of electric circuit permits analysis of an electric system in terms of voltages and currents and permits calculation of such quantities as charge, field, energy, power etc. Both the field concept and circuit concept have their respective utilities. But whereas the field concept is more fundamental, the circuit concept is more practical. Of course, the two concepts are intimately related. Thus the circuit concept arises from the same experimental facts as does concept described by Maxwell's equations. However, the field theory in more general and exact in nature, whereas the circuit concept involves several approximations. But inspite of this basic limitation, circuit theory retains its utility. It is significant, no doubt, that the nature of these approximations be clearly understood.

1.2. Network Elements

The basic electrical quantities in terms of which we may describe the function of an electrical circuit are : charge and energy. A physical circuit serves to transfer and transform energy. This energy transfer is achieved through charge transfer. Thus in any electrical network, there takes place energy transfer (through charge transfer) from the point of supply (*i.e.* from the energy source) to a point of transformation or conversion, referred to as the load or the sink. Of course, in this process, energy may be stored. Evidently then a physical circuit must provide means for such transfer and transformation. Accordingly a physical circuit is constituted by (*i*) sources of energy (*ii*) circuit elements like resistors, capacitors, inductors (including mutual inductance) and (*iii*) connecting wires etc.

Network elements may be (*i*) active or passive (*ii*) unilateral or bilateral (*iii*) linear or non-linear (*iv*) lumped or distributed. An electrical network is simply an interconnected aggregate of network elements of assorted nature. Network theory studies the behaviour of the entire network as a whole with respect to specified terminals and not the behaviour of the elements alone. The details of these elements are not of direct consequence. However, since behaviour of entire network depends directly on the behaviour of the elements, these network elements deserve careful consideration. Accordingly these network elements will be carefully classified and individually studies.

Active elements. An energy source, *i.e.* a voltage source or a current source, is said to be an active elements. Vacuum tubes and transistors are also active elements but they are not ideal energy sources.

Passive elements. An element, which is not an energy source, is a passive element. Thus a passive element serves to transform or store energy. Resistors, inductors and capacitors form typical passive elements.

Bilateral and unilateral elements. Bilateral elements are those elements which transmit equally well in either direction. Unilateral elements on the other hand, transmit widely unequally in the two directions. Elements made of high conductivity materials are in general, bilateral, while vacuum tubes, crystal rectifiers and metal rectifiers are unilateral elements.

Lumped and distributed elements. Physically separate elements such as resistors, capacitors and inductors are referred to as lumped elements. On the other hand, network elements which are inseparable for analytical purposes are called distributed elements. Thus a transmission line has distributed resistance, capacitance and inductance along its length.

Linear and non-linear elements. A linear element is one which is governed by a linear differential equation for all values of applied stimulus. Failing this, the element is said to be non-linear.

1.3. Scope of Network Analysis and Network Synthesis

Depending upon the character of the constituent elements, network systems may be classified into 3 basic categories namely, class A, class B and class C.

Class A network system is one in which all constituent elements are linear. An element (or a network system of elements) is said to be linear when its behaviour can be governed by linear differential equation. Thus for any given network system, let θ_i be the stimulus (or input) as a function of time and let θ_o be the corresponding response (or output) also expressed as a function of time. Now if the stimulus is increased to $k.\ \theta_i$, where k is a constant, the network system will be said to be linear if the response (or output) is $k.\ \theta_o$. Thus $k\theta_i$ and $k\theta_o$ form an admissible pair of stimulus and response functions for the linear system. Again if $(\theta_{i1}, \theta_{o1})$ and $(\theta_{i2}, \theta_{o2})$ denote any two admissible input-output pair functions for a network, then if the network is linear, then $(k_1\ \theta_{i1} + k_2\ \theta_{i2}, k_1\ \theta_{o1} + k_2\ \theta_{o2})$ will also form an admissible input-output pair function, where k_1 and k_2 are constants.

If one or more elements of the network are non-linear, the network degenerates to either class B or class C type. If the non-linear element/elements can be linearized atleast over a limited range of operation, the network system is said to be of class B type. On the other hand, if the non-linear elements cannot be linearized even over the limited range of operation, the network is said to be of class C type. The present work deals only with linear network system.

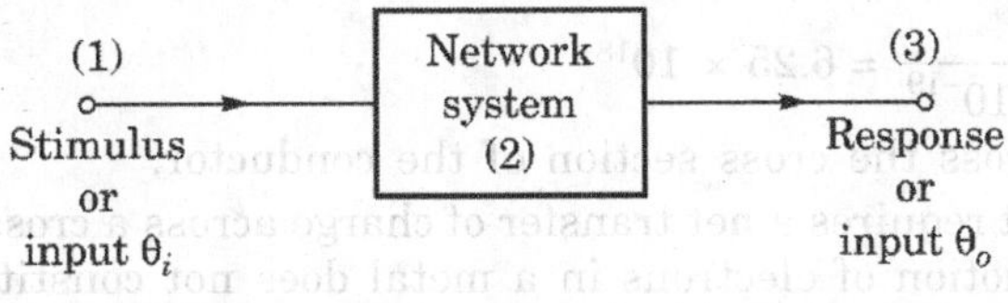

Fig. 1.1. The essential factors involved in network theory.

The study of linear network systems may be divided into two main heads : network analysis and network synthesis. Network analysis consists in finding the response (or output), when the stimulus (or input) and the network system components are given. On the other hand, network synthesis consists in finding the network system, which will give the prescribed output for a given stimulus (or input). Thus with reference to Fig. 1.1, network analysis and network synthesis are given by the following :

Network analysis : Given (1) and (2), to find (3).

Network synthesis : Given (1) and (3), to find (2).

This work deals with analysis of network composed of linear bilateral elements, mainly of the lumped type. However, some attention is afforded to analysis of network consisting of distributed linear bilateral elements as well. Finally synthesis of one port L-C networks is taken up.

1.4. Electric Charge and Electric Current

Electric charge and energy form the two most fundamental electrical quantities.

The basic unit of charge is the charge of an electron. But this charge is very small. Hence a larger unit of charge is used in practice. In M.K.S. system, coulomb is the unit of charge. An electron has a negative charge of 1.601×10^{-19} coulomb.

Charge of a particle or body may be positive or negative. Like charges repel each other while unlike charges attract each other. If there be two charges spaced a distance d apart, then the force of attraction or repulsion is inversely proportional to the square of the distance d between them.

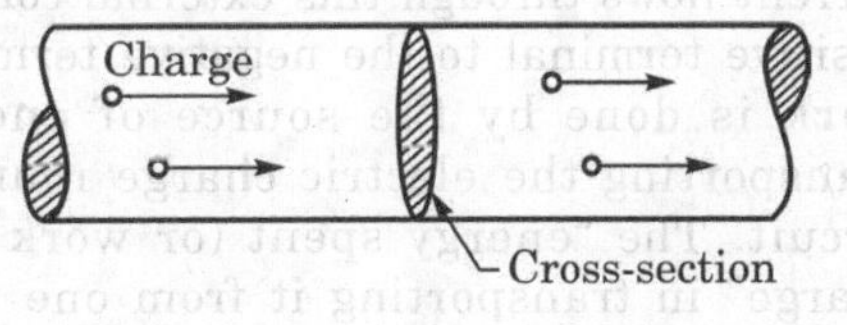

Fig. 1.2. Motion of charge in a conductor.

The charges may be at rest or may be in motion. A charge in motion constitutes an electric current. An electric current is defined as the "time rate of net motion of electric charge across a given cross sectional area". Thus con-sider the cross-section A of a conductor shown in Fig. 1.2. Electrons flow across this cross-section from say left to right. This constitutes an electrons current from left to right within the conductor. The conventional electric current, being the time rate of flow of positive charge will be considered to be flowing in the opposite direction, *i.e.* from right to left within the conductor.

Expressed mathematically, current i is given by

$$i = \frac{dq}{dt} \qquad \text{...(1.1)}$$

where q is the charge in motion and t is the time.

If the charge q is in coulombs and the time i is in seconds, the current is in amperes.

The charge of an electron is 1.601×10^{-19} coulomb. Hence current of one ampere signifies motion of

$$\frac{1}{1.601 \times 10^{-19}} = 6.25 \times 10^{18}$$

electrons per second across the cross section of the conductor.

An electric current requires a net transfer of charge across a cross-section in one direction. Accordingly a random motion of electrons in a metal does not constitute a current.

1.5. Electric Energy : Electrical Potential

Energy forms another basic electrical quantity. A conceptual scheme commonly used is the "conservation of energy" which states that energy cannot either be created or destroyed, but can only be converted in form. Thus electrical energy can be obtained from various sources on transformation. Electrical energy may be obtained by :

(*i*) *Magnetic induction.* As in a rotating generator. Mechanical energy of rotation is converted into electric energy.

(*ii*) *Voltaic method.* As in electric batteries converting chemical energy into electric energy.

(*iii*) *Electrostatic method.* As in friction machines like Van de Graaf generator converting mechanical energy into electric energy.

(*iv*) *Thermo-electric method.* Producing electricity by heating the junction of dissimilar metals like bismuth and copper. Heat energy is converted into electric energy.

(*v*) *Photo-electric method.* Converting light energy into electric energy by letting light fall on photo-electric devices.

Whatever be the source of creation of electric energy, the source or generator has two terminals, referred to as positive and negative terminal in Fig. 1.3. If now the two terminals are connected by an external conductor, then electric current flows through this external conductor from the positive terminal to the negative terminal. Of course, work is done by the source of energy supply in transporting the electric charge round the external circuit. The "energy spent (or work done) per unit charge" in transporting it from one terminal to the other is called the "potential" (or voltage).

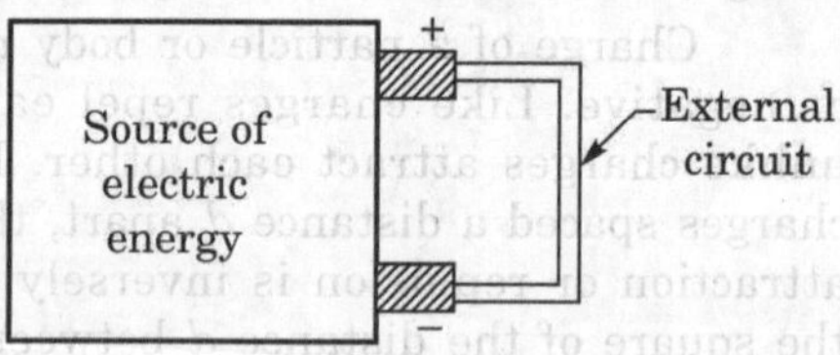

Fig. 1.3. Source of electric energy.

Thus mathematically, voltage v in volts is given by,

$$v = \frac{w}{q} \qquad ...(1.2)$$

where w is the work done (or energy spent) expressed in joules and q is the charge transported in coulombs.

In the above treatment, we have considered the potential of one terminal of a source with respect to the order. As a general case, we may consider any two points say P_1 and P_2. Then the potential of point P_2 with respect to that of point P_1 is the amount of work done in moving a unit positive charge from point P_1 to point P_2. We may as well define the potential of a point as the amount of work done in moving a unit positive charge from infinity to that point. If the unit charge is one coulomb, the work done is expressed in joules, then the potential is given is joules/coulomb, *i.e.*, in volts. In practice, however, the absolute potential of a point is of little significance. In most of the applications in Electrical Engineering, we are interested in the potential difference between two points.

Thus if w joules of work is done in moving q coulombs of positive charge from point P_1 to point P_2, the potential of P_2 with respect to that of P_1 in volts is given by Eq. (1.2).

Considering the same two points, let the charge transported be increased from q to $(q + dq)$. Then the work done in transportation also gets increased say from w to $(w + dw)$. Now since the potential difference has remainded unaltered,

$$v = \frac{w + dw}{q + dq} \quad \text{...(1.3)}$$

From Eqs. (1.2) and (1.3),

$$v = \frac{dw}{dq} \quad \text{...(1.4)}$$

The time rate of transfer of energy is called power. Thus power is given by,

$$p = \frac{dw}{dt} = \frac{dvq}{dt} \text{ from Eq. (1.2)}$$

$$= v.\frac{dq}{dt} \text{ if } v \text{ is constant}$$

$$= vi \quad \text{...(1.5)}$$

The M.K.S. unit of power is watt. Energy is given by integral equations

$$w = \int pdt = \int vi \,.\, dt \quad \text{...(1.6)}$$

1.6. R, L, C Parameters

Any network consists of one or more of the following passive elements : resistors, inductors and capacitors. Under ideal circumstances, resistors, inductors and capacitors are pure elements. Thus, an ideal resistor possesses only resistance and no inductance or capacitance. Similarly, in ideal cases, inductors and capacitors possess only inductance and capacitance respectively. In practice, ideal elements hardly ever exist. A physical resistor possesses not only resistance but also inductance and capacitance. Similarly a physical inductor possesses resistance and capacitance besides inductance and a physical condenser possesses resistance and inductance besides capacitance. A pure resistance obeys definite laws relating the voltage across it and the current through it. Similarly a pure inductance and pure capacitance follow different laws relating the associated voltage and current. These three elements *viz.* resistance, inductance and capacitance thus form the basic network elements or network parameters in terms of which any network may be expressed by replacing every physical passive network element by its equivalent network parameters. Then the response of the entire network may be calculated since we know :

(*i*) the response of each idealized network element and

(*ii*) the arrangement of these elements in the network.

Accordingly we proceed to study the current-voltage behaviour and other properties of these basic network parameters namely resistance, inductance and capacitance represented respectively by R, L and C.

1.7. The Resistance Parameter

Passage of electric current through a material results in collisions of the electrons with other atomic particles. These collisions may be elastic or inelastic. An inelastic collision results in change in the internal energy of the colliding particles and a corresponding loss in the total energy of the colliding particles. The loss in energy per unit charge manifests itself as potential drop across the material. This amount of energy lost depends upon the physical properties of a given substance.

For a given conductor, Ohm's law (Eq. 1.7) relates the current, voltage and resistance :

$$v = Ri \quad \text{...(1.7)}$$

where R is the resistance of the conductor in ohms,
v is the voltage drop across the resistor,
and i is the current in amperes.

Eq. (1.7) may be alternatively be written as :

$$v = R \cdot \frac{dq}{dt} \quad \text{...(1.8)}$$

or

$$q = \frac{1}{R}\int_0^t v\,dt \quad \text{...(1.9)}$$

Eq. (1.7) is sometimes written as :

$$i = Gv \quad \text{...(1.10)}$$

where G is the conductance of the conductor and equals $\frac{1}{R}$.

In the M.K.S. system, the unit of resistance is the ohm and that of conductance is mho or Siemen.

The energy lost by the electrons in passage through a conductor dissipates as heat. Resistance thus forms an energy dissipative ele-ment. At a given temperature, resistance of a conductor remains con-stant. In network analysis, resistance is assumed to remain constant, *i.e.* the temperature is assumed to remain constant.

Power absorbed in a resistor is given by,

$$P = vi \quad \text{...(1.11)}$$

where v, i and P are expressed in volts, amperes and watts respectively.

Eq. (1.11) may alternatively be put as :

$$P = \frac{v^2}{R} = i^2 \cdot R \quad \text{...(1.12)}$$

Power P indicates the time rate at which energy is absorbed in the system.

Hence energy lost in a resistance in time t is given by,

$$W = \int_0^t P dt = Pt = i^2\, Rt = \frac{v^2}{R} t \quad \text{...(1.13)}$$

where v is in volts, R is in ohms, t is in seconds and energy W is in joules.

Example 1.1. *A solid copper sphere 8 cm in diameter is deprived of 10^{12} electrons. Calculate the charge of the sphere in coulomb and the sign of the charge.*

Solution. The charge removed

$$= -10^{12} \times q \text{ coulomb} = -10^{12} \times 1.601 \times 10^{-19} \text{ coulomb}$$

$$= -1.601 \times 10^{-7} \text{ coulomb.}$$

Hence net charge on the sphere is positive and is equal to the charge removed in magnitude. Thus the charge on the sphere = + 1.601 × 10^{-7} coulomb.

Example 1.2. *A conductor carries a current of 1.2 amperes. Find the number of electrons that pass past its cross-section per second.*

Solution. Charge flow across the cross-section

$$= 1.2 \text{ coulomb/second.}$$

Charge of an electron = 1.6 × 10^{-19} coulomb.

Hence the number of electrons that flow past the cross-section per second = $\frac{1.2}{1.6 \times 10^{-19}}$

= 7.5 × 10^{18}.

Example 1.3. *The current in a conductor varies according to the equation = $3e^{-t}$ amp. for t greater than zero and is zero for t less than zero. Find the total charge in coulomb that passes through the conductor.*

Solution. $$\frac{dq}{dt} = i^3 e^{-t}$$

Hence $$q = \int_{t=0}^{t=\infty} i\,dt = \int_0^\infty 3e^{-t}\,dt = \left[-3e^{-t}\right]_0^\infty = [0 - 3(-1)] = 3 \text{ coulombs}$$

Example 1.4. *Current of three amperes flows through a resistor of 20 ohms. Find : (i) the power absorbed in the resistor ; (ii) energy dissipated in resistor per minute ; and (iii) charge flow through the resistor per minute.*

Solution. Power $P = i^2 \times R = (3)^2 \times 20 = 180$ watts

Energy dissipated per minute

$$P \times t = 180 \times 60 = 10{,}800 \text{ joules.}$$

Charge flow per minute

$$= q = i \times t = 3 \times 60 = 180 \text{ coulombs.}$$

1.8. The Inductance Parameter

In the year 1820, Oerstead observed that the needle of a mag-netic compass got deflected when current flowed in a neighbouring conductor. This showed that the effect was related to magnetism. He also discovered that the force was directed at right angles to the conductor for carrying the current. French physicist Andre Ampere, in the same year measured this force caused by the current in the conductor and derived a mathematical equation relating the force with the current, charge, distance etc.

With reference to Fig. 1.4, the magnetic field intensity, *i.e.*, the force per unit magnetic pole due to the current *i* in length *dl* of the conductor at a point *P* distant *r* from the conductor length *dl* is given by

$$dB = \frac{\mu i \cos\alpha \, dl}{4\pi r^2} \qquad ...(1.14)$$

where μ is the magnetic permeability of the medium in which the magnetic field exists.

∝ is the angle that the line joining point with length *dl* makes with the normal to the conductor drawn form *P*,

or $$B = \frac{\mu i \cos\alpha}{4\pi r^2}\, dl \qquad ...(1.14\ a)$$

From Eq. (1.14) it may be seen that the magnetic field density in constant at any fixed distance from the conductor. As a conceptual aid, solid lines with arrow-heads may be drawn to give the direction of *B* as Fig. 1.4 (*b*). These lines are referred to as the "magnetic field density lines" or the "lines of force".

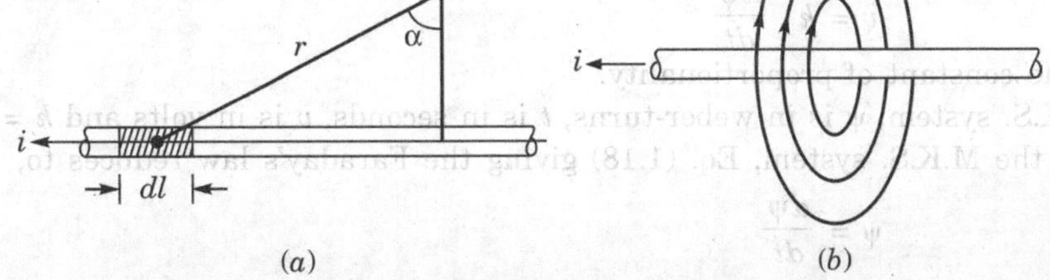

Fig. 1.4. The magnetic field of current carrying conductor.

Fig. 1.5 (*a*) shows cross section of a current carrying conductor along with the lines of force. Circular lines of force indicate that the magnetic field density is constant at constant distance from the conductor. The positions of the lines may be found experimentally by moving a point magnetic pole from place to place in space, while a magnetic compass will show the direction.

The magnetic flux is given by,

$$\phi = \int_S B \cos \theta \, ds \quad ...(1.15)$$

where θ is the angle between the surface of integration and the field density *B*.

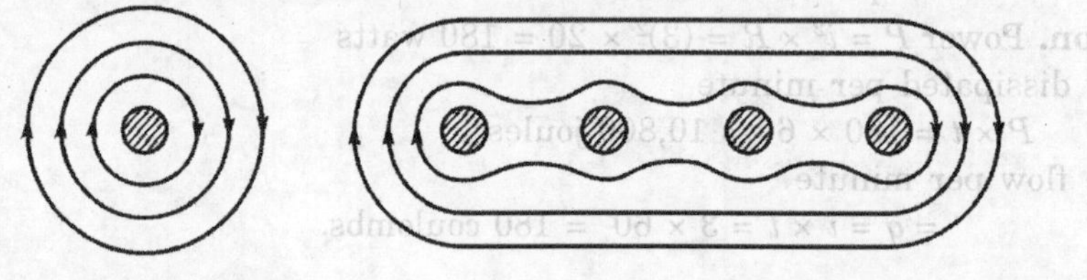

(*a*) Magnetic field of a single conductor. (*b*) Magnetic field of *N* parallel conductors.

Fig. 1.5. Magnetic fields of a single conductor and *N* parallel conductors.

Let us next consider the case of *N* parallel conductor as shown in Fig. 1.5 (*b*) carrying currents in such directions that the magnetic fluxes add. The $N\phi$ flux linkages are said to exist.

The flux linkage is then given by,

$$\psi = N\phi = N \int_S B \cos \theta \, ds \quad ...(1.16)$$

In case, however, only ϕ_1 lines of flux link N_1 conductors, ϕ_2 lines of flux link N_2 conductors and so on, then the total flux linkage is the algebraic sum of these flux linkages and is, therefore, given by

$$\psi = \sum_{j=1}^{j=n} N_j \phi_j \quad ...(1.17)$$

If the magnetic field density *B* remains constant, then the total flux linkage ψ also remains constant. If, however, the magnetic field density at any point is varying with time, then a voltage is induced in a conductor placed at the point. This experimental discovery was made by Faraday. He placed conducting circuits in close proximity and found that when the magnetic field produced by one circuit is altered, voltage is induced in the second circuit. A change in the magnetic field may be produced in the following two ways : (*i*) By moving the conductor in space or (*ii*) by changing the current with time.

Faraday found that the voltage induced is proportional to the time rate of change of flux linkage. Thus Faraday's law states that,

$$v = k \cdot \frac{d\psi}{dt} \quad ...(1.18)$$

where *k* is the constant of proportionality.

In M.K.S. system, ψ is in weber-turns, *t* is in seconds, *v* is in volts and $k = 1$.

Hence the M.K.S. system, Eq. (1.18) giving the Faraday's law reduces to,

$$\psi = \frac{d\psi}{dt} \quad ...(1.19)$$

Eq. (1.19) may be put in the following integral form :

$$\psi = \int v\,dt \quad \text{...(1.20)}$$

Thus flux linkage ψ is time integral of voltage v.
But from Eq. (1.1)

$$\theta = \int i\,dt \quad \text{...(1.21)}$$

i.e. the charge q is the time integral of current i.

By comparing Eqs. (1.20) and (1.21) we see that what flux linkage ψ is to voltage v, charge q is to current i.

Substituting the value of B from Eq. [1.14 (a)] into Eq. (1.16), we get

$$\psi = N\int\left(\int \frac{\mu\, i \cos\alpha\, dl}{4\pi r^2}\right) ds \quad \text{...(1.22)}$$

Making the assumption that i is constant throughout the length of the conductor, it may be removed from the integral. Hence, we get

$$\psi = \left[N\int\left(\int \frac{\mu \cos\alpha\, dl}{4\pi r^2}\right) ds\right] i \quad \text{...(1.23)}$$

The integral $N\int\left(\int \frac{\mu \cos\alpha\, dl}{4\pi r^2}\right) ds$ is defined as the "inductance parameter" or the coefficient of inductance and may be computed mathematically for simple systems of current carrying conductors or may be obtained experimentally by measuring ψ and i.

If the flux linkage ψ and the current i refer to the same physical system, the parameter is called the self-inductance and is symbolised by letter L. Then from Eq. (1.23),

$$\psi = Li \quad \text{...(1.24)}$$

where

$$L = N\int\left(\int \frac{\mu \cos\alpha\, dl}{4\pi r^2}\right) ds \quad \text{...(1.25)}$$

On the other hand, if a current i_1 in one circuit produces flux linkage ψ_2 in another circuit, the parameter is called the "mutual inductance", symbolized by letter M. We then get

$$\psi_2 = M_{21} \cdot i_1 \quad \text{...(1.26)}$$

Substituting Eq. (1.24) into Eq. (1.19), we get

$$v = \frac{d}{dt}(Li) \quad \text{...(1.27)}$$

If the inductance L does not vary with time, Eq. (1.27) reduces to,

$$v = L\frac{d}{dt} \quad \text{...(1.28)}$$

Eq. (1.28) on integration yields,

$$i = 1/L \int v\,dt \quad \text{...(1.29)}$$

For mutual inductance,

$$v = \frac{d}{dt}(Mi) \quad \text{...(1.30)}$$

If the mutual inductance M does not vary with time,

$$v = M\frac{di}{dt} \quad \text{...(1.31)}$$

Eq. (1.31) may be put in the following integral form :

$$i = \frac{1}{M}\int v dt \qquad \text{...(1.32)}$$

The M.K.S. unit of inductance is henry.

Eq. (1.28) may also be written as

$$v = L\frac{d}{dt}\left(\frac{dq}{dt}\right)$$

$$= L \cdot \frac{d^2q}{dt^2} \qquad \text{...(1.33)}$$

From the relation $\psi = Li$, we see that the product Li cannot change instantaneously, since an instantaneous change in ψ would mean an infinitely large voltage, which is an impossibility in any physical circuit. Let the product Li or ψ change by finite amount in interval of time $\Delta t = t_2 - t_1$ as shown in Fig. 1.6. Then time interval Δt cannot be zero. Eq. (1.20) may be put in the definite integral form :

$$\psi = \psi_0 + \int_0^t v dt \qquad \text{...(1.34)}$$

The integral portion of this equation can not have a finite value in zero time with finite v, *i.e.*

$$\lim_{t \to 0} \int_0^t v dt = 0 \quad v \neq \infty \qquad \text{...(1.35)}$$

This integration process is shown in Fig. 1.7 as summation of infinitesimal areas, v in height and dt in width. The interval from $t = 0$ to $t = t_1$ must be greater than zero for any area to be summed.

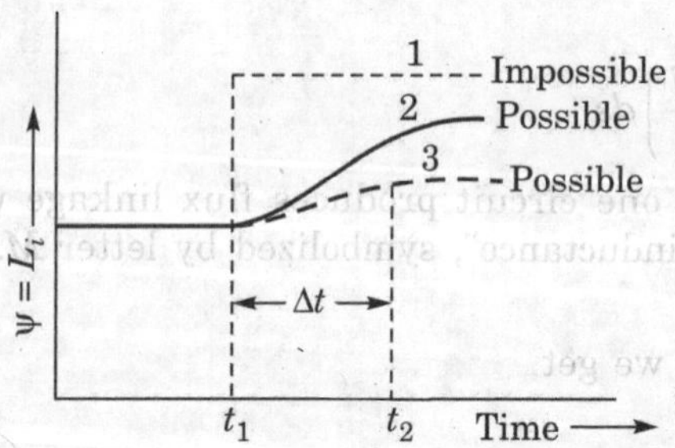

Fig. 1.6 Change of Li with time.

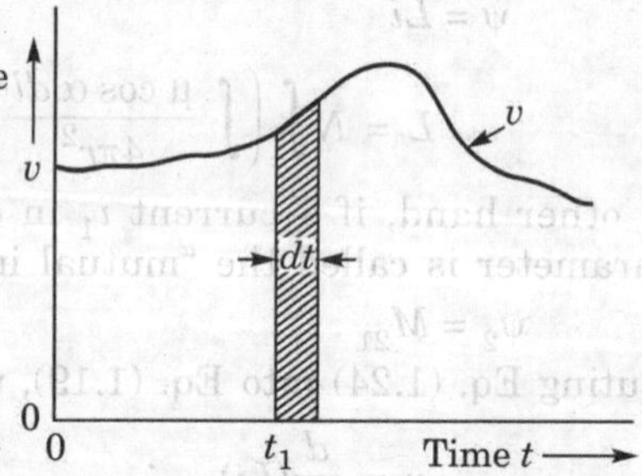

Fig. 1.7. Integration of voltage.

Eq. (1.35) aids in visualizing the requirement that the flux linkage ψ in an inductive system cannot change in zero time. Of course, either inductance L or current i may change instantaneously so as to maintain the product of L and i constant,

i.e. provided $\quad L_1 i_1 = L_2 . i_2 \qquad$ ...(1.36)

where subscripts 1 and 2 refer to conditions existing at time t_1 and t_2 extremely close to each other. This is called the "principle of constant flux linkage" and is similar to the "principle of conservation of momentum" in mechanics.

Thus in mechanics, Newton's law of force gives :

Force $\qquad F = \frac{d}{dt} Mv \qquad$ ...(1.37)

where M is the mass, v is the velocity and Mv is the momentum.

Momentum Mv of a system cannot change instantaneously.

From Eq. (1.36) we conclude the "if inductance remains constant, current cannot change instantaneously".

Power in an inductive element is given by,

$$P = vi = Li\frac{di}{dt} \qquad ...(1.38)$$

If L is in henry, i is in amperes and t in seconds, then power P is in watts.

Hence energy in an inductance is given by,

$$W = \int Pdt = \int Li\frac{di}{dt}dt$$

$$= \int Lidi = \frac{1}{2}Li^2 \qquad ...(1.39)$$

If L and i are respectively in henrys and amperes, then energy W is in joules.

Eq. (1.39) may be put as :

$$W = \frac{1}{2}\frac{\psi^2}{L} \text{ joules} \qquad ...(1.40)$$

This energy W is said to be "stored in the magnetic field" set up by the current through the inductor element. In this regard, inductance is analogous to mass or inertia in a mechanical system.

Example 1.5. *The current in a 3 henry inductor varies as shown in following figure. Find the following quantities after the current has flown for two seconds : (i) flux linkage in the system (ii) the time rate of change of flux linkages in the system and (iii) the quantity of charge having passed through the inductor.*

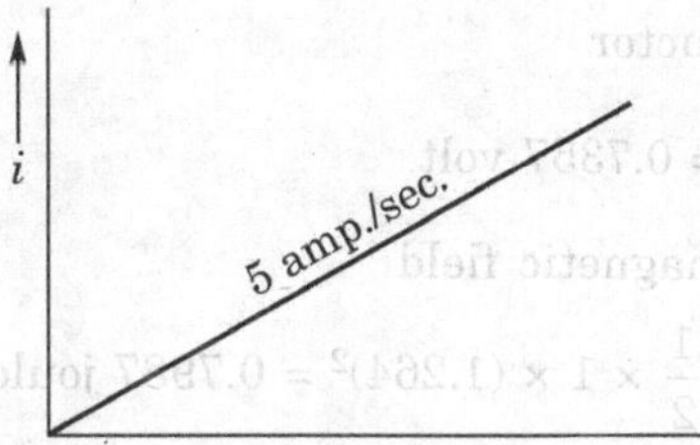

Solution. (*i*) After 2 seconds, current i = 1 amp.

Hence flux linkages $\psi = Li$

$= 3$ henry × 1 amp. = 3 henry-amp. = 3 weber-turn.

(*ii*) After 2 seconds, di/dt still remains constant at the value 0.5 amp/second.

Hence $$\frac{d\psi}{dt} = L\frac{di}{dt}$$

= 3 henry × 0.5 amp/sec. = 1.5 weber-turns/sec.

(*iii*) During 2 seconds, the charge that has passed through the inductor is given by,

$$q = \int_0^2 idi = \int_0^2 kt\, dt = \left[\frac{1}{2}kt^2\right]_0^2$$

where $k = 0.5$ amp/sec.

Hence $q = \frac{1}{2} \times 0.5 \text{ amp/sec} \times (2 \text{ sec})^2 = 1 \text{ amp/sec} = 1$ coulomb.

Example 1.6. *In the given circuit, switch K is closed at time t = 0. The current in the circuit is given by the equation : $i = 2(1 - e^{-t})$ amp, t > 0. At time t = 1 second, find (i) value of current (ii) rate of change of current (iii) total flux linkage (iv) rate of change of flux linkages (v) voltage across the inductor (vi) voltage across the resistor (vii) energy stored in the magnetic field of the inductor (viii) rate at which energy is being stored in the magnetic field of the inductor (ix) rate at which energy is being dissipated as heat and (x) rate at which the battery is supplying the energy.*

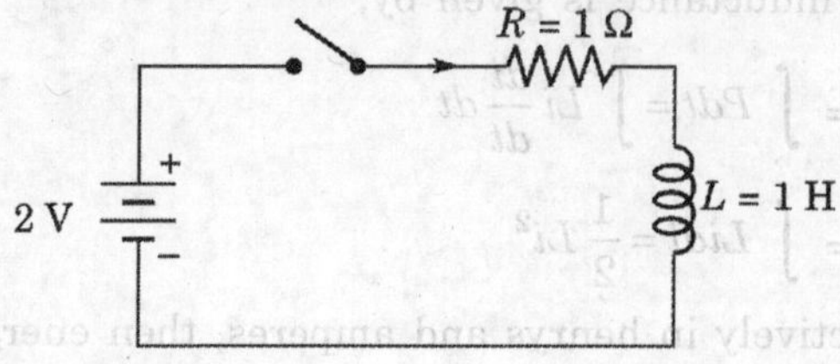

Solution.

At time $t = 1$ second,

(*i*) $i = 2(1 - e^{-t})$ amp. $= 2\left(1 - \frac{1}{e}\right) = 1.264$ amp.

(*ii*) $\frac{di}{dt} = 2(-e^{-t})(-1) = 2e^{-t} = 2e^{-1} = 0.7357$ amp/sec.

(*iii*) Total flux linkages

$= Li = 1$ henry $\times$ 1.264 amp. = 1.264 weber turns.

(*iv*) Rate of change of flux linkage

$= L\frac{di}{dt} = 1$ henry $\times$ 1.7357 amp/sec. = 0.7357 weber-turn/sec.

(*v*) Voltage across the inductor

$= \frac{d}{dt}(Li) = 0.7357$ volt.

(*vi*) Energy stored in the magnetic field

$= \frac{1}{2}Li^2 = \frac{1}{2} \times 1 \times (1.264)^2 = 0.7987$ joule.

(*vii*) Voltage across the resistor

$= i \times R = 1.264$ amp $\times$ 1 ohm = 1.264 volts.

(*viii*) Rate of storage of energy in the magnetic field

= Voltage across the inductor × Current = 0.7357 × 1.264 watt

= 0.93 watt.

(*ix*) Rate of energy dissipation in resistor

= Power in resistor = Voltage across resistor × Current

= 1.264 volts × 1.264 amp. = 1.597 watts.

(*x*) Rate of supply of energy by battery

$= \frac{d}{dt}$ (energy) = Voltage × Current

= 2 × 1.264 watts = 2.528 watts.

Example 1.7. *The following figure gives the variation of current i in an inductor of 2 henry. Calculate the voltage across the inductor and the charge in inductor at time t = 1 and 1.5 seconds.*

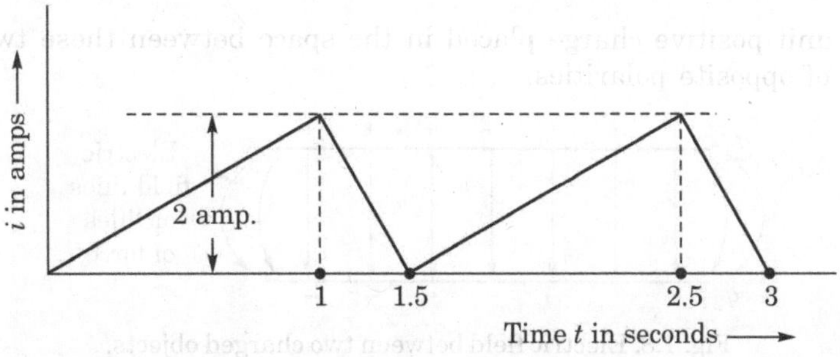

Solution. During time $t = 0$ to $t = 1$, current $i = 2t$ amps and $\frac{di}{dt} = 2$ amp/sec.

Voltage across the inductor

$$= L\frac{di}{dt} = 2 \times 2 = 4 \text{ volts}$$

Charge $q = \int idt = \int 2t\,dt = t^2$

At, $t = 1,\ q = (1)^2 = 1$ coulomb.

During $t = $ to $t = 1.5$ seconds,

$$\frac{di}{dt} = \frac{-2 \text{ amps.}}{0.5 \text{ sec.}} = -4 \text{ amps./sec.}$$

Voltage across the inductor

$$= L\frac{di}{dt} = 2(-4) = -8 \text{ volts.}$$

Current $i = 2 - 4(t - 1) = (6 - 4t)$

At time $t = 1.5$ seconds, charge q is given by

$$q = 1 + \int_{1.0}^{1.5} idt = 1 + \int_{1.0}^{1.5} (6 - 4t)\,dt = 1 + \left[\frac{(6-4t)^2}{2}\left(-\frac{1}{4}\right)\right]_{1.0}^{1.5} = 1.5 \text{ coulombs.}$$

1.9. The Capacitance Parameter

If there be charges q_1 and q_2 on two objects, placed say a distance r apart, as shown in Fig. 1.8, there results a force between the two objects. This forms a fundamental property of nature. Further it is found that the like charges repel while unlike charges attract each other. The force of attraction F is given by the relation,

$$F = \frac{-q_1 q_2}{4\pi\varepsilon r^2} \qquad ...(1.41)$$

where F is the force in newtons,

r is the distance in metres between the two point charges q_1 and q_2,

q_1 and q_2 are charges expressed in coulombs,

and ε is the permittivity (For free space, $\varepsilon = 8.854 \times 10^{-12}$ Farad per metre in M.K.S. units).

Eq. (1.41) is true for point charges only. The same may be applied to find the force between two objects and geometry or known charge distribution by vectorially adding all the forces.

Consider a unit positive charge placed in the space between these two objects carrying charges q_1 and q_2 of opposite polarities.

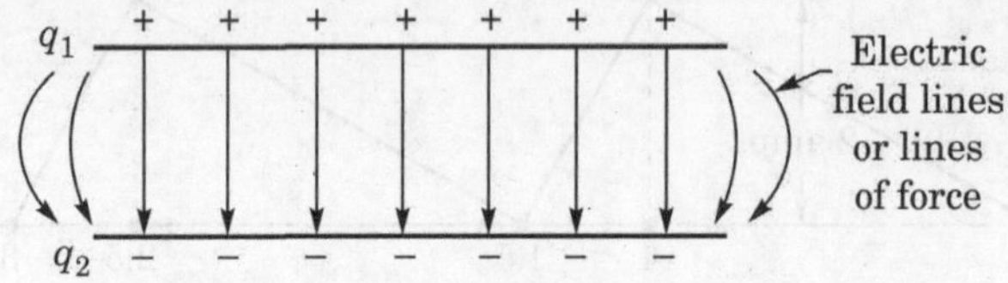

Fig. 1.8. Electric field between two charged objects.

The force exerted on this unit positive charge is vector quantity and is called the "electric field". If $q_1 = q_2 = q$ say, then the electric field is given by

$$E = \frac{F}{q} \qquad ...(1.42)$$

As a conceptual aid, often electric field is represented by line drawn in the direction of the field, *i.e.,* in the direction in which force will be exerted on a unit positive charge. Fig. 1.8 gives such electric field line or lines of force for parallel plane plates carrying charges q_1 and q_2. It may, of course, be borne in mind that these lines of force are simply conceptual aids and are not actually present.

The voltage v between the plates, *i.e.* the work done in moving a unit charge from one plate to the other is given by,

$$v = \int E \cos\theta \, dt \qquad ...(1.43)$$

where dr is the increment of distance between the plates.

and θ is the angle between the force and the direction of movement of r.

Substituting the value of force F from Eq. (1.41) into Eq. (1.43) and putting $q_1 = q_2 = q$, we get

$$v = \int \frac{q \cos\theta}{4\pi\varepsilon r^2} dr \qquad ...(1.44)$$

or

$$v = \left(- \int \frac{\cos\theta}{4\pi\varepsilon r^2} dr \right) q \qquad ...(1.45)$$

The quantity within the brackets may be evaluated for simple geometry of the plates or bodies carrying charges and may be obtained experimentally by measuring q and v. For a given geometry, the integral is a constant and is called "elastance", denoted by the letter S. Hence from Eq. (1.45)

$$v = Sq \qquad ...(1.46)$$

where

$$S = -\int \frac{\cos\theta}{4\pi\varepsilon r^2} dr \qquad ...(1.47)$$

The reciprocal of elastance is the capacitance denoted by letter C.

Thus

$$C = \frac{1}{S} \qquad ...(1.48)$$

Hence from Eqs. (1.46) and (1.48), we get

$$q = Cv \quad ...(1.49)$$

If q is in coulombs and v is the volts, capacitance C is given in "farads". The unit of elastance is daraf (farad spelled backwards). The quantity C, *i.e.* the capacitance forms a circuit parameter of the system.

Let there be an initial charge q_0 on the system, shown in Fig. 1.8 and let the charge increase linearly with time at the rate of k coulombs/second. Then charge on the system at any time t is given by,

$$q = q_0 + kt \quad ...(1.50)$$

The current is then given by,

$$i = \frac{dq}{dt} = \frac{d}{dt}(q_0 + kt)$$

or

$$i = k \quad ...(1.51)$$

We thus conclude that the current in a capacitive system is independent of the initial charge on the system but depends entirely on the rate of accumulation of charge.

Starting once again from the equation

$$i = \frac{dq}{dt}, \text{ we get}$$

$$dq = i\,dt \quad ...(1.52)$$

On integration $\int_{q_0}^{q} dq = \int_0^t i\,dt$

$$d = q_0 + \int_0^t i\,dt \quad ...(1.53)$$

From Eq. (1.52) we see that the total charge q on a capacitive system is equal to the initial charge q_0 plus the additional charge

$\int_0^t i\,dt$ deposited by the flow of current i for time t.

In order to find a relationship between current and voltage in capacitive system, we revert to the equation $q = Cv$. Current i is given by,

$$i = \frac{dq}{dt} = \frac{d}{dt}(Cv) \quad ...(1.54)$$

If the capacitance C does not vary with time, then

$$i = C\frac{dv}{dt} \quad ...(1.55)$$

On the other hand, if C is a time varying quantity, then we get

$$i = \frac{d}{dt}(Cv) = C\frac{dv}{dt} + v\frac{dC}{dt} \quad ...(1.56)$$

Equations (1.55) and (1.56) give current i in terms of v or its derivative.

Similary from Eq. (1.48), we get

$$v = \frac{q}{C} = \frac{1}{C}\int i\,dt = S\int i\,dt \quad ...(1.57)$$

Equation (1.57) gives voltage v across the capacitive system in terms of (*i*) integral of current i and (*ii*) circuit capacitance C or elastance S.

Voltage of a capacitive system cannot change instantaneously. Let us assume that the product Cv of a capacitive system has changed instantaneously.

Then

$$\frac{d}{dt}(Cv) = \infty \quad \text{or} \quad \frac{dq}{dt} = \infty \quad \text{or} \quad i = \infty.$$

We thus see that an instantaneous change in product Cv implies an infinite current, a physical impossibility. Thus with reference to Fig. 1.9, if the q or product Cv changes by a finite amount in time Δt, then this Δt cannot be made zero. Thus curve 1 is inadmissible while curves 2 and 3 are admissible.

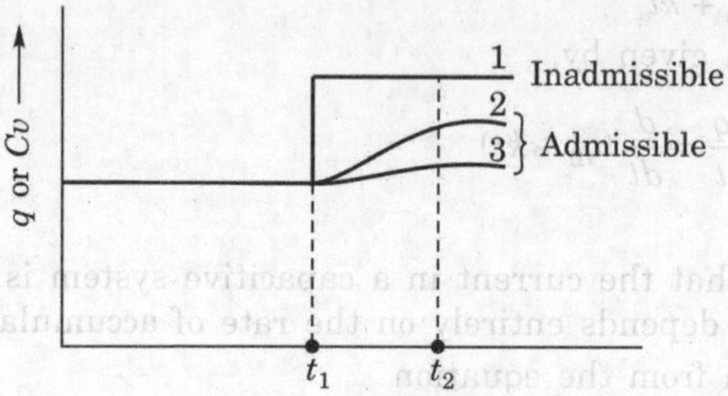

Fig. 1.9. Change of q or Cv with time.

We have already seen that,

$$q = q_0 + \int_0^t i\,dt \qquad ...(1.53)$$

With reference to Eq. (1.53), the above statement implies that for any finite value of current i, *i.e.* for $i = \infty$.

$$\lim_{t \to 0} \int_0^t i\,dt = 0 \qquad ...(1.58)$$

Fig. 1.10 shows a plot of current i as a function of time t for an arbitrary capacitive system. The area under the curve gives the charge added to the system, *i.e.* the quantity $\int_0^t i\,dt$. The integration process then amounts to summation of infinitesimal areas i in height and dt in width. Eq. (1.58), then implies that the interval from $t = 0$ to $t = t_1$ must be greater than zero for any area to be summed.

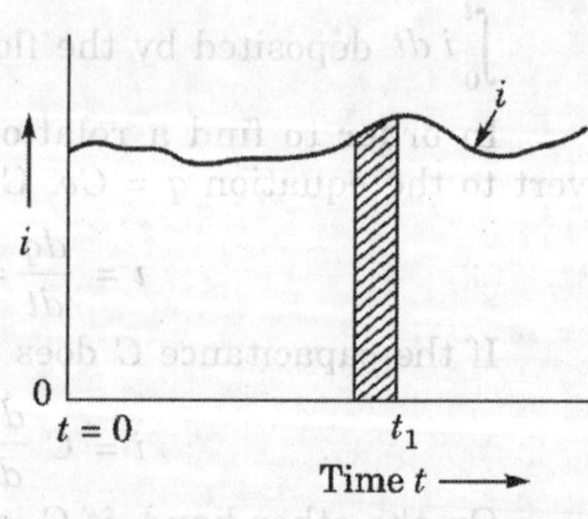

Fig. 1.10. Summation of current i to give addition of charge.

Thus we clearly establish that the product Cv or charge q in a capacitive system cannot either increase or decrease in zero time. But in most of the systems, capacitance does not change with time. Hence the above discussion establishes that "the voltage of a capacitive system cannot change instantaneously."

Assuming that capacitance C of a capacitor is time invariant, power in the capacitive element is given by the relation,

$$P = vi = vC\frac{dv}{dt} \text{ watts} \qquad ...(1.59)$$

and the energy E is given by,

$$E = \int P dt = \int vC dv$$

$$= \frac{1}{2} Cv^2 \text{ joules} \quad ...(1.60)$$

This energy E is stored in the electric field set up by the charges on the capacitive elements. If, however, voltage v is constant and capacitance C is time variant, then power in the capacitive element is given by,

$$P = vi = V\frac{dq}{dt}$$

$$= V \cdot V\frac{dc}{dt} \text{ watts} \quad ...(1.61)$$

and energy E is given by,

$$B = \int Pdt = \int V^2 dc = V^2 c \quad ...(1.62)$$

Example 1.8. *A condenser has one plate so rotated that the capacitance varies as shown in the following figure. A battery of constant voltage 10 volts is connected across the condenser. Find (i) current during time t = 0 to t = 1 second, (ii) Charge accumulated across the condenser at t = 1 second (iii) power in the condenser at t = 1 second and (iv) energy stored in the condenser at t = 1 second.*

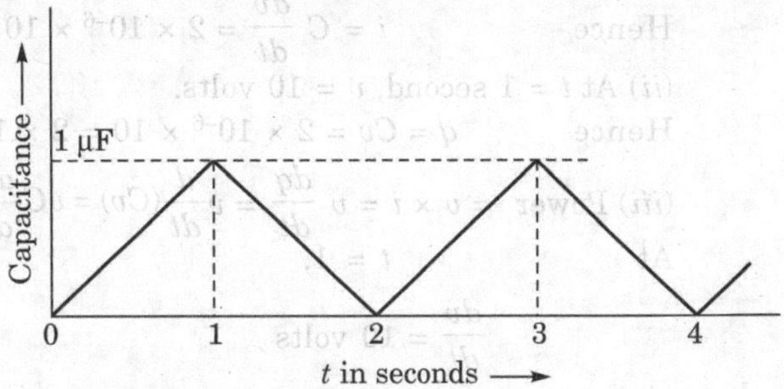

Solution.

(*i*) Current $\quad i = \dfrac{dq}{dt} = \dfrac{d}{dt}(cV) = V\dfrac{dc}{dt}$

During time $t = 0$ to $t = 1$,

$$\frac{dc}{dt} = 1 \text{ μ F/sec}$$

Hence $\quad i = V \times 1$ μF/sec

$= 10$ volts $\times 10^{-6}$ Farad/sec $= 10^{-5}$ amp.

(*ii*) $\quad q = cv$

At $\quad t = 1$ second

$c = 1$ μF.

Hence $q = 10^{-6}$ Farad $\times$ 10 volts $= 10^{-5}$ coulombs.

(*iii*) $\quad$ Power $P = Vi = V \cdot \dfrac{dq}{dt} = V \cdot \dfrac{d}{dt}(cV) = V^2 \cdot \dfrac{dc}{dt}$

$$\frac{dc}{dt} = 1 \text{ μF/sec.}$$

Hence during time $t = 0$ to $t = 1$ second.

Power $= V^2 \times 1$ μF/sec $= (10^2) \times 10^{-6}$ watt $= 10^{-4}$ watt.

(*iv*) Energy stored $= \displaystyle\int Pdt = \int V^2\, dc = V^2 c$

At $\quad t = 1$ sec, $c = 1$ μF.

Hence energy $= (10)^2 \times 10^{-6} = 10^{-4}$ joule.

Example 1.9. *To a 2μF condenser is applied a voltage of the form shown in the following figure. Find (i) the current during time t = 0 to t = 1 second, (ii) charge accumulated across the condenser at t = 1 second, (iii) power in the condenser at t = 1 second and (iv) energy stored in the condenser at t = 1 second.*

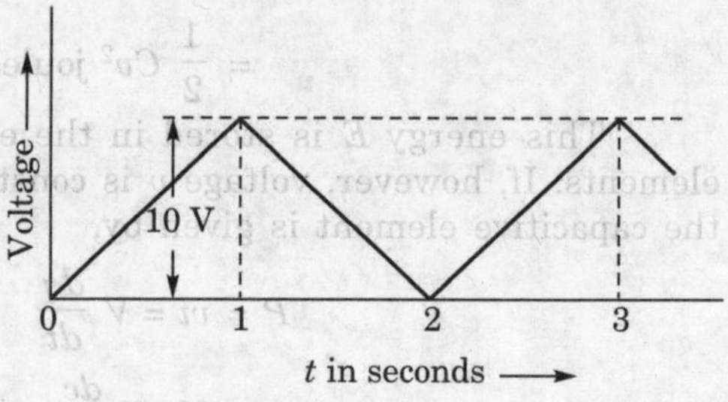

Solution.

(*i*) Current $i = \dfrac{dq}{dt} = \dfrac{d}{dt}(Cv) = V\dfrac{dv}{dt}$

During time $t = 0$ to $t = 1$ second

$$\frac{dv}{dt} = \frac{10 \text{ volts}}{1 \text{ sec}} = 10 \text{ volts/sec.}$$

Hence $i = C\dfrac{dv}{dt} = 2 \times 10^{-6} \times 10$ amp. = 20 μA.

(*ii*) At $t = 1$ second, $v = 10$ volts.

Hence $q = Cv = 2 \times 10^{-6} \times 10 = 2 \times 10^{-5}$ coulomb

(*iii*) Power $= v \times i = v\dfrac{dq}{dt} = v\dfrac{d}{dt}(Cv) = vC\dfrac{dv}{dt}$

At $t = 1$,

$$\frac{dv}{dt} = 10 \text{ volts}$$

and $v = 10$ volts/sec.

Hence power $= 10 \times 2 \times 10^{-6} \times 10 = 2 \times 10^{-4}$ watts.

(*iv*) Energy stored $= \displaystyle\int P dt = \int vC\frac{dv}{dt}\,.\,dt = \int vC\,dv = C\int v\,dv = \frac{1}{2}Cv^2$

At $t = 1$ second,

$$\text{energy} = \frac{1}{2} \times 2 \times 10^{-6} \times (10)^2 = 10^{-4} \text{ joule.}$$

Example 1.10. *A current shown in the following figure flows through a 10 μF condenser. Calculate voltage, charge, power and energy stored at time t = 1 and 2 seconds.*

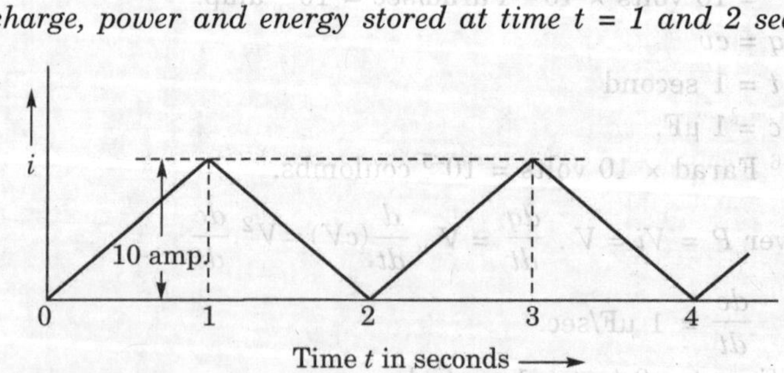

Solution. $q = Cv$

Hence $v = \dfrac{1}{C}q = \dfrac{1}{C}\displaystyle\int i\,dt$

During time t = 0 to t = 1 second,

$i = 10\,t$ amps, where t is in seconds.

Hence $v = \dfrac{1}{C}\displaystyle\int 10\,t\,dt = \frac{10}{C}\cdot\frac{t^2}{2} = \frac{5t^2}{C}$

At $t = 1$ second,

$$v = \frac{5}{10^{-5}} = 5 \times 10^5 \text{ volts.}$$

Charge $\quad q = \int i\, dt = \int 10\, t = 10\,\frac{t^2}{2} = 5 \times 1 = 5$ coulombs.

Power $\quad = vi = \frac{5t^2}{C} \times 10\, t = \frac{50t^3}{C}$

At $t = 1$ second,

$$\text{Power} = \frac{50}{10^{-5}} = 5 \times 10^6 \text{ watts}$$

$$\text{Energy} = \int P\, dt = \int \frac{50t^3}{C}\, dt = \frac{50}{C} \cdot \frac{t^4}{4} = \frac{25t^4}{2C}$$

At $t = 1$ second,

$$\text{Energy} = \frac{25}{2 \times 10^{-5}} = 12.5 \times 10^5 \text{ joules.}$$

During time $t = 1$ to $t = 2$ seconds :

$$i = 10 - 10\,(t - 1) = 20 - 10t$$

Charge $\quad q = q_{t-1} + \int i\, dt = 5 + \int (20 - 10t)\, dt = 5 + \left[20t = 5t^2\right]_{t=1}^{t=t}$

At $t = 2$, $q = 5 + [(40 - 20) - (20 - 5)] = 10$ coulombs.

Hence at $t = 2$ seconds,

$$v = \frac{q}{C} = \frac{10}{10^{-5}} = 10^6 \text{ volts.}$$

$$\text{Power} = vi = 10^{-6} \times 0 = 0$$

$$\text{Energy} = \int P\, dt = \int vi\, dt$$

$$= E_{t=1} + \int_{t=1}^{t=2} (20 - 10t)\,\frac{1}{C}\,(5 + 20t - 5t^2)\, dt$$

$$= 12.5 \times 10^5 + \frac{50}{C}\int_{t=1}^{t=2} (2 - t)\,(1 + 4t - t^2)\, dt$$

$$= 12.5 \times 10^5 + \frac{50}{C}\int (2 + 7t - 6t^2 + t^3)\, dt$$

$$= 12.5 \times 10^5 \times \frac{50}{C}\left[2t + \frac{7t^2}{2} - 2t^3 + \frac{t^4}{4}\right]_{t=1}^{t=2}$$

$$= 12.5 \times 10^5 + 50 \times 10^5\,[2.25] = 10^5\,(12.5 + 112.5) = 125 \times 10^5 \text{ joules.}$$

1.10. Energy Sources

By energy source, used in this context, is meant a device for generating electrical energy. Of course such generation of electrical energy is done by transformation from some other type of energy. Energy sources form active network elements.

Energy sources are classified in accordance with their current-voltage characteristics. Thus we have two types of energy sources. One category of energy sources approximate "ideal voltage sources" while the other category of sources approximate "ideal current sources".

Ideal voltage source. An ideal voltage source generates volt-age of a given time variation but neither the magnitude nor the time variation of the generated voltage changes with the magnitude of the current drawn from it. Thus the terminal voltage of this source remains constant for all values of output current from zero current condition to blunt short circuit. Evidently such a performance can be achieved by an energy source only when it has zero internal resistance, inductance and capacitance. The symbol for ideal voltage surce is generally a circle with polarity marks + and – denoting the positive and negative terminals of the source as shown in Fig. 1.11(*a*) and (*b*). The lower case letter v indicates a time varying source while the upper case letter V indicates a time invariant source. An approximate time variation of voltage is sometimes sketched within the circle. Thus the symbol having ~ placed within the circle indicates a source of sinusoidal voltage. However a battery is generally symbolized as in Fig. 1.11 (*c*).

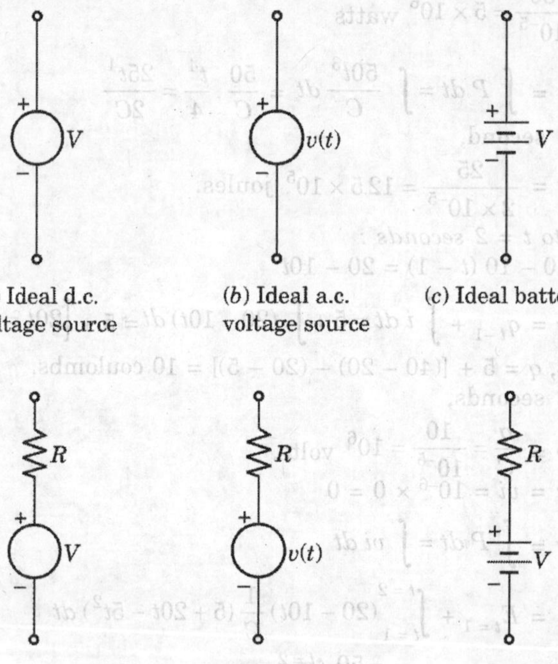

(*a*) Ideal d.c. voltage source (*b*) Ideal a.c. voltage source (*c*) Ideal battery

(*d*) Practical d.c. voltage source (*e*) Practical a.c. voltage source (*c*) Practical battery

Fig. 1.11. Symbols for ideal and practical voltage source.

Almost all practical voltage sources fall short of the ideal and their terminal voltage falls with increase in the output current. However in most of the cases, a practical voltage source may be approximated as an ideal voltage source with a series resistance in case of d.c. sources or with a series impedance (usually inductor) in the case of a.c. voltage source. This series resistor then accounts for the fall in terminal voltage with increase of output current. Symbol for a practical voltage source is accordingly the same as for an ideal voltage source with a series resistor R (or impedance Z) as shown in Fig. 1.11(*d*), (*e*) and (*f*).

Ideal current source. An ideal current source generates current of a given time variation but neither the magnitude nor the time variation of the generated current changes with the load. Thus the output current of this source remains constant for all values of load ranging from zero resistance to infinite resistance. If this ideal current source gives zero output current, the source reduces to just an open circuit. The requirement of constant current in an ideal current source can be satisfied only provided it has zero internal resistance, inductance and capacitance. The symbol for ideal current source is generally a circle with an associated arrow indicating the positive direction of current flow as shown in Fig. 1.12 (*a*) and (*b*). In this case also, the lower case letter *i* or *i* (*t*) indicates the time varying source while the upper case letter *I* indicates the time invariant source. Again approximate time variation of current may be sketched within the circle. Sometimes a rectangle instead of a circle is used to symbolize current source, in order to clearly differentiate it from voltage source.

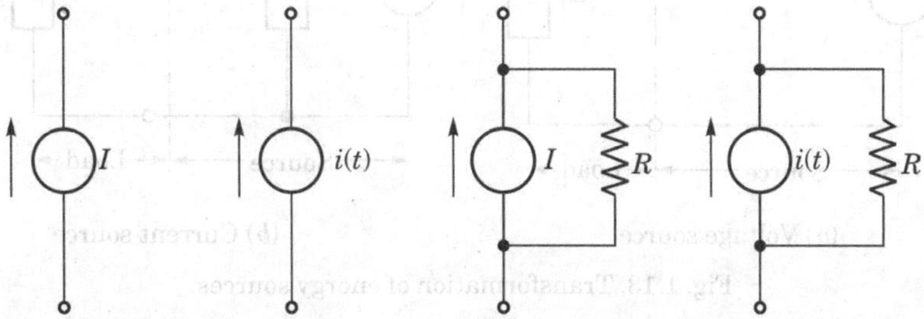

(*a*) Ideal d.c. current source (*b*) Ideal a.c. current source (*c*) Practical d.c. current source (*c*) Practical a.c. current source

Fig. 1.12. Symbols for ideal and practical current sources.

Again all practical current sources fall short of the ideal and their output current falls with the increase of load resistance (or impedance). Accordingly a practical current generator may be approximated as an ideal current generator with a shunt resistor in case of d.c. current source or a shunt impedance in case of a.c. current source. This shunt resistor then accounts for the fall of output load current with increase of load resistance. Symbol for a practical current source is the same as that for the corresponding ideal current source with a shunt resistance (impedance) as shown in Fig. 1.12 (*c*) and (*d*).

Photo-electric cell and pentode vacuum tube amplifiers form practical current generators of common occurrence in electronic circuits.

Although ideal current and voltage sources form two altogether different types of sources, practical sources cannot be so distinctly classified. In fact any source with suitable associated regulator circuit may be made to behave as constant voltage generator or constant current generator, closely approaching the ideal condition in either of the cases. The distinction made here is primarily for facility in network analysis and any particular energy source is treated either as a voltage source or a current source depending upon which type facilitates analysis of the network under consideration. Thus a practical voltage source may be transformed into its equivalent practical current source or *vice versa.*

1.11. Transformation of Energy Sources

Any practical energy source may be represented by either constant voltage source or constant current source. It is possible, therefore, to transform a practical voltage source into a current source and *vice versa*. Thus in Fig. 1.13 parts (*a*) and (*b*) show respectively the constant voltage source and constant current source with associated internal impedances Z_v and Z_i respectively. Each source drives a current through the load impedance Z_l.

Then with the voltage source connected to the load impedance Z_l, load current I_v through Z_l is given by,

$$I_v = \frac{V}{Z_v + Z_l} \qquad \text{...(1.63)}$$

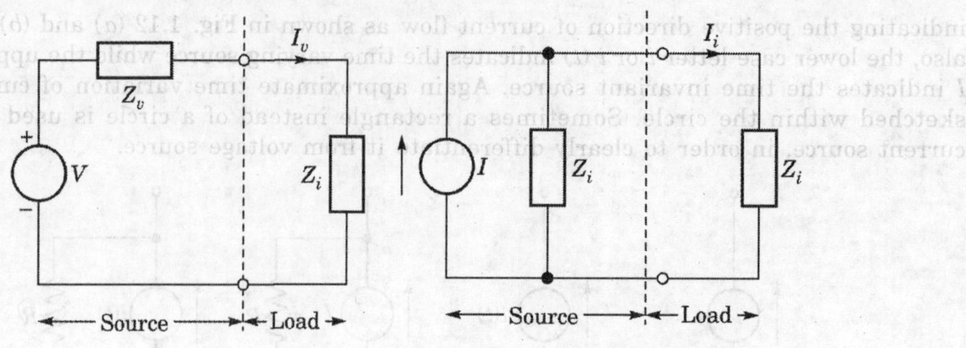

(a) Voltage source (b) Current source

Fig. 1.13. Transformation of energy sources.

With current source connected to Z_l, the load current I_i through Z_l is given by,

$$I_i = \frac{Z_i}{Z_i + Z_l}\,.\,I \qquad ...(1.64)$$

If the two energy sources are equivalent, then the load current I_v and I_i must be equal. Equating I_v to I_i, from Eqs. (1.63) and (1.64), we get

$$\frac{V}{Z_v + Z_l} = \frac{Z_i T}{Z_i + Z_l} \qquad ...(1.65)$$

Also $$V = Z_i\,.I \qquad ...(1.66)$$

From Eqs. (1.65) and (1.66)

$$Z_v + Z_l = Z_i + Z_l$$

or $$Z_v = Z_i.$$

Thus a constant voltage source of voltage V and series impedance Z may be equated to a constant current source of current I in parallel with an impedance Z, where $I = V/Z$.

1.12. Approximations in Circuit Representation

We have so far discussed the response of pure circuit elements namely resistance, inductance and capacitance. In analysing electrical systems we utilize the circuit concept and represent a physical system in terms of network parameters. The physical system involved may be an antenna, a transmission line or an electric motor. For the purpose of analysis, we study the properties of the physical system and replace it by equivalent circuit parameters. In so doing we put an inductor in the equivalent network if we observe the system to possess inductive effect. Similarly we may put in the equivalent network, a resistance and capacitance to represent resistive and capacitive effect respectively. These various elements then correspond to the various effects observed. Their magnitudes and placement in the equivalent network is also carefully decided.

Thus in an equivalent network, we account for all the large or prominent effects observed in the system. But there always remain a few smaller or secondary effects which often remain unrepresented in the equivalent electrical network. Thus an approximation has been made in representing the physical system. Obviously this lowers the accuracy of the results obtained after making calculations based on these approximate equivalent circuit.

To what extent should approximations be made ? Putting it otherwise, to what limit should the secondary effects be included in the equivalent network ? This decision entails engineering judgements and should be made considering the values of these secondary effects relative to the principal effects and the order of accuracy desired.

Again in the case of commercial components, such as resistors, inductors and capacitors, approximations are often involved in their representation in the equivalent circuit. Thus an inductor never behaves as a pure inductance. In most circumstances, it possesses unwanted resistive as well as capacitive effects. In several cases, these unwanted parasitic effects may be neglected in the equivalent network. Whether such an approximation should be made or not again forms an engineering decision.

In deriving expressions for *R*, *L* and *C* parameters, done in the earlier articles, we have assumed that (*i*) the charge does not vary with the dimensions of the conductor and (*ii*) the current does not vary with the length or the cross-sectional area of the conductor. These assumptions are not true for periodic currents flowing for brief intervals of time. Parameters calculated for these charged conditions will differ from the general parameter calculated under assumption of uniform current and charge. For accurate results, these parameters should be calculated for each type of current waveform. However, in most of the cases, an approximation is made that parameter values are the same as for non-varying or static conditions.

Further it is assumed that the system is linear. This forms a good approximation for most of the elements operating within their nominal operating range. Even vacuum tube, though basically non-linear, are considered linear for certain analysis if operated over a restricted range.

Again we assume the elements to be bilateral and lumped. Also as an approximation we assume that there is no interaction between electric and magnetic field, *i.e.* there is no radiation of energy.

1.13. Mutual Inductance

When two or more inductors are placed close together, there may result a mutual interaction of the magnetic fields to these inductors. This results in the mutual inductance parameters. We will first examine the case of two inductors mutually coupled and then subsequently examine the general case of n (n is an integer > 1) inductors mutually coupled.

1.13.1. Two Mutually Coupled Inductors and Dot Convention

Fig. 1.14 (*a*) shows two inductors wound on a common core. The magnetic field produced by current i_1 flowing in one coil, say coil 1 induces a voltage in the other coil. The coils are then said to be coupled and the windings constitute a transformer. The diagram also shows the detailed distribution of the windings on the core. Fig. 1.14 (*b*) gives the corresponding circuit diagram. Knowing the details of transformer construction for a given current i_1 in one coil, it is possible to compute magnitude and direction of the voltage induced in the other winding. The need for giving detailed construction as on a blue print is obviated by using the characterizing factor namely the coefficient of mutual inductance *M*. Manufacturers usually mark one end of each winding with a dot or some other symbol. These dots are equivalent to details of construction as far as the direction of the magnetic fluxes caused by currents entering the coils at the dotted ends are concerned, *i.e.* as far as the voltage directions are concerned. We will now discuss the meaning of these dot markings.

In Fig. 1.14 (*a*), a time varying voltage source of voltage $e_s(t)$ is connected to the winding 1-1 (now called the primary winding). At given instant of time, the voltage e_s has the polarity shown in Fig. 1.14 (*a*). The resulting current i_1 in the primary flows in the direction shown and enters the primary winding at the end marked with a dot.

The resulting phenomena are outlined below in steps :

(*i*) *Field.* The current i_1 in primary winding 1-1 causes a magnetic field which is chiefly concentrated along the axis of the coil.

This field is given by,

$$dB = \frac{\mu i_1 dl \cos \alpha}{4\pi r^2} \qquad ...(1.67)$$

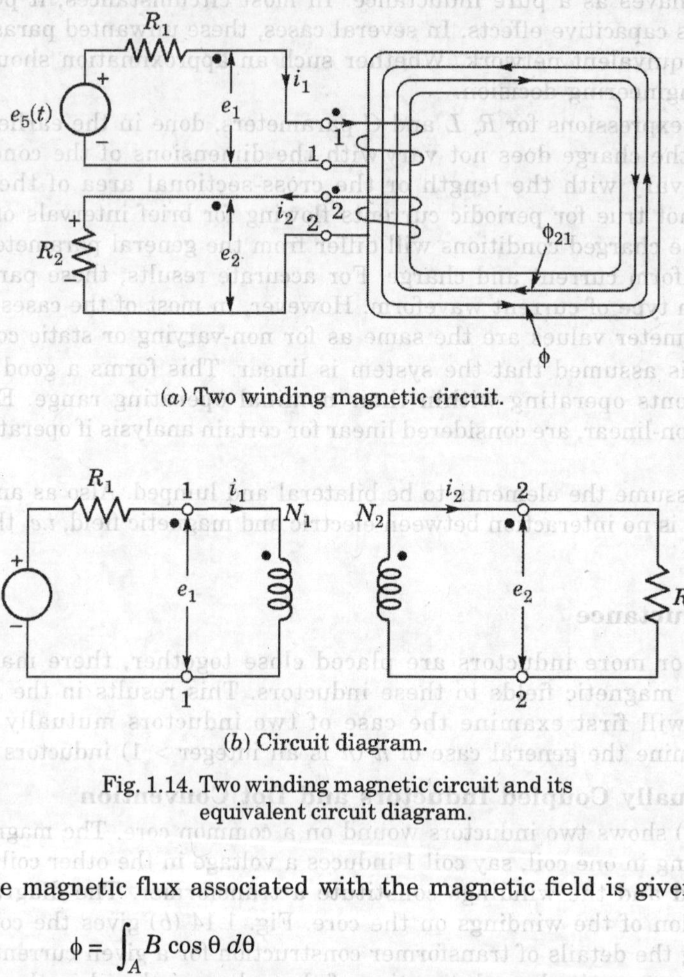

(*a*) Two winding magnetic circuit.

(*b*) Circuit diagram.

Fig. 1.14. Two winding magnetic circuit and its equivalent circuit diagram.

(*ii*) *Flux*. The magnetic flux associated with the magnetic field is given by,

$$\phi = \int_A B \cos \theta \, d\theta \qquad ...(1.68)$$

Direction of this flux is determined by the right handed screw rule, *i.e.* if the current is along the longitudinal motion of the screw, the flux is in the direction given by the circular motion of the screw. Of course almost the entire flux is confined to the magnetic core. Applying the above rule, the flux in the core is in direction shown by the arrow giving ϕ_{21}.

(*iii*) *Flux linkage*. The flux produced in the core due to current in the winding 1-1 links with the winding 2-2. Let the flux which so links with winding 2-2 be denoted by ϕ_{21}, where the subscripts 2 and 1 correspond to the order "effect-cause".

In this case, the same flux ϕ_{21} links with both the windings 1-1 and 2-2.

The magnitude of flux linkage with winding 1-1 is :

$$\psi_1 = N_1 . \phi_{21} \qquad ...(1.69)$$

where N_1 is the number of turns on the primary winding 1-1.

By Faraday's law, flux linkage ψ_1 is related with the voltage e_1 at terminals 1-1 by the relation :

$$\phi_1 = \int e_1 \, . \, dt \qquad ...(1.70)$$

From Eqs. (1.69) and (1.70), we get

$$\phi_{21} = \frac{\psi_1}{N_1} = \frac{1}{N_1}\int e_1 \, dt \qquad ...(1.71)$$

(*iv*) *Voltage induced in the secondary.* Since I_1 is a time varying quantity, ϕ_{21} is also time varying. Hence a voltage is induced in winding 2-2.

Flux linkage in winding 2-2 = $\psi_2 = N_2 \, \phi_{21}$ ...(1.72)

Hence according to Faraday's law, voltage e_2 induced in the winding 2-2 is given by,

$$e_2 = \frac{d\psi_2}{dt} \qquad ...(1.73)$$

The coefficient of mutual inductance relates flux linkage ψ_2 in the secondary winding 2-2 with the current i_1 in the primary winding 1-1.

Thus $\qquad \psi_2 = M_{21} \, . \, i_1$ ...(1.74)

Hence $\qquad e_2 = \dfrac{d\psi_2}{dt} = M_{21} \, . \, \dfrac{di_1}{dt}$ ...(1.75)

provided M_{21} is time invariant.

(*v*) *Direction of induced voltage.* The law regarding the direction of the induced voltage was established by the German physicist Lenz in 1834. Lenz's law estates that "the voltage induced in a coil by a time variant flux establishes a current in the coil in such a direction as to oppose the change in the initial flux which induced this voltage". The flux ϕ_{21} caused by current i_1 is directed clockwise in the core of the coils and this flux is increasing at the instant under consideration. The flux ϕ_{12} produced by current i_2 in coil 2-2 due to induced voltage v_2 in coil 2-2 must oppose the flux ϕ_{21}. Hence by right hand screw rule the current i_2 must flow in the direction shown by arrow head in Fig. 1.14. The reason why the induced flux ϕ_{12} must nccessarily oppose the incident flux ϕ_{21} is quite apparent. If ϕ_{12} aids the flux ϕ_{21}, another increasing current would be induced in the coil 1-1 and so on forming a vicious, cycle to produce infinite current. This is against the principle of conservation of energy.

(*iv*) *Dot convention.* The induced current i_2 flows out of the top end of the winding. Hence top end of winding 2-2 becomes positive and is marked with a dot. Thus with a time varying voltage applied at terminals 1-1, when the dotted end of winding 1-1 is positive, the dotted end of winding 2-2 is also positive. Thus the dotted ends of coils become positive (or negative) concurrently. If the positions of source and load are interchanged, *i.e.*, the source is connected to winding 2-2 and the load is connected to winding 1-1, a step-by-step analysis will show that an increasing current flowing in the dotted terminal of coil 2-2 makes the upper end of coil 1-1 positive and hence the dotted end. Thus the dotted ends of coils become concurrently positive irrespective of the positions of the driving source and the load.

Again let us suppose that the source voltage has at any instant of time polarity reverse to that shown in Fig. 1.14 so that a current flows out of the dot. Then by inspection or by step-by-step analysis we may establish that the dotted terminal of winding 2-2 becomes negative.

We thus conclude that :

Current flowing into the dot on one winding includes a voltage in the other winding making the dotted end positive.

Or

Current flowing out of the dot on one winding induces a voltage in the other winding making the dotted end negative.

Or

Current simultaneously flowing into (or simultaneously flowing out of) dots on winding induce flux in the core which are additive.

1.13.2. Three Mutually Coupled Inductors

We have already studies two mutually coupled inductors. We now proceed to consider the case of several inductors magnetically coupled.

Fig. 1.15 (*a*) shows three mutually coupled inductors L_1 L_2 and L_3. The currents entering these coils are i_1, i_2 and i_3 respectively.

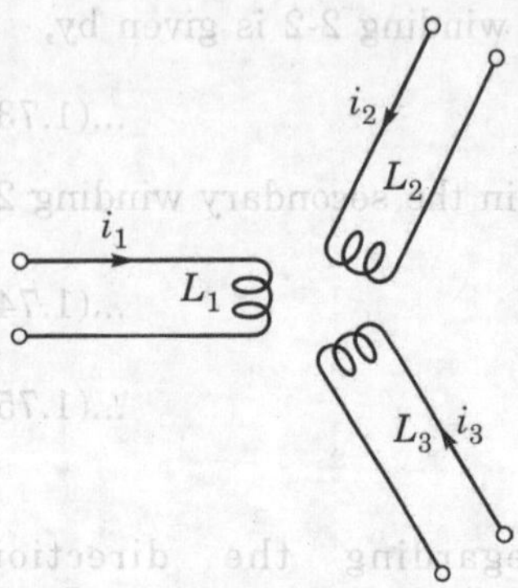

Fig. 1.15. Three magnetically coupled coils.

To facilitate understanding, we assume i_2 and i_3 to be zero and consider the effect of i_1 alone on the system. This current produces magnetic field B and a magnetic flux ϕ_1 whole of which links with the coil L_1 itself. The flux linkage ψ_1 produced with coil L_1 is related with the current i_2 in accordance with the relation :

$$.\psi_1 = L_{11} \cdot i_1 \qquad ...(1.76)$$

where L_{11} is the self-inductance of coil L_1.

Out of the total magnetic flux ϕ_1, a part ϕ_{21} links with N_2 turns of coil L_2 producing the flux linkage ϕ_{21}, so that

$$\psi_{21} = N_2 \cdot \phi_{21} \qquad ...(1.77)$$

where ϕ_{21} depends upon the mutual inductance M_{21}.

Eq. (1.77) may be put as : $\psi_{21} = M_{21} \cdot i_1$ ...(1.78)

where M_{21} is the mutual inductance between coils L_1 and L_2. The subscripts 2, 1 are placed in the order "effect, cause". Thus M_{21} gives the mutual inductance relating the cause *i.e.* the current i_1 in coil L_1 to effect *i.e.* flux linkage ψ_{21} in coil L_2.

Similarly flux linkage ψ_{31} with coil L_3, due to current i_1 in coil L_1 is given by,

$$\psi_{31} = M_{31} \cdot i_1 \qquad ...(1.79)$$

In general there will be either sources or loads connected to each of the coils so that current flows in each of the coils. We assume that the current directions and winding senses of the three coils are such that the flux linkages of any coil caused by all the coils are additive.

Then the total flux linkage ψ_1 in say coil L_1 is the sum of the flux linkages ψ_{11}, ψ_{12} and ψ_{13} where ψ_{11} ($= L_{11}\, i_1$) is the flux linkage produced by the current i_1 in the coil L_1 itself, and ψ_{12} ($= M_{12} \cdot i_2$) and ψ_{13} ($= M_{13}\, i_3$) are the flux linkages produced by the current i_2 and i_3 flowing in the coils L_2 and L_3 respectively. Thus,

$$\psi_1 = L_{11} \cdot i_1 + M_{12} \cdot i_2 + M_{13} \cdot i_3 \qquad ...(1.80)$$

Similarly for coil L_2, flux linkages ψ_2 is given by,

$$\psi_2 = M_{21} \cdot i_1 + L_{22}\, i_2 + M_{23}\, i_3 \qquad ...(1.81)$$

and for coil L_3, flux linkages ψ_3 is given by,

$$\psi_3 = M_{31} \cdot i_1 + M_{32}\, i_2 + L_{33}\, i_3 \qquad ...(1.82)$$

Assuming inductance parameters (both self and mutual) to be time invariant, by Faraday's law, the voltage induced in each, being the time rate of change of flux linkage, is given by,

$$e_1 = L_{11} \cdot \frac{di_1}{dt} + M_{12} \cdot \frac{di_2}{dt} + M_{13} \cdot \frac{di_3}{dt} \qquad ...(1.83)$$

$$e_2 = M_{21} \cdot \frac{di_1}{dt} + L_{22} \cdot \frac{di_2}{dt} + M_{23} \cdot \frac{di_3}{dt} \qquad ...(1.84)$$

and $$e_3 = M_{31} \cdot \frac{di_1}{dt} + M_{32} \cdot \frac{di_2}{dt} + L_{33} \cdot \frac{di_3}{dt} \qquad \text{...(1.85)}$$

When more than two coils are magnetically coupled, the magnetic flux induced by any one coil is related with that of every other by the usual dot convention. Of course dots of different shapes such as ● ■ ▮ ▲ etc. are used for each pair of coils. This scheme, however, has the drawback of confusion resulting from the use of a large number of similar dots. As an alternative to the use of dots for giving the information regarding the direction of resulting magnetic flux, or induced voltage, the same information may be contained in the sign of the coefficient of mutual inductance. This system is preferable to the dot system when the number of magnetically coupled coils is large. Of course, both systems have their advantages peculiar to certain problems and hence both systems are extensively used.

EXERCISE

1.1. 5×10^{11} electrons are removed from a solid copper sphere of diameter 6 cm. Find the charge of the sphere in coulombs and its sign. [**Ans.** $+ 8 \times 10^{-20}$ coulomb]

1.2. In a copper conductor, 3×10^{-18} electrons/second move past its cross-sectional area. Find the current in amperes. [**Ans.** 0.48 ampere]

1.3. A copper conductor carries a current of 400 mA. Find the net flow of electrons past any cross-section of the conductor per second. [**Ans.** 2.5×10^{18}]

1.4. In a copper conductor, there are 5×10^{22} free electrons in 1 cubic centimetre and the current density is 240 amp/cm^2. Find the mean electron drift in cm/second. [**Ans.** 0.03 cm/sec]

1.5. The current in a circuit varies according to the equation $i = 5 \sin \omega t$ amp., where $\omega = 2\pi \times 10^3$ radians/second. Find the charge in coulombs that passes through the circuit during the interval current i is positive. [**Ans.** 1.59×10^{-3} coulomb]

1.6. The current in a circuit varies as shown in the diagram. Calculate the charge in coulombs that passes through the circuit in one second. [**Ans.** 5 coulombs]

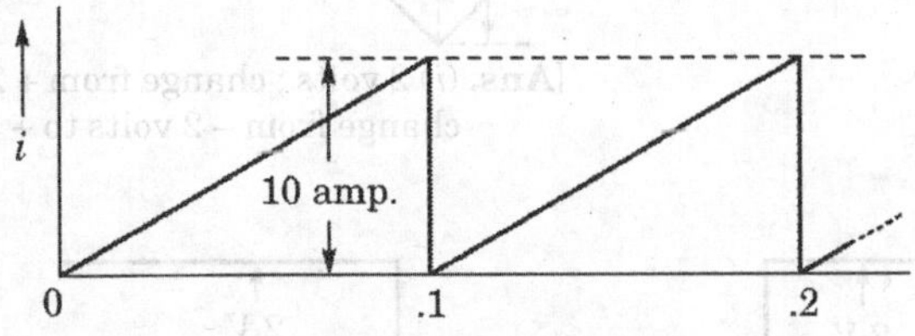

1.7. An energy source is connected to a circuit resulting in a current i of 5 amperes. The voltage difference across the output terminals of the source is 50 volts. Calculate (*i*) the power drawn from the source (*ii*) the energy supplied by the source in one minute (*iii*) charge transported in a minute.
[**Ans.** (*i*) 250 watts (*ii*) 15,000 joules (*iii*) 300 coulombs]

1.8. A current of 2 amperes flows through a resistor of 10 ohms. Find (*i*) the power absorbed in the resistor (*ii*) energy dissipated in the resistor per minute and (*iii*) charge flow through the resistor per minute.
[**Ans.** (*i*) 40 watts (*ii*) 2400 joules (*iii*) 120 coulombs]

1.9. Find the maximum current that may be allowed through a 40 ohm, 10 watt resistor. With this maximum current, find the energy lost in the resistor in 5 minutes. [**Ans.** 0.5 amp ; 3000 joules]

1.10. The current in a 2-henry inductor varies as shown in the following figure. Find (*i*) the flux linkage in the system after one second (*ii*) the time rate of change of flux linkages in the system after 10 seconds and (*iii*) the quantity of charge having passed through the inductor after 4 seconds.

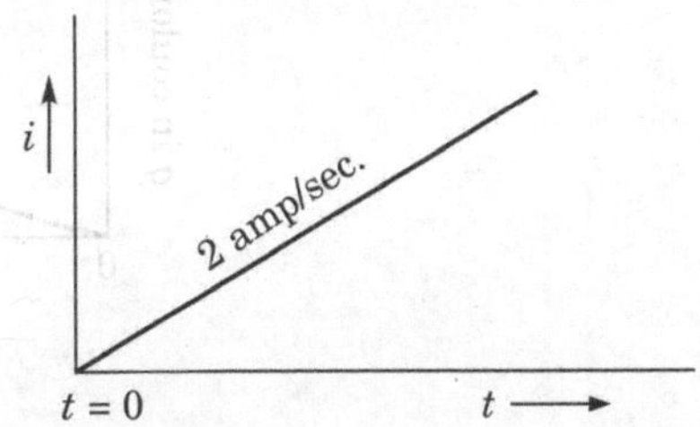

[**Ans.** (*i*) 4 weber-turns (*ii*) 4 weber turns/sec (*iii*) 16 coulombs]

1.11. In the given circuit, the switch S is closed at time $t = 0$. The current in the circuit is given by the equation : $t = 2\,(1 + e^{-t/2})$ amp. $t > 0$. At time $t = 2$ seconds, find : (*i*) value of current (*ii*) rate of change of current (*iii*) total flux linkages (*iv*) rate of change of flux linkages (*v*) voltage across the inductor (*vi*) energy stored in the magnetic field (*vii*) voltage across the resistor (*viii*) rate at which energy is being stored in the magnetic field of the inductor (*ix*) rate of dissipation of energy as heat (*x*) rate of supply of energy by the battery.

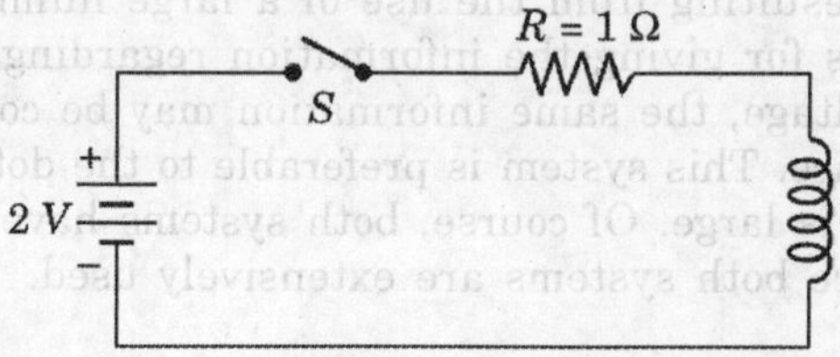

[**Ans.** (*i*) 1.264 amps (*ii*) 0.368 amp/sec (*iii*) 2.258 weber-turns (*iv*) 0.736 weber-turn/sec (*v*) 0.736 volt (*vi*) 1.6 joules (*vii*) 1.264 volts (*viii*) 0.93 watts (*ix*) 1.6 watts (*x*) 2.528 watts]

1.12. The following figure gives the variation of current i in an inductor of 1 henry. Plot the waveforms of charge stored in the magnetic field and the voltage across the inductor. Calculate voltage across the inductor and charge stored at time $t = 1, 2, 3$ and 4 seconds.

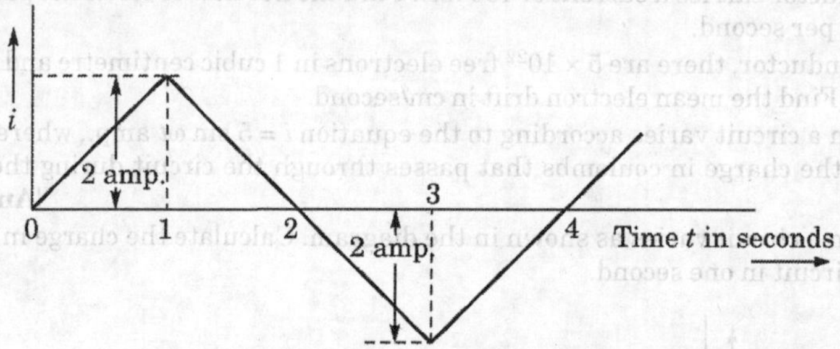

[**Ans.** (*i*) 2 volts ; change from + 2 volts to – 2 volts ; – 2 volts ; change from – 2 volts to + 8 volts (*ii*) 1, 2, 1, 0 coulomb]

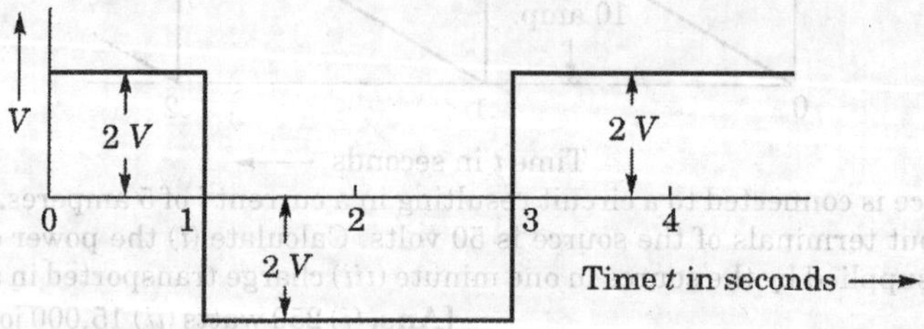

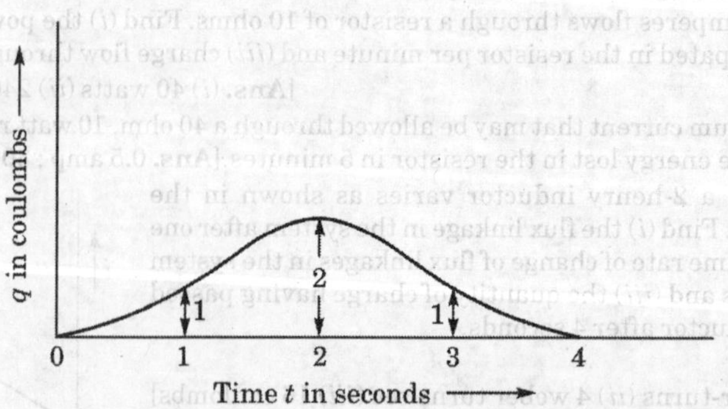

1.13. A condenser consists of two plates, one of which rotates so that the capacitance between the plates is given by the equation :

$$C = C_0 (1 - \cos \omega t)$$

A battery of constant voltage V volts is connected across the condenser. Find the expression for the current through the condenser.

[**Ans.** $i = VC_0 \, \omega \sin \omega t$]

1.14. A voltage $v = 10 \sin 2\pi \times 10^3 t$ is applied across a condenser C of 1 μF. Calculate (*i*) the amplitude of current through it (*ii*) maximum charge across the condenser (*iii*) maximum energy stored in the capacitor (*iv*) maximum power in the capacitor.

[**Ans.** (*i*) 62.8 mA (*ii*) 10^{-5} coulomb (*iii*) 5×10^{-5} joule (*iv*) 7.962×10^{-9} watt]

1.15. In the given circuit, the capacitor has been charged to a voltage of 10 volts and at time $t = 0$, switch S is closed. The resulting current in the circuit is known to be of the form $i = e^{-t}$ amp for $t > 0$. At time $t = 1$ sec, calculate : (*i*) rate of change of voltage v across capacitor C (*ii*) charge on the capacitor (*iii*) time rate of change of product Cv (*iv*) voltage across the condenser (*v*) energy stored in the electric field of the capacitor (*vi*) voltage across the resistor (*vii*) rate at which energy is being taken from the electric field of the capacitor (*viii*) rate at which energy is being dissipated as heat in the resistor.

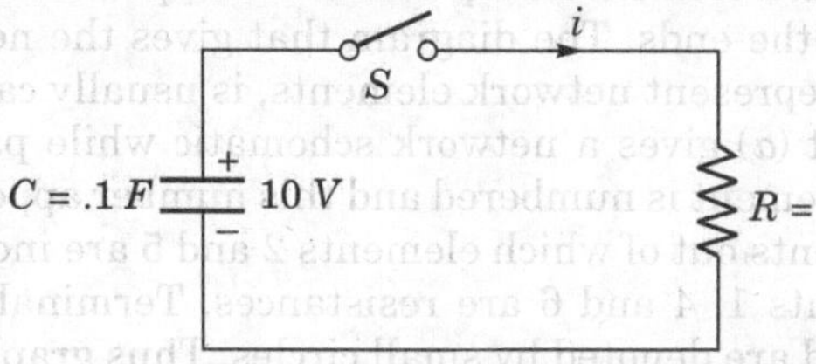

[**Ans.** (*i*) 3.68 volts/sec (*ii*) 0.632 coulomb (*iii*) 0.368 amp (*iv*) 0.32 volts (*v*) 1.997 joule (*vi*) 3.68 volts (*vii*) 1.37 watts (*viii*) 1.37 watts]

2

Network Topology or Network Geometry

2.1. The Graph of a Network

The network geometry or network topology concerns itself with the manner in which various elements in a network are ground and interconnected at their terminals and disregards entirely their values and types. Then each element irrespective of its type and value is simply represented by a line with small circles at the ends. The diagram that gives the network geometry and uses lines with dots at the ends to represent network elements, is usually called "a graph" of the given network. Thus in Fig. 2.1 part (*a*) gives a network schematic while part (*b*) gives its graph. To facilitate identification, each element is numbered and this number appears in the graph. Network of Fig. 2.1 (*a*) has in all 7 elements out of which elements 2 and 5 are inductances, elements, 3 and 7 are capacitances and elements 1, 4 and 6 are resistances. Terminals common to two or more elements are called "nodes" and are denoted by small circles. Thus graph of Fig. 2.1 (*b*) contains in all five nodes.

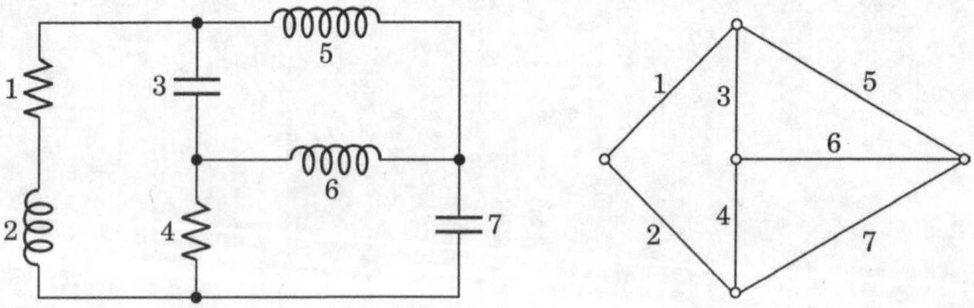

(*a*) Network schematic (*b*) Graph of the network

Fig. 2.1. A network schematic and its graph.

If network contains inductively coupled parts as in Fig. 2.2 (*a*) the corresponding graph shows these parts separately. Fig. 2.2 (*b*) gives the graph of network shown in Fig. 2.2 (*a*) and consists of two separate parts.

Usually separate parts are coalesced into one parts by permit-ting one node in each of the separate parts to become coincident as in Fig. 2.2 (*c*). By this measure, however, the constraint imposed is that the coalesced nodes have the same potential. This reduces the number of nodes and at the same time does not modify the currents and voltage in various branches.

2.2. "Tree" of a Network

The study of a graph of a network reveals the number of closed paths along which currents can flow. Such closed paths are essential for the flow of current. However, we may disallow flow of current by removing a few branches from the graph. The residual graph after removal of branches to disallow and closed path is called a "tree".

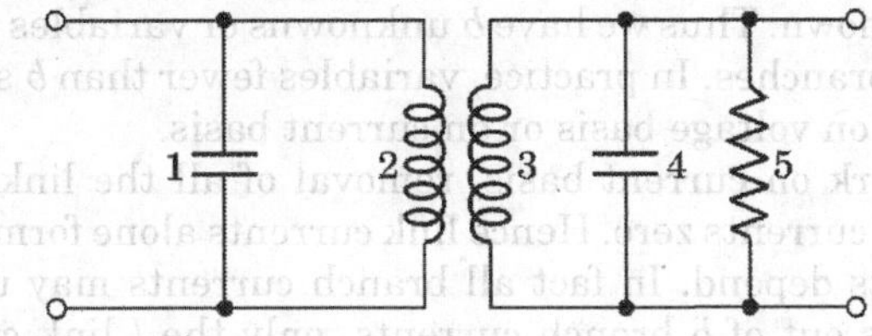

(*a*) Network schematic containing inductively coupled parts.

(*b*) Graph (*c*) Modified graph

Fig. 2.2. Schematic of a network containing inductively coupled parts and its graphs.

This removal of branches may be done in various ways. Fig. 2.3 (*a*) gives a graph while Fig 2.3 (*b*) and (*c*) give two of the numerous possible trees. In each tree, the residual branches so forming the tree

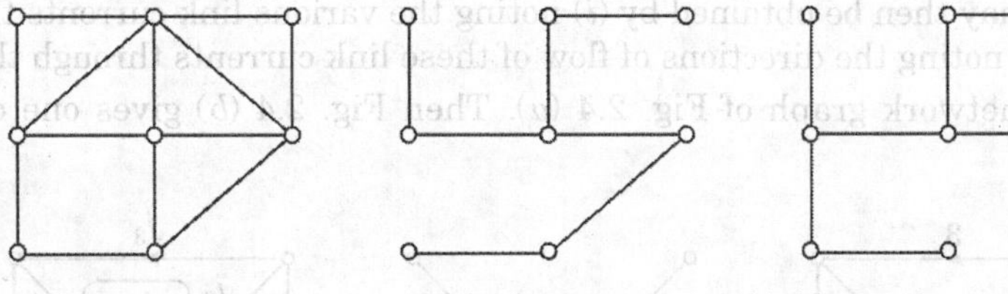

(*a*) A graph (*b*) A tree (*c*) Alternative tree

Fig. 2.3. A graph and two possible trees.

are just sufficient in number to connect all the nodes. Thus a tree may more precisely be defined as, any set of branches in the original graph, just sufficient in number to connect all the nodes.

If n_t denotes the total number of nodes, it may readily be seen that the minimum number of branches required to connect all the nodes is $(n_t - 1)$ and there results no closed paths. If there exist in the graph, branches exceeding $(n_t - 1)$, then there is bound to result a closed path. Thus we have,

$$n = n_t - 1 \quad \text{...(2.1)}$$

where n is the number of tree branches
and n_t is the total number of nodes.

The remaining branches are called "links". Let l be the number of links. Then

$$b = l + n \quad \text{...(2.2)}$$

where b is the total number of branches in the graph.

2.3. Network Variables

A network consists of not only the passive elements of various types but also sources of energy. A complete knowledge of the response of a network consists in knowing the currents and voltages in each of its branches. But each branch current is related to the branch voltage through the branch impedance. Thus branch current multiplied by branch impedance equals the branch voltage. Hence the response of a network is completely known if either all the branch currents or all the branch voltages are known. Thus we have b unknowns or variables in assessing the response of a network consisting of b branches. In practice, variables fewer than b suffice to characterise the network equilibrium, either on voltage basis or on current basis.

In analysing a network on current basis, removal of all the links destroys all the closed paths and renders all branch currents zero. Hence link currents alone form the independent current on which all branch currents depend. In fact all branch currents may uniquely be expressed in terms of link currents. Thus out of b branch currents, only the l link currents are independent while the remaining n tree branch currents form dependent currents. The minimum number of variables or unknowns involved in analysing a network on current basis is, therefore, l. The exact branches constituting the links vary with the choice of the tree.

Analysing a network on the voltage basis forcing the tree branch voltages to be zero makes all branch voltages zero. Hence tree branch voltages alone form the independent variables and it is possible to express uniquely the link voltages in terms of these tree branch voltages. Thus out of b branch voltages, only the n $(= n_t - 1)$ tree branch voltages are independent. The minimum number of variables or unknowns involved in the analysis of a network on the voltage basis is, therefore, n.

Thus we see that currents and voltages in all the branches of a network are completely known if we know l $(= b - n)$ link currents or n $(= b - l)$ tree branch voltages.

2.4. Link Currents ; Tie-set Schedules

To any tree of a graph, addition of a link result in a closed path or loop and a circulatory current or the "link current". There result, therefore, l link currents in a network. The current in any branch of the graph may then be obtained by (*i*) noting the various link currents that flow through the branch and (*ii*) by noting the directions of flow of these link currents through the branch.

Consider the network graph of Fig. 2.4 (*a*). Then Fig. 2.4 (*b*) gives one of the numerous possible trees.

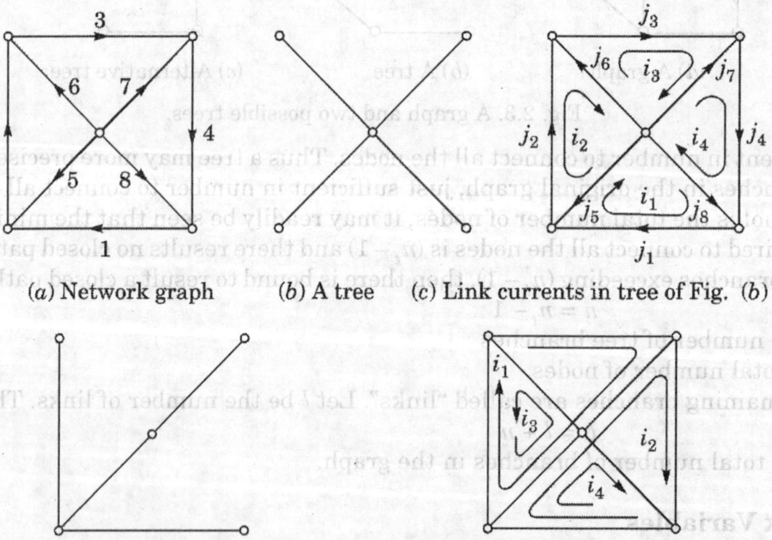

(*a*) Network graph (*b*) A tree (*c*) Link currents in tree of Fig. (*b*)

(*d*) Alternative tree (*e*) Link currents in trees of Fig. (*d*)

Fig. 2.4. Graph, tree and link currents of a network

The branch in the graph of Fig. 2.4 (*a*) have been numbered. Let j_1, j_2 ......, j_3 be the branch currents and let the arrow heads show the arbitrarily chosen directions of flow of these currents. In the tree of Fig. 2.4 (*b*) branches, 5, 6, 7 and 8 constitute the tree branches while branches 1, 2, 3 and

4 form the links. Addition of link 1 results in the formation of a closed loop and flow of link current i_1 shown in Fig. 2.4 (*c*). This link current i_1 traverses the branches 1, 5 and 8. These set of branches forming the closed loop on which the link current circulates, is called a "tie-set". The arrow head shows the direction of link current i_1. This direction is so chosen that the link current i_1 is confluent with current j_1 in the link 1.

Similarly addition of links 2, 3 and 4 result in flow of link currents i_1, i_3 and i_4 respectively. These link currents i_2, i_3 and i_4 are also confluent with the branch currents j_2, j_3 and j_4 respectively. Study of Fig. 2.4 (*c*) reveals that the branch current j_1 is identical with the link current i_1. The other branch currents j_2, j_3 and j_4 are similarly identical with the respective link currents i_2, i_3 and i_4.

Thus, we have

$$j_1 = i_1 \,;\, j_2 = i_2 \,;\, j_3 = i_3$$

and $$j_4 = i_4 \qquad ...(2.3)$$

The remaining branch currents may as well be expressed in terms of link currents i_1 to i_4. Thus a study of Fig. 2.4 (*a*) and (*c*) reveals the following relations :

$$j_5 = i_2 - i_1 \qquad ...(2.4\ a)$$

$$j_6 = i_3 - i_2 \qquad ...(2.4\ b)$$

$$j_7 = i_4 - i_3 \qquad ...(2.4\ c)$$

$$j_8 = i_1 - i_4 \qquad ...(2.4\ d)$$

Fig. 2.4 (*d*) shows another tree. Here branches 1, 2, 5 and 7 form the tree branches whereas branches 3, 4, 6 and 8 form the links. Addition of link 3 results in formation of a closed loop and flow of link current i_1 as shown in Fig. 2.4 (*e*). This link current i_1 is chosen to be confluent with the branch current j_3. Similarly addition of links 4, 6 and 8 result in flow of link currents i_2, i_3 and i_4 respectively which are confluent with branch currents j_4, j_6 and j_8 respectively. Study of Fig. 2.4 (*a*) and (*e*) reveals that currents i_1, i_2, i_3 and i_4 are identical with the branch currents j_3, j_4, j_6 and j_8 respectively.

Thus we have

$$j_3 = i_1 \qquad ...(2.5\ a)$$

$$j_4 = i_2 \qquad ...(2.5\ b)$$

$$j_6 = i_3 \qquad ...(2\text{-}5\ c)$$

$$j_8 = i_4 \qquad ...(2.5\ d)$$

The other tree branch currents may also be expressed in terms of link currents. Thus a study of Fig. 2.4 (*a*) and (*e*) reveals the following relations :

$$j_1 = i_2 + i_4 \qquad ...(2.6\ a)$$

$$j_2 = i_1 - i_3 \qquad ...(2.6\ b)$$

$$j_5 = i_1 - i_2 - i_3 - i_4 \qquad ...(2.6\ c)$$

and $$j_7 = i_2 - i_1 \qquad ...(2.6\ d)$$

This method of writing the tree branch currents in terms of the link currents may become very tedious and confusing if the network geometry is complex. For a given network tree, a systematic way of indicating the links is through use of a schedule. Table 2.1 gives the schedule for graph of Fig. 2.4 (*a*) using tree of Fig. 2.4 (*b*) and hence for the links shown in Fig. 2.4 (*c*).

Table 2.1

Tie-set Schedule

Link No.	*Branch number*							
	1	*2*	*3*	*4*	*5*	*6*	*7*	*8*
1	+ 1	0	0	0	− 1	0	0	+ 1
2	0	+ 1	0	0	+ 1	− 1	0	0
3	0	0	+ 1	0	0	+ 1	− 1	0
4	0	0	0	+ 1	0	0	+ 1	− 1

The link numbers 1, 2, 3 and 4 entered in the first column pertain to the four loops formed by adding the links 1, 2, 3 and 4 respectively to cause the four link currents i_1, i_2, i_3, i_4. Link current i_1 flows through the set branches 1, 5 and 8 forming a tie-set and does not flow through the branches 2, 3, 4, 6, and 7. Hence in the first row, enter zeros below the branch numbers 2, 3, 4, 6 and 7. Further link current i_1 is confluent with branch currents j_1 and j_8 and counterfluent with the branch current j_5. This is indicated by entering in the first row symbol + 1 below branch numbers 1 and 8 and entering symbol number − 1 below branch number 5. Similarly link current i_2 is confluent with branch currents j_2 and j_5 and is counterfluent with branch current j_6. Hence in the second row of the schedule, + 1 is entered below branch numbers 2 and 5 and − 1 is entered below branch number 6. Zeros are entered below branch numbers 3, 4, 7 and 8 since the link current i_2 does not flow through these branches. Similar entries are made in rows 3 and 4 for link currents i_3 and i_4. Each row of the schedule indicates elements of one tie set, *i.e.* the set of branches over which the corresponding link current flows. The entire schedule consisting of rows corresponding to different tie-sets is called a "tie-set schedule".

Having written the schedule, we can now use this schedule to write with no effort the equations giving the branch currents in terms of the link currents, by simply reading the columns of the schedule. Thus column 1 gives equation for j_1 in terms of link currents. In column 1, there is only one entry namely + 1 in row 1. Hence the desired equation is :

$$j_1 = i_1 \quad \text{...(2.7 a)}$$

Similarly reading the other columns, we get

$$j_2 = i_2 \quad \text{...(2.7 b)}$$
$$j_3 = i_3 \quad \text{...(2.7 c)}$$
$$j_4 = i_4 \quad \text{...(2.7 d)}$$
$$j_5 = -i_1 + i_2 \quad \text{...(2.7 e)}$$
$$j_6 = -i_2 + i_3 \quad \text{...(2.7 f)}$$
$$J_7 = -i_3 + i_4 \quad \text{...(2.7 g)}$$
$$j_8 = -i_4 + i_1 \quad \text{...(2.7 h)}$$

Equations (2.7) agree with equation (2.4).

This schedule has been constructed by rows, *i.e.* by noting the geometrical structure for the closed paths for various link currents. The results obtained is the set of equations giving branch currents in terms of link currents. It is also possible to construct the schedule by columns, *i.e.* by using the set of equations expressing branch currents in terms of link currents obtained by inspection. In that case, by reading the rows of the schedule, geometrical structure of the closed path traversed by the link currents may be obtained. Thus this tie-set schedule provides a compact and effective means of depicting the geometrical structure of the closed path as well as the algebraic relations giving the branch currents in terms of link currents.

Equations (2.7) give eight equations in four variables i_1, i_2, i_3 and i_4. This appears to be inconsistent. However, it may readily be seen that out of these eight equations, four equations namely equations 2.7 (*a*) to (*d*) are identities and there are only four independent equations namely equations 2.7 (*e*) to (*h*) in four variables. Thus equations (2.7) form a consistent set.

Thus ignoring Eqs. 2.7 (*a*) to (*d*), the remaining Eqs. 2.7 (*e*) to 2.7 (*h*) may be separated out to form an independent sub-set as given below :

$$j_5 = -i_1 + i_2 \quad \text{...(2.8 a)}$$

$$j_6 = -i_2 + i_3 \quad \text{...(2.8 b)}$$

$$j_7 = -i_3 + i_4 \quad \text{...(2.8 c)}$$

$$j_8 = -i_4 + i_1 \quad \text{...(2.8 d)}$$

Equations (2.8) may be solved to express link current i_1 to i_4 in terms of branch currents j_5 to j_8.

If the network is laid upon a plane or spherical surface without crossed branches. Then any tie-set forms a boundary dividing the entire network into two portions. Now if the branches forming this tie-set shrink longitudinally so as to reduce ultimately to a dot, then the network is a sort of "tied off' in the same manner as a fish net tied off by a draw string and the two portions of the total network are effectively separated except for a common node. It is this interpretation that has led to the use of the tie-set.

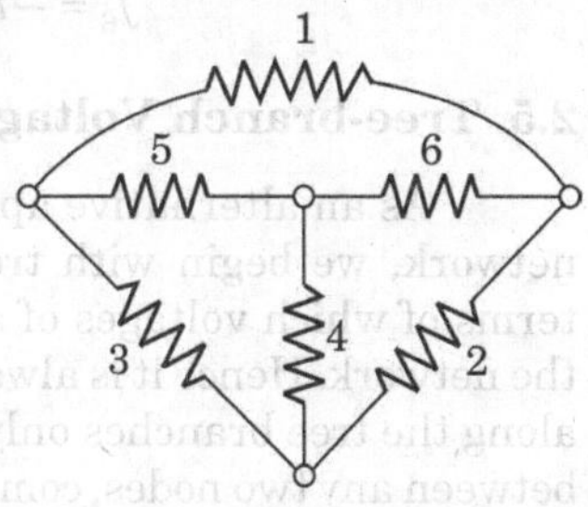

Example 2.1. *For the given network, draw the graph and a tree. Show the link currents on the graph and write the tie-set schedule for the tree. Write the equations for the branch currents and in terms of the link currents and write separately the independent equations.*

Solution.

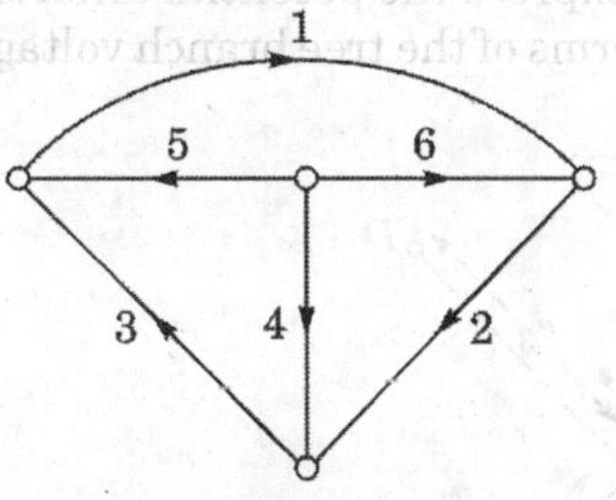

Graph

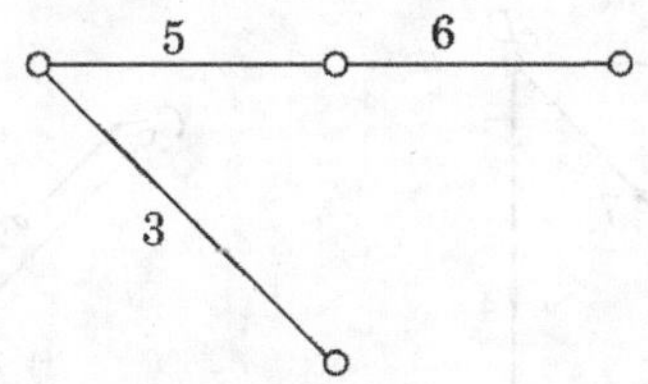

Tree

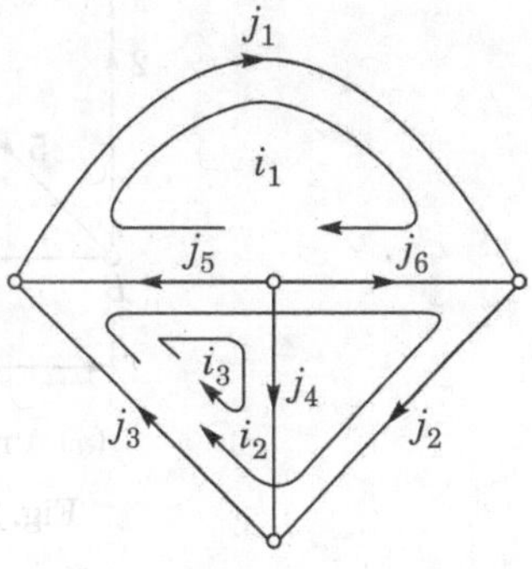

n_t = number of nodes = 4

n = number of tree branches = $n_t - 1 = 3$

b = total number of branches = 6

l = number of links = number of independent loop currents $= b - n = 6 - 3 = 3$

In the chosen tree, the links taken in order of branches 1, 2 and 4.

Tie-set Schedule

Link No.	Branch No.					
	1	*2*	*3*	*4*	*5*	*6*
1	+1	0	0	0	+1	−1
2	0	+1	+1	0	−1	+1
3	0	0	+1	+1	−1	0

The equations giving the branch currents in terms of independent link currents may be read from the rows of this schedule. These are :

$$j_1 = i_1$$
$$j_2 = i_2$$
$$j_3 = i_2 + i_3$$
$$j_4 = i_3$$
$$j_5 = i_1 - i_2 - i_3$$
$$j_6 = -i_1 + i_2.$$

Out of these equations the following three equations form identities :

$$j_1 = i_1 ; j_2 = i_2 ; j_4 = i_3.$$

The remaining equations are independent. There are :

$$j_3 = i_1 + i_3$$
$$j_5 = i_1 - i_2 - i_3$$
$$j_6 = -i_1 + i_2.$$

2.5. Tree-branch Voltages ; Cut-set Schedule

As an alternative approach to the problem of finding the branch voltages and currents in a network, we begin with treating the tree branch voltages as a set of independent variables in terms of which voltages of all branches may be expressed. Tree branches connect all the nodes in the network. Hence it is always possible to trace the path from one node to another node by travelling along the tree branches only. Accordingly it is possible to uniquely express the potential difference between any two nodes, commonly called the "node-pair voltage" in terms of the tree branch voltages.

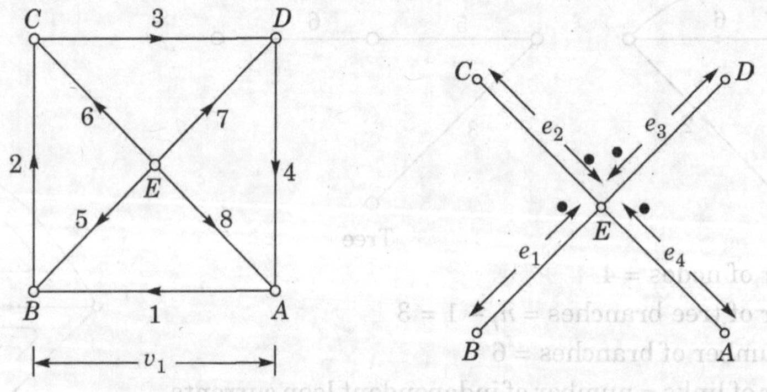

(a) A network graph (b) A tree

Fig. 2.5. A network graph, tree and tree-branch voltages.

We again consider the network graph of Fig. 2.4 (*a*) and the tree of Fig. 2.4 (*b*) redrawn in Fig. 2.5. Let v_1, v_2, ..., v_8 be the voltages of branches 1, 2, ..., 8 respectively. Current i_1 flows through branch 1 to make node *A* positive with respect to the node *B*. Hence we choose to designate v_1 as the voltage of node *A* with respect to that of node *B*. Potentials v_2, ..., v_8 are similarly chosen considering the assumed direction of flow of the pertinent branch currents. Branches 5, 6, 7 and 8 constitute the tree branches and the voltages v_5, v_6, v_7 and V_8 form a set of independent variables. In order to distinguish these from dependent branch voltages, let these be designated as e_1, e_2, e_3 and e_4 respectively. Thus, we have

$$\left.\begin{aligned} e_1 &= v_5 \\ e_2 &= v_6 \\ e_3 &= v_7 \\ \text{and} \quad e_4 &= u_8 \end{aligned}\right\} \qquad \text{...(2.9)}$$

The remaining branch voltages *i.e.* the link voltages may now be expressed in terms of the tree branch voltages e_1, e_2, e_3 and e_4. Thus inspection of Fig. 2.5 (*a*) yields,

$$v_1 = e_1 - e_4 \qquad \text{...(2.10 a)}$$

$$v_2 = e_2 - e_1 \qquad \text{...(2.10 b)}$$

$$v_3 = e_3 - e_2 \qquad \text{...(2.10 c)}$$

and

$$v_4 = e_4 - e_3 \qquad \text{...(2.10 d)}$$

In case of complicated network, this method of writing the branch voltage in terms of tree-branch voltages may become quite involved and confusing. Hence we may, as in the case of analysis on the link current basis, write a schedule, referred to as the cut-set schedule. Table 2.2 gives the cut-set schedule for the graph of Fig. 2.5 (*a*) and the tree of Fig. 2.5 (*b*).

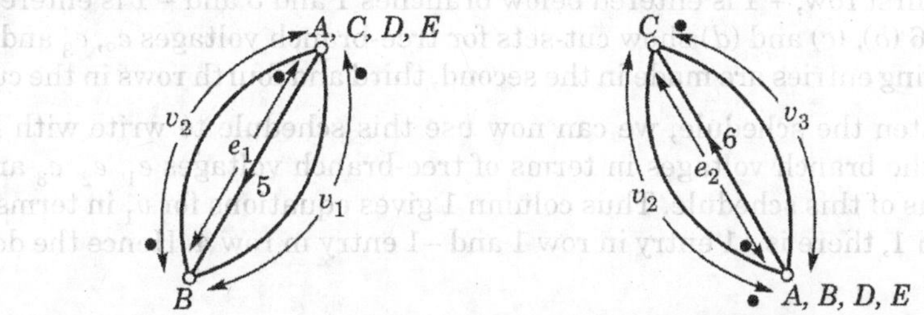

(*a*) Cut-set of tree-branch voltage e_1. (*b*) Cut-set of tree-branch voltage e_2.

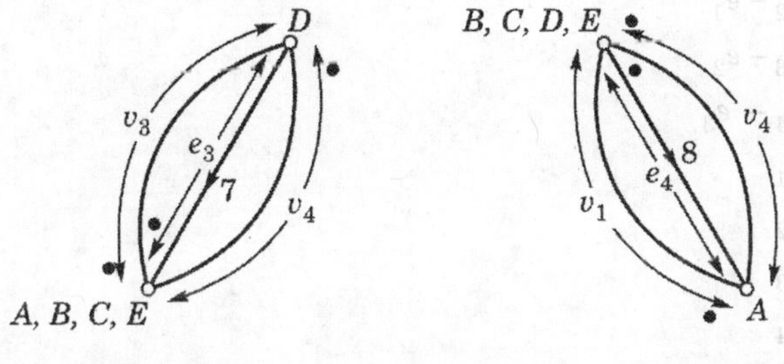

(*c*) Cut-set of tree-branch voltage e_3. (*d*) Cut-set of tree-branch voltage e_4.

Fig. 2.6. Cut-set for tree-branch voltages in the graph of Fig. 2.5 (*a*).

The tree branch voltage numbers 1, 2, 3 and 4 entered in the first column of the schedule pertain to the four branches 5, 6, 7 and 8 respectively. In order to fill the first row, *i.e.* the row corresponding to the tree-branch voltage e_1, we consider all tree-branches to be short circuited except the branch 5 corresponding to the tree-branch voltage e_1. This act simultaneously short circuits, links 3 and 4 as well and the tree of Fig. 2.5 (*a*) reduces to the form shown in Fig. 2.6 (*a*). The remaining set of branches referred to as a cut set, is analogous to a tie set in the analysis on the current basis.

Table 2.2
Cut-set Schedule

Tree branch voltage	*Branch number*							
No.	*1*	*2*	*3*	*4*	*5*	*6*	*7*	*8*
1	+ 1	− 1	0	0	+ 1	0	0	0
2	0	+ 1	− 1	0	0	+ 1	0	0
3	0	0	+ 1	− 1	0	0	+ 1	0
4	− 1	0	0	+ 1	0	0	0	+ 1

Thus in the first row, all entries will be zero except those for branches 1, 2 and 5. A study of Fig. 2.6 (*a*) reveals that v_1 and v_5 have the same polarity as e_1, while v_2 has the opposite polarity. Accordingly in the first row, + 1 is entered below branches 1 and 5 and – 1 is entered below branch 2. Similarly Fig. 2.6 (*b*), (*c*) and (*d*) show cut-sets for tree-branch voltages e_2, e_3 and e_4 respectively and the corresponding entries are made in the second, third and fourth rows in the cut-set schedule.

Having written the schedule, we can now use this schedule to write with little effort the quotations giving the branch voltages in terms of tree-branch voltages e_1, e_2, e_3 and e_4 by simply reading the columns of this schedule. Thus column 1 gives equations for v_1 in terms of tree-branch voltages. In column 1, there is +1 entry in row 1 and –1 entry in row 4. Hence the desired equation is :

$$v_1 = e_1 - e_4 \qquad ...(2.11\ a)$$

Similarly reading the other columns of the schedule, we get

$$v_2 = e_2 - e_1 \qquad ...(2.11\ b)$$

$$v_3 = e_3 - e_2 \qquad ...(2.11\ c)$$

$$v_4 = e_4 - e_3 \qquad ...(2.11\ d)$$

$$v_5 = e_1 \qquad ...(2.11\ e)$$

$$v_6 = e_2 \qquad ...(2.11\ f)$$

$$v_7 = e_3 \qquad ...(2.11\ g)$$

$$v_8 = e_4 \qquad ...(2.11\ h)$$

Equations (2.11) agree with equations (2.9) and (2.10).

This cut-set schedule has been constructed by rows, *i.e.* by noting the group of branches that get energized when any particular tree-branch voltage is the only non-zero one among all the tree-branch voltages. The result obtainable is the set of equations giving branch voltages in terms of tree-branch voltages. It is also possible, to construct this schedule by columns, *i.e.* by using the set of equations giving branch voltages in terms of the tree-branch voltages obtained by inspection. In that case, by reading the rows of the schedule information regarding the branches energized by tree-branch voltages may be obtained. Whatever be the method of construction, this cut-set schedule provides a compact and effective means of depicting the cut-set, *i.e.* branches energized by different tree-branch voltages and also the algebraic relations giving the branch voltages in terms of the tree branch voltages.

Equations (2.11) obtained by reading the columns of this schedule are eight in number. But there are only 4 independent vari-ables, namely the tree-branch voltages e_1, e_2, e_3 and e_4. This appears to be inconsistent. But it may readily be seen that out of these 8 equations, four equations, namely equations 2.11 (*e*) to (*h*) are identities whereas only four equations namely Eqs. 2.11 (*a*) to (*d*) are independent. This is consistent with the number of independent variables.

If all but one of the tree-branches are short circuited, then all the nodes in the network get divided into the groups ; all the nodes in one group concentrate at one end of the non-short circuited tree-branch while all the nodes in the other group concentrate at the other end of this branch. If now we hold these two groups of nodes separately, one in each hand, and pull our hands apart, then the residual branches joining the two groups get stretched if considered to possess elasticity. These stretched branches constitute the pertinent "cut-set". If the stretched branches are cut, the original network graph gets cut into two parts, one in each hand. This interpretation has led to the use of name "cut-set".

Example 2.2. *For the given network, draw the graph and a tree. Select suitable tree-branch voltages and write the cut-set schedule. Write equations for the branch voltages in terms of tree branch voltages.*

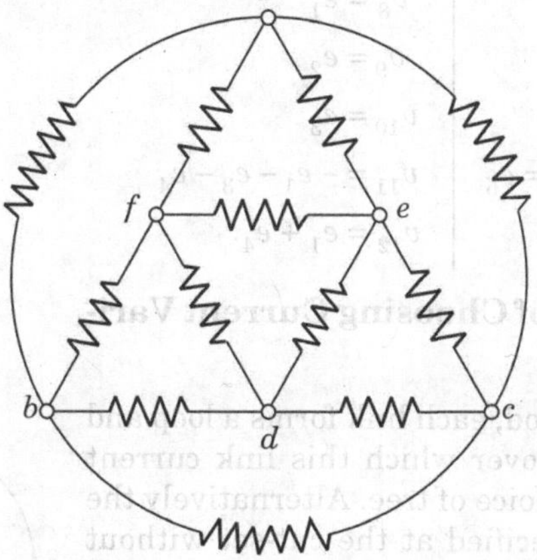

Solution.

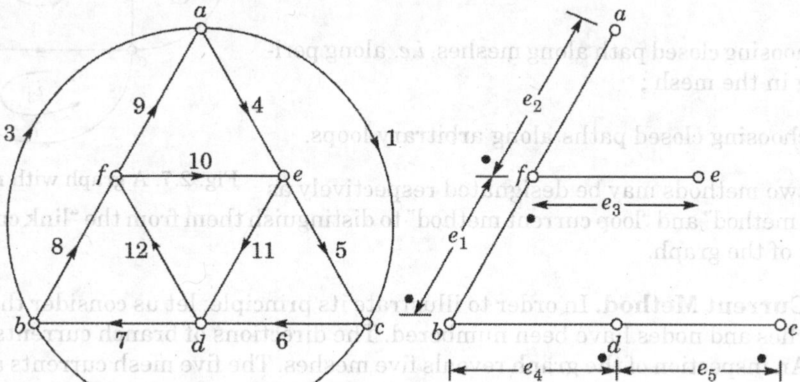

Graph Tree

n_t = number of nodes = 6

n = number of tree branches = 6 – 1 = 5

Cut-set Schedule

Tree-branch voltage number	*Branch number*											
	1	*2*	*3*	*4*	*5*	*6*	*7*	*8*	*9*	*10*	*11*	*12*
1	−1	0	1	0	−1	0	0	1	0	0	−1	1
2	−1	0	1	−1	0	0	0	0	1	0	0	0
3	0	0	0	1	−1	0	0	0	0	1	−1	0
4	−1	1	0	0	−1	0	1	0	0	0	−1	1
5	−1	1	0	0	−1	1	0	0	0	0	0	

Desired equations are :

$v_1 = -e_1 - e_2 - e_4 - e_5$	$v_7 = e_4$
$v_2 = e_4 + e_5$	$v_8 = e_1$
$v_3 = e_1 + e_2$	$v_9 = e_2$
$v_4 = -e_2 + e_3$	$v_{10} = e_3$
$v_5 = -e_1 - e_3 - e_4 = e_5$	$v_{11} = -e_1 - e_3 - e_4$
$v_6 = e_5$	$v_{12} = e_1 + e_4$

2.6. Mesh Current Method of Choosing Current Variables

In the link current method, each link forms a loop and the tie-set or the closed path over which this link current flows is determined from the choice of tree. Alternatively the set of closed paths may be specified at the cut-set without reference to a tree. The choice of closed paths may be done in two ways :

(*i*) by choosing closed path along meshes, *i.e.* along periphery opening in the mesh ;

(*ii*) by choosing closed paths along arbitrary loops.

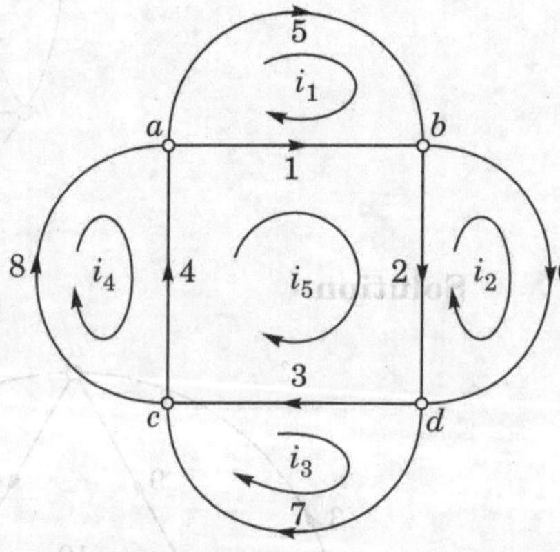

Fig. 2.7. A graph with mesh currents.

These two methods may be designated respectively as "mesh current method" and "loop current method" to distinguish them from the "link current method" using the tree of the graph.

Mesh Current Method. In order to illustrate its principle, let us consider the graph of Fig. 2.7. The branches and nodes have been numbered. The directions of branch currents are shown by arrow heads. An inspection of the graph reveals five meshes. The five mesh currents are designated i_1 to i_5 and the direction of all mesh currents have been arbitrarily chosen as clockwise. Tie-set schedule may be constructed for this choice of mesh currents in the same general way as done for link currents. This is given below :

Table 2.3

Tie-set Schedule

Mesh No.	*Branch number*							
	1	*2*	*3*	*4*	*5*	*6*	*7*	*8*
1	– 1	0	0	0	1	0	0	0
2	0	– 1	0	0	0	1	0	0
3	0	0	– 1	0	0	0	1	0
4	0	0	0	– 1	0	0	0	1
5	1	1	1	1	0	0	0	0

The columns of this schedule yield,

$$\left.\begin{aligned} j_1 &= -i_1 + i_5 \\ j_2 &= -i_2 + i_5 \\ j_3 &= -i_3 + i_5 \\ j_4 &= -i_4 + i_5 \\ j_5 &= i_1 \\ j_6 &= i_2 \\ j_7 &= i_3 \\ j_8 &= i_4 \end{aligned}\right\} \qquad \text{...(2.12)}$$

These same equations could, of course, be written straightway by inspection through noting the mesh currents that flow through each of the different branches. Thus through branch 1, current i_5 flows in the same direction as j_1 while mesh current i_1 flows in the opposite direction. Hence, $j_1 = -i_1 + i_5$. This agrees with Eqs. (2.12). Similarly we may obtain expression for branch currents j_2 to j_8.

Thus we see that we may obtain a set of equations relating the branch currents with mesh currents without the aid of a tree. But in a more complex network, the use of a tree and link currents is very helpful.

2.7. Loop Current Method

The independent currents, in terms of which branch currents may be expressed, may alternatively be chosen as currents flowing along arbitrarily chosen loops. Such loop currents must, of course be chosen carefully to be sufficient in number and should at the same time be independent. This may be ensured by the following two means :

(*i*) Ensuring that all branches have participated in forming the closed paths for the loop currents. This requirement ensures the sufficiency of loop currents but does not ensure independence of loop currents.

(*ii*) Ensuring that successive closed paths selected for different loop currents involve at least one branch that is not part of any of the previously selected paths.

Before accepting any choice of loop currents as adequate and independent it may also be verified that the number of loops is equal to $(b - n)$ where b is the total number of branches in the network and n is the number of node-pair, *i.e.* $n = (n_t - 1)$. Here n_t gives total number of nodes.

It is evident that the method of choosing the set of loops is not by trial and error. The choice is not evident by inspection. However there exists a straight forward procedure for checking a given choice. Thus the chosen set of loops is independent "if the l rows of the associated tie-set schedule are independent".

This condition is satisfied "if it is possible to find in this schedule, a subset of l independent columns, *i.e.* l independent equations among those expressing branch currents in terms of loop currents"

The simplest means of making this check among the columns is to pick-up those columns which corresponds to the links of any three. If these are independent then the loops chosen are independent.

The chosen set of equations will be independent if they have unique solutions. This may usually be found by inspections. Alternatively we assess the determinant of these equations. This determinant must be non-zero if the equations are to be independent.

Thus the condition for independence of arbitrarily selected set of closed paths is "non-zero value of determinant formed from the subset of columns corresponding to the links of a chosen tree".

As an illustration consider the network graph of Fig. 2.7. The arbitrarily chosen loop currents are shown in Fig. 2.8. The choice of loop currents is made in such a way that (*i*) all branches have been included (*ii*) at least one new branch is included in each loop and (*iii*) number of loops is equal to $l = (6 - n) = 5$.

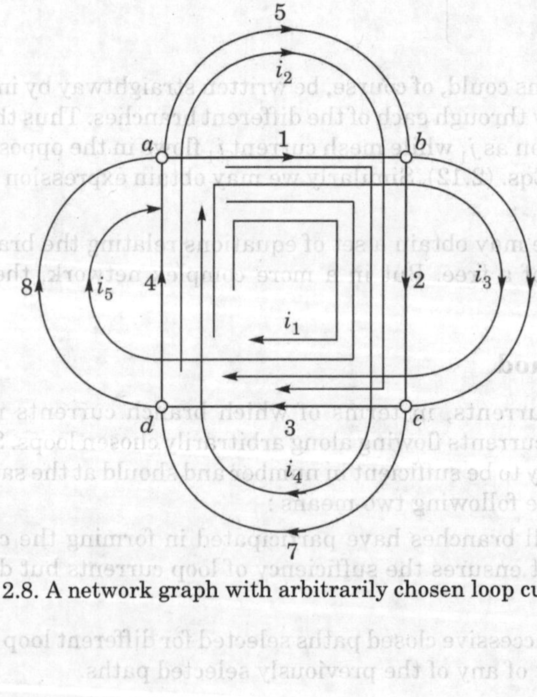

Fig. 2.8. A network graph with arbitrarily chosen loop currents.

Table 2.4
Tie-set Schedule

Loop No.	*Branch number* 1	2	3	4	5	6	7	8
1	1	1	1	1	0	0	0	0
2	0	1	1	1	1	0	0	0
3	1	0	1	1	0	1	0	0
4	1	1	0	1	0	0	1	0
5	1	1	1	0	0	0	0	1

The equations giving branch currents in terms of loop currents are :

$$\left.\begin{aligned} j_1 &= i_1 + i_3 + i_4 + i_5 & j_5 &= i_2 \\ j_2 &= i_1 + i_2 + i_4 + i_5 & j_6 &= i_3 \\ j_3 &= i_1 + i_2 + i_3 + i_5 & j_7 &= i_4 \\ j_4 &= i_1 + i_2 + i_3 + i_4 & j_8 &= i_5 \end{aligned}\right\} \quad ...(2.13)$$

In order to verify the independence of loop currents, let us pick up the link currents corresponding to any tree. Let the tree be as shown in Fig. 2.9. Then branch numbers, 2, 5, 6, 7 and 8 constitute the links. The corresponding equations picked up from Eqs. (2.13) are :

$$\left.\begin{aligned} j_2 &= i_1 + i_2 + i_4 + i_5 \\ j_5 &= i_2 \\ j_6 &= i_3 \\ j_7 &= i_4 \\ j_8 &= i_5 \end{aligned}\right\} \quad ...(2.14)$$

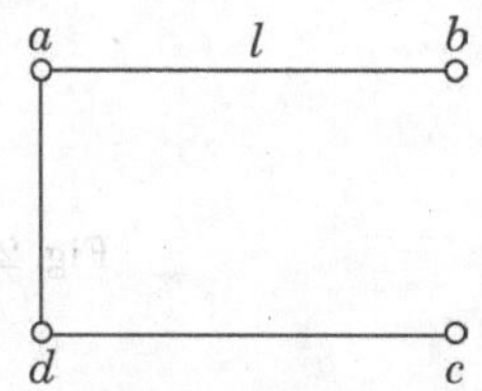

Fig. 2.9. Tree of graph of Fig. 2.8.

Inspection of Eqs. (2.14) indicates that these equations are independent. Hence the loop currents are independent.

2.8. Node Pair Voltage Method

One method of choosing voltage variables has already been discussed. In this method, the tree branch voltages themselves were treated as the independent voltage variables. Alternatively we may use arbitrarily chosen node pair voltages as the voltage variables without any reference to the tree.

To illustrate the principle of this method, let us again consider the network graph of Fig. 2.7 redrawn in Fig. 2.10 (*a*). The node-pair voltage variables are indicated in Fig. 2.10 (*b*) by arrows. The number of variables so chosen obviously must be $n = n_t - 1$, where n_t is the total number of nodes. Thus in the network graph under consideration, the node pair voltages are three in number and are designated as e_1, e_2 and e_3. Here e_1 is the voltage of node *a* with respect to that of node *d*. Similarly e_2 is the voltage of node *c* with respect to that of node *d* and e_3 is voltage of node *b* with respect to that of node *c*.

With this choice of node-pair voltage as the voltage variables, we construct the cut-set schedule given in Table 2.5. In this schedule, an additional column has been provided to give the picked-up nodes. Thus with reference to Fig. 2.7, if e_1 is regarded as the only non-zero node pair voltage, nodes *b*, *c* and *d* coincide at the tail end of e_1, whereas node *a* alone occupies the tip end. Hence cut-set 1 is found through picking up node *'a'* alone with all other nodes considered to be fixed and noting the set of branches in the network that get stretched. In this case, the branches so stretched are 1, 4, 5 and 8. Node pair voltage e_1 tends to send current through these branches diverging from node 'a'. But in Fig. 2.7, assumed positive directions of currents in branches 1 and 5 are divergent from node 'a' while those of currents in branches 4 and 8 are convergent. Hence in the first row, we enter the symbol

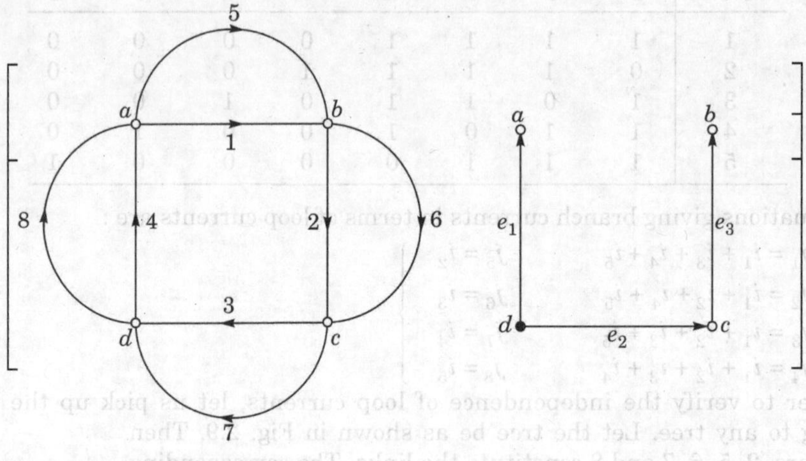

(*a*) Network graph (*b*) Arbitrarily chosen node pair voltages

Fig. 2.10. Network graph and arbitrarily chosen node-pair voltages.

Table 2.5
Cut-set Schedule

Node-pair	*Branch Number*								*Picked-up*
No.	*1*	*2*	*3*	*4*	*5*	*6*	*7*	*8*	*Nodes*
1	+ 1	0	0	–1	+1	0	0	– 1	*a*
2	0	– 1	+ 1	0	0	– 1	+ 1	0	*b*
3	– 1	+ 1	0	0	– 1	+ 1	0	0	*c*

$$v_5 = v_1 = e_1 - e_2 \quad \text{...(2.15 a)}$$

$$v_6 = v_2 = -e_2 + e_3 \quad \text{...(2.15 b)}$$

$$v_7 = v_3 = e_2 \quad \text{...(2.15 c)}$$

$$v_8 = v_4 = -e_1 \quad \text{...(2.15 d)}$$

+ 1 below branch numbers 1 and 5, and the symbol – 1 below branch numbers 4 and 8. All other entries are zero. Similar procedure is adopted for rows 2 and 3. Reading the columns of this cut-set schedule, we get

Now we select any three independent equations from this group and solve them. This selection may be done by inspection. However, the quickest and surest way to spot an independent subset among Eqs. (2.15) is the selection of tree in the associated network graph. The remaining equations will then yield the expressions for the link voltages in terms of the tree branch voltages.

2.9. Node-to-datum Voltage Method

This method consists of selected an arbitrarily selected node as the reference node and selecting as variables the potential of all other nodes with respect to the potential of this reference node. These voltages of all other nodes with respect to the reference or datum node are referred to as "node-to-datum" voltages or simply node voltages. This method of selecting node voltage variables is analogous to the method of selecting mesh current variables.

To illustrate the principle of this method, we again refer to the network graph of Fig. 2.10 (*a*) redrawn in Fig. 2.11 (*a*). The node-to- datum voltages are indicated in Fig. 2.11 *(b)* by arrows. Since node-to-datum voltage arrows form a tree like structure, these node-to-datum voltages always form an independent set.

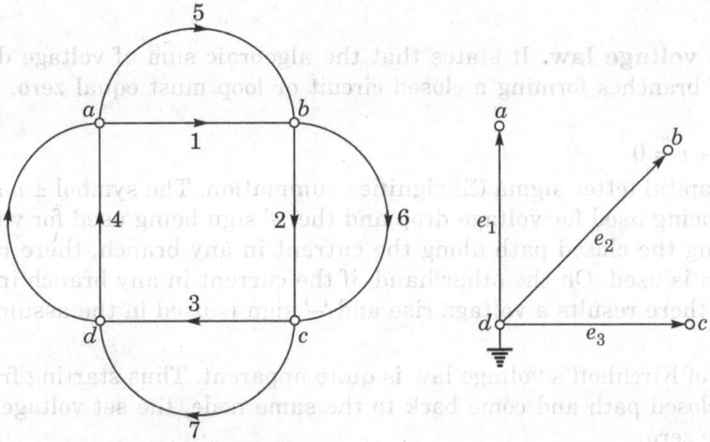

(*a*) Network graph (*b*) Node-to-datum voltages variables

Fig. 2.11. A network graph and node-to-datum voltage variables.

The cut-set schedule is constructed in the usual manner. In this method, however, it is relatively easy to find a cut-set since setting all but one node voltage to zero causes all the nodes except the pertinent node coincide at the datum. The cut-set schedule so formed is shown in Table 2.6.

Table 2.6

Cut-set Schedule

Node No.	*Branch Number*								*Picked-up Nodes*
	1	*2*	*3*	*4*	*5*	*6*	*7*	*8*	
1	+ 1	0	0	− 1	+ 1	0	0	− 1	*a*
2	− 1	+ 1	0	0	− 1	+ 1	0	0	*b*
3	0	− 1	+ 1	0	0	− 1	+ 1	0	*c*

Reading the columns of this schedule, we get

$$v_5 = v_1 = e_1 - e_2 \quad ...(2.16\ a)$$

$$v_6 = v_2 = e_2 - e_3 \quad ...(2.16\ b)$$

$$v_7 = v_3 = e_3 \quad ...(2.16\ c)$$

$$v_8 = v_4 = - e_1 \quad ...(2.16\ d)$$

We have to select from Eqs. (2.16) a subset of 3 independent equations. For this we use a tree and select out of Eqs. (2.16), equations giving voltages of tree branches. The solution of this independent subset gives values of node voltages e_1, e_2 and e_3 in terms of tree branch voltages. The remaining of Eqs. (2.16) then yield the expressions for the link voltages in terms of the tree-branch voltages.

2.10. The Kirchhoff's Laws

Having arrived at the set of independent variables on either the voltage basis or the current basis, we proceed to express the equilibrium of the network in terms of these. To achieve this we make use of Kirchhoff's voltage and current laws : Kirchhoff's voltage law is used when currents are chosen as variables while Kirchhoff's current law is used when voltages are chosen as variables.

Kirchhoff's voltage law. It states that the algebraic sum of voltage drops (or voltage rises) in any set of branches forming a closed circuit or loop must equal zero. Symbolically we write:

$$\Sigma + v = 0 \qquad ...(2.17)$$

The Greek capital letter sigma (Σ) signifies summation. The symbol $\pm\, v$ signifies voltage drops, the '+' sign being used for voltage drop and the '–' sign being used for voltage rise. Thus while we move along the closed path along the current in any branch, there results a voltage drop so that '+' sign is used. On the other hand, if the current in any branch in opposite to the direction of travel, there results a voltage rise and '–' sign is used in the assumption of voltage drops.

The validity of Kirchhoff's voltage law is quite apparent. Thus starting from any node, as we travel along a closed path and come back to the same node, the set voltage drop or the net voltage rise must be zero.

With reference to the network graph of Fig. 2.12, as we travel clockwise along the closed periphery of the graph starting from node d, summation of voltage drop must be zero in accordance with Kirchhoff's voltage law. Thus, we get

$$v_1 + v_2 + v_3 + v_4 - v_{27} - v_{16} + v_{15} + v_{14} + v_{13} + v_{17} = 0 \qquad ...(2.18)$$

where any branch voltage v_n is the voltage drop along the branch current. Thus v_3 is the voltage drop from node b to node c, *i.e.* it equals voltage of node b minus the voltages of node c.

Kirchhoff's current law. This law states that algebraic sum-mation of branch current confluent at any node must equal zero. Symbolically we may write :

$$\Sigma + j = 0 \qquad ...(2.19)$$

The Greek letter Σ (sigma) signifies summation while $\pm\, j$ signifies currents confluent at the nodes, the '+' sign being used for currents divergent from the node while '–' sign being used for currents convergent at the node. Thus with the application of Kirchhoff's current law to node 'a' in the graph of Fig. 2.12, we get

$$j_2 - j_1 - j_{18} = 0 \qquad ...(2.20)$$

Thus Kirchhoff's current law states that "the net current diverging from any node is zero".

Eq. (2.20) may as well be written as,

$$j_1 + J_{18} - j_2 = 0 \qquad ...(2.21)$$

Thus Kirchhoff's current law may alternatively be put as, "The net current convergent at any node equals zero".

Eq. (2.20) may also be written as :

$$j_2 = j_1 + j_{18} \qquad ...(2.22)$$

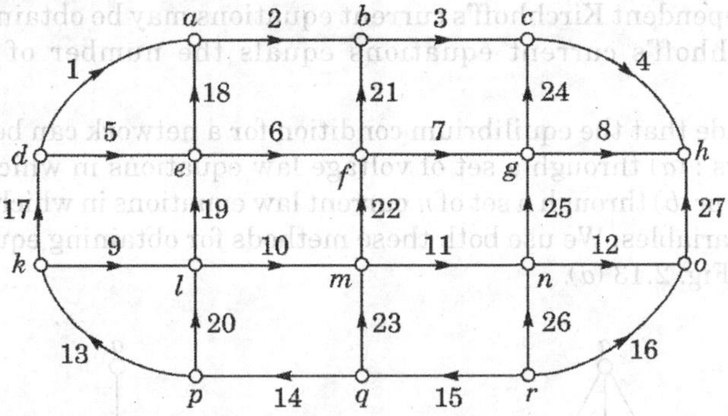

Fig. 2.12. A network graph.

Thus alternatively Kirchhoff's current law states that "the sum of the currents convergent at any node equals the sum of the currents divergent from it".

In fact Kirchhoff's current law is nothing but an expression for the principle of conservation of charge. Thus it signifies that "the charge cannot accumulate at any node". Since the principle of conservation of charge is true, Kirchhoff's current law is true as well.

Further Kirchhoff's current law applies not only to a node but to any group of nodes as a subgraph.

Thus with reference to the graph of Fig. 2.12, application of Kirchhoff's current law to nodes *a, d* and *e* yields :

$$j_2 - j_1 - j_{18} = 0 \quad \text{...(2.23)}$$

$$j_5 + j_1 - j_{17} = 0 \quad \text{...(2.24)}$$

and $$j_6 + j_{18} - j_5 - j_{19} = 0 \quad \text{...(2.25)}$$

Addition of these three equations yields :

$$j_2 + j_6 - j_{17} - j_{19} = 0 \quad \text{...(2.26)}$$

If we enclose nodes *a, d* and *e* and connecting branches *i.e.* branches 1, 5 and 18 in a box, then Currents divergent from this box are j_2 and j_6 while currents convergent on this box are j_{17} and j_{19}.

Hence net current divergent from box is $(j_2 + j_6 - j_{17} - j_{19})$. This is zero in accordance with Eq (2.26). Hence Kirchhoff's current law is true not only for a node but also for a subgraph contained in a box.

2.11. The Equilibrium Equations

The equilibrium equations are a set of equations that completely and uniquely determine the state of a network at any moment. They are, of course, written in terms of appropriately chosen current variables or voltage variables. In order that the equations be unique, the number of independent variables must equal the number of independent equations. Thus on the current basis, the number of independent currents is $l = b - (n_t - 1)$ and the same should be the number of independent equations. On the voltage basis, on the other hand, the number of independent voltage variables is $n = (n_t - 1)$ and this should, therefore, be the number of independent equations.

In the graph of Fig. 2.12, there are 27 branches and 16 nodes. Thus, $n_t = 16$ and $b = 27$. Hence $n = n_t - 1 = 16 - 1 = 15$ and $l = b - n = 27 - 15 = 12$. A study of this graph of Fig. 2.12 shows that there are 12 meshes. Hence the number of independent Kirchhoff's voltage equations will also be 12, *i.e.*, equal to *l*, the number of independent current variables. Also it may be seen that for two nodes, only one Kirchhoff's current equations may be obtained. Hence for n_t

nodes, $(n_t - 1) = n$ independent Kirchhoff's current equations may be obtained. Hence the number of independent Kirchhoff's current equations equals the number of independent voltage variables.

Thus we conclude that the equilibrium condition for a network can be expressed in either of the following two ways : (*a*) through a set of voltage law equations in which the currents are the independent variables or (*b*) through a set of *n* current law equations in which the node pair voltages are the independent variables. We use both these methods for obtaining equilibrium equations for the network graph of Fig. 2.13 (*a*).

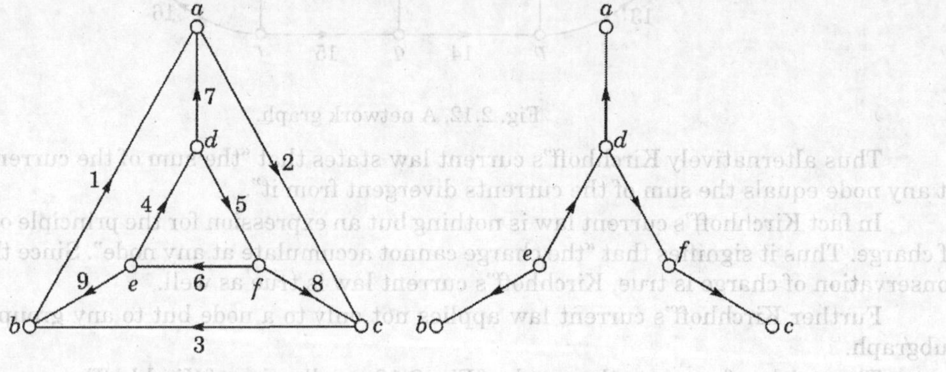

(*a*) A network graph (*b*) A tree

Fig. 2.13. A network graph and its tree.

Current variable method. For simplicity let us assume that all passive elements are resistive and let the resistance of these elements 1, 2......, 9 be $r_1, r_2......, r_9$ respectively. Then the equations relating the branch voltages and the branch currents are :

$$v_k = r_k j_k ...... \text{ for } k = 1, 2,......,9 \quad ...(2.27)$$

For the network graph of Fig. 2.13 (*a*), number of branches $b = 9$ and the number of nodes $n_t = 6$.

Hence number of node pairs $= n = n_t - 1 = 6 - 1 = 5$.

Also the number of links = number of link currents $= b - n = 9 - 5 = 4$.

Hence the number of independent current variables $= l = 4$.

For the tree of Fig. 2.13 (*b*), branches 1, 2, 3 and 9 form the links. Let the branch currents j_1, j_2, j_3 and j_6 in the links constitute the independent current variables i_1, i_2, i_3 and i_4 respectively. The tie-set schedule for the link currents i_1, i_2, i_3 and i_4 is constructed in the usual manner and is given in Table 2.7.

Table 2.7

Tie-set schedule

Link current	*Branch number*								
No.	*1*	*2*	*3*	*4*	*5*	*6*	*7*	*8*	*9*
1	1	0	0	−1	0	0	−1	0	1
2	0	1	0	0	−1	0	1	−1	0
3	0	0	1	1	1	0	0	1	−1
4	0	0	0	1	1	1	0	0	0

Kirchhoff's voltage law equations written for these loops are obtained by using coefficients in the rows of this schedule. Thus, we get

$$v_1 - v_4 - v_7 + v_9 = 0 \qquad \text{...(2.28 a)}$$

$$v_2 - v_5 + v_7 - v_8 = 0 \qquad \text{...(2.28 b)}$$

$$v_3 + v_4 + v_5 + v_8 - v_9 = 0 \qquad \text{...(2.28 c)}$$

$$v_4 + v_5 + v_6 = 0 \qquad \text{...(2.28 d)}$$

The columns of the same schedule express the branch currents in terms of the link currents. Thus, we get

$$\left.\begin{array}{l|l} j_1 = i_1 & j_6 = i_4 \\ j_2 = i_2 & j_7 = -i_1 + i_2 \\ j_3 = i_3 & j_8 = -i_2 + i_3 \\ j_4 = -i_1 + i_3 + i_4 & j_9 = i_1 - i_3 \\ j_5 = -i_2 + i_3 + i_4 & \end{array}\right\} \qquad \text{...(2.29)}$$

We now make two operations :

(*i*) Substitute in Eqs. (2.27) values of branch currents j_k in terms of link currents i_1 to i_4 as obtained from Eq. (2.29), and

(*ii*) Substitute values of branch voltages so obtained into Eqs. (2.28) to obtain l equations in l link currents.

Thus for the network graph of Fig. 2.13 (*a*), let all the branches be resistive and let their resistances be as below :

$$r_1 = r_2 = r_3 = 1 \text{ ohm.}$$
$$r_4 = r_5 = r_6 = 2 \text{ ohms.}$$
$$r_7 = r_8 = r_9 = 3 \text{ ohms.}$$

Then from Eq. (2.27), we get

$$\left.\begin{array}{lll} v_1 = j_1 ; & v_4 = 2j_4 ; & v_7 = 3j_7 \\ v_2 = j_2 ; & v_5 = 2j_5 ; & v_8 = 3j_8 \\ v_3 = j_3 ; & v_6 = 2j_6 ; & v_9 = 3j_9 \end{array}\right\} \qquad \text{...(2.30)}$$

Substituting values of $j_1, j_3 ......, j_9$ from Eqs. (2.29) into Eqs. (2.30), we get

$$\left.\begin{array}{lll} v_1 = i_1 ; & v_4 = 2(-i_1 + i_3 + i_4) ; & v_7 = 3(-i_1 + i_2) \\ v_2 = i_2 ; & v_5 = 2(-i_2 + i_3 + i_4) ; & v_8 = 3(-i_2 + i_3) \\ v_3 = i_3 ; & v_6 = 2i_4 ; & v_1 = 3(i_1 - i_3) \end{array}\right\} \qquad \text{...(2.31)}$$

Substituting values of branch voltages $v_1, ...\, v_9$ from Eqs. (2.31) into Eqs. (2.28), we get

$$i_1 - 2(-i_1 + i_3 + i_4) - 3(-i_1 + i_2) + 3(i_1 - i_3) = 0$$
$$i_2 - 2(-i_2 + i_3 + i_4) + 3(-i_1 + i_2) - 3(-i_2 - i_3) = 0$$
$$i_3 + 2(-i_1 + i_3 + i_4) + 2(-i_2 + i_3 + i_4) + 3(i_2 - i_3) = 0$$
$$2(-i_1 + i_3 + i_4) + 2(-i_2 + i_3 + i_4) + 2i_4 = 0$$

On rearranging these equations, we get

$$\left.\begin{array}{r} 9i_1 - 3i_2 - 5i_3 - 2j_4 = 0 \\ -3i_1 + 9i_2 - 5i_3 - 2i_4 = 0 \\ -5i_1 - 5i_2 + 11i_3 + 4i_4 = 0 \\ -2i_1 - 2i_2 + 4i_3 + 6i_4 = 0 \end{array}\right\} \qquad \text{...(2.32)}$$

These l equations in l independent variables may now be solved, in accordance with one of the methods outlined in the next article, to obtain values of currents i_1, i_2, i_3 and i_4, Eqs. (2.29) may then be used to obtain values of branch currents $j_1 j_2 ..., j_9$ and Eqs. (2.31) or (2.30) may be used to obtain values of branch voltages.

Voltage variable method. Again let us assume for simplicity that the branches be purely resistive and let the conductances of branches 1, 2, 3 etc. be g_2, g_2, etc. Then the equations relating the branch currents with branch voltages are :

$j_k = g_k . v_k$ for $k = 1, 2, ...b$ ...(2.33)

where branch conduc-tances g_1, g_1 etc. are reciprocals of branches resistance i_1, r_2 etc. respectively.

With reference to the graph of Fig. 2.13 (*a*) and tree of Fig. 2.13 (*b*), let the tree branch voltages v_9, v_4, v_5, v_8 and v_7 be identified respectively with the independent voltage variables e_1, e_2, e_3, e_4 and e_5. These are shown in Fig. 2.14.

Then the cut set schedule may be constructed as usual by rows, *i.e.* by noting the picked-up nodes pertinent to these four independent voltage variables. Table 2.8 gives the cut-set schedule.

Table 2.8

Cut-set Schedule

Independent tree branch voltage No.	*Brach number*									*Picked up Nodes*
	1	2	*3*	*4*	5	*6*	*7*	*8*	*9*	
1	– 1	0	1	0	0	0	0	0	1	*b*
2	1	0	– 1	1	0	– 1	0	0	0	*b, e*
3	0	1	– 1	0	1	– 1	0	0	0	*a, d, e, b*
4	0	1	– 1	0	0	0	0	1	0	*c*
5	1	– 1	0	0	0	0	1	0	0	*a*

Kirchhoff's current law equations for this choice of node pairs are readily obtained by using the coefficients in the rows of the cut-set schedule. Thus, we get

$$-j_1 + j_3 + j_9 = 0 \quad ...(2.34\ a)$$
$$j_1 - j_3 + j_4 - j_6 = 0 \quad ...(2.34\ b)$$
$$j_2 - j_3 + j_5 + j_6 = 0 \quad ...(2.34\ c)$$
$$j_2 - j_3 + j_8 = 0 \quad ...(2.34\ d)$$
$$j_1 - j_2 + j_7 = 0 \quad ...(2.34\ e)$$

The columns in the cut-set schedule express the branch voltages in terms of tree branch voltages. Thus, we get

$$\left.\begin{array}{ll} v_1 = -e_1 + e_2 + e_5 & v_6 = -e_2 - e_3 \\ & v_7 = e_5 \\ v_2 = e_2 + e_4 - e_5 & v_8 = e_4 \\ v_3 = e_1 - e_2 - e_3 - e_4 & v_9 = e_1 \\ v_4 = e_2 & \\ v_5 = e_3 & \end{array}\right\} \quad ...(2.35)$$

The branch conductances corresponding to the branch resistan-ces assumed earlier are :

$$g_1 = g_2 = g_3 = 1 \text{ mho}.$$

$$g_4 = g_5 = g_6 = 0.5 \text{ mho}$$
$$g_7 = g_8 = g_9 = 0.333 \text{ ohm}$$

Then from Eqs. (2.33), we get

$$\left.\begin{array}{lll} j_1 = v_1\,; & j_4 = 0.5\, v_4\,; & j_7 = 0.333\, v_7 \\ j_2 = v_2\,; & j_5 = 0.5\, v_5\,; & j_8 = 0.333\, v_8 \\ j_3 = v_3\,; & j_6 = 0.5\, v_6\,; & j_9 = 0.333\, v_9 \end{array}\right\} \qquad \text{...(2.36)}$$

Substituting the values of branch votages v_1 ...... , v_9 from Eqs. (2.35) into (2.36), we get

$$\left.\begin{array}{ll} j_1 = -e_1 + e_2 + e_5 & j_6 = 0.5\,(-e_2 - e_3) \\ j_2 = e_3 + e_4 - e_5 & j_7 = 0.333\, e_5 \\ j_3 = e_1 - e_2 - e_3 - e_4 & j_8 = 0.333\, e_4 \\ j_4 = 0.5\, e_2 & j_9 = 0.333\, e_1 \\ j_5 = 0.5\, e_3 & \end{array}\right\} \qquad \text{...(2.37)}$$

Substituting the values of branch currents from Eqs. (2.37) into Eqs. (2.34), we get

$$\left.\begin{array}{r} -(-e_1 + e_2 + e_5) + (e_1 - e_2 - e_3 - e_4) + 0.333\, e_1 = 0 \\ (-e_1 + e_2 + e_5) - (e_1 - e_2 - e_3 - e_4) + 0.5\, e_2 - 0.5\,(-e_2 - e_3) = 0 \\ (e_3 + e_4 + e_5) - (e_1 - e_2 - e_3 - e_4) + 0.5\, e_3 - 0.5\,(-e_2 - e_3) = 0 \\ (e_3 + e_4 + e_5) - (e_1 - e_2 - e_3 - e_4) + 0.333\, e_4 = 0 \\ (-e_1 + e_2 + e_5) - (e_2 + e_4 - e_5) + 0.333\, e_5 = 0 \end{array}\right\} \qquad \text{...(2.38)}$$

Rearranging Eqs. (2.38), we get

$$\left.\begin{array}{r} 2.333\, e_1 - 2\, e_2 - e_3 - e_4 - e_5 = 0 \\ -2e_1 + 3e_2 + 1.5\, e_3 + e_4 + e_5 = 0 \\ -e_1 + 1.5\, e_5 + 3e_3 + 2e_4 - e_5 = 0 \\ -e_1 + e_2 + 2e_3 + 2.333\, e_4 - e_5 = 0 \\ -e_1 + e_2 - e_3 - e_4 + 2.333\, e_5 = 0 \end{array}\right\} \qquad \text{...(2.39)}$$

These n equations in n independent variables may be solved to obtain values of e_1, e_2, e_3, e_4 and e_5. Eqs. (2.35) may then be used to obtain values of branch voltages v_1, v_2, ... v_9 and Eqs. (2.37) or (2.36) may be used to obtain values of branch current j_1, j_2, ..., j_9.

2.12. Parameter Matrices on the Loop Basis and Node Basis

Eq. (2.32) are written in a orderly form such that variables i_1 appear in the first column, variables i_2 in the second column and so on. Then the informations contained in Eqs. (2.32) are also contained with equal definiteness but with greater compactness in the matrix form given below. This matrix is known as the "loop parameter matrix".

$$[R] = \begin{bmatrix} 9 & -3 & -5 & -2 \\ -3 & 9 & -5 & -2 \\ -5 & -5 & 11 & 4 \\ -2 & -2 & 4 & 6 \end{bmatrix} \qquad \text{...(2.40)}$$

Similarly Eqs. (2.39) are written in an orderly form. Ths infor-mations contained in Eqs. (2.39) may be expressed with equal definite-ness and greater compactness in the matrix given below. This matrix is known as the "node-conductance parameter matrix".

$$[G] = \begin{bmatrix} 2.333 & -2 & -1 & -1 & -1 \\ -2 & 3 & 1.5 & 1 & 1 \\ -1 & 1.5 & 3 & 2 & -1 \\ -1 & 1 & 2 & 2.333 & -1 \\ -1 & 1 & -1 & -1 & 2.333 \end{bmatrix} \quad ...(2.41)$$

Use of matrix algebra may then be made to manipulate these equations to achieve the desired results.

Matrix concept also permits a greatly abbreviated method of designating loop and node-parameter values in numerical examples. Thus Eqs. (2.32) may be written in the common symbolic form given below :

$$\left.\begin{aligned} r_{11} \cdot i_1 + r_{12} \cdot i_2 + ...+ r_{1l} \cdot i_l &= 0 \\ r_{21} \cdot i_1 + r_{22} \cdot i_2 + ...+ r_{2l} \cdot i_l &= 0 \\ ... \quad ... \quad ... \quad ... \quad & ... \\ r_{l1} \cdot i_1 + r_{l2} \cdot i_2 + ...+ r_{ll} \cdot i_l &= 0 \end{aligned}\right\} \quad ...(2.42)$$

Here coefficients of variables are denoted by symbol r_{11}, r_{12}, r_{22} etc. The subscript 12 appended to r signifies that the coefficients appear in the first row and the second column. Thus any coefficient r_{sk}, signifies a coefficient appearing in the sth row and the kth column.

Then the matrix corresponding to Eqs. (2.32) may be written as,

$$[R] = \begin{bmatrix} r_{11} & r_{12} & \cdots & r_{1l} \\ r_{21} & r_{22} & \cdots & r_{2l} \\ r_{31} & r_{32} & \cdots & r_{3l} \\ \cdots & \cdots & \cdots & \cdots \\ r_{l1} & r_{l2} & \cdots & r_{ll} \end{bmatrix} \quad ...(2.43)$$

Similarly a set of node equation like Eqs. (2.39) may symbolically be written as below :

$$\left.\begin{aligned} g_{11} \cdot e_1 + g_{12} \cdot e_2 + ... + g_{1n} \cdot e_n &= 0 \\ g_{21} \cdot e_1 + g_{22} \cdot e_2 + ... + g_{2n} \cdot e_n &= 0 \\ ... \quad ... \quad ... \quad & ... \\ g_{n1} \cdot e_1 + g_{n2} \cdot e_2 + ... + g_{nn} \cdot e_n &= 0 \end{aligned}\right\} \quad ...(2.44)$$

The matrix corresponding to Eqs. (2.44) may be written as

$$[G] = \begin{bmatrix} g_{11} & g_{12} & \cdots & g_{1n} \\ g_{21} & g_{22} & \cdots & g_{2n} \\ \cdots & \cdots & \cdots & \cdots \\ g_{n1} & g_{n2} & \cdots & g_{nn} \end{bmatrix} \quad ...(2.45)$$

Eqs. (2.42) may be identified with Eqs. (2.32) provided that

$$r_{11} = 9, r_{12} = -3, r_{13} = -5 \text{ etc.} \quad ...(2.46)$$

Thus in order to write Eq. (2.32) symbolically we write Eq. (2.41) and Eq. (2.46) giving values of terms r_{sk}. This procedure is obviously arduous and space consuming. Matrix representation of Eqs. (2.40) evidently provides a greatly compact method of writing loop-parameter values. This has become possible because row and column position of a number identifies it as a specific r_{sk} value. It is then not necessary to write equations like Eq. (2.46). Similar remarks apply to node conductance parameter matrix.

Symmetry of parameter matrices. A study of loop resistance parameter matrix of Eq. (2.40) or node conductance parameter matrix of Eq. (2.41) shows that there exists a "symmetry about the principal diagonal". Thus in the matrix given by Eq. (2.43), rewritten as Eq. (2.47) the principal diagonal is shown as that passing through the terms r_{11}, r_{22},......r_{ll}. Then terms r_{12} and r_{21} are symmetrically disposed with respect to the principal diagonal. It may be seen that values of r_{12} and r_{21} are equal. Similarly $r_{23} = r_{32}$, $r_{34} = r_{43}$ and so on.

$$= R \begin{bmatrix} 9 & -3 & -5 & -2 \\ -3 & 9 & -5 & -2 \\ -5 & -5 & 11 & 4 \\ -2 & -2 & 4 & 6 \end{bmatrix} \qquad ...(2.47)$$

Principal Diagonal

In general we may write,

$$r_{sk} = r_{ks} \qquad ...(2.47\ a)$$

Similar symmetry about the principal diagonal exists in the node conductance matrix given in Eqs. (2.41).

In the analysis based on current variables, it may be seen that a set of geometrically independent loops of closed paths is chosen in accordance with one of three methods outlined earlier for defining the current variables. For writting the Kirchhoff's voltage law equations again selection of a set of geometrically independent loops is done. This set of loops or closed paths for purpose of procedural convenience is, in general, chosen to be the same as the set of loops selected for defining the independent current variables. But this is not obligatory. If the same loops are used for both the purposes, *i.e.* for defining the loop currents and for writing the Kirchhoff's voltage law equations, then the resulting loop resistance parameter matrix is symmetrical, If, however, separate choice of loop currents is made, then the resulting matrix is not symmetrical.

Similarly on the node basis, it is required to choose a set of geometrically independent node pairs and their cut-sets once for defin-ing the node pair voltage variables and again for writing Kirchhoff's current law equations. These sets of node pairs are usually but not necessarily the same. In case these two sets of node pairs are the same then the resulting node conductance parameter matrix is symmetrical.

2.13. Simplified Procedure Applicable in Several Cases

Formal procedures for obtaining equilibrium equations on the loop-basis and node basis have been outlined above. However, most of the practical networks have such geometries that they are "mappable on a plane" *L*. In such a case, it is possible to obtain equilibrium equations following simpler procedure. These procedures can be best illustrated with the help of an example. Simple procedures on current basis and voltage basis are treated separately.

On current basis. Fig. 2.15 (*a*) gives a resistance network while Fig. 2.15 (*b*) gives its graph. The assumed directions of branch currents are also shown. Since the network is mappable on a plane, it is possible to use the meshes as the geometrically independent set of closed loops. There are three meshes in this graph and let i_1, i_2 and i_3 be the mesh currents all flowing clockwise in the meshes. Then for the simple geometry of the network, it is possible to write (*i*) the voltage law equations for the meshes and (*ii*) equations giving the branch currents

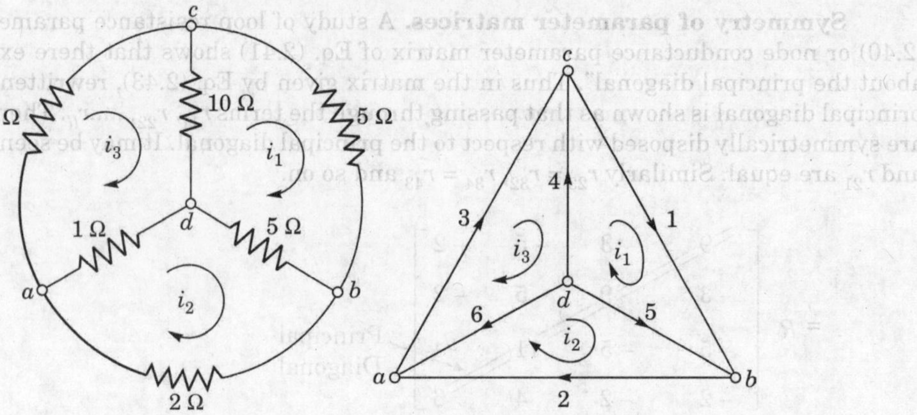

(*a*) A resistance network (*b*) The graph

Fig. 2.15. A resistance network and its graph.

in terms of mesh currents, directly without the need of any schedule. Thus for the graph shown, the Kirchhoff's voltage equations are :

$$\left.\begin{aligned} v_1 - v_5 + v_4 &= 0 \\ v_5 + v_2 - v_6 &= 0 \\ v_3 - v_4 + v_6 &= 0 \end{aligned}\right\} \qquad ...(2.48)$$

The branch currents in terms of the mesh currents are given by,

$$\left.\begin{aligned} j_1 &= i_1\,; \quad j_4 = i_1 - i_3 \\ j_2 &= i_2\,; \quad j_5 = i_2 - i_1 \\ j_3 &= i_3\,; \quad j_6 = i_3 - i_2 \end{aligned}\right\} \qquad ...(2.49)$$

Branch resistances are as below :

$$r_1 = 5\ \Omega,\ r_2 = 2\ \Omega,\ r_3 = 10\ \Omega,\ r_4 = 10\ \Omega,\ r_5 = 5\ \Omega,\ r_6 = 1\ \Omega \qquad ...(2.50)$$

Branch voltages are then given by,

$$\left.\begin{aligned} v_1 &= r_1 \cdot j_1 = r_1 \cdot i_1 = 5i_1 \\ v_2 &= r_2 \cdot j_2 = r_2 \cdot i_2 = 2i_2 \\ v_3 &= r_3 \,.\, j_3 = r_3 \,.\, i_3 = 10i_3 \\ v_4 &= r_4 \cdot j_4 = r_4\,(i_1 - i_3) = 10\,(i_1 - i_3) \\ v_5 &= r_5 \cdot j_5 = r_5\,(i_2 - i_1) = 5\,(i_2 - i_1) \\ v_6 &= r_6 \cdot j_6 = r_6\,(i_3 - i_2) = (i_3 - i_2) \end{aligned}\right\} \qquad ...(2.51)$$

Substituting values of branch voltage from Eq. (2.51) into Eq. (2.48), we get

$$\left.\begin{aligned} 5i_1 - 5\,(i_2 - i_1) + 10\,(i_1 - i_3) &= 0 \\ 5(i_2 - i_1) - 2i_2 - (i_3 - i_2) &= 0 \\ 10i_3 - 10\,(i_1 - i_3) + (i_3 - i_2) &= 0 \end{aligned}\right\} \qquad ...(2.52)$$

On rerranging Eq. (2.52) yield,

$$20i_1 - 5i_2 - 10i_3 = 0 \qquad ...(2.53\ a)$$

$$-5i_1 + 8i_2 - i_3 = 0 \qquad ...(2.53\ b)$$

$$-10i_1 - i_2 + 21i_3 = 0 \qquad ...(2.53\ c)$$

The corresponding loop resistance parameter matrix is :

$$[R] = \begin{bmatrix} 20 & -5 & -10 \\ -5 & 8 & -1 \\ -10 & -1 & 21 \end{bmatrix} \quad ...(2.54)$$

Eq. (2.53) may now be solved to obtain values of independent mesh currents i_1, i_2 and i_3. These values may be substituted in Eqs. (2.49) and (2.52) to get values of branch currents and branch voltages respectively.

On voltage basis. The node-pair voltage variables are chosen as a node-to-datum set but because of the simplicity of the geometry of the network, it is possible to write (*i*) Kirchhoff's current law equations and (*ii*) equations giving the branch voltages in terms of node-to-datum voltages, directly without the need of a cut-set schedule. Thus in the network graph of Fig. 2.15 (*b*), node '*a*' is chosen as the datum node and let the potentials of nodes *b*, *c* and *d* be e_1, e_2 and e_3 respectively as shown in Fig. 2.16. Then the current law equations pertinent to nodes *b*, *c* and *d* are :

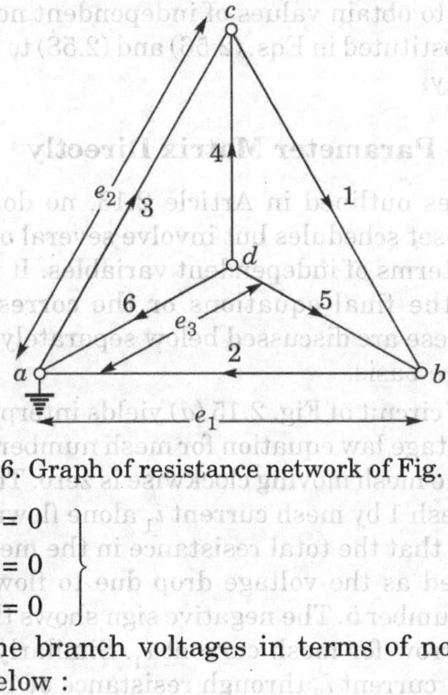

Fig. 2.16. Graph of resistance network of Fig. 2.15 (*a*).

$$\left.\begin{aligned} j_2 - j_1 - j_5 &= 0 \\ j_1 - j_3 - j_4 &= 0 \\ j_4 + j_5 + j_6 &= 0 \end{aligned}\right\} \quad ...(2.55)$$

The equations giving the branch voltages in terms of node-to-datum potentials are, by inspection of Fig. 2.15 (*b*), as below :

$$\left.\begin{aligned} v_1 &= e_2 - e_1 ; & v_4 &= e_3 - e_2 \\ v_2 &= e_1 ; & v_5 &= e_3 - e_1 \\ v_3 &= -e_2 ; & v_6 &= e_3 \end{aligned}\right\} \quad ...(2.56)$$

The branch conductances corresponding to the resistance values shown in Fig. 2.15 (*a*) are :

$g_1 = 0.2$ S, $g_2 = 0.5$ S, $g_3 = 0.1$ S, $g_4 = 0.1$ S, $g_5 = 0.2$ S, $g_6 = 1$ S ...(2.57)

Branch currents are then given by,

$$\left.\begin{aligned} j_1 &= g_1 \cdot v_1 = g_1 \cdot (e_2 - e_1) &&= 0.2\,(e_2 - e_1) \\ j_2 &= g_2 \cdot v_2 = g_2 \cdot e_1 &&= 0.5 e_1 \\ j_3 &= g_3 \cdot v_3 = g_3(-e_2) &&= 0.5 e_1 \\ j_4 &= g_4 \cdot v_4 = g_4(e_3 - e_2) &&= -0.1(e_3 - e_3) \\ j_5 &= g_5 \cdot v_5 = g_5(e_3 - e_1) &&= 0.2\,(e_3 - e_1) \\ j_6 &= g_6 \cdot v_6 = g_6 \cdot e_3 &&= e_3 \end{aligned}\right\} \quad ...(2.58)$$

Substituting the values of branch currents from Eq. (2.58) into Eq. (2.55), we get

$$\left.\begin{aligned} 0.5\, e_1 - 0.2\,(e_2 - e_1) - 0.2\,(e_3 - e_1) &= 0 \\ 0.2\,(e_2 - e_1) + 0.1\, e_2 - 0.1\,(e_3 - e_2) &= 0 \\ 0.1(e_3 - e_2) + 0.2\,(e_3 - e_1) + e_3 &= 0 \end{aligned}\right\} \quad ...(2.59)$$

On rearrangement Eq. (2.59) yield,

$$0.9e_1 - 0.2e_2 - 0.2e_3 = 0 \quad ...(2.60\ a)$$

$$-0.2e_1 + 0.4e_2 - 0.1e_3 = 0 \quad ...(2.60\ b)$$

$$-0.2e_1 - 0.1e_2 + 1.3e_3 = 0 \quad ...(2.60\ c)$$

The corresponding node conductance parameter matrix is

$$[G] = \begin{bmatrix} 0.9 & -0.2 & -0.2 \\ -0.2 & 0.4 & -0.1 \\ -0.2 & -0.1 & 1.3 \end{bmatrix} \quad ...(2.61)$$

Eq. (2.60) may be solved to obtain values of independent node-to-datum voltages e_1, e_2 and e_3. These values may then be substituted in Eqs. (2.56) and (2.58) to obtain values of branch voltages and branch currents respectively.

2.14. Method of Writing the Parameter Matrix Directly

The simplified procedures outlined in Article 2.13, no doubt, do away with the need of constructing the tie-set and cut-set schedules but involve several operations before arriving at the final independent equations in terms of independent variables. It is possible in the case of simple network geometries to write the final equations or the corresponding resistance matrix or conductance matrix directly. These are discussed below separately for the two cases of analysis on the current basis and the voltage basis.

Current Basis. Study of circuit of Fig. 2.15 (*a*) yields interpretation for the Eq. (2.53). Thus Eq. (2.53 *a*) is the Kirchhoff's voltage law equation for mesh number one. It states that the algebraic sum of all the voltage drops in the mesh moving clockwise is zero. The term 20 i_1 may be interpreted as the voltage drop caused in mesh 1 by mesh current i_1 alone flowing through a total resistance of 20 ohms. It may be readily seen that the total resistance in the mesh is 20 ohms. The second term namely $-5i_2$ may be interpreted as the voltage drop due to flow of mesh current i_2 through a resistance of 5 Ω in the branch number 5. The negative sign shows that this voltage drop is negative with respect to the reference arrow for mesh current i_1. Similarly the term $-10i_3$ is the voltage drop caused by the flow of mesh current i_3 through resistance of 10 Ω of branch number 4.

Equation (2.53 *b*) similarly expresses the fact that the algebraic sum of the voltage drops caused in mesh 2 by the various mesh currents equals zero. If any coefficient happen to be zero, it simply signifies that the pertinent mesh current does not flow through any branch of the mesh. Similar remarks apply to Eq. (2.53 *c*).

This physical interpretation permits us to write the loop resistance parameter matrix (2.54) directly. Thus the coefficient on the principal diagonal are respectively the total resistance values on the contours of the meshes 1, 2, 3 etc. Any other coefficient say a term r_{sk} has a value equal to the resistance of the branch common to meshes *s* and *k*. Its algebraic sign is plus if the mesh currents flow in the same direction through the common branch and it is minus if these mesh currents flow in the opposite directions.

It may also be seen that if all the mesh currents are chosen to have consistently clockwise (or consistently anti-clockwise) direction, then the algebraic signs of all non-diagonal coefficients in the loop resistance matrix are negative.

Voltage Basis. A simple physical interpretation may as well be given to the node equilibrium equations obtained on the node-to-datum basis. Thus Eq. (2.60 *a*) is the Kirchhoff's current law equation for node '*b*'. The first term in this equation namely 0.9 e_1 may be represented as the current divergent from node '*b*' caused by the node-to-datum voltage e_1 alone acting through total conductance of 0.9 S, constituted by conductances 0.5 S, 0.2 S and 0.2 S of branches 2, 5 and 1 respectively divergent from node *b* and acting in parallel. The second term in Eq. (2.60 *a*) namely – $0.2e_2$ may be interpreted as the current divergent from node *b* caused by node-to-datum voltage e_2 of node *c* alone flowing through the conductance of 0.2 S of branch number 1, which is common to nodes *b* and *c*. The negative sign appears because the current $0.2e_2$ cause by voltage e_2 is actually convergent at node *b*, *i.e.* opposite to current 0.9 e_1 divergent from node *b*. Similarly the term – 0.2 e_4 is the algebraic value of the current divergent from node *b* caused by node-to-datum voltage e_3 of node *b* flowing through conductance of 0.2 S of branch number 5.

Eq. (2.60 *b*) similarly expresses that the algebraic sum of the currents divergent from node *c* caused by node-to-datum voltages e_1, e_2 and e_3 equals zero. If any coefficient happens to be zero, it simply signifies that the pertinent node-to-datum voltage does not cause any current to be divergent from this node, *i.e.* the node does not have a branch common with this node *c*. Similar remarks apply to Eq. (2.60 *c*).

This physical interpretation permits us to write the node conductance parameter matrix Eq. (2.64) directly. Thus the coefficients on the principal diagonal are respectively the total values, *i.e* sum of the branch conductances divergent from nodes *b*, *c* and *d*. Any other coefficient, say a term g_{sk}, has a value equal to the conductance of the branches common to the node numbers *s* and *k*. Its algebraic sign is plus if the current in the common branch caused due to node-to-datum voltage e_k is divergent from node *s* and the sign is minus if the current is convergent at node *s*. But if all the node pair voltage variables are chosen as a node to datum set, then evidently no such non-diagonal coefficient will have minus sign.

2.15. Sources

In the discussion so far, energy sources were deliberately kept out of network. In fact, for understanding the network topology, choice of independent variable and formation of equilibrium equations based thereon, sources have no role to play. But if there were no sources, there would be no currents and voltages in the network elements. Solution of equations like (2.54) or (2.60) would yield all voltages and currents to be zero. Source must be included in the network. The equilibrium equations then get altered so as to include these. The way in which the source voltages or currents enter into the equilibrium equations, depends on how sources are inserted in a given passive network. Following are the two means of doing this :

(*i*) *Pliers method or Cut method.* This method is used for insertion of a voltage source and consists in inserting the voltage source into the gap formed by cutting a branch, as with pliers.

(*ii*) *Soldering iron method or Tie method.* This method is used for insertion of a current source and consists in connecting the current sources terminals to a selected node-pair, as is done with a soldering iron.

If a voltage source is connected across a node pairs, it becomes necessary to revise the network geometry with the end result that the voltage sources again appear only in series with the branches. Similarly if a current source is connected in series with a branch, it becomes necessary to revise the network geometry with the end result that current sources again appear only in parallel with branches *i.e.* across node pairs.

Thus consider the network graph of Fig. 2.17 (*a*) in which a voltage e_s appears in parallel with branch 4 of the network. Part (*b*) of Fig. 2.17 gives the resultant change in network geometry and the revised source arrangement. In Fig. 2.17 (*a*), branch 4 is rendered trivial by having source of voltage e_s in its parallel since the value of branch voltage v_4 is forced to be equal to e_3. Hence v_4 no longer remains unknown. Thus values of v_4 and j_4 remain fixed irrespective of what happens in the rest of network. Accordingly in the analysis we may as well remove branch 4 and e_s alone appears as a connecting link between nodes a and b. As an alternative we may remove the voltage source e_s from across nodes a and b and place it in series with each of the two branches 5 and 6 resulting in revised equivalent graph of Fig. 2.17 (*b*). Now the potentials of nodes c and d relative to that of nodes "*a*" are the same in Fig. 2.17 (*b*) as in Fig. 2.17 (*a*). Hence the branch voltages and currents in the graph of Fig. 2.17 (*b*) must be the same as in the graph of part (*a*), except that the branch 4 has been omitted. We may as well conclude that placing a voltage source across a branch amounts to placing a short circuit across it. As an alternative to the arrangement in Fig. 2.17 (*b*), we may place the voltage source in series with the branches confluent at "*a*" *i.e.* in branches 2 and 3.

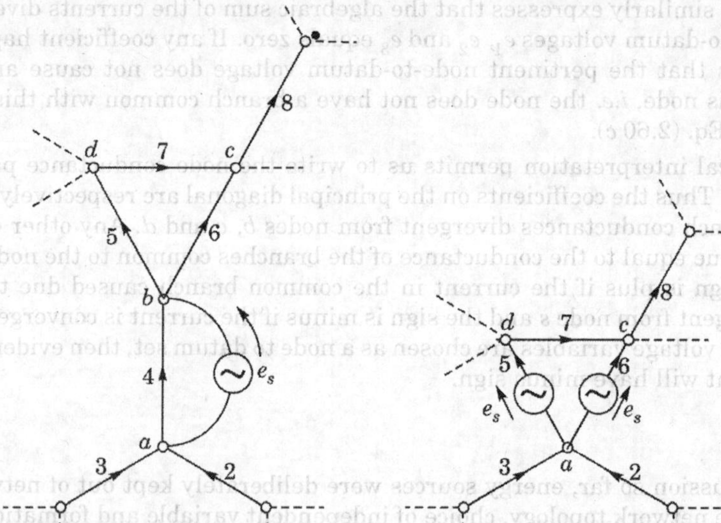

(*a*) A network graph. (*b*) Equivalent revised graph.

Fig. 2.17. A network graph with a voltage source across a branch and its equivalent revised graph.

Fig. 2.18 (*a*) gives a network graph in which a current source i, appears in series with branch 5 while Fig. 2.18 (*b*) gives the resultant change in network geometry and the revised source arrangement. In Fig. 2.18 (*a*), the branch 5 is rendered trivial by having a current source of current i_3 in its series since the current i_5 is forced to be equal to i_4. Hence i_5 is no longer unknown. Values of i_5 as well as v_s remain fixed irrespective of what happens in the rest of the network. Hence we may remove branch 5 and let current source i_s, alone bridge the node pair *a*-*b*. As an alternative we may remove source i_s from across node pair *a*-*b* and place it across each of the three branches 4, 6 and 7 connecting nodes a and b resulting in revised equivalent graph of Fig. 2.18 (*b*). The equivalence of this revised graph to the original graph of Fig. 2.18 (*a*) is evident by inspection since the same amount of source current still leaves node "*a*" and enters node "*b*", while no net source current either enters or leaves the nodes c and d. We may as well conclude that placing a current source in series with a branch amounts to open circuiting or removing the branch from the graph.

Thus we may summarise that no change in network geometry is necessitated if voltage source appear only in series with the branches and current sources appear only in parallel with the branches or across the node pairs. On the other hand, the network geometry is altered if a voltage source is placed in parallel with a branch or a current source is placed in series with a branch.

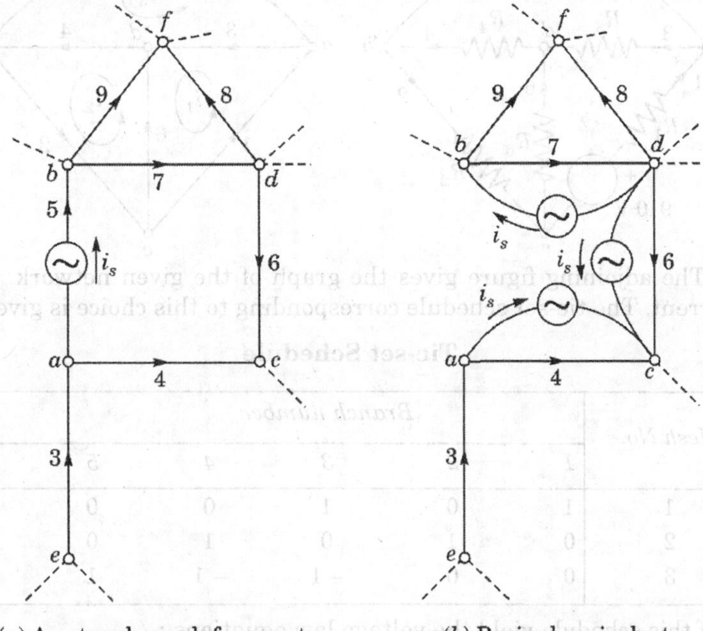

(a) A network graph fragment. (b) Revised equivalent.

Fig. 2.18. A network graph fragment involving a current source in series with a branch and its equilvalent revised graph.

An individual branch in a network may not contain any source or it may be associated with a current source or a voltage source or both. Thus let us consider the branch number k between nodes a and b, associated with a current source i_s in parallel and a voltage source e_s in series. Let v_k be the net voltage drop in the branch and j_k be the net current. Then for the reference directions shown in Fig. 2.19 the voltage drop in the passive link $a'b$ is $(v_k + e_s)$ and the current in it is $(j_k + i_s)$. Let the passive element $a'b$ of this branch have impedance Z and admittance y. Then we have

$$(v_k + e_s) = Z\,(j_k + i_s) \qquad ...(2.62)$$

or

$$(j_k + i_s) = y\,(v_k + e_s) \qquad ...(2.63)$$

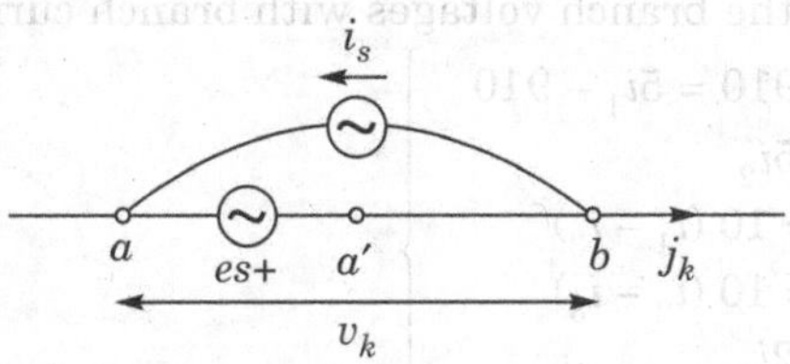

Fig. 2.19. A branch associated with current and voltage sources.

Example 2.3. *For the given resistive network write a tie-set schedule and equilibrium equations on the current basis. Obtain values of branch voltages. Given that* $R_1 = 5\ \Omega$, $R_2 = 5\ \Omega$, $R_3 = R_4 = R_6 = 10\ \Omega$, $R_5 = 2\ \Omega$.

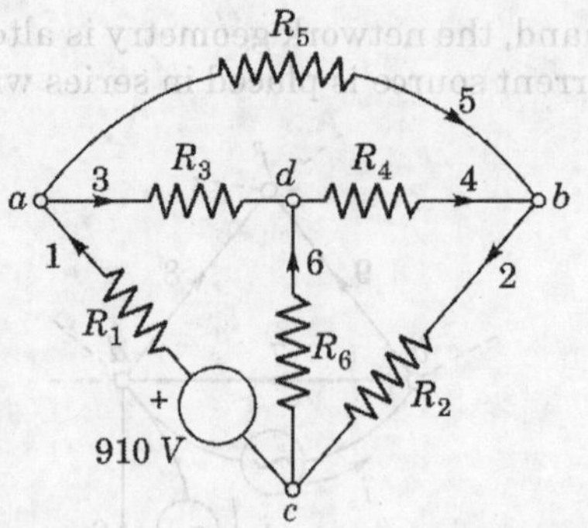

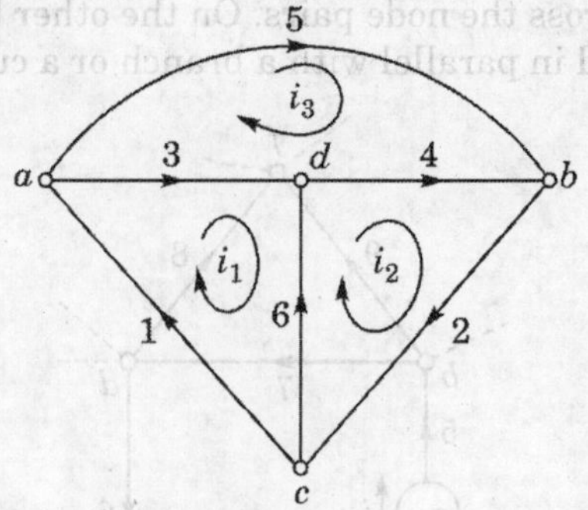

Solution. The adjoining figure gives the graph of the given network. Also shown is the choice of mesh current. The tie-set schedule corresponding to this choice is given below :

Tie-set Schedule

Mesh No.	*Branch number*					
	1	*2*	*3*	*4*	*5*	*6*
1	1	0	1	0	0	– 1
2	0	1	0	1	0	1
3	0	0	– 1	– 1	1	0

The rows of this schedule yield the voltage law equations :

$$v_1 + v_3 - v_6 = 0 \qquad ...(1a)$$

$$v_2 + v_4 + v_6 = 0 \qquad ...(1b)$$

$$-v_3 - v_4 + v_5 = 0 \qquad ...(1c)$$

The columns yield the following equations giving branch current in terms of mesh currents

$$\left.\begin{aligned} j_1 &= i_1 \\ j_2 &= i_2 \\ j_3 &= i_1 - i_3 \\ j_4 &= i_2 - i_3 \\ j_5 &= i_3 \\ j_6 &= -i_1 + i_2 \end{aligned}\right\} \qquad ...(2)$$

The equations relating the branch voltages with branch currents are :

$$\left.\begin{aligned} v_1 &= 5j_1 - 910 = 5i_1 - 910 \\ v_2 &= 5j_2 - 5i_2 \\ v_3 &= 10j_3 = 10\,(i_1 - i_3) \\ v_4 &= 10j_4 = 10\,(i_2 - i_3) \\ v_5 &= 2j_5 = 2i_3 \\ v_6 &= 10j_6 = 10\,(-i + i_2) \end{aligned}\right\} \qquad ...(3)$$

Substituting values of branch voltages from Eqs. (3) into Eqs. (1), we get

$$\left.\begin{aligned} (5i_1 - 910) + 10\,(i_1 - i_3) - 10\,(-i_1 + i_2) &= 0 \\ 5i_2 + 10\,(i_2 - i_3) + 10\,(-i_1 + i_2) &= 0 \\ -10\,(i_1 - i_3) - 10\,(i_2 - i_3) + 2i_3 &= 0 \end{aligned}\right\} \qquad ...(4)$$

Rearranging Eqs. (4), we get

$$\left.\begin{aligned} 25i_1 - 10i_2 - 10i_3 &= 910 \\ -10i_1 + 25i_2 - 10i_3 &= 0 \\ -10i_1 - 10i_2 + 22i_3 &= 0 \end{aligned}\right\} \quad ...(5)$$

Solution of Eqs. (5) yields :

$$i_1 = 90 \text{ amp.} ; i_2 = 64 \text{ amp. and } i_3 = 70 \text{ amp.}$$

Substitution of values of mesh current in Eqs. (2) yields

$$j_1 = i_1 = 90 \text{ amperes}$$
$$j_2 = i_2 = 64 \text{ amperes}$$
$$j_3 = i_1 - i_3 = 90 - 70 = 20 \text{ amperes}$$
$$j_4 = i_2 - i_3 = 64 - 70 = 6 \text{ amperes}$$
$$j_5 = i_3 = 70 \text{ amperes}$$
$$j_6 = i_2 - i_1 = 64 - 90 = -26 \text{ amperes.}$$

Substitution of the values of branch currents into Eqs. (3) yields :

$$v_1 = 5i_1 - 910 = 450 - 910 = -460 \text{ volts}$$
$$v_2 = 5j_2 = 5 \times 64 = 320 \text{ volts}$$
$$v_3 = 10j_3 = 10 \times 20 = 200 \text{ volts}$$
$$v_4 = 10j_4 = 10 \times (-6) = -60 \text{ volts}$$
$$v_5 = 2j_5 = 2 \times 70 = 140 \text{ volts}$$
$$v_6 = 10j_6 = 10(-26) = -260 \text{ volts.}$$

Example 2.4. *For the resistance network of Ex. 2.3, write a cut-set schedule and equilibrium equations on voltage basis. Hence obtain values of branch voltages and branch currents.*

Solution. Let node c be the reference node and let the potentials of a, b and d be e_1, e_2 and e_3 respectively with respect to that of the reference node c. Then the cut-set schedule for this choice of voltage variables is as below :

Node	*Branch number*						*Picked-up*
No.	*1*	*2*	*3*	*4*	*5*	*6*	*nodes*
1	– 1	0	1	0	1	0	*a*
2	0	1	0	1	– 1	0	*b*
3	0	0	– 1	1	0	– 1	*d*

The rows of this cut-set schedule give the current law equations. Thus :

$$\left.\begin{aligned} -j_1 + j_3 + j_5 &= 0 \\ j_2 + j_4 - j_5 &= 0 \\ -j_3 + j_4 - j_6 &= 0 \end{aligned}\right\} \quad ...(1)$$

The columns of the schedule yield the branch voltages in terms of node-to-datum voltages. Thus,

$$\left.\begin{aligned} v_1 &= -e_1 & \qquad v_4 &= -e_2 + e_3 \\ v_2 &= e_2 & v_5 &= e_1 - e_2 \\ v_3 &= e_1 - e_3 & v_6 &= -e_3 \end{aligned}\right\} \quad ...(2)$$

The equations giving branch currents in terms of branch voltages and node-to-datum voltages are :

$$\left.\begin{aligned} j_1 &= g_1(v_1+910) = 0.2\,(v_1+910) \\ &= 0.2\,(-e_1+910) \\ j_2 &= g_2 \,.\, v_2 = 0.2v_2 = 0.2e_2 \\ j_3 &= v_3 \,.\, v_3 = 0.1v_3 = 0.1\,(e_1-e_3) \\ j_4 &= g_4 \,.\, v_4 = 0.1v_4 = 0.1\,(-e_2+e_3) \\ j_5 &= g_5 \,.\, v_5 = 0.5v_5 = 0.5\,(e_1-e_2) \\ j_6 &= g_6 \,.\, v_6 = 0.5v_6 = 0.5\,(-e_3) \end{aligned}\right\} \quad ...(3)$$

Substituting values of branch currents from Eq. (3) into Eq. (1), we get

$$\left.\begin{aligned} -0.2\,(-e_1+910) + 0.1\,(e_1-e_3) + 0.5\,(e_1-e_2) &= 0 \\ 0.2e_2 - 0.1\,(-e_2+e_3) - 0.5\,(e_1-e_2) &= 0 \\ -0.1\,(e_1-e_3) + 0.1\,(-e_2+e_3) - 0.5\,e_3 &= 0 \end{aligned}\right\} \quad ...(4)$$

Rearranging Eq. (4), we get

$$\left.\begin{aligned} 0.8e_1 - 0.5e_2 - 0.1e_3 &= 182 \\ -5e_1 + 0.8e_2 - 0.1e_3 &= 0 \\ -0.1e_1 - 0.1e_2 + 0.3e_3 &= 0 \end{aligned}\right\} \quad ...(5)$$

Solution of Eqs. (5) yields,

$$e_1 = 460 \text{ volts} \,;\, e_3 = 320 \text{ volts and } e_3 = 260 \text{ volts}$$

Substitution of values of e_1, e_2 and e_3 in Eqs. (2) yields,

$$v_1 = -e_1 = -460 \text{ volts}$$
$$v_2 = e_2 = 320 \text{ volts}$$
$$v_3 = e_1 - e_3 = (460-260) = 200 \text{ volts}$$
$$v_4 = e_3 - e_2 = 260 - 320 = -60 \text{ volts}$$
$$v_5 = e_1 - e_2 = 460 - 320 = 140 \text{ volts}$$
$$v_6 = -e_3 = -260 \text{ volts.}$$

These values agree with those obtained in the analysis on current basis done in Ex. 2.3.

Substitution of values of v_1 to v_6 into Eqs. (5) yields :

$$j_1 = 0.2\,(v_1+910) = 0.2\,(-460+910) = 90 \text{ amperes}$$
$$j_2 = 0.2v_2 = 64 \text{ amperes}$$
$$j_3 = 0.1v_3 = 20 \text{ amperes}$$
$$j_4 = 0.1v_4 = -6 \text{ amperes}$$
$$j_5 = 0.5v_5 = 70 \text{ amperes}$$
$$j_6 = 0.1v_6 = -26 \text{ amperes.}$$

These values of a branch currents also agree with those obtained in the analysis on current basis done in Ex. 2.3.

Example 2.5. *In the given network obtain values of branch currents and branch voltages by the current variables method.*

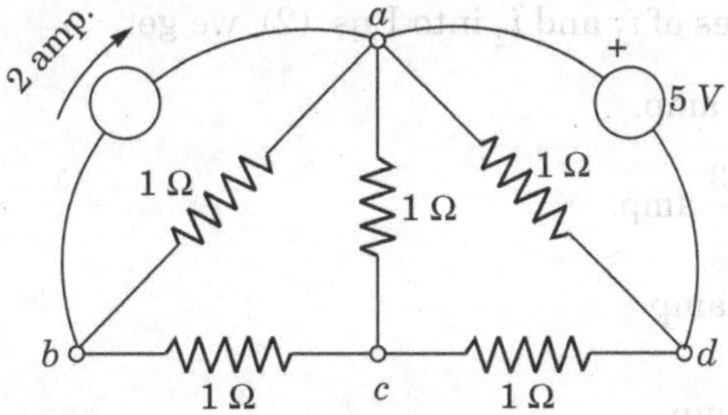

Solution. The graph of this network is shown adjacent. The branches have been numbered and the directions of branch currents have been indicated. Since the voltage source comes in shunt with 1 Ω resistor of branch 3, this resistor has been omitted from the graph.

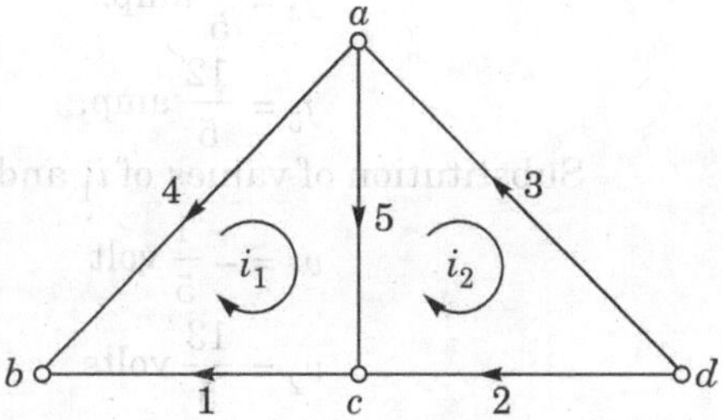

Let i_1 and i_3 be the mesh currents. Then the tie-set schedule corresponding to this choice is given below :

Mesh	*Branch number*				
No.	*1*	*2*	*3*	*4*	*5*
1	1	0	0	– 1	1
2	0	1	– 1	0	– 1

The rows of this tie-set schedule give the following voltage law equations :

$$\left.\begin{aligned} v_1 - v_4 + v_5 &= 0 \\ v_2 - v_3 - v_5 &= 0 \end{aligned}\right\} \quad ...(1)$$

The columns of schedule give the branch currents in terms of mesh currents. Thus, we get

$$\left.\begin{aligned} j_1 &= i_1 \\ j_2 &= i_2 \\ j_3 &= -i_2 \\ j_4 &= -i_1 \\ j_5 &= i_1 - i_2 \end{aligned}\right\} \quad ...(2)$$

The equations relating the branch voltages with branch currents are :

$$\left.\begin{aligned} v_1 &= r_1 \cdot j_1 = j_1 = i_1 \\ v_2 &= r_2 \cdot j_1 = j_2 = i_2 \\ v_3 &= -5 \\ v_4 &= r_4 (j_4 + 2) = j_4 + 2 = -i_1 + 2 \\ v_5 &= r_5 \cdot j_5 = j_5 = (i_1 - i_2) \end{aligned}\right\} \quad ...(3)$$

Substituting the values of branch voltages from Eqs. (3) into Eqs. (1), we get

$$\left.\begin{aligned} i_1 - (-i_1 + 2) + (i_1 - i_2) &= 0 \\ i_2 - (-5) - (i_1 - i_2) &= 0 \end{aligned}\right\} \quad ...(4)$$

On rearrangement, Eqs. (4) yield,

$$\left.\begin{aligned} 3i_1 - i_2 &= 2 \\ -i + 2i_2 &= -5 \end{aligned}\right\} \quad ...(5)$$

Solution of Eqs. (5) yields :

$$i_1 = -\frac{1}{5} \text{ amp}, \; i_2 = \frac{-13}{5} \text{ amp.}$$

Substituting the values of i_1 and i_2 into Eqs. (2), we get

$$j_1 = \frac{-1}{5} \text{ amp.}$$

$$j_2 = \frac{-13}{5} \text{ amp.}$$

$$j_3 = \frac{13}{5} \text{ amp.}$$

$$j_4 = \frac{1}{5} \text{ amp.}$$

$$j_5 = \frac{12}{5} \text{ amp.}$$

Substitution of values of i_1 and i_2 in Eqs. (3) yields :

$$v_1 = -\frac{1}{5} \text{ volt}$$

$$v_2 = \frac{13}{5} \text{ volts}$$

$$v_3 = -5 \text{ volts}$$

$$v_4 = \left(\frac{1}{5} + 2\right) = \frac{11}{5} \text{ volts}$$

$$v_5 = \frac{12}{5} \text{ volts.}$$

Since the current in branch 4 is 1/5 amp, the current through 1 Ω resistor in branch 4 is (2 + 1/5) = 11/5 amps. Further, since the voltage drop across 1 ohm resistor in branch 3 is 5 volts, the current through it = 5 amp. and the current through 5 volts source is $\left(5 + \frac{13}{5}\right) = \frac{38}{5}$ amperes.

Hence the current in the various branches are as shown in the following diagram.

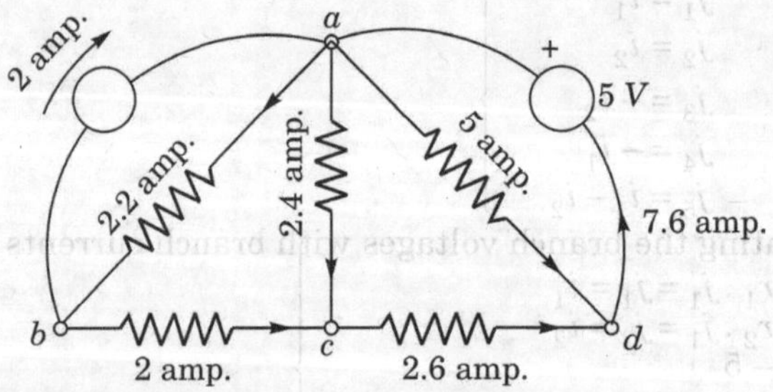

2.16. Methods of Solution of Equilibrium Equations

There are two principal methods of solving equilibrium equations not involving integrals or differentials, *i.e.* equilibrium equations for resistive network only. These methods are : (*i*) systematic elimination method and (*ii*) method using determinants.

2.16.1. Systematic Elimination Method

Consider the equilibrium equations of example 2.3 rewritten below.

$$\left.\begin{aligned} 25i_1 - 10i_2 - 10i_3 &= 910 \\ -10i_1 + 25i_2 - 10i_3 &= 0 \\ -10i_1 - 10i_2 + 22i_3 &= 0 \end{aligned}\right\} \quad ...(2.64)$$

A simple and straight forward method of solving a set of simultaneous equations like Eqs. (2.64) consists in systematically eliminating variables until we arrive at an equation containing a single variable. Having obtained the value of one variable, its value may be substituted in an equation containing two variables including this. This gives the value of the second variable. This process of substitution of values of variables in proper equations may be continued until all variables have been assessed.

Since only the numerical coefficients enter into the computation, we may omit symbols i_1, i_2 etc. altogether and consider only the numerical matrix of eqn. (2.65).

$$\begin{bmatrix} 25 & -10 & -10 & 910 \\ -10 & 25 & -10 & 0 \\ -10 & -10 & 22 & 0 \end{bmatrix} \quad \text{...(2.65)}$$

The steps involved in this systematic elimination method are given below :

(i) Eliminate i_1 from all but the first of these equations. With reference to matrix (2.65) this elimination amounts to eliminating second and third elements in the first column. The second element in the first column (symbolized by a_{21}) may be eliminated by adding to the elements of the second row, the respective α-multiplied elements of the first row

where $\alpha = -\dfrac{a_{21}}{a_{11}}$, *i.e.,* $\alpha = \dfrac{-(-10)}{25} = \dfrac{2}{5}$

The resulting new second row reads :

$$0 \qquad 21 \qquad 14 \qquad 364 \quad \text{...(2.66)}$$

Similarly the new third row is formed by adding to the element of the row, the respective α-multiplied element of the first row

where $\alpha = \dfrac{-a_{31}}{a_{11}}$, *i.e.,* $\alpha = \dfrac{-(-10)}{25} = \dfrac{2}{5}$

The resulting new third row reads :

$$0 \qquad -14 \qquad 18 \qquad 364 \quad \text{...(2.67)}$$

The transformed new matrix reads :

$$\begin{bmatrix} 25 & -10 & -10 & 910 \\ 0 & 21 & -14 & 364 \\ 0 & -14 & 18 & 364 \end{bmatrix} \quad \text{...(2.68)}$$

(ii) Eliminate i_2 from all but the first two equations corresponding to the new matrix (2.68). This may be done by adding to the third row, the respective α-multiplied elements of the second row where $\alpha = \dfrac{-a_{32}}{a_{22}}$, *i.e.,* $\alpha = \dfrac{(-14)}{21} = \dfrac{2}{3}$. The resulting new third row reads :

$$0 \qquad 0 \qquad \frac{26}{3} \qquad \frac{1820}{3} \quad \text{...(2.69)}$$

The new matrix now becomes :

$$\begin{bmatrix} 25 & -10 & -10 & 910 \\ 0 & 21 & -14 & 364 \\ 0 & 0 & \dfrac{26}{3} & \dfrac{1820}{3} \end{bmatrix} \quad \text{...(2.70)}$$

The last row in matrix (2.70) represents the equation,

$$\frac{26}{3} i_3 = \frac{1820}{3} \qquad \text{...(2.71)}$$

Hence $$i_3 = \frac{1820}{26} \qquad \text{...(2.72)}$$

The second row in matrix (2.70) represnts the equation :

$$21i_2 - 14i_3 = 364 \qquad \text{...(2.73)}$$

Substituting the value of i_3 from Eq. (2.72) into Eq. (2.73), we get

$$21i_2 = 364 + 14 \times 70 = 1344$$

Hence $$i_2 = \frac{1344}{21} = 64 \qquad \text{...(2.74)}$$

Finally substituting the values of i_2 and i_3 from Eqs. (2.72) and (2.74) into first of Eqs. (2.64), we get

$$25i_1 - 10(64) - 10(70) = 910$$

Hence $i_1 = 90$

This method of finding the variables through transformation of equations to eliminative variables involves a minimum of lost motion. Hence it is the best method to apply in numerical problems.

2 16.2. Method Using Determinants

This method involves greater amount of computation than the systematic elimination method. This has, however, the advantage that it permits expressing the solutions in a compact symbolic form. From these solutions in the symbolic form one may derive important characteristics of the networks.

Let the set of equations in variables $x_1, x_2, ..., x_n$ be written in the form :

$$\left.\begin{array}{l} a_{11} \cdot x_1 + a_{12} \cdot x_2 + \ldots\ldots + a_{1n} \cdot x_n = y_1 \\ a_{21} \cdot x_1 + a_{22} \cdot x_2 + \ldots\ldots + a_{2n} \cdot x_n = y_2 \\ \ldots \quad \ldots \quad \ldots \quad \ldots \\ a_{n1} \cdot x_1 + a_{n2} \cdot x_2 + \ldots\ldots + a_{nn} \cdot x_n = y_n \end{array}\right\} \qquad \text{...(2.75)}$$

The "determinants" of this system of equation is written in the form :

$$\Delta = \begin{vmatrix} a_{11} & a_{12} & \ldots & a_{1n} \\ a_{21} & a_{22} & \ldots & a_{2n} \\ \ldots & \ldots & \ldots & \ldots \\ a_{n1} & a_{n2} & \ldots & a_{nn} \end{vmatrix} \qquad \text{...(2.76)}$$

The appearance of a determinant is similar to the corresponding matrix except that the arrays of coefficients is enclosed between two vertical lines instead of between square brackets. However, its algebraic significance is entirely different from that of the matrix. If there be n equations in n variables, the determinant has n^2 elements and it is said to be of the order n.

The value of a second order determinant is given by,

$$\Delta = \begin{vmatrix} a_{11} & a_{12} \\ a_{21} & a_{22} \end{vmatrix} = a_{11} \cdot a_{22} - a_{12} \cdot a_{21} \qquad \text{...(2.77)}$$

The value of third order determinant is given in two basic forms : (*i*) expansion by rows and (*ii*) expansion by columns. The value of a third order determinant, expanding it by rows is given below :

$$\Delta = \begin{vmatrix} a_{11} & a_{12} & a_{13} \\ a_{21} & a_{22} & a_{23} \\ a_{31} & a_{32} & a_{33} \end{vmatrix} \qquad ...(2.78)$$

$$= a_{11} (a_{22} . a_{33} - a_{32} . a_{23}) + a_{12} (a_{23} . a_{31} - a_{21} . a_{33}) + a_{13} (a_{21} . a_{32} - a_{31} . a_{22}) \qquad ...(2.79)$$

$$= a_{11} (a_{22} . a_{33} - a_{32} . a_{23}) - a_{12} (a_{21} . a_{33} - a_{23} . a_{31}) + a_{13} (a_{21} . a_{32} - a_{31} . a_{22}) \qquad ...(2.80)$$

The total number of terms in the expansion of a determinant of nth order are n !.

The "minor" of any element a_{jk} of a determinant is the determinant which remains when, the column and the row containing the element a_{jk} are deleted. Thus in the determinant (2.78), the minor of the element a_{11} is

$$M_{11} = \begin{vmatrix} a_{22} & a_{23} \\ a_{32} & a_{33} \end{vmatrix} \qquad ...(2.81)$$

The value of M_{11} is given by,

$$M_{11} = (a_{22} . a_{33} - a_{32} . a_{23}) \qquad ...(2.82)$$

The cofactor of an element a_{jk} of a determinant is the minor of the element rearranged by columns and row taken is cyclic order starting from the column and row following the erased ones. Thus cofactor of element a_{11} is,

$$C_{11} = \begin{vmatrix} a_{22} & a_{23} \\ a_{32} & a_{33} \end{vmatrix} = (a_{22} . a_{33} - a_{32} . a_{23}) \qquad ...(2.83)$$

Thus $M_{11} = C_{11}$, *i.e.* minor of element a_{11} is equal to cofactor of element a_{11}.

In the determinant (2.78), the minor of element a_{12} is,

$$M_{12} = \begin{vmatrix} a_{21} & a_{23} \\ a_{31} & a_{33} \end{vmatrix} = (a_{21} . a_{33} - a_{23} . a_{31}) \qquad ...(2.84)$$

while the cofactor of element a_{12} is,

$$C_{12} = \begin{vmatrix} a_{23} & a_{21} \\ a_{33} & a_{31} \end{vmatrix} = (a_{23} . a_{31} - a_{21} . a_{33}) \qquad ...(2.85)$$

Thus $\qquad M_{12} = -C_{12}$.

It may be seen that the minor of any element a_{jk} is related to the cofactor of the same element by the relation :

$$C_{jk} = (-1)^{j+k} . M_{jk} \qquad ...(2.86)$$

Thus expansions (2.79) and (2.80) of a third order determinant may be written as :

$$\Delta = \begin{vmatrix} a_{11} & a_{12} & a_{13} \\ a_{21} & a_{22} & a_{23} \\ a_{31} & a_{32} & a_{33} \end{vmatrix}$$

$$= a_{11} . C_{11} + a_{12} . C_{12} + a_{13} . C_{13} \qquad ...(2.87)$$

$$= a_{11} . M_{11} - a_{12} . M_{12} + a_{13} . M_{13} \qquad ...(2.88)$$

The third order determinant (2.78) may as well be expanded by columns. Thus,

$$\Delta = \begin{vmatrix} a_{11} & a_{12} & a_{13} \\ a_{21} & a_{22} & a_{23} \\ a_{31} & a_{32} & a_{33} \end{vmatrix}$$

$$= a_{11}\,(a_{22}\,.\,a_{33} - a_{23}\,.\,a_{32}) + a_{21}\,(a_{32}\,.\,a_{13} - a_{12}\,.\,a_{33}) + a_{31}\,(a_{12}\,.\,a_{23} - a_{22}\,.\,a_{13}) \quad ...(2.89)$$

$$= a_{11}\,(a_{22}\,.\,a_{33} - a_{23}\,.\,a_{32}) - a_{21}\,(a_{12}\,.\,a_{33} - a_{32}\,.\,a_{13}) + a_{31}\,(a_{12}\,.\,a_{23} - a_{22}\,.\,a_{13}) \quad ...(2.90)$$

In terms of cofactor and minors, the expansion of a third order determinant by column may be written as :

$$\Delta = \begin{vmatrix} a_{11} & a_{12} & a_{13} \\ a_{21} & a_{22} & a_{23} \\ a_{31} & a_{32} & a_{33} \end{vmatrix}$$

$$= a_{11}\,.\,C_{11} + a_{21}\,.\,C_{21} + a_{31}\,.\,C_{31} \quad ...(2.91)$$

$$= a_{11}\,.\,M_{11} - a_{21}\,.\,M_{21} + a_{31}\,.\,M_{31} \quad ...(2.92)$$

In general, determinant of order n is equal to the sum of the product of the elements in any row or column multiplied by their corresponding $(n - 1)$ order cofactors. This method of expansion by cofactors or minors is of great significance in case of determinants of order higher than the third.

Determinant of the third order may often be conveniently expanded by a method known as the "Rule of Sarrus". According to this rule, we write down the three columns and then repeat the first two columns as shown below :

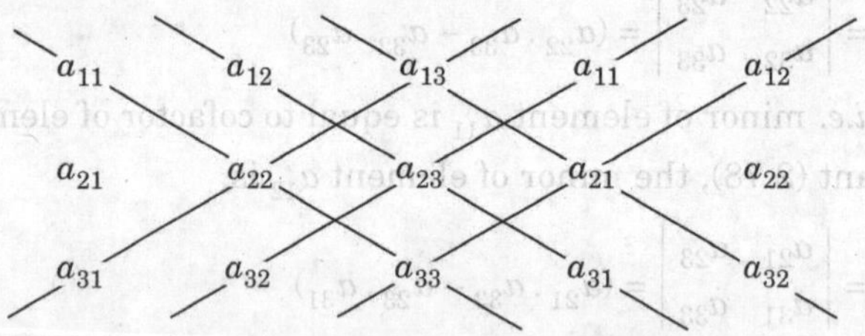

Then the products of the elements on the lines running to the right from top to bottom give the positive terms in the expansion while the product of the elements on the lines running to the right from bottom to top give the negative terms. Thus

$$D = (a_{11}\,.\,a_{22}\,.\,a_{33} + a_{12}\,.\,a_{23}\,.\,a_{31} + a_{13}\,.\,a_{21}\,.\,a_{32}) - (a_{31}\,.\,a_{22}\,.\,a_{13} + a_{32}\,.\,a_{23}\,.\,a_{11} + a_{33}\,.\,a_{21}\,.\,a_{12}) \quad ...(2.93)$$

Properties of Determinants. The following are the important properties of determinants.

(*i*) The value of a determinant remains unaltered if row are changed to columns and columns to rows :

$$\text{Thus} \quad \begin{vmatrix} a_1 & b_1 & c_1 \\ a_2 & b_2 & c_2 \\ a_3 & b_3 & c_3 \end{vmatrix} = \begin{vmatrix} a_1 & a_2 & a_3 \\ b_1 & b_2 & b_3 \\ c_1 & c_2 & c_3 \end{vmatrix} \quad ...(2.94)$$

(*ii*) The sign of determinant is altered, if two rows (or two columns) of determinant are interchanged.

$$\text{Thus} \quad \begin{vmatrix} b_1 & a_1 & c_1 \\ b_2 & a_2 & c_2 \\ b_3 & a_3 & c_3 \end{vmatrix} = - \begin{vmatrix} a_1 & b_1 & c_1 \\ a_2 & b_2 & c_2 \\ a_3 & c_3 & c_3 \end{vmatrix} \quad ...(2.95)$$

(*iii*) The determinant vanishes, if two rows (or two columns) of a determinant are identical.

Thus $$\begin{vmatrix} a_1 & a_1 & c_1 \\ a_2 & a_2 & c_2 \\ a_3 & a_3 & c_3 \end{vmatrix} = 0 \quad ...(2.96)$$

(*iv*) The determinant gets multiplied by a factor p, if each element of any row (or any column of determinant is multiplied by the factor p).

Thus $$\begin{vmatrix} pa_1 & pb_1 & pc_1 \\ a_2 & b_2 & c_2 \\ a_3 & b_3 & c_3 \end{vmatrix} = p\begin{vmatrix} a_1 & b_1 & c_1 \\ a_2 & b_2 & c_2 \\ a_3 & b_3 & c_3 \end{vmatrix} \quad ...(2.97)$$

(*v*) If each element of any row (or any column) of a determinant consists of the algebraic sum of r terms, the determinant is equivalent to the sum of r other determinants in each of which the elements consist of single terms.

Thus $$\begin{vmatrix} a_1+l_1-n_1 & b_1 & c_1 \\ a_2+l_2-n_2 & b_2 & c_2 \\ a_3+l_3-n_3 & b_3 & c_3 \end{vmatrix} = \begin{vmatrix} a_1 & b_1 & c_1 \\ a_2 & b_2 & c_2 \\ a_3 & b_3 & c_3 \end{vmatrix} + \begin{vmatrix} l_1 & b_1 & c_1 \\ l_2 & b_2 & c_2 \\ l_3 & b_3 & c_3 \end{vmatrix} - \begin{vmatrix} n_1 & b_1 & c_1 \\ n_2 & b_2 & c_2 \\ n_3 & b_3 & c_3 \end{vmatrix} \quad ...(2.98)$$

(*vi*) If the elements of any row (or any column) are increased or diminished by equimultiples of the corresponding elements of any other row (or column), the value of the determinant is unaltered.

Thus $$\begin{vmatrix} a_1+mb_1+nc_1 & b_1 & c_1 \\ a_2+mb_2+nc_2 & b_2 & c_2 \\ a_3+mb_3+nc_3 & b_3 & c_3 \end{vmatrix} = \begin{vmatrix} a_1 & b_1 & c_1 \\ a_2 & b_2 & c_2 \\ a_3 & b_3 & c_3 \end{vmatrix} \quad ...(2.99)$$

Solution of a system of linear equations by means of determinants. Let Eq. (2.75) be the set of equations and let the constants y_1, y_2 etc. be transferred to the left hand side so that the equations may be written as below :

$$\left.\begin{aligned} &a_{11}\cdot x_1 + a_{12}\cdot x_2 + a_{13}\cdot x_3 + \ldots\ldots + a_{1n}\cdot x_n + Z_1 = 0 \\ &a_{21}\cdot x_1 + a_{22}\cdot x_2 + a_{23}\cdot x_3 + \ldots\ldots + a_{2n}\cdot x_n + Z_2 = 0 \\ &\ldots \quad \ldots \quad \ldots \quad \ldots \quad \ldots \\ &a_{n1}\cdot x_1 + a_{n2}\cdot x_2 + a_{n3}\cdot x_3 + \ldots\ldots + a_{nn}\cdot x_n + Z_n = 0 \end{aligned}\right\} \quad ...(2.100)$$

Then it may be proved that,

$$\frac{(-1)^n x_1}{\Delta_1} = \frac{x_2}{\Delta_2} = \frac{(-1)^n \cdot x_3}{\Delta_3} = \ldots = \frac{1}{\Delta_0} \quad ...(2.101)$$

where Δ_0 is the system determinant formed by coefficients when we omit the column of the absolute terms ; Δ_1 is the determinant formed by the coefficients when we omit the column of terms involving variable x_1 and so on, subject to the condition that the columns follow one another in cyclic order.

To illustrate the method of solution of linear equations by using determinants, let us once again consider the equilibrium equations (2.64) rewritten below :

$$\left.\begin{aligned} 25i_1 - 10i_2 - 10i_3 - 10 &= 0 \\ -10i_1 + 25i_2 - 10i_3 + 0 &= 0 \\ -10i_1 - 10i_2 + 22i_3 + 0 &= 0 \end{aligned}\right\} \quad ...(2.102)$$

Then $$\frac{-i_1}{\Delta_1} = \frac{i_2}{\Delta_2} = \frac{-i_3}{\Delta_3} = \frac{1}{\Delta_4} \quad ...(2.103)$$

where $$\Delta_1 = \begin{vmatrix} -10 & -10 & -10 \\ 25 & -10 & 0 \\ -10 & 22 & 0 \end{vmatrix}$$

$$= -10\,(0-0) - (-10)\,(0-0) + (-10)\,(25 \times 22 - 100) = -4500$$

$$\Delta_2 = \begin{vmatrix} -10 & -10 & 25 \\ -10 & 0 & -10 \\ 22 & 0 & -10 \end{vmatrix} = 3200$$

$$\Delta_3 = \begin{vmatrix} -10 & 25 & -10 \\ 0 & -10 & 25 \\ 0 & -10 & -10 \end{vmatrix} = -3500$$

$$\Delta_0 = \begin{vmatrix} 25 & -10 & -10 \\ -10 & 25 & -10 \\ 10 & -10 & 22 \end{vmatrix} = 4550$$

Hence $$i_1 = \frac{-\Delta_1}{\Delta_0} = \frac{4500}{4550} = \frac{90}{91}$$

$$i_2 = \frac{\Delta_2}{\Delta_0} = \frac{3200}{4550} = \frac{64}{91}$$

$$i_3 = \frac{\Delta_3}{\Delta_0} = \frac{3500}{4550} = \frac{10}{13}$$

Cramer's Rule. An easier way of remembering and applying determinant method of solution of linear equations is through the so called "Cramer's Rule". Thus again consider the equation (2.75) reproduced below :

$$\left.\begin{aligned} a_{11}.x_1 + a_{12}.\,x_2 + a_{13}.x_3 + \ldots\ldots + a_{1n}.x_n &= y_1 \\ a_{21}.x_1 + a_{22}.x_2 + a_{23}.x_3 + \ldots\ldots + a_{2n}.x_n &= y_2 \\ a_{n1}.x_1 + a_{n2}.x_2 + a_{n3}.x_3 + \ldots\ldots\ a_{nn}.x_n &= y_n \end{aligned}\right\} \quad ...(2.104)$$

Then according to Cramer's Rule ;

$$\frac{x_1}{D_1} = \frac{x_2}{D_2} = \ldots = \frac{x_n}{D_n} = \frac{1}{\Delta_0} \quad ...(2.105)$$

where Δ_0 is the system determinant formed by coefficients of variables x_1 to x_n and is, therefore, given by,

$$\Delta_0 = \begin{vmatrix} a_{11} & a_{12} & \cdots & a_{1n} \\ a_{21} & a_{22} & \cdots & a_{2n} \\ \cdots & \cdots & \cdots & \cdots \\ a_{n1} & a_{n2} & \cdots & a_{nn} \end{vmatrix} \quad ...(2.106)$$

D_1 is the determinant formed by replacing the jth column of the system determinant by the column of absolute term, *i.e.* $y_1, y_2 \ldots\ldots y_n$.

To illustrate the method of solution of equations by Cramer's Rule, let us again consider the equilibrium equation (2.102) rewritten below :

$$\left.\begin{aligned} 25i_1 - 10i_2 - 10i_3 &= 10 \\ -10i_1 + 25i_2 - 10i_3 &= 0 \\ -10i_1 - 10i_2 + 22i_3 &= 0 \end{aligned}\right\} \qquad ...(2.107)$$

Then $$\Delta_0 = \begin{vmatrix} 25 & -10 & -10 \\ -10 & 25 & -10 \\ -10 & -10 & 22 \end{vmatrix} = 4550$$

$$D_1 = \begin{vmatrix} 10 & -10 & -10 \\ 0 & 25 & -10 \\ 0 & -10 & 22 \end{vmatrix} = 4550$$

$$D_2 = \begin{vmatrix} 25 & -10 & -10 \\ -10 & 0 & -10 \\ -10 & 0 & -22 \end{vmatrix} = 3200$$

$$D_3 = \begin{vmatrix} 25 & -10 & 10 \\ -10 & 25 & 0 \\ -10 & -10 & 2 \end{vmatrix} = 3500$$

Hence $$i_1 = \frac{D_1}{\Delta_0} = \frac{4500}{4550} = \frac{90}{91}$$

$$i_2 = \frac{D_2}{\Delta_0} = \frac{3200}{4550} = \frac{64}{91}$$

$$i_3 = \frac{D_3}{\Delta_0} = \frac{3500}{4550} = \frac{10}{13}.$$

Example 2.6. *For a certain 3-loop network, equilibrium equa-tions are :*

$$14i_1 - 2i_2 - 3i_3 = 2$$
$$-2i_1 + 2i_2 - 2i_3 = 0$$
$$-3i_1 - 2i_2 + 4.5i_3 = 0$$

Solve these equations to obtain values of currents i_1, i_2 and i_3 following the method of (a) systematic elimination and (b) determinants.

Solution. (*a*) *Systematic elimination method.* The system matrix may be written as :

$$\begin{bmatrix} 14 & -2 & -3 & 0 \\ -2 & 2 & -2 & 0 \\ -3 & -2 & 4.5 & 0 \end{bmatrix} \qquad ...(i)$$

Adding to the second row, the first row multiplied by $-\left(\frac{-2}{14}\right)$ and adding to the third row, the first row multiplied by $-\left(\frac{-3}{14}\right)$, we get the following revised matrix.

$$\begin{bmatrix} 14 & -2 & -3 & -2 \\ 0 & \frac{12}{7} & \frac{-17}{7} & \frac{2}{7} \\ 0 & \frac{-17}{7} & \frac{27}{7} & \frac{3}{7} \end{bmatrix} \qquad ...(ii)$$

In matrix (*ii*), adding to the third row, the second row multiplied by $-\frac{(-17/7)}{(12/7)}$, *i.e.*, $\frac{17}{12}$, we get the following new matrix :

$$\begin{bmatrix} 14 & -2 & -3 & -2 \\ 0 & \frac{12}{7} & \frac{-17}{7} & \frac{2}{7} \\ 0 & 0 & \frac{5}{12} & \frac{5}{6} \end{bmatrix} \qquad \text{...(iii)}$$

The third row of matrix (*iii*) reads

$$\frac{5}{12} i_3 = \frac{5}{6}$$

Hence $i_3 = 2.$

The second row of matrix (*iii*) reads :

$$\frac{12}{7} i_2 - \frac{17}{7} i_3 = \frac{2}{7}$$

or $12i_2 - 17i_3 = 2$

Hence $12i_2 = 2 + (17 \times 2)$

Hence $i_2 = 3.$

Substituting the values of i_2 and i_3 in the first equilibrium equation :

$$14i_1 - 2\,(3) - 3\,(2) = 2$$

Hence $i_1 = 1.$

(*b*) *Determinant Method.*

$$\frac{i_1}{D_1} = \frac{i_2}{D_2} = \frac{i_3}{D_3} = \frac{1}{\Delta_0}$$

$$\Delta_0 = \begin{vmatrix} 14 & -2 & -3 \\ -2 & 2 & -2 \\ -3 & -2 & 4.5 \end{vmatrix}$$

$$= 14\,(9 - 4) \; - 2(-9 - 6) + (-3)\,(4 + 6) = 10$$

$$D_1 = \begin{vmatrix} 2 & -2 & -3 \\ 0 & 2 & -2 \\ 0 & -0 & 4.5 \end{vmatrix} = 2\,(9 - 4) = 10$$

$$D_2 = \begin{vmatrix} 14 & 2 & -3 \\ -2 & 0 & -2 \\ -3 & 0 & 4.5 \end{vmatrix} = -2\,(-9 - 6) = 30$$

$$D_3 = \begin{vmatrix} 14 & -2 & 2 \\ -2 & 2 & 0 \\ -3 & -2 & 0 \end{vmatrix} = 2\,(4 + 6) = 20$$

Hence $i_1 = \frac{D_1}{\Delta_0} = \frac{10}{10} = 1, \qquad i_2 = \frac{D_2}{\Delta_0} = \frac{30}{10} = 3$

$$i_3 = \frac{D_3}{\Delta_0} = \frac{20}{10} = 2.$$

Example 2.7. *For the given resistive network write a tie-set schedule and obtain equilibrium equations on the current basis. Solve these equations and hence calculate values of branch currents and branch voltages.*

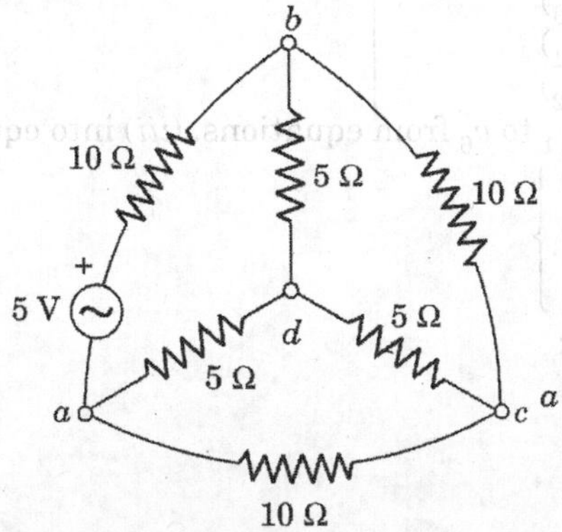

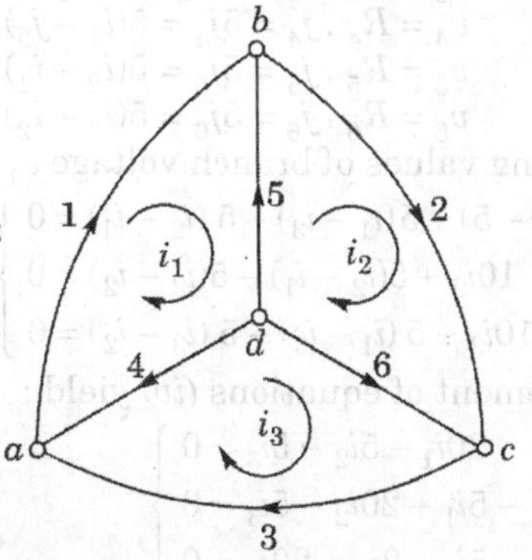

Solution. The adjoining figure gives the graph of the given network. Let the branches be numbered as shown. The graph also gives the assumed directions of branch currents. Let i_1, i_2 and i_3 be the mesh currents chosen as the independent variables and let all three be assumed to flow clockwise. It may be readily seen that the number of independent current variables is three.

No. of nodes $n_t = 4$

Node pairs $= n_t - 1 = 4 - 1 = 3$

No. of branches $b = 6.$

Hence no. of independent loops

$= l = b - n = 6 - 3 = 3.$

The tie-set schedule corresponding to this choice of mesh current as shown.

Tie-set Schedule

Mesh No.	*Branch number* 1	2	3	4	5	6
1	1	0	1	1	− 1	0
2	0	1	0	0	1	− 1
3	0	0	1	− 1	0	1

The rows of this schedule yield the voltage law equations :

$$\left.\begin{aligned} v_1 + v_4 - v_5 &= 0 \\ v_2 + v_5 - v_6 &= 0 \\ v_3 - v_4 + v_6 &= 0 \end{aligned}\right\} \quad ...(i)$$

The columns of this schedule give the branch currents in terms of mesh currents. Thus :

$$\left.\begin{aligned} j_1 &= i_1 & \quad j_4 &= i_1 - i_3 \\ j_2 &= i_2 & \quad j_5 &= -i_1 + i_2 \\ j_3 &= i_3 & \quad j_6 &= -i_2 + i_3 \end{aligned}\right\} \quad ...(iii)$$

[Note. The equations (*i*) and (*ii*) could, of course, be written down directly by inspection without the use of tie-set schedule.]

The branch voltages are then given by,

$$\left.\begin{aligned} v_1 &= R_1 \cdot j_1 - 5 = 10j_1 - 5 = 10i_1 - 5 \\ v_2 &= R_2 \cdot j_2 = 10j_2 = 10i_2 \\ v_3 &= R_3 \cdot i_3 = 10j_3 = 10i_3 \\ v_4 &= R_4 \cdot j_4 = 5j_4 = 5(i_1 - j_3) \\ v_5 &= R_5 \cdot j_5 = 5j_5 = 5(i_2 - i_1) \\ v_6 &= R_6 \cdot j_6 = 5j_6 = 5(i_3 - i_2) \end{aligned}\right\} \quad ...(iii)$$

Substituting values of branch voltage v_1 to v_6 from equations. *(iii)* into equations *(i)*, we get

$$\left.\begin{aligned} (10i_1 - 5) + 5(i_1 - i_3) - 5(i_2 - i_1) &= 0 \\ 10i_2 + 5(i_2 - i_1) - 5(i_3 - i_2) &= 0 \\ 10i_3 + 5(i_1 - i_3) - 5(i_3 - i_2) &= 0 \end{aligned}\right\} \quad ...(iv)$$

Rearrangement of equations *(iv)* yield :

$$\left.\begin{aligned} 20i_1 - 5i_2 - 5i_3 &= 0 \\ -5i_1 + 20i_2 - 5i_3 &= 0 \\ -5i_1 - 2i_2 + 20i_3 &= 0 \end{aligned}\right\} \quad ...(v)$$

On simplification equation *(v)* yield :

$$\left.\begin{aligned} 4i_1 - i_2 - i_3 &= 1 \\ -i_1 + 4i_2 - i_3 &= 0 \\ -i_1 - i_2 + 4i_3 &= 0 \end{aligned}\right\} \quad ...(vi)$$

Then $\dfrac{i_1}{D_1} = \dfrac{i_2}{D_2} = \dfrac{i_3}{D_3} = \dfrac{1}{\Delta_0}$

$$\Delta_0 = \begin{vmatrix} 4 & -1 & -1 \\ -1 & 4 & -1 \\ -1 & -1 & 4 \end{vmatrix} = 4(16 - 1) - (-1)(-4 - 1) + (-1)(1 + 4) = 50$$

$$D_1 = \begin{vmatrix} 1 & -1 & -1 \\ 0 & 4 & -1 \\ 0 & -1 & 4 \end{vmatrix} = (16 - 1) = 15$$

$$D_2 = \begin{vmatrix} 4 & 1 & -1 \\ -1 & 4 & -1 \\ -1 & 0 & -4 \end{vmatrix} = -1(-4 - 1) = 5$$

$$D_3 = \begin{vmatrix} 4 & -1 & 1 \\ -1 & 4 & 0 \\ -1 & -1 & 0 \end{vmatrix} = 1(1 + 4) = 5$$

Hence $i_1 = \dfrac{D_1}{\Delta_0} = \dfrac{15}{50} = 0.3$ amp.

$i_2 = \dfrac{D_2}{\Delta_0} = \dfrac{5}{50} = 0.1$ amp.

$i_3 = \dfrac{D_3}{\Delta_0} = \dfrac{5}{50} = 0.1$ amp.

Substituting value of i_1, i_2 and i_3 in equation *(ii)*, we get

$j_1 = i_1 = 0.3$ amp. $\quad j_4 = i_1 - i_3 = +0.3 - 0.1 = 0.2$ amp.

$j_2 = i_2 = 0.1$ amp. $\quad j_5 = i_2 - i_1 = 0.1 - 0.3 = -0.2$ amp.

$j_3 = i_3 = 0.1$ amp. $\quad j_6 = i_3 - i_2 = 0.1 - 0.1 = 0.$

From equations (*iii*), we get

$$v_1 = 10i - 5 = 3 - 5 = -2 \text{ volts}$$
$$v_2 = 10i_2 = 10 \times 0.1 = 1 \text{ volt}$$
$$v_3 = 10i_3 = 10 \times 0.1 = 1 \text{ volt}$$
$$v_4 = 5(i_1 - i_3) = 5(0.3 - 0.1) = 1 \text{ volt}$$
$$v_5 = 5(i_3 - i_1) = 5(0.1 - 0.3) = -1 \text{ volt}$$
$$v_6 = 5(i_3 - i_2) = (0.1 - 0.1) = 0 \text{ volt.}$$

Example 2.8. *For the resistive network of Ex. 2.7, write a cut-set shedule and obtain equilibrium equations on the voltage basis. Solve these equations and hence calculate values of branch currents and branch voltages.*

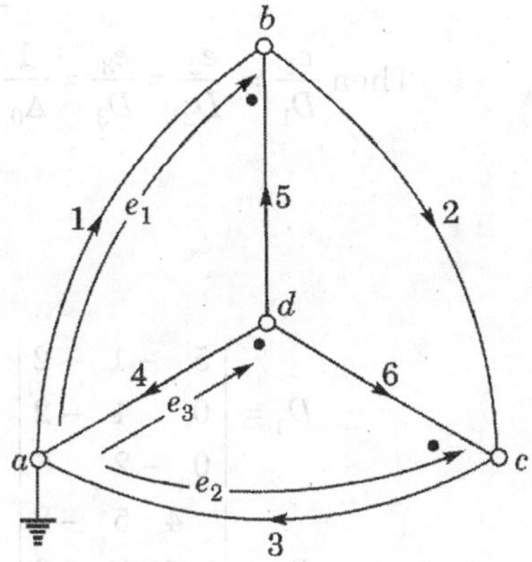

Solution. The adjoining figure shows the graph of the given network. Let the branches be num-bered as shown. The graph also gives the assumed directions of branch currents. Let node '*a*' be taken as the reference node or the datum node and e_1, e_2 and e_3 be the voltages of nodes be *b*, *c* and *d* respectively with respect to that of the reference node *a*.

The cut-set schedule cor-responding to this choice of node-to-datum voltage e_1, e_2 and e_3 is given here.

Cut-set Schedule

Node-to-datum pair No.	Branch number					
	1	2	3	4	5	6
1	– 1	1	0	0	– 1	0
2	0	– 1	1	0	0	– 1
3	0	0	0	1	1	1

The rows of this schedule yield the current law equations.

$$\left.\begin{aligned} -j_1 + j_2 - j_5 &= 0 \\ -j_2 + j_3 - j_6 &= 0 \\ j_4 + j_5 + j_6 &= 0 \end{aligned}\right\} \quad ...(i)$$

The columns of this schedule yield the branch voltages in terms of node-to-datum voltages. Thus

$$\left.\begin{aligned} v_1 &= -e_1 & v_4 &= e_3 \\ v_2 &= e_1 - e_2 & v_5 &= -e_1 - e_3 \\ v_3 &= e_2 & v_6 &= -e_2 + e_3 \end{aligned}\right\} \quad ...(ii)$$

The branch currents are given by :

$$\left.\begin{aligned} j_1 &= G_1(v_1 + 5) &&= 0.1(v_5 + 5) &&= -0.1(5 + e_1) \\ j_2 &= G_2 v_2 &&= 0.1v_2 &&= 0.1(e_1 - e_2) \\ j_3 &= G_3 v_3 &&= 0.1v_3 &&= 0.1e_2 \\ j_4 &= G_4 v_4 &&= 0.2v_4 &&= 0.2e_3 \\ j_5 &= G_5 v_5 &&= 0.2v_5 &&= 0.2(e_3 - e_1) \\ j_6 &= G_6 v_6 &&= 0.2v_6 &&= 0.2(e_3 - e_2) \end{aligned}\right\} \quad ...(iii)$$

Substituting values of branch currents j_1 to j_6 from Eqs. (*iii*) into Eqs. (*i*), we get

$$\left.\begin{aligned} -0.1(5-e_1)+0.1(e_1-e_2)-0.2(e_3-e_1)&=0\\ -0.1(e_1-e_2)+0.1e_2-0.2(e_3-e_2)&=0\\ 0.2e_3+0.2(e_3-e_1)+0.2(e_3-e_2)&=0 \end{aligned}\right\} \quad ...(iv)$$

On rearrangement and simplification Eqs. (*iv*) yield :

$$\left.\begin{aligned} 4e_1-e_2-2e_3&=5\\ -e_1+4e_2-2e_3&=0\\ -2e_1-2e_3+6e_3&=0 \end{aligned}\right\} \quad ...(v)$$

Then $\dfrac{e_1}{D_1}=\dfrac{e_2}{D_2}=\dfrac{e_3}{D_3}=\dfrac{1}{\Delta_0}$

$$\Delta_0=\begin{vmatrix} 4 & -1 & -2\\ -1 & 4 & -2\\ -2 & -2 & 6 \end{vmatrix}$$

$$= 4(24-4)-(-1)(-6-4)+(-2)(2+8)=50$$

$$D_1=\begin{vmatrix} 5 & -1 & -2\\ 0 & 4 & -2\\ 0 & -2 & 6 \end{vmatrix}=(24-4)=100$$

$$D_2=\begin{vmatrix} 4 & 5 & -2\\ -1 & 0 & -2\\ -2 & 0 & 6 \end{vmatrix}=-5(-6-4)=50$$

$$D_3=\begin{vmatrix} 4 & -1 & 5\\ -1 & 4 & 0\\ -2 & -2 & 0 \end{vmatrix}=5(2+8)=50$$

Hence $e_1=\dfrac{D_1}{\Delta_0}=\dfrac{100}{50}=2$ volts

$e_2=\dfrac{D_2}{\Delta_0}=\dfrac{50}{50}=1$ volt

$e_3=\dfrac{D_3}{\Delta_0}=\dfrac{50}{50}=1$ volt.

Hence from Eqs. (*ii*), we get

$v_1=-e_1=-2$ volts

$v_2=e_1-e_2=(2-1)=1$ volt

$v_3=e_2=1$ volt

$v_4=e_3=1$ volt

$v_5=(e_3-e_1)=(1-2)=-1$ volt

$v_6=(e_3-e_2)=(1-1)=0.$

From Eqs. (*iii*), we get

$j_1=0.1(5-e_1)=0.1(5-2)=0.3$ amp

$j_2=0.1(e_1-e_2)=0.1(2-1)=0.1$ amp

$j_3=0.1\,e_2=0.1$ amp

$j_4=0.2\,e_3=0.2$ amp

$j_5=0.2(e_3-e_1)=0.2(1-2)=-0.2$ amp

$j_6=0.2(e_3-e_2)=0.2(1-1)=0$ amp.

2.17. Ladder Network

There are several networks where short cut methods may be employed in numerical computation. Fig. 2.20 gives an unbalanced ladder network using resistive components only. The resistance values are also given. It is required to find the branch voltages and branch currents for a given excitation voltage e_s.

This network may be analysed by the conventional methods but hereunder is given a short cut method which may be specially used for this network. Thus at the outset we disregared the value of e_3 but assume that e_4 the potential of node 4 with respect to the common reference node R is 1 volt. We then proceed to find the value of voltage e_s.

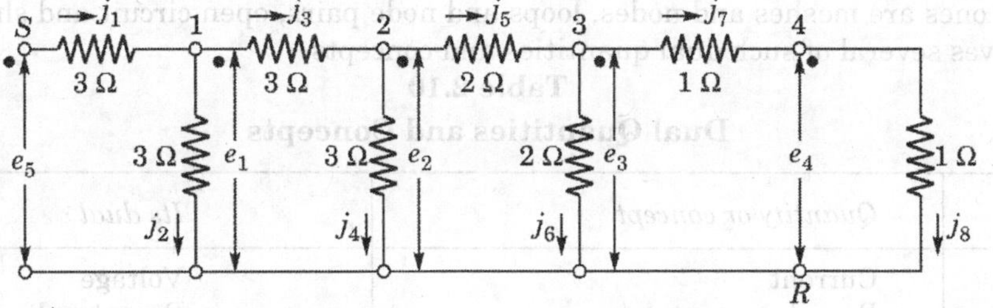

Fig. 2.20. Unbalanced ladder network.

If $e_4 = 1$, then $v_8 = 1$ volt and $j_7 = j_8 = \dfrac{1 \text{ volt}}{1 \text{ ohm}} = 1$ amp.

$$v_7 = 1 \text{ amp} \times 1\ \Omega = 1 \text{ volt.}$$

$$v_6 = e_3 = e_4 + v_7 = 1 + 1 = 2 \text{ volts}$$

$$j_6 = \frac{e_3}{2\ \Omega} = \frac{2 \text{ volts}}{2 \text{ ohms}} = 1 \text{ amp.}$$

$$j_5 = j_6 + j_7 = 1 + 1 = 2 \text{ amps.}$$

$$v_5 = 2j_5 + 4 \text{ volts.}$$

$$v_4 = e_2 = v_5 + e_3 = 4 + 2 = 6 \text{ volts.}$$

$$j_4 = \frac{v_4}{3 \text{ ohms}} = \frac{6 \text{ volts}}{3 \text{ ohms}} = 2 \text{ amp.}$$

$$j_3 = j_4 + j_5 = 2 + 2 = 4 \text{ amps.}$$

$$v_3 = 3j_3 + 12 \text{ volts.}$$

$$v_2 = e_1 = v_3 + e_2 = 12 + 6 = 18 \text{ volts.}$$

$$j_2 = \frac{v_2}{3} = \frac{12 \text{ volts}}{3 \text{ ohms}} = 6 \text{ amps.}$$

$$j_1 = j_2 + j_3 = 6 + 4 = 10 \text{ amps.}$$

$$v_1 = 3j_1 = 30 \text{ volts.}$$

$$e_s = v_1 + e_1 = 30 + 18 = 48 \text{ volts.}$$

Thus an input voltage of 48 volts produces a voltage of 1 volt at the output. If now the driving voltage is 10 volts, the output voltage is $\dfrac{10}{48} = 0.2083$ volt. All branch currents and branch voltages may now be obtained by multiplying the previous values by the factor 0.2083. Also the so-called "input resistance" of the network is $\dfrac{e_s}{j_1} = \dfrac{48 \text{ volts}}{10 \text{ amps}} = 4.8$ ohms.

It may be seen that this method is far shorter than the conventional loop or node analysis.

2.18. Duality

In the discussions regarding the selection of current and voltage variables in the analysis on the loop and node bases respectively, we come across a number of similarities and analogies between the proce-dure. Essentially the same sequence of ideas and procedures charac-terise both the loop and the node methods. The principal quantities and concepts involved in the two methods form pairs. Each of the quantity in such a pair thus plays a dual role. These quantities or concepts forming a pair are called "dual" quantities or concepts. Each in the pair is said to be the dual of the other in the pair. Thus current and voltage from dual quantities. Among dual concepts, the most fundamental ones are meshes and nodes, loops and node pairs, open circuit and short circuit etc. Table 2.10 gives several of such dual quantities and concepts.

Table 2.10

Dual Quantities and Concepts

S.No.	*Quantity or concept*	*Its dual*
1.	Current	Voltage
2.	Branch current	Branch voltage
3.	Mesh	Node
4.	Loop	Node pair
5.	Loop current	Node pair voltage
6.	Mesh current	Node voltage
7.	Number of independent loop l	Number of independent node pair n
8.	Link	Tree branch
9.	Link current	Tree branch current
10.	Tie set	Cut set
11.	Short circuit	Open circuit
12.	Shunt paths	Series paths

In Table 2.10, the quantities in the second column are associated with the loop method of analysis whereas the quantities in the third column are associated with the node method of analysis. However, it may be seen that duality is strictly a mutual relationship and any pair of quantities in the table can be interchanged.

Duality of Graphs and Networks. If the characterisation of one network graph on the loop basis yields result identical to those obtained for the characterisation of another network graph on the node basis, then the two networks are said to be duals. Dual graphs neces-sarily have the same number of branches while the number of tree branches in one equals the number of links in the other. This amounts to saying that the number of independent node pair in one equals the number of independent loops in the other. If the networks are duals then the equations expressing the branch currents in terms of loop currents for one network are identical in form with the equations expressing the branch voltages in terms of node pair voltages for the dual network. Thus these sets of equations for the two dual graphs may be interchanged if the letter j and i in one are replaced by e and v respectively in the other.

To illustrate the principle of finding the dual of a graph, *i.e.,* dual of a network only topologically, let us consider the network graph of Fig. 2.21 (*a*). It is required to draw the dual of this graph.

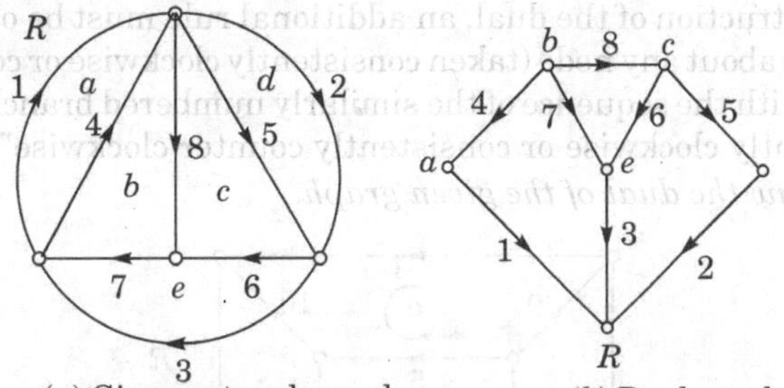

(*a*) Given network graph (*b*) Dual graph

Fig. 2.21. Given graph and its dual.

The given graph has five meshes and three independent code pairs, *i.e.* a total of four nodes. Hence the dual graph must have five node pairs (*i.e.* a total of 6 nodes) and 3 meshes. Further the total number of branches must be the same in each graph. The procedure for drawing the dual then is as follows (*i*) set down 5 small circles as nodes, one for each mesh in the given graph of Fig. 2.21 (*a*), (*ii*) put an extra small circle to act as the datum node and let it be numbered as *R*. (*iii*) assign each of these 5 nodes to one of the five meshes in the given graph. Thus number the meshes in the given graph as *a, b, c, d* and *e*, and number the 5 circles or nodes in the dual as shown in Fig. 2.21 (*b*). (*iv*) for each mesh in the given graph note the tie-set, *i.e.* the branches over which the mesh current flows and draw in the dual graph at the corresponding node, branches forming a cut set corresponding to this tie set in this given graph. Thus for say loop *a* in the given graph the branches forming the tie set are branches 1 and 4. Hence in the dual, at node *a* draw two branches and number them 1 and 4 as shown in Fig. 2.21 (*b*). Similarly for loop *b* the branches forming the tie set are 4, 7 and 8 and hence these branches are confluent at node *b* in the dual graph and so on. In this operation branch 4 joins nodes *a* and *b* in the dual graph. The actual process of drawing the graph then simply consists in noting in the given graph, the loop *s* and *k* to which any branch *j* is common and then in the dual graph, drawing the branch *j* to connect the nodes *s* and *k*. In the given graph, such branches common to two meshes are branches 4, 5, 6, 7 and 8. (*v*) The remaining branches, *i.e.* branches 1, 2 and 3 which are not common to two meshes in the original graph, must form a tie set that must be identical with the cut set of the dual graph associated with reference node *R*. Hence in the dual graph, these branches 1, 2 and 3 must converge at the reference node. This reference graph *R* in the dual may be assigned to the loop formed by the periphery of the given graph and this loop may be treated at the reference loop.

Next we put reference arrows on the branches in the dual graph. Thus in the original graph, as we travel along the mesh *a* in clockwise direction, this traversal is confluent with the arrow of branch 1 and is counterfluent with the arrow of branch 4. Hence in the dual graph, we attach reference arrow to branch 1 to make the current divergent from the node *a* and attach reference arrow to branch 4 to make the current convergent on the node *a*. Same procedure is adopted for all the meshes. Thus confluency and counterfluency of a current in clockwise traversal is correlated with the divergence and convergence respectively at the pertinent node. As an alternative, the traversal could be counter-clock-wise, consistently for all the meshes. Such a step will merely reverse all the reference arrows in the dual graph.

The graph of Fig. 2.21 (*b*) so obtained is a dual of the graph of Fig. 2.21 (*a*). Now if we proceed to find the dual to the graph of Fig. 2.21 (*b*) through the process outlined above, we reobtain graph of Fig. 2.21 (*a*). Thus the graphs of Fig. 2.21 (*a*) and (*b*) are duals of each other in every respect. In certain cases, however starting from a graph say we arrive at a dual graph *B,* the dual of which is not the original graph *A*. Even then graph *B* is said to be dual of graph *A* and yields current or voltage relations, similar to voltage or current relations in graph *A*. If, however, we want to ensure that a graph *C* which is dual of graph *A* be such that the dual of *C* is the original graph A, then in the construction of the dual, an additional rule must be observed. This rule is that "the sequence of branches about any node (taken consistently clockwise or consistently anticlockwise) is chosen to be identical with the sequence of the similarly numbered branches around the respective mesh traversed consistently clockwise or consistently counter clockwise".

Example 2.9. *Draw the dual of the given graph.*

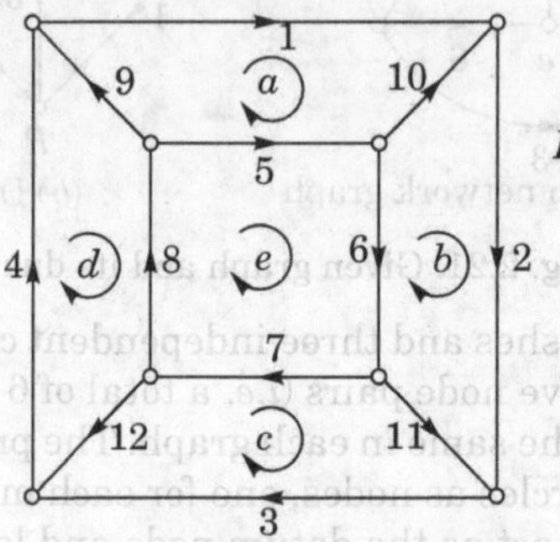

Solution. Let the mesh currents be chosen as shown in the graph and let these meshes be designated as *a, b, c, d* and *e*. Let *R* be the reference mesh. Then in the dual graph there will be 5 nodes *a, b, c, d* and *e*, and there will be a reference node *R*.

Considering mesh *a* in the given graph, mesh current is confluent with the branch currents 1 and 9, and counterfluent with branch currents 10 and 5. Hence in the dual graphs, branch currents 1 and 9 are divergent from node *a* and branch currents 10 and 5 are convergent at node *a*. Further in the dual graph branches are placed in the order 1, 10, 5 and 9 traversing anti-clockwise. Similar procedure is adopted for other nodes. The resulting dual graph is as shown. The dual graph is not mappable on a plane but mappable on a sphere. The anticlockwise order of branches at the nodes may be seen looking into the pertinent node from within the body of the solid represented by the graph.

2.19. Wye-Delta (Y – Δ) Transformation

In the systematic elimination method (Art. 2.16.1) a physical significance may be given to elimination of each variable. Thus if the equilibrium equations involve mesh current variables, then the number of these variables equals the number of meshes and elimination of one mesh current variable may then be given physical interpretation as equivalent to elimination of one mesh from the network graph. Similarly if the equilibrium equations involve node-voltage variables, then elimination of one node voltage variables may be interpreted as elimination of one node from the network graph.

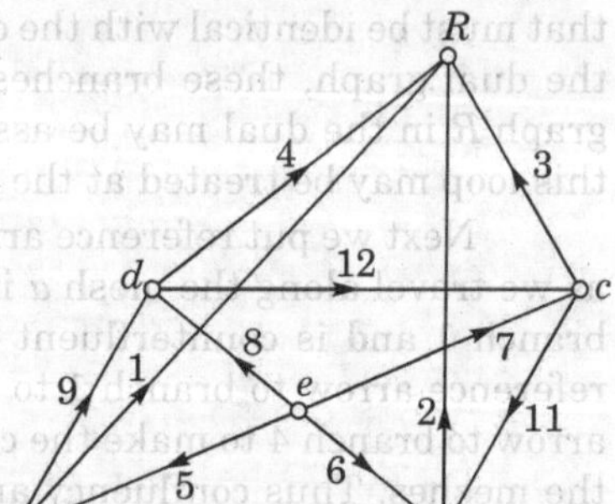

Dual graph

Wye-to-delta transformation. Consider the resistive network fragment in the *Y*(Wye) form shown in Fig. 2.22 *(a)*. This involves three branches and 4 nodes. The number on the branches give the branch conductances in mhos. Let e_1, e_2, e_3 and e_4 be the potential of nodes 1, 2, 3 and 4 with respect to some reference nodes not shown.

By simplified procedure outlined in Article 2.13, we may directly write the four equilibrium equations for this wye-network fragment only involving 4 node-voltage variables e_1, e_2, e_3 and e_4. The rest of the network may be disregarded for the moment. Thus, we get,

$$\left.\begin{aligned} 2e_1 + 0e_2 + 0e_3 - 2e_4 &= 0 \\ 0e_1 + 2e_2 + 0e_3 - 2e_4 &= 0 \\ 0e_1 + 0e_2 + 6e_3 - 6e_4 &= 0 \\ -2e_1 - 2e_2 - 6e_3 + 10e_3 &= 0 \end{aligned}\right\} \quad ...(2.108)$$

The corresponding conductance matrix is :

$$[G] = \left.\begin{bmatrix} 2 & 0 & 0 & -2 \\ 0 & 2 & 0 & -2 \\ 0 & 0 & 6 & -6 \\ -2 & -2 & -6 & 10 \end{bmatrix}\right\} \quad ...(2.109)$$

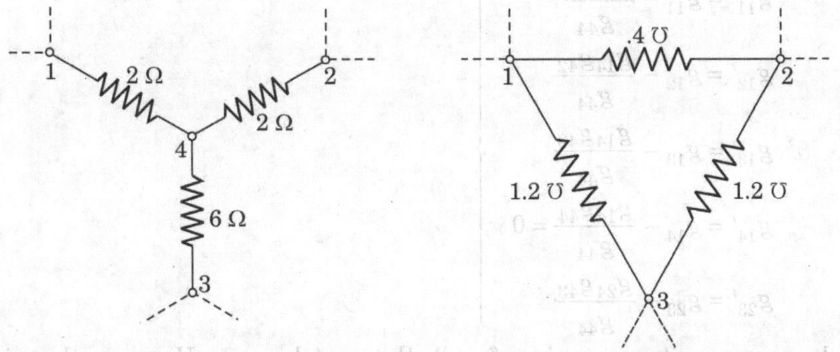

(*a*) Wye-network fragment (*b*) Delta-netwrok equivalent to the Wye-network fragment of (*a*)

Fig. 2.22. Wye-network fragment and its equivalent delta network fragment.

Now suppose we decide to eliminate variable e_4 from these equations. This may be achieved if we through proper manipulation, reduce to zero the first three elements in the fourth column. This may be done by adding to the elements of thc first, second and third row respectively the $\left(\frac{2}{10}\right), -\left(\frac{2}{10}\right)$ and $\left(\frac{6}{10}\right)$ multiplied elements of the fourth row. This results in the following conductance matrix :

$$[G] = \begin{pmatrix} 1.6 & -0.4 & -1.2 & 0 \\ -0.4 & 1.6 & -1.2 & 0 \\ -1.2 & -1.2 & 1.2 & 0 \\ -2 & -2 & -6 & 10 \end{pmatrix} \quad ...(2.110)$$

Disregarding the fourth row, we may now pick-up the first three rows and form the new node conductance matrix G'' corresponding to three equations in three variables e_1, e_2 and e_3. Thus, we have

$$[G''] = \begin{pmatrix} 1.6 & -0.4 & -1.2 \\ -0.4 & 1.6 & -1.2 \\ -1.2 & -1.2 & 2.4 \end{pmatrix} \quad ...(2.111)$$

Through this process, node 4 has been removed from the rest of the network without affecting the remaining node potentials. The network geometry to which the conductance matrix (2.111) relates is shown in Fig. 2.22 (*b*). The numerical values on the branches give the branch conductances in mhos. The truth of this may be verified by writing the node conductance matrix for this network and verifying that it is the same as that given by (2.111).

It may thus be seen that the delta-network fragment of Fig. 2.22 (*b*) is equivalent to the wye-network fragment of Fig. 2.22 (*a*) in so far as we may replace one by the other without disturbing the behavior of the entire network, of which either the wye or the delta network forms a fragment.

By a careful study of the procedure adopted in transforming the matrix (2.109), characterising the wye-network into the matrix (2.111) characterising the delta network, we may evolve a direct procedure for transformation of the wye network of Fig. 2.22 (*a*) into the delta network of Fig. 2.22 (*b*). Let g_{sk} denote the element located in the *s*th row and k_{th}. column of matrix [*G*], and let g_{sk}' denote the similar element in the matrix [*G*″]. Then the following relations giving the elements of [*G*″] in terms of the elements of [*G*] become evident from the study of the manipulations outlined above :

$$\left.\begin{aligned} g_{11}' &= g_{11} - \frac{g_{14}g_{41}}{g_{44}} \\ g_{12}' &= g_{12} - \frac{g_{14}g_{42}}{g_{44}} \\ g_{13}' &= g_{13} - \frac{g_{14}g_{43}}{g_{44}} \\ g_{14}' &= g_{14} - \frac{g_{14}g_{44}}{g_{44}} = 0 \\ g_{23}' &= g_{23} - \frac{g_{24}g_{43}}{g_{44}} \end{aligned}\right\} \qquad \text{...(2.112)}$$

Similarly we may write expressions for all other g_{sk}' elements. However, there is no need to do so since the delta network of Fig. 2.22 (*b*) may be completely constructed if we know the elements g_{12}', g_{13}' and g_{23}' alone. The negatives of these three element give the conductances of the branches linking the nodes to which the subscripts refer.

We now note that is matrix [*G*], the elements g_{12}, g_{13} and g_{23} are all zero. Hence from Eq. (2.112), we get

$$\left.\begin{aligned} -g_{12}' &= \frac{g_{14}g_{42}}{g_{44}} \\ -g_{13}' &= \frac{g_{14}g_{43}}{g_{44}} \\ -g_{23}' &= \frac{g_{24}g_{43}}{g_{44}} \end{aligned}\right\} \qquad \text{...(2.113)}$$

The quantities $-g_{12}'$, $-g_{13}'$ and $-g_{23}'$ give the conductances of branches in the delta network of Fig. 2.22 (*b*) in terms of conductances of the equivalent wye network.

The wye to delta transformation is pictorially summarised in Fig. 2.23. The *g*'s with the lower case literal subscripts give the conductances of branches in the wye network whereas the *g*'s with the upper case literal subscripts give the conductances of the branches in the equivalent delta network.

Equations relating g_{AB}, g_{BC} and g_{CA} with g_a, g_b and g_c may be obtained directly from Eq. (2.113). There are :

$$g_{AB} = \frac{g_a \cdot g_b}{g_a + g_b + g_c} \qquad \text{...(2.114 a)}$$

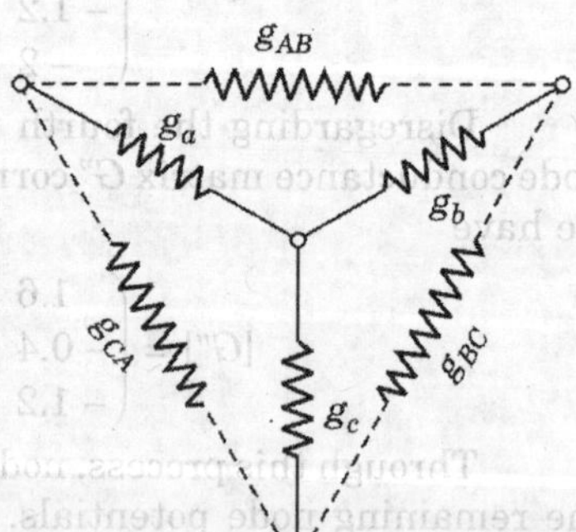

Fig. 2.23. Pictorial representation of the wye-to-delta transformation

$$g_{BC} = \frac{g_b \cdot g_c}{g_a + g_b + g_c} \qquad \text{...(2.114 b)}$$

$$g_{CA} = \frac{g_c \cdot g_a}{g_a + g_b + g_c} \qquad \text{...(2.114 c)}$$

Thus the rule for wye to delta transformation may be stated as "the product of the adjacent two conductances divided by the sum of all the three conductances".

Delta-to-wye (∇ – Y) Transformation. Consider the resistive network fragment in the delta (∇) form shown in Fig. 2.24 (*a*). This involves 3 branches, 3 nodes and 4 mesh currents. Let the branch resistance be r_1, r_2 and r_3 and let i_1, i_2, i_3 and i_4 be the independent mesh currents.

By the simplified procedure, we may directly write the four equilibrium equations for this delta network fragment only involving independent mesh currents i_1, i_2, i_3 and i_4. Thus, we get

$$\left.\begin{aligned} r_1.i_1 + 0.i_2 + 0.i_3 - r_1.i_4 &= 0 \\ 0.i_1 + r_2.i_2 + 0.i_3 - r_2.i_4 &= 0 \\ 0.i_1 + 0.i_2 + r_3.i_3 - r_3.i_4 &= 0 \\ -r_1.i_1 - r_2.i_2 - r_3.i_3 + (r_1 + r_2 + r_3)\, i_4 &= 0 \end{aligned}\right\} \qquad \text{...(2.115)}$$

The corresponding resistance matrix is :

$$[R] = \begin{pmatrix} r_1 & 0 & 0 & -r_1 \\ 0 & r_2 & 0 & -r_2 \\ 0 & 0 & r_3 & -r_3 \\ -r_1 & -r_2 & -r_3 & r_{44} \end{pmatrix} \qquad \text{...(2.116)}$$

where $r_{44} = r_1 + r_2 + r_3$ ...(2.117)

Now the variable i_4 may be eliminated from Eq. (2.116) by adding to the elements of the first, second and third rows respectively and $\frac{r_1}{r_{44}}$, $\frac{r_2}{r_{44}}$ and $\frac{r_3}{r_{44}}$ multiplied elements of the last row. In the resulting resistance matrix $[R']$ then, the first three elements in the fourth column are zeros. Considering only the first three rows of this matrix, we get three equations involving three independent variables i_1, i_2 and i_3, *i.e.* the variable i_4 has been eliminated. The new resistance matrix $[R'']$ corresponding to these three equation is then,

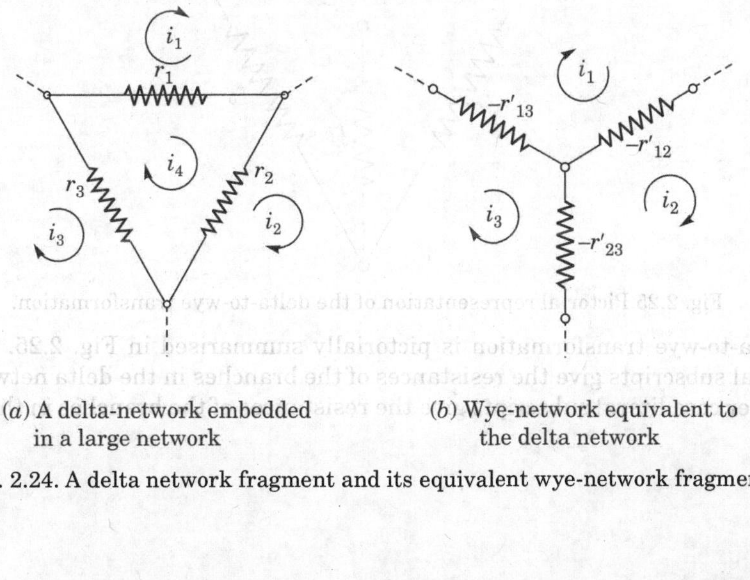

(*a*) A delta-network embedded in a large network

(*b*) Wye-network equivalent to the delta network

Fig. 2.24. A delta network fragment and its equivalent wye-network fragment.

$$[R'] = \begin{pmatrix} r_{11}' & r_{12}' & r_{13}' \\ r_{21}' & r_{22}' & r_{23}' \\ r_{31}' & r_{32}' & r_{33}' \end{pmatrix} \quad ...(2.118)$$

where
$$\left.\begin{aligned} r_{12}' &= 0 + \frac{r_1}{r_{44}}.(-r_2) \\ r_{13}' &= 0 + \frac{r_1}{r_{44}}.(-r_3) \\ r_{23}' &= 0 + \frac{r_2}{r_{44}}.(-r_3) \end{aligned}\right\} \quad ..(2.119)$$

The rest of the terms may similarly be written in accordance with the above procedure.

Through this process, mesh 4 has been removed from the rest of the network without affecting the remaining node potentials. The network geometry to which the resistance matrix (2.118) refers is shown in Fig. 2.24 (*b*). The branches are shown to have resistance $-r_{12}'$, $-r_{13}'$ and $-r_{23}'$. If we write the loop resistance matrix for this network, we arrive at the matrix (2.118). Hence the wye network fragment of Fig. 2.24 (*b*) is equivalent to the delta network fragement of Fig. 2.24 (*a*) in so far as we may replace one by the other without disturbing the behaviour of the entire network.

The branch resistance of equivalent wye network may be directly expressed in terms of the branch resistance of the delta network by utilizing the Eq. (2.119). Thus,

$$\left.\begin{aligned} -r_{12}' &= \frac{r_1 r_2}{r_1 + r_2 + r_3} \\ r_{13}' &= \frac{r_1 r_3}{r_1 + r_2 + r_3} \\ r_{23}' &= \frac{r_2 r_3}{r_1 + r_2 + r_3} \end{aligned}\right\} \quad ..(2.120)$$

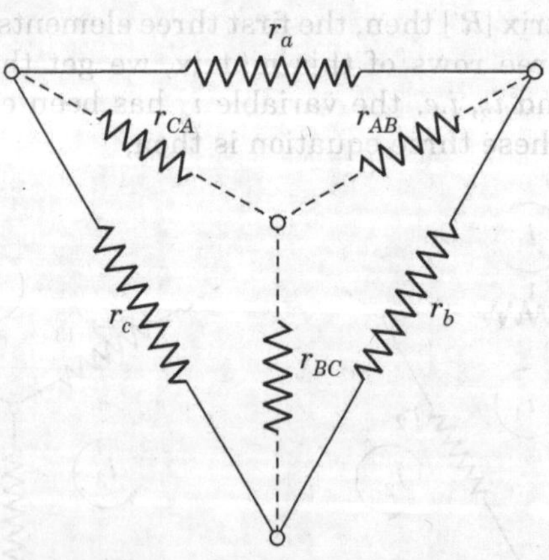

Fig. 2.25 Pictorial representation of the delta-to-wye transformation.

The delta-to-wye transformation is pictorially summarised in Fig. 2.25. The *r*'s with the lower case literal subscripts give the resistances of the branches in the delta network whereas the *r*'s with the upper case literal subscripts give the resistances of the branches in the equivalent wye network.

Equations relating r_{AB}, r_{BC} and r_{CA} with r_a, r_b and r_c may be obtained directly from Eq. (2.220). These are :

$$r_{AB} = \frac{r_a r_b}{r_a + r_b + r_c} \quad \text{...(2.221 a)}$$

$$r_{BC} = \frac{r_b r_c}{r_a + r_b + r_c} \quad \text{...(2.221 b)}$$

$$r_{CA} = \frac{r_a r_c}{r_a + r_b + r_c} \quad \text{...(2.221 c)}$$

The rule for delta-to-wye transformation may be stated as "the product of the adjacent two resistance divided by the sum of all the three resistances".

3

Step Function Response of Simple R-L and R-C Circuits

3.1. First Order Differential Equations

Eq. (3.1) gives a simple first order differential equation :

$$a_0 = \frac{di}{dt} + a_1 \,.\, i = 0 \qquad ...(3.1)$$

where a_0 and a_1 are constants.

Eq. (3.1) is of the first order since the highest order derivative namely *di/dt* is of the first order. The order of the differential equation is reckoned from the highest order derivative contained in it. Thus Eq. (3.2) given below is a differential equation of *n*th order :

$$a_0 \frac{d^n i}{dt^n} + a_1 \cdot \frac{d^{n-1} i}{dt^{n-1}} + \cdots + a_{n-1} \frac{di}{dt} + a_n i = C \qquad ...(3.2)$$

The degree of an equation is the power to which the highest order derivative appear after all possible algebraic reduction. Thus Eq. (3.2) is a *n*th order differential equation of first degree.

In Eq. (3.2) above, *t* is the independent variable where *i* is the dependent variable.

Linear and non-linear differential equation. A differential equations is said to be linear if the dependent variable and all its derivatives are of first degree. All other equations are said to be non-linear.

Ordinary differential equations. A differential equation is said to be ordinary if it contains only total derivatives (and not partial derivatives). On the order hand, if the differential equation contains partial derivatives also, it is said to be partial differential equation.

Homogeneous differential equation. The differential equation such as (3.2) is said to be homogeneous if the term *C* (term free of in dependent variable or their derivatives) is zero. Thus differential equation (3.2) becomes homogeneous if $C = 0$. If *C* is not zero, the differential equation is said to be non-homogeneous.

We will here consider circuits whose differential equations are "ordinary linear differential equations with constant coefficients".

Thus Eq. (3.3) gives one such equation for an electrical network.

$$a_0 \frac{d^n i}{dt^n} + a_1 \cdot \frac{d^{n-1} i}{dt^{n-1}} + \cdots + a_{n-1} \cdot \frac{di}{dt} + a_n \,.\, t = v(t) \qquad ...(3.3)$$

This is an ordinary linear differential equation of *n*th order.

Here *v (t) is* the time-varying source voltage and this *v (t)* may be called the *forcing function.* This voltage *v (t)* results in the *response* namely current *i* which forms the dependent variable.

3.2. R-L Circuit

Consider the *R-L* network of Fig. 3.1. Let initially the switch *K* be at position number 1.

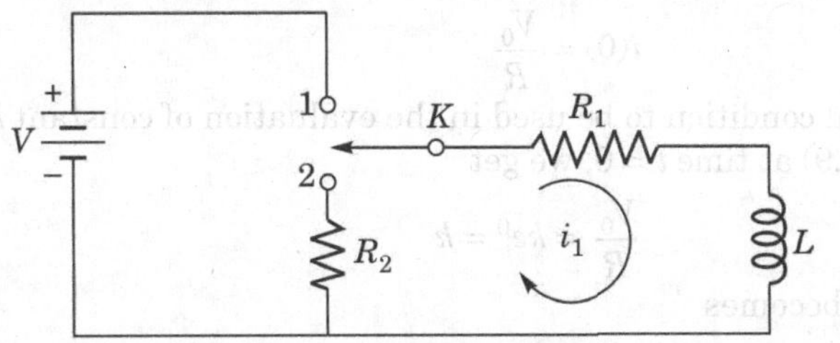

Fig. 3.1. Simple *R-L* Circuit.

In this condition, the network is assumed to be in a known state, *i.e.* all voltage and currents are known. At the instant of time designated $t = 0$, the switch *K* is moved from position 1 to 2. The objective of this analysis is to obtained equation for current, voltage, charge etc. in terms of time measured from the reference time $t = 0$, *i.e.* from the time switch *K* is moved from position 1 to position 2.

After time $t = 0$, application of Kirchhoff's voltage law to *R-L* network yields :

$$L\frac{di}{dt} + R_i = 0 \qquad ...(3.4)$$

Eq. (3.4) is a first order homogeneous linear differential equation with constant coefficients. Eq. (3.4) may be solved by separating the variables.

Thus Eq. (3.4) may be rearranged as :

$$\frac{di}{dt} = -\frac{R}{L}dt \qquad ...(3.5)$$

On integration, Eq. (3.5) yields,

$$l_n i = -\frac{R}{L}t + l_n k \qquad ...(3.6)$$

where *k* is a constant.

Eq. (3.6) may be a put as,

$$l_n i = l_n e^{-\frac{Rt}{L}} + l_n k \qquad ...(3.7)$$

$$= l_n (k.e^{-\frac{Rt}{L}}) \qquad ...(3.8)$$

On taking anti-logarithm, we get

$$i = k.e^{-\frac{Rt}{L}} \qquad ...(3.9)$$

Eq. (3.9) is the network response or network solution. The solution of a network should give an expression for the independent variable (*i* in this case) in terms of dependent variable and the expression should be free of derivatives. Thus Eq. (3.9) gives the solution of the given network of the Fig. 3.1. The validity of this solution may be verified by substituting the value of *i* as given by Eq. (3.9) into Eq. (3.4).

The solution as given by Eq. (3.9) is called the "General Solution" since the value of costant *k* has not been found. If the value of constant *k* is found and substituted in Eq. (3.9), the resulting solution is called the "Particular Solution". Thus whereas the general solution as given by Eq. (3.9) applies to any general solution for the given network, the particular solution meets the specifications of a particular problem.

Now the general solution as given by Eq. (3.9) gives the nature of the current *i* as determined by the circuit components *L* and *R*. In order to find the value of constant of integration we have to look into the initial conditions. We know that because of the presence of inductor L, the current i through the LR circuit just before switching must be the same as just before switching.

Just before switching at $t = 0$, the current is given by,

$$i(0) = \frac{V_0}{R} \quad ...(3.10)$$

This is the initial condition to be used in the evaluation of constant k. Thus putting current i equal to V_0/R in Eq. (3.9) at time $t = 0$, we get

$$\frac{V_0}{R} = ke^0 = k \quad ...(3.11)$$

Hence Eq. (3.9) becomes

$$i = \frac{V_0}{R} e^{-\frac{Rt}{L}}. \quad ...(3.12)$$

Eq. (3.12) gives the particular solution.

3.3. Solution of a Non-homogeneous Equation Using Integrating Factor

Let the given non-homogeneous equation be,

$$\frac{di}{dt} + Pi = Q \quad ...(3.13)$$

where P is a constant and Q may be either a function of the independent variable t or a constant.

Now let us multiply the Eq. (3.13) by a quantity e^{Pt}, called the integrating factor.

The resulting equation is,

$$e^{Pt}\frac{di}{dt} + Pie^{Pt} = Qe^{Pt} \quad ...(3.14)$$

We know that,

$$d\,(xy) = x\,dy + y\,dx \quad ...(3.15)$$

Letting $x = i$

and $y = e^{Pt}$, Eq. (3.15) yields,

$$\frac{d}{dt}(i.e^{Pt}) = e^{Pt}\frac{di}{dt} + i \cdot P \cdot e^{Pt} \quad ...(3.16)$$

Combining Eqs. (3.14) and (3.16), we get

$$\frac{d}{dt}(i.e^{Pt}) = Q\,e^{Pt} \quad ...(3.17)$$

Integrating Eq. (3.17), we get

$$i.e^{Pt} = \int Q\,e^{Pt}\,dt + k \quad ...(3.18)$$

or

$$i = e^{-Pt}\int Q\,e^{Pt}\,dt + k\,.\,e^{-Pt} \quad ...(3.19)$$

Value of i as given by Eq. (3.19) consists of two parts :

(*i*) $e^{-Pt}\int Q e^{Pt}\,dt$ called the *particular integral* and

(*ii*) $k.e^{-Pt}$, called the *complementary function.*

It may be noted that the particular integral does not contain the constant of integration k. On the other hand, the complementry function does not depend on the forcing function Q.

In the case of a network, P is a positive constant whose value depends on the network parameters. Quantity Q is either the forcing function or a derivative thereof.

In the limit as time, t approaches infinity, the complementry function must approach zero, since P is a positive constant.

Thus $$\underset{t\to\infty}{\text{Lt}}\ k.e^{-Pt} = 0 \qquad ...(3.20)$$

Hence as time t approaches infinity, the value of current i becomes,

$$i(\infty) = \underset{t\to 0}{\text{Lt}}\ i(t) = \underset{t\to 0}{\text{Lt}} = e^{-Pt}\int Q\,e^{Pt}\,dt \qquad ...(3.21)$$

Thus as time t approaches infinity, the complementry function approaches zero but the particular integral, in general, does not approach zero. The value of particular integral, at time $t = \infty$ is called the *steady-state value* of independent variable. For a non-zero steady state value to reach, it is necessary that the particular integral contains no exponential function.

In electrical network, the general nature of the steady state value i_{ss} is given by,

$$i_{ss} = k_1 + k_2 \sin(\omega t + \phi) \qquad ...(3.22)$$

where k_1 and k_2 are constants.

Now with reference to the general solution given by Eq. (3.19), let the particular integral and the complementry function be indicated by i_p and i_c respectively. Then Eq. (3.19) may be written as,

$$i = i_p + i_c \qquad ...(3.23)$$

Now as stated earliar the particluar integral i_p constitutes the steady state value i_{ss} whereas the complementary function i_c is nothing but a decaying exponential for positive value of constant P. This complementary function ke^{-Pt} is conventionally called the *transient* part of the solution and may be indicated by i_t.

Hence the complete solution may be written as,

$$i = i_{ss} + i_t \qquad ...(3.24)$$

Out of these two values, the steady state value remains the same at time $t = \infty$ as at $t = 0$. This steady state value i_{ss} thus establishes itself at time $t = 0$ itself. The transient value must, therefore, adjust itself to account for the response at $t = 0$ and at other times.

Such a division of the response i into two parts namely the steady state value i_{ss} and the transient part i_t is entirely arbitrary but is of great utility in visualising the nature of current variation.

With reference to Eq. (3.12) giving the current in the circuit of Fig. 3.1 after the switch S is moved from position 1 to position 2, the resulting current i consists only of the exponentially decaying component $\frac{V}{R}e^{-\frac{Rt}{L}}$. This corresponds to the transient part. The steady state value is zero. Thus at time $t = 0$, the total current becomes $\frac{V}{R}$.

3.4. Step Voltage Response of Series R.L. Circuit

With reference to the network of Fig. 3.1, let the switch K be moved from position 2 to position 1 at time $t = 0$. This amounts to applying to the R-L network a d.c. step voltage of value V volts.

On applying Kirchhoff's voltage law to the network, we get

$$L\frac{di}{dt} + Ri = V_0 \qquad ...(3.25)$$

or $$\frac{di}{dt} + \frac{R}{L} i = \frac{V_0}{L} \qquad ...(3.26)$$

Comparing Eq. (3.26) with Eq. (3.13), gives us the values of P and Q.

Thus $$P = \frac{R}{L} \quad \text{and} \quad Q = \frac{V_0}{L}.$$

Hence the solution of this equation as given by Eq. (3.19) becomes,

$$i = e^{-Pt} \int Qe^{Pt}\, dt + k \,.\, e^{-Pt} \qquad ...(3.19)$$

Substituting the values of P and Q, we get

$$i = e^{-\frac{Rt}{L}} \int \frac{V_0}{L} . e^{\frac{Rt}{L}}\, dt + k.e^{-\frac{Rt}{L}} \qquad ...(3.27)$$

or $$i = e^{-\frac{Rt}{L}} . \frac{V_0}{L} . e^{\frac{Rt}{L}} . \frac{L}{R} + k.e^{-\frac{Rt}{L}} \qquad ...(3.28)$$

or $$i = \frac{V_0}{R} + k.e^{-\frac{Rt}{L}} \qquad ...(3.29)$$

Eq. (3.29) gives the general solution of the network.

Here constant k remains to be evaluated. In order to evaluate constant k, we make use of the initial condition that the current i is zero before the switching action and it must remain zero just after switching because of the presence of inductor L.

Hence Eq. (3.29) yields,

$$0 = \frac{V_0}{R} + k.e^0 \qquad ...(3.30)$$

Hence $$k = -\frac{V_0}{R} \qquad ...(3.31)$$

On substituting this value of k in Eq. (3.29), we get

$$i = \frac{V_0}{R} - \frac{V_0}{R} e^{-\frac{Rt}{L}}$$

or $$i = \frac{V_0}{R}\left[1 - e^{-\frac{Rt}{L}}\right] \qquad ...(3.32)$$

This is the particular solution.

In Eq. (3.32), $\frac{V_0}{R}$ is the steady part i_{ss} of the solution while $\frac{-V_0}{R} e^{-\frac{Rt}{L}}$ is the transient part i_t of the solution. Fig. 3.2 shows the nature of variation of these two parts and also the variation of the sum i with time.

It may be seen that at $t = 0$, the steady state portion, i_{ss} is established at the value V_0/R. But at $t = 0$, total current i being zero, the transient portion i_t must adjust to value $\frac{-V_0}{R}$ at $t = 0$.

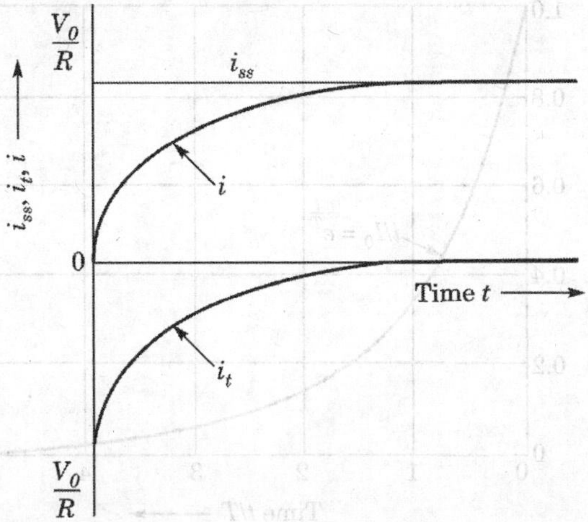

Fig. 3.2. Steady state and transient portions of the total current in the network of Fig. 3.1.

3.5. Time Constant

Eq. (3.12) gives the particular solution of Eq. (3.4).

Eq. (3.12) may be rewritten as,

$$i = I_0 e^{-t/T} \quad \text{...(3.33)}$$

where I_0 is the initial value of current, *i.e.* current at time $t = 0$ and equals V/R.

and $$T = \frac{L}{R}.$$

This ratio $\frac{L}{R}$ is called the "time-constant" of the R-L circuit.

Eq. (3.33) may be written as,

$$\frac{i}{I_0} = e^{-t/T} \quad \text{...(3.34)}$$

Then Eq. (3.34) gives the form of solution obtainable for all homogeneous first-order linear differential equations. Quantities T_0 and T will have different values for different equations or different problems.

It is of interest to study the physical significance of the term time constant.

Thus at time $t = T$, *i.e.* after a time interval equal to one time constant, the value of i in accordance with Eq. (3.34) is given by

$$\frac{i_{(T)}}{I_0} = e^{-1} = 0.37 \quad \text{...(3.35)}$$

Thus current reduces to 37% of its initial value after a time interval equal to one time constant.

Similarly by putting $t = 4T$ in Eq. (3.34), we find that the current reduces to about 2% of its initial value I_0 after a time interval equal to 4 time constants. Fig. 3.3 shows the variation of current ratio i/I_0 with time t/T.

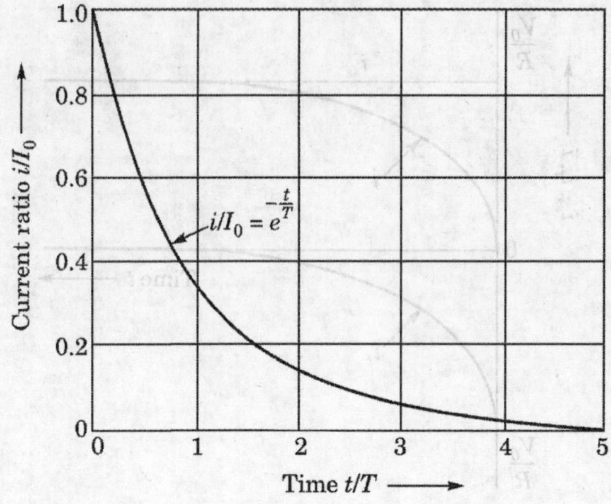

Fig. 3.3. Variation of current ratio i/I_0 with time.

Eq. (3.32) gives the particular solution of Eq. (3.26) which is a first-order linear non-homogeneous differential equation with a steady forcing function V. This Eq. (3.32) may be written as,

$$\frac{i}{I_0} = (1 - e^{-t/T}) \qquad \text{...(3.36)}$$

where I_0 is the steady state value of current and equal V_0/R,
and T is the time constant which equals L/R.

Then Eq. (3.36) gives the form of solution obtainable for all non-homogeneous first order linear differential equations.

At time $t = T$, *i.e.* after a time interval equal to one time constant, the value of current i in accordance with Eq. (3.36) is given by,

$$\frac{i_{(T)}}{I_0} = (1 - e^{-1}) = 0.63 \qquad \text{...(3.37)}$$

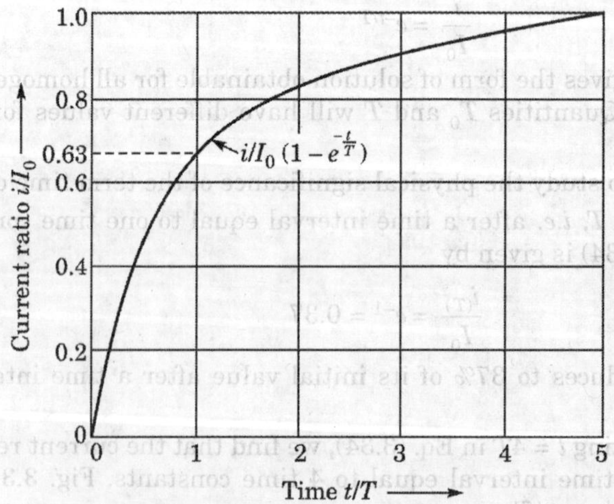

Fig. 3.4. Variation of current ratio i/I_0 with time.

Thus the current reaches 63% of its steady state value in one time constant. Similarly by putting $t = 4T$ in Eq. (3.36), we find that the current rises to approximately 98% of its final value in 4 time constants. Fig. 3.4 shows the nature of variation of current ratio i/I_0 with time t/T.

Thus we find that the time constant is a useful quantity in comparing the behaviour of different systems. It is conveniently possible to measure the time interval of an exponential function to decrease to 37% of its initial value (or increase to 67% of its final value) and these time intervals may be used for comparison of different systems.

3.6. Step Voltage Response of Series R-C Circuit

Case I. Let the switch k be initially at position 1. In this condition, the network is assumed to be in a known state, *i.e.* all voltages and currents are known. At an instant of time say $t = 0$, switch K be moved from position 1 to position 2.

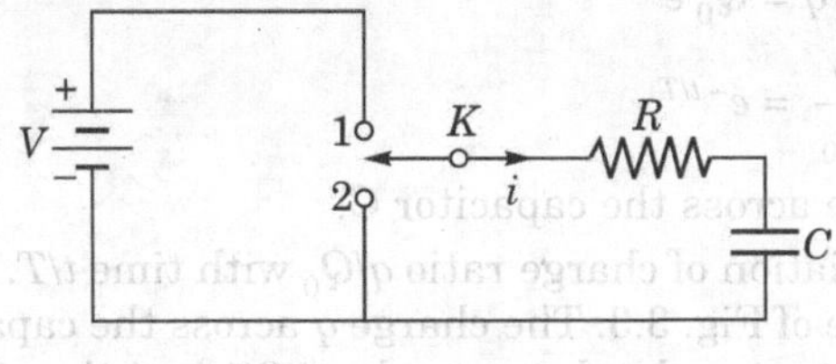

Fig. 3.5. Series *R-C* circuit.

After switching has been done, application of Kirchhoff's voltage law to the network yields,

$$\frac{1}{C}\int i\,dt + Ri = 0 \qquad \text{...(3.38)}$$

Eq. (3.38) may be rewritten as,

$$R\frac{dq}{dt} + \frac{q}{C} = 0 \qquad \text{...(3.39)}$$

Separating the variables, Eq. (3.39) may be written as,

$$-\frac{1}{RC}dt = \frac{dq}{q} \qquad \text{...(3.40)}$$

Integrating both sides,

$$-\frac{1}{RC}\int dt = \int \frac{dq}{q} \qquad \text{..(3.41)}$$

or

$$-\frac{t}{RC} = \ln q + \ln k \qquad \text{...(3.42)}$$

where ln k is the constant of integration.

Eq. (3.42) may be put as,

$$q = Re^{-\frac{t}{RC}} \qquad \text{...(3.43)}$$

Constant k may be evaluated from the initial condition. Before switching at $t = 0$, the charge q across the capacitor C is given by,

$$q_{(t=0)} = VC \qquad \text{...(3.44)}$$

Now as the impressed voltage V is suddenly removed (without opening the circuit) from the *RC* circuit, the charge across the capacitor must remain the same as just before switching.

Hence putting $q = VC$ at time $t = 0$ in Eq. (3.43), we get

$$k = VC \qquad \text{...(3.45)}$$

Substituting this value of k in Eq. (3.43), we get

$$q = VCe^{-\frac{t}{RC}} \qquad \text{...(3.46)}$$

or
$$v_C = \frac{q}{C} = V.e^{-\frac{t}{RC}} \qquad \text{...(3.47)}$$

where v_C is the voltage across the capacitor C at time t.

Eq. (3.47) gives the particular solution.

The product RC has dimensions of ohm × farads which may be shown equal to seconds. This products RC is called the "time constant" of the RC network and may be indicated by T.

Eq. (3.46) may be written as,

or
$$q = Q_0\, e^{-t/T} \qquad \text{...(3.48)}$$

or
$$\frac{q}{Q_0} = e^{-t/T} \qquad \text{...(3.49)}$$

where Q_0 is the initial charge across the capacitor C.

Fig. 3.6 shows the variation of charge ratio q/Q_0 with time t/T. This curve (actually plotting $e^{-t/T}$) is the same as the curve of Fig. 3.3. The charge q across the capacitor C reduces to 37% of its initial value in one time constant and reduces to about 2% in 4 time constants.

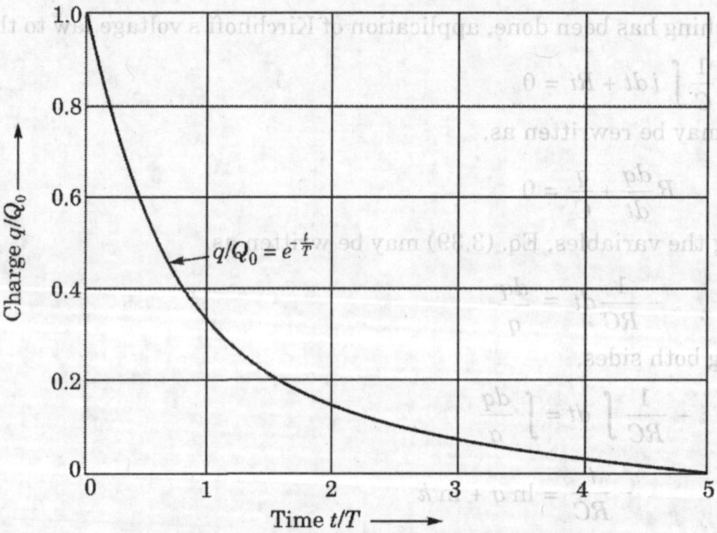

Fig. 3.6. Variation of charge ratio q/Q_0 with time.

Case II. Let initial the switch K be at position 2. Under this condition, there is no charge on capacitor C and there is no voltage across it. Let the switch K be moved from position 2 to position 1 at time t = 0. The entire voltage V now gets applied to R-C circuit.

Application of Kirchhoff's voltage law to this circuit yields,

$$Ri + \frac{1}{C} i\, dt = V \qquad \text{...(3.50)}$$

On differentiation, Eq. (3.50) yields,

$$R\frac{di}{dt} + \frac{i}{C} = 0 \qquad ...(3.51)$$

On separating the variables, we get

$$(-RC)\frac{di}{i} = dt \qquad ...(3.52)$$

On integration Eq. (3.52) gives,

$$-RC \ln = t + k \qquad ...(3.53)$$

where k is the constant of integration.

This value of constant k may be obtained by using the initial conditions.

Thus before the switch is put to position 1, the charge across the capacitor C is zero. Hence just after switching, at $t = 0$, the charge q and voltage v_c across capacity C must remain zero. Hence the entire voltage V drops across R. Hence initial current equals V/R.

Substituting this initial condition in Eq. (3.53), we get

$$-RC \ln^{V/R} = k \qquad ...(3.54)$$

Substituting this value of k in Eq. (3.53)

$$-RC \ln i = t - RC \ln^{V/R} \qquad ...(3.55)$$

or

$$\ln \frac{i}{V/R} = \frac{-t}{RC}$$

or

$$\frac{i}{V/R} = e^{-t/RC}$$

or

$$i = \frac{V}{R} . e^{-t/RC} \qquad ...(3.56)$$

$$i = Ie^{-t/T} \qquad ...(3.57)$$

where $I (= V/R)$ is the initial current, *i.e.* current at $t = 0$ and $T (= RC)$ is the time constant.

The voltage drop across resistor R equals Ri and has the same form as the current. Thus voltage v_R across R is given by,

$$v_R = IRe^{-t/T} \qquad ...(3.58)$$

$$= V . e^{-t/T} \qquad ...(3.59)$$

The voltage across capacitor C may be obtained by using the relation,

$$v_C = \frac{1}{C}\int i\, dt \qquad ...(3.60)$$

Alternatively

$$v_C = V - V_R$$

$$= V - Ve^{-t/T}$$

$$= V[1 - e^{-t/T}] \qquad ...(3.61)$$

Charge across the capacitor at time t is given by,

$$q = Cv_c = CV\,[1 - e^{-t/T}] \qquad ...(3.62)$$

Eq. (3.62) giving the solution for the network may be put as follows :

$$q = CV - CVe^{-t/T} \qquad ...(3.63)$$

$$= q_{ss} + q_t \qquad ...(3.64)$$

where q_{ss} is the steady state value of the charge and q_t is the transient part of the charge.

The transient part of the charge q namely $- CVe^{-t/T}$ increases with time and equals zero at time $t = \infty$. Thus the total charge q across the capacitor C is zero initially and equal CV at $t = \infty$.

Fig. 3.7 shows the steady state part q_{ss} and the transient part q_t of the total charge q across the capacitor plotted as a function of time t.

Eq. (3.62) may be rewritten as

$$\frac{q}{Q_0} = [1 - e^{-t/T}] \qquad ...(3.65)$$

where Q_0 is the final charge (steady state charge CV) across the capacitor C.

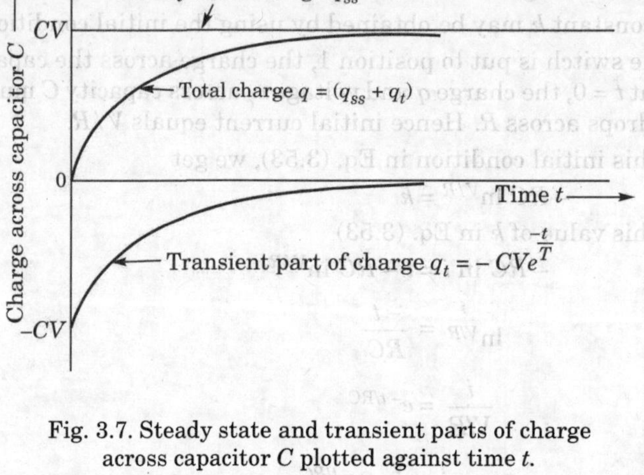

Fig. 3.7. Steady state and transient parts of charge across capacitor C plotted against time t.

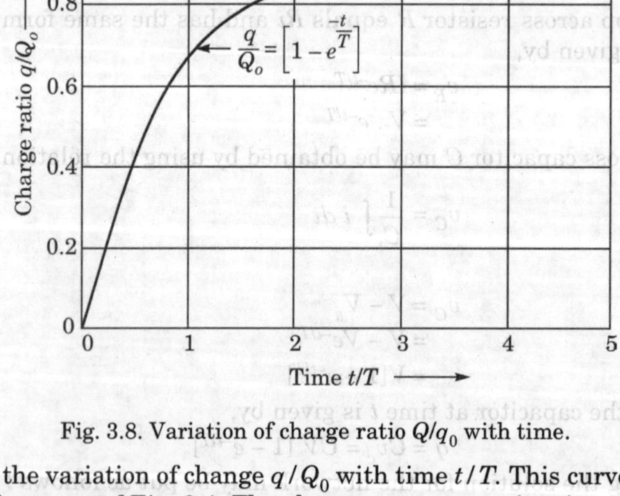

Fig. 3.8. Variation of charge ratio Q/q_0 with time.

Fig. 3.8 shows the variation of change q/Q_0 with time t/T. This curve (actually plotting $1 - e^{t/T}$) is the same as the curve of Fig. 3.4. The charge across capacitor increase to 63% of its final value in one time constant and increases to about 98% in 4 time constants.

3.7. Principal of Superposition

Fig. 3.9 shows a series R-L circuit placed in series with n voltage sources all placed in series.

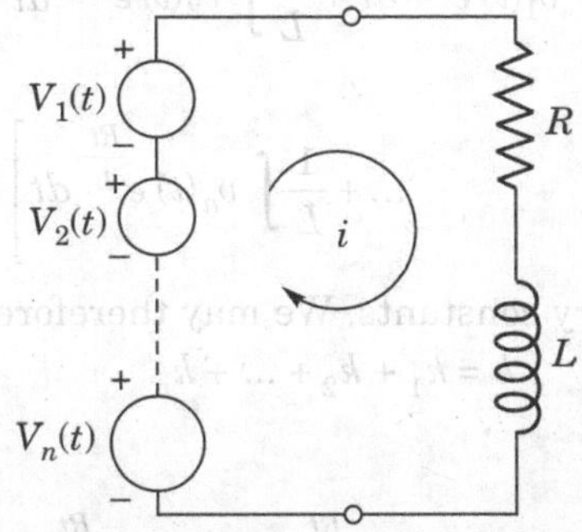

Fig. 3.9. R-L series circuit in series with n voltage sources.

The application of Kirchhoff's voltage law yields,

$$L\frac{di}{dt} + Ri = v_1(t) + v_2(t) + \ldots + v_n(t) \quad \ldots(3.66)$$

or

$$\frac{di}{dt} + \frac{R}{L}i = \frac{1}{L}[v_1(t) + v_2(t) + \ldots + v_n(t)] \quad \ldots(3.67)$$

Eq. (3.67) is a first linear non-homogeneous differential equation. Its general solution is,

$$i = e^{-Pt}\int Qe^{Pt}\,dt + k.e^{-Pt} \quad \ldots(3.68)$$

where $P = \dfrac{R}{L}$ and $Q = \dfrac{1}{L}[v_1(t) + v_2(t) + \ldots + v_n(t)]$

or

$$i = e^{-Pt}\int \frac{1}{L}[v_1(t) + v_2(t) + \ldots + v_n(t)]\,e^{Rt/L}\,dt + k.e^{-Rt/L} \quad \ldots(3.69)$$

In this solution given by Eq. (3.68), the particular integral $e^{-Pt}\int Qe^{+Pt}\,dt$ depends on the nature of the forcing function voltages. Hence the particular integral is often called the "forced response". On the other hand, the complementary function $k.e^{-Pt}$ does not depend on the forcing function Q except that the constant of integration k is evaluated from the magnitude of the forcing function at $t = 0$ and also from the circuit condition prevailing. Hence the complementary function is called the "free response". Thus the total response can be considered to be consisting of two parts namely forced response and free response. Thus the two parts of the solution of the differential equation may be defined by the following 3 sets of terms :

(1) Particular Integral	Complementary Function
$e^{-Pt}\int Qe^{-Pt}\,dt$	ke^{-Pt}
(2) Steady State Response	Transient Response
(3) Forced Response	Free Response.

All the three sets of terms are used in Electrical Engineering.

Now in the circuit of Fig. 3.9, suppose we remove and replace by short circuits all voltage sources, except $v_1(t)$. The response under this condition is,

$$t_1 = e^{-\frac{Rt}{L}}\int \frac{1}{L}v_1(t)\,e^{\frac{Rt}{L}}\,dt + k_1 \cdot e^{\frac{-Rt}{L}} \quad \ldots(3.70)$$

Response of each of the remaining voltage source is similar to that given by Eq. (3.70).

The total response is the sum of the individual responses and is given by,

$$i_1 + i_2 + ... + i_n = e^{-\frac{Rt}{L}} \left[\frac{1}{L} \int v_1(t)\, e^{\frac{Rt}{L}}\, dt + \frac{1}{L} \int v_2(t)\, e^{\frac{Rt}{L}}\, dt + ... \right.$$

$$\left. ... + \frac{1}{L} \int v_n(t)\, e^{\frac{Rt}{L}}\, dt \right] + (k_1 + k_2 + ... + k_n)\, e^{-\frac{Rt}{L}} \quad ...(3.71)$$

Now k_1, k_2 etc. are arbitrary constants. We may therefore use,

$$k = k_1 + k_2 + ... + k_n \quad ...(3.72)$$

Hence $i_1 + i_2 + ... + i_n$

$$= e^{-\frac{Rt}{L}} \int \frac{1}{L} (v_1 + v_2 + ... + v_n)\, e^{\frac{Rt}{L}}\, dt + k_1 . e^{\frac{-Rt}{L}} \quad ...(3.73)$$

This equation is identical with Eq. (3.69) which is applicable to the combined forcing functions.

Thus we conclude that the total response of a linear network in identical with that obtained by considering each source individually with all other sources short circuited and then summing these individual responses. This principle is known as the "Principle of Supperposition". The principle holds goods for any linear network for any number of voltages located anywhere in the network and not necessarily in series as shown in Fig. 3.9. Of course, the principle of superposition cannot be applied to non-linear systems.

Example 3.1. *In the given circuit, switch K is initially at position 1. On the steady state having reached, switch K is changed to position 2. Find the particular solution for the current in the circuit. Also find the voltage across R_1 and L at time t.*

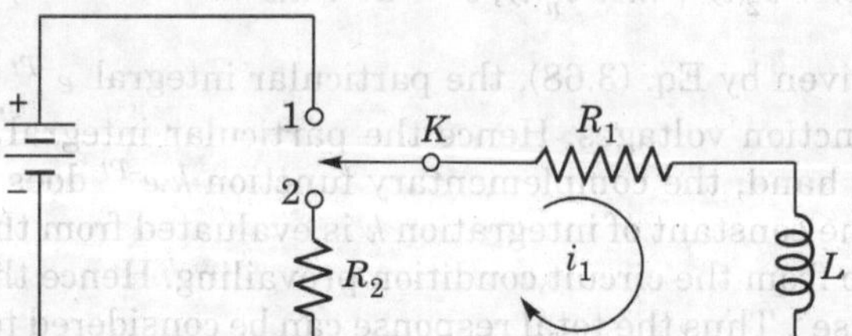

Solution. With switch K at position 2, application of Kirchhoff's voltage law yield,

$$i(R_1 + R_2) + L\frac{di}{dt} = 0 \quad ...(1)$$

Separating the variables,

$$\frac{di}{i} = -\frac{R_1 + R_2}{L} dt \quad ...(2)$$

Integrating equation (2), we get

$$\ln i = -\frac{(R_1 + R_2)\, t}{L} + \ln k$$

or

$$\ln i/k = \frac{-(R_1 + R_2)\, t}{L}$$

Hence $$i = k.e^{-\frac{(R_1 + R_2)t}{L}} \quad ...(3)$$

Constant k may be evaluated from the initial condition that at $t = 0$, after switching to position 2, current i at $t = 0$ after switching is the same as before switching and equals $\frac{V}{R_1}$.

Substituting this value at $t = 0$ in Eq. (3), we get

$$\frac{V}{R_1} = k.e^0 = k.$$

Putting $k = \frac{V}{R_1}$ in Eq. (3), we get the following particular solution for current,

$$i = \frac{V}{R_1} e^{-\frac{(R_1 + R_2 t}{L}} \quad ...(4)$$

Voltage across R_1 at time t is given by,

$$v_1 = i \times R_1 = V e^{-\frac{(R_1 + R_2)t}{L}}$$

Voltage across L at time t is given by,

$$v_L = L\frac{di}{dt} = L\frac{d}{dt}\left[\frac{V}{R_1} e^{-\frac{(R_1 + R_2)t}{L}}\right]$$

$$= L\frac{V}{R_1}.e^{-\frac{(R_1 + R_2)}{L}}\left[-\frac{R_1 + R_2}{L}\right]$$

$$= -V\left(\frac{R_1 + R_2}{R_1}\right) e^{-\frac{(R_1 + R_2)t}{L}}$$

Example 3.2. *In the given circuit, let the switch K be initially in position 2. On steady state condition having reached, switch K is changed to position 1. Find the particular solution for the current in the circuit. Also find expressions for the voltage across resistor R_1 and inductor L.*

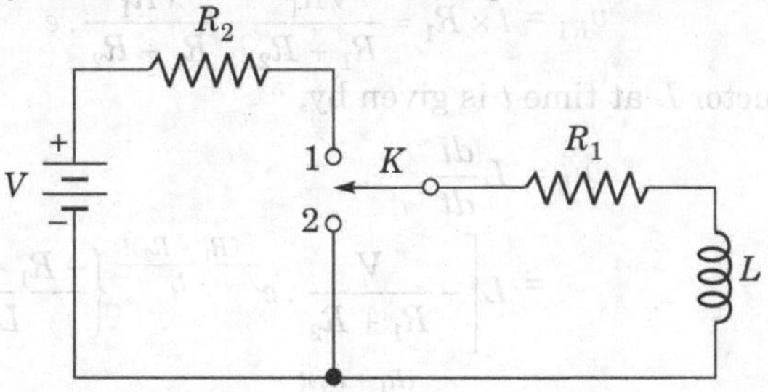

Solution. With switch K at position 1, application of Kirchhoff's voltage law yields,

$$Ri + L\frac{di}{dt} = V \quad ...(1)$$

where $R = R_1 + R_2$

Eq. (1) may be written as,

$$\frac{di}{dt} + \frac{R}{L}i = \frac{V}{L} \quad ...(2)$$

Eq. (2) is a linear non-homogeneous equation of the first order and its solution is,

$$i = e^{-Pt} \int Qe^{P}\, dt + k.e^{-Pt} \quad ...(3)$$

where $P = \frac{R}{L}$

and $Q = \frac{V}{L}$

Eq. (3) may be written as,

$$i = e^{-\frac{Rt}{L}} \int \frac{V}{L} . e^{\frac{RT}{L}}\, dt + k\, e^{-\frac{Rt}{L}}$$

$$= \frac{V}{L} e^{-\frac{Rt}{L}} . e^{\frac{Rt}{L}} . \frac{L}{R} + k\, e^{-\frac{Rt}{L}}$$

or

$$i = \frac{V}{R} + k\,.\,e^{-\frac{Rt}{L}} \quad ...(4)$$

Constant k may be evaluated from the initial condition that at $t = 0$ after switching to position 1 current i remains the same as before, *i.e* remains zero. This results because of the presence of inductor L.

Substituting $i = 0$ at $t = 0$ in Eq. (4), we get

$$0 = \frac{V}{R} + k.e^{0}$$

Hence

$$k = -\frac{V}{R}.$$

Hence that particular solution is,

$$i = \frac{V}{R_1 + R_2} - \frac{V}{R_1 + R_2} e^{-\frac{(R_1 + R_2)t}{L}} \quad ...(5)$$

Hence voltage across resistor R_1 at time t is given by,

$$v_{R1} = i \times R_1 = \frac{VR_1}{R_1 + R_2} - \frac{VR_1}{R_1 + R_2} . e^{-\frac{(R_1 + R_2)t}{L}}$$

Voltage across inductor L at time t is given by,

$$v_L = L\frac{di}{dt}$$

$$= L\left[-\frac{V}{R_1 + R_2} . e^{-\frac{(R_1 + R_2)t}{L}} \left\{ \frac{-R_1 + R_2}{L} \right\} \right]$$

$$= V . e^{-\frac{(R_1 + R_2)t}{L}} \quad ...(6)$$

Example 3.3. *Find the value of integrating factor S which when multiplied to differential equation,*

$$\frac{di}{dt} + P\,(t)\, i = Q\,(t)$$

makes the left hand side of the equation equal to the derivative $\frac{di}{dt}$ *(Si). Using this integrating factor, find the solution of the given differential equation.*

Solution. On multiplying the left hand side of the given equation by the integrating factor *S*, we get

$$\frac{d}{dt}(Si) = S\frac{di}{dt} + P(t)\,Si \qquad ...(1)$$

But the expansion of derivative $\frac{d}{dt}(Si)$ is given by

$$\frac{d}{dt}(Si) = S\frac{di}{dt} + i\frac{ds}{dt} \qquad ...(2)$$

Hence from Eqs. (1) and (2) we get

$$P(t)\,Si = i\,.\frac{ds}{dt}$$

Hence $$\frac{ds}{S} = \mathrm{P}(t)\,dt \qquad ...(3)$$

Integrating Eq. (3), we get

$$\ln S = \int Pdt \quad \text{or} \quad S = e^{\int Pdt} \qquad ...(4)$$

Multiplying the given equation by the integrating factor $e^{\int Pdt}$, we get

$$\frac{di}{dt}.e^{\int Pdt} + P(t)\,i.e^{\int Pdt} = Q(t)\,e^{\int Pdt}$$

or $$\frac{d}{dt}\left[i\,.\,e^{\int Pdt}\right] = Q\,e^{\int Pdt} \qquad ...(5)$$

Integrating Eq. (5), we get,

$$i.e^{\int Pdt} = \int Q\,e^{\int Pdt}\,dt + k$$

Hencc $$i = e^{\int -Pdt}\int Q\,e^{\int Pdt}\,dt + k.e^{\int Pdt}$$

Example 3.4. *In the circuit shown in the following figure, capacitor C_1 is initially charged to a voltage V_0. At time t = 0, switch K is closed. Obtain expressions for (i) current (ii) charge across C_1 and (iii) charge and voltage across C_2, as functions of time. If $C_1 = C_2 = 1\ \mu F$, $V_0 = 10$ volts and R = 10 ohms, calculate after time t = 10 μ-second, (i) current (ii) voltage across R (iii) charge across C_1 and (iv) voltage across C_2.*

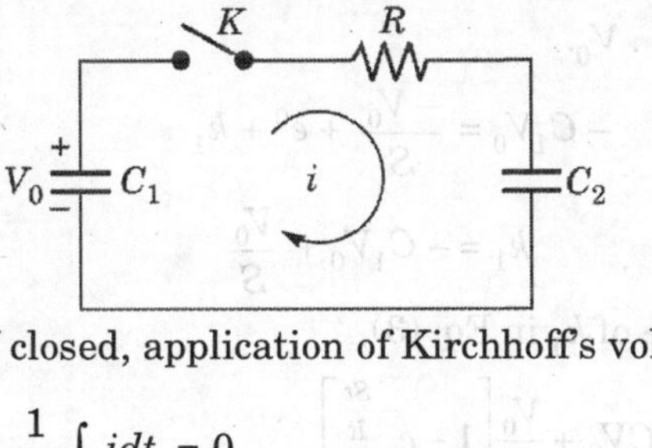

Solution. With switch *K* closed, application of Kirchhoff's voltage law yields,

$$iR + \frac{1}{C_1}\int idt + \frac{1}{C_2}\int idt = 0$$

or $$(S_1 + S_2)\int idt + iR = 0$$

On differentiation, we get

$$(S_1 + S_2)\, idt = -Rdi$$

Separating the variables,

$$\frac{-(S_1 + S_2)}{R}\, dt = \frac{di}{i}$$

On integration, we get $\frac{-(S_1 + S_2)t}{R} t + \ln k = \ln i$

or $$\ln i = \ln k + \ln e^{-\frac{(S_1 + S_2)t}{R}}$$

where ln k is the constant of integration.

Hence $$i = k \, . \, e^{-\frac{(S_1 + S_2)t}{R}} \qquad ...(1)$$

...General solution.

Constant k may be evaluated from the initial condition. Thus at time $t = 0$, voltage across capacitor $C_1 = V_0$ and it cannot change instantaneously. Also voltage across C_2 at $t = 0$ is zero.

Hence entire voltage V_0 drops in resistor R.

Hence $V_0 = I_0 R$ where I_0 is the initial current at, $t = 0$

Substituting this value of I_0 in Eq. (1), we get

$$\frac{V_0}{R} = ke^0 = k.$$

Hence we get the following particular solution,

$$i = \frac{V_0}{R} e^{-\frac{(S_1 + S_2)t}{R}} \qquad ...(2)$$

Charge across C_1 at time t is given by,

$$q_1 = \int i\, dt + k_1 = \int \frac{V_0}{R} . e^{-\frac{St}{R}} dt + k_1$$

where $$S = S_1 + S_2$$

or $$q_1 = \frac{V_0}{R} . e^{\frac{St}{R}} \left(-\frac{R}{S} \right) + k_1 = -\frac{V_0}{S} e^{-\frac{St}{R}} + k_1 \qquad ...(3)$$

At time $t = 0$, $q_1 = -C_1 . V_0$.

Hence $$-C_1 V_0 = \frac{-V_0}{S} + e^0 + k_1$$

Hence $$k_1 = -C_1 V_0 + \frac{V_0}{S}$$

Substituting this value of k_1 in Eq. (3),

$$q_1 = -CV_0 + \frac{V_0}{S}\left[1 - e^{-\frac{St}{R}} \right] \qquad ...(4)$$

Charge across C_2 given by,

$$q_2 = \int i\, dt = \int \frac{V_0}{R} e^{-\frac{St}{R}} dt + k_2 \qquad ...(5)$$

$$= \frac{-V_0}{S} e^{-\frac{St}{R}} + k_2$$

At time $t = 0$, $q_2 = 0$.

Hence $0 = \frac{-V_0}{S} e^0 + k_2$ or $k_2 = \frac{V_0}{S}$

Substituting this value of k_2 in Eq. (5), we get

$$q_2 = \frac{V_0}{S}\left[1 - e^{-\frac{St}{R}}\right] \quad ...(6)$$

Voltage across C_2 is given by,

$$v_{c2} = q_2 S_2 = \frac{V_0 S_2}{S}\left[1 - e^{-\frac{St}{R}}\right]$$

Substituting the numerical values,

Current $i = \frac{V_0}{R} . e^{-\frac{(S_1 + S_2)t}{R}}$

$$= \frac{10 \text{ volts}}{10 \text{ ohms}}\left[e^{-\frac{(10^6 + 10^6) \times 10 \times 10^{-6}}{10}}\right]$$

$= 0.135$ amp.

Voltage across $R = i \times R = 0.135 \times 10 = 1.35$ volts.

Charge across $C_1 = -C_1 V_0 + \frac{V_0}{S}\left[1 - e^{-\frac{St}{R}}\right]$

$$= 10^{-6} \times 10 + \frac{10}{2 \times 10^6} [1 - e^{2}] \text{ coulomb}$$

$= 5.675$ μ-coulomb.

$$q_2 = \frac{V_0}{S}\left[1 - e^{-\frac{St}{R}}\right] = \frac{10}{2 \times 10^6}[1 - 0.135] \text{ coulomb}$$

$= 4.325$ μ-coulomb.

Example 3.5. *In the given circuit, switch K is closed at time t = 0, the steady condition having reached previously. Obtain expression for the current in the circuit at any time t. If $R_1 = R_2 = 100$ ohms, V = 10 volts, and L = 1 henry, calculate at time t = 5 milliseconds, (i) current i (ii) voltage droop across R_2 and (iii) voltage across L.*

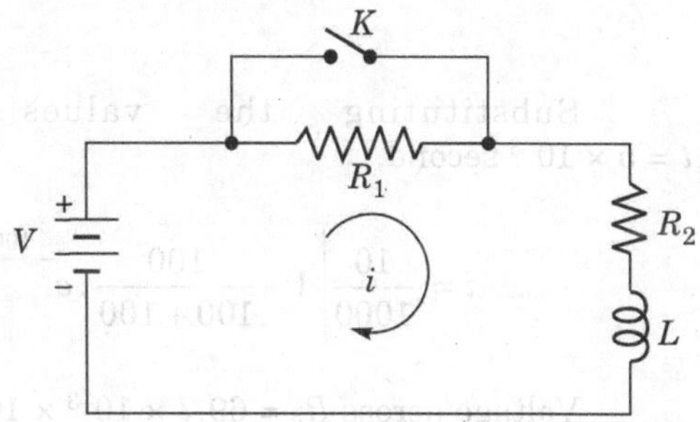

Solution. With switch *K* closed, application of Kirchhoff's voltage law yields,

$$L\frac{di}{dt} + R_2 i = V \quad ...(1)$$

or

$$\frac{di}{dt} + i\left(\frac{R_2}{L}\right) = \left(\frac{V}{L}\right) \quad ...(2)$$

Eq. (2) is a non-homogeneous first order linear differential equation.

The integrating factor is $e^{\frac{R_2 t}{L}}$.

Multiplying both sides of Eq. (2) by this integrating factor and integrating, we get

$$i = e^{-\frac{Rt}{L}} \int \left(\frac{V}{L}\right) e^{\frac{R_2 t}{L}} \, dt + k \, . \, e^{-\frac{R_2 t}{L}}$$

$$= e^{-\frac{R_2 t}{L}} \left(\frac{V}{L}\right) e^{\frac{R_2 t}{L}} \, . \, \frac{L}{R_2} + k \, . \, e^{-\frac{R_2 t}{L}}$$

or $$i = \frac{V}{R_2} + k \, . \, e^{-\frac{R_2 t}{L}} \qquad \text{...(3)}$$

...General solution.

Initial Condition. Just before closing the switch, the steady state condition has been reached, *i.e.* the current through the coil is $\frac{V}{R_1 + R_2}$. On closing the switch, the current through the coal L cannot change instantaneously. Hence after the switch K is closed, at time $t = 0$, current i still equals $\frac{V}{R_1 + R_2}$.

Substituting $i = \frac{V}{R_1 + R_2}$ at $t = 0$ in Eq. (3), we get

$$\frac{V}{R_1 + R_2} = \frac{V}{R_2} + k \, e^0$$

Hence $$k = \frac{V}{R_1 + R_2} - \frac{V}{R_2} = \frac{-VR_1}{R_1 + R_2}.$$

Substituting this value of k; in Eq. (3), we get

$$i = \frac{V}{R_2}\left[1 - \frac{R}{R_1 + R_2} e^{-\frac{R_2 t}{L}}\right] \qquad \text{...(4)}$$

...Particular solution

Substituting the values of various components and putting $t = 5 \times 10^{-3}$ second,

$$i = \frac{10}{1000}\left[1 - \frac{100}{100 + 100} \, . \, e^{-\frac{100 \times 5 \times 10^{-3}}{1}}\right] \text{ amp} = 69.7 \text{ mA.}$$

Voltage across $R_2 = 69.7 \times 10^{-3} \times 100 = 6.97$ volts

Voltage across $L = 10 - 6.97 = 3.03$ volts.

Example 3.6. *In the given circuit, switch K is closed at time t = 0. Obtain expression for the current i(t).*

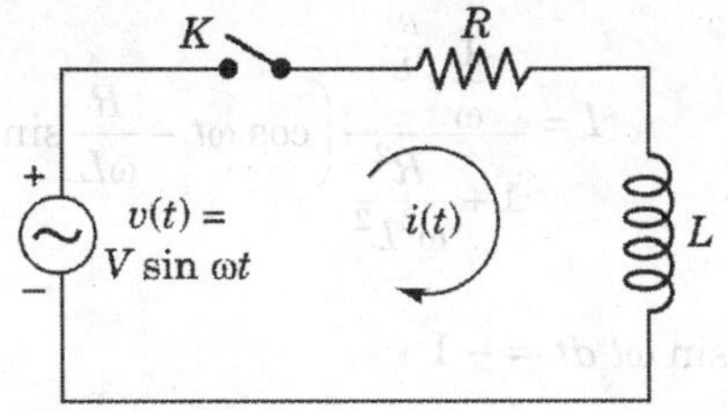

Solution. Application of Kirchhoff's voltage law yields

$$L\frac{di}{dt} + Ri = V \sin \omega t$$

or
$$\frac{di}{dt} + \left(\frac{R}{L}\right) i = \frac{V}{L} \sin \omega t \qquad \text{...(1)}$$

Eq. (1) is non-homogeneous first order linear differential equation.

The integrating factor

$$F = e^{Pt} = e^{\frac{Rt}{L}}.$$

Multiplying Eq. (1) by the integrating factor F, we get

$$\frac{d}{dt}\left(i.e^{\frac{RT}{L}}\right) = e^{\frac{Rt}{L}} \cdot \frac{V}{L} \sin \omega t$$

On integration, we get

$$i = e^{-\frac{Rt}{L}} \int e^{\frac{Rt}{L}} \frac{V}{L} \omega t \, dt + k\, e^{-\frac{Rt}{L}} \qquad \text{...(2)}$$

Let
$$I = -\int e^{\frac{Rt}{L}} . \sin \omega t \, dt \qquad \text{...(3)}$$

Then $I = \int e^{\frac{Rt}{L}} . \frac{1}{\omega} d \cos \omega t$

$$= \frac{1}{\omega} e^{\frac{Rt}{L}} \cos \omega t - \frac{R}{\omega L} \int \cos \omega t \, e^{\frac{Rt}{L}} \, dt$$

$$= \frac{1}{\omega} e^{\frac{Rt}{L}} \cos \omega t - \frac{R}{\omega L}\left[\int e^{\frac{Rt}{L}} . \frac{1}{\omega} d(\sin \omega t)\right]$$

$$= \frac{1}{\omega} e^{\frac{Rt}{L}} \cos \omega t - \frac{R}{\omega L}\left[\frac{1}{\omega} e^{\frac{Rt}{L}} \sin \omega t - \frac{R}{\omega L}\int e^{\frac{RT}{L}} \sin \omega t \, dt\right]$$

$$= \frac{1}{\omega} e^{\frac{Rt}{L}}\left[\cos \omega t - \frac{R}{\omega L} \sin \omega t\right] - \frac{R_2}{\omega^2 L^2} I$$

or
$$I\left[1 + \frac{R^2}{\omega^2 L^2}\right] = \frac{1}{\omega} e^{\frac{Rt}{L}}\left(\cos \omega t - \frac{R}{\omega L} \sin \omega t\right)$$

Hence
$$I = \frac{\frac{1}{\omega} e^{\frac{Rt}{L}}}{1 + \frac{R^2}{\omega^2 L^2}} \left(\cos \omega t - \frac{R}{\omega L} \sin \omega t \right)$$

Hence
$$\int e^{\frac{Rt}{L}} \sin \omega t \, dt = -1$$

$$= \frac{e^{\frac{Rt}{L}} \left(\frac{R}{L} \sin \omega t - \omega \cos \omega t \right)}{\frac{R^2}{L^2} + \omega^2}$$

Hence
$$i = \frac{V}{L} e^{-\frac{Rt}{L}} \frac{e^{\frac{Rt}{L}} \left(\frac{R}{L} \sin \omega t - \omega \cos \omega t \right)}{\left(\frac{R}{L} \right)^2 + \omega^2} + k.e^{-\frac{Rt}{L}}$$

$$= \frac{V}{R^2 + \omega^2 L^3} [R \sin \omega t - \omega L \cos \omega t] + k \,.\, e^{-\frac{Rt}{L}} \qquad \text{...(4)}$$

...General solution

Initial condition. At time $t = 0$, $i = V = \sin \theta = 0$.
Hence from Eq. (4),

$$0 = \frac{V}{R^2 + \omega^2 L^2} (-\omega L) + k$$

Hence
$$k = \frac{\omega L V}{R^2 + \omega^2 L^2}$$

Substituting this value of k; in Eq. (4), we get

$$i = \frac{V}{R^2 + \omega^2 L^2} [R \sin \omega t - \omega L \cos \omega t] + \frac{\omega L V}{R^2 + \omega^2 L^2} e^{-\frac{Rt}{L}}$$

$$= \frac{V}{R^2 + \omega^2 L^2} \left[(R \sin \omega t - \omega L \cos \omega t) + \omega L \, e^{-\frac{Rt}{L}} \right]$$

...Particular solution.

Example 3.7. *In the given circuit, the relay is adjusted to operate with a current of 7 mA. Switch K is closed at time t = 0. It is found that the relay operates at t = 0.2 second. Find (1) inductance L of the relay coil and (ii) equation for current i (t).*

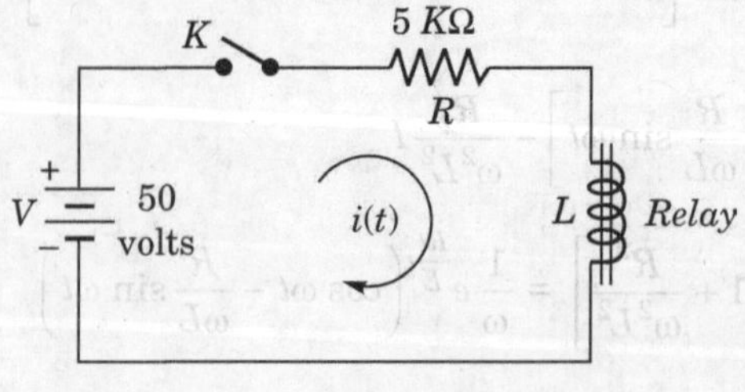

Solution. Application of Kirchhoff's voltage law to the closed loop yields,

$$L\frac{di}{dt} + Ri = V \qquad \text{...(1)}$$

or
$$\frac{di}{dt} + \left(\frac{R}{L}\right)i = \frac{V}{L} \qquad \text{...(2)}$$

Eq. (2) is a non-homogeneous first order linear differential equation and its solution is,

$$l = e^{-Pt}\int Q\, e^{Pt}\, dt + k\, e^{-Pt}$$

where $P = \dfrac{R}{L}$ and $Q = V/L$.

Hence
$$i = e^{-\frac{Rt}{L}} \int \frac{V}{L} e^{\frac{Rt}{L}}\, dt + k\, .\, e^{-\frac{Rt}{L}}$$

or
$$i = \frac{V}{R} + k.\, e^{-\frac{Rt}{L}} \qquad \text{...(3)}$$

...General solution.

The initial condition is that at $t = 0$, $i = 0$.

Hence
$$0 = \frac{V}{R} + k.\, e^{0} = \frac{V}{R} + k.$$

Hence
$$k = -\frac{V}{R}.$$

Substituting the value of k in Eq. (3), we get

$$i = \frac{V}{R}\left[1 - e^{\frac{Rt}{L}}\right] \qquad \text{...(4)}$$

...Particular solution.

At $t = 0.2$ second, $i = 7$ mA.

Hence
$$7 \times 10^{-3} = \frac{50}{5000}\left[1 + e^{-\frac{5000 \times 0.2}{L}}\right]$$

or
$$\left(1 - e^{-\frac{1000}{L}}\right) = 7 \times 10^{-3} \times 100 = 0.7$$

or
$$e^{-\frac{1000}{L}} = 1 - 0.7 = 0.3$$

Hence
$$L = 833 \text{ H}.$$

Hence equation (4) becomes,

$$i = \frac{50}{5000}\left[1 - e^{\frac{-5000\, t}{833}}\right]$$

or
$$i = 0.01\, [1 - e^{-6.02\, t}].$$

EXERCISES

3.1. In the given circuit, switch K is moved from position 1 to position 2 at time $t = 0$, steady-state current having previously established in the R-L circuit. Find the particular solution for the current in the circuit after $t = 0$. Calculate at time $t = 5$ milli-seconds, values of (*i*) current (*ii*) voltage across resistor R_1 and (*iii*) voltage across inductor L.

[Ans. $i = e^{-10t}$; 0.9535 amp ; 9.535 volts ; 19.07 volts]

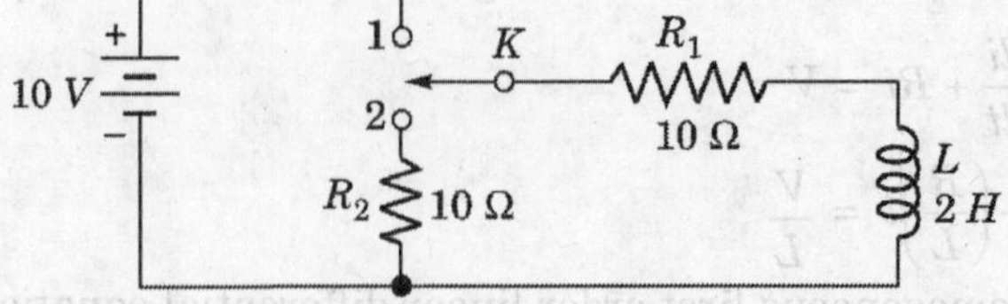

3.2. In the circuit of example 3.2, $V = 20$ volts, $R_1 = 10\ \Omega$, $R_2 = 10\ \Omega$ and $K = 1$ henry. Switch K is changed from position 2 to position 1 at $t = 0$, steady state condition having established prior to switching. Find expression for the particular solution for the current in the circuit. Calculate at time $t = 3$ milli-seconds, values of (*i*) current (*ii*) voltage across R_1 and (*iii*) voltage across L.

$$\left[\textbf{Ans. } i = \frac{V}{R_1 + R_2} - \frac{V}{R_1 + R_2} . e^{-\frac{(R_1 + R_2)t}{L}}\right.$$

(*i*) 0.0581 amp. (*ii*) 0.581 volts. (*iii*) 18.84 volts]

3.3. In the given network $V_0 = 10$ V, $R = 1\ \Omega$ and $L = 1$ henry. Switch K is closed at time $t = 0$. Assume that the steady state condition has reached prior to switching. Find expression for total particular solution for current i (*i*) through the circuit. [**Ans.** $i(t) = 10 - 10\ e^{-t}$]

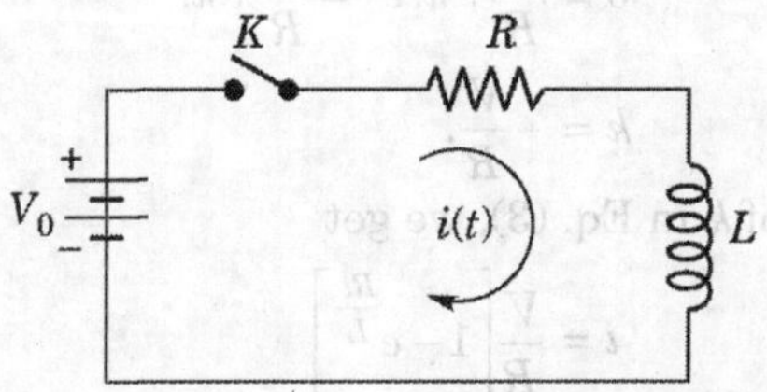

3.4. In the given network, switch K is closed at time $t = 0$. The waveform is observed on a C.R.O. as shown. The initial value of current is thus found to be 25 mA. The transient disappears, *i.e.* reduces to 2% of its initial value after time 0.1 second. Obtained (*i*) value of resistor R (*ii*) value of capacitor C and (*iii*) expression for current $i(t)$.

[**Ans.** (*i*) 8 kΩ (*ii*) 3.125 μF (*iii*) $i(t) = 25 \times 10^{-3}\ e^{-40t}$]

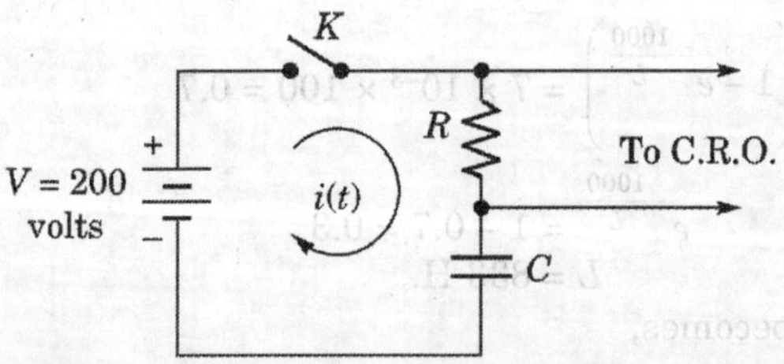

3.5. In the circuit of Example 3.5 switch K is opened at time $t = 0$, the steady state having been attained previously. Obtain expression for the current in the circuit at any time t. $R_1 = R_2 = 10\ \Omega$, $V = 20$ volts and $L = 2$ henry calculate at time $t = 4$ milli-seconds the following quantities: (*i*) current (*ii*) voltage across R_2 and (*iii*) voltage across L.

[**Ans.** (*i*) 1.961 amp., (*ii*) 19.61 volts, (*iii*) 19.22 volts]

4

Initial Conditions

4.1. Characteristics of Various Network Elements

On solving first order differential equation we first obtain the general solution which contains one arbitrary constant. On solving a differential equation of higher order, the number of arbitrary constants equals the order of the equation. These arbitrary constants are required to be evaluated for obtaining the particular solution. For evaluating these arbitrary constants we must have additional knowledge about the network described by the differential equation. It is then required to form a set of simultaneous equations one of which gives the general solution while the remaining give the values of voltages, current charge etc. or the derivatives of these quantities at the instant of switching. The number of these additional equations equals the number of unknowns. These additional equations thus describe the "Initial condition", *i.e* the conditions prevailing at time $t = 0+$.

Now before switching action takes place, the various elements of the network may already have voltage across their terminals or currents through them. Initial values of these voltages or currents before switching action (*i.e.* at time $t = 0$) have to be evaluated. Next we must know how each voltage and current changes when the switching is done. Knowing the values of voltage and currents at $t = 0-$ and knowing the changes introduced by switching action, we can find the initial values of currents and voltages just after switching, *i.e.* at time $t = 0+$. These additional equations giving the initial values of currents and voltages and their derivatives may be solved simultaneously with the general equation to give the values of constants.

Before formulating the initial conditions in networks, we first consider effect of switching action on resistors, inductors and capacitors.

(A) *Resistor.* In the case of an ideal resistor of value say R ohms, the voltage v is related to the current i through the Ohm's law $v = iR$. On application of a step voltage across the resistor, the resulting current i has the same shape as the applied voltage as shown in Fig. 4.1.

Thus as the voltage across a resistor change instantaneously, the current through it also changes instantaneously and *vice versa*.

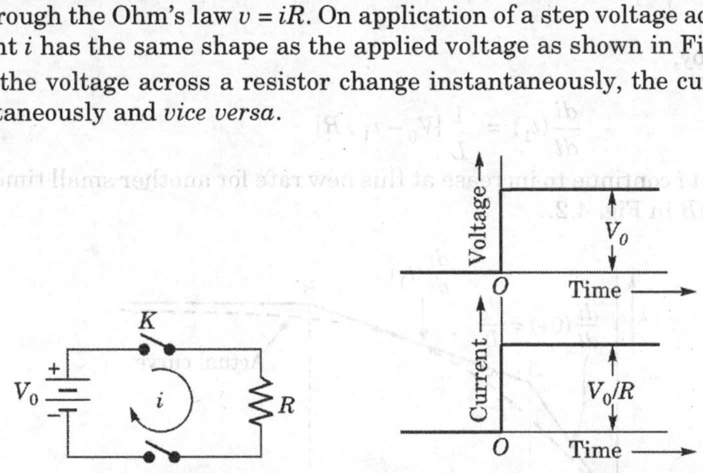

(*a*) Resistor circuit. (*b*) Response to step input voltage.

Fig. 4.1. Response of resistor to step input voltage.

(*B*) *Inductor*. The current through an inductor cannot change instantaneously. Accordingly energy source on being suddenly connected to an inductor will not cause current to flow initially. Thus inductor acts as open circuit for the newly applied energy at the instant of switching. However any current I_0 already flowing in the inductor before the switching action will continue to flow. Hence initially at time $t = 0+$, the inductor may be considered as a current source of current I_0.

(*C*) *Capacitor*. In a system of fixed capacitance, the voltage cannot change instantaneously. Since $v = q/c$, zero charge corresponds to zero voltage. Thus for a suddenly applied energy source a capacitor is equivalent to a short circuit. Hence on connecting an uncharged capacitor to an energy source, a current flows instantaneously. Further with an initial charge say q_0 in the system, the capacitor is equivalent to a voltage source of value $v_0 = q_0/c$.

4.2. Initial Values of Derivatives

Consider a series *R-L* circuit connected suddenly to a constant voltage source V_0.

Then application Kirchhoff's voltage law yields,

$$L\frac{di}{dt} + Ri = V_0 \quad \text{...(4.1)}$$

or

$$\frac{di}{dt} = \frac{1}{L}[V_0 - iR] \quad \text{...(4.2)}$$

Eq. (4.2) gives the variation of derivative $\frac{di}{dt}$ with current *i*. For an inductor, on switching in the supply voltage V_0 (*i.e.* at time $t = 0+$), current *i* must be zero. Hence from Eq. (4.2), we get

$$\frac{di}{dt}(0+) = \frac{V_0}{L} \quad \text{...(4.3)}$$

Eq. (4.3) shows that the slope $\frac{di}{dt}$ of the current *i* at time $t = 0+$ is positive and has a magnitude of V_0/L. Thus initially the current *i* increases linearly at the rate V_0/L and may be considered to continue to do so for a small time interval say t_1. Then after time interval t_1, the new value of current is $i_1 . \frac{V_0}{L} t_1$. At this time, in accordance with Eq. (4.2), the time rate of change of current $\frac{di}{dt}$ is given by,

$$\frac{di}{dt}(t_1) = \frac{1}{L}[V_0 - i_1 . R] \quad \text{...(4.4)}$$

Let the current *i* continue to increase at this new rate for another small time interval t_1 to t_2 as shown by region *AB* in Fig. 4.2.

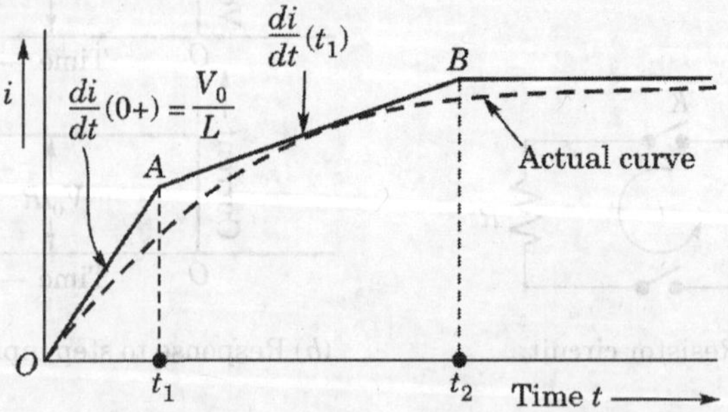

Fig. 4.2. Rate of change of current in an *R-L* circuit.

This process may be continued to give a graph showing the variation of current i with time t thus producing a graphical interpretation of the solution of the differential equation (4.2). As the time intervals t_1, t_2 etc. are reduced the approximate curve $OABC$ ... approaches the actual curve.

Thus we conclude that the first derivative represents the slope of the curve plotting the dependent variable (i in this case) as a function of independent variable (t in this case). Similarly the second derivative $\frac{d^2i}{dt^2}$ represents 'the rate of change of slope with time t'.

4.3. Procedure for Evaluating Initial Conditions

The procedure generally followed for evaluating initial conditions consists in following two steps in sequence :

(A) Solving for the initial values of the variables namely currents and voltages at $t = 0 +$.

(B) Solving for the derivatives of variables at $t = 0 +$. These are discussed below :

(A) *Solving for initial values of variables at t = 0 +.* This may be done by obtaining from the network schematic a new schematic of an equivalent network for $t = 0 +$, in accordance with the following rules :

(*i*) Replace every inductor by an open circuit or by a current generator having source current equal to that flowing at time $t = 0 +$.

(*ii*) Replace every capacitor by short circuit or by a voltage generator having source voltage v_0 equal to q_0/c if there is an initial charge q_0.

(*iii*) Leave every resistor in the network unchanged.

(B) *Solving for the initial values of derivatives at t = 0 +.* The details and the order of mathematical manupulation involved in solving for the derivatives will be different of each different case and can be best understood from the method followed in different cases studies below.

4.4. Initial Conditions in the Case of a Series RLC Network

Fig. 4.3 shows a series RLC network connected to a d.c. voltage source V_0 at time $t = 0$. It is assumed that no voltage has been applied to the given passive network prior to time $t = 0$. It is required to find $i(0 +), \frac{di}{dt}(0 +)$ and $\frac{d^2i}{dt^2}(0 +)$.

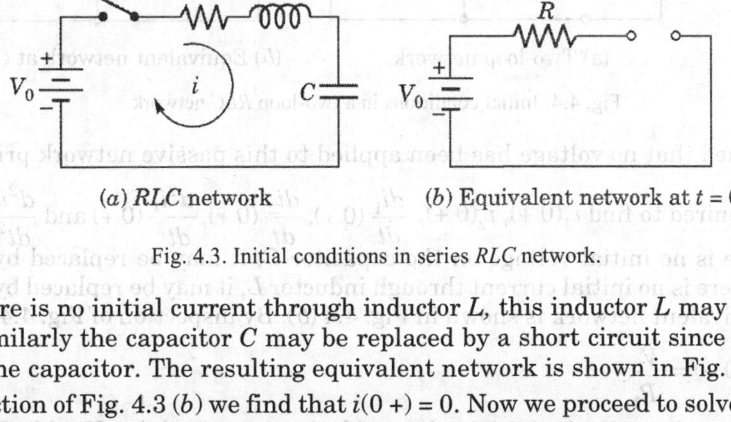

(*a*) *RLC* network (*b*) Equivalent network at $t = 0$

Fig. 4.3. Initial conditions in series *RLC* network.

Since there is no initial current through inductor L, this inductor L may be replaced by an open circuit. Similarly the capacitor C may be replaced by a short circuit since there is no initial voltage across the capacitor. The resulting equivalent network is shown in Fig. 4.3 (*b*).

By inspection of Fig. 4.3 (*b*) we find that $i(0 +) = 0$. Now we proceed to solve for initial values of derivatives. Applying Kirchhoff's voltage law to the network, we get

$$L\frac{di}{dt} + Ri + \frac{1}{C}\int i\,dt = V_0 \qquad ...(4.5)$$

Since this equation holds in general, it also holds at time $t = 0+$. Now the value of i is known to be zero at $t = 0+$. Also the quantity $\frac{1}{C}\int i\,dt$ is known to be zero at $t = 0+$ since this term is the voltage across the capacitor C.

Substituting $i = 0$ and $\frac{1}{C}\int i\,dt = 0$ at $t = 0+$, we get from Eq. (4.5),

$$\frac{di}{dt}(0+) = \frac{V_0}{L} \qquad ...(4.6)$$

In order to find the second derivative $\frac{d^2i}{dt^2}(0+)$, Eq. (4.5) may be differentiated to get,

$$L\frac{d^2i}{dt^2} + R\frac{di}{dt} + \frac{i}{C} = 0 \qquad ...(4.7)$$

Now we know that $\frac{di}{dt}(0+) = \frac{V_0}{L}$ and $i(0+) = 0$. Hence from Eq. (4.7), we get

$$L\frac{d^2i}{dt^2}(0+) + R\cdot\frac{V_0}{L} + 0 = 0$$

Hence $$\frac{d^2i}{dt^2}(0+) = -\frac{RV_0}{L}$$

4.5. Initial Conditions in the Case of a Typical Two-mesh RLC Circuit

Let the two-loop network of Fig. 4.4 (a) be connected to the d.c. supply V_0 by closing the switch at time $t = 0$.

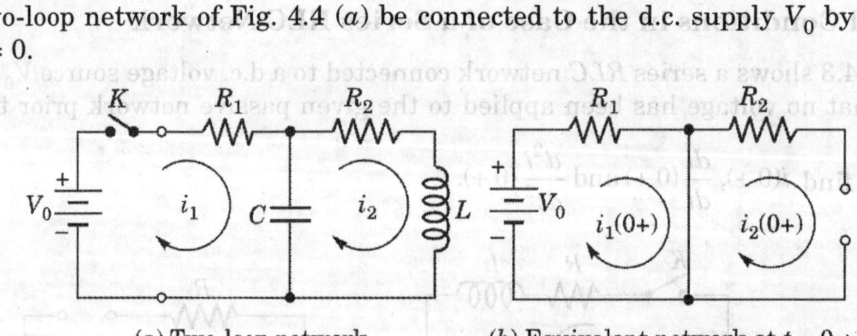

(a) Two-loop network. (*b*) Equivalent network at $t = 0+$.

Fig. 4.4. Initial conditions in a two-loop *RLC* network.

It is assumed that no voltage has been applied to this passive network prior to closing the switch K. It is required to find $i_1(0+)$, $i_2(0+)$, $\frac{di_1}{dt}(0+)$, $\frac{di_2}{dt}(0+)$, $\frac{d^2i_1}{dt^2}(0+)$ and $\frac{d^2i_2}{dt^2}(0+)$.

Since there is no initial voltage on the capacitor C, it may be replaced by a short circuit. Similarly since there is no initial current through inductor L, it may be replaced by an open circuit. The resulting equivalent network is shown in Fig. 4.4 (b). By inspection of Fig. 4.4 (b), we find that $i_2(0+) = 0$ and $i_1(0+) = \frac{V_0}{R_1}$.

Now we proceed to solve for initial values of derivatives. Applying Kirchhoff's voltage law to the network of Fig. 4.4 (a), we get

$$\frac{1}{C}\int (i_1 - i_2)\,dt + R_1 i_1 = V_0 \qquad ...(4.8)$$

and $$\frac{1}{C}\int (i_1 - i_2)\,dt + R_2 i_2 + L\frac{di_2}{dt} = 0 \qquad ...(4.9)$$

Eqs. (4.8) and (4.9) for loops I and II respectively are general equations. Hence they hold good for time $t = 0+$ as well. Now we know that $i(0+) = \frac{V_0}{R_1}$ and $i_2(0+) = 0$. Also the quantity $\frac{1}{C}\int (i_1 - i_2)\,dt$ is known to be zero at time $t = 0+$, since this term gives the voltage across capacitor C and capacitor acts as a short circuit at $t = 0+$.

Substituting $\frac{1}{C}\int (i_1 - i_2)\,dt = 0$ and $R_2\, i_2 = 0$ at time $t = 0+$ in Eq. (4.9), we get

$$\frac{di_2}{dt}(0+) = 0 \qquad ...(4.10)$$

In order to evaluate $\frac{di_1}{dt}(0+)$, we first differentiate Eq. (4.8), to get

$$\frac{i_1 - i_2}{C} + R_1\frac{di_1}{dt} = 0 \qquad ...(4.11)$$

...General equation

At time $t = 0+$, $i_2(0+) = 0$, $i_1(0+) = \frac{V_0}{R_1}$

Hence $$R_1 \cdot \frac{di_1}{dt}(0+) = -\frac{1}{C}\left[\frac{V_0}{R_1}\right]$$

or $$\frac{di_1}{dt}(0+) = -\frac{1}{R_1 C}\cdot\frac{V_0}{R_1} = -\frac{V_0}{CR_1^2} \qquad ...(4.12)$$

In order to evaluate the second derivative $\frac{d^2 i_1}{dt^2}(0+)$ we differentiate Eq. (4.11) to get,

$$\frac{d^2 i_1}{dt^2} = -\frac{1}{R_1 C}\left[\frac{di_1}{dt} - \frac{di_2}{dt}\right] \qquad ...(4.13)$$

...General equation

Hence at $t = 0+$, we get

$$\frac{d^2 i_1}{dt^2}(0+) = -\frac{1}{R_1 C}\left[-\frac{V_0}{R_1 C} - 0\right]$$

or $$\frac{d^2 i_1}{dt_2}(0+) = \frac{V_0}{t} \qquad ...(4.14)$$

In order to evaluate $\frac{d^2 i_2}{dt^2}(0+)$ we differentiate Eq. (4.9) to get,

$$\frac{1}{C}[i_2 - i_1] + R_2\frac{di_2}{dt} + L\frac{d^2 i_2}{dt_2} = 0$$

or $$\frac{d^2 i_2}{dt^2} = \frac{1}{L}\left[\frac{i_1 - i_2}{C} - R_2 \cdot \frac{di_2}{dt}\right] \qquad \text{...(4.15)}$$

Hence at time $t = 0 +$.

$$\frac{d^2 i_2}{dt^2}(0+) = \frac{1}{L}\left[\frac{V_0}{CR_1} - R \times 0\right]$$

or $$\frac{d^2 i_2}{dt^2}(0+) = \frac{V_0}{LCR_1}. \qquad \text{...(14.6)}$$

4.6. Initial Conditions in a Typical Three-mesh RLC Network

In the network of Fig. 4.5, steady state conditions is reached with switch K open. At time $t = 0$, switch K is closed. It is required to find the initial values of the loop currents i_1, i_2 and i_3.

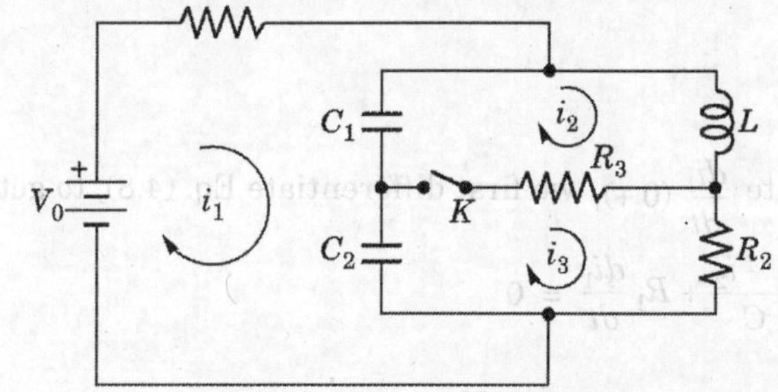

Fig. 4.5. Network with initial charges and currents.

We first proceed to find the currents and voltages in the network at time $t = 0 -$, *i.e.* just before the switch K is closed.

Under steady state condition, inductor L behaves as short circuit and capacitors C_1 and C_2 behave as open circuits. Hence the current through inductor L at $t = 0 -$ will be,

$$i_L(0-) = i_{R_2}(0-) = \frac{V_0}{R_1 + R_2} \qquad \text{...(4.17)}$$

The total voltage drop across the capacitors will be the same as the voltage drop across R_2. Thus

$$vC_1 + vC_2 = \frac{R_2 V_0}{R_1 + R_2} \qquad \text{...(4.18)}$$

Since the two capacitors C_1 and C_2 are connected in series, the charges on these must be equal. Hence, we have

$$q_1 = q_2$$

or $$C_1 v_{c_1} = C_2 v_{c_2}$$

Hence $$\frac{V_{c_1}}{V_{c_2}} = \frac{C_2}{C_1} = \frac{S_1}{S_2} \qquad \text{...(4.19)}$$

...General equation

From Eqs. (4.18) and (4.19), we get

$$v_{c_1} = \frac{R_2 V_0}{R_1 + R_2} \cdot \frac{S_1}{S_1 + S_2} \qquad \text{...(4.20)}$$

and $$v_{c_2} = \frac{R_2 V_0}{R_1 + R_2} \cdot \frac{S_2}{S_1 + S_2} \qquad ...(4.21)$$

In order to find the currents i_1, i_2 and i_3 at $t = 0+$, we draw the equivalent network resulting at $t = 0+$. This is shown in Fig. 4.6.

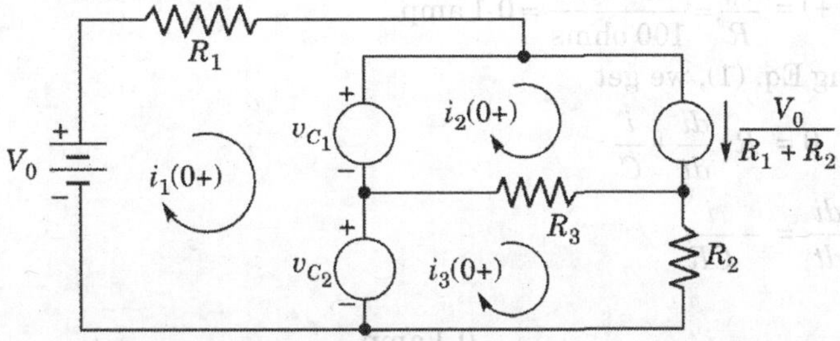

Fig. 4.6. Network equivalent to that of Fig. 4.5 at $t = +0$.

Application of Kirchhoff's voltage law to the loop containing V_0, R_1, v_{c_1} and v_{c_2} gives

$$R_1 i_1(0+) = V_0 - v_{c_1} - v_{c_2}$$

$$= V_0 - \frac{R_2 V_0}{R_1 + R_2} \cdot \frac{S_1}{S_1 + S_2} - \frac{R_2 V_0}{R_1 + R_2} \cdot \frac{S_2}{S_1 + S_2} = \frac{V_0 R_1}{R_1 + R_2}$$

Hence $$i_1(0+) = \frac{V_0}{R_1 + R_2} \qquad ...(4.22)$$

Current through the inductor L cannot change instantaneously.

Hence $$i_2(0+) = i_L(0+) = i_L(0-) = \frac{V_0}{R_1 + R_2} \qquad ...(4.23)$$

Further the voltage across the capacitor cannot change instantaneously. Hence pertaining to voltage v_{C_2} across capacitor C_2.

$$v_{c_2} = R_2 i_3(0+) R_3[i_3(0+) - I_2(0+)]$$

$$= i_3(0+)[R_2 + R_3] - i_2(0+) \, . \, R_3$$

Hence $i_3(0+)[R_2 + R_3] = v_{c_2} + R_3 i_2(0+)$

$$= \frac{R_2 V_0}{R_1 + R_2} \frac{S_2}{S_1 + S_2} + R_3 \cdot \frac{V_0}{R_1 + R_2}$$

Hence $$i_3(0+) = \frac{1}{R_2 + R_3} \cdot \frac{V_0}{R_1 + R_2}\left[\frac{R_2 S_2}{S_1 + S_2} + R_3\right] \qquad ...(4.24)$$

Example 4.1. *In the given circuit switch K is closed at $t = 0$. Find the values of i, di/dt and d^2i/dt^2 at $t = 0+$. Given that $V_0 = 10$ volts $R = 100$ ohms and $C = 1$ μF.*

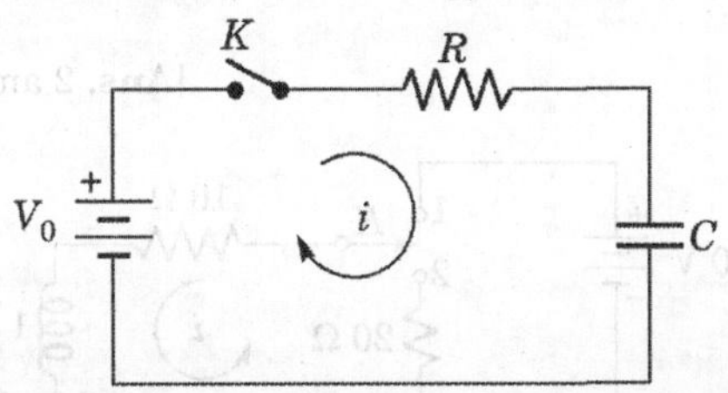

Solution. On applying Kirchhoff's voltage law to the circuit, we get

$$V_0 = Ri + \frac{1}{C}\int idt \qquad ...(1)$$

...General equation

At $t = 0+$, capacitor acts as a short circuit.

Hence $\quad i(0+) = \frac{V_0}{R} = \frac{10 \text{ volts}}{100 \text{ ohms}} = 0.1 \text{ amp.}$

Differentiating Eq. (1), we get

$$0 = R.\frac{di}{dt} + \frac{i}{C}$$

or

$$\frac{di}{dt} = -\frac{i}{CR} \qquad ...(2)$$

At $\quad t = 0+,$

$$\frac{di}{dt}(0+) = -\frac{i}{CR}.i(0+) = -\frac{0.1 \text{ amp}}{(10^{-6} \times 100) \text{ sec.}}$$

$$= -10^3 \text{ amp/sec.}$$

Differentiating Eq. (2), we get

$$\frac{d^2i}{dt^2} = -\frac{1}{CR}\frac{di}{dt} \qquad ...(3)$$

At $\quad t = 0+, \frac{d^2i}{dt^2}(0+) = -\frac{1}{CR}\left(\frac{di}{dt}\right)(0+)$

$$= -\frac{1}{10^{-6} \times 10}(-10^3) = 10^7 \text{ amp./sec./sec.}$$

EXERCISES

4.1. In the given circuit, switch K is closed at $t = 0$. Find the values of $i, \frac{di}{dt}$ and $\frac{d^2 i}{dt^2}$ at $t = 0+$. [**Ans.** 0, 10 amp/sec, – 1000 amp/sec^2]

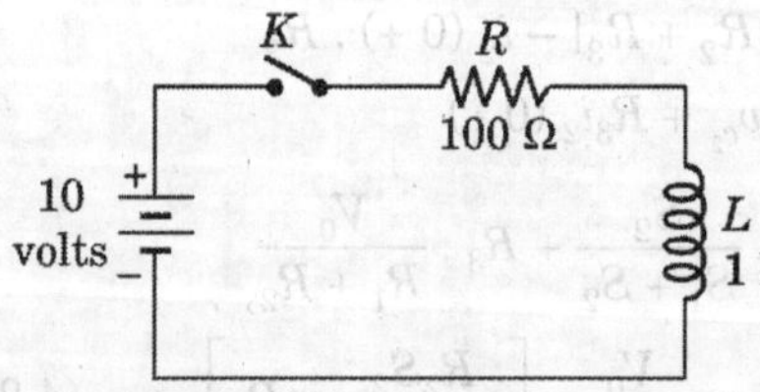

4.2. In the given circuit, switch K is changed from position 1 to position 2 at time $t = 0$, steady state condition having reached before switching. It is required to find $i, \frac{di}{dt}$ and $\frac{d^2i}{dt^2}$ at $t = 0+$.

[**Ans.** 2 amp. – 60 amp/sec. + 1800 amp/sec^2]

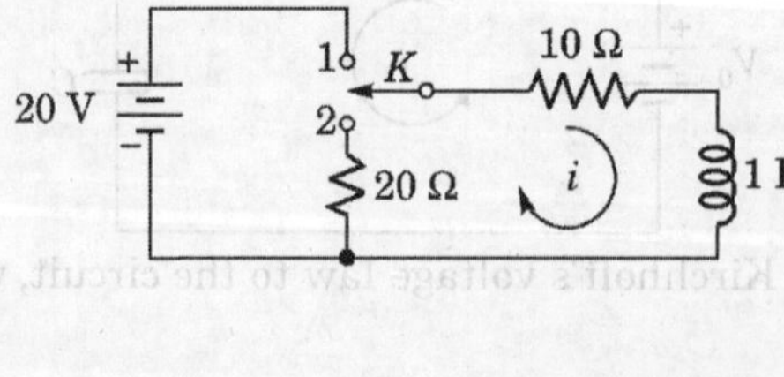

4.3. In the given circuit, switch K is changed from position 1 to position 2 at $t = 0$, steady state condition having reached before switching. It is required to find $i, \frac{di}{dt}$ and $\frac{d^2i}{dt^2}$ at $t = 0+$.

$\left[\textbf{Ans. } 1 \text{ amp} ; -\frac{10^5}{3} \text{ amp/sec} ; \frac{10^{10}}{9} \text{ amp/sec}^2\right]$

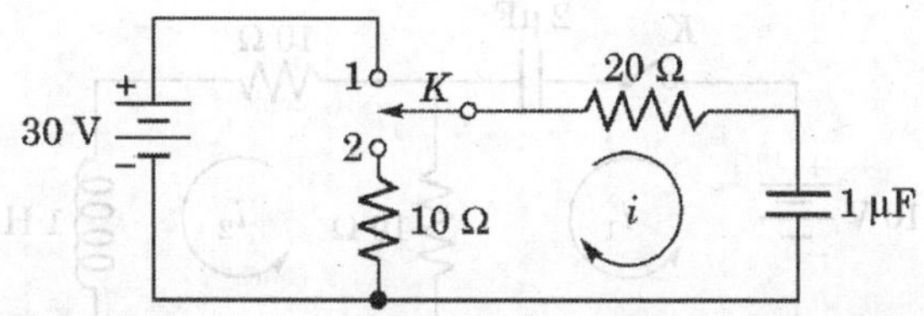

4.4. In the given circuit, switch K is changed from position 1 to position 2 at time $t = 0$, steady state condition having reached before switching. It is required to find $i, \frac{di}{dt}, \frac{d^2i}{dt^2}$ and $\frac{d^3i}{dt^3}$ at $t = 0+$.

[**Ans.** 0, – 10 amp/sec, 10 amp/sec^2 ; 10^7 amp/sec^3]

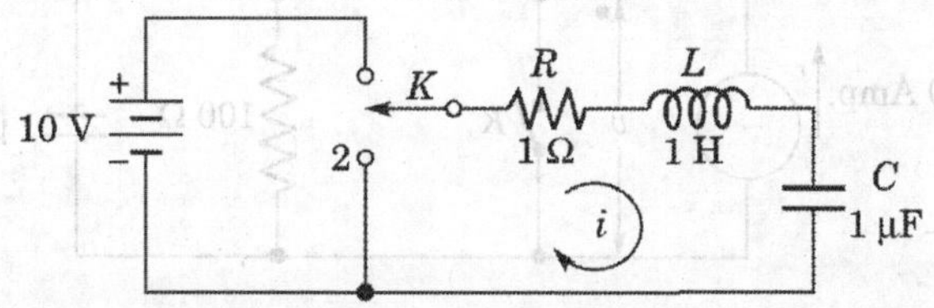

4.5. In the given circuit, switch K is changed from position 1 to position 2 at time $t = 0$, steady state condition having reached before switching. Find the values of $i, \frac{di}{dt}$ and $\frac{d^2i}{dt^2}$ at time $t = 0+$.

[**Ans.** 2 amp ; – 20 amp/sec ; – 1,999,800 amp/sec^2]

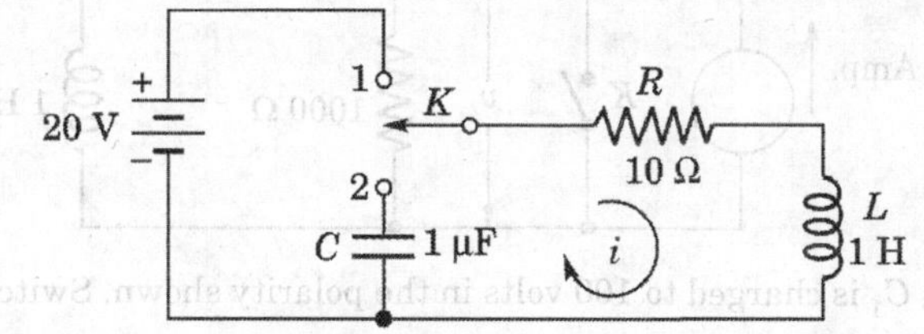

4.6. In the given circuit, switch K is changed from position 1 to position 2 at $t = 0$, the steady state condition having reached before switching. Find the values of $i, \frac{di}{dt}$ and $\frac{d^2i}{dt^2}$ at time $t = 0+$.

[**Ans.** 0, – 40 amp/sec ; 800 amp/sec^2]

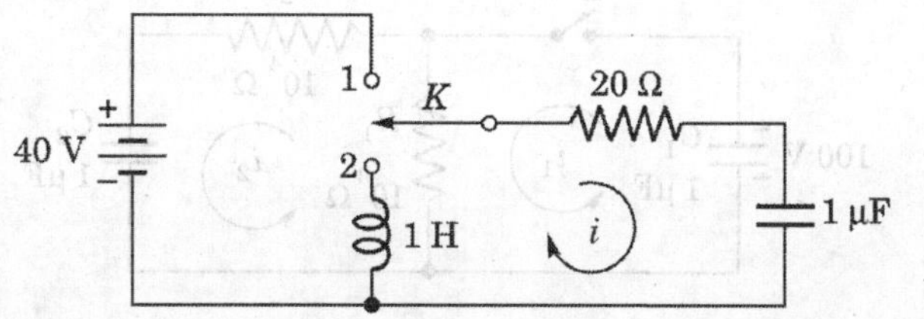

4.7. In the given circuit, switch K is closed at time $t = 0$. Find the values of $i_1, i_2, \frac{di}{dt}, \frac{di_2}{dt}, \frac{d^2i_1}{dt^2}$ and $\frac{d^2i_2}{dt^2}$ at time $t = 0+$.

[**Ans.** 1 amp ; 0 ; – 49,990 amp/sec^2 ; 10 amp/sec ; – 49,995 × 10^5 amp/sec^2 ; – 500,100 amp/sec^2]

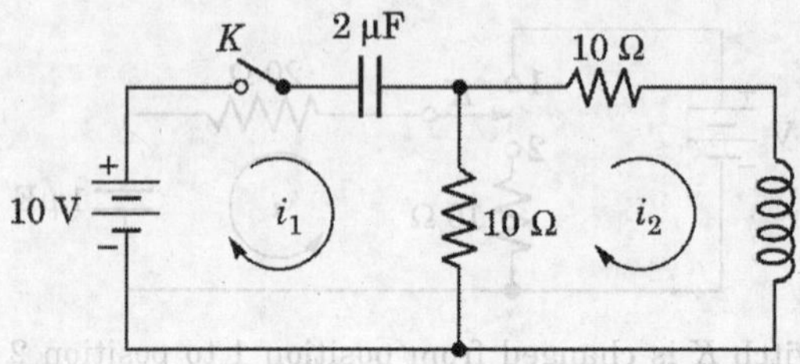

4.8. In the given circuit switch K is opened at $t = 0$. Find the values of v, $\frac{dv}{dt}$ and $\frac{d^2v}{dt^2}$ at $t = 0+$. [**Ans.** 0, 10^7 volts/sec, -10^{11} volts/sec^2]

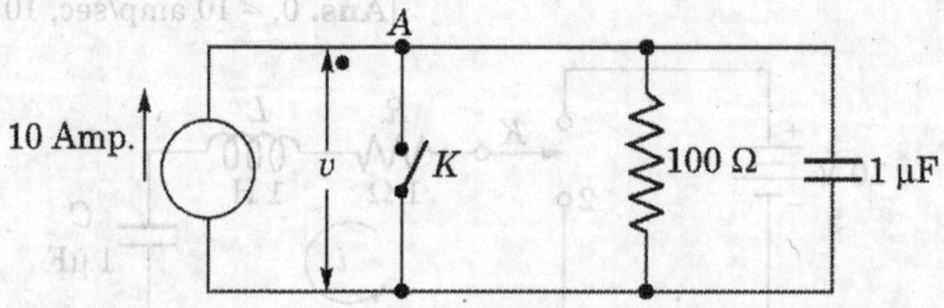

4.9. In the given circuit, switch K is opened at time $t = 0$. Find the values of v, $\frac{dv}{dt}$ and $\frac{d^2v}{dt^2}$ at $t = 0+$.

[**Ans.** 2000 volts ; -2×10^6 volts/sec ; 2×10^9 volts/sec^2]

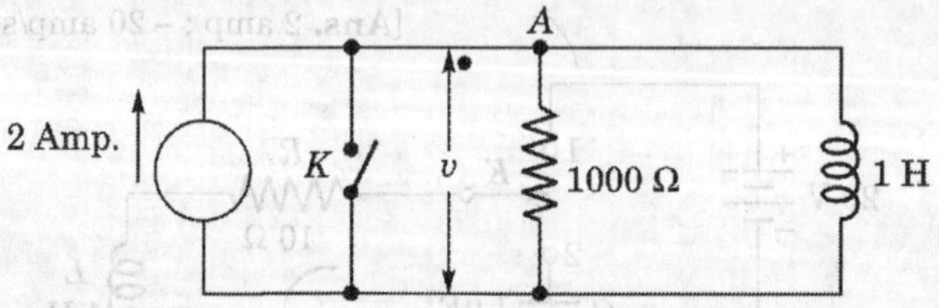

4.10. In the given circuit, C_1 is charged to 100 volts in the polarity shown. Switch K is closed at time $t = 0$. Find the value of $i_1, i_2, \frac{di_1}{dt}, \frac{di_2}{dt}, \frac{d^2i_1}{dt^2}$ and $\frac{d^2i_2}{dt^2}$ at $t = 0+$.

[**Ans.** 0.02 amp ; 0.01 amp ; – 5 amp/sec ; – 3 amp/sec ; 1300 amp/sec^2 ; 800 amp/sec^2]

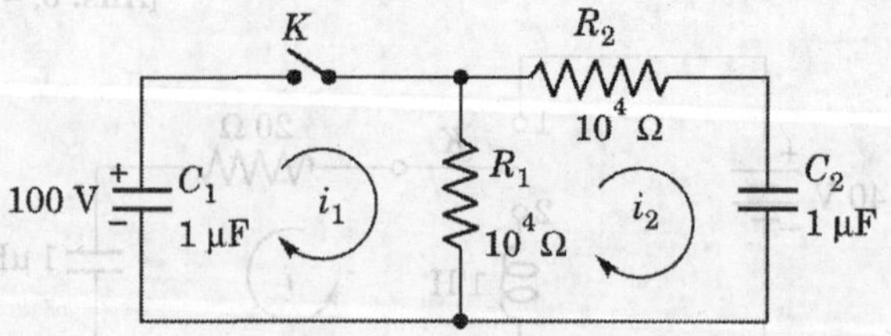

4.11. In the given circuit, swtich K is closed at time $t = 0$. Prove that at $t = 0+$, $\frac{di_1}{dt}$ equals $\frac{V_0}{R}\left[\omega \cos \omega t - \frac{\sin \omega t}{RC}\right]$ while $\frac{di_2}{dt}$ equals $\frac{V_0 \sin \omega t}{L}$.

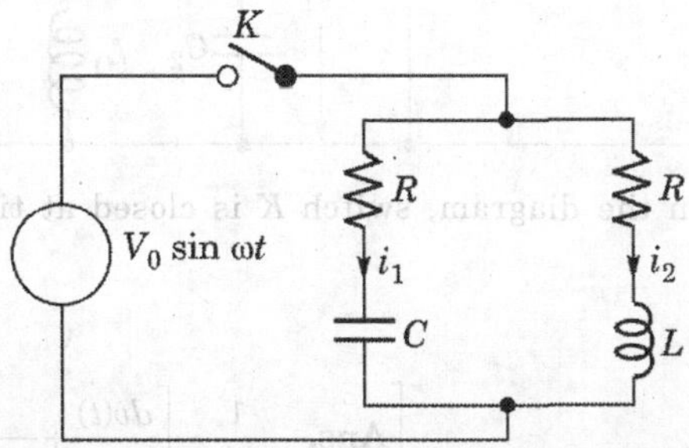

4.12. In the given circuit, steady state condition is reached with the switch K open. At time $t = 0$ switch K is closed. Write the integro-differential equations for the network after the switch is closed. Find the vdtage v_c across capacitor C and current i_2 through inductor L at time $t = 0-$. Find the values of $i_1, i_2, \frac{di_1}{dt}$ and $\frac{di_2}{dt}$ at $i = 0+$.

[**Ans.** 5 volts ; 0.5 amp ; 0.5 amp ; 0.5 amp ; – 5000 amp/sec ; 5 amp/sec]

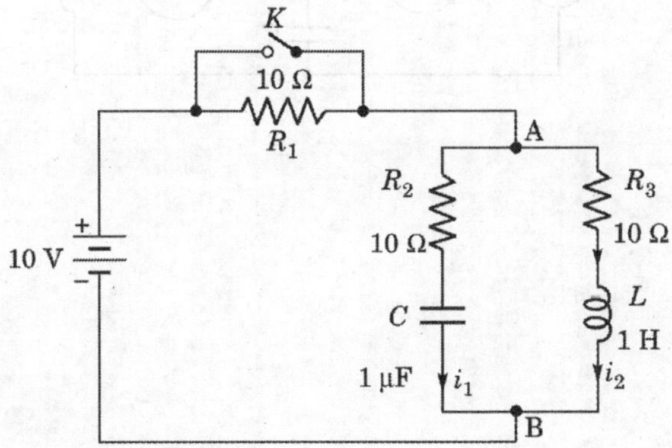

4.13. In the given circuit, switch K is opened at $t = 0$. Find the values of $v_1, v_2, \frac{dv_1}{dt}$ and $\frac{dv_2}{dt}$ at t time $t = 0-$.

[**Ans.** 100 volts, 0, 1000 volts/sec, 0]

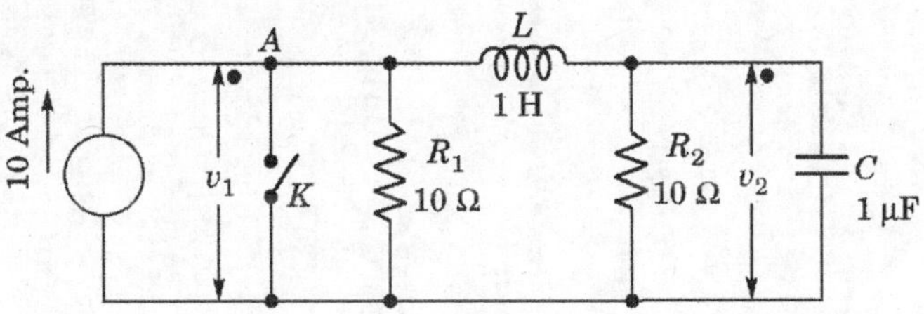

4.14. In the given network, switch K is closed at $t = 0$. Find the value of $\frac{dv_2}{dt}$ at $t = 0+$. [**Ans.** Zero]

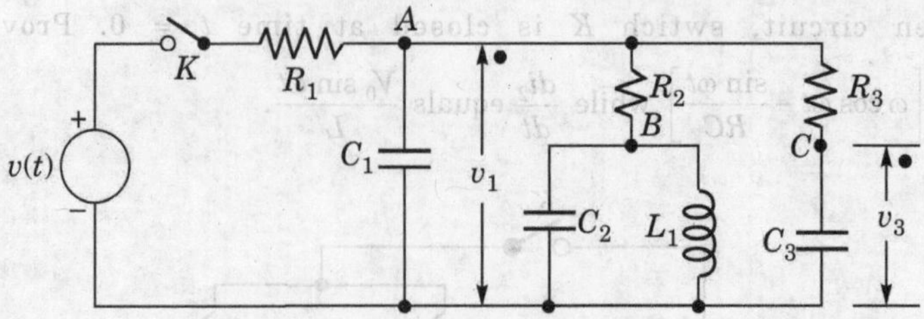

4.15. In the network shown in the diagram, switch K is closed at time $t = 0$. Find expressions for $\frac{di_1}{dt}(0+)$ and $\frac{di_2}{dt}(0+)$.

$$\left[\textbf{Ans. } \frac{1}{R_1+R_3}\left[\frac{dv(t)}{dt}+\frac{v(t)}{R_1+R_2}\left\{-\frac{1}{C}+\frac{R_3^2}{S}\right\}\right];\ \frac{R_3}{L}\cdot\frac{v(t)}{R_1+R_3}\right]$$

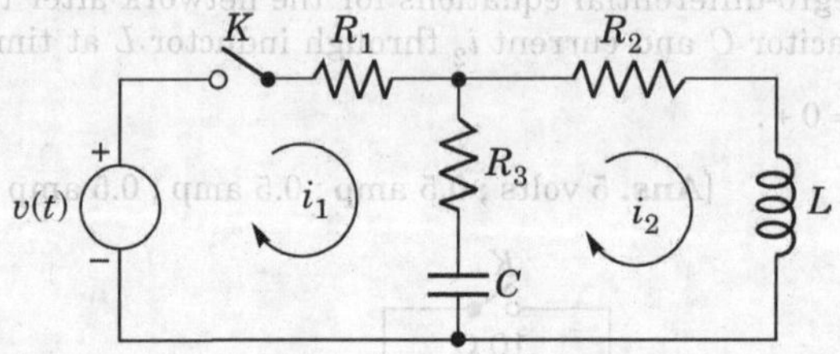

5

Network Analysis Involving Second and Higher Order Differential Equations

5.1. Introduction

In chapter 3 we have studies step function response of simple *R-L* and *R-C* networks. Such an analysis involves linear differential equations of first order with constant coefficients. The mathematical procedure outlined in chapter 3 for solving the network is called the *classical method* of solution. Similar classical method may be adopted for solving differential equations of higher order. The classical method of solution has advantage that it permits better understanding of the differential equations and the requirements of a solution. On the other hand, the operational method using the *Laplace transformation* affords expeditions mathematical computation in most cases. Accordingly we here deal only briefly with the solution of networks involving linear differential equations of higher order. Cases which can more easily be handled with the help of Laplace transformation are not considered here.

Further before taking up the analysis of an actual network, it is desirable to take up the solution of a second order linear homogeneous differential equation with constant coefficients.

5.2. Step Function Response of Series R-C Circuit

This involves a second order homogeneous linear differential equation. Accordingly we first take up the solution of this equation.

Eq. (5.1) gives a second order homogeneous linear differential equation with constant coefficient in its general form :

$$a_0 \cdot \frac{d^2i}{dt^2} + a_1 \cdot \frac{di}{dt} + a\, i = 0 \qquad ...(5.1)$$

Evidently the solution of this differential equation has to be such that the solution itself, its first derivative and its second derivative, each multiplied by a suitable coefficient, add up to zero. Obviously such a thing is possible only if the solution is of exponential form. Thus let the solution be :

$$i\,(t) = Ke^{st} \qquad ...(5.2)$$

where K and s are constants and may be real, imaginary or complex.

Hence $$\frac{di}{dt} = Kse^{st} \qquad ...(5.3)$$

and $$\frac{d^2i}{dt^2} = Ks^2e^{st} \qquad ...(5.4)$$

Substituting these values of $i, \frac{di}{dt}$ and $\frac{d^2i}{dt^2}$ in Eq. (5.1), we get

$$a_0\, s^2\, Ke^{st} + a_1 \cdot sKe^{st} + a_2\, Ke^{st} = 0 \qquad ...(5.5)$$

For finite values of t, $K.e^{st}$ can never become zero. Hence Eq. (5.5) may be put as,

$$a_0 s^2 + a_1 . s + a_2 = 0 \quad ...(5.6)$$

Eq. (5.6) then gives the requirement for Ke^{st} to be the solution. Eq. (5.6) is called the *Characteristic Equation* or *Auxiliary Equation.*

The two roots of this quadratic equation are,

$$s_1, s_2 = \frac{-a_1}{2a_0} \pm \frac{1}{2a_0}\sqrt{a_1^2 - 4a_0 a_2} \quad ...(5.7)$$

Hence the two forms of exponential solution of given second order homogeneous linear differential equation are :

$$i_1 = K_1 . e^{s_1 t} \quad ...[5.8\ (a)]$$

and

$$i_2 = K_2 . e^{s_2 t} \quad ...[5.8\ (b)]$$

Since i_1 and i_2 each represents a solution of the differential equation (5.1), their sum is also a solution. Thus i_3 represents a solution where

$$i_3 = i_1 + i_2 \quad ...(5.9)$$

The truth of this may be verified by substituting the value of i_3 into Eq. (5.1). Thus, we get

$$a_0 \frac{d^2}{dt^2}(i_1 + i_2) + a_1 . \frac{d}{dt}(i_1 + i_2) + a_2(i_1 + i_2) = 0 \quad ...(5.10)$$

or

$$\left(a_0 . \frac{d^2 i}{dt^2} + a_1 . \frac{di_1}{dt} + a_2 i_1 \right) + \left(a_0 . \frac{d^2 i_2}{dt^2} + a_1 . \frac{di_2}{dt} + a_2 . i_1 \right) = 0 \quad ...(5.11)$$

or

$$0 + 0 = 0.$$

Hence i_3 represents a solution of Eq. (5.1). Thus the general solution of the differential Eq. (5.1) is,

$$i = K_2 . e^{s_1 t} + K_2 . e^{s_2 t} \quad ...(5.12)$$

Values of s_1 and s_2 as determined by Eq. (5.7) may be real, imaginary or complex depending upon the values of coefficients a_0, a_1 and a_2 in the given second order homogeneous equation.

We now take up the d.c. step voltage response of a series *R-L-C* circuit.

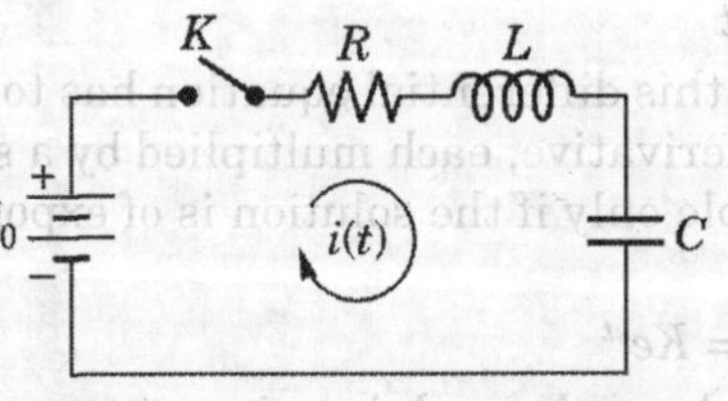

Fig. 5.1. Series *R-L-C* circuit.

Fig. 5.1 shows a series *R-L-C* circuit to which a d.c. voltage V_0 is suddenly applied. Then application of Kirchhoff's voltage law to the circuit yields.

$$L\frac{di}{dt} + Ri + \frac{1}{C}\int i\, dt = V_0 \quad ...(5.13)$$

Differentiating Eq. (5.13), we get

$$L\frac{d^2 i}{dt^2} + R . \frac{di}{dt} + \frac{i}{C} = 0 \quad ...(5.14)$$

The characteristic equation is,

$$LS^2 + RS + \frac{1}{C} = 0 \qquad ...(5.15)$$

The roots of this quadratic equation are given by,

$$S_1, S_2 = -\frac{R}{2L} \pm \frac{1}{2L}\sqrt{R^2 - 4\frac{L}{C}} \qquad ...(5.16)$$

Then the general solution is,

$$i(t) = K_2\, e^{s_1 t} + K_2 e \,.\, e^{s_2 t} \qquad ...(5.17)$$

The final form of the solution depends upon whether $R^2 > \frac{4L}{C}$ or $R^2 = \frac{4L}{C}$ or $R^2 < \frac{4L}{C}$. The three cases are considered below :

Case (A). $R^2 > \frac{4L}{C}$

In this case, the quantity $\left(R^2 - \frac{4L}{C}\right)$ is positive. Hence the roots S_1 and S_2 are real.

The arbitrary constants K_1 and K_2 may then be evaluated from the knowledge of the initial conditions.

If the switch is closed at time $t = 0$, $i(0+) = 0$, since the current in the inductor cannot change instantaneously. Also the voltage across the capacitor cannot change instantaneously. Hence at $t =$ $0+$, $\frac{1}{C}\int i\, dt$ is zero.

Hence at $t = 0+$, in Eq. (5.13) voltage drop Ri as well as $\frac{1}{C}\int i\, dt$ are zero.

Hence $$L\frac{di}{dt}(0+) + 0 + 0 = V_0 \qquad ...(5.18)$$

or $$\frac{di}{dt}(0+) = \frac{V_0}{L} \qquad ...(5.19)$$

Thus the two initial conditions are $i(0+) = 0$ and $\frac{di}{dt}(0+) = \frac{V_0}{L}$.

Substitution of the initial condition $i(0+) = 0$ in the general solution (5.17) yields,

$$K_1 + K_2 = 0 \qquad ...(5.20)$$

On differentiation, Eq. (5.15) yields,

$$\frac{di}{dt} = S_1 K_1 e^{s_1 t} + S_2 K_2{}^{s_2 t} \qquad ...(5.21)$$

Substitution of the initial condition $\frac{di}{dt}(0+) = \frac{V_0}{L}$ in Eq. (5.21) yields,

$$S_1 K_1 + S_2 K_2 = \frac{V_0}{L} \qquad ...(5.22)$$

Equations (5.20) and (5.22) may be solved simultaneously to give,

$$K_1 = \frac{V_0/L}{S_1 - S_2} \quad ...(5.23)$$

and

$$K_2 = \frac{V_0/L}{S_2 - S_1} \quad ...(5.24)$$

Hence the particular solution of Eq. (5.14) is,

$$i(t) = \frac{V_0/L}{S_1 - S_2}\left[e^{s_1 t} - e^{s_2 t}\right] \quad ...(5.25)$$

where S_1 and S_2 are given by Eq. (5.16).

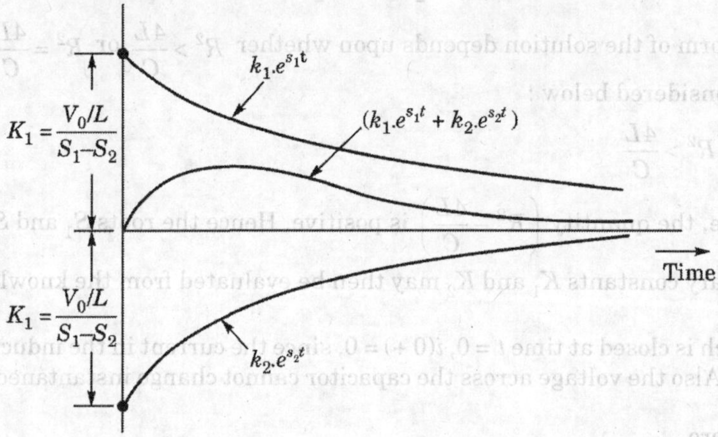

Fig. 5.2. Current *versus* time curves for series *R-L-C* circuit for $R_2 > \frac{4L}{C}$.

Fig. 5.2 gives the nature of the curves giving the variation of separate $K_1 \cdot e^{s_1 t}$ and $K_2 \cdot e^{s_2 t}$ with time t and also the variation of total current $(K_1 \cdot e^{s_1 t}$ and $K_2 \cdot e^{s_2 t})$ with time.

Case (B). $R^2 = \frac{4L}{C}$

Here quantity $\left(R^2 - \frac{4L}{C}\right)$ is zero. Hence the roots of characteristic equation (5.15) are real and equal (say each equal to S).

Then the solution as given by Eq. (5.27) becomes,

$$i(t) = (K_1 + K_2)e^{st} \quad ...(5.26)$$

or

$$i(t) = K \cdot e^{st} \quad ...(5.27)$$

where $K = K_1 + K_2$.

This is not a complete form of the solution since the general solution of a second order differential equation must contain two arbitrary constants. Hence the solution $i(t) = Ke^{st}$ must be modified. Let us assume that the solution is,

$$i(t) = y \cdot e^{st} \quad ...(5.28)$$

where y is a quantity to be determined.

Substituting this solution into Eq. (5.25) we arrive at the following requirement that y satisfies the differential equation,

$$\frac{d^2y}{dt^2} = 0 \qquad \text{...(5.29)}$$

On two successive integrations, Eq. (5.29) leads to the relation,

$$y = K_1 + K_2 t \qquad \text{...(5.30)}$$

Hence the solution in this case of repeated roots is,

$$i(t) = K_1 \,.\, e^{st} + K_2 t e^{st} \qquad \text{...(5.31)}$$

where $S = \dfrac{-R}{2L}$ ...(5.32)

In this case also the initial conditions are $i(0+) = 0$ and

$$\frac{di}{dt}(0+) = \frac{V_0}{L}.$$

Substitution of the initial conditions $i(0+) = 0$ in the general solution (5.31) yields,

$$K_1 = 0 \qquad \text{...(5.33)}$$

Hence Eq. (5.31) reduces to the following form :

$$i(t) = K_2 . t . e^{st} \qquad \text{...(5.34)}$$

On differentiation Eq. (5.34) yields,

$$\frac{di}{dt} = K_2[e^{st} + tse^{st}] \qquad \text{...(5.35)}$$

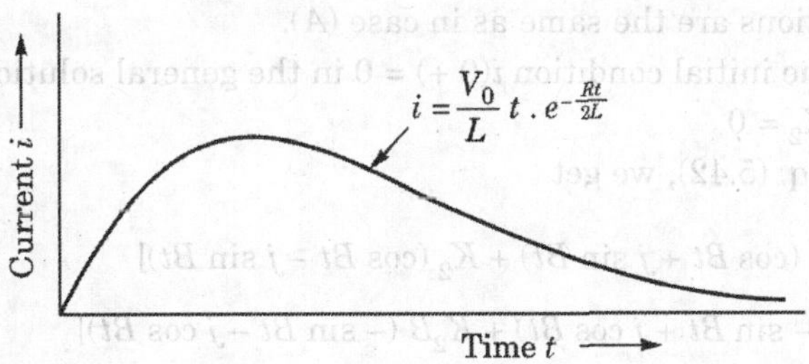

Fig. 5.3. Current *versus* time curve for a series *R-L-C* circuit, for $R^2 = \dfrac{4L}{C}$.

Substitution of the initial condition $\dfrac{di}{dt}(0+) = \dfrac{V_0}{L}$ in Eq. (5.35) yields,

$$K_2 = \frac{V_0}{L} \qquad \text{...(5.36)}$$

On substituting this value of K_2 in Eq. (5.34), we get the following particular solution.

$$i(t) = \frac{V_0}{L} te^{st} \qquad \text{...(5.37)}$$

$$= \frac{V_0}{L} t \,.\, e^{\frac{-R}{2L}t} \qquad \text{...(5.38)}$$

Fig. 5.3 gives the nature of the curve giving variation of the current $\dfrac{V_0}{L} t \cdot e^{\overline{(-R/2L)t}}$ with time.

Case (C). $R^2 < \dfrac{4L}{C}$.

In this case the quantity $\left(R^2 - \dfrac{4L}{C}\right)$ is negative. Hence the roots of characteristic equation (5.15) are complex and are given by,

$$S_1 = A + jB \quad \text{...[5.39 (a)]}$$
$$S_2 = A - jB \quad \text{...[5.39 (b)]}$$

where $A = \dfrac{-R}{2L}$

and $B = \dfrac{\sqrt{\dfrac{4L}{C} - R^2}}{2L}$

Hence the general solution becomes,

$$t(t) = K_1 \cdot e^{(A + jB)t} + K_2 \cdot e^{(A - jB)t} \quad \text{...(5.40)}$$

or $$i(t) = e^{At}[K_1 \cdot e^{jBt} + K_2 \cdot e^{-jBt}] \quad \text{...(5.41)}$$

Now $$e^{jBt} = \cos Bt + j \sin Bt$$

and $$e^{-jBt} = \cos Bt - j \sin Bt$$

Hence Eq. (5.41) may be put as,

$$i = e^{At}[K_1(\cos Bt + j \sin Bt) + K_2(\cos Bt - j \sin Bt)] \quad \text{...(5.42)}$$

The initial conditions are the same as in case (*A*).

Substitution of the initial condition $i(0 +) = 0$ in the general solution (5.42) yields,

$$K_1 + K_2 = 0 \quad \text{...(5.43)}$$

Differentiating Eq. (5.42), we get

$$\frac{di}{dt} = Ae^{At} [K_1 \cdot (\cos Bt + j \sin Bt) + K_2 (\cos Bt - j \sin Bt)]$$
$$+ e^{At}[K_1B (- \sin Bt + j \cos Bt) + K_2B (- \sin Bt - j \cos Bt)] \quad \text{...(5.44)}$$

Putting $\dfrac{di}{dt} = \dfrac{V_0}{L}$ at time $t = 0 +$, in Eq. (5.44), we get

$$\frac{V_0}{L} = A(K_1 + K_2) + jB(K_1 - K_2) \quad \text{...(5.45)}$$

$$= jB(K_1 - K_2)$$

Since $K_1 + K_2 = 0$

$$\frac{V_0}{L} = j2BK_1 \quad \text{...(5.47)}$$

Hence $$K_1 = \frac{V_0}{j2BL} \quad \text{...(5.48)}$$

and $$K_2 = \frac{-V_0}{j2BL} \quad \text{...(5.49)}$$

Substituting these values of K_1 and K_2 in Eq. (5.42), we get

$$i(t) = e^{At}\left[\frac{V_0}{j2BL}(\cos Bt + \sin Bt) - \frac{V_0}{j2BL}(\cos(Bt - \sin Bt)\right]$$

$$= e^{At}\frac{V_0}{BL}\sin Bt \qquad \text{...(5.50)}$$

Substituting these values of A and B in Eq. (5.20), we get

$$i(t) = \frac{V_0}{L}\cdot\frac{2L}{\sqrt{\frac{4L}{C} - R^2}}\,e^{-\frac{Rt}{2L}}\,.\sin\left(\frac{\sqrt{\frac{4L}{C} - R^2}}{2L}\right)_t$$

$$= \frac{V_0 e^{-\frac{Rt}{2L}}}{\sqrt{\frac{L}{C} - \frac{R^2}{4}}}\,.\sin\left(\sqrt{\frac{1}{LC} - \frac{R^2}{4L^2}}\right)_t \qquad \text{...(5.51)}$$

Thus in this case the current contains a sinusoidally oscillating component.

If the exponential component $e^{-\frac{Rt}{RL}}$ were absent, the current i would be purely sinusoidal with natural angular frequency given by,

$$\omega_n = \sqrt{\frac{1}{LC} - \frac{R^2}{4L^2}} \text{ radians/second} \qquad \text{...(5.52)}$$

The frequency expressed in cycles/second is,

$$f_n = \frac{\omega_n}{2\pi} = \frac{1}{2\pi}\sqrt{\frac{1}{LC} - \frac{R^2}{4L^2}} \qquad \text{...(5.53)}$$

This frequency f_n is called the "natural frequency" of oscillation since it depends only on the elements of the circuit and is independent of the applied voltage.

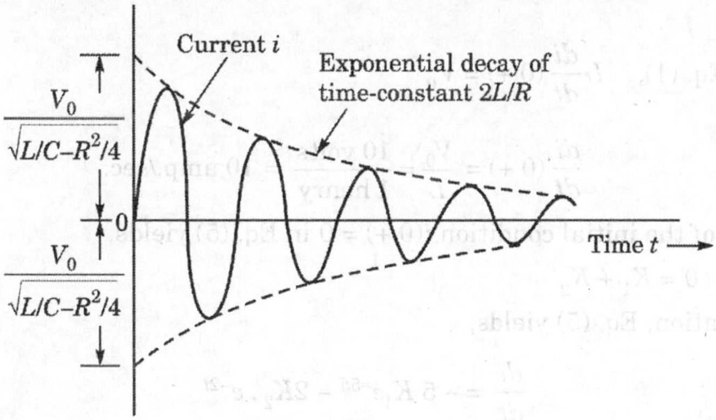

Fig. 5.3. Current *versus* time curve for a series R-L-C circuit for $R^2 < \frac{4L}{C}$.

The exponential term $e^{-Rt/2L}$ constitutes the 'damping factor' and results in successive current maxima to have decreasing amplitudes. Fig. 5.4 shows the variation of this current $i(t)$ with time t.

Example 5.1. *In the circuit of Fig. 5.1, switch K is closed at t = 0, R = 7 Ω, L = 1 henry, C = 0.1 Farad and V_0 = 10 volts. Obtain the general solution and the particular solution for current i(t). Obtain the value of current at time t = 0 second.*

Solution. Application of Kirchhoff's voltage law to the series network yields,

$$L\frac{di}{dt} + Ri + \frac{1}{C}\int i\,dt = V_0 \qquad ...(1)$$

On differentiation, we get

$$L\frac{d^2i}{dt^2} + R\frac{di}{dt} + \frac{i}{C} = 0 \qquad ...(2)$$

The characteristic equation is

$$LS^2 + RS + \frac{1}{C} = 0 \qquad ...(3)$$

Substituting the values of L, R and C, Eq. (3) becomes,

$$S^2 + 7S + 10 = 0 \qquad ...(4)$$

Roots of this quadratic equation are :

$$S_1, S_2 = -\frac{7}{2} \pm \frac{1}{2}\sqrt{(7)^2 - 4 \times 10}$$

$$= -5 \text{ or } -2.$$

Hence the general solution is,

$$i(t) = K_1 \cdot e^{-5t} + K_2 \cdot e^{-2t} \qquad ...(5)$$

Current in inductor L cannot change instantaneously. Similarly the voltage drop across the capacitor C cannot change instantaneously.

Hence $\quad i(0+) = 0 \quad$ and $\quad \frac{1}{C}\int i\,dt = 0$

Hence from Eq. (1), $\quad L\frac{di}{dt}(0+) = V_0$

or $$\frac{di}{dt}(0+) = \frac{V_0}{L} = \frac{10 \text{ volts}}{1 \text{ henry}} = 10 \text{ amp./sec.}$$

Substitution of the initial condition $i(0+) = 0$ in Eq. (5) yields,

$$0 = K_1 + K_2 \qquad ...(6)$$

On differentiation, Eq. (5) yields,

$$\frac{di}{dt} = -5\,K_1 e^{-55} - 2K_2 \cdot e^{-2t} \qquad ...(7)$$

Substitution of the initial condition $\frac{di}{dt}(0+) = 10$ amp./sec. in Eq. (7) yields,

$$10 = -5K_1 - 2K_2 \qquad ...(8)$$

On solving Eqs. (6) and (8) simultaneously, we get

$$K_1 = \frac{-10}{3} \text{ and } K_2 = \frac{10}{3}$$

Hence the particular solution is,

$$i(t) = \frac{-10}{3} e^{-5t} + \frac{10}{3} e^{-2t} \quad ...(9)$$

At $t = 0.1$ second,

$$i = \frac{10}{3} [e^{-.2} - e^{-.5}] \text{ amp.}$$

$$= 0.712 \text{ amp.}$$

Example 5.2. *In the series RLC network of Fig. 5.1, $V_0 = 10$ volts, $L = 1$ henry, $R = 2$ ohms and $C = 1/5$ farad. Switch K is closed at time $t = 0$. It is required to obtain the particular solution for $i(t)$. Calculate the value of current $i(t)$ at time $t = 0.1$ second.*

Solution. Application of Kirchhoff's voltage law to the series circuit yields,

$$\frac{di}{dt} + 2i + \frac{1}{2} \int i\, dt = V_0 \quad ...(1)$$

On differentiation we get,

$$\frac{d^2i}{dt^2} + 2\frac{di}{dt} + 5i = 0 \quad ...(2)$$

Let the solution to equation (2) be

$$i(t) = K.e^{st}$$

Then the characteristic equation becomes,

$$S^2 + 2S + 5 = 0 \quad ...(3)$$

Roots of this equadratic equation are :

$$S_1, S_2 = \frac{-2}{2} \pm \frac{1}{2}\sqrt{4 - 4 \times 5}$$

$$= -1 \pm j2$$

Hence the general solution is,

$$i(t) = K_1 . e^{(-1+j2)t} + K_2 . e^{(-1-j2)t}$$

$$= e^{-t}[K_1 . e^{j2t} + K_2 . e^{-j2t}] \quad ...(4)$$

$$= e^{-t}[K_1(\cos 2t + j \sin 2t) + K_2(\cos 2t - j \sin 2t)]$$

$$= e^{-t}[K_3 \cos 2t + K_4 \sin 2t] \quad ...(5)$$

where $K_3 = K_1 + K_2$

and $K_4 = j(K_1 - K_2)$.

Now the first initial condition is that $i(0+) = 0$ since the current in the inductor cannot change instantaneously.

Also $\frac{1}{C}\int idt = 0$ since the voltage drop in a capacitor cannot change instantaneously.

Hence at $t = 0+$, from Eq. (1) we get,

$$\frac{di}{dt}(0+) = V_0 = 10 \text{ amp/sec.}$$

Substitution of the initial condition $i(0+) = 0$ in Eq. (5) yields,

$$i(0+) = 0 = e^{-0}[K_3 \cos 0 + K_4 \sin 0]$$

Hence $K_3 = 0$.

On differentiation Eq. (5) yields,

$$\frac{di}{dt} = e^{-t}[-2K_3 \sin 2t + 2K_4 \cos 2t]$$
$$-e^{-t}[K_3 \cos 2t + K_4 \sin 2t]$$
$$= e^{-t}[\sin 2t(-2K_3 - K_4) + \cos 2t(2K_4 - K_3)] \quad ...(6)$$

Substitution of the initial condition $di/dt\ (0+) = 10$ in Eq. (6) yields,

$$\frac{di}{dt}(0+) = 10 = e^{-0}[\sin 0(-2K_3 - K_4) + \cos 0\,(2K_4 - K_3)]$$

or
$$10 = 2K_4 - K_3$$
$$= 2K_4$$

Hence $K_4 = 5$.

Hence particular solution is,

$$i(t) = 5e^{-t} \sin 2t$$

At $t = 0.1$ second,

$$i(t) = 5e^{-1} \sin 0.2 = \frac{5}{1.11} \sin 11° 27'$$
$$= 0.897 \text{ amp.}$$

5.3. Response of a Parallel R-L-C Network to a Step D.C. Current

Fig. 5.5 shows a parallel R-L-C circuit to which a d.c. current I_0 is suddenly applied.

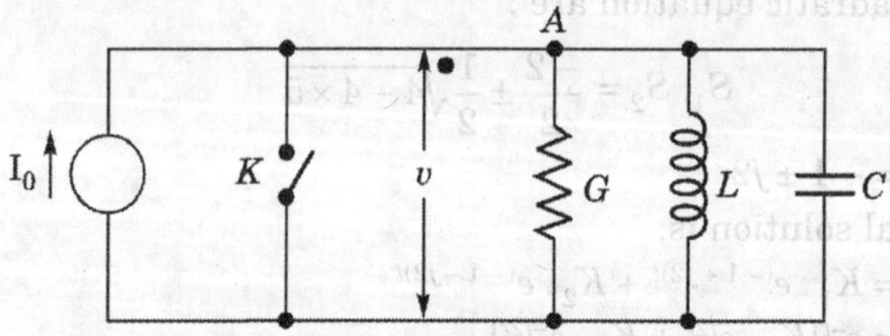

Fig. 5.5. Parallel R-L-C Network.

Let switch K be opened at time $t = 0$. Application of Kirchhoff's current law to node 4 yields,

$$C\frac{dv}{dt} + Gv + \frac{1}{L}\int v\,dt = I_0 \quad ...(5.54)$$

On differentiation, Eq. (5.54) yields,

$$C\frac{d^2v}{dt^2} + G.\frac{dv}{dt} + \frac{v}{L} = 0 \quad ...(5.55)$$

Let the solution of this Eq. (5.55) be

$$v(t) = Ke^{st} \quad ...(5.56)$$

Then
$$\frac{dv}{dt} = KSe^{st} \quad ...(5.57)$$

and $$\frac{d^2v}{dt^2} = KS^2e^{st} \quad ...(5.58)$$

Substitution of the values of v, $\frac{dv}{dt}$ and $\frac{d^2v}{dt^2}$ from Eqs. (5.56), (5.57) and (5.58) into Eq. (5.55) yields the following characteristic equation,

$$CS^2 + GS + \frac{1}{L} = 0 \quad ...(5.59)$$

The roots of this quadratic equation are given by,

$$S_1, S_2 = -\frac{G}{2C} \pm \frac{1}{2C}\sqrt{G^2 - 4\frac{C}{L}} \quad ...(5.60)$$

Then the general solution is,

$$v(t) = K_1 \cdot e^{s_1t} + K_2 \cdot e^{s_2t} \quad ...(5.61)$$

The final form of the solution depends upon whether $G^2 > \frac{4C}{L}$ or $G^2 = \frac{4C}{L}$ or $G^2 < \frac{4C}{L}$. These three cases are considered below. The treatment is similar to that given in article 5.3 for a series *R-L-C* network.

Case A. $G^2 > \frac{4C}{L}$.

In this case the quantity $\left(G^2 - \frac{4C}{L}\right)$ is positive. Hence the roots S_1 and S_2 are real.

The arbitrary constants K_1 and K_2 may then be evaluated from the knowledge of the initial conditions.

If the switch K is opened at time $t = 0$, $v(0+) = 0$ since the voltage across the capacitor C cannot change instantaneously. Also the current in the inductor cannot change instantaneously. Hence at $t = 0+$, $\frac{1}{L}\int v\,dt$ is zero.

Hence at time $t = 0+$, in Eq. (5.54) current Gv as well as the current $\frac{1}{L}\int v\,dt$ are zero.

Hence $$C\frac{dv}{dt}(0+) + 0 + 0 = I_0 \quad ...(5.62)$$

or $$\frac{dv}{dt}(0+) = \frac{I_0}{C} \quad ...(5.63)$$

Thus the two initial conditions are $v(0+) = 0$

and $$\frac{dv}{dt}(0+) = \frac{I_0}{C}.$$

Substitution of this initial condition $v(0+) = 0$ in the general solution (5.61) yields,

$$0 = K_1 + K_2 \quad ...(5.64)$$

On differentiation Eq. (5.61) yields,

$$\frac{dv}{dt} = K_1S_1\, e^{s_1t} + K_2S_2e^{s_2t} \quad ...(5.65)$$

Substitution of the initial condition $\frac{dv}{dt}(0+) = \frac{I_0}{C}$ in Eq. (5.65) yields,

$$S_1K_1 + S_2K_2 = \frac{I_0}{C} \qquad ...(5.66)$$

Eqs. (5.64) and (5.66) may be solved simultaneously to give,

$$K_1 = \frac{I_0/C}{S_1 - S_2} \qquad ...(5.67)$$

and
$$K_2 = -\frac{I_0/C}{S_1 - S_2} \qquad ...(5.68)$$

On substituting values of K_1 and K_2 as given by Eqs. (5.67) and (5.68) into Eq. (5.61), we get the following particular solution,

$$v(t) = \frac{I_0/C}{S_1 - S_2}[e^{s_1t} - e^{s_2t}] \qquad ...(5.69)$$

This solution is the same as the solution for the series *RLC* network as given by Eq. (5.25) except that the term I_0/C appear instead of V_0/L. Hence curves in Fig. 5.2 apply in this case also. The intercept on the *y*-axis by the curves giving $K_1e^{s_1t}$ and $K_2e^{s_2t}$ are however $\frac{I_0/C}{S_1 - S_2}$ each.

Case (B). $G^2 = \frac{4C}{L}$.

In this case, the quantity $\left(G^2 - \frac{4C}{L}\right)$ is zero. Hence the root of characteristic equation (5.59) are real and equal.

Hence the solution in this case of repeated roots is,

$$v(t) = K_1.e^{st} + K_2te^{st} \qquad ...(5.70)$$

where $S = \frac{-G}{2C}$

In this case also the initial conditions are $v(0+) = 0$ and

$\frac{dv}{dt}(0+) = I_0/C$.

Substitution of the initial condition $v(0+) = 0$ in the general solution (5.70) yields,

$$0 = K_1 \qquad ...(5.71)$$

Hence Eq. (5.70) reduces to the following form :

$$v(t) = K_2t.e^{st} \qquad ...(5.72)$$

On differentiation Eq. (5.72) yields,

$$\frac{dv}{dt} = K_2[e^{st} + ts\, e^{st}] \qquad ...(5.73)$$

Substitution of the initial condition $\frac{dv}{dt}(0+) = \frac{I_0}{C}$ in Eq. (5.73) yields,

$$K_2 = \frac{I_0}{C} \qquad (5.74)$$

On substituting this value of K_2 in Eq. (5.72) we get the following particular solution,

$$v(t) = \frac{I_0}{C} te^{st} \qquad ...(5.75)$$

$$= \frac{I_0}{C} te^{-\frac{Gt}{2C}} \qquad ...(5.76)$$

The curve giving the variation of voltage v,

$$\left(= \frac{I_0}{C} te^{-\frac{Gt}{2C}} \right)$$

with time t is similar to the curve given in Fig. 5.3.

Case (C). $G^2 < \frac{4C}{L}$.

In this case the quantity $\left(G^2 - \frac{4C}{L}\right)$ is negative. Hence the roots of the characteristic equation (5.59) are complex and are given by,

$$S_1 = A + jB \qquad ...(5.77)$$

and

$$S_2 = A - jB \qquad ...(5.78)$$

where $A = -\frac{G}{2C}$

and $B = \frac{\sqrt{\frac{4C}{L} - G^2}}{2C}$

Hence the general solution becomes,

$$v(t) = K_1 e^{(A + jB)t} + K_2 e^{(A - jB)t} \qquad ...(5.79)$$

or

$$v(t) = e^{At} [K_1 e^{jBt} + K_2 . e^{-jBt}] \qquad ...(5.80)$$

$$= e^{At} [K_1(\cos Bt + j \sin Bt) + K_2(\cos Bt - j \sin Bt)] \qquad ...(5.81)$$

Substitution of the initial condition $v(0 +) = 0$ in the general solution (5.81) yields,

$$K_1 + K_2 = 0 \qquad ...(5.82)$$

Differentiating Eq. (5.81) we get,

$$\frac{dv}{dt} = Ae^{At}[K_1(\cos Bt + j \sin Bt) + K_2(\cos Bt - j \sin Bt)]$$

$$+ e^{At}[K_1B(- \sin Bt + j \cos Bt) + K_2B(- \sin Bt - j \cos Bt)] \qquad ...(5.83)$$

On putting the initial condition $\frac{dv}{dt}(0 +) = \frac{I_0}{C}$ in Eq. (5.83), we get

$$\frac{I_0}{C} = A(K_1 + K_2) + jB(K_1 - K_2) \qquad ...(5.84)$$

$$= jB(K_1 - K_2) \qquad ...(5.85)$$

since $(K_1 + K_2) = 0$.

or

$$\frac{I_0}{C} = j2BK_1 \qquad ...(5.85)$$

or $$K_1 = \frac{I_0}{j2BC} \qquad ...(5.86)$$

and $$K_2 = \frac{-I_0}{j2BC} \qquad ...(5.87)$$

Substituting these values of K_1 and K_2 in Eq. (5.81), we get

$$v(t) = e^{At}\left[\frac{I_0}{j2BC}(\cos Bt + j\sin Bt) - \frac{I_0}{j2BC}(\cos Bt - j\sin Bt)\right]$$

$$= e^{At}\frac{I_0}{BC}\sin Bt \qquad ...(5.88)$$

Substituting the values of A and B in Eq. (5.88), we get

$$v(t) = \frac{I_0}{C}\cdot\frac{2C}{\sqrt{\frac{4C}{L} - G^2}}\, e^{-\frac{Gt}{2C}} \sin\left(\frac{\sqrt{\frac{4C}{L} - G^2}}{2C}\right)t$$

or $$v(t) = \frac{I_0\, e^{-\frac{Gt}{2C}}}{\sqrt{\frac{C}{L} - \frac{G^2}{4}}} \sin\left(\sqrt{\frac{1}{LC} - \frac{G^2}{4C^2}}\right)t \qquad ...(5.89)$$

This voltage $v(t)$ is thus a sinusoidally oscillating voltage whose amplitude is not constant but reduces exponentially with time constant $\frac{2C}{G}$.

The angular frequency of the sinusoidal voltage is given by,

$$\omega_n = \sqrt{\frac{1}{LC} - \frac{G^2}{4C^2}} \text{ radian/sec} \qquad ...(5.90)$$

The curve giving the variation of voltage $v(t)$ with time t is similar to that given in Fig. 5.4.

Example 5.3. *In the circuit of Fig. 5.5, switch K is opened at $t = 0$. It is given that $R = 1/7$ ohm, $L = 1/12$ henry, $C = 1$ farad and $I_0 = 10$ amperes. Obtain the particular solution for $v(t)$. Calculate the value of voltage v at time $t = 0.1$ second.*

Solution. Application of Kirchhoff's current law to the node A yields,

$$C\frac{dv}{dt} + Gv + \frac{1}{L}\int v\,dt = I_0 \qquad ...(1)$$

On differentiation we get,

$$C\frac{d^2v}{dt^2} + G\frac{dv}{dt} + \frac{v}{L} = 0 \qquad ...(2)$$

Let the solution of Eq. (2) be,

$$v(t) = Ke^{st} \qquad ...(3)$$

Substitution of v and its derivative from Eq. (3) into Eq. (2) gives the following characteristic equation,

$$CS^2 + GS + \frac{1}{L} = 0 \quad ...(4)$$

or $$S^2 + 7S + 12 = 0 \quad ...(5)$$

or $$(S + 3)(S + 4) = 0$$

Hence $S_1 = -3$

and $S_2 = -4.$

Hence the general solution is,

$$v(t) = K_1.e^{-3t} + K_2.e^{-4t} \quad ...(6)$$

At $$t = 0+, v(0+) = 0 \quad ...(7)$$

Also $\frac{1}{L}\int vdt = 0$ at $t = 0+$.

Hence from Eq. (1),

$$C\frac{dv}{dt}(0+) = I_0$$

or $$\frac{dv}{dt}(0+) = \frac{I_0}{C} = \frac{10}{1} = 10 \text{ volts/sec.}$$

Substitution of the initial condition $v(0+) = 0$ in Eq. (6) yields,

$$0 = K_1 + K_2 \quad ...(8)$$

On differentiation Eq. (6) yields,

$$\frac{dv}{dt} = (-3)K_1.e^{-3t} - 4K_2e^{-4t} \quad ...(9)$$

Substitution of the initial condition $\frac{dv}{dt}(0+) = 10$ volts/sec. in Eq. (9) yields,

$$10 = -3K_1 - 4K_2$$

or $$3K_1 + 4K_2 = -10 \quad ...(10)$$

Solving Eqs. (8) and (10) simultaneously we get,

$$K_1 = 10$$

and $$K_2 = -10$$

Hence the particular solution is,

$$v(t) = 10\,e^{-3t} - 10\,e^{-4t} \quad ...(11)$$

At $t = 0.1$ second

$$v(t) = 10(e^{-3} - e^{-4}) = 0.7 \text{ volt.}$$

Example 5.4. *In the circuit of Fig. 5.5, C = 1 farad, R = $\frac{1}{6}$ ohm, L = $\frac{1}{9}$ henry and I_0 = 4 amp. Switch K is opened at time t = 0. Obtain the particular solution for v(t). Calculate the value of voltage v at t = 0.1 and 0.2 second.*

Solution. Application of Kirchhoff's current law to node *A* yields,

$$C\frac{dv}{dt} + Gv + \frac{1}{L}\int v\,dt = I_0 \quad ...(1)$$

On differentiation, we get

$$C\frac{d^2v}{dt^2} + G.\frac{dv}{dt} + \frac{v}{L} = 0 \qquad ...(2)$$

or
$$\frac{d^2v}{dt^2} + 6\frac{dv}{dt} + 9v = 0 \qquad ...(3)$$

Let the solution be $v(t) = K.e^{st}$ ...(4)

Substitution of values of v and its derivatives as obtained from Eq. (4) into Eq. (3) yields the following characteristic equation :

$$S^2 + 6S + 9 = 0 \qquad ...(5)$$

This equation has repeated roots, each equal to – 3. Hence the solution of the equation in this case of repeated roots has to be as follows :

$$v(t) = K_1.e^{-3t} + K_2te^{-3t} \qquad ...(6)$$

At $t = 0 +$, $v(0 +) = 0$ since there can be no instantaneous change in the voltage across a capacitor. Similarly at $t = 0 +$, $\frac{1}{L}\int v\,dt$ is zero since there can be no instantaneous change in the current through an inductor.

Hence from Eq. (1),

$$C\frac{dv}{dt}(0 +) = I_0.$$

or
$$\frac{dv}{dt}(0 +) + \frac{I_0}{C} = \frac{4}{1} = 4 \text{ volts/second.}$$

Substitution of the initial condition $v(0 +) = 0$ in Eq. (6) yields,

$$K_1 = 0.$$

On differentiation Eq. (6) yields,

$$\frac{dv}{dt} = (-3)\,K_1\,e^{-3t} + (-3)\,K_2t\,e^{-3t} + K_2e^{-3t}$$

or
$$\frac{dv}{dt} = e^{-3t}\,[-3K_1 - 3K_2t + K_2] \qquad ...(7)$$

Substitution of the initial condition $\frac{dv}{dt}(0 +) = 4$ volts/second in Eq. (7) yields,

$$4 = K_2.$$

Hence the particular solution becomes,

$$v(t) = 4t\,e^{-3t} \qquad ...(8)$$

At $t = 0.1$ second, $v(t) = 4 \times 0.1 \times e^{-3.0} = 0.296$ volt

At $t = 0.2$ second, $v(t) = 4 \times 0.2 \times e^{-6} = 0.44$ volt.

Example 5.5. *In the circuit of Fig. 5.5, C = 1 farad, R = 0.5 Ω, L = 0.5 henry and I_0 = 2 amp. Switch K is opened at time t = 0. Obtain the particular solution for v(t). Assume that there is no initial charge across the capacitor C.*

Solution. Application of Kirchhoff's current law to node A (Fig. 5.5) yields,

$$C\frac{dv}{dt} + Gv + \frac{1}{L}\int v\,dt = I_0 \qquad ...(1)$$

On differentiation we get,

$$C\frac{d^2v}{dt^2}+G\frac{dv}{dt}+\frac{v}{L}=0 \qquad ...(2)$$

Substitution of values of C, G and L yields

$$\frac{d^2v}{dt^2}+2\frac{dv}{dt}+2v=0 \qquad ...(3)$$

Let the solution be : $v(t) = K e^{st}$ ...(4)

Substitution of values of v and its derivatives as obtained from Eq. (4) into Eq. (3) yields the following characteristic equation :

$$S^2 + 2S + 2 = 0 \qquad ...(5)$$

Roots of this quadratic equation are :

$$S_1, S_2 = -\frac{2}{2} \pm \frac{1}{2}\sqrt{4-8} = -1 \pm j$$

Hence the general solution is,

$$v(t) = K_1.e^{(-1+j)t} + K_2.e^{(-1-j)t}$$

or $$v(t) = e^{-t}[K_1 e^{jt} + K_2 e^{-jt}] = e^{-t}[K_1(\cos t + j \sin t) + K_2(\cos t + j \sin t)]$$

$$= e^{-t}[\cos t(K_1 + K_2) + \sin t\,(jK_1 - jK_2)]$$

$$= e^{-t}[K_3 \cos t + K_4 \sin t] \qquad ...(6)$$

Now since the voltage across capacitor C cannot change instantaneously, we have $v(0+) = 0$. This is initial condition.

Also $\frac{1}{L}\int v\,dt = 0$ at time $t = 0+$, since there can be no instantaneous change in current through an inductor.

Hence from Eq. (1) at $t = 0+$, we get $C\frac{dv}{dt}(0+) = I_0$

or $$\frac{dv}{dt}(0+) = \frac{I_0}{C} = \frac{2 \text{ amp.}}{1 \text{ farad}} = 2 \text{ volts/sec.}$$

This is the second initial condition.

Substitution of the initial condition $v(0+) = 0$ in Eq. (6) yields,

$$v(0+) = 0 = e^0\,[K_3 + 0]$$

or $$K_3 = 0 \qquad ...(7)$$

Hence Eq. (6) reduces to,

$$v(t) = K_4 e^{-t} \sin t \qquad ...(8)$$

On differentiation Eq. (8) yields,

$$\frac{dv}{dt} = K_4 e^{-t}\,[\cos t - \sin t] \qquad ...(9)$$

Substitution of initial condition $\frac{dv}{dt}(0+) = 2$ in Eq. (9) yields,

$$2 = K_4\,[\cos 0]$$

or $$K_4 = 2.$$

Hence the particular solution is,

$$v(t) = 2e^{-t} \sin t.$$

Example 5.6. *In the given circuit, capacitor C has an initial voltage $v_c(-0) = 10$ volts and at the same instant, current in the inductor L is zero. Switch K is closed at time t = 0. Obtain expression for the voltage v(t) across the inductor L.*

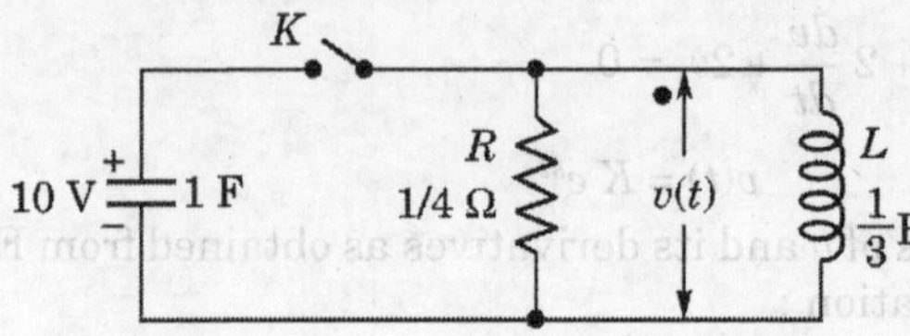

Solution. Application of Kirchhoff's current law to the circuit yields,

$$C\frac{dv}{dt} + Gv + \frac{1}{L}\int v dt = 0 \qquad ...(1)$$

On differentiation,

$$C\frac{d^2v}{dt^2} + G.\frac{dv}{dt} + \frac{v}{L} = 0. \qquad ...(2)$$

The characteristic equation is,

$$CS^2 + GS + \frac{1}{L} = 0 \qquad ...(3)$$

Substituting values of C, G and L, we get

$$S^2 + 4S + 3 = 0 \qquad ...(4)$$

or

$$(S + 1)(S + 3) = 0 \qquad ...(5)$$

Hence the general solution is,

$$v(t) = K_1.e^{-t} + K_2.e^{-3t} \qquad ...(6)$$

At time $t = 0+$, $v(0+) = 10\ V$ and $\frac{1}{L}\int v\, dt = 0.$

Hence from Eq. (1),

$$C\frac{dv}{dt}(0+) + 40 = 0$$

Hence $\frac{dv}{dt}(0+) = \frac{-40}{C} = -40$ volts/sec.

From Eq. (6) on differentiation,

$$\frac{dv}{dt} = -K_1e^{-t} - 3K_2e^{-3t} \qquad ...(7)$$

Substitution $v(0+) = 10$ at $t = 0$ in Eq. (6),

$$10 = K_1 + K_2 \qquad ...(8)$$

Substituting $\frac{dv}{dt}(0+) = -40$ at $t = 0$ in Eq. (7),

$$-40 = -K_1 - 3K_2 \qquad ...(9)$$

Solving Eqs. (7) and (8), we get, $K_1 = -5$ and $K_2 = 15$. Hence the expression for $v(t)$ becomes,

$$v(t) = -5e^{-t} + 15e^{-3t}.$$

Example 5.7. *In the given circuit, with switch K closed, steady state condition is reached. Now at time t = 0, switch K is opened. Obtain expression for the current i_L through the inductor.*

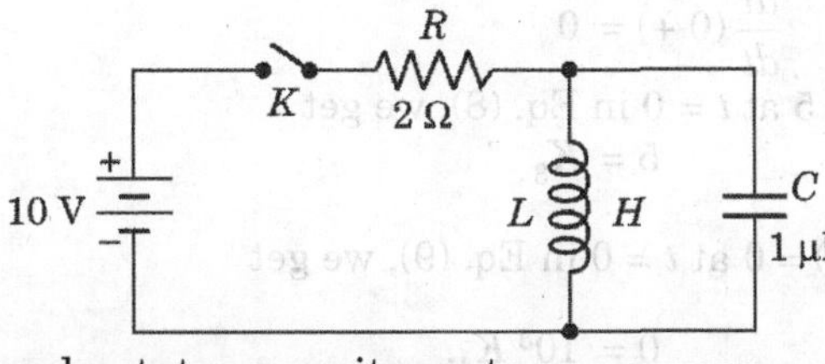

Solution. Under steady state, capacitor acts as an open circuit while inductor L acts as short circuit. Hence the circuit reduces to the form shown in the figure.

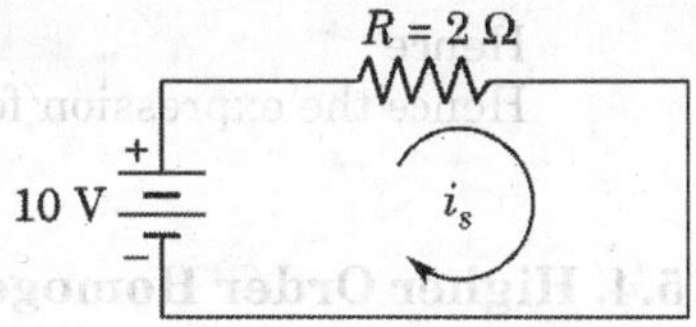

Hence current i_s under steady state is $= \dfrac{10\ V}{2\ \Omega} = 5$ amp. The entire battery voltage of 10 volts drops across resistor R. Voltage across capacitor C is zero and the current through inductor is 5 amp.

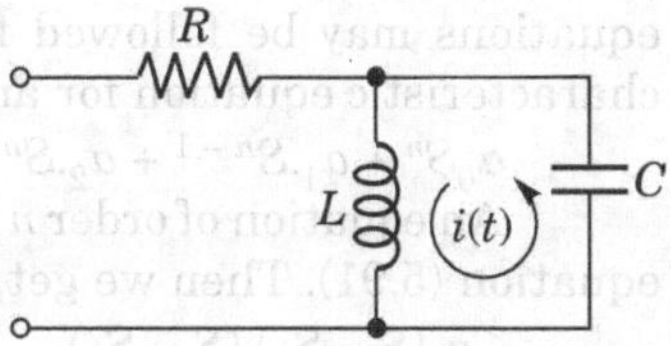

With Switch K opened. The circuit reduces to the form given below. The current through inductor L continues to flow. But now this current flows through capacitor C. Let this current be $i(t)$.

Then application of Kirchhoff's law to this L-C circuit yields,

$$L\frac{di}{dt} + \frac{1}{C}\int i\,dt = 0 \qquad ...(1)$$

or
$$\frac{d^2i}{dt^2} + \frac{i}{LC} = 0 \qquad ...(2)$$

or
$$\frac{d^2i}{dt^2} + 10^6 i = 0 \qquad ...(3)$$

The characteristic equation is,

$$S^2 + 10^6 = 0 \qquad ...(4)$$

or
$$S^2 = -10^6$$

Hence $S_1, S_2 = \pm j10^3$ ...(5)

Hence $i(t) = K_1 e^{j10^{3t}} + K_2 e^{-j10^{3t}}$ ...(6)

$$= K_1(\cos 10^{3t} + j\sin 10^{3t}) + K_2(\cos 10^{3t} - j\sin 10^{3t}) \qquad ...(7)$$

$$= \cos 10^{3t}(K_1 + K_2) + \sin 10^{3t}(jK_1 - jK_2)$$

$$= K_3 \cos 10^{3t} + K_4 \sin 10^{3t} \qquad ...(8)$$

where $K_3 = K_1 + K_2$ and $K_4 = j(K_1 - K_2)$.

Hence $\dfrac{di}{dt} = -10^3 K_3 \sin 10^{3t} + 10^3 K_4 \cos 10^{3t}$ ...(9)

At time $t = 0+$, $i(0+) = 5$ amp.

Also voltage $\frac{1}{C}\int idt$ across C remains zero at time $t = 0+$, since it cannot instantaneously. Hence from Eq. (1),

$$L\frac{di}{dt}(0+) = 0$$

or

$$\frac{di}{dt}(0+) = 0$$

Substituting $i(0+) = 5$ at $t = 0$ in Eq. (8), we get

$$5 = K_3 \qquad ...(10)$$

Substituting $\frac{di}{dt}(0+) = 0$ at $t = 0$ in Eq. (9), we get

$$0 = 10^3 K_4.$$

Hence $K_4 = 0.$

Hence the expression for current $i(t)$ through L becomes.

$$i(t) = 5 \cos 10^{3t}$$

5.4. Higher Order Homogeneous Differential Equations

The method of solution discussed so far for solving first-order and second-order differential equations may be followed for solving higher-order differential equations. Eq. (5.91) gives the characteristic equation for an nth order homogeneous differential equation

$$a_0S^n + a_1.S^{n-1} + a_2.S^{n-2} + ... + a_{n-2}S^2 + a_{n-1}S + a_n = 0 \qquad ...(5.91)$$

An equation of order n has n roots. These roots may be found by factorising the characteristic equation (5.91). Then we get,

$$a_0(S - S_1)(S - S_2) ... (S - S_n) = 0 \qquad ...(5.92)$$

Each of the above roots $S_1, S_2, ... S_n$ gives rise to a factor of the form $K_1e^{S_1t}$ in the solution. The sum of all these factors gives the solution of the differential equation. Thus we get the following solution :

$$i = K_1.e^{S_1t} + K_1.e^{S_2t} + ... + K_{n-1}.e^{S_{n-1}} + K_ne^{S_nt} \qquad ...(5.93)$$

Thus the problem of solving a higher-order homogeneous differential equation consists primarily in finding the roots of the characteristic equation.

Usually the process of finding the roots in the case of higher-order differential equation is quite involved. Fortunately, however, some simplification exist since the coefficients of Eq. (5.9) are *positive* and *real*. This property of coefficients results because these coefficients are made up of the system parameters *R, L* and *C*. Since *R, L* and *C* must be positive and real, the coefficients in Eq. (5.91) must also be positive and real.

The possible roots may belong to one of the following three possible forms : (*i*) real roots (*ii*) imaginary roots and (*iii*) complex roots. Here under we analyse the nature of the roots for characteristic equations of different orders.

First-order characteristic equation. Let the characteristic equation be,

$$a_0S + a_1 = 0 \qquad ...(5.94)$$

The root is

$$S = -\frac{a_1}{a_0}.$$

The root is thus real and negative because the coefficient a_0 and a_1 are always real and positive.

Second-order characteristic equation. Let the characteristic equation be,

$$a_0S^2 + a_1S + a_2 = 0 \qquad ...(5.95)$$

The roots are then given by

$$S_1, S_2 = \frac{-a_1}{2a_0} \pm \frac{1}{2a_0}\sqrt{a_1^{\,2} - 4a_0a_2} \qquad ...(5.96)$$

In this case, these roots may be either real, imaginary or complex. If the roots are complex, these roots must occur in conjugate pairs.

Third-order characteristic equation. We have seen that complex roots must occur in conjugate pairs. Hence in this case, at least one root must be real. The remaining two roots may be either both real or a conjugate pair of complex roots.

Fourth-order characteristic equation. In this case, following possibilities regarding the nature of roots occur :

(*a*) Four real roots (*b*) Two real and two roots forming a conjugate complex pair (*c*) Two sets of conjugate complex roots.

Thus the following rules apply in respect of the nature of roots :

(*i*) Complex roots must occur in conjugate pairs.

(*ii*) In the case of characteristic equation of odd order, at least one root is real. The remaining roots may be real or may occur in conjugate complex pairs.

(*iii*) In the case of characteristic equation of even order, the roots may be real or occur in conjugate complex pairs.

5.5. Solution of Non-homogeneous Differential Equations

A linear differential equation becomes non-homogeneous when the right hand side of the equation is non zero and constitutes some forcing function or derivative thereof. Thus Eq. (5.97) is a non-homogeneous linear second order differential equation.

$$\frac{d^2i}{dt^2} = 7\frac{di}{dt} + 10i = v(t) \qquad ...(5.97)$$

The solution of this non-homogeneous equation contains in part the solution of the corresponding homogeneous equation. Thus putting $v\ (t) = 0$, the corresponding homogeneous equation becomes,

$$\frac{d^2i}{dt^2} = 7\frac{di}{dt} + 10i = 0 \qquad ...(5.98)$$

The complete solution of this homogeneous equation is,

$$i_c = K_1 \cdot e^{-2t} + K_2\, e^{-5t} \qquad ...(5.99)$$

Let some function i_P satisfy the non-homogeneous equation (5.97). Then $(i_P + i_C)$ is also a solution of the non-homogeneous Eq. (5.97) because substitution of either K_1e^{-2t} or K_2e^{-5t} for i into Eq. (5.97) would add nothing to the right hand side of the equation. Thus the solution of homogeneous differential equation constitutes a part of the corresponding homogeneous differential equation. This part is called the *complementary function* while the remaining part of the solution is the *particular integral.*

Thus the total solution i of a non-homogeneous differential equation is given by,

$$i = i_P + i_C \qquad ...(5.100)$$

The complementary function for any given non-homogeneous differential equation may be found by the method outlined in the last article. The particular integral i_p may be found by the method given in the following article.

5.6. Particular Integral by the Method of Undetermined Coefficients

In the differential equation for an electric circuit, the term $v(t)$ constitutes the driving force or the derivative thereof. The types of waveform which this driving force in practical electric circuits may assume are rather limited. Thus $v(t)$ may be :

(*i*) a constant, (*ii*) sin ωt, cos ωt, Kt, $e^{-\alpha t}$ or (*iii*) product of these terms or (*iv*) linear combinations of these terms to give square waves, pulses etc.

Several methods are possible for determining the particular integral. If the driving force belongs to one of the practical forms mentioned above, then the method of *undetermined coefficients* is particularly suited.

The method of undetermined coefficients in general form consists in the following steps :

(*i*) Selecting trial functions of all possible forms that might satisfy the given differential equations. Table 5.1 gives the required form of trial functions.

(*ii*) Each of these trial functions is assigned an undetermined coefficient.

(*iii*) The sum of all these trial functions is substituted into the differential equation and a set of linear algebraic equations is obtained on equating coefficients of like functions in the equation resulting from this substitution.

(*iv*) The undetermined coefficients are then determined by solving this set of algebraic equations. If any trial function is not a solution, its coefficient will come out to be zero on solving this set of equations.

Table 5.1 : Choice of Trial Solution

Factor in v (t)	*Choice of the Particular Integral*
Constant	A
$a_1 t^n$	$t^n \left[B_0 + \frac{B_1}{t} + \frac{B_2}{t^2} + ... \frac{B_{n-1}}{t^{n-1}} + \frac{B_n}{t^n} \right]$
$a_2 e^{mt}$	$C e^{mt}$
$a_3 \cos \omega t$, $a_4 \sin \omega t$	$D \cos \omega t + E \sin \omega t$
$a_5 t^n e^{mt} \cos \omega t$, $a_6 t^n e^{mt} \sin \omega t$	$[F_0 t^n + F_1 t^{n-1} ...... + F_{n-1} t + F_n] e^{mt} \cos \omega t + [G_0 t^n + G_1 . t^{n-1} + ... + G_{n-1} t + G_n] e^{mt} \sin \omega t$

Through above procedure, the particular integral is obtained. The values of the undetermined coefficient obtained on solving the equations depends upon the circuit parameters and driving force parameters. No arbitrary constants are involved in the particular integral.

However before proceeding with the determination of the particular integral it is necessary to find the complementary function first. Each part of this complementary function is compared with the driving force $v(t)$. The rules for selection of trial function as given by Table 5.1 should be modified if these two functions have terms of the same mathematical form. If a term in any of the trial integrals already exists in the complementary function, it becomes necessary to modify the term by multiplying it by t before using it. If such a term in the trial integral appears K times in the complementary function, the term should be multiplied by t^k.

Once the particular integral has been determined the total solution may be obtained by adding this particular integral to the complementary function.

The particular solution may be obtained by evaluating the constants in the complementary function, making use of the initial conditions. Care must, however, be taken that the initial conditions are applied to the total solution and not to the complementary function alone except when the particular integral is zero *i.e.* when the driving force $v(t)$ is zero.

Some of these cases are taken up the following articles.

5.7. Response of R-L Circuit to Exponential Driving Force

Consider the series R-L circuit of Fig. 5.6 to which a driving force voltage $v(t) = V e^{-\alpha t}$ is applied. V and α are constants. It is required to find the total solution.

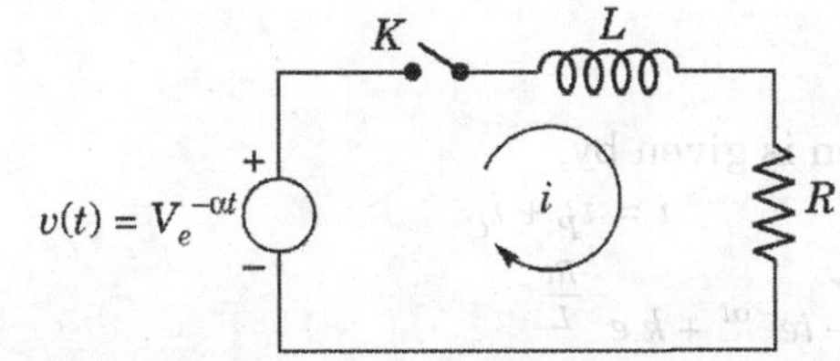

Fig. 5.6. R-L series circuit with exponential driving force voltage.

Applying Kirchhoff's voltage law to the network, we get

$$L\frac{di}{dt} + Ri = V e^{-\alpha t} \qquad ...(5.101)$$

or $$\frac{di}{dt} + \frac{R}{L}i = \frac{V}{L}e^{-\alpha t} \qquad ...(5.102)$$

The characteristic equation is,

$$S + \frac{R}{L} = 0 \qquad ...(5.103)$$

Hence the complementary function is,

$$i_C = K.e^{-\frac{Rt}{L}} \qquad ...(5.104)$$

Making use of Table 5.1, the trial solution for the particular integral is,

$$i_P = Ae^{-\alpha t} \qquad ...(5.105)$$

where A is the undetermined coefficient.

Case (a). $\alpha \neq \frac{R}{L}$

In this case, we may make use of the trial solution given by Eq. (5.105).
Substituting this trial solution into the differential equation (5.102), we get

$$-\alpha A e^{-\alpha t} + \frac{R}{L}A e^{-\alpha t} = \frac{V}{L}e^{-\alpha t} \qquad ...(5.106)$$

or $$A = \frac{V}{R - \alpha L}, \alpha \neq \frac{R}{L} \qquad ...(5.107)$$

The total solution is then given by,

$$i = i_P + i_C.$$

$$= \frac{V}{R - \alpha L}e^{-\alpha t} + k\,e^{-\frac{Rt}{L}}, \alpha \neq \frac{R}{L} \qquad ...(5.108)$$

The arbitrary constant K may be evaluated making use of the initial condition.

Case (B). $\alpha = \frac{R}{L}$.

In this case, the form of trial solution is,

$$i_P = Ate^{-\alpha t} \quad ...(5.109)$$

Substituting this trial solution into the differential equation, we get

$$A[-\alpha te^{-\alpha t} + e^{-\alpha t}] + \alpha Ate^{-\alpha t} = \frac{V}{L}e^{-\alpha t} \quad ...(5.110)$$

or

$$A = \frac{V}{L} \quad ...(5.111)$$

Hence the total solution is given by,

$$i = i_P + i_C$$

$$= \frac{V}{L}te^{-\alpha t} + k\,e^{-\frac{Rt}{L}} \quad ...(5.112)$$

$$= e^{-\alpha t} + \left[k + \frac{V}{L}t\right] \quad ...(5.113)$$

Example 5.6. *An exponential voltage v (t) = 10e^{-t} is suddenly applied at time t = 0 to series R-L circuit consisting of resistor R = 1 Ω and inductor L = 0.5 Henry. Obtain the particular solution for current i (t) through the circuit.*

Solution. Application of Kirchhoff's voltage law to the network yields,

$$L\frac{di}{dt} + Ri = 10e^{-t}$$

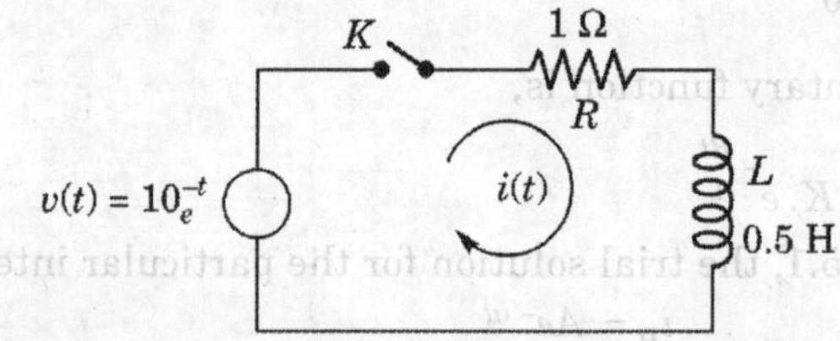

or

$$\frac{di}{dt} + \frac{R}{L}i = \frac{10}{L}e^{-t}$$

or

$$\frac{di}{dt} + 2i = 20e^{-t} \quad ...(1)$$

The characteristic equation is,

$$S + 2 = 0 \quad ...(2)$$

Hence the complementary function is,

$$i_c = k_1\,e^{-2t} \quad ...(3)$$

The trial solution for the particular integral is,

$$i_p = k_2\,e^{-t} \quad ...(4)$$

This is not of the same form as the complementary function i_C and is, therefore, admissible. Substituting the trial solution as given by Eq. (4) and its derivative into Eq. (1), we get

$$-K_2\,e^{-t} + 2\,K_2\,e^{-t} = 20e^{-t} \quad ...(5)$$

Hence $\quad K_2 = 20$

Hence the particular integral is given by,

$$i_P = 20e^{-t} \quad ...(6)$$

The total solution is then given by,

$$i(t) = i_C + i_P$$
$$= K_1 e^{-2t} + 20e^{-t} \qquad ...(7)$$

The constant K_1 may be evaluated making use of the initial conditions.

Initial conditions. There can be no instantaneous change in current through inductor L. Initially current through L is zero. Hence at time $t = 0+$, $i(0) = 0$.

Hence from Eq. (7) at $t = 0+$,

$$0 = K_1 e^0 + 20e^0$$

or

$$K_1 = -20$$

Hence the particular solution is,

$$i(t) = -20e^{-2t} + 20e^{-t}.$$

Example 5.7. *An exponential voltage $v(t) = 4e^{-2t}$ is suddenly applied at time $t = 0$ to a series R-L circuit consisting of $R = 2\ \Omega$ and $L = 1$ Henry. Find the particular solution for the current $i(t)$ through the circuit. Assume zero current through the inductor L before switching.*

Solution. Application of Kirchhoff's voltage law to the circuit yields,

$$L\frac{di}{dt} + Ri = 4e^{-2t} \qquad ...(1)$$

or

$$\frac{di}{dt} + \frac{R}{L}i = \frac{4}{L}e^{-2t}$$

or

$$\frac{di}{dt} + 2i = 4e^{-2t} \qquad ...(2)$$

The characteristic equation is,

$$S + 2 = 0 \qquad ...(3)$$

Hence the complementary function is,

$$i_C = K_1 e^{-2t} \qquad ...(4)$$

Since the form of driving function is the same as that of the complementary function, the trial solution for the particular integral is,

$$i_P = K_2 te^{-2t} \qquad ...(5)$$

Substituting of this trial solution into the differential equation (2) yields,

$$K_2 t(-2) e^{-2t} + K_2 e^{-2t} + 2K_2 te^{-2t} = 4e^{-2t} \qquad ...(6)$$

or

$$K_2 e^{-2t} = 4e^{-2t}$$

Hence $K_2 = 4$.

The particular integral is, therefore, as below :

$$i_P = 4t\, e^{-2t} \qquad ...(7)$$

The total solution is,

$$i(t) = i_C + i_P$$
$$= K_1 \cdot e^{-2t} + 4te^{-2t} \qquad ...(8)$$

Initial condition at $t = 0+$, $i(t) = 0$

Substituting $i(t) = 0$

at time $t = 0+$, in Eq. (8), we get

$$0 = K_1 e^0 + 0$$

Hence $K_1 = 0$

Hence the particular solution is,

$$i(t) = 4te^{-2t}$$

5.8. Response of R-L Circuit to Step Sinusoidal Voltage

Let a sinusoidal voltage $v(t) = V \sin(\omega t + \theta)$ be suddenly applied at time $t = 0$ to the series R-L circuit of Fig. 5.7. V and θ are constants. It is required to find to the total solution for current $i(t)$

Application of Kirchhoff's voltage law to the network yields,

$$L\frac{di}{dt} + Ri = V \sin(\omega t + \theta) \quad \text{...(5.114)}$$

or

$$\frac{di}{dt} + \frac{R}{L}i = \frac{V}{L} \sin(\omega t + \theta)$$

The corresponding characteristic equation is,

$$S + \frac{R}{L} = 0 \quad \text{...(5.115)}$$

Hence the complementary function is,

$$i_C = K e^{-\frac{Rt}{L}} \quad \text{...(5.116)}$$

From Table 5.1, the trial solution for the particular integral is,

$$i_P = A \cos(\omega t + \theta) + B \sin(\omega t + \theta) \quad \text{...(5.117)}$$

where A and B are undetermined coefficients.

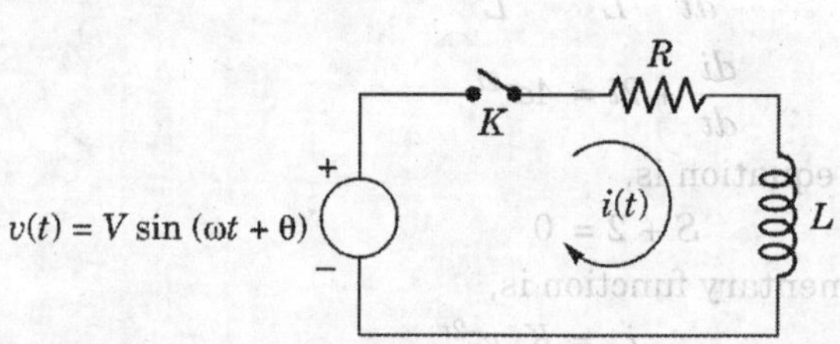

Fig. 5.7. R-L series circuit with step sinusoidal voltage.

On substituting this solution given by Eq. (5.117) into differential equation (5.114) we get,

$$-\omega LA \sin(\omega t + \theta) + \omega LB \cos(\omega t + \theta) + R[A \cos(\omega t + \theta) + B \sin(\omega t + \theta)]$$
$$= V \sin(\omega t + \theta) \quad \text{...(5.118)}$$

In Eq. (5.118) equating the coefficients of like functions we get the following two equations,

$$RB - \omega LA = V \quad \text{...(5.119)}$$

and

$$RA + \omega LB = 0 \quad \text{...(5.120)}$$

Solving Eqs. (5.119) and (5.120) we get the following values of A and B :

$$A = -\frac{\omega LV}{R^2 + \omega^2 L^2} \quad \text{...(5.121)}$$

and

$$B = \frac{VR}{R^2 + \omega^2 L^2} \quad \text{...(5.122)}$$

Substituting these values of A and B in Eq. (5.117) we get the following particular integral,

$$i_P = \frac{-\omega LV}{R^2 + \omega^2 L^2} \cos(\omega t + \theta) + \frac{VR}{R^2 + \omega^2 L^2} \sin(\omega t + \theta) \quad \text{...(5.123)}$$

Eq. (5.123) may be put as

$$i_P = \frac{V}{\sqrt{R^2 + \omega^2 L^2}} \sin\left(\omega t + \theta - \tan^{-1}\frac{\omega L}{R}\right) \quad ...(5.124)$$

The total solution is, therefore, given by,

$$i = i_P + i_C$$

$$= \frac{V}{\sqrt{R^2 + \omega^2 L^2}} \sin\left(\omega t + \theta - \tan^{-1}\frac{\omega L}{R}\right) + Ke^{-\frac{Rt}{L}} \quad ...(5.125)$$

Constant K may be evaluated making use of the initial conditions.

Thus if the switch K is closed at time $t = 0$, the initial current is zero because of the presence of inductor. Hence from Eq. (5.125),

$$\frac{V}{\sqrt{R^2 + \omega^2 L^2}} \sin\left(\theta - \tan^{-1}\frac{\omega L}{R}\right) + K = 0 \quad ...(5.126)$$

Hence $K = -\dfrac{V}{\sqrt{R^2 + \omega^2 L^2}} \sin\left(\theta - \tan^{-1}\dfrac{\omega L}{R}\right)$ ...(5.127)

Substituting this value of K in Eq. (5.125) we get the following particular solution

$$i = \frac{V}{\sqrt{R^2 + \omega^2 L^2}}\left[\underbrace{\sin\left(\omega t + \theta - \tan^{-1}\frac{\omega L}{R}\right)}_{\text{Steady State Response}} - \underbrace{\sin\left(\theta - \tan^{-1}\frac{\omega L}{R}\right)e^{-\frac{Rt}{L}}}_{\text{Transient Response}}\right] \quad ...(5.128)$$

Now if angle θ representing the angle of the sinusoid at the instant of closing the switch equals $\tan^{-1}\dfrac{\omega L}{R}$, then from Eq. (5.127) we see that the constant K becomes zero *i.e.* the transient part i_C of the total response becomes zero. Thus by closing the switch at the proper instant, the transient may be eliminated.

Example 5.8. *In the circuit of Fig. 5.7, the applied voltage is v (t) = 10 sin (10^4 t + π/6)., R = 2 Ω and L = .01 henry. Voltage v (t) is applied at time t = 0. Obtain the particular solution for current i (t) through the circuit. Assume zero initial current through the inductor L.*

Solution. Application of Kirchhoff's voltage law to the network yields,

$$L\frac{di}{dt} + Ri = 10 \sin(\omega t + \theta) \quad ...(1)$$

where $\omega = 10^4$ radians/second

and $\theta = \pi/6$ radian.

$$\frac{di}{dt} + \frac{R}{L}i = \frac{10}{L}\sin(\omega t + \theta) \quad ...(2)$$

$$\frac{di}{dt} + 200i = 10^3 \sin\left(10^{4t} + \frac{\pi}{6}\right) \quad ...(3)$$

The characteristic equation is,

$$S + 200 = 0 \quad ...(4)$$

Hence the complementary function is,

$$i_C = Ke^{-200t} \quad ...(5)$$

The trial solution for the particular integral is,

$$i_P = A\cos(\omega t + \theta) + B\sin(\omega t + \theta) \quad ...(6)$$

where A and B undeterminated coefficients.

On substituting this value of i_P into Eq. (1) we get,

$$-\omega LA\sin(\omega t + \theta) + \omega LB\cos(\omega t + \theta) + R[A\cos(\omega t + \theta) + B\sin(\omega t + \theta)]$$
$$= 10\sin(\omega t + \theta) \quad ...(7)$$

In Eq. (7) equating the coefficients of like functions we get the following two equations.

$$RB - \omega LA = 10 \quad ...(8)$$
$$RA + \omega LB = 0 \quad ...(9)$$

Solving Eqs. (8) and (9) simultaneously we get,

$$A = -\frac{10\omega L}{R^2 + \omega^2 L^2}$$

$$B = \frac{10R}{R^2 + \omega^2 L^2}$$

Hence $$i_P = \frac{-10\omega L}{R^2 + \omega^2 L^2}\cos(\omega t + \theta) + \frac{10R}{R^2 + \omega^2 L^2}\sin(\omega t + \theta) \quad ...(10)$$

$$= \frac{10}{\sqrt{R^2 + \omega^2 L^2}}\sin\left(\omega t + \theta - \tan^{-1}\frac{\omega L}{R}\right) \quad ...(11)$$

$$= \frac{10}{10^2}\sin\left(\omega t + \theta - \tan^{-1}\frac{10^4 \times 10^{-2}}{2}\right)$$

$$= 0.1\sin(\omega t + \theta - \tan^{-1} 50)$$

$$i(t) = i_C + i_P$$
$$= Ke^{-200t} + 0.1\sin(\omega t + \theta - \tan^{-1} 50) \quad ...(12)$$

At time $t = 0, +, i(0+) = 0$.

Hence from Eq. (12),

$$0 = K + 0.1\sin(\theta - \tan^{-1} 50)$$

or $$K = -0.1\sin(\theta - \tan^{-1} 50)$$

Hence the particular solution is,

$$i(t) = -0.1\sin(\theta - \tan^{-1} 50)\,e^{-200t} + 0.1\sin(\omega t + \theta - \tan^{-1} 50)$$

On substituting the values,

$$i(t) = 0.08559\,e^{-200t} + 0.1\sin(\omega t - 58° 51')$$

5.9. Response of Series R-C Circuit to Step Sinusoidal Voltage

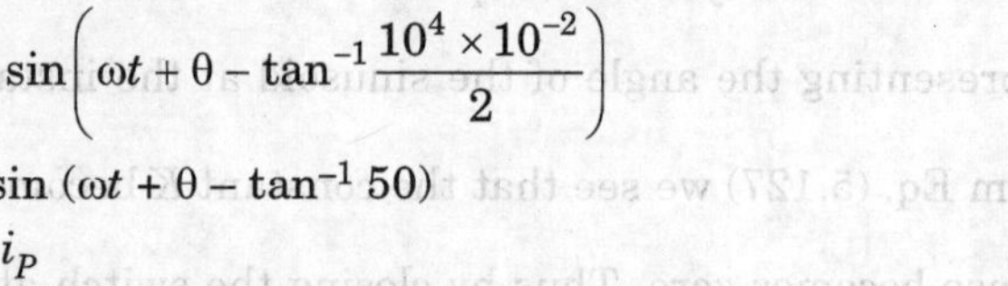

Fig. 5.8. *R-C* Series circuit with step sinusoidal voltage.

Let a sinusoidal voltage $v(t) = V \sin(\omega t + \theta)$ be suddenly applied at time $t = 0$ to the series R-C circuit of Fig. 5.8. V and θ are constants. It is required to find the total solution for the current $i(t)$.

Application of Kirchhoff's voltage law to the network yields,

$$Ri + \frac{1}{C}\int i\,dt = V \sin(\omega t + \theta) \qquad ...(5.129)$$

On differentiating and dividing by R, Eq. (5.129) yields,

$$\frac{di}{dt} + \frac{i}{RC} = \frac{\omega V}{R} \cos(\omega t + \theta) \qquad ...(5.130)$$

From Table 5.1, the trial solution for the particular integral is,

$$i_P = A\cos(\omega t + \theta) + B \sin(\omega t + \theta) \qquad ...(5.131)$$

where A and B are undetermined coefficients.

On substituting this solution given by Eq. (5.131) into differential equation (5.130) we get,

$$-\omega A \sin(\omega t + \theta) + \omega B \cos(\omega t + \theta) + \frac{A}{RC}\cos(\omega t + \theta) + \frac{B}{RC}\sin(\omega t + \theta)$$

$$= \frac{\omega V}{R}\cos(\omega t + \theta) \qquad ...(5.132)$$

In Eq. (5.132), equating the coefficients of like functions, we get the following two equations :

$$\frac{A}{RC} + \omega B = \frac{\omega V}{R} \qquad ...(5.133)$$

and

$$\frac{B}{RC}\theta - \omega A = 0 \qquad ...(5.134)$$

Solving Eqs. (5.133) and (5.134) we get the following values of A and B,

$$A = \frac{\omega CV}{1 + \omega^2 C^2 R^2} \qquad ...(5.135)$$

and

$$B = \frac{\omega^2 C^2 RV}{1 + \omega^2 C^2 R^2} \qquad ...(5.136)$$

Substituting these values of A and B in Eq. (5.131), we get the following particular integral,

$$i_P = \frac{\omega CV}{1 + \omega^2 C^2 R^2}\cos(\omega t + \theta) + \frac{\omega^2 C^2 RV}{1 + \omega^2 C^2 R^2}\sin(\omega t + \theta) \qquad ...(5.137)$$

Eq. (5.137) may be put as,

$$i_P = \frac{V}{\frac{1}{\omega^2 C^2} + R^2}\left[\frac{1}{\omega C}\cos(\omega t + \theta) + R\sin(\omega t + \theta)\right] \qquad ...(5.138)$$

or

$$i_P = \frac{V}{\sqrt{R^2 + \frac{1}{\omega^2 C^2}}}\cos(\omega t + \theta - \tan^{-1}\omega CR) \qquad ...(5.139)$$

The complementary function is given by,

$$i_C = Ke^{\frac{-t}{RC}} \quad \text{...(5.140)}$$

Hence the total solution is as below :

$$i = i_P + i_C$$

$$= \frac{V}{\sqrt{R^2 + \frac{1}{\omega^2 C^2}}} \cos(\omega t + \theta - \tan^{-1} \omega CR) \, Ke^{\frac{-t}{RC}} \quad \text{...(5.141)}$$

Constant K may be evaluated from the initial conditions. Thus if the switch K is closed at time $t = 0$, the initial voltage across C is zero.

Hence from Eq. (5.129),

$$Ri(0+) + 0 = V \sin \theta$$

or

$$i(0+) = \frac{V}{R} \sin \theta \quad \text{...(5.142)}$$

Substituting this initial condition into Eq. (5.141), we get

$$\frac{V}{R} \sin \theta = \frac{V}{\sqrt{R^2 + \frac{1}{\omega^2 C^2}}} \cos(\theta - \tan^{-1} \omega CR) + K$$

Hence

$$K = \frac{V}{R} \sin \theta - \frac{V}{\sqrt{R^2 + \frac{1}{\omega^2 C^2}}} \cos(\theta - \tan^{-1} \omega CR) \quad \text{...(5.144)}$$

In this case also, by proper choice of angle θ *i.e.* by properly selecting the instant of closing the switch, constant K may be made zero *i.e.*, the transient may be eliminated.

Example 5.9. *In the circuit of Fig. 5.8, the applied voltage is $v(t) = 5 \sin(10^5 t + \pi/6)$, $R = 1\ \Omega$ and $C = 0.1\ \mu F$. Obtain the particular solution for current $i(t)$ through the circuit. Switch K is closed at time $t = 0$. Assume zero initial charge across the capacitor C.*

Solution. Application of Kirchhoff's voltage law to the network yields,

$$Ri + \frac{1}{C}\int i\,dt = 5 \sin(\omega t + \theta) \quad \text{...(1)}$$

where $\omega = 10^7$ radians/second

and $\theta = \pi/6$ radian

or

$$\frac{di}{dt} + \frac{i}{RC} = \frac{5\omega}{R} \cos(\omega t + \theta) \quad \text{...(2)}$$

The trial solution for the particular integral is

$$i_P = A \cos(\omega t + \theta) + B \sin(\omega t + \theta) \quad \text{...(3)}$$

where A and B are undetermined coefficients.

On substitution of this trial solution into Eq. (2), we get

$$-\omega A \sin(\omega t + \theta) + \omega B \cos(\omega t + \theta) + \frac{A}{RC} \cos(\omega t + \theta)$$

$$+ \frac{B}{RC} \sin(\omega t + \theta) = \frac{5\omega}{R} \cos(\omega t + \theta) \quad \text{...(4)}$$

In Eq. (4), equating the coefficients of like functions we get the following two equations,

$$\frac{A}{RC} + \omega B = \frac{5\omega}{R} \quad \text{...(5)}$$

and $$\frac{B}{RC} - \omega A = 0 \quad ...(6)$$

Solving Eqs. (5) and (6) we get,

$$A = \frac{5\omega C}{1+\omega^2C^2R^2} \quad ...(7)$$

and $$B = \frac{5\omega^2C^2R}{1 + \omega^2C^2R^2} \quad ...(8)$$

Substituting these values of A and B in Eq. (3) we get,

$$i_P = \frac{5\omega C}{1+\omega^2C^2R^2}\cos(\omega t+\theta) + \frac{5\omega^2C^2R}{1+\omega^2C^2R^2}\sin(\omega t+\theta) \quad ...(9)$$

$$= \frac{5}{\sqrt{R^2+\frac{1}{\omega^2C^2}}}\cos(wt + q - \tan^{-1} wCR)$$

The complementary function is given by,

$$i_C = Ke^{-\frac{t}{RC}} \quad ...(10)$$

Hence the total solution is as below :

$$i = i_P + i_C = \frac{5}{\sqrt{R^2+\frac{1}{\omega^2C^2}}}\cos(\omega t+\theta-\tan^{-1}\omega CR) + Ke^{-\frac{t}{RC}} \quad ...(11)$$

At time $t = 0$, the initial voltage across C is zero. Hence from Eq. (1),

$$R \,.\, i(0+) + 0 = 5\sin 0$$

or $$i(0+) = \frac{5}{R}\sin\theta \quad ...(12)$$

Substituting this initial condition into Eq. (11) we get,

$$\frac{5}{R}\sin\theta = \frac{5}{\sqrt{R^2+\frac{1}{\omega^2C^2}}}\cos(\theta-\tan^{-1}\omega CR) + K \quad ...(13)$$

Hence $$K = \frac{5\sin\theta}{R} - \frac{5}{\sqrt{R^2+\frac{1}{\omega^2C^2}}}\cos(\omega - \tan^{-1}\omega CR) \quad ...(14)$$

Substituting the values of R, θ, ω and C we get,

$$K = \frac{5\sin 30°}{1} + \frac{5}{\sqrt{1+10^4}}\cos[30° - \tan^{-1}(10^{-2})] = 2.457$$

Hence the particular solution is,

$$i(t) = \frac{10}{10^2}\cos(10^5t + 29°\,24') + 2.457\,e^{-\frac{t}{10^{-7}}} = 0.05\cos(10^5t + 29°\,24') + 2.457\,e^{-10^7 t}$$

5.10. Response of Series R-C Circuit of Exponential Driving Force Voltage

Fig. 5.9 gives a series *R-C* circuit to which a driving force voltage $v(t) = Ve^{-\alpha t}$ is applied. V and α are constants. It is required to find the total solution.

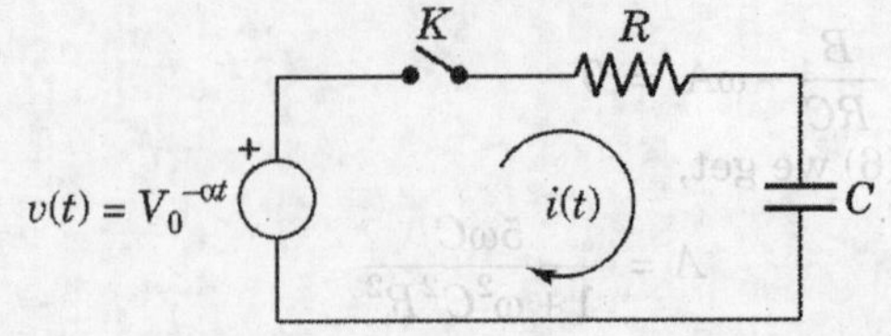

Fig. 5.9. *R-C* series circuit with exponential driving force voltage.

Applying Kirchhoff's voltage law to the network we get,

$$Ri + \frac{1}{C}\int i\,dt = Ve^{-\alpha t} \quad ...(5.145)$$

On differentiating and dividing by *R*, Eq. (5.145) yields,

$$\frac{di}{dt} + \frac{i}{RC} = \frac{-\alpha V}{R}e^{-\alpha t} \quad ...(5.146)$$

The characteristic equation is,

$$S + \frac{1}{RC} = 0 \quad ...(5.147)$$

Hence the complementary function is,

$$i_C = K\,e^{-\frac{t}{RC}} \quad ...(5.148)$$

Making use of Table 5.1, the trial solution for the particular integral is,

$$i_P = Ae^{-\alpha t} \quad ...(5.149)$$

where *A* is the undetermined coefficient.

Case (a). $\alpha \neq \frac{1}{RC}$.

In this case, we make use of the trial solution given by Eq. (5.149).

Substituting this trial solution into the differential equation (5.146) we get,

$$-\alpha\,Ae^{-\alpha t} + \frac{1}{RC}Ae^{-\alpha t} = \frac{-\alpha V}{R}e^{-\alpha t} \quad ...(5.150)$$

or

$$A = \frac{V}{R - \frac{1}{\alpha C}}, \quad \alpha \neq \frac{1}{RC} \quad ...(5.151)$$

Total solution is then given by,

$$i = i_P + i_C$$

$$= \frac{V}{R - \frac{1}{\alpha C}}e^{-\alpha t} + K.e^{-\frac{t}{RC}}, \alpha \neq \frac{1}{RC} \quad ...(5.152)$$

The arbitrary constant *K* may be evaluated making use of the initial conditions

Case (b). $\alpha = \frac{1}{RC}$

In this case, the form of trial solution is,

$$i_P = Ate^{-\alpha t} \quad ...(5.153)$$

Substituting this trial solution into the differential equation (5.146) we get,

$$A\left[-\alpha te^{-\alpha t} + e^{-\alpha t}\right] + \alpha\,Ate^{-\alpha t} = \frac{-\alpha V}{R}e^{-\alpha t} \quad ...(5.154)$$

or $$A = \frac{-\alpha V}{R} \quad ...(5.155)$$

Hence the total solution is given by,

$$i = i_P + i_C$$

$$= \frac{-\alpha V}{R} te^{-\alpha t} = K.e^{-\frac{t}{RC}}$$

or $$i = e^{-\alpha t}\left[K - \frac{\alpha V}{R}t\right] \quad ...(5.156)$$

Example 5.10. *An exponential voltage v (t) = 8 e^{-t} is suddenly applied at time t = 0 to a series R-C circuit comprising of resistor R = 2 Ω and capacitor C = 0.25 farad. Obtain the particular solution for current i (t) through the circuit. Assume zero initial charge across the capacitor C.*

Solution. Application of Kirchhoff's voltage law to the network yields,

$$Ri + \frac{1}{C}\int i\,dt = 8e^{-t} \quad ...(1)$$

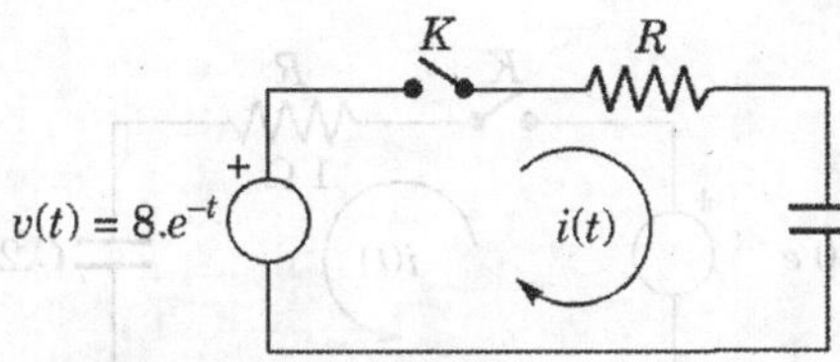

On differentiation and division by R we get,

$$\frac{di}{dt} + \frac{i}{RC} = -\frac{8}{R}e^{-t}$$

or $$\frac{di}{dt} + 2i = -4\,e^{-t} \quad ...(2)$$

The corresponding characteristic equation is,

$$S + 2 = 0 \quad ...(3)$$

Hence the complementary function is,

$$i_C = Ke^{-2t} \quad ...(4)$$

The trial solution for the particular integral is,

$$i_P = Ae^{-t} \quad ...(5)$$

Substituting this value of i_P in Eq. (2) we get,

$$-Ae^{-t} + 2Ae^{-t} = -4\,e^{-t} \quad ...(6)$$

Hence $A = -4.$

Hence particular integral is,

$$i_P = -4e^{-t} \quad ...(7)$$

The total general solution is

$$i(t) = i_P + i_C = -4e^{-t} + Ke^{-2t} \quad ...(8)$$

Initial Condition. Since the initial charge across capacitor C is zero, at time $t = 0+$, voltage across C must ramain zero. Thus at $i = 0 + \frac{1}{C}\int i\,dt = 0$. Hence from Eq. (1).

$$R\,.\,i(0+) + 0 = 8$$

Hence $\quad i(0+) = \frac{8}{R} = 4$

Hence in Eq. (8) putting $i(0+) = 4$ and $t = 0$, we get

$$4 = -4 + K$$

Hence $\quad K = 8.$

Hence the total particular solution becomes,

$$i(t) = 8e^{-2}t - 4e^{-t}.$$

Example 5.11. *An exponential voltage $v(t) = 20\, e^{-4t}$ is suddenly applied at time $t = 0$ to a series R-C circuit comprising of resistor $R = 1\ \Omega$ and capacitor $C = 0.25$ farad. Obtain the particular solution for the current $i(t)$ in the circuit. Assume that steady state condition has reached in the circuit before this voltage is applied.*

Solution. Application of Kirchhoff's voltage law to the circuit yields,

$$Ri + \frac{1}{C}\int i\,dt = 20e^{-4t} \quad ...(1)$$

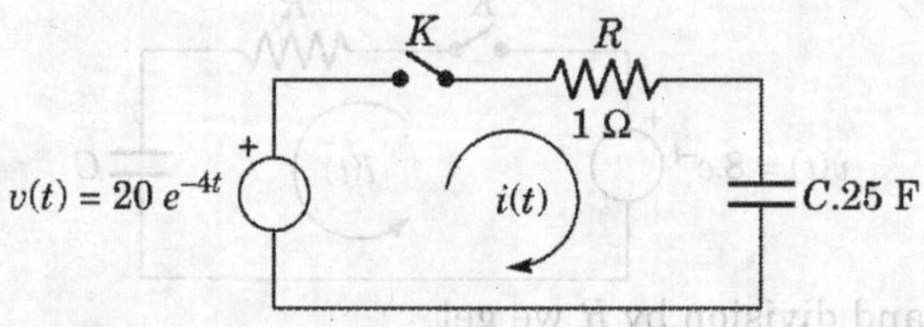

On differentiation and division by R, we get

$$\frac{di}{dt} + \frac{i}{RC} = \frac{-80}{R}e^{-4t}$$

or

$$\frac{di}{dt} + 4i = -80e^{-4t} \quad ...(2)$$

The corresponding characteristic equation is

$$S + 4 = 0 \quad ...(3)$$

Hence the complementary function is

$$i_C = Ke^{-4t} \quad ...(4)$$

Since the form of complementary function is the same as that of the driving voltage, the trial function for particular integral is,

$$i_P = Ate^{-4t} \quad ...(5)$$

Substituting this value of i_P in Eq. (2), we get

$$(-4)\,Ate^{-4t} + Ae^{-4t} + 4\,Ate^{-4t} = -80e^{-4t} \quad ...(6)$$

Hence $\quad A = -80.$

Hence $\quad i_P = -80te^{-4t} \quad ...(7)$

Total general solution becomes,

$$i(t) = i_P + I_C = -80te^{-4t} + Ke^{-4t} \quad ...(8)$$

Initial condition. Before switching, steady state condition is reached, *i.e.*, voltage across C is zero. Hence after switching voltage across capacitor C must remain zero.

Thus at $t = 0+, \frac{1}{C}\int idt = 0.$

Hence from Eq. (1),

$$R \cdot i(0+) + 0 = 20$$

or

$$i(0+) = \frac{20}{R} = 20$$

Hence in Eq. (8) putting $i(0+) = 4$ when $t = 0$, we get

$$20 = -0 + K$$

or

$$K = 20$$

Hence the particular solution is

$$i(t) = 20e^{-4t} - 80te^{-4t} = 20e^{-4t}[1 - 4t].$$

5.11. Response of Series R-L-C Circuit as Related to the S-plane Location of Roots

We have already discussed solution of second order homogeneous differential equation. Here we again take up the same, discussing the form of the response release to the location of the roots of the characteristic equation in the complex S plane. We take up the specific case of a series R-L-C circuit excited by a voltage source $v(t)$ as shown in Fig. 5.10.

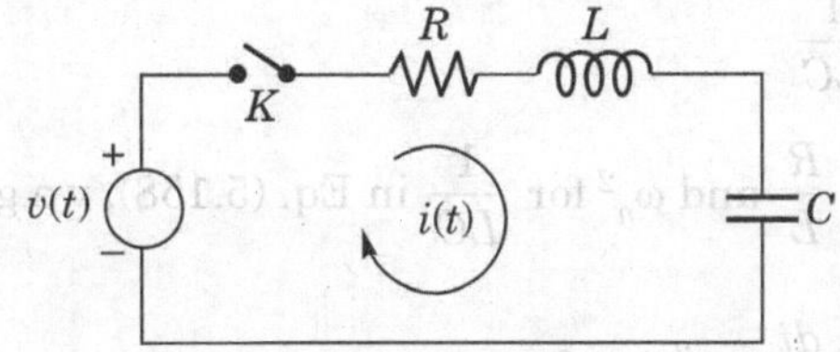

Fig. 5.10. Series R-L-C network.

Application of Kirchhoff's voltage law to this series circuit yields,

$$L\frac{di}{dt} + Ri + \frac{1}{C}\int idt = v(t) \quad ...(5.157)$$

On differentiation and division by L, we get

$$\frac{d^2i}{dt^2} + \frac{R}{L}\cdot\frac{di}{dt} + \frac{i}{LC} = \frac{1}{L}\frac{dv(t)}{dt} \quad ...(5.158)$$

The corresponding homogeneous equation is of second order and is as below,

$$\frac{d^2i}{dt^2} + \frac{R}{L}\frac{di}{dt} + \frac{1}{LC}i = 0 \quad ...(5.158\ a)$$

Eq. (5.158 a) then enable us to find the complementary function, while the particular integral may be obtained using the method given in article 5.7.

Here we take up only the second order homogeneous equation (5.158 a) and study the location of roots of the corresponding characteristic equation.

The characteristic equation is then as below :

$$S^2 + \left(\frac{R}{S}\right)S + \frac{1}{LC} = 0 \quad ...(5.159)$$

The roots of this quadratic equation are :

$$S_1, S_2 = -\frac{R}{2L} \pm \sqrt{\left(\frac{R}{2L}\right)^2 - \frac{R}{LC}} \quad ...(5.160)$$

Let Rc be the specific value of resistance R which causes the radical term in the above equation to vanish. The resistance Rc is called the "critical resistance".

Evidently then, $$\left(\frac{R_C}{2L}\right)^2 = \frac{1}{LC} \quad ...(5.161)$$

Hence $$R_C = 2\sqrt{\frac{C}{L}} \quad ...(5.162)$$

Let the ratio of actual resistance R to this critical resistance R_C called the "damping ratio", be denoted by ζ, (lower case Greek letter zeta).

Then $$\zeta = \frac{R}{R_C} = \frac{R}{2}\sqrt{\frac{C}{L}} \quad ...(5.163)$$

Further let $$\omega_n = \frac{1}{\sqrt{LC}} \quad ...(5.164)$$

where ω_n, is the *undamped natural angular frequency*.

The dimension of ω are $(\text{time})^{-1}$. Hence ω_n is correct being called a frequency.

Then the product $2\,\zeta\,\omega_n$ is given by,

$$2\,\zeta\,\omega_n = 2\frac{R}{2}\sqrt{\frac{C}{L}}\,\frac{1}{\sqrt{LC}} = \frac{R}{L} \quad ...(5.165)$$

Also $$\omega_n^{\,2} = \frac{1}{LC} \quad ...(5.166)$$

Substituting $2\,\zeta\,\omega_n$ for $\dfrac{R}{L}$ and $\omega_n^{\,2}$ for $\dfrac{1}{LC}$ in Eq. (5.158), we get

$$\frac{d^2i}{dt^2} + (2\,\zeta\,\omega_n)\frac{di}{dt} + \omega_n^2\, i = 0 \quad ...(5.167)$$

Eq. (5.167) gives the *standard form* of second order homogeneous linear differential equation.

Eq. (5.167) is the same as Eq. (5.158 *a*) except that here we have used two new constants ζ and ω_n instead of the coefficients R, L and C. These new constants ζ and ω_n render convenient the interpretation of the geometry of the root locations in the S-plane. Further these two new constants are significant in understanding the response of the network.

Another quantity of significance in the study of electrical circuits is the *Circuit Q* or *Quality factor*. The Q of an RLC series circuit is given by the relation,

$$Q = \frac{\omega_n L}{R} \quad ...(5.168)$$

Using the terms Q and ω_n, Eq. (5.158 *a*) may be put in the following form,

$$\frac{d^2i}{dt^2} + \frac{\omega_n}{Q}\frac{di}{dt} + \omega_n^2\, i = 0 \quad ...(5.169)$$

Thus $$Q = \frac{1}{2\zeta} \quad ...(5.170)$$

Referring back to Eq. (5.167) the corresponding characteristic equation is,

$$S^2 + 2\zeta\,\omega_n S + \omega_n^{\,2} = 0 \quad ...(5.171)$$

The roots of this equation are,

$$S_1, S_2 = -\,\zeta\,\omega_n \pm \omega_n\sqrt{\zeta^2 - 1} \quad ...(5.172)$$

Hence the general solution is as below :

$$i(t) = K_1 e^{\left[-\zeta\omega_n + \omega_n\sqrt{\zeta^2-1}\right]t} + K_2 e^{\left[-\zeta\omega_n + \omega_n\sqrt{\zeta^2-1}\right]t} \quad ...(5.173)$$

As the damping ratio ζ varies from zero to infinite, *i.e.* as R varies from zero to infinity, the nature of roots S_1, S_2 of the characteristic equation (5.171) undergo radical change. It is of interest to study the form of roots and also the locus of these roots on a complex S-plane as the damping ratio ζ varies from zero to infinity.

This study may be split into the following three different categories :

Case *(i) Underdamped circuit* $\zeta < 1$; Roots are complex and *conjugate.*

Case *(ii) Critically damped circuit* ; $\zeta = 1$; *Roots are real* and *repeated.*

Case *(iii) Over-damped circuit* ; $\zeta > 1$; *Roots are real.*

These three cases are studied here separately.

Case *(i) Under-damped circuit* ; $\zeta > 1$. In this case the roots are,

$$S_1, S_2 = -\zeta\,\omega_n \pm j\,\omega_n\sqrt{1-\zeta^2} \quad ...(5.174)$$

ζ being less than unity, the roots are complex and conjugate.

Let us define the complex root by the relation,

$$S = \sigma + j\,\omega \quad ...(5.175)$$

where σ (lower case Greek letter sigma) is the real part of S and ω is the imaginary part.

For a given value of ζ less than 1, Fig. 5.11 shows the location of roots S_1, S_2 of the characteristic equation in complex S-plane.

The real part of the root is

$$\sigma = -\zeta\,\omega_n \quad ...(5.176)$$

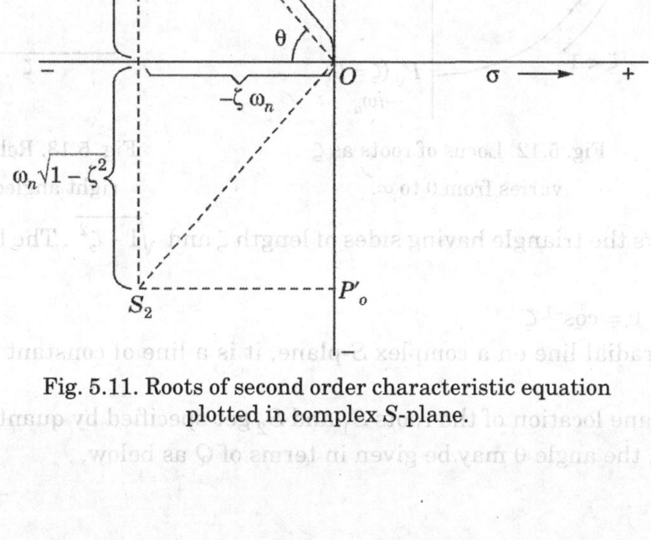

Fig. 5.11. Roots of second order characteristic equation plotted in complex S-plane.

The imaginary part of the root is,

$$\omega = \pm\, \omega_n \sqrt{1-\zeta^2} \qquad ...(5.177)$$

It may be seen that the real parts of the roots S_1 and S_2 have the same value namely $-\zeta\,\omega_n$ while the imaginary parts differ only in their sign.

Further we find that

$$\sigma^2 + \omega^2 = \zeta^2\, \omega_n^{\ 2} + \omega_n^{\ 2}(1-\zeta^2) = \omega_n^{\ 2} \qquad ...(5.178)$$

Hence the locus of the roots in the complex S-plane is a circle of radius ω_n. For a given value of ω_n, this locus is formed as ζ varies from 0 to 1. This locus is shown in Fig. 5.12.

For $\zeta = 0$, S_1, $S_2 = \pm j\, \omega_n$ ...(5.179)

Both the roots S_1 and S_2 are purely imaginary and represented by points P_0 and P_0' in Fig. 5.12.

At $\zeta = 1$, the roots are real and repeated, each being equal to $-\omega_n$. Hence the circular locus of root extends from P_0 and P_0' corresponding to $\zeta = 0$ to point P_1 corresponding to $\zeta = 1$.

Let θ_1 be the angle of either root measured from the $-\sigma$ axis.

$$\text{Then} \quad \theta = \tan^{-1} \frac{\omega_n \sqrt{1-\zeta^2}}{\omega_n\, \zeta} = \tan^{-1} \frac{\text{Imaginary part}}{\text{Real part}} \qquad ...(5.180)$$

$$\text{or} \quad \theta = \tan^{-1} \frac{\sqrt{1-\zeta^2}}{\zeta}$$

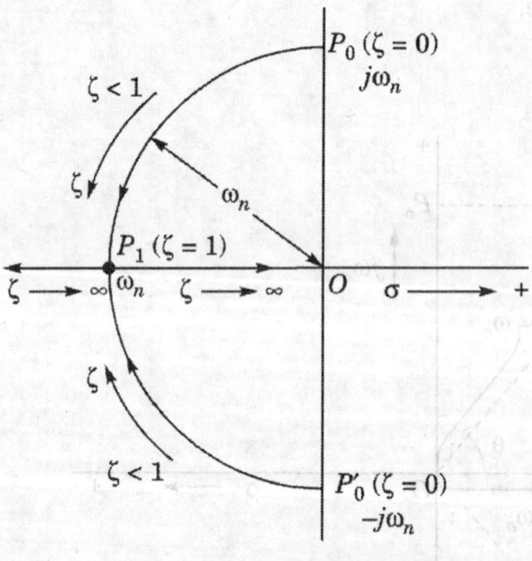

Fig. 5.12. Locus of roots as ζ varies from 0 to ∞.

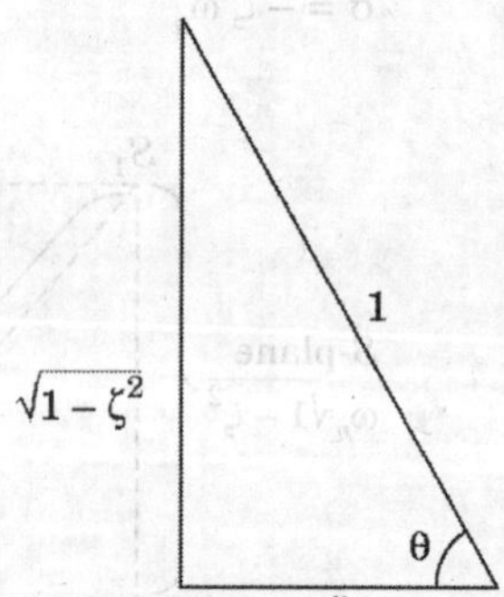

Fig. 5.13. Relationship in a right angled triangle.

Fig. 5.13 shows the triangle having sides of length ζ and $\sqrt{1-\zeta^2}$. The hypotenuse is then of unit length.

Hence $\quad \theta = \cos^{-1} \zeta$ ...(5.182)

If we draw a radial line on a complex S-plane, it is a line of constant ζ with ω_n increasing radially outwards.

Thus the S-plane location of the roots S_1 and S_2 get specified by quantities ω_n and ζ.

Alternatively, the angle θ may be given in terms of Q as below,

$$\theta = \cos^{-1}\frac{1}{2Q} \quad ...(5.183)$$

Case *(ii) Critically Damped Circuit ; ζ = 1.* With $\zeta = 1$, the imaginary part of the roots vanishes and the two roots are repeated, *i.e.* they have the same value $-\omega_n$.

Thus with $\zeta = 1, S_1 = S_2 = -\omega_n$ ...(5.184)

Point P_1 in Fig. 5.13 gives the locus of the roots for $\zeta = 1$.

Case *(iii) Overdamped Circuit ; ζ > 1.* In this case, the roots are given by,

$$S_1, S_2 = \omega_n(-\zeta \pm \sqrt{\zeta^2 - 1}) \quad ...(5.185)$$

ζ being greater than 1, both roots are real. With large value of ζ such that $1 << \zeta^2$, the roots approach 0 and $-2\zeta\,\omega_n$ as ζ increases. Fig. 5.12 shows this separation of the real roots for $\zeta > 1$.

5.12. General Solution in Terms of ζ, ω_n and Q

The general solution, as given by Eq. (5.173) assumes different forms for different categories of value of ζ outlined above. This reveals the nature of response for different categories of value of ζ. We here take up study of this general solution for different categories of values of ζ.

Case *(i) Underdamped Circuit : ζ, < 1 ; Q >* $\frac{1}{2}$. In this case the roots as given by Eq. (5.172) may be put as,

$$S_1, S_2 = \zeta\omega_n \pm j\,\omega_n\sqrt{1-\zeta^2} \quad ...(5.186)$$

where ζ is less than unity. The roots are now complex conjugates.

Hence the general solution is,

$$i = e^{-\zeta\omega_n t}\left[K_1 e^{j\omega_n\sqrt{1-\zeta^2}\;t} + K_2 e^{-j\omega_n\sqrt{1-\zeta^2}\;t}\right] \quad ...(5.187)$$

But Euler's equation gives,

$$e^{\pm jx} = \cos x \pm j\sin x \quad ...(5.188)$$

Hence Eq. (5.187) may be put as,

$$i = e^{-\zeta\omega_n t}[K_1\{\cos(\omega_n\sqrt{1-\zeta^2}\,t) + j\sin(\omega_n\sqrt{1-\zeta^2}\,t)\}$$
$$+ K_2\{\cos(\omega_n\sqrt{1-\zeta^2}t) - j\sin\omega_n\sqrt{1-\zeta^2}t)\}$$

or $\quad i = e^{-\zeta\omega_n t}\,[K_3\cos(\omega_n\sqrt{1-\zeta^2}t) + K_4\sin(\omega_n\sqrt{1+\zeta^2}t)]$ ...(5.189)

where $K_3 = K_1 + K_2$ ...(5.190)

and $K_4 = j(K_1 - K_2)$ ...(5.191)

Here K_3 and K_4 are also arbitrary constants of integration. Now Eqs. (5.190) and (5.191) may be written in the following form :

$$K_3 = K\sin\phi \quad ...(5.192)$$

and $$K_4 = K\cos\theta \quad ...(5.193)$$

Substituting the above values of K_3 and K_4 in Eq. (5.189), we get

$$i = Ke^{-\zeta\omega_n t}[\sin\phi\cos(\omega_n\sqrt{1-\zeta^2}t) + \cos\phi\sin(\omega_n\sqrt{1-\zeta^2}t) \quad ...(5.194)$$

or $$i = Ke^{-\zeta\omega_n t}\sin(\omega_n\sqrt{1-\zeta^2}\,t + \phi) \quad ...(5.195)$$

Through this manipulation we have transformed Eq. (5.189) containing two sinusoids into Eq. (5.195) containing only one sinusoid. Similarly the two arbitrary constants K_3 and K_4 have been replaced by two new constants namely K and ϕ.

From Eqs. (5.190) and (5.191) we get the following two equations giving the values of new arbitrary constants K and ϕ in terms in constants K_3 and K_4

$$K = \sqrt{K_3^2 + K_4^2} \quad ...(5.196)$$

and $$\phi = \tan^{-1}\frac{K_3}{K_4} \quad ...(5.197)$$

The quantity $e^{-\zeta\omega_n t}$ appearing in Eqs. (5.189) and (5.195) is called *damping factor* while the quantity $\zeta\omega_n$ is called the *decrement factor* or *attenuation factor*.

From Eq. (5.195) we see that the resulting current is multiplication of two terms : *(i)* exponential term $e^{-\zeta\omega_n t}$ *(ii)* sinusoidal term of angular frequency say ω.

Then $$\omega = \omega_n\sqrt{1-\zeta^2} \quad ...(5.198)$$

The frequency ω is called the actual angular frequency. When $\zeta = 0$, *i.e.* with $R = 0$ (zero damping) the radical term in the expression (5.198) for ω reduces to unity. Thus with zero damping angular frequency equals ω_n. Accordingly ω_n is called the *undamped natural angular frequency.* With the addition of damping, *i.e.* with non-zero value of R or ζ, the frequency of oscillation reduces to a value $\omega_n\sqrt{1-\zeta^2}$. Higher the value of ζ, more is the damping and more is the reduction in the angular frequency.

Case *(ii) Critically damped circuit* : $\zeta = 1$; $Q = \frac{1}{2}$. In this case, the two roots become identical. Hence with these repeated roots, the general solution becomes.

$$i = (K_1 + K_2 t)\, e^{-\omega_n t} \quad ...(5.199)$$

The limit of the quantity $t\,e^{-\omega_n t}$ as time tends to infinity may be found by l'Hospital's rule. The quantity $t\,e^{-\omega_n t}$ may be written as $\frac{t}{e^{\omega_n t}}$. Then differentiation of the numerator and the denominator with respect to t shows that,

$$\lim_{t\to\infty} t\,e^{-\omega_n t} = 0 \quad ...(5.200)$$

Case *(iii) Overdamped Circuit* ; $\zeta = 1$; $Q = \frac{1}{2}$. In this case, the general solution is the same as given by Eq. (5.173) reproduced below,

$$i = e^{-\zeta\omega_n t}[K_1 e^{\omega_n\sqrt{\zeta^2 - 1}t} + K_2\, e^{-\omega_n\sqrt{\zeta^2 - 1}t}] \quad ...(5.201)$$

The general solution as given by Eq. (5.201) may alternatively be put in a more convenient form involving hyperbolic functions.

We make use of the following relations,

$$e^{-x} = \cosh x + \sinh x \quad ...(5.202)$$

and $$e^{-x} = \cosh x - \sinh x \quad ...(5.203)$$

Hence Eq. (5.201) may be put as,

$$i = e^{-\zeta\omega_n t}\;[K_1 \cosh(\omega_n\sqrt{\zeta^2 - 1}t) + K_1 \sinh(\omega_n\sqrt{\zeta^2 - 1}t)$$
$$+ K_2 \cosh(\omega_n\sqrt{\zeta^2 - 1}t) - K_2 \sinh(\omega_n\sqrt{\zeta^2 - 1}t) \quad ...(5.204)$$

or $$i = e^{-\zeta\omega_n t}\;[K_5 \cosh(\omega_n\sqrt{\zeta^2 - 1}t) + K_6 \sinh(\omega_n\sqrt{\zeta^2 - 1}t)] \quad ...(5.205)$$

where $K_5 = K_1 + K_2$

and $K_6 = K_1 - K_2$ ...(5.207)

Thus we have converted Eq. (5.201) involving two arbitrary constants K_1 and K_2 into Eq. (5.205) involving two other constants K_5 and K_6.

5.13. Particular Solution in Terms of ζ and ω_n

For a given network the arbitrary constants involved in the general solution may be evaluated from the knowledge of the initial conditions. This is now taken up for the series *RLC* circuit of Fig. 5.10, with switch *K* closed at time $t = 0$. The evaluation on the constants in the general solution is taken up for the three cases discussed separately.

Case (*i*) *Under-damped circuit* ; $\zeta < 1$. In this case $R < R_c$.

The general solution is given by Eq. (5.189).

At $t = 0$ +, the current through the inductor is zero. Hence from Eq. (5.189),

$$0 = e^{-\zeta\omega_n t}[K_3 \cos(\omega_n\sqrt{1-\zeta^2}t) + 0]$$

Hence $K_3 = 0$ ...(5.208)

Putting $K_2 = 0$ in Eq. (5.189), we have

$$i = K_4 e^{-\zeta\omega_n t} \sin(\omega_n\sqrt{1-\zeta^2}t) \quad ...(5.209)$$

Differentiating Eq. (5.209) with respect to *t,* we get

$$\frac{di}{dt} = K_4 e^{-\zeta\omega_n t}[\omega_n\sqrt{1-\zeta^2} \cos(\omega_n\sqrt{1-\zeta^2}t) - \zeta\omega_n \sin(\omega_n\sqrt{1-\zeta^2}t)] \quad ...(5.210)$$

Kirchhoff's voltage law applied to the circuit of Fig. 5.10 gives,

$$L\frac{di}{dt} + Ri + \frac{1}{C}\int idt = V_0 \quad ...(5.211)$$

At $t = 0 +, \frac{1}{C}\int idt = 0$ and also $Ri = 0$

Hence from Eq. (5.211),

$$L\frac{di}{dt}(0+) + 0 + 0 = V_0$$

Hence $\frac{di}{dt}(0+) = \frac{V_0}{L}$ ...(5.212)

Hence at time $t = 0$ +, Eq. (5.210) becomes,

$$\frac{V_0}{L} = K_4[\omega\sqrt{1-\zeta^2}] \quad ...(5.213)$$

Hence $$K_4 = \frac{V_0}{\omega L\sqrt{1-\zeta^2}}$$

Substituting this value of K_4 in Eq. (5.209) we get the following particular solution

$$i = \frac{V_0}{\omega L\sqrt{1-\zeta^2}} e^{-\zeta\omega_n t} \sin(\omega_n\sqrt{1-\zeta^2}t) \quad ...(5.214)$$

Fig. 5.14 shows the variation of current i with time t for the given circuit with less than critical damping. In fact the current i is a sinusoid of angular frequency $\omega_n\sqrt{1-\zeta^2}$ radians/second and amplitude that reduces exponentially with time. The initial value of the amplitude is $\dfrac{V_0}{\omega L\sqrt{1-\zeta^2}}$ and the time constant of exponential decay of amplitude is $\zeta\omega_n$. Fig. 5.14 also shows the time variation of term $\dfrac{V_0}{\omega L\sqrt{1-\zeta^2}}e^{-\zeta\omega_n t}$. The instantaneous current i is a multiplication of this with $\sin(\omega_n\sqrt{1-\zeta^2}\,t)$.

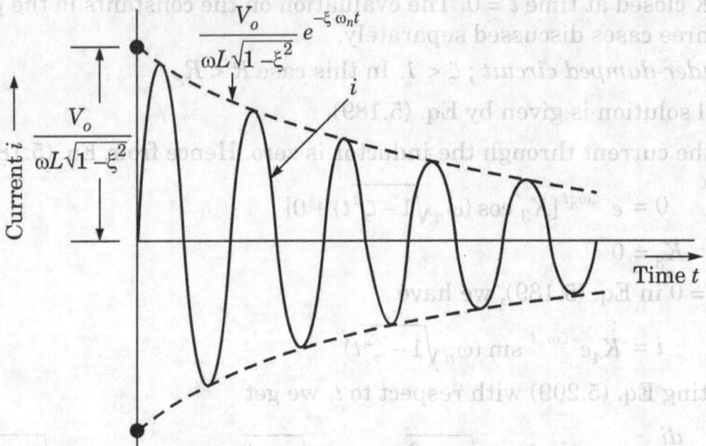

Fig. 5.14. Variation of current i with time t for under-damped circuit.

The attenuation factor (decrement factor) $\zeta\omega_n$ determines the rate of decay of oscillations. As the resistance R approaches zero, the oscillations become undamped and constant amplitude oscillations result.

The sinusoidal variation of current i, as given by Eq. (5.214) is equivalent to physical phenomenon of exchange of energy between the electric energy storage element (capacitor C) and magnetic energy storage element (inductor L). Thus on closing the switch K, magnetic energy is stored in magnetic field of the inductor. With decreasing current, this energy is returned to the electric field. In this process, part of the energy is dissipated in the resistor R so that the total energy decreases with each cycle. Ultimately the entire energy gets dissipated and the current reduces to zero. If the resistance R is zero, constant amplitude sinusoidal current results. In physical circuits resistance R (however small) is always present. Hence dissipation of energy with consequent damped oscillations always results. However, if by some means, energy lost per cycle through dissipation in resistance R is replenished, then the oscillations are sustained. This is the principle of oscillators used for producing a.c. power at audio and radio frequencies.

Case *(ii) Critically Damped Circuit.* In critically damped circuit, $\zeta = 1$, *i.e.* $R = R_C$. The general solution is given by Eq. (5.199) reproduced below :

$$i = (K_1 + K_2 t)e^{-\omega_n t} \qquad ...(5.215)$$

At $t = 0+$, $i(0+) = 0$ because of inductor L. The quantity $\left(\dfrac{1}{C}\right)\displaystyle\int i\,dt = 0$ at $t = 0+$ since the charge on the capacitor C cannot change instantaneously.

Hence from Eq. (5.211), at time $t = 0+$,

$$L\frac{di}{dt}(0+) + 0 + 0 = V_0$$

Hence $$\frac{di}{dt}(0+) = \frac{V_0}{L} \qquad ...(5.216)$$

Putting $i(0+) = 0$ in Eq. (5.215), we get at $t = 0+$,

$$0 = (K_1 + 0)e^{-0}$$

or $$K_1 = 0.$$

Hence Eq. (5.215) reduces to the following form

$$i = K_1 t\, e^{-\omega_n t} \qquad ...(5.217)$$

Differentiating Eq. (5.217), we get

$$\frac{di}{dt} = K_2[t(-\omega_n)\, e^{-\omega_n t} + e^{-\omega_n t}]$$

or $$\frac{di}{dt} = K_2\, e^{-\omega_n t}[1 - \omega_n t] \qquad ...(5.218)$$

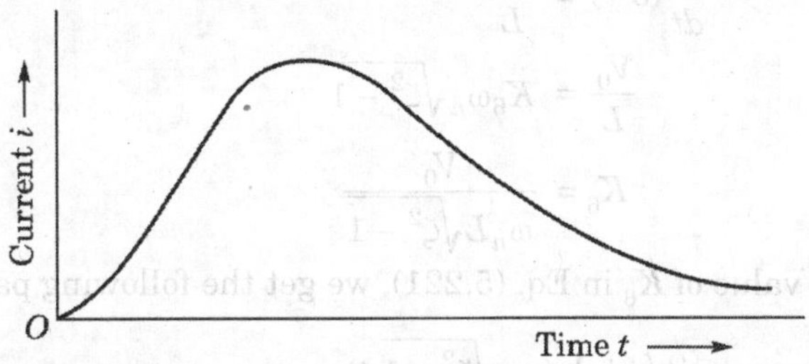

Fig. 5.15. Variation of current i with time t for critically damped circuit.

At time $t = 0+$,

$$\frac{di}{dt}(0+) = \frac{V_0}{L} = K_2 \qquad ...(5.219)$$

Substituting this value of K_2 into Eq. (5.217) yields the following particular solution

$$i = \frac{V_0}{L}.\, t\, e^{-\omega_n t} \qquad ...(5.220)$$

Fig. 5.15 shows the variations of i with time t in the case of critically damped circuit.

Case *(iii) Over damped Circuit* : $\zeta > 1$. In this case $R > R_c$.

The general solution is given by Eq. (5.205).

At $t = 0+$, current through the inductor L is zero.

Hence form Eq. (5.205),

$$0 = K_5 \cosh(\omega_n \sqrt{\zeta^2 - 1}\, t)$$

Hence $K_5 = 0$.

Putting $K_5 = 0$ in Eq. (5.205), we have

$$i = K_6 e^{-\zeta\omega_n t} \sinh(\omega_n \sqrt{\zeta^2 - 1}\, t) \qquad ...(5.221)$$

Also the term, $$\frac{1}{C}\int i\, dt = 0 \quad \text{at} \quad t = 0+.$$

Also $$Ri = 0 \quad \text{at} \quad t = 0+.$$

Hence from Eq. (5.221),

$$L\frac{di}{dt}(0+) = V_0$$

or $$\frac{di}{dt}(0+) = \frac{V_0}{L} \quad ...(5.222)$$

Constant K_6 may be evaluated from the initial condition as given by Eq. (5.222).

Now differentiating Eq. (5.221) with respect to time t, we get

$$\frac{di}{dt} = K_6 e^{-\zeta\omega_n t}[\omega_n\sqrt{\zeta^2-1}\cosh(\omega_n\sqrt{\zeta^2-1}\,t) - \zeta\omega_n \sinh(\omega_n\sqrt{\zeta^2-1}\,t)] \quad ...(5.223)$$

As t approaches zero, hyperbolic cosine term approaches unity while hyperbolic sine term approaches zero.

Hence $$\frac{di}{dt}(0+) = K_6\omega_n\sqrt{\zeta^2-1} \quad ...(5.224)$$

But $$\frac{di}{dt}(0+) = \frac{V_0}{L}$$

Hence $$\frac{V_0}{L} = K_6\omega_n\sqrt{\zeta^2-1}$$

Hence $$K_6 = \frac{V_0}{\omega_n L\sqrt{\zeta^2-1}} \quad ...(5.225)$$

Substituting this value of K_6 in Eq. (5.221), we get the following particular solution,

$$i = \frac{V_0}{\omega_n L\sqrt{\zeta^2-1}}\, e^{-\zeta\omega_n t}\sinh(\omega_n\sqrt{\zeta^2-1}\,t) \quad ...(5.226)$$

Fig. 5.16 shows the variation of current i with time t in the case of overdamped circuit.

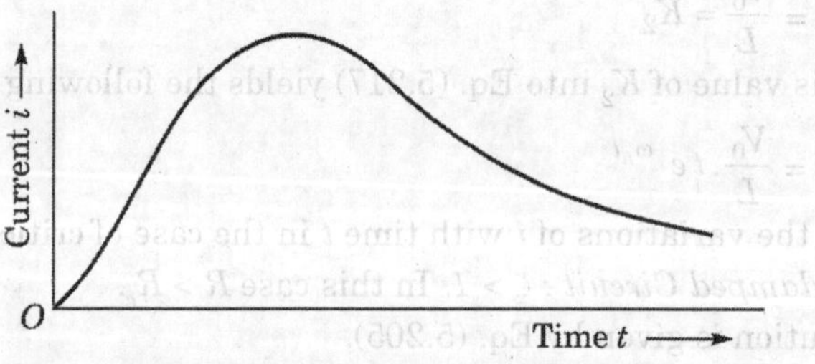

Fig. 5.16. Variation of current i with time t for overdamped circuit.

5.14. Summary of the Response of a Network Involving Second Order Characteristic Equation

We have discussed at length response of network involving second order linear differential equation. In case the equation is homogeneous, characteristic equation may be put in the form,

$$S^2 + a_1 S + a_2 = 0 \quad ...(5.227)$$

where a_1 and a_2 are real and positive constants. Eq. (5.227) may alternatively be put in the following standard form involving ζ and ω_n,

$$S^2 + 2\,\zeta\omega\, S + \omega_n^2 = 0 \quad ...(5.228)$$

In case the equation is non-homogeneous, we first find the complementary function assuming the driving force to be zero and then let the characteristic equation be given by Eq. (5.227) or Eq. (5.228).

Table 5.2

Response of network involving second order characteristic equation $S^2 + a_1S + a_2 = 0$ with a_1 and a_2 being real positive constants

Case	*Relation among coefficients*	*Nature of roots*	*Descriptive name*	*Solution*	*Graph of response*
(*i*)	$a_1^2 < 4a_2$ $\zeta < 1$ $R < R_C$	Conjugate complex roots with real parts negative $S_1, S_2 = \sigma_1 \pm j\omega_1$ $= -\zeta\omega_n \pm j\omega_n\sqrt{1-\zeta^2}$	Under-damped circuit	$i = e^{\sigma_1 t}[K_1 \cos \omega_1 t + K_2 \sin \omega_1 t]$ or $i = Ke^{\sigma_1 t} \sin(\omega_1 t + \phi)$	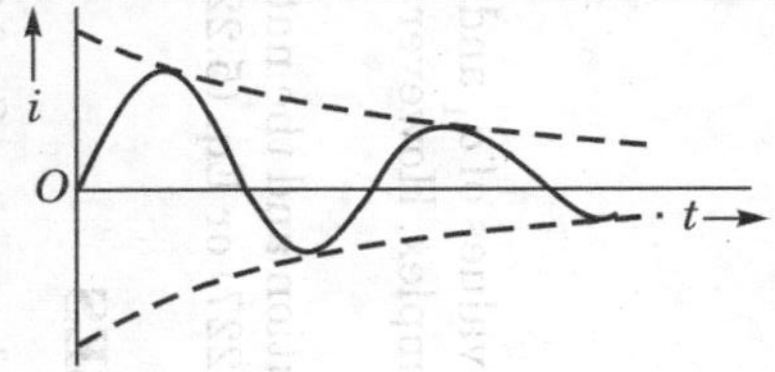
(*ii*)	$a_1^2 > 4a_2$ $\zeta > 1$ $R > R_C$	Negative, real and equal roots. $S_1 = S_2 = \sigma_1 = -\omega_n$	Critically damped circuit	$i = (K_1 + K_2)e^{-\omega_n t}$	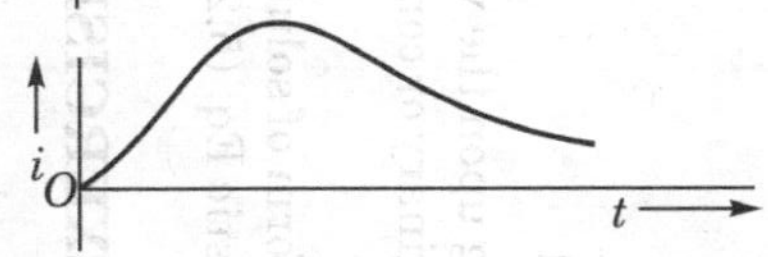
(*iii*)	$a_1^2 > 4a_2$ $\zeta > 1$ $R > R_C$	Negative, real and unequal roots. $S_1, S_2 = \sigma_1 \pm j\omega_1$ $= -\zeta\omega_n \pm j\omega_n\sqrt{1-\zeta^2}$	Over-damped circuit	$i = K_1e^{S_1 t} + Ke^{S_2 t}$ or $i = e^{\sigma_1 t}[K_1e^{\omega_1 t} + K_2e^{-\omega_1 t}]$ or $i = e^{\sigma_1 t} + [K_3 \cosh \omega_1 t + K_4 \sinh \omega_1 t]$	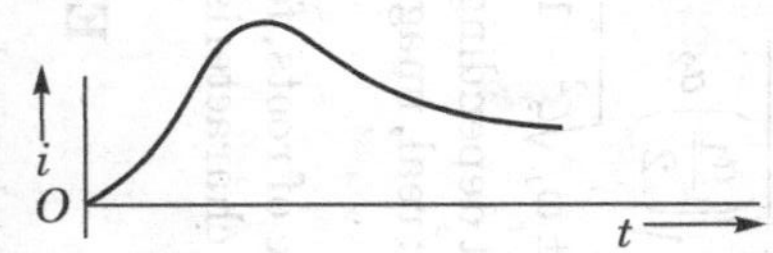
(*iv*)	$a_1 = 0$ $a_2 \neq 0$	Conjugate imaginary ..... $S_1, S_2 = \pm j\omega_1$ $= \pm j\omega_n\sqrt{1-\zeta^2}$	Oscillatory	$i = K_1 \cos \omega_1 t + K_2 \sin \omega_1 t$ or $i = K_1 \sin(\omega_1 t + \phi)$	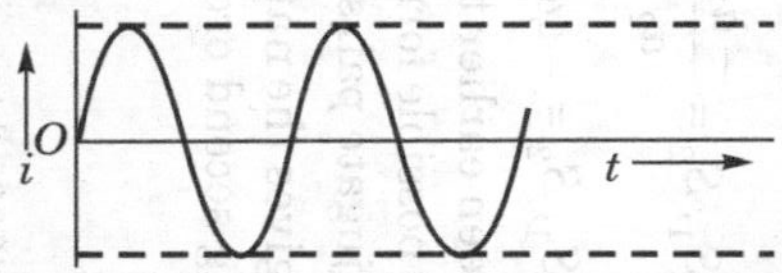

The roots are then given by either of the following two equations.

$$S_1, S_2 = \frac{-a_1}{a_2} \pm \sqrt{\left(\frac{a_1}{2}\right) a_2} \quad ...(5.229)$$

$$S_1, S_2 = -\zeta\omega_n \pm \omega_n\sqrt{\zeta^2 - 1} \quad ...(5.230)$$

We have seen earlier that depending upon the values of a_1 and a_2, these roots may take any of following three possible forms : real, imaginary or complex. However in case the roots are complex, they occur in conjugate pairs.

Table 5.2 gives the nature of roots, form of solution and the nature of response curve for the network involving second order characteristic Eq. (5.227) or Eq. (5.228).

EXERCISES

5.1. A step d.c.olf 20 vd to a series ductor L = 1 henry and capacitor C = 0.05 farad. Obtaal solution citor C is initially uncharged obtain particular solion for current i (t).

[**Ans.** $i(t) = K_1 e^{-5t} - K_2 e^{-4t}$; $i(t) = -20e^{-5t} + 20^{-4t}$]

5.2. A d.c. voltage of 10 volts is suddenly applied to a series circuit consisting of resistor $R = 10\ \Omega$, inductor L = 1 henry and capacitor C = 0.04 farad. The capacitor is initially uncharged. Obtain the particular solution for current i (t) in the circuit. [**Ans.** $i(t) = 10te^{-5t}$]

5.3. In the series RLC network of Fig. 5.1, V_0 = 5 volts. L = 1 Henry, $R = 4\ \Omega$ and C = 0.2 farad. Switch K is closed at time t = 0. It is required to obtain the particular solution for i (t). [**Ans.** $i(t) = 5e^{-t} \sin t$]

5.4. Show that $i = Ke^{-3t}$ and $i = Ke^{-t}$ are solutions of the differential equation

$$\frac{d^2i}{dt^2} + 4\frac{di}{dt} + 3i = 0.$$

5.5. Show that $i = Ke^{-2t}$ and $i = Kte^{-2t}$ are solutions of the differential equation

$$\frac{d^2i}{dt^2} + 4\frac{di}{dt} + 4i = 0.$$

5.6. Find the general solution for each of the following equations :

(*i*) $\frac{d^2i}{dt^2} + 6\frac{di}{dt} + 8i = 0$ (*ii*) $\frac{d^2i}{dt^2} + 7\frac{di}{dt} + 10i = 0$

(*iii*) $\frac{d^2i}{dt^2} + 4\frac{di}{dt} + 3i = 0$ (*iv*) $\frac{d^2i}{dt^2} + 6\frac{di}{dt} + 9i = 0$

(*v*) $\frac{d^2i}{dt^2} + 12\frac{di}{dt} + 36i = 0$ (*vi*) $\frac{d^2i}{dt^2} + 2\frac{di}{dt} + 3i = 0$.

[**Ans.** (*i*) $i(t) = K_1 e^{-4t} + K_2 e^{-2t}$
(*ii*) $i(t) = K_1 e^{-5t} + K_2 e^{-2t}$
(*iii*) $i(t) = K_1 e^{-3t} + K_2 e^{-t}$
(*iv*) $i(t) = K_1 e^{-3t} + K_2 te^{-3t}$
(*v*) $i(t) = K_1 e^{-6t} + K_2 te^{-6t}$
(*vi*) $i(t) = K_1 e^{(-1+j\sqrt{2})t} + K_3 e^{(-1-j\sqrt{2})t}$]

5.7. Find the particular solution of the equations of Problem 6 subject to the following initial conditions :

$$i(0+) = 0 \text{ and } \frac{di}{dt}(0+) = 10.$$

[**Ans.** (*i*) $i(t) = -5e^{-4t} + 5e^{-2t}$
(*ii*) $i(t) = -\frac{10}{3}e^{-5t} + \frac{10}{3}e^{-2t}$
(*iii*) $i(t) = -5e^{-3t} + 5e^{-t}$
(*iv*) $i(t) = 10te^{-3t}$
(*v*) $i(t) = 10te^{-6t}$
(*vi*) $i(t) = 5\sqrt{2}e^{-t}\sin\sqrt{2}t$]

5.8. Find the particular solution for each of the following equation subject to the initial conditions that $i(0+) = 2$ and $\frac{di}{dt}(0+) = 0$.

(*i*) $\frac{d^2i}{dt^2} + 6\frac{di}{dt} + 5i = 0$ (*ii*) $\frac{d^2i}{dt^2} + 10\frac{di}{dt} + 25i = 0$ (*iii*) $\frac{d^2i}{dt^2} + 4\frac{di}{dt} + 5i = 0$

[**Ans.** (*i*) $i(t) = -\frac{1}{2}e^{-5t} + \frac{5}{2}e^{-t}$, (*ii*) $i(t) = 2e^{-5t} + 10te^{-5t}$
(*iii*) $i(t) = e^{-2t}[2\cos t + 4\sin t]$

5.9. A current source of 4 amperes is suddenly connected to a parallel *R-L-C* circuit at time $t = 0$. Obtain the particular solution for voltage $v(t)$ across the element. Given that $R = 0.2\ \Omega$, $L = \frac{1}{6}$ henry and $C = 1$ farad. Assume that there is no initial charge across the capacitor *C*.

[**Ans.** $v(t) = 4e^{-2t} - 4e^{-3t}$]

5.10. A current source of 5 amperes is suddenly connected to a parallel *R-L-C* circuit at time $t = 0$. Obtain the particular solution for voltage $v(t)$, across the circuit elements. Given that $R = \frac{1}{3}$ ohm, $L = \frac{1}{2}$ henry and $C = 1$ farad. Assume that there is no initial charge across the capacitor *C*. [**Ans.** $v(t) = 5e^{-t} - 5e^{-3t}$]

5.11. In thc circuit of Fig. 5.5, $C = 1$, farad, $R = \frac{1}{4}$ ohm, $L = \frac{1}{4}$ henry and $I_0 = 10$ amp. Switch *K* is opened at time $t = 0$. Obtain the particular solution for $v(t)$. Assume zero initial charge across the capacitor *C*. [**Ans.** $v(t) = 10t\,e^{-2t}$]

5.12. A current source of 8 amperes is suddenly connected to a parallel *R-L-C* circuit a time $t = 0$. Obtain the particular solution for voltage $v(t)$ across the circuit element. Given that $R = 1/8$ ohm, $L = 1/16$ henry and $C = 1$ farad. Assume that there is no initial charge across capacitor *C* and no initial current in inductor *L* before switching.

[**Ans.** $v(t) = 8t\,e^{-4t}$]

5.13. In the circuit of Fig. 5.5, $C = 1\ \mu F$, $R = 0.5\ \Omega$, $L = 0.2$ henry and $I_0 = 4$ amp. Switch *K* is opened at time $t = 0$. Obtain the particular solution for voltage $v(t)$ across the elements. Assume zero initial charge across the capacitor *C* and zero initial current in inductor *L* before switching.

[**Ans.** $v(t) = 2\,e^{-t}\sin 2t$]

5.14. A d.c. current source of 8 amp. is suddenly connected to a parallel *R-L-C* network at time $t = 0$. Obtain the particular solution for voltage $v(t)$ across the circuit elements. Given that $R = 1/8\ \Omega$, $L = 0.1$ henry,
a n d
$C = 2$ farads. Assume zero initial charge across capacitor *C* and zero initial current through inductor *L*.
[**Ans.** $v(t) = 4\,e^{-2t}\sin t$]

5.15. Solve the differential equations :

(*i*) $\frac{d^3i}{dt^3} + 3\frac{d^2i}{dt^2} + 4\frac{di}{dt} + 2i = 0$ (*ii*) $2\frac{d^3i}{dt^3} + 7\frac{d^2i}{dt^2} + 7\frac{di}{dt} + 2i = 0$

[**Ans.** (*i*) $i(t) = K_1e^{-t} + K_2e^{-\frac{(3+j\sqrt{3})t}{2}} + K_3e^{\frac{-(3+j\sqrt{3})t}{2}}$

$$(ii)\ i(t) = K_1e^{-t} + K_2e^{-2t} + K_3e^{-\frac{t}{2}}]$$

5.16. Solve the differential equation,

$$2\frac{d^3i}{dt^3} + 11\frac{d^2i}{dt^2} + 18\frac{di}{dt} + 9i = 0$$ subject to the initial condition that $i(0+) = 0$,

$$\frac{di}{dt}(0+) = 2 \text{ and } \frac{d^2i}{dt^2}(0+) = -2 \quad [\textbf{Ans. } i(t) = 6e^{-t} + 2e^{-3t} - 8e^{-\frac{3t}{2}}]$$

5.17. The response of a network is given by $i(t) = K_1 t\, e^{-3t}\ t \geq 0$

Find the instant at which $i(t)$ attains a maximum value. $\left[\textbf{Ans. } t = \frac{1}{3} \text{ second}\right]$

5.18. The response of a network is given by, $i(t) = K_1\, e^{-4t}\ K_2\, e^{-3t}\ t \geq 0$
Proves that $i(t)$ reaches a maximum at a time,

$$t = \ln\frac{4K_1}{3K_2}.$$

5.19. In the given circuit, capacitor C has an initial voltage $v_c\ (0-) = 5$ volts and at the same instant, the current in the inductor L is zero. Switch K is closed at time $t = 0$. Obtain expression for the voltage $v(t)$. [**Ans.** $v(t) = -10^{-2t} + 15\, e^{-3t}$]

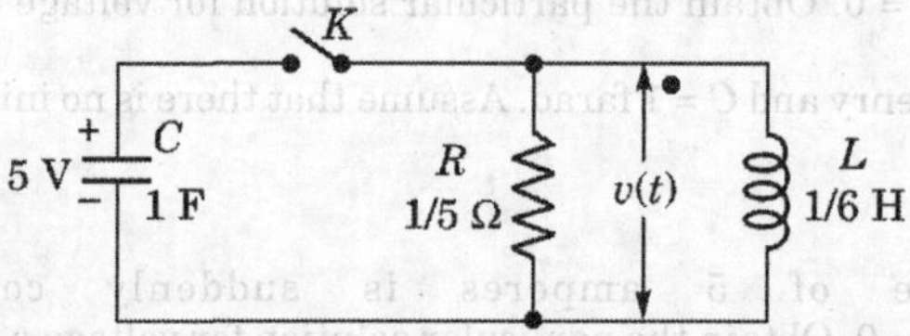

5.20. Solve the following non-homogeneous linear differential equations for $t \geq 0$.

(a) $\frac{d^2i}{dt^2} + 4\frac{di}{dt} + 4i + 2$ (b) $\frac{d^2i}{dt^2} + 4\frac{di}{dt} + 3i = 3t$ (c) $\frac{d^2i}{dt^2} + 4\frac{di}{dt} + 2i = e^{-3t}$

(d) $\frac{d^2i}{dt^2} + 5\frac{di}{dt} + 4i = e^{-t}$ (e) $\frac{d^2v}{dt^2} + 4\frac{dv}{dt} + 3v = e^{-2t} + e^{-t}$ (f) $\frac{d^2v}{dt^2} + 3\frac{dv}{dt} + 2v = te^{-3t}$

(g) $\frac{d^2i}{dt^2} + 5\frac{di}{dt} + 6i = 4 \sin 4t$

[**Ans.** (a) $i(t) = K_1e^{-2t} - K_2te^{-2t} + \frac{1}{2}$

(b) $i(t) = K_1e^{-t} + K_2e^{-3t} + t\frac{4}{3}$

(c) $i(t) = K_1e^{-t} - K_2e^{-2t} + \frac{1}{2}e^{-3t}$

(d) $i(t) = K_1e^{-t} - K_2e^{-2t}\frac{1}{3}te^{-3t}$

(e) $v(t) = K_1e^{-t} + K_2e^{-3t} + \frac{1}{2}te^{-t} - e^{-2t}$

(f) $v(t) = K_1e^{-t} + K_2e^{-3t} + \frac{1}{2}t\, e^{-2t} + \frac{3}{4}e^{-3t}$

(g) $i(t) = K_1e^{-2t} + K_2e^{-3t} - .16 \cos 4t - .08 \sin 4t$]

5.21. An exponential voltage $v(t) = 4e^{-3t}$ is applied at time $t = 0$ to a series R-C circuit consisting of a resistor $R = 0.5\ \Omega$ and inductor $L = 0.25$ henry. Obtain the particular solution for current $i(t)$ through the circuit. Assume zero current through the inductor before the application of voltage $v(t)$. [**Ans.** $i(t) = 16\ (e^{-2t} - e^{-3t})$]

5.22. An exponential voltage $v(t) = 2e^{-4t}$ is applied at time $t = 0$ to a series R-L circuit comprising a reristor or $R = 4\ \Omega$ and inductor $L = 1$ henry. Obtain the particular solution for current $i(t)$ through the circuit. Assume zero current through the inductor before switching. **[Ans.** $i\ (t) = 2te^{-4t}$]

5.23. A sinusoidal voltage $v(t) = 4 \sin\left(10^6 t + \frac{\pi}{4}\right)$ is suddenly applied at time $t = 0$ to a series *R-L* circuit comprising of resistor $R = 1\ \Omega$ and inductor $L = 1$ mH. Obtain the total particular solution for the current $i\ (t)$ through the circuit. Assume zero initial current through the inductor L before switching.

[Ans. $i\ (t) = 0.028\ e^{-1000t} + 0.04 \sin (10^5 t - 44°\ 26')$]

5.24. In the circuit of Fig. 5.8, voltage $v\ (t) = 6 \sin\left(10^4 t + \frac{\pi}{4}\right)$ is connected at time $t = 0$ to the series *R-C* circuit consisting of $R = 10\ \Omega$ and $C = 0.5\ \mu F$. Obtain the particular solution for the current $i\ (t)$ through the circuit. Assume zero initial charge across the capacitor.

[Ans. $i\ (t) = 0.03 \cos (10^{4t} + 41°\ 08') + 0.0198\ e^{-2 \times 10^5 t}$]

5.25. An exponential voltage $v\ (t) = 10e^{-2t}$ is applied at time $t = 0$ to a series *R-C* circuit comprising of resistor $R = 2\ \Omega$ and capacitor $C = 0.1$ farad. Obtain the particular solution for current $i\ (t)$ through the circuit. Assume zero initial charge across the capacitor. **[Ans.** $i\ (t) = 7.5\ e^{-5t} - 3e^{-2t}$]

5.26. An exponential voltage $v\ (t) = 4e^{-5t}$ is applied at time $t = 0$ to a series *R-C* circuit comprising of resistor $R = 0.2\ \Omega$ and capacitor $C = 1$ farad. Obtain particular solution for current $i\ (t)$ through the circuit. Assume that steady state condition has reached in the *R-C* circuit before application of the exponential voltage. **[Ans.** $i\ (t) = 20\ e^{-5t}\ (1 + 20t)$]

6

Network Analysis Using Laplace Transformation

6.1. Introduction

The classical method of network analysis discussed so far becomes quite involved when used for network involving higher order differential equations. Accordingly it is usually preferred to use Laplace transformation for solving such differential equations.

Before Laplace transformation method of solving differential equation came into vogue, Heaviside's Operational Calculus was widely used. However, today Laplace transformation is popularly used. It has the following advantages over the classical method :

(*i*) The solution of the differential equation gets greatly simplified.

(*ii*) The method yields in a single operation the complete solution, *i.e.* both the particular integral and the complementary function.

(*iii*) Initial conditions get automatically specified in the transformed equation whereas in the classical method, these initial conditions have to be separately specified.

(*iv*) Finally the initial conditions get included in the problem in the first step in the analysis rather than in the last step.

The process of using Laplace transformation is similar to the process of using logarithms which is also a type of transformation. Use of logarithms simplifies operations such as multiplication, division, raising quantities to power, finding roots etc. Thus consider the case of multiplication using logarithms. Let us take two numbers, 24.45 and 15.14. We are required to find the product of these numbers using logarithms. We first transform these two numbers by taking their logarithms. These logarithms are then added. The sum of logarithms so obtained has little meaning by itself. Next we perform the *inverse transformation, i.e.* we find the antilogarithm of this sum. This yields the desired product of the given two numbers. The time involved in this manipulation using logarithms is usually less than that needed in direct multiplication. Fig. 6.1 gives the flow sheet of the operation involved in finding the product of the given two numbers using logarithms.

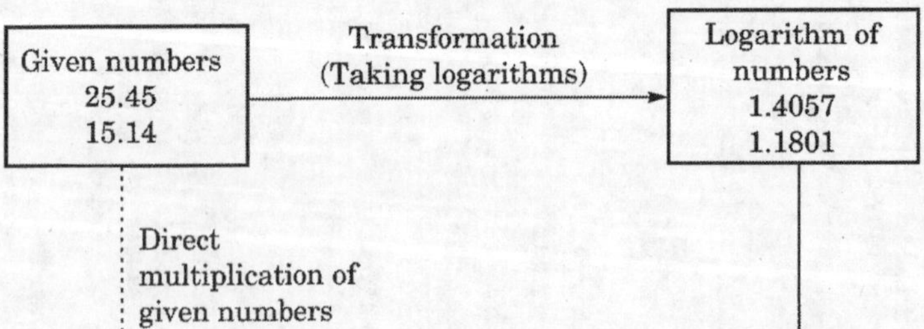

Fig. 6.1. Flow sheet of operations in multiplication using logarithm.

The process of solving differential equation using Laplace transformation is illustrated diagrammatically by the flow sheet of Fig. 6.2 and consists of the following steps :

(*i*) For the given integro-differential operation, find the corresponding *Laplace transform*, making use of the table of Laplace transform. The process of finding the Laplace transform actually involves mathematical manipulation but time may be saved by simply making use of table of Laplace transforms.

(*ii*) Initial conditions are then inserted and the transform is manipulated algebraically. This yields the *revised transform*.

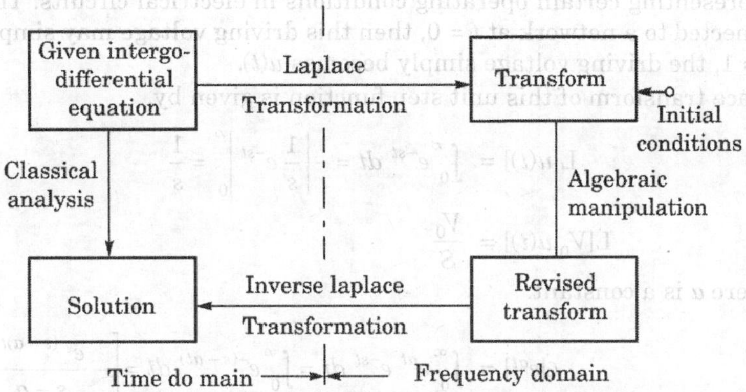

Fig. 6.2. Flow diagram of operation in solving a network using Laplace transformation.

(*iii*) Finally we find the *inverse Laplace transform* of the revised transform again making use of the table of Laplace transforms. This yields the desired complete solution. The time involved in this manipulation using Laplace transformation is usually much less than that needed in solution by classical method.

6.2. The Laplace Transformation

For a given function of time $f(t)$, the Laplace transform equals time integration from zero to infinity of $f(t)e^{-st}$, where s is a complex number equal to $(\sigma + j\omega)$. Laplace transform is generally denoted by the letter $\mathcal{L}$. The Laplace transform of $f(t)$ is generally designated $F(s)$. Thus we have

$$\mathcal{L}[f(t)] = F(s) = \int_0^\infty f(t)\, e^{-st}\, dt \qquad ...(6.1)$$

Thus the letter $\mathcal{L}$ simply signifies "the Laplace transform of". Not all functions $f(t)$ are Laplace transformable. For a function $f(t)$ to be Laplace transformable, it is necessary that

$$\int_0^\infty |f(t)|\, e^{-\sigma_1 t}\, dt < \infty \qquad ...(6.2)$$

for a real positive σ_1.

For physical networks, $f(t)$ is such that this condition is readily satisfied.

Evaluation of $\mathcal{L}[f(t)]$, *i.e.* $F(s)$ for a given function $f(t)$ may be done by usual method. This is usually not very involved. Further, having once obtained the Laplace transform of a function, it is not necessary to obtain it again for a second problem. In fact what we do is to simply prepare a table giving Laplace transform for typical functions $f(t)$. This table may then be used for finding Laplace transforms in the future. Thus

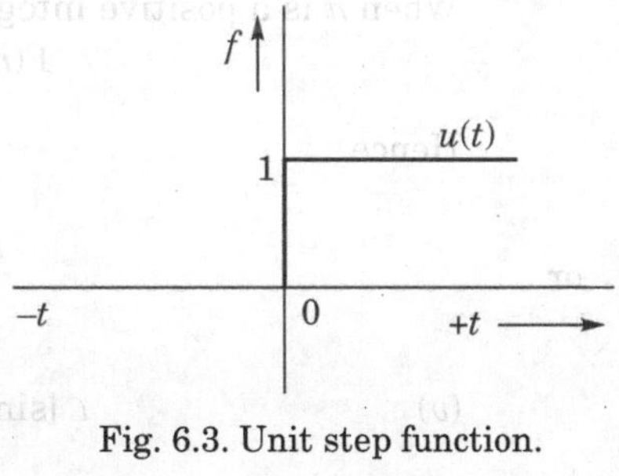

Fig. 6.3. Unit step function.

corresponding to any time function $f(t)$ there exists the corresponding transform $F(s)$. The functions $f(t)$ and $F(s)$ thus constitute a *transform pair*.

We here find the Laplace transform of a few typical time functions.

(*i*) *Unit step function*. Fig. 6.3 shows a unit step function $f = u(t)$.

This unit step function is described by the equation,

$$\left.\begin{aligned} f(t) &= 1, \quad t \geq 0 \\ &= 0, \quad < 0 \end{aligned}\right] \qquad ...(6.3)$$

This unit step function may be denoted by $u(t)$. This notation of unit step function is very convenient in representing certain operating conditions in electrical circuits. Thus if a battery of voltage V_0 is connected to a network at $t = 0$, then this driving voltage may simply be represented by $V_0\, u(t)$. If $V_0 = 1$, the driving voltage simply becomes $u(t)$.

Now Laplace transform of this unit step function is given by,

$$\mathrm{L}[u(t)] = \int_0^\infty e^{-st}\, dt = -\left| \frac{1}{s} e^{-st} \right|_0^\infty = \frac{1}{s} \qquad ...(6.4)$$

Hence,
$$\mathrm{L}[V_0\, u(t)] = \frac{V_0}{S} \qquad ...(6.5)$$

(*ii*) e^{at}; where a is a constant.

$$\mathcal{L}[e^{at}] = \int_0^\infty e^{at}\, e^{-st}\, dt = \int_0^\infty e^{-(s-at)}\, dt = \left[-\frac{e^{-(s-a)t}}{s-a} \right]_0^\infty$$

$$= \frac{1}{s-a},\ \sigma_1 > a \qquad ...(6.6)$$

Thuse e^{st} and $\frac{1}{s-a}$ constitute a transform pair.

(*iii*)
$$t\mathrm{L}[t] = \int_0^\infty t\, e^{-st}\, dt = \frac{1}{s^2}\int_0^\infty (st)\, e^{-st}\, d(st) = \frac{1}{s^2}\int_0^\infty x\, e^{-x}\, dx$$

where $x = st$

$$= \frac{1}{s^2} \qquad ...(6.7)$$

(*iv*)
$$t^n\mathrm{L}[t^n] = \int_0^\infty t^n\, e^{-st}\, dt = \frac{1}{s^{n+1}}\int_0^\infty (st)^n\, e^{-st}\, d(st)$$

$$= \frac{1}{s^{n+1}}\int_0^\infty x^n\, e^{-x}\, dx \text{, where } x = st$$

$$= \frac{\Gamma(n+1)}{s^{n+1}} \qquad ...(6.8)$$

When n is a positive integer,

$$\Gamma(n+1) = n\,!$$

Hence
$$\mathcal{L}[t^n] = \frac{n\,!}{s^{n+1}} \qquad ...(6.9)$$

or
$$\frac{\mathcal{L}\,[t^n]}{n\,!} = \frac{1}{s^{n+1}} \qquad ...(6.10)$$

(*v*)
$$\mathcal{L}\,[\sinh at] = \mathcal{L}\left[\frac{e^{at} - e^{-at}}{2}\right] = \frac{1}{2}\left[\frac{1}{s-a} - \frac{1}{s+a}\right] \qquad ...(6.11)$$

$$= \frac{a}{s^2 - a^2} \qquad \text{...(6.12)}$$

(vi) $$\mathcal{L}\,[\cosh at] = \mathcal{L}\left[\frac{e^{at} - e^{-at}}{2}\right] \qquad \text{...(6.13)}$$

$$= \frac{1}{2}\left[\frac{1}{s-a} + \frac{1}{s+a}\right] = \frac{a}{s^2 - a^2}$$

(vii) $$\sin at \text{L}\,[\sinh jat] = \frac{ja}{s^2 + a^2}$$

But $$\sinh jat = j \sin at$$

Hence, $$\text{L}\,[\sin at] = \frac{a}{s^2 + a^2} \qquad \text{...(6.14)}$$

(viii) $$\cos at \text{L}\,[\cosh jat] = \frac{s}{s^2 + a^2}$$

But $$\cosh jat = \cos at$$

Hence $$\text{L}\,[\cos at] = \frac{s}{s^2 + a^2} \qquad \text{...(6.15)}$$

6.3. Inverse Laplace Transformation

This consists in finding the time function *f(t)* from the function *F(s)*. The inverse Laplace transformation is given by the *complex inversion integral.*

$$f(t) = \frac{1}{2\pi j}\int_{\sigma_1 - j\infty}^{\sigma_1 + j\infty} F(s)e^{st}\, ds \qquad \text{...(6.16)}$$

where σ is the real part of *s*.

This is a contour integral in which the path of integration, called the Bromwich path, is along the vertical line $s = \sigma_1$ from $-j\infty$ to $+j\infty$ as shown in Fig. 6.4.

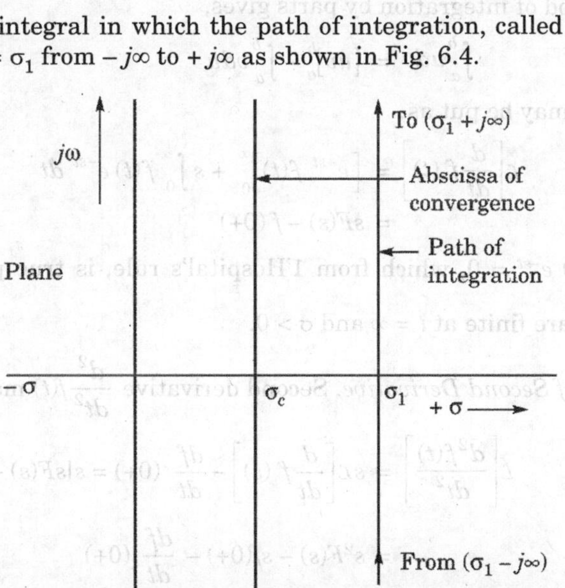

Fig. 6.4. Path of integration in the inverse Laplace transformation.

For proper evaluation of the inversion integral, it becomes necessary that σ_1 be greater than certain minimum σ_o, called the *abscissa of convergence*. With reference to Laplace transform of Eq. (6.6) this quantity abscissa of convergence is the same as quantity a.

However it becomes unnecessary to use, inversion integral in most cases because of the uniqueness of the Laplace transformation, *i.e.* there cannot be more than one different functions having the same Laplace transformation $F(s)$. Thus all that is necessary is to pick up from the table of Laplace transforms the function $f(t)$ corresponding to the given function $F(s)$.

Symbol $\mathcal{L}^{-1}$ is generally used to denote the inverse Laplace transformation. Thus we may write,

$$\mathcal{L}^{-1}[\mathcal{L}\{f(t)\}] = \mathcal{L}^{-1}[F(s)] = f(t) \quad ...(6.17)$$

6.4. Important Theorems Regarding Laplace Transformation

(*i*) *Laplace Transform of Linear Combinations.* Let $f_1(t)$ and $f_2(t)$ be two functions of time and let a and b be two constants.

Then $\mathcal{L}[af_1(t) + bf_2(t)]$

$$= \int_0^\infty [af_1(t) + bf_2(t)]e^{-st}\,dt = a\int_0^\infty f_1(t)e^{-st}\,dt + b\int_0^\infty f_2(t)e^{-st}\,dt$$

$$= aF_1(s) + bF_2(s) \quad ...(6.18)$$

(*ii*) *Transform of First Derivative.* Let the given derivative be $\dfrac{d}{dt}f(t)$.

Then $$\mathcal{L}\left[\frac{d}{dt}f(t)\right] = \int_0^\infty \frac{d}{dt}f(t)e^{-st}\,dt \quad ...(6.19)$$

Let $$u = e^{-st} \text{ and } dv = df(t) \quad ...(6.20)$$

Then $$du = -se^{-st}\,dt \quad ...(6.21)$$

and $$v = f(t) \quad ...(6.22)$$

Hence the method of integration by parts gives,

$$\int_a^b u\,dv = [uv]_a^b - \int_a^b v\,du \quad ...(6.23)$$

Then Eq. (6.19) may be put as,

$$\mathcal{L}\left[\frac{d}{dt}f(t)\right] = \left[e^{-st}f(t)\right]_0^\infty + s\int_0^\infty f(t)\,e^{-st}\,dt$$

$$= sF(s) - f(0+) \quad ...(6.24)$$

provided that $\lim\limits_{t\to\infty} f(t)\,e^{-st} = 0$, which from 1'Hospital's rule, is true provided that $f(t)$ and its successive derivatives are finite at $t = \infty$ and $\sigma > 0$.

(*iii*) *Transform of Second Derivative.* Second derivative $\dfrac{d^2}{dt^2}f(t)$ may be put as $\dfrac{d}{dt}\left[\dfrac{d}{dt}f(t)\right]$.

Then $$\mathcal{L}\left[\frac{d^2f(t)}{dt^2}\right] = s\mathcal{L}\left[\frac{d}{dt}f(s)\right] - \frac{df}{dt}(0+) = s[sF(s) - f(0+)] - \frac{df}{dt}(0+)$$

$$= s^2F(s) - sf(0+) - \frac{df}{dt}(0+) \quad ...(6.25)$$

Continuing in this fashion, the Laplace transform for the nth derivative is,

$$\mathcal{L}\frac{d^n f(t)}{dt^n} = s^n F(s) - s^{n-1} f(0+) - s^{n-2}\frac{df}{dt}(0+) - \ldots\ldots - \frac{d^{n-1}f}{dt^{n-1}}(0+) \qquad \ldots(6.26)$$

(iv) Laplace Transform of an integral. Let the given integral be $\int_0^t f(t)d(t)$.

Then $$\mathcal{L}\left[\int_0^t f(t)dt\right] = \int_0^\infty \left[\int_0^t f(t)dt\right] e^{-st}\, dt \qquad \ldots(6.27)$$

The integration may be done by parts.

Thus let $$u = \int_0^t f(t)dt$$

and $$dv = e^{-st}\, dt \qquad \ldots(6.28)$$

Hence $$du = f(t)dt$$

and $$v = -\frac{1}{s} e^{-st}\, dt \qquad \ldots(6.29)$$

On integrating by parts, we get

$$\mathcal{L}\left[\int_0^t f(t)dt\right] = \left[-\frac{e^{-st}}{s}\int_0^t f(t)dt\right]_0^\infty + \frac{1}{s}\int_0^\infty f(t)\, e^{-st}\, dt \qquad \ldots(6.30)$$

For $t = \infty$, quantity e^{-st} becomes zero and for $t = 0$, $\int_0^\infty f(t)\, e^{-st}\, dt$ becomes zero. Hence the first term on the right hand side of Eq. (6.30) vanishes.

Hence, we get $$\mathcal{L} = \left[\int_0^t f(t)dt\right] = \frac{F(s)}{s} \qquad \ldots(6.31)$$

Alternatively,

Let $$\phi(t) = \int_0^t f(t)\, dt \qquad \ldots(6.32)$$

Then $$\phi'(t) = \frac{d\phi}{dt} = f(t)$$

and $$\phi(0) = 0.$$

Then from Eq. (6.24).

$$\mathcal{L}\{f(t)\} = \mathcal{L}\{\phi'(t)\} = s\mathcal{L}\,[\phi(t)]$$

for $$\mathcal{L}\left[\int_0^t f(t)dt\right] = \frac{1}{s}\,[\mathcal{L}f(t)] = \frac{F(s)}{s} \qquad \ldots(6.33)$$

From Eq. (6.31), we see that the division of the transform of a function by s corresponds to integration of that function from 0 to t.

(v) Replacement of parameter s by $(s - b)$. If we replace s by $(s - b)$ in the transform $F(s)$, where b is some constant, then

$$F(s-b) = \int_0^\infty e^{-(s-b)t} f(t)\, dt \qquad \ldots(6.34)$$

$$= \int_0^\infty e^{-st}\,[e^{bt} f(t)]\, dt \qquad \ldots(6.35)$$

$$= \mathcal{L}\,[e^{bt} f(t)] \qquad \ldots(6.36)$$

Thus replacement of the parameter s by $(s - b)$ in a transform corresponds to the multiplication of the original function $f(t)$ by e^{bt}.

Eq. (6.36) is referred to as the exponential shift. This immediately yields the following new Laplace Transforms :

From Eq. (6.10),

$$\mathcal{L}\,(e^{bt}\,t^n] = \frac{\Gamma(n+1)}{(s-b)^{n+1}} \qquad ...(6.37)$$

When $n = 1$,

$$\mathcal{L}\,[e^{at}\,t] = \frac{1}{(s-b)^2} \qquad ...(6.37\ a)$$

From Eq. (6.14),

$$\mathcal{L}\,[e^{bt}\sin at] = \frac{a}{(s-b)^2 + a^2} \qquad ...(6.38)$$

From Eq. (6.15),

$$\mathcal{L}\,[e^{bt}\cos at] = \frac{s-b}{(s-b)^2 + a^2} \qquad ...(6.39)$$

From Eq. (6.12),

$$\mathcal{L}\,[e^{bt}\sinh at] = \frac{a}{(s-b)^2 - a^2} \qquad ...(6.40)$$

From Eq. (6.13),

$$\mathcal{L}\,[e^{bt}\cosh at] = \frac{s-b}{(s-b)^2 - a^2} \qquad ...(6.41)$$

(*vi*) *Inverse Laplace of derivative of* $F(s)$. On differentiating Eq. (6.1) with respect to s, we get

$$\frac{dF(s)}{ds} = F'(s) = \int_0^\infty \frac{d}{ds}\,[e^{-st}\,f(t)dt \qquad ...(6.42)$$

$$= \int_0^\infty e^{-st}[-t\,f\,(t)]dt = \mathcal{L}\,[-t\,f\,(t)] \qquad ...(6.43)$$

Similarly

$$F''s = \frac{d}{ds^2}\,F(s) = \mathcal{L}[t^2\,f(t)] \qquad ...(6.44)$$

In general,

$$F^{(n)}\,(s) = \frac{d}{ds^n}\,F(s) = \mathcal{L}(-t)^n\,f(t)] \qquad ...(6.45)$$

Eq. (6.45) immediately yields the following new Laplace transforms :

From Eq. (6.14),

$$\mathcal{L}\,[t\sin at] = -\frac{d}{ds}\left[\frac{a}{s^2+a^2}\right] = \frac{2as}{(s^2+a^2)^2} \qquad ...(6.46)$$

From Eq. (6.15),

$$\mathcal{L}\,[t\cos at] = -\frac{d}{ds}\left[\frac{s}{s^2+a^2}\right] = \frac{s^2-a^2}{(s^2+a^2)^2} \qquad ...(6.47)$$

From Eq. (6.12),

$$\mathcal{L}\,[t\sinh at] = -\frac{d}{ds}\left[\frac{a}{s^2-a^2}\right] = \frac{2as}{(s^2-a^2)^2} \qquad ...(6.48)$$

From Eq. (6.13),

$$\mathcal{L}\,[t\cosh at] = -\frac{d}{ds}\left[\frac{s}{s^2-a^2}\right] = \frac{s^2+a^2}{(s^2-a^2)^2}$$

6.5. Application of Laplace Transformation in Analysing Simple Networks

Here we take up the analysis of a few simple networks making use of Laplace transformation and the theorems regarding Laplace transformation.

(*A*) **Step Response of Series R-L Circuit.** Consider the series *R-L* circuit of Fig. 6.5. Let the switch *K* be closed at time $t = 0$.

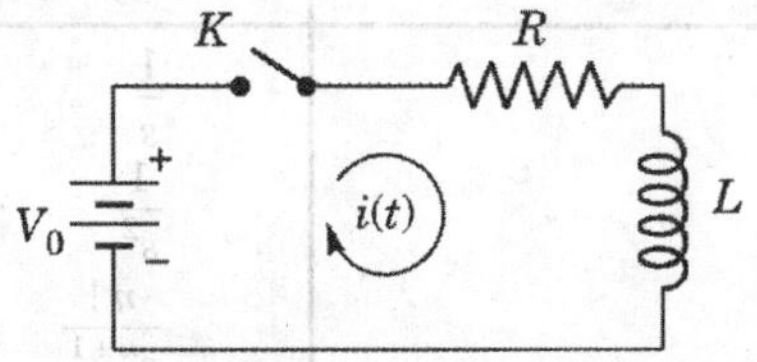

Fig. 6.5. Series *R-L* circuit.

Application of Kirchhoff's voltage law to the circuit yields the following differential equation:

$$L\frac{di}{dt} + Ri = V_0\, u(t) \quad ...(6.49)$$

The corresponding Laplace transform equation is,

$$L\,[SI(s) - i(0+)] + RI\,(s) = \frac{V_0}{s} \quad ...(6.50)$$

We now insert the initial condition.

Because of the presence of inductance L, $(0\ +) = 0$. Inserting this initial condition in Eq. (6.50), we get

$$Is\,[R + Ls] = \frac{V_0}{s}$$

Hence
$$I(s) = \frac{V_0}{L}\cdot\frac{1}{s\left(s+\dfrac{R}{L}\right)} \quad ...(6.51)$$

Now inverse Laplace transform of $\dfrac{1}{s(s-a)}$ from the Table of Laplace transforms is, $-\dfrac{1}{a}[1 - e^{at}]$. In this case $a = -\dfrac{R}{L}$. Hence Eq. (6.51) yields.

$$i(t) = \frac{V_0}{L}\left(-\frac{1}{-R/L}\right)\left[1 - e^{-\frac{Rt}{L}}\right] = \frac{V_0}{L}\left[1 - e^{-\frac{Rt}{L}}\right] \quad ...(6.52)$$

This is the same solution as given by Eq. (3.32) obtained by classical method. It may be noted that Eq. (6.52) gives the complete solution directly. Here $\dfrac{V_0}{R}$ is the steady state response, *i.e.* the particular integral while $-\dfrac{V_0}{R}e^{-\frac{Rt}{L}}$ is the transient response, *i.e.* the complementary function.

Alternatively. With reference to Eq. (6.51) instead of using the Laplace transform table to find the inverse Laplace transform for the function $\dfrac{1}{s(s + R/L)}$, we may break the quantity $\dfrac{V_0}{s(s + R/L)}$ into several parts. Thus let,

$$\frac{V_0/L}{s\left(s+\dfrac{R}{L}\right)} = \frac{K_1}{s} + \frac{K_2}{\left(s+\dfrac{R}{L}\right)} \quad ...(6.53)$$

where K_1 and K_2 are unknown coefficients. Eq. (6.53) may be put as,

Table 6.1. Table of Laplace Transforms

$f(t)$	$F(s)$
$1, u(t)$	$\frac{1}{s}$
t	$\frac{1}{s^2}$
t^n (n is integer)	$\frac{n!}{s^{n+1}}$
e^{at}	$\frac{1}{s-a}$
te^{at}	$\frac{1}{(s-a)^2}$
$t^n e^{at}$	$\frac{n!}{s-a)^{n+1}}$
$\frac{e^{bt}-e^{at}}{(a-b)}$	$\frac{1}{(s-a)(s-b)}$
$\frac{e^{-at}}{(b-a)(c-a)}+\frac{e^{-bt}}{(a-b)(c-b)}\frac{e}{(a-c)(b-c)}$	$\frac{1}{(s+a)(s+b)(s+c)}$
$1-e^{at}$	$\frac{1}{s}-\frac{1}{s-a}=\frac{-a}{s(s-a)}$
$\sin at$	$\frac{a}{s^2+a^2}$
$\cos at$	$\frac{s}{s^2+a^2}$
$\sinh at$	$\frac{a}{s^2-a^2}$
$\cosh at$	$\frac{s}{s^2-a^2}$
$e^{-at}\sin \omega t$	$\frac{\omega}{(s+a)^2+\omega^2}$
$e^{-at}\cos \omega t$	$\frac{s+a}{(s+a)^2+\omega^2}$
$\sin(\omega t+\theta)$	$\frac{s\sin\theta+\omega\cos\theta}{s^2+\omega^2}$
$\cos(\omega t+\theta)$	$\frac{s\cos\theta-\omega\sin\theta}{s^2+\omega^2}$
$1-\cos at$	$\frac{1}{s}-\frac{s}{s^2+a^2}=\frac{a^3}{s(s^2+a^2)}$
$t\sin at$	$\frac{2as}{(s^2+a^2)^2}$
$t\cos at$	$\frac{s^2-a^2}{(s^2+a^2)^2}$
$t\sinh at$	$\frac{2as}{(s^2-a^2)^2}$
$t\cosh at$	$\frac{s^2+a^2}{(s^2-a^2)^2}$

$$\frac{V_0/L}{s\left(s+\dfrac{R}{L}\right)} = \frac{K_1\left(s+\dfrac{R}{L}\right)+K_2 s}{s(s+R/L)} \qquad \text{...(6.54)}$$

Hence $$\frac{V_0}{L} = K_1\left(s+\frac{R}{L}\right)+K_2 s \qquad \text{...(6.55)}$$

Equating coefficients of like functions, we get the following algebraic equations,

$$\left.\begin{aligned} K_1\frac{R}{L} &= \frac{V_0}{L} \\ K_1+K_2 &= 0 \end{aligned}\right\} \qquad \text{...(6.56)}$$

and

Equations (6.56) yield,

$$K_1 = \frac{V_0}{R} \text{ and } K_2 = -\frac{V_0}{R} \qquad \text{...(6.57)}$$

Substituting these values of K_1 and K_2 into Eq. (6.53), we get

$$\frac{V_0/L}{s(s+R/L)} = \frac{V_0}{R}\cdot\frac{1}{s}-\frac{V_0}{R}\cdot\frac{1}{s+R/L} \qquad \text{...(6.58)}$$

Hence $$I(s) = \frac{V_0}{R}\left[\frac{1}{s}-\frac{1}{s+R/L}\right] \qquad \text{...(6.59)}$$

Taking the inverse Laplace transformation, we get

$$i(t) = \frac{V_0}{R}\left[\mathcal{L}^{-1}\left(\frac{1}{s}\right)-\mathcal{L}^{-1}\left\{\frac{1}{s+\dfrac{R}{L}}\right\}\right] \qquad \text{...(6.60)}$$

$$= \frac{V_0}{R}\left[1-e^{-\frac{Rt}{L}}\right] \qquad \text{...(6.61)}$$

Eq. (6.61) gives the complete particular solution

(*B*) **Step Response of Series *R-C* Circuit.** Consider next the series *R-C* circuit of Fig. 6.6. Let the switch be closed at time $t = 0$. Application of Kirchhoff's voltage law to the circuit yields the following integro-differential equation :

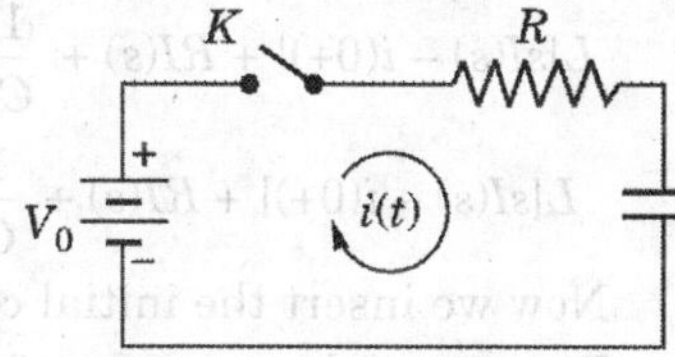

Fig. 6.6. Series *R-C* circuit.

$$\frac{1}{C}\int_{-\infty}^{t} idt + Ri = V_0 u(t) \qquad \text{...(6.62)}$$

This may be put as,

$$\frac{1}{C}\int_{0}^{t} idt + \frac{1}{C}\int_{-\infty}^{t} idt + Ri = V_0 \cdot u(t) \qquad \text{...(6.63)}$$

The corresponding Laplace transform equation becomes

$$\frac{1}{C}\left[\frac{I(s)}{s}\right]+\frac{1}{C}\,\mathcal{L}\,[q(0+)] + RI(s) = V_0\frac{1}{s}$$

or $$\frac{1}{C}\left[\frac{I(s)}{s}+\frac{q(0+)}{s}\right] + RI(s) = \frac{V_0}{s} \qquad \text{...(6.64)}$$

Now $q(0+)$ is the charge on the capacitor C at time $t = 0+$. If the capacitor in initially uncharged, then $q(0+) = 0$. Hence Eq. (6.64) reduces to the following form :

$$I(s)\left[\frac{1}{Cs}+R\right] = \frac{V_0}{s} \quad \text{...(6.65)}$$

Hence $$I(s) = \frac{V_0/R}{s+\dfrac{1}{RC}} \quad \text{...(6.66)}$$

Eq. (6.66) gives, what may be called, the revised transform. On taking the inverse Laplace transform Eq. (6.66) may be put as,

$$\mathcal{L}^{-1}[I(s)] = \mathcal{L}^{-1}\left[\frac{V_0/R}{s+\dfrac{1}{RC}}\right] \quad \text{...(6.67)}$$

or $$i(t) = \frac{V_0}{R}e^{-\frac{t}{RC}} \quad \text{...(6.68)}$$

Eq. (6.68) is the complete particular solution.

(*C*) **Step Response of Series R-L-C circuit.** In the series *R-L-C* circuit of Fig. 6.7, let the switch *K* be closed at time $t = 0$, applying a d.c. voltage V_0 to the circuit. Application of Kirchhoff's voltage law to the circuit then yields the following integro-differential equation.

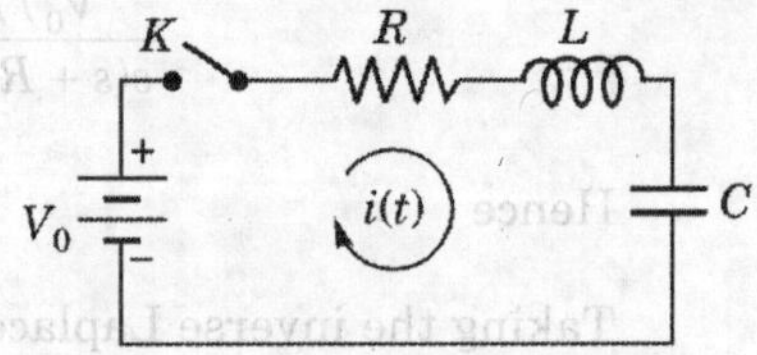

Fig. 6.7. Series *R-L-C* circuit.

$$L\frac{di}{dt}+Ri+\frac{1}{C}\int_{-\infty}^{t} idt = V_0 \,.\, u(t) \quad \text{...(6.69)}$$

This may be put as

$$L\frac{di}{dt}+Ri+\frac{1}{C}\int_{-\infty}^{t} idt+\frac{1}{C}\int_{0}^{t} idt = V_0 \,.\, u(t) \quad \text{...(6.70)}$$

The corresponding Laplace transform equation becomes,

$$L[sI(s)-i(0+)]+RI(s)+\frac{1}{C}\mathcal{L}q(0+)+\frac{1}{C}.\frac{I(s)}{s} = \frac{V_0}{s} \quad \text{...(6.71)}$$

or $$L[sI(s)-i(0+)]+RI(s)+\frac{1}{C}.\frac{q(0+)}{s}+\frac{1}{C}\frac{I(s)}{s} = \frac{V_0}{s} \quad \text{...(6.72)}$$

Now we insert the initial conditions.

Because of the presence of inductor L, $i(0+) = 0$. Further $q(0+)$ is the charge on the capacitor C at $t = 0+$. If the capacitor is initially uncharged, then $q = (0+) = 0$. Substituting these two initially conditions in Eq. (6.72), we get

$$Ls \,.\, I(s)+R \,.\, I(s)+\frac{I(s)}{Cs} = \frac{V_0}{s} \quad \text{...(6.73)}$$

or $$I(s)\left[Ls+R+\frac{1}{Cs}\right] = V_0\frac{1}{s} \quad \text{...(6.74)}$$

Hence $$I(s) = \frac{V_0}{\left[Ls^2+Rs+\dfrac{1}{C}\right]} \quad \text{...(6.75)}$$

$$= \frac{V_0}{L(s-s_1)(s-s_2)} \quad \text{...(6.76)}$$

where s_1, s_2 are the roots of the equation,

$$Ls^2 + Rs + \frac{1}{C} = 0 \qquad ...(6.77)$$

Thus

$$s_1, s_2 = \frac{-R}{2L} \pm \frac{1}{2L}\sqrt{R^2 - 4\frac{L}{C}} \qquad ...(6.78)$$

On taking the inverse Laplace transform, Eq. (6.76), yields

$$i(t) = \frac{V_0 / L}{(s_1 - s_2)}[e^{s_1 t} - e^{s_2 t}] \qquad ...(6.79)$$

(*D*) **Step Response of Parallel R-L-C Circuit.** In the parallel *R-L-C* circuit of Fig. 6.8, let the switch *K* be opened at time $t = 0$, thus connecting the d.c. current source I_0 to the circuit. Application of Kirchhoff's current law to the circuit yields the following integro-differential equation,

$$C\frac{dv}{dt} + Gv + \frac{1}{L}\int_{-\infty}^{t} vdt = I_0 \,.\, u(t) \qquad ...(6.80)$$

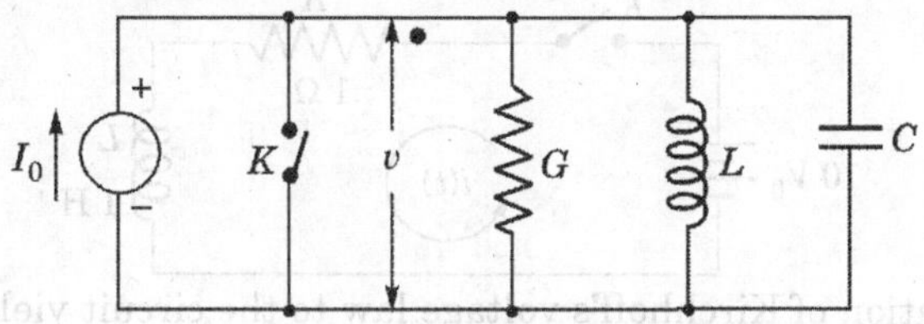

Fig. 6.8. Parallel *R-L-C* Circuit.

This may be put as,

$$C\frac{dv}{dt} + Gv + \frac{1}{L}\int_{-\infty}^{0} vdt + \frac{1}{L}\int_{0}^{t} vdt = I_0 . u(t) \qquad ...(6.81)$$

The corresponding Laplace transform equation is,

$$C[s \,.\, V(s) - v(0+)] + G \,.\, V(s) + \frac{1}{L} \,.\, \psi(0+) + \frac{1}{L}.\frac{V(s)}{s} = \frac{I_0}{s} \qquad ...(6.82)$$

where $\psi(0+)$ is the flux linkage and equals $Li(0+)$.

Now we insert the initial conditions.

Because of the presence of capacitor *C*, $v(0+) = 0$ since the voltage across a capacitor cannot change intantaneously. Also the current in the inductor *L* during the time interval $-\infty$ to 0 is zero. Hence $\psi(0+)$ is zero. Substituting these two initial conditions in Eq. (6.82), we get

$$C \,.\, sV(s) + G \,.\, V(s) + \frac{1}{Ls}V(s) = \frac{1}{s} \,.\, I_0 \qquad ...(6.83)$$

or

$$V(s)\left[Cs + G + \frac{1}{Ls}\right] = \frac{I_0}{s} \qquad ...(6.84)$$

Hence

$$V(s) = \frac{I_0}{\left(Cs^2 + Gs + \frac{1}{L}\right)} \qquad ...(6.85)$$

$$= \frac{I_0}{C\left(s^2 + \frac{G}{C}s + \frac{1}{LC}\right)} \qquad ...(6.86)$$

$$= \frac{I_0}{C(s - s_1)(s - s_2)} \qquad ...(6.87)$$

where s_1, s_2 are the roots of the equation,

$$Cs^2 + Gs + \frac{1}{L} = 0 \quad \text{...(6.88)}$$

Then $$s_1, s_2 = \frac{-G}{2c} \pm \frac{1}{2C}\sqrt{G^2 - 4\frac{C}{L}} \quad \text{...(6.89)}$$

On taking the inverse Lapalace transform Eq. (6.87) yields,

$$v(t) = \frac{I_0 / C}{s_1 - s_2}\left[e^{s_1 t} - e^{s_2 t}\right] \quad \text{...(6.90)}$$

This is the same as Eq. (5.69) obtained through classical analysis.

Example 6.1. *In the given circuit switch K is closed at time t = 0. There is no current through L prior to switching. Obtain the particular solution for i(t)*

(**Note:** *This is the same as exercise 3.3 of chapter 3.*)

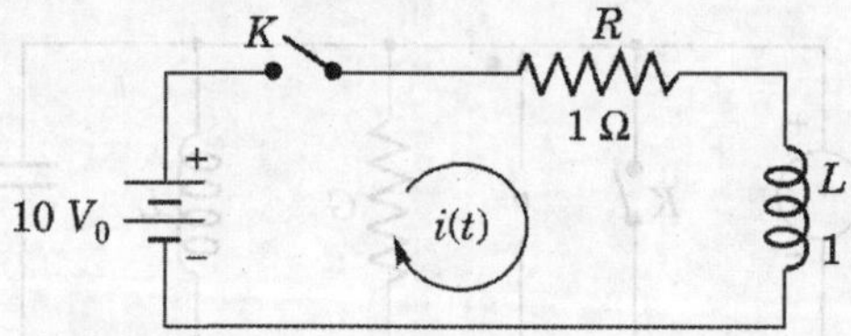

Solution. Application of Kirchhoff's voltage law to the circuit yields,

$$L\frac{di}{dt} + Ri = 10\,u(t) \quad \text{...(1)}$$

$$\frac{di}{dt} + i = 10\,u(t)$$

The corresponding Laplace transform equation is,

$$s\,I(s) - i(0+) + I(s) = 10\frac{1}{s} \quad \text{...(2)}$$

Since the current in the inductor cannot change instantaneously, we have $i(0+) = 0$. Putting this initial condition in Eq. (2), we get

$$I(s)[1 + s] = 10\frac{1}{s} \quad \text{...(3)}$$

or $$I(s) = \frac{10}{s(s+1)} \quad \text{...(4)}$$

On taking inverse Laplace transform Eq. (4) yields,

$$i(t) = 10\left[-\frac{1}{-1}\right][1 - e^{-t}] = 10\,[1 - e^{-t}].$$

Example 6.2. *In the given circuit switch K is moved from position 1 to position 2 at time t = 0, the steady-state current having previously*

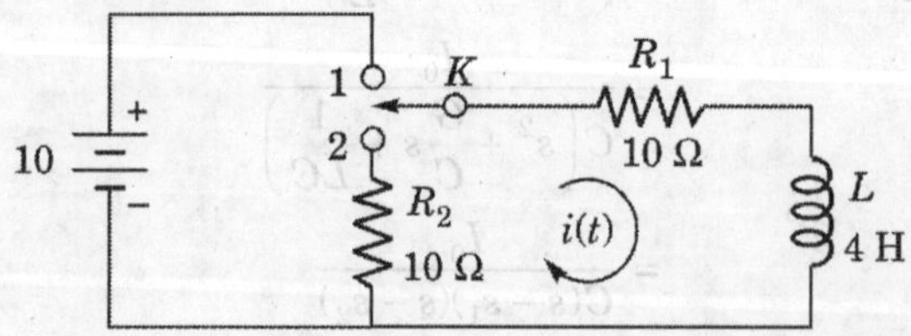

established in the R-L circuit. Find the particular solution for the current i(t) after switching.

Solution. Application of Kirchhoff's voltage law to the circuit with switch K in position 2 yields,

$$L\frac{di}{dt} + R_1 i + R_2 i = 0 \qquad ...(1)$$

or

$$4\frac{di}{dt} + 20\,i = 0 \qquad ...(2)$$

or

$$\frac{di}{dt} + 5\,i = 0$$

The corresponding Laplace transform equation is,

$$s\,I(s) - i(0+) + 5\,I(s) = 0 \qquad ...(3)$$

or

$$I(s)(s+5) = i(0+) \qquad ...(4)$$

Now current at $t = 0-$ is $\frac{10}{R_1} = \frac{10}{10} = 1$ ampere. After switching the current $i(0+)$ must also be 1 ampere because of the presence of inductor L.

Thus Eq. (4) becomes,

$$I(s) = \frac{1}{s+5} \qquad ...(5)$$

On taking inverse Laplace transform, we get

$$i(t) = e^{-5t}.$$

Example 6.3. *In the given circuit, switch K is closed at time t = 0. Obtain particular solution for current i(t) after the switch is closed. Assume that there is no charge the capacitor C before switching.*

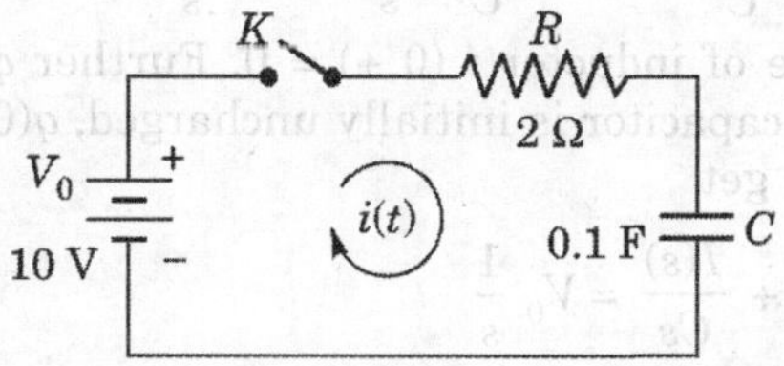

Solution. Application of Kirchhoff's voltage law to the circuit yields the following equation :

$$\frac{1}{C}\int_{-\infty}^{t} i\,dt + Ri = V_0 \,.\, u(t) \qquad ...(1)$$

This may be put as,

$$\frac{1}{C}\int_{-\infty}^{t} i\,dt + \frac{1}{C}\int_{-\infty}^{0} i\,dt + Ri = V_0 \,.\, u(t) \qquad ...(2)$$

The corresponding Laplace transform equation is :

$$\frac{1}{C}\cdot\frac{I(s)}{s} + \frac{1}{C}\,\mathcal{L}\,[q(0+)] + R\,I(s) = V_0\frac{1}{s} \qquad ...(3)$$

Now $q(0+)$ is the charge on the capacitor C at time $i = 0+$. Since the charge at $t = 0-$ is zero, the charge at $t = 0+$ is also zero since the charge across a capacitor cannot change instantaneously. Thus $q(0+) = 0$.

Hence Eq. (3) reduces to the following form :

$$I(s)\left[\frac{1}{Cs}+R\right] = V_0\,\frac{1}{s}$$

or $$I(s) = \frac{V_0/R}{s+\dfrac{1}{RC}} \quad ...(4)$$

Taking the inverse Laplace transform,

$$i(t) = \frac{V_0}{R}\,.\,e^{-\frac{t}{RC}} = \frac{10\text{ V}}{2\,\Omega}e^{-\frac{t}{2\times 0.1}}$$

or $$i(t) = 5\,e^{-5t}$$

Example 6.4. *In the circuit of Fig. 6.7, $V_0 = 10$ volts, $R = 5\,\Omega$. $L = 1$ H and $C = 0.25$ farad. The switch K is closed at time $t = 0$. Obtain the particular solution for cuttent $i(t)$ through the series circuit. Assume that there is zero current through inductor L and zero charge across capacitor C before switching.*

Solution. Application of Kirchhoff's law to the circuit yield the following equation :

$$L\frac{di}{dt}+Ri+\frac{1}{C}\int_{-\infty}^{t} i\,dt = V_0 u(t) \quad ...(1)$$

This may be put as,

$$L\frac{di}{dt}+Ri+\frac{1}{C}\int_{-\infty}^{t} i\,dt+\frac{1}{C}\int_{0}^{t} i\,dt = V_0\,u(t) \quad ...(2)$$

The corresponding Laplace transform equation is,

$$L[sI(s)-i(0+)+R\,I(s)+\frac{1}{C}\,\mathcal{L}\,q(0)+\frac{1}{C}\cdot\frac{I(s)}{s} = V_0\cdot\frac{1}{s} \quad ...(3)$$

Because of the presence of inductor $i\ (0+) = 0$. Further $q(0+)$ is the charge across the capacitor at $t = 0+$. Since the capacitor is initially uncharged, $q(0+) = 0$. substituting these two initial conditions in Eq. (3), we get

$$Ls\,I(s)+R.I(s)+\frac{I(s)}{Cs} = V_0\,\frac{1}{s} \quad ...(4)$$

or $$I(s)\left[Ls+R+\frac{1}{Cs}\right] = V_0\,\frac{1}{s} \quad ...(5)$$

Hence $$I(s) = \frac{V_0}{\left(Ls^2+Rs+\dfrac{1}{C}\right)} \quad ...(6)$$

Substituting the values of L, R, C and V_0, we get

$$I(s) = \frac{10}{s^2+5s+4}$$

$$= \frac{10}{(s+1)\,(s+4)} \quad ...(7)$$

Taking the inverse Laplace transform, we get

$$i(t) = \frac{10}{-1-(-4)}\,[e^{-t} - e^{-4t}] = \frac{10}{3}\,[e^{-t} - e^{-4t}]$$

Example 6.5. *A step d.c. voltage of 8 volts is applied at time t = 0 to a series R-L-C. Circuit consisting of a resistor of 4 ohms, inductor L = 1 Henry and Capacitor C = 0.25 Farad. Obtain the particular solution for the current i(t) through the circuit. Assume zero current through inductor L and zero charge across the capacitor C before switching.*

Solution. Application of Kirchhoff's voltage law to the circuit yields the following equation :

$$L\frac{di}{dt} + Ri + \frac{1}{C}\int_{-\infty}^{t} idt = V_0 u(t) \quad ...(1)$$

This may be put as

$$L\frac{di}{dt} + Ri + \frac{1}{C}\int_{-\infty}^{t} idt + \frac{1}{C}\int_{0}^{t} idt = V_0 u(t) \quad ...(2)$$

The corresponding Laplace transform equation is,

$$L[sI(s) - i(0+)] + RI(s) + \frac{1}{C}\,\mathcal{L}q(0+) + \frac{1}{C}\int_{0}^{t} idt = V_0 u(t) \quad ...(3)$$

Because of the presence of inductor L, $i(0+) = 0$

Because of the presence of capacitor C, $q(0+) = 0$.

Substituting these initial conditions in Eq. 3, we get,

$$LsI(s) + RI(s) + \frac{1}{C}\frac{I(s)}{s} = V_0 \cdot \frac{1}{s} \quad ...(4)$$

or

$$I(s)\left[Ls + R + \frac{1}{Cs}\right] = V_0\,\frac{1}{s} \quad ...(5)$$

Hence

$$I(s) = \frac{V_0}{\boxed{Ls^2 + Rs + \frac{1}{C}}} \quad ...(6)$$

Substituting the values of L, R, C and V_0, we get

$$I(s) = \frac{8}{s^2 + 4s + 4}$$

$$= \frac{8}{(s+2)(s+2)}$$

Taking the inverse Laplace transform, we get

$$i(t) = 8te^{-2t}.$$

Example 6.6. *A step d.c. current of 5 amperes is applied at time t = 0 to a parallel R-L-C circuit consisting of resistor R = $\frac{1}{7}$ ohms, inductor L = 0.1 Henry and capacitor C = 1 Farad. Obtain the particular solution for voltage v(t) across the circuit. Assume zero charge across the capacitor C.*

Solution. The circuit is the same as given in Fig. 6.8. Application of Kirchhoff's current law to the circuit yields the following equation :

$$C\frac{dv}{dt} + Gv + \frac{1}{L}\int_{-\infty}^{t} vdt = I_0\, u(t) \quad ...(1)$$

This may be put as,

$$C\frac{dv}{dt} + Gv + \frac{1}{L}\int_{-\infty}^{t} vdt + \frac{1}{L}\int_{0}^{t} vdt = I_0 u(t) \quad ...(2)$$

This corresponding Laplace transform equation is,

$$C[s.V(s) - v(0+)] + GV(s) + \frac{1}{L}\mathcal{L}\int_{-\infty}^{0} vdt + \frac{1}{L}.\frac{V(s)}{s} = I_0\frac{1}{s} \quad ...(3)$$

Because of the presence of capacitor, $v(0+) = 0$ since the voltage across any capacitor cannot change instantaneously. Also the current in the inductor L during the time interval $-\infty$ to 0 is zero.

Hence $\frac{1}{L}\int_{-\infty}^{0} vdt$ is zero. Substituting there two initial conditions in Eq. (3), we get

$$CsV(s) + G.V(s) + \frac{1}{Ls}V(s) = \frac{1}{s}I_0 \quad ...(4)$$

or

$$V(s) = \frac{I_0}{\left(Cs^3 + Gs + \frac{1}{L}\right)} \quad ...(5)$$

Substituting the values of G, C, L and I_0 in Eq. (5), we get

$$V(s) = \frac{5}{s^2 + 7s + 10} \quad ...(6)$$

$$= \frac{5}{(s+2)(s+5)} \quad ...(7)$$

Taking the inverse Laplace transform, we get

$$v(t) = \frac{5}{-2-(-5)}\,[e^{-2t} - e^{-5t}]$$

$$= \frac{5}{3}\,[e^{-2t} - e^{-5t}].$$

Example 6.7. *A step d.c. current of 6 amperes is applied to a parallel R-L-C circuit consisting of resistor $R = \frac{1}{4}\ \Omega$, inductor $L = \frac{1}{4}$ H and capacitor $C = 1$ Farad. Obtain the complete particular solution for voltage $v(t)$ across the capacitor. Assume zero initial charge across the capacitor and zero initial current through the inductor before application of the current.*

Solution. The circuit is the same as given in Fig. 6.8. Application of Kirchhoff's current law to the circuit yields the following equation :

$$C\frac{dv}{dt} + Gv + \frac{1}{L}\int_{-\infty}^{0} vdt = I_0\,u(t) \quad ...(1)$$

This may be put as,

$$C\frac{dv}{dt} + Gv + \frac{1}{2}\int_{-\infty}^{0} vdt + \frac{1}{L}\int_{0}^{t} vdt = I_0.u(t) \quad ...(2)$$

The corresponding Laplace transform equation is,

$$\mathcal{L}(sV(s) - v(0+)] + G\,V(s) + \frac{1}{L}\mathcal{L}\int_{0}^{t} vdt + \frac{1}{L}\frac{V(s)}{s} = I_0.\frac{1}{s} \quad ...(3)$$

Because of the presence of capacitor C, $v(0+) = 0$, since the voltage across any capacitor cannot change instantaneously. Also the current in the inductor L during the time interval $-\infty$ to 0 is zero.

Hence $\frac{-1}{L}\int_{-\infty}^{0} vdt$ is zero. Substituting these two initial conditions in Eq. (3), we get

$$Cs.V(s) + G\,V(s) + \frac{1}{Ls}.V(s) = I_0\frac{1}{s} \qquad ...(4)$$

or
$$V(s) = \frac{I_0}{Cs^2 + Gs + \dfrac{1}{L}} \qquad ...(5)$$

Substituting the values of C, G, L and I_0 in Eq. (5), we get

$$V(s) = \frac{6}{s^2 + 4s + 4} = \frac{6}{(s+2)(s+2)} \qquad ...(6)$$

Taking the inverse Laplace transform, we get

$$v(t) = 6te^{-2t}$$ **Ans.**

Example 6.8. *Solve Example 5.2 using Laplace transformation.*

Solution. Application of Kirchhoff's voltage law to the series circuit yields,

$$L\frac{di}{dt} + Ri + \frac{1}{C}\int_{-\infty}^{t} idt = V_0\,u(t) \qquad ...(1)$$

This may be put as

$$L\frac{di}{dt} + Ri + \frac{1}{C}\int_{-\infty}^{t} idt + \frac{1}{C}\int_{-\infty}^{t} i(dt) = V_0u(t) \qquad ...(2)$$

The corresponding Lapalce transform equation is,

$$L[sI(s) - i(0+)] + R.I(s) + \frac{1}{C}\,\mathcal{L}\,q(0+) + \frac{1}{C}.\frac{I(s)}{s} = V_0\frac{1}{s} \qquad ...(3)$$

Because of the presence of inductor L, $i(0+) = 0$. Further $q(0+)$ is the charge across the capacitor C at $t = 0+$. Since the capacitor is uncharged before switching, $q(0+) = 0$. Substituting these initial conditions in Eq. (3), we get

$$Ls.I(s) + R.I(s) + \frac{1}{Cs}.I(s) = V_0\frac{1}{s} \qquad ...(4)$$

Hence
$$I(s) = \frac{V_0}{Ls^2 + Rs + \dfrac{1}{C}} \qquad ...(5)$$

Substituting the values of V_0, L, R and C, we get

$$I(s) = \frac{10}{s^3 + 2s + 5} \qquad ...(6)$$

$$= \frac{10}{(s - s_1)(s - s_2)} \qquad ...(7)$$

where $s_1, s_2 = \frac{-2}{2} \pm \frac{1}{2}\sqrt{4 - 5 \times 4}$

$$= -1 \pm j2 \qquad ...(8)$$

Taking inverse Laplace transform, we get

$$i(t) = \frac{10}{(s_1 - s_2)}\,[e^{+s_1t} - e^{s_2t}] \qquad ...(9)$$

$$= \frac{10}{j4}\,[e^{(-1+j2t} - e^{(-1-j2)t}] \qquad ...(10)$$

$$= \frac{10}{j4}\,e^{-t}[e^{j2t} - e^{-j2t}] \qquad ...(11)$$

$$= \frac{5}{j2} e^{-t} [+ 2j \sin 2t] \quad ...(12)$$

$$= 5 e^{-t} \sin 2t.$$

Example 6.9. *In the given circuit switch K is opened at time t = 0. Obtain the complete particular solution for voltabe v(t) across the*

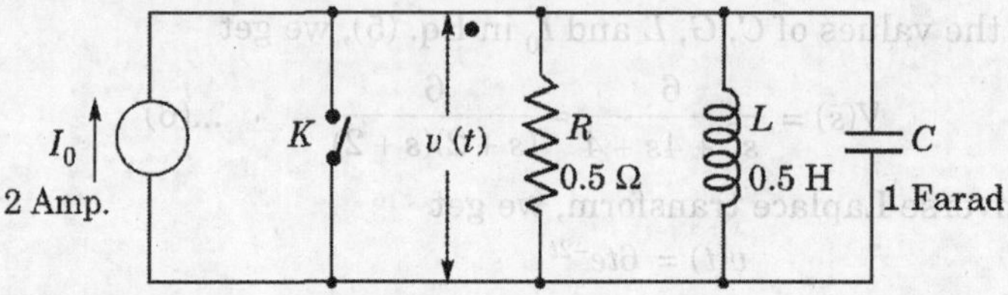

parallel circuit. Assume that there is no charge across the capacitor C and no current in inductor L before switching.

(**Note :** *This is the same problem as Example 5.5.*)

Solution. Application of Kirchhoff's current law to the circuit yields,

$$C\frac{dv}{dt} + Gv + \frac{1}{L}\int_{-\infty}^{t} vdt = I_0 \cdot u(t) \quad ...(1)$$

This may be put as,

$$C\frac{dv}{dt} + Gv + \frac{1}{L}\int_{-\infty}^{0} vdt + \frac{1}{L}\int_{0}^{t} vdt = I_0 \cdot u(t) \quad ...(2)$$

The corresponding Laplace transform equation is

$$C[s.V(s) - v(0+)] + G.V(s) \frac{1}{L} \mathcal{L}\int_{-\infty}^{0} vdt + \frac{1}{L}\cdot\frac{V(s)}{s} = I_0 \cdot \frac{1}{s} \quad ...(3)$$

Because of the presence of capacitor C, $v(0+) = 0$, since the voltage across any capacitor cannot change instantaneously. Also the current in the inductor L at time $t = 0-$ is zero, *i.e.* $\frac{1}{L}\int_{-\infty}^{0} vdt$ is zero. Substituting these two initial conditions in Eq. (3), we get

$$CsV(s) + G.V(s) + \frac{1}{Ls} \cdot V(s) = I_0 \cdot \frac{1}{s} \quad ...(4)$$

or

$$V(s) = \frac{I_0}{Cs^2 + Gs + \frac{1}{L}} \quad ...(5)$$

Substituting the values of G, C, L and I_0 in Eq. (5), we get

$$V(s) = \frac{2}{s^2 + 2s + 2} \quad ...(6)$$

$$= \frac{2}{(s - s_1)(s - s_2)} \quad ...(7)$$

where $s_1, s_2 = \frac{-2}{2} \pm \frac{1}{2}\sqrt{4 - 8} = -1 \pm j$

Taking inverse Laplace transform, we get

$$i(t) = \frac{2}{s_1 - s_2}[e^{s_1 t} - e^{s_2 t}]$$

$$= \frac{2}{2j}\,[e^{(-1+j)t} - e^{(-1-j)t}] = \frac{2}{2j}\,e^{-t}\,[e^{jt} - e^{-jt}]$$

$$= \frac{2\,e^{-t}}{2j}\,.\,2j \sin t = 2\,e^{-t} \sin t.$$

6.6. Use of Partial Function Expansion in Analysis Using Laplace Transformation

In the analysis of a network by Laplace transformation we first write the integro-differential equation for the given network. The resulting differential equation in its general form is as follows :

$$a_0 \cdot \frac{d^n i}{dt^n} + i_1 \cdot \frac{d^{n-1} i}{dt^{n-1}} + \ldots.. + a_{n-1} \cdot \frac{di}{dt} + a_n \cdot i = v(t) \quad \ldots(6.91)$$

The corresponding Laplace transform equation may be put as,

$$I(s) = \frac{\mathcal{L}[v(t) + \text{Initial condition terms}}{a_0 s^n + a_1 . s^{n-1} + \ldots.. + a_{n-1} s + a_n} \quad \ldots(6.92)$$

In general this Laplace transform equation is a quotient of polynomial in s.

Thus we may write,

$$I(s) = \frac{N(s)}{D(s)} \quad \ldots(6.93)$$

where $N(s)$ and $D(s)$ are polynomials in s.

It may be noted that $D(s) = 0$ is nothing but the characteristic equation in classical method.

In general, the transform expression for $I(s)$ namely $\frac{N(s)}{D(s)}$ is required to be split into simpler terms before use of Laplace transform table may be made to obtain the Inverse Laplace transform.

Before the partial fraction expansion is done, it is necessary to ensure that the order of the polynomial $N(s)$ is less than the order of the polynomial $D(s)$. If the order of the polynomial $N(s)$ equals or exceeds that of $D(s)$, then we divide the numerator by the denominator to obtain an expansion of the following form :

$$\frac{N(s)}{D(s)} = A_0 + A_1 . s + A_2 . s^2 + \ldots\ldots + A_{n-d} s^{n-d} + \frac{N_1(s)}{D(s)} \quad \ldots(6.94)$$

where n is the order of the numerator and d is the order of the denominator.

Now the principle of a partial fraction expansion may be applied on the term $\frac{N_1(s)}{D(s)}$.

The first step consists in factorising the denominator polynomial $D(s)$.

Thus
$$D(s) = a_0 s^d + a_1 s^{d-1} + \ldots\ldots + a_{d-1} s + a_d$$
$$= a_0\,(s - s_1)\,(s - s_2)\,\ldots.. + (s - s_d) \quad \ldots(6.95)$$

where $s_1, s_2, \ldots\ldots, s_d$ are the d roots of the equation $D(s) = 0$.

These roots may assume the following three possible forms :

(*i*) real and simple roots

(*ii*) conjugate complex roots

(*iii*) multiple roots.

If the roots are real and simple, then the partial fraction expansion is as follows :

$$\frac{N_1(s)}{(s - s_1)(s - s_2)\ldots(s - s_d)} = \frac{K_1}{s - s_1} + \frac{K_2}{s - s_2} + \ldots.. + \frac{K_d}{s - s_d} \quad \ldots(6.96)$$

where K_1, K_2, etc. are real constants, called *residues*.

If the roots are such that two roots form a complex conjugate pair, then the partial fraction expansion is as follows :

$$\frac{N_1(s)}{D_1(s)(s-\alpha-j\beta)(s-\alpha+j\beta)} = \frac{K_1}{(s-\alpha-j\beta)} + \frac{K_1'}{(s-\alpha+j\beta)} + \ldots \quad \ldots(6.97)$$

where K_1 and K_1' form complex conjugate pair.

Thus when the roots form a conjugate pair, the partial fraction expansion coefficients also form a conjugate pair.

If the roots are repeated r times, then the partial fraction expansion is as follows :

$$\frac{N_1(s)}{(s-s_1)^r} = \frac{K_1}{(s-s_1)} + \frac{K_2}{(s-s_2)} + \ldots\ldots + \frac{K_d}{(s-s_d)^r} \quad \ldots(6.98)$$

Similar terms will appear for another repeated root, if any.

6.7. Heaviside's Partial Fraction Expansion Theorem

This theorem provides the method for evaluation of coefficients in K_1, K_2 etc. in the partial fraction expansion.

Case A. **Real and simple roots.** Reverting to the case of real and simple roots, partial fraction expansion is given by Eq. (6.96) reproduced here :

$$\frac{N_1(s)}{D(s)} = \frac{K_1}{s-s_1} + \frac{K_2}{s-s_2} + \ldots\ldots + \frac{K_d}{s-s_d} \quad \ldots(6.99)$$

The coefficients $K_1, K_2, \ldots\ldots, K_d$ are required to be evaluated. Then any coefficient say K_p is given by multiplying the quotient $\frac{N_1(s)}{D(s)}$ by the denominator of coefficient K_p, *i.e.* by the factor $(s - s_p)$ and setting s to the roots s_p. Thus coefficient K_p is given by,

$$K_p = \left[\frac{N_1(s)}{D(s)}(s-s_p)\right]_{s=s_p} \quad \ldots(6.100)$$

Case B. **Repeated roots.** Let there be r repeated roots each equal to s_p. Let then,

$$\frac{N_1(s)}{D(s)} = \frac{P(s)}{(s-s_p)^r} = \frac{K_1}{s-s_p} + \frac{K_2}{(s-s_p)^2} + \ldots + \frac{K_n}{(s-s_p)^n} + \ldots\ldots + \frac{K_r}{(s-s_p)^n} \quad \ldots(6.101)$$

where n is any term in the partial fraction expansion and is less than r.

$P(s)$ is given by,

$$P(s) = \frac{N_1(s)}{D(s)} \cdot (s-s_p)^r \quad \ldots(6.102)$$

Multiplying Eq. (6.101) by quantity $(s - s_p)^r$, we get

$P(s) = K_1 (s - s_p)^{r-1} + K_2(s - s_p)^{r-2} + \ldots K_{r-1} (s - p) + K_r$ ...(6.103)

Now if we let $s = s_p$, all terms on the right hand side of Eq. (6.103) vanish except the term K_r. This gives the value of K_r as,

$$K_r = [\,P(s)\,]_{s=s_p} \quad \ldots(6.104)$$

Now on differentiating Eq. (6.103) once with respect to s, term K_r vanishes but the coefficient K_{r-1} remains without a multiplying function of s. In this differential equation if we let $s = s_p$, all terms on the right hand side of the differential equation disappear except the term K_{r-1}. This gives the value of K_{r-1}.

$$K_{r-1} = \left[\frac{dP(s)}{ds}\right]_{s=s_p} \quad \ldots(6.105)$$

By successive differentiation we may thus find value of each of the coefficients K_1, K_2 etc.

The general term K_n may be obtained by differentiating Eq. (6.103), $(r - n)$ times and letting $s = s_p$. Then we get

$$K_n = \frac{1}{(r-n)!}\left[\frac{d^{r-n}\,P(s)}{ds^{r-n}}\right]_{s=s_p} \qquad \text{...(6.106)}$$

or

$$K_n = \frac{1}{(r-n)!}\left[\frac{d^{r-n}}{ds^{r-n}}\right]\left\{\frac{N_1(s)}{D(s)}(s-s_p)^r\right\}_{s=s_p} \qquad \text{...(6.107)}$$

Example 6.10. *Current I(s) in a network is given by*

$$I(s) = \frac{2s+5}{s^2+5s+6}$$

It is required to expand this quotient of polynomials by the method of partial fractions.

Solution. The quotient of polynomials may be put as,

$$\frac{2s+5}{s^2+5s+6} = \frac{2s+5}{(s+2)(s+3)} = \frac{K_1}{s+2} + \frac{K_2}{s+3} \qquad \text{...(1)}$$

To find K_1, we multiply Eq. (1) by $(s + 2)$. Thus we get

$$\frac{(2s+5)(s+2)}{(s+2)(s+3)} = K_1 + K_2\,\frac{s+2}{s+3} \qquad \text{...(2)}$$

or

$$\frac{2s+5}{s+3} = K_1 + K_2\,.\,\frac{s+2}{s+3} \qquad \text{...(3)}$$

Letting $s = -2$, we get

$$K_1 = \frac{2(-2)+5}{(-2)+3} = 1 \qquad \text{...(4)}$$

To find K_2 we multiply Eq. (1) by $(s + 3)$. Thus, we get

$$\frac{(2s+5)}{(s+2)} = K_1\,.\,\frac{s+3}{s+2} + K_3 \qquad \text{...(5)}$$

Putting $s = -3$, we get

$$K_2 = \frac{2(-3)+5}{(-3)+2} \qquad \text{...(6)}$$

Hence, we get

$$\frac{2s+5}{s^2+5s+6} = \frac{1}{s+2} + \frac{1}{s+3} \qquad \text{...(7)}$$

Example 6.11. *Current I(s) in a network is given by*

$$I(s) = \frac{s+3}{(s+1)^2}\,.$$

It is required to expand this quotient of polynomials by the method of partial fractions.

Solution. In this case, the denominator has repeated factor $(s + 1)$. Hence the quotient of polynomials may be put as,

$$\frac{s+3}{(s+1)^2} = \frac{K_1}{s+1} + \frac{K_2}{(s+1)^2} \qquad \text{...(1)}$$

On multiplying by $(s + 1)^2$, Eq. (1) yields,

$$(s+3) = K_1(s+1) + K_2 \qquad \text{...(2)}$$

Putting $s = -1$, in Eq. (2), we get

$$K_2 = (-1+3) = 2 \qquad \text{...(3)}$$

Differentiating Eq. (2) with respect to s yields,

$$\frac{d(s+3)}{ds} = K_1 . \frac{d(s+1)}{ds} \qquad \text{...(4)}$$

Hence $K_1 = 1$.

Hence the partial fraction expansion is,

$$\frac{s+3}{(s+1)^2} = \frac{1}{s+1} + \frac{2}{(s+1)^2}$$

Example 6.12. *Let a quotient of polynomials that results on Laplace transformation of a network equation be* $\frac{1}{s^2+4s+8}$. *It is required to expand this quotient of polynomials be the method of partial fraction.*

Solution. The quotient of polynomials may be put as,

$$\frac{1}{s^2+4s+8} = \frac{K_1}{(s+2+2j)} + \frac{K_2}{(s+2-j2)} \qquad \text{...(1)}$$

Multiplying Eq. (1) by $(s + 2 + j2)$, we get

$$\frac{1}{s+2-j2} = K_1 + K_2 . \frac{s+2+j2}{s+2-j2} \qquad \text{...(2)}$$

Putting $s = -2 - j2$ in Eq. (2), we get

$$\frac{1}{-2-j2+2-j2} = K_1$$

or

$$K_1 = \frac{1}{4j} = \frac{j}{4} \qquad \text{...(3)}$$

Similarly multiplying Eq. (1) by $(s + 2 - j2)$, we get

$$\frac{1}{s+2+j2} = K_1 . \frac{s+2-j2}{s+2+j2} + K_2 \qquad \text{...(4)}$$

Putting $s = -2 + j2$ in Eq. (4), we get

$$\frac{1}{-2+j2+2+j2} = K_2$$

$$K_2 = \frac{-j}{4} \qquad \text{...(5)}$$

Hence the desired expansion is,

$$\frac{1}{s^2+4s+8} = \frac{j\frac{1}{4}}{s+2+j2} - \frac{j\frac{1}{4}}{s+2-j2} \qquad \text{...(6)}$$

Example 6.13. *Let the quotient of polynomials resulting on Laplace transformation of a network equation be* $\frac{2s^2+5s+2}{(s+1)^3}$. *It is required to expand this quotient of polynomials by the method of partial fractions.*

Solution. The quotient of polynomials may be written as,

$$\frac{2s^2+5s+2}{(s+1)^3} = \frac{K_1}{(s+1)} + \frac{K_2}{(s+1)^2} + \frac{K_3}{(s+1)^3} \qquad ...(1)$$

Multiplying Eq. (1) by $(s + 1)^3$, we get

$$P(s) = (2s^2 + 5s + 2)$$
$$= K_1(s + 1)^2 + K_2(s + 1) + K_3 \qquad ...(2)$$

Putting $s = -1$, in Eq. (2), we get

$$K_3 = (2 - 5 + 2) = -1 \qquad ...(3)$$

Differentiating Eq. (2) with respect to s, we get

$$(4s + 5) = 2K_1 (s + 1) + K_2 \qquad ...(4)$$

Putting $s = -1$ in Eq. (4), we get

$$K_2 = (-4 + 5) = 1 \qquad ...(5)$$

Differentiating Eq. (4) with respect to s, we get

$$4 = 2K_1$$

Hence $K_1 = 2.$

Hence the partial fraction expansion is given by,

$$\frac{2s^2+5s+2}{(s+1)^3} = \frac{2}{s+1} + \frac{1}{(s+1)^2} - \frac{1}{(s+1)^3}.$$

Example 6.14. *The quotient of polynomials resulting on Laplace transformation of a network equation is* $\frac{2s+3}{(s+1)^2(s+2)}$. *It is required to expand this quotient of polynomials by the method of partial fractions.*

Solution. In this case the polynomial in the denominator contains both simple and repeated roots. Hence a combination of both rules of partial fraction expansion may be used.

Thus let, $$\frac{2s+3}{(s+1)^2(s+2)} + \frac{K_1}{(s+1)} + \frac{K_2}{(s+1)^2} + \frac{K_3}{(s+2)} \qquad ...(1)$$

Multiplying Eq. (1) by $(s + 2)$, we have

$$\frac{(2s+3)}{(s+1)^2} = \frac{K_1(s+2)}{(s+1)} + \frac{K_2(s+2)}{(s+1)^2} + K_3 \qquad ...(2)$$

Putting $s = -2$ in Eq. (2), we get

$$K_3 = \frac{(-4+3)}{(-2+1)} = -1 \qquad ...(3)$$

Next, multiplying Eq. (1) by $(s + 1)^2$, we get

$$\frac{(2s+3)}{(s+2)} = K_1(s+1) + K_2 + K_3\frac{(s+1)^2}{(s+2)} \qquad ...(4)$$

Putting $s = -1$ in Eq. (4), we get

$$K_2 = \frac{-1+3}{-1+2} = 1 \qquad ...(5)$$

Differentiating Eq. (4) with respect to s, we get

$$\frac{(s+2)2-(2s+3)}{(s+2)^2} = K_1 + K_3 \cdot \frac{2(s+2)(s+1)-(s+1)^2}{(s+2)^2} \qquad ...(6)$$

or
$$\frac{1}{(s+2)^2} = K_1 + K_3 \cdot \frac{(s+1)(s+3)}{(s+2)^2} \quad ...(7)$$

Putting $s = -1$ in Eq. (7), we get

$$K_1 = \frac{1}{(-1+2)^2} = 1 \quad ...(8)$$

Hence the partial fraction expansion is given by,

$$\frac{(2s+3)}{(s+1)^2(s+2)} = \frac{1}{s+1} + \frac{1}{(s+1)^2} - \frac{1}{(s+2)}.$$

Example 6.15. *Find the inverse Laplace transform of each of the following function F(s) :*

(a) $\frac{2s+3}{s^2+3s}$ (b) $\frac{2s^2+6s+5}{(s+1)^2(s+2)}$ (c) $\frac{3s^2+4}{s(s^2+4)}$.

Solution.

(a)
$$\frac{2s+3}{s^2+3s} = \frac{2s+3}{s(s+3)} = \frac{K_1}{s} + \frac{K_2}{s+3} \quad ...(1)$$

Multiplying Eq. (1) by s, we get

$$\frac{2s+3}{(s+3)} = K_1 + \frac{sK_2}{s+3} \quad ...(2)$$

Putting $s = 0$ in Eq. (2), we get

$$1 = K_1$$

Multiplying Eq. (1) by $s + 3$, we get ...(3)

$$\frac{2s+3}{s} = K_1 \cdot \frac{s+3}{s} + K_2 \quad ...(4)$$

Putting $s = -3$ in Eq. (4), we get

$$\frac{-6+3}{-3} = K_2 \text{ or } K_2 = 1.$$

Hence
$$\frac{2s+3}{s^2+3s} = \frac{1}{s} + \frac{1}{s+3} \quad ...(5)$$

Hence
$$\mathcal{L}^{-1}\frac{2s+3}{s^2+3s} = \mathcal{L}^{-1}\frac{1}{s} + \mathcal{L}^{-1}\frac{1}{s+3} = 1 + e^{-3t}$$

(b) Let
$$\frac{2s^2+6s+5}{(s+1)^2(s+2)} = \frac{K_1}{s+1} + \frac{K_2}{(s+1)^2} + \frac{K_3}{s+2} \quad ...(1)$$

Multiplying Eq. (1) by $(s + 2)$, we get

$$\frac{(2s^2+6s+5)}{(s+1)^2} = K_1\frac{s+2}{s+1} + K_2\frac{s+2}{(s+1)^2} + K_3 \quad ...(2)$$

Putting $s = -2$ in Eq. (2), we get

$$\frac{2(4)-12+5}{(-2+1)^2} = K_3$$

or
$$K_3 = 1 \quad ...(3)$$

Next multiplying Eq. (1) by $(s + 1)^2$, we get

$$\frac{2s^2+6s+5}{s+2} = K_1(s+1) + K_2 + K_3 \cdot \frac{(s+1)^2}{s+2} \quad ...(4)$$

Putting $s = -1$ in Eq. (4), we get

$$\frac{+2-6+5}{-1+2} = K_2$$

or $$K_2 = 1 \qquad ...(5)$$

Differentiating Eq. (4) with respect to s, we get

$$\frac{(s+2)(4s+6)-(2s^2+6s+5)}{(s+2)^2} = K_1 + K_3 \cdot \frac{(s+2)(2s+2)-(s+1)^2}{(s+2)^2}$$

or $$\frac{2s^2+8s+7}{(s+2)^2} = K_1 + K_3 \frac{(s+1)(2s+3)}{(s+2)^2} \qquad ...(6)$$

Putting $s = -1$ in Eq. (6), we get

$$\frac{2-8+7}{(s+2)^2} = K_1 \quad \text{or} \quad K_1 = 1 \qquad ...(7)$$

Hence $$\frac{2s^2+6s+5}{(s+1)^2(s+2)} = \frac{1}{s+1} + \frac{1}{(s+1)^2} + \frac{1}{s+2} \qquad ...(8)$$

Hence $$\mathcal{L}^{-1} \frac{2s^2+6s+5}{(s+1)^2(s+2)} = e^{-t} + te^{-t} + e^{-2t}$$

(*c*) Let $$\frac{3s+4}{s(s^2+4)} = \frac{K_1}{s} + \frac{K_2}{s+j2} + \frac{K_3}{s-j2} \qquad ...(1)$$

Multiplying Eq. (1) by s, we get

$$\frac{3s^2+4}{(s^2+4)} = K_1 + K_2 \cdot \frac{s}{s+2j} + K_2 \cdot \frac{s}{s-2j} \qquad ...(2)$$

Putting $s = 0$ in Eq. (2), we get

$$\frac{4}{4} = K_1 \quad \text{or} \quad K_1 = 1 \qquad ...(3)$$

Multiplying Eq. (1) by $(s + j2)$, we get

$$\frac{(3s^2+4)}{s(s-j2)} = K_1 \cdot \frac{s+j2}{s} + K_2 + K_3 \cdot \frac{s+j2}{s-j2} \qquad ...(4)$$

Putting $s = -j2$ in Eq. (4), we get

$$K_2 = \frac{3(-4)+4}{-j2(-j2-j2)} = \frac{-8}{-8} = 1 \qquad ...(5)$$

Multiplying Eq. (1) by $(s - j2)$, we get

$$\frac{(3s^2+4)}{s(s+j2)} = K_1 \cdot \frac{s-j2}{s} + K_2 \cdot \frac{s-j2}{s+j2} + K_3 \qquad ...(6)$$

Putting $s = j2$ in Eq. (6), we get

$$K_3 = \frac{3(-4)+4}{j2(j2+j2)} = \frac{-8}{-8} = 1 \qquad ...(7)$$

Hence $$\frac{3s^2+4}{s(s^2+4)} = \frac{1}{s} + \frac{1}{s+j2} + \frac{1}{s-j2} \qquad ...(8)$$

Hence $$\mathcal{L}^{-1}\left[\frac{3s^2+4}{s(s^2+4)}\right] = \mathcal{L}^{-1}\left(\frac{1}{s}\right) + \mathcal{L}^{-2}\left(\frac{1}{s+j2}\right) + \mathcal{L}^{-1}\left(\frac{1}{s-j2}\right)$$

...(9)

$$= 1 + e^{-j2t} + e^{+j2t} \quad ...(10)$$

$$= 1 + 2\cos 2t \quad ...(11)$$

Example 6.16. *Using Laplace transformation, solve the following differential equation :*

$$\frac{d^2i}{dt^2} + 4 \cdot \frac{di}{dt} + 8i = 8u(t)$$

Given that $i(0+) = 3$ *and* $\frac{di}{dt}(0+) = -4.$

Solution. The Laplace transformation of this differential equation is

$$\left[s^2I(s) - si(0+) - \frac{di}{dt}(0+)\right] + 4[sI(s) - i(0+)] + 8I(s) = 8\frac{1}{s} \quad ...(1)$$

or
$$I(s)[s^2 + 4s + 8] = \frac{8}{s} + si(0+) + \frac{di}{dt}(0+) + 4i(0+) \quad ...(2)$$

Putting $i(0+) = 3$ and $\frac{di}{dt}(0+) = -4$ in Eq. (2), we get

$$I(s)[s^2 + 4s + 8] = \frac{8}{s} + 3s + 8$$

$$= \frac{3s^2 + 8s + 8}{s} \quad ...(3)$$

or
$$I(s) = \frac{3s^2 + 8s + 8}{s(s^2 + 4s + 8)} \quad ...(4)$$

This equation may be expanded by the method of partial fractions. Thus let,

$$I(s) = \frac{3s^2 + 8s + 8}{s(s^2 + 4s + 8)} = \frac{K_1}{s} + \frac{K_2}{s + 2 + j2} + \frac{K_3}{s + 2 - j2} \quad ...(5)$$

To evaluate K_1 we multiply Eq. (5) by s. Thus, we get

$$\frac{3s^2 + 8s + 8}{s^2 + 4s + 8} = K_1 + \frac{K_2 s}{s^2 + 2 + j2} + K_3 \cdot \frac{s}{s + 2 - j2} \quad ...(6)$$

Putting $s = 0$ in Eq. (6), we get

$$K_1 = \frac{8}{8} = 1 \quad ...(7)$$

To evaluate K_2, we multiply Eq. (5) by $(s + 2 + j2)$. Thus we get

$$\frac{(3s^2 + 8s + 8)}{s(s + 2 - j^2)} = K_1 \cdot \frac{s + 2 + j2}{s} + K_2 + K_3 \frac{s + 2 + j2}{s + 2 - j2} \quad ...(8)$$

Putting $s = (-2 - j2)$ in Eq. (8), we get

$$K_2 = \frac{3(-2 - j2)^2 + 8(-2 - j2) + 8}{(-2 - j2)(-2 - j2 + 2 - j2)} = 1 \quad ...(9)$$

To evaluate K_3, we multiply Eq. (5) by $(s + 2 - j2)$. Thus, we get

$$\frac{3s^2 + 8s + 8}{s(s + 2 + j2)} = K_1 \cdot \frac{s + 2 - j2}{s} + K_2 \cdot \frac{s + 2 - j2}{s + 2 + j2} + K_3 \quad ...(10)$$

Putting $s = (-2 + j2)$ in Eq. (10), we get

$$K_3 = \frac{3(-2+j2)^2 + 8(-2+j2) + 8}{(-2+j2)(-2+j2+2+j2)} = 1 \qquad ...(11)$$

Hence the complete partial fraction expansion becomes,

$$I(s) = \frac{1}{s} + \frac{1}{s+2+j2} + \frac{1}{s+2-j2} \qquad ...(12)$$

On inverse Laplace transformation Eq. (12) yields,

$$i(t) = 1 + e^{(-2-j2)t} + e^{(-2+j2)t}$$

$$= 1 + e^{-2t}[e^{-j2t} + e^{j2t}] \qquad ...(13)$$

$$= 1 + 2e^{-2t} \cos 2t \qquad ...(14)$$

6.8. Response of Series R-L Circuit to Exponential Driving Voltage

The exponential driving force voltage $V_0 e^{-\alpha t}$ is applied to the series *R-L* circuit at time $t = 0$ by closing the switch *K*. V_0 and α are constants. It is required to find the particular solution for current $i(t)$ using Laplace transformation.

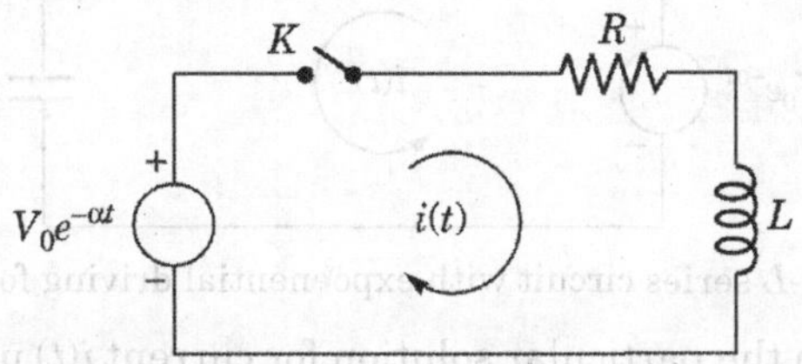

Fig. 6.9. *R-L* series circuit with exponential driving voltage.

Application of Kirchhoff's voltage law to the network yields

$$L \frac{di}{dt} + Ri = V_0 e^{-\alpha t} \qquad ...(6.108)$$

On Laplace transformation Eq. (6.108) becomes,

$$L[s.I(s) - i(0+)] + R.I(s) = V_0 \cdot \frac{1}{s+\alpha} \qquad ...(6.109)$$

Initial conditions. There is no current through inductor before closing the switch *K*. Hence the current remains zero at time $t = 0+$, *i.e.* $i(0+) = 0$.

Substituting this initial condition in Eq. (6.109), we get

$$I(s)\,[Ls + R] = \frac{V_0}{s+\alpha} \qquad ...(6.110)$$

or

$$I(s) = \frac{V_0}{(s+\alpha)(Ls+R)} = \frac{V_0}{L} \cdot \frac{1}{(s+\alpha)\left(s + \frac{R}{L}\right)} \qquad ...(6.111)$$

Case (A) $\alpha \neq R/L$.

In this case, Eq. (6.111) on inverse Laplace transformation yields,

$$i(t) = \frac{V_0}{L} \cdot \frac{1}{-\alpha + R/L}\left[e^{-\alpha t} - e^{-\frac{Rt}{L}}\right] \qquad ...(6.112)$$

$$= \frac{V_0}{R - \alpha L}\left[e^{-\alpha t} - e^{-\frac{Rt}{L}}\right] \qquad ...(6.113)$$

Case (B) $\alpha = R/L$.

In this case, Eq. (6.111) becomes,

$$I(s) = \frac{V_0}{L} \cdot \frac{1}{(s+\alpha)^2} \qquad ...(6.114)$$

On inverse Laplace transformation Eq. (6.114) yields

$$i(t) = \frac{V_0}{L} \,.\, i.e.^{-\alpha t} \qquad ...(6.115)$$

6.9. Response of Series R-C Circuit to Exponential Driving Voltage

The exponential driving voltage $V_0 e^{-\alpha t}$ is applied to the series *R-C* circuit at time $t = 0$ by closing the switch *K*. V_0 and α are constants.

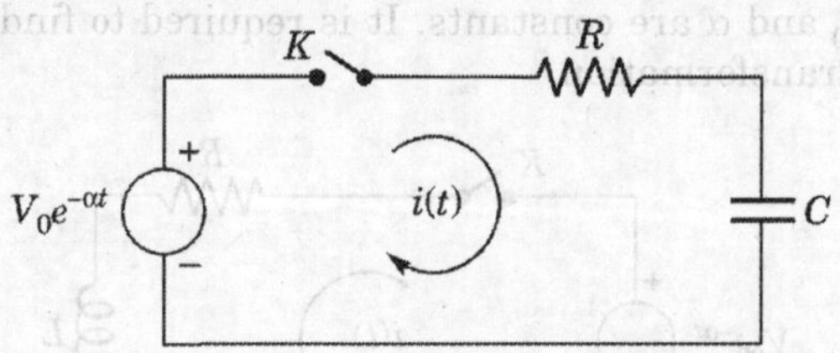

Fig. 6.10. *R-L* series circuit with expoenential driving force voltage.

It is required to obtain the particular solution for current $i(t)$ using Laplace transformation.

Application of Kirchhoff's voltage law to the network yields,

$$Ri + \frac{1}{C}\int_{-\infty}^{t} i dt = V_0 e^{-\alpha t} \qquad ...(6.116)$$

or
$$Ri + \frac{1}{C}\int_{-\infty}^{t} i dt + \frac{1}{C}\int_{0}^{t} i dt = V_0 e^{-\alpha t} \qquad ...(6.117)$$

On Laplace transformation Eq. (6.117) becomes,

$$R.I(s) + \frac{1}{C}\cdot\frac{q(0+)}{s} + \frac{1}{C}\cdot\frac{I(s)}{s} = V_0 \cdot \frac{1}{s+\alpha} \qquad ...(6.118)$$

Initial condition. There is no initial charge across capacitor *C* before switching, *i.e.* at time $t = 0-$. Further the charge across *C* cannot charge instantaneously. Hence $q(0+) = 0$. Substituting this initial condition in Eq. (6.118), we get

$$I(s)\left[R + \frac{1}{Cs}\right] = \frac{V_0}{s+\alpha} \qquad ...(6.119)$$

or
$$I(s) = \frac{V_0 s}{(s+\alpha)\left(Rs + \frac{1}{C}\right)}$$

$$= \frac{V_0}{R} \cdot \frac{s}{(s+\alpha)\left(s + \frac{1}{CR}\right)} \qquad ...(6.120)$$

Case (A) $\alpha \neq 1/CR$.

Let
$$\frac{s}{(s+\alpha)\left(s+\frac{1}{CR}\right)} = \frac{K_1}{s+\alpha} + \frac{K_2}{s+\frac{1}{CR}} \quad ...(6.121)$$

Multiplying Eq. (6.121) by $(s + \alpha)$ and putting $s = -\alpha$, we get

$$K_1 = \frac{s}{s+\frac{1}{CR}} = \frac{-\alpha}{-\alpha+\frac{1}{CR}} = \frac{\alpha}{\alpha-\frac{1}{CR}} = \frac{\alpha . CR}{\alpha CR - 1} \quad ...(6.122)$$

Multiplying Eq. (6.121) by $\left(s+\frac{1}{CR}\right)$ and putting $s = -\frac{1}{CR}$, we get

$$K_2 = \frac{s}{s+\alpha} = \frac{-\frac{1}{CR}}{-\frac{1}{CR}+\alpha} = \frac{\frac{1}{CR}}{\frac{1}{CR}-\alpha} = \frac{1}{1-\alpha CR} \quad ...(6.123)$$

Hence Eq. (6.120) becomes,

$$I(s) = \frac{V_0}{R}\left[\frac{\alpha CR}{\alpha CR - 1} \cdot \frac{1}{s+\alpha} + \frac{1}{1-\alpha CR} \cdot \frac{1}{s+\frac{1}{CR}}\right]$$

$$= \frac{V_0}{R} \cdot \frac{1}{\alpha CR - 1}\left[\frac{\alpha CR}{s+\alpha} - \frac{1}{s+\frac{1}{CR}}\right] \quad ...(6.124)$$

On inverse Laplace transformation, we get

$$i(t) = \frac{V_0}{R(\alpha CR - 1)}\left[\alpha CR . e^{-\alpha t} - e^{-\frac{t}{CR}}\right] \quad ...(6.125)$$

Case (B) $\alpha = \frac{1}{CR}$

In this case Eq. (6.120) becomes,

$$I(s) = \frac{V_0}{R} \frac{s}{(s+\alpha)^2} \quad ...(6.126)$$

Let
$$\frac{s}{(s+\alpha)^2} = \frac{K_1}{s+\alpha} + \frac{K_2}{(s+\alpha)^2} \quad ...(6.127)$$

Multiplying Eq. (6.127) by $(s + \alpha)^2$, we get

$$s = K_1(s+\alpha) + K_2 \quad ...(6.128)$$

Putting $s = -\alpha$ in Eq. (6.128), we get

$$K_2 = -\alpha \quad ...(6.129)$$

Differentiating Eq. (6.128) with respect to s, we get

$$1 = K_1 + 0.$$

Thus
$$K_1 = 1 \quad ...(6.130)$$

Hence
$$\frac{s}{(s+\alpha)^2} = \frac{1}{s+\alpha} - \frac{\alpha}{(s+\alpha)^2}$$

Hence Eq. (6.126) becomes,

$$I(s) = \frac{V_0}{R}\left[\frac{1}{s+\alpha} - \frac{\alpha}{(s+\alpha)^2}\right] \quad \text{...(6.131)}$$

On inverse Laplace transformation Eq. (6.131) yields,

$$i(t) = \frac{V_0}{R}\,[e^{-\alpha t} - \alpha\, t\, e^{-\alpha t}]$$

$$= \frac{V_0}{R}\, e^{-\alpha t}[1 - \alpha t] \quad \text{...(6.132)}$$

6.10. Response of Series R-L-C Circuit to Exponential Driving Voltage

The exponential driving voltage $V_0\, e^{-\alpha t}$ is applied to the series *R-L-C* circuit at time $t = 0$ by closing the switch *K*. V_0 and α are constants. It is required to obtain the particular solution for current $i(t)$ using Laplace transformation.

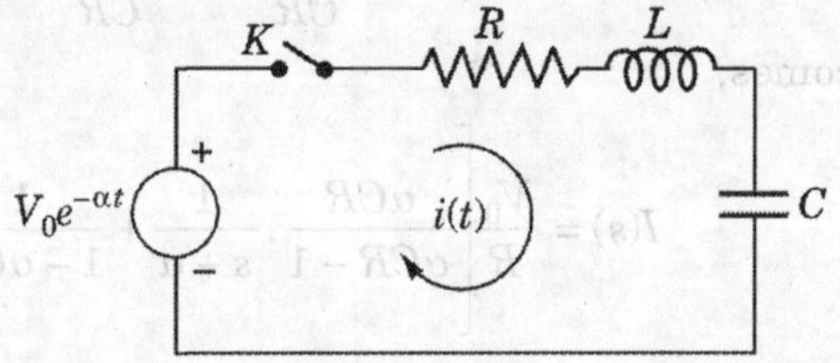

Fig. 6.11. *R-L-C* series circuit with exponential driving voltage.

Application of Kirchhoff's voltage law to the network yields,

$$L\frac{di}{dt} + Ri + \frac{1}{C}\int_{-\infty}^{0} i\, dt + \frac{1}{C}\int_{0}^{t} i\, dt = V_0 e^{-\alpha t} \quad \text{...(6.133)}$$

On Laplace transformation Eq. (6.133) yields,

$$L[sI(s - i(0+)] + R.I(s) + \frac{1}{C}\frac{q(0+)}{s} + \frac{1}{C}.\frac{I(s)}{s} = V_0\frac{1}{s+\alpha} \quad \text{...(6.134)}$$

Initial conditons. There is zero current through the inductor before closing the switch *K*. Hence the current remains zero after closing the switch at $t = 0+$, *i.e.* $i(0+) = 0$. Also there is no initial charge across the capacitor *C* before closing the switch *K*. Hence charge *q* remains zero at time $t = 0+$, *i.e.* $q(0+) = 0$.

Substituting these initial conditions in Eq. (6.134), we get

$$I(s)\left[Ls + R + \frac{1}{Cs}\right] = V_0\frac{1}{s+\alpha} \quad \text{...(6.135)}$$

or

$$I(s) = \frac{V_0}{(s+\alpha)\left(Ls + R + \frac{1}{Cs}\right)} \quad \text{...(6.136)}$$

$$= \frac{V_0}{(s+\alpha)\left[Ls^2 + Rs + \frac{1}{C}\right]} \quad \text{...(6.137)}$$

$$= \frac{V_0}{L} \cdot \frac{s}{(s+\alpha)\left(s^2 + \frac{R}{L}s + \frac{1}{CL}\right)} \qquad ...(6.138)$$

$$= \frac{V_0}{L} \cdot \frac{s}{(s+\alpha)(s-s_1)(s-s_2)} \qquad ...(6.139)$$

where s_1, s_2 are the roots of the quadratic equation,

$$s^2 + \frac{R}{L}s + \frac{1}{LC} = 0 \qquad ...(6.140)$$

and are given by,

$$s_1, s_2 = -\frac{R/L}{2} \pm \frac{1}{2}\sqrt{\frac{R^2}{L^2} - 4\frac{1}{LC}} \qquad ...(6.141)$$

Eq. (6.139) may be put as,

$$I(s) = \frac{V_0}{L}\left[\frac{K_1}{s+\alpha} + \frac{K_2}{s-s_1} + \frac{K_3}{s-s_2}\right], -a\ ^1 s_1\ ^1 s_2 \qquad ...(6.142)$$

Constants K_1, K_2 and K_3 may be determined by the method of partial fractions.

On inverse Laplace transformation Eq. (6.142) yields,

$$i(t) = \frac{V_0}{L}\,[K_1.e^{-\alpha t} + K_2 e^{s_1 t} + K_3\, e^{s_2 t}] \qquad ...(6.143)$$

6.11. Response of Parallel R-L-C Circuit to Exponential Driving Current

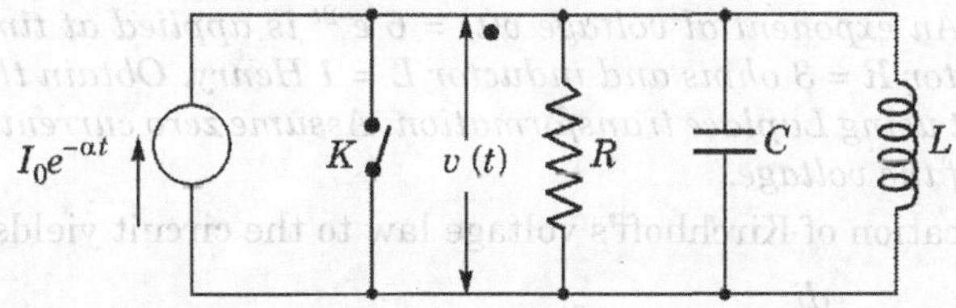

Fig. 6.12. *R-L-C* parallel circuit with exponential driving current.

An exponential driving current $I_0e^{-\alpha t}$ is applied to the parrallel *R-L-C* circuit at time $t = 0$ by opening the switch *K*. I_0 and α are constants. It is required to obtain the particular solution for voltage $v(t)$ across the parallel circuit using Laplace transformation.

Application of Kirchhoff's current law to the network yields,

$$C\frac{dv}{dt} + Gv + \frac{1}{L}\int_{-\infty}^{0} vdt + \frac{1}{L}\int_{0}^{t} vdt = I_0e^{-\alpha t} \qquad ...(6.144)$$

The corresponding Laplace transform equation is,

$$C[s.V(s) - v(0+)] + G\,.\,V(s) + \frac{1}{L}\,\mathcal{L}\,\psi(0) + \frac{1}{L}.\frac{V(s)}{s} = \frac{I_0}{s+\alpha} \qquad ...(6.145)$$

Initial condition. Because of the presence of capacitor *C*, $v(0+) = 0$ since the voltage across a capacitor cannot change instantaneously. Also the current in the inductor *L* during the time interval $-\infty$ to 0 is zero. Hence $\psi(0+)$ is zero. Substituting these initial conditions in Eq. (6.145), we get

$$V(s)\left[Cs + G + \frac{1}{Ls}\right] = \frac{I_0}{s+\alpha} \qquad ...(6.146)$$

or $$V(s) = \frac{I_0}{(s+\alpha)\left(Cs + G + \frac{1}{Ls}\right)} \quad ...(6.147)$$

$$= \frac{I_0}{C} \cdot \frac{s}{(s+\alpha)\left(s^2 + \frac{G}{s} + \frac{1}{LC}\right)} \quad ...(6.148)$$

$$= \frac{I_0}{C} \cdot \frac{s}{(s+\alpha)(s-s_1)(s-s_2)} \quad ...(6.149)$$

where s_1, s_2 are the roots of the equation,

$$s^2 + \frac{G}{C}s + \frac{1}{LC} = 0 \quad ...(6.150)$$

Thus $$s_1, s_2 = -\frac{G}{2C} \pm \frac{1}{2}\sqrt{\frac{G^2}{C^2} - \frac{4}{LC}} \quad ...(6.151)$$

Eq. (6.149) may be put as,

$$V(s) = \frac{I_0}{C}\left[\frac{K_1}{s+\alpha} + \frac{K_2}{s-s_1} + \frac{K_3}{s-s_2}\right], -\alpha \neq s_1 \neq s_2 \quad ...(6.152)$$

Terms K_1, K_2 and K_3 may be determined by the method of partial fractions.

On inverse Laplace transformation, Eq. (6.152) yields,

$$i(t) = \frac{I_0}{C}[K_1\, e^{-\alpha t} + K_2\, e^{s_1 t} + K_3\, e^{s_2 t}] \quad ...(6.153)$$

Example 6.17. *An exponential voltage $v(t) = 6\, e^{-2t}$ is applied at time $t = 0$ to a series R-L circuit comprising resistor $R = 3$ ohms and inductor $L = 1$ Henry. Obtain the complete solution for current i(t) in the circuit using Laplace transformation. Assume zero current through the inductor L before the application of the voltage.*

Solution. Application of Kirchhoff's voltage law to the circuit yields,

$$L\frac{di}{dt} + Ri = 6e^{-2t} \quad ...(1)$$

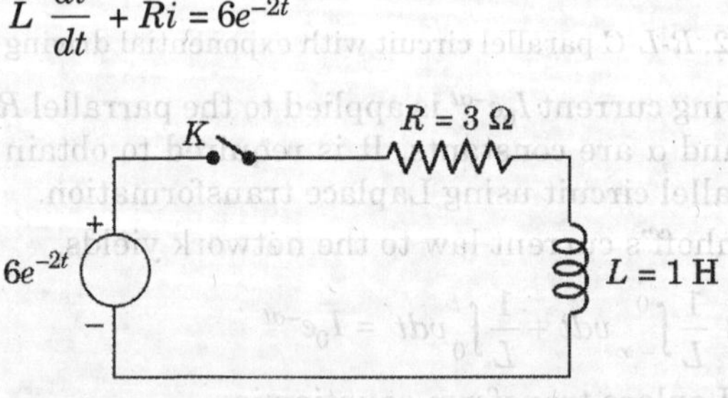

On Laplace transformation Eq. (1) yields,

$$L[s.I(s) - i(9+)] + R.I(s) = \frac{6}{s+2} \quad ...(2)$$

Initial condition. Because of the presence of inductor L, $i(0+) = 0$.

Substituting this initial condition in Eq. (2), we get

$$I(s)\ [Ls + R] = \frac{6}{s+2}$$

or
$$I(s) = \frac{6}{(s+2)(Ls+R)} \quad ...(3)$$

$$= \frac{6}{(s+2)(s+3)} \quad ...(4)$$

On inverse Lapalce transformation Eq. (4) yields,

$$i(t) = \frac{6}{-2-(-3)}[e^{-2t} - e^{-3t}]$$

or
$$i(t) = 6[e^{-2t} - e^{-3t}].$$ **Ans.**

Example 6.18. *An exponential voltage $v(t) = 5e^{-t}$ is applied at time $t = 0$ to a series R-C circuit comprising resistor $R = 5\ \Omega$ and capacitor $C = 0.1$ Farad. Using Laplace transformation obtain the complete particular solution for current i(t) through the circuit. Assume zero charge across the capacitor before application of the driving voltage.*

Solution. Application of Kirchhoff's voltage law to the circuit yields,

$$Ri + \int_{-\infty}^{0} idt + \frac{1}{C}\int_0^t idt = 5e^{-t} \quad ...(1)$$

On Laplace transformation Eq. (1) yield,

$$R.I(s) + \frac{1}{C}.\frac{q(0+)}{s} + \frac{1}{C}.\frac{I(s)}{s} = 5.\frac{1}{s+1} \quad ...(2)$$

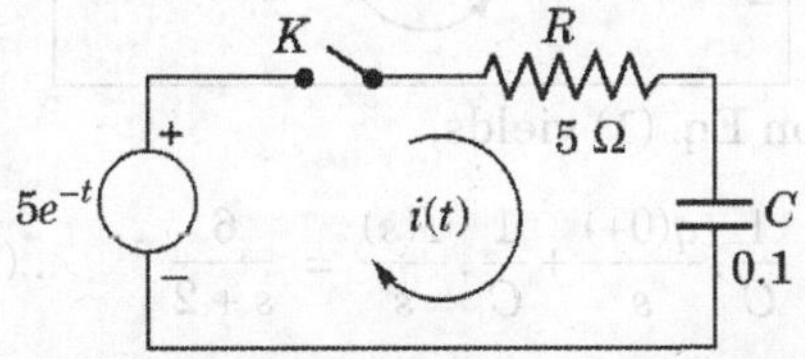

Initial condition. There is no initial charge across the capacitor. But the charge across the capacitor cannot change instantaneously. Hence $q(0+) = 0$. Substituting this initial condition in Eq. (2), we get

$$I(s)\left[R + \frac{1}{Cs}\right] = \frac{5}{s+1} \quad ...(3)$$

or
$$I(s) = \frac{5}{s+1}.\frac{1}{R+\frac{1}{s}} = \frac{5s}{(s+1)\left(s+\frac{1}{CR}\right)}$$

$$= \frac{s}{(s+1)(s+2)} \quad ...(4)$$

Let
$$\frac{s}{(s+1)(s+2)} = \frac{K_1}{s+1} + \frac{K_2}{s+2} \quad ...(5)$$

Multiplying Eq. (5) by $(s + 1)$ and putting $s = -1$, we get

$$K_1 = \frac{2}{s+2} = \frac{-1}{-1+2} = -1 \quad ...(6)$$

Multiplying Eq. (5) by $(s + 2)$ and putting $s = -2$, we get

$$K_2 = \frac{s}{s+1} = \frac{-2}{-2+1} = 2 \qquad ...(7)$$

Hence $$\frac{s}{(s+1)(s+2)} = \frac{2}{s+2} - \frac{1}{s+1} \qquad ...(8)$$

Hence $$I(s) = \frac{2}{s+2} - \frac{1}{s+1} \qquad ...(9)$$

On inverse Laplace transformation, Eq. (9) yields,

$$i(t) = 2e^{-2t} - e^{-t}.$$ **Ans.**

Example 6.19. *In the series R-L-C circuit of Fig. 6.11, R = 5 Ω, L = 1 H and C = 0.25 Farad. Driving voltage is $6e^{-2t}$. Switch K is closed at time t = 0. Obtain complete particular solution for current i(t) in the circuit using Laplace transformation. Assume zero current through inductor L and zero charge across capacitor C before closing the switch K.*

Solution. Application of Kirchhoff's voltage law to the circuit yields,

$$L\frac{di}{dt} + Ri + \frac{1}{C}\int_{-\infty}^{0} idt + \frac{1}{C}\int_{0}^{t} idt = 6e^{-2t} \qquad ...(1)$$

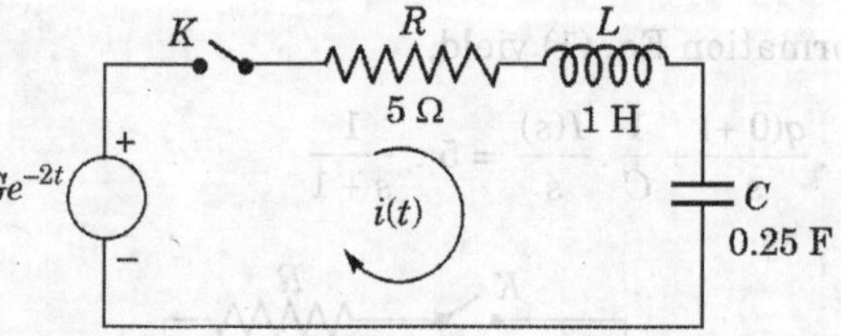

On Laplace transformation Eq. (1) yields,

$$L[s.I(s) - i(0+)] + R.I(s) + \frac{1}{C}\cdot\frac{q(0+)}{s} + \frac{1}{C}\cdot\frac{I(s)}{s} = \frac{6}{s+2} \qquad ...(2)$$

Initial conditions. At time $t = 0+$, current $i(0+)$ must be the same as at time $t = 0-$ because of the presence of inductor L. Thus $i(0+) = 0$. Further at $t = 0+$, charge $q(0+)$ across capacitor must be the same as at time $t = 0-$. Thus $q(0+) = 0$.

Substituting these initial conditions in Eq. (2), we get

$$I(s)\left[Ls + R + \frac{1}{Cs}\right] = \frac{6}{s+2} \qquad ...(3)$$

or $$I(s) = \frac{6}{(s+2)\left(Ls + R + \frac{1}{Cs}\right)}$$

$$= \frac{6}{L}\cdot\frac{s}{(s+2)\left(s^2 + \frac{R}{L}s + \frac{1}{CL}\right)} \qquad ...(4)$$

Substituting values of L, R and C in Eq. (4), we get

$$I(s) = \frac{6s}{(s+2)(s^2+5s+4)}$$

$$= \frac{6s}{(s+1)(s+2)(s+4)} \quad ...(5)$$

Let $$\frac{6s}{(s+1)(s+2)(s+4)} = \frac{K_1}{s+1} + \frac{K_2}{s+2} + \frac{K_3}{s+4} \quad ...(6)$$

Multiplying Eq. (6) by $(s + 1)$ and putting $s = -1$, we get

$$K_1 = \frac{6s}{(s+2)(s+4)} = \frac{-6}{(-1+2)(-1+4)} = -2 \quad ...(7)$$

Multiplying Eq. (6) by $(s + 2)$ and putting $s = -2$, we get

$$K_2 = \frac{6s}{(s+1)(s+4)} = \frac{-12}{(-2+1)(-2+4)} = \frac{-12}{-2} = 6 \quad ...(8)$$

Multiplying Eq. (6) by $(s + 4)$ and putting $s = -4$, we get

$$K_3 = \frac{6s}{(s+1)(s+2)} = \frac{-24}{(-4+1)(-4+2)} = \frac{-24}{6} = -4 \quad ...(9)$$

Hence $$I(s) = \frac{-2}{s+2} + \frac{6}{s+2} - \frac{4}{s+4} \quad ...(10)$$

On inverse Laplace transformation,

$$i(t) = -2e^{-t} + 6e^{-2t} - 4e^{-4t}.$$ **Ans.**

Example 6.20. *In the parallel R-L-C circuit of Fig. 6.12, $R = 0.2\ \Omega$, $L = \frac{1}{6}$ Henry and $C = 1$ Farad. Driving current is $4e^{-t}$ ampere. Switch K is opened at time $t = 0$. Obtain complete particular solution for voltage $v(t)$ across the parallel circuit. Assume zero current through inductor L and zero charge across capacitor C before switch K is opened.*

Solution. Application of Kirchhoff's current law to the circuit yields,

$$C\frac{dv}{dt} + Gv + \frac{1}{L}\int_{-\infty}^{0} v\,dt + \frac{1}{L}\int_{0}^{t} v\,dt = 4e^{-t} \quad ...(1)$$

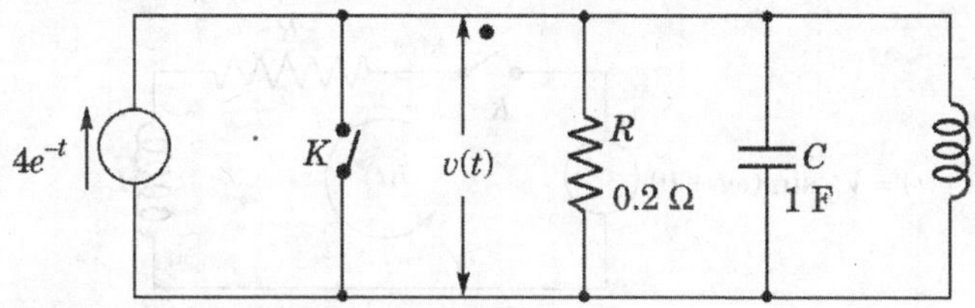

On Laplace transformation Eq. (1) yields,

$$C[s.V(s) - v(0+)] + G\,.\,V(s) + \frac{1}{L}\cdot\frac{\psi(0+)}{s} + \frac{1}{L}\cdot\frac{V(s)}{s} = \frac{4}{s+1} \quad ...(2)$$

Initial conditions. Because of the presence of capacitor C, $v(0+) = 0$ since the voltage across a capacitor cannot change instantaneously. Also the current in the inductor during the time interval $-\infty$ to 0 is zero, *i.e.* $\psi(0-) = 0$. Hence $\psi(0+) = 0$, since flux linkage in an inductor cannot change instantaneously.

Substituting these initial conditions in Eq. (2), we get

$$V(s)\left[Cs + G + \frac{1}{Ls}\right] = \frac{4}{s+1} \quad ...(3)$$

or $$V(s) = \frac{4}{(s+1)\left(Cs + G + \frac{1}{Ls}\right)}$$

$$= \frac{4}{C} \frac{s}{(s+1)\left(s^2 + \frac{G}{C}s + \frac{1}{LC}\right)} \quad ...(4)$$

$$= \frac{4s}{(s+1)(s^2 - 5s + 6)}$$

$$= \frac{4s}{(s+1)(s+2)(s+3)} \quad ...(5)$$

Let $$\frac{4s}{(s+1)(s+2)(s+3)} = \frac{K_1}{s+1} + \frac{K_2}{s+2} + \frac{K_3}{s+3} \quad ...(6)$$

Multiplying Eq. (6) by $(s + 1)$ and putting $s = -1$, we get

$$K_1 = \frac{4s}{(s+2)(s+3)} = \frac{-4}{(-1+2)(-1+3)} = -2 \quad ...(7)$$

Multiplying Eq. (6) by $(s + 2)$ and putting $s = -2$, we get

$$K_2 = \frac{4s}{(s+1)(s+3)} = \frac{-8}{(-2+1)(-2+3)} = 8 \quad ...(8)$$

Multiplying Eq. (6) by $(s + 3)$ and putting $s = -3$, we get

$$K_2 = \frac{4s}{(s+1)(s+2)} = \frac{-12}{(-3+1)(-3+2)} = -6 \quad ...(9)$$

Hence $$V(s) = \frac{-2}{s+1} + \frac{8}{s+2} - \frac{6}{s+3} \quad ...(10)$$

On inverse Laplace transformation Eq. (10) yields,

$$v(t) = -2e^{-t} + 8e^{-2t} - 6e^{-3t}.$$ **Ans.**

6.12. Response of Series R-L Circuit to Step Sinusoidal Driving Voltage

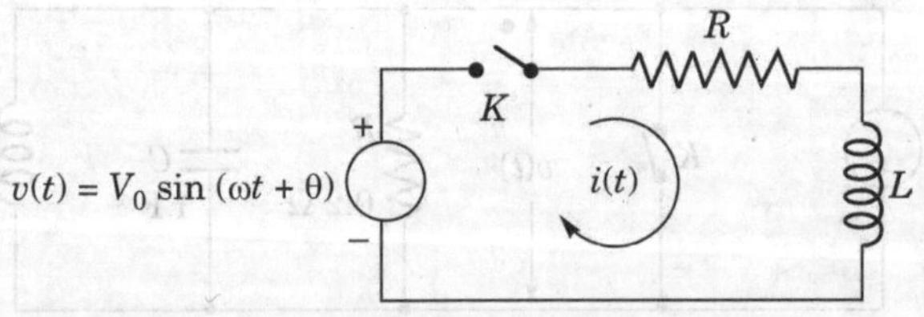

Fig. 6.13. Series *R-L* circuit with sinusoidal driving voltage.

Sinusoidal driving voltage $v(t) = V_0 \sin(\omega t + \theta)$ is applied to series *R-L* circuit at time $t = 0$ by closing the switch *K*. V_0, ω and θ are constants. It is required to find the complete particular solution for current $i(t)$ using Laplace transformation.

Application of Kirchhoff's voltage law to the series circuit of Fig. 6.13 yields,

$$L\frac{di}{dt} + Ri = V_0 \sin(\omega t + \theta) \quad ...(6.154)$$

On Laplace transformation Eq. (6.154) yields,

$$L.[I(s) - i(0+)] + R.I(s) = V_0 \cdot \frac{s \sin\theta + \omega\cos\theta}{s^2 + \omega^2} \quad ...(6.155)$$

Initial condition. There is no current through the inductor before closing the switch, *i.e.* $i(0-) = 0$. Since the current in an inductor cannot change instantaneously, $i(0+) = 0$.

Substituting this initial condition in Eq. (6.155), we get

$$I(s)[Ls + R] = \frac{V_0(s \sin \theta + \omega \cos \theta)}{s^2 + \omega^2} \quad \text{...(6.156)}$$

or

$$I(s) = \frac{V_0(s \sin \theta + \omega \cos \theta)}{(s^2 + \omega^2)(Ls + R)} \quad \text{...(6.157)}$$

$$= \frac{V_0}{L} \cdot \frac{(s \sin \theta + \omega \cos \theta)}{(s + j\omega)(s - j\omega)\left(s + \dfrac{R}{L}\right)} \quad \text{...(6.158)}$$

Let

$$\frac{s \sin \theta + \omega \cos \theta}{\left(s + \dfrac{R}{J}\right)(s + j\omega)(s - j\omega)} = \frac{K_1}{s + \dfrac{R}{L}} + \frac{K_2}{s + j\omega} + \frac{K_3}{s - j\omega} \quad \text{...(6.159)}$$

Multiplying Eq. (6.159) by $\left(s + \dfrac{R}{L}\right)$ and putting $s = -\dfrac{R}{L}$, we get

$$K_1 = \frac{\left(-\dfrac{R}{L} \sin \theta + \omega \cos \theta\right)}{\dfrac{R^2}{L^2} + \omega^2} \quad \text{...(6.160)}$$

Multiplying Eq. (6.159) by $(s + j\omega)$ and putting $s = -j\omega$, we get

$$K_2 = \frac{(-j\omega) \sin \theta + \omega \cos \theta}{\left(-j\omega + \dfrac{R}{L}\right)(-j\omega - j\omega)} = \frac{\omega \cos \theta - j\omega \sin \theta}{-2j\omega\left(\dfrac{R}{L} - j\omega\right)}$$

$$= \frac{\sin \theta + j \cos \theta}{2\left(\dfrac{R}{L} - j\omega\right)} \quad \text{...(6.161)}$$

Multiplying Eq. (6.159) by $(s - j\omega)$ and putting $s = +j\omega$, we get

$$K_3 = \frac{j\omega \sin \theta + \omega \cos \theta}{(j\omega + j\omega)\left(\dfrac{R}{L} + j\omega\right)} = \frac{j\omega(\sin \theta - j \cos \theta)}{j2\omega\left(\dfrac{R}{L} + j\omega\right)}$$

$$= \frac{\sin \theta - j \cos \theta}{2\left(\dfrac{R}{L} + j\omega\right)} \quad \text{...(6.162)}$$

On inverse Laplace transformation Eq. (6.158) yields,

Hence

$$i(t) = \frac{V_0}{L}\left[K_1 e^{-\frac{Rt}{L}} + K_2 e^{-j\omega t} + K_3 e^{+j\omega t}\right] \quad \text{...(6.163)}$$

$$= \frac{V_0}{R^2 + \omega^2 L^2}[-R \sin q + wL \cos q]\, e^{-\frac{Rt}{L}}$$

$$+ \frac{V_0}{2}\left[\frac{\sin\theta + j\cos\theta}{(R - j\omega L)}(\cos \omega t - j\sin \omega t) + \frac{\sin\theta - j\cos\theta}{R + j\omega L}(\cos \omega t + j \sin \omega t)\right] \quad \text{...(6.164)}$$

$$= \frac{V_0}{\sqrt{R^2+\omega^2L^2}} \sin\left(\theta - \tan^{-1}\frac{\omega L}{R}\right) e^{-\frac{Rt}{L}}$$

$$+ \frac{V_0}{2} \cos wt \left[\frac{\sin\theta + j\cos\theta}{R - j\omega L} + \frac{\sin\theta - j\cos\theta}{R + j\omega L}\right]$$

$$-j\frac{V_0}{2} \sin wt \left[\frac{\sin\theta + j\cos\theta}{R - j\omega L} - \frac{\sin\theta - j\cos\theta}{R + j\omega L}\right] \quad ...(6.165)$$

$$= \frac{-V_0}{\sqrt{R^2+\omega^2L^2}} \sin\left(\theta - \tan^{-1}\frac{\omega L}{R}\right) e^{-\frac{Rt}{L}}$$

$$+ V_0 \cos wt \frac{R\sin\theta - \omega L\cos\theta}{R^2+\omega^2 L^2}$$

$$+ V_0 \sin wt \frac{R\cos\theta + \omega L\cos\theta}{R^2+\omega^2L^2} \quad ...(6.166)$$

$$= \frac{-V_0}{\sqrt{R^2+\omega^2L^2}} \sin\left(\theta - \tan^{-1}\frac{\omega L}{R}\right) e^{-\frac{Rt}{L}}$$

$$+ \frac{V_0}{R^2+\omega^2L^2}\left[\cos\omega t\sqrt{R^2+\omega^2L^2}\sin\left(\theta - \tan^{-1}\frac{\omega L}{L}\right)\right.$$

$$\left. + \sin wt\sqrt{R^2+\omega^2L^2}\cos\left(\theta - \tan^{-1}\frac{\omega L}{R}\right)\right]$$

$$= \frac{-V_0}{\sqrt{R^2+\omega^2L^2}} \sin\left(\theta - \tan^{-1}\frac{\omega L}{R}\right) e^{-\frac{Rt}{L}}$$

$$+ \frac{V_0}{\sqrt{R^2+\omega^2L^2}} \sin\left(\omega t + \theta - \tan^{-1}\frac{\omega L}{R}\right) \quad ...(6.167)$$

Eq. (6.167) is the same as Eq. (5.128) obtained by classical method.

6.13. Response of Series R-C Circuit to Step Sinusoidal Voltage

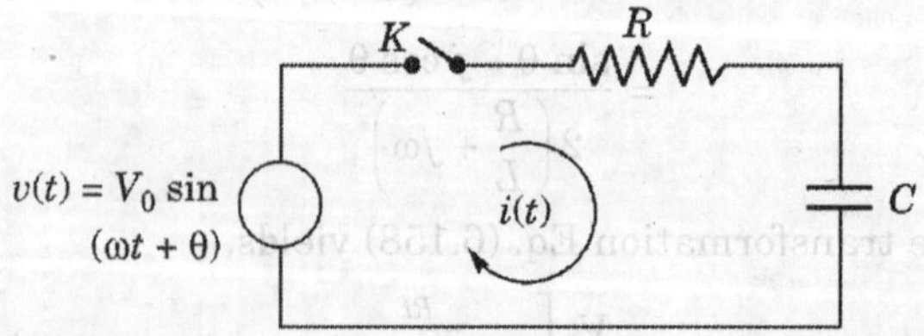

Fig. 6.14. *R-C* series circuit with step sinusoidal voltage.

Sinusoidal voltage $v(t) = V\sin(\omega t + \theta)$ is applied to series *R-C* circuit at time $t = 0$ by closing the switch *K*. V_0, ω and θ are constants. It is required to find complete particular solution for current $i(t)$ using Laplace transformation.

Application of Kirchhoff's voltage law to the series *R-C* circuit of Fig. 6.14 yields,

$$Ri + \frac{1}{C}\int_{-\infty}^{0} idt + \frac{1}{C}\int_{0}^{t} idt = V_0 \sin(\omega t + \theta) \qquad \text{...(6.168)}$$

On Laplace transformation, we get

$$.I(s) + \frac{1}{C}\cdot\frac{q(0+)}{s} + \frac{1}{C}\cdot\frac{I(s)}{s} = V_0 \cdot \frac{s\sin\theta + \omega\cos\theta}{s^2+\omega^2} \qquad \text{...(6.169)}$$

Initial condition. There is no charge across the capacitor at time $t = 0$. There cannot be any instantaneous change in charge across a capacitor. Hence $q(0+) = 0$.

Substituting this initial codition in Eq. (6.169), we get

$$I(s)\left[R + \frac{1}{Cs}\right] = V_0 \frac{[s\sin\theta + \omega\cos\theta]}{s^2+\omega^2} \qquad \text{...(6.170)}$$

Hence
$$I(s) = \frac{V_0[s\sin\theta + \omega\cos\theta]}{(s^2+\omega^2)\left(R + \frac{1}{Cs}\right)} = \frac{V_0}{R}\cdot\frac{s(s\sin\theta+\omega\cos\theta)}{\left(s+\frac{1}{CR}\right)(s+j\omega)(s-j\omega)} \qquad \text{...(6.171)}$$

Let
$$\frac{s(s\sin\theta+\omega\cos\theta)}{\left(s+\frac{1}{CR}\right)(s+j\omega)(s-j\omega)} = \frac{K_1}{s+\frac{1}{CR}} + \frac{K_2}{s+j\omega} + \frac{K_3}{s-j\omega} \qquad \text{...(6.172)}$$

Multiplying Eq. (6.172) by $\left(s+\frac{1}{CR}\right)$ and putting $s = -\frac{1}{CR}$, we get

$$K_1 = \frac{\left(\frac{1}{RC}\right)\left(\frac{1}{CR}\sin\theta + \omega\cos\theta\right)}{\left(\frac{1}{C^2R^2}+\omega^2\right)} = \frac{\frac{1}{CR}\left(\frac{1}{CR}\sin\theta - \omega\sin\theta\right)}{\frac{1}{C^2R^2}+\omega^2} \qquad \text{...(6.173)}$$

Multiplying Eq. (6.172) by $(s+j\omega)$ and putting $s = -j\omega$, we get

$$K_2 = \frac{(-j\omega)(-j\omega\sin\theta+\omega\cos\theta)}{(-j\omega-j\omega)\left(-j\omega+\frac{1}{CR}\right)} = \frac{\omega\cos\theta - j\,\omega\sin\theta}{2\left(\frac{1}{CR}-j\omega\right)} = \frac{(\cos\theta - j\sin\theta)}{2\left(\frac{1}{\omega CR}-j\right)} \qquad \text{...(6.174)}$$

Multiplying Eq. (6.172) by $(s-j\omega)$ and putting $s = +j\omega$, we get

$$K_3 = \frac{(j\omega)(j\omega\sin\theta+\omega\cos\theta)}{(j\omega+j\omega)\left(j\omega+\frac{1}{CR}\right)} - \frac{(\cos\theta + j\sin\theta)}{2\left(\frac{1}{\omega RC}+j\right)} \qquad \text{...(6.175)}$$

On inverse Laplace transformation Eq. (6.171) yields,

$$i(t) = \frac{V_0}{R}\left[K_1 e^{\frac{-t}{RC}} + K_2 e^{-j\omega t} + K_3 e^{+j\omega t}\right] \qquad \text{...(6.176)}$$

The coefficient of first term on the right hand side

$$= \frac{V_0}{R}\cdot\frac{\left(\frac{1}{C^2R^2}+\omega^2\right)\sin\theta - \omega^2\sin\theta - \frac{\omega\cos\theta}{CR}}{\frac{1}{C^2R^2}+\omega^2} \qquad \text{...(6.177)}$$

$$= \frac{V_0}{R}\sin\theta - \frac{V_0}{R^2+\frac{1}{\omega^2C^2}}\left[R\sin\theta + \frac{1}{\omega C}\cos\theta\right]$$

$$= \frac{V_0}{R} \sin \theta - \frac{V_0}{\sqrt{R^2 + \frac{1}{\omega^2 C^2}}} \cos (q - \tan^{-1} wCR) \quad ...(6.178)$$

The sum of the second and third terms

$$= \frac{V_0}{2R}\left[\frac{e^{-j\theta t}\, e^{-j\omega t}}{\left(\frac{1}{\omega CR} - j\right)} + \frac{e^{j\theta t}\, e^{j\omega t}}{\left(\frac{1}{\omega CR} - j\right)}\right]$$

$$= \frac{V_0}{2R}\left[\frac{\frac{1}{\omega CR}\left\{e^{-j(\omega t + \theta)} + e^{+j(\omega t + \theta)}\right\} + j\left\{e^{-j(\omega t + \theta)} - e^{+j(\omega t + \theta)}\right\}}{\frac{1}{\omega^2 C^2 R^2} + 1}\right]$$

$$= \frac{V_0}{2\left(R^2 + \frac{1}{\omega^2 C^2}\right)}\left[\frac{1}{\omega C} \cdot 2 \cos (\omega t + \theta) + 2R \sin (\omega t + \theta)\right]$$

$$= \frac{V_0}{\left(R^2 + \frac{1}{\omega^2 C^2}\right)}\left[\frac{1}{\omega C} \cos (\omega t + \theta) + R \sin (\omega t + \theta)\right]$$

$$= \frac{V_0}{\sqrt{\left(R^2 + \frac{1}{\omega^2 C^2}\right)}} \cos (\omega t + \theta - \tan^{-1} \omega CR) \quad ...(6.179)$$

Hence complete solution is,

$$i(t) = \left[\frac{V_0}{R} \sin \theta - \frac{V_0}{\sqrt{R^2 + \frac{1}{\omega^2 C^2}}} \cos (\theta - \tan^{-1} \omega CR)\right] e^{-\frac{t}{Rt}}$$

$$+ \frac{V_0}{\sqrt{R^2 + \frac{1}{\omega^2 C^2}}} \cos (\omega t + \theta - \tan^{-1} \omega RC) \quad ...(6.180)$$

This is the same solution as given by Eqs. (5.141) and (5.144) obtained through classical method.

6.14. Response of Series R-L-C Circuit to Step Sinusoidal Voltage

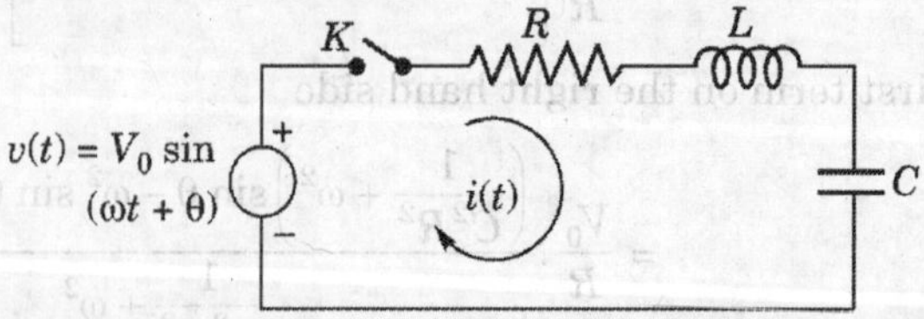

Fig. 6.15. Series *R-L-C* circuit with step sinusoidal voltage.

Sinusoidal voltage $v(t) = V_0 \sin (\omega t + \theta)$ is applied to series *R-L-C* circuit at time $t = 0$ by closing the switch *K*. V_0, ω and θ are constants. It is required to find the complete particular solution for current $i(t)$ using Laplace transformation.

Application of Kirchhoff's voltage law to the series R-L-C circuit of Fig. 6.15 yields,

$$L\frac{di}{dt} + Ri + \frac{1}{C}\int_{-\infty}^{0} idt + \frac{1}{C}\int_{0}^{t} idt = V_0 \sin(\omega t + \theta) \qquad ...(6.181)$$

On Laplace transformation Eq. (6.181) yields,

$$L[Cs.I(s) - i(0+)] + ... + RI(s) + \frac{1}{C}\cdot\frac{I(s)}{s} = V_0\frac{s\sin\theta + \omega\cos\theta}{s^2+\omega^2} \qquad ...(6.182)$$

Initial conditions. There is zero current through the inductor before closing the switch K. Hence the current remains zero at $t = 0+$ after closing the switch K, *i.e.* $i(0+) = 0$. Also there is no initial charge across the capacitor C at $t = 0-$. Hence charge remains zero at time $t = 0+$, *i.e.* $q(0+) = 0$.

Substituting these initial conditions in Eq. (6.182), we get

$$I(s)\left[Ls + R + \frac{1}{Cs}\right] = \frac{v_0[s\sin\theta + \omega\cos\theta]}{s^2+\omega^2} \qquad ...(6.183)$$

or

$$I(s) = \frac{V_0 s[s\sin\theta + \omega\cos\theta]}{L(s^2+\omega^2)\left(s^2 + \frac{R}{L}s + \frac{1}{LC}\right)} \qquad ...(6.184)$$

$$= \frac{V_0}{L}\cdot\frac{s(s\sin\theta + \omega\cos\theta)}{(s+j\omega)(s-j\omega)(s-s_1)(s-s_2)} \qquad ...(6.185)$$

where s_1, s_2 are the roots of the quadratic equation :

$$\left(s^2 + \frac{R}{L}C + \frac{1}{LC} = 0\right) \qquad ...(6.186)$$

Thus

$$s_1, s_2 = -\frac{R/L}{2} \pm \frac{1}{2}\sqrt{\frac{R^2}{L^2} - \frac{4}{LC}} \qquad ...(6.187)$$

Let

$$\frac{s(s\sin\theta + \omega\cos\theta)}{(s+j\omega)(s-j\omega)(s-s_1)(s-s_2)} = \frac{K_1}{s-s_1} + \frac{K_2}{s-s_2} + \frac{K_3}{s+j\omega} + \frac{K_4}{s-j\omega} \qquad ...(6.188)$$

Multiplying Eq. (6.188) by $(s - s_1)$ and putting $s = s_1$, we get

$$K_1 = \frac{s_1(s_1\sin\theta + \omega\cos\theta)}{(s_1+j\omega)(s_1-j\omega)(s_1-s_2)} \qquad ...(6.189)$$

Multiplying Eq. (6.188) by $(s - s_2)$ and putting $s = s_2$, we get

$$K_2 = \frac{s_1(s_2\sin\theta + \omega\cos\theta)}{(s_1+j\omega)(s_2-j\omega)(s_2-s_1)} \qquad ...(6.190)$$

Multiplying Eq. (6.188) by $(s + j\omega)$ and putting $s = j\omega$, we get

$$K_2 = \frac{-j\omega(-j\omega\sin\theta + \omega\cos\theta)}{(-j\omega - j\omega)(-j\omega - s_1)(-j\omega - s_2)} = \frac{\omega(\cos\theta - j\sin\theta)}{2(s_1+j\omega)(s_2+j\omega)} \qquad ...(6.191)$$

Multiplying Eq. (6.188) by $(s - j\omega)$ and putting $s = +j\omega$, we get

$$K_4 = \frac{j\omega(j\omega\sin\theta + \omega\cos\theta)}{(j\omega + j\omega)(j\omega - s_1)(j\omega + s_2)} = \frac{\omega(\cos\theta + j\sin\theta)}{2(s_1 - j\omega)(s_2 - j\omega)} \qquad ...(6.192)$$

Hence

$$i(t) = \frac{V_0}{L}\left[K_1.e^{s_1t} + K_2\,e^{s_2t}\right] + \frac{V_0}{L}\left[K_3e^{-j\omega t} + K_4e^{+j\omega t}\right] \qquad ...(6.193)$$

Sum of the terms within first bracket

$$= \frac{V_0}{L} \cdot \frac{s_1(s_1 \sin\theta + \omega\cos\theta)}{(s_1^2 + \omega^2)\sqrt{\dfrac{R^2}{L^2} - \dfrac{4}{LC}}} e^{s_1 t} - \frac{V_0}{L} \cdot \frac{s_2(s_2 \sin\theta + \omega\cos\theta)}{(s_2 + \omega^2)\sqrt{\dfrac{R^2}{L^2} - \dfrac{4}{LC}}} \quad ...(6.194)$$

This constitutes the transient response of the network.

Sum of the terms within the second bracket on the right hand side Eq. (6.193)

$$= \frac{V_0}{2L}\left[\frac{\omega e^{-j\theta} \cdot e^{-j\omega t}}{(s_1 + j\omega)(s_2 + j\omega)} + \frac{\omega^{+j\theta} e^{-j\omega t}}{(s_1 - j\omega)(s_2 - j\omega)}\right]$$

$$= \frac{V_0\omega}{2L}\left[\frac{e^{-j(\omega t + \theta)}}{(s_1 + j\omega)(s_2 + j\omega)} + \frac{e^{+j\omega(\omega t + \theta)}}{(s_1 - j\omega)(s_2 - j\omega)}\right]$$

$$= \frac{V_0\omega}{2L(s_1^2 + \omega^2)(s_2^2 + \omega^2)} [e^{-j(\omega t + \theta)}.(s_1 s_2 - \omega^2 + j\omega s_1 + j\omega s_2) + e^{j(\omega t + \theta)}.(s_1 s_2 - \omega^2 + j\omega s_1 + j\omega s_2)]$$

$$= \frac{V_0\omega}{2L(s_1^2 + \omega^2)(s_2^2 + \omega^2)} [(s_1 s_2 - \omega^2)\, 2\cos(\omega t + \theta) - (\omega s_1 + \omega s_2)\, 2\sin(\omega t + \theta)]$$

$$= \frac{V_0\omega}{L} \cdot \frac{1}{(s_1^2 + \omega^2)(s_2^2 + \omega^2)} \times \left[\left(\frac{1}{LC} - \omega^2\right)\cos(\omega t + \theta) - \left(-\frac{\omega R}{L}\right)\sin(\omega t + \theta\right]$$

$$= \frac{V_0\omega}{L} \cdot \frac{\left[\dfrac{\omega R}{L}\sin(\omega t + \theta) - \left(\omega^2 - \dfrac{1}{LC}\right)\cos(\omega t + \theta)\right]}{(s_1^2 + \omega^2)(s_2^2 + \omega^2)}$$

$$= \frac{V_0\omega}{L} \cdot \frac{1}{(s_1^2 + \omega^2)(s_2^2 + \omega^2)} \sin\left[\omega t + \theta - \tan^{-1}\left(\frac{\omega L \dfrac{-1}{\omega C}}{R}\right)\right] \times \frac{\omega}{L}\sqrt{R^2 + \left(\omega L - \frac{1}{\omega C}\right)^2}$$

$$= \frac{V_0\omega^2}{L} \cdot \frac{1}{(s_1^2 + \omega^2)(s_2^2 + \omega^2)} \sin\left[\omega t + \theta - \tan^{-1}\left(\frac{\omega L \dfrac{-1}{\omega C}}{R}\right)\right] \times \sqrt{R^2 + \left(\omega L - \frac{1}{\omega C}\right)^2}$$

$$= \frac{V_0}{\sqrt{R^2 + \left(\omega L - \dfrac{1}{\omega C}\right)^2}} \sin\left[\omega t + \theta - \tan^{-1}\left(\frac{\omega L - \dfrac{1}{\omega C}}{R}\right)\right] \quad ...(6.195)$$

This constitutes the steady-state response of the series *R-L-C* network to a step sinusoidal voltage.

Example 6.21. *A sinusoidal voltage 25 sin 10 t is applied at time t = 0 to a series R-L circuit comprising resistor R = 5 Ω and inductor L = 1 henry. By the method of Laplace transformation, find current i(t). Assume zero current through inductor before application of voltage.*

Solution. Application of Kirchhoff's voltage law to the series circuit yields,

$$L\frac{di}{dt} + Ri = 25 \sin 10t \qquad \text{...(1)}$$

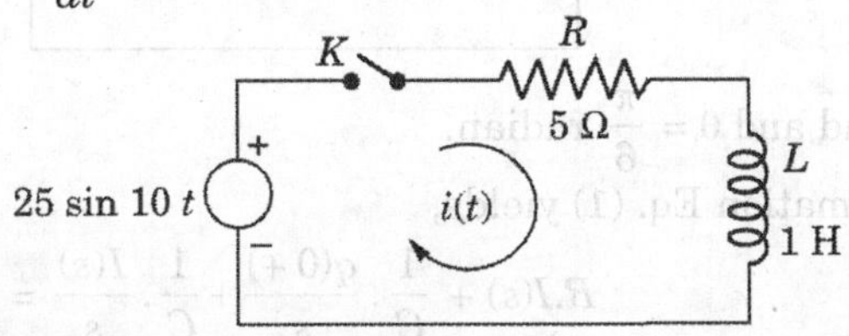

On Laplace transformation Eq. (1) yields,

$$L[s.I(s) - i(0+)] - R.I(s) = 25\frac{10}{s^2+100} \qquad \text{...(2)}$$

Initial condition. There is no current through the inductor before closing the switch *K*, *i.e.* $i(0-) = 0$. Hence presence of inductor *L* causes $i(0+) = 0$.

Substituting $i(0+) = 0$ in Eq. (2), we get

$$I(s)(Ls + R) = \frac{250}{s^2+100} \qquad \text{...(3)}$$

or

$$I(s) = \frac{250}{(s+5)(s^2+100)} \qquad \text{...(4)}$$

$$= \frac{250}{(s+5)(s+j10)(s-j10)} \qquad \text{...(5)}$$

On inverse Laplace transformation Eq. (5) yields,

$$i(t) = 250\left[\frac{e^{-5t}}{(j10-5)(-j10-5)} + \frac{e^{-j10t}}{(5-j10)(-j10-j10)} + \frac{e^{+j10t}}{(5+j10)(j10+j10)}\right]$$

$$= 250\left[\frac{e^{-5t}}{125} + \frac{e^{-j10t}}{-100-(j+2)} + \frac{e^{+j10t}}{100(j-2)}\right]$$

$$= 2e^{-5t} - \frac{1}{2}(2-j)\,e^{-j10t} - \frac{1}{2}(2+j)e^{j10t}$$

$$= 2e^{-5t} - \frac{1}{2}j(e^{j10t} - e^{-j10t}) - (e^{j10t} + e^{-j10t})$$

$$= 2e^{-5t} + \sin 10t\ 2\cos 10t$$

$$= 2e^{-5t} + \sqrt{5}\sin(10t - \tan^{-1} 2) \quad \textbf{Ans.}$$

Example 6.22. *In the circuit of Fig. 6.14, the applied voltage is* $v(t) = 10 \sin\left[\tan t + \frac{\pi}{6}\right]$, *R = 1 Ω and K = 1 farad. Using Laplace transformation, find complete particular solution for current i(t). Switch K is closed at time t = 0. Assume zero charge across the capacitor before switching.*

Solution. Application of Kirchhoff's voltage law to circuit yields,

$$Ri + \frac{1}{C}\int_{-\infty}^{0} idt + \int_{0}^{t} idt = 10 \sin (\omega t + \theta) \quad ...(1)$$

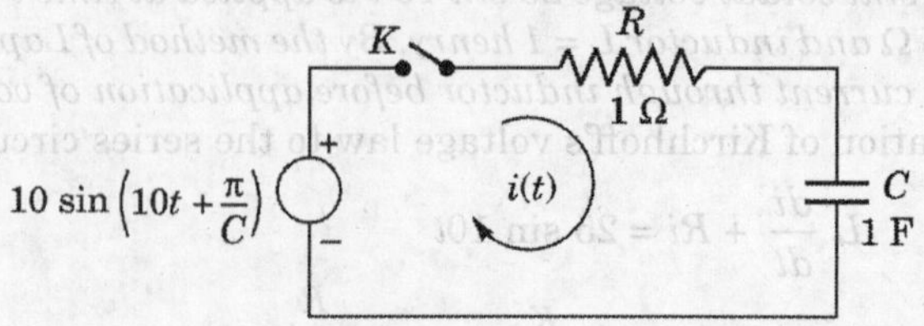

where ω = 10 radians/second and $\theta = \frac{\pi}{6}$ radian.

On Laplace transformation Eq. (1) yields,

$$R.I(s) + \frac{1}{C}.\frac{q(0+)}{s} + \frac{1}{C}.\frac{I(s)}{s} = 10 . \frac{s \sin\theta + \omega\cos\theta}{s^2+\omega^2} \quad ...(2)$$

Initial condition. There is no charge across the capacitor C at time $t = 0$. There cannot be any instantaneous change in charge across a capacitor. Hence $q(0+) = 0$.

Substituting this initial condition in Eq. (2), we get

$$I(s)\left[R + \frac{1}{Cs}\right] = 10\,\frac{s\sin\theta + \omega\cos\theta}{s^2+\omega^2} \quad ...(3)$$

or

$$I(s) = \frac{10\,(s\sin\theta + \omega\cos\theta)}{(s^2+\omega^2)\left(R + \frac{1}{Cs}\right)} \quad ...(4)$$

$$= \frac{10}{R}.\frac{s(s\sin\theta + 10\cos\theta)}{(s+j\omega)(s-j\omega)\left(s + \frac{1}{CR}\right)}$$

or

$$I(s) = \frac{10}{1}.\frac{s(s\sin\theta + 10\cos\theta)}{(s+j\omega)(s-j\omega)(s+1)} \quad ...(5)$$

Let, $$\frac{s(s\sin\theta + 10\cos\theta)}{(s+1)(s+j10)(s-j10)} = \frac{K_1}{s+1} + \frac{K_2}{s+j10} + \frac{K_3}{s-j10} \quad ...(6)$$

Multiplying Eq. (6) by $(s + 1)$ and putting $s = -1$, we get

$$K_1 = \frac{(-1)(-\sin\theta + 10\cos\theta)}{(-1+j10)(-1-j10)} = \frac{\sin\theta - 10\cos\theta}{(1+j10)(1-j10)}$$

$$= \frac{\frac{1}{2} - 10\sqrt{3/2}}{101} = \frac{1-10\sqrt{3}}{202} \quad ...(7)$$

Multiplying Eq. (6) by $(s + j10)$ and putting $s = -j10$, we get

$$K_2 = \frac{-j10(-j10\sin\theta + 10\cos\theta)}{(-j10+1)(-j10-j10)} = \frac{10(\cos\theta - j\sin\theta)}{2(1-j10)}$$

$$= \frac{10}{202}(1+j10)(\cos\theta - j\sin\theta) = \frac{10}{202}(1+j10)e^{-j\theta} \quad ...(8)$$

Multiplying Eq. (6) by $(s - j10)$ and putting $s = +j10$, we get

$$K_2 = \frac{j10(j10\sin\theta + 10\cos\theta)}{(j10+1)(j10+j10)} = \frac{10(\cos\theta + j\sin\theta)}{2(1+j10)}$$

$$= \frac{10}{202}(1-j10)e^{+j\theta} \quad ...(9)$$

On inverse Laplace transformation Eq. (5) yields,

$$i(t) = [K_1e^{-t} + K_2e^{-j10t} + K_3e^{j10t}] \quad ...(10)$$

$$= \frac{10}{202}(1-10\sqrt{3})e^{-t} + \frac{100}{202}(1+j10)e^{-j(10t+\theta)} + \frac{100}{202}(1-j10)e^{+j(10t+\theta)} \quad ...(11)$$

The last two terms on the right hand side Eq. (11),

$$= \frac{100}{202}[\{e^{j(10t+\theta)} + e^{-j(10t+\theta)}\} - j10\{e^{j(10t+\theta)} - e^{-j(10t+\theta)}\}]$$

$$= \frac{100}{202}[2\cos(10t+\theta) - j10(2j)\sin(10t+\theta)]$$

$$= \frac{200}{202}[\cos(10t+\theta) + 10\sin(10t+\theta)]$$

$$= \frac{100}{\sqrt{101}}\cos(10t+\theta-\tan^{-1}10) \quad ...(12)$$

$$= \frac{100}{\sqrt{101}}\cos(10t + 30^\circ - 84^\circ\,18') = \frac{100}{\sqrt{101}}\cos(10t - 54^\circ\,18')$$

Hence, $i(t) = \frac{5}{101}(1-10\sqrt{3})e^{-t} + \frac{100}{\sqrt{101}}\cos(10t - 54^\circ\,18')$. **Ans.**

EXERCISES 6

6.1. In the circuit of Fig. 6.5, $V_0 = 4$ volts, $R = 2\ \Omega$ and $L = 0.5$ henry. Switch K is closed at time $t = 0$. Find the total particular solution for current $i(t)$ through the network. Assume the circuit to be unenergised before closing the switch K. **[Ans.** $i(t) = 2(1 - e^{-4t})$**]**

6.2. In the circuit of Fig. 6.6, $V_0 = 6$ volts, $R = 10\ \Omega$ and $C = 0.05$ farad. Switch K is closed at time $t = 0$. Find the total particular solution for current $i(t)$ through the network after switching. Assume zero charge across the capacitor before switching. **[Ans.** $i(t) = 0.6e^{-2t}$**]**

6.3. In the circuit of Fig. 6.7, $V_0 = 4$ volts, $L = 2$ H, $R = 9\ \Omega$ and $C = \frac{1}{7}$ Farad. Switch K is closed at time $t = 0$. Obtain the particular solution for current $i(t)$ through the series circuit. Assume zero current through the inductor L and zero charge across the capacitor C before switching.

$$\left[\textbf{Ans. } i(t) = \frac{4}{5}\left(e^{-t} - e^{\frac{-7t}{2}}\right)\right]$$

6.4. A step d.c. voltage of 4 volts is applied to a series R-L-C circuit consisting of a resistor $R = 4\ \Omega$, inductor $L = 4$ H and capacitor $C = 1$ Farad. Obtain the particular solution for the current $i(t)$ through the circuit. Assume zero current through the inductor L and zero charge across the capacitor C before switching.

$$\left[\textbf{Ans. } i(t) = t\,e^{\frac{-t}{2}}\right]$$

6.5. Solve Example 5.1 using Laplace transformation method.

6.6. A step d.c. current of 10 amp. is applied at time $t = 0$ to a parallel R-L-C circuit consisting of a resistor $R = 0.2\ \Omega$, inductor $L = \frac{1}{6}$ H and capacitor $C = 1$ farad. Obtain the particular solution for voltage $v(t)$ across the circuit. Assume zero initial charge across capacitor C and zero initial current through inductor L. **[Ans.** $v(t) = 10(e^{-2t} - e^{-3t})$**]**

6.7. A step d.c. current of 1 amp. is applied at time $t = 0$ to a parallel R-L-C circuit comprising a resistor $R = 2.5\ \Omega$ inductor $L = 1$ H and capacitor $C = 0.1$ farad. Obtain the complete particular solution for voltage $v(t)$ across the circuit. Assume zero initial charge across capacitor C and zero initial current through the inductor L before application of current. [**Ans.** $v(t) = 200\, t\, e^{-10t}$]

6.8. In the series R-L-C circuit of Fig. 6.7, $v_0 = 8$ volts, $L = 1$ henry, $R = 3\ \Omega$ and $C = 0.2$ farad. Switch K is closed at time $t = 0$. Obtain the complete particular solution for current $i(t)$ through the series circuit. Assume zero current through the inductor L and zero charge across the capacitor C before switching.

$$\left[\textbf{Ans. } i(t) = 4 \sin 2t\, e^{\frac{-3t}{2}}\right]$$

6.9. In the parallel R-L-C circuit of Fig. 6.8, $I_0 = 5$ amp., $L = 0.2$ H, $C = 2$ F and $R = 0.5$ ohm. Switch K is opened at time $t = 0$. Obtain the complete particular solution for the voltage $v(t)$ acros the parallel network. Assume zero current through inductor L and and zero voltage across capacitor C before switching.

$$\left[\textbf{Ans. } v(t) = \frac{5}{3} e^{\frac{-t}{2}} \sin \frac{3t}{2}\right]$$

6.10. Work Exercise 5.9 using Laplace transformation method.

6.11. Work Exercise 5.10 using Laplace transformation method.

6.12. In the given network switch K is closed at time $t = 0$. Capacitor C is initially charged to a voltage of 10 volts. Using Laplace transformation method, solve for current $i(t)$.[**Ans.** $i(t) = +2\, e^{-t}$]

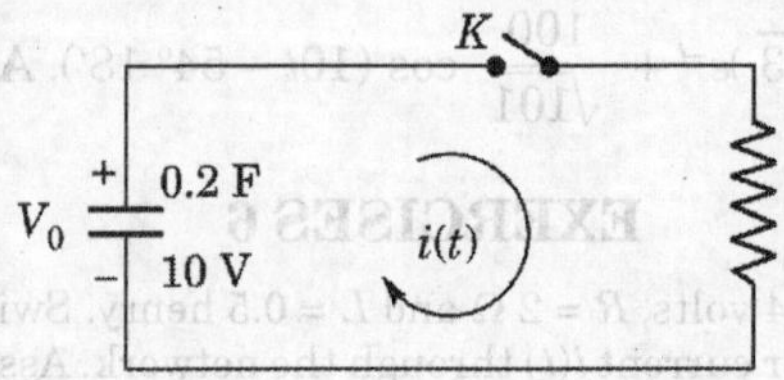

6.13. In the given network, switch K is closed at time $t = 0$. Capacitor C is initially charged to V_0 volts. Using Laplace transformation method obtain expression for current $i(t)$. If $V_0 = 10$ volts, $L = 2$ H and $C = 2$ farad, solve for $i(t)$.

$$\left[\textbf{Ans. } i(t) = V_0 \sqrt{\frac{C}{L}} \sin \sqrt{LC}\, t \,;\, i(t) = 10 \sin 2t\right]$$

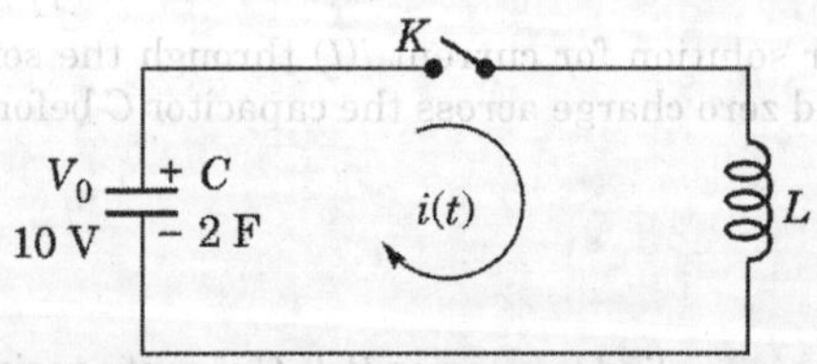

6.14. In the given circuit, the steady-state condition is reached with switch K in position 1. Later on at time $t = 0$, switch K is moved from position 1 to 2. Using Laplace transformation, obtain expression for current $i(t)$ in the L-C circuit. If $V_0 = 10$ volts, $R = 2\ \Omega$, $C = 0.1$ farad and $L = 1$ mH, solve for current $i(t)$.

$$\left[\textbf{Ans. } i(t) = \frac{V_0}{R} \cdot \cos\left(\frac{1}{\sqrt{LC}} t\right);\, i(t) = 5 \cos 100\, t\right]$$

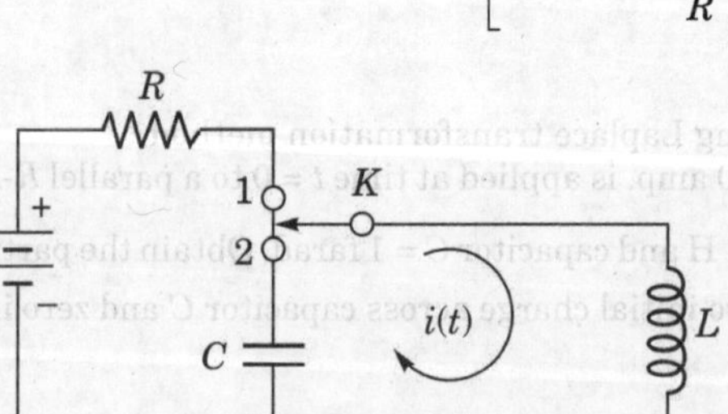

6.15. Work Example 5.6 using Laplace transformation method.

6.16. Work Example 5.7 using Laplace transformation method.

6.17. Verify the following equations by completing a partial fraction expansion :

(i) $\dfrac{-2}{s^2-1} = \dfrac{1}{s+1} - \dfrac{1}{s-1}$ (ii) $\dfrac{3s+5}{s^2+3s+2} = \dfrac{1}{s+2} + \dfrac{2}{s+1}$

(iii) $\dfrac{2s^2+6s+2}{s^3+3s^2+2s} = \dfrac{1}{s} + \dfrac{2}{s+1} - \dfrac{1}{s+2}$ (iv) $\dfrac{s^3+s^2+1}{s^2+s-2} = \dfrac{1}{s} + \dfrac{1}{s-1} + \dfrac{1}{s+2}$

(v) $\dfrac{2(s+2)}{s^2+1} = \dfrac{1+j2}{s+j} + \dfrac{1-j2}{s-j}$ (vi) $\dfrac{s+4}{(s+2)^2} = \dfrac{1}{s+2} + \dfrac{2}{(s+2)^2}$

(vii) $\dfrac{2s^2+3s-1}{(s+2)(s+1)^2} = \dfrac{1}{s+2} + \dfrac{1}{s+1} + \dfrac{2}{(s+1)^2}$ (viii) $\dfrac{2s^3+3s^2+5s+2}{s^2(s+1)^2} = \dfrac{1}{s} + \dfrac{2}{s^2} + \dfrac{1}{s+1} - \dfrac{2}{(s+1)^2}$

(ix) $\dfrac{3s^2-3s^2+4s+4}{s^2(s+1)^2} = \dfrac{1}{s} + \dfrac{1}{s^2} + \dfrac{1-j}{s+j2} + \dfrac{1+j}{s-j2}$

6.18. Expand the following functions by the method of partial function :

(i) $F(s) = \dfrac{2s^2+13s+3}{s(s^2+4s+3)}$ $\left[\textbf{Ans. } F(s) = \dfrac{1}{s} + \dfrac{2}{s+1} + \dfrac{3}{s+3}\right]$

(ii) $F(s) = \dfrac{2s^2-s-2}{s^2(s+1)(s+3)}$ $\left[\textbf{Ans. } F(s) = \dfrac{1}{s} - \dfrac{1}{s^2} + \dfrac{1}{s+1} - \dfrac{2}{s+2}\right]$

(iii) $F(s) = \dfrac{s^2+3s+1}{(s+1)^3}$ $\left[\textbf{Ans. } F(s) = \dfrac{1}{s+1} + \dfrac{1}{(s+1)^2} - \dfrac{1}{(s+1)^3}\right]$

(iv) $F(s) = \dfrac{2s^2+9s^2+12s+8}{s(s+2)^3}$ $\left[\textbf{Ans. } F(s) = \dfrac{1}{s} + \dfrac{1}{s+2} - \dfrac{1}{(s+1)^2} - \dfrac{2}{(s+2)^3}\right]$

6.19. Find the inverse Laplace transform of each of the following values of $F(s)$:

(i) $\dfrac{s+5}{(s+1)(s+3)}$ [**Ans.** $2e^{-t} - e^{-3t}$] (ii) $\dfrac{s}{(s+1)^2(s+2)}$ [**Ans.** $e^{-2t} + 2te^{-3t} - e^{-t}$]

(iii) $\dfrac{4s^2+3s+2}{(s+2)(s^2+1)}$ [**Ans.** $2e^{-2t} + j2\sin t$] (iv) $\dfrac{4s^2+6s+2}{(s)(s^2+2s+2)}$ [**Ans.** $2 + e^{-t}(e^{jt} + e^{-jt})$]

6.20. Solve the differential equations given in Exercise 5.7 using Laplace transformation method.

6.21. Solve the differential equation given in Exercise 5.8 using Laplace transformation method.

6.22. In the given circuit, capacitor C is initially charged to 10 volts as shown. At time $t = 0$, switch K is closed. Find the current $i(t)$ using Laplace transformation method.

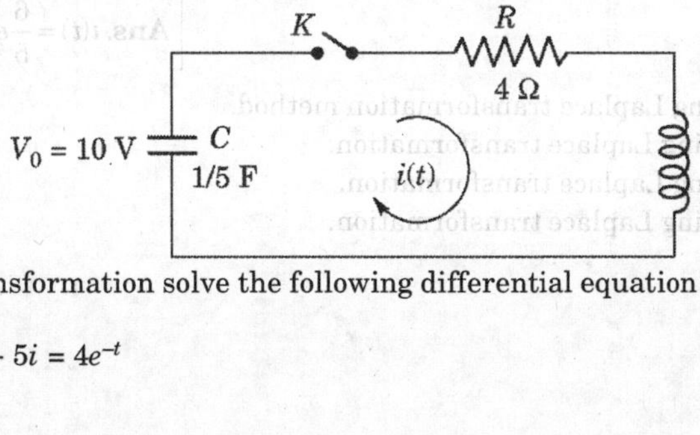

6.23. Using Laplace transformation solve the following differential equation :

$$\frac{d^2i}{dt^2} + 2\frac{di}{dt} + 5i = 4e^{-t}$$

Given that $i(0+) = 3$ and $\frac{di}{dt}(0+) = -3$. [**Ans.** $i(t) = e^{-t}(1 + 2\cos 2t)$]

6.24. Solve the following equations using Laplace transformation :

(i) $\frac{d^2i}{dt^2} - 4t = e^{3t}$ $\left[\textbf{Ans. } i(t) = \frac{1}{16}e^{-2t} - \frac{1}{16}e^{2t} + \frac{1}{4}te^{2t} + K_1 \cosh 2t + K_2 \sinh 2t\right]$

(ii) $\frac{d^2i}{dt^2} + 4\frac{di}{dt} + 3i = 5$ $\left[\textbf{Ans. } \frac{5}{3} + K_3e^{-t} + K_4e^{-3t}\right]$

6.25. Work Exercise 5.21 using Laplace transformation method.
6.26. Work Exercise 5.22 using Laplace transformation method.
6.27. Work Example 5.10 using Laplace transformation method.
6.28. Work Example 5.11 using Laplace transformation method.
6.29. Work Exercise 5.25 using Laplace transformation method.
6.30. Work Exercise 5.26 using Laplace transformation method.
6.31. An exponential voltage $4e^{-3t}$ is applied at time $t = 0$ to a series R-L-C circuit comprising $R = 4\ \Omega$, $L = 1$ H and $C = \frac{1}{3}$ farad. Obtain complete particular solution for the current $i(t)$ using Laplace transformation. Assume zero current through inductor L and zero charge across capacitor C before application of this exponential voltage.

[**Ans.** $i(t) = -e^{-t} + e^{-3t} + 6t\,e^{-3t}$]

6.32. An exponential current e^{-2t} amp. is applied at time $t = 0$ to a parallel R-L-C circuit comprising $R = \frac{1}{3}$ Ω, $L = 0.5$ henry and $C = 1$ farad. Using Laplace transformation obtain complete solution for voltage $v(t)$ across the parallel circuit. Assume zero current through the inductor L and zero charge across the capacitor C before application of current.

[**Ans.** $v(t) = -e^{-t} + e^{-2t} + 2t\,e^{-2t}$]

6.33. An exponential current $4e^{-t}$ amp. is applied at time $t = 0$ to a parallel R-L circuit comprising resistor $R = 1\ \Omega$ and inductor $L = \frac{1}{3}$ henry. Using Laplace transformation, obtain complete solution for voltage $v(t)$ across the parallel circuit. Assume zero current in the inductor L before application of current. [**Ans.** $v(t) = -2e^{-t} + 6e^{-3t}$]

6.34. An exponential current $2e^{-3t}$ is applied at time $t = 0$ to a parallel R-C circuit comprising resistor $R = \frac{1}{2}$ Ω and capacitor $C = 1$ farad. Using Laplace transformation, obtain complete particular solution for voltage $v(t)$ across the network. Assume zero charge across the capacitor before the application of current. [**Ans.** $v(t) = 2e^{-2t} - 2e^{-3t}$]

6.35. A sinusoidal voltage $12 \sin 8t$ is applied at time $t = 0$ to a series R-L circuit comprising resistor $R = 4\ \Omega$ and inductor $L = 1$ henry. By the method of Lapalce transformation, find current $i(t)$. Assume zero current through inductor before application of voltage.

$$\left[\textbf{Ans. } i(t) = \frac{6}{5}e^{-4t} + \frac{3}{\sqrt{5}}\sin(8t - \tan^{-1} 2)\right]$$

6.36. Work Example 5.8 using Laplace transformation method.
6.37. Work Exercise 5.23 using Laplace transformation.
6.38. Work Example 5.9 using Laplace transformation.
6.39. Work Exercise 5.24 using Laplace transformation.

7

Laplace Transform of Special Signal Waveforms

7.1. Introduction

So far we have studied the response of R-L-C networks to excitations or signals of simple waveforms such as step d.c., exponential and sinusoidal. Now we study the response of networks to signals of more complicated waveforms, such as (*a*) rectangular pulse (*b*) pulse of sine wave (*c*) square wave (*d*) ramp function (*e*) modified ramp function etc. Fig. 7.1 shows the above named waveforms. The signals may be either non-recurring or recurring. Thus rectangular pulse and sinewave

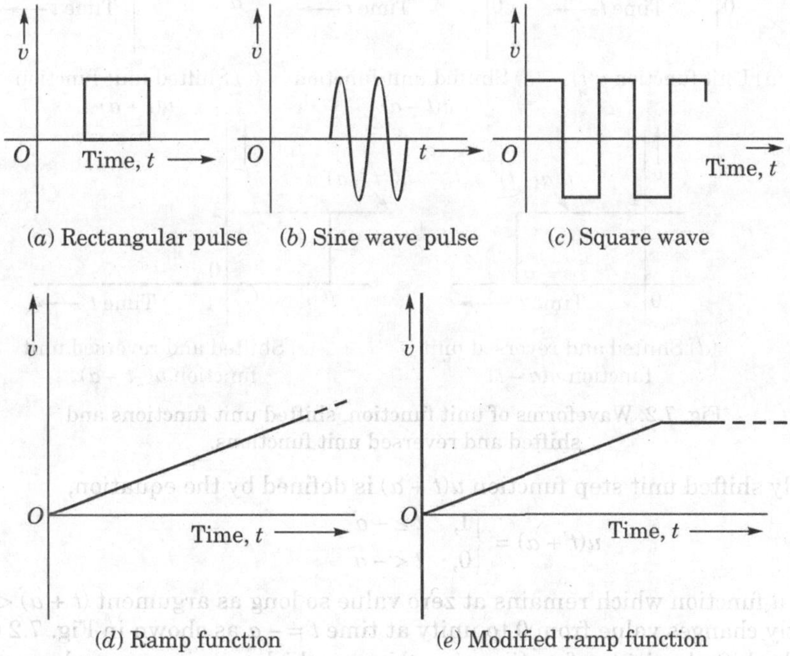

Fig. 7.1. Waveforms of a few typical excitations.

pulse constitute non-recurring signals, *i.e.* signals which occur during an interval of time and become zero for all other time. The square wave exists for all time after switching and thus constitutes a recurring signal. On the other hand, ramp and unit step functions constitute basic building blocks in terms of which other waveform may be expressed.

7.2. Response to Shifted Unit Step Function

The unit step function has already been defined earlier. It is given by the equation,

$$u(t) = \begin{cases} 1, & t \geq 0 \\ 0, & t < 0 \end{cases} \qquad \text{...(7.1)}$$

Thus the function remains at value zero until time $t = 0$ and suddenly changes its value from 0 to unity at time $t = 0$ as shown in Fig. 7.2 (*a*).

Consider next the shifted unit function defined by the equation

$$u(t-a) = \begin{cases} 1, & t \geq 0 \\ 0, & t < 0 \end{cases} \qquad \text{...(7.2)}$$

This is a function which remains at zero value until $t = a$ and abruptly changes value from 0 to unity at time $t = a$ as shown in Fig. 7.2 *(b)*. The quantity $(t - a)$ is called the *argument* of the function *u*. Thus the unit step function has unit value when the argument $(t - a)$ is positive and has zero value when the argument $(t - a)$ is negative.

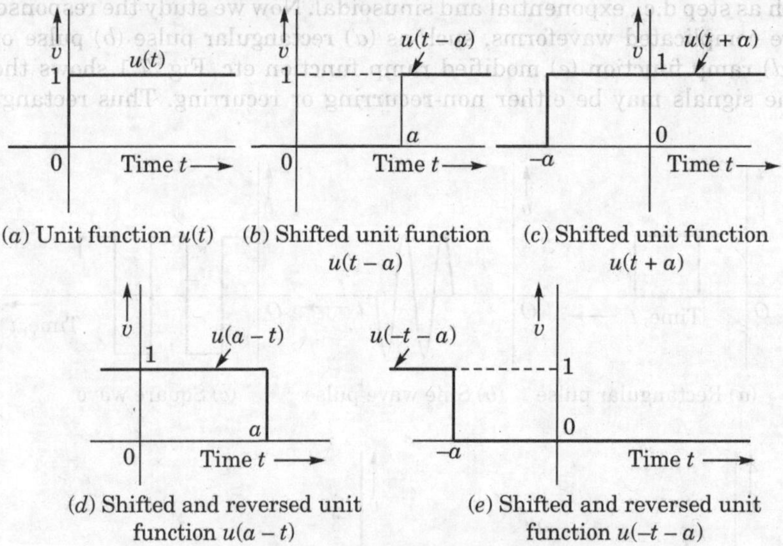

(*a*) Unit function $u(t)$ (*b*) Shifted unit function $u(t-a)$ (c) Shifted unit function $u(t+a)$

(*d*) Shifted and reversed unit function $u(a-t)$ (*e*) Shifted and reversed unit function $u(-t-a)$

Fig. 7.2. Waveforms of unit function, shifted unit functions and shifted and reversed unit functions.

Similarly shifted unit step function $u(t + a)$ is defined by the equation,

$$u(t+a) = \begin{cases} 1, & t \geq -a \\ 0, & t < -a \end{cases} \qquad \text{...(7.3)}$$

Thus is a function which remains at zero value so long as argument $(t + a) < 0$, *i.e.* time $t < -a$ and abruptly changes value from 0 to unity at time $t = -a$ as shown in Fig. 7.2 (*c*).

Similarly shifted unit step function $u(a - t)$ is one which remains zero so long as the argument $(a - t)$ is negative, *i.e.* as long as the argument $(a - t) < 0$ or $t > a$ and abruptly becomes unit and remains so for positive values of argument $(a - t)$, *i.e.* for $t < a$. This function is given by equation,

$$u(a-t) = \begin{cases} 1, & t \leq a \\ 0, & t > a \end{cases} \qquad \text{...(7.4)}$$

Function $u(a - t)$ is shown in Fig. 7.2 (*d*).

Finally the shifted unit step function $u(-t - a)$ is one which remains zero as long as the argument $(-t - a)$ is negative, *i.e.* as long as $-a - t < 0$ or $t > -a$ and abruptly becomes unit at $t = -a$ and remains so for $t < -a$. This function is given by equation,

$$u(-t-a) = \begin{cases} 1, & t \le -a \\ 0, & t > -a \end{cases} \qquad ...(7.5)$$

Function $u(-t-a)$ is shown in Fig. 7.2 (*e*).

Laplace transform of unit step functions. Now we find the Laplace transform of various unit step functions described above.

(*i*) $u(t)$ $$\mathcal{L}\,u(t) = \int_0^\infty 1 \,.\, e^{-st}\, dt = \left[\frac{-e^{-st}}{s}\right]_0^\infty = \frac{1}{s}$$

Thus $$\mathcal{L}\,u(t) = \frac{1}{s} \qquad ...(7.6)$$

(*ii*) $u(t-a)$ $$\mathcal{L}\,u(t-a) = \int_0^\infty 1 \,.\, e^{-st}\, dt = \left[\frac{-e^{-st}}{s}\right]_0^\infty = e^{-as}\,.\left(\frac{1}{s}\right)$$

Thus $$\mathcal{L}\,u(t-a) = e^{-as}\left(\frac{1}{s}\right) \qquad ...(7.7)$$

(*iii*) $u(t+a)$ $$\mathcal{L}\,u(t+a) = \int_{-a}^\infty 1 \,.\, e^{-st}\, dt = \left[\frac{-e^{-st}}{s}\right]_{-a}^\infty = e^{as}\left(\frac{1}{s}\right)$$

Thus $$\mathcal{L}\,u(t+a) = e^{as}\,.\left(\frac{1}{s}\right) \qquad ...(7.8)$$

Comparative study of Eqs. (7.6) and (7.7) shows that shifting of unit step function from one beginning at time $t = 0$ that beginning at time $t = a$ results in multiplying the Laplace transform by e^{-as}. Alternatively we may state that multiplication of function$1/s$ by e^{-as} results is shifting the inverse Laplace transform from $u(t)$, *i.e.* one beginning at $t = 0$ to $u(t-a)$, *i.e.* one beginning at $t = a$.

7.3. Shifting Theorem

Let any time function $f(t)$ be delayed by time a. Then this time function $f(t)$ so delayed may be represented by $f(t-a).u(t-a)$.

We now proceed to find the Laplace transform of this function $f(t-a).u(t-a)$.

Let $$F(s) = \int_0^\infty f(t)e^{-st}\, dt \qquad ...(7.9)$$

Then $F(s)$ is also given by $$F(s) = \int_0^\infty f(t')e^{-st'}\, dt' \qquad ...(7.10)$$

where t' is any new variable.

Let $t' = t - a$. Then Eq. (7.10) yields,

$$F(s) = \int_0^\infty f(t-a)\, e^{-s(t-a)}\, d(t-a) = \int_a^\infty f(t-a)\, e^{-s(t-a)}\, dt \qquad ...(7.11)$$

$$= e^{as} \int_a^\infty f(t-a)\, e^{-st}\, dt \qquad ...(7.12)$$

Now in Eq. (7.12) the lower limit of integration may be changed from a to 0 if $f(t-a)$ is multiplied by $u(t-a)$.

Thus $$F(s) = e^{as} \int_0^\infty f(t-a)\,.u(t-a)e^{-st}\, dt \qquad ...(7.13)$$

$$= e^{as}\, \mathcal{L}\, [f(t-a).u(t-a)] \qquad ...(7.14)$$

or $$\mathcal{L}\, [f(t-a).u(t-a)] = e^{-as}\, \mathcal{L}f(t) \qquad ...(7.15)$$

Conversely, $$\mathcal{L}^{-1}[e^{-as}F(s)] = f(t-a).u(t-a) \qquad ...(7.16)$$

Eq. (7.15) states that Laplace transform of any function delayed by time interval a is e^{-as} times the transform of the function. This result is called the *Real translation theorem* or *the shifting theorem*.

Translation in the s-domain. Let $f(t)$ be any function of time t and let its Laplace transform be $F(s)$. Now if s is translated to $(s-a)$, the Laplace transform becomes $F(s-a)$. It is required to find the inverse Laplace transform of this function.

To do so we write the Laplace transform for a new variable s' equal to $(s-a)$.

Thus $$f(t) = \mathcal{L}^{-1}\, F(s') \qquad ...(7.16\ a)$$

or $$F(s') = \int_0^\infty f(t)\, e^{-s't}\, dt \qquad ...(7.16\ b)$$

$$= \int_0^\infty f(t).e^{-(s-a)t}\, dt \qquad ...(7.16\ c)$$

$$= \int_0^\infty f(t).e^{-(s-a)t}\, dt \qquad ...(7.16\ d)$$

$$= \int_0^\infty f(t)e^{-st}\, e^{-st}\, dt \qquad ...(7.16\ e)$$

where $f'(t) = f(t).\, e^{at}$ ...(7.16 *f*)

Eq. (7.16 *e*) may be put as,

$$F(s') = \mathcal{L}\, f'(t) \qquad ...(7.16\ g)$$

$$= \mathcal{L}\, f(t)e^{at} \qquad ...(7.16\ h)$$

Thus, we get $$\mathcal{L}\, f(t)\, e^{at} = F(s-a) \qquad ...(7.16\ i)$$

or $$f(t)\, e^{at} = \mathcal{L}^{-1}\, F(s-a) \qquad ...(7.16\ j)$$

7.4. Pulse as a Combination of Two Unit Step Functions

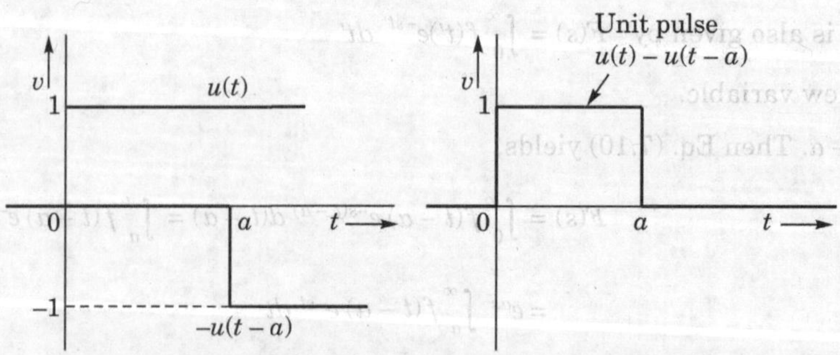

(*a*) Two unit step functions (*b*) Unit pulse

Fig. 7.3. Summation of two unit step functions to produce a unit pulse of duration *a*.

Combinations of unit step functions with suitable shifting may be made to represent various other signals. Thus consider a function $f(t)$ as the sum of two unit step functions $u(t)$ and $-u(t-a)$ as given by the following equation :

$$f(t) = u(t) - u(t-a) \quad ...(7.17)$$

Fig. 7.3 (a) shows these two functions while Fig. 7.3 (b) shows the sum. The resultant function has a unit value from $t = 0$ to $t = a$ and has zero value for all other value of time t. This constitutes a pulse of duration a and magnitude unity and beginning at time $t = 0$.

In general, addition of two step functions $V_0u(t-a)$ and $-V_0u(t-b)$ results in pulse of magnitude V_0, of duration $(b-a)$ and beginning at time $t = a$.

7.5. Pulse Response of a Series R-L Circuit

A driving pulse of width a and magnitude V_0 is applied to a series R-L circuit at $t = 0$ by closing the switch K (circuit of Fig. 7.4).

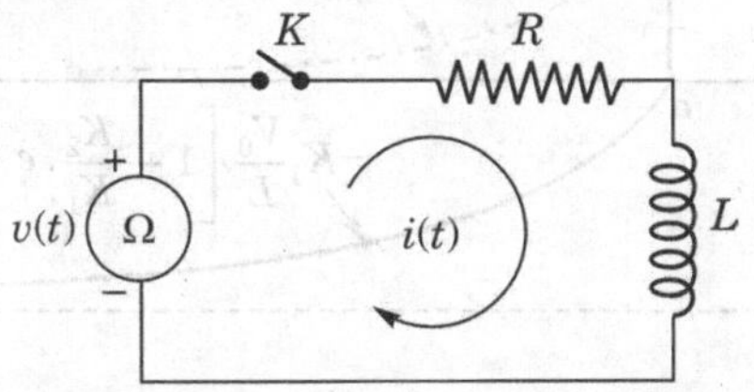

Fig. 7.4. Series R-L circuit with driving pulse voltage.

The driving pulse is then given by,

$$v(t) = V_0[u(t) - u(t-a)] \quad ...(7.18)$$

Using Eq. (7.7), the Laplace transform of $v(t)$ is given by,

$$V(s) = \frac{V_0}{s}[1 - e^{-as}] \quad ...(7.19)$$

Application of Kirchhoff's voltage law to the given circuit yields,

$$L\frac{di}{dt} + Ri = v(t) \quad ...(7.20)$$

On Laplace transformation, we get,

$$L[sI(s) - i(0+)] + R.I(s) = \frac{V_0}{s}[1 - e^{-as}] \quad ...(7.21)$$

The initial current $i(0+) = 0$. Substituting this value of $i(0+)$ in Eq. (7.21), we get

$$I(s)[Ls + R] = \frac{V_0}{s}[1 - e^{-as}] \quad ...(7.22)$$

Hence

$$I(s) = \frac{V_0[1 - e^{-as}]}{s(Ls + R)} \quad ...(7.23)$$

$$= (1 - e^{-as})\frac{V_0}{L}\left[\frac{K_1}{s} + \frac{K_2}{s + R/L}\right] \quad ...(7.24)$$

$$= \frac{V_0}{L}\left[\frac{K_1}{s} + \frac{K_2}{s + R/L} - \frac{K_1e^{-as}}{s} - \frac{K_2e^{-as}}{s + R/L}\right] \quad ...(7.25)$$

On inverse Laplace transformation,

$$i(t) = \frac{V_0}{L}\left[K_1.u(t) + K_2.e^{-\frac{Rt}{L}}.u(t) - K_1.u(t-a) - K_2.u(t-a).e^{\frac{-R(t-a)}{L}} \right] \quad ...(7.26)$$

$$= \frac{K_1V_0}{L}\left[u(t)\left(1+\frac{K_2}{K_1}e^{-\frac{Rt}{L}}\right) - u(t-a)\left(3+\frac{K_3}{K_1}.e^{-\frac{R(t-a)}{L}}\right)\right] \quad ...(7.27)$$

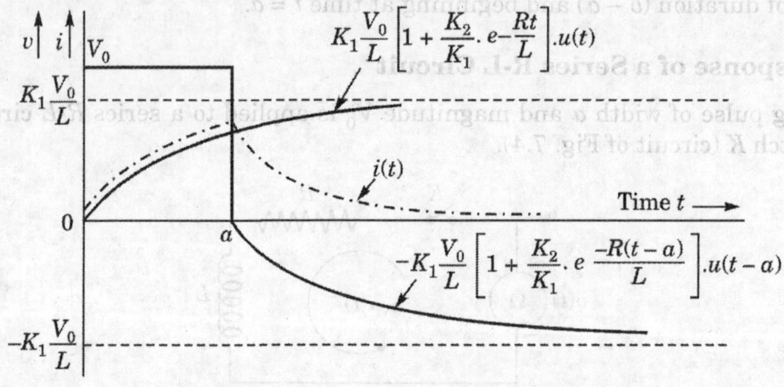

Fig. 7.5. Response of series R-L circuit to driving pulse voltage.

The third and the fourth terms of Eq. (7.26) are shifted in time by a and are opposite in sign with the first and the second terms.

Fig. 7.5 gives the waveforms of the driving pulse voltage, the resulting two parts of the response and the overall response.

7.6. Pulse Response of Series R-C Circuit

Fig. 7.6 shows a series R-C circuit to which a driving pulse voltage of width a and magnitude V_0 is applied at time $t = 0$ by closing the switch K.

The driving voltage is given by,

$$v(t) = V_0[u(t) - u(t-a)] \quad ...(7.28)$$

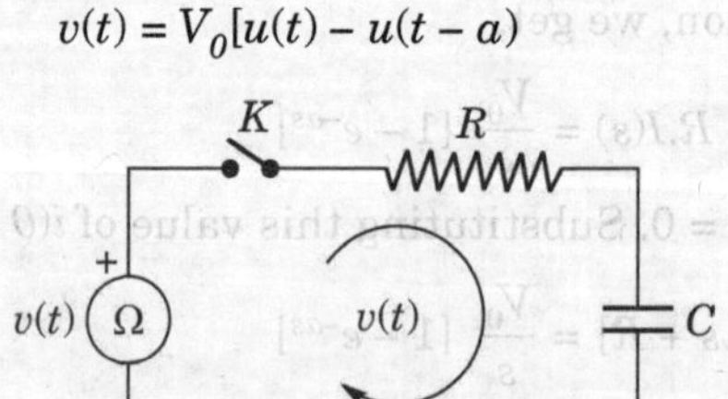

Fig. 7.6. Series R-C circuit with driving pulse voltage.

Application of Kirchhoff's voltage law to the circuit of Fig. 7.6 yields,

$$Ri + \frac{1}{C}\int_{-\infty}^{t} idt = v(t) \quad ...(7.29)$$

On Laplace transformation Eq. (7.29) yields,

$$RI(s) + \frac{1}{C}\frac{q(0+)}{s} + \frac{1}{C}\cdot\frac{I(s)}{s} = \frac{V_0}{s}[1 - e^{-as}] \quad ...(7.30)$$

But $q(0+) = 0$. Hence Eq. (7.30) yields,

$$I(s)\left[R + \frac{1}{Cs}\right] = \frac{V_0}{s}[1 - e^{-as}] \quad ...(7.31)$$

or

$$I(s) = \frac{V_0}{s}\cdot\frac{1 - e^{-as}}{R + \frac{1}{Cs}} \quad ...(7.32)$$

or

$$I(s) = \frac{V_0}{R}\cdot\frac{1 - e^{-as}}{s + \frac{1}{RC}} \quad ...(7.33)$$

$$= \frac{V_0}{R}\left[\frac{1}{s + \frac{1}{RC}} - \frac{e^{-as}}{s + \frac{1}{RC}}\right] \quad ...(7.34)$$

On inverse Laplace transformation, we get

$$i(t) = \mathcal{L}^{-1} I(s) = \frac{V_0}{R}\left[u(t)\,.\,e^{-\frac{1}{RC}} - u(t-a)\,.\,e^{-\frac{(t-a)}{RC}}\right] \quad ...(7.35)$$

Here the second term in Eq. (7.35) is shifted in time by a and is opposite in sign with the first term.

Fig. 7.7 shows the waveforms of the driving pulse voltage, the resulting two parts of the response and the resultant response.

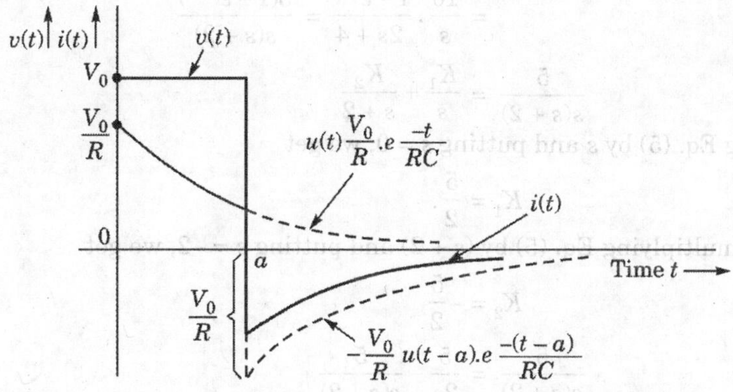

Fig. 7.7. Response of series R-C circuit to driving pulse voltage.

7.7. Scaling Theorem

This is a theorem that relates scale changes, *i.e.* multiplication by a positive constant in the s or frequency domain to the corresponding changes in scale in the t or time domain.

In a time-variant function $f(t)$, let scale change be introduced to form a new function $f(t/t_0)$, where t_0 is a positive constant.

$$\text{Then } \mathcal{L}[f(t/t_0)] = \int_0^\infty f(t/t_0)e^{-st}\,dt \quad ...(7.36)$$

$$= t_0 \int_0^{\infty} f(t/t_0)\, e^{-(t_0 s)t/t_0} d(t/t_0) \qquad ...(7.37)$$

$$= t_0 \int_0^{\infty} f(T)\, e^{-t_0 sT}\, dT \qquad ...(7.38)$$

where $T = t/t_0$

Eq. (7.37) may be put as,

$$\mathcal{L}\,[f(t/t_0)] = t_0 F(t_0 s) \qquad ...(7.40)$$

On inverse Laplace transformation Eq. (7.40) yields,

$$\mathcal{L}^{-1}\, F(t_0 s) = \frac{f(t/t_0)}{t_0} \qquad ...(7.41)$$

Example 7.1. *A pulse voltage of width a and magnitude 10 volts is applied at time t = 0 to series R-L circuit consisting of resistance R = 4 Ω and inductor L = 2 henrys. Find the current i(t). Assume zero current through the inductor L before application of voltage pulse.*

Solution. Application of Kirchhoff's voltage law to the circuit yields,

$$L\frac{di}{dt} + Ri = 10[u(t) - u(t-a)] \qquad ...(1)$$

On Laplace transformation, we get

$$L[s.I(s) - i(0+)] + R\,.\,I(s) = \frac{10}{s}\,[1 - e^{-as}] \qquad ...(2)$$

But $i(0+) = 0$. Hence Eq. (2) yields,

$$I(s) = \frac{10}{s}\cdot\frac{1-e^{-as}}{Ls+R} \qquad ...(3)$$

$$= \frac{10}{s}\cdot\frac{1-e^{-as}}{2s+4} = \frac{5(1-e^{-as})}{s(s+2)} \qquad ...(4)$$

Let $$\frac{5}{s(s+2)} = \frac{K_1}{s} + \frac{K_2}{s+2} \qquad ...(5)$$

Multiplying Eq. (5) by s and putting $s = 0$, we get

$$K_1 = \frac{5}{2}.$$

Similarly, multiplying Eq. (5) by $(s+2)$ and putting $s = -2$, we get

$$K_2 = -\frac{5}{2}$$

Hence $$\frac{5}{s(s+2)} = \frac{5}{2s} - \frac{5}{s(s+2)}$$

Hence Eq. (4), becomes

$$I(s) = \frac{5}{2}\left[\frac{1}{s} - \frac{1}{s+2} - \frac{e^{-as}}{s} + \frac{e^{-as}}{s+2}\right] \qquad ...(6)$$

On inverse Laplace transformation, we get

$$i(t) = \mathcal{L}^{-1}\, I(s) = \frac{5}{2}\,[u(t) - u(t)\,.\,e^{-2t} - u(t-a) + u(t-a)e^{-2(t-a)}].$$

Ans.

Example 7.2. A *voltage pulse of width b and magnitude 8 volts is applied at time t = 0 to a series R-C circuit comprising a resistor R = 1 Ω and capacitor C = $\frac{1}{4}$ farad. Find the current i(t). Assume zero charge across the capacitor C before application of voltage pulse.*

Solution. Application of Kirchhoff's voltage law to the circuit yields,

$$Ri + \frac{1}{C}\int_{-\infty}^{t} idt = 8[u(t) - u(t-b)] \quad ...(1)$$

On Laplace transformation Eq. (1) yields,

$$R.I(s) + \frac{1}{C}\cdot\frac{q(0+)}{s} + \frac{1}{C}\cdot\frac{I(s)}{s} = \frac{8}{s}[1 - e^{-bs}] \quad ...(2)$$

But $q(0+) = 0$. Hence Eq. (2) yields,

$$I(s) = \frac{8(1-e^{-bs})}{s\left(R + \frac{1}{Cs}\right)} \quad ...(3)$$

$$= \frac{8}{Rs + \frac{1}{C}}(1 - e^{-bs}) = \frac{8}{s+4}(1 - e^{-bs}) \quad ...(4)$$

$$= \frac{8}{s+4} - \frac{8e^{-bs}}{s+4} \quad ...(5)$$

On inverse Laplace transformation Eq. (5) yields,

$$i(t) = 8[u(t) \,.\, e^{-4t} - u(t-b) \,.\, e^{-4(t-b)}]. \quad \textbf{Ans.}$$

Example 7.3. *Let the Laplace transform equation for current in a network be,*

$$I(s) = \frac{2}{s(s+2)}$$

Find the corresponding current i(t) in the time domain. Using scaling theorem, find the current i(t) for

$$I(s) = \frac{2}{(3s)(3s+2)}.$$

Solution.

Let $$\frac{2}{s(s+2)} = \frac{K_1}{s} + \frac{K_2}{s+2} \quad ...(1)$$

Then multiplying Eq. (1) by s and putting $s = 0$, we get

$$K_1 = 1.$$

Similarly multiplying Eq. (1) by $(s + 2)$ and putting $s = -2$, we get

$$K_2 = -1.$$

Hence $$I(s) = \frac{2}{s(s+2)} = \frac{1}{s} - \frac{1}{s+2} \quad ...(2)$$

On inverse Laplace transformation Eq. (2) yields,

$$i(t) = 1 - e^{-2t} \quad ...(3)$$

Now $$I(s) = \frac{2}{(3s)(3s+2)} = I(3s) \quad ...(4)$$

Using scaling theorem,

$$\mathcal{L}^{-1}I_1(s) = \mathcal{L}^{-1}I(3s) = \frac{1}{3}[i(t/3)] = \frac{1}{3}[1 - e^{-2t/3}]. \quad \textbf{Ans.}$$

7.8. Ramp Function and Impulse Function

Ramp function. If a time variant current or voltage increases linearly with time, it is known as a *ramp function or a linear ramp.*

Thus consider a unit step voltage applied to an inductor L. Then the inductor current is given by,

$$i_L = \frac{1}{L}\int_{-\infty}^{t} v_L \, dt \qquad ...(7.42)$$

Now $v_L = u(t)$.

If $i_L(0+) = 0$, then

$$i_L = \frac{t}{L} \text{ for } t > 0 \qquad ...(7.43)$$

Thus this response current constitutes a ramp function.

Similarly if a unit step current is applied to a capacitor C, then the capacitor voltage is given by,

$$v_c = \frac{1}{C}\int_{-\infty}^{t} i_c \, dt \qquad ...(7.44)$$

Now $i_c = u(t)$.

If $v_c(0+) = 0$, then

$$v_c = \frac{t}{C} \qquad ...(7.45)$$

This response voltage also constitutes a ramp function.

Impulse Function. If a function has only one non-zero value and if this value is infinite, then this function is known as an *impulse function.*

Thus consider a unit step current applied to an inductor L. Then the inductor voltage is given by,

$$v_L = L \cdot \frac{di_L}{dt} \qquad ...(7.46)$$

Now $i_L = u(t)$. Hence the derivative $\frac{di_L}{dt}$ has zero value for all time except the instant $t = 0$ when stepping occurs. At this instant, derivative $\frac{di_L}{dt}$, being the slope of current i_L becomes infinite. Thus the response voltage constitutes an impulse function.

Similarly if a unit step voltage is applied to a capacitor C then the capacitor current is given by,

$$i_c = C \cdot \frac{dv_c}{dt} \qquad ...(7.47)$$

Now v_c is $u(t)$. Hence the derivative dv_c/dt has zero value for all time except the instant $t = 0$ when the step occurs. At this instant the derivative dv_c/dt, being the slope of the voltage v_c, becomes infinite. Thus the response current constitutes an impulse function.

Fig. 7.8 shows the ramp, step and impulse functions. If a ramp function is differentiated it results in the step function and this step function on further differentiation results in impulse function. If Fig. 7.8, these functions are arranged from top to bottom in this order. Conversely if an

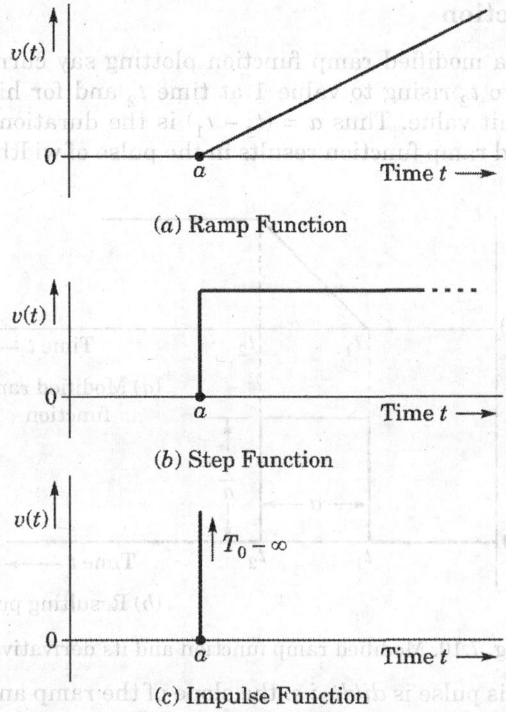

Fig. 7.8. Ramp, step and impulse functions.

impulse function is integrated it results in a step function and this step function on further integration results in ramp function. Thus in Fig. 7.8 proceeding from bottom to top the function are arranged in order they are obtained through integration.

7.9. Unit Ramp Function

Fig. 7.9 (*a*) shows a unit step function. On integration this results in unit ramp function of Fig. 7.9 (*b*). On second and third integration we get functions shown in Fig. 7.9 (*c*) and (*d*) respectively. Conversely starting from the waveform in Fig. 7.9 (*d*), on first, second and third differentiation, we get back functions shown in Fig. 7.9 (*c*), (*b*) and (*a*) respectively. Thus all the four functions shown in Fig. 7.9 are intimatly related and arise from the unit step function. Hence in a way all these four functions are unit functions.

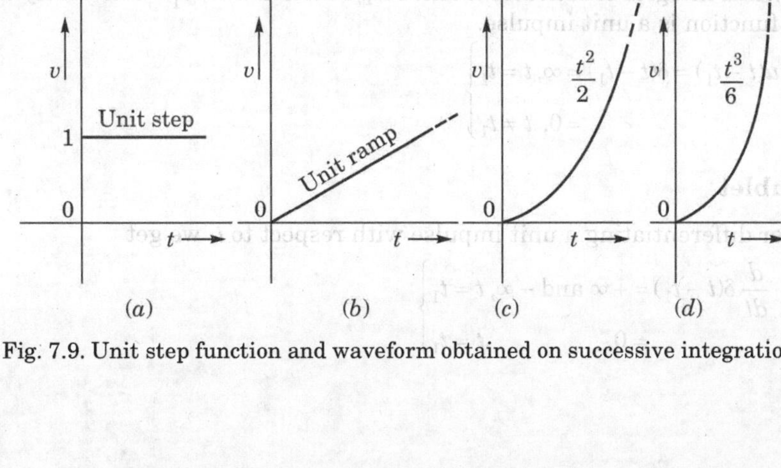

Fig. 7.9. Unit step function and waveform obtained on successive integration.

7.10. Unit Impulse Function

Fig. 7.10 (*a*) shows a modified ramp function plotting say current *i*. This is a true ramp function for the period t_1 to t_2 rising to value 1 at time t_2 and for higher values of time t_2 the function has a constant unit value. Thus $a = (t_2 - t_1)$ is the duration of the ramp function. On differentiation this modified ramp function results in the pulse of width *a* and height 1/*a* as shown in Fig. 7.10 (*b*).

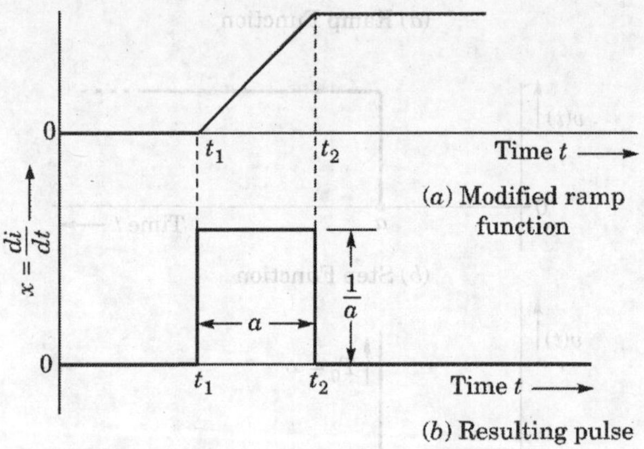

Fig. 7.10. Modified ramp function and its derivative.

The magnitude of this pulse is *di*/*dt*, *i.e.* the slope of the ramp and the duration of the pulse is $a = (t_2 - t_1)$. From Fig. 7.10 (*a*), the slope *di*/*dt* of ramp function equals the height 1 divided by the duration *a* of the ramp. Thus

$$x = \frac{di}{dt} = \frac{1}{a} \qquad ...(7.48)$$

The area of the pulse is $a \times 1/a = 1$, for all values of *a*. Now as *a* is reduced, the width of pulse reduces while its magnitude increases. Finally as *a* approaches zero, (*i*) the modified ramp function approaches a unit step function and (*ii*) the pulse approaches zero width and infinite height maintaining its area equal to one. In the limit, the pulse becomes what may be called a *unit pulse*. Unit impulse is denoted by $\delta(t - t_1)$, where t_1 is the instant of time at which this pulse occurs.

Now if we integrate this unit impulse with respect to time *t*, we get

$$\left.\begin{aligned}\int_{-\infty}^{t} \delta(i - t_1)\, dt &= 1 \text{ for } t \geq t_1 \\ &= 0 \text{ for } t < t_1\end{aligned}\right\} \qquad ...(7.49)$$

Evidently this integral constitutes a unit step function $u(t - t_1)$. Conversely time-derivative of the unit step function is a unit impulse.

$$\text{Thus } \left.\begin{aligned}\frac{d}{dt} u(t - t_1) = \delta(t - t_1) &= \infty, t = t_1 \\ &= 0, \ t \neq t_1\end{aligned}\right\} \qquad ...(7.50)$$

7.11. Unit Doublet

On further differentiating a unit impulse with respect to *t*, we get

$$\left.\begin{aligned}\frac{d}{dt}\delta(t - t_1) &= +\infty \text{ and } -\infty, t = t_1 \\ &= 0, \qquad t \neq t_1\end{aligned}\right\} \qquad ...(7.51)$$

The function $d/dt\ \delta(t - t_1)$ is called a *unit doublet*. The name doublet is given to it since it is obtained from the function shown in Fig. 7.11 (*a*) by letting *C* approach zero.

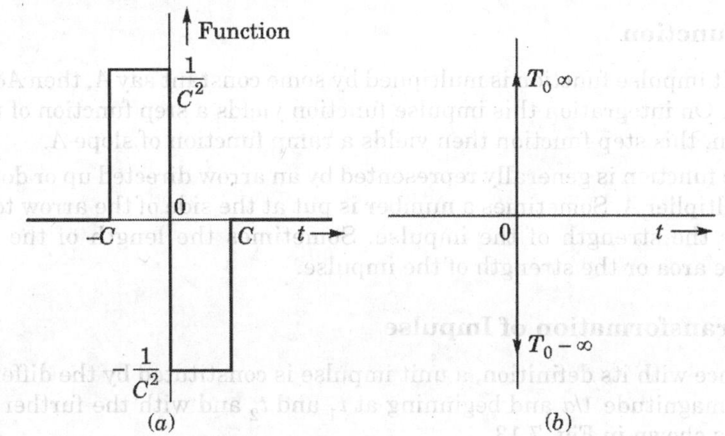

Fig. 7.11. Function shown in (*a*) which as *C* approaches zero constitutes the unit doublet of (*b*).

Now we may extend the sequence of Fig. 7.9 to include the unit impulse and the unit doublet. This is shown in Fig. 7.12.

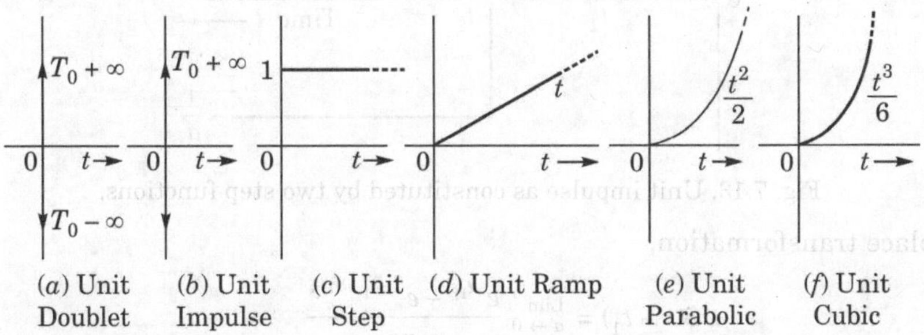

Fig. 7.12. Waveforms of unit step function and its derivatives and integrals.

7.12. Response of Inductor and Capacitor to Unit Impulse

Let a unit impulse of voltage be applied to an inductor. Then the resulting current is given by,

$$i_L = \frac{1}{L}\int_{-\infty}^{t} \delta(t-a)\,dt = \frac{1}{L}\,u(t-a) \qquad \text{...(7.52)}$$

We thus find that a unit impulse of voltage applied to an inductor *L* results instantaneously in current 1/*L* amperes. Ordinary the current in an inductor does not change instantaneously. This instantaneous creation of current 1/*L* amperes thus constitutes on unusual behaviour of an inductor but this results because the driving voltage in the form of an impulse is also an unusual one.

Similarly when a unit impulse of current is applied to a capacitor *C*, the resulting voltage across the capacitor is given by,

$$v_c = \frac{1}{C}\int_{-\infty}^{t} \delta(t-a)dt = \frac{1}{C}\,.\,u(t-a) \qquad \text{...(7.53)}$$

We thus find that a unit impulse of current applied to a capacitor C results in $1/C$ volts to appear instantaneously across the capacitor C.

7.13. Impulse Function

When a unit impulse function is multiplied by some constant say A, then $A\delta(t)$ represents an impulse of area A. On integration this impulse function yields a step function of magnitude A. On further integration, this step function then yields a ramp function of slope A.

An impulse function is generally represented by an arrow directed up or down depending up the sign of the multiplier A. Sometimes a number is put at the side of the arrow to denote the area of the impulse or the strength of the impulse. Sometimes the length of the arrow is chosen proportional to the area or the strength of the impulse.

7.14. Laplace Transformation of Impulse

In accordance with its definition, a unit impulse is constituted by the difference of two step functions each of magnitude $1/a$ and beginning at t_1 and t_2 and with the further provision that a approaches zero as shown in Fig. 7.13.

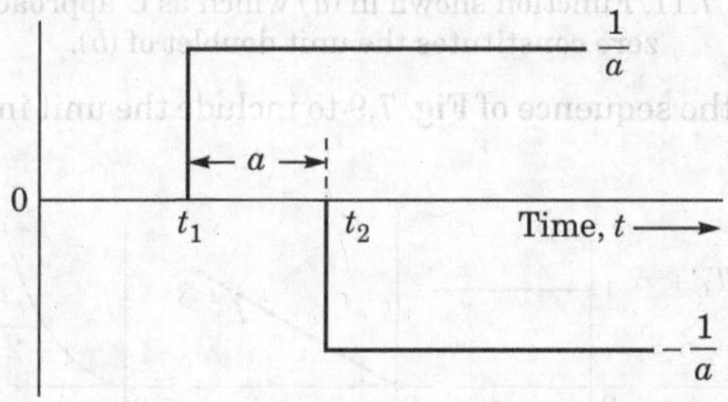

Fig. 7.13. Unit impulse as constituted by two step functions.

On Laplace transformation,

$$\mathcal{L}\,\delta(t-t_1) = \lim_{a\to 0} \frac{e^{-t_1 s} - e^{-t(t_1+a)s}}{as} \quad ...(7.55)$$

where $a = t_2 - t_1$ ...(7.56)

This limit may be obtained by l'Hospital rule. This gives us,

$$\mathcal{L}\,\delta(t-t_1) = e^{-t_1 s} \quad ...(7.57)$$

Here t_1 is the instant at which the unit impulse appears. When $t_1 = 0$, *i.e.* when the unit impulse occurs at $t = 0$,

$$\mathcal{L}\,\delta(t) = 1 \quad ...(7.58)$$

Alternatively, $$\mathcal{L}\,\delta(t) = \mathcal{L}\left[\frac{di}{dt}u(t)\right] = s\,\mathcal{L}\,[u(t)] = s\cdot\frac{1}{s} = 1 \quad ...(7.59)$$

and $$\mathcal{L}\,\delta(t-t_1) = \mathcal{L}\left[\frac{d}{dt}u(t-t_1)\right] = s\,\mathcal{L}[u(t-t_1)] = s\cdot\frac{e^{-t_1 s}}{s} = e^{-t_1 s} \quad ...(7.60)$$

7.15. Laplace Transform of Ramp Functions

A unit ramp function occurring at $t = 0$ denoted by $r(t)$ equals $\int_0^t u(t)dt$.

Hence $$\mathcal{L}[r(t)] = \mathcal{L}\left[\int_0^t u(t)dt\right] = \frac{1}{s}\,\mathcal{L}\,[u(t)] = \frac{1}{s^2} \quad ...(7.61)$$

An unit ramp function occurring at $t = a$ is denoted by $r(t - a)$ and equals $\int_0^t u(t-a)\,dt$.

Hence $$\mathcal{L}\,[r(t-a)] = \mathcal{L}\left[\int_0^t u(t-a)\,dt\right] = \frac{1}{s}\,\mathcal{L}\,u(t-a)$$

$$= \frac{1}{s}\cdot\frac{1}{s}\cdot e^{-as} = \frac{e^{-as}}{s^2} \quad ...(7.62)$$

Similarly ramp function of slope occurring at $t = 0$ equals $K\int_0^t u(t)\,dt$.

Hence its Laplace transform is given by,

$$\mathcal{L}\,[K\,.\,r(t)] = \mathcal{L}\left[K\int_0^t u(t)\,dt\right] = K\mathcal{L}\left[\int_0^t u(t)\,dt\right] = \frac{K}{s^2} \quad ...(7.63)$$

Finally a ramp of slope K occurring at time $t = a$ is denoted by $K\,.\,r(t-a)$ and equals K. $\int_0^t u(t-a)\,dt$.

Hence its Laplace transform is given by,

$$\mathcal{L}\,[K.r(t-a)] = K\,\mathcal{L}\,[r(t-a)] = \frac{K.e^{-as}}{s^2} \quad ...(7.64)$$

7.16. Laplace Transform of Unit Doublet Function

Unit doublet occurring at time t_1 is given by,

$$\delta'(t - t_1) = \frac{d}{dt}\,.\,\delta(t - t_1) \quad ...(7.65)$$

where $\delta(t - t_1)$ is the unit impulse occurring at time $t = t_1$. Its Laplace transform is given by,

$$\mathcal{L}[\delta'(t-t_1)] = \mathcal{L}\left[\frac{d}{dt}\,.\,\delta(t-t_1)\right] = s\mathcal{L}\delta(t-t_1) - [\delta(t-t_1)]^{t=0}$$

$$= s\mathcal{L}\delta(t - t_1) = s\;e^{-t_1 s} \quad ...(7.66)$$

Hence $$\mathcal{L}\delta'(t) = s \quad ...(7.67)$$

Finally Laplace transform of a doublet of magnitude K occurring at $t = t_1$ is given by,

$$\mathcal{L}\,[K\delta'(t-t_1)] = K\mathcal{L}\,[\delta'(t-t_1)] = Ks\;e^{-t_1 s} \quad ...(7.68)$$

7.17. Summary of Laplace Transforms of Different Unit Functions

From the above study we find that the Laplace transforms of all units functions occurring at $t = 0$ are in the form $1/s^n$. Further when one unit function is obtained from another on differentiation, the new transform is obtained from the first by multiplying by s. Thus Laplace transform of unit ramp function is $1/s^2$. On differentiation we get unit step function whose Laplace transform is $\frac{1}{s}\left(=\frac{1}{s^2}\times s\right)$. On further differentiation we get unit impulse whose Laplace transform is $1\left(=\frac{1}{s}\times s\right)$. On further differentiation we get unit doublet whose Laplace transform is s $(= 1 \times s)$. Finally on differentiation of unit doublet function we get unit triplet function whose Laplace transform is s^2 $(= s \times s)$. This technique may be continued to get new transforms. Thus a unit parabolic function is obtained on integration of unit ramp function. Hence its Laplace transform is obtained by multiplying by 1/s the transform of unit ramp function. This equals $\frac{1}{s} \times \frac{1}{s^2} = \frac{1}{s^2}$. These results are given in Table 7.1.

Table 7.1

Laplace Transforms of Unit Functions Occurring at $t = 0$

Unit Function	*Symbol*	*Laplace Transform*
Unit parabolic function	$p(t)$	$\frac{1}{s^3}$
Unit Ramp Function	$r(t)$	$\frac{1}{s^2}$
Unit Step Function	$u(t)$	$\frac{1}{s}$
Unit Impulse Function	$\delta(t)$	1
Unit Doublet Function	$\delta'(t)$	s
Unit Triplet Function	$\delta''(t)$	s^2

On delaying the start of any of these unit functions from time $t = 0$ to time $t = a$, the Laplace transform gets multiplied by e^{-as}. Thus Table 7.2 shows these unit functions and their Laplace transforms.

Table 7.2

Laplace Transforms of Unit Functions Occurring at $t = 0$

Delayed Unit Function	*Symbols*	*Laplace Transforms*
Unit Parabolic Function	$p(t-a)$	$\frac{1}{s^2} . e^{-as}$
Unit Ramp Function	$r(t-a)$	$\frac{1}{s^2} . e^{-as}$
Unit Step Function	$u(t-a)$	$\frac{1}{s} e^{-as}$
Unit Impulse Function	$\delta(t-a)$	e^{-as}
Unit Doublet Function	$\delta'(t-a)$	$s.e^{-as}$
Unit Triplet Function	$\delta''(t-a)$	$s^2 e^{-as}$

Example 7.4. *The network of Example 7.1 is driven by unit impulse at time t = 0. Find the current i(t).*

Solution. With unit impulse driving voltage Kirchhoff's law yields,

$$L\frac{di}{dt} + Ri = \delta(t) \quad ...(1)$$

On Laplace transformation, we get

$$L[s.I(s) - i(0+)] + R.I(s) = 1 \quad ...(2)$$

But $\quad i(0+) = 0$

Hence Eq. (2) yields,

$$I(s)[Ls + R] = 1 \quad ...(3)$$

or

$$I(s) = \frac{1}{Ls + R} = \frac{1}{L(s + R/L)} \quad ...(4)$$

On substituting values of L and R,

$$I(s) = \frac{1}{2} \cdot \frac{1}{s+2} \quad ...(5)$$

On invere Laplace transformation, we get

$$i(t) = \frac{1}{2} \cdot e^{-2t} \quad ...(6)$$

Note. Eq. (6) giving the response of an R-L circuit to unit impulse driving voltage shows that the response to an impulse is governed by the constants of the network.

Example 7.5. *The network of Example 7.2 is driven by a unit impulse voltage at time t = 0. Find the current i(t). Given that charge q(0 +) across capacitor C is zero.*

Solution. With unit impulse driving voltage applied at time $t = 0$, Kirchhoff's law yields,

$$Ri + \frac{1}{C}\int_{-\infty}^{t} idt = \delta(t) \quad ...(1)$$

or

$$Ri + \frac{1}{C}\int_{-\infty}^{0} idt + \frac{1}{C}\int_{0}^{t} idt = \delta(t) \quad ...(2)$$

On Laplace transformation Eq. (2) yields,

$$R.I(s) + \frac{1}{C} \cdot \frac{q(0+)}{s} + \frac{1}{C} \cdot \frac{I(s)}{s} = 1 \quad ...(3)$$

Now $q(0+) = 0$

Hence Eq. (3) yields,

$$I(s)\left[R + \frac{1}{Cs}\right] = 1 \quad ...(4)$$

Hence

$$I(s) = \frac{1}{R + \frac{1}{Cs}} = \frac{1}{R} \frac{s}{s + \frac{1}{RC}} \quad ...(5)$$

On substituting values of R and C, we get

$$I(s) = \frac{s}{s+4} = 1 - \frac{4}{s+4} \quad ...(6)$$

On inverse Laplace transformation, we get

$$i(t) = \delta(t) - 4e^{-4t}. \quad \textbf{Ans.}$$

Example 7.6. *Find the response current of a series R-L circuit consisting of resistor R = 3 Ω and inductor L = 1 henry when each of the following driving force voltage is applied :*

(*i*) *unit ramp voltage r (t – 2),*

(*ii*) *unit impulse voltage δ(t – 2),*

(*iii*) *unit step voltage u(t – 2),*

(*iv*) *unit doublet δ′(t – 2) and*

(*v*) *pulse of width 'a' and magnitude 1 volt beginning at time t = 2 seconds.*

Solution. (*i*) Unit ramp voltage $r(t-2)$.

Application of Kirchhoff's voltage law to the circuit yields,

$$L\frac{di}{dt} + Ri = r(t-2) \quad ...(1)$$

On Laplace transformation, we get

$$L[s.I(s) - i(0+)] + R.I(s) = \frac{1}{s^2} e^{-2s} \quad ...(2)$$

But $i(0+) = 0.$

Hence Eq. (2) yields,

$$I(s)[R + Ls] = \frac{e^{-2s}}{s^2} \quad ...(3)$$

Hence $$I(s) = \frac{e^{-2s}}{s^2\,(Ls + R)} = \frac{e^{-2s}}{s^2(s+3)} \quad ...(4)$$

Let $$\frac{1}{s^2(s+3)} = \frac{K_1}{s} + \frac{K_2}{s^2} + \frac{K_3}{s+3} \quad ...(5)$$

Multiplying Eq. (5) by $(s + 3)$ and putting $s = -3$, we get

$$K_2 = \frac{1}{(-3)^2} = \frac{1}{9}$$

Multiplying Eq. (5) by s^2, we get

$$\frac{1}{s+3} = K_1 s + K_2 + \frac{K_3 s^2}{s+3} \quad ...(6)$$

Putting $s = 0$ in Eq. (6), we get

$$K_2 = \frac{1}{3}.$$

Differentiating Eq. (6) with respect to s, we get

$$\frac{-1}{(s+3)^2} = K_1 + K_3 \cdot \frac{(s+3)(2s) - s^2(1)}{(s+3)^2} \quad ...(7)$$

Putting $s = 0$ in Eq. (7), we get

$$K_1 = -\frac{1}{9}.$$

Hence $$I(s) = \frac{-e^{-2s}}{9s} + \frac{e^{-2s}}{3s^2} + \frac{e^{-2s}}{9(s+3)} \quad ...(8)$$

On inverse Laplace transformation, we get

$$i(t) = -\frac{1}{9}\,u(t-2) + \frac{1}{3}\,r(t-2) + \frac{1}{9}\,e^{-3(t-2)} \,.\, u(t-2) \quad ...(9)$$

(*ii*) *Unit Impulse Voltage* $\delta(t - 2)$. In this case,

$$L\,\frac{di}{dt} + Ri = \delta(t-2) \quad ...(10)$$

Hence $$I(s) = \frac{e^{-2s}}{Ls + R} = \frac{e^{-2s}}{s+3} \quad ...(11)$$

On inverse Laplace transformation,

$$i(t) = e^{-3(t-2)} \,.\, u(t-2) \quad ...(12)$$

(*iii*) *Unit Step Voltage u(t – 2).* In this case,

$$I(s)\,[Ls + R] = \mathcal{L}\,u(t-2)$$

$$= \frac{e^{-2s}}{s} \quad ...(13)$$

Hence $$I(s) = \frac{e^{-2s}}{s(Ls + R)} = \frac{e^{-2s}}{s(s+3)} \quad ...(14)$$

Let $$\frac{1}{s(s+3)} = \frac{K_1}{s} + \frac{K_2}{s+3} \quad ...(15)$$

Multiplying Eq. (15) by s and putting $s = 0$, we get

$$K_1 = \frac{1}{3}$$

Similarly multiplying Eq. (15) by $(s + 3)$ and putting $s = -3$, we get

$$K_2 = -\frac{1}{3}$$

Hence $$I(s) = e^{-2s}\left[\frac{1}{3s} - \frac{1}{3(s+3)}\right] \quad ...(16)$$

On inverse Laplace transformation Eq. (16) yields,

$$i(t) = \frac{1}{3}\, u(t-2) - \frac{1}{3}\, e^{-3(t-2)} \,.\, u(t-2) \quad ...(17)$$

$$= +\frac{1}{3}\, u(t-2)\, [1 - e^{-3(t-2)}] \quad ...(18)$$

(iv) Unit Doublet Voltage $\delta'(t-2)$. In this case, the Laplace transform equation for the network is,

$$I(s)[Ls + R] = \mathcal{L}\, \delta'(t-2)$$

$$= s \,.\, e^{-2s} \quad ...(19)$$

Hence $$I(s) = \frac{se^{-2s}}{s+3} = e^{-2s}\left[1 + \frac{3}{s+3}\right] \quad ...(20)$$

On inverse Laplace transformation Eq. (20) yields

$$i(t) = \delta(t-2) \,.\, u(t-2) - 3e^{-(t-2)} \,.\, u(t-2)$$

$$= u(t-2)[\delta(t-2) - 3e^{-3(t-2)}] \quad ...(21)$$

(v) Pulse of width 'a', magnitude 1 volt beginning at $t = 2$. In this case, the Kirchhoff's voltage law applied to the circuit yields,

$$L\frac{di}{dt} + Ri = u(t-2) - u(t-2-a) \quad ...(22)$$

On Laplace transformation, we get

$$L[s.I(s) - i(0)] + R\, I(s) = \left[\frac{1}{s} \,.\, e^{-2s} - \frac{1}{s} \,.\, e^{-(2+a)s}\right]$$

Putting $i(0+) = 0$, we get

$$I(s)[Ls + R] = \frac{1}{s} \,.\, [e^{-2s} - e^{-(2+a)s}]$$

Hence $$I(s) = [e^{-2s} - e^{-(2+a)s}] \,.\, \frac{1}{s(s+3)} = [e^{-2s} - e^{-(2+a)s}] \,.\, \left[\frac{1}{3s} - \frac{1}{3(s+3)}\right]$$

$$= \frac{1}{3}\left[\frac{e^{-2s}}{s} - \frac{e^{-(2+a)s}}{s} - \frac{e^{-2s}}{s+3} + \frac{e^{-(2+a)s}}{s+3}\right]$$

On inverse Laplace transformation, we get

$$i(t) = \frac{1}{3}\, [u(t-2) - u(t-2-a) - e^{-3(t-2)} \,.\, u(t-2) + e^{-3(t-2-a)} \,.\, u(t-2-a)].$$

Example 7.7. *Find the current $i(t)$ in a series R-C circuit consisting of $R = 2\ \Omega$ and $C = \frac{1}{4}$ farad when each of the following driving force voltage is applied : (i) ramp voltage $2r(t-3)$, (ii) step voltage $2u(t-3)$, (iii) impulse voltage $2\delta(t-3)$ and (iv) double voltage $2\delta'(t-3)$.*

Solution. *With ramp voltage $2r(t-3)$.* Application of Kirchhoff's voltage law to the circuit yields,

$$Ri + \frac{1}{C}\int_{-\infty}^{t} idt \;=\; 2r\,(t-3) \qquad ...(1)$$

On Laplace transformation, we get

$$R\,I(s) + \frac{1}{C}\cdot\frac{q(0+)}{s} + \frac{1}{s}\cdot\frac{I(s)}{s} \;=\; 2\,.\frac{1}{s^2}\,e^{-3s} \qquad ...(2)$$

But $\qquad q(0+) = 0.$

Hence Eq. (2) yields,

$$I(s)\left[R + \frac{1}{Cs}\right] = \frac{2e^{-3s}}{s^2} \qquad ...(3)$$

or

$$I(s) = \frac{2e^{-3s}}{s\left(2+\dfrac{4}{s}\right)} = \frac{e^{-3s}}{s(s+2)} \qquad ...(4)$$

Let

$$\frac{1}{s(s+2)} = \frac{K_1}{s} + \frac{K_2}{s+2} \qquad ...(5)$$

Multiplying Eq. (5) by s and putting $s = 0$, we get

$$K_1 = -\frac{1}{2}$$

Multiplying Eq. (5) by $(s + 2)$ and putting $s = -2$, we get

$$K_2 = -\frac{1}{2}$$

Hence

$$I(s) = \frac{1}{2}\left[\frac{e^{-3s}}{s} - \frac{e^{-3s}}{s+2}\right] \qquad ...(6)$$

On inverse Laplace transformation,

$$i(t) = 2\,.\,u(t-3) - \frac{1}{2}\,e^{-2(t-3)}\,.\,u(t-3) \qquad ...(7)$$

(ii) With Step Voltage 2u(t – 3). In this case, Laplace transform equation for the cicruit is,

$$I(s)\left[R + \frac{1}{Cs}\right] = 2\,.\,\frac{1}{s}\,e^{-3s} \qquad ...(8)$$

Hence

$$I(s) = \frac{2e^{-3s}}{s\left(2+\dfrac{4}{s}\right)} = \frac{e^{-3s}}{s+2} \qquad ...(9)$$

On inverse Laplace transformation Eq. (9) yields,

$$i(t) = e^{-2(t-3)}\,.\,u(t-3) \qquad ...(10)$$

(iii) With Impulse Voltage 2δ(t – 3). In this case, Laplace transform equation is,

$$I(s)\left[R + \frac{1}{Cs}\right] = 2e^{-3s} \qquad ...(11)$$

Hence

$$I(s) = \frac{2e^{-3s}}{2+\dfrac{4}{s}} = \frac{se^{-3s}}{(s+2)} = e^{-3s}\left[1 - \frac{2}{s+2}\right] \qquad ...(12)$$

On inverse Laplace transformation, Eq. (12) yields,

$$i(t) = \delta(t-3) - 2e^{-2(t-3)}\,.\,u(t-3) \qquad ...(13)$$

(iv) With doublet Voltage 2δ′ (t – 3). In this case the Laplace transform equation is,

$$I(s)\left(R + \frac{1}{Cs}\right) = 2se^{-3s} \qquad ...(14)$$

Hence $$I(s) = \frac{2se^{-3s}}{2+\dfrac{4}{s}} = \frac{s^2e^{-3s}}{s+2}$$

or $$I(s) = e^{-3s}\left[s - 2 + \frac{4}{s+2}\right] = s\,.\,e^{-3s} - 2e^{-3s} + 4.\ \frac{e^{-3s}}{s+2} \quad ...(15)$$

On inverse Laplace transformation, we get

$$i(t) = \delta'(t-3) - 2\delta\,(t-3) + 4e^{-2(t-3)},\ t \geq 3 \quad ...(16)$$

Example 7.8. *Find the current i(t) in a series R-L-C circuit comprising resistor R = 5 Ω, inductor L = 1 henry and capacitor C = $\frac{1}{4}$ farad when each of the following driving force voltage is applied : (i) ramp voltage 12r(t – 2) ; (ii) step voltage 3u(t – 3), (iii) impulse voltage 3δ(t – 1) and (iv) double voltage 2δ′(t – 3).*

Solution. *(i) With ramp voltage r(t – 2).* The Kirchhoff's voltage law equation for the circuit is,

$$L\,\frac{di}{dt} + \frac{1}{C}\int_{-\infty}^{t} idt\ + Ri = 12r\,(t-2) \quad ...(1)$$

On Laplace transformation, we get

$$L[s.I(s) - i(0+)] + \frac{1}{C}\,.\,\frac{q(0+)}{s} + \frac{1}{C}\,.\,\frac{I(s)}{s} + R.I(s) = \frac{12}{s^2}\,.e^{-2s} \quad ...(2)$$

But $i(0+) = q(0+) = 0$.
Hence Eq. (2), yields

$$I(s) = \frac{12e^{-2s}}{s^2\left(Ls + R + \dfrac{1}{Cs}\right)} = \frac{12e^{-2s}}{s(s^2+5s+4)} = \frac{12e^{-2s}}{s(s+1)(s+4)} \quad ...(3)$$

Let $$\frac{2}{s(s+1)(s+4)} = \frac{K_1}{s} + \frac{K_2}{s+1} + \frac{K_3}{s+4} \quad ...(4)$$

Multiplying Eq. (4) by s and putting $s = 0$, we get

$$K_1 = \frac{12}{4} = 3.$$

Multiplying Eq. (4) by $(s + 1)$ and putting $s = -1$, we get

$$K_2 = \frac{12}{(-1)(-1+4)} = -4.$$

Multiplying Eq. (4) by (s + 4) and putting $s = -4$, we get

$$K_3 = \frac{12}{(-4)(-4+1)} = +1.$$

Hence $$I(s) = \frac{3e^{-2s}}{s} - \frac{4e^{-2s}}{s+1} + \frac{e^{-2s}}{s+4} \quad ...(5)$$

On inverse Laplace transformation, we get

$$i(t) = 3u(t-2) - 4e^{-(t-2)} + e^{-4(t-2)},\ t \geq 2 \quad ...(6)$$

(ii) With Step Voltage 3u(t – 3). Laplace transform equation in this case is,

$$I(s)\left[Ls + R + \frac{1}{Cs}\right] = \frac{3e^{-3s}}{s} \quad ...(7)$$

or $$I(s) = \frac{3e^{-3s}}{s\left(Ls + R + \frac{1}{Cs}\right)} = \frac{3e^{-3s}}{(s^2+5s+4)} = \frac{3e^{-3s}}{(s+1)(s+4)} \quad ...(8)$$

Let $$\frac{3}{(s+1)(s+4)} = \frac{K_1}{s+1} + \frac{K_2}{s+4} \quad ...(9)$$

Multiplying Eq. (9) by (s + 1) and putting s = – 1, we get

$$K_1 = \frac{3}{-1+4} = 1.$$

Multiplying Eq. (9) by (s + 4) and putting s = – 4, we get

$$K_2 = \frac{3}{-4+1} = -1$$

Hence $$I(s) = e^{-3s}\left[\frac{1}{s+1} - \frac{1}{s+4}\right] = \frac{e^{-3s}}{s+1} - \frac{e^{-3s}}{s+4} \quad ...(10)$$

On inverse Laplace transformation, we get

$$i(t) = e^{-(t-3)} - e^{-4(t-3)}, t \geq 3 \quad ...(11)$$

(*iii*) *With Impulse Voltage 3δ(t – 1).* Laplace transform equation in this case is,

$$I(s)\left[Ls + R + \frac{1}{Cs}\right] = \mathcal{L}\, 3\delta(t-1) = 3e^{-s} \quad ...(12)$$

Hence $$I(s) = \frac{3e^{-s}}{s+5+\frac{1}{s}} = \frac{3se^{-s}}{(s+1)(s+4)} \quad ...(13)$$

Let $$\frac{3s}{(s+1)(s+4)} = \frac{K_1}{s+1} + \frac{K_2}{s+4} \quad ...(14)$$

Multiplying Eq. (14) by (s + 1) and putting s = – 1, we get

$$K_1 = \frac{3(-1)}{-1+4} = -1.$$

Multiplying Eq. (14) by (s + 4) and puttings = – 4, we get

$$K_2 = \frac{3(-4)}{-4+1} = 4.$$

Hence $$I(s) = e^{-8}\left[\frac{-1}{s+1} + \frac{4}{s+4}\right] = \frac{4e^{-s}}{s+4} - \frac{e^{-s}}{s+1} \quad ...(15)$$

On Laplace transformation Eq. (15) yields,

$$i(t) = 4 \,.\, e^{-4(t-1)} - e^{-(t-1)}, t \geq 1 \quad ...(16)$$

(*iv*) *With Doublet Voltage 2δ′ (t –* 3). Laplace transform equation is

$$I(s)\left[Ls + R + \frac{1}{Cs}\right] = \mathcal{L}\, 2\delta'(t-3) = 2se^{-3s} \quad ...(17)$$

Hence $$I(s) = \frac{2se^{-3s}}{Ls + R + \frac{1}{Cs}} = \frac{2s^2e^{-3s}}{s^2+5s+4} \quad ...(18)$$

$$= e^{-3s}\left[2 - \frac{10s+8}{s^2+5s+4}\right] \quad ...(19)$$

Let $$\frac{10s+8}{(s^3+5s+4)} = \frac{K_1}{s+1} + \frac{K_2}{s+4} \qquad ...(20)$$

Multiplying Eq. (20) by (s + 1) and putting s = – 1, we get

$$K_1 = \frac{-10+8}{-1+4} = -\frac{2}{3}$$

Mutliplying Eq. (20) by (s + 4) and putting s = – 4, we get

$$K_2 = \frac{-40+8}{(-4+1)} = \frac{32}{3}$$

Hence $$I(s) = 2e^{-3s} - e^{-3s}\left[-\frac{2}{3}.\frac{1}{s+1} + \frac{32}{3}.\frac{1}{s+4}\right] \qquad ...(21)$$

$$= 2e^{-3s}\ \frac{2}{3}.\frac{e^{-3s}}{s+1} - \frac{32}{3}.\frac{e^{-3s}}{s+4} \qquad ...(22)$$

On inverse Laplace transformation, we get

$$i(t) = 2\delta(t-3) + \frac{2}{3}.e^{-(t-3)} - \frac{32}{3}.e^{-4(t-3)},\ t \geq 3 \qquad ...(23)$$

7.18. Synthesis of a Few Typical Waveforms and Their Laplace Transforms

The step function, impulse function, ramp function etc. constitute the basic functions which may be combined properly to build other waveforms. For illustration we start again with a pulse function. In Article 7.2 we have seen how a pulse of unit amplitude extending from $t = 0$ to $t = a$ may be formed by taking difference between two step functions. Similarly by taking difference between two step functions $u(t-a)$ and $u(t-b)$ we may form a unit pulse extending from $t = a$ to $t = b$ as shown in Fig 7.14 (*a*). This pulse may be represented by the relation :

$$v(t) = u(t-a) - u(t-b) \qquad ...(7.69)$$

The same unit pulse may alternatively be formed by suitable combination of unit step functions $u(b-t)$ and $u(a-t)$ *as* given by Eq. (7.70) and illustrated in Fig. 7.14 (*b*).

$$v(t) = u(b-1) - u(a-1) \qquad ...(7.70)$$

Finally the same unit pulse may be formed by multiplication of two unit steps $u(b-t)$ and $u(t-a)$ as given by Eq. (7.71) and illustrated in Fig. 7.14(*c*).

$$v(t) = u(b-t)\ .\ u(t-a) \qquad ...(7.71)$$

This technique of synthesis may be used to form a variety of waveforms starting from well known and simple functions. A few of these are considered here.

(*A*) *Half cycle of sinewave starting from t = 0.*

Fig. 71.5 (*a*) shows a sinewave of unit amplitude and periodic time T seconds and defined for all positive values of time t as given by the relation :

$$v_1 = \sin 2\pi\ \frac{t}{T}\ .\ u(t) \qquad ...(7.72)$$

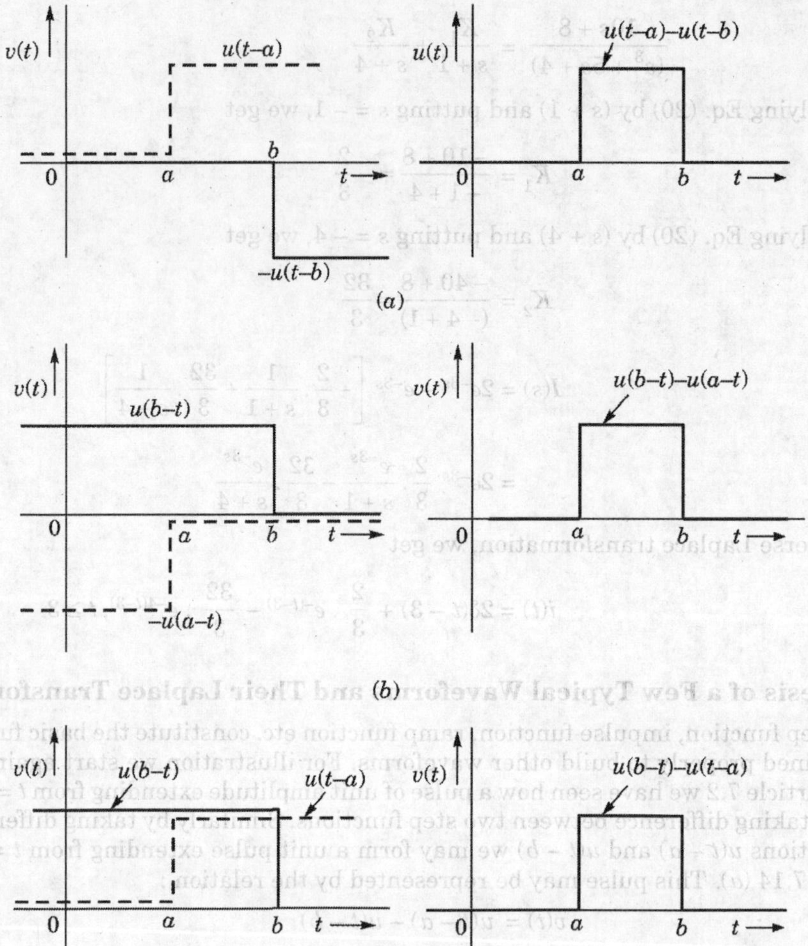

Fig. 7.14. Combination of various unit step functions to form a unit pulse extending from $t = a$ to $t = b$.

Fig. 7.15 (*b*) shows the same sinewave shifted by time $T/2$ seconds. This shifted sinewave is defined by the relation,

$$v_2 = \sin \frac{2\pi}{T}\left(t - \frac{T}{2}\right) . u\left(t - \frac{T}{2}\right) \quad ...(7.73)$$

On adding these two waveforms we get the desired half cycle of the sinewave shown in Fig. 7.15 (*c*) and given by the relation,

$$v(t) = \sin \frac{2\pi t}{T} . u(t) + \sin \frac{2\pi}{T}\left(t - \frac{T}{2}\right) . u\left(t - \frac{T}{2}\right) \quad ...(7.74)$$

On Laplace transformation making use of the shifting theorem, Eq. (7.74) yields,

$$V(s) = \frac{\dfrac{2\pi}{T}}{s^2 + \left(\dfrac{2\pi}{T}\right)^2}\left[1 + e^{-\frac{T}{2}s}\right] \quad ...(7.75)$$

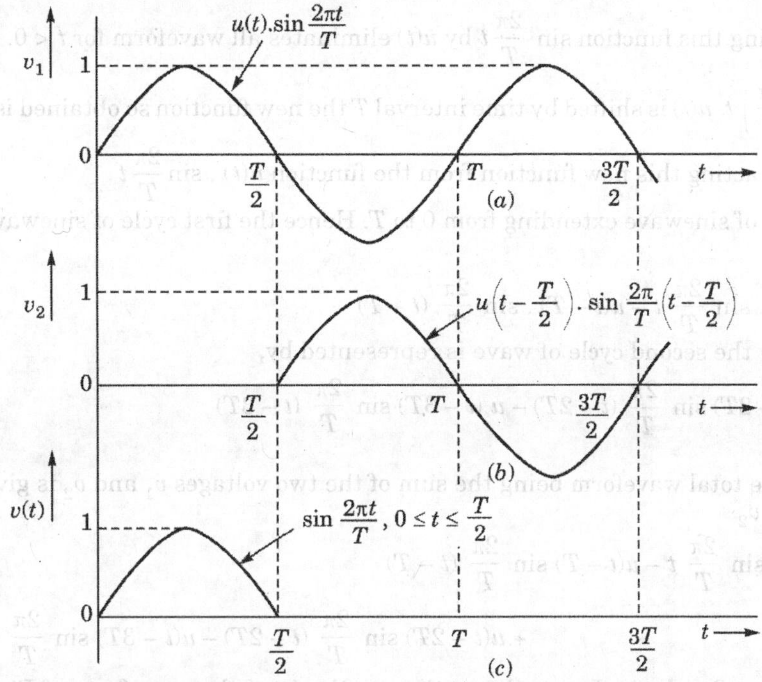

Fig. 7.15. Synthesis of a half cycle of sinewave or a sinusoidal pulse.

To simplify the expressions, let us take the periodic time T as 2 seconds. Then Eqs. (7.74) and (7.75) reduce to the following forms :

$$v(t) = \sin \pi t \,.\, u(t) + \sin \pi\,(t-1)\,.\,u(t-1) \qquad ...(7.76)$$

and

$$V(s) = \frac{\pi}{s^2+\pi^2}\,(1+e^{-t}) \qquad ...(7.77)$$

(B) Two cycles of sinewave extending from 0 to T and 2T to 3T

Consider next the waveform shown in Fig. 7.16. It consists of two cycles of sinusoidal voltage, one extending from 0 to T and the other extending from $2T$ to $3T$. The voltage has zero value at all other times from $t = -\infty$ *to* $t = +\infty$.

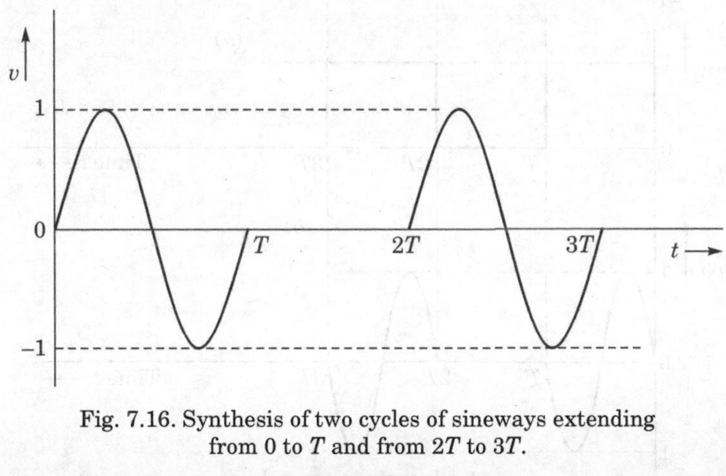

Fig. 7.16. Synthesis of two cycles of sineways extending from 0 to T and from $2T$ to $3T$.

Now function sin $(2\pi/T)t$ has the waveform shown in the interval 0 to T but the function sin $(2\pi/T)t$ exists for all other time.

Multiplying this function $\sin \frac{2\pi}{T} t$ by $u(t)$ eliminates all waveform for $t < 0$. Now if this new function $\sin \left(\frac{2\pi}{T}\right) t . u(t)$ is shifted by time interval T the new function so obtained is $u(t-T). \sin \frac{2\pi}{T}$ $(t - T)$. On subtracting this new function from the function $u(t) . \sin \frac{2\pi}{T} t$ we get the cycle of sinewave extending from 0 to T. Hence the first cycle of sinewave of Fig. 7.16 is represented by,

$$v_1 = u(t) . \sin \frac{2\pi}{T} t - u(t-T) . \sin \frac{2\pi}{T} (t-T) \quad ...(7.78)$$

Similarly the second cycle of wave is represented by,

$$v_2 = u(t-2T) \sin \frac{2\pi}{T} (t-2T) - u(t-3T) \sin \frac{2\pi}{T} (t-3T) \quad ...(7.79)$$

Hence the total waveform being the sum of the two voltages v_1 and v_2 is given by,

$$v = v_1 + v_2$$

$$= u(t) \sin \frac{2\pi}{T} t - u(t-T) \sin \frac{2\pi}{T} (t-T)$$

$$+ u(t-2T) \sin \frac{2\pi}{T} (t-2T) - u(t-3T) \sin \frac{2\pi}{T} (t-3T) \quad ...(7.80)$$

Alternative Synthesis. In an alternative synthesis of the waveform of Fig. 7.16, we may consider the function to be the product of two waveforms : (*a*) continuous sinewave shown in Fig. 7.17 (*a*) and (*b*) two gate functions shown in Fig. 7.17 (*b*). The resulting function is shown in Fig. 7.17 (*c*).

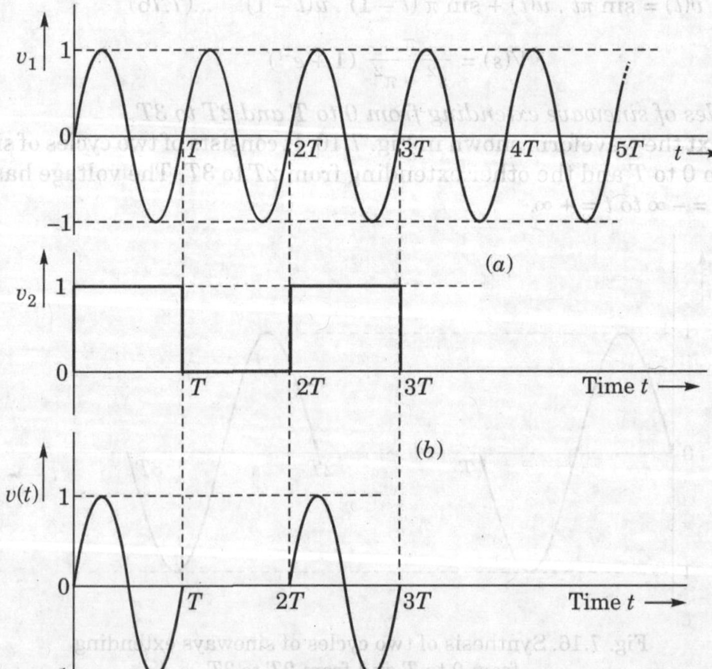

(c) Two sinewave pulses

Fig. 7.17. Synthesis of two sinewave pulses.

Consider the first gate which is a pulse starting at time $t = 0$ and ending at time $t = T$. Thus the duration of this gate is T. This gate may be represented as,

$$\bigcap_{0,\,T(t)} = u(t) - u(t - T) \qquad ...(7.81)$$

Similarly the second gate is a pulse starting at $t = 2T$ and ending at time $t = 3T$. The duration of this gate also is T. This gate may be represented by $\bigcap_{2T,\,T(t)}$ and is given by,

$$\bigcap_{2T,\,T(t)} = u(t - 2T) - u(t - 3T) \qquad ...(7.82)$$

Hence the waveform of Fig. 7.17 (c) may be described as,

$$v(t) = \sin\left(\frac{2\pi}{T}t\right)\left[\bigcap_{0,\,T(t)} + \bigcap_{2T,\,T(t)}\right] \qquad ...(7.83)$$

Similarly the waveform of Fig. 7.15 may be represented as,

$$v(t) = \sin\left(\frac{2\pi}{T}t\right)\left[\bigcap_{0,\,T/2(t)}\right] \qquad ...(7.84)$$

(C) *Isosceles Triangle.* Fig. 7.18 (a) shows an isosceles triangle of unit height and duration $2a$ seconds. This triangle may be constructed from properly selected ramp functions. Thus consider the three ramp functions of Fig. 7.18 (b). The first ramp function starts from $t = 0$ and has slope of $\frac{1}{a}$ and may be represented by $\frac{1}{a} \cdot r(t)$. The third ramp function starts from $t = 2a$ and has slope of $\frac{1}{a}$ and

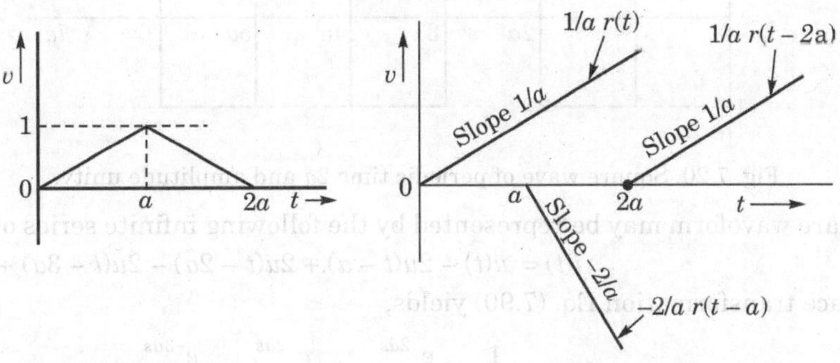

(a) Isosceles triangle (b) Three ramp functions resulting in the isosceles triangle.

Fig. 7.18. Synthesis of an isosceles triangular pulse from ramp functions.

may be represented by $1/a.r(t - 2a)$. The given triangle is simply the addition of the three ramp functions.

The isosceles triangular pulse of Fig. 7.18 (a) starting at $t = 0$ and of duration $2a$ may be denoted $\Lambda_{0,\,2a}(t)$ where Λ is the Greek letter *lambda*. Accordingly this triangular function is given by the equation,

$$\Lambda_{0,\,2a(t)} = \frac{1}{a} \cdot r(t) - \frac{2}{a} \cdot r(t - a) + \frac{1}{a} \cdot r(t - 2a) \qquad ...(7.85)$$

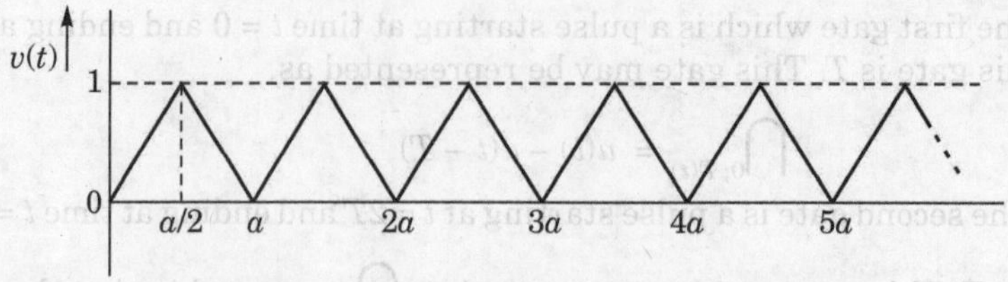

Fig. 7.19. Saw-tooth waveform of periodic time a.

Following this notation saw-tooth waveform of Fig. 7.19 with periodic time of each saw tooth equal to a may be represented by the infinite series.

$$v(t) = \Lambda_{0,\,a} + \Lambda_{a,\,a} + \Lambda_{2a,\,a} + \ldots\ldots \quad \ldots(7.86)$$

Laplace transformation of the triangular waveform of Fig. 7.18 (a) described by Eq. (7.85) is,

$$V(s) = \frac{1}{a}\cdot\frac{1}{s^2} - \frac{2}{a}\cdot\frac{e^{-as}}{s^2} + \frac{1}{a}\cdot\frac{e^{-2as}}{s^2} \quad \ldots(7.87)$$

$$= \frac{1}{as^2}\,[1 - 2e^{-as} + e^{-2as}] \quad \ldots(7.88)$$

$$= \frac{(1 - e^{-as})^2}{as^2} \quad \ldots(7.89)$$

(*D*) *Square Wave.* Fig. 7.20 shows a square wave of amplitude unity and periodic time $2a$.

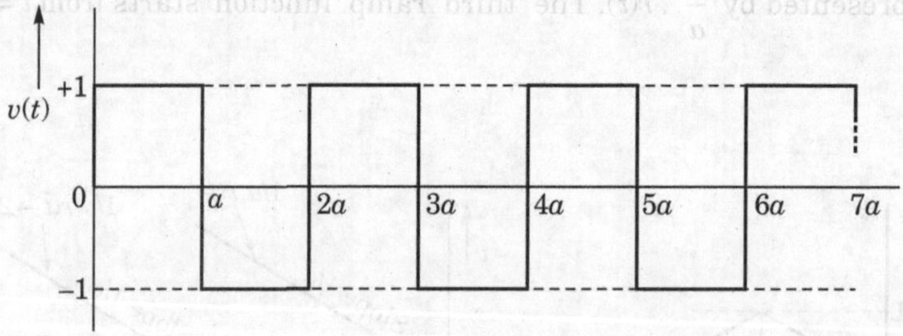

Fig. 7.20. Square wave of periodic time $2a$ and amplitude unity.

This square waveform may be represented by the following infinite series of step functions,

$$i(t) = u(t) - 2u(t - a).+ 2u(t - 2a) - 2u(t - 3a) + \ldots\ldots \quad \ldots(7.90)$$

On Laplace transformation Eq. (7.90) yields,

$$V(s) = \frac{1}{s} - 2\frac{e^{-2as}}{s} + 2\cdot\frac{e^{-2as}}{s} - 2\frac{e^{-3as}}{s} + \ldots\ldots \quad \ldots(7.91)$$

$$= \frac{1}{s}\left[1 - 2e^{-as}\left(1 - e^{-as} + e^{-2as} - e^{-3as} + \ldots\ldots\right)\right] \quad \ldots(7.92)$$

But $\quad 1 - e^{-as} + e^{-2as} - e^{-3as} = \ldots\ldots + \dfrac{1}{1 + e^{-as}} \quad \ldots(7.93)$

Hence Eq. (7.92) yields,

$$V(s) = \frac{1}{s}\left[1 - \frac{2e^{-as}}{1 + e^{-as}}\right] \quad \ldots(7.94)$$

$$= \frac{1}{s}\cdot\frac{1 - e^{-as}}{1 + e^{-as}} \quad \ldots(7.95)$$

$$= \frac{1}{s} \tanh \frac{as}{2} \qquad \text{...(7.96)}$$

7.19. Transform of any Function that Repeats Itself

Let $f(t)$ be any function of time t.

Let then $\qquad f(t + nT) = f(t) \qquad$ ...(7.97)

where n is a positive or negative integer and T is the periodic time.

The Laplace transform of any such function is,

$$F(s) = \int_0^\infty f(t)e^{-st}\, dt$$

$$= \int_0^T f(t)e^{-st}\, dt + \int_T^{2T} f(t)e^{-st}\, dt + \int_{2T}^{3T} f(t)e^{-st}\, dt + \ldots\ldots \qquad \text{...(7.98)}$$

Now function $[f(t)]_T^{2T}$ is nothing but the function $[f(t)]_0^T$ shifted by time interval T. Hence by shifting theorem the Laplace transform $\int_T^{2T} f(t)e^{-st}\, dt$ is nothing but the transform $\int_0^T f(t)e^{-st}\, dt$ multiplied by e^{-st}. Thus $\int_T^{2T} f(t)e^{-st}\, dt$ equals $e^{-sT}\int_0^T f(t)e^{-st}\, dt$. Similarly transform $\int_{2T}^{3T} f(t)e^{-st}\, dt$ equals $e^{-2sT}\int_0^T f(t)e^{-st} dt$. Similar remarks apply for function $f(t)$ existing during other intervals of time. Hence Eq. (7.98) yields,

$$F(s) = (1 + e^{-sT} + e^{-2sT} + \ldots\ldots) \int_0^T f(t)e^{-st} dt \qquad \text{...(7.99)}$$

$$= \frac{1}{1 - e^{-sT}} \int_0^T e^{-st} f(t)\, dt \qquad \text{...(7.100)}$$

Now if $f(t)$ exists only from 0 to T, $\int_0^T e^{-st} f(t)\, dt$ represents the Laplace transform of $f(t)$. Let it be denoted by $F_1(s)$. Then Eq. (7.100) yields,

$$F(s) = \frac{1}{1 - e^{-Ts}} F_1(s) \qquad \text{...(7.101)}$$

Eq. (7.101) relates the transform $F(s)$ of any periodic function to the transform $F_1(s)$ of the first cycle only. This is the general principle used in finding the Laplace transform of square wave in the last article.

7.20. Train of Pulses of Width *a* and Periodic Time *T*

Fig. 7.21 shows a train of pulses of width a, amplitude A and periodic time T. The first pulse begins at time $t = 0$, the second at T and so on.

The first pulse is given by the equation,

$$v_1(t) = A\, [u(t) - u(t - a)] \qquad \text{...(7.102)}$$

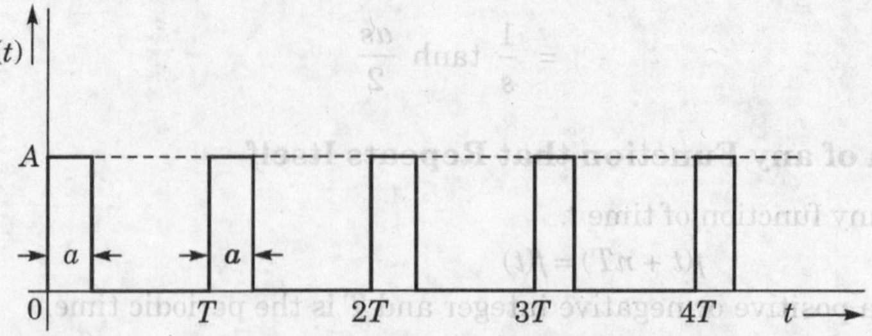

Fig. 7.21. Train of pulses of width a and periodic time T.

Its Laplace transform equation is,

$$V_1(s) = A \cdot \frac{1}{s}[1 - e^{-as}] \qquad ...(7.103)$$

The second, third etc. pulses are similar to the first pulse except that they are shifted by time intervals T, $2T$ etc. Hence using the property discussed in Article 7.20 for periodic waves, the Laplace transform equation for this train pulses is as follows :

$$V(s) = V_1(s) \cdot \frac{1}{1 - e^{-Ts}} \qquad ...(7.104)$$

$$= A \cdot \frac{1}{s} \cdot \frac{1 - e^{-as}}{a - e^{-Ts}} \qquad ...(7.105)$$

7.21. Train of Unit Impulses of Periodic Time *T*

Fig. 7.22 shows a train of unit impulses spaced T units of time apart. Area of each impulse is unity and the first impulse occurs at time $t = 0$. A train of impulses may be represented by Russian letter Ш, pronounced as 'sh' (as in "short"). If the periodic time is T, the symbol used is $\text{Ш}_T(t)$. Thus we have,

$$\text{Ш}_T(t) = \delta(t) + \delta(t - T) + \delta(t - 2T) + \ldots\ldots \qquad ...(7.106)$$

or

$$\text{Ш}_T(t) = \sum_{n=0}^{n=\infty} \delta(t - nT) \qquad ...(7.107)$$

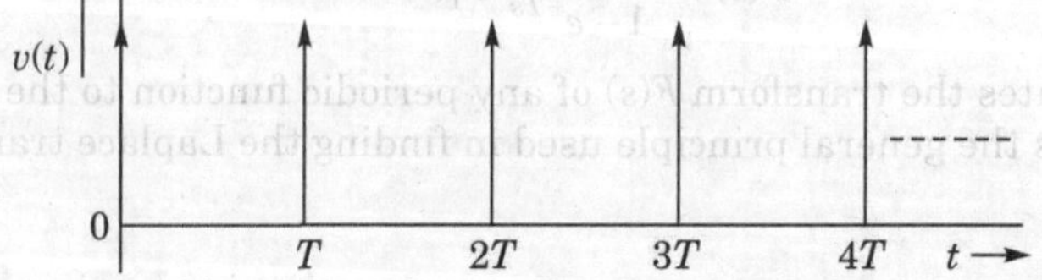

Fig. 7.22. Train of unit impulses.

Let $f(t)$ be any function of time t. Then the product of $\text{Ш}_T(t)$ is given by the relation,

$$f^*(t) = f(t) \cdot \text{Ш}_T(t) \qquad ...(7.108)$$

Function $f^*(t)$ represents a *discrete sampled function, i.e.* a function which has a non-zero value only at times $t = nT$, n being an integer. Now at time $t = nT$, *i.e.* at $(n + 1)$th impulse, the function $f^*(t)$ is in the form of an impulse of area equal to $f(nT)$. This area $f(nT)$ is often called the weight of the function and the function $f^*(t)$ is called a weighted impulse train.

A few examples of discrete sampled function are given below :

Consider the function $f_1(t)$ given by the relation,

$$f_1(t) = kt \quad \text{...(7.109)}$$

where k is a constant.

This is a straight line through the origin with slope equal to k. When multiplied by $\text{Ш}_T(t)$, this results $f_1^*(t)$ given by the relation

$$f_1^*(t) = kt \,.\, \text{Ш}_T(t) \quad \text{...(7.110)}$$

Weighted impulse train $f_1^*(t)$ as given by Eq. (7.110) is shown in Fig. 7.23.

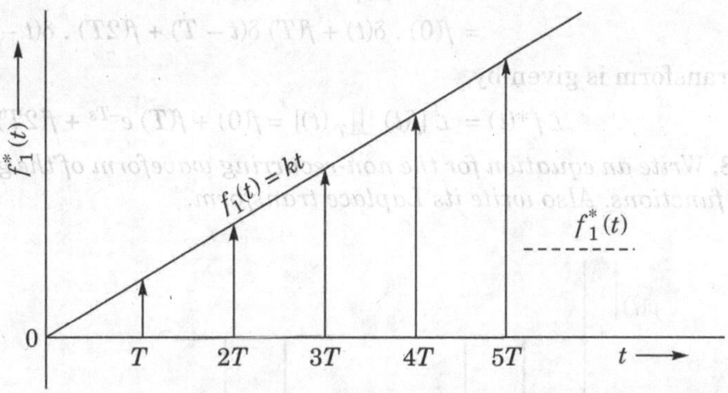

Fig. 7.23. Impulse train $kt \,.\, \text{Ш}_T(t)$

Next consider the function $f_2(t)$ given by the relation

$$f_2(t) = A \sin \frac{2\pi}{T_1} t \quad \text{...(7.111)}$$

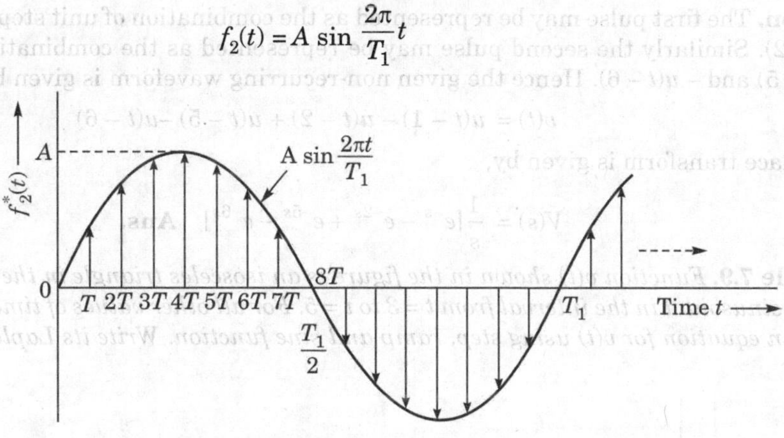

Fig. 7.24. Impulse train $A \sin \left(\frac{2\pi}{T_1} t\right) . \text{Ш}_T(t)$

This is a sinewave of amplitude A and periodic time T_1. When multiplied *by* $\text{Ш}_T(t)$ this results in $f_2^*(t)$ given by the relation,

$$f_2^*(t) = A \sin \left(\frac{2\pi}{T_1} t\right) . \text{Ш}_T(t) \quad \text{...(7.112)}$$

Weighted impulse train $f_2{}^*(t)$ as given by Eq. (7.112) is shown in Fig. 7.24 for $T_1 = 16T$.

Laplace transform of $\text{Ш}_T(t)$ may be obtained by computing the transform of each of the terms of series given by Eq. (7.106). Thus

$$\text{Ш}_T(s) = \mathcal{L}\,[\text{Ш}_T(t)] = \mathcal{L}\,[\delta(t) + \delta(t - T) + \delta(t - 2T) + \ldots\ldots] \qquad \ldots(7.113)$$

$$= 1 + e^{-Ts} + e^{-2Ts} + \ldots\ldots \qquad \ldots(7.114)$$

By using Eq. (7.101), Eq. (7.114) may be put as,

$$\text{Ш}_T(t) = \frac{1}{1 - e^{-Ts}} \qquad \ldots(7.115)$$

Consider next the weighted impulse train $f(t)\,.\text{Ш}_T(t)$ given by,

$$f^*(t) = f(t).\ \text{Ш}_T(s)$$

$$= f(0)\,.\,\delta(t) + f(T)\,\delta(t - T) + f(2T)\,.\,\delta(t - 2T) + \ldots\ldots \qquad \ldots(7.116)$$

Its Laplace transform is given by,

$$\mathcal{L}\,f^*(t) = \mathcal{L}\,[f(t)\ \text{Ш}_T(t)] = f(0) + f(T)\,e^{-Ts} + f(2T)\,e^{-2Ts} + \ldots \qquad \ldots(7.117)$$

Example 7.8. *Write an equation for the non-recurring waveform of the given figure as linear combination of step functions. Also write its Laplace transform.*

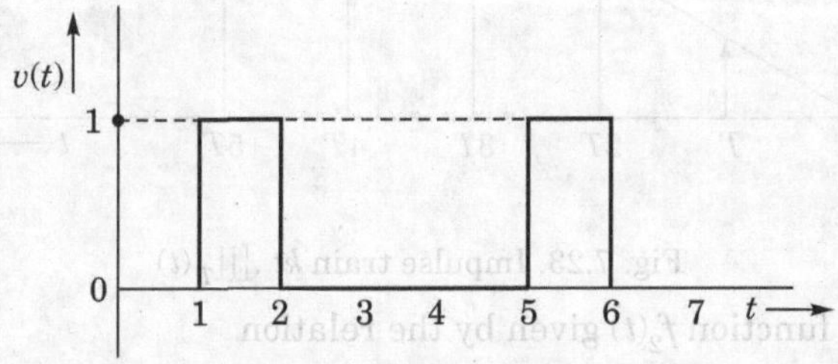

Solution. The first pulse may be represented as the combination of unit step functions $u(t - 1)$ and $- u(t - 2)$. Similarly the second pulse may be represented as the combination of unit step functions $u(t - 5)$ and $- u(t - 6)$. Hence the given non-recurring waveform is given by,

$$v(t) = u(t - 1) - u(t - 2) + u(t - 5) - u(t - 6)$$

Its Laplace transform is given by,

$$V(s) = \frac{1}{s}[e^{-s} - e^{-2s} + e^{-5s} - e^{-6s}] \quad \textbf{Ans.}$$

Example 7.9. *Function v(t) shown in the figure is an isosceles triangle in the interval from t = 1 to t = 2 and sinusoidal in the interval from t = 3 to t = 5. For all other values of time t, the function is zero. Write an equation for v(t) using step, ramp and sine function. Write its Laplace transform.*

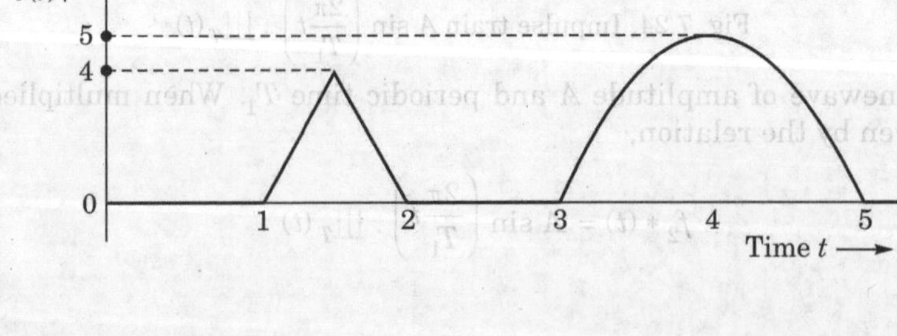

Solution. The given isosceles triangle is a linear combination of following three ramp functions : (*i*) $8r(t-1)$ of slope 8 volts/sec, (*ii*) $-16r(t-1.5)$ of slope -16 volts sec and (*iii*) $8r(t-2)$ of slope 8 volts/sec. These are shown in figure above.

Hence equation for isosceles triangle is,

$$v_1(t) = 8r(t-1) - 16r(t-1.5) + 8r(t-2)$$

The given half cycle of sinewave of periodic time $T = 4$ seconds, of amplitude 5 second and beginning at $t = 3$ second may be considered to be formed by linear combination of following two sinewaves :

(*i*) $5 \sin \frac{2\pi}{4}(t-3) \,.\, u(t-3)$ and (*ii*) $5 \sin \frac{2\pi}{4}(t-5) \,.\, u(t-5)$.

Hence equation for half cycle of sinewave is,

$$v_2(t) = 5 \sin \frac{2\pi}{4}(t-3) \,.\, u(t-3) + 5 \sin \frac{2\pi}{4}(t-5) \,.\, u(t-5)$$

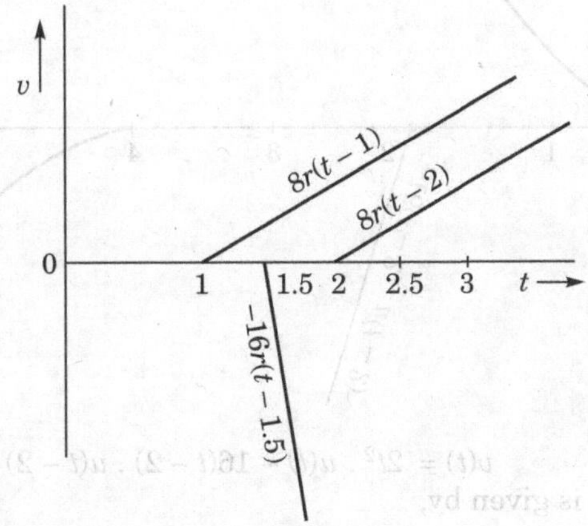

Hence the equation for the complete function is,

$$v(t) = 8[r(t-1) - 2r(t-1.5) + r(t-2)]$$
$$+ 5\left[\sin \frac{2\pi}{4}(t-3) \,.\, u(t-3) + \sin \frac{2\pi}{4}(t-5) \,.\, u(t-5)\right]$$

Hence
$$V(s) = \frac{8}{s^2}[e^{-s} - 2e^{-1.5s} + e^{-2s}]$$
$$+ 5\frac{\pi/2}{s^2 + \left(\frac{\pi}{2}\right)^2}[e^{-3s} + e^{-5s}]$$

Example 7.10. *The parabolic voltage pulse v(t) shown in the figure occurs only once. Write an equation for v(t) using functions multiplied by appropriately delayed step functions. Write its Laplace transform.*

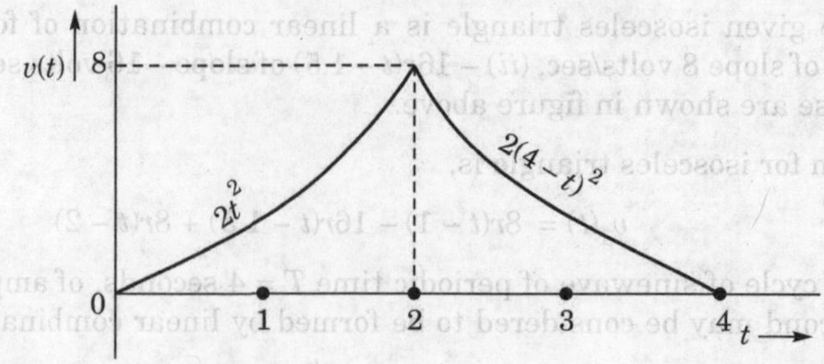

Solution. The given function may be put as the sum of the three functions shown below :

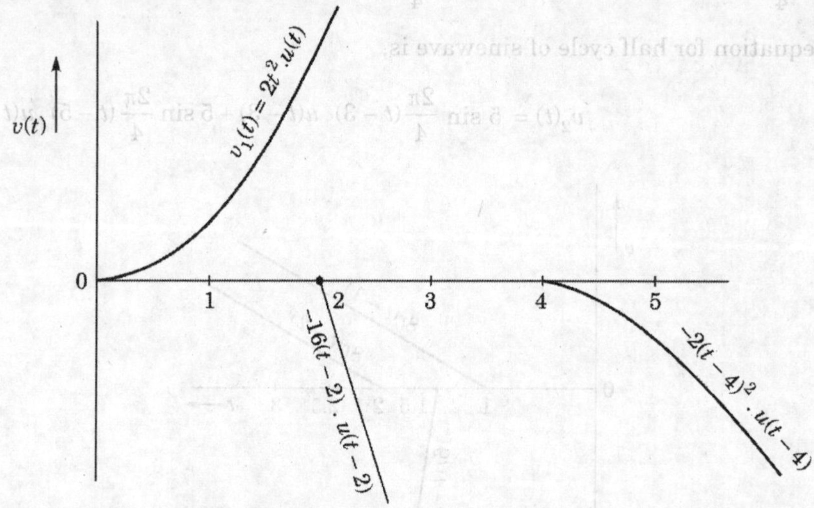

Thus $$v(t) = 2t^2 \,.\, u(t) - 16(t-2) \,.\, u(t-2) - 2(t-4)^2 \,.\, u(t-4)$$

Its Laplace transform is given by,

$$V(s) = \frac{4}{s^3} - 16\frac{1}{s^2}e^{-2s} - 4\frac{1}{s^2} \,.\, e^{-4s} = \frac{4}{s^3}(1 - e^{-4s}) - \frac{16}{s^2}\, e^{-2s}$$

Example 7.11. *A voltage pulse of magnitude 6 volts and dura-tion 3 seconds extending from t = 3 seconds to t = 6 seconds is applied to a series R-L circuit consisting of R = 6 Ω and L = 2H. Obtain the current i(t). Also calculate the voltage across L and R.*

Solution. Application of Kirchhoff's voltage law to the circuit yields,

$$L\frac{di}{dt} + Ri = 6[u(t-3) - u(t-6)] \quad \text{...(1)}$$

On Laplace transformation, we get

$$L[s.I(s) - i(0+)] + R.I(s) = \frac{6}{s}[e^{-3s} - e^{-6s}] \quad \text{...(2)}$$

But $$i(0+) = 0.$$

Hence $$I(s)[Ls + R] = \frac{6}{s}[e^{-3s} - e^{-6s}] \quad \text{...(3)}$$

or $$I(s) = \frac{6}{s} \,.\, \frac{e^{-3s} - e^{-6s}}{Ls + R} = \frac{6}{s} \,.\, \frac{(e^{-3s} - e^{-6s})}{(2s+6)} = (e^{-3s} - e^{6s})\left[\frac{1}{s} - \frac{1}{s+3}\right] \quad \text{...(4)}$$

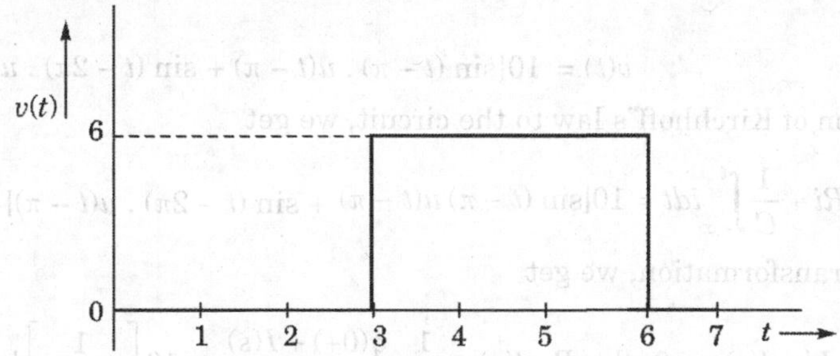

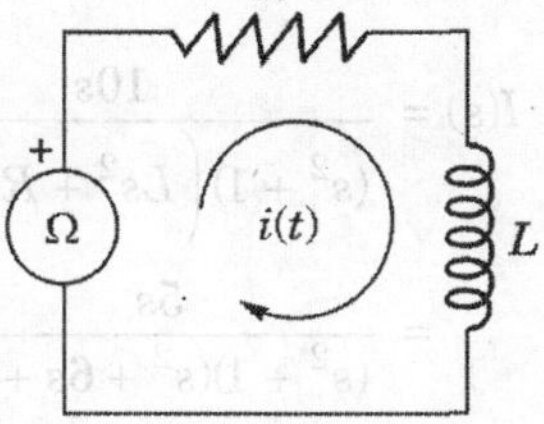

On inverse Laplace transformation Eq. (4) yields,

$$i(t) = u(t-3) - u(t-6) - e^{-3(t-3)} \,.\, u(t-3) + e^{-3(t-6)}\, u(t-6)$$

$$= u(t-3)[1 - e^{-3(t-3)}] - u(t-6)[1 - s^{-3(t-6)}] \qquad ...(5)$$

Voltage across the inductor is given by,

$$v_L = L \,.\, \frac{di}{dt} = 2[u(t-3)\{-(-3)e^{-3(t-3)}\} - u\,(t-6)\,\{-(-3)e^{-3(t-6)}\}]$$

$$= 6u(t-3)e^{-3(t-3)} - 6u(t-6)\, e^{-3(t-6)}$$

Example 7.12. *A half cycle of sinewave of amplitude 10 volts, periodic time 2π seconds, extending from t = π seconds t = 2π seconds (as shown in the figure) is applied to a series R-L-C circuit consisting of resistance R = 12 Ω inductor L = 2 H and capacitor C = 0.1 farad. Find the current i(t).*

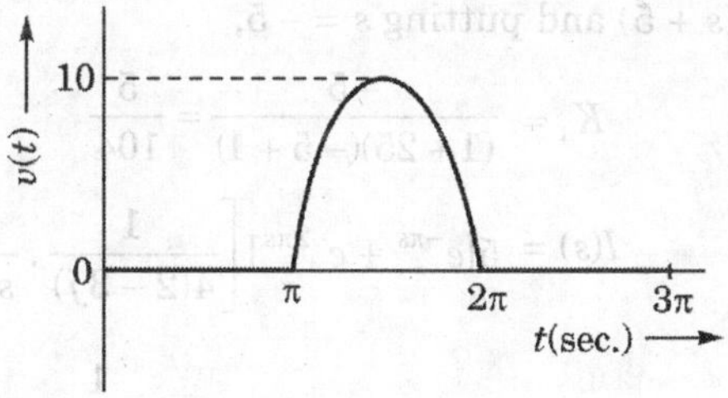

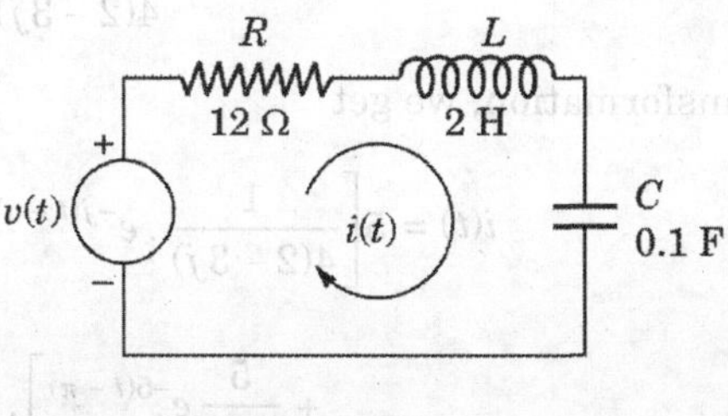

Solution.

$$v(t) = 10[\sin (t - \pi) . u(t - \pi) + \sin (t - 2\pi) . u(t - 2\pi)] \quad ...(1)$$

On application of Kirchhoff's law to the circuit, we get

$$L\frac{di}{dt} + Ri + \frac{1}{C}\int_{-\infty}^{t} idt = 10[\sin (t - \pi)\, u(t - \pi) + \sin (t - 2\pi) . u(t - \pi)] \quad ...(2)$$

On Laplace transformation, we get

$$L[s .I(s) - i(0+)] + R . I(s) + \frac{1}{C} . \frac{q(0+) + I(s)}{s} = 10\left[\frac{1}{s^2+1}\right][e^{-\pi s} + e^{-2\pi s}] \quad ...(3)$$

But $i(0+) = q(0+) = 0$.

Hence Eq. (3) yields,
$$I(s) = \frac{10s}{(s^2+1)\left(Ls^2 + Rs + \frac{1}{C}\right)}[e^{-\pi s} + e^{-2\pi s}] \quad ...(4)$$

$$= \frac{5s}{(s^2+1)(s^2+6s+5)}[e^{-\pi s} + e^{-2\pi s}] \quad ...(5)$$

Let
$$\frac{s}{(s^2+1)(s^2+6s+5)} = \frac{K_1}{s+j} + \frac{K_2}{s-j} + \frac{K_3}{s+1} + \frac{K_4}{s+5} \quad ...(6)$$

Multiplying Eq. (6) by $(s + j)$ and putting $s = -j$,

$$K_1 = \frac{-j}{-2j(1-j)(5-j)} = \frac{1}{4(2-3j)}$$

Multiplying Eq. (6) by $(s - j)$ and putting $s = +j$,

$$K_2 = \frac{+j}{2j(1+j)(5+j)} = \frac{1}{4(2+3j)}$$

Multiplying Eq. (6) by $(s + 1)$ and putting $s = -1$,

$$K_3 = \frac{-1}{(-1+j)(-1-j)(-1+5)} = \frac{-1}{8}$$

Multiplying Eq. (6) by $(s + 5)$ and putting $s = -5$,

$$K_4 = \frac{-5}{(1+25)(-5+1)} = \frac{5}{104}$$

Hence
$$I(s) = 5[e^{-\pi s} + e^{-2\pi s}]\left[\frac{1}{4(2-3j)} . \frac{1}{s+j} + \frac{1}{4(2-3j)} . \frac{1}{s-j} - \frac{1}{8} . \frac{1}{s+1} + \frac{5}{104} . \frac{1}{s+5}\right]$$

On inverse Laplace transformation, we get

$$i(t) = 5\left[\frac{1}{4(2-3j)} . e^{-j(t-\pi)} + \frac{1}{4(2+3j)} e^{j(t-\pi)} - \frac{1}{8} e^{-j(t-\pi)} + \frac{5}{104} e^{-5(t-\pi)}\right] . u(t-\pi) + 5\left[\frac{1}{4(2-3j)} . e^{-j(t-2\pi)}\right.$$

$$+ \frac{1}{4(2+3j)} e^{+j(t-2\pi)} - \frac{1}{8} e^{-(t-2\pi)} + \frac{5}{104} e^{-5(t-2\pi)} \Bigg] . u(t-2\pi)$$

Example 7.13. *Voltage having waveform of* **truncated ramp** *as shown in the figure is applied to an R-L network consisting of resistor R = 3 Ω and inductor L = 1 henry. The rise time t_0 = 2μ seconds. Find the current i(t)*

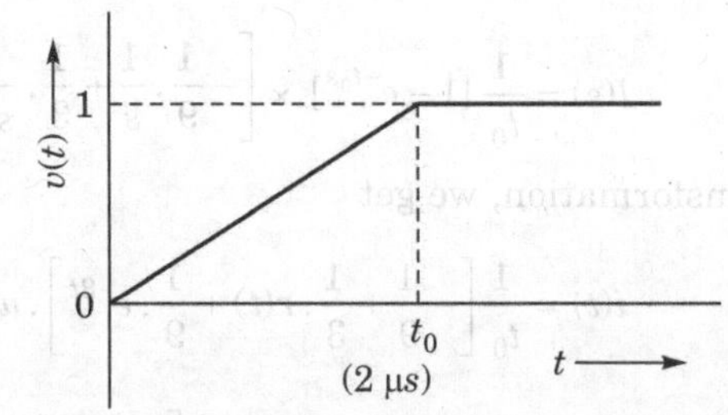

Solution. The truncated ramp may be considered to be formed by the following two ramps:

(*i*) a ramp voltage starting at time $t = 0$ and having slope $= \frac{1}{t_0}$. This may be represented by $\frac{1}{t_0} r(t)$.

(*ii*) a ramp voltage starting at time $t = t_0$ and having slope $= -\frac{1}{t_0}$. This may be represented by $-\frac{1}{t_0} r(t - t_0)$.

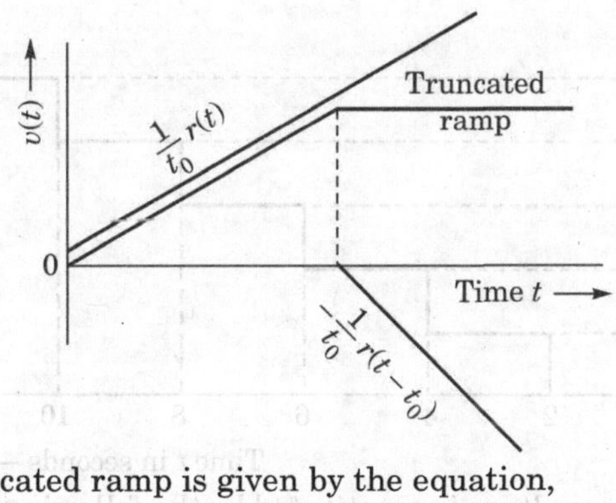

Hence the given truncated ramp is given by the equation,

$$v(t) = \frac{1}{t_0} r(t) - \frac{1}{t_0} r(t - t_0) \quad ...(1)$$

Application of Kirchhoff's voltage law to the given network yields,

$$L\frac{di}{dt} + Ri = v(t) \quad ...(2)$$

On Laplace transformation, we get

$$L[s \,.\, I(s) - i(0+)] + R \,.\, I(s) = \frac{1}{t_0}\left[\frac{1}{s^2} - \frac{1}{s^2} e^{-t_0 s}\right] \quad ...(3)$$

But $i(0+) = 0$.

Hence Eq. (3) yields,

$$I(s)[Ls + R] = \frac{1}{t_0} \,.\, \frac{1}{s^2} [1 - e^{-t_0 s}] \quad ...(4)$$

or $$I(s) = \frac{1}{t_0 s^2}[1 - e^{-t_0 s}]\frac{1}{s+3} \quad ...(5)$$

By method of partial fraction, we get

$$\frac{1}{s^2(s+3)} = -\frac{1}{9}\cdot\frac{1}{s} + \frac{1}{3}\cdot\frac{1}{s^2} + \frac{1}{9}\cdot\frac{1}{s+3} \quad ...(6)$$

Hence $$I(s) = \frac{1}{t_0}[1 - e^{-t_0 s}] \times \left[-\frac{1}{9}\cdot\frac{1}{s} + \frac{1}{3}\cdot\frac{1}{s^2} + \frac{1}{9}\cdot\frac{1}{s+3}\right] \quad ...(7)$$

On inverse Laplace transformation, we get

$$i(t) = \frac{1}{t_0}\left[-\frac{1}{9} + \frac{1}{3}\,.\,r(t) + \frac{1}{9}\,.\,e^{-3t}\right].\,u(t)$$

$$-\frac{1}{t_0}\left[-\frac{1}{9} + \frac{1}{3}r(t - t_0) + \frac{1}{9}e^{-3(t-t_0)}\right].\,u(t - t_0)$$

where $t_0 = 2 \times 10^{-6}$ sec.

Example 7.14. *A staircase voltage shown in the figure is applied to an R-L network consisting* of L = 1 H and R = 2 Ω. *Write equation for the staircase in terms of step function. Find the current i(t). Draw the waveform of current i(t).*

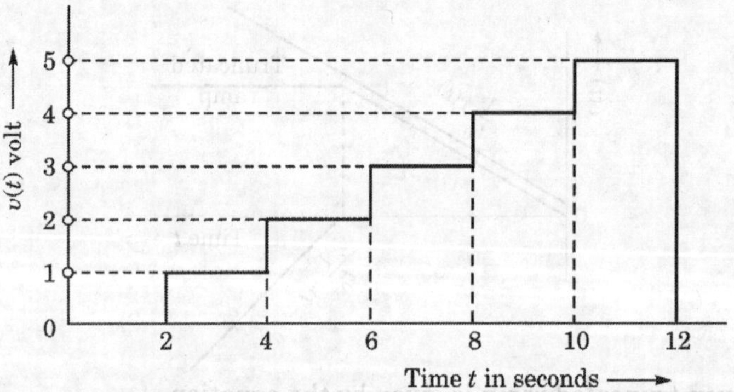

Solution. The staircase voltage is constituted by the following : (*i*) a unit step voltage at t = 2 seconds, (*ii*) further unit step voltages at t = 4, t = 6, t = 8 and t = 10 seconds and (*iii*) a negative step voltage of magnitude 5 volts at t = 12 seconds.

Hence the given staircase voltage may be represented by the equation,

$$v(t) = u(t - 2) + u(t - 4) + u(t - 6) + u(t - 8) + u(t - 10) - 5u(t - 12) \quad ...(1)$$

On application of Kirchhoff's voltage law to the *R-L* circuit, we get

$$Ri + L\frac{di}{dt} = v(t) \quad ...(2)$$

On Laplace transformation Eq. (2) yields,

$$R.I(s) + L[s.I(s) - i(0+)] = \frac{1}{s}[e^{-2s} + e^{-4s} + e^{-6s} + e^{-8s} + e^{-10s} - 5e^{-12s}] \quad ...(3)$$

But $i(0+) = 0$

Hence $I(s) = \frac{1}{s(s+2)}[e^{-2s} + e^{-4s} + e^{-6s} + e^{-8s} + e^{-10s} + 5e^{-12s}]$ ...(4)

$$= \frac{1}{2}\left[\frac{1}{s} - \frac{1}{s+2}\right][e^{-2s} + e^{-4s} + e^{-6s} + e^{-8s} + e^{-10s} - 5e^{-12s}] \quad ...(5)$$

On inverse Laplace transformation Eq. (5) yields,

$$i(t) = \frac{1}{2}[1 - e^{-2(t-2)}].u(t-2) + \frac{1}{2}[1 - e^{-2(t-4)}].u(t-4)$$

$$+ \frac{1}{2}[1 - e^{-2(t-6)}].u(t-6) + \frac{1}{2}[1 - e^{-2(t-8)}].u(t-8)$$

$$+ \frac{1}{2}[1 - e^{-2(t-10)}]u(t-10) - \frac{5}{2}[1 - e^{-2(t-12)}].u(t-12) \quad ...(6)$$

The waveform of current $i(t)$ is as shown in the following figure.

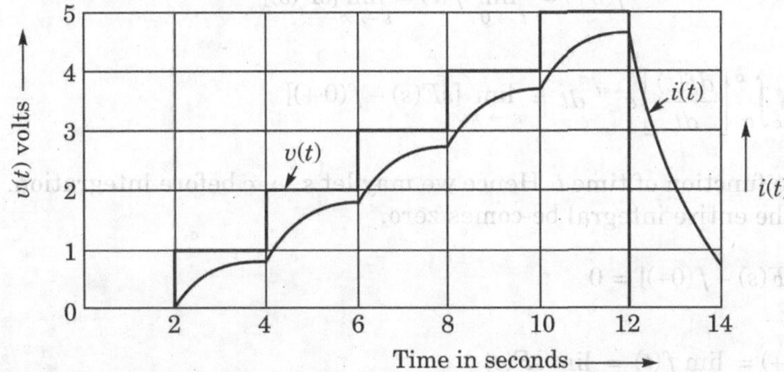

Example 7.15. *The given figure shows the output voltage of a fullwave rectifier. The amplitude is V_0 and the duration of each half cycle of sinewave is 1 second. Show that the Laplace transform of this function is given by,*

$$V(s) = V_0 \frac{\pi}{s^2 + \pi^2} \coth \frac{s}{2}.$$

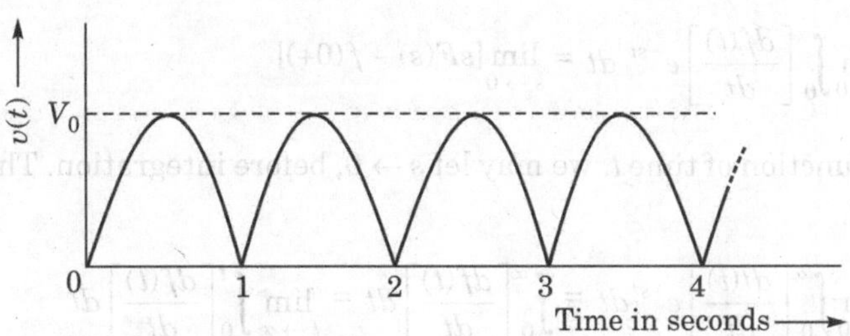

Solution. The first half cycle of sinewave is given by the equation,

$$v_1(t) = V_0 \sin \pi t.u(t) + V_0 \sin \pi(t-1).u(t-1) \quad ...(1)$$

On Laplace transformation Eq. (1) yields,

$$V_1(s) = V_0\left(\frac{\pi}{s^2 + \pi^2}\right) + V_0 \cdot \left(\frac{\pi}{s^2 + \pi^2}\right)e^{-s}$$

or $$V_1(s) = V_0 \frac{\pi}{s^2 + \pi^2} \cdot (1 + e^{-s}) \qquad ...(2)$$

Hence the Laplace transformation of the whole waveform is,

$$V(s) = \frac{1}{1 - e^{-s}} \cdot V_1(s) = V_0 \frac{\pi}{s^2 + \pi^2} \cdot \frac{1 + e^{-s}}{1 - e^{-s}} = V_0 \cdot \frac{\pi}{s^2 + \pi^2} \cdot \coth \frac{s}{2}.$$

7.22. The Initial and Final Values Theorem

For a given transform function $F(s)$, it is often required to find the initial and the final values of the corresponding response function $f(t)$. This may be done directly making use of the two theorems, one giving the initial value of $f(t)$ and the other giving the final value of $f(t)$.

Initial Value Theorem. This theorem states that if $f(t)$ and its first derivative are Laplace transformable, then

$$f(0+) = \lim_{t \to 0+} f(t) = \lim_{s \to \infty} [sF(s)] \qquad ...(7.118)$$

Proof. $$\lim_{s \to \infty} \int_0^{\infty} \left[\frac{df(t)}{dt}\right] e^{-st}\, dt = \lim_{s \to \infty} [sF(s) - f(0+)] \qquad ...(7.119)$$

Now s is not a function of time t. Hence we may let $s \to \infty$ before integration. This makes e^{-st} equal zero. Thus the entire integral be-comes zero.

Hence $$\lim_{s \to \infty} [sF(s) - f(0+)] = 0 \qquad ...(7.120)$$

or $$f(0+) = \lim_{t \to 0} f(t) = \lim_{t \to 0} sF(s) \qquad ...(7.118)$$

Final Value Theorem. This theorem states that if $f(t)$ and its first derivatives are Laplace transformable, then

$$\lim_{t \to \infty} f(t) = \lim_{s \to 0} sF(s) \qquad ...(7.121)$$

Proof. $$\lim_{s \to 0} \int_0^{\infty} \left[\frac{df(t)}{dt}\right] e^{-st}\, dt = \lim_{s \to 0} [sF(s) - f(0+)] \qquad ...(7.122)$$

s not being a function of time t, we may let $s \to 0$, before integration. This makes e^{-st} equal 1. Hence we get,

$$\lim_{s \to 0} \int_0^{\infty} \left[\frac{dt(t)}{dt}\right] e^{-st} dt = \int_0^{\infty} \left[\frac{df(t)}{dt}\right] dt = \lim_{t \to \infty} \int_0^{t} \left[\frac{df(t)}{dt}\right] dt$$

$$= \lim_{t \to \infty} [f(t) - F(0+)] \qquad ...(7.123)$$

Combining Eqs. (7.122) and (7.123), we get the required result namely

$$\lim_{t \to \infty} f(t) = \lim_{s = 0} sF(s) \qquad ...(7.121)$$

Exception to this theorem. Equation (7.121) requires that all the roots in the denominator of

$sF(s)$ have negative real parts failing which limiting values of $f(t)$ with $t \to \infty$ does not exist. Thus with sinusoidal excitation, $\lim_{t \to \infty}$ (sin ωt) does not have a definite value while the roots in the denominator of $sF(s)$ result on inverse Laplace transformation in term e^{∞} which is infinite. Hence Eq. (7.121) does not apply for sinusoidal excitation.

Example 7.16. *Find the value of i(0+) using the Initial value theorem, for the Laplace transform given below,*

$$I(s) = \frac{2s+3}{(s+1)(s+3)}$$

Verify the result by solving for i(t).

Solution. Applying the initial value theorem,

$$i(0+) = \lim_{s \to \infty} \frac{s(2s+3)}{(s+1)(s+3)} = \lim_{s \to \infty} \frac{2s^2+3s}{s^2+4s+3} = 2.$$

Thus $i(0+)$ has been obtained directly without the need of solving for $i(t)$. However the correctness of this result may be verified by solving for $i(t)$ and putting $t = 0$.

Thus the given transform may be put as,

$$\frac{2s+3}{(s+1)(s+3)} = \frac{K_1}{s+1} + \frac{K_1}{s+3} \quad ...(1)$$

Multiplying Eq. (1) by $(s + 1)$ and putting $s = -1$, we get

$$K_1 = \frac{-2+2}{-1+3} = \frac{1}{2}$$

Similarly multiplying Eq. (1) by $(s + 3)$ and putting $s = -3$, we get

$$K_2 = \frac{-6+3}{-1+3} = \frac{+3}{2}$$

Hence $$I(s) = \frac{1}{2(s+1)} + \frac{3}{2} \cdot \frac{1}{s+3} \quad ...(2)$$

On inverse Laplace transformation

$$i(t) = \frac{1}{2} e^{-t} + \frac{3}{2} - e^{-3t} \quad ...(3)$$

At time $t = 0$, $i(0+) = \frac{1}{2} + \frac{3}{2} = 2$

This agrees with the value obtained by using the Initial Value Theorem.

Example 7.17. *For the following Laplace transform find the value of i(t) = ∞ making use of final value theorem :*

$$I(s) = \frac{s+6}{s(s+3)}.$$ *Verify the result by solving for i(t).*

Solution. For the given transform,

$$sI(s) = \frac{s+6}{s+3}$$

Making use of Final Value Theorem,

$$\lim_{t \to \infty} i(t) = \lim_{s \to 0} sI(s)$$

$$= \lim_{s \to 0} \frac{s+6}{s+3} = 2.$$

Verification.

Let $$\frac{s+6}{s(s+3)} = \frac{K_1}{s} + \frac{K_2}{s+3} \quad ...(1)$$

Multiplying Eq. (1) by s and putting $s = 0$, we get

$$K_1 = \frac{6}{3} = 2.$$

Multiplying Eq. (1) by $(s + 2)$ and putting $s = -2$, we get

$$K_2 = \frac{-3+6}{-3} = -1$$

Hence $$I(s) = \frac{2}{s} - \frac{1}{s+3} \quad ...(2)$$

One inverse Laplace transformation,

$$i(t) = 2u(t) - e^{-st} \quad ...(3)$$

$$\lim_{t \to \infty} i(t) = 2 - 0 = 2.$$

This agrees with the result obtained through use of final value theorem.

7.23. The Convolution Integral

Let $F_1(s)$ and $F_2(s)$ be the Laplace transforms of functions $f_1(t)$ and $f_2(t)$ respectively. Then the inverse Laplace transform of product $F_1(s)\,F_2(s)$ may be obtained from the *Convolution* of $f_1(t)$ and $f_2(t)$ as given by the equation,

$$f(t) = \mathcal{L}^{-1}\,[F_1(s)\,F_2(s)] = \int_0^t f_1(\tau) f^2(t-\tau)\,d\tau \quad ...(7.124)$$

$$= \int_0^t f_2(\tau) f_1(t-\tau)\,d\tau \quad ...(7.125)$$

where τ is a dummy variable for t.

The integrals in Eq. (7.124) and (7.125) are called *convolution integrals.*

Convolution of functions $f_1(t)$ and $f_2(t)$ is indicated by the follow-ing notation

$$f(t) = f_1(t) * f_2(t) \quad ...[7.126(a)]$$

$$= f_2(t) * f_1(t) \quad ...[1.126(b)]$$

where $$f_2(t) * f_2(t) = \int_0^t f_1(t-\tau)\,f_2(\tau)\,d\tau \quad ...[7.127(a)]$$

and $$f_2(t) * f_1(t) = \int_0^t f_2(t-\tau)\,f_1(\tau)\,d\tau \quad ...[7.127(b)]$$

Thus we may write,

$$F(s) = F_1(s)F_2(s) = \mathcal{L}[f_1(t) * f_2(t)] = \mathcal{L}[f_2(t) * f_1(t)] \quad ...(7.128)$$

Derivation. Let the Laplace transform integrals $F_1(s)$ and $F_2(s)$ involve dummy variables x and y as given below :

$$F_1(s) = \int_0^{\infty} f_1(x)\, e^{-sx}\, dx \quad ...(7.129)$$

and

$$F_2(s) = \int_0^{\infty} f_2(y)\, e^{-sy}\, dy \quad ...(7.130)$$

Now integral $F_1(s)$ is constant with respect to the variable y while $F_2(s)$ is constant with respect to the variable x. Hence we may write,

$$F(s) = F_1(s)\, F_2(s) = \int_0^{\infty}\int_0^{\infty} f_1(x)\, f_2(y)\, e^{-s(x+y)}\, dxdy \quad ...(7.131)$$

Now we change the variable and introduce new variables t and τ defined by the relations :

$$t = x + y \quad ...(7.132)$$

and

$$\tau = y \quad ...(7.133)$$

The product $dx\, dy$ and $d\tau\, dt$ are related by the Jacobin by the following relation :

$$dx\, dy = \left| \frac{\partial x}{\partial \tau}\frac{\partial y}{\partial t} - \frac{\partial x}{\partial t}\cdot\frac{\partial y}{\partial \tau}\, d\tau\, dt \right| \quad ...(7.134)$$

On evaluating the partial derivatives using Eqs. (7.132) and (7.133), we get

$$\left| \frac{\partial x}{\partial \tau}\frac{\partial y}{\partial t} - \frac{\partial x}{\partial t}\cdot\frac{\partial y}{\partial \tau} \right| = 1$$

Hence Eq. (7.134) yields,

$$dx\, dy = d\tau\, .\, dt \quad ...(7.135)$$

Thus the differential area $dx\, dy$ in the first system of variables is the same as the differential area $d\tau\, dt$ in the new system of variables.

In order to rewrite Eq. (7.131) in terms of new variables τ and t we must also determine the new limits of integration.

Now using the variables x and y, the integration extends from 0 to infinity for both variables x and y.

Further $\quad t = x + y = \tau + x \quad ...(7.136)$

But since the smallest value of x is zero, it is required to consider only $t \geq \tau$ or consider τ upto t. The equation $\tau = t$ may be represented by a straight line through the origin in the $\tau - t$ plane having a slope of 45° as shown in Fig. 7.25.

Now in order to integrate the area between the line $\tau = t$ and $\tau = 0$ we are required to make the following two integrations : (*i*) first we integrate from $\tau = 0$ to $\tau = t$ and (*ii*) then we integrate from $t = 0$ to $t = \infty$.

Having ascertained the limits of integration and having estab-lished that $d\tau\, dt$ is equal to $dy\, dx$, we now rewrite Eq. (7.131) in terms of variables t and τ as below :

$$F(s) = \int_{t=0}^{t=\infty}\left[\int_{\tau=0}^{\tau=t} f_1(t-\tau)\, f_2(\tau)\, d\tau\right] e^{-st}\, dt \quad ...(7.137)$$

On inverse Laplace transformation Eq. (7.137) yields,

$$f(t) = \mathcal{L}^{-1}[F_1(s)\,F_2(s)] = \int_0^t f_1(t-\tau)\,f_2(\tau)\,d\tau = f_1(t) * f_2(t) \qquad \text{...(7.138)}$$

If we interchange $f_1(t)$ and $f_2(t)$, the above deviation yields,

$$f(t) = \mathcal{L}^{-1}[F_1(s)\,F_2(s)] = \int_0^t f_2(t-\tau)\,f_1(\tau)\,d\tau = f_2(t) * f_1(t) \qquad \text{...(7.139)}$$

Eqs. (7.138) and (7.139) are the same as Eqs. (7.125) and (7.124) respectively.

The convolution may be interpreted in terms of the following four physical processes : (*i*) folding (*ii*) translating (*iii*) multiplying and (*iv*) integrating. The German word describing these 4 processes is Faltung. According the convolution integral is also called *Faltung integral.*

The above mentioned 4 steps involved in the convolution may be best illustrated through an example. Thus let,

$$F_1(s) = \frac{1}{s^2} \qquad \text{...(7.140)}$$

and

$$F_2(s) = \frac{1}{s+2} \qquad \text{...(7.141)}$$

Hence

$$f_1(t) = r(t) \qquad \text{...(7.142)}$$

and

$$f_2(t) = e^{-2t}.u(t) \qquad \text{...(7.143)}$$

We wish to evaluate $f(t)$ or $\mathcal{L}^{-1}[F_1(s)\,F_2(s)]$ by convolution *i.e.* we wish to determine,

$$f(t) = f(t) * f_2(t) = \int_0^t r(t-\tau)\,e^{-2r}\,d\tau \qquad \text{...(7.144)}$$

The various steps involved in convolving these two function are shown in Fig. 7.26. Thus functions $f_1(t)$ and $f_2(t)$ are shown in Fig. 7.26 (*a*) while functions $f_1(\tau)$ and $f_2(\tau)$ are shown in Fig. 7.26 (*b*).

Folding. Next step consists in finding the functions $f_1(-\tau)$ and $f_2(-\tau)$. Graphs of these are obtained on folding about the $\tau = 0$ axis the graphs in Fig. 7.26 (*b*). The resulting graphs are shown in Fig. 7.26 (*c*).

Translating. Next step consists in translating the functions $f_1(-\tau)$ and $f_2(-\tau)$ for some specific value of t. This results in new functions $f_1(t-\tau)$ and $f_2(t-\tau)$ drawn in Fig. 7.26 (*d*).

Multiplication. Next step consists in multiplying the functions $f_1(t-\tau)$ and $f_2(\tau)$ to get the function $f_1(t-\tau)\,f_2(\tau)$ and to multiply the function $f_2(t-\tau)$ with $f_1(\tau)$ to get the function $f_2(t-\tau)\,f_1(\tau)$. These two resulting functions are drawn in Fig. 7.26 (*e*). These functions resulting on multiplication are the same as the functions within the integral sign in Eqs. (7.125) and (7.124).

Integration. Next step consists in integrating the cross-hetched area to yield the functions

$$\int_0^t f_1(t-\tau)\,f_2(\tau)\,d\tau \text{ and } \int_0^t f_2(t-\tau)\,f_1(\tau)\,d\tau \text{ respectively.}$$

For the selected value of t, these integrals are nothing but the convolution integrals of Eqs. (7.125) and (7.124). Both of these represent the same function. Thus,

$$f(t) = f_1(t) * f_2(t) = f_2(t) * f_1(t).$$

If the process is repeated for various values of t and the function $f(t)$ plotted against t, we get curves shown in Fig. 7.26 (*f*).

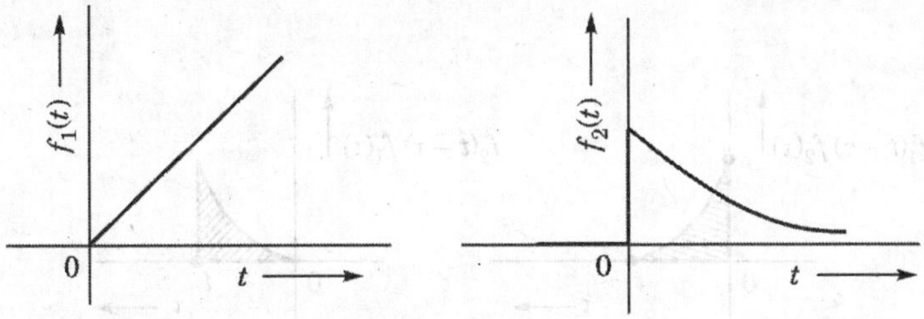

(a) Functions of variable t.

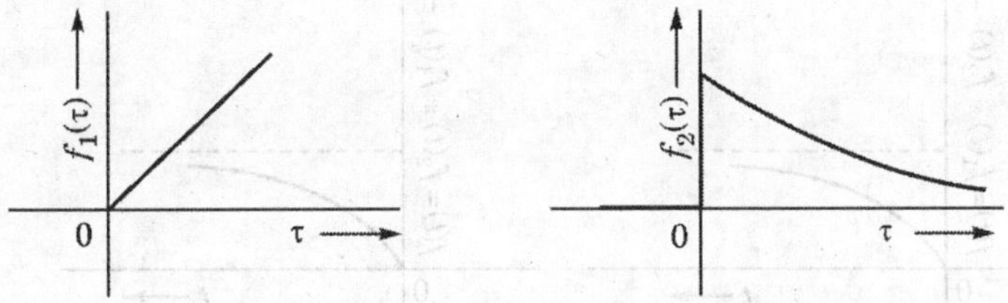

(b) Functions of dummy variable τ.

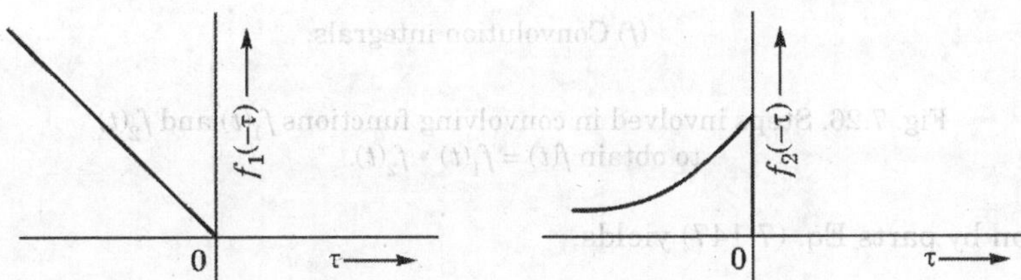

(c) Folded functions of variable τ.

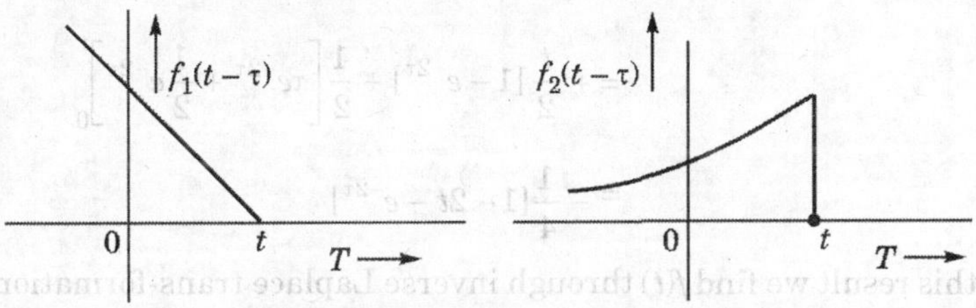

(c) Folded and translated functions.

For the given examples, integration of Eq. (7.144) is given below :

$$f(t) = \int_0^t e^{-2r} r(t - \tau)\, d\tau \quad ...(7.145)$$

$$= \int_0^t e^{-2r} r(t - \tau)\, d\tau \quad ...(7.146)$$

$$f(t) = t\int_0^t e^{-2r}\, d\tau - \int_0^t e^{-2t}\, \tau\, d\tau \quad ...(7.147)$$

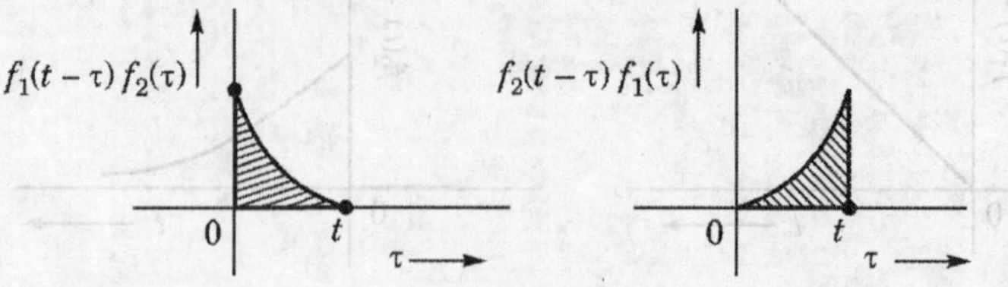

(*e*) Multiplied functions.

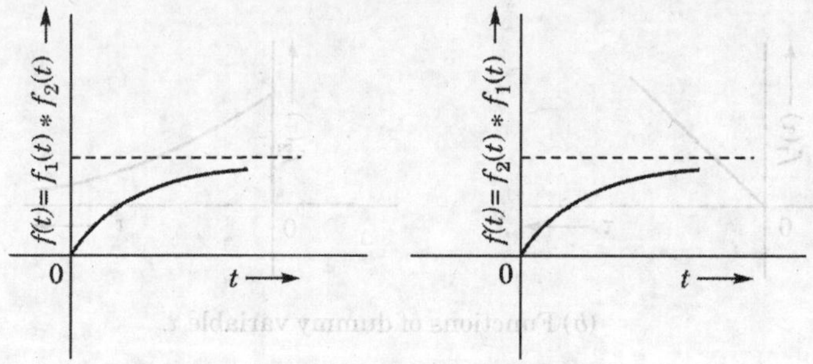

(*f*) Convolution integrals.

Fig. 7.26. Steps involved in convolving functions $f_1(t)$ and $f_2(t)$ to obtain $f(t) = f_1(t) * f_2(t)$.

Integration by parts Eq. (7.147) yields,

or
$$f(t) = t\left[\frac{e^{-2\tau}}{-2}\right]_0^t - \left[\tau \,.\, \frac{e^{-2\tau}}{(-2)} - \int \frac{e^{-2\tau}}{(-2)}\,d\tau\right]_0^t$$

$$= +\frac{t}{2}\,[1 - e^{-2\tau}] + \frac{1}{2}\left[\tau e^{-2\tau} + \frac{1}{2}e^{-2\tau}\right]_0^t$$

$$= -\frac{1}{4}[1 - 2t - e^{-2\tau}] \qquad ...(7.148)$$

To verify this result we find $f(t)$ through inverse Laplace trans-formation of products of $F_1(s)$ and $F_2(s)$.

This
$$F(s) = F_1(s)\,.\,F_2(s) = \frac{1}{s^2(s+2)} \qquad ...(7.149)$$

Let
$$\frac{1}{s^2(s+2)} = \frac{K_1}{s} + \frac{K_2}{s^2} + \frac{K_3}{s+2} \qquad ...(7.150)$$

Multiplying Eq. (7.150) by s^2, we get

$$\frac{1}{s+2} = K_1 s + K_2 + \frac{K_3 s^2}{s+2} \qquad ...(7.151)$$

Putting $s = 0$ in Eq. (7.151), we get

$$K_2 = \frac{1}{2}.$$

Differentiating Eq. (7.151) with respect to s, we get

$$K_1 + K_3 \cdot \frac{(s+2)\,2s - s^2}{(s+2)^2} = \frac{-1}{(s+2)^2} \qquad ...(7.152)$$

Putting $s = 0$ in Eq. (7.152), we get

$$K_1 = \frac{-1}{4}$$

Multiplying Eq. (7.150) by $(s + 2)$ and putting $s = -2$, we get

$$K_3 = \frac{1}{(s+2)^2} = \frac{1}{4}$$

Hence

$$F(s) = -\frac{1}{4}\cdot\frac{1}{s} + \frac{1}{2}\cdot\frac{1}{s^2} + \frac{1}{4}\cdot\frac{1}{s+2} \qquad ...(7.153)$$

On inverse Laplace transformation Eq. (7.153) yields,

$$f(t) = -\frac{1}{4} + \frac{1}{2}\cdot t + \frac{1}{4}\cdot e^{-2t}$$

$$= -\frac{1}{4}[1 - 2t - e^{-2t}] \qquad ...(7.153\ a)$$

Thus the value of $f(t)$ as given by Eq. (7.148) found on convolution agrees with the value as given by Eq. (7.154) obtained through inverse transformation of product $F_1(s)\,.\,F_2(s)$.

7.24. Convolution as a Summation

In certain applications we are required to replace the convolution integral by a finite summation. Let the convolution integral be given by the equation,

$$f(t) = \int_0^t f_1(\tau)\, f_2(t-\tau)\, d\tau \qquad ...(7.154)$$

Let then the infinitesimal $\delta\tau$ be replaced by a time interval of finite width T and let $nT = \tau$ where n is an integer. Then Eq. (7.154) may be written as a summation as below :

$$f(t) = T \sum_{n=0}^{n=k} f_1(nT)\, f_2(t - nT) \qquad ...(7.155)$$

where $KT \le t < (K+1)T$ ...(7.156)

where K is one of the values of the integer n.

Eq. (7.155) may be expressed as below :

$$f(t) = T[f_1(0)\, f_2(t) + f_1(T) f_2(t-T) + f_1(2T)\, f_2(t-2T) + ...] \qquad ...(7.157)$$

Fig. 7.27 shows the waveforms of the individual terms in Eq. (7.157) namely the terms $Tf_1(0)\, f_2(T)$, $Tf_1(T)\, f_2(t-T)$, $Tf_1(2T)\, f_2(t-2T)$ etc. Each of these terms, *i.e.* term $Tf_1(nT)\, f_2(t-nT)$ is the impulse response of maximum value $Tf_1(nT)$ shifted by interval nT along the t-axis. On summation of these terms, there results the function $f(t)$. Evidently the order of accuracy of the approximation depends on how small T is chosen. The smaller the value of T, the better is the accuracy. In the limit T equals $d\tau$ and then the result is exact.

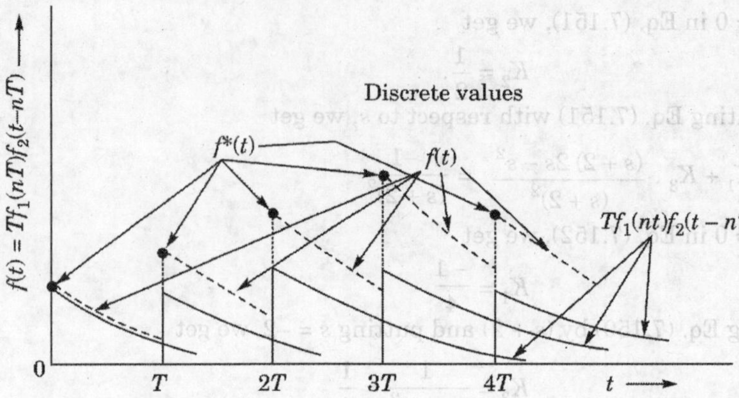

Fig. 7.27. Continuous response $f(t)$ and discrete values of response evaluated on considering convolution as a summation.

The values of $f(t)$ are calculated for discrete values of time t namely for KT, where K is an integer. Let these discrete values of $f(t)$ be indicated by $f*(t)$. Then

$$f*(t) = f(KT) = T\sum_{n=0}^{n=k} f_1(nT)\, f_2(K-n)T \qquad ...(7.158)$$

Here the asterisk represents a discrete sampled function, *i.e.* Eq. (7.158) is not a continuous function but holds for integral values of K. On the other hand, Eq. (7.155) may be used to compute $f(t)$ for all continuous values of time t. Both $f*(t)$ and $f(t)$ are plotted in Fig. 7.27.

EXERCISES

7.1. A pulse voltage of width a and magnitude 3 volts is applied at $t = 0$ to a series R-L circuit consisting of resistor $R = 3\ \Omega$ and inductor $L = 1$ henry. Find the current $i(t)$.

[**Ans.** $i(t) = u(t)\,(1 - e^{-3t}) - u(t-a).(1 - e^{-3(t-a)})$]

7.2. A voltage pulse of width 2 seconds and magnitude 4 volts is applied at time $t = 0$ to a series R-C circuit comprising a resistor $R = 2\ \Omega$ and capacitor $C = 0.1$ Farad. Find the current $i(t)$.

[**Ans.** $i(t) = 2\{u(t).e^{-5t} - u(t-a)\,e^{-5(t-a)}\}$]

7.3. A network consisting of resistor $R = 4\ \Omega$ and inductor $L = 1$ H is driven by a unit impulse at time $t = 3$ seconds. Find the current $i(t)$. [**Ans.** $i(t) = e^{-4(t-3)}\,.\,u(t-3)$]

7.4. A network consisting of a series combination of resistor $R = 1\ \Omega$ and capacitor $C = 0.2$. Farad is driven by a unit impulse $\delta(t-3)$. Find the current $i(t)$. [**Ans.** $i(t) = \delta(t-3) - 5e^{-5(t-3)}$]

7.5. Find the response of a series R-L circuit consisting of a resistor $R = 8\ \Omega$ and inductor $L = 2$ H when a parabolic function $2p(t-3)$ starting at $t = 3$ seconds is applied to it.

$$\left[\textbf{Ans. } i(t) = \frac{1}{64}\{4u(t-3) - 4r(t-3) + 16p(t-3) - e^{-4(t-3)}\}, t > 3\right]$$

7.6. Find the current in a series R-L circuit consisting of a resistor $R = 6\ \Omega$ and inductor $L = 3$ H when each of the following driving force voltage, each starting at time $t = 4$ seconds, is applied : (*i*) ramp function $3t(i-4)$. (*ii*) step function $3u(t-4)$, (*iii*) impulse function $3\delta(t-4)$, (*iv*) doublet function $3\delta'(t-4)$.

[**Ans.** (*i*) $i(t) = \frac{1}{4}\{-u(t-4) + 2r(t-4) + e^{-2(t-4)}u(t-4)\}$

(*ii*) $i(t) = \frac{1}{2}\{u(t-4) - e^{-2(t-4)}\,.\,u(t-4)$

(iii) $i(t) = e^{-2(t-4)} \cdot u(t-4)$

(iv) $i(t) = \delta(t-4) - 2e^{-2(t-4)}$]

7.7. Find the current $i(t)$ in a series R-C circuit comprising resistor $R = 1\ \Omega$ and capacitor $C = 0.2$ Farad when each of the following driving force voltage is applied: (i) ramp voltage $3r(t-1)$ (ii) step voltage $2u(t-2)$, (iii) impulse voltage $4\delta(t)$ and (iv) doublet voltage $\delta'(t-3)$.

[**Ans.** (i) $i(t) = \frac{3}{5} u(t-1)\{1 - e^{-5(t-1)}\}$

(ii) $i(t) = 2u(t-2)\, e^{-5(t-2)}$

(iii) $i(t) = 4\{\delta(t) - 5e^{-5t}\}$

(iv) $i(t) = \delta'(t-3) - 5\delta(t-3) + 25u(t-3)e^{-5(t-3)}$]

7.8. Find the current $i(t)$ in a series R-L-C circuit comprising of resistor $R = 3\ \Omega$, inductor $L = 1$ Henry and capacitor $C = \frac{1}{2}$ Farad, when each of the following driving force voltage is supplied : (i) ramp voltage $2(r(t-1)$, (ii) step voltage $u(t-3)$, (iii) impulse voltage $\delta(t-2)$ and (iv) doublet $\delta'(t-2)$.

[**Ans.** (i) $i(t) = u(t-1) - 2e^{-(t-1)} \cdot u(t-1) + e^{-2(t-1)} \cdot u(t-1)$

(ii) $i(t) = e^{-(t-3)} \cdot u(t-3) - e^{-2(t-3)} \cdot u(t-3)$

(iii) $i(t) = 2e^{-2(t-2)} \cdot u(t-2) - e^{-(t-2)} \cdot u(t-2)$

(iv) $i(t) = \delta(t-2) + e^{-(t-2)} \cdot u(t-2) + 4e^{-2(t-2)} \cdot u(t-2)$]

7.9. Write the equation for the waveform shown in the figure in terms of linear combinations of step functions. Also write its Laplace transform.

[**Ans.** (1) $v(t) = 8\{u(t-2) - u(t-4)\} - 6\{u(t-5) - u(t-6)\}$

$$V(s) = \frac{8}{s}\{e^{-2s} - e^{-4s}\} - \frac{6}{s}\{e^{-5s} - e^{-6s}\})$$

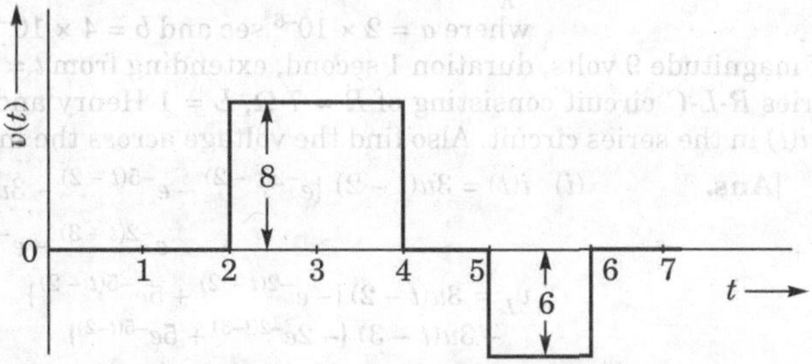

7.10. The voltage waveform shown in the figure is sinusoidal during the interval $t = 2$ to $t = 4$ seconds and is a pulse during the interval $t = 5$ to $t = 6$ seconds. For all others values of time t, $v(t)$ is zero. Write an equation for this voltage $v(t)$ and write its Laplace transform.

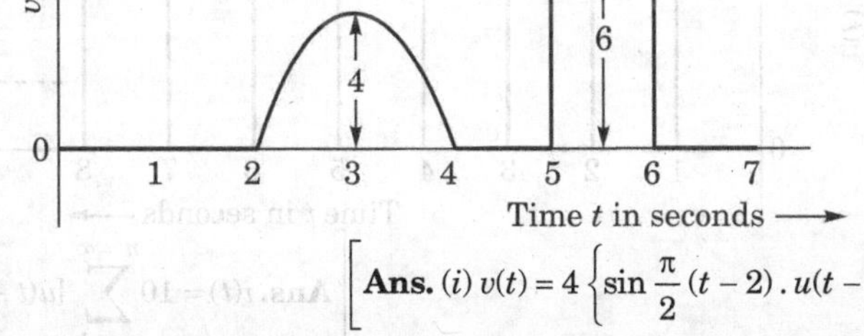

$$\left[\textbf{Ans.}\ (i)\ v(t) = 4\left\{\sin\frac{\pi}{2}(t-2) \cdot u(t-2) - \sin\frac{\pi}{2}(t-4) \cdot u(t-4)\right\}\right.$$

$$+ 6\{u(t-5) - u(t-6)\}$$

$$(ii)\ V(s) = \frac{2\pi}{s^2 + \left(\frac{\pi}{2}\right)^2}\{e^{-2s} - e^{-4s}\} + \frac{6}{s}\{e^{-5s} - e^{-6s}\}\Bigg]$$

7.11. **A voltage pulse of magnitude 8 volts and duration 2 seconds extending from $t = 2$ seconds to $t = 4$ seconds is applied to a series R-L network consisting of $R = 2\ \Omega$ and $L = 1$ Henry. Obtain the current $i(t)$. Also calculate the voltages across inductor L and resistor R.**

[Ans.
$$(i) = 4u(t-2)\{1 - e^{-2(t-2)} - 4u(t-4).\{1 - e^{-2(t-4)}\}]$$
$$v_L = 8\{u(t-2)\ e^{-2(t-2)} - u(t-4) - e^{-2(t-2)}\}$$
$$v_R = 8u(t-2)\{1 - e^{-2(t-2)}\} - 8u(t-4)\{1 - e^{-2(1-4)}\}]$$

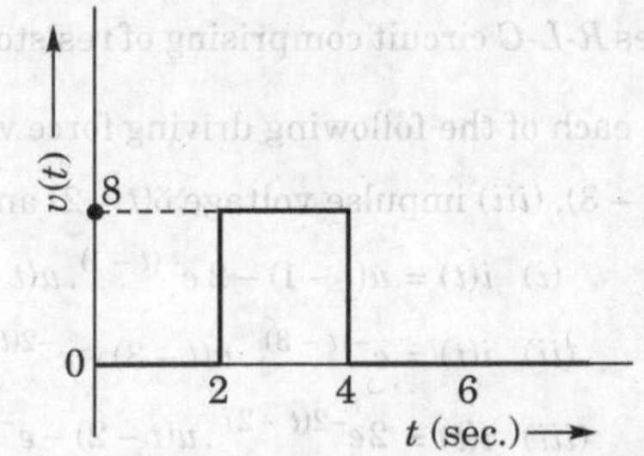

7.12. **A voltage pulse of magnitude 8 volts, duration 2 μ-sec extending from time $t = 2$ μ sec to $t = 4$ μ sec is applied to a series R-C circuit consisting of resistor $R = 100\ \Omega$ and capacitor $C = 0.01$ μF. Obtain (*i*) the current $i(t)$, (*ii*) voltage v_C across the capacitor C and (*iii*) voltage v_R across the resistor R.**

[Ans.
$$(i)\ i(t) = 0.08\{u(t-a)\ e^{-10^6(t-a)} - u(t-b)\ e^{-10^6(t-b)}\}$$
$$(ii)\ v_C = 8\{u(t-a) - u(t-a)\ e^{-10^6(t-a)} - u(t-b) + u(t-b)\ e^{-10^6(t-b)}\}$$
$$(iii)\ v_R = 8\{u(t-a\}\ e^{-10^6(t-a)} - u(t-b) - e^{-10^6(t-b)}\}$$
where $a = 2 \times 10^{-6}$ sec and $b = 4 \times 10^{-6}$ sec.]

7.13. **A voltage pulse of magnitude 9 volts, duration 1 second, extending from $t = 2$ seconds to $t = 3$ seconds is applied to a series R-L-C circuit consisting of $R = 7\ \Omega$, $L = 1$ Henry and $C = 0.1$ Farad. Find the resulting current $i(t)$ in the series circuit. Also find the voltage across the inductor L and capacitor C.**

[Ans.
$$(i)\ i(t) = 3u(t-2)\ \{e^{-2(t-2)} - e^{-5(t-2)} - 3u(t-3)$$
$$e^{-2(t-3)} - e^{-5(t-3)}\}$$
$$v_L = 3u(t-2)\{-e^{-2(t-2)} + 5e^{-5(t-2)}\}$$
$$-\ 3u(t-3)\ \{-2e^{-2(t-3)} + 5e^{-5(t-2)}\}$$
$$v_C = 3u(t-2)\{3 - 5e^{-2(t-2)} + 2e^{-5(t-2)}\}$$
$$-\ 3u(t-3)\ \{3 - 5e^{-2(t-3)} + 2e^{-5(t-3)}\}$$

7.14. **A train of voltage pulses of magnitude 9 volts duration 1 second each and periodic time 2 seconds with first pulse beginning at $t = 1$ second (as shown in the adjoining figure) is applied to a series R-L circuit consisting of a resistor $R = 1\ \Omega$ and inductor $L = 0.1$ Henry. Obtain the current $i(t)$.**

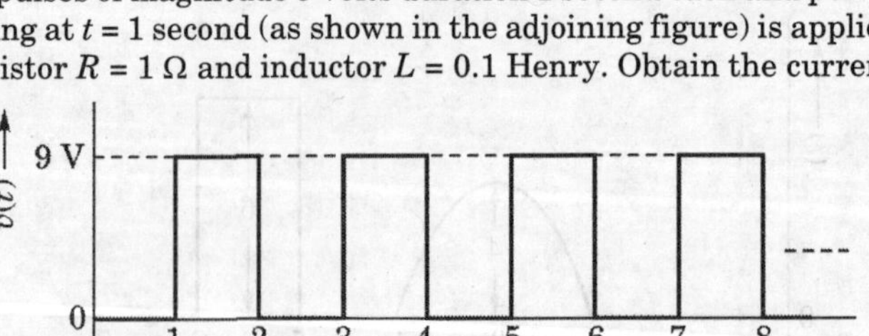

$$\left[\ \textbf{Ans. } i(t) = 10\sum_{n=1}^{n=\infty}\ [u(t-1)\{1 - e^{-10(t-1)}\}(-1)^{n+1}\ \right]$$

7.15. One cycle of sinewave voltage of amplitude 10 volts and periodic time π seconds extending from $t = \pi$ seconds to $t = 2\pi$ seconds (as shown in the figure) is applied to series R-L circuit consisting of resistor $R = 3\ \Omega$ and inductor $L = 1$ Henry. Find the current $i(t)$ and the voltage v_L across the inductor L.

$$\left[\textbf{Ans. } i(t) = 20\left[\frac{-1}{4(2+j5)}.e^{-j2(t-\pi)} - \frac{1}{4(2-j5)}.e^{+j2(t-\pi)} + \frac{1}{29}e^{-5(t-\pi)}\right] \times u(t-\pi) - 20\right.$$

$$\left.\left[\frac{-1}{4(2+j5)}.e^{-j2(t-2\pi)} - \frac{1}{4(2-j5)}.e^{+j2(t-2\pi)} + \frac{1}{29}e^{-5(t-2\pi)}\right].u(t-2\pi)\right]$$

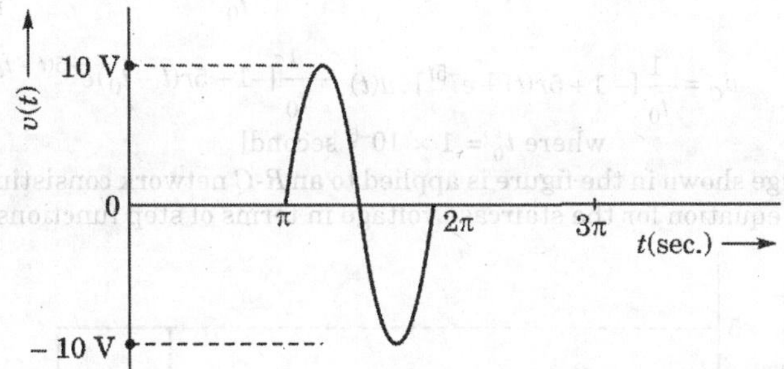

7.16. Half cycle of sinewave voltage of amplitude 5 volts and periodic time π seconds extending from $t = \pi/2$ seconds to $t = \pi$ seconds (as shown in the figure) is applied to a series R-C circuit consisting of resistor $R = 2\ \Omega$ and capacitor $C = 0.5$ Farad. Find (*i*) the current $i(t)$ and (*ii*) voltage v_C across the capacitor C.

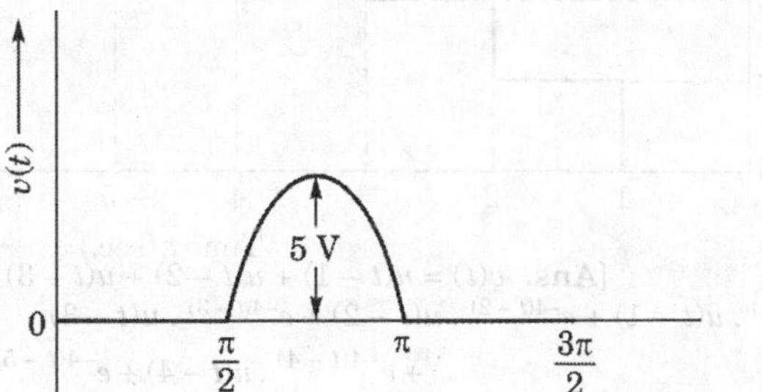

$$\left[\textbf{Ans. } (i)\ i(t) = 5\left[\frac{1}{2(1-j2)}e^{-j2\left(t-\frac{\pi}{2}\right)} + \frac{1}{2(1+j2)}e^{+j2\left(t-\frac{\pi}{2}\right)} - \frac{1}{5}e^{-\left(t-\frac{\pi}{2}\right)}\right]\right.$$

$$\times u\left(t-\frac{\pi}{2}\right) - 5\left[\frac{1}{2(1-j2)}e^{-j2(t-\pi)} + \frac{1}{2(1+j2)}e^{+j2(t-\pi)} - \frac{1}{5}e^{-(t-\pi)}\right].u(t-\pi)$$

$$(ii)\ v_C = 10\left[-\frac{1}{4(2+j)}e^{-j2\left(t-\frac{\pi}{2}\right)} - \frac{1}{4(2-j)}e^{-j2\left(t-\frac{\pi}{2}\right)} + \frac{1}{5}e^{-\left(t-\frac{\pi}{2}\right)}\right]$$

$$\left.\times u\left(t-\frac{\pi}{2}\right) - 10\left[-\frac{1}{4(2+j)}e^{j2(t-\pi)} - \frac{1}{4(2-j)}e^{+j2(t-\pi)} + \frac{1}{5}e^{-(t-\pi)}\right].u(t-\pi)\right]$$

7.17. A voltage having waveform of truncated ramp as shown in the figure is applied to an R-C network consisting of $R = 1\ \Omega$ and capacitor $C = 0.2$ Farad. The rise time $t_0 = 1\ \mu$ sec. Find the current $i(t)$. Also find the voltage across the capacitor C.

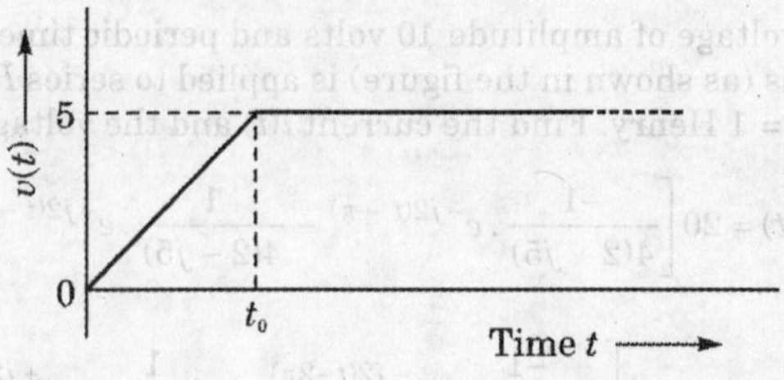

[**Ans.** (*i*) $i(t) = \frac{1}{t_0}[1 - e^{-5t}] \,.\, u(t) - \frac{1}{t_0}[1 - e^{-5(t - t_0)}] \,.\, u(t - t_0)$

$$v_C = \frac{1}{t_0}[-1 + 5r(t) + e^{-5t}] \,.\, u(t) - \frac{1}{t_0}[-1 + 5r(t - t_0)e^{-5(t - t_0)}] \,.\, u(t - t_0)$$

where $t_0 = 1 \times 10^{-6}$ second]

7.18. A staircases voltage shown in the figure is applied to an *R-C* network consisting of $R = 1\ \Omega$ and $C = 0.25$ Farad. Write the equation for the staircase voltage in terms of step functions. Find the current $i(t)$.

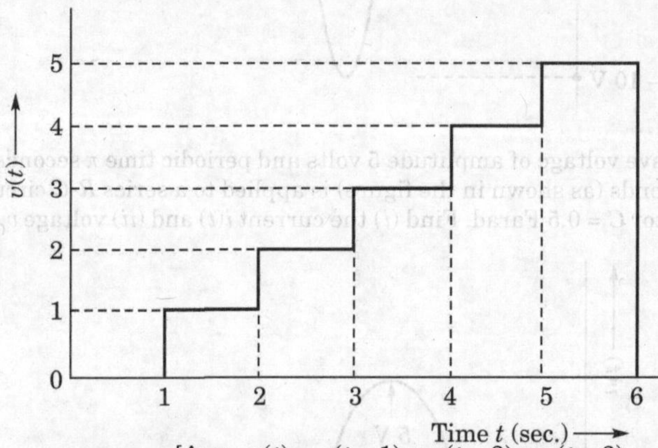

[**Ans.** $v(t) = u(t - 1) + u(t - 2) + u(t - 3) + u(t - 4) + u(t - 5) - 5u(t - 6)$

$i(t) = e^{-4(t-1)} \,.\, u(t - 1) + e^{-4(t-2)} \,.\, u(t - 2) + e^{-4(t-3)} \,.\, u(t - 3)$

$+ e^{-4(t-4)} \,.\, u(t - 4) + e^{-4(t-5)} \,.\, u(t - 5) - 5e^{-4(t-6)} \,.\, u(t - 6)$]

7.19. Given figure shows a raised ramp function voltage. Write its equation and determine its Laplace transform.

$$\left[\textbf{Ans. } v(t) = 4u(t - t_0) + Kr(t - t_0);\ V(s) = e^{-t_0 s}\left\{\frac{4}{s} + \frac{K}{s^2}\right\}\right]$$

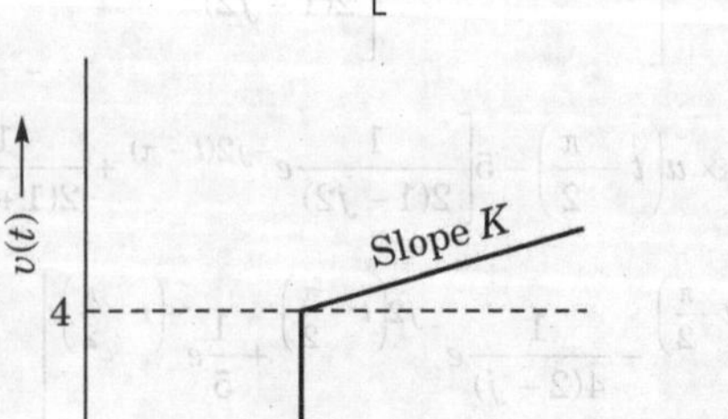

7.20. A linearly varying voltage is given by the equation,

$$v(t) = K(t - t_0)\, u(t).$$

Plot this function and find its Laplace transform.

[**Ans.** (*i*) Plot is a straight line of slope *K* cutting the time axis at t_0 and the voltage axis at $-kt_0$.

$$(ii)\ V(s) = \frac{K}{s^2}[1 - t_0 s]$$

7.21. Show that the Laplace transform of the given square wave is $V(s) = \dfrac{A}{s\left[1 - e^{-\frac{as}{2}}\right]}$

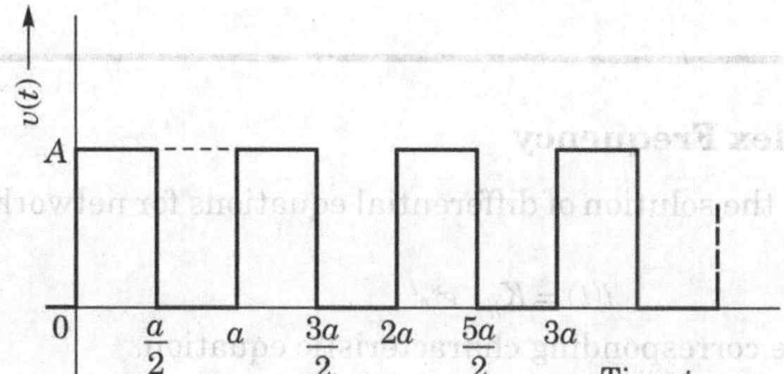

7.22. **The following figure shows a sweep voltage of periodic time T and amplitude V_0. Find its Laplace transform.**

$$\left[\textbf{Ans. } V(s) = \frac{V_0}{T}\cdot\frac{1}{s^2} - \frac{V_0}{s}\cdot\frac{e^{-Ts}}{(1 - e^{-Ts})}\right]$$

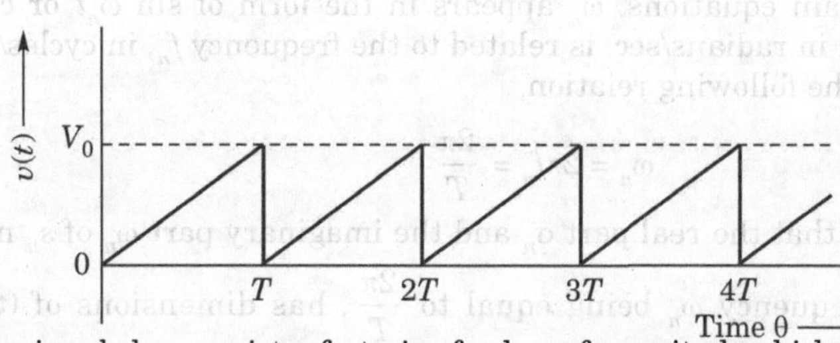

7.23. **The waveform given below consists of a train of pulses of magnitude which decays exponentially. Find the Laplace transform $F(s)$.**

$$\left[\textbf{Ans. } F(s) = \frac{V_0}{(s+2)\,(1 + e^{-(2+s)})}\right]$$

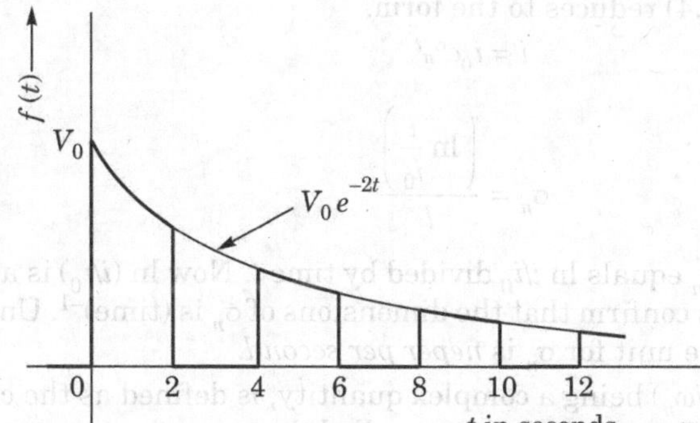

7.24. Find $L^{-1}[F_1(s)\,F_2(s)]$ by using convolution for the following functions :

(a) $F_1(s) = \dfrac{1}{s+2}$, $F_2(s) = \dfrac{1}{s+2}$ (b) $F_1(s) = \dfrac{1}{s+3}$, $F_2(s) = \dfrac{1}{s+2}$

[**Ans.** (a) $f(t) = te^{-2t}$ (b) $f(t) = \dfrac{4}{3}u(t)\,[1 + 3te^{-3t} - e^{-3t}]$

8

Transform Impedance and Admittance Functions

8.1. Concept of Complex Frequency

We have seen that the solution of differential equations for networks is of the following form in time domain :

$$i(t) = K_n \cdot e^{s_n t} \quad ...(8.1)$$

where s_n is the root of the corresponding characteristic equation.

s_n is, in general, a complex number and may therefore be expressed as,

$$s_n = \sigma_n + j\omega_n \quad ...(8.2)$$

σ_n is the real part of s_n while ω_n is the imaginary part. ω_n is expressed in radians per second and may be referred to as the radian frequency.

In the time domain equations, ω_n appears in the form of sin $\omega_n t$ or cos $\omega_n t$. The radian frequency ω_n, expressed in radians/sec. is related to the frequency f_n, in cycles/sec. or the periodic time T (in seconds) by the following relation,

$$\omega_n = 2\pi f_n = \frac{2\pi}{T} \quad ...(8.3)$$

Eq. (8.2) implies that the real part σ_n and the imaginary part ω_n of s_n must have identical dimensions. Radian frequency ω_n being equal to $\frac{2\pi}{T}$, has dimensions of $(\text{time})^{-1}$. Hence the dimensions of σ_n must also be $(\text{time})^{-1}$ or the unit of σ_n must be "some quantity per unit time".

Now Eq. (8.1) may be put as,

$$i = i_0(e^{\sigma_n t} \cdot e^{j\omega_n t}) \quad ...(8.4)$$

σ_n here appears as an exponential factor.

If ω_n is zero, Eq. (8.4) reduces to the form,

$$i = i_0 e^{\sigma_n t} \quad ...(8.5)$$

or

$$\sigma_n = \frac{\left(\ln \frac{i}{i_0}\right)}{l} \quad ...(8.6)$$

Thus we see that σ_n equals ln i/i_0 divided by time t. Now ln (i/i_0) is a dimensionless quantity and from Eq. (8.6) we thus confirm that the dimensions of σ_n is $(\text{time})^{-1}$. Unit for Natural logarithm ln (i/i_0) is neper. Hence the unit for σ_n is *neper per second.*

The root s_n $(= \sigma_n + j\omega_n)$ being a complex quantity, is defined as the complex frequency. Thus complex frequency s_n consists of a real part σ_n called the *neper frequency* and an imaginary part ω_n called the *radian frequency* (or real frequency).

8.2. Physical Significance of Complex Frequency

The complex frequency $s_n (= \sigma_n + j\omega_n)$ appears in the exponential $e^{s_n t}$ in Eq. (8.1) giving the solution of a differential equation. Physical significance of complex frequency s_n may be studied for the following three cases :

Case A. *Zero Radian Frequency*

In this case $$s_n = \sigma_n + j0 \quad ...(8.7)$$

Hence Eq. (8.1) reduces to,

$$i(t) = K_n e^{\sigma_n t} \quad ...(8.8)$$

If σ_n is positive, *i.e.* $\sigma_n > 0$, then the exponential $K_n e^{\sigma_n t}$ increases exponentially.

If σ_n is negative, *i.e.* $\sigma_n < 0$, then the exponential funtion $K_n e^{\sigma_n t}$ decreases exponentially.

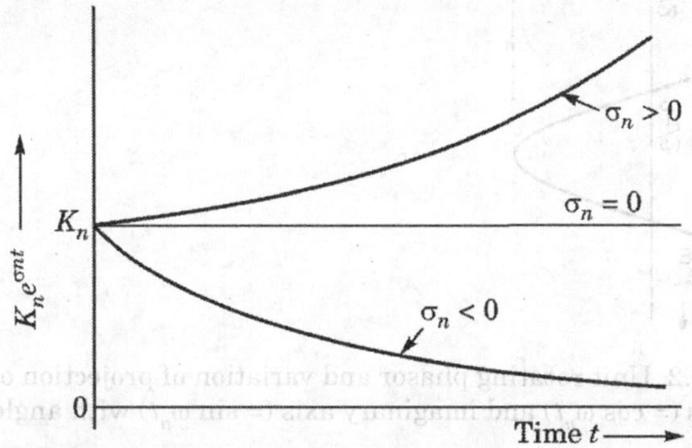

Fig. 8.1. Variation of exponential term $K_n e^{\sigma_n t}$ with time t for positive, zero and negative values of σ.

If $\sigma_n = 0$ so that $s_n = 0 + j0$, the exponential term $K_n e^{s_n t}$ simply reduces to K_n, *i.e.* it becomes time invariant signifying that the resulting current $i(t)$ is a d.c. current. Fig. 8.1 shows the variation of exponential term $K_n e^{\sigma_n t}$ with time t for the above three cases of $\sigma_n > 0$, $\sigma_n < 0$ and $\sigma_n = 0$.

Case B. *Zero Neper Frequency*

In this case, $$s_n = 0 + j\omega_n \quad ...(8.9)$$

Hence Eq. (8.1) reduces to the following form,

$$i(t) = K_n e^{+j\omega_n t} = K_n (\cos \omega_n t + j \sin \omega_n t) \quad ...(8.10)$$

The exponential $e^{+j\omega_n t}$ may be interpreted in terms of a physical model of a rotating phasor of unit length. The direction of rotation of this phasor is determined by the sign of $j\omega_n t$, anticlockwise (or positive) rotation for positive sign and clockwise (or negative) rotation for negative sign. The rate of rotation of the phasor equals ω_n radians/second.

For positive or anti-clockwise rotation, the real part of $e^{+j\omega_n t}$ or the projection on the real axis equals $\cos \omega_n t$, while the imaginary part of $e^{+j\omega_n t}$ or the projection on the imaginary axis, equals $\sin \omega_n t$. This is shown in Fig. 8.2.

The variation of exponential function $e^{+j\omega_n t}$ with time is thus sinusoidal and hence constitutes the case of sinusoidal steady state.

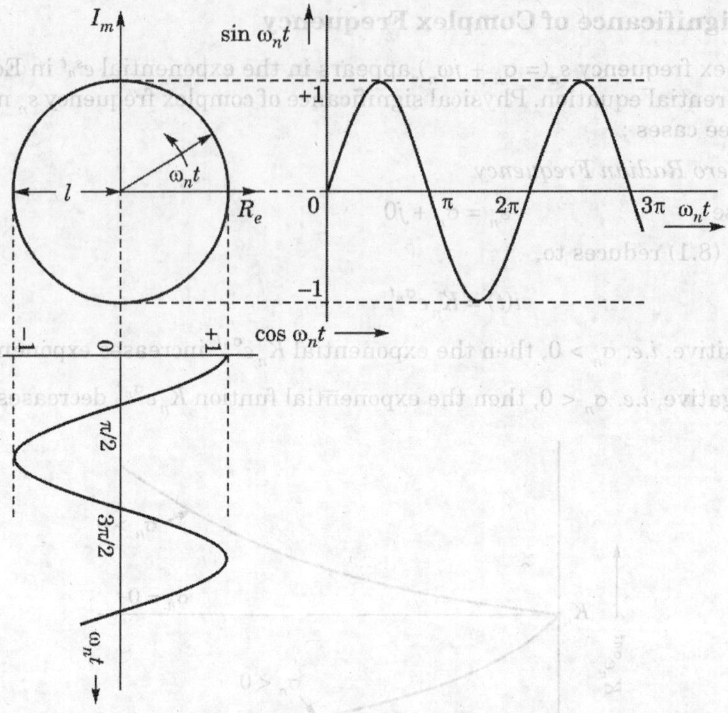

Fig. 8.2. Unit rotating phasor and variation of projection on real axis (= cos $\omega_n t$) and imaginary axis (= sin $\omega_n t$) with angle $\omega_n t$.

Case C. *General Case*

In general, both σ_n and ω_n are non-zero. Hence the frequency is complex and is given by,

$$s_n = \sigma_n + j\omega_n \quad ...(8.11)$$

Hence

$$i(t) = K_n \cdot e^{s_n t} = K_n e^{(\sigma_n + j\omega_n)\,t}$$

$$= K_n e^{\sigma_n t} \cdot e^{j\omega_n t} \quad ...(8.12)$$

Eq. (8.12) shows that with complex frequency, the time variation of response $i(t)$ is the product of the response for $s_n = \sigma_n + j0$ and the response for $s_n = 0 + j\omega_n$. The response $e^{\sigma_n t}$ for the case of neper frequency alone ($s^n = \sigma_n + j0$) is an exponentially increasing or decaying function. The response $e^{j\omega_n t}$ for the case of radian frequency alone ($s_n = 0 + j\omega_n$) may be represented by a rotating phasor. The product $e^{\sigma_n t} \cdot e^{j\omega_n t}$ may then be visualised as a rotating phasor whose magnitude is not constant at unity but changes continuously with time. Fig. 8.3 shows two such phasor models.

The instantaneous magnitude of phasor is e^{σ_n} [taking k_n in Eq. (8.12) to be unity]. The projection of this rotating phasor on the real axis,

$$R_e(e^{s_n t}) = e^{\sigma_n t} \cos \omega_n t \quad ...(8.13)$$

The projection on the imaginary axis is,

$$I_m(e^{s_n t}) = e^{\sigma_n t} \sin \omega_n t \quad ...(8.14)$$

It may be readily seen that these projections on the real and imaginary axes, for negative value of σ_n, constitute sinusoids of real frequency ω_n with amplitude decaying exponentially as shown in Fig. 8.4 (*a*). On the other hand for $\sigma_n > 0$, the resulting projections on the real and imaginary axis are oscillations with amplitude increasing exponentially as shown in Fig. 8.4(*b*).

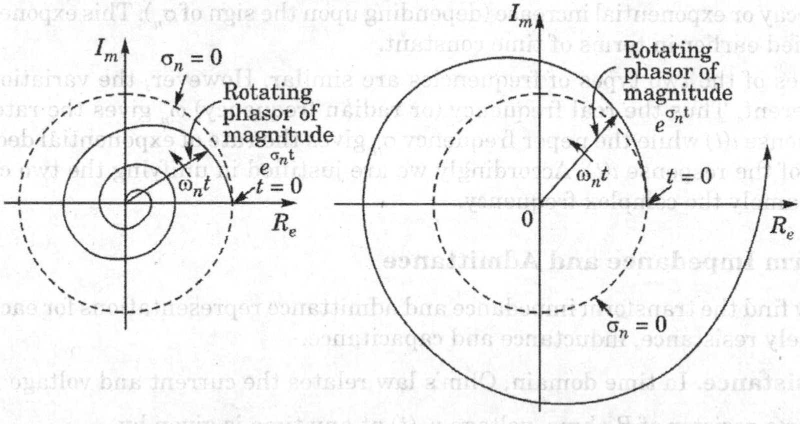

(*a*) σ_n negative (*b*) σ_n positive

Fig. 8.3. Exponentially varying rotating phasor.

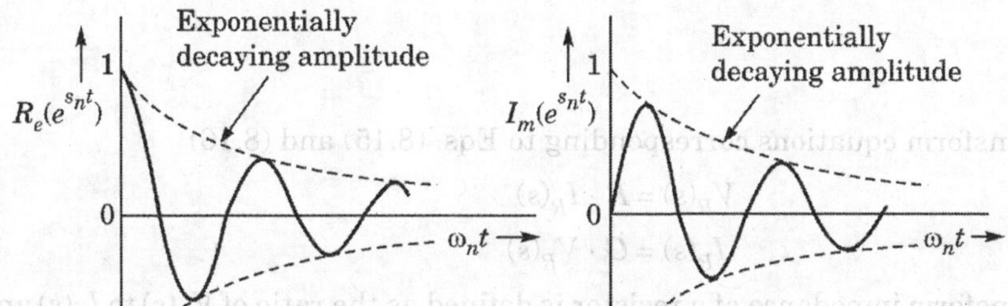

(*i*) Projection on real axis (*ii*) Projection on imaginary axis

(*a*) Projections on real and imaginary axes for $\sigma_n < 0$.

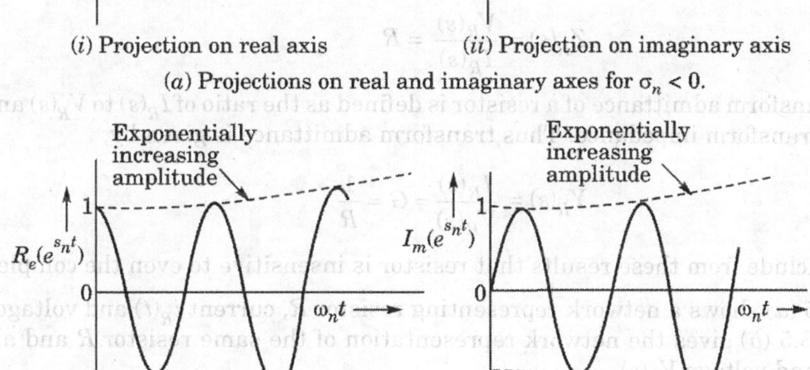

(*i*) Projection on real axis (*ii*) Projection on imaginary axis

(*b*) Projections on real and imaginary axes for $\sigma_n > 0$.

Fig. 8.4. Projections of rotating phasor $e^{snt} \cdot e^{jwnt}$ on real and imaginary axes.

We thus see that,

(*i*) the imaginary part ω_n of complex frequency s_n constitutes the radian (or real) frequency and governs the sinusoidal oscillations.

(*ii*) the real part σ_n of the complex frequency namely the neper frequency governs the exponential decay or exponential increase (depending upon the sign of σ_n). This exponential variation has been studied earlier in terms of time constant.

The roles of the two types of frequencies are similar. However, the variations which they cause are different. Thus the real frequency (or radian frequency) ω_n gives the rate of sinusoidal change of response $i(t)$ while the neper frequency σ_n gives the rate of exponential decay or increase of magnitude of the response $i(t)$. Accordingly we are justified in unifying the two concepts under one heading namely the complex frequency.

8.3. Transform Impedance and Admittance

We now find the transform impedance and admittance representations for each of the circuit elements namely resistance, inductance and capacitance.

(*A*) **Resistance.** In time domain, Ohm's law relates the current and voltage in a resistor.

Thus for a resistor of R ohms, voltage $v_R(t)$ at any time is given by,

$$v_R(t) = R \cdot i_R(t) \qquad ...(8.15)$$

or

$$I_R(t) = G \cdot v_R(t) \qquad ...(8.16)$$

where $G = \dfrac{1}{R}$ ...(8.17)

The transform equations corresponding to Eqs. (8.15) and (8.16)

are,

$$V_R(s) = R \cdot I_R(s) \qquad ...(8.18)$$

and

$$I_R(s) = G \cdot V_R(s) \qquad ...(8.19)$$

The transform impedance of a resistor is defined as the ratio of $V_R(s)$ to $I_R(s)$ and is therefore given by,

$$Z_R(s) = \frac{V_R(s)}{I_R(s)} = R \qquad ...(8.20)$$

The transform admittance of a resistor is defined as the ratio of $I_R(s)$ to $V_R(s)$ and is therefore reciprocal of transform impedance. Thus transform admittance is given by,

$$Y_R(s) = \frac{I_R(s)}{V_R(s)} = G = \frac{1}{R} \qquad ...(8.21)$$

We conclude from these results that resistor is insensitive to even the complex frequency.

Fig. 8.5 (*a*) shows a network representing resistor R, current $i_R(t)$ and voltage $v_R(t)$ in time domain. Fig. 8.5 (*b*) gives the network representation of the same resistor R and also transform current $I_R(s)$ and voltage $V_R(s)$.

(*B*) **Inductance.** In time domain, the following equation relates the current $i_L(t)$ in an inductor L to the voltage $v_L(t)$ across it.

$$v_L(t) = L \cdot \frac{di_L(t)}{dt} \qquad ...(8.22)$$

or

$$i_L(t) = \frac{1}{L}\int_{-\infty}^{t} v_L(t)\, dt \qquad ...(8.23)$$

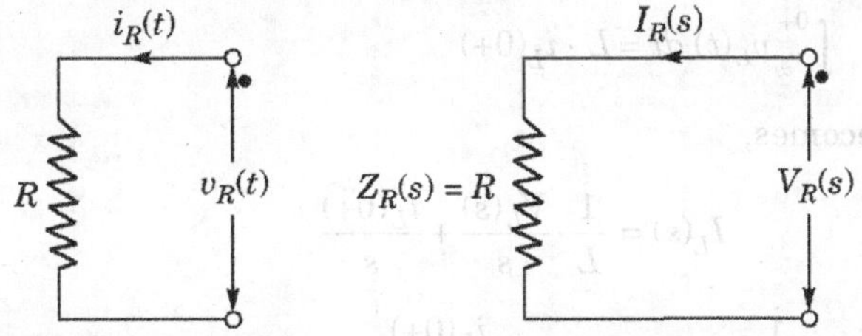

(a) Resistor in time domain (b) Transform representation of resistor

Fig. 8.5. Resistor and its transform impedance representation.

Laplace transform equation corresponding to Eq. (8.22) is,

$$V_L(s) = L[sI_L(s) - i_L(0+)] \quad ...(8.24)$$

Eq. (8.24) may be rearranged as below,

$$Ls\, I_L(s) = V_L(s) + Li_L(0+) \quad ...(8.25)$$

In Eqs. (8.24) and (8.25), $V_L(s)$ is the Laplace transform of the applied voltage $v_L(t)$ and $Li_L(0+)$ is the transform voltage caused by the initial current $i_L(0+)$ present in the inductor at time $t = 0+$.

Let $$V_1(s) = V_L(s) + L \cdot i_L(0+) \quad ...(8.26)$$

Then Eq. (8.25) becomes, $Ls\, I_L(s) = V_1(s)$ ...(8.27)

$V_1(s)$ is the total transform voltage across the inductor. Hence the transform impedance of the inductor L being the ratio of transform voltage $V_1(s)$ to transform current $I_L(s)$ is given by,

$$Z_L(s) = \frac{V_1(s)}{I_L(s)} = Ls \quad ...(8.28)$$

Fig. 8.6 (a) shows the time domain network representation of inductor L, current $i_L(t)$ through it and applied voltage $v_L(t)$.

Here $i_L(t)$ includes the initial current $i_L(0+)$. Fig. 8.6 (b) gives the transform representation of same inductor L in terms of impedance using Eq. (8.25).

Laplace transform equation corresponding to Eq. (8.23) is,

$$I_L(s) = \frac{1}{L}\left[\frac{V_L(s)}{s} + \frac{\int_{-\infty}^{+0} v_L(t)\,dt}{s}\right] \quad ...(8.29)$$

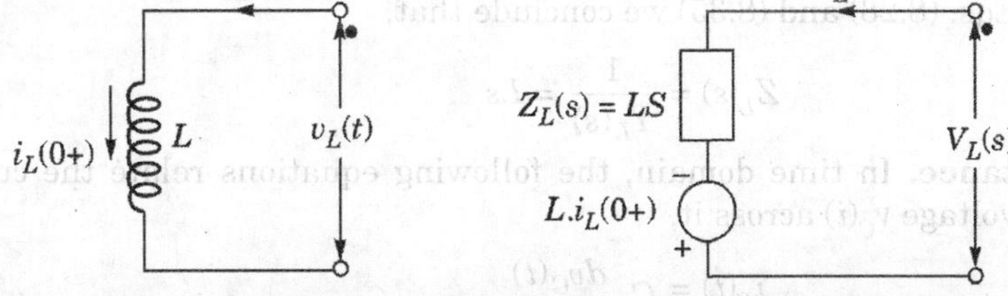

(a) Inductor with initial current $i_L(0+)$ (b) Transform representation of inductor

Fig. 8.6. Inductor with initial current and its transform representation in terms of impedance.

But $$\int_{-\infty}^{0+} v_L(t)\,dt = L \cdot i_L(0+) \qquad ...(8.30)$$

Hence Eq. (8.29) becomes,

$$I_L(s) = \frac{1}{L} \cdot \frac{V_L(s)}{s} + \frac{i_L(0+)}{s} \qquad ...(8.31)$$

or $$\frac{1}{Ls} V_L(s) = I_L(s) - \frac{i_L(0+)}{s} \qquad ...(8.32)$$

In Eq. (8.32), $I_L(s)$ is the Laplace transform of the applied current $i_L(t)$ and $\frac{i_L(0+)}{s}$ is the transform current caused by the initial current $i_L(0+)$ in the inductor.

Let $$I_1(s) = I_L(s) - \frac{i_L(0+)}{s} \qquad ...(8.33)$$

Then Eq. (8.32) becomes,

$$\frac{1}{Ls} V_L(s) = I_L(s) \qquad ...(8.34)$$

$I_1(s)$ is the total transform current through the inductor L. Hence the transform admittance of the inductor L being the ratio of transform current $I_1(s)$ to transform voltage $V_L(s)$ is given by,

$$Y_L(s) = \frac{I_1(s)}{V_L(s)} = \frac{1}{Ls} \qquad ...(8.35)$$

Fig. 8.7 (*a*) shows the time domain representation of inductor L with initial current $iL(0+)$. Current $i_L(t)$ includes the initial current $i_L(0+)$. Fig. 8.7 (*b*) gives the transform representation of the same inductor L in terms of transform admittance using Eq. (8.32).

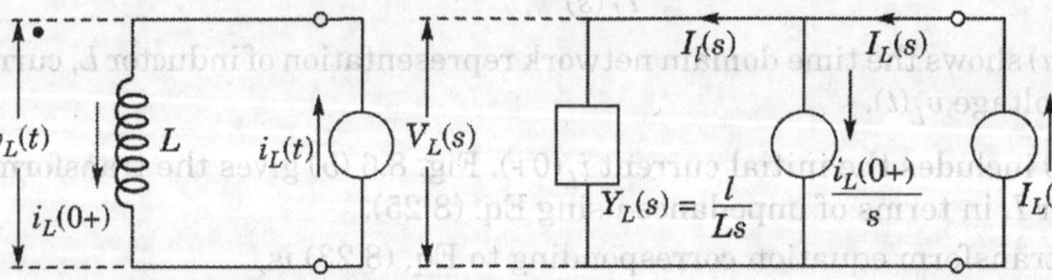

(*a*) Time domain representation of inductance L with initial current $i_L(0+)$ (*b*) Transform representation of inductor with initial current $i_L(0+)$

Fig. 8.7. Time domain and transform representations of inductor in terms of admittance

Combining Eqs. (8.28) and (8.35) we conclude that,

$$Z_L(s) = \frac{1}{Y_L(s)} = Ls \qquad ...(8.36)$$

(*C*) **Capacitance.** In time domain, the following equations relate the current $i_C(t)$ in a capacitor C to the voltage $v_C(i)$ across it,

$$i_C(t) = C \cdot \frac{dv_C(t)}{dt} \qquad ...(8.37)$$

or $$v_C(t) = \frac{1}{C}\int_{-\infty}^{t} i_C(t)\,dt \quad ...(8.38)$$

Laplace transform equation corresponding to Eq. (8.38) is,

$$V_C(s) = \frac{1}{C}\left[\frac{I_C(s)}{s} + \frac{q(0+)}{s}\right] \quad ...(8.39)$$

where $q(0+)$ is the initial charges across the capacitor and

$$\frac{q(0+)}{C} = v_C(0+)$$

is the initial voltage across the capacitor.

In Eq. (8.39), $\frac{q(0+)}{Cs}$ or $\frac{V_C(0+)}{s}$ is the transform voltage caused by initial voltage $v_C(0+)$ across capacitor C at time $t = 0+$.

Eq. (8.39) may be rearranged as,

$$\frac{1}{Cs}\cdot I_C(s) = V_C(s) - \frac{v_C(0+)}{s} \quad ...(8.40)$$

Let $$V_1(s) = V_C(s) - \frac{v_C(0+)}{s} \quad ...(8.41)$$

Then Eq. (8.40) becomes,

$$\frac{1}{Cs} I_C(s) = V_1(s) \quad ...(8.42)$$

$V_1(s)$ is the total transform voltage across the capacitor. Hence the transform impedance of the capacitor C, being the ratio of transform voltage $V_1(s)$ to transform current $I_C(s)$ is given by,

$$Z_C(s) = \frac{V_1(s)}{I_C(s)} = \frac{1}{Cs} \quad ...(8.43)$$

Fig. 8.8 (*a*) shows the time domain representation of capacitor C with initial voltage $v_C(0+)$ across it. Voltage $V_1(s)$ includes the initial voltage $v_C(0+)$. Fig. 8.8 (*b*) gives the transform representation of the same capacitor in terms of transform impedance using Eq. (8.40).

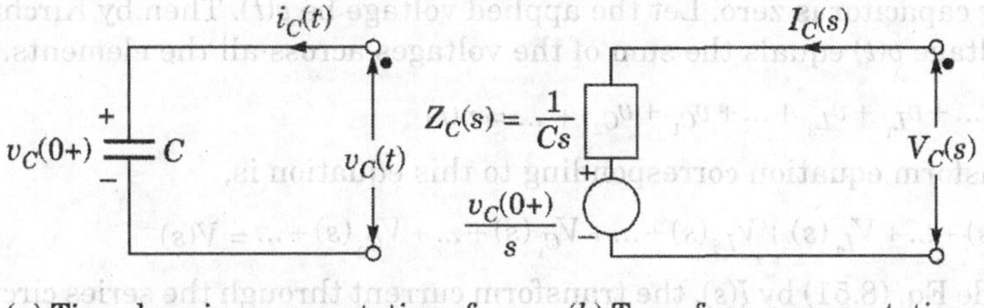

(*a*) Time domain representation of capacitor C with initial voltage $v_C(0+)$ (*b*) Transform representation of capacitor C with initial voltage $v_C(0+)$

Fig. 8.8. Time domain and transform representations of capacitor in terms of impedance.

Transform equation corresponding to Eq. (8.37) is,

$$I_C(s) = C[sV_C(s) - v_C(0+)] \quad ...(8.44)$$

or $$CsV_C(s) = I_C(s) + C\,v_C(0+) \quad ...(8.45)$$

Let the current through the admittance $Y_C(s)$ of capacitor C be designated as $I_1(s)$. Then

$$I_1(s) = I_C(s) + C\, v_C(0+) \qquad ...(8.46)$$

Then Eq. (8.45) may be put as,

$$Cs\, V_C(s) = I_1(s) \qquad ...(8.47)$$

Hence the transform admittance of the capacitor C, being the ratio of transform current $I_1(s)$ to transform voltage $V_C(s)$ is given by,

$$Y_C(s) = \frac{I_1(s)}{V_C(s)} = Cs \qquad ...(8.48)$$

Fig. 8.9 (a) shows the time domain representation of capacitor C with initial voltage $v_C(0+)$ across it. Fig. 8.9 (c) gives the transform representation of the same capacitor in terms of admittance using Eq. (8.46).

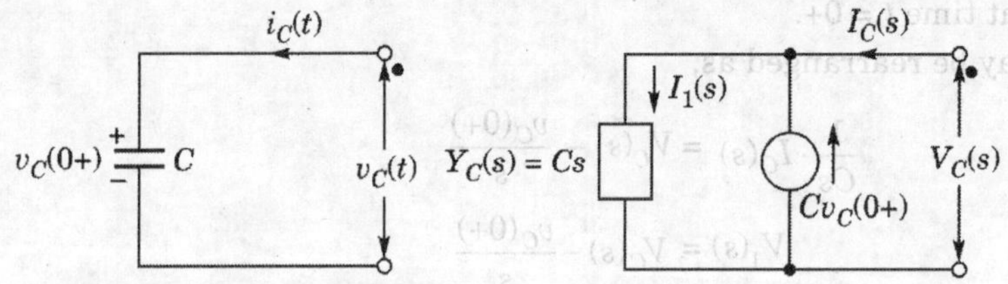

(a) Capacitor C with initial voltage $v_C(0+)$

(b) Transform representation of capacitor C with initial voltage $v_C(0+)$

Fig. 8.10. Capacitor with initial voltage and its transform representation in terms of admittance.

Combining Eqs. (8.43) and (8.48), we get

$$Z_c(s) = \frac{1}{Y_c(s)} = \frac{1}{Cs} \qquad ...(8.49)$$

8.4. Series and Parallel Combinations of Elements

Fig. 8.10 (a) shows a series combination of resistors $R_1, R_2, ...$, inductors $L_1, L_2, ...$ and capacitors $C_1, C_2, ...$ For simplification let us assume that initial current in every inductor is zero and initial charge across every capacitor is zero. Let the applied voltage be $v(t)$. Then by Kirchhoff's voltages law, the applied voltage $v(t)$ equals the sum of the voltages across all the elements. Thus, we get

$$v_{R_1} + v_{R_2} + ... + v_{L_1} + v_{L_2} + ... + v_{C_1} + v_{C_2} + ... = v(t) \qquad ...(8.50)$$

Laplace transform equation corresponding to this equation is,

$$v_{R_1}(s) + V_{R_2}(s) + ... + V_{L_1}(s) + V_{L_2}(s) + ... + V_{C_1}(s) + ... + V_{C_2}(s) + ... = V(s) \qquad ...(8.51)$$

Now we divide Eq. (8.51) by $I(s)$, the transform current through the series circuit. Each term on the left hand side of Eq. (8.51) on being divided by $I(s)$ results in corresponding transform impedance. Hence, we get

$$Z_{R_1}(s) + Z_{R_2}(s) + ... + Z_{L_1}(s) + Z_{L_2}(s) + ... + Z_{C_1}(s) + Z_{C_2}(s) + ... = Z(s) \qquad ...(8.52)$$

or

$$\sum_{K=1}^{K=n} Z_K(s) = Z(s) \qquad ...(8.53)$$

where n is the total number of elements of all kinds in series.

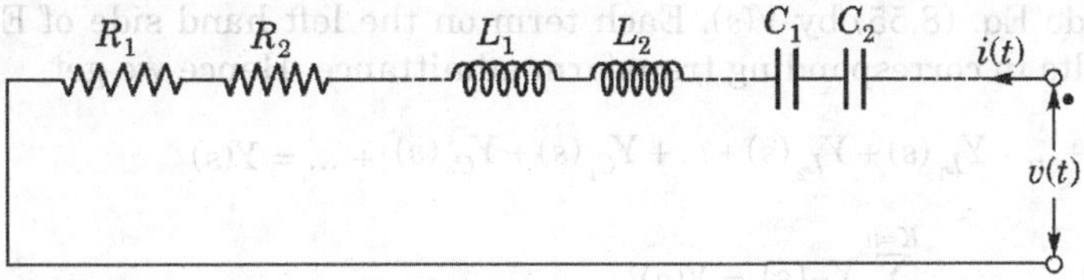

(*a*) Series circuit containing resistors, inductors and capacitors.

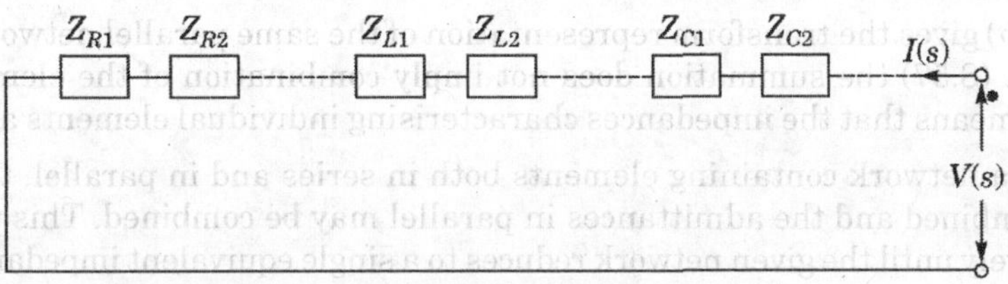

(*b*) Corresponding transform representation.

Fig. 8.10. Series *R-L-C* circuit and corresponding transform representation.

Fig. 8.10 (*b*) gives the transform representation of the same series network and represents Eq. (8.52). In Eq. (8.53), the summation does not imply combination of elements themselves. It simply means that the impedances characterising the individual elements are being summed.

Fig. 8.11 (*a*) shows a parallel combination of resistors of conductance G_1, G_2,.., inductors L_1, L_2,... and capacitors C_1, C_2,.... Here again we assume that the inductors have zero initial currents and capacitors have zero initial charges. Let $v(t)$ be the applied voltage. This is common to all the elements.

Then application of Kirchhoff's current law to the circuit yields,

$$i_{R_1}(t) + i_{R_2}(t) + \ldots + i_{L_1}(t) + i_{L_2}(t) + \ldots + i_{C_1}(t) + i_{C_2}(t) + \ldots = i(t) \qquad \ldots(8.54)$$

where $i(t)$ is the total current drawn by the parallel circuit as shown in Fig. 8.11 (*a*).

Transform equation corresponding to Eq. (8.54) is as below,

$$I_{R_1}(s) + I_{R_2}(s) + \ldots + I_{L_1}(s) + I_{L_2}(s) + \ldots + I_{C_1}(s) + I_{C_2}(s) + \ldots = I(s) \qquad ..(8.55)$$

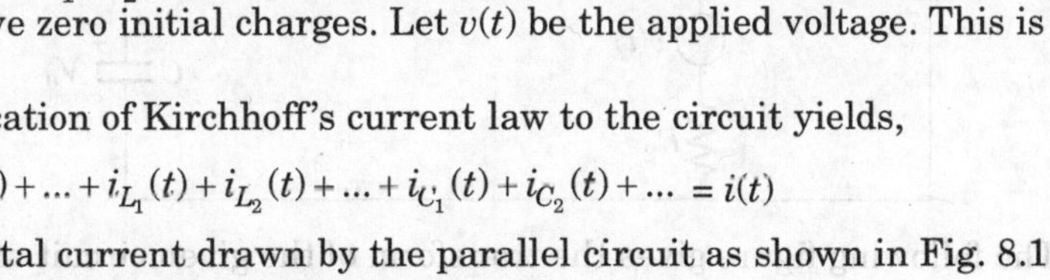

(*a*) Parallel circuit containing resistors, inductors and capacitors.

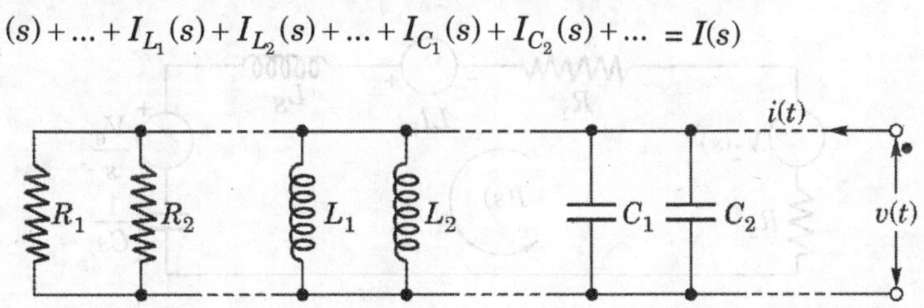

(*b*) Corresponding transform representation.

Fig. 8.11. Shunt *R-L-C* circuit and its transform representation.

Next we divide Eq. (8.55) by *V*(*s*). Each term on the left hand side of Eq. (8.55) on being divided by *V*(*s*) results in corresponding transform admittance. Hence we get

$$Y_{R_1}(s) + Y_{R_2}(e) + \ldots + Y_{L_1}(s) + Y_{L_2}(s) + \ldots + Y_{C_1}(s) + Y_{C_2}(s) + \ldots = Y(s) \qquad \ldots(8.56)$$

or

$$\sum_{K=1}^{K=n} Y_K(s) = Y(s) \qquad \ldots(8.57)$$

where *n* is the total number of elements of all kinds in parallel.

Fig. 8.11 (*b*) gives the transform representation of the same parallel network and represents Eq. (8.56). In Eq. (8.57) the summation does not imply combination of the elements themselves. Rather it simply means that the impedances characterising individual elements are being summed.

In case of a network containing elements both in series and in parallel, the impedances in series may be combined and the admittances in parallel may be combined. This procedure may be adopted successively until the given network reduces to a single equivalent impedance or admittance.

Example 8.1. *In the given circuit switch K is moved from position 1 to position 2 at time t = 0. At time t = 0 –, the current through inductor L is I_0 and voltage across capacitor C is V_0 in the polarity shown. At time t = 0+, voltage source v(t) and resistor R_2 get connected to the R-L-C circuit. Find the transform current I(s) and current i(t).*

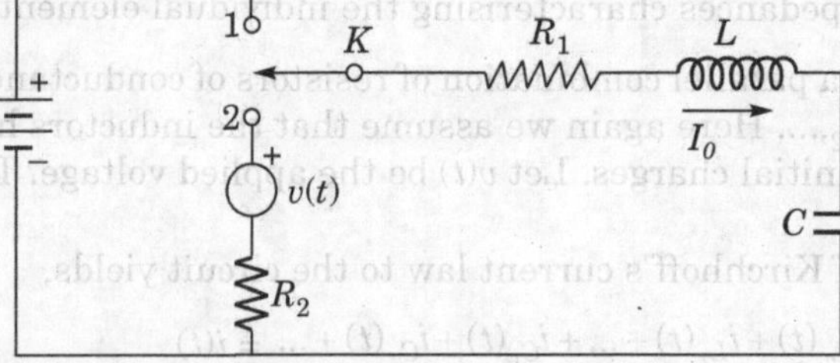

Solution. The following figure gives the transform of the given circuit after the swtich *K* is moved from position 1 to position 2.

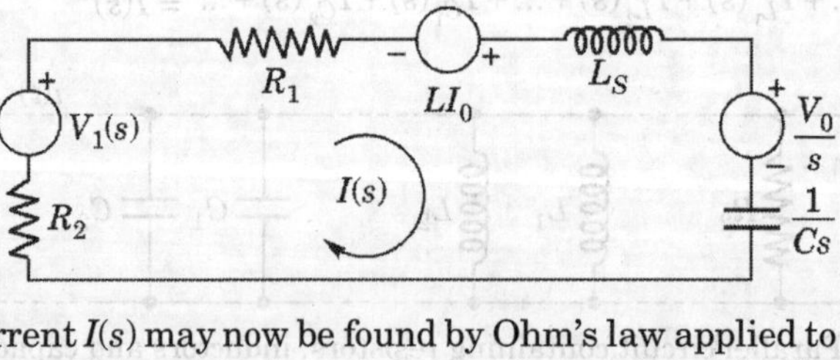

The transform current *I*(*s*) may now be found by Ohm's law applied to this transform network. Thus the transform current *I*(*s*) equals the total transform voltage in the network divided by the total transform impedance.

Now total transform voltage in the network is given by,

$$V(s) = V_1(s) + LI_0 - \frac{V_0}{s}$$

The total transform impedance is given by,

$$Z(s) = R_1 + R_2 + Ls + \frac{1}{Cs}$$

Hence the transform current is given by,

$$I(s) = \frac{V(s)}{Z(s)} = \frac{V_1(s) + LI_0 - \dfrac{V_0}{s}}{R_1 + R_2 + Ls + \dfrac{1}{Cs}}$$

This transform equation may now be expanded by partial fraction method and on inverse Laplace transformation, we get *i*(*t*).

Note. It may be noted that this solution does not require writing the differential equation in the time domain and at the same time all the initial conditions are automatically included in it.

Example 8.2. *In the given circuit, switch K is moved from position 1 to position 2 at time t = 0. At time t = 0–, the current through inductor L is I_0 and the voltage across capacitor C is V_0 in the polarity shown. At time t = 0+, current source i(t) and resistor R_2 get connected to the R_1-L-C parallel circuit. Find the voltage V(s) and v(t) across the R_1-L-C parallel circuit.*

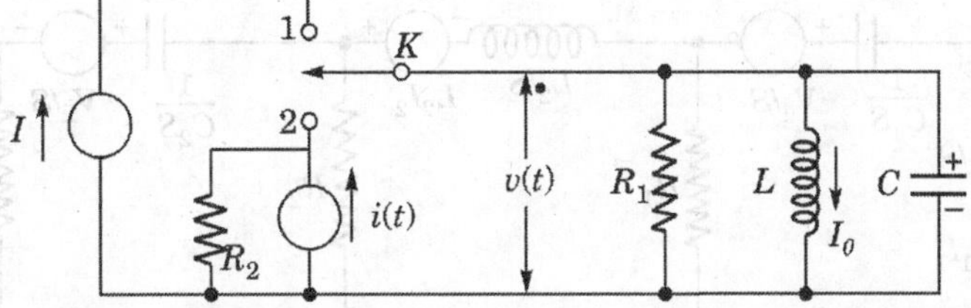

Solution. The following figure gives the transform network corresponding to the given network with switch *K* moved to position 2.

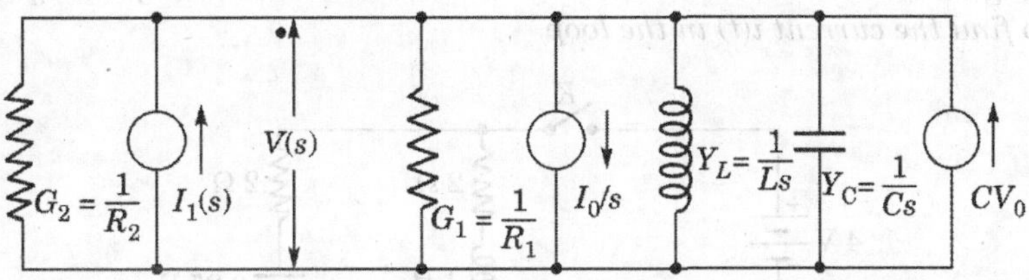

The transform voltage *V*(*s*) may now be found by Ohm's law applied to this transform network. Thus the transform voltage *V*(*s*) equals the total transform current in the network divided by the total transform admittance.

Total transform current in the network is given by,

$$I(s) = I_1(s) - \frac{I_0}{s} + CV_0 \quad ...(1)$$

Total transform admittance is given by,

$$Y(s) = G_1 + G_2 + \frac{1}{Ls} + Cs \quad ...(2)$$

Hence the transform voltage is given by,

$$V(s) = \frac{I(s)}{Y(s)} = \frac{I_1(s) + CV_0 - I_0/s}{G_1 + G_2 + \dfrac{1}{Ls} + Cs} \quad ...(3)$$

Above transform equation may now be expanded by the method of partial fractions and on inverse Laplace transform, we get $v(t)$.

Example 8.3. *In the given network, initial currents and voltages are present at time t = 0 as a result of removal of active elements. Draw the transform network for analysis on the loop basis.*

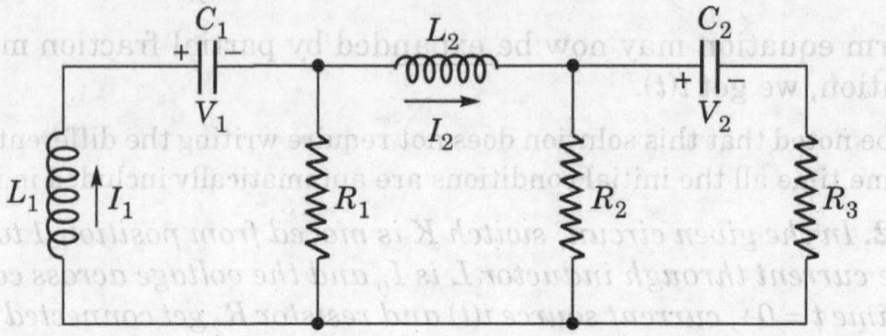

Solution. For analysis on the loop basis, each network element is replaced by its transform impedance and equivalent voltage source if any. Thus we get the transform network shown below.

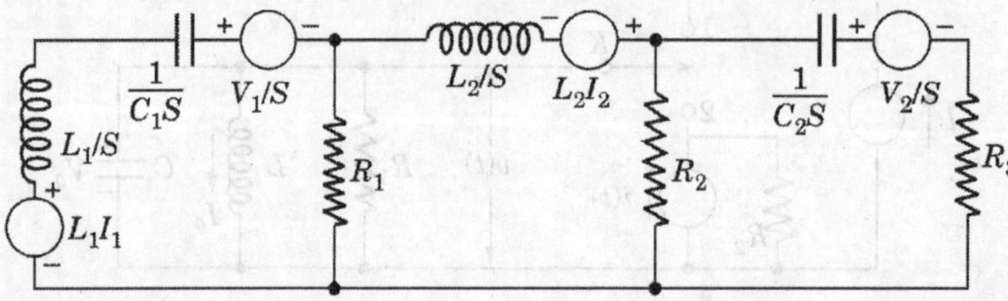

Example 8.4. *In the given network, switch K is opened at time t = 0, the steady state having established previously. With switch K open, draw the transform network for analysis on the loop basis, representing all elements and all initial conditions. Write the transform equation for current in the loop. Also find the current i(t) in the loop.*

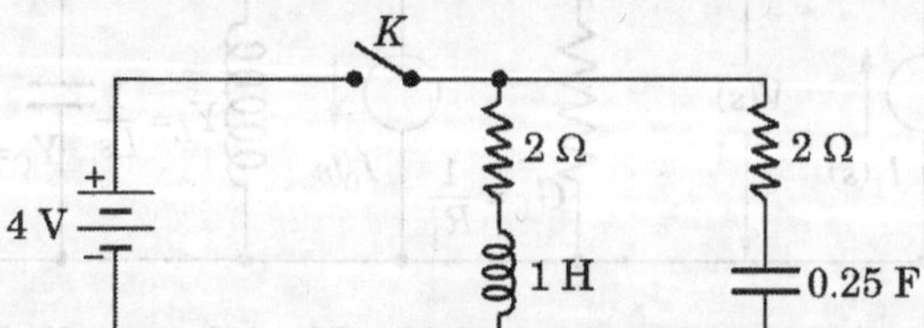

Solution. Under the steady state with switch K closed, current through inductor is 2 amp. and that through the capacitor is zero. The voltage across the capacitor equals the driving voltage *i.e.* 4 volts d.c. Hence the corresponding transform network is as shown.

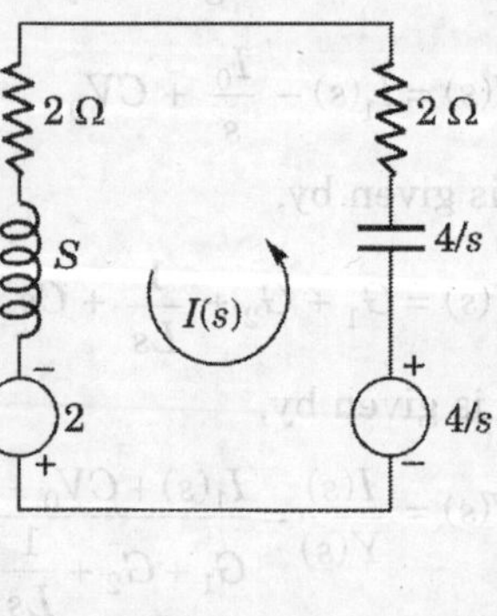

Hence $I(s) = \dfrac{V(s)}{Z(s)} = \dfrac{2+4/s}{2+2+s+4/s} = \dfrac{2(s+2)}{(s+2)^2} = \dfrac{2}{s+2}$

Hence $i(t) = 2e^{-2t} \cdot u(t)$.

Example 8.5. *For the R-C network shown in the figure, find the transform impedance Z(s) in the form of a quotient of polynomials of s.*

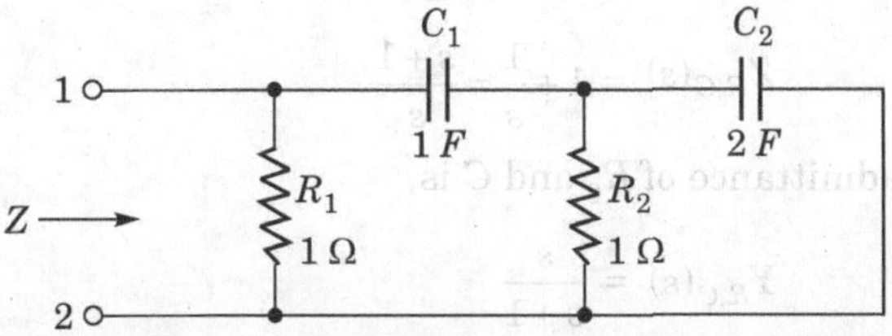

Solution. Transform network corresponding to the given network is as below.

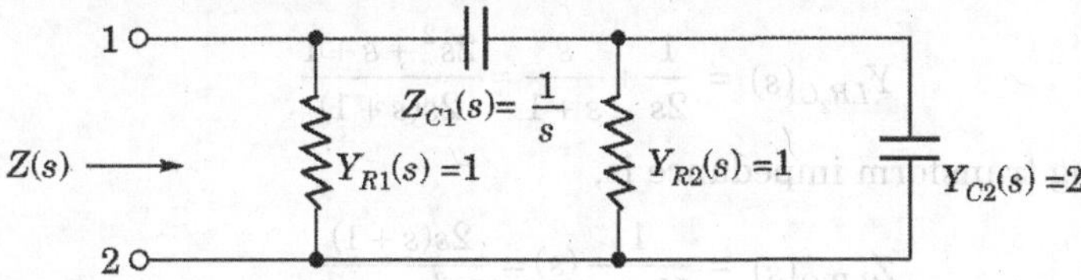

$$Y_{R_2C_2}(s) = Y_{R_2}(s) + Y_{C_2}(s) = 1 + 2s$$

$$Z_{R_2C_2}(s) = \frac{1}{2s+1}$$

$$Z_{C_1R_2C_2}(s) = Z_{C_1}(s) + Z_{R_2C_2}(s) = \frac{1}{s} + \frac{1}{2s+1} = \frac{3s+1}{s(2s+1)}$$

or $$Y_{C_1R_2C_2}(s) = \frac{s(2s+1)}{3s+1}$$

$$Y(s) = Y_{R_1}(s) + Y_{C_1R_2C_2}(s) = 1 + \frac{s(2s+1)}{3s+1} = \frac{2s^2+4s+1}{3s+1}$$

Hence $$Z(s) = \frac{1}{Y(s)} = \frac{3s+1}{2s^2+4s+1}.$$

Example 8.6. *The network shown in the diagram is initially relaxed i.e. with zero current through the inductor and zero charge across the capacitor. Switch K is closed at time t = 0. Find the transform current I(s) drawn from the generator.*

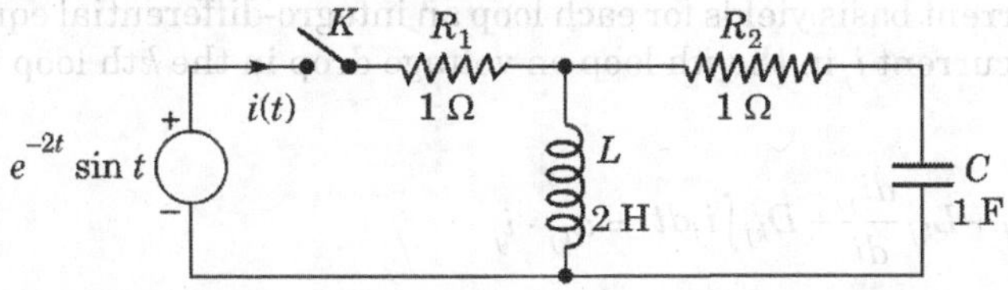

Solution. The transform network corresponding to the given network is as below :

Transform admittance of inductor is $Y_L(s) = \dfrac{1}{2s}$

Transform impedance of R_2 and C is given by,

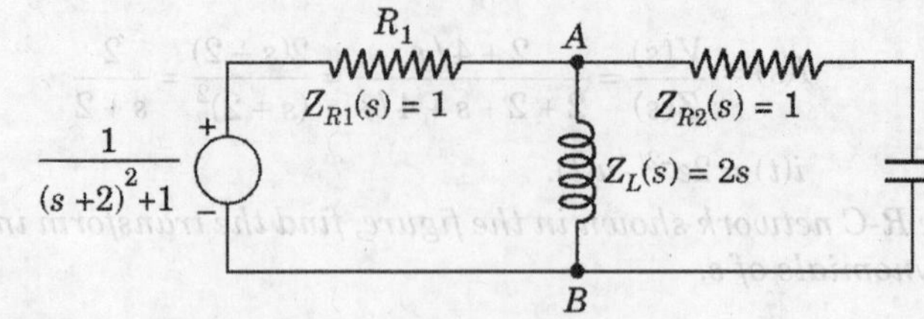

$$Z_{R_2C}(s) = 1 + \frac{1}{s} = \frac{s+1}{s}$$

Hence transform admittance of R_2 and C is,

$$Y_{R_2C}(s) = \frac{s}{s+1}$$

Transform admittance of L in parallel with R_2 and C is,

$$Y_{LR_2C}(s) = \frac{1}{2s} + \frac{s}{s+1} = \frac{2s^2+s+1}{2s(s+1)}$$

Corresponding transform impedance is,

$$Z_{LR_2C}(s) = \frac{1}{Y_{LR_2C}}(s) = \frac{2s(s+1)}{2s^2+s+1}$$

Total impedance offered to the source is,

$$Z(s) = 1 + \frac{2s(s+1)}{2s^2+s+1} = \frac{4s^2+3s+1}{2s^2+s+1}$$

Hence current $\quad I(s) = \frac{V(s)}{Z(s)} = \frac{2s^2+s+1}{[(s+2)^2+1]\,[4s^2+3s+1]}$

8.5. General Network Analysis for Passive Elements

In Chapter 2, we have dealt with the general network analysis for resistive network. The same general methods of network analysis either on current basis or on voltage basis may be used for analysing any network involving all types of passive network elements namely resistors, capacitors, and inductors (including mutual inductances). The methods of analysis on current basis and voltage basis are considered below :

8.5.1. General Network Analysis on Current Basis

Analysis on current basis yields for each loop an integro-differential equation of the following type giving effects of current i_j in the jth loop on voltage drop in the kth loop where j and k are any integers.

$$R_{kj} \cdot i_j + L_{kj}\frac{di_j}{di} + D_{kj}\int i_j dt = a_{kj} \cdot i_j \qquad ...(8.58)$$

where R_{kj}, L_{kj} and D_{kj} are respectively the total resistance, total inductance and total elastance common to loops k and j.

Eq. (8.58) may be written as,

$$\left(R_{kj} + L_{kj}\frac{d}{dt} + D_{kj}\int dt\right)i_j = a_{kj} \cdot i_j \quad ...(8.59)$$

This symbolism implies that the variable i_j is operated upon by multiplication by R_{kj}, multiplicated by L_{kj} and differentiation, and finally multiplication by D_{kj} and integration. Thus all these three operations taken together constitute the symbol a_{kj}.

Eq. (8.59) gives the voltage drop in loop k caused by current i_j in loop j. The total voltage drop in loop k equals the voltage drops caused in loop k by currents flowing in every loop say from 1 to l where l is the total number of loop currents. Mathematically this may be obtained by letting j have all values from 1 to l. This total voltage drop in passive elements in loop k caused by all the currents from 1 to l must equal the total voltage rise caused by energy sources within loop k. Let this voltage rise be v_k. Then application of Kirchhoff's voltage law to the loop gives,

$$\sum_{j=1}^{j=l} a_{kj} \cdot i_j = v_k ...(8.60)$$

Similar equations my be written for every other loop. Thus general equations for all the loops in a network may be written in the most concise form as below.

$$\sum_{j=1}^{l} a_{kj} \cdot i_j = v_k,\ k = 1, 2, ...\ l. \quad ...(8.61)$$

This concise expression may be expanded and put in the form of following set of equations.

$$a_{11} \cdot i_1 + a_{12} \cdot i_2 + a_{13} \cdot i_3 + ... + a_{1l} \cdot i_l = v_1 \quad ...(8.62.1)$$

$$a_{21} \cdot i_1 + a_{22} \cdot i_2 + a_{23} \cdot i_3 + ... + a_{2l} \cdot i_l = v_2 \quad ...(8.62.2)$$

....

$$a_{l1} \cdot i_1 + a_{l2} \cdot i_2 + a_{l3} \cdot i_3 + ... + a_{ll} \cdot i_l = v_l \quad ...(8.62.3)$$

These equations may be written in the form of a chart or schedule which lays emphasis on the operator coefficients a_{11}, a_{12} etc. This is given below.

		Coefficients of					
Eq. No.	*Voltage*	i_1	i_2	i_3	i_4	...	i_l
1	v_1	a_{11}	a_{12}	a_{13}	a_{14}	...	a_{1l}
2	v_2	a_{21}	a_{22}	a_{23}	a_{24}	...	a_{2l}
—	...	...	...	...	...	...	...
l	v_l	a_{l1}	a_{l2}	a_{l3}	a_{l4}	...	a_{l1}

If all loop currents i_1 to i_l are chosen consistently clockwise or consistently counter-clockwise, then all coefficients $a_{11}, a_{22}, a_{33} ... a_{ll}$ are positive and all other coefficients are negative. Of course, in most cases, many coefficients are zero.

The chart given above and the corresponding set of equations (8.62) may be written in compact form to give the following matrix equation.

$$\begin{bmatrix} v_1 \\ v_2 \\ v_3 \\ \cdots \\ v_l \end{bmatrix} = \begin{bmatrix} a_{11} & a_{12} & a_{13} & \cdots & a_{1l} \\ a_{21} & a_{22} & a_{23} & \cdots & a_{2l} \\ a_{31} & a_{32} & a_{33} & \cdots & a_{3l} \\ \cdots & \cdots & \cdots & \cdots & \cdots \\ a_{l1} & a_{l2} & a_{l3} & \cdots & a_{ll} \end{bmatrix} \begin{bmatrix} i_1 \\ i_2 \\ i_3 \\ \vdots \\ i_l \end{bmatrix} \qquad \text{...(8.63)}$$

Eq. (8.63) may be written symbolically as below :

$$[V] = [A]\ [I] \qquad \text{...(8.64)}$$

Here $[V]$ and $[I]$ are *column* matrices whereas $[A]$ is a *square* matrix.

Example 8.7. *Write Kirchhoff's voltage law equation for the given network.*

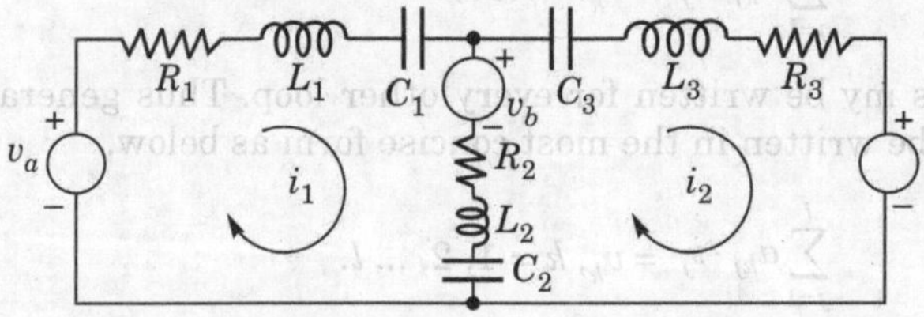

Solution. Let i_1 and i_2, taken clockwise, be the loop currents. Then application of Kirchhoff's law gives,

$$\sum_{j=1}^{2} a_{kj} \cdot i_j = v_k,\ k = 1, 2 \qquad \text{...(1)}$$

Eq. (1) may be expanded to give,

$$a_{11} \cdot i_1 + a_{12} \cdot i_2 = v_1 \qquad \text{...(2)}$$

and

$$a_{21} \cdot i_1 + a_{22} \cdot i_2 = v_2 \qquad \text{...(3)}$$

The operator coefficients a_{11}, a_{12}, a_{21} and a_{23} may be found by inspection of the given network. Thus we get,

$$a_{11} = (R_1 + R_2) + (L_1 + L_2)\ \frac{d}{dt} + (D_1 + D_2) \int dt \qquad \text{...(4)}$$

$$a_{22} = (R_2 + R_3) + (L_2 + L_3)\ \frac{d}{dt} + (D_2 + D_3) \int dt \qquad \text{...(5)}$$

$$a_{12} = a_{21} = -\left(R_2 + L_2 \frac{d}{dt} + D_2 \int dt \right) \qquad \text{...(6)}$$

The voltage terms v_1 and v_2 are given by,

$$v_1 = v_a - v_b \qquad \text{...(7)}$$

$$v_2 = v_b - v_c \qquad \text{...(8)}$$

8.5.2. General Network Analysis on Voltage Basis. Analysis on voltage basis yields for each node, an integro-differential equation of the following type giving effects of node voltages v_j of the

jth node on current in the kth node where j and k are any integers

$$G_{kj} \cdot v_j + C_{kj} \frac{dv_j}{dt} + \frac{1}{L_{kj}} \int v_j \, dt = b_{kj} \cdot v_j \qquad \text{...(8.65)}$$

where G_{kj}, L_{kj}, and C_{kj}, are respectively the total resistance, total inductance and total capacitance common to nodes k and j.

Eq. (8.65) may be written as,

$$\left[G_{kj} + C_{kj} \frac{d}{dt} + \frac{1}{L_{kj}} \int dt \right] v_j = b_{kj} \cdot v_j \qquad \text{...(8.66)}$$

This symbolism implies that the variable b_{kj} is operated upon by multiplication by G_{kj}, multiplication by C_{kj} and differentiation and finally multiplication by $\frac{1}{L_{kj}}$ and integration. Thus all these three operations taken together constitute the symbol b_{kj}.

Eq. (8.66) gives the current divergent at node k caused by voltage v_j of node j. The total current divergent at node k equals the current divergent at node k resulting from node voltages at nodes 1 to n where n is the total number of node-to-datum voltages ($n = n_t - 1$, where n_t is the total number of nodes).

Mathematically this may be obtained by letting j have all values from 1 to n. This total current divergent at node k caused by all the node-to-datum voltages from 1 to n must equal the total current convergent at node k caused by energy sources energising node k. Let this convergent current be i_k. Then application of Kirchhoff's current law to the node k yields :

$$\sum_{j=1}^{n} b_{kj} \cdot v_j = i_k \qquad \text{...(8.67)}$$

Similar equations may be written for every other node. These equations for all the nodes in a network may be written in the most concise form as below :

$$\sum_{j=1}^{n} b_{kj} \cdot v_j = i_k, \; k = 1, 2, \ldots n \qquad \text{...(8.68)}$$

This concise expression may be expanded and put in the form of following set of equations.

$$b_{11} \cdot v_1 + b_{12} \cdot v_2 + b_{13} \cdot v_3 + \ldots + b_{1n} \cdot v_n = i_1 \qquad \text{...(8.69.1)}$$

$$b_{21} \cdot v_1 + b_{22} \cdot v_2 + b_{23} \cdot v_3 + \ldots + b_{2n} \cdot v_n = i_2 \qquad \text{...(8.69.2)}$$

$$\ldots \quad \ldots \quad \ldots \quad \ldots \quad \ldots$$

$$b_{n1} \cdot v_1 + b_{n2} \cdot v_2 + b_{n3} \cdot v_3 + \ldots + b_{nn} \cdot v_n = i_n \qquad \text{...(8.69.3)}$$

Eqs. (8.69) may be written in compact form to give the following matrix equation,

$$\begin{bmatrix} i_1 \\ i_2 \\ \ldots \\ i_n \end{bmatrix} = \begin{bmatrix} b_{11} & b_{12} & b_{13} & \cdots & b_{1n} \\ b_{21} & b_{22} & b_{23} & \cdots & b_{2n} \\ \ldots & \ldots & \ldots & \ldots & \ldots \\ b_{n1} & b_{n2} & n_{n3} & \cdots & b_{nn} \end{bmatrix} \begin{bmatrix} v_1 \\ v_2 \\ \ldots \\ v_n \end{bmatrix} \qquad \text{...(8.70)}$$

In applying Eq. (8.69) to networks, it is not necessary to simplify the network by combining the elements. Thus at node *j*, the capacitance C_{jj} is the sum of the capacitances connected to node *j i.e.* the capacitance from node *j* to ground with all other nodes grounded. Similarly C_{kj} is the sum of all the capacitances connected between node *j* and node *k i.e.* the capacitances from node *j* to node *k* with all other nodes grounded.

Similar remarks apply for inverse inductance $\frac{1}{L}$ and for conductance *G*.

Generally the same convention for positive current is followed in node equations for a network. Thus for every node, all currents convergent at the node may be taken as positive and all currents divergent from the node may be taken as negative. If the same convention regarding positive current is followed for all the nodes, then the sign of coefficients $b_{11}, b_{22}, \ldots b_{nn}$ will be positive and sign of all other coefficients will be negative.

Example 8.8. *Write Kirchhoff's current law equation for the given network.*

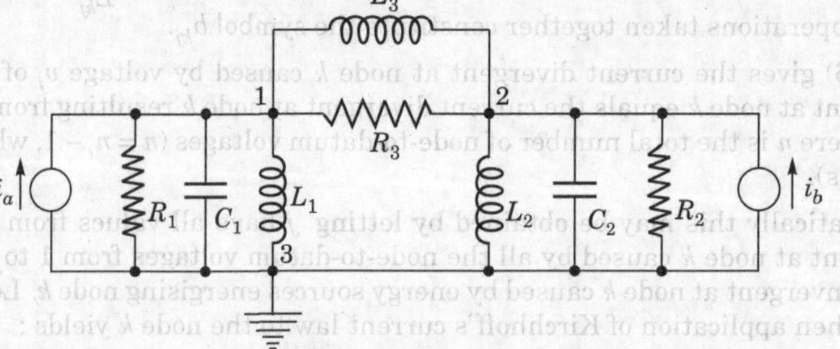

Datum node

Solution. Here there are in all 3 nodes namely nodes 1, 2 and 3. Let node 3 be taken as the datum node. Let voltages of nodes 1 and 2 with respect to node 3 be v_1 and v_2. Then application of Kirchhoff's current law to the nodes 1 and 2 yields the following equations :

$$b_{11} \cdot v_1 + b_{12} \cdot v_2 = i_1 \qquad \ldots(1)$$

$$b_{21} \cdot v_1 + b_{22} \cdot v_2 = i_2 \qquad \ldots(2)$$

where
$$b_{11} = G_1 + G_3 + C_1 \frac{d}{dt} + \left(\frac{1}{L_1} + \frac{1}{L_3}\right)\int dt \qquad \ldots(3)$$

$$b_{22} = G_2 + G_3 + C_2 \cdot \frac{d}{dt} + \left(\frac{1}{L_2} + \frac{1}{L_3}\right)\int dt \qquad \ldots(4)$$

$$b_{12} = b_{21} = -\left[G_3 + \frac{1}{L_3}\int dt\right] \qquad \ldots(5)$$

$$i_1 = i_a \qquad \ldots(6)$$

and
$$i_2 = i_b \qquad \ldots(7)$$

8.6. General Network Analysis Using Laplace Transformation

Last article gives the method of writing a set of integro- differential equations for a general network using the "*a*" and "*b*" coefficients. Thus in general, using the analysis on loop basis, the coefficient a_{kj} is given by,

$$a_{kj} = R_{kj} + L_{kj}\,\frac{d}{dt} + D_{kj}\int dt \qquad \text{...(8.71)}$$

The corresponding matrix is given by,

$$[A] = \begin{bmatrix} a_{11} & a_{12} & a_{13} & \cdots & a_{1l} \\ a_{21} & a_{22} & a_{23} & \cdots & a_{2l} \\ a_{31} & a_{32} & a_{33} & \cdots & a_{3l} \\ \cdots & \cdots & \cdots & \cdots & \cdots \\ a_{l1} & a_{l2} & a_{l3} & \cdots & a_{ll} \end{bmatrix} \qquad \text{...(8.72)}$$

Similarly using the analysis on the node basis, the coefficient b_{kj} is given by,

$$b_{kj} = G_{kj} + C_{kj}\,\frac{d}{dt} + \frac{1}{L_{kj}}\int dt \qquad \text{...(8.73)}$$

The corresponding matrix is given by

$$[B] = \begin{bmatrix} b_{11} & b_{12} & b_{13} & \cdots & b_{1n} \\ b_{21} & b_{22} & b_{23} & \cdots & b_{2n} \\ b_{31} & b_{32} & b_{33} & \cdots & b_{3n} \\ \cdots & \cdots & \cdots & \cdots & \cdots \\ b_{n1} & b_{n2} & b_{n3} & \cdots & b_{nn} \end{bmatrix} \qquad \text{...(8.74)}$$

In the Laplace transform equivalent, the a-coefficients become impedance terms $Z(s)$ plus initial condition sources while the b-coefficients become admittance terms $Y(s)$ plus initial condition sources. Thus the transform form of Eqs. (8.62) is as below :

$$\begin{aligned} Z_{11}(s)\cdot I_1(s) + Z_{12}(s)\cdot I_2(s) + \ldots + Z_{1l}(s)\cdot I_l(s) &= V_1(s) + V_{01}(s) \\ Z_{21}(s)\cdot I_1(s) + Z_{22}(s)\cdot I_2(s) + \ldots + Z_{2l}(s)\cdot I_l(s) &= V_2(s) + V_{02}(s) \\ \ldots \quad \ldots \quad \ldots \quad \ldots \quad & \ldots \quad \ldots \\ Z_{l1}(s)\cdot I_1(s) + Z_{l2}(s)\cdot I_2(s) + \ldots + Z_{ll}(s)\cdot I_l(s) &= V_l(s) + V_{0l}(s) \end{aligned} \qquad \text{...(8.75)}$$

Eqs. (8.75) may be written in the matrix equation form given below :

$$\begin{bmatrix} Z_{11}(s) & Z_{12}(s) & \cdots & Z_{1l}(s) \\ Z_{21}(s) & Z_{22}(s) & \cdots & Z_{2l}(s) \\ \cdots & \cdots & \cdots & \cdots \\ Z_{l1}(s) & Z_{l2}(s) & \cdots & Z_{ll}(s) \end{bmatrix} \begin{bmatrix} I_1(s) \\ I_2(s) \\ \cdots \\ I_l(s) \end{bmatrix} = \begin{bmatrix} V_1(s) \\ V_2(s) \\ \cdots \\ V_l(s) \end{bmatrix} + \begin{bmatrix} V_{01}(s) \\ V_{02}(s) \\ \cdots \\ V_{0l}(s) \end{bmatrix} \qquad \text{...(8.76)}$$

Eq. (8.75) may be put more compactly as below :

$$[Z]\,[I] = [V] + [V_0] = [V'] \qquad \text{...(8.77)}$$

Here $[I]$ and $[V']$ are column matrices while $[Z]$ is a square matrix.

On node basis the transform form of Eq. (8.69) is as below :

$$\left.\begin{aligned} Y_{11}(s)\cdot V_1(s) + Y_{12}(s)\cdot V_2(s) + \ldots + Y_{1n}(s)\cdot V_n(s) &= I_1(s) + I_{01}(s) \\ Y_{21}(s)\cdot V_1(s) + Y_{22}(s)\cdot V_2(s) + \ldots + Y_{2n}(s)\cdot V_n(s) &= I_2(s) + I_{02}(s) \\ \ldots \quad \ldots \quad \ldots \quad \ldots \quad & \ldots \quad \ldots \end{aligned}\right] \qquad \text{...(8.78)}$$

Eqs. (8.78) may be written in the matrix equation form given below :

$$\begin{bmatrix} Y_{11}(s) & Y_{12}(s) & \cdots & Y_{1n}(s) \\ Y_{21}(s) & Y_{22}(s) & \cdots & Y_{2n}(s) \\ \cdots & \cdots & \cdots & \cdots \\ Y_{n1}(s) & Y_{n2}(s) & \cdots & Y_{nn}(s) \end{bmatrix} \begin{bmatrix} V_1(s) \\ V_2(s) \\ \cdots \\ V_n(s) \end{bmatrix} = \begin{bmatrix} I_1(s) \\ I_2(s) \\ \cdots \\ I_n(s) \end{bmatrix} + \begin{bmatrix} I_{01}(s) \\ I_{02}(s) \\ \cdots \\ I_{0n}(s) \end{bmatrix} \quad \text{...(8.79)}$$

Eq. (8.79) may be put more compactly as below,

$$[Y][V] = [I] + [I_0] = [I'] \quad \text{...(8.80)}$$

Solution of Eqs. (8.75) or (8.78) may be found by Cramer's rule.

For Eqs. (8.75), Cramer's rule yields,

$$I_1(s) = \frac{D_1}{\Delta},\ I_2(s) = \frac{D_2}{\Delta}, ...,\ I_l(s) = \frac{D_l}{\Delta} \quad \text{...(8.81)}$$

where Δ is the system determinant given by,

$$\Delta = \begin{bmatrix} Z_{11}(s) & Z_{12}(s) & \cdots & Z_{1l}(s) \\ Z_{21}(s) & Z_{22}(s) & \cdots & Z_{2l}(s) \\ \cdots & \cdots & \cdots & \cdots \\ Z_{l1}(s) & Z_{l2}(s) & \cdots & Z_{li}(s) \end{bmatrix} \quad \text{...(8.82)}$$

D_j is the determinant formed by replacing the jth column of Z-coefficient by column $V_1'(s), V_2'(s) \ldots V_l'(s)$ where $V_j'(s)$ equals $V_j(s) + V_{0j}(s)$.

For third order equations *i.e.* for $l = 3$, Eqs. (8.81) yield,

$$I_1(s) = \frac{D_1}{\Delta} = \frac{1}{\Delta}[V_1'(s)\cdot\Delta_{11} + V_2'(s) + \Delta_{21} + V_3'(s)\cdot\Delta_{31}] \quad \text{...(8.83)}$$

$$I_2(s) = \frac{D_2}{\Delta} = \frac{1}{\Delta}[V_1'(s)\cdot\Delta_{12} + V_2'(s) + \Delta_{22} + V_3'(s)\cdot\Delta_{32}] \quad \text{...(8.84)}$$

$$I_3(s) = \frac{D_3}{\Delta} = \frac{1}{\Delta}[V_1'(s)\cdot\Delta_{13} + V_2'(s)\cdot\Delta_{23} + V_3'(s)\cdot\Delta_{33}] \quad \text{...(8.85)}$$

where Δ_{11}, Δ_{21} etc. are the co-factors corresponding to terms $Z_{11}(s)$, $Z_{21}(s)$ etc.

It may be noted here that $V_j'(s)$ is a summation of voltages $V_j(s)$ and $V_{0j}(s)$ where $V_j(s)$ is the transform of all voltage sources in loop j and $V_{0j}(s)$ is the transform voltage representation of all initial conditions in loop j. This summation must, however, be made considering the polarity of every source with respect to the reference direction of the loop current $I_j(s)$. Further current sources, if any, must first be transformed into equivalent voltage source before the summation is done.

Similarly for Eq. (8.78), Cramer's rule yields,

$$V_1(s) = \frac{D_1}{\Delta},\ V_2(s) = \frac{D_2}{\Delta}, ...,\ V_n(s) = \frac{D_n}{\Delta} \quad \text{...(8.86)}$$

where Δ is the system determinant given by,

$$\Delta = \begin{vmatrix} Y_{11}(s) & Y_{12}(s) & \cdots & Y_{1n}(s) \\ Y_{21}(s) & Y_{22}(s) & \cdots & Y_{2n}(s) \\ \cdots & \cdots & \cdots & \cdots \\ Y_{n1}(s) & Z_{n2}(s) & \cdots & Y_{nn}(s) \end{vmatrix} \quad \text{...(8.87)}$$

D_j is the determinant formed by replacing the jth column of Y-coefficients by the column $I'_1(s), I'_2(s),..., I'_n(s)$ where $I'_j(s)$ equals $I_j(s) + I_{0j}(s)$.

For third order equations *i.e.* for $n = 3$, Eqs. (8.86) yield,

$$V_1(s) = \frac{D_1}{\Delta} = \frac{1}{\Delta}[I'_1(s)\cdot\Delta_{11} + I'_2(s)\cdot\Delta_{21} + I'_3(s)\cdot\Delta_{31}] \quad ...(8.88)$$

$$V_2(s) = \frac{D_2}{\Delta} = \frac{1}{\Delta}[I'_1(s)\cdot\Delta_{12} + I'_2(s)\cdot\Delta_{22} + I'_3(s)\cdot\Delta_{32}] \quad ...(8.89)$$

$$V_3(s) = \frac{D_3}{\Delta} = \frac{1}{\Delta}[I'_1(s)\cdot\Delta_{13} + I'_2(s)\cdot\Delta_{23} + I'_3(s)\cdot\Delta_{33}] \quad ...(8.90)$$

where Δ_{11}, Δ_{21}, etc. are the cofactors corresponding to terms $Y_{11}(s)$, $Y_{21}(s)$ etc.

In the above equations, $I'_j(s)$ is the summation of currents $I_j(s)$ and $I_{0j}(s)$ where $I_j(s)$ is the transform of all current sources at node j and $I_{0j}(s)$ is the transform current representation of all initial conditions at node j. This summation must however, be made considering the polarity of every source. Further voltage sources, if any, must first be transformed into equivalent current sources before the summation is done.

Example 8.9. *In the given network switch K is closed at time t = 0. There is no initial current in any inductor and no initial charge across any capacitor. Draw the transform network and write equilibrium equation on loop current basis.*

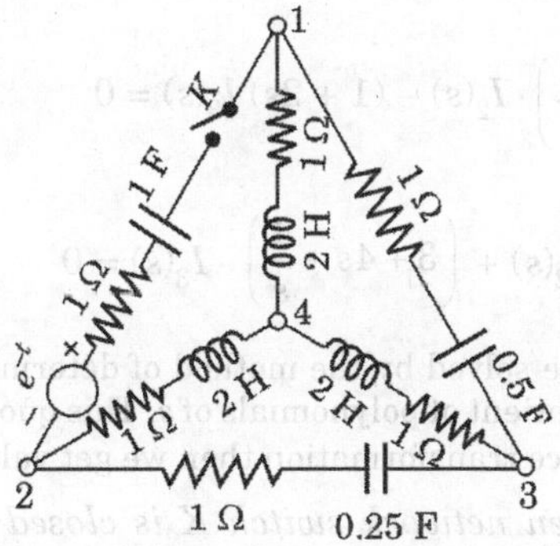

Solution. The transform network is a given on page 367.

Let $I_1(s)$, $I_2(s)$ and $I_3(s)$ be the loop currents as shown. Then application of Kirchhoff's voltage law to the loops gives the following equilibrium equations.

$$Z_{11}(s)\cdot I_1(s) + Z_{12}(s)\cdot I_2(s) + Z_{13}(s)\cdot I_3(s) = \frac{1}{s+1} \quad ...(1)$$

$$Z_{21}(s)\cdot I_1(s) + Z_{22}(s)\cdot I_2(s) + Z_{23}(s)\cdot I_3(s) = 0 \quad ...(2)$$

$$Z_{31}(s)\cdot I_1(s) + Z_{32}(s)\cdot I_2(s) + Z_{33}(s)\cdot I_3(s) = 0 \quad ...(3)$$

where $Z_{11}(s) = 3 + 4s + \frac{1}{s}$

$$Z_{22}(s) = 3 + 4s + \frac{2}{s}$$

$$Z_{33}(s) = 3 + 4s + \frac{4}{s}$$

$$Z_{12}(s) = Z_{21}(s) = -(1 + 2s)$$
$$Z_{13}(s) = Z_{31}(s) = -(1 + 2s)$$
$$Z_{23}(s) = Z_{32}(s) = -(1 + 2s)$$

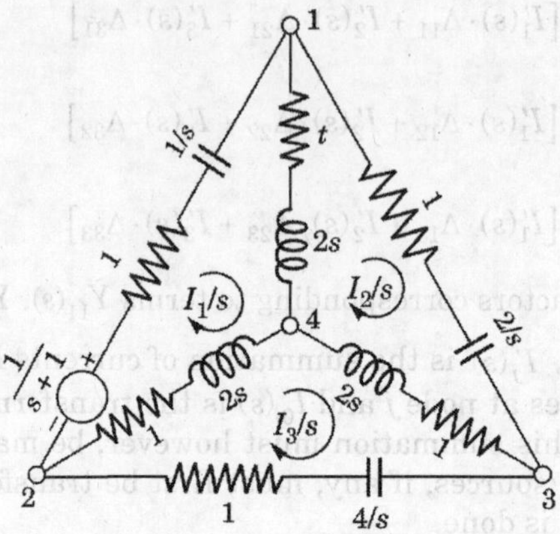

Substituting the values of coefficient into Eqs. (1) to (3), we get

$$\left(3 + 4s + \frac{1}{s}\right) I_1(s) - (1 + 2s)\, I_2(s) - (1 + 2s)\, I_3(s) = \frac{1}{s+1} \qquad ...(4)$$

$$-(1 + 2s)\, I_1(s) + \left(3 + 4s + \frac{2}{s}\right) \cdot I_2(s) - (1 + 2s)\, I_3(s) = 0 \qquad ...(5)$$

$$-(1 + 2s)\, I_1(s) - (1 + 2s) \cdot I_2(s) + \left(3 + 4s + \frac{4}{s}\right) \cdot I_3(s) = 0 \qquad ...(6)$$

Note. These equations may be solved by the method of determinants to get values of $I_1(s)$, $I_2(s)$ and $I_3(s)$, each expressed in the form of quotient of polynomials of s. This quotient may be simplified by the method of partial fractions. On inverse Laplace transformation then we get values of $i_1(t)$, $i_2(t)$ and $i_3(t)$.

Example 8.10. *In the given network switch K is closed at time $t = 0$. There is no initial current in the inductor and no initial charges across the capacitors. Draw the transform network corresponding to the given network and write equilibrium equations on the loop basis. Solve these equations to express $I_1(s)$, $I_2(s)$ and $I_3(s)$ as quotients of polynomials of s.*

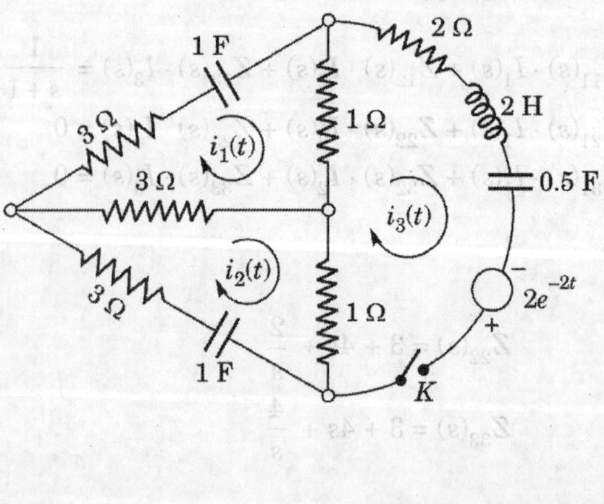

Solution. The transform network is as follows :

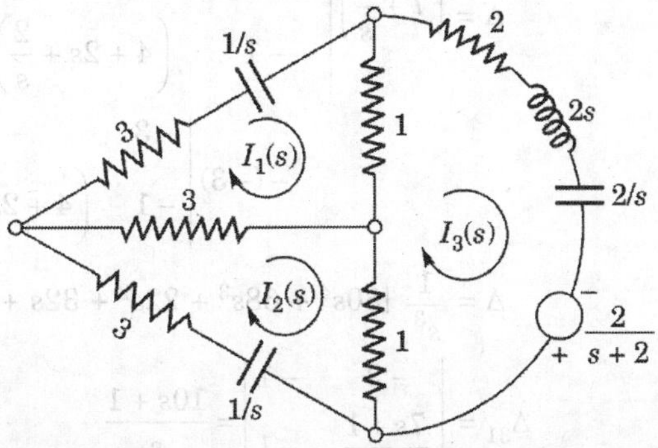

Let $I_1(s)$, $I_2(s)$ and $I_3(s)$ be the transform loop currents. All impedance elements have been replaced by their transform impedances. Application of Kirchhoff's voltage law to the 3 loops yields the following three equilibrium equations,

$$\left(7+\frac{1}{s}\right)I_1(s) - 3I_2(s) - I_3(s) = 0 \quad ...(1)$$

$$-3I_1(s) + \left(7+\frac{1}{s}\right)I_2(s) - I_3(s) = 0 \quad ...(2)$$

$$-I_1(s) - I_2(s) + \left(4+2s+\frac{2}{s}\right)I_3(s) = \frac{2}{s+2} \quad ...(3)$$

System determinant is an below :

$$\Delta = \begin{vmatrix} \left(7+\frac{1}{s}\right) & -3 & -1 \\ -3 & \left(7+\frac{1}{s}\right) & -1 \\ -1 & -1 & \left(4+2s+\frac{2}{s}\right) \end{vmatrix} \quad ...(4)$$

Then

$$I_1(s) = \frac{D_1}{\Delta} = \frac{1}{\Delta}\left[(0\times\Delta_{11}) + (0\times\Delta_{21}) + \frac{2}{s+2}\cdot\Delta_{31}\right]$$

$$= \frac{2}{s+2}\cdot\frac{\Delta_{31}}{\Delta} \quad ...(5)$$

$$I_2(s) = \frac{D_2}{\Delta} = \frac{1}{\Delta}\left[(0\times\Delta_{12}) + (0\times\Delta_{21}) + \frac{2}{s+2}\cdot\Delta_{33}\right]$$

$$= \frac{2}{s+2}\cdot\frac{\Delta_{32}}{\Delta} \quad ...(6)$$

$$I_3(s) = \frac{D_3}{\Delta} = \frac{1}{\Delta}\left[(0\times\Delta_{31}) + (0\times\Delta_{32}) + \frac{2}{s+2}\cdot\Delta_{33}\right]$$

$$= \frac{2}{s+2}\cdot\frac{\Delta_{32}}{\Delta} \quad ...(7)$$

$$\Delta = \left(7+\frac{1}{s}\right)\begin{vmatrix} \left(7+\frac{1}{s}\right) & -1 \\ -1 & \left(4+2s+\frac{2}{s}\right) \end{vmatrix} - (-3)\begin{vmatrix} -3 & -1 \\ -1 & \left(4+2s+\frac{2}{s}\right) \end{vmatrix} + (-1)\begin{vmatrix} -3 & -1 \\ \left(7+\frac{1}{s}\right) & -1 \end{vmatrix}$$

or
$$\Delta = \frac{1}{s^3}\,[80s^4 + 68s^3 + 22s^2 + 32s + 2]$$

$$\Delta_{31} = \begin{vmatrix} -3 & -1 \\ \frac{7s+1}{s} & -1 \end{vmatrix} = \frac{10s+1}{s}$$

$$\Delta_{32} = (-1)\begin{vmatrix} \frac{7s+1}{s} & -1 \\ -3 & -1 \end{vmatrix} = \frac{10s+1}{s}$$

$$D_{23} = \begin{vmatrix} \frac{7s+1}{s} & -3 \\ -3 & \frac{7s+1}{s} \end{vmatrix} = \frac{40s^2+14s+1}{s^2}$$

Hence
$$I_1(s) = \frac{2}{s+2}\cdot\frac{10s+1}{s}\cdot\frac{s^3}{80s^4+68s^3+22s^2+32s+2}$$

$$= \frac{(10s+1)s^2}{(s+2)(40s^4+34s^3+11s^2+16s+1)}$$

$$I_2(s) = \frac{2}{s+2}\cdot\frac{10s+1}{s}\cdot\frac{s^3}{80s^4+68s^3+22s^2+32s+2} = I_1(s)$$

$$I_3(s) = \frac{2}{s+2}\cdot\frac{40s^2+14s+1}{s^2}\cdot\frac{s^3}{80s^4+68s^3+22s^2+32s+2}$$

$$= \frac{(40s^2+14s+1)s}{(s+2)(40s^2+34s^3+11s^2+16s+1)}$$

8.7. Superposition Principle (Superposition Theorem)

From Eq. (8.83) it is apparent that in order to determine the current $I_1(s)$ we may consider each of the transform voltage sources $V_1'(s)$, $V_2'(s)$ and $V_3'(s)$ one at a time and then add their individual responses to get $I_1(s)$. Similar remarks apply for $I_2(s)$ and $I_3(s)$. This is nothing but the *principle of Superposition.*

The principle of superposition involves following two properties (*i*) the property of additivity and (*ii*) the property of homogeneity in linear networks.

Additivity Property. In a linear network having a number of independent sources (including initial condition sources), the overall response equals the sum of the responses of each individual source with all other sources made inoperative *i.e.* reduced to zero voltage or zero current.

This property is apparent from Eqs. (8.83) to (8.85).

Homogeneity Property. If all source voltages or currents are multiplied by any constant, the response gets multiplied by the same constant.

8.8. Principle of Reciprocity (Reciprocity Theorem)

Eqs. (8.83) to (8.85) give the transform loop currents $I_1(s)$, $I_2(s)$ and $I_3(s)$ in a three loop network. Similar equations may be written for any general network involving say l loops. Assuming the network to be initially relaxed, the transform current in kth loop is given by,

$$I_k(s) = \frac{1}{\Delta}[\Delta_{1k} \cdot V_1(s) + \Delta_{2k} \cdot V_2(s) + ... + \Delta_{lk} \cdot V_l(s)] \quad ...(8.91)$$

Now if all voltages excepting $V_j(s)$ are zero, then Eq. (8.86) reduces to the following simple form,

$$I_k(s) = \frac{\Delta_{jk}}{\Delta} V_j(s) \quad ...(8.92)$$

Again assuming the network to be initially relaxed, the transform current in the jth loop is given by,

$$I_j(s) = \frac{1}{\Delta} [\Delta_{1j} \cdot V_1(s) + \Delta_{2j} \cdot V_2(s) + ... + \Delta_{ij} \cdot V_l(s)] \quad ...(8.93)$$

Now if all voltages excepting $V_k(s)$ are zero, then Eq. (8.93) reduces to the following simple form,

$$I_j(s) = \frac{\Delta_{kj}}{\Delta} \cdot V_k(s) \quad ...(8.94)$$

Fig. 8.12 gives two networks for which Eqs. (8.92) and (8.94) apply. These figures show the loop numbers j and k only. All other loops are enclosed in the block schematically representing the network.

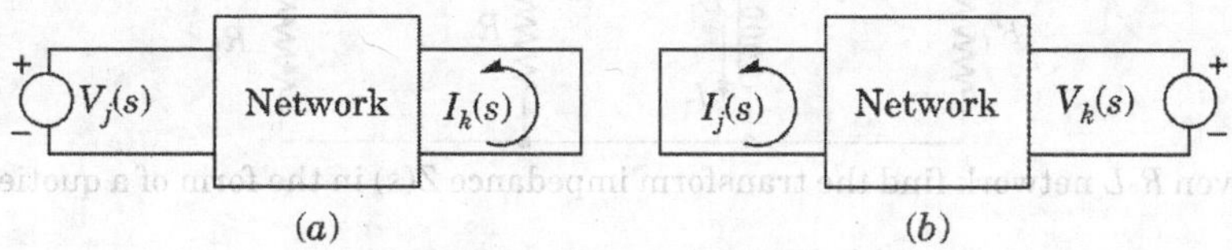

Fig. 8.12. Networks illustrating the principle of reciprocity.

In network of Fig. 8.12 (*a*) transform voltage $V_j(s)$ in the jth loop produces transform current $I_k(s)$ in the kth loop and this current is equal to $\frac{\Delta_{jk}}{\Delta}$ times the applied voltage. Now if $V_j(s)$ is transferred to loop k as shown in Fig. 8.12 (*b*) and $V_k(s)$ is made equal to $V_j(s)$, then the value of transform current $I_j(s)$ in loop j is $\frac{\Delta_{kj}}{\Delta}$ times the applied voltage. If matrix [Z] is symmetrical, then

$$\Delta_{jk} = \Delta_{kj} \quad ...(8.95)$$

Then current $I_j(s)$ equals the current $I_k(s)$.

In general, for a network with symmetrical impedance matrix,

$$\frac{I_k(s)}{V_j(s)} = \frac{I_j(s)}{V_k(s)} \quad ...(8.96)$$

From Eq. (8.96) we infer that the ratio of the response transform to the excitation transform remains the same when we interchange the positions of response and excitation in the network. This is the *principle of reciprocity*. The networks for which this principle holds are called reciprocal networks.

For a network to be reciprocal it is evident that the following conditions must be satisfied :

(*i*) the network should be initially relaxed

(*ii*) only linear elements should be present in the network

and (*iii*) dependent or controlled sources even if linear must be absent in order that the matrix [*Z*] is symmetrical.

EXERCISE

8.1. In the given network, switch *K* is closed at time $t = 0$. At time $t = 0-$, the voltages indicated in the circuit are present on the two capacitors. Draw the transform network, for analysis on the loop basis, representing all elements and all initial conditions.

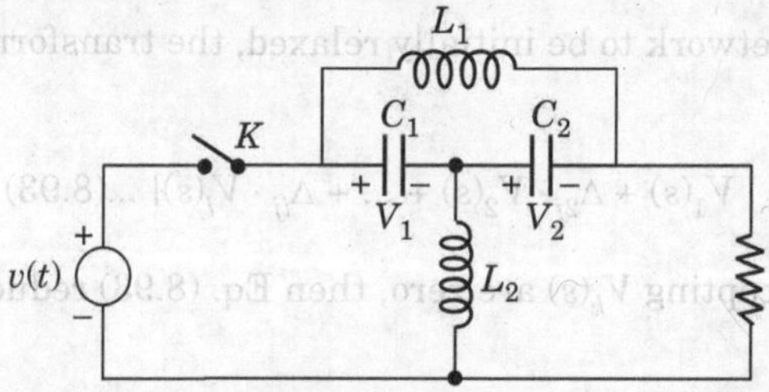

8.2. In the given network, initial currents and voltages are present at time $t = 0$ as a result of removal of active elements. Draw the transform network for analysis on the loop basis, representing all elements and all initial conditions.

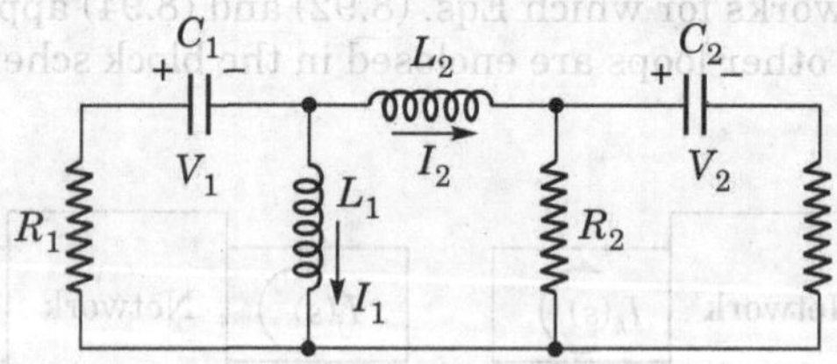

8.3. For the given *R-L* network find the transform impedance *Z*(*s*) in the form of a quotient of polynomials of *s*.

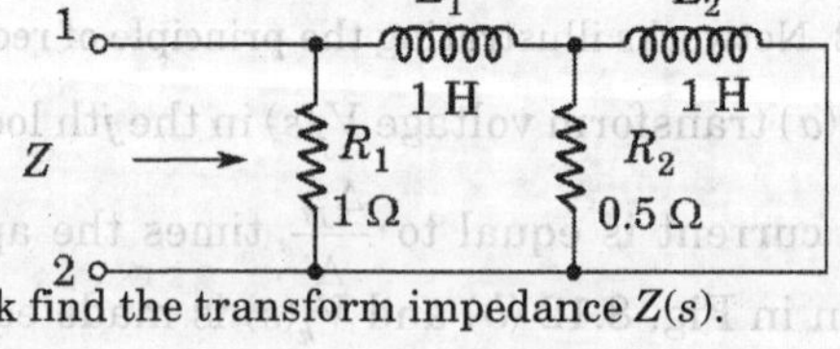

$$\left[\textbf{Ans. } Z(s) = \frac{s(s+2)}{s^2+3s+1}\right]$$

8.4. For the given *L-C* network find the transform impedance *Z*(*s*).

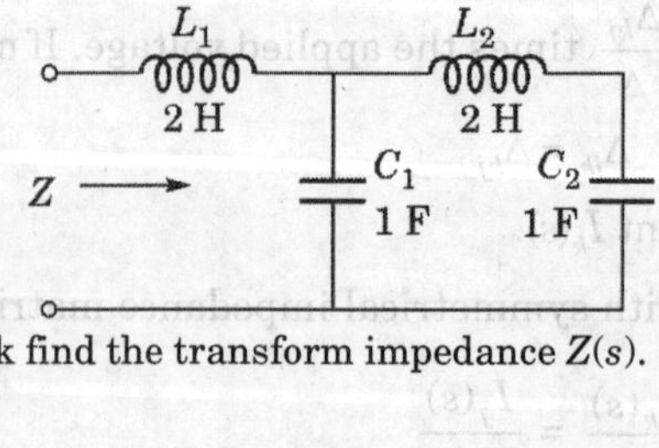

$$\left[\textbf{Ans. } Z(s) = \frac{4s^4+6s^2+1}{2s(s^2+1)}\right]$$

8.5. For the given *R-L* network find the transform impedance *Z*(*s*).

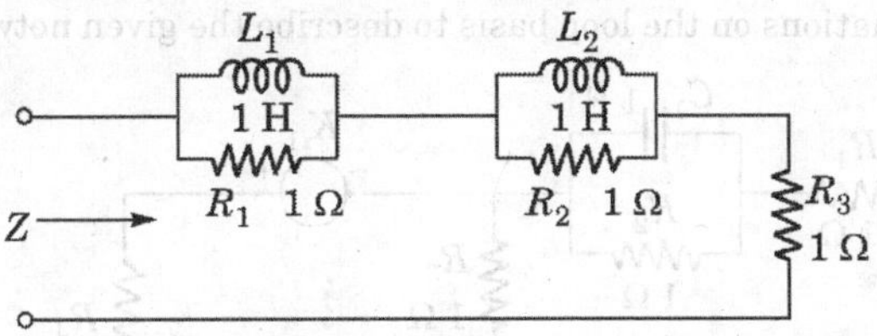

$$\left[\textbf{Ans. } Z(s) = \frac{3s+1}{s+1}\right]$$

8.6. For the *R-L-C* circuit given below, find the transform impedance $Z(s)$.

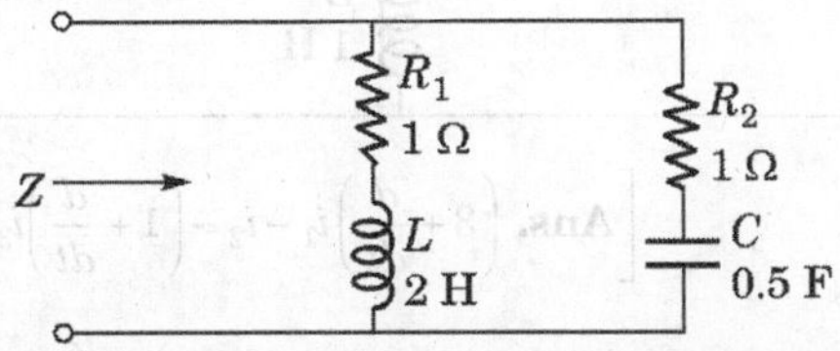

$$\left[\textbf{Ans. } Z(s) = \frac{(2s+1)(s+2)}{2(s^2+s+1)}\right]$$

8.7. The given network is initially relaxed. Switch *K* is closed at time $t = 0$. Find the transform current $I(s)$ drawn from the generator.

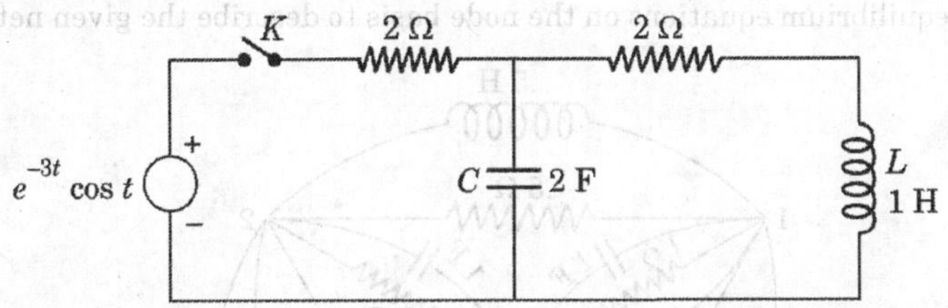

$$\left[\textbf{Ans. } I(s) = \frac{(s+3)(2s^2+4s+1)}{(s^2+6s+10)(4s^2+9s+4)}\right]$$

8.8. In the given network switch *K* is closed at time $t = 0$. The initial current through inductor *L* is 1 Ampere and the initial voltage across capacitor *C* is 2 volts as shown. Draw the transform network showing all initial conditions. Find the transform current $I(s)$ that flows through the series circuit.

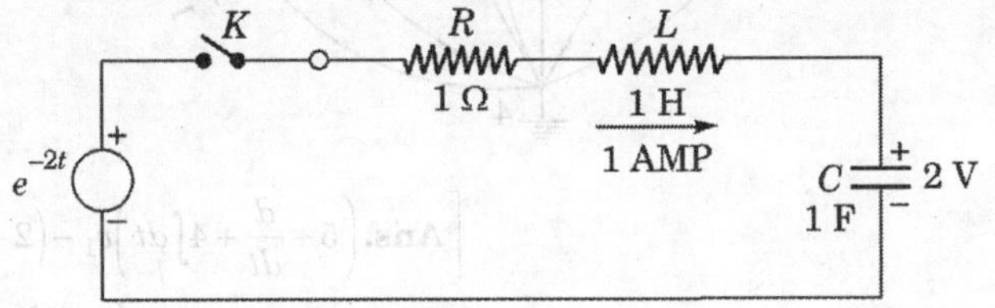

$$\left[\textbf{Ans. } I(s) = \frac{s^2+s-4}{(s+2)(s^2+s+4)}\right]$$

8.9. In the given network, switch *K* is closed at time $t = 0$. The initial current through inductor $L = 2$ amperes and the initial voltage across capacitor is 2 volts as shown in the diagram. Draw the transform network showing all the initial conditions. Find the transform voltage $V(s)$ across the parallel network.

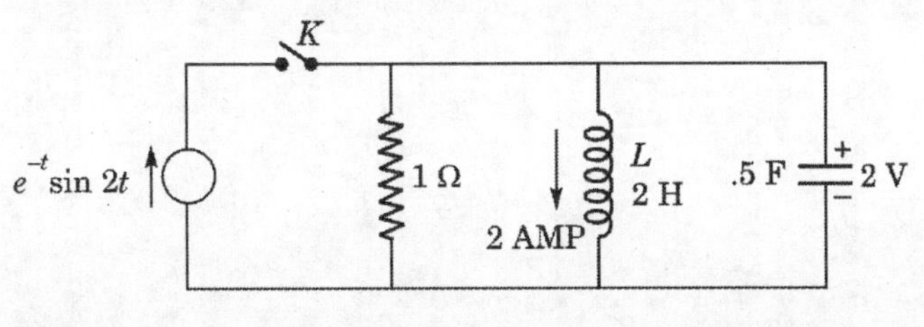

$$\left[\textbf{Ans. } V(s) = \frac{2(s^2+3s+10)}{(s^2+2s+5)(s+1)^2}\right]$$

8.10. Write a set of Equilibrium equations on the loop basis to describe the given network.

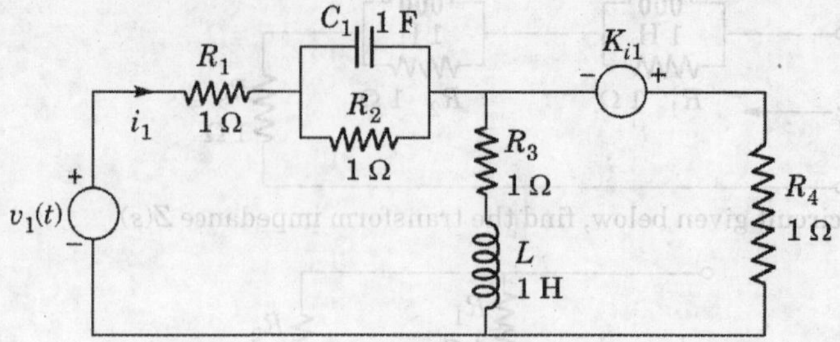

$$\left[\textbf{Ans. } \left(3+\frac{d}{dt}\right)i_1 - i_2 - \left(1+\frac{d}{dt}\right)i_3 = v_1(t) - i_1 + \left(1+\int dt\right)i_2 - 0 = 0\right.$$

$$\left. -\left(1+k_1+\frac{d}{dt}\right)i_1 + 0 + \left(2+\frac{d}{dt}\right)i_3 = 0.\right]$$

8.11. Write a set of equilibrium equations on the node basis to describe the given network.

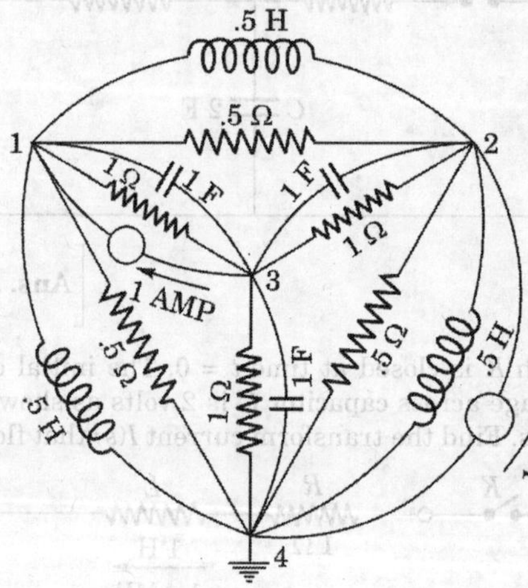

$$\left[\textbf{Ans. } \left(5+\frac{d}{dt}+4\int dt\right)v_1 - \left(2+2\int dt\right)v_2 - \left(1+\frac{d}{dt}\right)v_3 = 1\right.$$

$$-\left(2+2\int dt\right)v_1 + \left(5+\frac{d}{dt}+4\int dt\right)v_2 - \left(1+\frac{d}{dt}\right)v_3 = 1$$

$$\left. -\left(1+\frac{d}{dt}\right)v_1 - \left(1+\frac{d}{dt}\right)v_2 + \left(3+3\frac{d}{dt}\right)v_3 = -1\right]$$

9

Network Theorems

9.1. Introduction

Chapters 2 and 8 give the methods of network analysis which are general in nature. These methods may be used for any network. Solution of equilibrium equations in such methods enables us to find currents and voltages in all branches of the network. Several network problems, however, involve only a restricted analysis. Thus it may be required to find branch current and branch voltage of only one branch in the network or putting it alternatively, to find the current, voltage and power in a load impedance connected across given two terminals of a network. Another problem involving restricted analysis may be to establish conditions for maximum transfer of power from a given network to a given load. For such restricted analysis, although the general methods of analysis may be used, the desired results may be obtained more expeditiously and conveniently through use of certain network theorems. Some of the important network theorems are treated in this chapter.

9.2. Superposition Theorem

This theorem states that in a linear network containing several sources, (including the initial condition sources), the overall response (loop current or node voltage) at any point in the network equals the sum of the responses of each individual source considered separately with all other sources made inoperative *i.e.* replaced by impedances equal to their internal impedances.

Proof of Superposition Theorem. For analysis on the loop basis, the proof of superposition theorem has already been given in Article 8.7.

Thus on loop basis, Eq. (8.75) reproduced below give the equilibrium equations for a l-loop network.

$$\left.\begin{aligned} Z_{11}(s)\cdot I_1(s)+Z_{12}(s)\cdot I_2(s)+...+Z_{1l}(s)\cdot I_l(s) &= V_1(s)+V_{01}(s)\\ Z_{21}(s)\cdot I_1(s)+Z_{22}(s)\cdot I_2(s)+...+Z_{2l}(s)\cdot I_l(s) &= V_2(s)+V_{02}(s)\\ ...\quad ...\quad ... &\quad ...\quad ...\\ Z_{l1}(s)\cdot I_1(s)+Z_{l2}(s)\cdot I_2(s)+...+Z_{ll}(s)\cdot I_l(s) &= V_l(s)+V_{0l}(s) \end{aligned}\right\} \quad ...(9.1)$$

Here $V_1(s)$, $V_2(s)$ ... are the source voltages while $V_{01}(s)$, $V_{02}(s)$ etc. are the initial condition voltages.

Solution of Eqs. (9.1) may be found by Cramer's rule. Thus we get

$$I_1(s)=\frac{D_1}{\Delta},\ I_2(s)=\frac{D_2}{\Delta},\ ...,\ I_l(s)=\frac{D_l}{\Delta} \quad ...(9.2)$$

where Δ is the system determinant given by,

$$\Delta=\begin{vmatrix} Z_{11}(s) & Z_{12}(s) & \cdots & Z_{1l}(s)\\ Z_{21}(s) & Z_{22}(s) & \cdots & Z_{2l}(s)\\ \cdots & \cdots & & \cdots\\ Z_{l1}(s) & Z_{l2}(s) & \cdots & Z_{ll}(s) \end{vmatrix} \quad ...(9.3)$$

D_j is the determinant formed by replacing the jth column of Z-coefficient in the determinants Δ by the column $V_1'(s), V_2'(s) \ldots V_l'(s)$ where $V_j'(s)$ equals $V_j(s) + V_{0j}(s)$.

Thus current in the jth loop is given by,

$$I_j(s) = \frac{D_j}{\Delta} = \frac{1}{\Delta}\left[V_1'(s)\cdot\Delta_{1j} + V_2'(s)\cdot\Delta_{2j} + \ldots + V_l(s)\cdot\Delta_{ij}\right] \quad \ldots(9.4)$$

From Eq. (9.4) it is apparent that in order to determine the current $I_j(s)$ we may consider each of the voltage sources $V_1'(s), V_2'(s) \ldots V_l'(s)$ one at a time and then add their individual responses to get $I_j(s)$. This constitutes the proof of the superposition theorem for analysis on the current basis.

Similar proof of superposition theorem may be given for analysis on the voltage basis. Thus on voltage basis, equilibrium equations for a network having n node-to-datum voltages are as below :

$$\left.\begin{aligned} Y_{11}(s)\cdot V_1(s) + Y_{12}(s)\cdot V_2(s) + \ldots + Y_{1n}(s)\cdot V_n(s) &= I_1(s) + I_{01}(s) \\ Y_{21}(s)\cdot V_1(s) + Y_{22}(s)\cdot V_2(s) + \ldots + Y_{2n}(s)\cdot V_n(s) &= I_2(s) + I_{02}(s) \\ \ldots \qquad \ldots \qquad \ldots \qquad & \ldots \qquad \ldots \\ Y_{n1}(s)\cdot V_1(s) + Y_{n2}(s)\cdot V_2(s) + \ldots + Y_{nn}(s)\cdot V_n(s) &= I_n(s) + I_{0n}(s) \end{aligned}\right\} \quad \ldots(9.5)$$

Here $I_1(s), I_2(s), \ldots, I_n(s)$ are the source voltages while $I_{01}(s), I_{02}(s), \ldots, I_{0n}(s)$ are the initial condition equivalent current sources.

Solution of Eqs. (9.5) may be found by Cramer's by rule. Thus we get,

$$V_1(s) = \frac{D_1}{\Delta},\ V_2(s) = \frac{D_2}{\Delta}, \ldots, V_n(s) = \frac{D_n}{\Delta} \quad \ldots(9.6)$$

where Δ is the Y-coefficient system determinant given by,

$$\Delta = \begin{vmatrix} Y_{11}(s) & Y_{12}(s) & \cdots & Y_{1n}(s) \\ Y_{21}(s) & Y_{22}(s) & \cdots & Y_{2n}(s) \\ \cdots & \cdots & \cdots & \cdots \\ Y_{n1}(s) & Y_{n2}(s) & \cdots & Y_{nn}(s) \end{vmatrix} \quad \ldots(9.7)$$

D_j is the determinant formed by replacing the jth column of Y-coefficients in the determinant Δ by the column $I_1'(s), I_2'(s), \ldots I_n'(s)$ where $I_j'(s)$ equals $I_j(s) + I_{0j}(s)$. Thus voltage at the jth node is given by,

$$V_j(s) = \frac{D_j}{\Delta} = \frac{1}{\Delta}\left[I_1'(s)\cdot\Delta_{1j} + I_2'(s)\cdot\Delta_{2j} + \ldots + I_n'(s)\cdot\Delta_{nj}\right] \quad \ldots(9.8)$$

Eq. (9.8) constitutes the proof of the superposition theorem for analysis on the voltage basis.

Significance of Superposition Theorem. The superposition theorem is of significance since it permits the solution of the network without setting up large number of simultaneous equations. Only one source need be considered at a time. Further if new voltages are introduced into the network, it obviates the need of solving the network afresh.

Example 9.1. *In the network shown in the diagram, making use of the superposition theorem, determine the current flowing in the resistors R_1, R_2 and R_3 and the potential of point A relative to point B.*

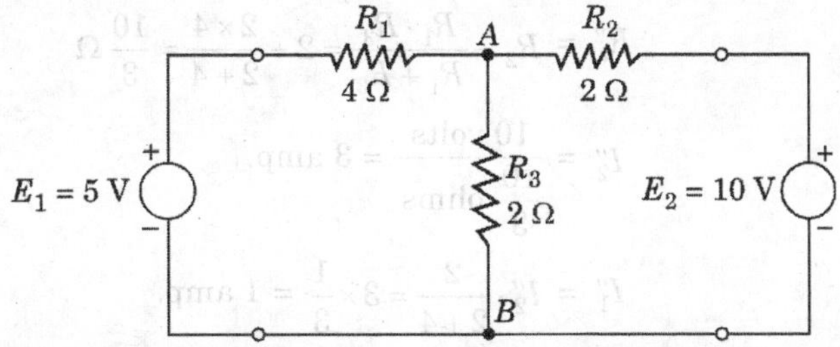

Solution. Considering the voltage source E_1 alone and short circuiting the voltage source E_2, the network reduces to the form shown in Fig. (*a*). Let the currents I_1', I_2' and I_3' flow as shown in the figure.

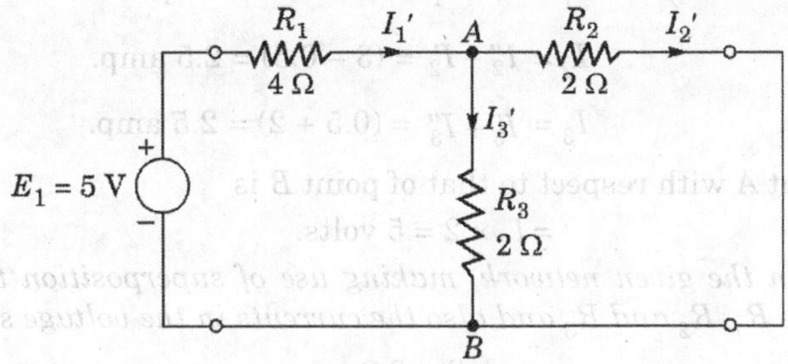

Fig. (*a*)

The total resistance of the network to the source E_1 is,

$$R_t' = R_1 + \frac{R_2 \cdot R_3}{R_2 + R_3} = 4 + \frac{2 \times 2}{2 + 2} = 5\ \Omega$$

Hence current $$I_1' = \frac{5 \text{ volts}}{5 \text{ ohm}} = 1 \text{ amp.}$$

$$I_2' = I_1' \cdot \frac{2}{2+2} = 0.5 \text{ amp.}$$

$$I_3' = I_1' \cdot \frac{2}{2+2} = 0.5 \text{ amp.}$$

Next considering the voltage source E_2 alone and short circuiting the voltage source E_1, the network reduces to the form shown in Fig. (*b*).

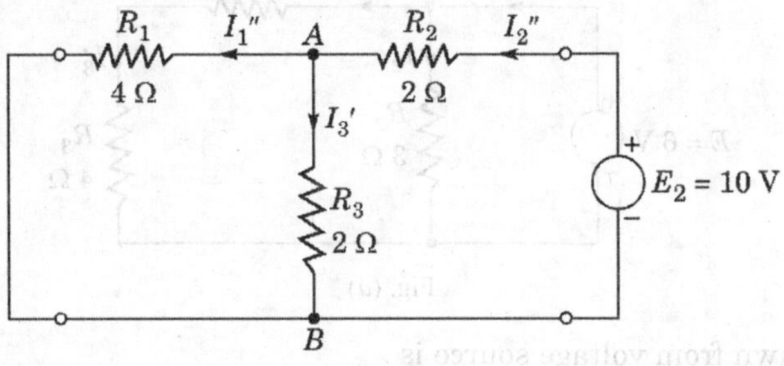

FIg. (*b*)

The total resistance of the network to source E_2 is,

$$R_t'' = R_2 + \frac{R_1 \cdot R_3}{R_1 + R_3} = 2 + \frac{2 \times 4}{2+4} = \frac{10}{3}\ \Omega$$

Hence
$$I_2'' = \frac{10 \text{ volts}}{\frac{10}{3} \text{ ohms}} = 3 \text{ amp.}$$

$$I_1'' = I_2'' \cdot \frac{2}{2+4} = 3 \times \frac{1}{3} = 1 \text{ amp.}$$

$$I_3'' = I_1'' - I_2'' = (3 - 1) = 2 \text{ amp.}$$

When both source voltages E_1 and E_2 are considered, then by Superposition theorem,

$$I_1 = I_1' - I_1'' = (1 - 1) = 0 \text{ amp.}$$

$$I_2 = I_2'' - I_2' = (3 - 0.5) = 2.5 \text{ amp.}$$

$$I_3 = I_3' + I_3'' = (0.5 + 2) = 2.5 \text{ amp.}$$

Potential of point A with respect to that of point B is

$$= I_3 \times 2 = 5 \text{ volts.}$$

Example 9.2. *In the given network, making use of superposition theorem, determine the currents in the resistors R_1, R_2 and R_3 and also the currents in the voltage source E.*

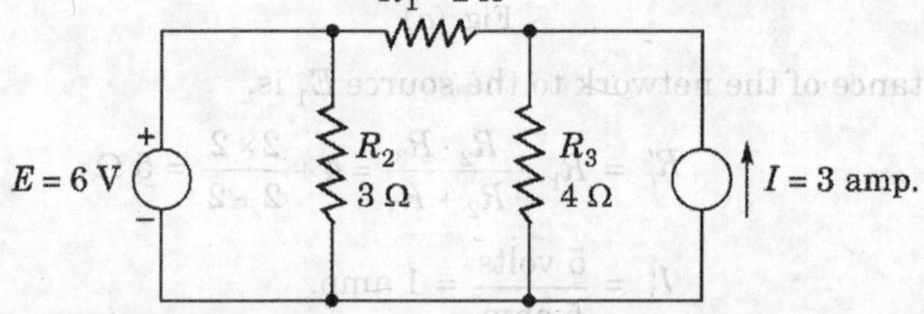

Solution. Considering the voltage source E alone and open circuiting the current source I, the network reduces to that shown in Fig. (*a*).

Then
$$I_2' = \frac{6 \text{ volts}}{3 \text{ ohms}} = 2 \text{ amp.}$$

$$I_1' = I_3' = \frac{6 \text{ volts}}{6 \text{ ohms}} = 1 \text{ amp.}$$

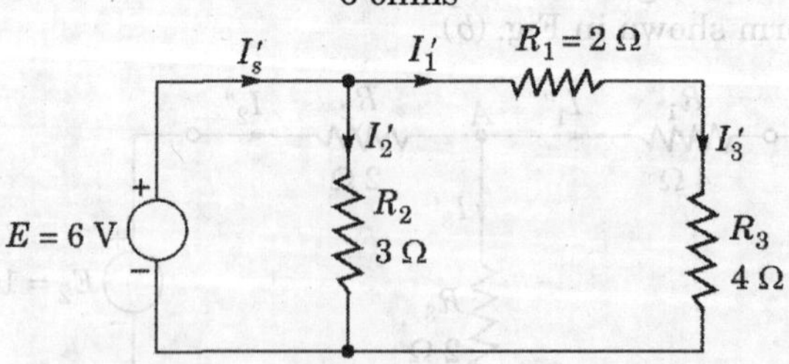

Fig. (*a*)

The current drawn from voltage source is

$$I_3' = I_1' + I_2' = (1 + 2) = 3 \text{ amp.}$$

Next considering the current source I alone and short circuiting the voltage source E, the network reduces to that shown in Fig. (*b*).

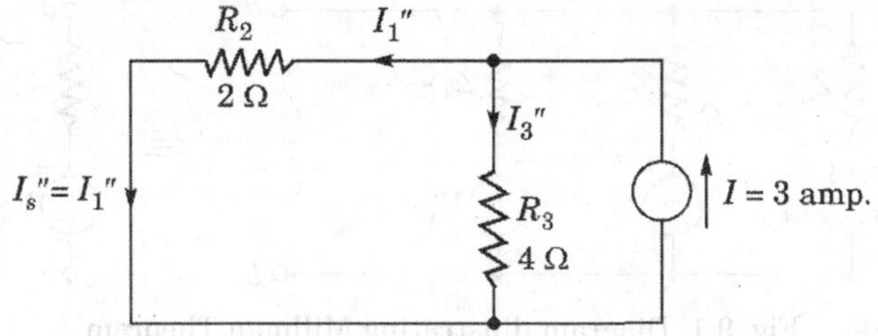

Fig. (b)

Then current $$I_1'' = I \cdot \frac{4}{4+2} = \frac{3 \times 4}{6} = 2 \text{ amp.}$$

$$I_3'' = I \times \frac{2}{4+2} = \frac{3 \times 2}{6} = 1 \text{ amp.}$$

Current through R_2 is zero since a short circuit has been placed across it.

Current through voltage source

$$= I_1'' = 2 \text{ amp.}$$

When both the sources are considered, then by superposition theorem,

$$I_1 = I_1' - I_1'' = (1 - 2) = -1 \text{ amp.}$$

Thus 1 amp. current flows through R_1 from right to left,

$$I_2 = I_2' + 0 = 2 \text{ amp.}$$

$$I_3 = I_3' + I_3'' = 1 + 1 = 2 \text{ amp.}$$

Current through voltage source is,

$$I_s = I_s' - I_s'' = 3 - 2 = 1 \text{ amp.}$$

Hence current distribution in the network is as shown in Fig. (c).

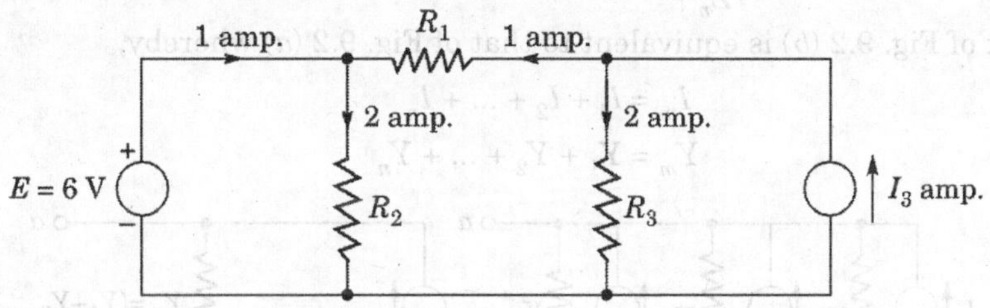

Fig. (c)

9.3. Millman Theorem

Millman theorem states that if n voltage sources $V_1, V_2, ..., V_n$ having internal impedances (or series impedances) $Z_1, Z_2, ..., Z_n$ respectively are connected in parallel as shown in Fig. 9.1, then these sources may be replaced by a single voltage source V_m having internal series impedance Z_m, where V_m and Z_m are given by the following equations :

$$V_m = \frac{V_1Y_1 + V_2Y_2 + V_3Y_3 + ...}{Y_1 + Y_2 + Y_3 + ...} \quad ...(9.9)$$

and $$Z_m = \frac{1}{Y_1 + Y_2 + Y_3} \quad ...(9.10)$$

where $Y_1, Y_2, Y_3, ..., Y_n$ are the admittances corresponding to $Z_1, Z_2, Z_3, ..., Z_n$.

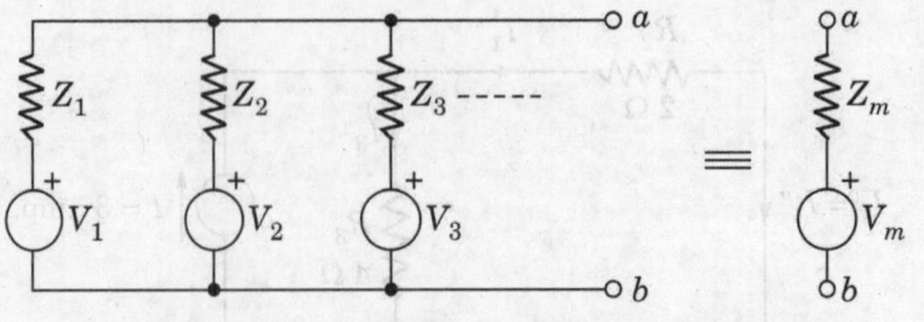

Fig. 9.1. Diagram illustrating Millman Theorem.

Proof of Millman Theorem. A voltage source V_1 with series impedance Z_1 may be replaced by a current source V_1Y_1 with shunt admittance $Y_1\left(=\dfrac{1}{Z_1}\right)$. Accordingly the network of Fig. 9.1 may be replaced by its equivalent network shown in Fig. 9.2 (*a*), where

$$\left.\begin{aligned} I_1 &= V_1 \cdot Y_1 \\ I_2 &= V_2 \cdot Y_2 \\ \ldots & \quad \ldots \\ I_n &= V_n \cdot Y_n \end{aligned}\right\} \qquad \ldots(9.11)$$

and

$$\left.\begin{aligned} Y_1 &= \frac{1}{Z_1} \\ Y_2 &= \frac{1}{Z_2} \\ Y_3 &= \frac{1}{Z_3} \\ \ldots & \quad \ldots \\ Y_n &= \frac{1}{Z_n} \end{aligned}\right\} \qquad \ldots(9.12)$$

Network of Fig. 9.2 (*b*) is equivalent to that of Fig. 9.2 (*a*) whereby,

$$I_m = I_1 + I_2 + \ldots + I_n \qquad \ldots(9.13)$$

and

$$Y_m = Y_1 + Y_2 + \ldots + Y_n \qquad \ldots(9.14)$$

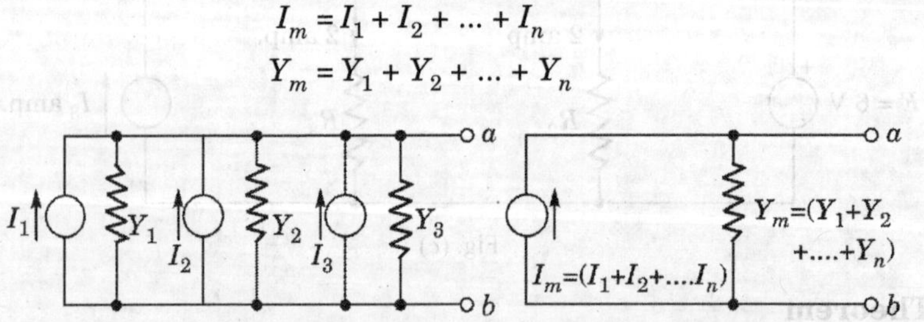

(*a*) Network equivalent to that of Fig. 9.1.

(*b*) Network equivalent to that of Fig. 9.2(*a*).

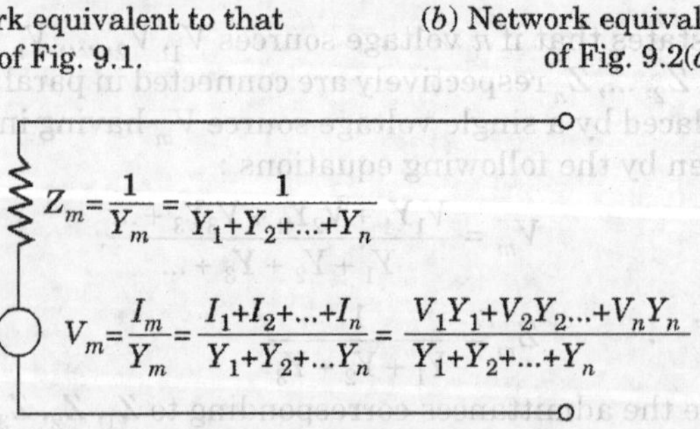

(*c*) Final equivalent circuit.

Fig. 9.2. Circuits equivalent to that of Fig. 9.1.

Reconverting the current source of Fig. 9.2 (*b*) into an equivalent voltage source, we arrive at the equivalent circuit of Fig. 9.2 (*c*) where,

$$Z_m = \frac{1}{Y_m} = \frac{1}{Y_1 + Y_2 + ... + Y_n} \quad ...(9.15)$$

and

$$V_m = \frac{I_m}{Y_m} = \frac{I_1 + I_2 + ... + I_n}{Y_1 + Y_2 + ... + Y_n} = \frac{V_1Y_1 + V_2Y_2 + ... + V_nY_n}{Y_1 + Y_2 + ... + Y_n} \quad ...(9.16)$$

Equations (9.15) and (9.16) give the same values of V_m and Z_m as Eqs. (9.9) and (9.10). This establishes the truth of Millman Theorem.

The above discussion describes Millman Theorem expressing impedances and energy sources in time domain. Same is true of Millman Theorem in frequency domain. Every impedance and energy source should then be expressed in frequency domain.

Example 9.3. *Using Millman Theorem, find the current in resistor R_3 in the given network*

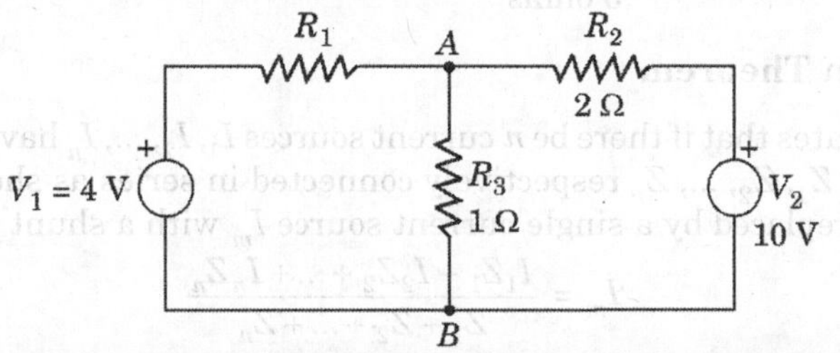

Solution. There are three shunt paths between nodes *A* and *B*. Applying Millman theorem to these shunt paths, the equivalent circuit between nodes *A* and *B* may be put as voltage source V_m in series with resistance R_m where

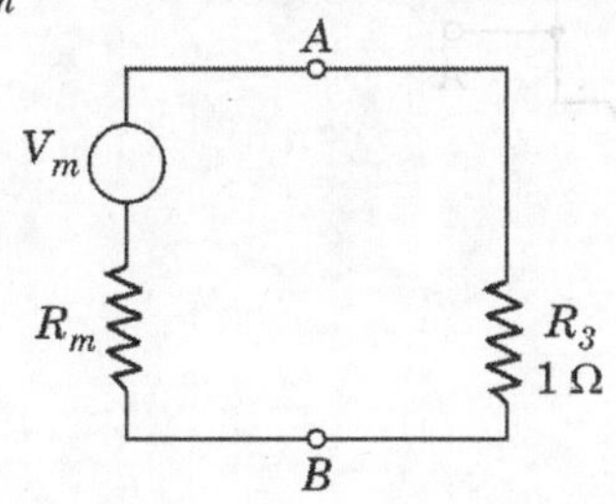

$$V_m = \frac{V_1 \cdot Y_1 + V_2 \cdot Y_2 + V_3 \cdot Y_3}{Y_1 + Y_2 + Y_3} = \frac{(4 \times 0.5) + (0 \times 1) + (10 \times 0.5)}{0.5 + 1 + 0.5}$$

$$= 3.5 \text{ volts}$$

$$R_m = \frac{1}{Y_1 + Y_2 + Y_3} = \frac{1}{0.5 + 1 + 0.5} = 0.5 \text{ ohm.}$$

Hence the voltage across resistor R_3 = 3.5 volts and the current through resistor $R_3 = \frac{3.5 \text{ volts}}{1 \text{ ohm}} = 3.5$ amp.

Alternatively

The two voltage sources V_1 and V_2 with series resistances R_1 and R_2 may be combined into one. The equivalent network is then as shown below :

Then by Millman theorem,

$$V_m = \frac{V_1Y_1 + V_2Y_2}{Y_1 + Y_2} = \frac{(4 \times 0.5) + (10 \times 0.5)}{0.5 + 0.5} = 7 \text{ volts}$$

$$R_m = \frac{1}{Y_1 + Y_2} = \frac{1}{0.5 + 0.5} = 1\ \Omega$$

Hence current through

$$R_3 = \frac{V_m}{R_m + R_3} = \frac{7 \text{ volts}}{(1 + 1) \text{ ohms}} = 3.5 \text{ amp.}$$

Example 9.4. *Using Millman Theorem find the current and voltage in resistor R_4 in the given network.*

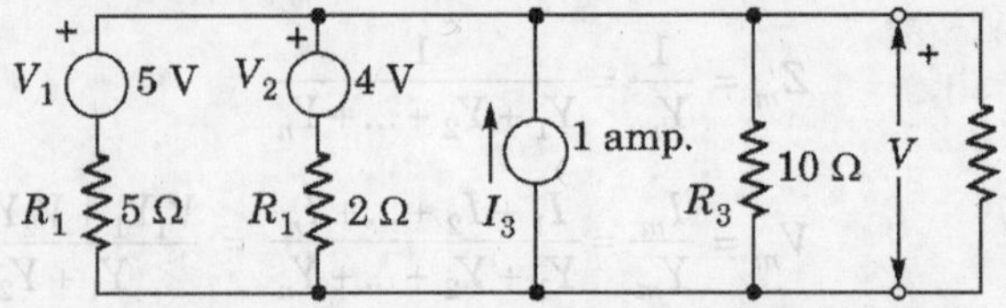

Solution. Current source I_3 with shunt resistor R_3 may be converted into equivalent voltage source V_3 with series resistor R_3 where $V_3 = I_3 \cdot R_3 = 1 \times 10 = 10$ volts.

Let V be the voltage across R_4. Then Millman Theorem yields,

$$V = \frac{V_1Y_1 + V_2Y_2 + V_3Y_3}{Y_1 + Y_2 + Y_3 + Y_4} = \frac{(5\times 0.2) + (4\times 0.5) + (10\times 0.1)}{0.2 + 0.5 + 0.1 + 0.2} = 4 \text{ volts}$$

$$\text{Hence current through } R_4 = \frac{4 \text{ volts}}{5 \text{ ohms}} = 0.8 \text{ Amp.}$$

9.4. Dual of Millman Theorem

This theorem states that if there be n current sources $I_1, I_2, \ldots, I_n$ having internal impedances (or shunt impedances) $Z_1, Z_2, \ldots, Z_n$ respectively connected in series as shown in Fig. 9.3 (a), then these sources may be replaced by a single current source I_m with a shunt impedance Z_m given by,

$$I_m = \frac{I_1Z_1 + I_2Z_2 + \ldots + I_nZ_n}{Z_1 + Z_2 + \ldots + Z_n} \qquad \ldots(9.17)$$

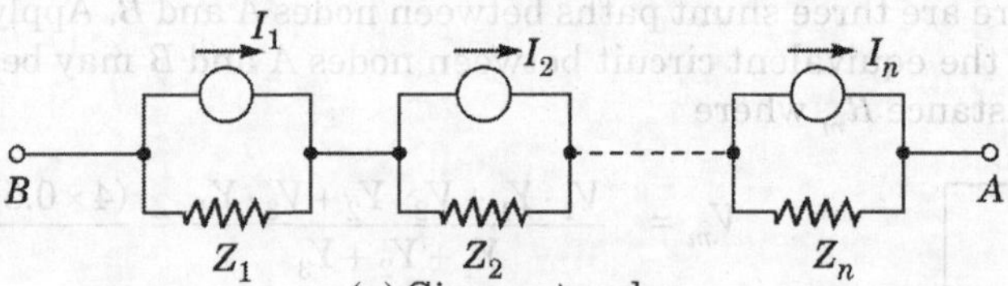

(a) Given network

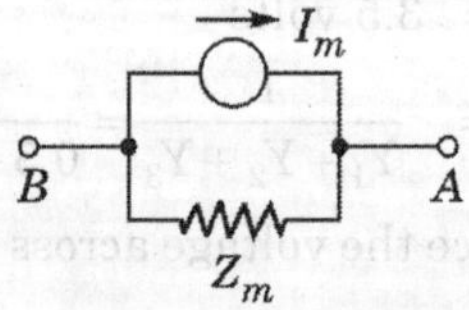

(b) Equivalent network

Fig. 9.3. Equivalent network as obtained by use of dual of Millman theorem.

$$Z_m = Z_1 + Z_2 + \ldots + Z_n \qquad \ldots(9.18)$$

Proof. This theorem may be proved by replacing each current source by its equivalent voltage source. Thus current source I_1 with shunt impedance Z_1 may be replaced by voltage source V_1 with series impedance Z_1 where $V_1 = I_1 \cdot Z_1$. Thus network of Fig. 9.4 (a) is equivalent to the network of Fig. 9.3 (a) where,

$$\left.\begin{aligned} V_1 &= I_1 \cdot Z_1 \\ V_2 &= I_2 \cdot Z_2 \\ \ldots & \;\ldots\; \ldots \\ V_n &= I_n \cdot Z_n \end{aligned}\right\} \qquad \ldots(9.19)$$

These voltage sources in series may be replaced by a single voltage source V_m in series with impedance Z_m as shown in Fig. 9.4 (*b*), where

$$V_m = V_1 + V_2 + ... + V_n \quad ...(9.20)$$

and

$$Z_m = Z_1 + Z_2 + ... + Z_n \quad ...(9.21)$$

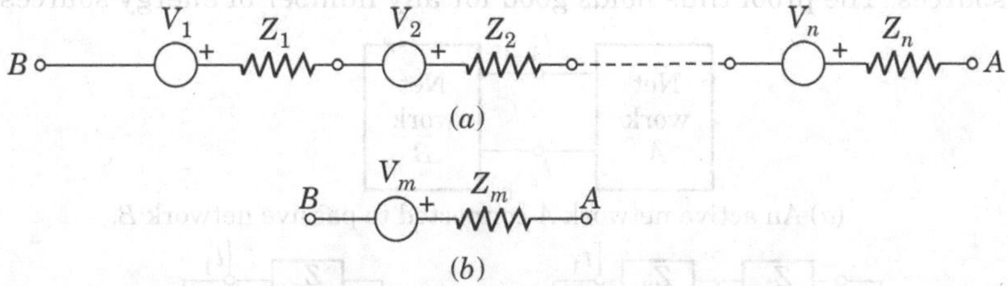

Fig. 9.4. Networks equivalent to that of Fig. 9.3 (*a*).

Finally this voltage source V_m of Fig. 9.4 (*b*) may be replaced by a current source I_m with shunt impedance Z_m resulting in equivalent circuit of Fig. 9.3 (*b*).

Here

$$I_m = \frac{V_m}{Z_m} \quad ...(9.22)$$

$$= \frac{V_1 + V_2 + ... + V_n}{Z_m} = \frac{I_1Z_1 + I_2Z_2 + ... + I_nZ_n}{Z_1 + Z_2 + ... + Z_n} \quad ...(9.23)$$

This establishes the truth of the Dual of Millman theorem.

9.5. Thevenin's Theorem

Several networks involve a number of voltage or current sources. One is often interested in finding the correct values of voltage and current in a restricted portion of the network rather than in all the branches of the network. Then one replaces the actual sources of energy by a single "equivalent voltage source" or by a single "equivalent current source" acting at a terminal pair. The term "equivalent" implies that we will obtain the same voltages and currents throughout the network as those obtained in the network with the actual sources present. Thevenin's and Norton's theorems provide methods of source transformation whereby distributed sources of both voltage type and current type may be replaced by an equivalent source acting at the desired point. Analysis of the complete network is thus obtained.

Thevenin's theorem states the current I_l which flows from a given linear active network *A* (with initial currents and voltages) to a passive network *B* (not inductively coupled to network *A*), usually referred to as the load, is the same as one which flows to the same network *B* when connected to a network (called Thevenin's equivalent of network *A*) constituted by a voltage source V_{oc} with internal impedance Z_g where,

V_{oc} is the open circuited voltage of network *A* at load terminals and Z_g is the impedance of network *A* seen looking back from the load terminals with all energy sources replaced by their internal impedances.

Proof of Thevenin's Theorem

Fig. 9.5 (*a*) shows two networks *A* and *B* of which network *A* is composed of linear passive elements and contains either independent or controlled voltages and/or current sources. Further there may be present initial currents in inductors and initial voltages across capacitors. There exists no magnetic coupling between networks *A* and *B*. Network *B* contains only passive elements which are initially relaxed. Network *B* is generally referred to as the load.

Now any network may be reduced to an equivalent network in *T* or π configuration with a suitable voltage source. Thus network *A* may be represented by its equivalent network shown in Fig. 9.5 (*b*). If there exist more than one energy source, then in accordance with the principle of superposition, each such energy source may be considered separately. Each such source along with passive elements of network A may then be reduced to the simple network of Fig. 9.5 (b). All voltage sources V_1, V_2 ..., placed in series in network of Fig. 9.5 (b) may then be combined together and replaced by a single voltage source V. Impedance elements Z_1, Z_2 and Z_3 remain the same for all the energy sources. The proof thus holds good for any number of energy sources.

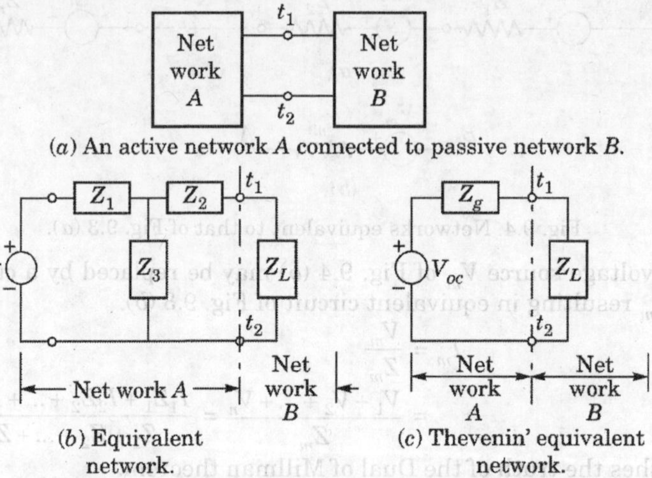

(a) An active network A connected to passive network B.

(b) Equivalent network.

(c) Thevenin' equivalent network.

Fig. 9.5. An active network and its Thevenin's equivalent.

Similarly the passive network B may be replaced by a single impedance Z_l as shown in Fig. 9.5 (b).

Let the resulting current to network B be I_l.

Solution of network of Fig. 9.5 (b) yields,

$$I_l = \frac{V \cdot Z_3}{Z_1Z_2 + Z_2Z_3 + Z_1Z_3 + Z_l(Z_1 + Z_3)} \quad ...(9.24)$$

Eq. (9.24) may be rearranged in the following form,

$$I_l = \frac{VZ_3/(Z_1 + Z_3)}{\dfrac{Z_1Z_2 + Z_2Z_3 + Z_1Z_3}{Z_1 + Z_3} + Z_l} \quad ...(9.25)$$

This current I_l is the same as would flow through Z_l if Z_l were connected to a voltage source of voltage V_{eq} and internal impedance Z_{eq} given respectively by,

$$V_{eq} = \frac{VZ_3}{Z_1 + Z_3} \quad ...(9.26)$$

and
$$Z_{eq} = \frac{Z_1Z_2 + Z_2Z_3 + Z_1Z_3}{Z_1 + Z_3} \quad ...(9.27$$

If the network A were open circuited *i.e.* Z_l is removed, the open circuit voltage V_{oc} at the terminals $t_1 - t_2$ of the network A is given by,

$$V_{oc} = V\frac{Z_3}{Z_1 + Z_3} \quad ...(9.28)$$

and if Z_l is removed and the voltage source V is replaced by a short circuit, the impedance offered by network A looking back from terminals $t_1 - t_2$ is given by,

$$Z_g = Z_2 + \frac{Z_1Z_3}{Z_1 + Z_3} = \frac{Z_1Z_2 + Z_2Z_3 + Z_1Z_3}{Z_1 + Z_3} \quad ...(9.29)$$

Comparison of Eqs. (9.26) and (9.27) with Eqs. (9.28) and (9.29) respectively shows that $V_{oc} = V_{eq}$ and $Z_g = Z_{eq}$. Thus the current I_l which flows through the load Z_l connected to network A is the same as one which flows through Z_l when connected to a voltage source whose voltage is the open circuit voltage V_{oc} of the network A and whose internal impedance is the impedance Z_g of the network A looking back from the load terminals $t_1 - t_2$ with the voltage and current sources replaced by their internal impedances. This prove the validity of Thevenin's theorem.

Example 9.5. *Find the current and voltage in resistor R_2 in the network of Example 9.3 using Thevenin's theorem.*

Solution. In order to find the open circuit voltage across terminals A and B we open circuit the network at terminals A and B *i.e.* we remove R_3. The resulting circuit is then as shown in Fig. (*a*).

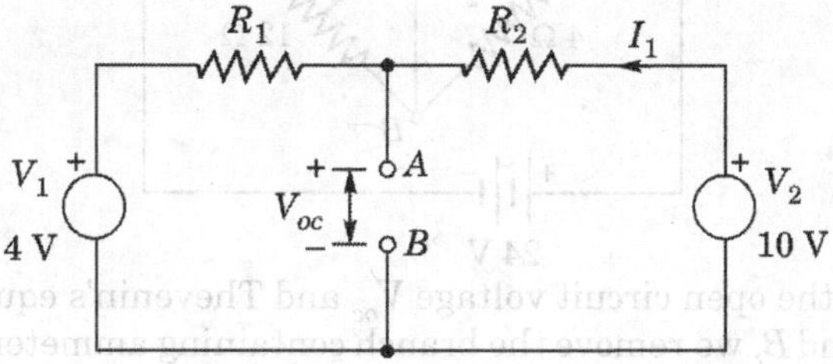

Fig. (*a*)

Let a current I_1 flow in the series circuit constituted by V_1, V_2, R_1 and R_2. Application of Kirchhoff's voltage law to the series circuit yields,

$$10 - 4 - I_1(R_1 + R_2) = 0$$

or
$$I_1(2 + 2) = 6$$

Hence
$$I_1 = 1.5 \text{ amp.}$$

Hence open circuit voltage V_{oc} between terminals A and B is given by,

$$V_{oc} = V_2 - I_2R_2 = 10 - (1.5 \times 2) = 7 \text{ volts.}$$

The internal impedance Z_g of Thevenin's equivalent voltage source may be obtained by short-circuiting the ideal voltage source V_1 and V_2 and finding the impedance offered by the network across the terminals A and B. This network is shown in Fig. (*b*).

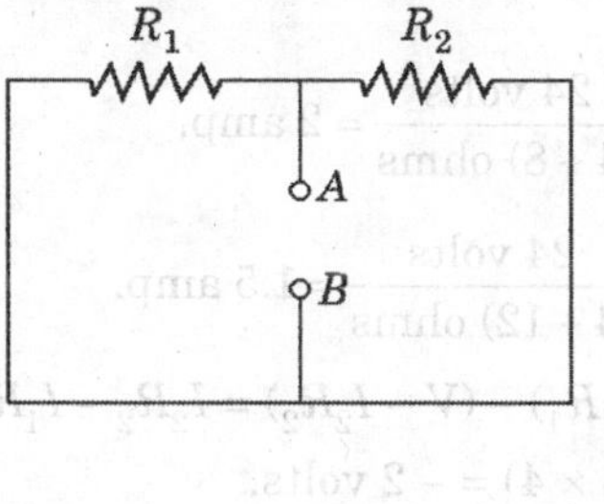

Fig. (*b*)

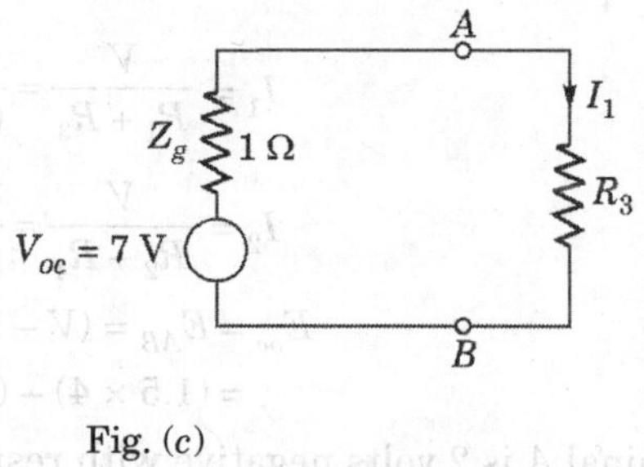

Fig. (*c*)

Then
$$Z_g = \frac{R_1R_2}{R_1 + R_2} = \frac{2 \times 2}{2 + 2} = 1\ \Omega.$$

Thevenin's equivalent voltage source is then as shown in Fig. (*c*).

Hence current $I_l = \dfrac{V_{oc}}{R_3 + Z_g} = \dfrac{7 \text{ volts}}{(1+1) \text{ ohms}} = 3.5 \text{ amp.}$

The voltage across $R_3 = I_l \times R_3 = (3.5 \times 1) = 3.5$ volts.

Example 9.6. *Using Millman theorem find the current in the ammeter A of resistance 3 Ω connected in the unbalanced Wheatstone bridge shown in the following figure.*

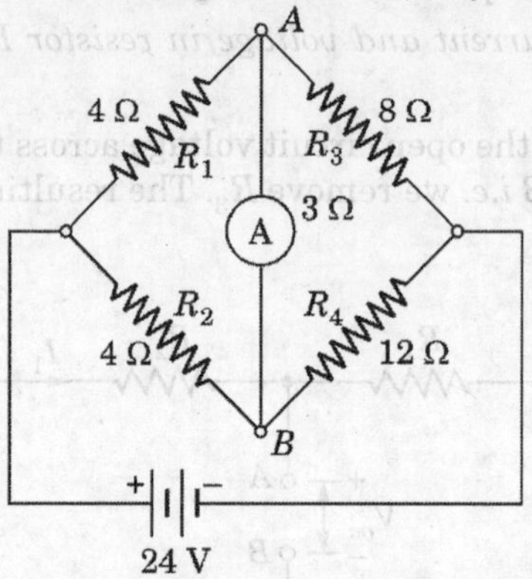

Solution. To find the open circuit voltage V_{oc} and Thevenin's equivalent source impedance Z_g between terminals *A* and *B*, we remove the branch containing ammeter *A*. The resulting network is shown in Fig. (*a*).

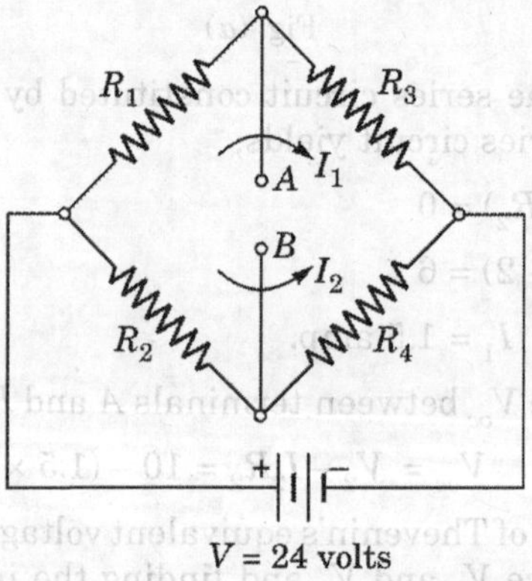

Fig. (*a*)

In Fig. (*a*) let current I_1 flow through resistors R_1 and R_3 and let current I_2 flow through resistors R_2 and R_4.

Then $$I_1 = \frac{V}{R_1 + R_3} = \frac{24 \text{ volts}}{(4+8) \text{ ohms}} = 2 \text{ amp.}$$

and $$I_2 = \frac{V}{R_2 + R_4} = \frac{24 \text{ volts}}{(4+12) \text{ ohms}} = 1.5 \text{ amp.}$$

Hence $$E_{oc} = E_{AB} = (V - I_1R_1) - (V - I_2R_2) = I_2R_2 - I_1R_1$$
$$= (1.5 \times 4) - (2 \times 4) = -2 \text{ volts.}$$

Thus terminal *A* is 2 volts negative with respect to terminal *B*.

In order to find the internal impedance Z_g of the equivalent Thevenin's voltage source, we replace all sources by their internal impedances. Then the network reduces to the form shown in Fig. (*b*).

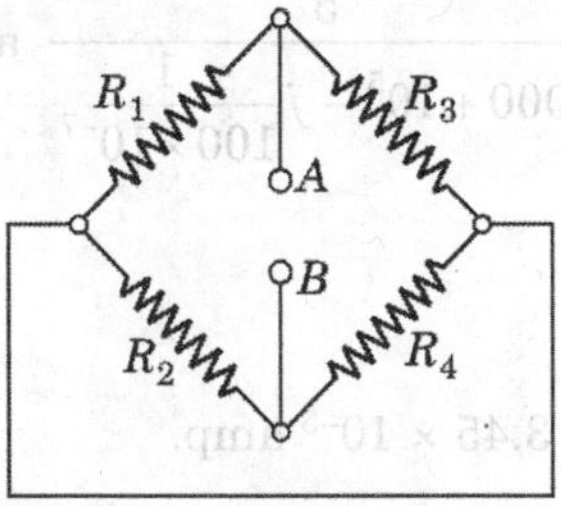

Fig. (b)

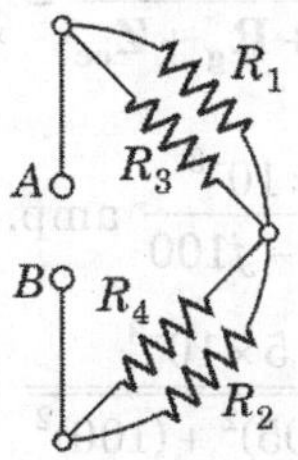

Fig. (c)

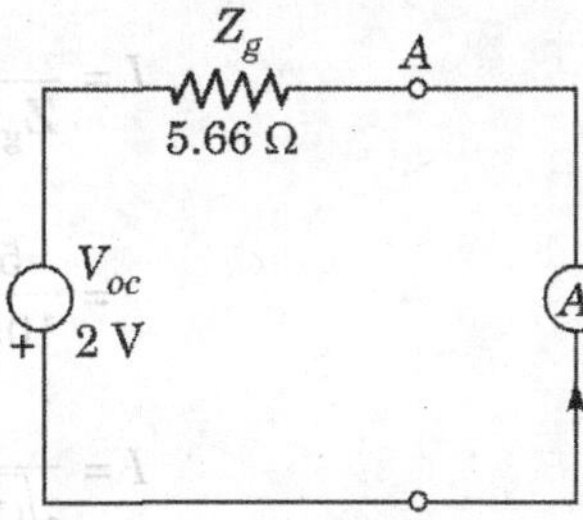

Fig. (d)

Fig. (d)

Network in Fig. (b) may be redrawn as in Fig. (c).

Then $$Z_g = \frac{R_1R_2}{R_1 + R_3} + \frac{R_2R_4}{R_2 + R_4} = \frac{4\times 8}{4+8} + \frac{4\times 12}{4+12} = 5.66\ \Omega$$

Hence Thevenin's equivalent circuit may be drawn as shown in Fig. (d). Hence current I that flows in the ammeter A from terminal B to A is given by,

$$I = \frac{V_{oc}}{Z_g + 3} = \frac{2 \text{ volts}}{(5.66+3) \text{ ohms}} = 0.2308 \text{ amp.}$$

Example 9.7. *Using Thevenin's theorem, find the magnitude and phase angle of current in the resistor R_g and the voltage V_{AB} across R_g in the network shown below :*

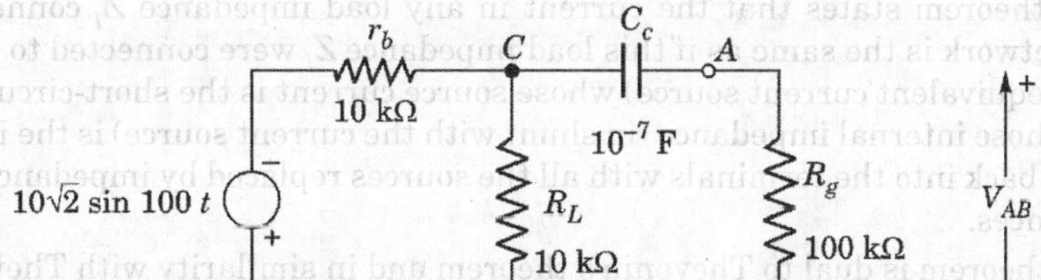

Solution. We apply Thevenin's theorem to the network excluding the branch containing resistor R_g and capacitor C_c *i.e.* to the network shown in Fig. (a).

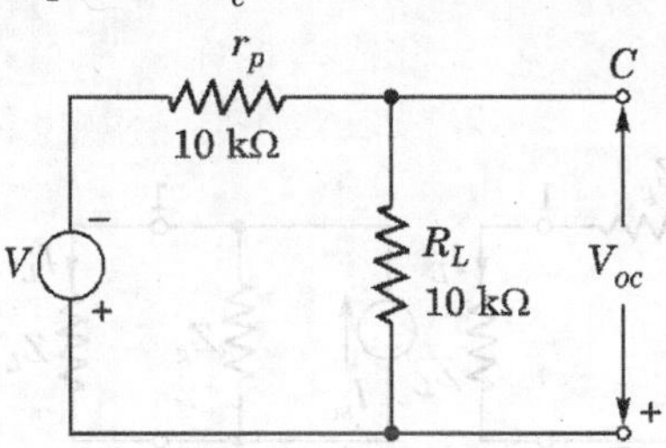

Fig. (a)

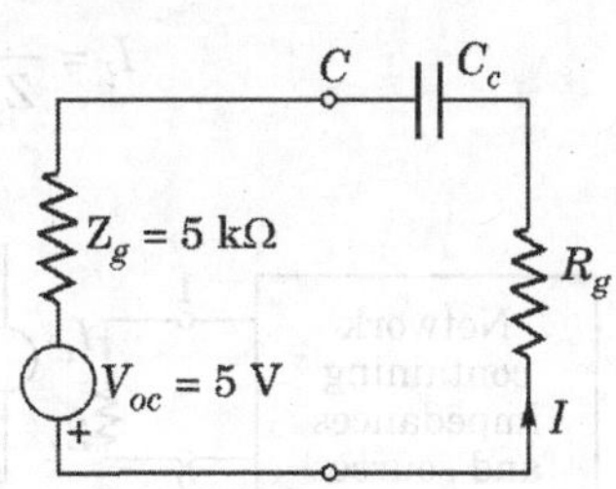

Fig. (b)

Then $$V_{oc} = \frac{V \cdot r_p}{R_l + r_p} = \frac{10 \times 10^4}{(10+10)\,10^3} = 5 \text{ volts}$$

$$Z_g = \frac{r_p \cdot R_l}{r_p + R_l} = \frac{10^4 \times 10^4}{10^4 + 10^4} = 5 \times 10^6\ \Omega$$

Fig. (b) then gives the Thevenin's equivalent voltage source connected to the load constituted by C_c and R_g. Current I is then given by,

$$I = \frac{\mathbf{V_{oc}}}{\mathbf{Z_g} + \mathbf{R_g} + \mathbf{Z_{cc}}} = \frac{5}{5000 + 10^5 - j\dfrac{1}{100 \times 10^{-7}}} \text{ amp.}$$

$$= \frac{5 \times 10^{-3}}{105 - j100} \text{ amp.}$$

Magnitude $$I = \frac{5 \times 10^{-3}}{\sqrt{(105)^2 + (100)^2}} = 3.45 \times 10^{-5} \text{ amp.}$$

Phase angle of current $I = \tan^{-1} \dfrac{100}{105} = 43.6°$

Voltage $\mathbf{V}_{AB}$ across R_g is given by,

$$\mathbf{V}_{AB} = -\mathbf{I.R}_g = \frac{-5 \times 10^{-3} \times 10^5}{105 - j100} = \frac{-500}{105 - j100}$$

Magnitude $$V_{AB} = \frac{500}{\sqrt{(105)^2 + (100)^2}} = 3.45 \text{ volts}$$

Phase angle of voltage $V_{AB} = 180° + \tan^{-1} \dfrac{100}{105} = 233.6°.$

9.6. Norton's Theorem

Norton's theorem states that the current in any load impedance Z_l connected to the two terminals of a network is the same as if this load impedance Z_l were connected to a current source (called Norton's equivalent current source) whose source current is the short-circuit current at the terminals and whose internal impedance (in shunt with the current source) is the impedance of the network looking back into the terminals with all the sources replaced by impedances equal to their internal impedances.

Norton's theorem is dual to Thevenin's theorem and in similarity with Thevenin's theorem, holds good for the current in the load impedance only and not for currents within the network. The truth of Norton's theorem may be established starting from Thevenin's equivalent voltage source. Thus Fig. 9.6 (*b*) gives the Thevenin's equivalent form for network of Fig. 9.6 (*a*).

Then $$I_l = \frac{V_{oc}}{Z_g + Z_l} \quad ...(9.30)$$

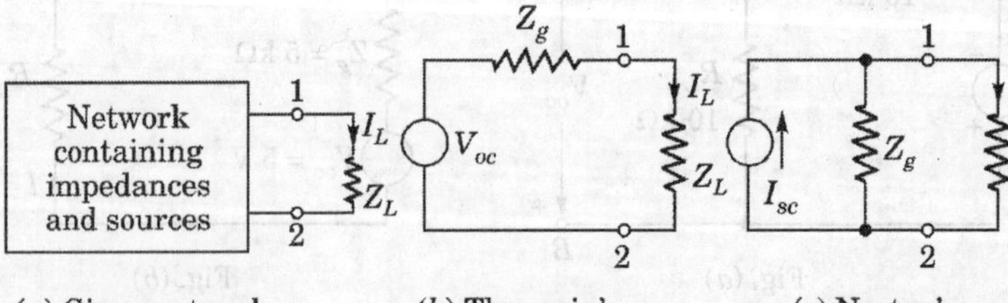

(*a*) Given network. (*b*) Thevenin's equivalent form. (*c*) Norton's equivalent form.

Fig. 9.6. Norton's equivalent network.

On short-circuiting terminals 1 and 2,

$$I_{sc} = \frac{V_{oc}}{Z_g} \quad ...(9.31)$$

In Fig. 9.6 (*c*), the current through Z_l is given by,

$$I_l = \frac{I_{sc} \cdot Z_g}{Z_g + Z_l} \qquad \text{...(9.32)}$$

Combining Eqs. (9.31) and (9.32), we get

$$I_l = \frac{V_{oc}}{Z_g + Z_l} \qquad \text{...(9.33)}$$

Hence $I_l' = I_l$. Hence the network of Fig. 9.6 (*c*) is equivalent to the network of Fig. 9.6 (*b*) and hence is equivalent to the given network of Fig. 9.6 (*a*). This establishes the truth of Norton's theorem.

Example 9.8. *Using Norton's theorem find the current in the load-resistor R_l in the network shown below.*

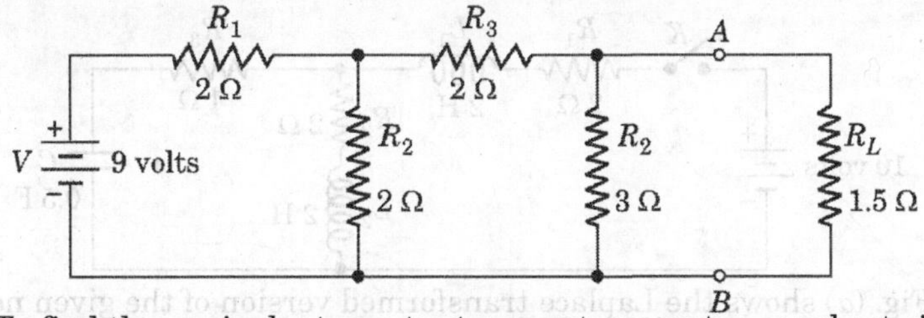

Solution. To find the equivalent constant current generator, we short-circuit terminals *A*-*B*. The circuit then reduces to the form shown in Fig. (*a*).

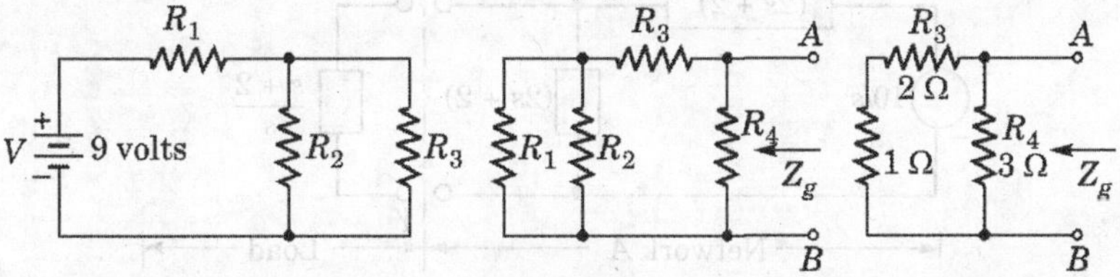

Fig. (*a*) Fig. (*b*) Fig. (*c*)

Total resistance offered to voltage source *V* is then,

$$R_l = R_1 \frac{R_2 \times R_3}{R_2 + R_3} = 2 + \frac{2 \times 2}{2 + 2} = 3\ \Omega$$

Hence current drawn from voltage source

$$V = \frac{9 \text{ volts}}{3 \text{ ohms}} = 3 \text{ amp.}$$

The current through the short circuit $= 3 \times \dfrac{R_2}{R_2 + R_3} = \dfrac{3 \times 2}{2 + 2} = 1.5$ amp.

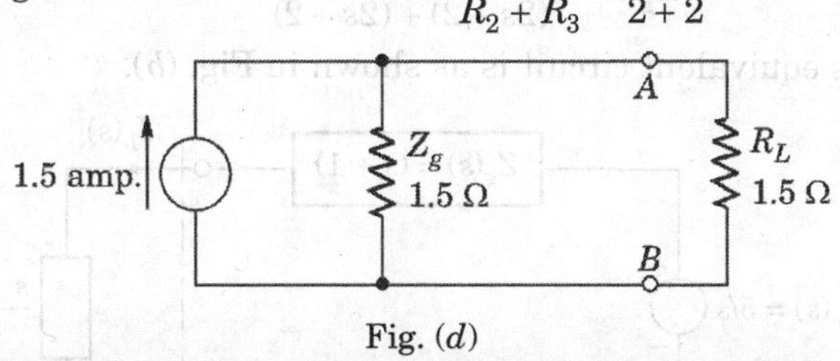

Fig. (*d*)

The impedance of this Norton's equivalent current generator Z_g is found by open circuiting terminals *A*-*B* and looking into the network with voltage source *V* short circuited as shown in Fig. (*b*). R_1 and R_2 in parallel yield a resistance of 1 Ω as shown in Fig. (*c*).

Hence $$Z_g = \frac{R_4(R_3+1)}{R_4+(R_3+1)} = \frac{3(2+1)}{3+2+1} = 1.5\ \Omega$$

Hence Norton's equivalent current source is constituted by a current source of 1.5 amp. with shunt resistance of 1.5 Ω as shown in Fig. (*d*).

Hence current through load resistor $R_1 = 1.5 \times \frac{1.5}{1.5+1.5} = 0.75$ amp.

9.7. Thevenin's Theorem and Norton's Theorem in Frequency Domain

In Frequency domain, Thevenin's theorem and Norton's theorem may be stated and proved in precisely the same way as done in articles 9.5 and 9.6 for time domain. Use of these theorems in frequency domain problems becomes clear from the following solved examples.

Example 9.9. *The given network is in relaxed state until time t = 0 when switch K is closed. Using Thevenin's theorem, find the current i(t) in the resistor R_3.*

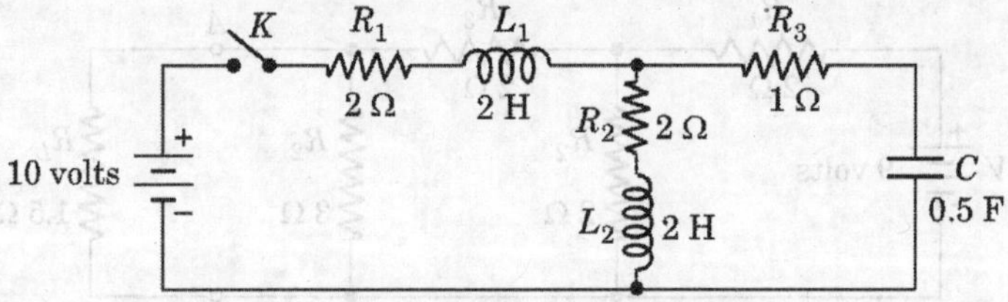

Solution. Fig. (*a*) shows the Laplace transformed version of the given network.

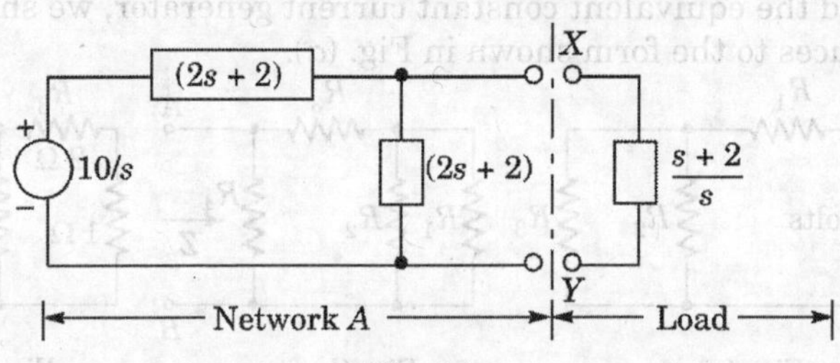

Fig. (*a*)

We apply Thevenin's theorem to the network *A* lying to the left on chain dotted line *XY*. Open circuit transform voltage is given by,

$$V_{oc}(s) = \frac{\left(\frac{10}{s}\right)(2s+2)}{(2s+2)+(2s+2)} = \frac{5}{s}$$

The impedance of network *A* with the voltage source short circuited is,

$$Z_g(s) = \frac{(2s+2)(2s+2)}{(2s+2)+(2s+2)} = s+1.$$

Hence Thevenin's equivalent circuit is as shown in Fig. (*b*).

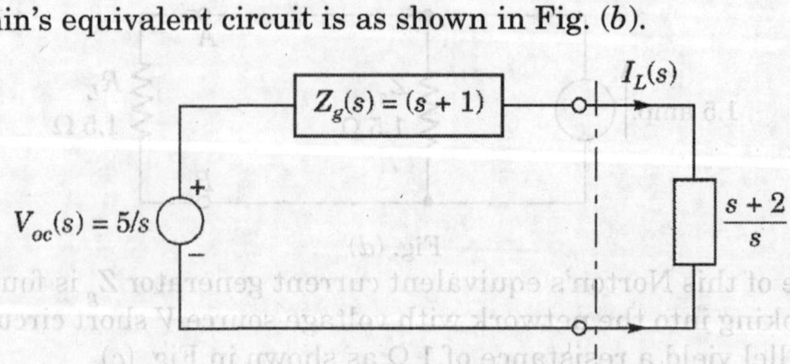

Fig. (*b*)

Hence transform current $I_l(s)$ through the load is,

$$I_l(s) = \frac{V_{oc}(s)}{Z_l(s) + Z_l(s)} = \frac{5/s}{(s+1) + \left(\frac{s+2}{s}\right)} = \frac{5}{(s+1)^2 + (1)^2}$$

On inverse Laplace transformation, we get

$$i_l(t) = 5e^{-t} \sin t.$$

Example 9.10. *In the given network capacitor C_1 is charged to 10 volts in the polarity shown. Capacitor C_2 is initially uncharged. At time t = 0, switch K is closed. Using Thevenin's theorem find the current in resistor R_2.*

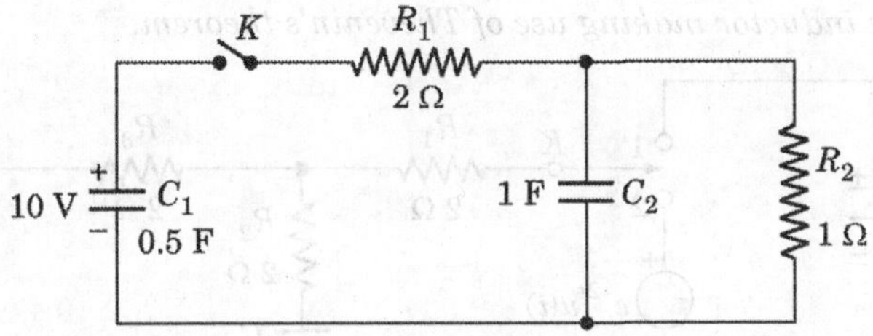

Solution. The transform network corresponding to the given network is shown in Fig. (*a*).

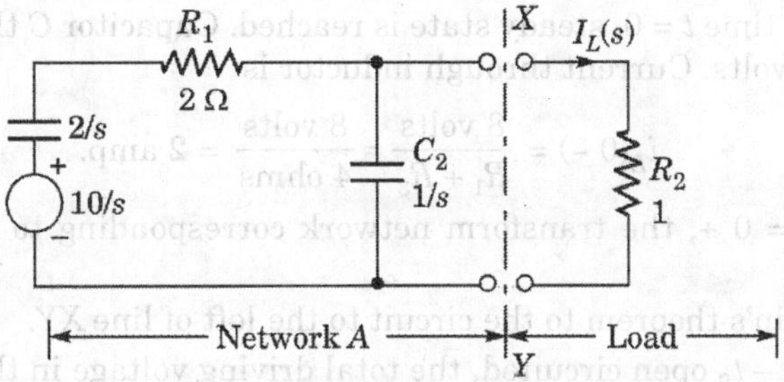

Fig. (*a*)

We apply Thevenin's theorem to the network to the left of the line *XY i.e.* to network *A*. Then the open circuit transform voltage is given by,

$$V_{oc}(s) = \frac{(10/s)(1/s)}{\frac{1}{s} + 2 + \frac{2}{s}} = \frac{10}{s(2s+3)}$$

The impedance of network *A* with the voltage source short circuited is,

$$Z_g(s) = \frac{\left(2 + \frac{2}{s}\right)\cdot\frac{1}{s}}{2 + \frac{2}{s} + \frac{1}{s}} = \frac{(2s+2)}{s(2s+3)}$$

Hence transform current through R_2 is,

$$I_l(s) = \frac{V_{oc}(s)}{Z_g(s) + R_2} = \frac{\frac{10}{s(2s+3)}}{\frac{2s+2}{s(2s+3)} + 1} = \frac{5}{(s+2)\left(s + \frac{1}{2}\right)}$$

On partial fraction expansion, we get

$$I_l(s) = \frac{10}{s}\left[\frac{1}{s+\frac{1}{2}} - \frac{1}{s+2}\right]$$

On inverse Laplace transformation,

$$i_l(t) = \frac{10}{2}\left[e^{-\frac{t}{2}} - e^{-2t}\right]$$

Example 9.11. *In the given network, switch K is in position 1 until steady state is reached. Switch K is moved to position 2 at time t = 0. With switch in position 2, determine the transform of the current through the inductor making use of Thevenin's theorem.*

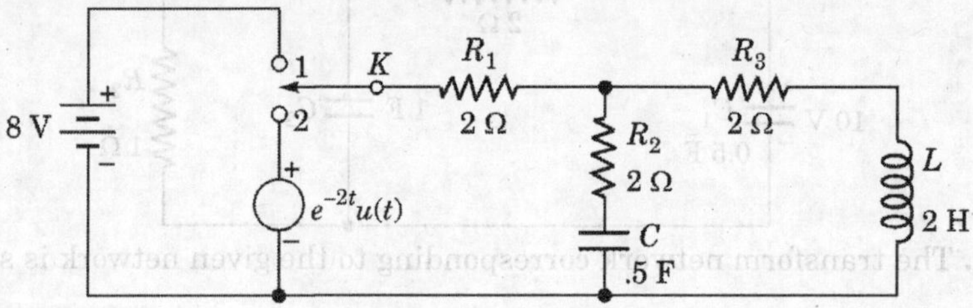

Solution. Before time $t = 0$, steady state is reached. Capacitor C then has zero current and it gets charged to full 8 volts. Current through inductor is

$$i_L(0-) = \frac{8 \text{ volts}}{R_1 + R_3} = \frac{8 \text{ volts}}{4 \text{ ohms}} = 2 \text{ amp.}$$

Hence at time $t = 0+$, the transform network corresponding to the given network is as shown in Fig. (*a*).

We apply Thevenin's theorem to the circuit to the left of line *XY*.

With terminals $t_1 - t_2$ open circuited, the total driving voltage in the closed loop is,

$$V(s) = \frac{1}{s+2} - \frac{8}{s} = \frac{-(7s+16)}{s(s+2)}$$

Impedance of the closed loop is,

$$Z(s) = 2 + 2 + \frac{2}{s} = \frac{2(2s+1)}{s}$$

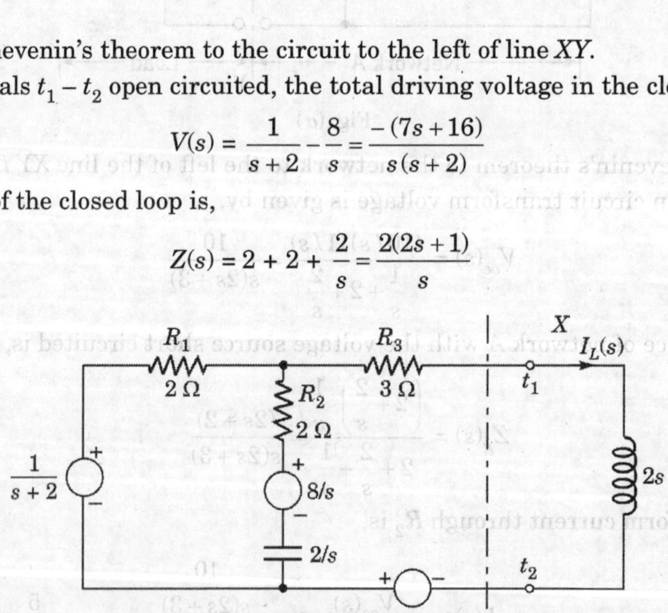

Fig. (*a*)

Hence current through the closed loop is,

$$I(s) = \frac{V(s)}{Z(s)} = \frac{-\dfrac{(7s+16)}{s(s+2)}}{\dfrac{2(2s+1)}{s}} = \frac{-(7s+1)}{2(s+2)(2s+1)}$$

Hence open circuit transform voltage between terminals $t_1 - t_2$ is,

$$V_{oc} = 4 + \frac{1}{s+2} - R_1\left[-\frac{(7s+16)}{2(s+2)(2s+1)}\right]$$

$$= \frac{4s+9}{s+2} + \frac{2(7s+16)}{2(s+2)(2s+1)} = \frac{8s^2+29s+25}{(s+2)(2s+1)}$$

The impedance of the network A with voltage source short circuited is,

$$Z_g(s) = 2 + \frac{(2)\left(2+\dfrac{2}{s}\right)}{2+2+\dfrac{2}{s}} = \frac{2(3s+2)}{(2s+1)}$$

transform load impedance $Z_l(s) = 2s$.

Hence transform current through inductor is,

$$I_l(s) = \frac{V_{oc}(s)}{Z_g(s)+Z_l(s)} = \frac{\dfrac{8s^2+29s+25}{(s+2)(2s+1)}}{\dfrac{2(3s+2)}{2s+1}+2s} = \frac{8s^2+29s+25}{4(s+2)(s^2+25+1)}$$

Example 9.12. *In the given network, there is no initial current through the inductors and no initial voltage across the capacitor. Switch K is closed at time t = 0. Using Norton's theorem find the current through the inductor L_2.*

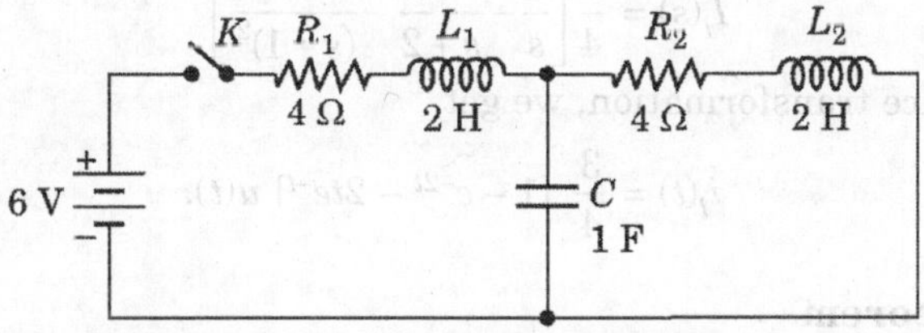

Solution. The transform network corresponding to the given network is shown in Fig. (*a*).

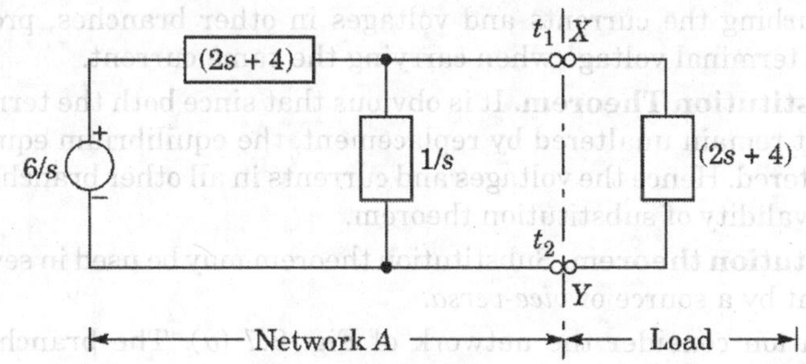

Fig. (*a*)

We apply Norton's theorem to the network A lying to the left of line X-Y.

Then looking from terminals $t_1 - t_2$ into network A with voltage source $\frac{6}{s}$ short circuited, we get the following value of Norton's equivalent circuit impedance,

$$Z_g(s) = \frac{(2s+4)\frac{1}{s}}{(2s+4)+\frac{1}{s}} = \frac{2s+4}{2s^2+4s+1}.$$

On short circuiting terminals $t_1 - t_2$, the resulting short circuit current is given by,

$$I_g(s) = \frac{6}{s} \cdot \frac{1}{2s+4} = \frac{3}{s(s+2)}$$

Hence Norton's equivalent circuit is as shown in Fig. (*b*).

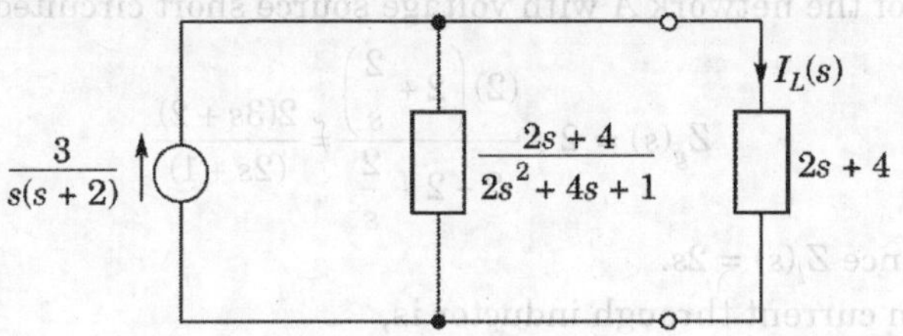

Fig. (*b*)

Hence current through inductor L_2 is given by,

$$I_l(s) = \frac{3}{s(s+2)} \cdot \frac{2s+4}{2s^2+4s+1} \cdot \frac{1}{\frac{2s+4}{2s^2+4s+1}+(2s+4)} = \frac{3}{2s(s+2)\,(s+1)^2}$$

This equation is expanded by the partial fractions to give,

$$I_l(s) = \frac{3}{4}\left[\frac{1}{s} - \frac{1}{s+2} - \frac{1}{(s+1)^2}\right]$$

On inverse Laplace transformation, we get

$$i_l(t) = \frac{3}{4}\,[1 - e^{-2t} - 2te^{-t}]\,u(t).$$

9.8. Substitution Theorem

Substitution theorem states that any branch in a network may be substituted by a new branch without disturbing the currents and voltages in other branches, provided that the new branch has the same terminal voltage when carrying the same current.

Proof of Substitution Theorem. It is obvious that since both the terminal voltage as well as the branch current remain unaltered by replacement, the equilibrium equations for the entire network remain unaltered. Hence the voltages and currents in all other branches remain unaltered. This establishes the validity of substitution theorem.

Use of Substitution theorem. Substitution theorem may be used in several cases to replace an impedance element by a source or *vice-versa*.

As an illustration consider the network of Fig. 9.7 (*a*). The branch m in this network constituted by 4 Ω impedance carries a current of 0.5 amp. Then in accordance with the substitution theorem any one of the branches shown in Fig. 9.7 (*b*) may replace the branch m in the network of Fig. 9.7 (*a*). In general, if the voltage V_m across the branch m in network may be represented by equation,

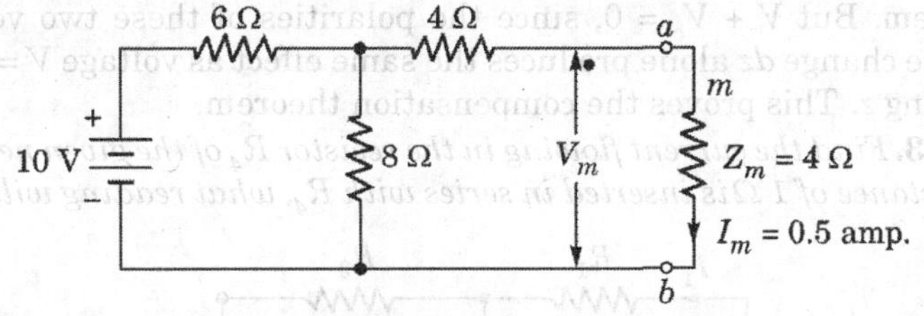

(a) Given network

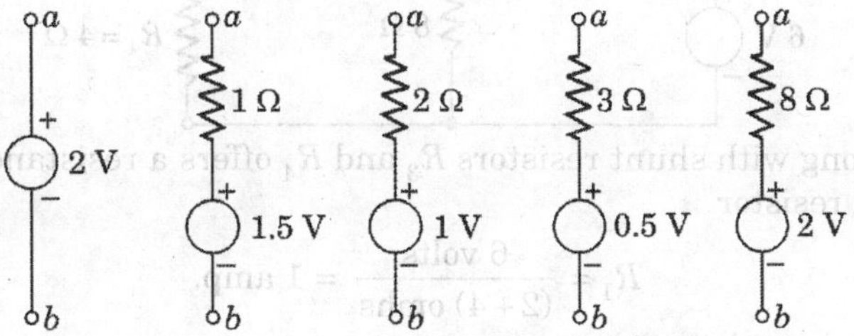

(b) Branches equivalent to branch m of Fig. (a).

Fig. 9.7. Illustration of substitution theorem.

$$V_m = Z_m \cdot I_m + V \qquad ...(9.34)$$

then this branch m may be substituted by another such that voltage across it is given by,

$$V_m = Z'_m \cdot I_m + V' \qquad ...(9.35)$$

i.e. when Z'_m and V' are so chosen that V_m and I_m are the same as in the branch m of the original network.

9.9. Compensation (Alternation) Theorem

In a linear network if any impedance Z carrying a current I is changed to a value $(Z + dz)$, then the currents in all the branches of the network change and the current increment produced in any branch equals that produced by a voltage source of voltage $I.\ dz$ placed in series with the altered impedance.

Proof of Compensation Theorem. Consider the linear network of Fig. 9.8 (*a*), one branch of which is shown outside the box representing the remaining network. An additional impedance dz is introduced into this branch and let a compensating voltage $V_c = I.\ dz$ be inserted in the branch in the polarity shown simultaneously with the insertion of impedance dz. Then the current in this branch remains unaltered at the value I since the voltage drop $I.\ dz$ in the impedance dz is compensated by a voltage rise $V_c = I.\ dz$ in accordance with the substitution theorem.

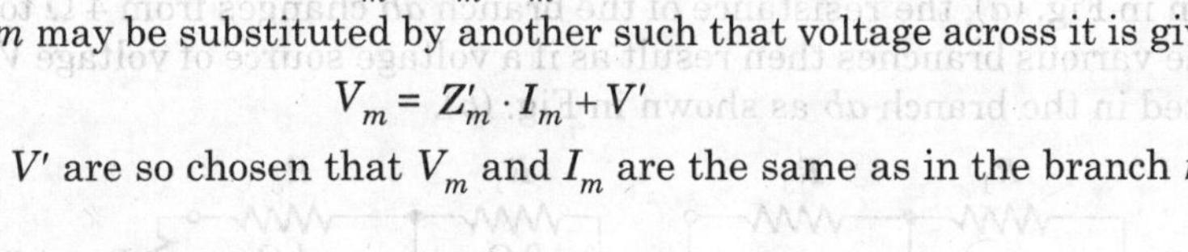

(a) (b)

Fig. 9.8. Circuits for proving the Compensation Theorem.

Next let another source of voltage $V = I.\ dz$ be introduced in the branch as shown in Fig. 9.8 (*b*). Then the current in every branch of the network will get modified in accordance with the superposition theorem. But $V + V_c = 0$, since the polarities of these two voltages are opposite. Hence the impedance change dz alone produces the same effect as voltage $V = I \cdot dz$ acting alone in this branch containing z. This proves the compensation theorem.

Example 9.13. *Find the current flowing in the resistor R_4 of the given network. If an ammeter having internal resistance of 1 Ω is inserted in series with R_4, what reading will this ammeter show?*

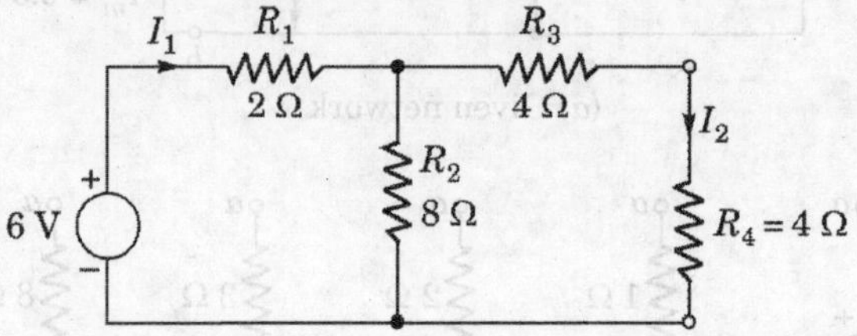

Solution. R_2 along with shunt resistors R_3 and R_4 offers a resistance of 4 Ω in series with R_1. Hence current I_1 in resistor

$$R_1 = \frac{6 \text{ volts}}{(2+4) \text{ omhs}} = 1 \text{ amp.}$$

Hence current I_2 in resistor.

$R_4 = I_1 \cdot \dfrac{8}{8+8}$ = 0.5 amp. An ideal (zero resistance) ammeter will then measure a current of 0.5 ampere in this branch. However, with the insertion of an ammeter of resistance 1 ohm in series with R_4 as shown in Fig. (*a*), the resistance of the branch *ab* changes from 4 Ω to 5 Ω. The changes in currents in the various branches then result as if a voltage source of voltage $V = I.\ dz = 0.5 \times 1 =$ 0.5 volt is inserted in the branch *ab* as shown in Fig. (*b*).

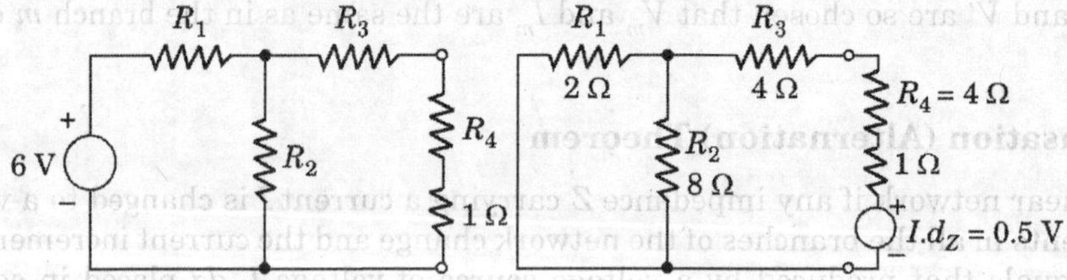

This voltage $I \cdot dz$ = 0.5 volt works into an impedance

$$= 5 + 4 + \frac{2 \times 8}{2 \times 8} = 10.6\ \Omega$$

Hence current drawn from this voltage source

$$= \frac{0.5 \text{ volt}}{10.6\ \Omega} = 0.0472 \text{ amp.}$$

This current is opposite to the current I_2 through resistor R_4 caused by 6 V source.
Hence the ammeter reading = (0.5 – 0.0472) = 0.4528 amp.

9.10. Compensation Theorem A

In any network, linear or non-linear, any impedance may be replaced by a voltage source of zero internal combustion and voltage equal to the instantaneous potential difference produced across the replaced impedance by the current flowing through it.

Fig. 9.9 (*a*) shows a network in which current I flows through the branch having impedance z. The currents and voltages in all the

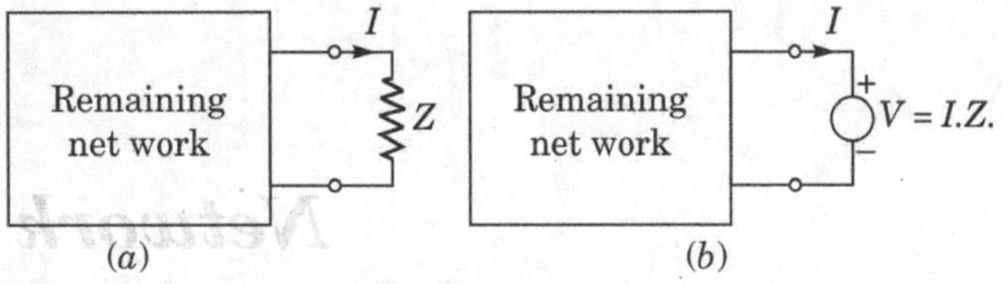

Fig. 9.9. Network illustrating the Compensation theorem A.

branches are completely determined by equations of Kirchoff's Laws. These equations do not get altered if the network is changed from that shown in Fig. 9.9 (a) to that in Fig. 9.9 (b). Hence this replacement cannot effect the current flowing in any branch of the network.

However, if any part of the network is changed, the value of V must also be changed. It may also be noted that the impedances in the network may be linear or non-linear and may be bilateral or unilateral.

EXERCISES

9.1. The given network is in relaxed state until time $t = 0$ when switch K is closed. Using Thevenin's theorem, find the current $i(t)$ in the resistor R_3.

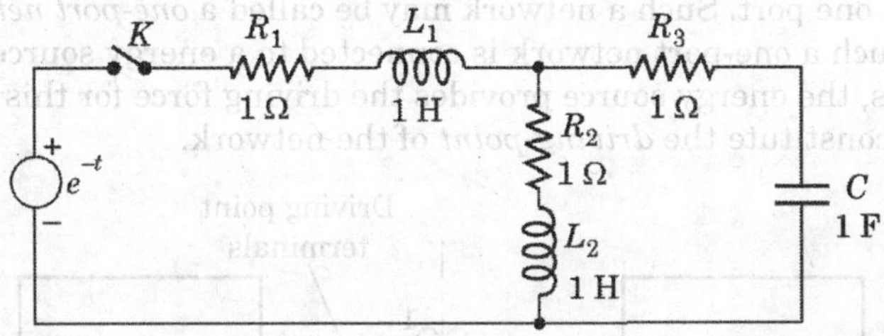

[**Ans.** $i(t) = (-2e^{-2t} + 2e^{-t} - te^{-t})\, u(t)$]

9.2. The capacitor C in the given network is initially charged to 2 volts in the polarity shown. Switch K is closed at time $t = 0$. Using Thevenin's theorem, find the current $i(t)$ in the resistor R_3.

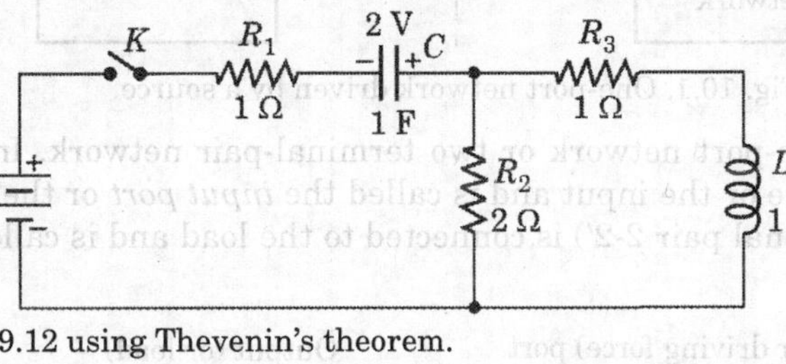

[**Ans.** $i(t) = 4te^{-t} \cdot u(t)$]

9.3. Solve example 9.12 using Thevenin's theorem.

9.4. In the given circuits, capacitors C_1 is charged to 8 volts in the polarity shown. Capacitors C_2 is initially uncharged. At time $t = 0$, switch K is closed. Using Thevenin's theorem, find the transform current in resistor R_2.

$$\left[\textbf{Ans. } i_l(s) = \frac{16}{2s^3 + 5s^2 + 5s + 2}\right]$$

10

Network Functions

10.1. Introduction

The concept of transform impedance and transform admittance has already been introduced in chapter eight. The same concept is further elaborated here. In addition, the concept of *transfer functions* relating currents and voltages in different sections of a network, is introduced. These functions are mathematically similar to the transform impedance or admittance functions and are included in the broader category of functions called the *Network functions.*

Terminal Pairs or Parts. Any network may be represented schematically by a rectangle or box as shown in Fig. 10.1. A network may be used for a variety of purposes. Thus consider its use as a load connected to some other network. In order to connect it to the active network, there must be available two terminals of this passive network. Fig. 10.1 shows a network with one pair of terminals 1-1′ or with one port. Such a network may be called a *one-port network* or *one terminal-pair network.* When such a one-port network is connected to a energy source or an active network at its pair of terminals, the energy source provides the driving force for this one-port network and the pair of terminals constitute the *driving-point* of the network.

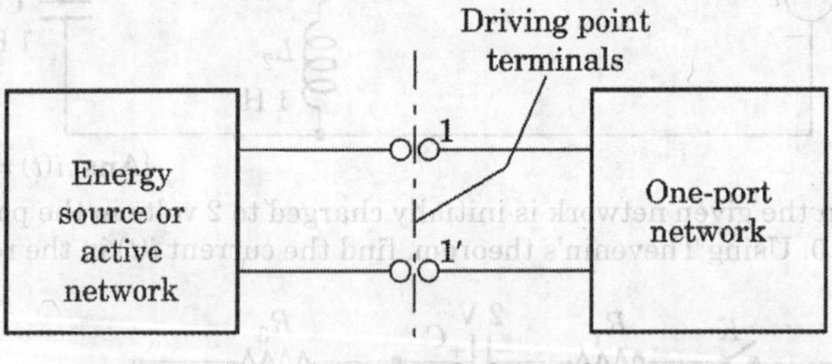

Fig. 10.1. One-port network driven by a source.

Fig. 10.2 shows a two-port network or two terminal-pair network. In this case, port 1 is connected to the driving force or the input and is called the *input port* or the *driving port.* On the other hand, port 2 (*i.e.* terminal pair 2-2′) is connected to the load and is called the *output port* or the *load port.*

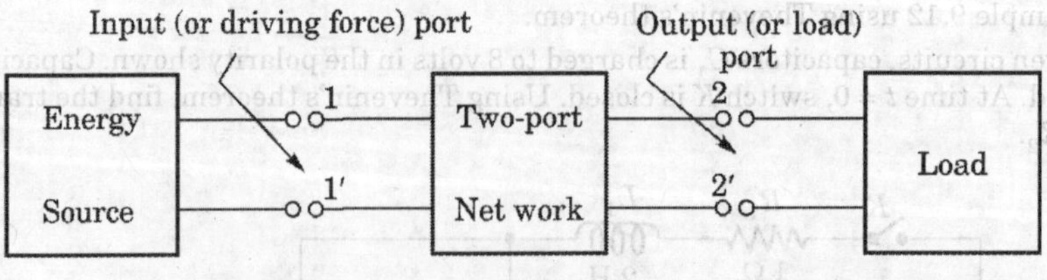

Fig. 10.2. Two-port network driven by an energy source.

Fig. 10.3 shows a general n-port network. Here driving force (energy source) may be connected to one or more ports and other networks may be connected at the remaining ports.

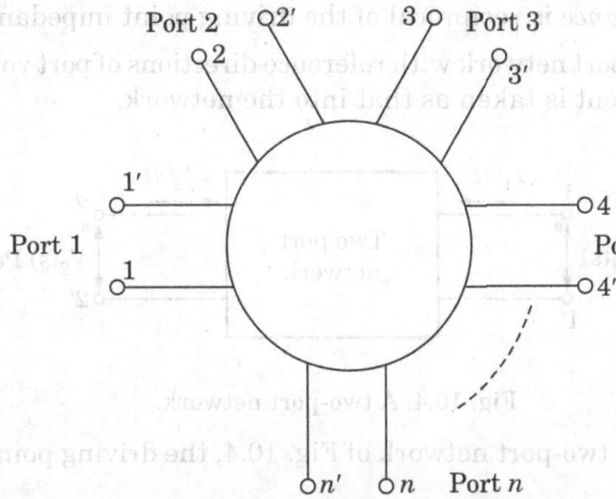

Fig. 10.3. General n-port network.

10.2. Network Functions for One-Port Network

For a one-port network in the zero or relaxed state (*i.e.* with no initial conditions) containing no internal voltage or current sources (except controlled sources), the transform impedance $z(s)$ at its port is defined as the ratio of the transform voltage $V(s)$ to the transform current $V(s)$ at the port.

Thus we may write,

$$Z(s) = \frac{V(s)}{I(s)} \quad \text{...(10.1)}$$

The transform admittance $Y(s)$ at the port is reciprocal of the transform impedance. Thus,

$$Y(s) = \frac{I}{Z(s)} = \frac{I(s)}{V(s)} \quad \text{...(10.2)}$$

10.3. Network Functions for a Two-Port Network

For a two-port network in the zero or relaxed state (*i.e.* with no initial conditions) containing no internal voltage or current sources (except controlled sources), the transform impedance $Z(s)$ at any port, say port 1, is defined as the ratio of transform voltage $V(s)$ at this port to the transform current $I(s)$ at either this port or the other port. Thus without specifying the port at which current $I(s)$ is considered, the transform impedance is given by,

$$Z(s) = \frac{V(s)}{I(s)} \quad \text{...(10.3)}$$

Transform admittance $Y(s)$ at any port being reciprocal of transform impedance is given by,

$$Y(s) = \frac{1}{Z(s)} = \frac{I(s)}{V(s)} \quad \text{...(10.4)}$$

If $V(s)$ and $I(s)$ pertain to the same port, then the transform impedance and transform admittance are specified as *driving point impedance* and *driving point admittance* respectively.

Thus for a two-port network in zero state with no internal energy sources, the *driving point impedance* is defined as the ratio of the transform voltage at any port to the transform current at the same port.

Driving point admittance is reciprocal of the driving point impedance at the same port.

Fig. 10.4 gives a two-port network with reference directions of port voltages and port currents. Reference direction for current is taken as that into the network.

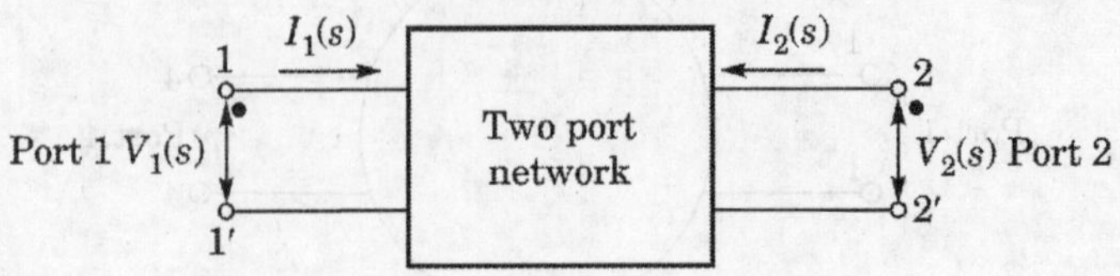

Fig. 10.4. A two-port network.

With reference to the two-port network of Fig. 10.4, the driving point impedance at port 1 is given by,

$$Z_{11}(s) = \frac{V_1(s)}{I_1(s)} \quad \text{...(10.5)}$$

While the driving point admittance at port 1 is given by,

$$Y_{11}(s) = \frac{I_1(s)}{V_1(s)} \quad \text{...(10.6)}$$

Transfer functions. Transfer functions, in general, relate a quantity at one part to a quantity at another port. Thus the transfer functions which relate voltages and currents may take the following forms :

(*a*) *voltage transfer ratio.* This is the ratio of voltage at one port to voltage at another port.

(*b*) *current transfer ratio.* This is the ratio of the current at one port to the current at another port.

(*c*) *transfer admittance.* This is the ratio of current at one port to voltage at another port.

(*d*) *transfer impedance.* This is the ratio of voltage at one port to current to another port.

Conventionally transfer function is defined as the ratio of an output quantity to an input quantity.

With reference to the two-port network of Fig. 10.4, the two output quantities are $V_2(s)$ and $I_2(s)$ while the two input quantities are $V_1(s)$ and $I_1(s)$. Thus for the two-port network, the four transfer functions are as below :

$$\left.\begin{aligned} Z_{21}(s) &= \frac{V_2(s)}{I_1(s)} \\ Y_{21}(s) &= \frac{I_2(s)}{V_1(s)} \\ G_{21}(s) &= \frac{V_2(s)}{V_1(s)} \\ \alpha_{21}(s) &= \frac{I_2(s)}{I_1(s)} \end{aligned}\right\} \quad \text{...(10.7)}$$

The transfer functions listed above have subscripts 2, 1 in the order *of effect cause*. Thus $Z_{21}(s)$ implies that the cause namely $I_1(s)$ has resulted in the effect namely $V_2(s)$.

In the following examples, we work out network functions for a few simple networks.

Example 10.1. *Find the transform impedance Z(s) of the given one-port network.*

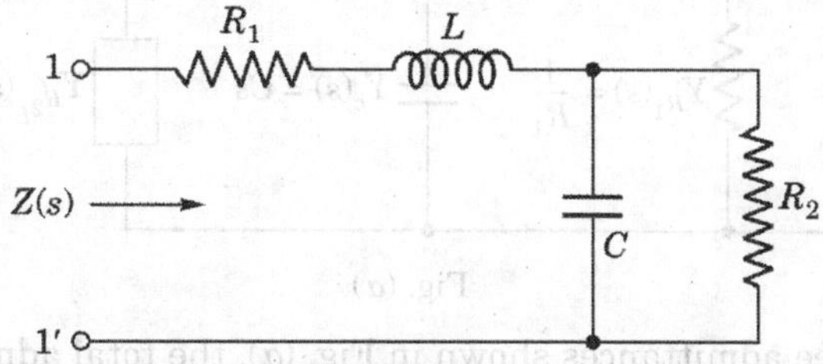

Solution. Transform network corresponding to the given network is shown in Fig. (*a*).

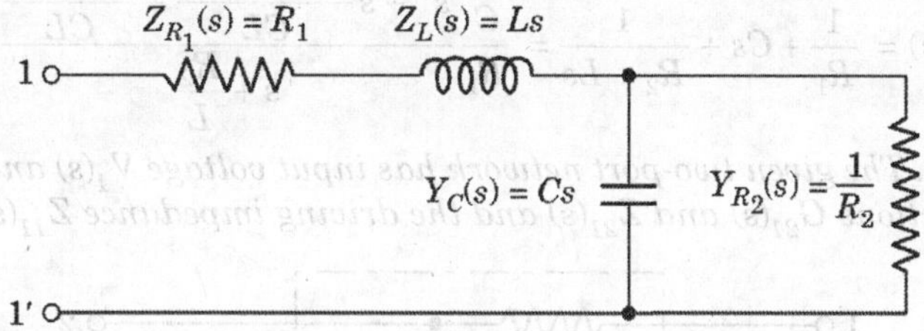

Fig. (*a*)

Transform admittances *CS* and $\dfrac{1}{R_2}$ may be combined together and the resulting series network is shown in Fig. (*b*).

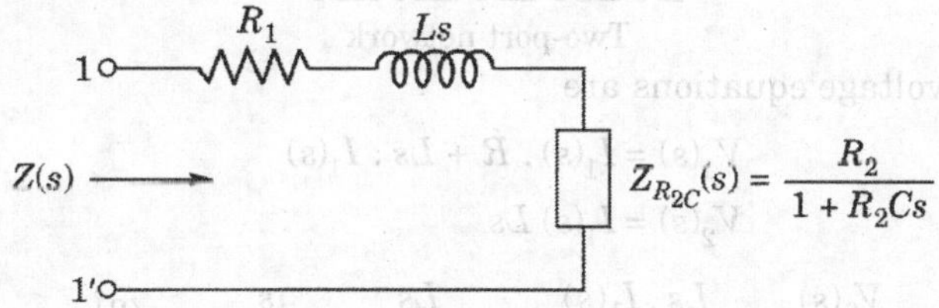

Fig. (*b*)

Hence the transform impedance *Z*(*s*) at the given port is,

$$Z(s) = R_1 + Ls + \frac{R_2}{1 + R_2\, Cs} = \frac{R_2LC\, s^2 + s(L + R_1R_2C) + (R_1 + R_2)}{1 + R_2\, Cs}$$

or
$$Z(s) = L\frac{s^2 + s\dfrac{L + R_1R_2C}{R_2LC} + \dfrac{R_1 + R_2}{R_2LC}}{s + \dfrac{1}{R_2C}}.$$

Example 10.2. *Find the transform impedance Z(s) of the given one-port network.*

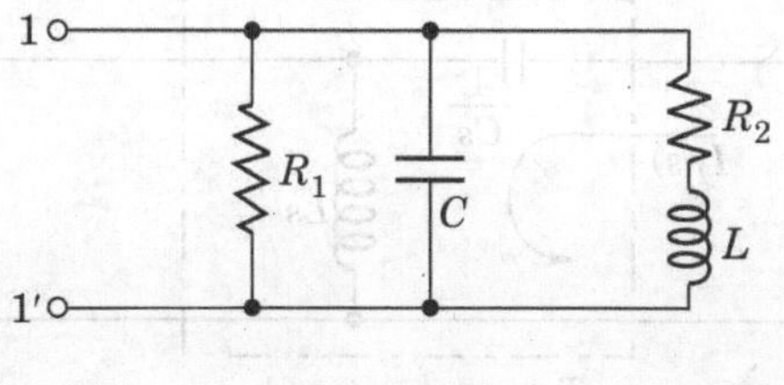

Solution. Transform network corresponding to the given network is shown in Fig. (*a*).

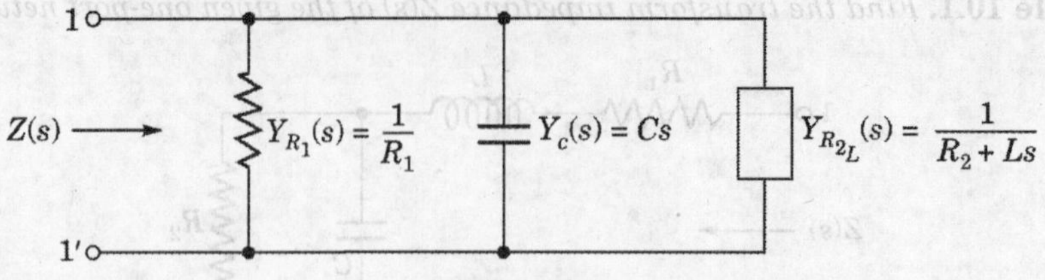

Fig. (*a*)

Combining the three admittances shown in Fig. (*a*), the total admittance at the port is

$$Y(s) = \frac{1}{R_1} + Cs + \frac{1}{R_2 + Ls} = \frac{C}{R_1} \frac{s^2 + s\frac{L + CR_1R_2}{CL} + \frac{R_1 + R_2}{CL}}{s + \frac{R_2}{L}}.$$

Example 10.3. *The given two-port network has input voltage $V_1(s)$ and output voltage $V_2(s)$. Find the transfer functions $G_{21}(s)$ and $Z_{21}(s)$ and the driving impedance $Z_{11}(s)$.*

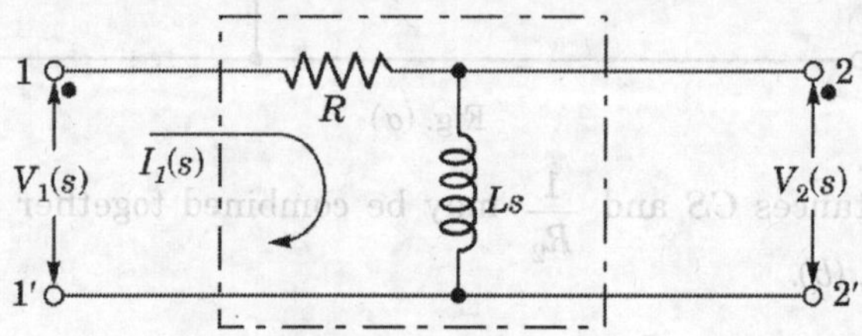

Two-port network

Solution. The voltage equations are

$$V_1(s) = I_1(s) \,.\, R + Ls \,.\, I_1(s) \qquad ...(1)$$

$$V_2(s) = I_1(s)\, Ls \qquad ...(2)$$

Hence $$G_{21}(s) = \frac{V_2(s)}{V_1(s)} = \frac{Ls \,.\, I_1(s)}{(R + Ls)\, I_1(s)} = \frac{Ls}{Ls + R} = \frac{s}{s + \frac{R}{L}} \qquad ...(3)$$

$$Z_{21}(s) = \frac{V_2(s)}{I_1(s)} = \frac{I_1(s) \cdot Ls}{I_1(s)} = Ls \qquad ...(4)$$

$$Z_{11}(s) = \frac{V_1(s)}{I_1(s)} = \frac{I_1(s)\,[Ls + R]}{I_1(s)} = Ls + R \qquad ...(5)$$

Example 10.4. *The given two-port network has input voltage $V_1(s)$ and output voltage $V_2(s)$. Find the transfer functions $G_{21}(s)$ and $Z_{21}(s)$ and the driving point admittance $Y_{11}(s)$.*

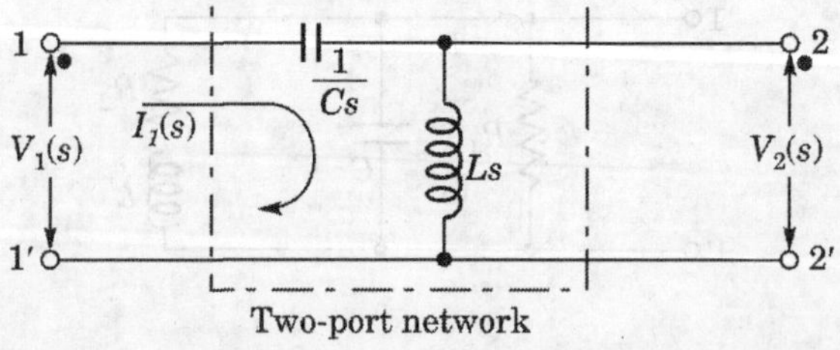

Two-port network

Solution. The voltage transform equations are :

$$V_1(s) = I_1(s)\left[\frac{1}{Cs} + Ls\right] \quad ...(1)$$

$$V_2(s) = I_1(s)\,.\,Ls \quad ...(2)$$

Hence transfer voltage ratio is,

$$G_{21}(s) = \frac{V_2(s)}{V_1(s)} = \frac{Ls}{Ls + \frac{1}{Cs}} = \frac{s^2}{s^2 + \frac{1}{LC}} \quad ...(3)$$

Transfer impedance $$Z_{21}(s) = \frac{V_2(s)}{I_1(s)} = \frac{I_1(s)\cdot Ls}{I_1(s)} = Ls \quad ...(4)$$

$$Y_{11}(s) = \frac{I_1(s)}{V_1(s)} = \frac{I_1 s}{I_1(s)\left[Ls + \frac{1}{Cs}\right]} = \frac{1}{L}\cdot\frac{s}{s^2 + \frac{1}{LC}} \quad ...(5)$$

Example 10.5. *For the given network, find the transfer functions $G_{21}(s)$, $Z_{21}(s)$ and driving point impedance $Z_{11}(s)$.*

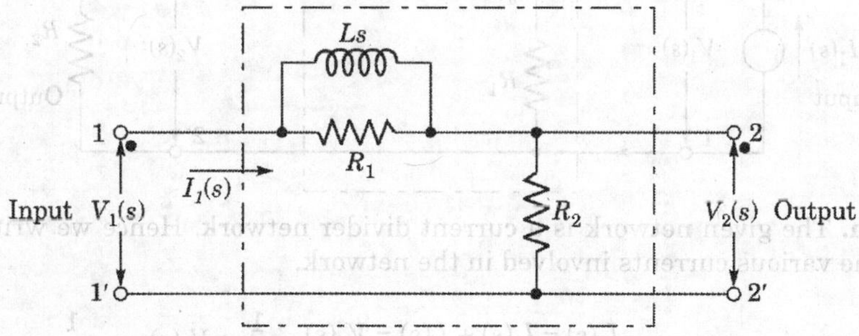

Solution. Transform impedances R_1 and Ls may be combined into an equivalent transform impedance $Z_{R_1L}(s)$ given by,

$$Z_{R_1L}(s) = \frac{1}{\frac{1}{R_1} + \frac{1}{Ls}} = \frac{R_1 Ls}{R_1 + Ls} \quad ...(1)$$

Now $$V_2(s) = I_1(s)\,.\,R_2 \quad ...(2)$$

and $$V_1(s) = I_1(s)\left[R_2 + \frac{R_1 Ls}{R_1 + Ls}\right] \quad ...(3)$$

Hence the transfer functions are as below :

$$G_{21}(s) = \frac{V_2(s)}{V_1(s)} = \frac{R_2}{R_2 + \frac{R_1 Ls}{R_1 + Ls}} = \frac{Ls + R_1}{Ls\left(\frac{R_1 + R_2}{R_2}\right) + R_1}$$

or $$G_{21}(s) = \frac{s + \dfrac{R_1}{L}}{s \, . \dfrac{R_1 + R_2}{R_2} + \dfrac{R_1}{L}} \qquad ...(4)$$

$$Z_{12}(s) = \frac{V_2(s)}{I_1(s)} = \frac{I_1(s) R_2}{I_1(s)} = R_2 \qquad ...(5)$$

$$Z_{11}(s) = \frac{V_1(s)}{I_1(s)} = R_2 + \frac{R_1 Ls}{R_1 + Ls} = \frac{s + \dfrac{R_1 R_2}{L(R_1 + R_2)}}{s + \left(\dfrac{R_1}{L}\right)} (R_1 + R_2) \qquad ...(6)$$

Example 10.6. *The given network is driven by a current source and is terminated by resistor R_2 at port 2. For this terminated 2-port network, calculate (a) transfer functions $G_{21}(s)$, $a_{21}(s)$, $Z_{21}(s)$, and $Y_{21}(s)$ and (b) driving point impedance $Z_{11}(s)$.*

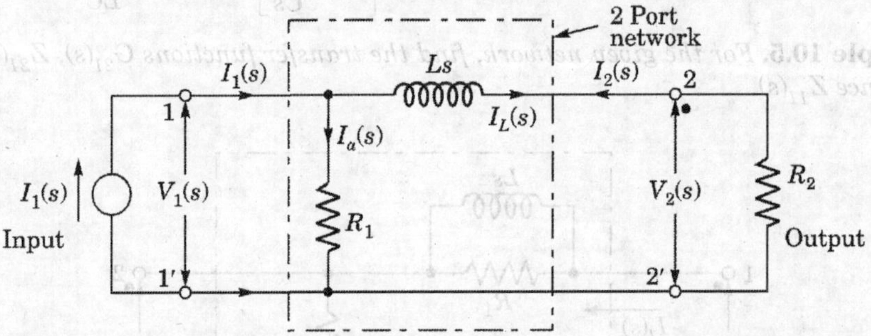

Solution. The given network is a current divider network. Hence we write the following equations for the various currents involved in the network.

$$I_1(s) = I_a(s) + I_l(s) = V_1(s) \, . \frac{1}{R_1} + V_1(s) \times \frac{1}{Ls + R_2} \qquad ...(1)$$

$$I_l(s) = \frac{I_1(s)\left(\dfrac{1}{Ls + R_2}\right)}{\dfrac{1}{R_1} + \dfrac{1}{Ls + R_2}} = I_1(s) \, . \frac{R_1}{L} \, . \frac{1}{s + \dfrac{R_1 + R_2}{L}} \qquad ...(2)$$

But $$I_2(s) = -\, I_l(s) \qquad ...(3)$$

Hence $$\alpha_{21}(s) = \frac{I_2(s)}{I_1(s)} = -\frac{R_1}{L} \frac{1}{s + \dfrac{R_1 + R_2}{L}} \qquad ...(4)$$

$$G_{21}(s) = \frac{V_2(s)}{V_1(s)} = \frac{I_l(s) R_2}{I_l(s)(R_2 + Ls)} = \frac{R_2}{L} \, . \frac{1}{s + \dfrac{R_2}{L}} \qquad ...(5)$$

$$G_{21}(s) = \frac{V_2(s)}{V_1(s)} = \frac{I_l(s) R_2}{I_1(s)} = \frac{R_1 R_2}{L} \, . \frac{1}{s + \dfrac{R_1 + R_2}{L}} \qquad ...(6)$$

$$G_{21}(s) = \frac{I_2(s)}{V_1(s)} = \frac{-I_l(s)}{I_l(s)[Ls + R_2]} = \frac{-1}{L} \cdot \frac{1}{s + \dfrac{R_2}{L}} \quad ...(7)$$

$$Z_{11}(s) = \frac{V_1(s)}{I_1(s)} = \frac{V_1(s)}{V_1(s)\left[\dfrac{1}{R_1} + \dfrac{1}{Ls + R_2}\right]} = \frac{R_1}{L} \cdot \frac{s + \dfrac{R_2}{L}}{s + \dfrac{R_1 + R_2}{L}} \quad ...(8)$$

10.4. Network Functions as a Quotient of Polynomials in s

We find that the expression for network function may, in general, be put in the form of a ratio of polynomials in s. Thus,

Network function

$$= \frac{P(s)}{Q(s)} = \frac{a_0 s^n + a_1 s^{n-1} + a_2 s^{n-2} + ... a_{n-1} s + a_n}{b_0 s^m + b_1 s^{m-1} + b_2 s^{m-2} + ... b_{m-1} s + b_m} \quad ...(10.8)$$

This ratio is a rational function of s when n and m are integers. In equation (10.8), n is the degree of the polynomial in the numerator while m is the degree of the polynomial in the denominator. The fact that the ratio of polynomials giving a network function is a rational function of s may be seen from equation (8.87) for analysis of a general network on current basis. This equation is reproduced below :

$$I_k(s) = \frac{\Delta_{jk}}{\Delta} V_j(s) \quad ...(10.9)$$

Hence the network function

$$\frac{I_k(s)}{V_j(s)} = \frac{\Delta_{jk}}{\Delta} \quad ...(10.10)$$

Hence Δ is the determinant of impedance matrix [Z] and is of order l, whereas Δ_{jk}, is a cofactor of Δ with row j and column k deleted and is, therefore, a determinant of order $(l - 1)$.

Now in determinant Δ, every element in its most general form is of the following nature :

$$Z_{jk} = R_{jk} + L_{jk} \cdot s + \frac{1}{C_{jk} \cdot s} \quad ...(10.11)$$

Hence the expression for Δ_{jk} and Δ will contain products, sums and quotients of terms of this type. Hence any network function $I_k(s)/V_j(s)$, being the ratio of determinants Δ_{jk} and Δ, will always be in the form of a rational quotient of polynomials of the type given by equation (10.8). This is true for all networks.

10.5. Poles and Zeros of Network Functions

We have seen that every network function may be expressed in the form of a quotient of polynomials in s. Thus let the network function be given by,

$$N(s) = \frac{P(s)}{Q(s)} = \frac{a_0 s^n + a_1 s^{n-1} + ... + a_{n-1} \cdot s + a_n}{b_0 s^m + b_1 \cdot s^{m-1} + ... + b_{m-1} s + b_m} \quad ...(10.12)$$

where coefficients a_0 to a_n and b_0 to b_m are real and positive for a network containing passive elements only and containing no controlled sources. Now the polynomial in the numerator is of degree n. Hence equation $P(s) = 0$ has n roots. Let these roots be $Z_1, Z_2, ..., Z_n$. Then numerator $P(s)$ may be written as the product of n linear factors $(s - Z_1)$, $(s - Z_2)$, ..., $(s - Z_n)$. Similarly the polynomial in the denominator is of degree m. Hence equation $Q(s) = 0$ has m roots. Let these roots be $p_1, p_2, ... p_m$. Then quantity $Q(s)$ may be written as the product of m linear factors $(s - p_1)$, $(s - p_2)$, ... $(s - p_m)$. Hence equation (10.12) giving the network function $N(s)$ may be written as,

$$N(s) = F\frac{(s - Z_1)(s - Z_2) ...... (s - Z_n)}{(s - p_1)(s - p_2) ...... (s - p_m)} \qquad ...(10.13)$$

where F is a constant called the scale factor.

Further terms Z_1, Z_2, ..., Z_n and also terms p_1, p_2, ..., . p_m are complex frequencies.

From the study of equation (10.13) we draw the following conclusions :

(i) When the variable s has value equal to any of the roots Z_1, Z_2, ..., Z_n, the network function $N(s)$ becomes zero. Hence these complex frequencies Z_1, Z_2, ..., Z_n are called the *zeros* of the network function.

(ii) When the variable s has any of the values p_1, p_2, ..., p_m, the network function $N(s)$ becomes infinite. Hence these complex frequencies p_1, p_2, ... p_m are called the poles of the network function.

Factors $(s - Z_1)$, $(s - Z_2)$ etc. in the numerator of equation (10.13) giving network function $N(s)$ are called the *zero factors,* while factors $(s - p_1)$, $(s - p_2)$ etc. in the denominator of equation (10.13) giving the network function $N(s)$ are called the *pole factors.*

From equation (10.13) we conclude that any network function is completely known if we know its zeros, poles and the scale factor F. Accordingly poles and zeros are very useful quantities in describing the behaviour of any network.

If a pole or zero is not repeated, it is said to be *simple* or *distinct*. On the other hand, if a pole or zero is repeated once, it is said to be *double*. Similarly if a pole or zero is repeated twice, it is said to be *triple.* In a general case, when r poles or zeros have the same value, that pole or zero is said to be of *multiplicity r*.

Poles and Zeros of Infinity and at Zero. Multiple poles and zeros are taken to be present at s equal to infinity, the degree or multiplicity depending upon the values of n and m. In this equation (10.12) when $n > m$, the pole at infinity is of degree or multiplicity $(n - m)$, so that the total number of poles also becomes n. Out of these n poles, m poles exist at finite values of complex frequency s while $(n - m)$ poles exist at $s = \infty$. Similarly when $n < m$, the zeros at infinity are of degree or multiplicity $(m - n)$ so that the total number of zero also becomes m. Out of these m zeros, n zeros exist at finite values of s while $(m - n)$ zeros exist at $s = \infty$.

Total Number of Zeros Equals Total Number of Poles. For any rational network function, counting poles and zero at zero and infinity, in addition to the poles and zeros at finite values of s, the total number of zeros is equal to the total number of poles. Thus consider the following network function,

$$N(s) = \frac{s(s+2)}{(s+3)(s+1+j1)(s+1-j1)} \qquad ...(10.14)$$

Here the network function has a zero at $s = 0$, and a zero at $s = -2$. Thus in all it has 2 zeros. The function has a pole each at $s = -3$, $s = -1 - j1$ and $s = -1 + j1$. Thus the number of poles equals 3. Hence there is included a zero at infinity in order to make the number of zeros equal the number of poles.

Fig. 10.5 shows that plot of poles and zeros of network function $N(s)$ as given by equation (10.14). Symbol O is generally used to indicate a zero while symbol X is used to indicate a pole.

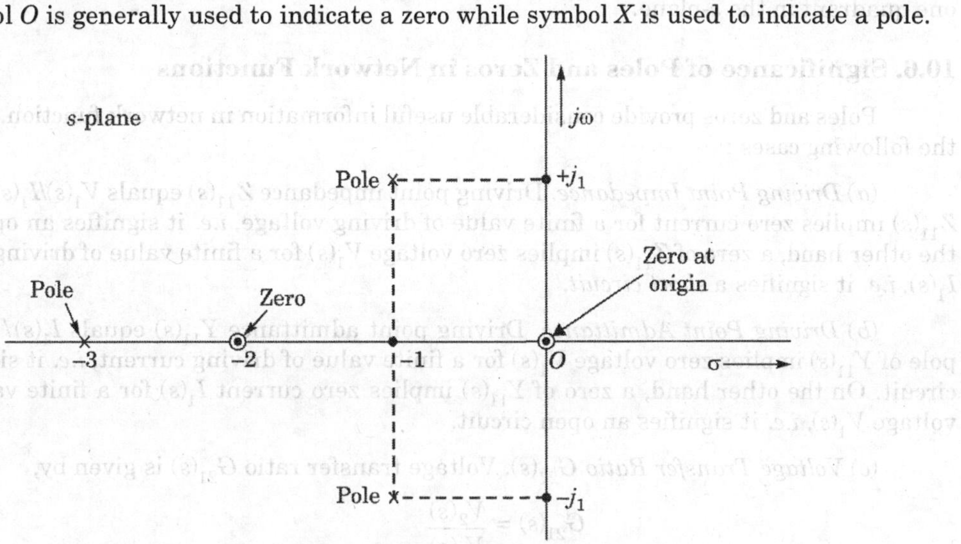

Fig. 10.5. Location of poles and zeros in network function of equation (10.14).

Three Dimensional Plot of Network Function. At poles, a network function becomes infinite while at zeros, it becomes zero.

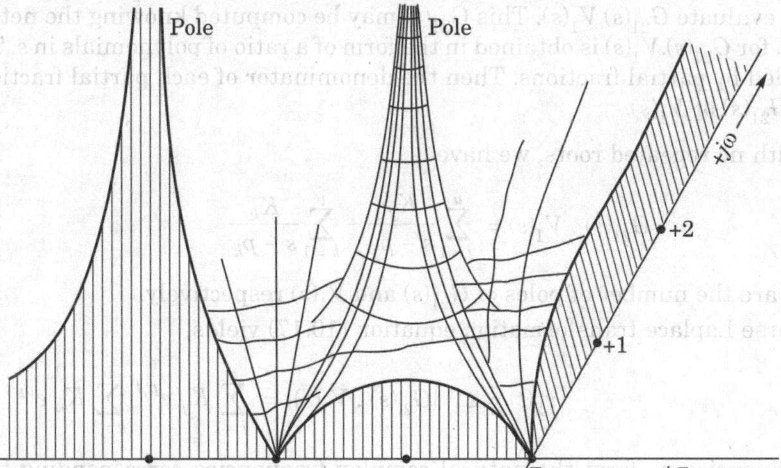

Fig. 10.6. Magnitude of network function of equation (10.14) plotted against complex frequency.

Accordingly poles and zeros constitute *critical frequencies.* At every other frequency, the network function has a finite non-zero value. Fig. 10.6 shows a three-dimensional plot of the magnitude of network function given by equation (10.14) as a function of complex frequency $s(= \sigma + j\omega)$ or only one quadrant in the s-plane.

10.6. Significance of Poles and Zeros in Network Functions

Poles and zeros provide considerable useful information in network function. Thus consider the following cases :

(*a*) *Driving Point Impedance*. Driving point impedance $Z_{11}(s)$ equals $V_1(s)/I_1(s)$. Hence a pole $Z_{11}(s)$ implies zero current for a finite value of driving voltage, *i.e.* it signifies an open circuit. On the other hand, a zero of $Z_{11}(s)$ implies zero voltage $V_1(s)$ for a finite value of driving point current $I_1(s)$, *i.e.* it signifies a *short circuit.*

(*b*) *Driving Point Admittance.* Driving point admittance $Y_{11}(s)$ equals $I_1(s)/V_1(s)$. Hence a pole of $Y_{11}(s)$ implies zero voltage $V_1(s)$ for a finite value of driving current, *i.e.* it signifies a short circuit. On the other hand, a zero of $Y_{11}(s)$ implies zero current $I_1(s)$ for a finite value of driving voltage $V_1(s)$, *i.e.* it signifies an open circuit.

(*c*) *Voltage Transfer Ratio* $G_{21}(s)$. Voltage transfer ratio $G_{21}(s)$ is given by,

$$G_{21}(s) = \frac{V_2(s)}{V_1(s)} \qquad ...(10.15)$$

Equation (10.15) may be written as,

$$V_2(s) = V_1(s) \, . \, G_{21}(s) \qquad ...(10.16)$$

In most of the network problems, the input voltage $V_1(s)$ or $v_1(t)$ in the time domain, is given and we are required to compute the output voltage or the response $V_2(s)$ or $v_2(t)$. In order to find $V_2(s)$, we must evaluate $G_{21}(s)\, V_1(s)$. This $G_{21}(s)$ may be computed knowing the network elements. The expression for $G_{21}(s).V_1(s)$ is obtained in the form of a ratio of polynomials in s. This expression may be expanded by partial fractions. Then the denominator of each partial fraction term gives a pole of either $G_{21}(s)$ or $V_1(s)$.

Thus with no repeated roots, we have

$$G_{21}(s) \, . \, V_1(s) = \sum_{j=1}^{u} \frac{K_j}{s - p_j} + \sum_{k=1}^{v} \frac{K_k}{s - p_k} \qquad ....(10.17)$$

where u and v are the number of poles of $G_{21}(s)$ and $V_1(s)$ respectively.

On Inverse Laplace transformation equation (10.17) yields,

$$v_2(t) = \mathcal{L}^{-1} \left[G_{21}(s) \, . \, V_1(s) \right] = \sum_{j=1}^{u} K_j \, e^{p_j t} \sum_{k=1}^{v} K_k \, e^{p_k t} \qquad ...(10.18)$$

The frequencies p_j, form the natural complex frequencies corresponding to what may be called, *free oscillations* and these depend entirely on the network function $G_{21}(s)$. On the other hand, frequencies p_k constitute the complex frequencies corresponding to the *forced oscillations* and these depend entirely on the driving force $V_1(s)$.

We conclude, therefore, that the poles determine the time variation of the response. Zeros on the other hand, determine the magnitudes of coefficients K_j and K_k in the partial fraction expansion and thus determine the magnitude of response.

(*d*) *Other Network Functions*. Significance of poles and zeros in other transfer functions namely $Y_{21}(s)$, $Z_{21}(s)$ and $\alpha_{21}(s)$ is the same as discussed above for voltage transfer ratio $G_{21}(s)$. In each of these transfer functions, poles determine the time variation of the response whereas zeros determine the magnitudes.

10.7. Restrictions on Locations of Poles and Zeros in Driving Point Functions

The restrictions which get imposed on the location of poles and zeros in driving point functions are discussed below :

(i) Coefficients in the Polynomials P(s) and Q(s) of $N(s) = \dfrac{(Ps)}{Q(s)}$ *must be real and positive.* We have already seen earlier that any network function may be put in the form of quotient of polynomials of s as below,

$$N(s) = \frac{P(s)}{Q(s)} = \frac{a_0 s^n + a_1 s^{n-1} + ... + a_n}{b_0 s^m + b_1 s^{m-1} + ... + b_m} \quad ...(10.19)$$

where coefficients a's and b's are real positive. Hence when s is real, $P(s)$ and $Q(s)$ will also be real. Such functions are called *real functions.*

(ii) Poles and zeros, if complex, must occur in Conjugate Pairs. Let polynomial $P(s)$ in equation (10.19) be a real function. Now let one of the zeros of $P(s)$ be complex. Let it be equal to $(-a - jb)$. Then its conjugate namely $(-a + jb)$ must also form a zero of the same polynomial $P(s)$, failing which $P(s)$ will have some complex coefficients. This may be established as below :

Let $P(s)$ contain only one pair of conjugate zeros namely $(-a - jb)$ and $(-a + jb)$. Then $P(s)$ is given by

$$P(s) = (s + a + jb)(s + a - jb) = (s + a)^2 + (b)^2 \quad ...(10.20)$$

or

$$P(s) = s^3 + 2as + (a^2 + b^2) \quad ...(10.21)$$

From equation (10.21), it is evident that $P(s)$ is real since a and b are real.

Next consider two complex zeros which are not conjugate. Let these be $(-a - jb)$ and $(-c - jd)$. Then the product $(s + a + jb)(s + c + jd)$, where $a \neq c$ and $b \neq -d$, will not have all real coefficients. Hence such zeros are inadmissible in network functions.

Thus we conclude that in a real network function, the zeros must either be real or must occur in conjugate pairs.

(iii) The real part of all Poles and Zeros must be either Negative or Zero. From equation (10.21) we further observe that in order to make $P(s)$ a real function, the second term namely $2as$ be positive. Hence 'a' must be positive. Hence the real part of all poles and zeros namely $(-a)$ must be negative.

This restriction that the real part of pole or zero be negative or zero, arises from the assumption that any network constituted by passive elements only, must be *stable, i.e.* the excitation due to any initial condition in any elements results in bounded output. By bounded output is meant an output which remains finite no matter how large time is made.

Thus when a voltage source $V(s)$ is applied to a one port network containing passive elements only, the resulting response is a current $I(s)$ at the input. Conversely a current source $I(s)$ as the excitation results in a voltage $V(s)$ across the port as the response. The network must be stable with either excitation current $I(s)$ of excitation voltage $V(s)$. Hence the conclusions drawn for say zeros will apply for poles as well and *vice versa.* Now let us consider the driving point impedance $Z(s)$. Let the denominator in the expression for $Z(s)$ contain the factor $(s - s_p)$, where $s_p = \sigma_p + j\omega_p$. This factor $(s - s_p)$ will cause a time domain response of the following form :

$$\text{Response} = K_p \cdot e^{s_p t} = K_p \cdot e^{\sigma_p t} \cdot e^{j\omega_p t} \quad ...(10.22)$$

Since the network function is real, the denominator must also contain factor $(s - s_p')$ where $s_p' = \sigma_p - j\omega_p$. The corresponding time domain response is given by,

$$\text{Response} = K_p' \cdot e^{s_p' t} = K_p' \cdot e^{\sigma_p t} \cdot e^{-j\omega_p t} \qquad ...(10.23)$$

Combining the two responses, the combined response is given by,

$$\text{Total response} = e^{\sigma_p t} \left[K_p \cdot e^{j\omega_p t} + K_p' \cdot e^{-j\omega_p t}\right] \qquad ...(10.24)$$

$$= K_0 e^{\sigma_p t} \cdot \sin(\omega_p t + \theta_p) \qquad ...(10.25)$$

From equation (10.25) we see that for the response to be bounded, all that is necessary is to have $\sigma_p \le 0$.

Thus we conclude that for a driving point impedance (or admittance) to be bounded, the poles (and zeros) should have negative or zero real part. Thus in s-plane all poles and zeros must lie in *left half of the s-plane* and none can lie in the *right half of the s-plane.* Of course, poles and zeros can lie on the boundry dividing the left half and the right half.

(*iv*) *If the Real Part of any Pole or Zero is Zero, then that Pole or Zero must be simple* (*not repeated*). We have seen that the real part of a complex pole or zero must be either negative or zero. Thus the real parts of poles and zero may have zero value, *i.e.* the poles and zeros may lie on the boundary dividing the left half of the s-place and right half of the s-plane. But the restriction offered is that such poles and zeros must be simple (not multiple or repeated). This restriction crops up because if the poles or zeros be of order n, then the time domain response contains term t^{n-1} and this term becomes infinite as time t increases to infinity.

Multiple poles and zeros may, however, exist at locations in the left half of the s-plane. If there exist n such multiple poles at any location, then such poles result in response of the form $t^{n-1} \cdot e^{-\sigma t}$ which constitutes a bounded response since,

$$\lim_{t \to \infty} t^{n-1} \cdot e^{-\alpha t} = 0 \qquad ...(10.26)$$

by 1′ Hospital's rule (for finite value of n).

(*v*) *Polynomial P*(*s*) *or Q*(*s*) *cannot have missing terms between those of highest and lowest order unless all even order terms or all odd order terms are missing.* From the earlier discussion we conclude that the polynomials $P(s)$ and $Q(s)$ in the expression for driving point function are constituted by the products of the following factors : (*i*) constant k (*ii*) $(s + a)$, where a is either zero or real and positive (*iii*) $(s^2 + bs + c)$ and (*iv*) $(s^2 + d)$ where b, c and d are real and positive. Hence polynomials $P(s)$ and $Q(s)$ formed by product of three factors will also have all coefficients which are real and positives since negative sign cannot appear through any mechanism. Further since negative sign cannot be introduced, there exists no chance of cancellation of a positive term with a negative term. Thus three is no possibility of a coefficient becoming zero through mechanism of cancellation of a positive term with a negative term. Thus polynomial $P(s)$ or $Q(s)$ as given by equation (10.19) has all coefficients *non-zero* except under the following two conditions :

(*i*) Polynomial composed of factors like $(s^2 + d)$ only. In that ease the polynomial contains only even order terms and is free of odd order terms.

(*ii*) Polynomial having a simple (not multiple) zero at the origin and all other factors of the type $(s^2 + d)$. In this case, polynomial formed by terms of type $(s^2 + d)$ is even polynomial but on multiplication by a single s, the polynomial becomes an odd polynomial, *i.e.* coefficients of all even order are zero.

We thus conclude that in a polynomial $P(s)$ or $Q(s)$ representing a driving point function, no coefficient may be zero, *i.e.* no term in the polynomial may be missing unless all the even order or all the odd order terms are missing.

(iv) The Degrees of P(s) and Q(s) may differ by Zero or One only. Consider the behaviour of a one port network at very high and at very low frequencies.

(a) At *very high frequencies*. At very high frequencies, the impedance of an inductor, $Z_L(s) = Ls$, is very large compared to the impedance of any other element and thus dominates the impedance function of the network. Hence the impedance function of the network may be represented by equivalent inductance L_{eq} as shown in Fig. 10.7 (*a*). Impedance $Z_c(s) = \frac{1}{Cs}$ of C is extremely small and may be neglected. Hence if the network does not contain L, then either the resistor will dominate the impedance function of the network or the equivalent network would be short circuit since impedance $\frac{1}{Cs}$ of C approaches zero as frequency s approaches infinity. Thus in this case, the impedance function may be represented by R_{eq} as shown in Fig. 10.7 (*b*), where R_{eq} may be finite or zero.

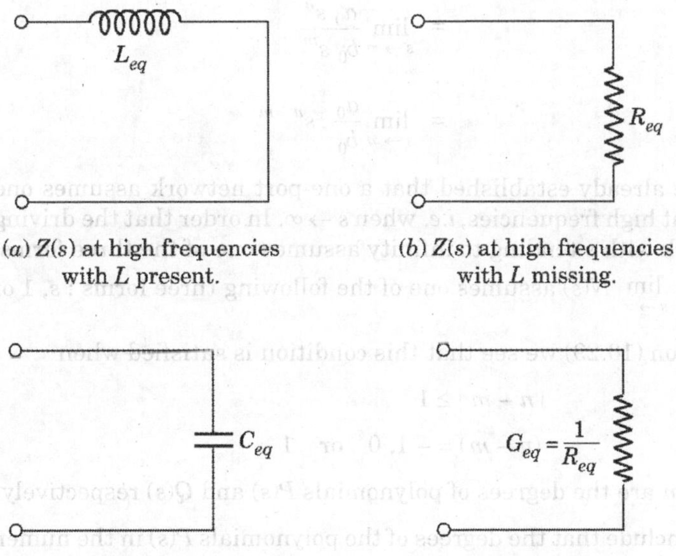

(*a*) $Z(s)$ at high frequencies with L present.

(*b*) $Z(s)$ at high frequencies with L missing.

(*c*) $Y(s)$ at high frequencies with C present.

(*d*) $Y(s)$ at high frequencies with C missing.

Fig. 10.7. High frequency equivalent networks for a one port network.

At very high frequencies, the admittance of a capacitor $Y_c(s) = Cs$, is very large compared to admittance of any other element and will thus dominate the admittance function of the network. Hence the admittance function of the network may be represented by equivalent capacitance C_{eq} as shown in Fig. 10.7 (*c*).

Admittance of L, $Y_L(s) = \frac{1}{Ls}$, is extremely small and may be neglected. Hence if the network does not contain C, then either the resistor will dominate the admittance function of the network or the equivalent network would be open circuit, since the admittance $\frac{1}{Ls}$ of L approaches zero as frequency s approaches infinity. Thus in this case, the admittance function may be represented by G_{eq} as shown in Fig. 10.7 (*d*) where G_{eq} may be finite or zero.

We thus see that equivalent representation of one port network at high frequencies involves at most one kind of element and will assume one of the forms shown in Fig. 10.7.

(*b*) *At Low Frequencies*. Conclusions similar to above may be drawn for impedance and admittance function of a one port network at low frequencies. Thus at low frequencies also, *i.e.* when s approaches zero, the equivalent representation of a one port network involves at most one kind of element.

Requisite conditions for a driving point voltage to assume equivalent representation of Fig. 10.7. We now explore the conditions under which driving point function of a general network assumes the equivalent representation of Fig. 10.7.

From equation 10.12, the value of driving point function $N(s)$ when $S \to \infty$ is given by,

$$\lim_{s \to \infty} N(s) = \lim_{s \to \infty} \frac{a_0 s^n + a_1 . s^{n-1} + ... + a_{n-1} . s + a_n}{b_0 s^m + b_1 . s^{m-1} + ... + a_{m-1} . s + a_m} \quad ...(10.27)$$

$$= \lim_{s \to \infty} \frac{a_0 \, s^n}{b_0 \, s^m} \quad ...(10.28)$$

$$= \lim_{s \to \infty} \frac{a_0}{b_0} . s^{n-m}$$

But we have already established that a one-port network assumes one of the three forms shown in Fig. 10.7 at high frequencies, *i.e.* when $s \to \infty$. In order that the driving point function $N(s)$ of a general network with s tending to infinity assumes one of the three forms shown in Fig. 10.7, it is necessary that $\lim_{s \to \infty} N(s)$ assumes one of the following three forms : s, 1 or $1/s$.

From equation (10.29) we see that this condition is satisfied when

$$| n - m | \geq 1 \quad ...(10.30)$$

or

$$(n - m) = -1, 0 \quad \text{or} \quad 1 \quad ...(10.31)$$

Here n and m are the degrees of polynomials $P(s)$ and $Q(s)$ respectively.

Hence we conclude that the degrees of the polynomials $P(s)$ in the numerator and $Q(s)$ in the denominator for a driving point function *may differ by one at most.*

(*viii*) *Lowest Degree terms in P(s) and Q(s) may differ in Degree by at most one*. At low frequencies, *i.e.* as s approaches zero, in $P(s)$ and $Q(s)$, the high degree terms such as s^n, s^{n-1}, s^m, s^{m-1} etc. are small and may be neglected. Hence network function $N(s)$ may be put as

$$N(s) = \frac{... + a_{n-1} s + a_n}{... + b_{m-1} s + b_n} \quad ...(10.32)$$

In order that the driving point function $N(s)$ of a network, with s tending to zero assume one of the four forms shown in Fig. 10.7, it is necessary that lim $\lim_{s \to 0} N(s)$ assume one of the following 3 forms : s, 1 or $\frac{1}{s}$. This condition may be satisfied in only three possible ways. We will now explore these three possibilities. As s approaches zero, all high order terms except $a_{n-1}\, s$, a_n, $b_{m-1}\, s$ and b_m

become zero.

Let $N(s)$ be a driving point impedance. Then the three possibilities are as below :

(a) $a_n = 0$ and $b_m \neq 0$,

Then
$$\lim_{s \to \infty} N(s) = \lim_{s \to 0} \frac{a_{n-1}}{b_{m-1} + \frac{b_m}{s}} \quad ...(10.33)$$

$$= \lim_{s \to 0} \frac{a_{n-1}}{b_{m-1}} \cdot \frac{1}{1 + \frac{b_m}{b_{m-1} \cdot s}} = \lim_{s \to 0} \frac{a_{n-1}}{b_m} s \quad ...(10.34)$$

Thus impedance $N(s)$ represents an inductor.

(b) $b_m = 0$ and $a_n \neq 0$.

Then
$$\lim_{s \to 0} N(s) = \lim_{s \to 0} \frac{a_{n-1} \cdot s + a_n}{b_{m-1} \cdot s} \quad ...(10.35)$$

$$= \lim_{s \to 0} \frac{a_{n-1}}{b_{m-1}} \cdot \left[1 + \frac{n_n}{a_{n-1} \cdot s}\right] \quad ...(10.36)$$

$$= \lim_{s \to 0} \frac{a_n}{b_{m-1}} \cdot \frac{1}{s} \quad ...(10.37)$$

Thus impedance $N(s)$ represents a capacitor.

(c) $a_n \neq 0$ and $b_m \neq 0$.

Then
$$\lim_{s \to 0} N(s) = \lim_{s \to 0} \frac{a_{n-1} + \frac{a_n}{s}}{b_{m-1} + \frac{b_m}{s}} \quad ...(10.38)$$

$$= \frac{a_n}{b_m} \quad ...(10.39)$$

Thus driving point impedance $N(s)$ becomes a constant which represents the impedance of a resistor.

Next let $N(s)$ be the driving point admittance.

Then the three possibilities are as below :

(a) $a_n = 0$ and $b_m \neq 0$.

Then in accordance with Eq. (10.34), admittance $N(s)$ when s approaches zero equals

$$\lim_{s \to 0} \frac{a_{n-1}}{b_m} s.$$

This represents a capacitor.

(b) $b_n = 0$ and $a_n \neq 0$.

Then in accordance with Eq. (10.37), admittance $N(s)$ when s approaches zero, equals

$$\lim_{s \to 0} \frac{a_n}{b_{m-1}} \cdot \frac{1}{s}$$

This represents an inductor.

(*c*) $a_n \neq 0$ and $b_m \neq 0$.

Then in accordance with Eq. (10.38), $N(s)$ represents a resistor.

In case (*a*) above, *i.e.* when $a_n = 0$ and $b_m \neq 0$, the term of lowest degree in $P(s)$ is $a_{n-1}.s$ while the term of lowest degree in $Q(s)$ is b_m. Thus term of lowest degree in numerator is one degree higher than the term of lowest degree in denominator.

Similarly we see that in case (*b*), the degree of lowest degree term in numerator is one lower than the degree of lowest degree term in denominator.

Finally in case (*c*), the terms of lowest degree in numerator and denominator are of the same degree.

We thus conclude that in any driving point function $N(s)$, the terms of lowest degree in the numerator and denominator *may differ in degree by at most one.*

Items (*i*) to (*vii*) above give the necessary conditions for driving point functions [with common factors in numerator $P(s)$ and denominator $Q(s)$ cancelled].

Viability of a few driving point functions are discussed in the following examples in the light of above discussions.

Example 10.7. *Verify whether the following expression for driving point impedance Z(s) is suitable for representing a passive one-port network*

$$Z(s) = \frac{s^4 + 2s^3 - 2s + 1}{s^3 + s^2 - 2s + 12}.$$

Solution. This function is not suitable for representing the impedance of a one port network for the following reasons :

(*a*) In the numerator one coefficient is negative.

(*b*) In the denominator one coefficient is negative.

(*c*) In the numerator one coefficient is missing.

(*d*) Denominator on factorisation equals $(s + 3)(s^2 - 2s + 4)$.

This has 2 poles of $Z(s)$ in the right half of *s*-plane.

Example 10.8. *Verify whether the following expression for driving point impedance is suitable for representing a passive one-port network*

$$Z(s) = \frac{s^2 + s + 2}{s^4 + 5s^3 + 6s^2}.$$

Solution. This function is not suitable for representing the impedance of a one-port network for the following reasons :

(*a*) The degree of numerator is 2 while that of the denominator is 4, a difference of 2 which is in excess of the maximum permitted different of 1.

(*b*) The denominator equals $s^2(s + 2)(s + 3)$. Thus there is a double pole at the origin in the *s*-plane which is not permitted.

Example 10.9. *Verify whether the following expression for the driving point impedance Z(s) is suitable for representing a passive one-port network*

$$Z(s) = \frac{s^2(s^2 - 2s + 6)}{(s + 3)}.$$

Solution. This function is not suitable for representing the driving point impedance of a one-port network for the following reasons :

(*a*) The term of the lowest degree in the numerator is of degree 2 while that in the denominator is zero, a difference of 2 which is in excess of the maximum permitted difference of one.

(*b*) The numerator has a factor s^2 indicating a double zero at the origin in the s-plane which is not permitted.

(*c*) The factor $(s^2 - 2s + 6)$ yields two poles of $Z(s)$ in the right half of the s-plane.

(*d*) The degree of numerator is 4 while that of denominator is one, a difference of 3 which is in excess of the maximum permitted difference of one.

10.8. Restrictions on Locations of Poles and Zeros for Transfer Functions

Now we consider the restrictions on locations of poles and zeros for transfer functions Z_{21}, Y_{21}, G_{21} and α_{21}. Some of these restrictions may be established using the same technique as used for driving point functions. Here again we refer to the 2-port network of Fig. 10.2. Let 1-1′ be the input port and 2-2′ be the output port. We connect the energy source at port 1-1′ and record the output voltage or current at port 2-2′.

The following restrictions are then found to apply to poles and zeros of various transfer functions :

(*i*) *The Real part of Poles must be negative or zero (but simple).* Now if the network is passive, application of step voltage or current will result in output response which is bounded. For the response to remain bounded we had earlier found that for a one-port network, the restriction is that the real part of the poles be negative or zero. In case this negative part is zero (including the origin), the poles must be simple (not multiple). The same restriction applies to the poles of transfer function of a two-port network. For a one-port network, these restrictions apply to zeros also because for a one-port network $Y(s) = \frac{1}{Z(s)}$.

For a two-port network however, in general,

$$Z_{12}(s) \neq \frac{1}{Y_{12}(s)} \quad \text{and} \quad G_{12} \neq \frac{1}{\alpha_{12}(s)}.$$

Hence these restrictions do not apply to zeros of the transfer functions of a two-port network. We thus summarise that for a transfer function :

(*i*) the poles must lie in the left half of the complex s-plane including the boundary (if simple).

(*ii*) the zeros may, however, lie in the right half plane provided they are conjugate if complex.

Transfer functions with zeros in the left half plane are called *minimum-phase transfer functions* while transfer functions with zeros in the right half plane are called *maximum-plane transfer functions.*

(*iii*) *For $G_{12}(s)$ and $\alpha_{21}(s)$, the Maximum Degree of $P(s)$ equals the degree of $Q(s)$.* Next we established the restriction regarding difference in degrees $P(s)$ and $Q(s)$ for the transfer function $N(s) = P(s)/Q(s)$. We established this for simple network namely T-and π-network shown in Fig. 10.8. We use the T-network of Fig. 10.8 (*a*) to establish properties of $G_{21}(s)$ and $Z_{21}(s)$ and use the π-network of Fig. 10.8 (*b*) to establish properties of $\alpha_{21}(s)$ and $Y_{21}(s)$.

Now in Fig. 10.8 (*a*) with output terminals 2-2′ open, Z_3 may be shorted without affecting G_{21}. Then for the T-network of Fig. 10.8 (*a*) for input voltage V_1 at port 1,

$$G_{21}(s) = \frac{V_2(s)}{V_1(s)} = \frac{Z_2(s)}{Z_1(s) + Z_2(s)} \qquad ...(10.40)$$

Similarly in Fig. 10.8 (*b*) with output terminals shorted $Y_3(s)$ may be opened without affecting $\alpha_{21}(s)$. Then with input current I_1 at port 1-1′, we have

$$\alpha_{21}(s) = \frac{I_2(s)}{I_1(s)} = \frac{Y_1(s)}{Y_1(s) + Y_2(s)} \qquad ...(10.41)$$

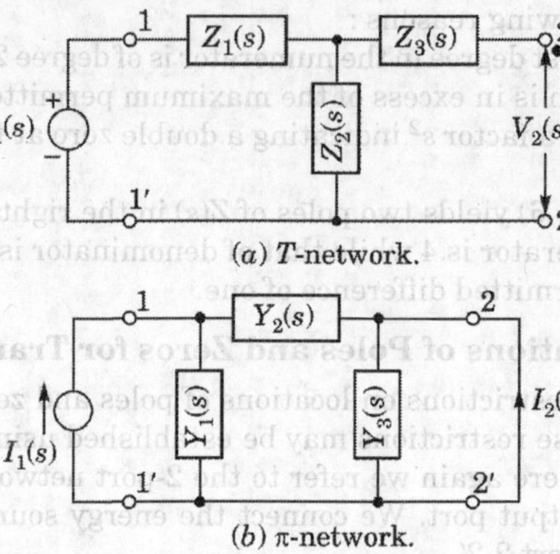

Fig. 10.8. *T*-and π-network structures representing a general two-port network.

Eqs. (10.40) and (10.41) are duals. Hence the results obtained for any one apply equally well to the other. For simplicity we deal with the *T*-network of Fig. 10.8 (*a*) and the results so obtained for $G_{21}(s)$ will then apply to $\alpha_{21}(s)$ as well.

In the last article we had established that for a one-port network as *s* approaches infinity, the entire network reduces essentially to an equivalent network in which only one kind of elements dominate.

Hence in the *T*-network of Fig. 10.8 (*a*) we consider Z_1, Z_2 and Z_3 to be constituted by one kind of elements only. But there are only two sub-networks namely Z_1 and Z_2 in the *T*-network of Fig. 10.8 (*a*) with output open circuited. Hence the following two possibilities exist :

(*a*) $Z_1(s)$ and $Z_2(s)$ are of the same kind. Then $G_{21}(s)$ becomes a constant and the network containing $Z_1(s)$ and $Z_2(s)$ serves simply as a potential divider independent of time. But since we are considering only the high frequency circuit of general sub-networks $Z_1(s)$ and $Z_2(s)$, *i.e.*, equivalent network when *s* approaches infinity, the voltage ratio $G_2(s)$ becomes constant only under the condition that the degree of $P(s)$ equals the degree of $Q(s)$.

(*b*) $Z_1(s)$ and $Z_2(s)$ are of different kinds. In this case it may be shown that, whatever be the nature of $Z_1(s)$ and $Z_2(s)$, whether inductor, capacitor or resistor the degree of numerator is equal to or less than the degree of denominator and it can never exceed the degree of denominator.

Same is true for current ratio $\alpha_{21}(s)$. Thus we conclude that in the expression for voltage transfer ratio $G_{21}(s)$ or current transfer ratio $\alpha_{21}(s)$, the degree of numerator may at the most equal the degree of denominator.

(*iii*) *For* $Z_{21}(s)$ *and* $Y_{21}(s)$*, the Maximum Degree of P(s) equals the degree of Q(s) plus one.* In order to study the properties of $Z_{21}(s)$ we make use of *T*-network of Fig. 10.8 (*a*) with a current source $I_1(s)$ connected to input port 1-1′ as shown in Fig. 10.9 (*a*). Similarly in order to study the properties of $Y_{21}(s)$, we make use of π-network of Fig. 10.8 (*b*) with a voltage source $V_1(s)$ connected to the input port 1-1′ as shown in Fig. 10.9 (*b*).

Now in Fig. 10.9 (*a*) with output terminals 2-2′ open, Z_3 may be shorted without affecting $Z_{12}(s)$. Then for the *T*-network of Fig. 10.9 (*a*) for the input current $I_1(s)$ at port 1, we get

$$Z_{21}(s) = \frac{V_2(s)}{I_1(s)} = \frac{Z_2(s) \cdot I_1(s)}{I_1(s)} = Z_2(s) \qquad \text{...(10.42)}$$

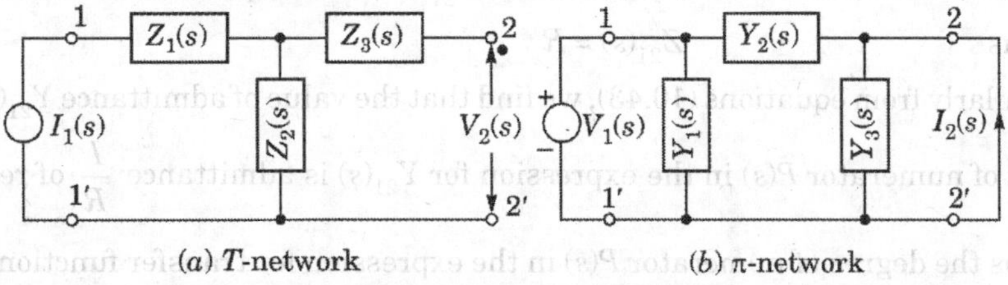

Fig. 10.9. *T*- and π-network structures representing a general two-port network.

Similarly in Fig. 10.9 (*b*) with output terminals 2-2′ short circuited, $Y_3(s)$ may be opened without affecting $Y_{21}(s)$. Then for the π-network of Fig. 10.9 (*b*) with the input voltage $V_1(s)$ at port 1, we get

$$Y_{21}(s) = \frac{I_2(s)}{V_1(s)} = \frac{-V_1(s) \cdot Y_2(s)}{V_1(s)} = -Y_2(s) \qquad \text{...(10.43)}$$

Equations (10.42) and (10.43) are dual. Hence the results obtained for any one, say $G_{21}(s)$ obtained using *T*-network of Fig. 10.9 (*a*) apply equals well to $Y_{21}(s)$ obtained on using π-network of Fig. 10.9 (*b*).

Now from Equation (10.42) we find that the value of impedance $Z_2(s)$ which maximises the degree of $P(s)$ in $Z_{21}(s)$ in impedance Ls of an inductor L. This is shown in Fig. 10.10 (*a*). Equation (10.42) then yields,

$$Z_{21}(s) = Z_2(s) = Ls \qquad \text{...(10.44)}$$

Similarly from equation (10.43) we find that the value of admittance $Y_2(s)$ which maximises the degree of numerator $P(s)$ in $Y_{21}(s)$ is admittance Cs of a capacitor C. This is shown in Fig. 10.10 (*b*). Equation (10.43) then yields,

$$Y_{21}(s) = -Y_2(s) = -Cs \qquad \text{...(10.45)}$$

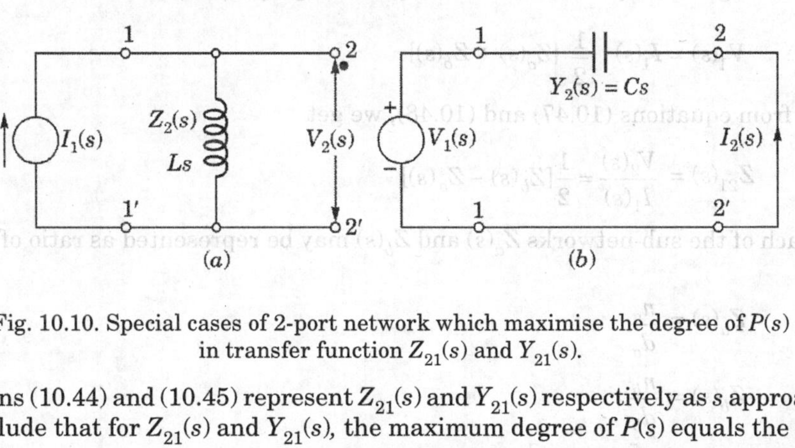

Fig. 10.10. Special cases of 2-port network which maximise the degree of $P(s)$ in transfer function $Z_{21}(s)$ and $Y_{21}(s)$.

Equations (10.44) and (10.45) represent $Z_{21}(s)$ and $Y_{21}(s)$ respectively as s approaches infinity. Hence we conclude that for $Z_{21}(s)$ and $Y_{21}(s)$, the maximum degree of $P(s)$ equals the degree of $Q(s)$ plus one.

(*iv*) *The degree of P(s) may be as small as zero and independent of the degree of Q(s).* Again we refer to equations (10.42) and (10.43) giving the expressions for $Z_{21}(s)$ and $Y_{21}(s)$ for a π-network and π-network equivalent circuits for general 2-port network.

From equations (10.42), we find that the value of impedance $Z_2(s)$ which minimises the degree of numerator $P(s)$ in the expression for $Z_{21}(s)$ is the impedance R of a resistor.

Thus $$Z_{21}(s) = R \qquad ...(10.46)$$

Similarly from equations (10.43), we find that the value of admittance $Y_{21}(s)$ which minimises the degree of numerator $P(s)$ in the expression for $Y_{21}(s)$ is admittance $\frac{I}{R}$ of resistor R.

Thus the degree of numerator $P(s)$ in the expression for transfer function $Z_{21}(s)$ and $Y_{21}(s)$ is zero irrespective of the degree of the denominator $Q(s)$.

It may be shown that the same is true for other transfer functions namely $G_{21}(s)$ *and* $\alpha_{21}(s)$.

(*v*) *Polynomial P(s) may have terms missing between the terms of lowest and highest degree and flow of the coefficients may be negative.* In order to establish this, we consider the symmetrical lattice network of Fig. 10.11 as representing the general 2-port network.

We apply current $I_1(s)$ at the input port 1. Then from Fig. 10.11 (*b*), we get

$$V_2(s) = V_1(s)\left[\frac{Z_b(s)}{Z_a(s)+Z_b(s)} - \frac{Z_a(s)}{Z_a(s)+Z_b(s)}\right] \qquad ...(10.47)$$

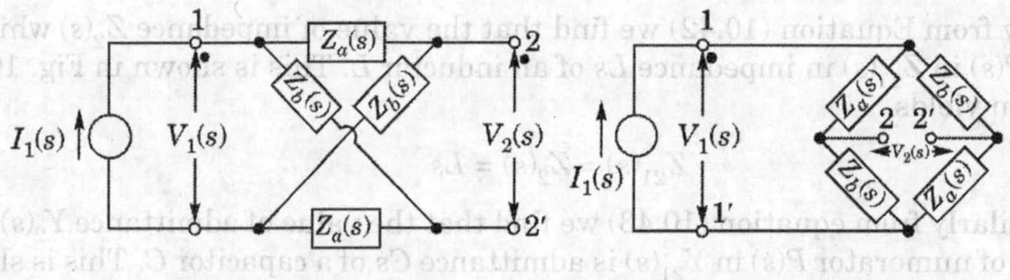

(*a*) Symmetrical lattice (*b*) Alternative arrangement

Fig. 10.11. Symmetrical lattice representing a general 2-port network.

But $$V_1(s) = I_1(s)\,.\,\frac{1}{2}\,[Z_a(s) + Z_b(s)] \qquad ...(10.48)$$

Hence from equations (10.47) and (10.48), we get

$$Z_{21}(s) = \frac{V_2(s)}{I_1(s)} = \frac{1}{2}[Z_b(s) - Z_a(s)] \qquad ...(10.49)$$

Now each of the sub-networks $Z_a(s)$ and $Z_b(s)$ may be represented as ratio of polynomials of s. Thus let

$$Z_a(s) = \frac{n_a}{d_a} \qquad ...(10.50)$$

and $$Z_b(s) = \frac{n_b}{d_b} \qquad ...(10.51)$$

Then $$Z_{21}(s) = \frac{1}{2}\left[\frac{n_b}{d_b} - \frac{n_a}{d_a}\right]$$

$$= \frac{1}{2}\left[\frac{n_b \cdot d_a - n_a \cdot d_b}{d_a \cdot d_b}\right] \qquad ...(10.52)$$

From equation (10.52) we conclude that the lowest possible degree in the numerator of $Z_{21}(s)$ may be zero. This situation corresponds to cancellation of all terms in s leaving only a constant term. This is the same property as *(iv)* established earlier using *T*-network form of equivalent circuit.

We also see from equation (10.52) that in the numerator polynomial of $Z_{21}(s)$, any term may be zero or negative. Similarly remark apply to other transfer functions.

(vi) The coefficients in the polynomial P(s) and Q(s) of N(s) = P(s) / Q(s) must be real and those of Q(s) must be positive. In similarly with the driving point functions the coefficients in the polynomials $P(s)$ and $Q(s)$ for transfer function $N(s)$ must be real. Further the coefficients in denominator polynomial $Q(s)$ must be positive. However the numerator polynomial $P(s)$ may have negative coefficients as seen from equation (10.52).

(vii) Poles and Zeros must be conjugate if imaginary or complex. This restriction for transfer functions is the same as in the case of driving point functions.

(viii) The polynomial Q(s) may not have any missing terms between the lowest and highest degree terms unless all even or all odd terms are missing. This restriction on denominator polynomial $Q(s)$ is the same as in the case of driving point functions.

The restrictions on the location of poles and zeros for transfer functions established above are summarised in Table 10.1.

Table 10.1

Restrictions on Pole and Zero Location in Transfer Functions

[With Common Factors in P(s) and Q(s) cancelled]

(i)	*(a)* The coefficients in the polynomials $P(s)$ and $Q(s)$ of $N(s) = P(s)/Q(s)$ must be real.
	(b) Coefficients in $Q(s)$ must be positive but some of the coefficients in $P(s)$ may be negative.
(ii)	Poles and zeros, if imaginary or complex, must be conjugate.
(iii)	*(a)* The real parts of poles must be zero or negative.
	(b) If the real part is zero (including the origin), then that pole must be simple (not multiple).
(iv)	The polynomial $Q(s)$ may not have any missing terms between the highest and the lowest degree terms, unless all even or all odd terms are missing.
(v)	The polynomial $P(s)$ may have terms missing between the lowest and highest degree terms.
(vi)	The degree of $P(s)$ may be as small as zero independent of the degree of $Q(s)$.
(vii)	For $G_{21}(s)$ and $\alpha_{21}(s)$, the maximum degree of $P(s)$ equals the degree of $Q(s)$.
(viii)	For $Z_{21}(s)$ and $Y_{21}(s)$, the maximum degree of $P(s)$ equals the degree of $Q(s)$ plus one.

10.9. Time Domain Response from Pole and Zero Plot

Pole and zero plot of a given network function gives useful information about the critical frequencies at which the network function is abnormal, *i.e.* either zero or infinite. At the same time, the time domain response of the given network may be assessed from the pole and zero plot of a network function and from the knowledge of the network sources. Thus let a driving voltage $V(s)$ be applied to a network having driving point admittance $Y(s)$. Then the resulting transform current $I(s)$ is given by,

$$I(s) = Y(s) \cdot V(s) = \frac{P(s)}{Q(s)} \qquad ...(10.53)$$

The ratio $P(s)/Q(s)$ may be put as,

$$\frac{P(s)}{Q(s)} = F \cdot \frac{(s - z_1)(s - z_2)......(s - z_n)}{(s - p_1)(s - p_2)......(s - p_m)} \quad ...(10.54)$$

We have seen earlier that the poles of this function determine the time-domain behaviour of the current $i(t)$. Further the zeros together with the poles and the scale factor F determine the magnitude of the each of terms of $i(t)$. This is elaborated here.

Let the damping ratio be ζ and the undamped natural frequency be ω_n for the given circuit. Then the poles and zeros of equation (10.54) expressed in terms of ζ and ω_n will have the following forms for different value of ζ.

$$s_1, s_2 = -\zeta\omega_n \pm j\omega_n\sqrt{1-\zeta^2} \quad \text{for } \zeta < 1 \quad ...(10.55)$$

$$s_1, s_2 = -\zeta\omega_n \pm \omega_n\sqrt{\zeta^2 - 1} \quad \text{for } \zeta > 1 \quad ...(10.56)$$

$$s_1, s_2 = -\omega_n \quad \text{for } \zeta = 1 \quad ...(10.57)$$

$$s_1, s_2 = \pm j\omega_n \quad \text{for } \zeta = 0 \quad ...(10.58)$$

Equation (10.55) gives the location of poles in the s-plane. For these poles, the time domain response in terms of ζ and ω_n is given by the following equation :

$$i(t) = K_1 \cdot e^{(-\zeta\omega_n + j\omega_n\sqrt{1-\zeta^2})t} + K_2 \cdot e^{(-\zeta\omega_n - j\omega_n\sqrt{1-\zeta^2})t} \quad ...(10.59)$$

$$= K_4 \cdot e^{-\zeta\omega_n t} \cdot \sin \omega_n\sqrt{1-\zeta^2}\, t \quad ...(10.60)$$

We also know that the contours of root s on the complex s-plane have the following properties for different values of parameters.

(*i*) For constant ω_n, the contours are circles of radius ω_n as shown in Fig. 10.12 (*a*).

(*ii*) For constant damping ratio ζ, contours are straight lines through the origin at angle $\theta = \cos^{-1}\zeta$ with negative real axis as shown in Fig. 10.12 (*b*).

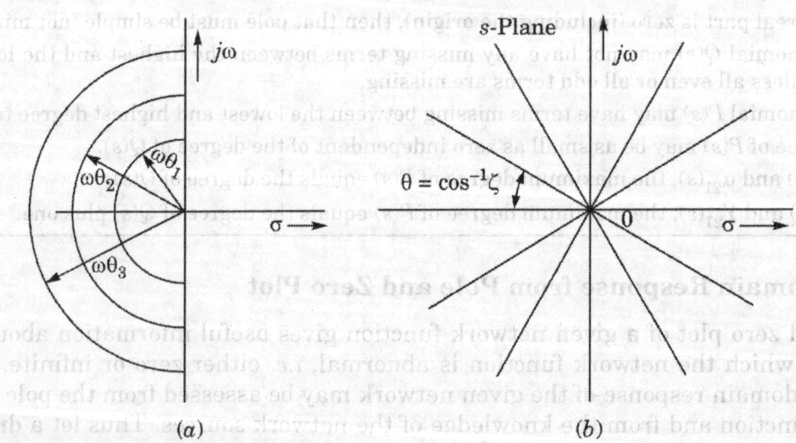

(*iii*) For constant damping $\zeta\omega_n$, contours are straight lines parallel to the $j\omega$ axis in the s-plane as shown in Fig. 10.12 (*c*).

(*iv*) For constant frequency $\omega_n\sqrt{1-\zeta^2}$, contours are straight lines parallel to the real axis in the s-plane as shown in Fig. 10.12 (*d*).

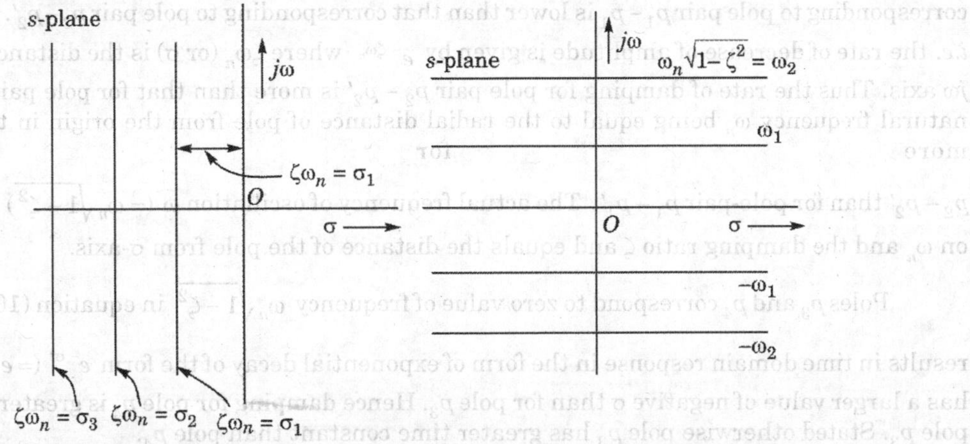

(c) Constant damping $\zeta\omega_n$ (d) Constant $\omega = \omega_n\sqrt{1-\zeta^2}$

Fig. 10.12. Contours of root s for constant parameter values in the s-plane.

In order to grasp the significance of these contours, let us consider the poles shown in Fig. 10.13. No zeros are included here for

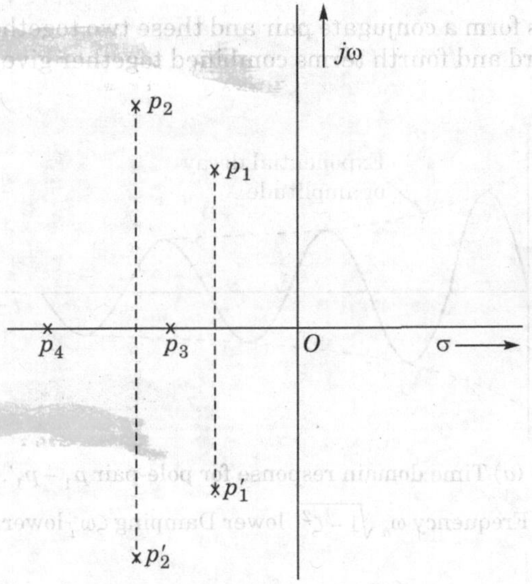

Fig. 10.13. An array of poles.

the sake of clarity. These sets of poles are consistent with the restrictions on the location of poles and zeros. Thus poles p_1 and p_1' constitute one conjugate pair. Similarly poles p_2 and p_2 constitute another pair. p_3 and p_4 form the remaining poles.

Now pair of poles p_1 and p_1' signify time domain response of the type given by equation (10.60). This response is in the form of a damped sinusoidal oscillation of frequency $\omega_n\sqrt{1-\zeta^2}$ which is the height of pole p_1 from σ-axis. Similarly the pair of poles p_2 and p_2' signify time domain response in the form of another damped oscillation of frequency equal to the height of the pole p_2 above the σ-axis. Evidently for the locations for poles chosen in Fig. 10.13, the frequency of oscillation corresponding to pole pair $p_1 - p_1$ is lower than that corresponding to pole pair $p_2 - p_2'$. The damping, *i.e.* the rate of decrease of amplitude is given by $e^{-\zeta\omega_n}$ where $\zeta\omega_n$ (or σ) is the distance of pole from $j\omega$ axis. Thus the rate of damping for pole pair $p_2 - p_2'$ is more than that for pole pair $p_1 - p_1'$. The natural frequency ω_n being equal to the radial distance of pole from the origin in the s-plane, is more for pole-pair $p_2 - p_2'$ than for pole-pair $p_1 - p_1'$. The actual frequency of oscillation ω $(= \omega_n\sqrt{1-\zeta^2})$ depends both on ω_n and the damping ratio ζ and equals the distance of the pole from σ-axis.

Poles p_3 and p_4 correspond to zero value of frequency $\omega_n\sqrt{1-\zeta^2}$ in equation (10.60) and each results in time domain response in the form of exponential decay of the form $e^{-\sigma t}$ $(= e^{-\zeta\omega_n t})$. Pole p_4 has a larger value of negative σ than for pole p_3. Hence damping for pole p_4 is greater than that for pole p_3. Stated otherwise pole p_3 has greater time constant than pole p_4.

The time domain response of each of the four poles (or pole pairs) for the poles of Fig. 10.13 is shown in Fig. 10.14 for arbitary amplitude of each response.

The total time domain response corresponding to the poles in Fig. 10.13 is obtained by adding these individual responses. Thus the total response is,

$$i(t) = K_1.e^{p_1 t} + K_2.e^{p_1' t} + K_3.e^{p_2 t} + K_4.e^{p_2' t} + K_5.e^{p_3 t} + K_6.e^{p_4 t} \quad ...(10.61)$$

Then first two terms form a conjugate pair and these two together give a damped sinusoidal response. Similarly the third and fourth terms combined together give another damped sinusoidal response.

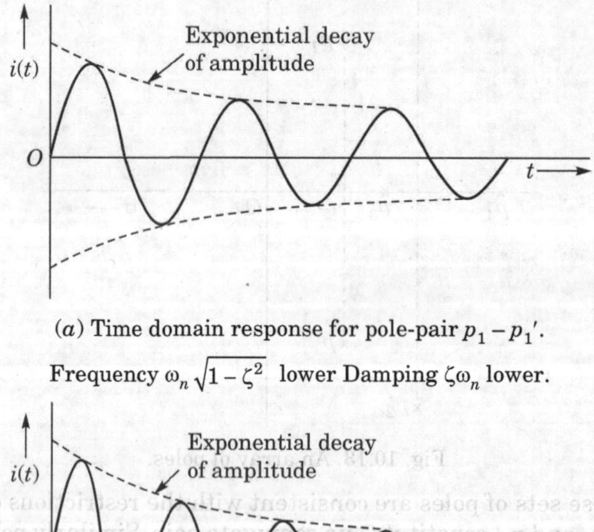

(*a*) Time domain response for pole-pair $p_1 - p_1'$.

Frequency $\omega_n\sqrt{1-\zeta^2}$ lower Damping $\zeta\omega_n$ lower.

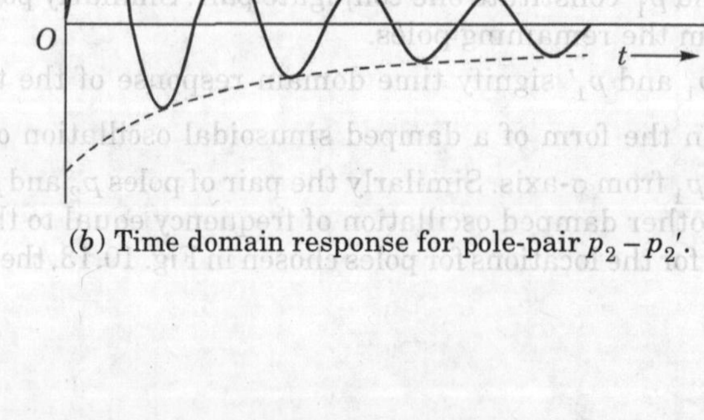

(*b*) Time domain response for pole-pair $p_2 - p_2'$.

Frequency $\omega_n \sqrt{1-\zeta^2}$ higher Damping $\zeta\omega_n$ higher.

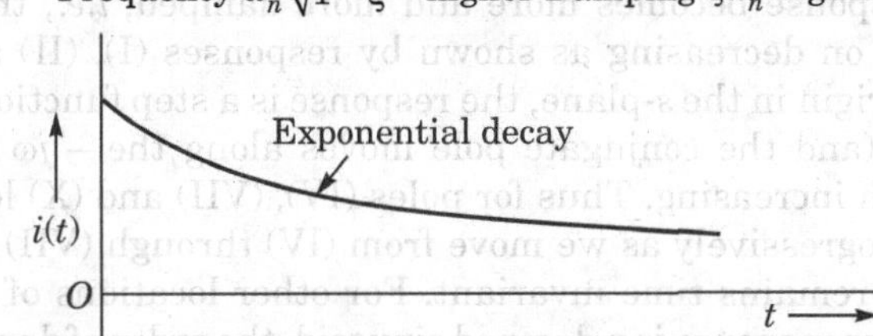

(*c*) Time domain response for pole p_3. Frequency σ (= $\zeta\omega_n$) lower.

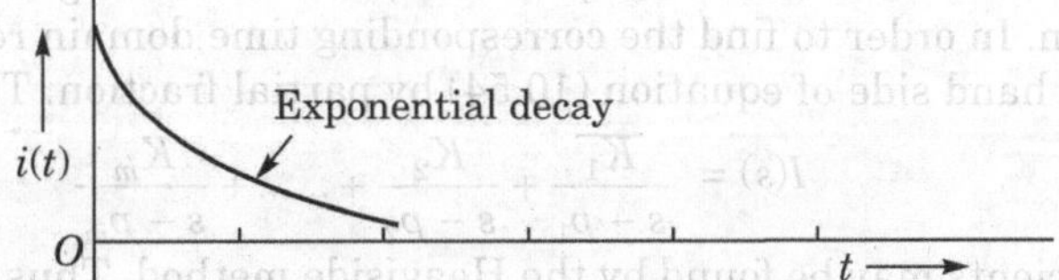

(*d*) Time domain response for pole p_4. Damping σ (= $\zeta\omega_n$) higher.

Fig. 10.14. Time domain response corresponding to poles (or pole pairs) of Fig. 10.13.

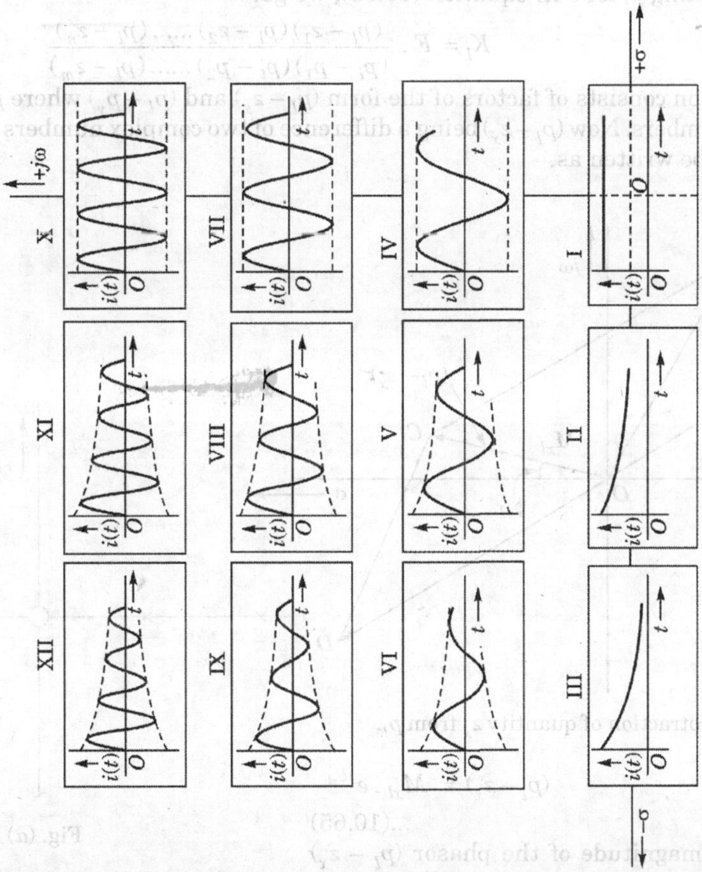

Fig. 10.15. Time domain response as dependent on the location of pole.

Poles lying on the σ-axis result in exponential response. As the pole moves more and more along the – σ axis, the response becomes more and more damped, *i.e.*, the time constant of the exponential response goes on decreasing as shown by responses (I), (II) and (III) shown in Fig. 10.15. For the pole at the origin in the *s*-plane, the response is a step function as shown As the pole moves along they *jω* axis (and the conjugate pole moves along the – *jω* axis), the frequency of sinusoidal response goes on increasing. Thus for poles (IV), (VII) and (X) located on the + *jω* axis, the frequency increases progressively as we move from (IV) through (VII) to (X). But since σ = 0, the amplitude of response remains time invariant. For other locations of poles namely (V), (VI), (VIII), (IX), (XI) and (XII), the response is a damped sinusoid, the order of damping and the frequency of sinusoid depending upon the location of pole.

Magnitude of terms in time domain response. Equation (10.54) gives the network function $I(s)$ in frequency domain. In order to find the corresponding time domain response, we expand the expression on the right hand side of equation (10.54) by partial fraction. Thus we get,

$$I(s) = \frac{K_1}{s - p_1} + \frac{K_2}{s - p_2} + ... + \frac{K_m}{s - p_m} \quad ...(10.62)$$

Any of the coefficients may be found by the Heaviside method. Thus the coefficient K_l of the *l*th factor is given by,

$$K_l = F\left[\frac{(s - z_1)(s - z_2) ...... (s - z_n)}{(s - p_1)(s - p_2) ...... (s - p_m)} . (s - p_l)\right]_{s = + p_l} \quad ...(10.63)$$

On substituting p_l for s in equation (10.63), we get

$$K_l = F . \frac{(p_l - z_1)(p_l - z_2) ...... (p_l - z_n)}{(p_l - p_1)(p_l - p_2) ...... (p_l - z_m)} \quad ...(10.64)$$

This equation consists of factors of the form $(p_l - z_x)$ and $(p_l - p_y)$ where p_l, p_y and z_x are all known complex numbers. Now $(p_l - z_x)$ being a difference of two complex numbers is another complex number and may be written as,

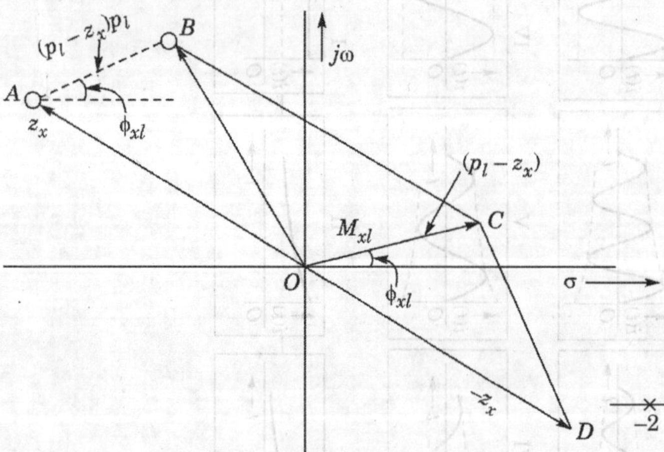

Fig. 10.16. Subtraction of quantity z_x from p_l.

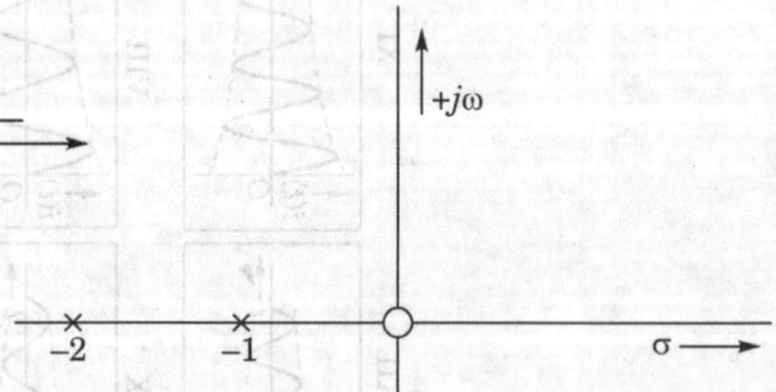

$$(p_l - z_x) = M_{xl} . e^{j\phi_{xl}} \quad ...(10.65)$$

Fig. (*a*)

where M_{xl} is the magnitude of the phasor $(p_l - z_x)$

and ϕ_{xl} is the phase angle of the same phasor. Similarly each factor $(p_l - p_y)$ in the denominator of equation (10.64) being a difference of two complex numbers, is another complex number and may be written as,

$$(p_l - p_y) = Q_{yl} \cdot e^{j\theta_{yl}} \qquad ..(10.66)$$

where Q_{yl} is the magnitude of the phasor $(p_l - p_y)$ and θ_{yl} is the phase angle of the same phasor.

Fig. 10.16 shows the difference of two complex quantities p_l and z_x in the s-plane. It may be readily seen that the difference $(p_l - z_x)$ is nothing but a phasor AB directed from z_x to p_l. The magnitude M_{xl} of this phasor is the distance from z_x to p_l while the phase along ϕ_{xl} is the angle of the line from z_x to p_l measured with respect to $\sigma = 0$ line. Similar remarks apply to phasor Q_{yl}.

Thus each factor in equation (10.64) may be expressed in terms of its magnitude and phase angle. Hence equation (10.64) may be written as,

$$K_l = F \cdot \frac{M_{1l} \cdot M_{2l} \cdot M_{3l} \, ... \, M_{nl}}{Q_{1l} \cdot Q_{2l} \cdot Q_{3l} \, ... \, Q_{ml}} \times e^{j[(\phi_{1l} + \phi_{2l} + ... + \phi_{nl}) - (\theta_{1l} + \theta_{2l} + ... \theta_{ml})]} \qquad ...(10.67)$$

Equation (10.67) gives the magnitude and phase angle of the coefficient K_l. Thus all the coefficients from K_1 to K_m may be evaluated by this technique.

Magnitudes M_{1l}, M_{2l} ...... and Q_{1l}, Q_{2l} ...... may be easily measured from a plot of poles and zeros on the s-plane.

Similarly, the phase angles ϕ_{1l}, ϕ_{2l} ...... and θ_{1l}, θ_{2l} ...... may also be measured from the plot of poles and zeros on the s-plane.

Thus the method of evaluating a network function say $I(s)$ as given by equation (10.62), using the poles and zeros consists in the following :

(*i*) Plot to scale on the s-plane, the poles and zeros of the network function $I(s) = P(s)/Q(x)$.

(*ii*) Measure or calculate the distances Q_{1l}, Q_{2l} ...... Q_{ml} of a given pole say p_l from each of the other finite poles.

(*iii*) Similarly measure or calculate the distances M_{1l}, M_{2l} ...... M_{nl} of the same pole p_l from each of the zeros.

(*iv*) Measure or calculate the angle of the line joining that pole p_l to each of the other finite poles and the zeros, giving

$$\theta_{1l}, \theta_{2l} \, ... \, \theta_{ml} \text{ and } \phi_{1l}, \phi_{2l}, \, ... \, \phi_{nl}.$$

(*v*) Substitute these quantities in equation (10.67) to evaluate K_l.

(*vi*) Similarly evaluate each of the coefficients from K_1 to K_m and substitute these values in equation (10.62) to evaluate the given network function $I(s)$.

Example 10.10. *Let the transform current I(s) in a network be given by the following equation:*

$$I(s) = \frac{2s}{(s+1)(s+2)}.$$

Plot the poles and zeros in the s-plane and hence obtain the time domain response.

Solution. Evidently the function has poles at – 1 and – 2 and a zero at the origin. The plot of poles and zeros is as shown in Fig. (*a*).

The function can be easily expanded by partial fractions and then the time domain response $i(t)$ may be found. But the time domain value $i(t)$ can also be evaluated using the plot of poles and zeros on s-plane.

Since factors $(s + 1)$ and $(s + 2)$ appear in the denominator polynomial, the time domain response will be,

$$i(t) = K_1 . e^{-t} + K_2.e^{-2}t \quad ...(1)$$

The coefficients K_1 and K_2 may be evaluated from the pole-zero plot. Thus for the plot of poles and zeros as given in Fig. (*a*), we get

$$M_{01} = 1 \text{ and } \qquad \phi_{01} = 180°$$

$$Q_{21} = 1 \text{ and } \qquad \theta_{21} = 0°.$$

Hence $$K_1 = F.\frac{M_{01} . e^{j\phi_{01}}}{Q_{2l} . e^{j\theta_{2l}}} = 2.\frac{e^{j180°}}{e^{j0°}} = 2e^{j180°} = -2.$$

Similarly, $$M_{02} = 2 \text{ and } \quad \phi_{02} = 180°$$

$$Q_{12} = 1 \text{ and } \qquad \theta_{12} = 180°.$$

$$K_2 = F.\frac{M_{02} . e^{j\phi_{02}}}{Q_{12} . e^{j\theta_{12}}} = 2\frac{2e^{j180°}}{1e^{j180°}} = 4.$$

Substituting the values of coefficients K_1 and K_2 into equation (1), we get

$$i(t) = -2e^{-t} + 4 . e^{-2t}.$$

10.10. Criterion for Stability of Active Network in terms of Root Locus Plot

So far, we have considered only passive network, *i.e.* networks containing no active elements. Such passive networks are stable, *i.e.*, have no poles on the right half of the *s*-plane. On the other hand, *active networks, i.e.* networks containing one or more controlled (or dependent) energy sources *are not always stable.* We proceed to determine the condition under which an active network is stable. This can be best done considering a typical active network. Fig. 10.17 shows an active network containing one controlled source of voltage KV_2, where K is a positive constant.

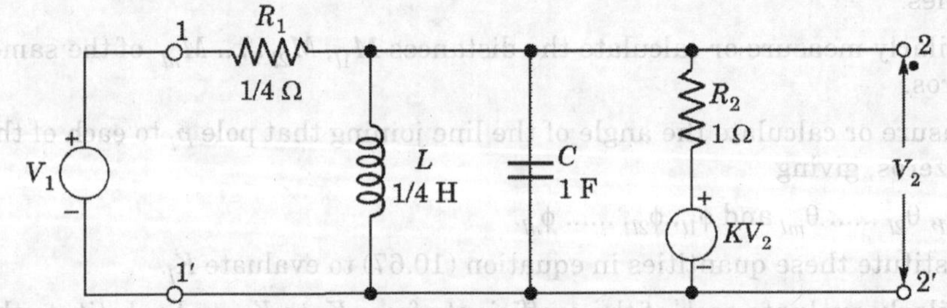

Fig. 10.17. Network with controlled source.

Corresponding transform network is as given in Fig. 10.18.

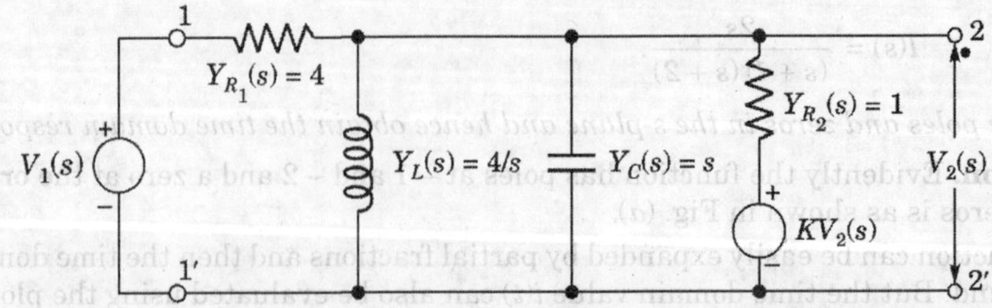

Fig. 10.18. Transform network corresponding to the network of Fig. 10.17.

Applying Millman Theorem to the circuit between nodes 2 and 2′, we get

$$V_2(s) = \frac{4 . V_1(s) + K . V_2(s)}{4 + \frac{4}{s} + s + 1} \quad ...(10.68)$$

or $$V_2(s)\left[s + 5 + \frac{4}{s}\right] = 4.V_1(s) + K.V_2(s)$$

or $$V_2(s)\left[s + (5 - K) + \frac{4}{s}\right] = 4 . V_1(s).$$

Hence $$G_{21}(s) = \frac{V_2(s)}{V_1(s)} = \frac{4}{s + (5 - K) + \frac{4}{s}} = 4 . \frac{s}{s^2 + (5 - K)s + 4} \quad ...(10.69)$$

From equation (10.69) we conclude that (*i*) there is a zero at the origin and (*ii*) the location of poles depends on the value of K.

Equations (10.69) may be put as,

$$G_{21}(s) = F . \frac{P(s)}{Q(s)} \quad ...(10.70)$$

where $$F = 4, P(s) = s$$

and $$Q(s) = s^2 + (5 - K)s + 4$$

Consider the roots of the equation

$$S + (5 - K)s + 4 = 0 \quad ...(10.71)$$

The roots are,

$$s = \frac{-(5-K)}{2} \pm \frac{1}{2}\sqrt{(5-K)^2 - 4 \times 4} \quad ...(10.72)$$

when $$K = 0,$$

$$s = -\frac{5}{2} \pm \frac{3}{2}$$

or $$s = -1, -4 \quad ...(10.73)$$

Thus for $K = 0$, *i.e.* with no controlled source, the poles of the network function $G_{21}(s)$, being -1 and -4, lie in the left half of the s-plane.

However as K increases, the poles move towards each other meeting at $\sqrt{(5-K)^2 - 16} = 0$, *i.e.* when $5 - K = \pm 4$. Taking the positive sign, the poles meet when $K = \pm 1$. In this case, the roots are -2 each.

Fig. 10.19 gives the locus of the roots of equation $Q(s) = 0$, *i.e.* equation (10.17). This plot called the *root locus plot* is extremely useful in the study of systems.

We see from this root locus plot that as K increases beyond the value 1, the locus of root is a circle. The poles are located on the imaginary axis at $+ j2$ and $- j2$ when $K = 5$. For value of K exceeding 5, the poles move into the positive half of the s-plane moving along the circle of radius 2 and centre at the origin. The poles meet each other again when $5 - K = -4$, *i.e.* when $K = 9$. In this case, the roots are $+ 2$ each.

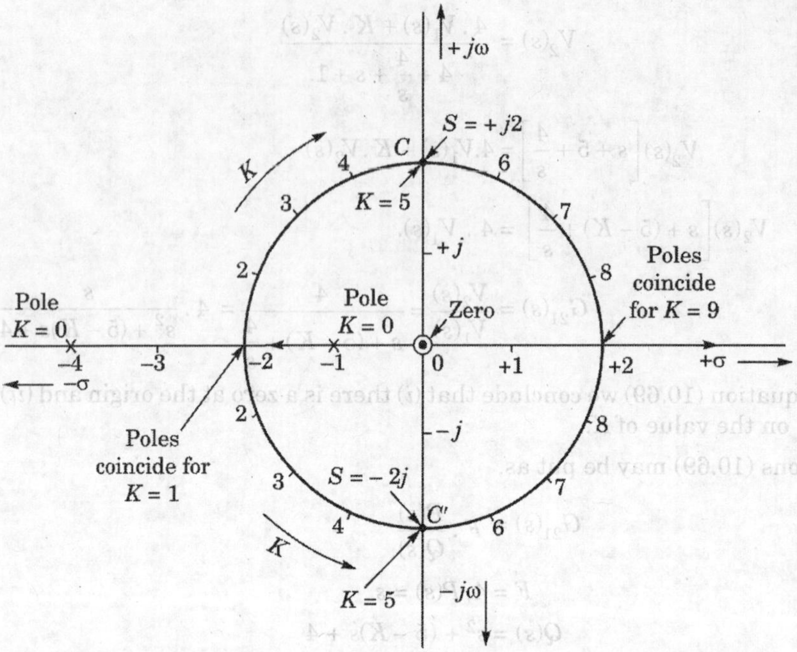

Fig. 10.19. Locus of the poles of the transfer function $G(s)$ as increases from 0 to infinity.

For $K > +9$, the poles again lie on the real axis but remain in the right half of the s-plane—one pole moving towards the origin and the other moving towards infinity.

Now as long as K is less than 5, the poles lie in the left half of the s-plane and the network is stable. At points C and C' in Fig. 10.19, the poles lie on the imaginary axis and the network is oscillatory in nature with no decay of amplitude. For values of K exceeding 5, the poles lie in the right half of the s-plane so that the network is unstable.

Thus as the poles move across the imaginary axis forming the critical boundary, the network passes from stable state to unstable state. Once the poles cross the imaginary axis, the network becomes unstable.

Stable System. Any active network or any general system is said to be stable if the transfer function has its poles confined to the left half of the s-plane and the imaginary axis. Thus if an active network oscillates with constant amplitude corresponding to the case of poles lying on the imaginary axis, it may be said to be stable.

Strictly Stable System. Any active network or any general system is said to be strictly stable if the transfer function has its poles confined to the left half of the s-plane only excluding the imaginary axis.

Thus a strictly stable active network excludes even the state of oscillation with constant amplitude with poles on the imaginary axis.

With reference to the responses shown in Fig. 10.15, requirement for a stable system is that *a bounded input must result in a bounded output*.

Accordingly in a stable network, any bounded input should not result in output of the form $t, t^2, e^t, t \sin \omega t, t \cos \omega t$ etc.

From Fig. 10.19 we see that the network of Fig. 10.17 is strictly stable for $K < 5$ and is stable for $K < 5$. With $K = 5$, the network oscillates with constant amplitude and with frequency ω_n equal to 2. For $K > 5$, the network oscillates with amplitude which continuously increases with time.

10.11. Criterion for Stability in Terms of Denominator Polynomial of Transfer Function : Routh Criterion

We have just seen that the locations of poles govern the stability of an active network. We may study the requirements of denominator polynomial $Q(s)$ of the transfer function.

Let the denominator polynomial be,

$$Q(s) = b_0 s^m + b_1 \cdot s^{m-1} + \ldots\ldots + b_m \quad \ldots(10.74)$$

Stability criterion then requires that the roots of equation $Q(s) = 0$ should not have positive (or zero) real parts. It may be readily seen that even if all the coefficients in $Q(s)$ are real and positive, some of the roots of equation $Q(s) = 0$ may have positive real parts. Thus consider the following polynomial :

$$Q(s) = (s + 3)(s^2 - s + 10) = s^3 + 2s^2 + 7s + 10 \quad \ldots(10.75)$$

All the coefficients in this polynomial are real and positive but inspite of this two of the roots have positive real parts.

We thus conclude that for stability of an active network it is not sufficient that all the coefficients of the denominator polynomial $Q(s)$ be real and positive.

We, therefore, look for the condition of the denominator polynomial which is both necessary and adequate for stability.

We revert to the study of equation $Q(s) = 0$. On factorisation this may be written as,

$$b_0(s - p_1)(s - p_2) \ldots\ldots (s - p_m) = 0 \quad \ldots(10.76)$$

On multiplication, these factors yield,

$$\begin{aligned} Q(s) = b_0 s^m &- b_0(p_1 + p_2 + \ldots\ldots + p_m) s^{m-1} \\ &+ b_0(p_1 p_2 + p_2 p_3 + \ldots\ldots) s^{m-2} \\ &- b_0(p_1 p_2 p_3 + p_2 p_3 p_4 + \ldots\ldots) s^{m-3} \\ &\ldots\ldots \quad \ldots\ldots \quad \ldots\ldots \\ &+ b_0(-1)^m p_1 p_2 \ldots\ldots p_m = 0 \end{aligned} \quad \ldots(10.77)$$

Equating the coefficients in Eq. (10.77) to those in Eq. (10.74), we get

$$\frac{b_1}{b_0} = -(p_1 + p_2 + \ldots p_m) = -\text{ Sum of the roots} \quad \ldots(10.78)$$

$$\frac{b_2}{b_0} = (p_1 p_2 + p_2 p_3 + \ldots\ldots)$$

$$= \text{Sum of the products of roots taken two at a time} \quad \ldots(10.79)$$

$$\frac{b_3}{b_0} = -(p_1 p_2 p_3 + p_2 p_3 p_4 + \ldots\ldots)$$

$$= \text{Sum of the products of roots taken three at a time} \quad \ldots(10.80)$$

and so on.

Finally $\frac{b_m}{b_0} = (-1)^m$ product of roots ...(10.81)

Now if all the roots p_1, p_2 etc. have negative real parts, then from Eqs. (10.78) to (10.81), it becomes clear that all the coefficients of Eq. (10.74) must have the same sign. Thus 'all coefficients having the same sign' forms a necessary condition for all roots to have negative real parts but it does not form a sufficient condition as seen from Eq. (10.75). We further see that *none of coefficients can have zero value* because zero value of a coefficient involves cancellation which in turn requires some root to have positive real parts.

We, therefore, look for the condition of the coefficients which is *both necessary and sufficient* for the roots to have negative real parts, *i.e.* the condition of the coefficients for stability.

Although the theory of stability of an active system was developed independently by various scientists and engineers such as Routh, Lyapunov, Hurwitz, Lienard, Chipart and Nyquist, the criterion for stability described below is usually called *Routh criterion of stability* and sometimes called *Routh Hurwitz criterion.*

The following steps are involved in applying the criterion.

Step I. This consists in picking up from the complete polynomial $Q(s)$, even numbered coefficients namely b_0, b_2, b_4 etc. forming one row and then picking up odd numbered coefficients namely b_1, b_3, b_5 etc. forming the second row. This is shown below :

First row of coefficients

$$Q(s) = b_0.s^m + b_1.s^{m-1} + b_2.s^{m-2} + b_3.s^{m-3} + b_4.s^{m-4} + b_5.s^{m-5} + \ldots\ldots\ldots$$

Second row of coefficients

These two rows of coefficients are arranged as below :

$$\left.\begin{array}{lllll} b_0 & b_2 & b_4 & b_6 & b_8\ldots \\ b_1 & b_3 & b_5 & b_7 & b_9\ldots \end{array}\right\} \begin{array}{l}\ldots\ldots \\ \ldots\ldots\end{array} \quad \ldots(10.83)$$

Step II. Complete the Routh-Hurwitz array (also sometimes called schedule or scheme).

For $m = 7$, the array is given by (10.84). This consists of $(m + 1)$, *i.e.* 8 rows. The first and the second rows are the same as given by (10.83).

$$\begin{array}{l|llll} s^7 & b_0 & b_2 & b_4 & b_6 \\ s^6 & b_1 & b_3 & b_5 & b_7 \\ s^5 & c_1 & c_3 & c_5 & \\ s^4 & d_1 & d_3 & d_5 & \\ s^3 & e_1 & e_3 & & \\ s^2 & f_1 & f_3 & & \\ s & g_1 & & & \\ s_0 & h_1 & & & \end{array} \quad \ldots(10.84)$$

The *c, d, e, f, g, h* entries in (10.84) are determined by the algorithm given below :

$$c_1 = \frac{\begin{vmatrix} b_0 & b_2 \\ b_1 & b_3 \end{vmatrix}}{b_1} = \frac{b_1 b_2 - b_0 b_3}{b_1} \quad \text{...(10.85)}$$

$$c_3 = \frac{\begin{vmatrix} b_0 & b_4 \\ b_1 & b_5 \end{vmatrix}}{b_1} = \frac{b_1 b_4 - b_0 b_5}{b_1} \quad \text{...(10.86)}$$

$$c_5 = \frac{\begin{vmatrix} b_0 & b_6 \\ b_1 & b_7 \end{vmatrix}}{b_1} = \frac{b_1 b_6 - b_0 b_7}{b_1} \quad \text{...(10.87)}$$

$$d_1 = \frac{\begin{vmatrix} b_1 & b_3 \\ c_1 & c_3 \end{vmatrix}}{c_1} = \frac{c_1 b_3 - c_3 b_1}{c_1} \quad \text{...(10.88)}$$

$$d_3 = \frac{\begin{vmatrix} b_1 & b_5 \\ c_1 & c_5 \end{vmatrix}}{c_1} = \frac{c_1 b_5 - c_5 b_1}{c_1} \quad \text{...(10.89)}$$

$$d_5 = \frac{\begin{vmatrix} b_1 & b_7 \\ c_1 & 0 \end{vmatrix}}{c_1} = \frac{c_1 b_7 - 0}{c_1} = b_7 \quad \text{..(10.90)}$$

and so on.

The algorithm is applied as below to give the Eqs. (10.85) to (10.90).

In order to determine any element in say the Kth row jth column of the array (10.84), we use four other elements of the two rows directly above this element, *i.e.* in row numbers $(K-1)$ and $(K-2)$. Out of these 4 elements 2 belong the column of the array, one from row No. $(K-1)$ and the other from row No. $(K-2)$. The remaining 2 elements belong to the column to the immediate right of the element, *i.e.* column No. $(j+1)$. These 4 elements then form a determinant like structure as given in Eqs. (10.85) to (10.90). The product of elements joined by a line with positive slope is given a positive sign while the product of elements joined by a line with negative slope is given a negative sign. The difference of these products is divided by the element of column 1 and row $(K-1)$. This process is repeated until we complete all the $(n+1)$ rows.

Step III. **Application of Criterion.** *The Routh-Hurwitz theorem states that the number of changes in the sign of the first column to the right of the vertical line in Routh Hurwitz array moving from top to bottom is equal to the number of roots of Q (s) = 0 with positive real parts.* But for a system to be stable, the roots of $Q(s) = 0$ must not have positive real parts.

Accordingly Routh-Hurwitz criterion for stability states that a network of system is stable, if and only if, there are no changes of sign in the first column of the Routh-Hurwitz array for the denominator polynomial $Q(s)$ of the transfer function describing the given network. This requirement is both necessary as well as sufficient for stability.

Now regarding the first column of the array, the following 3 possibilities exist.

Case (*i*) All the elements of first column are non-zero.

Case (*ii*) One or more elements of first column are zero but the remaining elements of the row containing a zero in the first column are non-zero.

Case (*iii*) One or more elements in the first column are zero and simultaneously all other remaining elements in the row containing this zero in the first column are also zero.

Following solved examples deal with all the three cases mentioned above.

Case I. Let the denominator polynomial of a transfer-function be given by

$$Q(s) = s^3 + 9s^2 + 26s + 4 \quad ...(10.91)$$

It is required to form the Routh array and verify the stability of the network.

The Routh array for the denominator polynomial is as below

$$\begin{array}{c|cc} s^3 & 1 & 26 \\ s^2 & 9 & 4 \\ s^1 & \frac{230}{9} & \\ s^0 & 4 & \end{array} \quad ...(10.92)$$

We see that there is no change in the sign of the elements in the first column of the array. Hence from Routh theorem, we conclude that there are no roots with positive real parts.

This may be verified by factorising the polynomial. Thus on factorisation, we get

$$Q(s) = s^3 + 9s^2 + 26s + 4 = (s + 2)(s + 3)(s + 4) \quad ...(10.93)$$

Hence the roots of the equation $Q(s) = 0$ are – 2, –3 and – 4. This agrees with the result obtained above by application of Routh criterion.

Case II. Let the denominator polynomial of a transfer function for a network be,

$$Q(s) = s^4 + s^3 + 3s^2 + 3s + 4 \quad ...(10.94)$$

It is required to form the Routh array and find the number of roots of equation $Q(s) = 0$ which have positive real parts.

The Routh array for this polynomial is as below :

$$\begin{array}{c|ccc} s^4 & 1 & 3 & 4 \\ s^3 & 1 & 3 & \\ s^2 & \alpha & 4 & \\ s^1 & 3 - \frac{4}{\alpha} & & \\ s^0 & 4 & & \end{array} \quad ...(10.95)$$

In this case the element of the first column, third row comes out to be zero but no other element in this third row is zero. With this element as zero, it becomes impossible to proceed further with forming the array. To overcome this difficulty, we replace the zero with the small quantity α as shown and then complete the array.

Now for small value of α, the fourth element of the first column becomes negative. Thus there are two changes of sign in the first column indicating that there are two roots of the equation $Q(s) = 0$ which have positive real parts.

Case III. Consider the following denominator polynomial of a transfer function for a network :

$$Q(s) = s^3 + 3s^2 + 3s + A \quad ...(10.96)$$

where A is adjustable.

The Routh array is as below :

$$\begin{array}{c|cc} s^3 & 1 & 3 \\ s^2 & 3 & A \\ s^1 & \dfrac{9-A}{3} & \\ s^0 & A & \end{array} \qquad ...(10.97)$$

From the study of the first column of this array, we see that the system is stable for $A < 9$ but is unstable for $A > 9$. Consider the case when $A = 9$. For $A = 9$, the Routh array (10.96) reduces to the following form :

$$\begin{array}{c|cc} s^3 & 1 & 3 \\ s^2 & 3 & 9 \\ s^1 & 0 & \\ s^0 & ? & \end{array} \qquad ...(10.98)$$

In this case, the entire third row has vanished and it becomes impossible to complete the array for the fourth row.

This difficulty can be overcome as below :

Let the index of the vanishing row be s^{r+1} and let the previous row of index s^r have non-zero elements $f_1, f_2, f_3, ...$

Let $$Q_1(s) = f_1 s^r + f_2 s^{r-2} + ... \qquad ...(10.99)$$

Then it may be shown that the polynomial $Q(s)$ contains the polynomial $Q_1(s)$. Then $Q(s)$ may be put as,

$$Q(s) = Q_1(s) \cdot Q_2(s) \qquad ...(10.100)$$

Knowing $Q(s)$ and $Q_1(s)$ we may find out $Q_2(s)$. We then apply Routh criterion to $Q_2(s)$.

In the given case, from the study of array (10.97),

$$Q_1(s) = 3s^2 + 9 = 3\,(s^2 + 3) \qquad ...(10.101)$$

Hence $$Q_2(s) = \frac{Q(s)}{Q_1(s)} = \frac{s^3 + 3s^2 + 3s + 9}{3(s^2 + 3)} = \frac{1}{3}(s + 3) \qquad ...(10.102)$$

Now the polynomial $Q_2(s)$, *i.e.* $\frac{1}{3}(s + 3)$ may be tested by inspection. The root is $s = -3$. The root of equation $Q_1(s) = 0$ are $s = \pm\sqrt{3}j$. These two roots are located on the imaginary axis which forms the boundary between stability and instability.

Of course, the array $Q(s)$ in this case could have been tested for stability using the method used in case (II). The method just outlined becomes essential whenever a row of two or more elements consists of zeros.

Example 10.11. *The denominator polynomial of a transfer function in given by,*

$$Q(s) = s^3 + s^2 + 2s + 24$$

Form the Routh array and verify the stability of the network.

Solution. The Routh array for this polynomial is as below :

$$\begin{array}{c|cc} s^3 & 1 & 2 \\ s^2 & 1 & 24 \\ s^1 & -22 & \\ s^0 & +24 & \end{array}$$

There are two changes in the sign of the elements in the first column, one from 1 to – 22 and the other from – 22 to 24. Hence there are two roots of equation $Q(s) = 0$ which have positive real parts. Hence the network is not stable.

Example 10.12. *The denominator polynomial of transfer function for a network is as below :*

$$Q(s) = s^4 + s^3 + 2s^2 + 2s + 12$$

Form the Routh array and verify for stability of the network.

Solution. The Routh array for this polynomial is as below :

$$\begin{array}{c|ccc} s^4 & 1 & 2 & 12 \\ s^3 & 1 & 2 & \\ s^2 & \alpha & 12 & \\ s^1 & 2 - \dfrac{12}{\alpha} & & \\ s^0 & 12 & & \end{array}$$

The element in the first column and third row is zero. But it may be put as α, where α is a very small number almost equal to zero. Hence the element $\left(2 - \dfrac{12}{\alpha}\right)$ is a negative number. Thus there are two changes in the sign of elements of first column. Hence there are two roots of equation $Q(s) = 0$ which have positive real parts. Hence the network is not stable.

Example 10.13. *The denominator polynomial of transfer function for a network is as below :*

$$Q(s) = s^3 + 2s^2 + 3s + A$$

where A is adjustable. Find the values of A for which the network is stable.

Solution. For the given polynomial, the Routh array is as below :

$$\begin{array}{c|cc} s^3 & 1 & 3 \\ s^2 & 2 & A \\ s^1 & \dfrac{6-A}{2} & \\ s^0 & A & \end{array}$$

From the study of the first column of this array, we see that when $A < 6$ term $\dfrac{6-A}{2}$ is positive and all terms in the first column are positive, *i.e.* there are no changes in signs of these elements. Hence the system is stable. When $A > 6$, term $\frac{6-A}{2}$ becomes negative so that there are two changes in the signs of the elements in the first column. Hence there are roots of equation $Q(s) = 0$ which have positive real parts. Hence the system is unstable.

When $A = 6$, the Routh array is as follows :

$$\begin{array}{c|cc} s^3 & 1 & 3 \\ s^2 & 2 & 6 \\ s^1 & \alpha & \\ s^0 & 6 & \end{array}$$

where α is a very small number almost equal to zero and is put instead of zero. In this case also, we find that there are no changes in the sign of the elements in the first column. Hence the system is stable.

Example 10.14. *Apply Routh criterion to the following equation and determine the number of roots (i) with positive real parts (ii) with zero real parts and (iii) with negative real parts*

$$s^2 + 6s^5 + 18s^4 + 38s^3 + 47s^2 + 52s + 30 = 0.$$

Solution. The Routh array for the polynomial is as below :

$$\begin{array}{c|ccc} s^6 & 1 & 8 & 47 \quad 30 \\ s^5 & 6 & 38 & 52 \\ s^4 & \frac{35}{3} & \frac{115}{3} & 80 \\ s^3 & \frac{128}{7} & \frac{256}{7} & \\ s^2 & 15 & 30 & \\ s^1 & 0 & 0 & \\ s^0 & ? & & \end{array}$$

In this case all the elements in the sixth row becomes zero and the array can be completed.

To proceed further we equate the given polynomial to the product of two polynomials $Q_1(s)$ and $Q_2(s)$, where $Q_1(s)$ is obtained from the 5th row of the above array.

Thus $$Q_1(s) = 15s^2 + 30 = 15(s^2 + 2)$$

Hence $$Q_2(s) = \frac{Q(s)}{Q_1(s)} = \frac{s^6 + 6s^5 + 18s^4 + 38s^3 + 47s^2 + 52s + 30}{15(s^2+2)}$$

$$= \frac{1}{15}[s^4 + 6s^3 + 16s^2 + 26s + 15].$$

Thus the given equation reduces to the following form :

$$(s^2 + 2)(s^4 + 6s^3 + 16s^2 + 26s + 15) = 0$$

The roots of equation $s^2 + 2 = 0$ are $s = \pm j\sqrt{2}$.

The nature of the roots of equation $s^4 + 6s^3 + 16s^2 + 26s + 15 = 0$ may be found by forming Routh array for this polynomial.

This is as below :

s^4	1	16 15
s^3	6	26
s^2	$\frac{35}{3}$	15
s^1	$\frac{128}{7}$	
s^0	15	

There are no changes in the sign of elements in the first column. Hence all the four roots have negative real parts.

Thus out of 6 roots, 4 roots have negative real parts while the remaining 2 roots have zero real parts.

Example 10.15. *Apply Routh criterion to the following equation and determine the number of roots (i) with positive real parts (ii) with zero real parts and (iii) with negative real parts*

$$s^5 + s^4 + 4s^3 + 24s^2 + 3s + 63 = 0.$$

Solution. The Routh array for this polynomial is as below :

s^5	1	4	3
s^4	1	24	63
s^3	−20	−60	
s^2	21	63	
s^1	0	0	
s^0	?		

In this case, all the elements in the fifth row have become zero and the array cannot be completed.

To proceed further, we equate the given polynomial to the product of two polynomial $Q_1(s)$ and $Q_2(s)$, where $Q_1(s)$ is obtained from the fourth row of the above array.

Thus $$Q_1(s) = 21s^2 + 63 = 21(s^2 + 3).$$

Hence $$Q_2(s) = \frac{Q(s)}{Q_1(s)} = \frac{s^5 + s^4 + 4s^3 + 24s^2 + 3s + 63}{21(s^2 + 3)} = \frac{1}{21}[s^3 + s^2 + s + 21].$$

Thus the given equation reduces to the following form :

$$(s^2 + 3)(s^3 + s^2 + s + 21) = 0.$$

The roots of equation $s^2 + 3 = 0$ are $s = \pm j\sqrt{3}$. These two roots have zero real parts.

The nature of the roots of equation $s^3 + s^2 + s + 21 = 0$ may be found by forming the Routh array for this polynomial. This is as below :

s^3	1	1
s^2	1	21
s^1	− 20	
s^0	21	

We find from this array that there are two changes in the sign of the elements in the first column. Hence there are two roots which have positive real parts. The remaining one root of this equation has negative real parts. Thus out of five roots of this equation, two have positive real parts, two have zero real parts and the remaining one has negative real parts.

EXERCISES

10.1. For the given resistive network determine the numerical value of (*i*) Z_n (*ii*) G_{21} (*iii*) Z_{21} (*iv*) Y_{21} and (*v*) α_{21}.

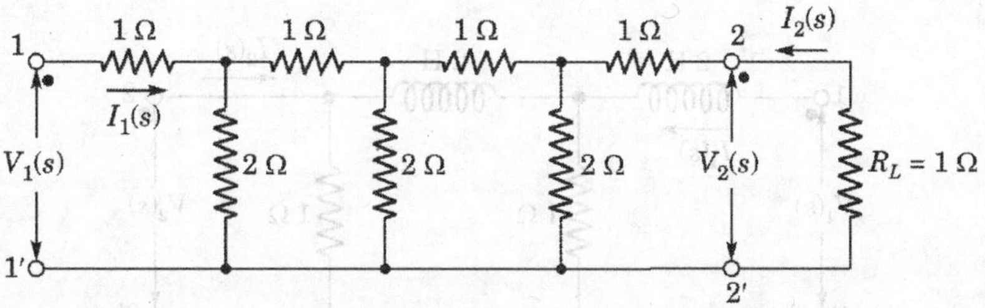

$$\left[\textbf{Ans. } Z_{11} = 2\,\Omega ; G_{21} = \frac{1}{16} ; Z_{21} = \frac{1}{8}\,\Omega ; Y_{21} = -\frac{1}{16} S ; \alpha_{21} = \frac{-1}{8}\right]$$

10.2. For the given 2-port network, determine the voltage ratio transfer function $G_{21}(s)$. If this network is terminated at port 2 with a 2 Ω resistor, find for this terminated 2 port network, the following network functions :

(*i*) $Z_{11}(s)$ (*ii*) $G_{21}(s)$ (*iii*) $Z_{21}(s)$ (*iv*) $Y_{21}(s)$ and (*v*) $a_{21}(s)$.

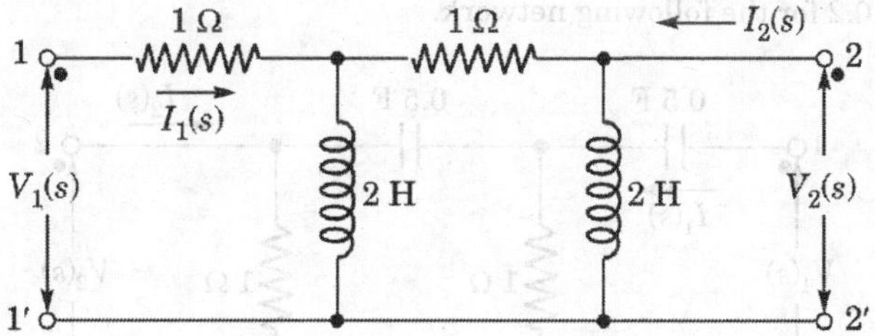

$$\left[\textbf{Ans. } \frac{4s^2}{(2s+1)^2} ; Z_{11}(s) = \frac{8s^2+7s+1}{2s^2+5s+1} ; Z_{21}(s) = \frac{4s^2}{2s^2+5s+1} ;\right.$$

$$\left. Y_{21} = \frac{-2s^2}{8s^2+7s+1} ; \alpha_{21}(s) = \frac{-2s^2}{2s^2+5s+1}\right]$$

10.3. Repeat exercise 10.2 for the following network.

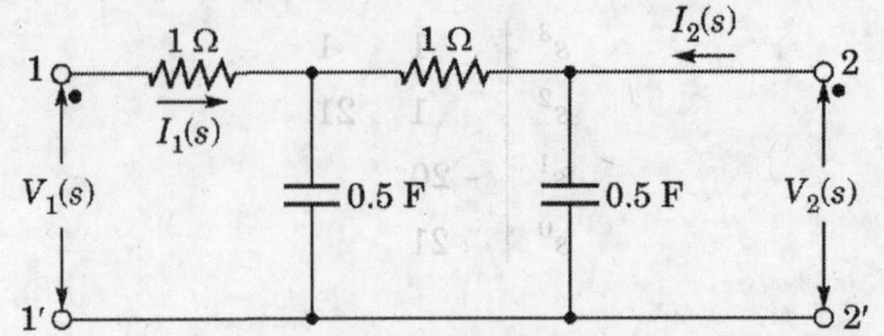

$$\left[\textbf{Ans. } \frac{4}{(s+2)^2};\ Z_{11}(s) = \frac{s^3+5s^2+6s+4}{s(s^2+3s+4)};\ Z_{21}(s) = \frac{4}{s^2+3s+4};\right.$$

$$\left. Y_{21}(s) = \frac{-2s}{s^3+5s^2+6s+4};\ \alpha_{21}(s) = \frac{-2}{s^2+3s+4} \right]$$

10.4. Repeat exercise 10.2 for the following network :

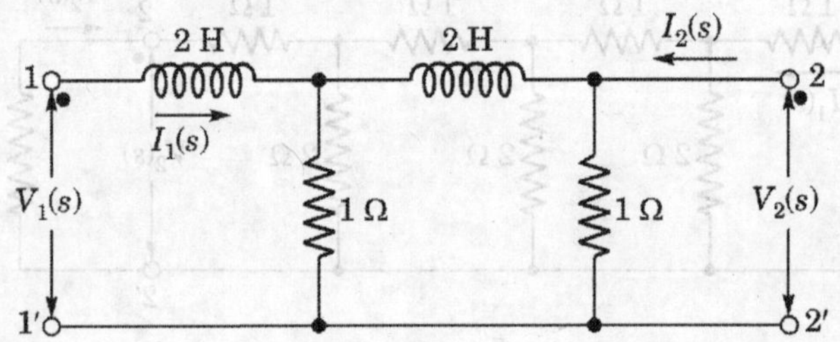

$$\left[\textbf{Ans. } \frac{1}{(2s+1)^2};\ Z_{11}(s) = \frac{12s^2+16s+2}{6s+5};\ Z_{21}(s) = \frac{3}{6s+5};\right.$$

$$\left. Y_{21}(s) = \frac{-1}{2s^2+16s+2};\ \alpha_{21}(s) = \frac{-1}{6s+5} \right]$$

10.5. Repeat exercise 10.2 for the following network.

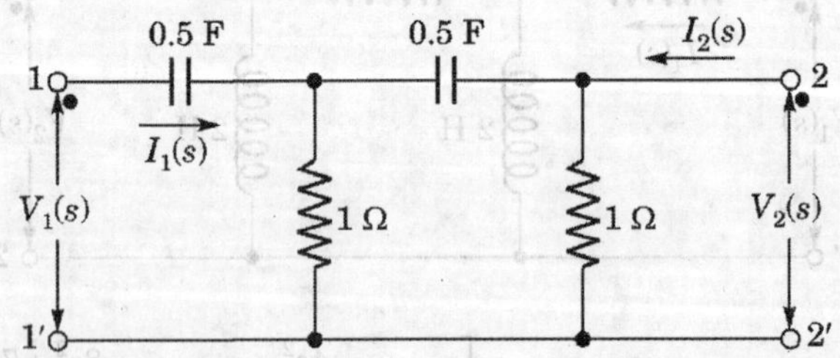

$$\left[\textbf{Ans. } \frac{s^2}{(s+2)^2};\ Z_{11}(s) = \frac{2s^2+16s+12}{s(5s+6)};\ Z_{21}(s) = \frac{2s}{2s+6};\right.$$

$$\left. Y_{21}(s) = \frac{-s^2}{2s^2+16s+12};\ \alpha_{21}(s) = \frac{-s}{5s+6} \right]$$

10.6. Repeat exercise 10.2 for the following network.

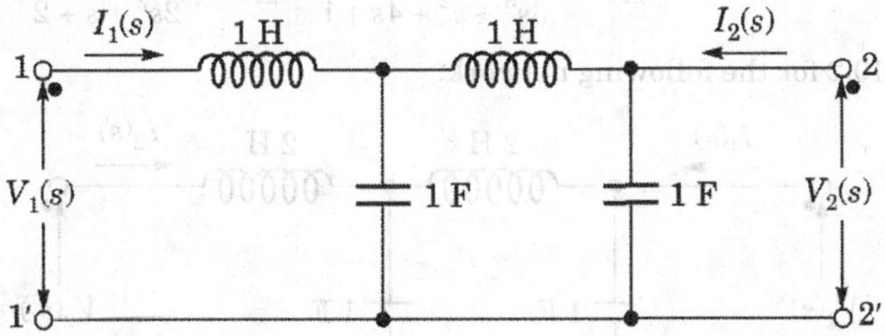

$$\left[\textbf{Ans. } \frac{1}{(s^2+1)^2};\ Z_{11}(s)=\frac{2s^4+s^3+6s^2+2s+2}{2s^3+s^2+4s+1};\right.$$

$$Z_{21}(s)=\frac{1}{2s^3+s^2+4s+1};\ Y_{21}(s)=\frac{-1}{2s^4+s^3+6s^2+2s+2};$$

$$\left.\alpha_{31}(s)=\frac{-1}{2s^3+s^2+4s+1}\right]$$

10.7. Repeat exercise 10.2 for the following network.

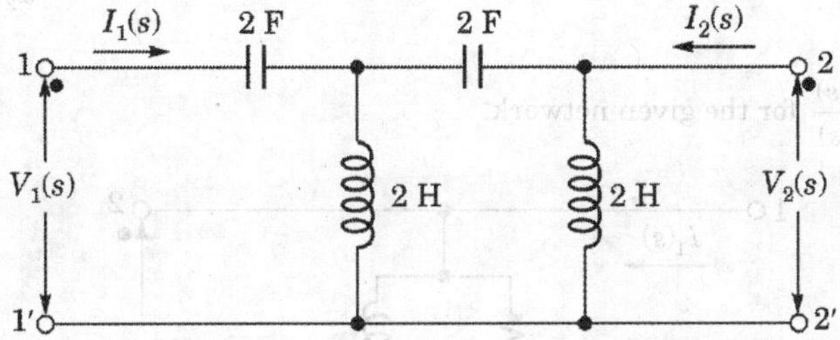

$$\left[\textbf{Ans. } \frac{16s^4}{(4s^2+1)^2};\ Z_{11}(s)=\frac{16s^4+8s^3+12s^2+s+1}{2s(4s^2+8s^2\ s+1)};\right.$$

$$Z_{21}(s)=\frac{8s^3}{4s^3+8s^2+s+1};\ Y_{21}(s)=\frac{-8s^4}{16s^4+8s^3+12s^2+s+1};$$

$$\left.\alpha_{21}(s)=\frac{-4s^3}{4s^3+8s^2+s+1}\right]$$

10.8. Repeat exercise 10.2 for the following network.

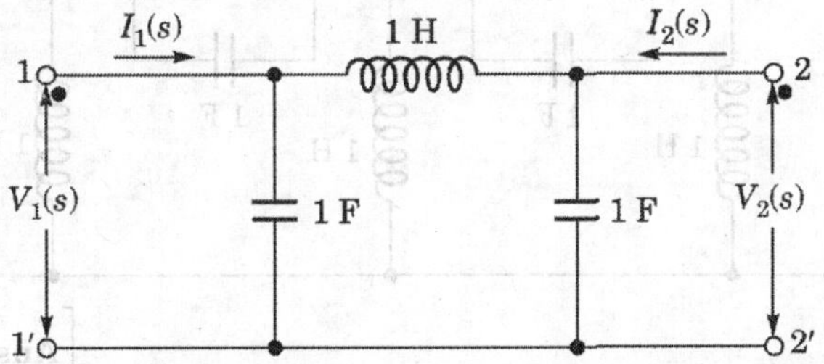

$$\left[\textbf{Ans. } \frac{1}{s^2+1};\ Z_{11}(s)=\frac{2s^2+s+2}{2s^3+s^2+4s+1};\right.$$

$$Z_{21}(s) = \frac{2}{3s^3 + s^2 + 4s + 1}; Y_{21}(s) = \frac{-1}{2s^2 + s + 2}; \alpha_{21}(s) = \frac{-1}{2s^3 + s^2 + 4s + 1}\Bigg]$$

10.9. Repeat exercise 10.2 for the following network.

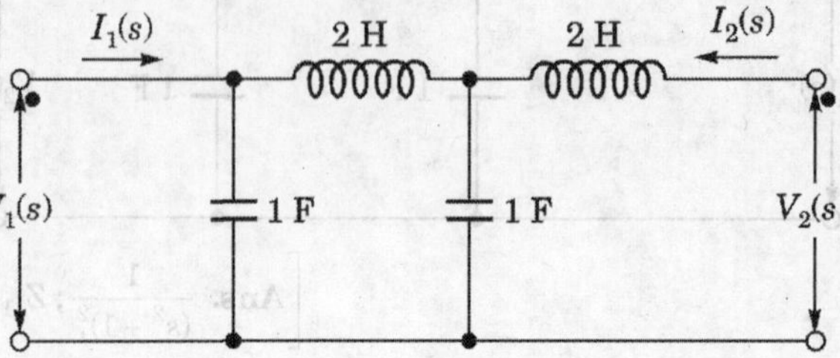

$$\left[\textbf{Ans. } \frac{1}{2s^2+1}; Z_{11}(s) = \frac{4s^2 + 8s + 2}{4s^3 + 10s^2 + 4s + 1};\right.$$

$$Z_{21}(s) = \frac{2}{3s^3 + 10s^2 + 4s + 1}; Y_{21}(s) = \frac{-1}{4s^2 + 8s + 2};$$

$$\left.\alpha_{21}(s) = \frac{-1}{4s^3 + 10s^2 + 4s + 1}\right]$$

10.10. Find $Z_{21}(s) = \dfrac{V_2(s)}{I_2(s)}$ for the given network.

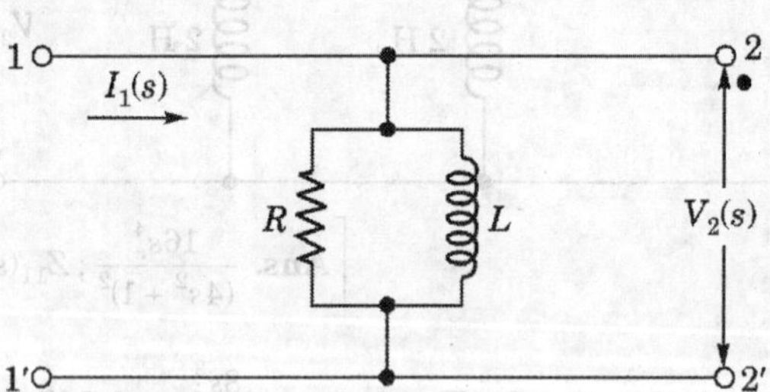

$$\left[\textbf{Ans. } Z_{21}(s) = \frac{SLR}{SL + R}\right]$$

10.11. For the given network find the voltage-ratio transfer function $G_{21}(s)$ and the transfer impedance $Z_{21}(s)$ $= \dfrac{V_2(s)}{I_1(s)}$.

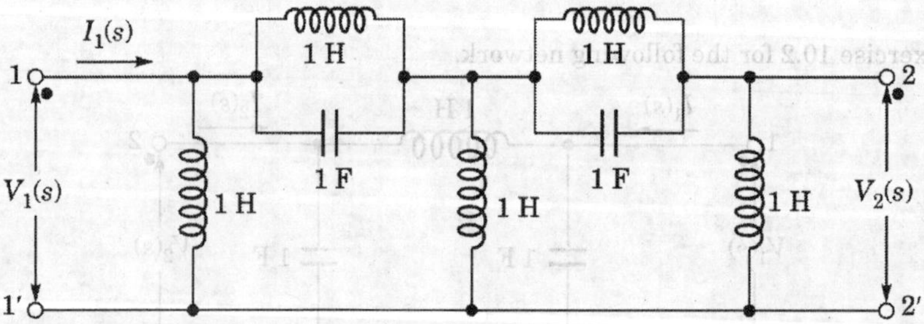

$$\left[\textbf{Ans. } Z_{21}(s) = \frac{(s^2+1)^2}{s^3 + 3s^2 + 2s + 5};\right.$$

$$\left.Z_{21}(s) = \frac{s(s^2+1)^2}{s^4 + 2s^3 + 7s^2 + 3s + 8}\right]$$

10.12. The given network is terminated at port 2 by a resistor of 1 Ω. Find the transfer admittance, $Y_{21}(s) = \dfrac{I_2(s)}{V_2(s)}$ for this terminated network.

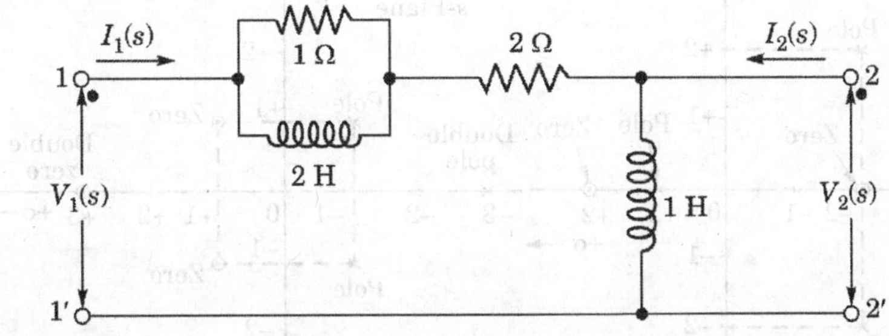

$$\left[\textbf{Ans. } Y_{21}(s) = \frac{-s(2s+1)}{8s^2+9s+2}\right]$$

10.13. For the given network, determine the ratio transfer function $G_{21}(s)$.

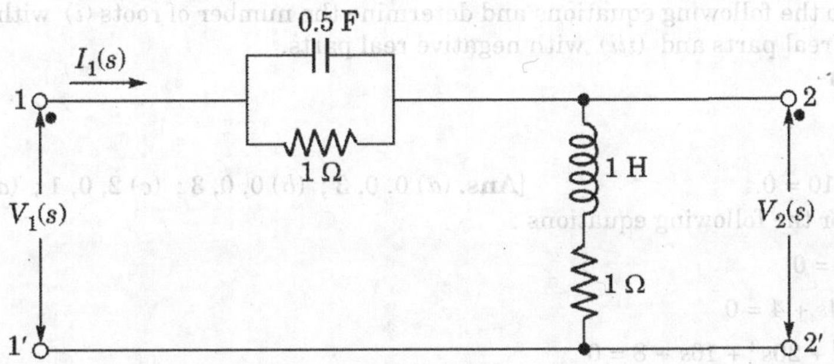

$$\left[\textbf{Ans. } G_{21}(s) = \frac{(s+1)(s+2)}{s^2+3s+4}\right]$$

10.14. Plot the poles and zeros in the s-plane for the following network functions :

(i) $F(s) = \dfrac{s^2+4s+3}{s^2+2s}$; (ii) $F(s) = \dfrac{(s+2)(s^2+9)}{(s^2+4)(s^2+4s+5)}$

(iii) $F(s) = \dfrac{(s^2-4)}{(s-1)(s^2+4s+8)}$ (iv) $F(s) = \dfrac{(s^2-2s+2)(s^2-6s+9)}{(s^2+2s+2)(s^2+6s+9)}$

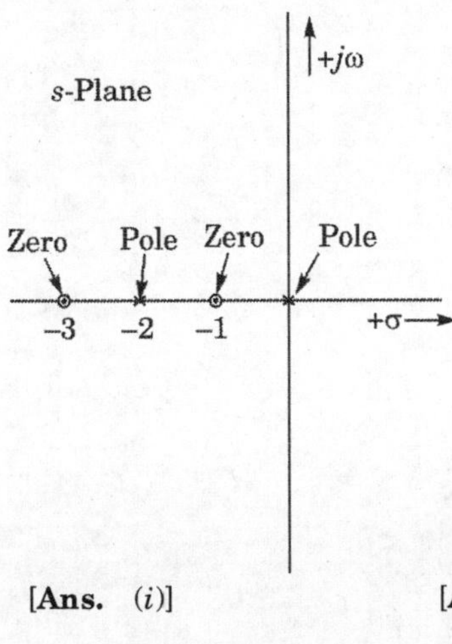

[**Ans.** (i)]

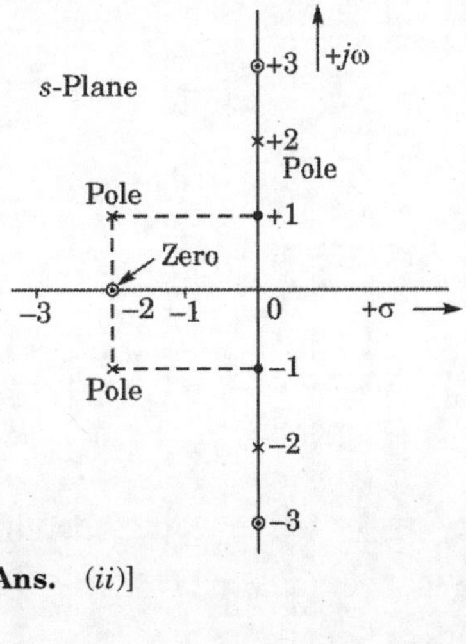

[**Ans.** (ii)]

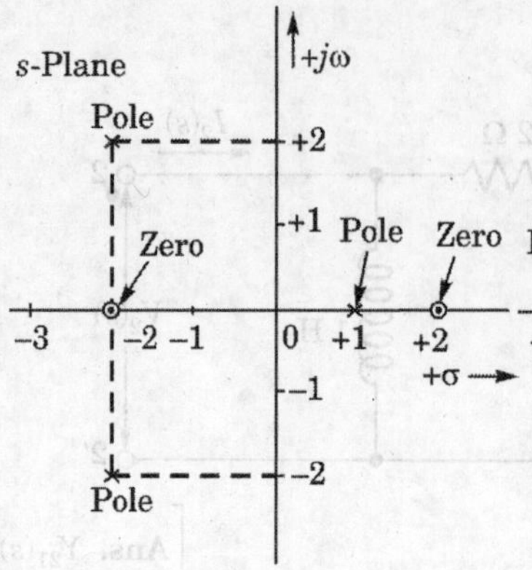

[**Ans.** (*iii*)]

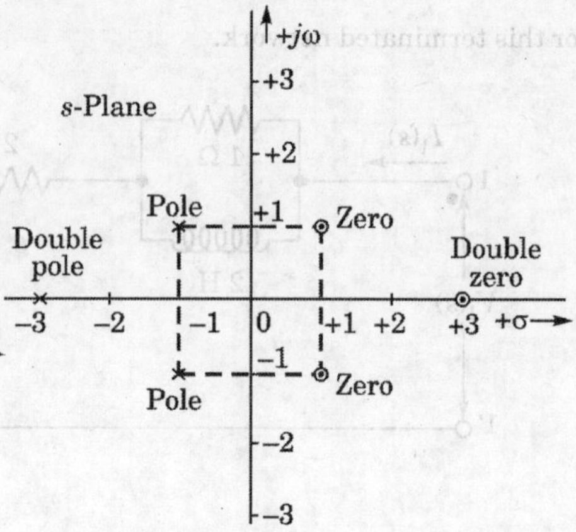

[**Ans.** (*iv*)]

10.15. Apply Routh criterion to the following equations and determine the number of roots (*i*) with positive real parts (*ii*) with zero real parts and (*iii*) with negative real parts.

(*a*) $2s^3 + 5s^2 + 3s + 3 = 0$

(*b*) $s^3 + 2s^2 + 5s + 2 = 0$

(*c*) $6s^3 + 2s^2 + 5s + 2 = 0$

(*d*) $s^4 + 2s^3 + 2s^2 + 6s + 10 = 0.$ [**Ans.** (*a*) 0, 0, 3 ; (*b*) 0, 0, 3 ; (*c*) 2, 0, 1 ; (*d*) 2, 0, 1]

10.16. Repeat exercise 10.15 for the following equations :

(*a*) $s^4 + s^3 + 2s^2 + 2s + 4 = 0$

(*b*) $s^5 + s^4 + 2s^3 + 2s^2 + 4s + 4 = 0$

(*c*) $s^6 + 5s^5 + 13s^4 + 21s^3 + 20s^2 + 16s + 8 = 0$

(*d*) $s^4 + 4s^3 + 8s^2 + 12s + 15 = 0.$ [**Ans.** (*a*) 2, 0, 2 ; (*b*) 2, 0, 3 ; (*c*) 0, 2, 4 ; (*d*) 0, 2, 2]

10.17. Repeat exercise 10.15 for the following equations :

(*a*) $s^6 + 5s^5 + 15s^4 + 28s^3 + 44s^2 + 36s + 36 = 0$

(*b*) $s^6 + s^5 - 4s^4 + 18s^3 + 17s^2 + 17s + 15 = 0$

(*c*) $s^6 - s^5 - 2s^4 + 4s^3 - 5s^2 + 21s + 30 = 0.$ [**Ans.** (*a*) 0, 2, 4 ; (*b*) 2, 2, 8 ; (*c*) 2, 2, 2]

11

Parameters of Two-port Network

11.1. Introduction

In the last chapter we have studied the network functions namely the driving point functions and the transfer function. These constitute the general network functions applicable to networks on which no restrictions have been imposed. In this chapter, we study certain special class of network functions useful in describing primarily two-port networks on which additional restrictions have been imposed. These restrictions may consist in short circuiting or open circuiting one of the two ports of the two-port network. These network functions or network parameters may also be generalised to describe an n-port network.

Fig. 11.1 shows a 2-port network with the following four variables: (*i*) Current I_1 and voltage V_1 at port 1 and (*ii*) Current I_2 and voltage V_2 at port 2. Only the two ports are shown available for external connections. Rest of the network is enclosed inside the box. There are other voltages and currents inside the box but these are not available for measurement.

Out of the four variables shown in Fig. 11.1, only two are independent while remaining two form the dependent variables and may be expressed in terms of the two independent variables and the

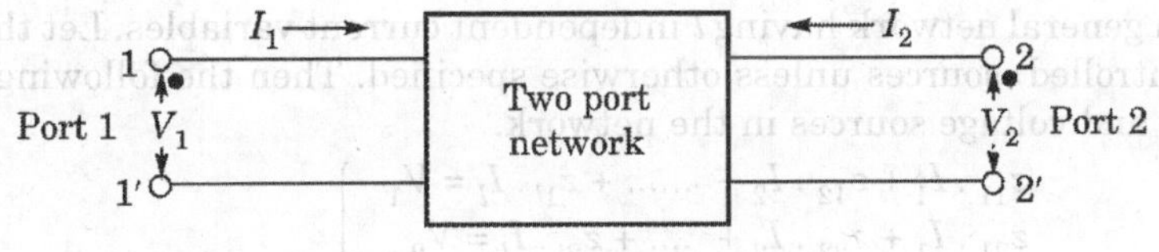

Fig. 11.1. A two-port network.

parameters of the given 2-port network. Thus suppose currents I_1 and I_2 form the independent variables. Then voltages V_1 and V_2 form the dependent variables and may be expressed in terms of I_1, I_2 and a set of network parameters called the "open circuit impedance parameters". Next if voltages V_1 and V_2 form the independent variables, then currents I_1 and I_2 form the dependent variables and may be expressed in terms of V_1, V_2 and a set of network parameters called "short circuit admittance parameters". Other important choices of independent variables are :

(*i*) V_2, I_2 ; (*ii*) $V_1 I_1$; (*iii*) I_1, V_2 and (*iv*) V_1, I_2. These define other network parameters namely "transmission parameters", inverse transmission parameters", "hybrid parameters" and "inverse hybrid parameters" respectively. Table 11.1 gives the above six combinations of independent variables and the equations giving the dependent variables in terms of independent variable and the corresponding network parameters.

Table 11.1
Two-Port Network Parameters

Variables			
Dependent Variables	*Independent Variables*	*Equations giving the dependent variables*	*Network Parameters*
V_1, V_2	I_1, I_2	$V_1 = z_{11} \cdot I_1 + z_{12} \cdot I_2$ $V_2 = z_{21} \cdot I_1 + z_{22} \cdot I_2$	Open circuit impedance parameter $z_{11}, z_{12}, z_{21}, z_{22}$
I_2, I_2	V_1, V_2	$I_1 = y_{11} \cdot V_1 + y_{12} \cdot V_2$ $V_2 = y_{21} \cdot V_1 + y_{22} \cdot V_2$	Short circuit admittance parameters $y_{11}, y_{12}, y_{21}, y_{22}$
V_1, I_1	V_2, I_2	$V_1 = AV_2 - BI_2$ $I_2 = CV_2 - DI_2$	Transmission parameters A, B, C, D
V_2, I_2	V_1, I_1	$V_2 = A'V_1 - B'I_1$ $I_2 = C'V_1 - D'I_1$	Inverse transmission parameters A', B', C', D'
V_1, I_2	I_1, V_2	$V_1 = h_{11} \cdot I_1 + h_{12} \cdot V_2$ $I_2 = h_{21} \cdot I_1 + h_{22} \cdot V_2$	Hybrid parameters h_{11}, h_{12}, h_{21}, h_{22}
I_1, V_2	V_1, I_2	$I_1 = g_{11} \cdot V_1 + g_{12} \cdot I_2$ $V_2 = g_{21} \cdot V_1 + g_{22} \cdot I_2$	Inverse hybrid parameters $g_{11}, g_{12}, g_{21}, g_{22}$

11.2. Short Circuit Admittance Parameters

Consider a general network having l independent current variables. Let the network be free of dependent (controlled) sources unless otherwise specified. Then the following equations relate the loop currents and voltage sources in the network.

$$\left.\begin{aligned} z_{11} \cdot I_1 + z_{12} \cdot I_2 + \;\ldots\ldots + z_{1l} \cdot I_l &= V_1 \\ z_{21} \cdot I_1 + z_{22} \cdot I_2 + \;\ldots. + z_{2l} \cdot I_l &= V_2 \\ \ldots. \qquad \ldots. \qquad & \ldots. \\ z_{l1} \cdot I_1 + z_{l2} \cdot I_2 + \;\ldots\ldots + z_{ll} \cdot I_l &= V_1 \end{aligned}\right\} \qquad \ldots(11.1)$$

Solving for currents, we get

$$I_1 = \frac{1}{\Delta}[\Delta_{11} \cdot V_1 + \Delta_{21} \cdot V_2 + \ldots\ldots + \Delta_{l1} \cdot V_l] \qquad \ldots(11.2)$$

$$I_2 = \frac{1}{\Delta}[\Delta_{12} \cdot V_1 + \Delta_{22} \cdot V_2 + \ldots\ldots + \Delta_{l2} \cdot V_l] \qquad \ldots(11.3)$$

etc.

where $\Delta_{11}, \Delta_{12}, \Delta_{21}$ etc. ...... are the cofactors of coefficients z_{11}, z_{12}, z_{21} etc. respectively in the system impedance determinant Δ.

Now the two port network of Fig. 11.1 forms a special case of this general network in which all voltage sources except V_1 and V_2 are zero. Thus $V_3 = V_4 = \ldots\ldots = V_l = 0$. Hence Eqs. (11.2) and (11.3) reduce to the following forms,

$$I_1 = \frac{\Delta_{11}}{\Delta} . V_1 + \frac{\Delta_{21}}{\Delta} . V_2 \quad ...(11.4)$$

and
$$I_2 = \frac{\Delta_{12}}{\Delta} . V_1 + \frac{\Delta_{22}}{\Delta} . V_2 \quad ...(11.5)$$

Dimensionally the ratios $\frac{\Delta_{11}}{\Delta}, \frac{\Delta_{21}}{\Delta}, \frac{\Delta_{12}}{\Delta}$ and $\frac{\Delta_{22}}{\Delta}$ are admittances. Hence we may use the coefficients $y_{11}, y_{12}, y_{21}, y_{22}$ respectively for denoting the ratio $\frac{\Delta_{11}}{\Delta}, \frac{\Delta_{21}}{\Delta}, \frac{\Delta_{12}}{\Delta}$ and $\frac{\Delta_{22}}{\Delta}$, *i.e.*, in general, introduce the notation,

$$y_{jk} = \frac{\Delta_{kj}}{\Delta} \quad ...[11.5(a)]$$

Then Eqs. (11.4) and (11.5) become,

$$I_1 = y_{11} . V_1 + y_{12} . V_2 \quad ...(11.6)$$

and
$$I_2 = y_{21} . V_1 + y_{22} . V_2 \quad ...(11.7)$$

Conventionally lower case letter y is used for these y-coefficients.

Short-circuit Constraint. Eqs. (11.6) and (11.7) are general equations for a general two-port network without any constraint imposed. For the purpose of defining the short circuit admittance parameters, we now impose suitable constraint namely short circuiting either port 1 or port 2.

With port 2 short circuited, *i.e.* with $V_2 = 0$, Eqs (11.6) and (11.7) yield,

$$y_{11} = \left.\frac{I_1}{V_1}\right|_{V_2 = 0} \quad ...(11.8)$$

$$y_{21} = \left.\frac{I_2}{V_1}\right|_{V_2 = 0} \quad ...(11.9)$$

Similarly with port 1 short circuited *i.e.* with $V_1 = 0$, Eqs. (11.6) and (11.7) yield,

$$y_{12} = \left.\frac{I_1}{V_2}\right|_{V_1 = 0} \quad ...(11.10)$$

$$y_{22} = \left.\frac{I_2}{V_2}\right|_{V_1 = 0} \quad ...(11.11)$$

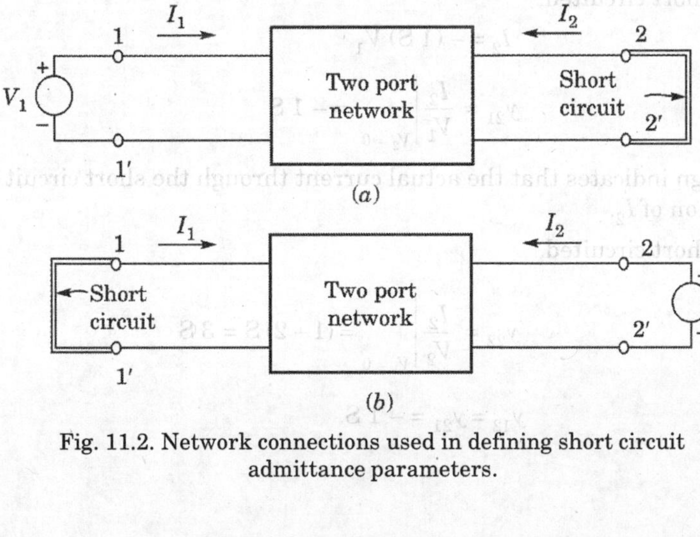

Fig. 11.2. Network connections used in defining short circuit admittance parameters.

Physically y_{11} is the driving point admittance at port 1 with port 2 short circuited. y_{21} is the transfer admittance at port 1 with port 2 short circuit. y_{11} and y_{21} may be computed from the circuit elements or may be measured making use of the circuit connection of Fig. 11.2 (*a*).

Similarly y_{22} is the driving point admittance at port 2 with port 1 short circuited and y_{12} is the transfer admittance at port 2 with port 1 short circuited. Parameters y_{22} and y_{12} be computed or measured making use of the circuit connection of Fig. 11.2 (*b*).

Since each of Eqs. (11.8) to (11.11) involve a short circuit at one port, these parameters y_{11}, y_{21}, y_{12} and y_{22} are called the short circuit admittance parameters or simply *y*-parameters.

Out of these four parameters, two namely y_{11} and y_{22} form the driving point short circuit admittances while the other two namely y_{12} and y_{21} for the short circuit transfer admittances.

If the network under study is *reciprocal*, then in accordance with the reciprocity principle,

$$\left.\frac{I_2}{V_2}\right|_{V_1=0} = \left.\frac{I_2}{V_1}\right|_{V_2=0} \qquad ...(11.12)$$

or

$$y_{12} = y_{21} \qquad ...(11.13)$$

Thus for a reciprocal network, only three *y*-parameters namely y_{11}, y_{22} and y_{21} (or y_{12}) are sufficient to fully specify the relationships between the currents and the voltages at the two ports.

Example 11.1. *Compute the short circuit admittance parameters for the resistive π-network given below :*

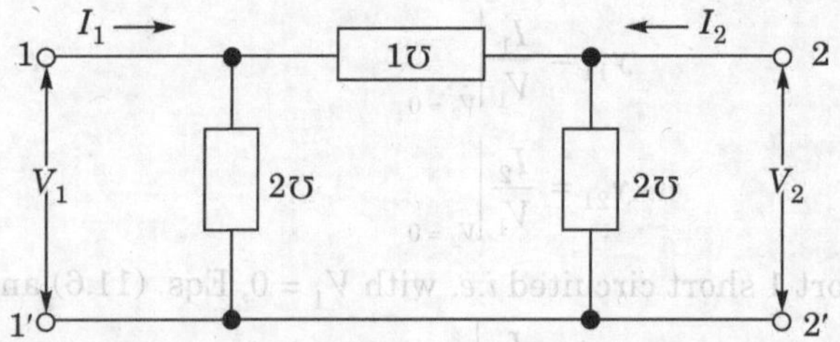

Solution. On short circuiting port 2, we get

$$y_{11} = \left.\frac{I_1}{V_1}\right|_{V_2=0} = (2 + 1) = 3 \text{ S}$$

With port 2 short circuited,

$$I_2 = -(1 \text{ S})\, V_1$$

Hence

$$y_{21} = \left.\frac{I_2}{V_1}\right|_{V_2=0} = -1 \text{ S}$$

The minus sign indicates that the actual current through the short circuit flows opposite to the reference direction of I_2.

With port 1 short circuited,

$$y_{22} = \left.\frac{I_2}{V_2}\right|_{V_1=0} = (1 + 2) \text{ S} = 3 \text{ S}$$

$$y_{12} = y_{21} = -1 \text{ S}.$$

Example 11.2. *Find the y-parameters for the given resistive network containing a controlled voltage.*

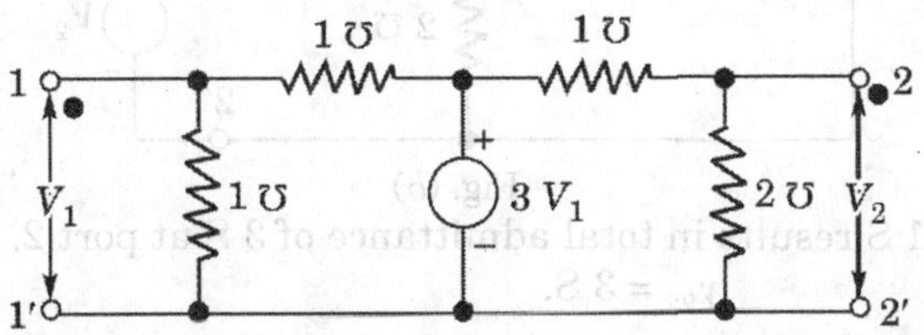

Solution. With port 2 short circuited, the circuit reduces to the following form :

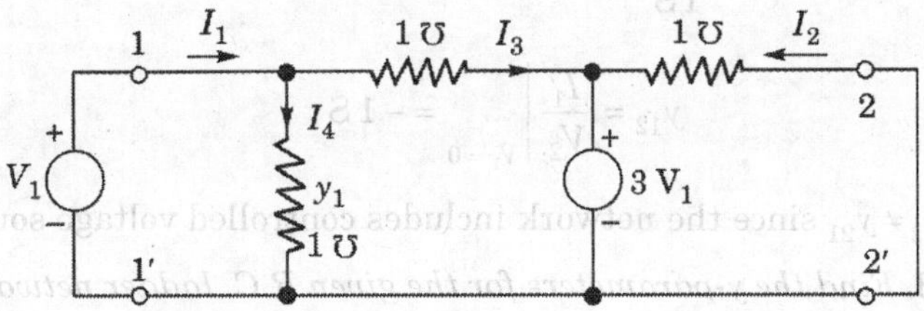

Then, we get

$$\frac{-I_2}{1\,\text{S}} = 3\,V_1 \qquad \text{...(1)}$$

$$\frac{I_3}{1\,\text{S}} + 3\,V_1 = V_1$$

or

$$2V_1 = -\,I_3 \qquad \text{...(2)}$$

Also

$$I_1 = I_4 + I_3 \qquad \text{...(3)}$$

and

$$V_1 = \frac{I_3}{1\,\text{S}} \qquad \text{...(4)}$$

From Eqs. (1) to (4), we get

$$I_1 = V_1 + I_3 = V_1 - 2V_1 = -\,V_1$$

Hence

$$y_{11} = \left.\frac{I_1}{V_1}\right|_{V_2 = 0} = -\,1\,\text{S}$$

and

$$y_{21} = \left.\frac{I_2}{V_1}\right|_{V_2 = 0} = \frac{-\,3V_1}{V_1} = -\,3\,\text{S}.$$

With port 1 short circuited, the circuit reduces to the form shown in Fig. (*a*).

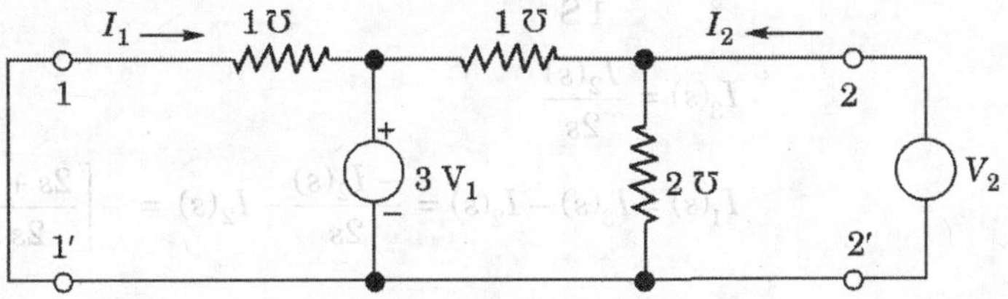

Fig. (*a*)

But since $V_1 = 0$, the voltage source $3\,V_1$ reduces to a short circuit. Hence the circuit reduces to the form shown in Fig. (*b*).

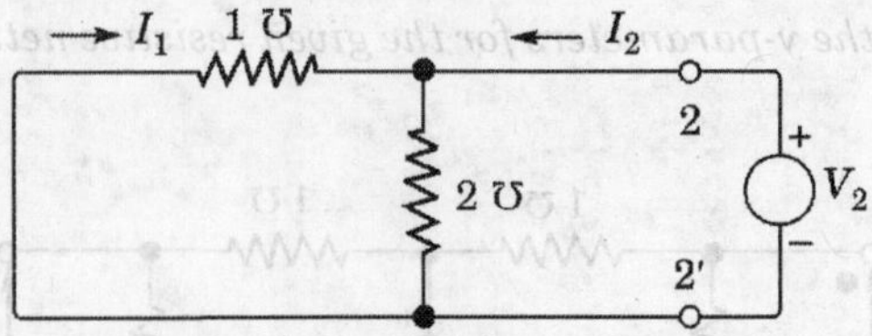

Fig. (*b*)

2 S in shunt with 1 S results in total admittance of 3 S at port 2.

Thus $$y_{22} = 3\ \text{S}.$$

Further $$\frac{-I_1}{1\ \text{S}} = V_2$$

Hence $$y_{12} = \left.\frac{I_1}{V_2}\right|_{V_1=0} = -1\ \text{S}$$

In this case $y_{12} \neq y_{21}$ since the network includes controlled voltage source.

Example 11.3. *Find the y-parameters for the given R.C. ladder network.*

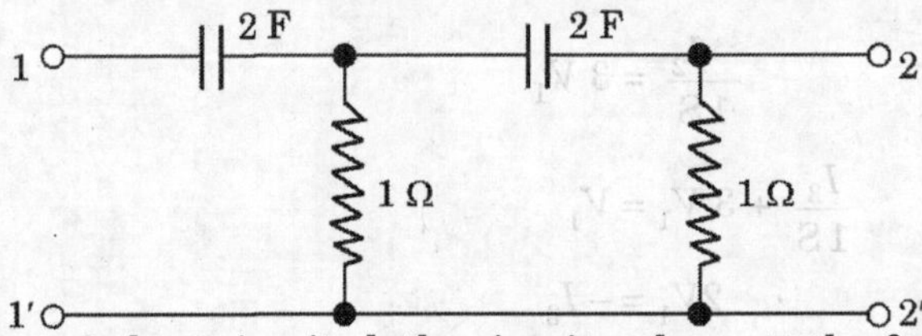

Solution. With port 2 short circuited, the circuit reduces to the from shown in Fig. (*a*).

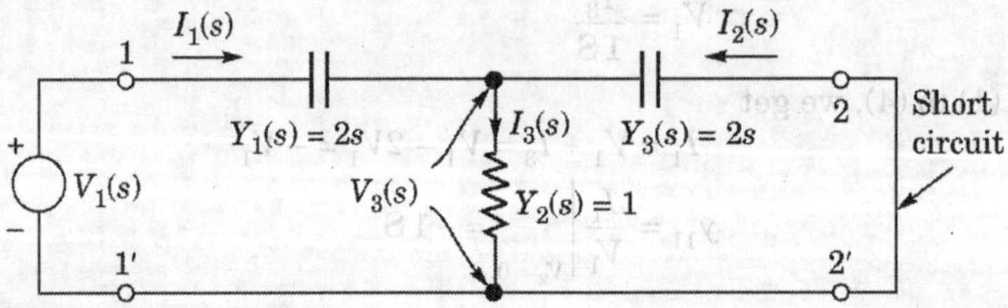

From Fig. (*a*), we get

$$V_3(s) = \frac{-I_2(s)}{2s} \qquad \text{...(1)}$$

Also $$V_3(s) = \frac{I_3(s)}{1\ \text{S}} \qquad \text{...(2)}$$

Hence $$I_3(s) = \frac{I_2(s)}{2s} \qquad \text{...(3)}$$

$$I_1(s) = I_3(s) - I_2(s) = \frac{-I_2(s)}{2s} - I_2(s) = -\left[\frac{2s+1}{2s}\right] I_2(s) \qquad \text{...(4)}$$

Hence $$V_1(s) = \frac{I_1(s)}{2s} - \frac{I_2(s)}{2s} = \frac{1}{2s}[I_1(s) - I_2(s)] \qquad \text{...(5)}$$

$$= \frac{1}{2s}\left[I_1(s) - I_1(s)\frac{2s}{2s+1}\right] = I_1(s)\frac{4s+1}{2s(2s+1)} \qquad \text{...(6)}$$

Hence $$y_{11}(s) = \left.\frac{I_1(s)}{V_1(s)}\right|_{V_2(s)=0} = \frac{2s(2s+1)}{2s+1} \qquad \text{...(7)}$$

$$y_{21}(s) = \left.\frac{I_2(s)}{V_1(s)}\right|_{V_2(s)=0} = \frac{-2s}{(2s+1)} \cdot \frac{2s(2s+1)}{(4s+1)} = \frac{-4s^2}{4s+1}.$$

With port 1 short circuited, the network reduces to the form shown in Fig. (*b*).

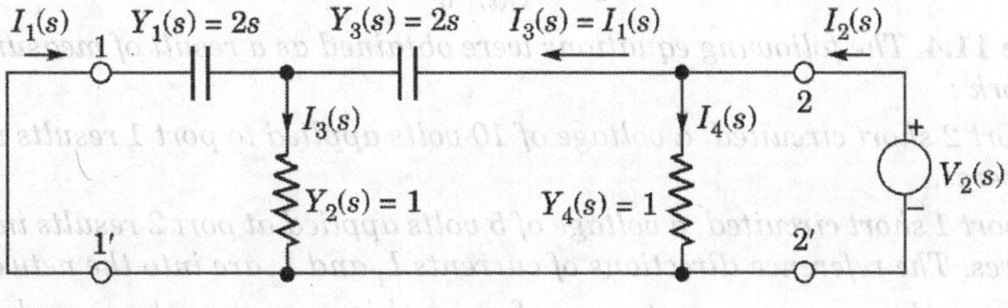

(*b*)

Then, we get the following relations :

$$V_3(s) = \frac{-I_1(s)}{Y_1(s)} = \frac{I_1(s)}{2s} \qquad \text{...(1)}$$

Also $$V_3(s) = \frac{I_3(s)}{Y_2(s)} = I_3(s) \qquad \text{...(2)}$$

$$V_2(s) = \frac{I_4(s)}{Y_4(s)} = I_4(s) \qquad \text{...(3)}$$

Also $$V_2(s) = [I_3(s) - I_1(s)]/2s - V_3(s) \qquad \text{...(4)}$$

$$I_4(s) = I_2(s) - [I_3(s) - I_1(s)] \qquad \text{...(5)}$$

From equations (1) to (5), we get

$$I_3(s) = \frac{-I_1(s)}{2s} \qquad \text{...(6)}$$

$$V_2(s) = I_4(s) = I_2(s) - I_3(s) + I_1(s) = I_2(s) + \frac{I_1(s)}{2s} + I_1(s)$$

$$= I_2(s) + I_1(s)\,\frac{2s+1}{2s} \qquad \text{...(7)}$$

But $$V_2(s) = V_3(s) + \frac{I_3(s) - I_1(s)}{2s} = I_3(s) + \frac{I_3(s) - I_1(s)}{2s} = \frac{(2s+1)I_3(s) - I_1(s)}{2s}$$

$$= -\frac{3s+1}{4s^2} I_1(s) \qquad \text{...(8)}$$

Hence $$y_{12}(s) = \left.\frac{I_1(s)}{V_2(s)}\right|_{V_1=0} = \frac{-4s^2}{4s+1} \qquad \text{...(9)}$$

Also from equations (7) and (8),

$$I_2(s) + I_1(s)\,\frac{2s+1}{2s} = -\frac{4s+1}{4s^2} I_1(s)$$

Hence $$I_2(s) = -\frac{4s^2 - 6s + 1}{4s^2} I_1(s)$$

Hence $$V_2(s) = \frac{4s+1}{4s^2} \frac{4s^2}{4s^2+6s+1} I_2(s) = \frac{3s+1}{4s^2+6s+1} I_2(s)$$

Hence $$y_{22} = \left. \frac{I_2(s)}{V_2(s)} \right|_{V_1(s)=0} = \frac{4s^2+6s+1}{4s+1}.$$

Example 11.4. *The following equations were obtained as a result of measurements made on a two port network :*

(i) with port 2 short circuited, a voltage of 10 volts applied to port 1 results in $I_1 = 5$ amperes and $I_2 = -2$ amperes.

(ii) with port 1 short circuited, a voltage of 5 volts applied at port 2 results in $I_1 = -1$ amperes and $I_2 = 2$ amperes. The reference directions of currents I_1 and I_2 are into the network.

Compute the y-parameters for this network and write the y-parameter equations. Compute the voltage across 10 Ω resistor connected across port 2.

Solution. The y-parameter equations are :

$$I_1 = y_{11} \cdot V_1 + y_{12} \cdot V_2 \quad ...(1)$$
$$I_2 = y_{21} \cdot V_1 + y_{22} \cdot V_2 \quad ...(2)$$

Hence $$y_{11} = \left. \frac{I_1}{V_2} \right|_{V_2=0} = \frac{5 \text{ amp.}}{10 \text{ volts}} = -0.5 \text{ S}$$

$$y_{21} = \left. \frac{I_2}{V_1} \right|_{V_2=0} = \frac{-2 \text{ amp.}}{10 \text{ volts}} = -0.2 \text{ S}$$

$$y_{22} = \left. \frac{I_2}{V_2} \right|_{V_1=0} = \frac{2 \text{ amp.}}{5 \text{ volts}} = 0.4 \text{ S}$$

$$y_{12} = \left. \frac{I_1}{V_2} \right|_{V_1=0} = \frac{-1 \text{ amp.}}{5 \text{ volts}} = -0.2 \text{ S}$$

Hence the y-parameter equations become :

$$I_1 = 0.5\, V_1 - 0.2\, V_2 \quad ...(3)$$
$$I_2 = -0.2\, V_1 + 0.4\, V_2 \quad ...(4)$$

Now if load resistor R_l = 10 Ω is connected across port 2 and voltage source of 10 volts is connected across port 1, then

$$V_1 = 10 \text{ volts} \quad ...(5)$$

and $$V_2 = -I_2, R_l = -10\, I_2 \quad ...(6)$$

Hence from equation (4), $I_2 = -2 + 0.4(-10\, I_2)$

Hence $I_2 - 0.4$ amp.

and $$V_2 = -10(-0.4) = +4 \text{ volts.}$$

11.3. Open Circuit Impedance Parameters

Consider a general network having n independent voltage variables. Let the network be free of dependent (controlled) sources unless otherwise specified. Then the following equations relate the voltage variables, admittances of network branches and the driving current sources.

$$\left.\begin{aligned} y_{11} . V_1 + y_{12} . V_2 + ... + y_{1n} . V_n &= I_1 \\ y_{21} . V_1 + y_{22} . V_2 + ... + y_{2n} . V_n &= I_2 \\ .... \quad .... \quad .... \quad .... \quad & .... \\ y_{n1} . V_1 + y_{n2} . V_2 + ... + y_{nn} . V_n &= I_n \end{aligned}\right\} \quad ...(11.14)$$

Solving for currents, we get

$$V_1 = \frac{1}{\Delta}[\Delta_{11} . I_1 + \Delta_{21} . I_2 + ... + \Delta_{n1} . I_n] \quad ...(11.15)$$

$$V_2 = \frac{1}{\Delta}[\Delta_{12} . I_1 + \Delta_{22} . I_2 + ... + \Delta_{n2} . I_n] \quad ...(11.16)$$

etc.

where Δ_{11}, Δ_{12}, Δ_{21} are the cofactors of coefficients y_{11}, y_{12}, y_{21} ...... respectively in the system admittance determinant Δ.

For the two port network of Fig. 11.1, equations (11.5) and (11.16) reduce to the following simple forms.

$$V_1 = \frac{\Delta_{11}}{\Delta} . I_1 + \frac{\Delta_{21}}{\Delta} . I_2 \quad ...(11.17)$$

and

$$V_2 = \frac{\Delta_{12}}{\Delta} . I_1 + \frac{\Delta_{22}}{\Delta} . I_2 \quad ...(11.18)$$

Dimensionally the ratio $\frac{\Delta_{11}}{\Delta}, \frac{\Delta_{12}}{\Delta}, \frac{\Delta_{21}}{\Delta}$ and $\frac{\Delta_{22}}{\Delta}$ are impedances. Hence we many use the coefficients z_{11}, z_{12}, z_{21} and z_{22} respectively for the ratios $\frac{\Delta_{11}}{\Delta}, \frac{\Delta_{21}}{\Delta}, \frac{\Delta_{12}}{\Delta}$ and $\frac{\Delta_{22}}{\Delta}$ *i.e.*, in general introduce the notation $z_{jk} = \frac{\Delta_{kj}}{\Delta}$, then equations (11.17) and (11.18) become,

$$V_1 = z_{11} . I_1 + z_{12} . I_2 \quad ...(11.19)$$

$$V_2 = z_{21} . I_1 + z_{22} . I_2 \quad ...(11.20)$$

Conventionally lower case letter z is used for these z-coefficients.

Open Circuit Constraint. Equations (11.19) and (11.20) are general equations for a two-port network without any constraint imposed. For the purpose of defining the open circuit impedance parameters we now impose suitable constraint namely open circuiting either port 1 or port 2.

With port 2 open circuited, *i.e.* with $I_2 - 0$, equations (11.19) and (11.20) yield,

$$z_{11} = \left.\frac{V_1}{I_1}\right|_{I_2 = 0} \quad ...(11.21)$$

$$z_{21} = \left.\frac{V_2}{I_1}\right|_{I_2 = 0} \qquad ...(11.22)$$

Similarly with port 1 open circuited, *i.e.* with $I_1 = 0$, equations (11.19) and (11.20) yield,

$$z_{12} = \left.\frac{V_1}{I_2}\right|_{I_1 = 0} \qquad ...(11.23)$$

and

$$z_{22} = \left.\frac{V_2}{I_2}\right|_{I_1 = 0} \qquad ...(11.24)$$

We may see that z_{11} is the *driving point impedance* at port 1 with port 2 *open circuited* and z_{21} is the *transfer impedance* at port 1 with port 2 open circuited.

z_{11} and z_{21} may be computed knowing the network elements or may be measured making use of the circuit connection of Fig. 11.3 (*a*).

Similarly z_{22} is the *driving point impedance* at port 2 with port 1 *open circuited* and z_{12} is the *transfer impedance* at port 2 with port 1 *open circuited.*

Parameters z_{22} and z_{12} may be computed from the values of circuit elements or may be measured making use of the circuit connections of Fig. 11.3 (*b*).

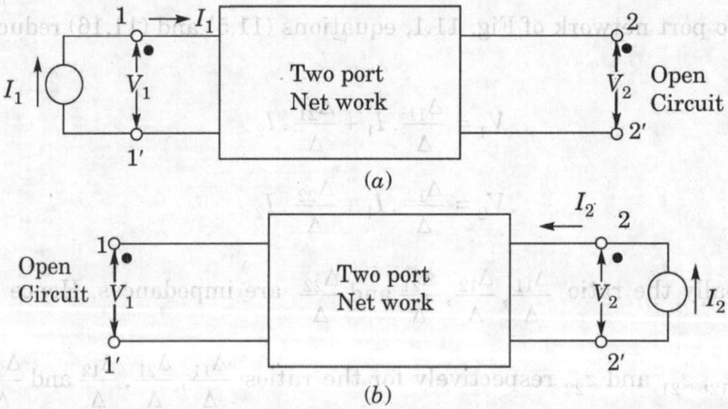

Fig. 11.3. Network connections used in defining open circuit impedance parameters.

Since each of the equations (11.21) to (11.24) involves an open circuit at one port, these parameters z_{11}, z_{21}, z_{12} and z_{22} are called *open circuit impedance parameters* or simply *z-parameters*. Out of these four two namely z_{11} and z_{22} form the open circuit driving point impedances while the remaining two namely z_{21} and z_{12} form the open circuit transfer impedances.

If the network under study is reciprocal, then in accordance with the reciprocity principle.

$$\left.\frac{V_2}{I_1}\right|_{I_2 = 0} = \left.\frac{V_1}{I_2}\right|_{I_1 = 0} \qquad ...(11.25)$$

or

$$z_{21} = z_{12} \qquad ...(11.26)$$

Thus for a reciprocal network, only three *z*-parameters namely z_{11}, z_{22} and z_{12} (or z_{21}) are sufficient in order to fully specify the relationships between currents and voltages at the two ports.

Example 11.5. *Compute the open circuit impedance parameters for the T-network given below:*

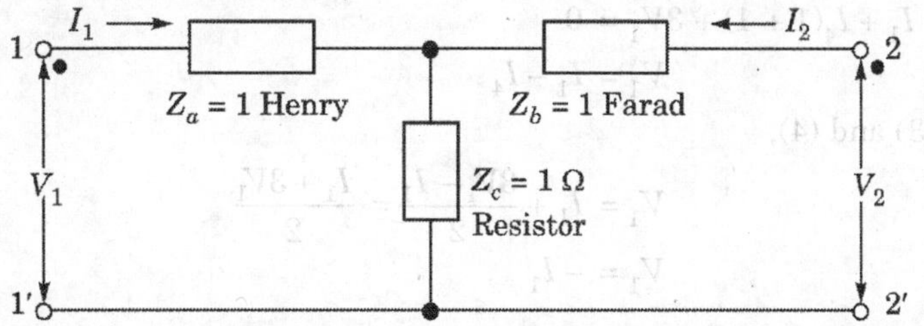

Solution. The transform network corresponding to the given network is given in Fig. (*a*).

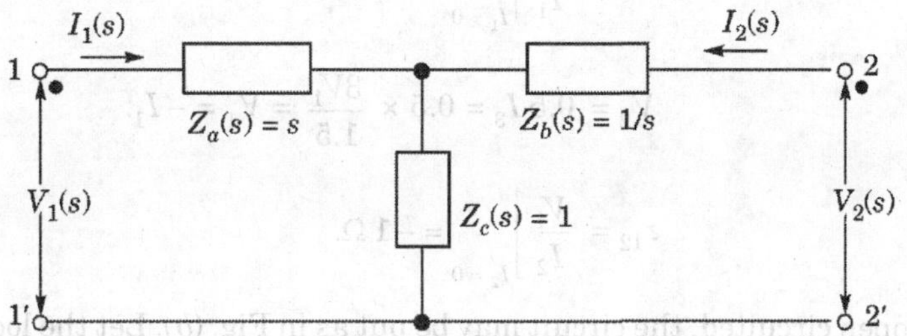

Fig. (*a*).

With port 2 open circuited, we get

$$z_{11} = \left.\frac{V_1(s)}{I_1(s)}\right|_{I_2(s)=0} = Z_a(s) + Z_c(s) = s + 1$$

$$z_{21} = \left.\frac{V_2(s)}{I_1(s)}\right|_{I_2(s)=0} = \frac{I_1(s)\,.\,Z_c(s)}{I_1(s)} = Z_c(s) = 1$$

$$z_{22} = \left.\frac{V_2(s)}{I_2(s)}\right|_{I_1(s)=0} = Z_b(s) + Z_c(s) = \frac{1}{s} + 1 = \frac{s+1}{s}$$

$$z_{12} = \left.\frac{V_1(s)}{I_2(s)}\right|_{I_1(s)=0} = \frac{I_2(s)\,.\,Z_c(s)}{I_2(s)} = Z_c(s) = 1.$$

Example 11.6. *Find the z-parameters for the resistive network of Example 11.2.*

Solution. With port 2 open circuited, the circuit may be put as in Fig. (*a*).

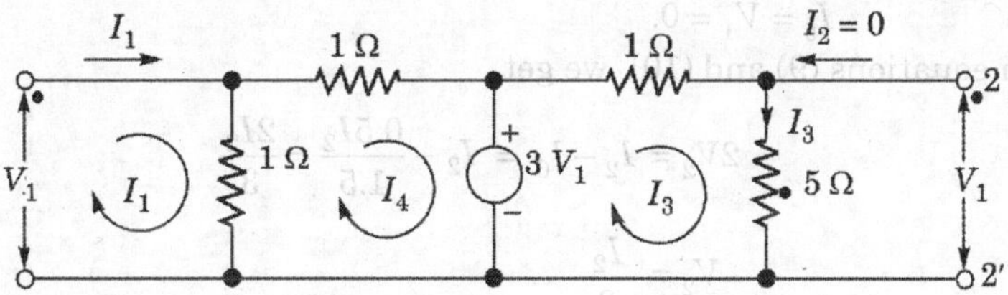

Fig. (*a*)

We then have,

$$V_2 = I_3 \times 0.5 \qquad \text{...(1)}$$

$$I_3(1 + 0.5) - 3V_1 = 0 \qquad \text{...(2)}$$

$$-I_1 + I_4(1+1) + 3V_1 = 0 \quad ...(3)$$

$$V_1 = I_1 - I_4 \quad ...(4)$$

From Eqs. (3) and (4),

$$V_1 = I_1 + \frac{3V_1 - I_1}{2} = \frac{I_1 + 3V_1}{2}$$

Hence $V_1 = -I_1$ ...(5)

Hence $z_{11} = \left.\frac{V_1}{I_1}\right|_{I_1=0} = -1\,\Omega$ ...(6)

Further $V_2 = 0.5\,I_3 = 0.5 \times \frac{3V_1}{1.5} = V_1 = -I_1.$

Hence $z_{12} = \left.\frac{V_1}{I_2}\right|_{I_2=0} = -1\,\Omega.$

With port 1 open circuited, the circuit may be put as in Fig. (*b*). Let the loop current be I_5 and I_6 as shown.

Then we have,

$$I_5 \times 1 = V_1 \quad ...(7)$$

$$2I_5 = 3V_1 \quad ...(8)$$

$$I_6(0.5+1) + 3V_1 = 0.5I_2 \quad ...(9)$$

and

$$0.5(I_2 - I_6) = V_2 \quad ...(10)$$

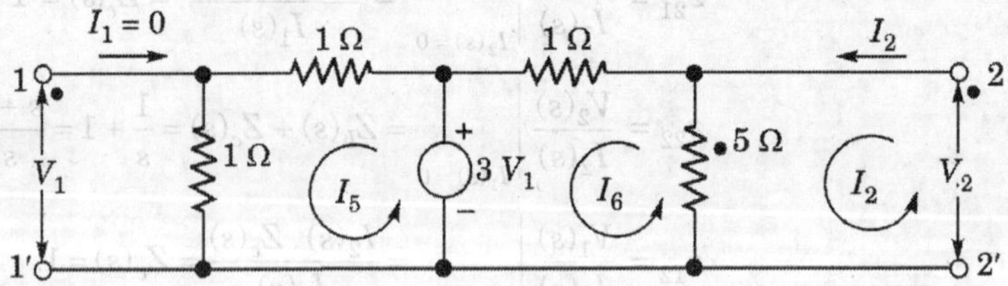

Fig. (*b*)

From equations (7) and (8), we get

$$I_5 = V_1 = 0.$$

Hence from equations (9) and (10), we get

$$2V_2 = I_2 - I_6 = I_2 - \frac{0.5I_2}{1.5} = \frac{2I_2}{3}$$

Hence $V_2 = \frac{I_2}{3}$

Hence $z_{22} = \left.\frac{V_2}{I_2}\right|_{I_1=0} = \frac{1}{3}\,\Omega$

$$z_{12} = \left.\frac{V_1}{I_2}\right|_{I_1=0} = 0.$$

Example 11.7. *Find the z-parameters for the R.C. ladder network of Example 11.3.*

Solution. With port 2 open circuited, the corresponding transform network is as shown in Fig. (*a*).

Then we have,

$$I_3(s) \,.\, 1 = V_2(s) \quad \text{...(1)}$$

$$I_3(s)\left[1 + \frac{1}{2s} + 1\right] = I_1(s) \quad \text{...(2)}$$

$$V_1(s) = I_1(s)\left[\frac{1}{2s} + 1\right] - I_3(s) \times 1 \quad \text{...(3)}$$

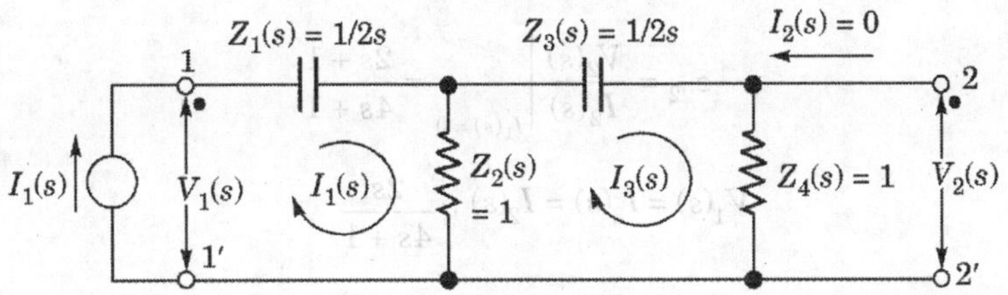

Fig. (*a*)

From equation (2),

$$I_3(s) \,.\, \frac{4s+1}{4s} = I_1(s)$$

or

$$I_3(s) = I_1(s) \,.\, \frac{2s}{4s+1} \quad \text{...(4)}$$

Hence

$$V_1(s) = I_1(s) \,.\, \frac{2s+1}{2s} - I_1(s) \,.\, \frac{2s}{4s+1} = I_1(s)\left[\frac{6s+1}{2s(4s+1)}\right] \quad \text{...(5)}$$

Hence

$$z_{11} = \left.\frac{V_1(s)}{I_1(s)}\right|_{I_2(s)=0} = \frac{6s+1}{2s(4s+1)}$$

Also

$$V_2(s) = I_3(s) = I_1(s) \,.\, \frac{2s}{4s+1} \quad \text{...(6)}$$

Hence

$$z_{21} = \left.\frac{V_2(s)}{I_1(s)}\right|_{I_2(s)=0} = \frac{2s}{4s+1}$$

With port 1 open circuited, the corresponding transform network is as shown in Fig. (*b*).

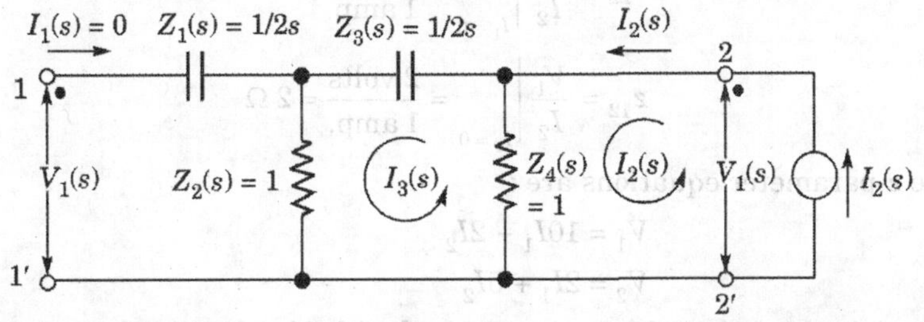

Fig. (*b*)

Then we have,

$$I_2(s) \,.\, 1 = V_1(s)$$

$$I_3(s) \,.\, \left[2 + \frac{1}{2s}\right] = I_2(s) \quad \text{...(8)}$$

$$V_3(s) = I_2(s) \,.\, 1 - I_3(s) \,.\, 1 \quad \text{...(9)}$$

From equation (8),

$$I_3(s) = I_2(s) \,.\, \frac{2s}{4s+1} \quad \text{...(10)}$$

Hence
$$V_2(s) = I_2(s) - I_3(s)$$

$$= I_2(s) - I_2(s) \,.\, \frac{2s}{4s+1} = \frac{2s+1}{4s+1} \,.\, I_2(s) \quad \text{...(11)}$$

Hence
$$z_{22} = \left.\frac{V_2(s)}{I_2(s)}\right|_{I_1(s)=0} = \frac{2s+1}{4s+1}$$

$$V_1(s) = I_3(s) = I_2(s) \,.\, \frac{2s}{4s+1}$$

Hence
$$z_{12}(s) = \left.\frac{V_1(s)}{I_2(s)}\right|_{I_1=0} = \frac{2s}{4s+1}.$$

Example 11.8. *The following results were obtained as a result measurements made on a 2-port resistive network :*

(i) With port 2 open circuited, a voltage of 10 volts applied at port 1 results in I_1 = 1 ampere and V_2 = + 2 volts,

(ii) With port 1 open circuited, a voltage of 5 volts applied at port 2 results in I_2 = I ampere and V_1 = + 2 volts.

Find the z-parametres for this network. With a 10 volts source connected across port I, find the voltage across 10 Ω resistor connected across port 2.

Solution.

$$z_{11} = \left.\frac{V_1}{I_1}\right|_{I_2=0} = \frac{10 \text{ volts}}{1 \text{ amp.}} = 10\ \Omega$$

$$z_{21} = \left.\frac{V_2}{I_1}\right|_{I_2=0} = \frac{2 \text{ volts}}{1 \text{ amp.}} = 2\ \Omega$$

$$z_{22} = \left.\frac{V_2}{I_2}\right|_{I_1=0} = \frac{5 \text{ volts}}{1 \text{ amp.}} = 5\ \Omega$$

$$z_{12} = \left.\frac{V_1}{I_2}\right|_{I_1=0} = \frac{2 \text{ volts}}{1 \text{ amp.}} = 2\ \Omega$$

Hence the z-parameter equations are :

$$V_1 = 10I_1 + 2I_2 \quad \text{...(1)}$$

$$V_2 = 2I_1 + 5I_2 \quad \text{...(2)}$$

With 10 Ω resistor connected across port 2 and with 10 volts source connected across port 1, we have

$$V_1 = 10 \text{ volts},$$

$$V_2 = -I_2 \cdot R_l = -10\, I_2.$$

The minus sign appears because the current I_2 flowing in the reference direction produces voltage $-V_2$.

Hence from equations (1) and (2), we have

$$10 = 10I_1 + 2I_2 \qquad ...(3)$$

and

$$-10I_2 = 2I_1 + 5I_2 \qquad ...(4)$$

Solving equations (3) and (4), we get

$$I_2 = \frac{-10}{73} \text{ amp.}$$

Hence voltage $$V_2 = -I_2 R_l = -\left(-\frac{10}{73}\right) \times 10 = \frac{100}{73} \text{ volts.}$$

11.4. Expressions for z-parameters in terms of y-parameters and vice versa

Equations (11.6) and (11.7) give the currents I_1 and I_2 in a 2-port network in terms of port voltages V_1 and V_2 and short circuit admittance parameters y_{11}, y_{12}, y_{21} and y_{22}.

On solving these equations for V_1 and V_2, we get

$$V_1 = \frac{y_{22}}{\Delta_y} \cdot I_1 - \frac{y_{12}}{\Delta_y} \cdot I_2 \qquad ...(11.27)$$

and

$$V_2 = \frac{-y_{21}}{\Delta_y} \cdot I_1 - \frac{y_{11}}{\Delta_y} \cdot I_2 \qquad ...(11.28)$$

where Δ_y is the admittance determinant and is given by,

$$\Delta_y = \begin{vmatrix} y_{11} & y_{12} \\ y_{21} & y_{22} \end{vmatrix} = y_{11} \cdot y_{22} - y_{12} \cdot y_{21} \qquad ...(11.29)$$

Comparing equations (11.27) and (11.28) with equations (11.19) and (11.20), we get

$$z_{11} = \frac{y_{22}}{\Delta_y} \qquad ...(11.30)$$

$$z_{22} = \frac{y_{11}}{\Delta_y} \qquad ...(11.31)$$

$$z_{12} = \frac{-y_{21}}{\Delta_y} \qquad ...(11.32)$$

and

$$z_{21} = \frac{-y_{12}}{\Delta_y} \qquad ...(11.33)$$

Similarly solving equations (11.19) and (11.20) for I_1 and I_2 and comparing these with equations (11.6) and (11.7), we get the following equations giving y-parameters in terms of z-parameters.

$$y_{11} = \frac{z_{22}}{\Delta_z} \qquad ...(11.34)$$

$$y_{22} = \frac{z_{11}}{\Delta_z} \qquad ...(11.35)$$

$$y_{12} = \frac{-z_{21}}{\Delta_z} \quad ...(11.36)$$

and
$$z_{21} = \frac{-z_{12}}{\Delta_z} \quad ...(11.37)$$

where Δz is the impedance determinant and is given by

$$\Delta_z = \begin{vmatrix} z_{11} & z_{12} \\ z_{21} & z_{22} \end{vmatrix} = z_{11} \cdot z_{22} - z_{12} \cdot z_{21} \quad ...(11.38)$$

From equations (11.32) and (11.37), we get

$$\Delta_y \cdot \Delta_x = \left(\frac{-y_{21}}{z_{12}}\right)\left(\frac{-z_{12}}{y_{21}}\right)$$

or
$$\Delta_y \cdot \Delta_z = 1 \quad ...(11.39)$$

Finally from equations (11.30) and (11.34), we get

$$z_{11} \cdot y_{11} = \frac{z_{22} \cdot y_{22}}{\Delta_y \cdot \Delta_z}$$

or
$$z_{11} \cdot y_{11} = z_{22} \cdot y_{22} \quad ...(11.40)$$

Example 11.9. *A two-port network has the following z-parameters : $z_{11} = 10\ \Omega$, $z_{22} = 12\ \Omega$, $z_{12} = z_{21} = 5\ \Omega$. Compute the y-parameters for the same network.*

Solution.
$$\Delta_z = z_{11} \cdot z_{22} - z^2_{12} = (10 \times 12) - (5)^2 = 95.$$

Hence
$$y_{11} = \frac{z_{22}}{\Delta_z} = \frac{12}{95} = 0.1263 \text{ S}$$

$$y_{22} = \frac{z_{11}}{\Delta_z} = \frac{10}{95} = 0.1053 \text{ S}$$

$$y_{12} = y_{21} = \frac{-z_{12}}{\Delta_z} = \frac{-5}{95} = -0.0526 \text{ S}.$$

11.5. Transmission Parameters (A, B, C, D Parameters)

The transmission parameters express voltage and current at port 1 in terms of voltage and current at port 2 as given by the following equations :

$$V_1 = A \cdot V_2 - B \cdot I_2 \quad ...(11.41)$$

$$I_1 = C \cdot V_2 - D \cdot I_2 \quad ...(11.42)$$

Here *A, B, C* and *D* are the *transmission parameters,* also sometimes called *ABCD parameters,* or *chain parameters* or *general circuit parameters.*

In equations (11.41) and (11.42), the negative sign in the second term is for I_2 and not for the parameters *B* and *D*. This negative sign arises from the fact that reference direction of I_2 as in Fig. 11.1 is opposite to that in power transmission problems.

Physical significance of these *ABCD* parameters becomes clear on studying the 2-port network under open circuit and short circuit conditions at port 2. This also enables us to express these *ABCD* parameters in terms of *z* and *y*-parameters.

Thus with port 2 open circuited *i.e.*, with $I_2 = 0$, equation (11.41) yields,

$$\frac{1}{A} = \left.\frac{V_2}{V_1}\right|_{I_2=0} = g_{21}\big|_{I_2=0} \qquad ...(11.43)$$

$$= \text{open circuit voltage gain} \qquad ...(11.44)$$

With port 2 short-circuited, *i.e.* with $I_2 = 0$, equation (11.41) yields,

$$-\frac{1}{B} = \left.\frac{I_2}{V_1}\right|_{V_2=0} = y_{21}\Big|_{V_2=0} \qquad ...(11.45)$$

$$= \text{short circuit transfer admittance } y_{21} \qquad ...(11.46)$$

With port 2 open-circuited, *i.e.* with $I_2 = 0$, equation (11.42) yields,

$$\frac{1}{C} = \left.\frac{V_2}{I_1}\right|_{I_2=0} = z_{21}\Big|_{I_2=0} \qquad ...(11.47)$$

$$= \text{open circuit transfer impedance } z_{21} \qquad ...(11.48)$$

Finally with port 2 short circuited, *i.e.* with $V_2 = 0$, equation (11.42) yields,

$$-\frac{1}{D} = \left.\frac{I_2}{I_1}\right|_{V_2=0} = \alpha_{21}\Big|_{V_2=0} \qquad ...(11.49)$$

$$= \text{short circuit current gain } \alpha_{21} \qquad ...(11.50)$$

The transmission parameters are frequently used in describing two-port networks arranged in cascade. Thus Fig. 11.4 shows two such networks N_m and N_n arranged in cascade.

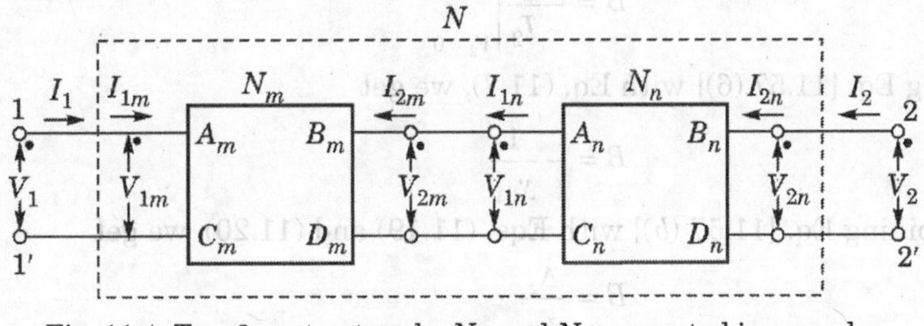

Fig. 11.4. Two 2-port networks N_m and N_n connected in cascade.

The *ABCD* parameter equations for these two networks in the matrix form are as below :

$$\begin{bmatrix} V_{1m} \\ I_{1m} \end{bmatrix} = \begin{bmatrix} A_m & B_m \\ C_m & D_m \end{bmatrix} \begin{bmatrix} V_{2m} \\ -I_{2m} \end{bmatrix} \qquad ...(11.51)$$

and

$$\begin{bmatrix} V_{1n} \\ I_{1n} \end{bmatrix} = \begin{bmatrix} A_n & B_n \\ C_n & D_n \end{bmatrix} \begin{bmatrix} V_{2n} \\ -I_{2n} \end{bmatrix} \qquad ...(11.52)$$

The complete network comprising these two networks in cascade is shown enclosed by the dashed line in Fig. 11.4. For this complete network, we have

$$\begin{bmatrix} V_1 \\ I_1 \end{bmatrix} = \begin{bmatrix} A & B \\ C & D \end{bmatrix} \begin{bmatrix} V_2 \\ -I_2 \end{bmatrix} \qquad ...(11.53)$$

But from Fig. 11.4 we see that,

$V_1 = V_{1m}$; $I_1 = I_{1m}$; $V_{2m} = V_{1n}$; $I_{2m} = -I_{1n}$; $I_{2n} = I_2$ and $V_{2n} = V_2$ ...(11.54)

We combine Eqs. (11.52), (11.53) and (11.54) to eliminate currents and voltages with subscript *m* or *n* and thus get,

$$\begin{bmatrix} A & B \\ C & D \end{bmatrix} = \begin{bmatrix} A_m & B_m \\ C_m & D_m \end{bmatrix} \begin{bmatrix} A_n & B_n \\ C_n & D_n \end{bmatrix} \quad ...(11.55)$$

Eq. (11.55) holds for two networks in cascade but it may be generalized for any number of two-port networks connected in cascade. Thus we find that the transmission parameter matrix for the overall network is simply the matrix product of the transmission parameter matrices of each of the two-port networks in cascade.

11.6. Expressions for ABCD Parameters in terms of z-parameters and y-parameters

From Eqs. (11.41) and (11.42), we get

$$A = \left. \frac{V_1}{V_2} \right|_{I_2 = 0} \quad ...(11.56)$$

Combining Eq. (11.56) with Eqs. (11.19) and (11.20), we get

$$A = \frac{z_{11}}{z_{21}} \quad ...(11.57)$$

Combining Eq. (11.56) with Eq. (11.7), we get

$$A = \frac{-y_{22}}{y_{21}} \quad ...[11.57(a)]$$

Similarly from Eqs. (11.41) and (11.42), we get

$$B = \left. \frac{V_1}{-I_2} \right|_{V_2 = 0} \quad ...[11.57\ (b)]$$

Combining Eq. [11.57 (6)] with Eq. (11.7), we get

$$B = -\frac{1}{y_{21}} \quad ...(11.58)$$

Also combining Eq. [11.57 (*b*)] with Eqs. (11.19) and (11.20), we get

$$B = \frac{\Delta_z}{z_{21}} \quad ...[11.59\ (a)]$$

$$= \frac{z_{11} \cdot z_{22} - z_{21} \cdot z_{12}}{z_{21}} \quad ...[11.59\ (b)]$$

Again from Eqs. (11.41) and (11.42), we get

$$C = \left. \frac{I_1}{V_2} \right|_{I_1 = 0} \quad ...(11.60)$$

Combining Eq. (11.60) with Eq. (11.20), we get

$$C = \frac{1}{z_{21}} \quad ...(11.61)$$

Combining Eq. (11.60) with Eqs. (11.6) and (11.7), we get

$$C = \frac{-\Delta_y}{y_{21}} \quad ...[11.62\ (a)]$$

$$= \frac{(y_{11} \cdot y_{22} - y_{12} \cdot y_{21})}{y_{21}} \quad ...[11.62\ (b)]$$

Finally from Eqs. (11.41) and (11.42), we get

$$D = \left. \frac{I_1}{-I_2} \right|_{V_2 = 0} \quad ...(11.63)$$

Combining Eq. (11.63) with Eq. (11.20), we get

$$D = \frac{z_{22}}{z_{21}} \quad ...(11.64)$$

Combining Eq. (11.63) with Eqs. (11.6) and (11.7), we get

$$D = \frac{-y_{11}}{y_{21}} \quad ...(11.65)$$

Thus we see that parameters A and D are dimensionless, B has dimensions of impedance and C has dimensions of admittance.

Also the determinant of Eqs. (11.41) and (11.42) is given by

$$\Delta = BC - AD \quad ...(11.66)$$

Substituting the values of parameters A, B, C and D, we get

$$\Delta = \left(\frac{-1}{y_{21}}\right)\left(\frac{-\Delta_y}{y_{21}}\right) - \left(\frac{-y_{22}}{y_{21}}\right)\left(-\frac{y_{11}}{y_{21}}\right)$$

$$= \frac{\Delta_y - y_{22} \cdot y_{11}}{y_{12} \cdot y_{21}} = \frac{y_{22} \cdot y_{11} - y_{12} \cdot y_{21} - y_{22} \cdot y_{11}}{y_{12} \cdot y_{21}} = -1.$$

Hence $AD - BC = 1$. ...(11.67)

Hence in a two-port bilateral network, if three out of four transmission parameters are known, then the fourth may be found out using Eq. (11.67).

11.7. Inverse Transmission Parameters

Eqs. (11.41) and (11.42) express V_1 and I_1 at port 1 in terms of V_2 and I_2 at port 2. Alternatively we may express V_2 and I_2 in terms of V_1 and I_1 as below :

$$V_2 = A'V_1 - B'I_1 \quad ...(11.68)$$

$$I_2 = C'V_1 - D'I_1 \quad ...(11.69)$$

Here A', B', C' and D' constitute the so called "Inverse Transmission parameters". Eqs. (11.68) and (11.69) apply to transmission in the direction opposite to that described by Eqs. (11.41) and (11.42). Because of similarity to Eqs. (11.68) and (11.69) with Eqs. (11.41) and (11.42), the $A'B'C'D'$ parameters have properties similar to $ABCD$ parameters.

Thus Eqs. (11.43) to (11.65) apply to $A'B'C'D'$ parameters if we interchange the subscripts 1 and 2. We may similarly show that for the inverse transmission parameters.

$$A'D' - B'C' = 1. \quad ...(11.70)$$

Example 11.10. *Find out ABCD parameters for the resistive n-network of Example 11.1.*

Solution. The circuit is redrawn as shown in Fig. (*a*).

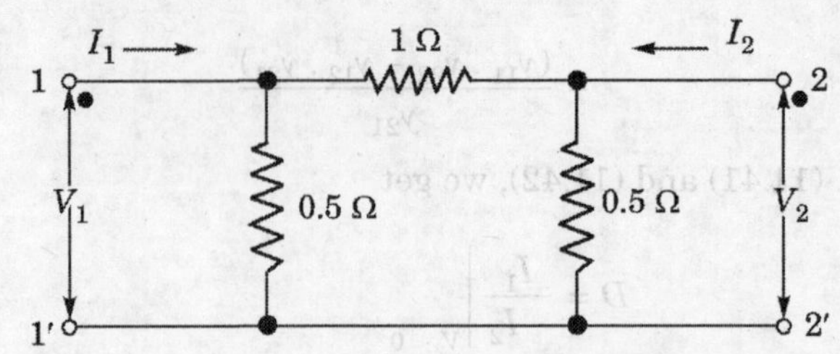

Fig. (*a*)

On short circuiting port 2, the circuit reduces to the form shown in Fig. (*b*)

$$V_1 = -I_2(1\ \Omega) = -I_2.$$

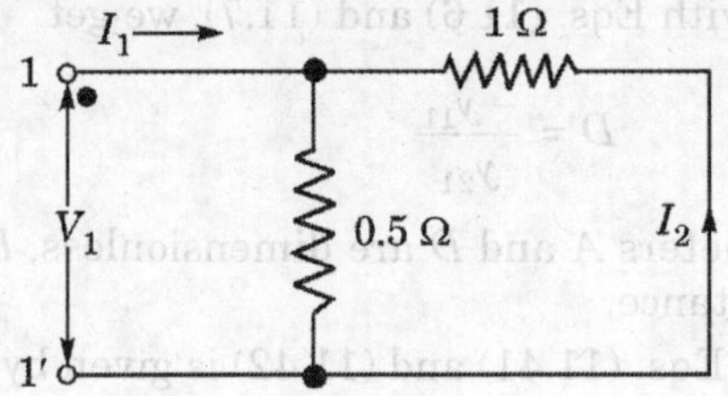

Fig. (*b*)

Hence
$$B = \left.\frac{-V_1}{I_2}\right|_{V_2=0} = 1\ \Omega$$

Also
$$I_1 = \frac{V_1}{0.5} + \frac{V_1}{1} = 3V_1 = -3I_2$$

Hence
$$D = \left.\frac{-I_1}{I_2}\right|_{V_2=0} = 3$$

With port 2 open circuited, we get $I_2 = 0$.

Let the currents be as shown in Fig. (*c*).

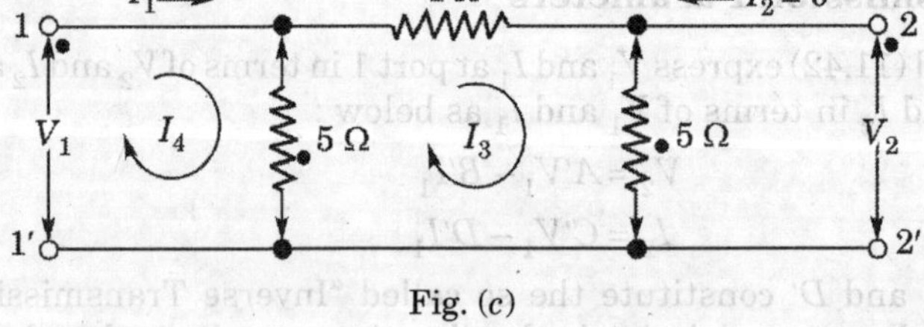

Fig. (*c*)

Then
$$I_4 = \frac{V_1}{0.5} = 2V_1$$

$$I_3 = \frac{V_1}{1.5} = \frac{2V_1}{3}$$

$$I_1 = I_3 + I_4 = 2V_1\left(1 + \frac{1}{3}\right) = \frac{8V_1}{3}$$

$$V_2 = I_3 \times 0.5 = 0.5 \times \frac{2V_1}{3} = \frac{V_1}{3}$$

Hence
$$A = \left.\frac{V_1}{V_2}\right|_{I_2=0} = 3$$

$$C = \left.\frac{I_1}{V_2}\right|_{I_2=0} = \frac{8V_1/3}{V_1/3} = 8\text{ S.}$$

Example 11.11. *Find the transmission parameters for the given R-C network.*

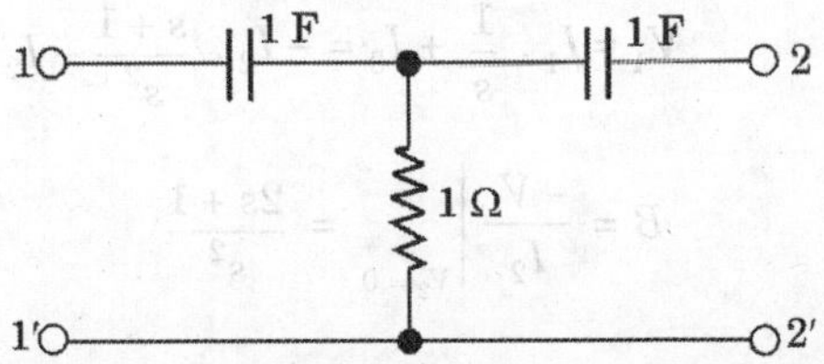

Solution. With port 2 open circuited, Fig. (*a*) below gives the current, voltages and impedances.

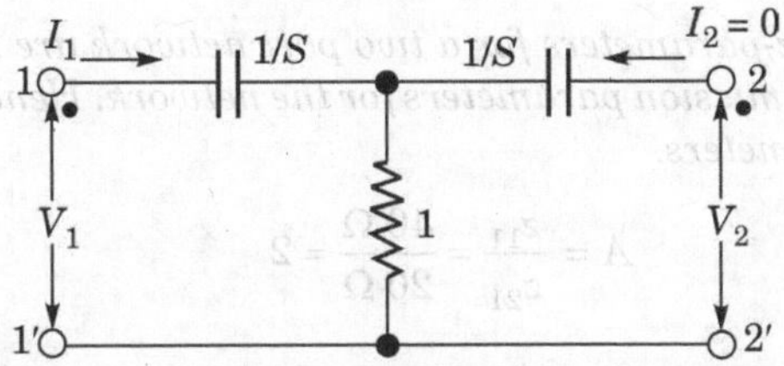

Fig. (*a*)

Then
$$I_2 = 0$$
$$I_1 = \frac{V_1}{1+\frac{1}{s}} = V_1 \cdot \frac{s}{s+1}$$
$$V_2 = I_1 \times 1\,\Omega.$$

Hence
$$A = \left.\frac{V_1}{V_2}\right|_{I_1=0} = \frac{I_1 \cdot \frac{s+1}{s}}{I_1} = \frac{s+1}{s}$$

and
$$C = \left.\frac{I_1}{V_1}\right|_{I_2=0} = \frac{I_1}{I_1} = 1\text{ S}$$

With port 2 short circuited, the circuit is as shown in Fig. (*b*).

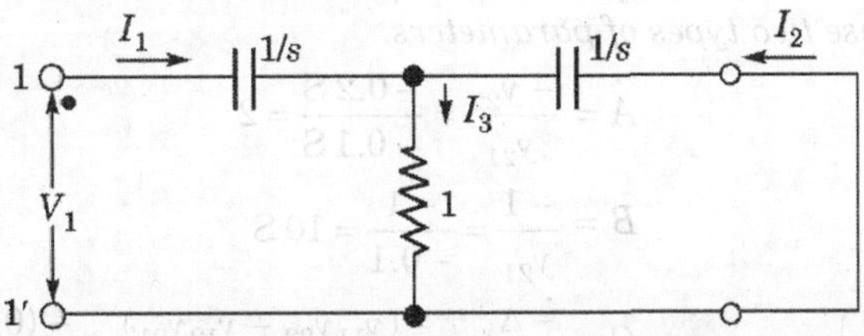

Fig. (*b*)

Then $$V_2 = 0$$

$$I_3 = -I_2 \cdot \frac{1}{s}$$

$$I_1 = I_3 - I_2 = I_2\left[-\frac{1}{s} - 1\right] = -I_2 \cdot \frac{s+1}{s}$$

$$V_1 = I_1 \cdot \frac{1}{s} + I_3 = -I_2 \cdot \frac{s+1}{s^2} - I_2 \cdot \frac{1}{s} = -I_2 \cdot \frac{2s+1}{s^2}$$

Hence $$B = \left.\frac{-V_1}{I_2}\right|_{V_2=0} = \frac{2s+1}{s^2}$$

$$D = \left.\frac{-I_1}{I_2}\right|_{V_2=0} = \frac{s+1}{s}.$$

Example 11.12. *The z-parameters for a two port network are : $z_{11} = 40\ \Omega$, $Z_{22} = 30\ \Omega$, $Z_{12} = Z_{21} = 20\ \Omega$. Compute the transmission parameters for the network. Hence write the network equations using these two types of parameters.*

Solution. $$A = \frac{z_{11}}{z_{21}} = \frac{40\ \Omega}{20\ \Omega} = 2$$

$$B = \frac{\Delta_z}{z_{22}} = \frac{z_{11} \cdot z_{22} - z_{12} \cdot z_{21}}{z_{21}} = \frac{(40 \times 30) - (20 \times 20)}{20} = 40\ \Omega$$

$$C = \frac{1}{z_{21}} = \frac{1}{20} = 0.05\ \text{S}$$

$$D = \frac{z_{22}}{z_{21}} = \frac{30\ \Omega}{20\ \Omega} = 1.5$$

Network equations using z-parameters are :

$$V_1 = 40I_1 + 20I_2$$
$$V_2 = 20I_1 + 30I_2$$

Similarly network equations using *ABCD* parameters are :

$$V_1 = 2V_2 - 40I_2$$
$$I_1 = 0.05V_2 - 1.5I_2.$$

Example 11.13. *The y-parameters of a two-port network are : $y_{11} = 0.4\ S$; $y_{22} = 0.2\ S$; $y_{12} = y_{21} = -0.1\ S$. Compute the transmission parameters of the network and write the equilibrium equations for the network using these two types of parameters.*

Solution. $$A = \frac{-y_{22}}{y_{21}} = \frac{-0.2\ \text{S}}{-0.1\ \text{S}} = 2$$

$$B = \frac{-1}{y_{21}} = \frac{-1}{-0.1} = 10\ \text{S}$$

$$C = \frac{-\Delta_y}{y_{21}} = \frac{-(y_{11}y_{22} - y_{12}y_{21})}{y_{21}} = \frac{-(0.4 \times 0.2 - 0.01)}{-0.1} = 0.7\ \text{S}$$

$$D = \frac{-y_{11}}{y_{21}} = \frac{-0.4\ \text{S}}{-0.1\ \text{S}} = 4$$

Network equation using y-parameters are :

$$I_1 = 0.4V_1 - 0.1V_2$$

$$I_2 = -0.1V_1 - 0.2V_2$$

Network equations using *ABCD* parameters are :

$$V_1 = 2V_2 - 10I_2$$

$$I_1 = 0.7V_2 - 4I_2$$

Example 11.14. *The z-parameters of a 2-port network are :* $z_{11} = 10\ \Omega$, $z_{22} = 8\ \Omega$, $z_{12} = z_{21} = 5\ \Omega$. *Compute the y-parameters and the ABCD parameters of the network and write sets of equations using (i) z-parameters, (ii) y-parameters and (iii) ABCD prameters.*

Solution.

$$y_{11} = \frac{z_{22}}{z_{11} \cdot z_{22} - z_{12} \cdot z_{21}} = \frac{8}{(10 \times 8) - (5)^2} = 0.1454\ \text{S}$$

$$y_{22} = \frac{z_{11}}{z_{11} \cdot z_{22} - z_{21} \cdot z_{21}} = \frac{10}{(10 \times 8) - (5)^2} = 0.1818\ \text{S}$$

$$y_{12} = y_{21} = \frac{-z_{12}}{z_{11} \cdot z_{22} - z_{12} \cdot z_{21}} = \frac{-5}{(10 \times 8) - (5)^2} = -0.0909\ \text{S}$$

$$A = \frac{z_{11}}{z_{21}} = \frac{10\ \Omega}{5\ \Omega} = 2$$

$$B = \frac{z_{11} \cdot z_{22} - z_{12} \cdot z_{21}}{z_{21}} = \frac{(10 \times 8) - (5)^2}{5} = 11\ \Omega$$

$$C = \frac{1}{z_{21}} = \frac{1}{5\ \Omega} = 0.2\ \text{S}$$

$$D = \frac{z_{22}}{z_{21}} = \frac{8\ \Omega}{5\ \Omega} = 1.6$$

Network equations using z-parameters are :

$$V_1 = 10I_1 + 5I_2$$

$$V_2 = 5I_1 + 8I_2$$

Network equations using y-parameters are :

$$I_1 = 0.1454V_1 - 0.0909V_2$$

$$I_2 = -0.0909V_1 + 0.1818V_2$$

Network equations using *ABCD* parameters are :

$$V_1 = 2V_2 - 11I_2$$

$$I_1 = 0.2V_2 - 1.6I_2.$$

11.8. Hybrid Parameters

Hybrid parameters find extensive use in transistor circuits. These parameters express the voltage V_1 at port 1 and current I_2 at port 2 in terms of I_1 and V_2 as given below :

$$V_1 = h_{11} . I_1 + h_{12} V_2 \quad ...(11.71)$$

$$I_2 = h_{21} . I_1 + h_{22} . V_2 \quad ...(11.72)$$

From these equations, the h-parameters may be defined under the conditions $I_1 = 0$ and $V_2 = 0$. Thus by letting $V_2 = 0$, *i.e.* short circuiting port 2, we have

$$h_{11} = \left.\frac{V_1}{I_1}\right|_{V_2 = 0} \quad ...(11.73)$$

$$h_{21} = \left.\frac{I_2}{I_1}\right|_{V_2 = 0} \quad ...(11.74)$$

Similarly by letting $I_1 = 0$, *i.e.* open circuiting port 1, we get

$$h_{12} = \left.\frac{V_1}{V_2}\right|_{I_1 = 0} \quad ...(11.75)$$

$$h_{22} = \left.\frac{I_2}{V_2}\right|_{I_1 = 0} \quad ...(11.76)$$

Obviously then,

h_{11} is the short-circuit input impedance or the driving point impedance at port 1.

h_{21} is the short circuit current gain.

h_{12} is the open circuit voltage gain in the reverse direction.

h_{22} is open circuit output admittance or the driving point admittance at port 2.

h_{21} and h_{12} are dimensionless.

h_{11} has the dimensions of an impedance.

h_{22} has the dimensions of an admittance.

Since these parameters are dimensionally mixed up, these are called "hybrid parameters".

In the case of a transistor, it is easy to make measurements to determine h_{11} and h_{21} by short circuiting port 2. On the other hand, it is more difficult to make measurements with port 2 open circuited. This is the reason why h-parameters are popularly used in representing transistors. Fig. 11.5 shows the h-parameter network which is equivalent to the general 2 port network.

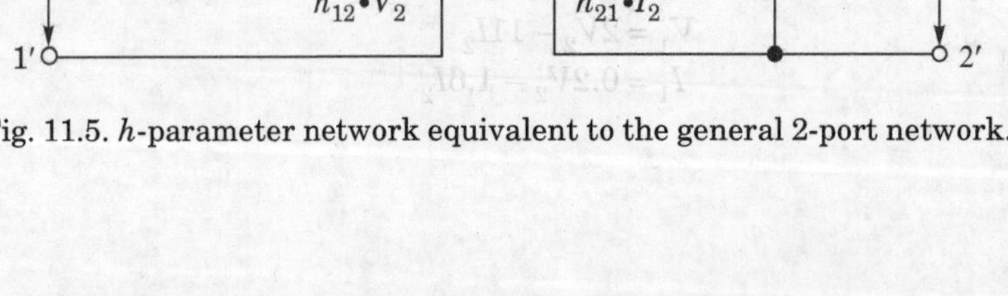

Fig. 11.5. h-parameter network equivalent to the general 2-port network.

11.9. Inverse Hybrid Parameter or g-parameters

Inverse hybrid parameters, also called *g*-parameters, express the current I_1 and voltage V_2 in terms of V_1 and I_2 as below :

$$I_1 = g_{11} \cdot V_1 + g_{12} \cdot I_2 \qquad ...(11.77)$$

$$V_2 = g_{21} \cdot V_1 + g_{22} \cdot I_2 \qquad ...(11.78)$$

From equations (11.77) and (11.78), we may give physical significance to the *g*-parameters. Thus,

$$g_{11} = \left.\frac{I_1}{V_1}\right|_{I_2 = 0} \qquad ...(11.79)$$

= open circuit input admittance or the driving point admittance at port 1 ...(11.80)

$$g_{21} = \left.\frac{V_2}{V_1}\right|_{I_2 = 0} \qquad ...(11.81)$$

= open circuit voltage ratio ...(11.82)

$$g_{12} = \left.\frac{I_1}{I_2}\right|_{V_1 = 0} \qquad ...(11.83)$$

= short circuit reverse current gain ...(11.84)

$$g_{22} = \left.\frac{V_2}{I_2}\right|_{V_1 = 0} \qquad ...(11.85)$$

= short circuit output impedance or the driving point impedance at port 2 ...(11.86)

Fig. 11.6 shows the *g*-parameter network which is equivalent to the general 2-port network.

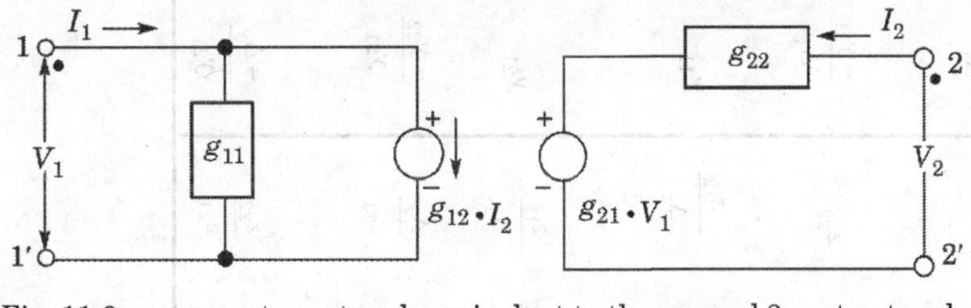

Fig. 11.6. *g*-parameter network equivalent to the general 2-port network.

11.10. Conversion of Parameter Sets

We have just studied six sets of parameters. Each has its own utility and is suited for certain specific applications. However, we often find it necessary to convert from one set of parameters to another. Through simple mathematical manipulation, it is possible to convert from any one set to any of the remaining sets. Table 11.2 gives the relationships between different sets of parameters. In this table, matrices placed in each of the rows are equivalent. The equivalence involves determinants Δ_x, Δ_y etc. where,

$$\Delta_x = z_{11} \cdot z_{22} - z_{12} \cdot z_{21}$$

$$\Delta_y = y_{11} \cdot y_{22} - y_{12} \cdot y_{21}$$

and so on.

Table 11.2. Conversion of Parameters

	$[z]$		$[y]$		$[ABCD]$		$[A'B'C'D']$		$[h]$		$[g]$	
$[z]$	z_{11}	z_{12}	$\frac{y_{22}}{\Delta_y}$	$\frac{-y_{22}}{\Delta_y}$	$\frac{A}{C}$	$\frac{\Delta_T}{C}$	$\frac{D'}{C'}$	$\frac{1}{C'}$	$\frac{\Delta_h}{h_{22}}$	$\frac{h_{12}}{h_{22}}$	$\frac{1}{g_{11}}$	$\frac{-g_{12}}{g_{11}}$
	z_{21}	z_{22}	$\frac{-y_{21}}{\Delta_y}$	$\frac{y_{11}}{\Delta_y}$	$\frac{1}{C}$	$\frac{D}{C}$	$\frac{\Delta_T'}{C'}$	$\frac{A'}{C'}$	$\frac{-h_{21}}{h_{22}}$	$\frac{1}{h_{22}}$	$\frac{g_{21}}{g_{11}}$	$\frac{\Delta_g}{h_{11}}$
$[y]$	$\frac{z_{22}}{\Delta_z}$	$\frac{-z_{12}}{\Delta_z}$	y_{11}	y_{12}	$\frac{D}{B}$	$\frac{-\Delta_T}{B}$	$\frac{A'}{B'}$	$\frac{-1}{B'}$	$\frac{1}{h_{11}}$	$\frac{-h_{12}}{h_{11}}$	$\frac{\Delta_g}{g_{22}}$	$\frac{g_{12}}{g_{22}}$
	$\frac{-z_{22}}{\Delta_z}$	$\frac{z_{12}}{\Delta_z}$	y_{21}	y_{22}	$\frac{-1}{B}$	$\frac{A}{B}$	$\frac{-\Delta_T'}{B'}$	$\frac{D'}{B'}$	$\frac{h_{21}}{h_{11}}$	$\frac{\Delta_h}{h_{11}}$	$\frac{-g_{21}}{g_{22}}$	$\frac{1}{g_{22}}$
$[ABCD]$	$\frac{z_{11}}{z_{21}}$	$\frac{\Delta_z}{z_{21}}$	$\frac{-y_{22}}{y_{21}}$	$\frac{-1}{y_{21}}$	A	B	$\frac{D'}{\Delta_T'}$	$\frac{B'}{\Delta_T'}$	$\frac{-\Delta_h}{h_{21}}$	$\frac{-h_{11}}{h_{21}}$	$\frac{1}{g_{21}}$	$\frac{g_{22}}{g_{21}}$
	$\frac{1}{z_{21}}$	$\frac{z_{22}}{z_{21}}$	$\frac{-\Delta_y}{y_{21}}$	$\frac{-y_{11}}{y_{21}}$	C	D	$\frac{C'}{\Delta_T'}$	$\frac{A'}{\Delta_T'}$	$\frac{-h_{22}}{h_{21}}$	$\frac{-1}{h_{21}}$	$\frac{g_{11}}{g_{21}}$	$\frac{\Delta_z}{\Delta_{21}}$

	[z]		[y]		[ABCD]		[A'B'C'D']		[h]		[g]	
[A'B'C'D']	$\frac{z_{22}}{z_{12}}$	$\frac{\Delta_z}{z_{12}}$	$\frac{-y_{11}}{y_{12}}$	$\frac{-1}{y_{12}}$	$\frac{D}{\Delta_T}$	$\frac{B}{\Delta_T}$	A'	B'	$\frac{1}{h_{12}}$	$\frac{h_{11}}{h_{12}}$	$\frac{-\Delta_g}{g_{12}}$	$\frac{-g_{22}}{g_{12}}$
	$\frac{1}{z_{12}}$	$\frac{z_{11}}{z_{12}}$	$\frac{-\Delta_y}{y_{12}}$	$\frac{-y_{22}}{y_{12}}$	$\frac{C}{\Delta_T}$	$\frac{A}{\Delta_T}$	C'	D'	$\frac{h_{22}}{h_{12}}$	$\frac{\Delta_h}{h_{12}}$	$\frac{-g_{11}}{g_{12}}$	$\frac{-1}{g_{12}}$
[h]	$\frac{\Delta_z}{z_{22}}$	$\frac{z_{12}}{z_{22}}$	$\frac{1}{y_{11}}$	$\frac{-y_{12}}{y_{11}}$	$\frac{B}{D}$	$\frac{\Delta_T}{D}$	$\frac{B'}{A'}$	$\frac{1}{A'}$	h_{11}	h_{12}	$\frac{g_{22}}{\Delta_g}$	$\frac{-g_{12}}{\Delta_g}$
	$\frac{-z_{21}}{z_{22}}$	$\frac{1}{z_{22}}$	$\frac{y_{21}}{y_{11}}$	$\frac{\Delta_y}{y_{11}}$	$\frac{-1}{D}$	$\frac{C}{D}$	$\frac{-\Delta_T'}{A'}$	$\frac{C'}{A'}$	h_{21}	h_{22}	$\frac{-g_{21}}{\Delta_g}$	$\frac{g_{11}}{\Delta_g}$
[g]	$\frac{1}{z_{11}}$	$\frac{-z_{12}}{z_{11}}$	$\frac{\Delta_y}{y_{22}}$	$\frac{y_{12}}{y_{22}}$	$\frac{C}{A}$	$\frac{-\Delta_T}{A}$	$\frac{C'}{D'}$	$\frac{-1}{D'}$	$\frac{h_{22}}{\Delta_h}$	$\frac{-h_{12}}{\Delta_h}$	g_{11}	g_{12}
	$\frac{z_{21}}{z_{11}}$	$\frac{\Delta_z}{z_{11}}$	$\frac{-y_{21}}{y_{22}}$	$\frac{1}{y_{22}}$	$\frac{1}{A}$	$\frac{B}{A}$	$\frac{\Delta_T'}{D'}$	$\frac{B'}{D'}$	$\frac{-h_{21}}{\Delta_h}$	$\frac{h_{11}}{\Delta_h}$	g_{21}	g_{22}

11.11. Conditions for Reciprocity of a Two-port Network

Table 11.3 gives the conditions, for the six sets of parameters, under which (*i*) a two-port passive network is reciprocal and (*ii*) a passive reciprocal two-port network is symmetrical *i.e.* the condition under which the ports may be interchanged without altering the port voltages and currents.

Table 11.3

Condition under which Passive Two-port Network is Reciprocal and Symmetrical

Parameters	*Conditions for Reciprocity*	*Condition for Electrical symmetry*
z	$z_{12} = z_{21}$	$z_{11} = z_{22}$
y	$y_{12} = y_{21}$	$y_{11} = y_{22}$
$ABCD$	$AD - BC = 1$	$A = D$
$A'B'C'D'$	$A'D' - B'C' = 1$	$A' = D'$
h	$h_{12} = -h_{21}$	$\Delta_h = 1$
g	$h_{12} = -g_{21}$	$\Delta_g = 1$

11.12. Input Impedance in terms of z-parameters and Load Impedance

Fig. 11.7 shows a two-port network at the input port of which a voltage V_1 is applied and at the output port of which a load impedance Z_l is connected.

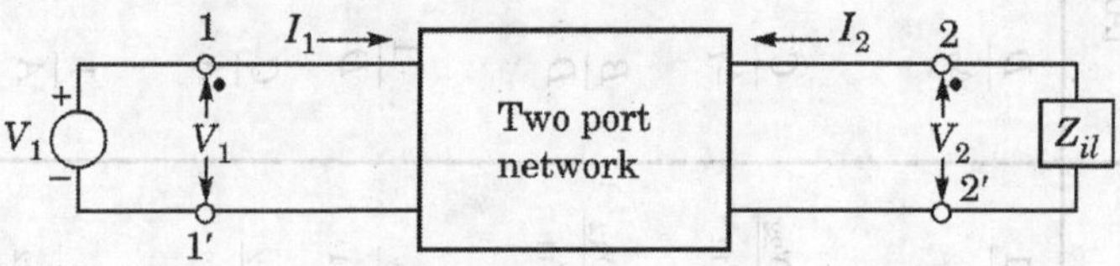

Fig. 11.7. Input impedance of a 2-port network.

The input impedance or the driving point impedance at port 1 is given by

$$Z_i = \frac{V_1}{I_1} \quad \text{...(11.87)}$$

while $$Z_l = \frac{V_2}{-I_1} \quad \text{...(11.88)}$$

But from Eq. (11.20), we get

$$z_{21} \cdot I_1 = V_2 - z_{22} \cdot I_2 \quad \text{...(11.89)}$$

$$= -I_2 Z_l - z_{22} \cdot I_2 \quad \text{...(11.90)}$$

Hence $$I_2 = \frac{-z_{21} \cdot I_1}{z_{22} + Z_l} \quad \text{...(11.91)}$$

Hence from Eq. (11.19)

$$z_{11} \cdot I_1 + z_{12}\left[\frac{-z_{21}}{z_{22} + Z_l}\right] I_1 = V_1$$

or $$I_1\left[\frac{z_{11} \cdot z_{22} - z_{12} \cdot z_{21} + z_{11} \cdot Z_l}{z_{22} + Z_l}\right] = V_1$$

Hence $$Z_i = \frac{V_1}{I_1} = \frac{z_{11} \cdot z_{22} - z_{12} \cdot z_{21} + z_{11} \cdot Z_l}{z_{22} + Z_l} \quad ...(11.92)$$

or $$Z_i = \frac{\Delta_z + z_{11} \cdot Z_l}{z_{22} + Z_l} \quad ...(11.93)$$

Thus an impedance Z_l connected at the output of a two-port network results in an impedance Z_i at the input terminals, *i.e.* there results a transformation of impedance.

Now if the output end is open circuited, *i.e.* Z_l is made infinite, the input impedance is

$$Z_{io} = \frac{\frac{\Delta_z}{Z_i} + z_{11}}{\frac{Z_2}{Z_l} + 1} = z_{11}$$

On the other hand, if the output end is short circuited, *i.e.* Z_l is made zero, then the input impedance is,

$$Z_{is} = \frac{\Delta_z}{z_{22}} = \frac{1}{y_{11}}.$$

11.13. Input Impedance in terms of y-Parameters and Load Admittance

With reference to the two-port network of Fig. 11.7, we have

Input impedance $$Z_i = \frac{V_1}{I_1} \quad ...(11.94)$$

while $$-I_2 = V_2 . Y_l \quad ...(11.95)$$

where Y_l is the load admittance and equals $\frac{1}{Z_l}$. Hence from Eq. (11.7), we get

$$y_{21} \cdot V_1 + y_{22}\left(\frac{-I_2}{Y_l}\right) = I_2 \quad ...(11.96)$$

or $$y_{21} \cdot V_1 = I_2\left[1 + \frac{y_{22}}{Y_l}\right] \quad ...(11.97)$$

Hence $$I_2 = \frac{y_{21} \cdot V_1}{1 + \frac{y_{22}}{Y_l}} \quad ...(11.98)$$

Hence from Eq. (11.6), we get

$$I_1 = y_{11} \cdot V_1 + y_{12}\left[-\frac{1}{Y_l} \cdot \frac{y_{21} \cdot V_1}{1 + \frac{y_{22}}{Y_l}}\right] \quad ...(11.99)$$

Hence input admittance is given by,

$$Y_i = \frac{I_1}{V_1} = \frac{(y_{11} \cdot y_{22} - y_{12} \cdot y_{21}) + y_{11} \cdot Y_l}{y_{22} + Y_l} \quad ...(11.100)$$

$$Y_i = \frac{\Delta y + y_{11} \cdot Y_l}{y_{22} + Y_l} \quad ...(11.101)$$

Input impedance

$$Z_i = \frac{1}{Y_i} = \frac{y_{22} + Y_l}{\Delta_y + y_{11} \cdot Y_l} \quad ...(11.102)$$

If the output port is open circuited, *i.e.* Y_l is made zero, then the input impedance is,

$$Z_{io} = \frac{y_{22}}{\Delta_y} = z_{11} \quad ...(11.103)$$

On the other hand, if the output port is short circuited *i.e.* Y_l is made infinite, the input admittance is

$$Y_{i8} = \left[\frac{\dfrac{\Delta_y}{Y_l} + y_{11}}{\dfrac{y_{22}}{Y_l} + 1} \right]_{Y_l = \infty} = y_{11} \quad ...(11.104)$$

11.14. Input Impedance in terms of ABCD Parameters and the Load Impedance

With reference to the 2-port network of Fig. 11.7, we have

$$Z_i = \frac{V_1}{I_1} \quad ...(11.105)$$

and
$$Z_l = \frac{-V_2}{I_2} \quad ...(11.106)$$

Then from Eqs. (11.41) and (11.42), we get

$$Z_i = \frac{V_1}{I_1} = \frac{AV_2 - BI_2}{CV_2 - DI_2} \quad ...(11.107)$$

Substituting the value of V_2 from Eqs. (11.106) into (11.107), we get

$$Z_f = \frac{A(-I_2 \cdot Z_l) - BI_2}{C(-I_2 \cdot Z_l) - DI_2}$$

or
$$Z_i = \frac{AZ_l + B}{CZ_l + D} \quad ...(11.108)$$

If the port 2 is open circuited, *i.e.* Z_l is made infinite, the input impedance is,

$$Z_{io} = \left[\frac{A + \dfrac{B}{Z_l}}{C + \dfrac{D}{Z_l}} \right]_{Z_i = \infty} = \frac{A}{C} \quad ...(11.109)$$

or
$$Z_{io} = \frac{z_{11}/z_{12}}{1/z_{12}} = z_{11} \quad ...(11.110)$$

On the other hand, if the output port is short circuited, *i.e.* Z_i is made zero, the input impedance is,

$$Z_{is} = \frac{B}{D} \quad ...(11.111)$$

or $$Z_{is} = \frac{-1/y_{12}}{-y_{11}/y_{12}} = \frac{1}{y_{11}} \quad ...(11.112)$$

11.15. Output Impedance in terms of z-parameters

Fig. 11.8 shows a two-port network at the output (*i.e.* port 2) of which a voltage V_2 is applied while an impedance Z_1 is connected across port 1. It is required to find the expression for the output impedance *i.e.* the driving point impedance at port 2.

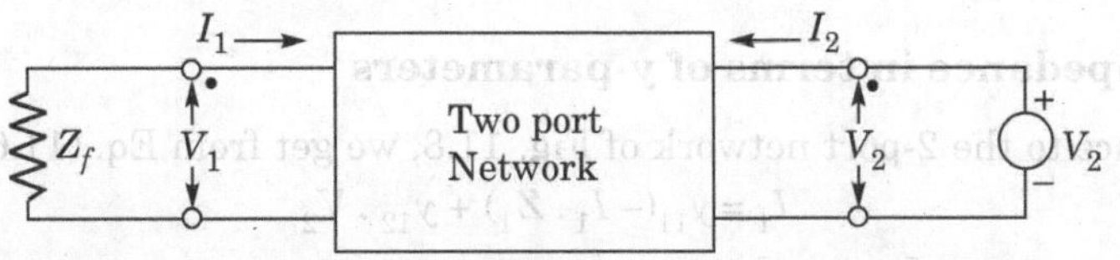

Fig. 11.8. The output impedance of a two-port network.

The output impedance is then,

$$Z_o = \frac{V_2}{I_2} \quad ...(11.113)$$

where $$Z_1 = \frac{V_1}{-I_1} \quad ...(11.114)$$

From Eq. (11.19),

$$z_{11} \cdot I_1 + z_{12} \cdot I_2 = -I_1 \cdot Z_1$$

or $$I_1(z_{11} + Z_1) = -I_1 \cdot z_{12}$$

or $$I_1 = -I_2 \cdot \frac{z_{12}}{z_{11} + Z_1} \quad ...(11.115)$$

Hence from Eq. (11.20), we get

$$z_{21}\left[-I_2 \cdot \frac{z_{12}}{z_{11} + Z_1}\right] + z_{22} \cdot I_2 = V_2.$$

Hence $$Z_o = \frac{V_2}{I_2} = z_{22} - \frac{z_{21} \cdot z_{12}}{z_{11} + Z_1}$$

$$= \frac{(z_{11}z_{22} - z_{12} \cdot z_{21}) + z_{22} \cdot Z_1}{z_{11} + Z_1} \quad ...(11.116)$$

or $$Z_o = \frac{\Delta_z + z_{22}\, Z_1}{z_{11} + Z_1} \quad ...(11.117)$$

The expression for output impedance Z_o as given by Eq. (11.117) is similar to the expression for input impedance Z_i given by Eq. (11.93) except that the ports have been exchanged so that Z_1 appears instead of Z_l and z_{11} and z_{22} appear in places of z_{22} and z_{11} respectively. Thus Eq. (11.117) could have been written from Eq. (11.93) by inspection.

With port 1 open circuited, *i.e.* with Z_1 made infinite, the output impedance is given by,

$$Z_{oo} = \left[\frac{\dfrac{\Delta_z}{Z_1} + z_{22}}{\dfrac{z_{11}}{Z_1} + 1}\right]_{Z_1 = \infty} = z_{22}$$

Thus with port 1 open circuited, the output impedance reduces to the open circuit driving point impedance at port 2.

With port 1 short circuited, *i.e.* with Z_1 made zero, the output impedance is given by,

$$Z_{os} = \frac{\Delta_z}{z_{11}} = \frac{1}{y_{22}}.$$

We thus see that with input end short circuited, the output admittance simply reduces to the short circuit driving point admittance at port 2.

11.16. Output Impedance in terms of y-parameters

With reference to the 2-port network of Fig. 11.8, we get from Eq. (11.6)

$$I_1 = y_{11}(-I_1 . Z_1) + y_{12} . V_2$$

or
$$I_1\left[1 + \frac{y_{11}}{Y_1}\right] = y_{12} . V_2$$

where Y_1 is the admittance of Z_1 and equals $\frac{1}{Z_1}$.

Hence
$$I_1 = V_2 \frac{y_{12} . Y_1}{Y_1 + y_{11}} \qquad ...(11.118)$$

From Eq. (11.7), we get

$$y_{21}\left(\frac{-I_1}{Y_1}\right) + y_{22} . V_2 = I_2$$

or
$$\frac{-y_{21}}{Y_1} . V_2 . \frac{y_{12} . Y_1}{y_{11} + Y_1} + y_{22} . V_2 = I_2$$

Hence the output admittance is given by,

$$Y_0 = \frac{I_2}{V_2} = y_{22} - \frac{y_{12} \cdot y_{21}}{y_{11} + Y_1} = \frac{(y_{11} \cdot y_{22} - y_{12} \cdot y_{21}) + y_{22} . Y_1}{y_{11} + Y_1}$$

$$= \frac{\Delta_y + y_{22} . Y_1}{y_{11} + Y_1} \qquad ...(11.119)$$

Or output impedance,
$$Z_o = \frac{1}{Y_o} = \frac{y_{11} + Y_1}{\Delta_y + y_{22} Y_1} \qquad ...(11.120)$$

Expression (11.120) giving the output impedance is similar to Eq. (11.102) given the input impedance except that the ports have been exchanged so that Y_1 appears instead of Y_l and y_{11} and y_{22} are also exchanged. Thus Eq. (11.120) could have been written from Eq. (11.102) by inspection.

With port 1 open circuited, *i.e.* with Y_1 made zero, the output impedance reduces to,

$$Z_{oo} = \frac{y_{11}}{\Delta_{11}} = z_{22}$$

Similarly with port 1 short circulated, *i.e.* with Y_1 made infinite, the output impedance reduces to $1/y_{22}$ or the output admittance becomes y_{22}.

11.17. Output Impedance in terms of ABCD Parameters

With reference to the 2-port network of Fig. 11.8, we have

Output impedance $$Z_o = \frac{V_2}{I_2}$$ ...(11.121)

and $$Z_1 = \frac{V_1}{-I_1}$$ ...(11.122)

From Eqs. (11.41) and (11.42), we get

$$-Z_1 = \frac{AV_2 - BI_2}{CV_2 - DI_2} = \frac{AZ_oI_2 - BI_2}{CZ_oI_2 - DI_2} = \frac{AZ_o - B}{CZ_o - D}$$

or $$-Z_1 CZ_o + Z_1 D = AZ_o - B$$

Hence $$Z_o = \frac{DZ_1 + B}{CZ_1 + A}$$ ...(11.123)

If port 1 is open circuited, *i.e.* Z_1 is made infinite, then the output impedance becomes,

$$Z_{oo} = \left[\frac{D + \frac{B}{Z_1}}{C + \frac{A}{Z_1}}\right]_{Z_1 = \infty} = \frac{D}{C}$$ ...(11.124)

$$= \frac{z_{22}/z_{12}}{1/z_{12}} = z_{22}$$ ...[11.124 (*a*)]

On the other hand, if port 1 is short circuited, *i.e.* Z_1 is made zero, then the output impedance becomes,

$$Z_{os} = \frac{B}{A} = \frac{-1/y_{12}}{y_{22}/y_{12}} = \frac{1}{y_{22}}$$ ...(11.125)

From Eqs. (11.109), to (11.112), we get

$$\frac{Z_{io}}{Z_{is}} = z_{11} \cdot y_{11} = \frac{AD}{BC}$$ ...(11.126)

Similarly from Eqs. (11.124) and (11.125), we get

$$\frac{Z_{oo}}{Z_{os}} = z_{22} \cdot y_{22} = \frac{AD}{BC}$$ ...(11.127)

Hence $$z_{11} \cdot y_{11} = z_{22} y_{22} = \frac{AD}{BC}$$ ...(11.128)

11.18. ABCD Parameters in Terms of Open Circuit and Short Circuit Impedances

From Eqs. (11.124) and (11.125), we get

$$Z_{oo} - Z_{os} = \frac{D}{C} - \frac{B}{A} = \frac{AD - BC}{AC} = \frac{1}{AC}$$

or $$AC = \frac{1}{Z_{oo} - Z_{os}}$$ ...(11.129)

From Eq. (11.109), we get

$$\frac{A}{C} = Z_{io} \qquad \text{...(11.130)}$$

Multiplying Eqs. (11.129) and (11.130) and taking the square root, we get

$$A = \pm \sqrt{\frac{Z_{io}}{Z_{oo} - Z_{os}}} \qquad \text{...(11.131)}$$

Dividing Eq. (11.129) by Eq. (11.130) and taking the square root, we get

$$C = \pm \frac{1}{\sqrt{Z_{io}(Z_{oo} - Z_{os})}} \qquad \text{...(11.132)}$$

Then from Eq. (11.125), we get

$$B = A \,.\, Z_{os} = \pm\, Z_{os}\sqrt{\frac{Z_{io}}{Z_{oo} - Z_{os}}} \qquad \text{...(11.133)}$$

From Eq. (11.124),

$$D = C\, Z_{oo} = \frac{\pm Z_{oo}}{\sqrt{Z_{io}(Z_{oo} - Z_{os})}} \qquad \text{...(11.134)}$$

Example 11.15. *The following equations give the voltages V_1 and V_2 at the two ports of a two-port network :*

$$V_1 = 5I_2 + 2I_2$$
$$V_2 = 2I_1 + I_2$$

A load resistor of 3 Ω is connected across port 2. Calculate the input impedance.

Solution. We have

$$V_1 = 5I_1 + 2I_2 \qquad \text{...(1)}$$

and

$$V_2 = 2I_1 - I_2 \qquad \text{...(2)}$$

But

$$V_2 = -I_2 \,.\, R_l = -3I_2 \qquad \text{...(3)}$$

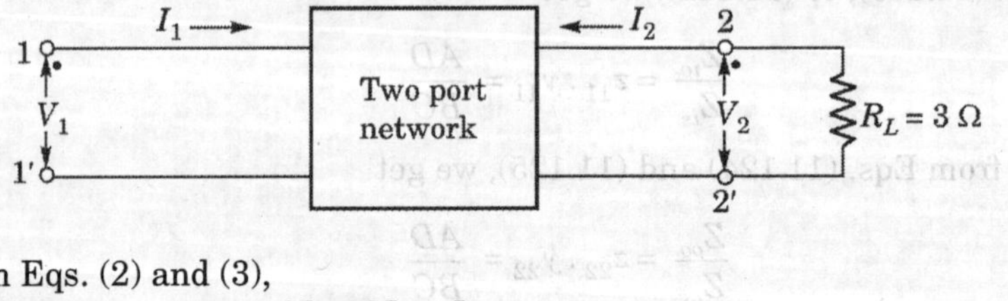

Hence from Eqs. (2) and (3),

$$-3I_2 = 2I_1 + I_2$$

or

$$I_2 = \frac{-I_1}{2} \qquad \text{...(4)}$$

Combining Eqs. (1) and (4), we get

$$V_1 = 5I_1 + 2\left(\frac{-I_1}{2}\right) = 4I_1.$$

Hence input impedance

$$Z_i = \frac{V_1}{I_1} = 4\,\Omega.$$

Example 11.16. *A two-port network has the following parameters : $z_{22} = 40\ \Omega, z_{11} = 30\ \Omega, y_{22} = 0.05$ S. Calculate the ABCD parameters of the network.*

Solution.

$$Z_{oo} = z_{22} = 40\ \Omega$$
$$Z_{io} = Z_{11} = 30\ \Omega$$

$$Z_{os} = \frac{1}{y_{22}} = \frac{1}{0.5\ \text{S}} = 20\ \Omega$$

But
$$Z_{io} = \frac{A}{C}$$

$$Z_{oo} = \frac{D}{C}$$

and
$$Z_{os} = \frac{B}{A}$$

Hence
$$Z_{oo} - Z_{os} = \frac{D}{C} - \frac{B}{A} = \frac{AD - BC}{AC} = \frac{1}{AC}$$

Hence
$$A = \pm\sqrt{\frac{Z_{io}}{Z_{oo} - Z_{os}}} = \pm\sqrt{\frac{30}{40 - 20}} = \pm 1.225$$

$$C = \pm\frac{1}{\sqrt{Z_{io}(Z_{oo} - Z_{os})}} = \pm\frac{1}{\sqrt{30(40 - 20)}} = \pm\ 0.0408\ \text{S}$$

$$B = A\ .\ Z_{os} = \pm\ 1.225 \times 20 = \pm\ 24.5\ \Omega$$
$$D = C\ .\ Z_{oo} = \pm\ 0.0408 \times 40 = \pm\ 1.636.$$

11.19. T-section Representation of a Two-port Network

Any two-port network may be represented by an equivalent *T*-network as shown in Fig. 11.9. Then the elements of this equivalent *T*-section may be conveniently expressed in terms of *z*-parameters or *ABCD* parameters. Conversely these parameters of the network may be expressed in terms of the elements of this equivalent *T*-network.

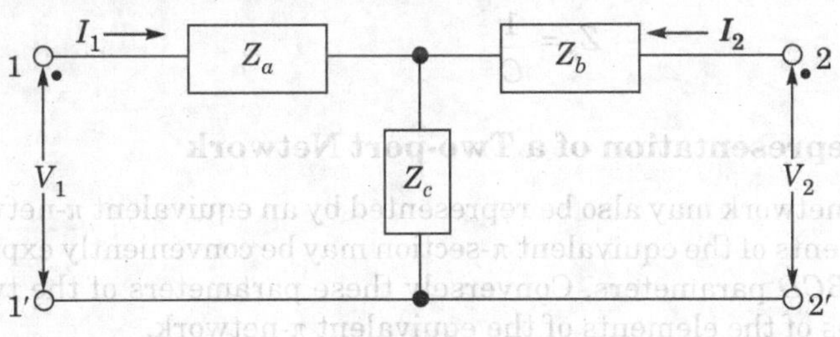

Fig. 11.9. *T*-section representation of a four terminal network.

(*a*) *z-parameters*

$$z_{11} = \left.\frac{V_1}{I_2}\right|_{I_2 = 0} = Z_a + Z_b \qquad ...(11.135)$$

$$z_{21} = \left.\frac{V_2}{I_1}\right|_{I_2 = 0} = Z_c \qquad ...(11.36)$$

$$z_{22} = \left.\frac{V_2}{I_2}\right|_{I_1=0} = Z_b + Z_c \quad ...(11.137)$$

and
$$z_{12} = \left.\frac{V_1}{I_2}\right|_{I_1=0} = Z_c \quad ...(11.138)$$

Then
$$Z_c = z_{12} = z_{21} \quad ...(11.139)$$
$$Z_a = z_{11} - z_{12} \quad ...(11.140)$$
$$Z_b = z_{22} - z_{12} \quad ...(11.141)$$

(b) ABCD parameters

Using Eqs. (11.135) to (11.138) in conjunction with Eqs. (11.57) (11.59 *b*), (11.61) and (11.64), we get

$$A = \frac{z_{11}}{z_{21}} = 1 + \frac{Z_a}{Z_c} = 1 + Z_a \,.\, Y_c \quad ...(11.142)$$

$$B = \frac{z_{11}\,.\,z_{22} - z_{12}\,.\,z_{21}}{z_{21}} = \frac{(Z_a + Z_c)(Z_b + Z_c) - Z_c^{\,2}}{Z_c}$$

$$= Z_a + Z_b + \frac{Z_a \cdot Z_b}{Z_c} \quad ...(11.143)$$

$$= Z_a + Z_b + Z_a \,.\, Z_b \,.\, Y_c \quad ...(11.144)$$

$$C = \frac{1}{Z_{12}} = \frac{1}{Z_c} = Y_c \quad ...(11.145)$$

and
$$D = \frac{z_{22}}{z_{12}} = \frac{Z_b + Z_c}{Z_c} = 1 + \frac{Z_b}{Z_c} = 1 + Z_b \,.\, Y_c \quad ...(11.146)$$

Conversely,
$$Z_a = \frac{(A-1)}{C} \quad ...(11.147)$$
$$Z_b = \frac{(D-1)}{C} \quad ...(11.148)$$

and
$$Z_c = \frac{1}{C} \quad ...(11.149)$$

11.20. π-section Representation of a Two-port Network

Any two-port network may also be represented by an equivalent π-network as shown in Fig. 11.10. Then the elements of the equivalent π-section may be conveniently expressed in terms of the *y*-parameters and *ABCD* parameters. Conversely these parameters of the two-port network may be expressed in terms of the elements of the equivalent π-network.

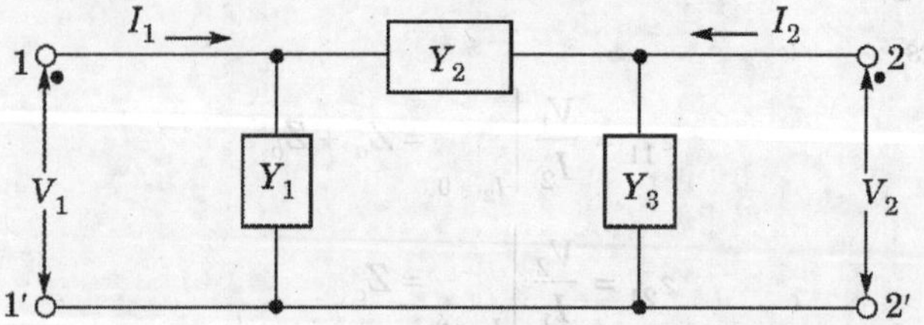

Fig. 11.10. π-section representation of a two-port network.

Then $$y_{11} = \left.\frac{I_1}{V_1}\right|_{V_2=0} = Y_1 + Y_2 \quad ...(11.150)$$

$$y_{21} = \left.\frac{I_2}{V_1}\right|_{V_2=0} = -Y_2 \quad ...(11.151)$$

$$y_{22} = \left.\frac{I_2}{V_2}\right|_{V_1=0} = Y_3 + Y_2 \quad ...(11.152)$$

$$y_{12} = \left.\frac{I_1}{V_2}\right|_{V_1=0} = -Y_2 \quad ...(11.153)$$

Then $$Y_1 = y_{11} + y_{21} \quad ...(11.154)$$

$$Y_2 = -y_{21} \quad ...(11.155)$$

and $$Y_3 = y_{22} + y_{21} \quad ...(11.156)$$

Also using Eqs. (11.150) to (11.153) in conjunction with Eqs. (11.57 *a*), (11.58) (11.62 *b*) and (11.65), we get

$$A = \frac{-y_{22}}{y_{21}} = \frac{Y_3 + Y_2}{Y_2} \quad ...(11.157)$$

$$B = -\frac{1}{y_{21}} = \frac{1}{Y_2} = Z_2 \quad ...(11.158)$$

$$C = \frac{y_{12} \cdot y_{21} - y_{11} \cdot y_{22}}{Y_{21}} = \frac{Y_2^2 - (Y_1 + Y_2)(Y_3 + Y_2)}{-Y_2}$$

or $$C = Y_1 + Y_3 + \frac{Y_1 \cdot Y_3}{Y_2} \quad ...(11.159)$$

and $$D = \frac{-y_{11}}{y_{21}} = \frac{Y_1 + Y_2}{Y_2} \quad ...(11.160)$$

Conversely, $$Y_1 = \frac{(D-1)}{B} \quad ...(11.161)$$

$$Y_2 = \frac{1}{B} \quad ...(11.162)$$

and $$Y_3 = \frac{(A-1)}{B} \quad ...(11.163)$$

Example 11.17. *The z-parameters for a two-port network are :* $z_{11} = 30\ \Omega$, $z_{22} = 40\ \Omega$, $z_{12} = z_{21} = 20\ \Omega$. *Find the equivalent T-network.*

Solution. Let Fig. 11.8 give the *T*-network equivalent to the given 2-port network.

Then $$z_{11} = \left.\frac{I_1}{I_1}\right|_{I_2=0} = Z_a + Z_c$$

$$z_{22} = \left.\frac{V_2}{I_2}\right|_{I_1=0} = Z_b + Z_c$$

$$z_{21} = \left.\frac{V_2}{I_1}\right|_{I_2=0} = Z_c$$

For the given network, we have

$$Z_c = z_{21} = z_{12} = 20\ \Omega$$
$$Z_a + Z_c = z_{21} = 30\ \Omega$$
$$Z_b + Z_c = z_{22} = 40\ \Omega$$

Hence we have $Z_c = 20\ \Omega$

$$Z_a = 30 - 20 = 10\ \Omega$$

and $Z_b = 40 - 20 = 20\ \Omega.$

Example 11.18. *The z-parameters of a 2-port network are : $z_{11} = 20\ \Omega$, $z_{22} = 30\ \Omega$, $z_{12} = z_{21}$; $= 10\ \Omega$. Find the y and ABCD parameters of the network. Also find its equivalent T-network.*

Solution.

$$y_{11} = \frac{z_{22}}{z_{11} \cdot z_{22} - z_{12} \cdot z_{21}} = \frac{30}{(20 \times 30) - (10)^2} = 0.06\ \text{S}$$

$$y_{22} = \frac{z_{11}}{z_{11} \cdot z_{22} - z_{12} \cdot z_{21}} = \frac{20}{600 - 100} = 0.04\ \text{S}$$

$$y_{21} = y_{12} = \frac{-z_{12}}{z_{11} \cdot z_{22} - z_{12} \cdot z_{21}} = \frac{-10}{600 - 100} = -0.2\ \text{S}$$

$$A = \frac{z_{11}}{z_{21}} = \frac{20}{10} = 2$$

$$B = \frac{\Delta_z}{z_{21}} = \frac{500}{10} = 50\ \Omega$$

$$C = \frac{1}{z_{21}} = \frac{1}{10\ \Omega} = 0.1\ \text{S}$$

$$D = \frac{z_{22}}{z_{21}} = \frac{30\ \Omega}{10\ \Omega} = 3$$

Let the elements of the equivalent T-network be Z_a, Z_b and Z_c as shown in Fig. 11.8.

Then

$$z_{11} = \left.\frac{V_1}{I_1}\right|_{I_2 = 0} = Z_a + Z_c$$

Hence $Z_a + Z_b = 20\ \Omega$

$$z_{22} = \left.\frac{V_2}{I_2}\right|_{I_1 = 0} = Z_b + Z_c$$

Hence $Z_b + Z_c = 30\ \Omega$

$$z_{21} = \left.\frac{V_2}{I_1}\right|_{I_2 = 0} = Z_c$$

Hence $Z_c = 10\ \Omega$

Hence we get the following values of T-network elements :

$$Z_c = 10\ \Omega$$
$$Z_b = 30 - Z_c = 30 - 10 = 20\ \Omega$$
$$Z_a = 20 - Z_c = 20 - 10 = 10\ \Omega.$$

Example 11.19. *Currents I_1 and I_2 entering at port 1 and 2 respectively of a two port network are given by the following equations :*

$$I_1 = 0.5\,V_1 - 0.2\,V_2$$
$$I_2 = -\,0.2\,V_1 + V_2$$

where V_1 and V_2 are the voltages of ports 1 and 2 respectively. Find the y, z and ABCD parameters for the network. Also find its equivalent π-network.

Solution. Let the equivalent π-network be as shown in Fig. 11.9. Then we have

$$y_{11} = \left.\frac{I_1}{V_1}\right|_{V_2 = 0} = 0.5\text{ S} = Y_1 + Y_2 \qquad ...(1)$$

$$y_{22} = \left.\frac{I_2}{V_2}\right|_{V_1 = 0} = 1\text{ S} = Y_2 + Y_3 \qquad ...(2)$$

$$y_{21} = \left.\frac{I_2}{V_1}\right|_{V_2 = 0} = -\,0.2\text{ S} = -\,Y_2 \qquad ...(3)$$

$$y_{21} = \left.\frac{I_1}{V_2}\right|_{V_1 = 0} = -\,0.2\text{ S} = -\,Y_2 \qquad ...(4)$$

From Eq. (4), $Y_2 = 0.2$ S.

From Eq. (1), $Y_1 = 0.5 - Y_2 = 0.5 - 0.2 = 0.3$ S

From Eq. (2), $Y_3 = 1 - Y_2 = 1 - 0.2 = 0.8$ S

$$z_{11} = \frac{y_{22}}{y_{11}\cdot y_{22} - y_{12}\cdot y_{21}} = \frac{1}{0.5 - (0.04)} = 2.174\ \Omega$$

$$z_{22} = \frac{y_{11}}{y_{11}\cdot y_{22} - y_{12}\cdot y_{21}} = \frac{0.5}{0.46} = 1.087\ \Omega$$

$$z_{12} = z_{21} = \frac{-\,y_{12}}{y_{11}\cdot y_{22} - y_{12}\cdot y_{21}} = \frac{0.2}{0.46} = 0.4348\ \Omega$$

$$A = \frac{-\,y_{22}}{y_{12}} = \frac{-1}{-0.2} = 5$$

$$B = \frac{-1}{y_{12}} = \frac{1}{0.2} = 5\ \Omega$$

$$C = \frac{-\,(y_{11}\cdot y_{22} - y_{12}\cdot y_{21})}{y_{12}} = \frac{-\,0.46}{-\,0.2} = 2.3\text{ S}$$

$$D = \frac{-\,y_{11}}{y_{12}} = \frac{-\,0.5\text{ S}}{-\,0.2\text{ S}} = 2.5.$$

11.21. T to π and π to T Transformations

Fig. 11.11 gives the *T*-network wherein Z_a, Z_b, and Z_c may either be simple impedances or the driving point impedance of one port network. Then by inspection we may write the following equations for the open circuit driving point and transfer impedances of this tee (*T*) network.

$$z_{11} = Z_a + Z_c = \frac{y_a + y_c}{y_a\cdot y_c} \qquad ...(11.164)$$

$$z_{22} = Z_b + Z_c = \frac{y_b + y_c}{y_b\cdot y_c} \qquad ...(11.165)$$

$$z_{12} = Z_{21} + Z_c = \frac{1}{y_c} \quad ...(11.166)$$

where y_a, y_b and y_c are the admittances corresponding to impedances Z_a, Z_b and Z_c respectively.

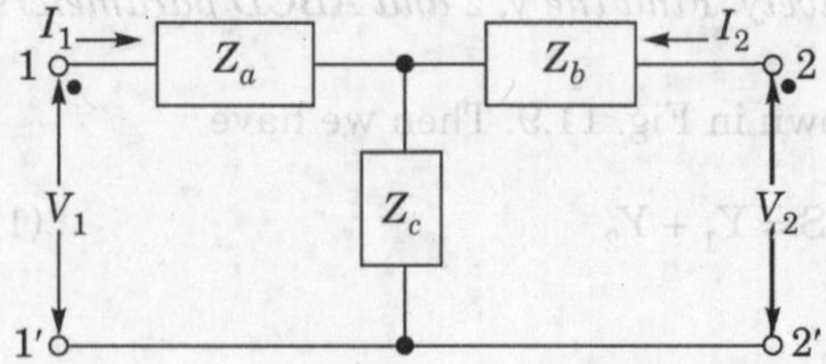

Fig. 11.11. (*a*) tee (*T*) network.

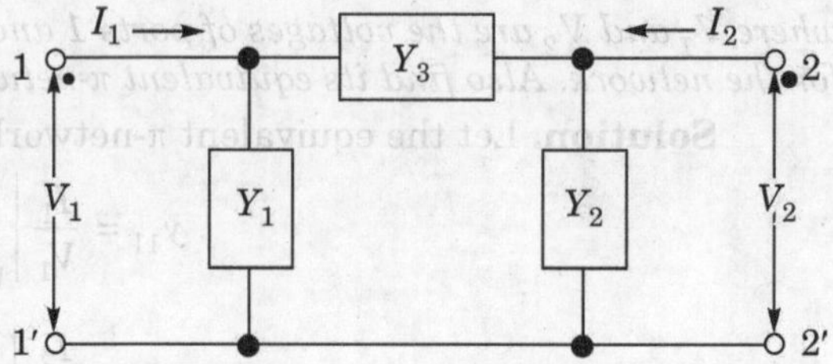

Fig. 11.12. (*a*) pi (π) network.

The *z*-determinant is then given by,

$$\Delta_z = Z_{11} \cdot Z_{22} - Z_{12}^2 = (Z_a + Z_c)(Z_b + Z_c) - Z_c^2$$

$$= Z_a \cdot Z_c + Z_b \cdot Z_c + Z_a \cdot Z_c \quad ...(11.167)$$

$$= \frac{y_a + y_b + y_c}{y_a \cdot y_b \cdot y_c} \quad ...(11.168)$$

Hence short circuit driving point and transfer admittances are given by,

$$y_{11} = \frac{z_{22}}{\Delta_z} = \frac{y_a(y_b + y_c)}{y_a + y_b + y_c} = \frac{y_a \cdot y_b}{y_a + y_b + y_c} + \frac{y_a \cdot y_c}{y_a + y_b + y_c} \quad ...(11.169)$$

$$y_{22} = \frac{z_{11}}{\Delta_z} = \frac{y_b(y_a + y_c)}{y_a + y_b + y_c} = \frac{y_a \cdot y_b}{y_a + y_b + y_c} + \frac{y_b \cdot y_c}{y_a + y_b + y_c} \quad ...(11.170)$$

and

$$y_{12} = y_{21} = \frac{-z_{12}}{\Delta_z} = \frac{-y_a \cdot y_b}{y_a + y_b + y_c} \quad ...(11.171)$$

Fig. 11.12 gives the pi (π) network wherein y_1, y_2 and y_3 may be simple admittances or the driving point admittances of one port networks. Then by inspection we may write the following equations for the short circuit driving point and transfer admittances in terms of the admittances y_1, y_2 and y_3 of the π-network.

$$y_{11} = y_1 + y_3 = \frac{(z_1 + z_3)}{z_1 \cdot z_3} \quad ...(11.172)$$

$$y_{22} = y_2 + y_3 = \frac{(z_2 + z_3)}{z_2 \cdot z_3} \quad ...(11.173)$$

and

$$y_{12} = y_{21} = -y_3 = -\frac{1}{z_3} \quad ...(11.174)$$

where z_1, z_2 and z_3 are the impedances corresponding to the admittances y_1, y_2 and y_3 respectively.

The *y*-determinant is given by,

$$\Delta_y = y_{11} \cdot y_{22} - y_{12} \cdot y_{21} = (y_1 + y_3)(y_2 + y_3) - y_3^2$$

$$= y_1 y_2 + y_2 y_3 + y_3 y_1 \quad ...(11.175)$$

$$= \frac{z_1 + z_2 + z_3}{z_1 \, z_2 \, z_3} \quad ...(11.176)$$

Hence open circuit driving point and transfer impedances of the network are given by,

$$z_{11} = \frac{y_{22}}{\Delta_y} = \frac{z_1(z_2 + z_3)}{z_1 + z_2 + z_3} = \frac{z_1 z_2}{z_1 + z_2 + z_3} + \frac{z_1 z_3}{z_1 + z_2 + z_3} \quad ...(11.177)$$

$$z_{22} = \frac{y_{11}}{\Delta_y} = \frac{z_1(z_1 + z_3)}{z_1 + z_2 + z_3} = \frac{z_1 z_2}{z_1 + z_2 + z_3} + \frac{z_2 z_3}{z_1 + z_2 + z_3} \quad ...(11.178)$$

$$z_{12} = \frac{-y_{12}}{\Delta_y} = \frac{z_1 z_2}{z_1 + z_2 + z_3} \quad ...(11.179)$$

A comparative study of Eqs. (11.172) to (11.179) for π-network with the Eqs. (11.164) to (11.171) shows that these are dual networks.

The conditions under which the T and π networks of Figs. 11.11 and 11.12 are equivalent may be obtained by comparison of equations characterising these networks. Thus Eqs. (11.164), (11.165) and (11.166) giving the open circuit driving point and transfer impedances of the T-network may be equated respectively with the Eqs. (11.177), (11.178) and (11.179) giving the open circuit driving point and transfer impedances of π-network. This equivalence yields,

$$Z_a = \frac{z_1 z_3}{z_1 + z_2 + z_3} \quad ...(11.180)$$

$$Z_b = \frac{z_2 z_3}{z_1 + z_2 + z_3} \quad ...(11.181)$$

and

$$Z_c = \frac{z_1 z_2}{z_1 + z_2 + z_3} \quad ...(11.182)$$

Similarly Eqs. (11.169), (11.170) and (11.171) giving the short circuit driving point and transfer admittances of the T-network may be equated respectively with Eqs. (11.172), (11.173) and (11.174) giving the short circuit driving point and transfer admittances of the π-network. This gives,

$$y_1 = \frac{y_a y_c}{y_a + y_b + y_c} \quad ...(11.183)$$

$$y_2 = \frac{y_b y_c}{y_a + y_b + y_c} \quad ...(11.184)$$

$$y_3 = \frac{y_a y_b}{y_a + y_b + y_c} \quad ...(11.185)$$

Eqs. (11.180), (11.181) and (11.182) enable us to transform a π-network into a T-network while Eqs. (11.183), (11.184) and (11.185) enable us to transform a T-network into a π-network Eqs. (11.180) to (11.182) and (11.183) to (11.185) providing means of transformation for π to T and from T to π configurations are duals proving again that T and π networks are dual of each other.

It may also be seen that the T and π-networks discussed above are structurally the same as the wye and delta networks respectively discussed earlier and the delta-wye transformation equations are equivalent to the π-T transformation equations. Hence the phrase "product of two adjacent divided by the sum of all three" still holds good. Similar remarks apply for wye-delta transformation and T-π transformation.]

Example 11.20. *Find the equivalent π-network for the given T-network.*

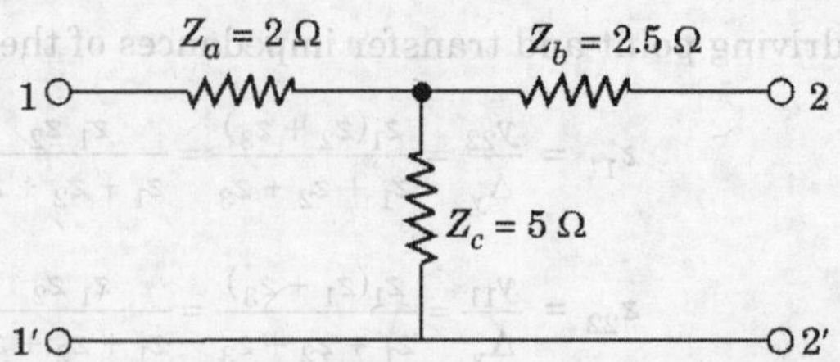

Solution. Let the equivalent π-network have y_3, as the series admittance and y_1 and y_2 as the shunt admittances as ports 1 and 2 respectively.

Then
$$y_a = \frac{1}{z_a} = \frac{1}{2\,\Omega} = 0.5\ \text{S}$$

$$y_b = \frac{1}{z_b} = \frac{1}{2.5\ \text{S}} = 0.4\ \text{S}$$

$$y_c = \frac{1}{z_c} = \frac{1}{5\ \Omega} = 0.2\ \text{S}$$

$$y_1 = \frac{y_a\, y_c}{y_a + y_b + y_c} = \frac{0.5 \times 0.2}{0.5 + 0.4 + 0.2} = \frac{1}{11}\ \text{S}$$

$$y_2 = \frac{y_b\, y_c}{y_a + y_b + y_c} = \frac{0.4 \times 0.2}{0.5 + 0.4 + 0.2} = \frac{0.8}{11}\ \text{S}$$

$$y_3 = \frac{y_a\, y_b}{y_a + y_b + y_c} = \frac{0.5 \times 0.4}{0.5 + 0.4 + 0.2} = \frac{2}{11}\ \text{S}$$

Hence
$$z_1 = \frac{1}{y_1} = 11\ \Omega$$

$$z_2 = \frac{1}{y_2} = 13.75\ \Omega$$

$$z_3 = \frac{1}{y_3} = 5.5\ \Omega$$

Example 11.21. *Find the equivalent T-network for the given π-network.*

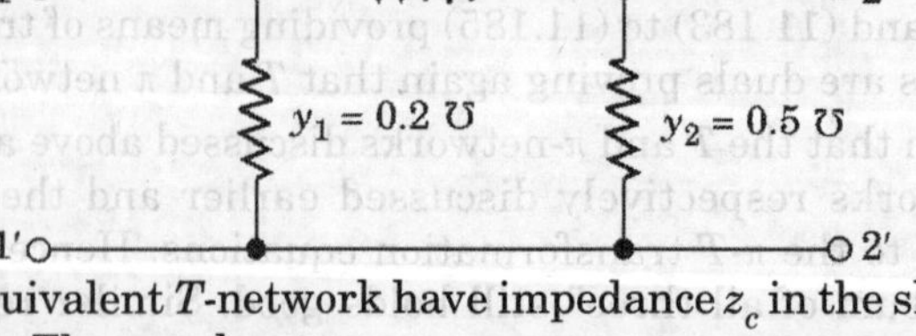

Solution. Let the equivalent T-network have impedance z_c in the shunt arm and impedances z_a and z_b in the series arms. Then we have,

$$z_1 = \frac{1}{y_1} = \frac{1}{0.2\ \text{S}} = 5\ \Omega$$

$$z_2 = \frac{1}{y_2} = \frac{1}{0.5\text{ S}} = 2\,\Omega$$

$$z_3 = \frac{1}{z_3} = \frac{1}{1\text{S}} = 1\,\Omega$$

Hence $$z_a = \frac{z_1 z_3}{z_1 + z_2 + z_3} = \frac{(5 \times 1)}{5 + 2 + 1} = 0.625\,\Omega$$

$$z_b = \frac{z_2 z_3}{z_1 + z_2 + z_3} = \frac{(2 \times 1)}{5 + 2 + 1} = 0.25\,\Omega$$

$$z_c = \frac{z_1 z_2}{z_1 + z_2 + z_3} = \frac{(5 \times 2)}{5 + 2 + 1} = 1.25\,\Omega$$

11.22. Image Impedances

In a two-port network, if two impedances Z_{i1} and Z_{i2} are such that Z_{i1} is the driving point impedance at port 1 with impedance Z_{i2} connected across the port 2 and Z_{i2} is the driving point impedance at port 2 with impedance Z_{i1} connected across the port 1, then the impedances Z_{i1} and Z_{i2} are called the "image impedances" of the network.

Image impedances may be expressed in terms of *ABCD* parameters.

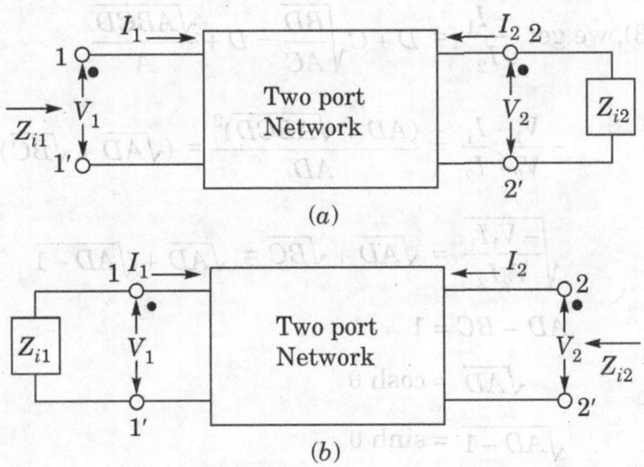

Fig. 11.13. Image impedance of a two-port network.

Fig. 11.13 (*a*) shows a two-port network with impedance Z_{i2} connected across port 2.

Then $$Z_{i1} = \frac{AV_2 - BI_2}{CV_2 - DI_2} \qquad ...(11.186)$$

But $$V_2 = -Z_{i2} \cdot I_2 \qquad ...(11.187)$$

Hence $$Z_{i1} = \frac{AZ_{i2} + B}{CZ_{i2} + D} \qquad ...(11.188)$$

Similarly from Fig. 11.13 (*b*), we get

$$Z_{i2} = \frac{DZ_{i1} + B}{CZ_{i1} + A} \qquad ...(11.189)$$

From Equations (11.188) and (11.189), we get

$$Z_{i1} = \sqrt{\frac{AB}{CD}} \quad ...(11.190)$$

and

$$Z_{i2} = \sqrt{\frac{BD}{AC}} \quad ...(11.191)$$

Equations (11.190) and (11.191) give the values of image impedances Z_{i1} and Z_{i2} in terms of *ABCD* parameters.

The two image parameters do not completely define a network. A third parameter, called the "image transfer parameter" is needed. This parameter may be obtained from the voltage and current ratios.

Let the image impedance Z_{i2} be connected across port 2. Then,

$$V_1 = AV_2 - BI_2 = \left[A + \frac{B}{Z_{i2}}\right] V_2 \quad ...(11.192)$$

$$I_1 = CV_2 - DI_2 = -[CZ_{i2} + D]\, I_2 \quad ...(11.193)$$

From Eq. (11.192), we get $\dfrac{V_1}{V_2} = A + B\sqrt{\dfrac{AC}{BD}} = A + \dfrac{\sqrt{ABCD}}{C}$ ...(11.194)

From Eq. (11.193), we get $\dfrac{-I_1}{I_2} = D + C\sqrt{\dfrac{BD}{AC}} = D + \dfrac{\sqrt{ABCD}}{A}$ ...(11.195)

Hence

$$-\frac{V_1}{V_2} \cdot \frac{I_1}{I_2} = \frac{(AD + \sqrt{ABCD})^2}{AD} = (\sqrt{AD} + \sqrt{BC})^2 \quad ...(11.196)$$

or

$$\sqrt{\frac{-V_1 I_1}{V_2 I_2}} = \sqrt{AD} + \sqrt{BC} = \sqrt{AD} + \sqrt{AD - 1} \quad ...(11.197)$$

since

$$AD - BC = 1$$

Let

$$\sqrt{AD} = \cosh\theta \quad ...(11.198)$$

Then

$$\sqrt{AD - 1} = \sinh\theta \quad ...(11.199)$$

Hence

$$\sqrt{\frac{-V_1 I_1}{V_2 I_2}} = \cosh\theta + \sinh\theta \quad ...(11.200)$$

$$= e^{\theta} \quad ...(11.201)$$

Hence

$$\theta = \log_e \sqrt{\frac{-V_1 I_1}{V_2 I_2}} \quad ...(11.202)$$

θ is called the "image transfer parameter".

The sign of θ is, however, ambiguous since either sign of θ will satisfy Equations (11.198) and (11.199). For the direction of propagation from port 1 to port 2, the magnitude of $V_1 I_1$ exceeds the magnitude of $V_2 I_2$ so that the real part of θ is positive. Further

$$V_1 = Z_{i1} \cdot I_1 \quad ...(11.203)$$

and

$$V_2 = -Z_{i2} \cdot I_2 \quad ...(11.204)$$

Hence Eq. (11.202) may be written as,

$$\theta = \frac{1}{2}\log_e \frac{Z_{i1}}{Z_{i2}} + \log_e \frac{I_1}{I_2} \quad ...(11.205)$$

θ may also be written as, $$\theta = \cosh^{-1}\sqrt{AD} \quad ...(11.206)$$

$$= \sinh^{-1}\sqrt{BC} \quad ...(11.207)$$

$$= \sinh^{-1}\sqrt{\frac{BC}{AD}} \quad ...(11.208)$$

11.23. Image Parameters in terms of Short Circuit and Open Circuit Impedances

From Eq. (11.190),

$$Z_{i1} = \sqrt{\frac{AB}{CD}}$$

But $$Z_{i0} = \frac{A}{C}$$

and $$Z_{is} = \frac{B}{D}$$

Hence $$Z_{i1} = \sqrt{Z_{i0}.Z_{is}} \quad ...(11.209)$$

Similarly $$Z_{i2} = \sqrt{\frac{BD}{AC}}$$

$$Z_{oo} = \frac{D}{C}$$

and $$Z_{os} = \frac{B}{A}$$

Hence $$Z_{i2} = \sqrt{Z_{oo}\,.\,Z_{os}} \quad ...(11.210)$$

From Eq. (11.208),

$$\theta = \tanh^{-1}\sqrt{\frac{BC}{AD}}$$

Hence $$\theta = \tanh^{-1}\sqrt{\frac{Z_{is}}{Z_{io}}} \quad ...(11.211)$$

$$= \tanh^{-1}\sqrt{\frac{Z_{os}}{Z_{oo}}} \quad ...(11.212)$$

Eqs. (11.209) to (11.212) permit determination of image parameters Z_{i1}, Z_{i2} and θ from physical measurements of open circuit and short circuit impedances.

Having measured open circuit impedance Z_{io} (or Z_{oo}) and short circuit impedance Z_{is} (or Z_{io}), in order to calculate image transfer parameter θ, we proceed as below :

Let $m = \sqrt{\frac{Z_{is}}{Z_{io}}}$, choosing the root with real part positive.

Then $$m = \sqrt{\frac{Z_{is}}{Z_{io}}} = \tanh\theta = \frac{e^{\theta} - e^{-\theta}}{e^{\theta} + e^{-\theta}} = \frac{e^{2\theta} - 1}{e^{2\theta} + 1}$$

Hence $$e^{2\theta} = \frac{1+m}{1-m} = r_e^{j\phi}$$

where r and ϕ may be computed from knowledge of m *i.e.* from the knowledge of Z_{is} and Z_{io}.

Hence $$\theta = \frac{1}{2}\log_e{}^r + j\left(\frac{\phi}{2} + n\pi\right),\ n = 1, 2, 3...... \qquad ...(11.213)$$

It may thus be seen that, in general, θ is a complex quantity. The real part of θ *i.e.* $\frac{1}{2}\log_e{}^r$ is called the "image attenuation" while the imaginary part *i.e.* $j\left(\frac{\phi}{2} + n\pi\right)$ is called the "image phase constant."

Example 11.22. *For the given 2-port network, calculate the z-parameters, ABCD parameters, open circuit and short circuit impedances and image parameters.*

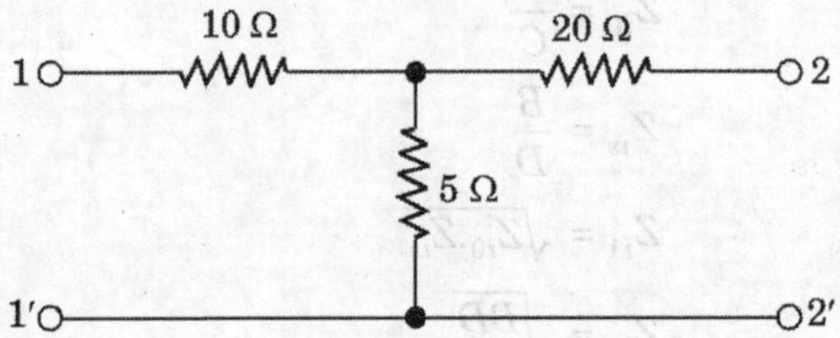

Solution. $$z_{11} = \left.\frac{V_1}{I_1}\right|_{I_1=0} = 10 + 5 = 15\ \Omega$$

$$z_{22} = \left.\frac{V_2}{I_2}\right|_{I_1=0} = 20 + 5 = 25\ \Omega$$

$$z_{21} = \left.\frac{V_2}{I_1}\right|_{I_2=0} = 5\ \Omega$$

$$z_{12} = \left.\frac{V_1}{I_2}\right|_{I_1=0} = 5\ \Omega$$

$$A = \frac{z_{11}}{z_{21}} = \frac{15\ \Omega}{5\ \Omega} = 3$$

$$B = \frac{z_{12}\,.\,z_{22} - z_{21}\,.\,z_{12}}{z_{21}} = \frac{(15 \times 25) - (25)}{5} = 70\ \Omega$$

$$C = \frac{1}{z_{21}} = \frac{1}{5\ \Omega} = 0.2\ \text{S}$$

$$D = \frac{z_{22}}{z_{21}} = \frac{25\ \Omega}{5\ \Omega} = 5$$

Open circuit impedance at port one = $Z_{io} = z_{11} = 15\ \Omega$. Short circuit impedance at port one is given by,

$$Z_{is} = \frac{1}{y_{11}} = \frac{\Delta_z}{z_{22}} = \frac{z_{11} \cdot z_{22} - z_{21} \cdot z_{22}}{z_{22}}$$

Substituting the values, $Z_{is} = \dfrac{(15 \times 25) - (25)}{25} = 14\ \Omega$

Open circuit impedance at port 2 = $Z_{oo} = z_{22} = 25\ \Omega$. Short circuit impedance at port 2 is given by,

$$Z_{os} = \frac{1}{y_{22}} = \frac{\Delta_z}{z_{11}} = \frac{z_{11} \cdot z_{22} - z_{21} \cdot z_{12}}{z_{11}}$$

Substituting the values, $Z_{os} = \dfrac{(15 \times 25) - (25)}{15} = 23.33\ \Omega$

Image parameters

$$Z_{i1} = \sqrt{\frac{AB}{CD}} = \sqrt{\frac{3 \times 70}{0.2 \times 5}} = 14.49\ \Omega$$

$$Z_{i2} = \sqrt{\frac{BD}{AC}} = \sqrt{\frac{50 \times 5}{3 \times 0.2}} = 24.15\ \Omega$$

$$\theta = \tanh^{-1} \sqrt{\frac{BC}{AD}}$$

Let $m = \sqrt{\dfrac{BC}{AD}}$

Then $m = \sqrt{\dfrac{70 \times 0.2}{3 \times 5}} = 0.9661$

But $m = \tanh \theta = \dfrac{e^{2\theta} - 1}{e^{2\theta} + 1}$

Hence $e^{2\theta} = \dfrac{1+m}{1-m} = \dfrac{1+0.9661}{1-0.9661} = 57.98$

Hence $\theta = \dfrac{1}{2} \log_e{}^{57.98} = 20.31.$

Example 11.23. *For a 2-port network, the following results are obtained on measurements : Driving point impedance at port 1 with port 2 open circuited and short circuited respectively are 30 Ω and 20 Ω. Driving point impedance at port 2 with port 1 open circuited and short circuited respectively are 40 Ω and 26.66 Ω. Calculate the image parameters.*

Solution. $Z_{i1} = \sqrt{Z_{io} \times Z_{is}} = \sqrt{30 \times 20} = 24.49\ \Omega$

$$Z_{i2} = \sqrt{Z_{oo} \times z_{os}} = \sqrt{40 \times 26.66} = 32.68\ \Omega$$

$$m = \sqrt{\frac{Z_{is}}{Z_{io}}} = \sqrt{\frac{20}{30}} = 0.8165$$

$$e^{2\theta} = \frac{1+m}{1-m} = \frac{1+0.8165}{1-0.8165} = 9.897$$

$$\theta = \frac{1}{2} \log_e{}^{9.897} = 1.147.$$

11.24. Symmetrical Networks

By symmetrical network is meant a network which is symmetrical with respect to the ports. For such a symmetrical network, the image impedance is the referred to as the *iteractive impedance* or *characteristic impedance* and is usually denoted by Z_o. The image transfer constant of a symmetrical network is called the *propagation constant* and is usually denoted by γ.

Because of the symmetry with respect to the two ports, we have

$$z_{11} = z_{22}$$

$$y_{11} = y_{22}$$

$$Z_{is} = Z_{os}$$

$$Z_{io} = Z_{oo}$$

and $$A = D.$$

Also $$Z_{i1} = Z_{i2} = Z_o = \sqrt{\frac{B}{C}} \quad ...(11.214)$$

and $$\theta = \gamma = \log_e \sqrt{\frac{-V_1 I_1}{V_2 I_2}} \quad ...(11.215)$$

$$= \log_e \sqrt{\frac{Z_a {I_1}^2}{V_o {I_2}^2}} = \log_e \frac{I_1}{I_2} \quad ...(11.216)$$

In general, the propagation constant γ is a complex quantity and let

$$\gamma = \alpha + j\beta \quad ...(11.217)$$

The real part of γ, namely α, is called the *attenuation constant* and is measured in nepers.

The imaginary part of γ, namely β, is called the *phase constant* and is measured in radians.

From Eq. (11.198), $$\gamma = \cosh^{-1} \sqrt{AD} = \cosh^{-1} A = \sinh^{-1} \sqrt{BC} \quad ...(11.218)$$

Z_0 and γ in terms of Open Circuit and Short Circuit Impedance. From Eqs. (11.209) and (11.210),

$$Z_o = \sqrt{Z_{is} . Z_{io}} = \sqrt{Z_{os} . Z_{oo}} \quad ...(11.219)$$

From Eq. (11.211) and (11.212),

$$\gamma = \tanh^{-1} \sqrt{\frac{Z_{is}}{Z_{io}}} = \tanh^{-1} \sqrt{\frac{Z_{os}}{Z_{oo}}} \quad ...(11.220)$$

ABCD parameters in terms of Z_0 and γ

From Eq. (11.218), $$A = D = \cosh \gamma \quad ...(11.221)$$

Also $$\sqrt{BC} = \sinh \gamma \quad ...(11.222)$$

Hence

From Eq. (11.214),

$$\sqrt{\frac{B}{C}} = Z_o \quad ...(11.223)$$

Hence $$B = Z_o \sinh \gamma \qquad ...(11.224)$$

and $$C = \frac{\sinh \gamma}{Z_o} \qquad ...(11.225)$$

Example 11.24. *For the symmetrical 2-port network given below, find the z and ABCD parameters. Hence or otherwise, find iterative impedance and propagation constant for this network.*

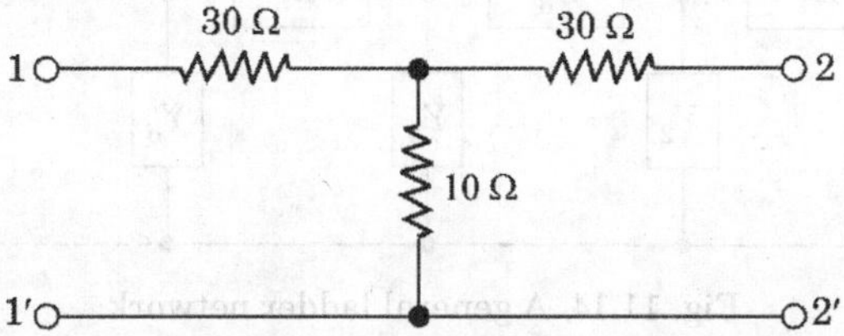

Solution.
$$z_{11} = \left.\frac{V_1}{I_1}\right|_{I_2 = 0} = 30 + 10 = 40\ \Omega$$

$$z_{22} = \left.\frac{V_2}{I_2}\right|_{I_1 = 0} = 30 + 10 = 40\ \Omega$$

$$z_{21} = \left.\frac{V_2}{I_1}\right|_{I_2 = 0} = 10\ \Omega$$

$$z_{12} = \left.\frac{V_1}{I_2}\right|_{I_1 = 0} = 10\ \Omega$$

$$A = \frac{z_{11}}{z_{21}} = \frac{40\ \Omega}{10\ \Omega} = 4$$

$$B = \frac{\Delta_z}{z_{21}} = \frac{z_{21} \cdot z_{22} - z_{12} - z_{12} \cdot z_{21}}{z_{21}} = \frac{(40)^2 - (10)^2}{10} = 150\ \Omega$$

$$C = \frac{1}{z_{21}} = \frac{1}{10\ \Omega} = 0.1\ \text{S}$$

$$D = \frac{z_{22}}{z_{21}} = \frac{40\ \Omega}{10\ \Omega} = 4$$

Interative impedance

$$Z_o = \sqrt{\frac{B}{C}} = \sqrt{\frac{150\ \Omega}{0.1\ \text{S}}} = 38.73\ \Omega$$

$$m = \sqrt{\frac{BC}{AD}} = \sqrt{\frac{150 \times 0.1}{4 \times 4}} = 0.9683$$

$$e^{2\gamma} = \frac{1+m}{1-m} = \frac{1 + 0.9683}{1 - 0.9583} = 62.07$$

Hence $$\gamma = \frac{1}{2} l_n^{62.07} = 2.065.$$

11.25. Ladder Network

Fig. 11.14 shows a general ladder network. If each of the impedances z_1, z_3 etc. and each of the admittances y_2, y_4 etc. represent only one element, then this ladder network is referred to as simple ladder. A general ladder, on the other hand, may contain arms which are complicated. Fig. 11.15 shows one such non-simple ladder network.

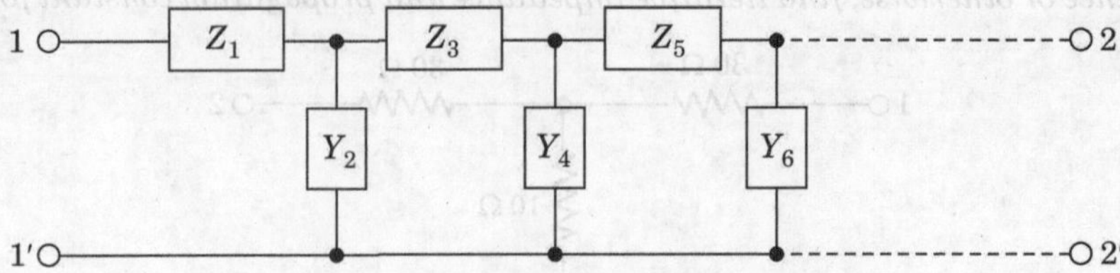

Fig. 11.14. A general ladder network.

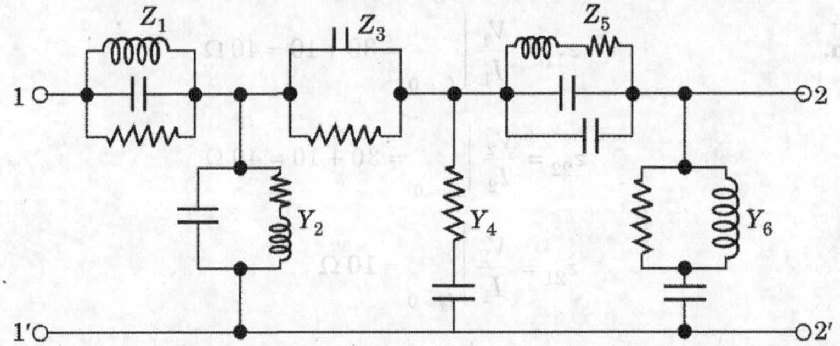

Fig. 11.15. A non-simple ladder network.

In describing a network, conventionally we indicate series arm by their impedances and shunt arms by their admittances.

We now take up the computation of the driving point functions for the ladder network of Fig. 11.14 considering only six elements *i.e.*, series arms of impedances z_1, z_3 and z_5, and shunt arms of admittances y_2, y_4 and y_6.

In order to find the driving point impedance at port 1, we start computation beginning at port 2 *i.e.* begin with y_6. Thus y_6 is inverted and combined with z_5. Next this sum is inverted and combined with y_4. This process is continued until all the arms have been included. Thus the driving point impedance at port 1 is given by,

$$z_{11} = z_1 + \cfrac{1}{y_2 + \cfrac{1}{z_3 + \cfrac{1}{y_4 + \cfrac{1}{z_5 + \cfrac{1}{y_6}}}}} \quad ...(11.226)$$

This equation constitutes the so called, *continued fraction.*

Transfer Function. For finding the transfer functions, we again start at the output port and then work backward applying Kirchhoff's current law and Kirchhoff's voltage law.

Example 11.25. *Find, the open circuit driving point impedance at port 1 of the following two-port network.*

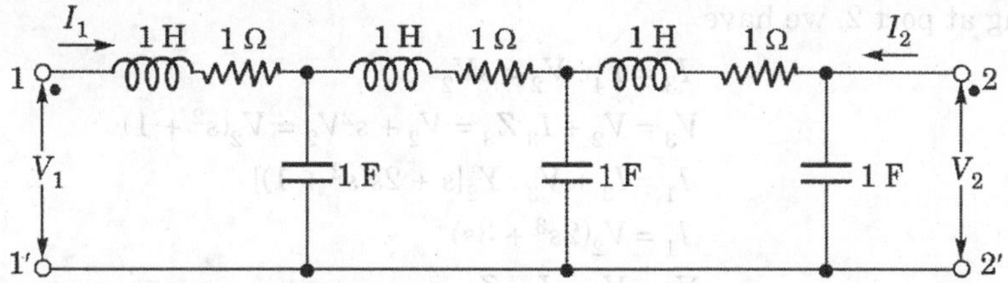

Solution. Corresponding Laplace transform network is as below:

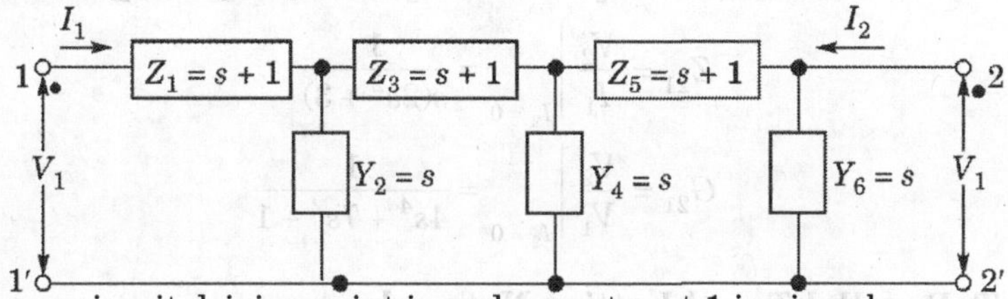

Then the open circuit driving point impedance at port 1 is given by

$$z_{11} = (s+1) + \cfrac{1}{s + \cfrac{1}{(s+1) + \cfrac{1}{s + \cfrac{1}{(s+1) + \cfrac{1}{s}}}}}$$

$$= \frac{s^6 + 6s^5 + 11s^4 + 13s^3 + 10s^2 + 5s + 1}{s^5 + 5s^4 + 5s^3 + 3s^2 + 3s}$$

Example 11.26. *Find the open circuit transfer impedance z_{21} i.e. V_2/I_1) and open circuit voltage ratio $G_{21}\left(\text{i.e. } \dfrac{V_2}{I_1}\right)$ for the following ladder network.*

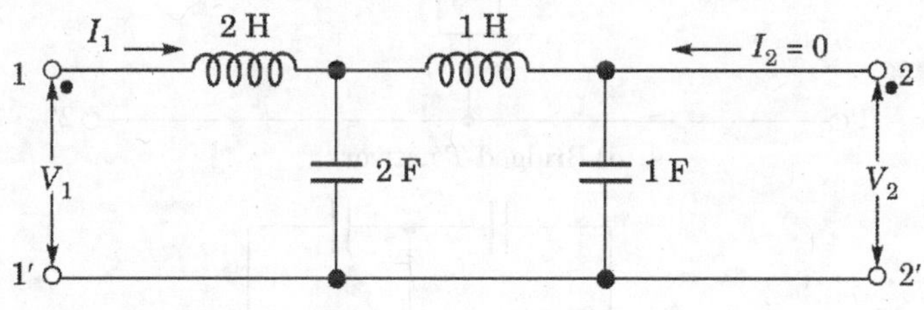

Solution. Corresponding Laplace transform network is as below :

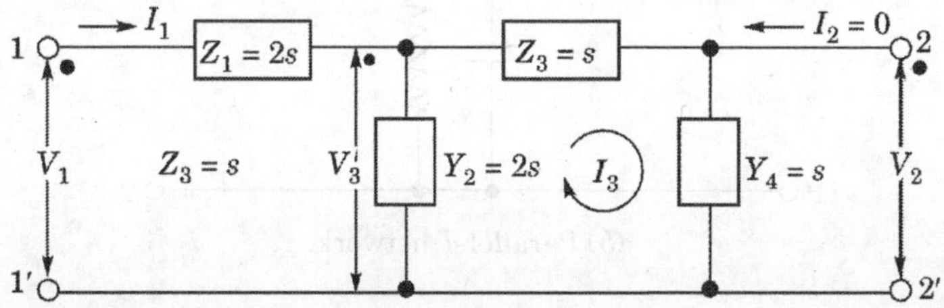

Beginning at port 2, we have

$$I_3 = Y_4 \,.\, V_2 = sV_2 \qquad ...(1)$$

$$V_3 = V_2 + I_3 Z_3 = V_2 + s^2 V_2 = V_2(s^2 + 1)$$

$$I_1 = I_3 + V_3 \,.\, Y_2 [s + 2s(s^2 + 1)]$$

or

$$I_1 = V_2(2s^3 + 3s) \qquad ...(2)$$

$$V_1 = V_3 + I_1 \,.\, Z_1$$

$$= V_2(s^2 + 1) + V_2(2s^2 + 3s) \,.\, 2s = V_2[4s^4 + 7s^2 + 1] \qquad ...(3)$$

Hence

$$Z_{21} = \left.\frac{V_2}{I_1}\right|_{I_2 = 0} = \frac{1}{s(2s^2 + 3)}$$

$$G_{21} = \left.\frac{V_2}{V_1}\right|_{I_2 = 0} = \frac{1}{4s^4 + 7s^2 + 1}.$$

11.26. Bridged-T, Parallel-T and Lattice Network

So far we have dealt with network functions of networks of the T, π or ladder configurations. We now take up a few other types of networks to which the methods outlined in the last article are not applicable.

Fig. 11.16 shows a bridged-T network, parallel-T-network and lattice network. The method described in the last article does not apply in the case of any of these networks because the current in the output depends upon voltages of a number of nodes instead of only one, thus resulting in a number of simultaneous equations. These simultaneous equations should be solved by the usual methods applied in node or loop analysis.

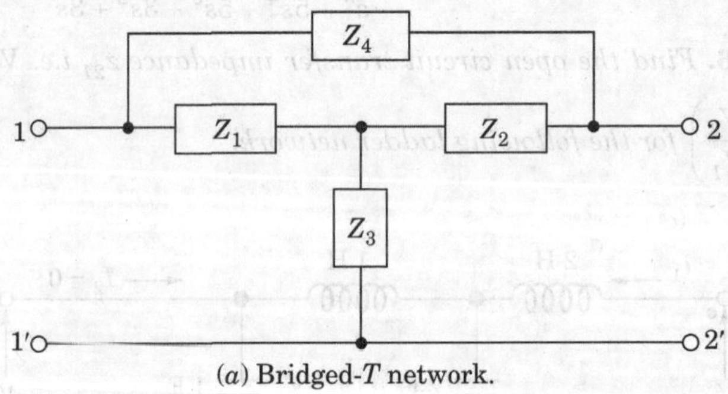

(*a*) Bridged-T network.

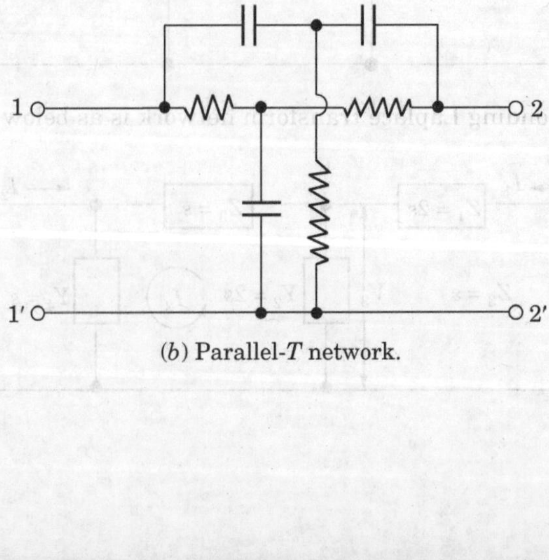

(*b*) Parallel-T network.

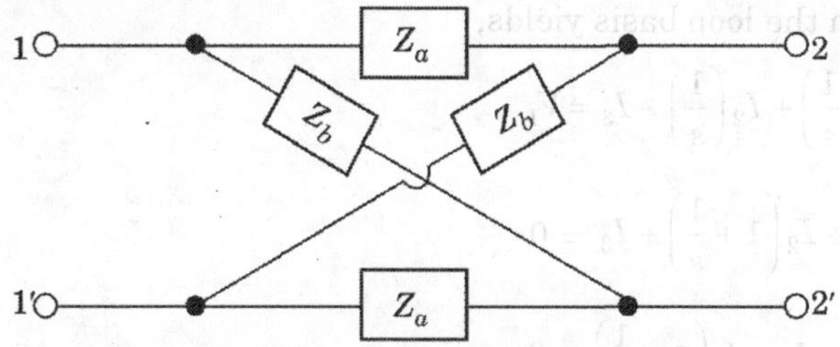

(*c*) Lattice network.

Fig. 11.16. A few non-ladder networks.

For such non-ladder networks, analysing either on node basis or on loop basis, the network function is expressed as a quotient of determinants. This we have already done in earlier study.

Thus in the analysis on the loop basis, the admittance function may be put as,

$$Y_{jk} = \frac{\Delta_{kj}}{\Delta} \qquad ...(11.227)$$

where Δ is the loop basis system determinant and Y may be replaced by y if the output port is short circuited.

In the analysis on the node basis, the impedance function may be put as,

$$Z_{jk} = \frac{\Delta'_{kj}}{\Delta'} \qquad ...(11.228)$$

where Δ' is the node basis system determinant and Z may be replaced by z if the output port is open circuited.

Also
$$G_{21} = \frac{V_2}{V_1} = \frac{\Delta'_{21}}{\Delta'_{11}} \qquad ...(11.229)$$

and
$$\alpha_{21} = \frac{I_2}{I_1} = \frac{\Delta_{21}}{\Delta_{11}} \qquad ...(11.230)$$

Example 11.27. *For the given bridged T-network, find the driving point admittance Y_{11} and transfer admittance Y_{21} with a 2 Ω load resistor connected across port 2.*

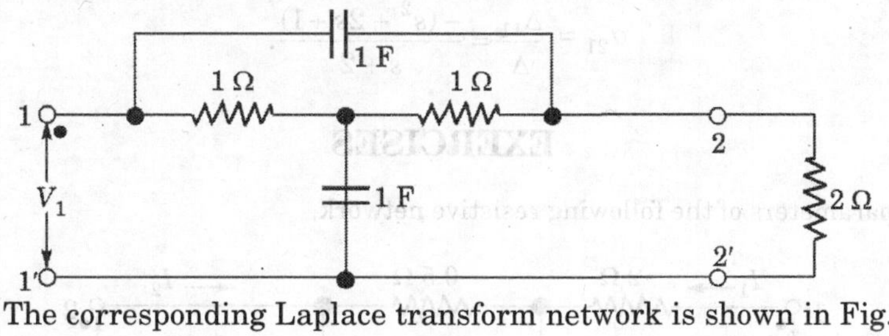

Solution. The corresponding Laplace transform network is shown in Fig. (*a*).

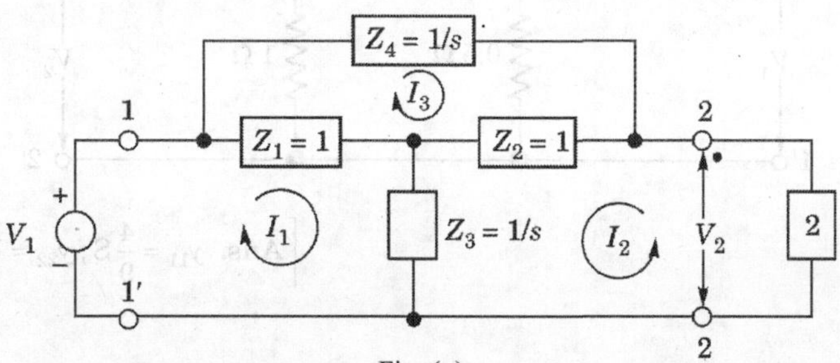

Fig. (*a*)

Then analysis on the loop basis yields,

$$I_1\left(1+\frac{1}{s}\right)+I_2\left(\frac{1}{s}\right)-I_3=V_1 \quad \text{...(1)}$$

$$I_1\left(\frac{1}{s}\right)+I_2\left(1+\frac{1}{s}\right)+I_3=0 \quad \text{...(2)}$$

$$I_1(-1)+I_2+I_3\left(2+\frac{1}{s}\right)=0 \quad \text{...(3)}$$

$$\Delta=\begin{vmatrix}\left(1+\frac{1}{s}\right) & \frac{1}{s} & -1\\ \frac{1}{s} & \left(1+\frac{1}{s}\right) & +1\\ -1 & +1 & \left(2+\frac{1}{s}\right)\end{vmatrix} \quad \text{...(4)}$$

$$=\frac{s+2}{s^2}$$

$$\Delta_{11}=\begin{vmatrix}\left(1+\frac{1}{s}\right) & +1\\ +1 & \left(2+\frac{1}{s}\right)\end{vmatrix}=\frac{s^2+3s+1}{s^2}$$

Hence $$Y_{11}=\frac{\Delta_{11}}{\Delta}=\frac{s^2+3s+1}{s+2}$$

$$\Delta_{12}=\begin{vmatrix}\frac{1}{s} & -1\\ +1 & \left(1+\frac{1}{s}\right)\end{vmatrix}=\frac{(s^2+2s+1)}{s^2}$$

Hence $$\alpha_{21}=\frac{\Delta_{11}}{\Delta}=\frac{-(s^2+2s+1)}{s+2}.$$

EXERCISES

11.1. Find the y-parameters of the following resistive network.

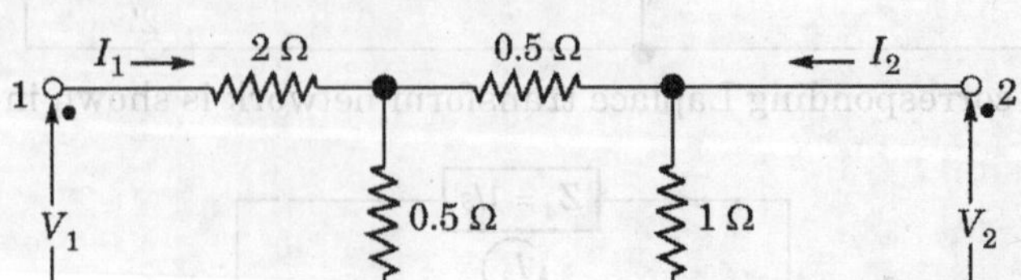

$$\left[\textbf{Ans.}\ y_{11}=\frac{4}{9}\,\text{S};\ y_{22}=\frac{19}{9}\,\text{S};\ y_{21}=y_{12}=-\frac{2}{9}\,\text{S}\right]$$

11.2. The given network contains a current controlled current source. For this network, find the *y*-parameters.

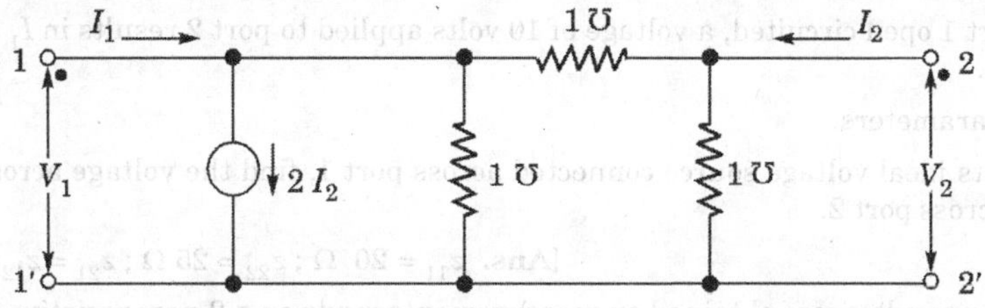

[**Ans.** $y_{11} = -2$ S ; $y_{22} = 2$ S ; $y_{21} = -1$ S ; $y_{12} = -1$ S]

11.3. Find the *z*-parameters of the resistive network of exercise 11.1.

$$\left[\textbf{Ans. } z_{11} = \frac{19}{8}\,\Omega\,;\ z_{22} = 0.5\,\Omega\,;\ z_{12} = y_{21} = 0.25\,\Omega\right]$$

11.4. Find the *z*-parameters for the network of exercise 11.2.

$$\left[\textbf{Ans. } z_{11} = \frac{2}{3}\,\Omega\,;\ z_{22} = 0\,;\ z_{12} = -1\,\Omega\,;\ z_{21} = \frac{1}{3}\,\Omega\right]$$

11.5. Find the *y*-parameters for the given bridged-*T* R.C. network.

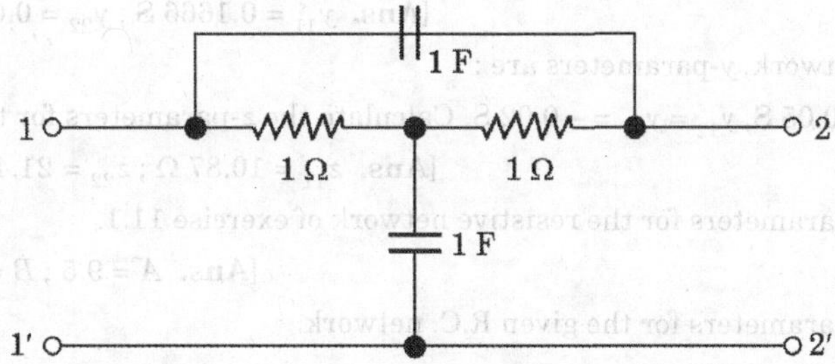

$$\left[\textbf{Ans. } z_{22}(s) = y_{11}(s) = \frac{s(2s+1)(s^2+3s+1)}{6s^2+15s^2+10s+2}\right.$$

$$\left. y_{21}(s) = y_{12}(s) = \frac{-s(2s+1)(s^2+2s+1)}{(6s^3+15s^2+10s+2)}\right]$$

11.6. Find the *z*-parameters for the bridged-*T* R.C. network of exercise 11.5.

$$\left[\textbf{Ans. } z_{11}(s) = z_{22}(s) = \frac{s^2+3s+1}{s(2s+1)}\right.$$

$$\left. z_{21}(s) = z_{12}(s) = \frac{(s^2+2s+1)}{s(2s+1)}\right]$$

11.7. The following equations give the currents at the two ports of a 2-port network :

$$I_1 = 0.2\,V_1 - 0.05\,V_2$$

$$I_2 = -0.05\,V_1 + 0.1\,V_2$$

Compute the *z*-parameters for the network. [**Ans.** $z_{11} = 5.714\ \Omega$; $z_{22} = 11.428\ \Omega$; $z_{12} = z_{21} = 2.857\ \Omega$]

11.8. The following results were obtained as a result of measurements made on a 2-port network :

(*i*) With port 2 open circuited, a voltage of 20 volts applied to port 1 results in I_1 = 1 amp. and V_1 = 3 volts.

(*ii*) With port 1 open circuited, a voltage of 10 volts applied to port 2 results in I_1 = 0.4 amp. and V_2 = 1.2 volts.

Find the *z*-parameters.

With a 5 volts ideal voltage source connected across port 1, find the voltage across the 20 Ω resistor connected across port 2.

[**Ans.** z_{11} = 20 Ω ; z_{22} = 25 Ω ; $z_{21} = z_{12}$ = 3 Ω ; 0.3367 volt]

11.9. The following results were obtained on measurements made on a 2-port resistive network :

(*i*) With port-2 short circuited, a voltage of 8 volts applied to port 1 results in I_1 = 1.6 amp. and I_2 = – 0.8 amp.

(*ii*) With port 1 short circuited, a voltage of 10 volts applied to port 2 results in I_1 = – 1 amp. and I_2 = 1.2 amp.

Find the *y*-parameters for the network.

With a 5 volts source connected across port 1, find the voltage across a 20 Ω load resistor connected across port 2.

[**Ans.** y_n = 0.2 S ; y_{22} = 0.12 S ; $y_{12} = y_{21}$ = – 0.1 S ; V_2 = 2.941 volts]

11.10. For a two-port network, *z*-parameters are : z_{11} = 20 Ω, z_{22} = 30 Ω, $z_{12} = z_{21}$ = 10 Ω. Calculate the *y*-parameters for the same network.

[**Ans.** y_{11} = 0.1666 S ; y_{22} = 0.04 S ; $y_{12} = y_{21}$ = – 0.02 S]

11.11. For a two port network, *y*-parameters are :

y_{11} = 0.1 S, y_{22} = 0.05 S, $y_{12} = y_{21}$ = – 0.02 S. Calculate the *z*-parameters for the same network.

[**Ans.** z_{11} = 10.87 Ω ; z_{22} = 21.47 Ω ; $z_{12} = z_{21}$ = 4.348 Ω]

11.12. Find the *ABCD* parameters for the resistive network of exercise 11.1.

[**Ans.** *A* = 9.5 ; *B* = 4.5 Ω. ; C = 4 S ; *D* = 2]

11.13. Find the *ABCD* parameters for the given R.C. network.

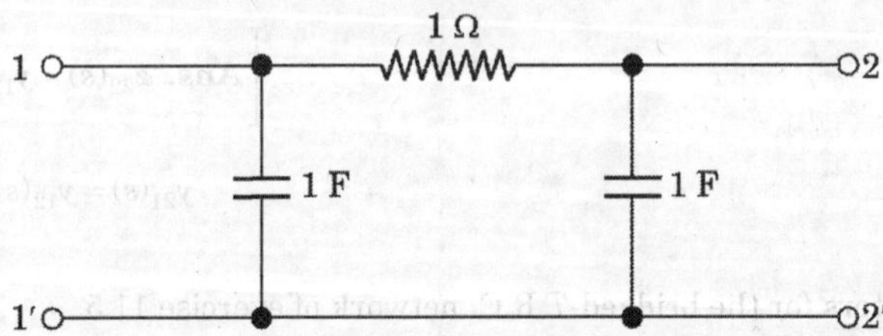

[**Ans.** *A* = *s* + 1 ; *B* = 1 ; *C* = *s*(*s* + 2) ; *D* = (*s* + 1)]

11.14. The *z*-parameters of a two-port network are : z_{11} = 30 Ω, z_{22} = 10 Ω, $z_{12} = z_{21}$ = 15 Ω. Calculate the transmission parameters for the network. Hence write the network equations using transmission parameters.

[**Ans.** *A* = 2 ; *B* = 5 ; *C* = 0.0666 S ; *D* = 0.666 ;
$V_x = 2\,V_2 - 5\,I_2$; $I_1 = 0.0666\,V_2 - 0.666\,I_2$]

11.15. The following equations give the currents I_1 and I_2, at the two ports of a two-port network :

$$I_1 = 0.25\,V_1 - 0.2\,V_2$$

$$I_2 = -0.2\,V_1 + 0.1\,V_1.$$

Calculate the *ABCD* parameters for the network. Hence write the network equations using the *ABCD* parameters.

[**Ans.** $A = 0.5$; $B = 5\ \Omega$; $C = -0.075$, $D = 1.25$; $V_1 = 0.5\ V_2 - 5\ I_1$, $I_1 = -0.075\ V_2 - 1.25\ I_1$]

11.16. The *z*-parameters of a two-port network are : $z_{11} = 5\ \Omega$, $z_{22} = 2\ \Omega$, $z_{12} = z_{21} = 3\ \Omega$. Load resistor of $4\ \Omega$ is connected across the output port *i.e.* port 2. Calculate the input impedance. [**Ans.** $Z_i = 3.5\ \Omega$]

11.17. The following results were obtained as a result of measurements on a two-port network :

(*i*) With port 2 open circuited, a voltage of 10 volts applied at port 1 resulted in current $I_1 = 2.5$ amperes and voltage $V_2 = 5$ volts.

(*ii*) With port 1 open circuited, a voltage of 10 volts applied at port 2 resulted in current $I_1 = 2$ ampere and voltage $V_1 = 4$ volts. Find the *z*-pararneters of the network and the elements of the equivalent *T*-network.

[**Ans.** $z_{11} = 4\ \Omega$; $z_{22} = 5\ \Omega$; $z_{12} = z_{21}\ 2\ \Omega$; $Z_a = 2\ \Omega$; $Z_b = 3\ \Omega$; $Z_c = 2\ \Omega$]

11.18. Voltage V_1 and V_2 at the ports of a 2-port network are given by

$$V_1 = 60\ I_1 + 20\ I_2$$
$$V_2 = 20\ I_1 + 40\ I_2.$$

Find the *z*, *y* and *ABCD* parameters of the network. Also find its equivalent *T*-network.

[**Ans.** $z_{11} = 60\ \Omega$; $z_{22} = 40\ \Omega$; $z_{12} = z_{21} = 20\ \Omega$.
$y_{11} = 0.02$ S ; $y_2 = 0.03$ S ; $y_{12} = y_{21} = 0.01$ S
$A = 3$; $B = 100\ \Omega$; $C = 0.05$ S, $D = 2$.
$Z_c = 20\ \Omega$, $Z_b = 20\ \Omega$, $Z_a = 40\ \Omega$]

11.19. The *y*-parameters of a two-port network are : $y_{11} = 0.4$ S, $y_{22} = 0.25$ S, $y_{12} = y_{21} = -0.2$ S. Find the *z* and *ABCD* parameters of the network. Also find its equivalent π- network.

[**Ans.** $z_{11} = 41.6\ \Omega$; $z_{22} = 6.66\ \Omega$; $z_{12} = z_{21} = 3.33\ \Omega$.
$A = 1.25$; $B = 5\ \Omega$; $C = 0.03$ S, $D = 2$.
$y_1 = 0.2$ S ; $y_2 = 0.2$ S ; $y_3 = 0.05$ S]

11.20. Find the equivalent π-network for the given *T*-network. [**Ans.** $z_1 = 40\ \Omega$, $z_2 = 16\ \Omega$, $z_3 = 8\ \Omega$]

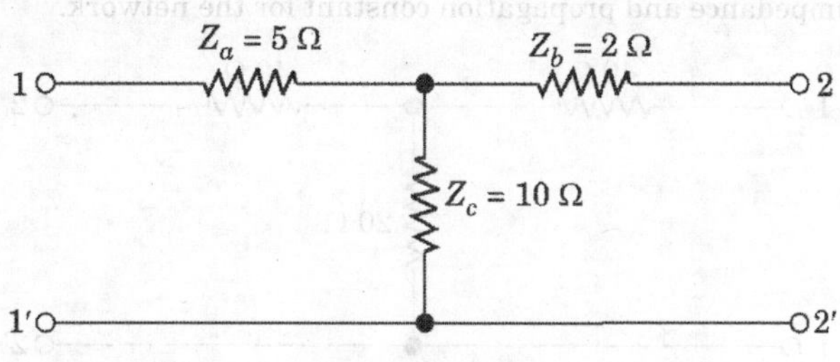

11.21. Find the equivalent *T*-network for the given π-network.

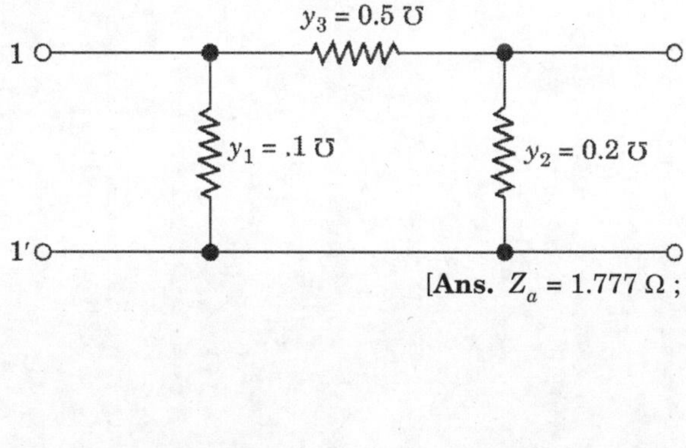

[**Ans.** $Z_a = 1.777\ \Omega$; $Z_b = 0.586\ \Omega$; $Z_c = 2.94\ \Omega$]

11.22. For the given two-port network, calculate the z-parameters and the image parameters.

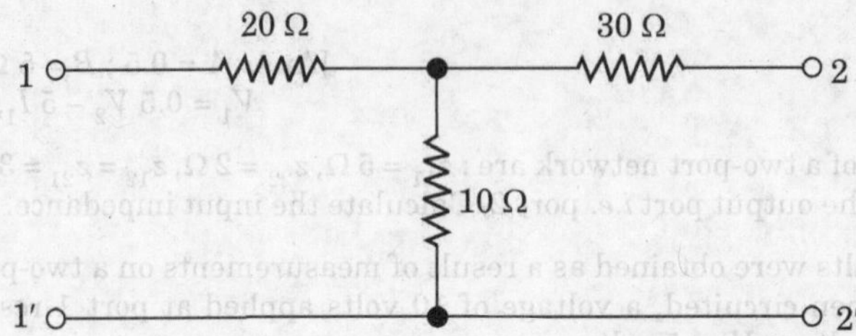

[**Ans.** $z_{11} = 30\ \Omega$; $z_{22} = 40\ \Omega$; $z_{12} = z_{21} = 10\ \Omega$
$Z_{i1} = 28.72\ \Omega$; $Z_{i2} = 38.3\ \Omega$; $\theta = 1.914$]

11.23. The z-parameters of a 2-port network are :

$z_{11} = 50\ \Omega$, $z_{22} = 30\ \Omega$ and $z_{12} = z_{21} = 20\ \Omega$.

Calculate the y parameters, *ABCD* parameters and the image parameters of the network.

[**Ans.** $y_{11} = 0.0273$ S ; $y_{22} = 0.0454$ S ; $y_{12} = y_{21} = -0.01818$ S
$A = 2.5$; $B = 55\ \Omega$; $C = 0.05$; $D = 1.5$
$Z_{i1} = 42.82\ \Omega$; $Z_{i2} = 25.69\ \Omega$; $\theta = 1.280$]

11.24. Derive expressions for the image parameters of a two-port network in terms of *ABCD* parameters. A two-port network has the following *ABCD* parameters : $A = 4$, $B = 50\ \Omega$, $C = 0.1$ S and $D = 2$. Calculate the image parameters of the network.

[**Ans.** $Z_{i1} = 31.61\ \Omega$; $Z_{i2} = 15.81\ \Omega$; $\theta = 0.7331$]

11.25. A two-port network has :

(*i*) at port 1, driving point impedances of 60 Ω. and 55 Ω with port 2 open circuited and short circuited respectively.

(*ii*) at port 2, driving point impedances 80 Ω and 73.33 Ω with port 1 open circuited and short circuited respectively.

Find the image parameters of the network. [**Ans.** $Z_{i1} = 57.45\ \Omega$; $Z_{i2} = 76.59\ \Omega$; $\theta = 1.914$]

11.26. For the given symmetrical network, find the z-parameter and *ABCD* parameters. Hence or otherwise, find the iterative impedance and propagation constant for the network.

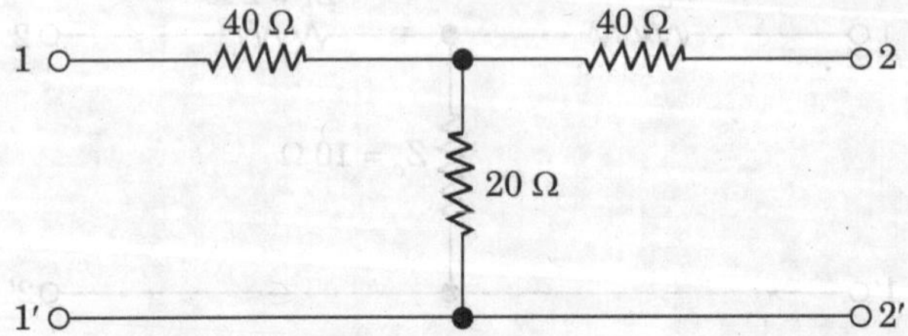

[**Ans.** $z_{11} = z_{22} = 60\ \Omega$; $z_{12} = z_{21} = 20\ \Omega$.
$A = D = 3$; $B = 160\ \Omega$; $C = 0.05$ S.
$Z_0 = 56.57\ \Omega$; $\gamma = 1.762$]

12

Sinusoidal Steady State Analysis

12.1. Introduction

Unlike all other waveforms, sinusoidal waveform has the special property that if a sinusoidal signal is applied to a network containing linear passive elements, then resulting current and voltage in every element of the network is bound to be sinusoidal *in the steady state.* However, this response may differ from the stimulus in its amplitude and phase angle.

This special property of the sinusoid results because :

(*i*) any sinusoid on differentiation or on integration yields another sinusoid of the same frequency.

Thus $$\frac{d}{dt} k \sin(\omega t + \phi) = \omega k \cos(\omega t + \phi) = \omega k \sin\left(\omega t + \frac{\pi}{2} + \phi\right) \qquad ...(12.1)$$

and $$\int k \sin(\omega t + \phi) = \frac{-k}{\omega} \cos(\omega t + \phi) = \frac{-k}{\omega} \sin\left(\omega t + \frac{\pi}{2} + \phi\right) \qquad ...(12.2)$$

(*ii*) Summation of sinusoids of the same frequency but different amplitudes and phase angles results in another sinusoid of the same frequency.

Thus $$k_1 \sin(\omega t + \phi_1) + k_2 \sin(\omega t + \phi_2) + ... = k_t \sin(\omega t + \phi_t) \qquad ...(12.3)$$

But $$e^{\pm j\omega t} = \cos \omega t \pm j \sin \theta \qquad ...(12.4)$$

Hence an exponential function e^{st} has a finite and non-zero steady state value only when $s = + j\omega$ or $- j\omega$.

Further sinusoidal time variations are of greatest occurrence in nature.

In this chapter, we deal with the calculation of sinusoidal steady state response only making use of the general solution obtained in the earlier chapters.

12.2. Sinusoidal Steady State Response

Let a voltage $v(t) = V_1 \sin \omega_1 t$ be applied to a network. Let $Y(s)$ be the admittance function of the network. Then the resulting response current is given by,

$$I(s) = Y(s) \cdot V(s) \qquad ...(12.5)$$

where $V(s)$ is the Laplace transform *of* $v(t)$.

then $$V(s) = V_1 \cdot \frac{\omega_1}{s^2 + \omega_1^2} \qquad ...(12.6)$$

where V_1 and ω_1 are real positive constants. Then Eq. (12.5) may be written as,

$$I(s) = \frac{\omega_1 V_1 . Y(s)}{s^2 + \omega_1^2} \qquad ...(12.7)$$

Network function $Y(s)$ itself may be expressed as a ratio of polynomials. Thus let,

$$Y(s) = \frac{P_1(s)}{Q_1(s)} \quad \text{...(12.8)}$$

Let $$Q_1(s) = (s - p_1)(s - p_2) \dots (s - p_m) \quad \text{...(12.9)}$$

where $p_1, p_2, \dots\dots p_m$ are the poles of $Y(s)$.

Then the response transform current $I(s)$ may be expressed in partial fraction form as below:

$$I(s) = \frac{\omega_1 V_1 \,.\, Y(s)}{s^3 + \omega_1^{\,2}} = \frac{k_1}{s - p_1} + \frac{k_2}{s - p_2} + \dots + \frac{k_m}{s - p_m} + \frac{k\omega}{s + j\omega_1} + \frac{k\omega'}{s - j\omega_1} \quad \text{...(12.10)}$$

Coefficients $k\omega$ and $k\omega'$ may be evaluated by the use of Heaviside method. Thus multiplying Eq. (12.10) by $(s + j\omega_1)$ and putting $s = -j\omega_1$, we get,

$$k\omega = \frac{\omega_1 V_1 Y(-j\omega_1)}{-j2\omega_1} \quad \text{...(12.11)}$$

where $Y(-j\omega_1)$ may be expressed in the polar form as $|\,Y_1\,|\,e^{-j\phi}$.

Hence Eq. (12.11) yields,

$$k\omega = \frac{V_1\,|\,Y_1\,|\,e^{-j\phi}}{-j2} \quad \text{...(12.12)}$$

Similarly $$k\omega' = \frac{\omega_1 V_1 Y(+j\omega_1)}{+j2\omega_1} = \frac{V_1\,|\,Y_1\,|\,e^{j\phi}}{j2} \quad \text{...(12.13)}$$

Substituting the values of $k\omega$ and $k\omega'$ as given by Eqs. (12.12) and (12.13) into equation (12.10), we get the following expression for the last two terms of $I(s)$,

$$\frac{k\omega}{s + j\omega_1} + \frac{k\omega'}{s - j\omega_1} = \frac{V_1\,|\,Y_1\,|}{j2}\left[\frac{e^{j\phi}}{s - j\omega_1} - \frac{e^{-j\phi}}{s + j\omega_1}\right] \quad \text{...(12.14)}$$

On inverse Laplace transformation, we get time domain response of the last two terms

$$= \frac{V_1\,|\,Y_1\,|}{j2}\left[e^{j\omega_1 t} \,.\, e^{j\phi} - e^{-j\omega_1 t} \,.\, e^{-j\phi}\right] = \frac{V_1\,|\,Y_1\,|}{j2}\left[e^{j(\omega_1 t + \phi)} - e^{-j(\omega_1 t + \phi)}\right]$$

$$= V_1\,|\,Y_1\,|\sin(\omega_1 t + \phi) \quad \text{...(12.15)}$$

Inverse Laplace transformation of Eq. (12.10) yields

$$i(t) = V_1\,|\,Y_1\,|\sin(\mathrm{w}_1 t + \mathrm{f}) = k_1 e^{p_1 t} + k_2 e^{p_2 t} + \dots + k_m e^{p_m t} \quad \text{...(12.16)}$$

But for passive network, the real part of each of the poles $p_1, p_2 \dots p_m$ is negative so that the exponential response $(k_1 e^{p_1 t} + k_2 e^{p_2 t} + \dots + k_m e^{p_m t})$ decays with time and becomes almost zero for large values of t. Thus after sufficiently long period of time, only the first term in Eq. (12.16), namely the term $V_1\,|\,Y_1\,|\sin(\omega_1 t + \phi)$ will exist. This constitutes the steady state response i_{ss}. Thus we have,

$$i_{ss} = V_1\,|\,Y_1\,|\sin(\omega_1 t + \phi) \quad \text{...(12.17)}$$

This steady state response $V_1\,|\,Y_1\,|\sin(\omega_1 t + \phi)$ has resulted from the excitation $V_1 \sin(\omega_1 t + \phi)$. Thus we observe that the excitation and the response differ in magnitude by multiplier $|\,Y_1\,|$ and in phase by angle ϕ. But $|\,Y_1\,|$ are ϕ nothing but the magnitude and phase angle of $Y(j\omega_1)$. Hence we conclude that the steady state response for sinusoidal excitation may be found by letting $s = j\omega$ in the network function relating excitation and the response.

12.3. The Sinusoid in relation to Exponential Functions e ± jωt

Consider a sinusoidal waveform of amplitude V given by the equation,

$$v = V \sin(\omega t + \phi) \qquad ...(12.18)$$

Here ω is the frequency in radians/second and φ is the phase angle of voltage v relative to the reference voltage v' given by,

$$v' = V \sin \omega t \qquad ...(12.19)$$

The periodic time of v is the time interval between two consecutive maxima or minima. Thus it may be reckoned from $\omega t = 0$ to $\omega t = 2\pi$ radians. Let the periodic time be ωT. Then $\omega T = 2\pi$

or $$T = \frac{2\pi}{\omega} \text{ second} \qquad ...(12.20)$$

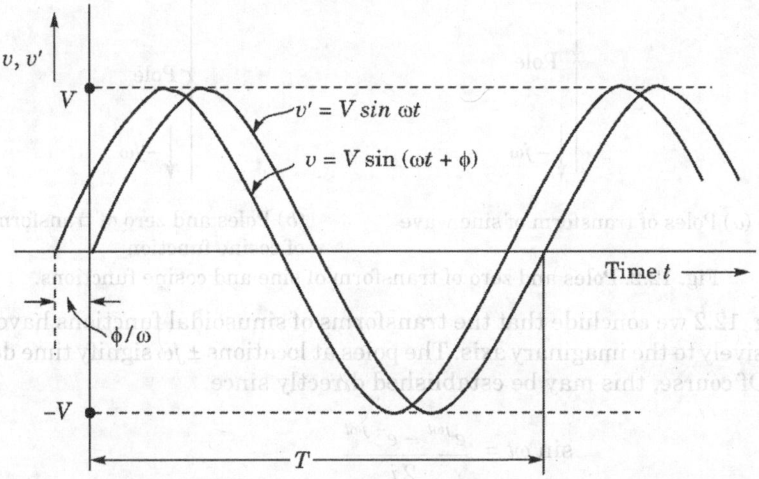

Fig. 12.1. Time variation of sinusoids of amplitude V and periodic time T.

Fig. 12.1 shows the time variation of voltages v and v'. Here φ/ω is the time displacement of sinusoid v relative to v' while φ is the phase angle of v' relative to v. If φ is positive, sinusoidal v passes through zero value (and goes positive) φ/ω seconds earlier then v' and then v is said to lead v' by φ/ω second or φ radians. On the other hand, if φ is negative, sinusoid v passes through a zero value φ/ω seconds later than v' and then v is said to lag v' by φ/ω seconds or φ radians.

Eq. (12.18) may be written as,

$$v = V \cos\left(\omega t + \phi - \frac{\pi}{\omega}\right) = V \cos(\omega t + \beta) \qquad ...(12.21)$$

where $$\beta = \phi - \frac{\pi}{2} \qquad ...(12.22)$$

Eq. (12.21) may be written as,

$$v = (V \cos \beta) \cos \omega t + (-V \sin \beta) \sin \omega t \qquad ...(12.23)$$

Now $v[= V \sin(\omega t + \phi)]$ is the general form of steady state response. Hence we conclude that the general form of signal may be put as the sum of sine and cosine functions.

Now $$\mathcal{L}(\sin \omega t) = \frac{\omega}{s^2 + \omega^2} \qquad ...(12.24)$$

and $$\mathcal{L}(\cos \omega t) = \frac{\omega}{s^2 + \omega^2} \qquad ...(12.25)$$

Fig. 12.2 shows the location of poles and zeros of Laplace transform of sine and cosine functions as given by Eqs. (12.24) and (12.25).

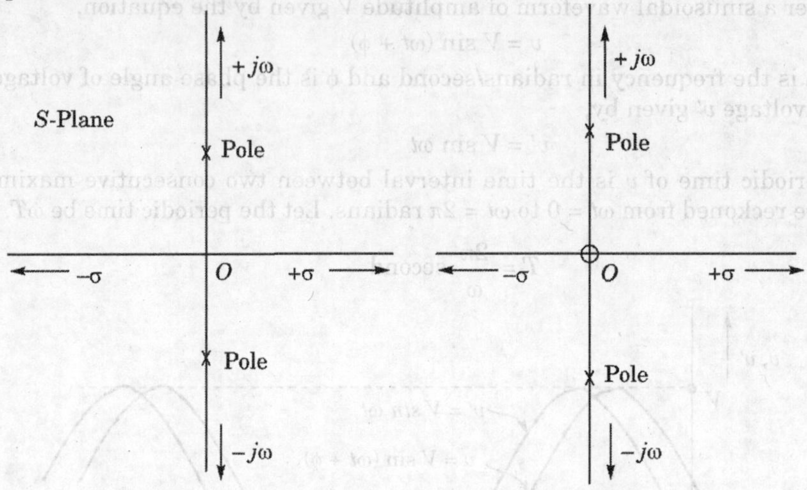

(a) Poles of transform of sine wave (b) Poles and zero of transform of cosine function

Fig. 12.2. Poles and zero of transform of sine and cosine functions.

From Fig. 12.2 we conclude that the transforms of sinusoidal functions have poles and zeros restricted exclusively to the imaginary axis. The poles at locations $\pm j\omega$ signify time domain responses $e^{+j\omega t}$ and $e^{-j\omega t}$. Of course, this may be established directly since

$$\sin \omega t = \frac{e^{j\omega t} - e^{-j\omega t}}{2j} \quad ...(12.26)$$

and

$$\cos \omega t = \frac{e^{j\omega t} - e^{-j\omega t}}{2} \quad ...(12.27)$$

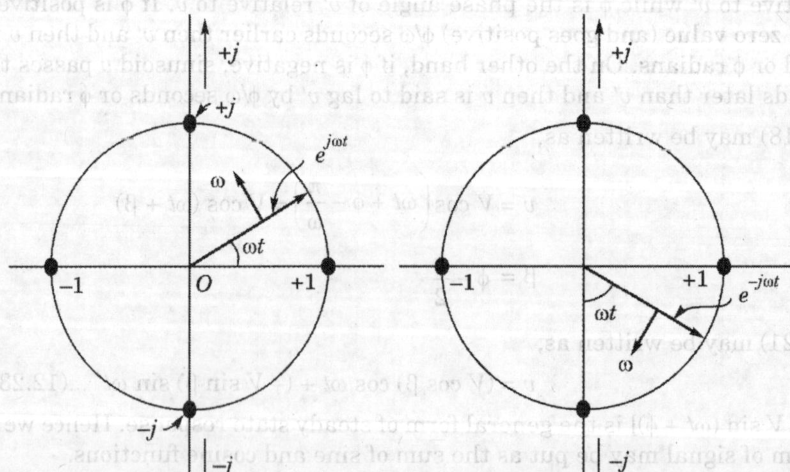

(a) rotating phasor representing the term $e^{j\omega t}$ (b) rotating phasor representing the term $e^{-j\omega t}$

Fig. 12.3. Rotating phasors representing the terms $e^{j\omega t}$ and $e^{-j\omega t}$.

The quantity $e^{j\omega t}$ may be represented by a unit rotating phasor rotating in the positive *i.e.* counterclockwise direction as shown in Fig. 12.3 (*a*). Similarly the term $e^{-j\omega t}$ may be represented by a unit rotating phasor rotating in the negative or clockwise direction as shown in Fig. 12.3 (*b*).

Then sin ωt, in accordance with Eq. (12.33) equals the difference of two rotating phasors each of magnitude $\frac{1}{2}$ and rotating in opposite directions. The factor $\frac{e^{j\omega t}}{2}$ is represented in Fig. 12.4 by a phasor *OA* of magnitude $\frac{1}{2}$ rotating in counterclockwise direction. The factor $\frac{-e^{j\omega t}}{2}$ is represented in Fig. 12.4 by a phasor *OB* of magnitude $\frac{1}{2}$ rotating in clockwise direction. These two are equal in magnitude and are symmetrically disposed with respect to the imaginary axis. The addition of the phasors $\frac{1}{2}e^{j\omega t}$ and $-\frac{1}{2}e^{-j\omega t}$ results in a phasor *OC* on the $+j$ axis as shown in Fig. 12.4. Multiplication of this combination $\frac{1}{2}[e^{j\omega t} - e^{-j\omega t}]$ by factor $\frac{1}{j}$ or $(-j)$ causes rotation of the phasor *OC* by 90° in the negative direction *i.e.* clockwise direction. This results in phasor *OD* which in accordance with Eq. (12.26) represents the function sin ωt.

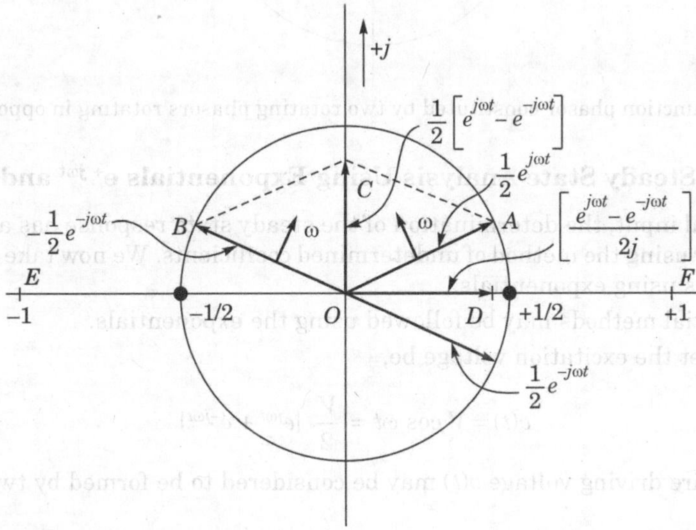

Fig. 12.4. Sine wave phasor constituted by two rotating phasors rotating in opposite directions.

Thus we see that the phasor for sin ωt always lies along the real axis. This is to be expected since sin ωt is a real number. However its magnitude varies between the limits – 1 and + 1 *i.e.* point *D* moves along the real axis between the points *E* to *F* as shown in Fig. 12.4. When $\omega t = 0$, sin ωt equals zero. On the other hand, when $\omega t = \frac{\pi}{2}$, sin ωt equals 1.

Fig. 12.5 shows the construction of phasor for cos ωt in terms of exponential factors. In Fig. 12.5, phasor *OA* represents the exponential factor $\frac{1}{2}e^{j\omega t}$ while phasor *OB* represents the exponential factor $\frac{1}{2}e^{-j\omega t}$ Summation of these two phasors gives a phasor OC which represents the factor

$\frac{1}{2}[e^{j\omega t} + e^{-j\omega t}]$. Hence from equation (12.27), this phasor OC represents the term cos ωt.

From Fig. 12.5 we see that phasor for cos ωt also always lies along the real axis. Its magnitude varies between the limits – 1 and + 1 *i.e.* point C in Fig. 12.5 moves along the real axis between the points E, corresponding to $\omega t = \pi$, and F corresponding to $\omega t = 0$. On the other hand, when $\omega t = \frac{\pi}{2}$ or $\frac{3\pi}{2}$, cos ωt has zero value.

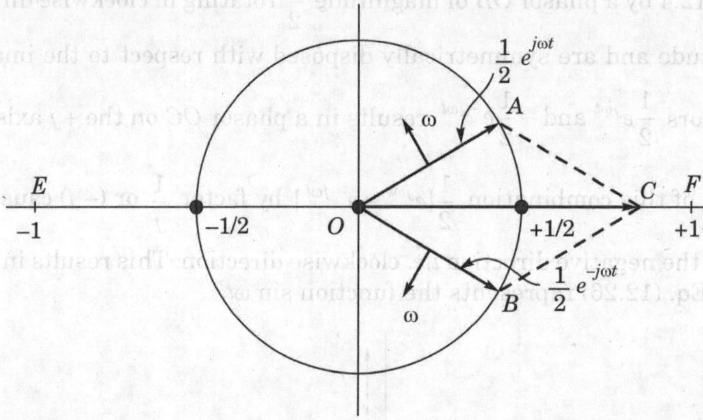

Fig. 12.5. Cosine function phasor constituted by two rotating phasors rotating in opposite directions.

12.4. Sinusoidal Steady State Analysis Using Exponentials $e^{+j\omega t}$ and $e^{-j\omega t}$

For sinusoidal input, the determination of the steady state response has already been done in an earlier chapter using the method of undetermined coefficients. We now take up the sinusoidal steady state analysis using exponentials.

Two differential methods may be followed using the exponentials.

Method I. Let the excitation voltage be,

$$v(t) = V \cos \omega t = \frac{V}{2}\,[e^{j\omega t} + e^{-j\omega t}] \qquad \text{...(12.28)}$$

Thus the entire driving voltage $v(t)$ may be considered to be formed by two driving voltage $\frac{V}{2}e^{j\omega t}$ and $\frac{V}{2}e^{-j\omega t}$.

For the given network we now find the steady state response making use of the method of undetermined coefficients for each of the two excitations $\frac{V}{2}e^{j\omega t}$ and $\frac{V}{2}e^{-j\omega t}$ considered separately.

Let these steady state responses be i_{ss1} and i_{ss2} respectively. Then the total steady state response i_{ss} is the summation of these two responses and is given by,

$$i_{ss} = i_{ss1} + i_{ss2} \qquad \text{...(12.29)}$$

Similar procedure may be followed for excitation V sin ωt considering this excitation V sin

ωt to be given by summation of two exponentials $e^{j\omega t}$ and $e^{-j\omega t}$ as given by the relation :

$$V \sin \omega t = \frac{V}{2j}\left[e^{j\omega t} - e^{-j\omega t}\right] \quad ...(12.30)$$

Method II. Let a driving voltage $v(t)$ be given by

$$v(t) = e^{j(\omega t + \phi)} \quad ...(12.31)$$

$$= V \cos(\omega t + \phi) + j\, V \sin(\omega t - \phi) \quad ...(12.32)$$

In actual practice, there exists no physical generator of complex numbers. The above assumption of voltage $v(t)$ as given by Eq. (12.32) is simply a mathematically aid in obtaining the desired result more conveniently.

Now let voltage $v(t)$ as given by Eq. (12.31) result in steady state response current $i(t)$. Further let $i_r(t)$ be the response due to the excitation $V \cos(\omega t + \phi)$ *i.e.* due to the real part of the total excitation $V e^{j(\omega t + \phi)}$ and let $i_m(t)$ be the response due to the excitation $V \sin(\omega t + \phi)$ *i.e.* due to the imaginary part of the total excitation.

Then by the principle of superposition, we get

$$i(t) = i_r(t) + j i_m(t) \quad ...(12.33)$$

Then $$i_r(t) = R_e[i(V)] \quad ...(12.34)$$

and $$i_m(t) = I_m[i(t)] \quad ...(12.35)$$

In Eq. (12.34) symbol R_e stands for *the real part of* and in Eq. (12.35) the symbol I_m stands for *the imaginary part of*.

Now Eq. (12.31) may be written as :

$$v(t) = Ve^{i\phi} \, . \, e^{j\omega t} \quad ...(12.36)$$

$$= \mathbf{V}e^{j\omega t} \quad ...(12.37)$$

where **V** is the complex number of magnitude V and phase angle ϕ.

Now superposition property of a linear network involves homogeneity property. Accordingly we may first compute the solution of the network using the excitation $e^{j\omega t}$ and then multiplying the response by $\mathbf{V}(= Ve^{j\phi})$ in order to get the response with excitation $\mathbf{V}e^{j\omega t}$.

The above discussion leads to the formulation of the following procedure for sinusoidal steady analysis for excitations $V \cos(\omega t + \phi)$ and $V \sin(\omega t + \phi)$,

(*i*) Find the response to the excitation $e^{j\omega t}$.

(*ii*) Multiply this response by $\mathbf{V} = Ve^{j\phi}$.

(*iii*) Express this product in the form $A + jB$. Then the real part A gives the desired steady state response due to the excitation $V \cos(\omega t + \phi)$ while the imaginary part B gives the steady state response due to the excitation $V \sin(\omega t + \phi)$.

12.5. Sinusoidal Steady State Analysis of a Series R-L Network

Fig. 12.6 shows a series *R-L* circuit to which excitation $v(t)$ equal to $V \cos \omega t$ is applied. It is required to find the steady state component of current in the series circuit.

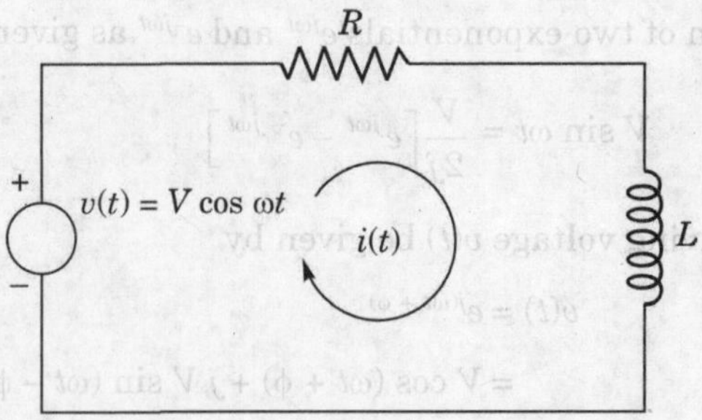

Fig. 12.6. Series *R-L* circuit with sinusoidal excitation.

The desired analysis may be done by either of the two methods outlined above. These are given below :

Method I. The driving voltage given by

$$v(t) = V \cos \omega t \qquad ...(12.38)$$

$$= \frac{V}{2}\left[e^{j\omega t} + e^{-j\omega t}\right] \qquad ...(12.39)$$

Thus the entire driving voltage $v(t)$ may be considered to be formed by two driving voltages namely $\frac{V}{2}e^{j\omega t}$ and $\frac{V}{2}e^{-j\omega t}$.

Considering only the voltage source $\frac{V}{2}e^{j\omega t}$, application of Kirchhoff's voltage law of the series network yields,

$$L\frac{di}{dt} + Ri = \frac{V}{2}e^{j\omega t} \qquad ...(12.40)$$

In order to solve this equation to find the steady state current, we make use of the method of undetermined coefficient and assume that the desired solution is of the following form

$$i_{ss1} = Ae^{j\omega t} \qquad ...(12.41)$$

where A is the undetermined coefficient.

Substituting the value of current $i(t)$ from Eq. (12.41) into Eq. (12.40), we get

$$j\omega LA + RA = \frac{V}{2} \qquad ...(12.42)$$

Hence

$$A = \frac{V/2}{R + j\omega L} \qquad ...(12.43)$$

Next we consider the voltage source $\frac{V}{2}e^{-j\omega t}$ and assume the desired response to be,

$$i_{ss2} = Be^{-j\omega t} \qquad ...(12.44)$$

Then we get,

$$B = \frac{V/2}{R - j\omega L} \qquad ...(12.45)$$

Then by the principle of superposition, the total steady state current i_{ss} is the summation of currents i_{ss1} and i_{ss2}.

Hence $i_{ss} = i_{ss1} + i_{ss2}$

$$= \frac{V}{2}\left[\frac{e^{j\omega t}}{R + j\omega L} + \frac{e^{-j\omega t}}{R - j\omega L}\right] \quad ...(12.46)$$

$$= \frac{V}{R^2 + \omega^2 L^2}[R \cos \omega t + \omega L \sin \omega t] \quad ...(12.47)$$

$$= \frac{V}{\sqrt{R^2 + \omega^2 L^2}} \cos\left(\omega t - \tan^{-1}\frac{\omega L}{R}\right) \quad ...(12.48)$$

Eq. (12.48) gives the desired result.

Method II. Let $e^{j\omega t}$ be the excitation.

Then application of Kirchhoff's voltage law to the network yields,

$$L\frac{di}{dt} + Ri = e^{j\omega t} \quad ...(12.49)$$

Let the steady state solution be,

$$i_s = Ae^{j\omega t} \quad ...(12.50)$$

where A is the undetermined coefficient.

Substitution of value of $i(t)$ as given by Eq. (12.50) into Eq. (12.51) yields,

$$j\omega LA\, e^{j\omega t} + RA\, e^{j\omega t} = e^{j\omega t}$$

or

$$\omega LA + RA = 1 \quad ...(12.51)$$

Hence

$$A = \frac{1}{R + j\omega L} \quad ...(12.52)$$

Hence

$$i_s = \frac{1}{R + j\omega L} \cdot e^{j\omega t} \quad ...(12.53)$$

With excitation $Ve^{j\omega t}$, the steady state current is

$$i_s = \frac{V}{R + j\omega L} e^{j\omega t} \quad ...(12.54)$$

Hence with excitation $V \cos \omega t$, the steady state response is given by,

$$i_{ss} = R_e\left[\frac{V}{(R + j\omega L)}\right] e^{j\omega t} \quad ...(12.55)$$

$$= R_e\left[\frac{V(\cos \omega t + j \sin \omega t)}{R + j\omega L}\right]$$

$$= R_e\left[\frac{V\,.\,(R \cos \omega t + \omega L \sin \omega L) - j(\omega L \cos \omega t + R \sin \omega t)}{R^2 + \omega^2 L^2}\right]$$

$$= \frac{V(R \cos \omega t + \omega L \sin \omega t)}{R^2 + \omega^2 L^2}$$

$$= \frac{V}{\sqrt{R^2 + \omega^2 L^2}} \cos\left(\omega t - \tan^{-1}\frac{\omega L}{R^2}\right)$$

12.6. Sinusoidal Steady State Analysis of a Parallel R-L Network

Fig. 12.7 shows a parallel *R-L* network to which excitation current $i(t) = I\cos(\omega_t + \phi)$ is applied. It is required to find the steady, state voltage across the *R-L* network.

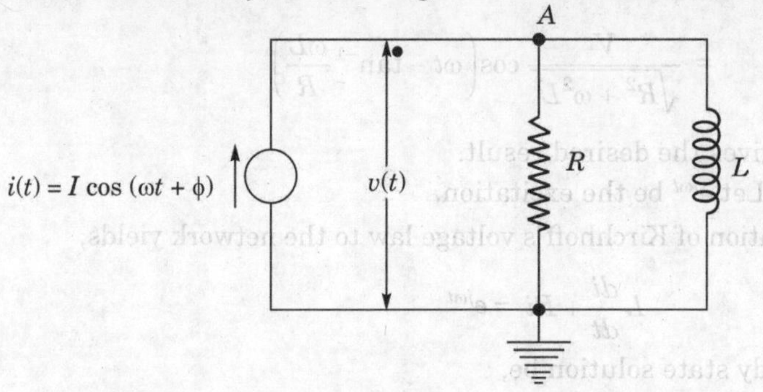

Fig. 12.7. Parallel *R-L* circuit with sinusoidal excitation.

The desired analysis may be done by either of the two methods outlined in article 12.4. These are given below.

Method I. The driving current is given by,

$$i(t) = I\cos(\omega t + \phi) \qquad \text{...(12.58)}$$

$$= \frac{I}{2}\left[ej^{(\omega t + \phi)} + e^{-j(\omega t + \phi)}\right] \qquad \text{...(12.59)}$$

Considering only the current source $\frac{I}{2}e^{(j\omega t + \phi)}$, application of Kirchhoff's current law to node *A* yields,

$$\frac{v}{R} + \frac{1}{L}\int_{-\infty}^{t} v\,dt = \frac{I}{2}e^{j(\omega t + \phi)} \qquad \text{...(12.60)}$$

Since the initial value found by integrating from $t = -\infty$ to $t = 0$ does not alter the steady state response, the lower limit in the integral does not enter into the evaluation. We may, therefore, write Eq. (12.60) in indefinite integral form as below :

$$\frac{v}{R} + \frac{1}{L}\int v\,dt = \frac{I}{2}e^{j(\omega t + \phi)} \qquad \text{...(12.61)}$$

Let the desired steady state solution be

$$v_{ss1} = A.e^{j(\omega t + \phi)} \qquad \text{...(12.62)}$$

where *A* is the undetermined coefficient. Substituting the value $v(t)$ from Eq. (12.62), into Eq. (12.61), we get

$$\frac{A}{R}e^{j(\omega t + \phi)} + \frac{1}{L}\frac{A}{j\omega}e^{j(\omega t + \phi)} = \frac{I}{2}e^{j(\omega t + \phi)}$$

or $$\frac{A}{R}+\frac{A}{j\omega L}=\frac{I}{2} \qquad ...(12.63)$$

Hence $$A=\frac{I/2}{\frac{1}{R}+\frac{1}{j\omega L}} \qquad ...(12.64)$$

Next we consider the current source $\frac{I}{2}e^{-j(\omega t+\phi)}$ and assume the steady state response to be given by,

$$v_{ss2}=B\,e^{-j(\omega t+\phi)} \qquad ...(12.65)$$

Then we get $$B=\frac{I/2}{\frac{1}{R}-\frac{1}{j\omega L}} \qquad ...(12.66)$$

Then by the principle of superposition, the total steady state voltage v_{ss} is the summation of voltages v_{ss1} and v_{ss2}.

Hence $v_{ss}=v_{ss1}+v_{ss2}$.

$$=\frac{I}{2}\left[\frac{e^{j(\omega t+\phi)}}{\frac{1}{R}+\frac{1}{j\omega L}}+\frac{e^{-j(\omega t+\phi)}}{\frac{1}{R}-\frac{1}{j\omega L}}\right] \qquad ...(12.67)$$

$$=\frac{1}{2\left(\frac{1}{R^2}+\frac{1}{\omega^2L^2}\right)}\times\left[\frac{1}{R}\left\{e^{j(\omega t+\phi)}+e^{-j(\omega t+\phi)}\right\}+j\frac{1}{\omega L}\left\{e^{j(\omega t+\phi)}-e^{-j(\omega t+\phi)}\right\}\right]$$

$$=\frac{I}{\frac{1}{R^2}+\frac{1}{\omega^2L^2}}\left[\frac{1}{R}\cos(\omega t+\phi)-\frac{1}{\omega L}\sin(\omega t+\phi)\right]$$

$$=\frac{I}{\sqrt{\frac{1}{R^2}+\frac{1}{\omega^2L^2}}}\cos\left(\omega t+\phi+\tan^{-1}\frac{R}{\omega L}\right) \qquad ...(12.68)$$

$$=\frac{I\cdot\omega LR}{\sqrt{R^2+\omega^2L^2}}\cos\left(\omega t+\phi+\tan^{-1}\frac{R}{\omega L}\right) \qquad ...(12.69)$$

Method II. Let $e^{j\omega t}$ be the excitation. Then application of Kirchhoff's law to the circuit yields,

$$\frac{v}{R}+\frac{1}{L}\int_{-\infty}^{t}v\,dt=e^{j\omega t} \qquad ...(12.70)$$

Again for reasons given in method I, we write Eq. (12.70) in indefinite integral form as below :

$$\frac{v}{R}+\frac{1}{L}\int v\,dt=e^{j\omega t} \qquad ...(12.71)$$

Let the desired steady state solution be,

$$v_{sst} = A\,e^{j\omega t} \qquad ...(12.72)$$

where A is the undetermined coefficient. Substituting the value of v as given by Eq. (12.27) into Eq. (12.71), we get

$$\frac{A.e^{j\omega t}}{R} + \frac{A.e^{j\omega t}}{j\omega L} = e^{j\omega t}$$

Hence
$$A = \frac{1}{\dfrac{1}{R} + \dfrac{1}{j\omega L}} \qquad ...(12.73)$$

Hence
$$v_{sst} = \frac{1}{\dfrac{1}{R} + \dfrac{1}{j\omega L}}\, e^{j\omega t} \qquad ...(12.74)$$

Hence the desired steady state response for excitation $I\cos(\omega t + \phi)$ is given by,

$$v_{ss} = R_e\left[Ie^{j\phi}\left(\frac{1}{\dfrac{1}{R} + \dfrac{1}{j\omega L}}\right)^{e^{j\omega t}}\right] \qquad ...(12.75)$$

On algebraic manipulation Eq. (12.75) yields,

$$v_{ss} = \frac{I\omega LR}{\sqrt{R^2 + \omega^2 L^2}} \cos\left(\omega t + \phi + \tan^{-1}\frac{R}{\omega L}\right) \qquad ...(12.76)$$

12.7. Sinusoidal Steady State Analysis using $R_e\, e^{j\omega t}$ or $I_m\, e^{j\omega t}$

As an alternative to the method discussed in article 12.4, we may find the sinusoidal steady state solution using the following identifies :

$$\cos \omega t = R_e\,.\, e^{j\omega t} \qquad ...(12.77)$$

$$\sin \omega t = I_m\,.\, e^{j\omega t} \qquad ...(12.78)$$

Thus if the excitation $V\cos(\omega t + \phi)$ is applied to say a series circuit, we may use the relation,

$$V\cos(\omega t + \phi) = R_e[V\,.\, e^{j(\omega t + \phi)}] \qquad ...(12.79)$$

$$= R_e[V\,.\, e^{j\phi}\,.\, e^{j\omega t}] \qquad ...(12.80)$$

$$= R_e[\mathbf{V}e^{j\omega t}] \qquad ...(12.81)$$

where
$$\mathbf{V} = V\,.\, e^{j\phi} \qquad ...(12.82)$$

For illustration, let us consider the series. R-L circuit of Fig. 12.6. Then application of Kirchhoff's law to the circuit yields,

$$L\frac{di}{dt} + Ri = R_e[Ve^{j\phi}\, e^{j\omega t}] \qquad ...(12.83)$$

By the method of undetermined coefficients, we assume the steady state solution to be,

$$i_{ss} = R_e[A\,.\, e^{j\omega t}] \qquad ...(12.84)$$

where A is the undetermined coefficient.

Substituting the value of i as given by Eq. (12.84) into Eq. (12.83), we get

$$L\frac{d}{dt}\left[R_e\left\{Ae^{j\omega t}\right\}\right] + R\left[R_e\left\{Ae^{j\omega t}\right\}\right] = R_e\left[Ve^{j\phi} \,.\, e^{j\omega t}\right] \quad ...(12.85)$$

We now make use of the following 3 rules of complex quantities :

$$R_e[k_1 f_1 + k_2 f_2] = k_1 \,.\, Ref_1 + k_2 Ref_2 \quad ...(12.86)$$

$$R_e\frac{df}{dt} = \frac{d}{d_t}(Ref) \quad ...(12.87)$$

and

$$R_e \int fdt = f(R_e \,.\, f)dt \quad ...(12.88)$$

Using these properties in Eq. (12.85), we get

$$R_e\left[A\left(L\frac{d}{dt} + R\right)e^{j\omega t}\right] = R_e[\mathbf{V}e^{k\omega t}] \quad ...(12.89)$$

or

$$R_e[\{A(R + j\omega L) - \mathbf{V}\}\, e^{j\omega t}] = 0 \quad ...(12.90)$$

This equation holds good for all values of time t and hence, we get

$$A(R + j\omega L) = \mathbf{V}$$

or

$$A = \frac{\mathbf{V}}{R + j\omega L} \quad ...(12.91)$$

Substituting this value of A in Eq. (12.84), we get the following steady state solution :

$$i_{ss} = R_e\left[\frac{\mathbf{V}}{R + j\omega L}\, e^{j\omega t}\right] \quad ..(12.92)$$

where $\mathbf{V}e = ve^{j\phi}$

Equation (12.92) reduces to Eq. (12.55) if ϕ is zero.

On algebraic manipulation, Eq. (12.92) yields,

$$i_{ss} = \frac{V}{\sqrt{R^2 + \omega^2 L^2}}\cos\left(\omega t + \phi - \tan^{-1}\frac{\omega L}{R}\right) \quad ...(12.93)$$

In case the excitation is $V \sin(\omega t + \phi)$, in the above analysis, everywhere we use I_m instead of R_e and arrive at the solution.

$$i_{ss} = \frac{V}{\sqrt{R^2 + \omega^2 L^2}}\sin\left(\omega t + \phi - \tan^{-1}\frac{\omega L}{R}\right) \quad ...(12.94)$$

General Series Network. Let us consider a general series network. From Eq. (12.81), excitation $V \cos(\omega t + \phi)$ may be written as,

$$V\cos(\omega t + \phi) = R_e\ [\mathbf{V}e^{j\omega t}] \quad ...(12.95)$$

where

$$\mathbf{V} = Ve^{j\phi} \quad ...(12.96)$$

Then from the above discussion, the steady state solution is of the form,

$$i_{ss} = R_e[\mathbf{I}e^{j\omega t}] \quad ...(12.97)$$

where $$\mathbf{I} = Ie^{j\theta} \quad ...(12.98)$$

Here excitation $V \cos(\omega t + \phi)$ has resulted in response i_{ss}. Hence we may write the following expression for the network impedance under sinusoidal steady state.

$$\mathbf{Z}(j\omega) = \frac{V \cos(\omega t + \phi)}{i_{ss}} = \frac{\mathbf{V}}{\mathbf{I}} \quad ...(12.99)$$

Hence from Eqs. (12.96) and (12.98), we get

$$\mathbf{Z}(j\omega) = \frac{Ve^{j\phi}}{Ie^{j\theta}} = \frac{V}{I} \cdot e^{j(\phi - \theta)} \quad ...(12.100)$$

Now this $\mathbf{Z}(j\omega)$, being the network impedance under sinusoidal steady state, forms a special category of Laplace transform network impedance $Z(s)$ in which $s = j\omega$.

Thus $$\mathbf{Z}(j\omega) = \left.\frac{V(s)}{I(s)}\right|_{s = j\omega} \quad ...(12.101)$$

Now Eq. (12.99) may be written in the following forms :

$$\mathbf{I}\mathbf{Z}(j\omega) = \mathbf{V} \quad ...(12.102)$$

or $$\mathbf{I} = \frac{\mathbf{V}}{\mathbf{Z}(j\omega)} \quad ...(12.103)$$

For a given network, once the current $\mathbf{I}$ is determined, then the steady state solution is given by,

$$i_{ss} = R_e[\mathbf{I}e^{j\omega t}] \quad ...(12.104)$$

Response i_{ss} may always be put in the form,

$$i_{ss} = \frac{\mathbf{V}}{|Z|} \cos(\omega t + \theta) \quad ...(12.105)$$

where V is the magnitude of $\mathbf{V}$ and $|Z|$ is the magnitude of $\mathbf{Z}(j\omega)$.

Here θ is the phase angle of current i_{ss} and is given by,

$$\theta = \phi - \text{phase angle of impedance } \mathbf{Z}(j\omega)$$

$$= \phi - \tan^{-1} \frac{I_m \mathbf{Z}(j\omega)}{R_e \mathbf{Z}(j\omega)} \quad ...(12.106)$$

12.8. Phasors and Phasor Diagrams

We have already made use of phasors in the sinusoidal steady state analysis. Now we employ the same for a general l-loop network having sinusoidal sources of the same frequency. It is required to find the steady state response in the network. As per methods already discussed earlier we may write in transform form l equations involving l independent loop currents. These equations may now be rewritten for the sinusoidal steady state by

(*i*) letting $s = j\omega$, where ω is the frequency of excitation of each source,

(*ii*) writing impedance function $Z_{jk}(j\omega)$ instead of $Z_{jk}(s)$, (*iii*) representing each loop voltage by a phasor of the form $V_j\, e^{j\omega t}$ and

(*iv*) representing each loop current by a phasor of the form $I_k\, e^{j\omega t}$

Then the l equations may be written as below :

$$\left.\begin{aligned} z_{11}(j\omega).\mathbf{I}_1 + z_{12}(j\omega).\mathbf{I}_1 + \ldots\ldots + \mathbf{Z}_{1l}(j\omega).\mathbf{I}_l &= \mathbf{V}_1 \\ z_{21}(j\omega).\mathbf{I}_1 + z_{22}(j\omega).\mathbf{I}_2 + \ldots\ldots + \mathbf{Z}_{2l}(j\omega).\mathbf{I}_l &= \mathbf{V}_2 \\ \ldots\ \ldots\ \ldots\ \ldots\ \ldots\ \ldots\ \ldots\ \ldots\ \ldots\ \ldots\ &\ldots \\ z_{l1}(j\omega).\mathbf{I}_1 + z_{l2}(j\omega).\mathbf{I}_2 + \ldots\ldots + \mathbf{Z}_{ll}(j\omega).\mathbf{I}_l &= \mathbf{V}_l \end{aligned}\right\} \qquad \ldots(12.107)$$

In each of these equations exponential $e^{j\omega t}$ has been cancelled. Having written Eq. (12.107), any loop current out of l loop currents $\mathbf{I}_1$ to $\mathbf{I}_l$ may be found through usual algebraic manipulation. The loop current $\mathbf{I}_k$ in the kth loop is then of the form,

$$\mathbf{I}_k = I_k\ .e^{j\theta k} \qquad \ldots(12.108)$$

From Eq. (12.108), knowing the magnitude I_k and phase angle θ_k, time domain response may be written as given in Eq. (12.109), provided that the excitation voltages are of the form.

$V_1 \cos(\omega t + \phi_1)$, $V_2 \cos(\omega t + \phi_2)$ etc.

$$k_k(t) = I_k\ .\ \cos(\omega t + \theta_k) \qquad \ldots(12.109)$$

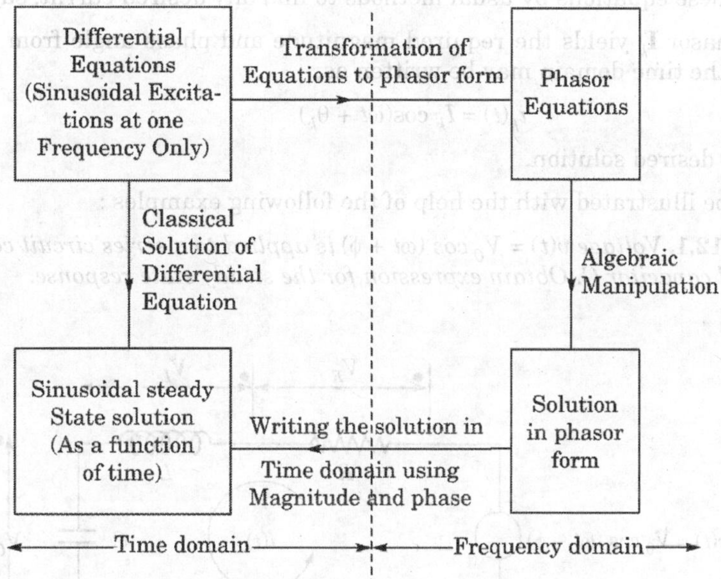

Fig. 12.8. Flow chart giving the method of obtaining the sinusoidal steady state response using phasors.

The flow chart of Fig. 12.8 gives the general method of sinusoidal steady state response using phasors. This flow chart is similar to the flow chart used earlier to depict the use of Laplace transformation. Evidently the method described by this chart can be used only when all source voltages are sinusoids of the same frequency and only steady state solution is desired.

The following steps are involved in this method of writing sinusoidal steady state response using phasors :

(*i*) Convert all the differential equations into Laplace transform equation form.

(*ii*) Put $s = j\omega$ in all these transform equations where ω is the angular frequency of each of the sinusoidal sources.

(iii) Set all initial conditions to zero, since initial conditions are immaterial in the determination of steady state solution.

(iv) Describe every source voltage in the cosine form such as,

$$v_j(t) = V_j \cos(\omega t + \phi_j) \qquad ...(12.110)$$

The corresponding phasor is,

$$\mathbf{V}_j = V_j\, e^{j\phi_j} \qquad ...(12.111)$$

Sine functions, if any may be converted to corresponding cosine functions using the following relations :

$$\sin(\omega t + \alpha) = \cos\left(\omega t + \alpha - \frac{\pi}{2}\right) \qquad ...(12.112)$$

or

$$\cos(\omega t + \alpha) = \sin\left(\omega t + \alpha - \frac{\pi}{2}\right) \qquad ...(12.113)$$

(v) The resulting set of equations is of the form given by Eqs. (12.107).

(vi) Solve these equations by usual methods to find any desired currnt, say current $\mathbf{I}_k$.

(vii) This phasor $\mathbf{I}_k$ yields the required magnitude and phase angle from which the steady state solution in the time domain may be written as,

$$i_k(t) = I_k \cos(\omega t + \theta_k) \qquad ...(12.114)$$

This is the desired solution.

This may be illustrated with the help of the following examples :

Example 12.1. *Voltage $v(t) = V_0 \cos(\omega t + \phi)$ is applied to a series circuit containing resistor R, inductor L and capacitor C. Obtain expression for the steady state response.*

Solution.

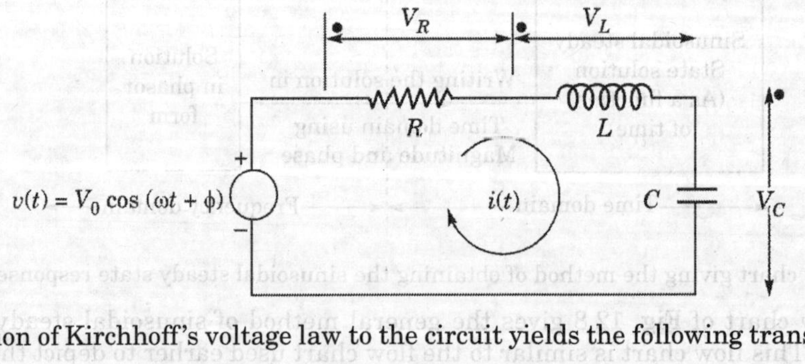

Application of Kirchhoff's voltage law to the circuit yields the following transform equation:

$$I(s)\,.\,Z(s) = V(s) \qquad ...(1)$$

or

$$I(s)\left[R + Ls + \frac{1}{CS}\right] = V(s) \qquad ...(2)$$

Under sinusoidal steady state, Eq. (2) may be put in the following phasor form,

$$\mathbf{I}\left[R + j\omega L + \frac{1}{j\omega C}\right] = V_o e^{j\phi} \qquad ...(3)$$

Hence $$\mathbf{I} = Ie^{j\phi_1} = \frac{V_o e^{j\phi}}{R + j\left(\omega L - \dfrac{1}{\omega C}\right)} \qquad \text{...(4)}$$

Hence magnitude $$I = \frac{V_o}{\sqrt{R_2 + \left(\omega L - \dfrac{1}{\omega C}\right)^2}} \qquad \text{...(5)}$$

and $$\theta_1 = \phi - \tan^{-1} \frac{\omega L - \dfrac{1}{\omega C}}{R} \qquad \text{...(6)}$$

Hence the expression for time domain response is,

$$i(t) = I \cos(\omega t + \theta_1) \qquad \text{...(7)}$$

where I and θ_1 are given by Eqs. (5) and (6) respectively.

Example 12.2. *Draw the phasor diagram for the network of Example 12.1.*

Solution. Let us take the applied voltage **V** as the reference in the sense that it is drawn at $\theta = 0$ in the complex plane as shown in the following figure. Then current **I** lags behind the voltage **V** by an angle θ_1, where θ_1, is given by Eq. (6) in Example 12.1. Thus phasor **I** may be drawn as shown. Voltage $\mathbf{V}_R$ being equal to $\mathbf{I}R$ is in phase with current **I** and is accordingly drawn along the phasor **I**. Its length equals IR.

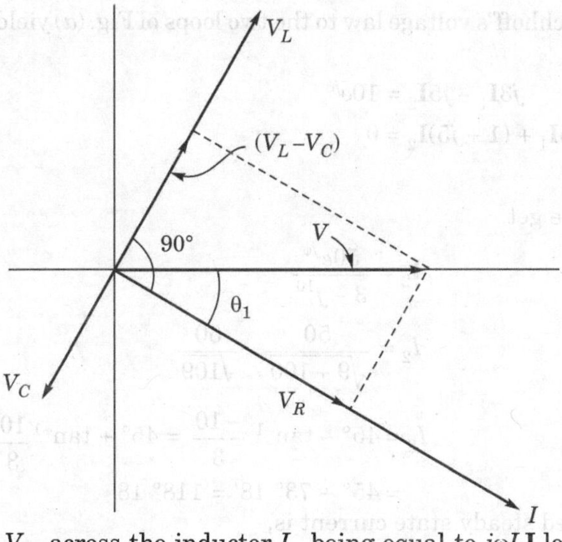

Similarly voltage V_L, across the inductor L, being equal to $j\omega L\mathbf{I}$ leads the current **I** by 90° and is, therefore, drawn accordingly. Finally voltage $\mathbf{V}_c$ across the capacitor C, being equal $\dfrac{I}{j\omega C}\left(= -j\dfrac{\mathbf{I}}{\omega C}\right)$ lags behind current **I** by 90° and is drawn in direction opposite to $\mathbf{V}_L$. Phasor $(\mathbf{V}_L - \mathbf{V}_C)$ on being added to V_R results in phasor **V** representing the applied voltage. We could have, alternatively, started construction of the phasor diagram by using any other reference say **I** but the final phasor diagram would still be the same expect that it stands rotated by angle θ_1.

Example 12.3. *In the given circuit, voltage v_1 is 10 cos* $\left(5t + \frac{\pi}{4}\right)$. *Find the current i_2 in the steady state. Draw the complete phasor diagram.*

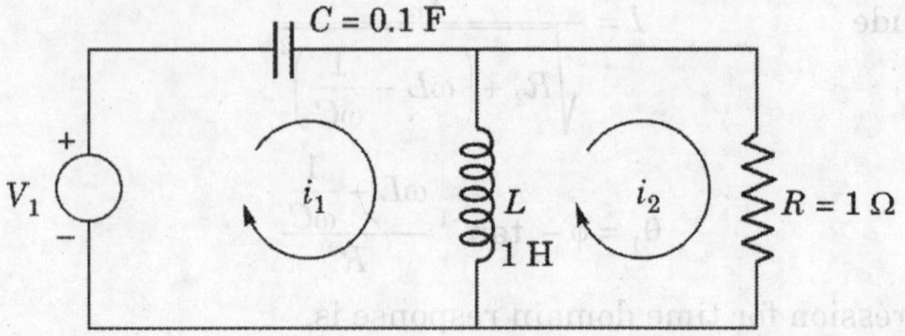

Solution. The impedance of each element and the voltage phasor as shown in Fig. (*a*).

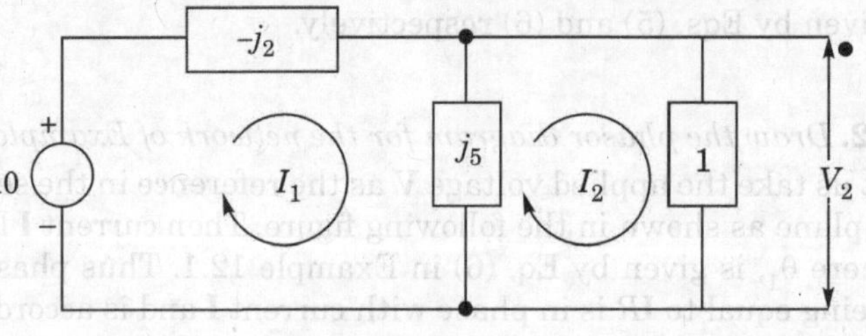

Fig. (*a*)

Application of Kirchhoff's voltage law to the two loops of Fig. (*a*) yields the following equations :

$$j3\mathbf{I}_1 - j5\mathbf{I}_2 = 10e^{j\phi} \qquad ...(1)$$

$$-j5\mathbf{I}_1 + (1 + j5)\mathbf{I}_2 = 0 \qquad ...(2)$$

where ϕ is $\pi/4$ radian.

Eliminating $\mathbf{I}_1$, we get

$$\mathbf{I}_2 = \frac{50e^{j\phi}}{3 - j^{10}} \qquad ...(3)$$

Magnitude $\qquad I_2 = \frac{50}{\sqrt{9 + 100}} = \frac{50}{\sqrt{109}}$

Phase angle of $\qquad I_2 = 45° - \tan^{-1}\frac{-10}{3} = 45° + \tan^{-1}\frac{10}{3}$

$$= 45° + 73°\ 18' = 118°\ 18'$$

Hence the required steady state current is,

$$i_2 = \frac{50}{\sqrt{109}} \cos\,(5t + 118°\ 18')$$

For drawing the phasor diagram we may select voltage V_2 as the reference. Phasor $\mathbf{I}_R$ indicating the current through this resistor R is then along the phasor $\mathbf{V}_2$ as shown. The phasor $\mathbf{I}_L$ indicating the current through inductor L lags $\mathbf{V}_2$ by 90°. Currents $\mathbf{I}_L$ and $\mathbf{I}_R$ have been combined to constitute the current $\mathbf{I}_{RL}$. This is the same as current $\mathbf{I}_C$ through the capacitor C. The voltage V_C across the capacitor C lags behind the current $\mathbf{I}_C$ by 90° $\left(\text{since } \mathbf{V}_C = \frac{\mathbf{I}_C}{j\omega C}\right)$ as shown. The applied voltage $\mathbf{V}_1$ is the phasor addition of $\mathbf{V}_C$ and $\mathbf{V}_2$. The phasor diagram shown here has been constructed using arbitrary lengths for each of the phasors and the actual values have been ignored. We may, however, construct a phasor diagram to scale using given and calculated values of phasors.

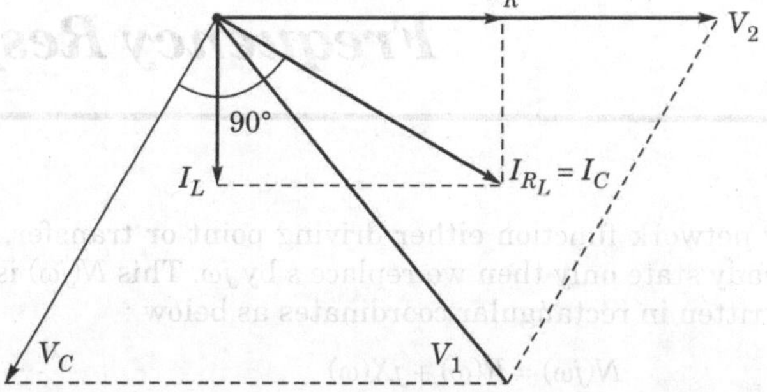

Fig. (*b*)

EXERCISES

12.1. Using the method of Article 12.4, solve the following differential equations for the steady state solution

(*a*) $\dfrac{di}{dt} + 3i = 2 \sin 3t$. (*b*) $\dfrac{di}{dt} + 2i = \cos t$ $\left[\textbf{Ans.}\ (a) \dfrac{2}{\sqrt{18}} \sin (3t - 45°)\,; (b) \dfrac{1}{\sqrt{5}} \cos\left(t - \tan^{-1}\dfrac{1}{2}\right)\right]$

12.2. Repeat Exercise 12.1 for the following differential equations :

(*a*) $\dfrac{di}{dt} + 2i = \cos\left(2t + \dfrac{\pi}{4}\right)$ (*b*) $\dfrac{di}{dt} + 4t = \sin (3t + 30°)$

(*c*) $\dfrac{d^2 i}{dt^2} + 3\dfrac{di}{dt} + i = \cos (2t + 45°)$

$\left[\textbf{Ans.}\ (a) \dfrac{1}{\sqrt{8}} \cos 2t\,; (b) \dfrac{1}{5} \sin\left(3t + 30° - \tan^{-1}\dfrac{3}{4}\right); \quad (c) \dfrac{-1}{3\sqrt{5}} \cos (2t + 45° + \tan^{-1} 2)\right]$

12.3. Voltage $v(t) = 10 \cos (10^3 t + 60°)$ is applied to a series circuit consisting of resistor $R = 10\ \Omega$, inductor $L = 0.02\ H$ and capacitor $C = 10^{-4}$ Farad. Find the steady current.

$\left[\textbf{Ans.}\ i(t) = \dfrac{1}{\sqrt{2}} \cos (10^3 t + 15°)\right]$

12.4. In the given circuit, the driving voltages is $v(t) = 5 \cos (10t + 45°)$. Find the current i_2 in the steady state.

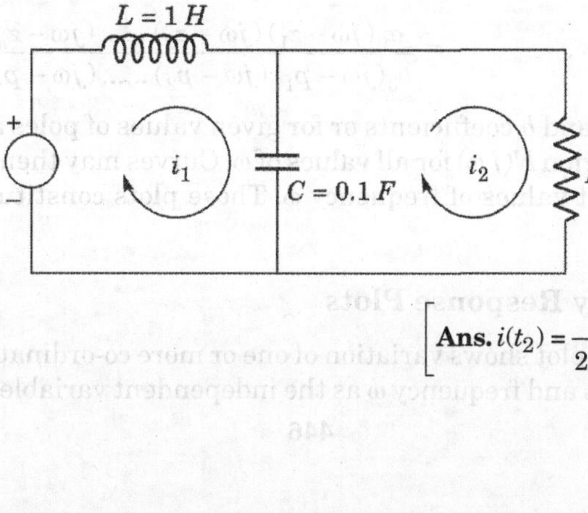

$\left[\textbf{Ans.}\ i(t_2) = \dfrac{5}{2\sqrt{106}} \cos\left(10t + 45° + \tan^{-1}\dfrac{5}{9}\right)\right]$

13

Frequency Response Plots

13.1. Introduction

Let $N(s)$ be any network function either driving point or transfer. Now if we restrict the study to sinusoidal steady state only then we replace s by $j\omega$. This $N(j\omega)$ is, in general, a complex function and may be written in rectangular coordinates as below :

$$N(j\omega) = R(\omega) + jX(\omega) \qquad ...(13.1)$$

where $R(\omega)$ is the real part of the network function $N(j\omega)$ while $X(\omega)$ is the imaginary part.

Alternatively $N(j\omega)$ may be written in the polar form as below :

$$N(j\omega) = | N(j\omega) | \, e^{j\phi(\omega)} \qquad ...(13.2)$$

where $| N(j\omega) |$ is the magnitude of the network function $N(j\omega)$ and $\phi(\omega)$ is the phase angle.

Evidently then $| N(j\omega) |$ and $\phi(\omega)$ may expressed in terms of $R(\omega)$ and $X(\omega)$ through the following equations :

$$\phi(\omega) = \tan^{-1} \frac{X(\omega)}{R(\omega)} \qquad ...(13.3)$$

and

$$| N(j\omega) | = \sqrt{[R(\omega)]^2 + [X(\omega)]^2} \qquad ...(13.4)$$

The general network function in transformed form is given by the following expression,

$$N(s) = \frac{a_0 \,.\, s^n + a_1 \,.\, s^{n-1} + ... + a_n}{b_0 \,.\, s^m + b_1 \,.\, s^{m-1} + ... + b_m} \qquad ...(13.5)$$

For sinusoidal steady state analysis, s may be replaced by $j\omega$ so that the expression for $N(s)$ may be put as,

$$N(j\omega) = \frac{a_0 (j\omega)^n + a_1 \,.\, (j\omega)^{n-1} + ... + a_n}{b_0 (j\omega)^m + b_1 \,.\, (j\omega)^{m-1} + ... + b_m} \qquad ...(13.6)$$

$$= \frac{a_0 (j\omega - z_1)(j\omega - z_2) ...... (j\omega - z_n)}{b_0 (j\omega - p_1)(j\omega - p_2) ...... (j\omega - p_m)}$$

For given values of a and b coefficients or for given values of poles and zeros, it is instructive to compute the network function $N(j\,\omega)$ for all values of ω. Curves may then be drawn giving variation of parts of $N(j\omega)$ for different values of frequency ω. These plots constitute the *frequency response plots.*

13.2. Types of Frequency Response Plots

A frequency response plot shows variation of one or more co-ordinates of the network function $N(j\omega)$ as dependent variables and frequency ω as the independent variable. The various co-ordinates that may be plotted are : $R(\omega)$, $X(\omega)$, $| N(j\omega) |$ and $\phi(\omega)$. Thus the various plots using only one co-ordinate are :

(*i*) $R(\omega)$ versus ω plot (*ii*) $X(\omega)$ versus ω plot

(*iii*) $| N(j\omega) |$ versus ω plot (*iv*) $\phi(\omega)$ versus ω plot.

It is also possible and a common practice to plot the magnitude and phase of the network function in polar coordinate system with frequency ω as the parameter. This is usually referred to as the complex loci.

Sometimes use is made of logarithmic coordinates in magnitude and phase plots resulting in what are called *Bode plots*.

In this article, we take up the study of use of linear coordinates in plots of magnitude and phase of the network function against frequency ω.

Fig. 13.1 gives these linear plots of the four parts of the network function namely $R(\omega)$, $X(\omega)$, $| N(j\omega) |$ and $\phi(\omega)$ as function of frequency ω. It may be readily seen that the magnitude $| N(j\omega) |$ and the real part $R(\omega)$ are even functions of ω while the phase angle $\phi(\omega)$ and the imaginary part $X(\omega)$ are odd functions of (ω). Thus all the information contained in the frequency range, from $\omega = -\infty$ to $\omega = 0$ is redundant since it is already contained in the plot for positive frequency range from $\omega = 0$ to $\omega = +\infty$. Hence it is customary to make use of the frequency range from 0 to ∞ only rather than the full range from $-\infty$ to $+\infty$. However in certain cases, for example in the application of Nyquist criterion, it becomes necessary to use the complete range of frequency from $-\infty$ to $+\infty$.

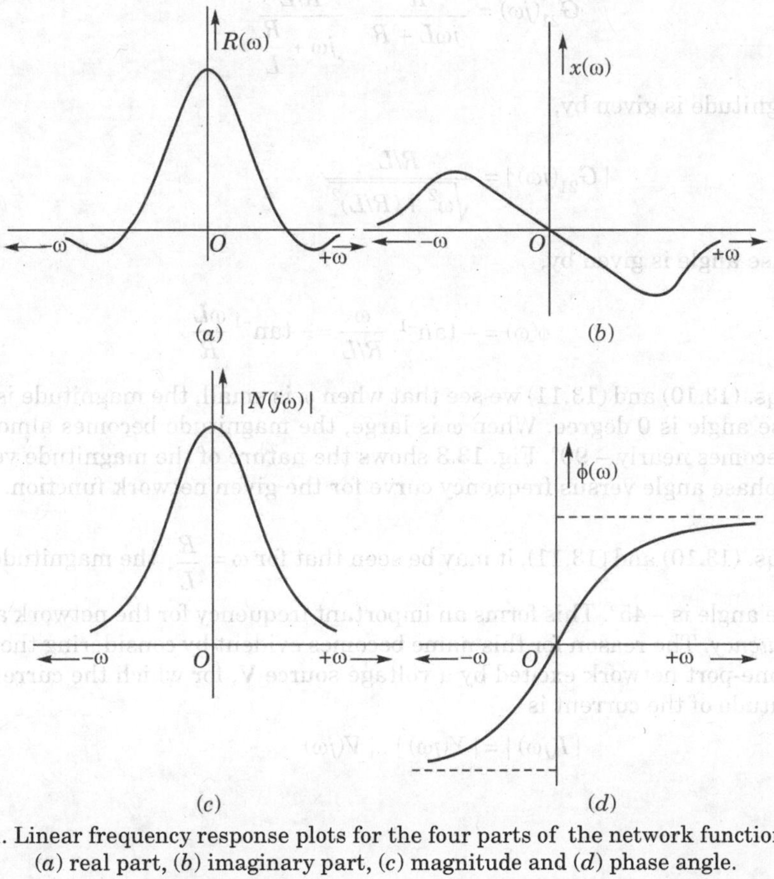

Fig. 13.1. Linear frequency response plots for the four parts of the network function $N(j\omega)$: (*a*) real part, (*b*) imaginary part, (*c*) magnitude and (*d*) phase angle.

Further we seldom use the $R(\omega)$ versus ω and $X(\omega)$ versus ω plots in Engineering applications. Hence these plots are not being considered any further. We discuss only the $|N(j\omega)|$ versus ω and $\phi(\omega)$ versus ω plots.

The Magnitude and the Phase Plots

The study of the nature of the magnitude and the phase plots may be best done with the help of a typical network. Thus consider the R-L network of Fig. 13.2.

The voltage ratio transfer function of this network is given by,

$$G_{21}(s) = \frac{V_2(s)}{V_1(s)} = \frac{R}{Ls + R} \qquad ...(13.8)$$

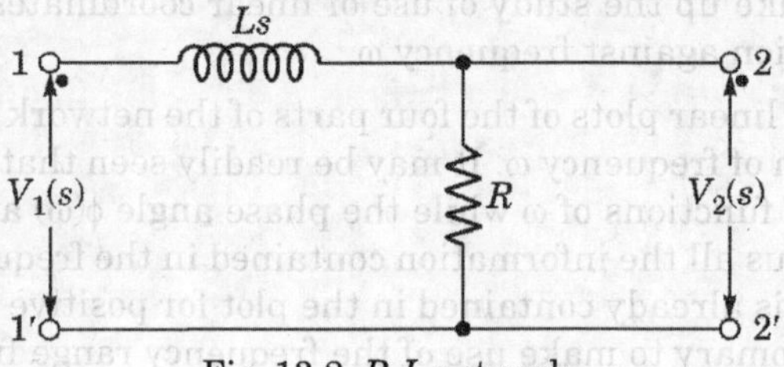

Fig. 13.2. R-L network.

For the sinusoidal steady state analysis, Eq. (13.8) takes the following form :

$$G_{21}(j\omega) = \frac{R}{j\omega L + R} = \frac{R/L}{j\omega + \dfrac{R}{L}} \qquad ...(13.9)$$

The magnitude is given by,

$$|G_{21}(j\omega)| = \frac{R/L}{\sqrt{\omega^2 + (R/L)^2}} \qquad ...(13.10)$$

The phase angle is given by,

$$\phi(\omega) = -\tan^{-1} \frac{\omega}{R/L} = -\tan^{-1} \frac{\omega L}{R} \qquad ...(13.11)$$

From Eqs. (13.10) and (13.11) we see that when ω is small, the magnitude is approximately 1 and the phase angle is 0 degree. When ω is large, the magnitude becomes almost zero and the phase angle, becomes nearly $-90°$. Fig. 13.3 shows the nature of the magnitude versus frequency curve and the phase angle versus frequency curve for the given network function.

From Eqs. (13.10) and (13.11), it may be seen that for $\omega = \dfrac{R}{L}$, the magnitude is $\dfrac{1}{\sqrt{2}} \approx 0.707$ while the phase angle is $-45°$. This forms an important frequency for the network and is called the *half power frequency*. The reason for this name becomes evident by considering the R-L network of Fig. 13.2 as a one-port network excited by a voltage source **V**, for which the current phasor is **I** = **YV**. The magnitude of the current is

$$|I(j\omega)| = |Y(j\omega)| \,.\, |V(j\omega)| \qquad ...(13.12)$$

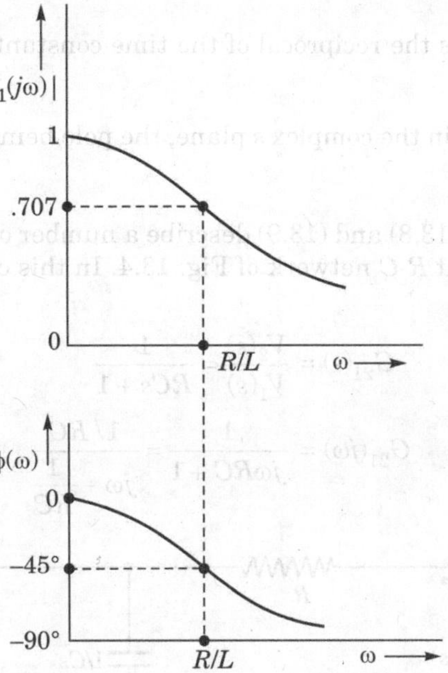

Fig. 13.3. Magnitude versus ω and phase angle versus ω curves of transfer function $G_{21}(j\omega)$ for the network of Fig. 13.2.

But the average power in the resistor R of the R-L combination is,

$$P = \frac{1}{2} |I(j\omega)|^2 \cdot R \qquad \text{...(13.13)}$$

Let ω_1 be the frequency at which $|I| = \frac{1}{\sqrt{2}} |I(j\omega)|_{\text{max.}}$ From Eq. (13.12), this obviously will be the frequency at which the admittance is $\frac{1}{\sqrt{2}}$ times its maximum value. Let P_m be the maximum power given by Eq. (13.13). Then

$$P_m = \frac{1}{2} |I(j\omega)|^2_{\text{max}} \cdot R \qquad \text{...(13.14)}$$

At frequency ω_1 the average power in the resistor is,

$$P_1 = \frac{1}{2} \times \frac{1}{2} |I(j\omega)|^2_{\text{max}} \cdot R = \frac{1}{2} P_m \qquad \text{...(13.15)}$$

Thus at frequency ω_1, the power in the resistor is *half* of the maximum value ; this justifies the name *half power frequency* given to this frequency. Thus the half power frequency is the frequency at which the magnitude of a network function, either driving point or transfer, reduces to $0.707 \left(\text{or } \frac{1}{\sqrt{2}} \right)$ of itrs maximum value.

Referring again to Eq. (13.9), we find that the half power frequency ω_1 is given by,

$$\omega_1 = \frac{R}{L} \qquad \text{...(13.16)}$$

We also see that $\frac{R}{L}$ is the reciprocal of the time constant T of the R-L network and is the negative of the pole location in the complex s plane, the pole being given by, $\sigma = -\frac{R}{L}$, as seen from Eq. (13.8).

Equations similar to (13.8) and (13.9) describe a number of 2-element R-L or R-C networks. Thus consider to two-element R-C network of Fig. 13.4. In this case, the equations corresponding to (13.8) and (13.9) are,

$$G_{21}(s) = \frac{V_2(s)}{V_1(s)} = \frac{1}{RCs+1} \quad \text{...[13.17 (a)]}$$

and

$$G_{21}(j\omega) = \frac{1}{j\omega RC+1} = \frac{1/RC}{j\omega + \frac{1}{RC}} \quad \text{...[13.17 (b)]}$$

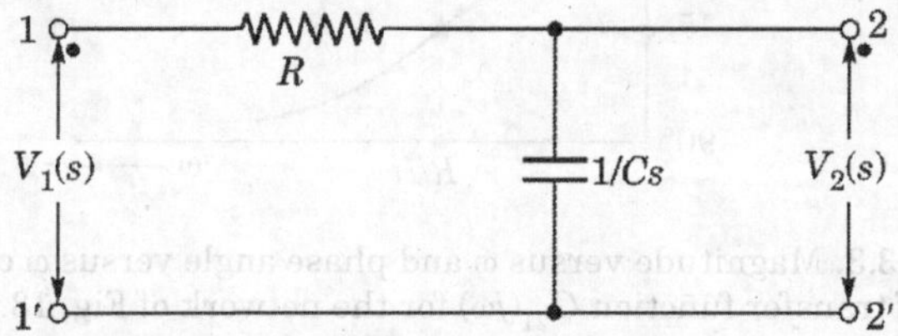

Fig. 13.4. Two-element R-C network.

In this case, the half power frequency ω_1 is $\frac{1}{RC}$.

In networks like those given in Figs. 13.2 and 13.4, the Eqs. (13.9) or [13.17 (*b*)] may be written in the following standard form :

$$G_{21}(j\omega) = \frac{1}{1 + j\frac{\omega}{\omega_1}} \quad \text{...(13.18)}$$

The equation may be used in the preparation of universal plots of magnitude versus frequency ratio ω/ω_1 and the phase angle versus ω/ω_1.

13.4. The Complex Loci

For a network function $N(j\omega)$ having the general form given by Eq. (13.7), we may express it in terms of the real and the imaginary parts $R(\omega)$ and $X(\omega)$, or in terms of the magnitude and phase angle $|N(j\omega)|$ and $\phi(\omega)$ respectively. All these parts will be functions of frequency ω. For a given value of frequency ω, a point say P represents the network function $N(j\omega) = R(\omega) + jX(\omega)$ on a complex $N(j\omega)$ plane as shown in Fig. 13.5. Now as the frequency ω is varied, the point P_m representing the network function $N(j\omega)$ moves tracing a locus on the complex frequency plane. The name complex locus is given to a single plot which describes the rectangular coordinates. $R(\omega)$ and $X(\omega)$ with ω as the parameter and simultaneously describes the polar coordinates $M(\omega)$ and $\phi(\omega)$ with ω as the parameter. Thus it is only one plot with two interpretations. Thus each point on the locus represents a phasor extending from the origin to the point for a specific value of ω. This phasor is of magnitude M(ω) and phase angle $\phi(\omega)$.

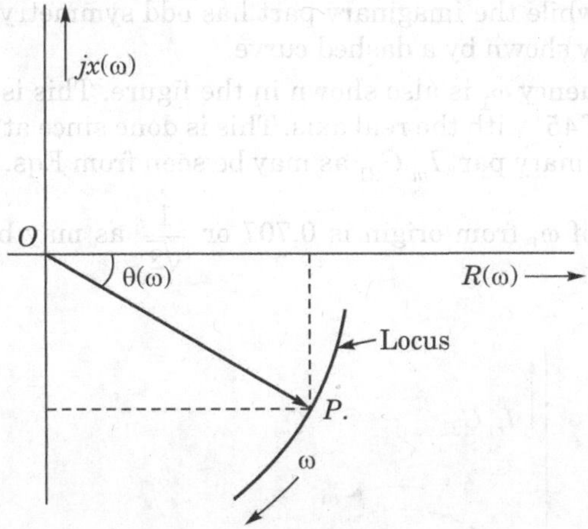

Fig. 13.5. Locus of the tip of the phasor of magnitude $M(\omega)$ and phase $\phi(\omega)$ as frequency ω varies.

Obviously the complex locus discussed above and depicted in Fig. 13.5 contains all the information as contained in the magnitude and phase plots of Fig. 13.1 (*c*) and (*d*) and nothing more. Thus there seems to be no specific advantage in using complex locus. However, there are several reasons why complex locus is preferred. The principal reason being that the use of complex locus is made in applying the "Nyquist criterion". Often complex locus is referred to as the *Nyquist plot.* The nature of the complex loci in a few typical cases is considered below.

13.5. Complex Locus for Two-element R-C Network

(*a*) *With Series Resistor and Shunt Capacitor*. Consider the *R-C* network of Fig. 13.4. Eq. [13.17 (*b*)] gives the transfer function $G_{21}(j\omega)$. Fig. 13.6 shows the complex locus for this network function. The locus starts at $(1 + j0)$ for $\omega = 0$, traces a semicircular path and reaches the origin as ω approaches ∞.

The fact that the locus is a circle may be verified by rationalising Eq. [13.17 (*b*)]. Thus Eq. [13.17 (*b*)] yields,

$$R_e G_{21} + j\, I_m\, G_{21} = \frac{1}{1 + j\omega RC} = \frac{1}{1 + \omega^2 R^2 C^2} = j \frac{RC\omega}{1 + R^2 \omega^2 C^2} \qquad \text{...(13.19)}$$

Thus
$$R_e\, G_{21} = \frac{1}{1 + \omega^2 R^2 C^2} \qquad \text{...(13.20)}$$

and
$$I_m\, G_{21} = -\frac{RC\omega}{1 + R^2 C^2 \omega^2} \qquad \text{...(13.21)}$$

From Eqs. (13.20) and (13.21), eliminating the parameter ω, we get the following relation between the real part $R_e\, G_{21}$ and the imaginary part $I_m\, G_{21}$.

$$\left(R_e G_{21} - \frac{1}{2}\right)^2 + (I_m\, G_{21})^2 = \left(\frac{1}{2}\right)^2 \qquad \text{...(13.22)}$$

This obviously is the equation of a circle of radius $\frac{1}{2}$ and centre at $R_e\, G_{21} = \frac{1}{2}$, $I_m\, G_{21} = 0$ as shown in Fig. 13.6.

The upper half of the circle pertains to the frequency range $\omega = -\infty$ to $\omega = -0$. This locus for the negative frequencies is the image of that for positive frequencies. This results because the real part

$R_e G_{21}$ has even symmetry while the imaginary part has odd symmetry. The locus for the negative frequency range is generally shown by a dashed curve.

The half power frequency ω_1 is also shown in the figure. This is obtained by drawing a line from origin making angle of 45° with the real axis. This is done since at ω_1, $RC\omega = 1$ so that the real part $R_e\, G_{21}$ equals the imaginary part $I_m\, G_{21}$ as may be seen from Eqs. (13.20) and (13.21). Each is equal to $\frac{1}{2}$. The distance of ω_1 from origin is 0.707 or $\frac{1}{\sqrt{2}}$ as may be seen from Eq. (13.18) by putting $\omega = \omega_1$.

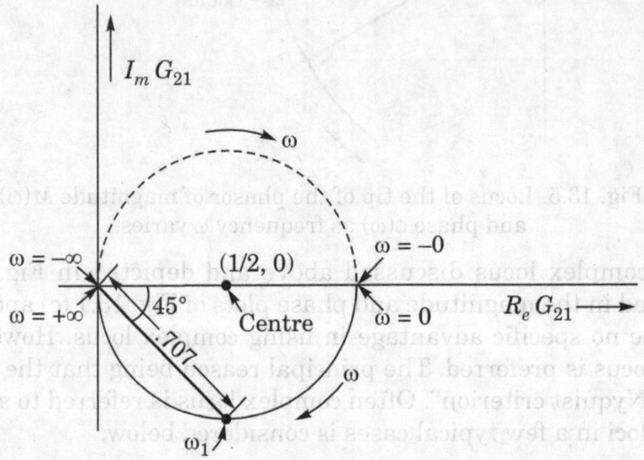

Fig. 13.6. Complex locus for the transfer function $G_{21}(j\omega)$ for network of Fig. 13.4.

(*b*) *With Series Capacitor and Shunt Resistor*. Fig. 13.7 gives the two-element *R-C* network with series capacitor and shunt resistor. The voltage ratio transfer function is then given by,

$$G_{21}(s) = \frac{R}{R + \dfrac{1}{Cs}} = \frac{s}{s + \dfrac{1}{RC}} \qquad ...(13.23)$$

For the sinusoidal steady state, G_{21} becomes,

$$G_{21}(j\omega) = \frac{j\omega}{j\omega + \dfrac{1}{RC}} \qquad ...(13.24)$$

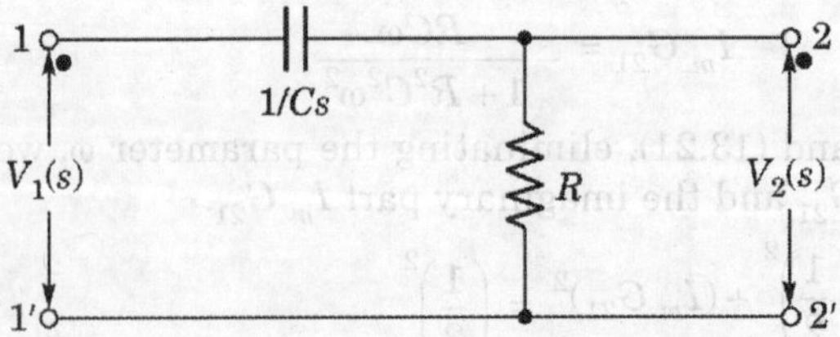

Fig. 13.7. Two-element *R-C* network with series capacitor and shunt resistor.

At $\omega = 0$, $G_{21}(j\omega) = 0$ and $\phi(\omega) = +90°$

At $\omega = \frac{1}{RC}$, $G_{21}(j\omega) = \frac{1}{\sqrt{2}}$ or 0.707 and $\phi(\omega) = +45°$

At $\omega = \infty$, $G_{21}(j\omega) = 1$ and $\phi(\omega) = 0°$.

For this network also, the locus of $G_{21}\,(j\omega)$ is a circle. This may be verified by rationalising Eq. (13.24).

Thus $$R_e\, G_{21} + jI_m\, G_{21} = 1 + \frac{1}{j\omega CR} = \frac{1}{1 - j\dfrac{1}{\omega CR}} = \frac{1}{1 + \dfrac{1}{\omega^3 R^2 C^2}} + j\frac{\dfrac{1}{\omega CR}}{1 + \dfrac{1}{\omega^2 C^2 R^2}} \quad ...(13.25)$$

Thus $$R_e\, G_{21} = 1 + \frac{1}{\omega^2 R^2 C^2} \quad ...(13.26)$$

and $$I_m\, G_{21} = \frac{\dfrac{1}{\omega CR}}{1 + \dfrac{1}{\omega^2 C^2 R^2}} \quad ...(13.27)$$

From Eqs. (13.26) and (13.27), eliminating the parameter ω, we get the following relation between the real part $R_e\, G_{21}$ and the imaginary part $I_m\, G_{21}$.

$$\left(R_e\, G_{21} - \frac{1}{2}\right)^2 + (I_m\, G_{21})^2 = \left(\frac{1}{2}\right)^2 \quad ...(13.28)$$

This is the same as Eq. (13.22) for the network of Fig. (13.4) Hence in this case also, the locus is circle of radius $\frac{1}{2}$ and centre at

$$R_e\, G_{21} = \frac{1}{2},\; I_m\, G_{21} = 0$$

as shown in Fig. 13.8.

In Fig. 13.8, the upper half of the circle pertains to the frequency range $\omega = 0$ to $\omega = \infty$ while the lower half, shown by a dashed curve, refers to the frequency range $\omega = -\infty$ to $\omega = -0$, and forms the image of the upper half.

The half power frequency ω_1 is also drawn in the figure. This is obtained, as usual, by drawing a line making an angle of 45° with the real axis as shown. The half power frequency in this case also equals $1/RC$.

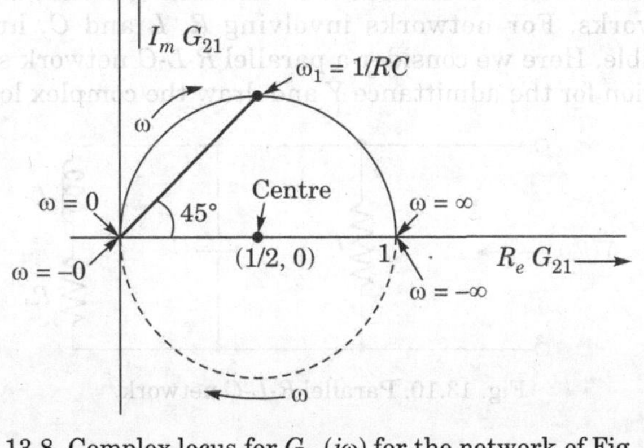

Fig. 13.8. Complex locus for $G_{21}(j\omega)$ for the network of Fig. 13.7

Fig. 13.9 gives the curves showing the variation of magnitude M_{21} and the phase angle ϕ_{21} with frequency ω for the network of Fig. 13.7.

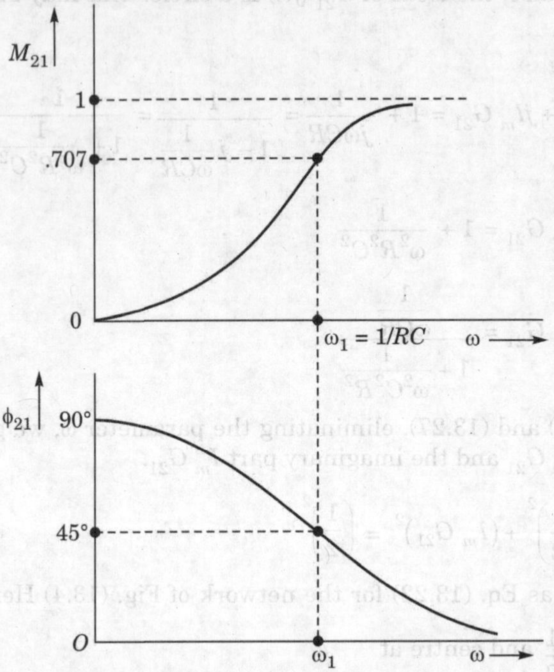

Fig. 13.9. Variation of magnitude M_{21} and phase angle ϕ_{21} with frequency ω.

On comparing the *R-C* circuits of Figs. 13.4 and 13.7, we find that,

(*i*) the output in network of Fig. 13.4 *lags* behind the input for all values of ω whereas the output in the network of Fig. 13.7 *leads* the input for all values of ω, and

(*ii*) the magnitude variations of the transfer function G_{21} (*j*ω) with frequency ω are inverse in the two cases *i.e.* for a constant input voltage V_1, the output voltage V_2 decreases with increase of frequency ω in the network of Fig. 13.4 and increases with frequency ω in the network of Fig. 13.7.

13.6. Complex Locus for Parallel R-L-C Network

So far we have considered two-element *R-C* networks. Similar, analysis could be done for two-element *R-L* networks. For networks involving *R, L* and *C*, huge varieties of circuit configurations are possible. Here we consider a parallel *R-L-C* network shown in Fig. 13.10. It is required to find expression for the admittance *Y* and draw the complex locus for this admittance.

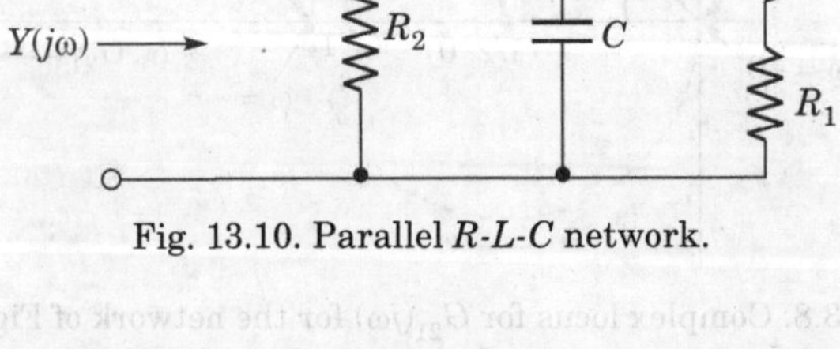

Fig. 13.10. Parallel *R-L-C* network.

This network may be considered to be formed by three sub-networks in parallel, (*i*) R_2 (*ii*) C (*iii*) R_1L. The total admittance of the complete network is the summation of the admittances of these individual subnetworks.

Thus the total admittance is given by,

$$Y(j\omega) = Y_{R_2}(j\omega) + Y_C(j\omega) + Y_{R_1-L}(j\omega) \quad ...(13.29)$$

Fig. 13.11 gives separately the complex loci for these three admittances $Y_{R_2}(j\omega)$, $Y_C(j\omega)$ and $Y_{R_1-L}(j\omega)$. Point by point phasor addition of all these three loci yields the composite locus for the admittance $Y(j\omega)$ of the entire network. For R_2, the admittance is $Y_{R_2} = \dfrac{1}{R_2}$ and it does not vary with frequency ω as shown in Fig. 13.11 (*a*). For C, the admittance is $Y_C = j\omega C$ so that the locus lies along the imaginary axis as shown in Fig. 13.11 (*b*). For subnetwork R_1-L, the admittance is given by,

$$Y_{R_1-L}(j\omega) = \frac{\dfrac{1}{L}}{j\omega + \dfrac{R_1}{L}} \quad ...(13.30)$$

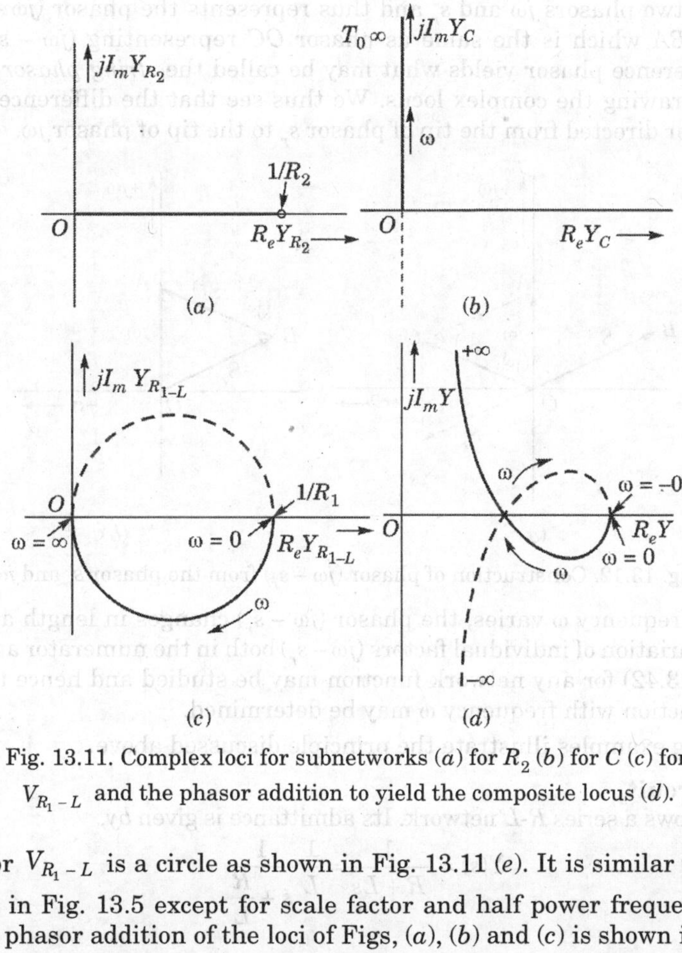

Fig. 13.11. Complex loci for subnetworks (*a*) for R_2 (*b*) for C (*c*) for V_{R_1-L} and the phasor addition to yield the composite locus (*d*).

The locus for V_{R_1-L} is a circle as shown in Fig. 13.11 (*e*). It is similar to the locus for *R-C* network as shown in Fig. 13.5 except for scale factor and half power frequency. The composite locus, which is the phasor addition of the loci of Figs, (*a*), (*b*) and (*c*) is shown in Fig. 13.11 (*d*).

This method of phasor addition of complex loci of subnetwork to yield the composite complex locus for the complete network may be applied to any given network provided that it is possible to express the driving point admittance or impedance of the entire network as the sum of the admittances or impedance of the sub-networks.

13.7. Plots drawn from s-plane Phasors

Any network function $N(s)$ may be put as,

$$N(s) = F\frac{(s-z_1)(s-z_2)\ldots\ldots(s-z_n)}{(s-p_1)(s-p_2)\ldots\ldots(s-p_m)} \qquad \ldots(13.31)$$

Under sinusoidal steady state, s may be replaced by $j\omega$ so that Eq. (13.31) may be put as,

$$N(s) = F\frac{(j\omega-z_1)(j\omega-z_2)\ldots\ldots(j\omega-z_n)}{(j\omega-p_1)(j\omega-p_2)\ldots\ldots(j\omega-p_m)} \qquad \ldots(13.32)$$

In the s-plane, each of the terms $j\omega$, $z_1, z_2, \ldots z_n$, or $p_1, p_2, \ldots p_m$ represents a phasor. Let $(j\omega - s_r)$ represent a general term in either the numerator polynomial or denominator polynomial. Now any such term $(j\omega - s_r)$ being the difference of two phasors $j\omega$ and s_r, is also a phasor. In general, s_r is a complex quantity while $j\omega$ is imaginary. These two phasors are represented in Fig. 13.12 by OA and OB respectively. Fig. 13.12 (*a*) shows the method of drawing the phasor OC which is the difference of these two phasors $j\omega$ and s_r and thus represents the phasor $(j\omega - s_r)$. Fig. 13.12 (*b*) shows the phasor BA which is the same as phasor OC representing $(j\omega - s_r)$. This method of construction of difference phasor yields what may be called the *string phasor diagram,* which is more suitable for drawing the complex locus. We thus see that the difference phasor $(j\omega - s_r)$ is nothing but a phasor directed from the tip of phasor s_r to the tip of phasor $j\omega$.

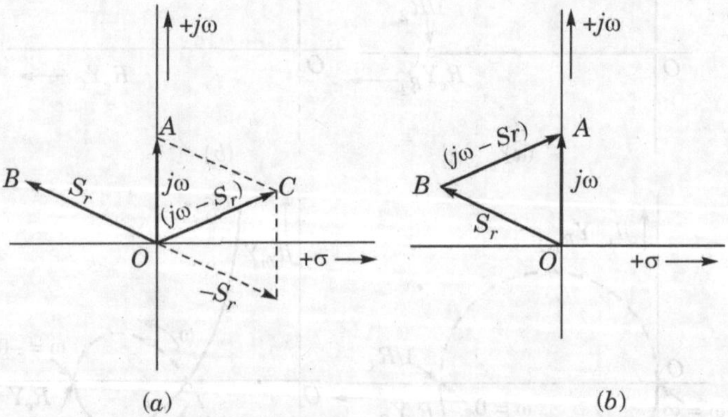

Fig. 13.12. Construction of phasor $(j\omega - s_r)$ from the phasor s_r and $j\omega$.

Now as the frequency ω varies, the phasor $(j\omega - s_r)$ changes in length and angle. With the variation of ω the variation of individual factors $(j\omega - s_r)$ both in the numerator and the denominator of the expression (13.42) for any network function may be studied and hence the variation of the overall network function with frequency ω may be determined.

The following examples illustrate the principle discussed above.

(A) Series R-L Circuit

Fig. 13.13 shows a series R-L network. Its admittance is given *by,*

$$Y(s) = \frac{1}{R+Ls} = \frac{1}{L}\,\frac{1}{s+\dfrac{R}{L}} \qquad \ldots(13.33)$$

or $$Y(j\omega) = \frac{1}{L}\,\frac{1}{j\omega + \frac{R}{L}} \qquad ...(13.34)$$

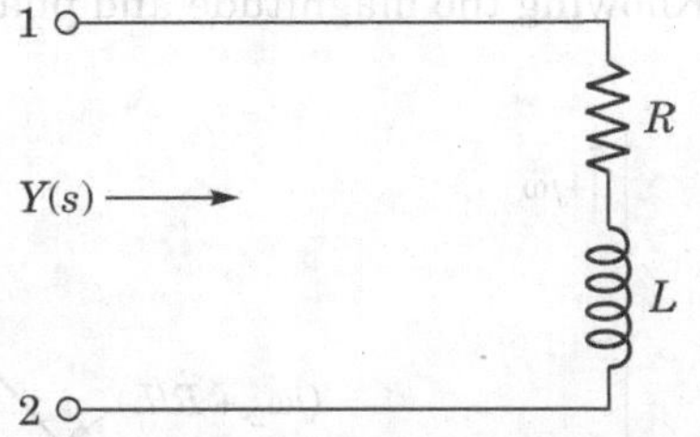

Fig. 13.13 Series *R-L* network.

This admittance $Y(s)$ has a pole at $s = -\frac{R}{L}$ and a zero at infinity. Fig. 13.14 shows the location of the pole at $-\frac{R}{L}$ and also shows the construction of the phasor representing $\left(j\omega + \frac{R}{L}\right)$ *i.e.* $\left[j\omega - \left(-\frac{R}{L}\right)\right]$.

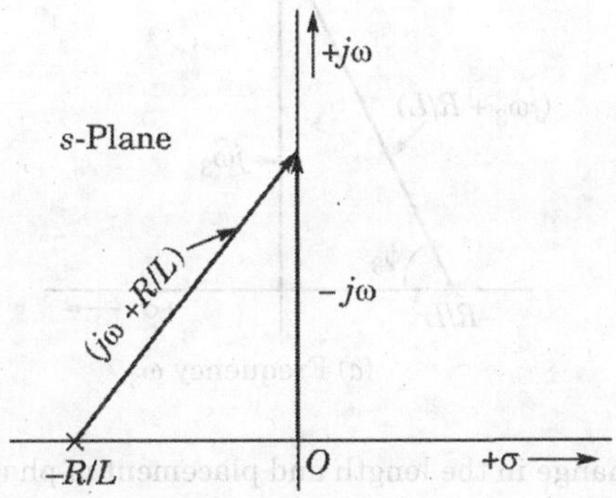

Fig. 13.14. Phasor representation of $\left(j\omega + \frac{R}{L}\right)$.

Now as the frequency ω increases from say ω_1 to ω_2, the phasor increases in length and alter its position as in Fig. 13.15. On further increase of frequency from ω_2 to ω_3, the phaseor $\left(j\omega + \frac{R}{L}\right)$ further increases in length and becomes more vertical as shown.

Now let $$L\left(j\omega + \frac{R}{L}\right) = Me^{\phi} \qquad ...(13.35)$$

where M is the magnitude and ϕ is the phase angle.

Then from Eq. (13.34), we get

$$Y(j\omega) = \frac{1}{M}e^{-j\phi} \qquad ...(13.36)$$

where $1/M$ is the magnitude of the admittance function and $-\phi$ is its phase angle.

It may be seen that when $\omega = 0$, $M = R$ so that the magnitude $\frac{1}{M} = \frac{1}{R}$ and the phase angle

$-\phi = 0$. At $\omega = \infty$, $M = \infty$ so that the magnitude $\dfrac{1}{M} = 0$ and the phase angle $-\phi = -90°$. Thus as ω increases from zero to ∞, magnitude of the admittance $Y(j\omega)$ changes from $1/R$ to 0 while the phase angle changes from 0 to — 90°. Knowing the magnitude and phase angle, the phasor.

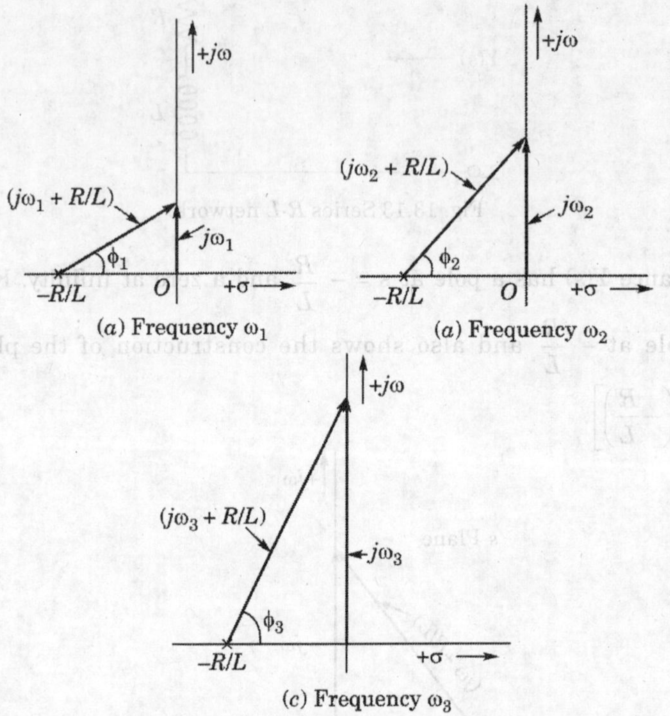

Fig. 13.15. Change in the length and placement of phasor $\left(j\omega + \dfrac{R}{L}\right)$ as ω increases from ω_1, through ω_2 to ω_3.

$$Y(j\omega) = R_e\, Y(j\omega) + jI_m\, Y(j\omega)$$

may be plotted for values of ω from 0 to ∞ to result in the complex locus shown in Fig. 13.16.

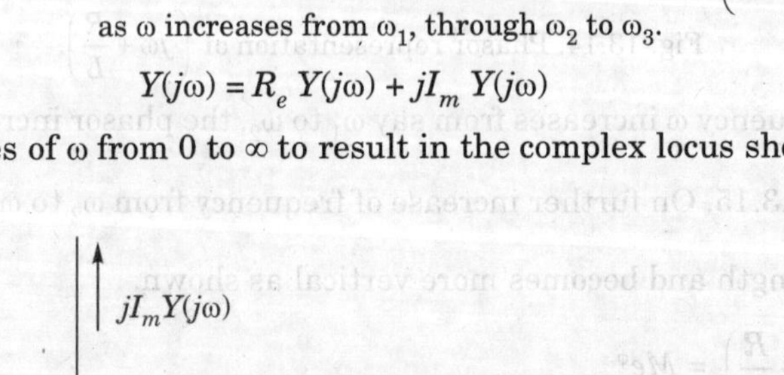

Fig. 13.16. Complex locus for Y($j\omega$) for series R-L network obtained through use of s-plane phasors.

(B) Series R-L-C Network

Fig. 13.17 shows a series *R-L-C* network. Its impedance $Z(s)$ is given by,

$$Z(s) = R + Ls + \frac{1}{Cs} \qquad ...(13.37)$$

Hence its transform impedance is,

$$Y(s) = \frac{s}{R + Ls + \dfrac{1}{Cs}} = \frac{1}{L} \cdot \frac{1}{s^2 + \dfrac{R}{L}s + \dfrac{1}{LC}} \qquad ...(13.38)$$

$$= \frac{1}{L} \cdot \frac{s}{(s - p_1)(s - p_1')} \qquad ...(13.39)$$

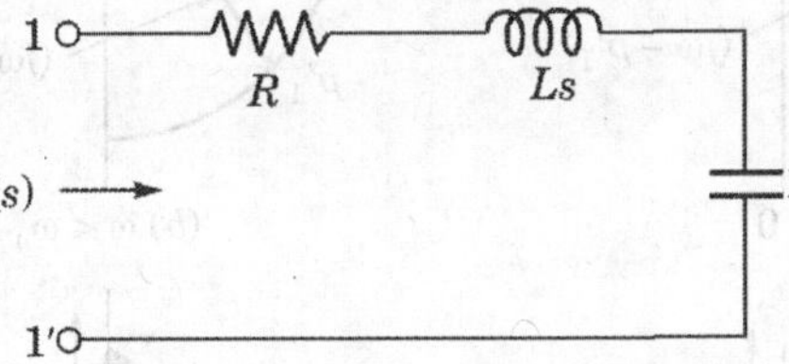

Fig. 13.17. Series *R-L-C* network.

In Eq. (13.39),

$$p_1, p_1' = -\frac{2}{2L} \pm j\sqrt{\frac{1}{LC} - \left(\frac{R}{2L}\right)^2} \qquad ...(13.40)$$

$$= -\zeta\omega_n \pm j\omega_n\sqrt{1 - \zeta^2} \qquad ...(13.41)$$

Here ω_n is the natural frequency of the network and equals $\dfrac{1}{\sqrt{LC}}$. Further ζ, is the damping ratio and equals $\dfrac{R}{2}\sqrt{\dfrac{C}{L}}$. The circuit is oscillatory when $\zeta < 1$. Considering this case alone, Eq. (13.41) gives the two poles p_1, p_1'. These poles are complex conjugates as shown in Fig. 13.8 and are located on a circle of radius ω_n. A line from the origin to the pole makes an angle of $\theta = \cos^{-1} \zeta$, with the negative real axis as shown in Fig. 13.17. Further there is a single zero at the origin.

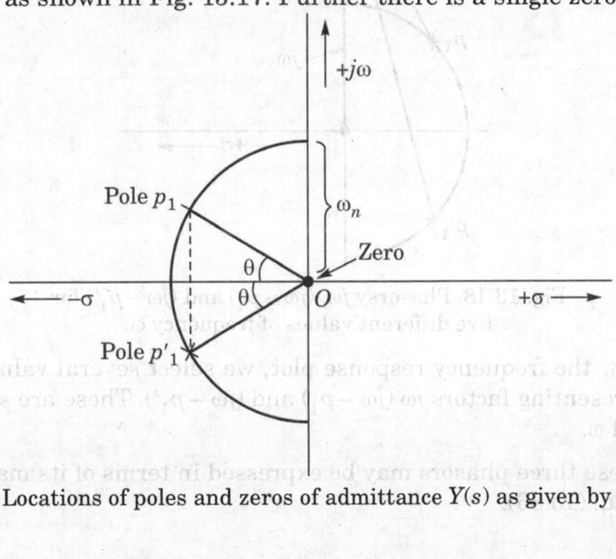

Fig. 13.17. Locations of poles and zeros of admittance $Y(s)$ as given by Eq. (13.38).

In the sinusoidal steady state, $s = j\omega$ so that Eq. (13.38) may be put as,

$$Y(j\omega) = \frac{1}{L} \cdot \frac{j\omega}{(j\omega - p_1)(j\omega - p_1')} \qquad ...(13.42)$$

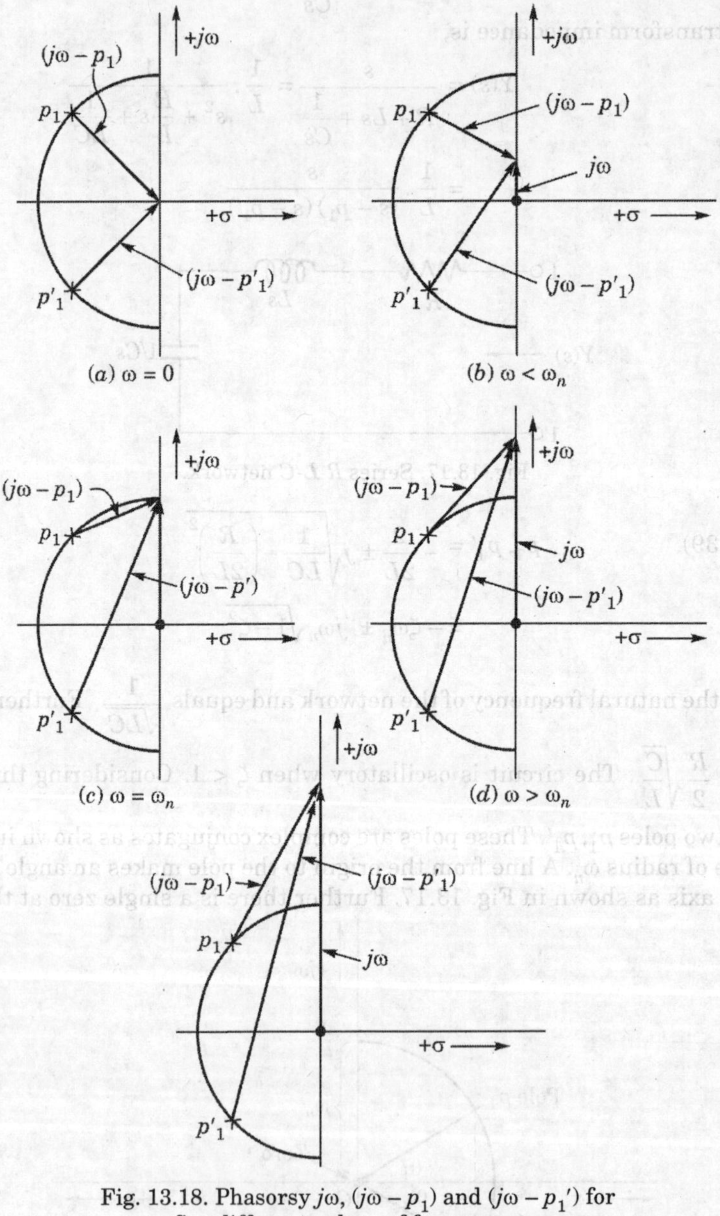

Fig. 13.18. Phasorsy $j\omega$, $(j\omega - p_1)$ and $(j\omega - p_1')$ for five different values of frequency ω.

In order to draw the frequency response plot, we select several values of frequency ω and draw the phasors representing factors $j\omega$ $(j\omega - p_1)$ and $(j\omega - p_1')$. These are shown in Fig. 13.18 for five different values of ω.

Now each of these three phasors may be expressed in terms of its magnitude and phase by equations similar to Eq. (13.36).

Thus $j\omega$ may be represented by,

$$j\omega = M_0 \; e^{+j\phi_0} \quad ...(13.43)$$

Similarly $(j\omega - p_1)$ and $(j\omega - p_1')$ may be expressed as,

$$(j\omega - p_1) = M_1 \, . \; e^{+j\phi_1} \quad ...(13.44)$$

and $$(j\omega - p_1') = M_1' \; e^{+j\phi_1'} \quad ...(13.45)$$

Then in accordance with Eq. (13.42), the entire admittance function $Y(j\omega)$ may be expressed in terms of these magnitudes and phases as below :

$$Y(j\omega) = F \, . \frac{M_0}{M_1 \, . \, M_1'} \, . \, e^{j(\phi_0 - \phi_1 - \phi_1')} \quad ...(13.46)$$

where F is the scale factor and equals $1/L$.

Eq. (13.46) may be put as

$$Y(j\omega) = Me^{j\phi} \quad ...(13.47)$$

where $$M = F \, . \frac{M_0}{M_1 \, . \, M_1'} \quad ...(13.48)$$

and $$= (\phi_0 - \phi_1 - \phi_1') \quad ...(13.49)$$

The maximum value of $| Y(j\omega) |$ results at a frequency close to one at which M_1 has minimum value *i.e.* the frequency at which the tip of the phasor $j\omega$ is closest to the pole p_1. At frequencies close to this frequency, M_1, changes rapidly while M_0 and M_1' change very slowly. The frequency at which $| \; Y(j\omega) \; |$ is maximum, is defined as the *frequency resonance.* Fig. 13.19 shows the magnitude M and the phase angle ϕ of the admittance $Y(j\omega)$ for five spot frequencies of Fig. 13.18. When frequency ω is continuously varied from 0 to ∞, the curves giving the nature of variation of magnitude M and phase angle ϕ with frequency ω are as shown in Fig. 13.19.

Now $I(j\omega)$ is equal to $Y(j\omega).V$. Hence the current $I(j\omega)$ varies directly as admittance $Y(j\omega)$ and the frequency of resonance is also the frequency of maximum current $I(j\omega)$.

From Eq. (13.37), admittance $Y(j\omega)$ may be written as,

$$Y(j\omega) = R + j\omega \, L = \frac{1}{j\omega C} \quad ...(13.50)$$

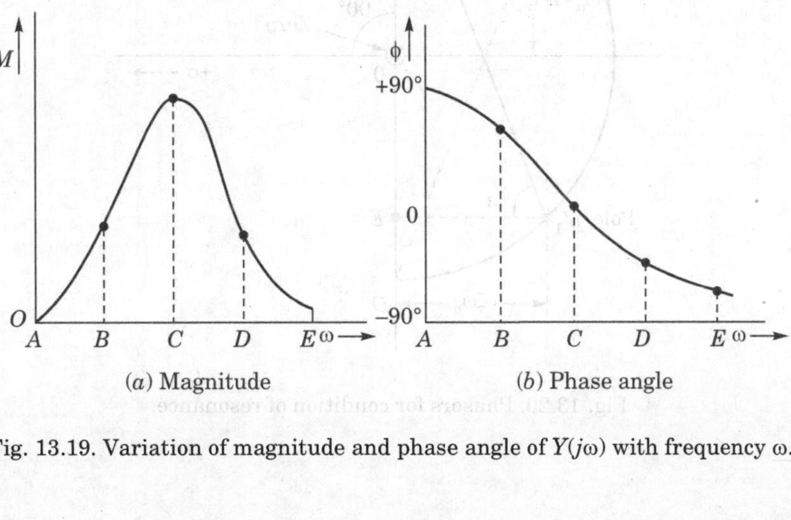

(*a*) Magnitude (*b*) Phase angle

Fig. 13.19. Variation of magnitude and phase angle of $Y(j\omega)$ with frequency ω.

Hence the magnitude may be written as,

$$Y(j\omega) = \frac{1}{\sqrt{R^2 + \left(j\omega L - \frac{1}{\omega C}\right)^2}} \qquad \text{...(13.51)}$$

From Eq. (13.51) we find that $| Y(j\omega) |$ has maximum value when

$$\omega L - \frac{1}{\omega C} = 0 \qquad \text{...(13.52)}$$

or

$$\omega = \frac{1}{\sqrt{LC}} = \omega_n \qquad \text{...(13.53)}$$

We thus find that resonance occurs at $\omega = \omega_n$, and not at frequency opposite to the pole on the $j\omega$ axis.

Fig. 13.20 gives in detail the various phasors for the condition of resonance. The phase angles of the phasors *BA* representing $(j\omega - p_1)$ and *CA* representing $(j\omega - p_1')$ have been marked as ϕ_1 and ϕ_1' respectively. The phasor *OA* from the zero at origin to $j\omega_n$ is along the $j\omega$ axis and has a constant phase angle of 90°. Further it may be seen that the sum of phase angles ϕ_1 and ϕ_1' is equal to 90° because the triangle *ABD* being inscribed in a semicircle, is a right angled triangle.

The total phase angle of the admittance function $Y(j\omega)$ is,

$$\phi = \phi_0 - \phi_1 - \phi_1'$$

$$= 90° - 90° = 0 \qquad \text{...(13.54)}$$

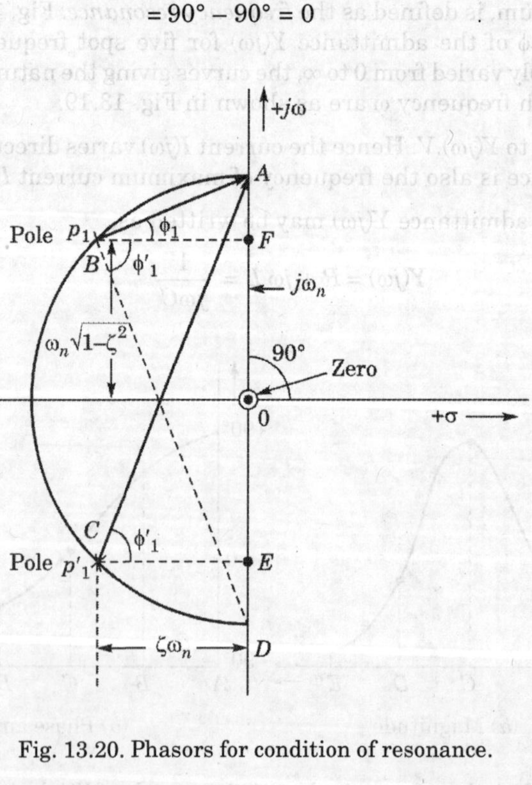

Fig. 13.20. Phasors for condition of resonance.

Thus the phase angle of admittance at resonance is zero. Further putting $\omega L = \dfrac{1}{\omega C}$ in Eq. (13.51), we find that the magnitude of admitance $Y(j\omega)$ at resonance is $1/R$. Hence the current $I(j\omega)$ at resonance is V/R.

The Circuit Q. The circuit Q or simply Q of a series RLC circuit is defined as the ratio of reactance of L or C at resonance frequency to the resistance R. Thus

$$Q = \frac{\omega_n L}{R} = \frac{1}{\omega_n CR} = \frac{1}{2} \cdot \frac{\omega_n}{R/2L} \qquad ...(13.55)$$

From Eq. (13.55) we conclude that a series RLC circuit with low R has high Q. The quantity $R/2L$ equals $\zeta\omega_n$. Hence Q may also be defined as

$$Q = \frac{1}{2} \cdot \frac{\omega_n}{\zeta\omega_n} = \frac{1}{2} \cdot \frac{\text{Length } OA}{\text{Length } CE} \qquad ...(13.56)$$

where lengths OA and CE refer to Fig. 13.20.

Hence we conclude that closer the poles p_1 and p_1' are to the $j\omega$ axis, the higher is the Q. Thus the Q of a given series RLC circuit may be obtained directly from the scale plot of the poles and zeros of the admittance or impedance function.

The circuit Q may alternatively be expressed as,

$$Q = \frac{1}{2\zeta} \qquad ...(13.57)$$

$$= \frac{1}{2\cos\theta} \qquad ...(13.58)$$

where θ is the angle of the line OB measured from the $-\sigma$ axis in Fig. 13.20.

From Eq. (13.57) we conclude the value of Q varies inversely at the damping ratio ζ.

Fig. 13.21 shows several curves giving the variation of magnitude of $Y(j\omega)$ with frequency ω for three different values of Q.

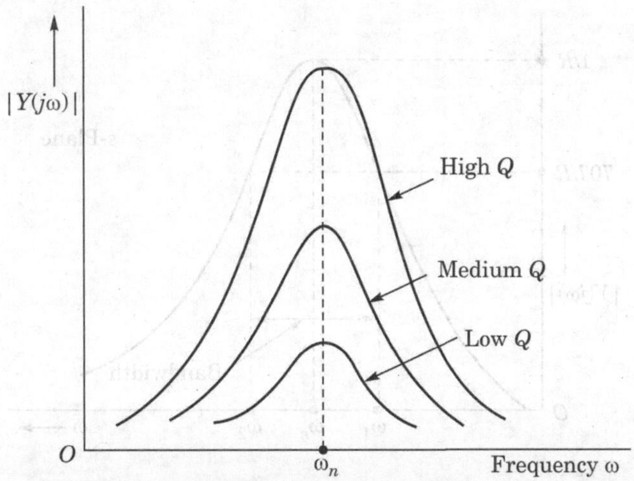

Fig. 13.21. Plots of magnitude $Y(j\omega)$ against frequency, with Q as the parameter.

An alternative means of describing the circuit Q is in terms of *half power frequencies.* The current in the series circuit at resonance is V/R. Now at half power frequencies, the current has the magnitude $\frac{1}{\sqrt{2}} \cdot \frac{V}{R}$ so that the power is half of that at resonance. This implies that the magnitude of admittance $|Y(j\omega)|$ must be $\sqrt{2}R$. Hence from Eq. (13.51) at a half power frequency, we have

$$\sqrt{R^2 + \left(\omega L - \frac{L}{\omega C}\right)^2} = \sqrt{2}R \quad \text{...(13.59)}$$

or

$$\left(\omega L - \frac{L}{\omega C}\right) = \pm R \quad \text{...(13.60)}$$

or

$$\omega^2 \pm \frac{R}{L} \frac{1}{LC} = 0 \quad \text{...(13.61)}$$

Hence

$$\omega = \mp \frac{R}{2L} \mp \sqrt{\left(\frac{R}{2L}\right)^2 + \frac{1}{LC}} \quad \text{...(13.62)}$$

In terms of damping ratio ζ, and undamped natural frequency ω_n, Eq. (13.62) may be put as,

$$\omega = \omega_n \left(\pm \zeta \pm \sqrt{\zeta^2 + 1}\right) \quad \text{...(13.63)}$$

Out of the four values of half power frequencies given by Eq. (13.63), let the two positive values be ω_1 and ω_2. Then we have

$$\omega_1, \omega_2 = \omega_n \left(\sqrt{\zeta^2 + 1} \pm \zeta\right) \quad \text{...(13.64)}$$

Then

$$\omega_1 \times \omega_2 = \omega_n^2 (\zeta^2 + 1 - \zeta^2)$$

or

$$\omega_1 \omega_2 = \omega_n^2 \quad \text{...(13.65)}$$

Thus ω_n is the geometrical mean of the two half power frequencies ω_1 and ω_2.

The frequency range between ω_1 and ω_2 is defined as the *half power bandwidth* or simply *bandwidth* of the series circuit and is usually indicated by B.

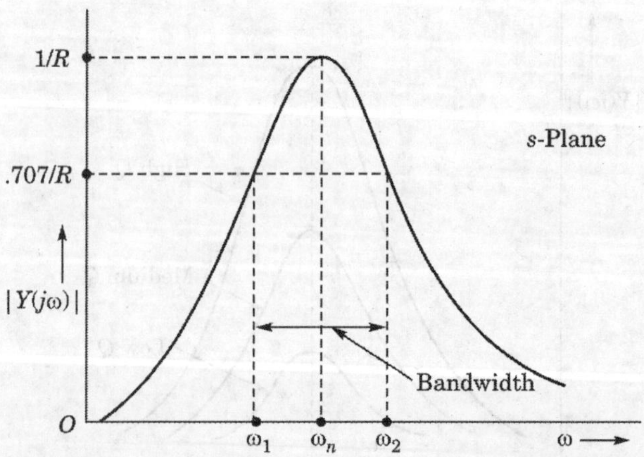

Fig. 13.22. Bandwidth shown on admittance versus frequency curve.

Fig. 13.22 shows the half power frequencies ω_1 and ω_2 and the bandwidth B on the curve giving magnitude $| Y(j\omega) |$ as a function of frequency ω.

Then $$B = \omega_2 - \omega_1 = 2\omega_n \zeta = \frac{\omega_n}{Q} \quad ...(13.66)$$

Thus the bandwidth varies inversely with the circuit Q.

Series *RLC* circuit having very high Q *i.e.* very low damping ratio ζ, is often used as a *frequency selector*. Then ζ^2 is negligibly small compared to 1. Hence from Eq. (13.64), we get

$$\omega_2 = \omega_n + \zeta\omega_n \quad ...(13.67)$$

and $$\omega_1 = \omega_n - \zeta\omega_n \quad ...(13.68)$$

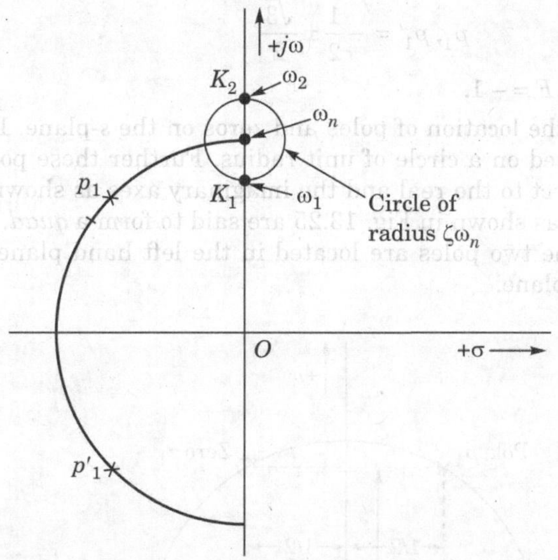

Fig. 13.23. Bandwidth defined by a circle of radius $\zeta\omega_n$, for high Q case.

Now with reference to Fig. 13.20, the quantity $\zeta\omega_n$ is indicated by distance BF *i.e.* the distance of the pole p_1 or p_1' from $j\omega$ axis. Then if we draw a circle of radius $\zeta\omega_n$ with centre at $(\zeta + j\omega_n)$, the points K_1 and K_2 where this circle crosses the $j\omega$ axis, give the locations of the half power frequencies as shown in Fig. 13.23. Hence the frequency range $K_1 K_2$ gives the bandwidth.

(c) Symmetrical Lattice

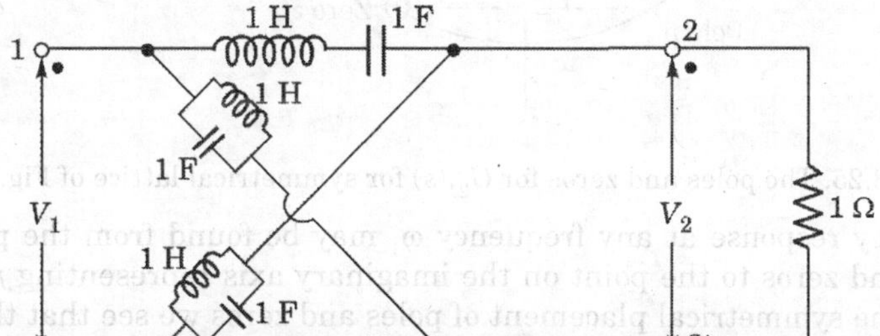

Fig. 13.24. A symmetrical lattice network.

Fig. 13.24 show as symmetrical lattice network. The voltage ratio transfer function $G_{21}(s)$ may be found by usual analysis. Thus for the given values, we get

$$G_{21}(s) = \frac{V_2(s)}{V_1(s)} = \frac{-(s^2 - s + 1)}{s^2 + s + 1} \quad ...(13.69)$$

Eq. (13.69) may be put as,

$$G_{21}(s) = (-1)\frac{(s - z_1)(s - z_1')}{(s - p_1)(s - p_1')} \quad ...(13.70)$$

The two zeros have the values,

$$z_1, z_1' = \frac{1}{2} \pm j\frac{\sqrt{3}}{2} \quad ...(13.71)$$

The two poles have the values,

$$p_1, p_1' = -\frac{1}{2} \pm \frac{\sqrt{3}}{2} \quad ...(13.72)$$

The scale factor is $F = -1$.

Fig. 13.25 shows the location of poles and zeros on the s-plane. It may be seen that these poles and zeros are located on a circle of unit radius. Further these poles and zeros are located symmetrically with respect to the real and the imaginary axes as shown in Fig. 13.25. The poles and zeros with locations as shown in Fig. 13.25 are said to form a *quad*. Evidently out of the four members of the quad, the two poles are located in the left hand plane while the two zeros are located in the right half plane.

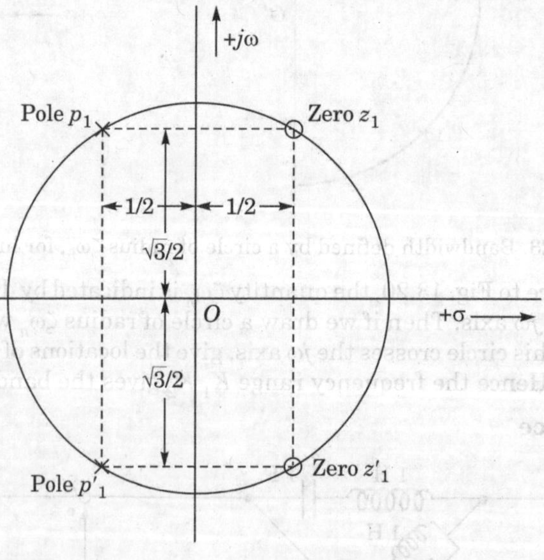

Fig. 13.25. The poles and zeros for $G_{21}(s)$ for symmetrical lattice of Fig. 13.24.

The frequency response at any frequency ω_1 may be found from the phasors drawn from each of the poles and zeros to the point on the imaginary axis representing $j\omega_1$ as shown in Fig. 13.26. Because of the symmetrical placement of poles and zeros we see that the magnitude of the phasor $(j\omega_1 - z_1)$ represented by CE in Fig. 13.26 is always equal to the magnitude of phasor $(j\omega_1 - p_1)$ represented by AE. Similarly the magnitude of phasor $(j\omega_1 - z_1')$ equals the magnitude of phasor $(j\omega_1 - p_1')$.

Hence from Eq. (13.70) we conclude that,

$$\left| \frac{V_2(j\omega)}{V_1(j\omega)} \right| = 1 \qquad ...(13.73)$$

Eq. (13.73) states that the magnitude of the output voltage is always equal to the magnitude of the input voltage for all values of frequency ω as shown in Fig. 13.27 (*a*). Hence this network constitutes what may be called an *all-pass network*. The phase of the transfer function $G_{21}(j\omega)$ equals the summation of the positive phase angles of the zero *phasors* $(j\omega - z_1)$ and $(j\omega - z_1')$ minus the phase angles of the pole phasors $(j\omega - p_1)$ and $(j\omega - p_1')$. Thus the phase angle of $G_{21}(j\omega)$ is,

$$\phi = (\phi_{z_1} + \phi'_{z_1}) - (\phi_{p_1} + \phi'_{p_1}) \qquad ...(13.74)$$

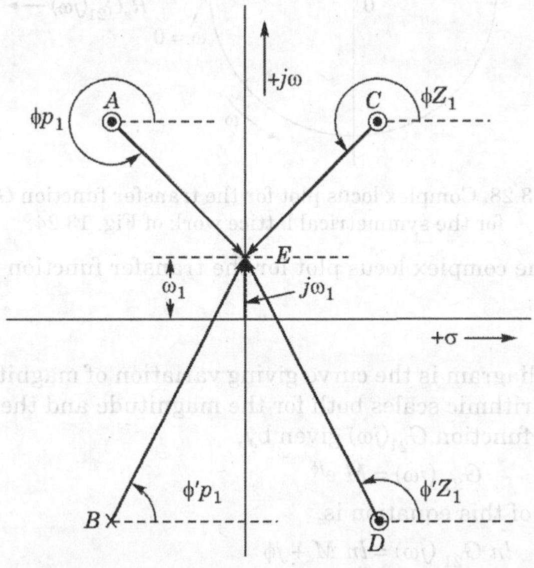

Fig. 13.26. Phasors used for finding the magnitude and phase angle of transfer function $G_{21}(s)$ for the network of Fig. 13.24.

The phase angles $\phi_{z_1}, \phi'_{z_1}, \phi_{p_1}$ and ϕ'_{p_1} are shown in Fig. 13.26.

At ω = 0, point *E* is at the origin and the phase angle ϕ of $G_{21}(j\omega)$ is zero. As ω increases, point *E* progressively moves upward along

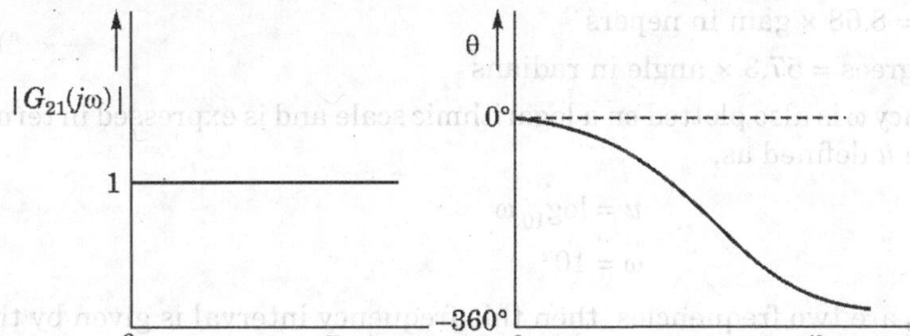

(*a*) Magnitude versus frequency (*b*) Phase angle versus frequency

Fig. 13.27. Magnitude versus frequency and phase versus frequency curves for transfer function $G_{21}(j\omega)$ for network of Fig. 13.24.

the imaginary axis and ϕ becomes more and more negative. At $\omega = \infty$, the phase angle ϕ becomes – 360° *i.e.* 0°. Fig. 13.27 (*b*) gives the phase angle versus frequency characteristic.

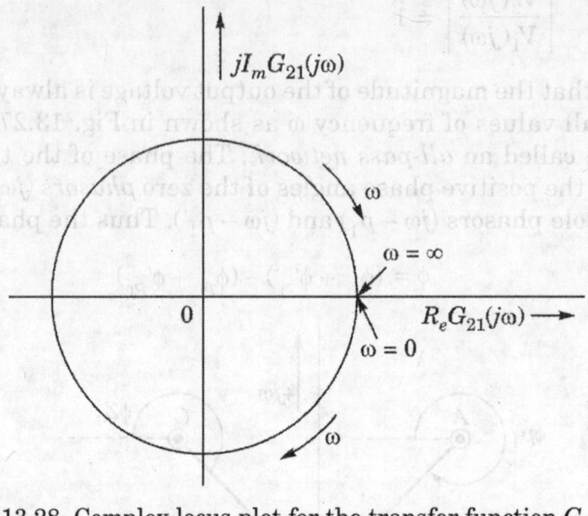

Fig. 13.28. Complex locus plot for the transfer function $G_{21}(j\omega)$ for the symmetrical lattice work of Fig. 13.24.

Fig. 13.28 shows the complex locus plot for the transfer function $G_{21}(j\omega)$.

13.8. Bode Diagrams

Bode plot or Bode diagram is the curve giving variation of magnitude of a network function with frequency using logarithmic scales both for the magnitude and the frequency. Thus consider the voltage ratio transfer function $G_{21}(j\omega)$ given by,

$$G_{21}(j\omega) = M e^{j\phi} \quad ...(13.75)$$

Natural logarithm of this equation is,

$$ln\ G_{21}(j\omega) = ln\ M + j\phi \quad ...(13.76)$$

where $ln\ M$ is the logarithmic gain or simply the *gain* in nepers and ϕ is the *phase angle* in radians.

Alternatively the gain may be expressed in decibels (*dB*).

Thus gain in $dB = 20 \log M$ ...(13.77)

Similarly more common unit for the phase angle ϕ is the degree. Following equations relate the decibels to nepers and degrees to radians.

gain in dB = 8.68 × gain in nepers ...(13.78)

angle in degrees = 57.3 × angle in radians ...(13.79)

The frequency ω is also plotted on a logarithmic scale and is expressed in terms of logarithmic frequency variable u defined as,

$$u = \log_{10} \omega \quad ...(13.80)$$

or

$$\omega = 10^u \quad ...(13.81)$$

If ω_1 and ω_2 are two frequencies, then this frequency interval is given by the equation,

$$u_2 - u_1 = \log^{\omega_2} - \log^{\omega_1} = \log^{\frac{\omega_2}{\omega_1}} \quad ...(13.82)$$

If $\frac{\omega_2}{\omega_1} = 2$, this frequency interval forms the octave.

If $\frac{\omega_2}{\omega_1} = 10$, the frequency interval is the *decade*.

Since Bode plot uses logarithmic scales for frequency, the slopes of straight lines in the Bode plot is expressed in terms of octave or decade.

Now we refer back to Eq. (13.7) giving the expression for transfer function $N(j\omega)$ in terms of zeros and poles. We further, for the sake of explicitness, assume that all the poles and zeros are distinct *i.e.* non-repeated.

Now let $z_1 = -\frac{1}{T_1}$, a real number.

Then $$(j\omega - z_1) = \frac{1}{T_1}(1 + j\omega\, T_1) \qquad ...(13.83)$$

On taking natural logarithms, Eq. (13.83) yields,

$$ln^{(j\omega - z_1)} = ln^{\frac{1}{T_1}} + ln\,|1 + j\omega\, T_1| + j\tan^{-1}\omega T_1 \qquad ...(13.84)$$

Using decibel notation, the first two terms in Eq. (13.84) equal

$$20\log^{\frac{1}{T_1}} + 20\log^{|1 + j\omega T_1|}\, dB \qquad ...(13.85)$$

The last term in Eq. (13.84) may be expressed in degrees as,

$$\phi = 57.3\tan^{-1}\omega T_1 \qquad ...(13.86)$$

These are the general forms which all factors in the numerator adopt.

Similarly for the denominator of Eq. (13.7), let $p_1 = -\frac{1}{t_1}$, $p_2 = -\frac{1}{t_2}$ etc. Then the magnitude of transfer function $N(j\omega)$ in decibels is given by,

$$|N(j\omega)| \text{ in } dB = 20\log\frac{a_0 t_1 t_2 \,......\, t_m}{b_0 T_1 T_2 \,......\, T_n} + 20\log|1 + j\omega T_1|$$

$$+ ... + 20\log|1 + j\omega T_n| - 20\log|1 + j\omega t_1| - ... - 20\log|1 + j\omega t_m| \qquad ...(13.87)$$

The phase angle of the transfer function $N(j\omega)$ is given by,

$$\phi(\omega) = 57.3\,(\tan^{-1}\omega T_1 + \tan^{-1}\omega T_2 + ... + \tan^{-1}\omega T_n$$
$$- 57.3\,(\tan^{-1}\omega t_1 + ... + \tan^{-1}\omega t_m) \qquad ...(13.88)$$

From Eq. (13.87) we find that (*i*) the first term is frequency invariant and (*ii*) all other terms are similar in form except for the value of T_1, T_2 etc. Similarly in Eq. (13.88), all terms are similar except for the values of T_1, T_2, etc.

We now take up a detailed study of the second term in Eq. (13.87) and the first term in Eq. (13.88). Having done this, the total magnitude and phase angle of the network function may be computed.

Magnitude of Factor 20 log | 1 + jωT$_1$ |

Let the magnitude of this factor be denoted by $|G_1|$. Then

$$|G| = 20\log|(1 + j\omega T_1)| = 20\log^{(1=\omega^2 T_1^2)^{1/2}} \quad ...(13.89)$$

For low frequencies, $\omega T_2 << 1$ so that the magnitude $|G_1|$ is given by,

$$|G_1| \approx 20\log^1 = 0\ dB \quad ...(13.90)$$

Thus the $|G_1|$ versus ω curve approaches the straight line asymptote having zero magnitude and zero slope.

For large values of ω, $\omega T_1 >> 1$, so that $|G_1|$ is given by,

$$|G_1| \approx 20\log \omega T_1\ dB \quad ...(13.91)$$

Thus for high frequencies, $|G_1|$ versus ω curve approaches another straight line AB asymptote as shown in Fig. 13.29. The slope of this straight line may be found from Eq. (13.91).

Thus the magnitude $|G_1|$ changes 6 dB as ω changes from $|\frac{1}{T_1}|$ to $\frac{2}{T_1}$. Hence the slope is 6 dB/octave. The overall magnitude $|N(j\omega)|$ will also vary similarly. Hence the slope of straight line in Bode plot is also the same *i.e.* 6 dB/octave. If the frequency ω changes from $1/T_1$ to $10/T_1$ *i.e.* by a decade, then the magnitude $|G_1|$ changes by 20 dB. Hence the slope of $|G_1|$ or $|N(j\omega)|$ may also be put as 20 dB/decade.

Frequency $\omega_1 = \frac{1}{T_1}$ is important since it is the frequency at which the two asymptotic curves defined by Eqs. (13.90) and (13.91) intersect. This frequency is referred to as the *break frequency* or the *corner frequency*. This is the reciprocal of the time constant and equals the half power frequency.

The magnitude of G_1 at the break frequency ω_1, in accordance with Eq. (13.89) is given by,

$$|G_1| = 20\log\sqrt{2}\ dB \approx 3\ dB \quad ...(13.92)$$

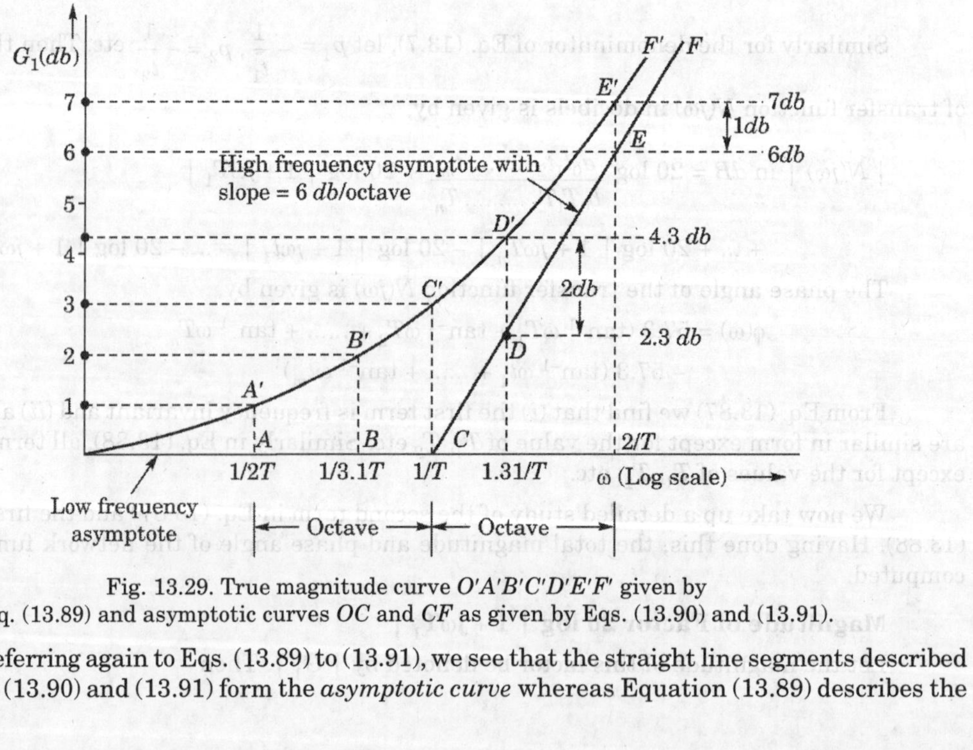

Fig. 13.29. True magnitude curve $O'A'B'C'D'E'F'$ given by Eq. (13.89) and asymptotic curves OC and CF as given by Eqs. (13.90) and (13.91).

Now referring again to Eqs. (13.89) to (13.91), we see that the straight line segments described by Equations (13.90) and (13.91) form the *asymptotic curve* whereas Equation (13.89) describes the true magnitude response curve. The values given by the two curves differ. Table 13.1 gives values given by the true response curve and the asymptotic curve for a number of values of ω.

Table 13.1

Frequency ω	*True Magnitude*	*Asymptotic Magnitude*	*Difference*
$\frac{1}{2T}$	1 *dB*	0 *dB*	1 *dB*
$\frac{1}{1.31T}$	2 *dB*	0 *dB*	2 *dB*
$\frac{1}{T}$	3 *dB*	0 *dB*	3 *dB*
$\frac{1.31}{T}$	4.3 *dB*	2.3 *dB*	2 *dB*
$\frac{2}{T}$	7 *dB*	6 *dB*	1 *dB*

This Table may be used to draw the true response curve *OC″ F′*. Thus with reference to Fig. 13.29, we may first draw the asymptotic curve *OCF* using Equations (13.90) and (13.91). Then knowing the difference as given by column 4 of Table 13.1, the true response curve may be drawn as shown in Fig. 13.29.

The procedure for drawing the true magnitude curve using Table 13.1 is as below :

(*i*) For the given value of *T*, we determine the break frequency $\omega = (1/T)$.

(*ii*) For this break frequency, we draw two asymptotic lines (*a*) one of zero slope extending towards lower frequencies and (*b*) another line of slope 6 *dB*/octave running towards higher frequencies.

(*iii*) At break point *C*, we plot a point *C′* 3 *dB* up. Similarly, at frequency $\frac{1}{1.31\,T}$ we plot a point *B′* 2 *dB* above point *B* ; at frequencies 1/2 *T* we plot a point *A′* 1 *dB* above point *A* ; a frequency $\frac{13.1}{T}$ we plot a point *D′* 2 *dB* above point *D* ; finally at frequency 2/*T* we plot a point *E′* 1 *dB* above point *E*.

(*iv*) We then join the points *A′*, *B′*, *C′*, *D′* and *E′* to yield the true magnitude curve.

(*v*) If a factor comes from a pole rather than from a zero in the network function *N*(*j*ω), then all values including the slope are negative.

The complete procedure for drawing a Bode plot from the knowledge of network function is elaborated below with the help of a typical example.

Complete Procedure for Drawing a Bode Plot

Let a network function be given by,

$$N(j\omega) = \frac{(1 + j\omega T_1)(1 + j\omega T_2)(1 + j\omega T_3)}{(1 + j\omega t_1)(1 + j\omega t_2)} \qquad \text{...(13.93)}$$

In Eq. (13.93), the zeros are $-\frac{1}{T_1}$ and $-\frac{1}{T_2}$ and the poles are $-\frac{1}{t_1}$ and $-\frac{1}{t_2}$. Thus knowing the zero say $-\frac{1}{T_1}$, we may find the corresponding break frequency using the relation $\omega_1 = \frac{1}{T_1}$. This is shown diagrammatically in Fig. 13.30. Thus by rotation in the s-plane, each zero or pole gives rise to corresponding break frequency.

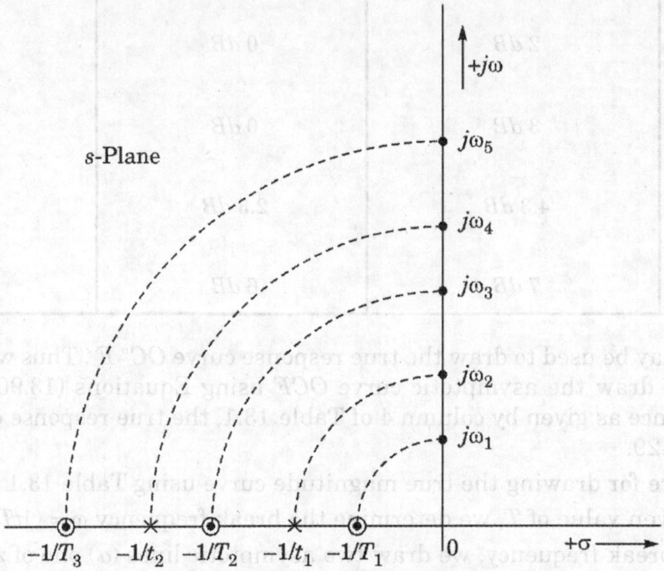

Fig. 13.30. Rotation of poles and zeros in the s-plane to yield corresponding break frequencies.

(A) First Order Factors. Now using Bode coordinates corresponding to each of the three factors in the numerator of Eq. (13.93), an asymptotic line is drawn having a slope of 6 *dB*/octave as shown in Fig. 13.31 (*a*). Similarly for each of the two factors in the denominator of Eq. (13.93) an asymptotic line is drawn having a slope of – 6 *dB*/octave as shown in Fig. 13.31 (*a*). Next the responses given by these asymptotic lines are added as required by Eq. (13.87) thereby yielding the asymptotic response of Fig. 13.31 (*b*).

The true responses for each of the four factors are obtained by the method discussed earlier and all these four true responses are added to yield the true response of the overall network function. This is given by the dotted line in Fig. 13.31 (*b*).

Next we draw the phase angle versus frequency curve. In Eq. (13.88) the first term is given by,

$$\phi_1 = 57.3 \tan^{-1} \omega T_1 \qquad \text{...(13.94)}$$

Table 13.2 gives the value of quantity $57.3 \tan^{-1} \omega T_1$ for different spot values of ω.

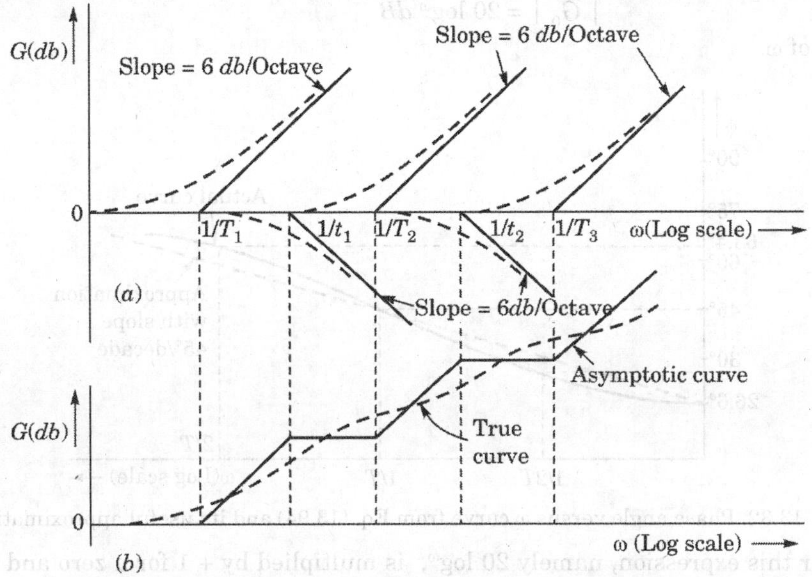

Fig. 13.31 (*a*). Response of individual factors in Eq. (13.93) and (*b*) overall response for the magnitude of $G(j\omega)$.

Table 13.2

Frequency ω (radians)	*57.3 tan⁻¹ ωT*
0	0°
$\frac{1}{2T}$	26.6°
$\frac{1}{\sqrt{3}T}$	30°
$\frac{1}{T}$	45°
$\sqrt{3}T$	60°
$2T$	63.4°
∞	90°

This table is used to draw the phase angle ϕ_1 versus ω curve corresponding to the first factor in the numerator of Eq. (13.93). In Fig. 13.32, the solid curve represents the ϕ_1 versus ω variation. A useful approximation to this curve is a straight line of slope 45° per decade passing through 45° at $\omega = \frac{1}{T}$ as shown by the dotted line in Fig. 13.32. As may be seen from Fig. 13.32, the maximum error introduced by this curve is less than 6° from $\omega = \frac{1}{T}$ to $\omega = \frac{10}{T}$. In case the phase angle ϕ arises from a pole factor, then ϕ must be multiplied by – 1.

(*b*) *Zero or Pole at the Origin*. A factor *s* in the network function *N*(*s*) represents a zero at the origin if present in the numerator and represents a pole at the origin if present in the denominator. The magnitude response of such a pole or zero at the origin is given by,

$$| G_0 | = 20 \log^{\omega} dB \qquad ...(13.95)$$

for all values of ω.

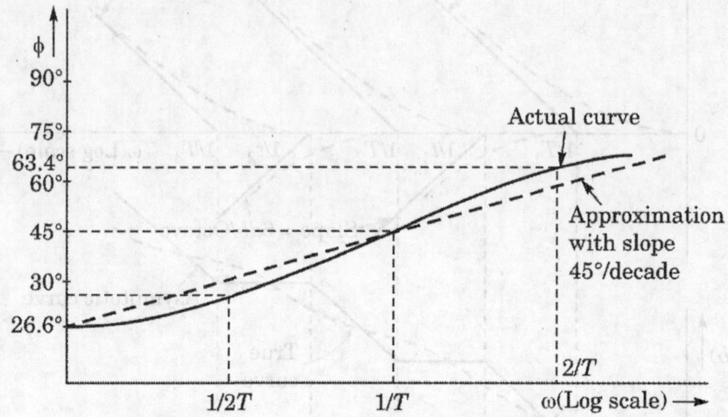

Fig. 13.32. Phase angle versus ω curve from Eq. (13.94) and its useful approximation.

Further this expression, namely 20 log$^{\omega}$, is multiplied by + 1 for a zero and by a – 1 for a pole. The phase angle contribution by such a faction is + 90° for a zero at the origin and – 90° for a pole at the origin.

(*c*) *Second Order Factors.* Finally let us consider the case when the network function $N(s)$ has poles or zeros which are complex conjugates. Then the factor $(1 + sT_1)$ or $(1 + j\omega T_1)$ in Eq. (13.83) is replaced by a second order factor given below,

$$M_1 = 1 + 2\,\zeta s T + s^2T^2 \qquad ...(13.96)$$

where ζ is the damping ratio.

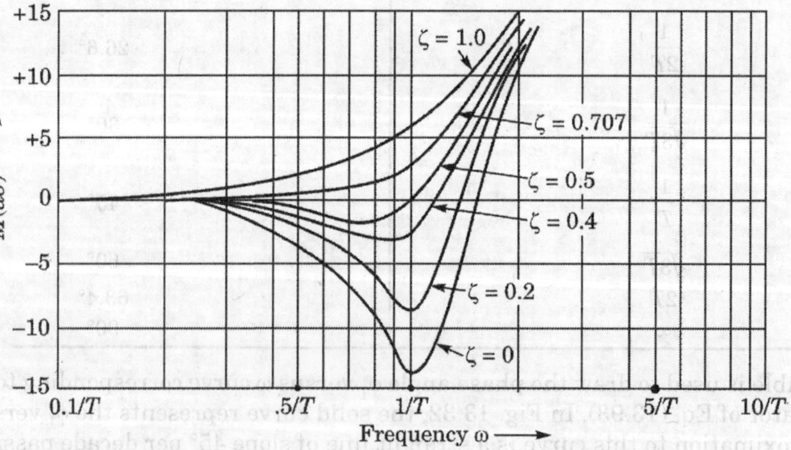

Fig. 13.33. Magnitude versus frequency curves given by Eq. (13.98) with ζ as the parameter.

For sinusoidal steady state consideration, Eq. (13.96) may by put as,

$$M_1 = 1 + 2\zeta j\omega T - \omega^2T^2 \qquad ...(13.97)$$

Magnitude of this factor is given by,

$$| M_1 | = 10 \log [(1 - \omega^2T^2) + (2\zeta\omega T)^2]\ dB \qquad ...(13.98)$$

The phase angle of the factor is given by

$$\phi = \tan^{-1} \frac{2\zeta\omega T}{1 - \omega^2 T^2} \qquad ...(13.99)$$

Fig. 13.33 shows the plot of magnitude $| M_1 |$ as a function of frequency ω with ζ as the parameter. Similarly Fig. 13.34 shows the plot of phase angle ϕ as function of frequency ω with ζ as the parameter.

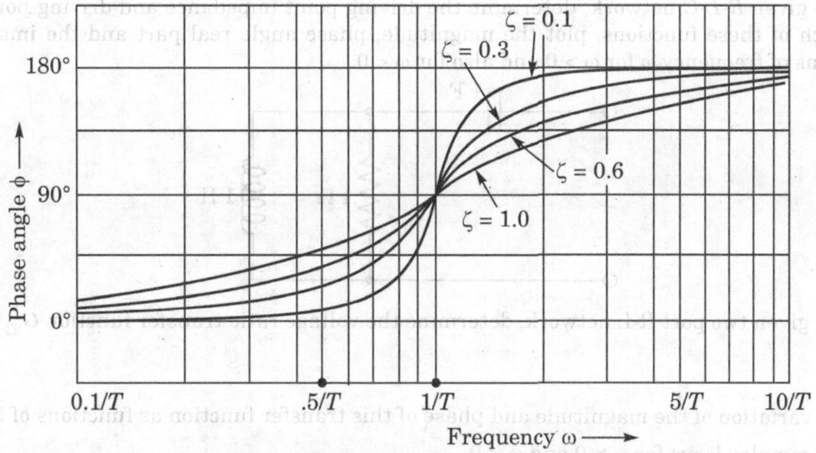

Fig. 13.34. Phase angle versus frequency curves given by Eq. (13.99), with ζ as the parameter.

From the study of Eqs. (13.98) and (13.99) and from the curves given in Figs. (13.33) and (13.34), the following useful deduction may be made regarding the use of these second order factors in the network function in constructing the Bode diagrams :

(*i*) In the magnitude versus frequency plot, the low frequency asymptote is the zero *dB* line as in the case of first order factor.

(*ii*) The high frequency asymptote is,

$$| M_1 | \approx 40 \log^{\omega T} dB \qquad ...(13.100)$$

This is a straight line of slope 12 *dB*/octave or 40 *dB*/decade.

(*iii*) The beak frequency *i.e.* the intersection of low frequency and high frequency asymptotes is $\omega_b = \dfrac{1}{T}$ for all values of ζ.

(*iv*) At the break frequency ω_b, value of M_1 is given by

$$M_1\left(\frac{1}{T}\right) = 20 \log^{2\zeta} dB \qquad ...(13.101)$$

$M_1\left(\dfrac{1}{T}\right)$ will have (*a*) zero value for $\zeta = 0.5$ (*b*) positive values for $\zeta > 0.5$ and (*c*) negative values for $\zeta < 0.5$.

(*v*) The phase angle ϕ increases from 0° at low frequencies to 180° at high frequencies and has the value 90° at the break frequency ω_b, for all values of damping ratio ζ.

(*vi*) The phase angle curve changes abruptly near the break frequency, the order of abruptness increasing with the reduction of the value of ζ.

(*uii*) For pole factors, all the equations used above should be multiplied by – 1.

In a general case, a network function $N(j\omega)$ may include first order factors, second order factors and zero or poles at the origin. The complete Bode diagrams may then be drawn combining the magnitude and phase responses of all the constituent factors.

EXERCISES

13.1. For the given *R-L-C* network, determine the driving point impedance and driving point admittance. For each of these functions, plot the magnitude, phase angle real part and the imaginary part as functions of frequency ω for ω > 0 and also for ω < 0.

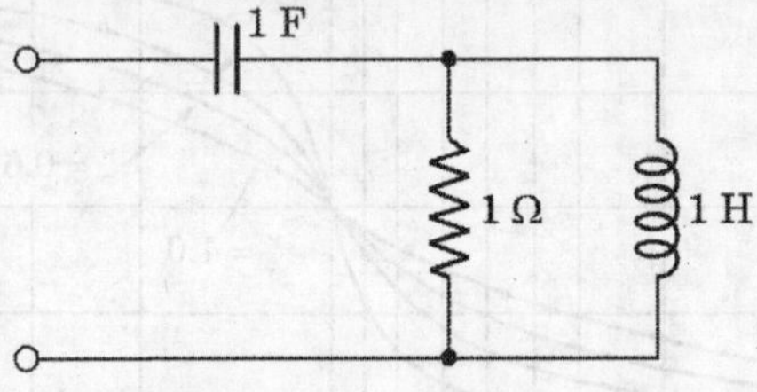

13.2. For the given two port R-L network, determine the voltage ratio transfer function $G_{21}(j\omega) = \dfrac{V_2(j\omega)}{V_1(j\omega)}$.

Plot

(*i*) the variation of the magnitude and phase of this transfer function as functions of frequency ω

(*ii*) the complex locus for ω > 0 and ω < 0.

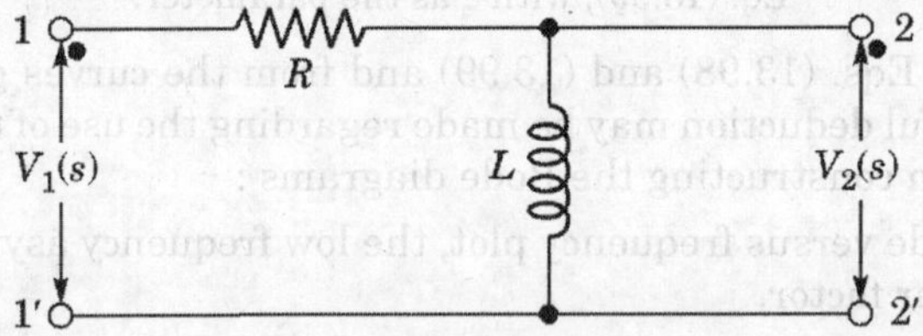

13.3. Repeat exercise 13.2 for the L-R two port network shown below :

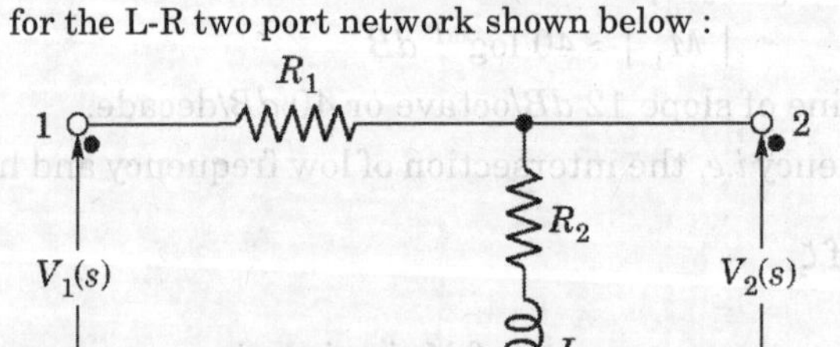

13.4. Analyse the four element network shown below to determine : (*a*) the locus of the driving point impedance of the network and (*b*) the locus of the driving point admittance of the network.

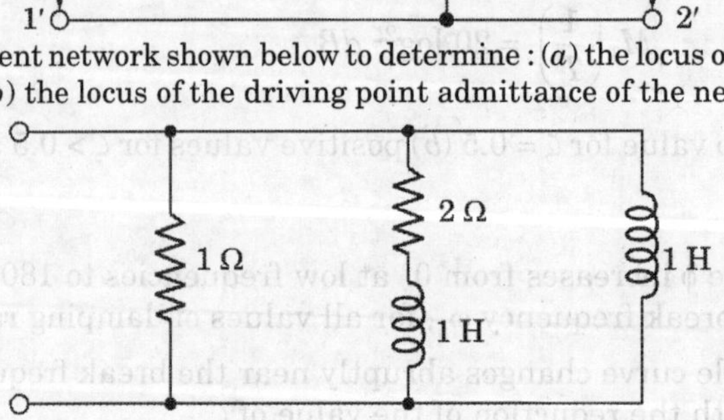

14

Input Power and Power Transfer

14.1. Introduction

Concepts of energy and power have already been discussed in the first chapter. These concepts are now being extended for use in analysis of one port and two-port networks operating in the sinusoidal steady state.

In this chapter, we first study the one port networks, followed by the study of two port networks, the latter involving the consideration of power transfer from the source to the load. Finally we consider the effect of inserting a new network in cascade with the two port network and determining the power loss or gain at the load due to this insertion.

14.2. Energy and Power in a One-port Network with Sinu-soidal Excitation

Fig. 14.1 shows a general one-port network consisting of elements which may be linear or non-linear, active of passive. Conventionally the reference direction for the flow of energy or power into the network is as shown in Fig. 14.1.

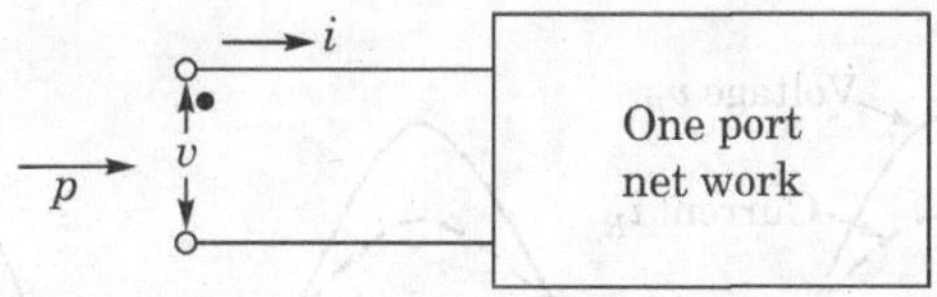

Fig. 14.1. One-port network.

Similarly the voltage and current reference directions are as shown in Fig. 14.1. For these reference directions the positive value of p implies flow of energy into the network and the negative value implies flow of energy out of the network.

Then the energy absorbed by the network in time interval from t_1 to t_2 is given by,

$$w = \int_{t_1}^{t_2} v(t) \,.\, i(t)\, dt \text{ joules} \qquad ...(14.1)$$

The rate, at which the energy is being absorbed, constitutes the power and is given by,

$$p = \frac{dw}{dt} = v(t) \,.\, i(t) \text{ watts} \qquad ...(14.2)$$

These have already been derived in Chapter 1.

Now we apply Eqs. (14.1) and (14.2) to the one port networks formed by single linear elements. The analysis is, however, restricted to sinusoidal steady state only.

(*a*) **Resistor R.** Let the one port network of Fig. 14.1 be formed by a single element formed by resistor R. Then voltage v is given by

$$v = Ri \qquad ...(14.3)$$

The energy absorbed by resistor is given by,

$$w_R = \int_{t_1}^{t_2} ri^2(t)\,.\,dt = \int_{t_1}^{t_2} \frac{v^2(t)}{R}\,dt \qquad ...(14.4)$$

The power is given by, $$p_R = R_i^{\,2}(t) = \frac{v^2(t)}{R} \qquad ...(14.5)$$

Let the sinusoidal current i be given by,

$$i = I_m \sin \omega t$$

and let us assume $t_1 = 0$. Then Eq. (14.4) yields,

$$\omega_R = \int_0^{t_2} RI_m^{\,2} \sin^2 \omega t\, dt = \frac{RI_m^2}{2}\int_0^{t_2} (1 - \cos 2\,\omega t)\, dt$$

$$= \frac{RI_m^2}{2}\left(t - \frac{\sin 2\omega t}{2}\right) \text{ joules} \qquad ...(14.6)$$

for any time $t = t_2$.

Similarly Eq. (14.5) yields, $$p_R = RI_m^{\,2} \sin^2 \omega t = \frac{RI_m^2}{2}\,(1 - \cos 2\,\omega t) \text{ watts} \qquad ...(14.7)$$

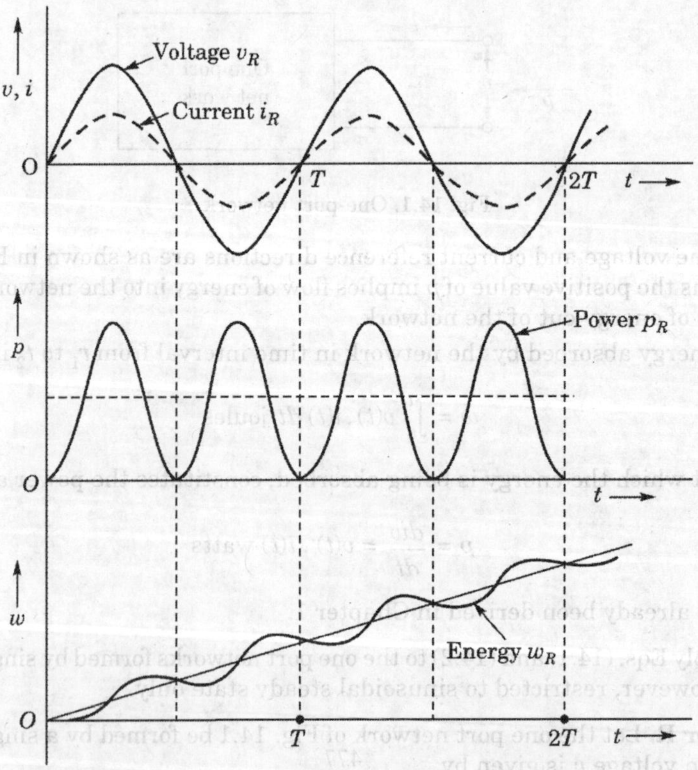

Fig. 14.2. Waveforms of voltage v, current i, power and energy w in resistor R with sinusoidal excitation.

Fig. 14.2 shows the time variation of voltage v_R, current i_R, energy w_R and power p_R for single element resistor. It may be seen from these curves that (*i*) the power p_R varies at a frequency twice that of voltage u_R or current i_R, (*ii*) the power p_R and energy w_R are always positive and (*iii*) the energy w_R increases continuously with increase of time t.

(*b*) **Inductor.** Next let the one port network of Fig. 14.1 be constituted by single element L. Then voltage v is given by,

$$v = L \cdot \frac{di}{dt} \qquad \text{...(14.8)}$$

Substituting this value of v in Eq. (14.1), we get

$$w_L = \int_{t_1}^{t_2} L \cdot \frac{di}{dt} \cdot i \, dt = \int_{t_1}^{t_2} Li \, dt$$

$$w_L = \frac{1}{2} L (i_2^2 - i_1^2) \text{ joules}$$

where i_1 and i_2 are the currents at time t_1 and t_2 respectively.

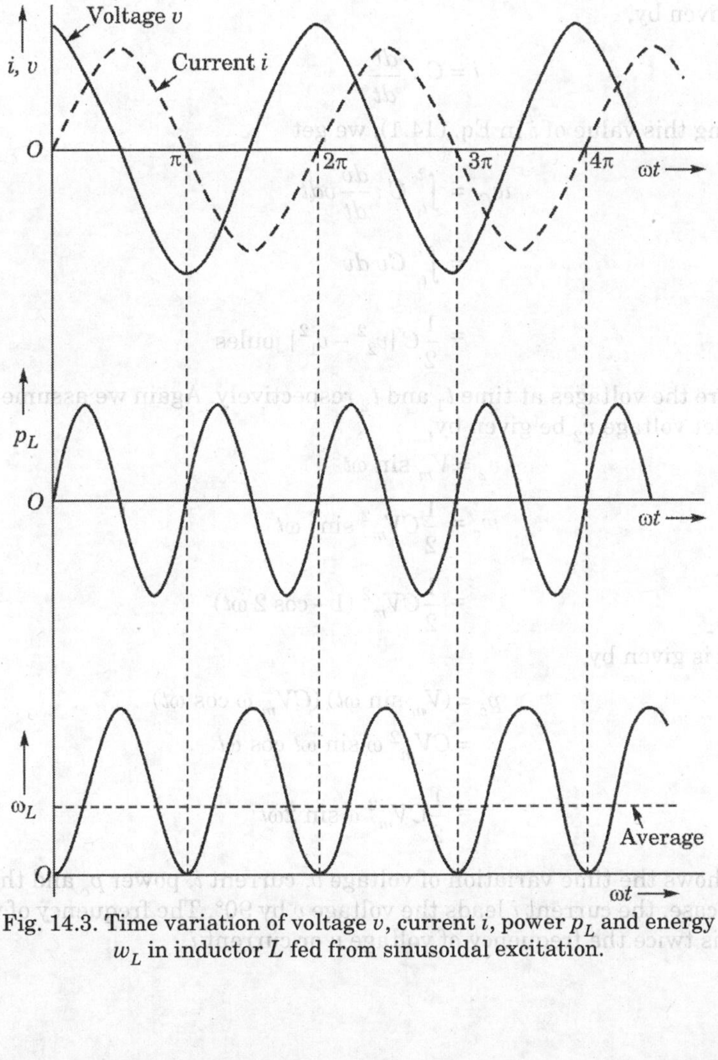

Fig. 14.3. Time variation of voltage v, current i, power p_L and energy w_L in inductor L fed from sinusoidal excitation.

If we assume the current i_1 at time t_1 to be zero and that the current i_2 is given by,

$$i_2 = I_m \sin \omega t \qquad ...(14.11)$$

then

$$w_L = \frac{1}{2} L I_m^2 \sin^2 \omega t \qquad ...(14.12)$$

$$= \frac{1}{4} L I_m^2 (1 - \cos 2\omega t) \qquad ...(14.13)$$

The power in the inductor is then,

$$p_L = vi = (L I_m \omega \cos \omega t)(I_m \sin \omega t) = L I_m^2 \omega \sin \omega t \cos \omega t$$

$$= \frac{1}{2} L I_m^2 \omega \sin 2\omega t \text{ watts} \qquad ...(14.14)$$

Fig. 14.3 shows the time variation of voltage v, current i, power p_L and energy w_L in the inductor. In this case, the current i lags behind the voltage v by 90°. Further the power p_L and energy w_L vary at a frequency twice that of v or i. However the maximum value of energy w_L remains the same for each cycle.

(*c*) **Capacitor.** Finally let the one port network of Fig. 14.1 be constituted by a capacitor C. The current i is given by,

$$i = C \cdot \frac{dv}{dt} \qquad ...(14.15)$$

Substituting this value of i in Eq. (14.1), we get

$$w_C = \int_{t_1}^{t_2} C \cdot \frac{dv}{dt} v dt$$

$$= \int_{t_1}^{t_2} Cv\, dv \qquad ...(14.16)$$

$$= \frac{1}{2} C [v_2^2 - v_1^2] \text{ joules} \qquad ...(14.17)$$

where v_1 and v_2 are the voltages at time t_1 and t_2 respectively. Again we assume voltage v_1 at time t_1 to be zero and let voltage v_2 be given by,

$$v_2 = V_m \sin \omega t \qquad ...(14.18)$$

Then

$$w_c = \frac{1}{2} C V_m^2 \sin^2 \omega t \qquad ...(14.19)$$

$$= \frac{1}{2} C V_m^2 (1 - \cos 2\omega t) \qquad ...(14.20)$$

The power is given by,

$$p_c = (V_m \sin \omega t)(C V_m \omega \cos \omega t) \qquad ...(14.21)$$

$$= C V_m^2 \omega \sin \omega t \cos \omega t \qquad ...(14.22)$$

$$= \frac{1}{2} C V_m^2 \omega \sin 2\omega t \qquad ...(14.23)$$

Fig. 14.4 shows the time variation of voltage v, current i, power p_c and the energy w_c in the capacitor. In this case, the current i leads the voltage v by 90°. The frequency of variation of power p_c and energy w_c is twice the frequency of voltage v or current i.

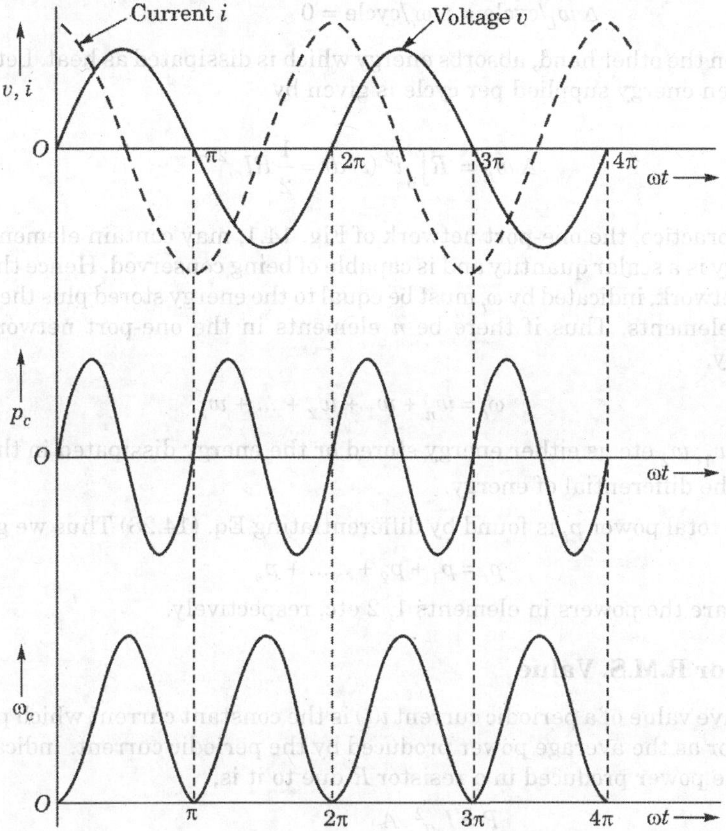

Fig. 14.4. Time variation of voltage v, current i, power p_c and energy w_c in a capacitor with sinusoidal excitation.

The following conclusions may be drawn from the study of single element networks with sinusoidal excitation.

(*i*) The energy and power variations in the inductor and the capacitor are of the same form.

(*ii*) The average power p over say n periods of time T seconds each equals the integral of p from $t = 0$ to $t = nT$ divided by nT. But the integral is zero for each cycle. Hence for inductor and capacitor, the average value of power is zero. This may be written as,

$$[p_L(t)]_{av} = [p_c(t)]_{av} = 0 \qquad ...(14.24)$$

For resistor, the average power is half of the peak value. Thus average power is given by,

$$[p_R(t)]_{av} = \frac{1}{2} I_m^{\ 2} R \qquad ...(14.25)$$

(*iii*) In accordance with the convention of sign given in Fig. 14.1 the positive power implies that energy is being supplied to the network while the negative power implies that energy is being returned by the network to the source. For passive network element, the energy returned cannot exceed the energy being supplied. Further in the cases of inductor and capacitor, the energy w becomes zero after each complete cycle of voltage or current. Thus we conclude that during each cycle, the energy supplied is returned in full. Thus we may write,

$$\Delta w_L/\text{cycle} = \Delta \omega_c/\text{cycle} = 0 \quad \text{...(14.26)}$$

Resistor, on the other hand, absorbs energy which is dissipated as heat. Let T be the periodic, time of v or i. Then energy supplied per cycle is given by

$$\Delta w_R = R\int_0^t i^2 (t)\, dt = \frac{1}{2} R I_m^{\ 2}\, T \quad \text{...(14.27)}$$

In actual practice, the one-port network of Fig. 14.1, may contain elements of all the three kinds. Now energy is a scalar quantity and is capable of being conserved. Hence the energy supplied to any one-port network, indicated by ω_t must be equal to the energy stored plus the energy dissipated in the resistive elements. Thus if there be n elements in the one-port network, then the total energy is given by,

$$\omega_t = w_n + w_1 + w_2 + \ldots + w_n \quad \text{...(14.28)}$$

where any term w_1, w_2 etc. is either energy stored or the energy dissipated in that element.

Power is the differential of energy.

Hence the total power p_t is found by differentiating Eq. (14.28) Thus we get,

$$p_t = p_1 + p_2 + \ldots\ldots + p_n \quad \text{...(14.29)}$$

where p_1, p_2 etc. are the powers in elements 1, 2 etc. respectively.

14.3. Effective or R.M.S. Value

The effective value of a periodic current $i(t)$ is the constant current which produces the same power in a resistor as the average power produced by the periodic current. Indicating the effective current by I_{eff}, the power produced in a resistor R due to it is,

$$P = I_{eff}^{\ 2} \,.\, A \quad \text{...(14.30)}$$

(A) Sinusoidal steady state. The average power produced in the resistor R by the sinusoidal current $i(t)$, in accordance with Eq. (14.25) is,

$$P_{av} = [p_R(t)]_{av} = \frac{1}{2} I_m^{\ 2} \,.\, R \quad \text{...(14.31)}$$

Equating p to p_{av}, we get

$$I_{eff} = \frac{I_m}{\sqrt{2}} \quad \text{...(14.32)}$$

Now for a resistor R, $p = \dfrac{V^2}{R}$ and $V_m = I_m \,.\, R$. Hence we get,

$$V_{eff} = \frac{V_m}{\sqrt{2}} \quad \text{...(14.33)}$$

(B) For non-sinusoidal periodic current. Let us here consider a current $i(t)$ of periodic time T. Then the average power is given by,

$$P_{av} = \left[\frac{1}{T}\int_{t_0}^{t_0 + T} R \,.\, i^2(t) \,.\, dt\right] \quad \text{...(14.34)}$$

Equating P as given by Eq. (14.30) to P_{av} as given by Eq. (14.34), we get

$$I_{eff} = \left[\frac{1}{T}\int_{t_0}^{t_0+T} i^2(t)\,dt\right]^{\frac{1}{2}} \quad ...(14.35)$$

Eq. (14.35) gives the general form of equation defining the effective value of any periodic function.

The effective value of voltage of periodic time T is similarly given by,

$$V_{eff} = \left[\frac{1}{T}\int_{t_0}^{t_0+T} v^2(t)\,dt\right]^{\frac{1}{2}} \quad ...(14.36)$$

Study of Eqs. (14.35) and (14.36) reveals that the operation of finding the effective value consists *in extracting the square root of the mean (average) of the squared function $i^2(t)$.*

Hence a name for effective value describing the above operation is the *root-mean-square* value, abbreviated as *r.m.s.*

Thus in sinusoidal steady state, Eqs. (14.32) and (14.33) may be written as

$$I_{rms} = I_{eff} = \frac{I_m}{\sqrt{2}} \approx .707 I_m \quad ...(14.37)$$

and

$$V_{rms} = V_{eff} = \frac{V_m}{\sqrt{2}} \approx .707\ V_m \quad ...(14.38)$$

The effective or the r.m.s. value is significant since most of the voltmeters and ammeters are designed to read these r.m.s. values. The peak value is then simply $\sqrt{2}$ times the r.m.s. value.

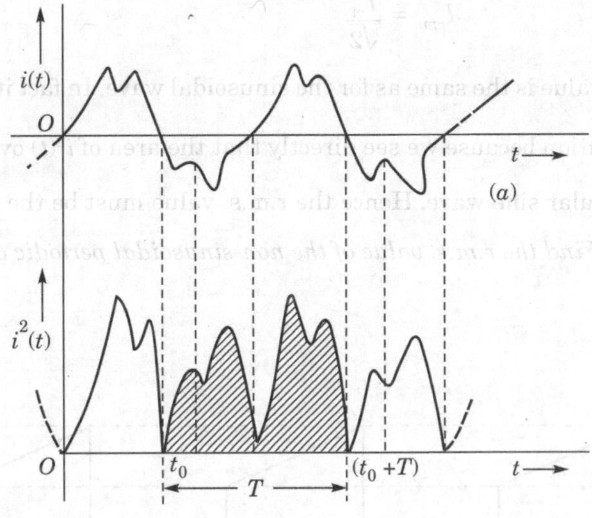

Fig. 14.5. Waveforms of $i^2(t)$ of part (*b*) used for computing the r.m.s. value of non-sinusoidal periodic current $i(t)$ of part (*a*).

The r.m.s. value of a non-sinusoidal periodic current $i(t)$ may be computed by making use of Eq. (14.35). Fig. 14.5 gives the operation. Thus Fig. 14.5 (*a*) gives the waveform of an arbitrary non-sinusoidal periodic current of periodic time T. Fig. 14.5 (*b*) shows the waveform of corresponding function $i^2(t)$. Then the shaded area of the function $i^2(t)$ in the time interval T is the integral of $i^2(t)$.

This area is then divided by the interval T and the square root of this quantity is computed giving the r.m.s. value of current $i(t)$.

Example 14.1. *Determine the r.m.s. value of the current shown in the diagram below, produced by a full wave rectifier.*

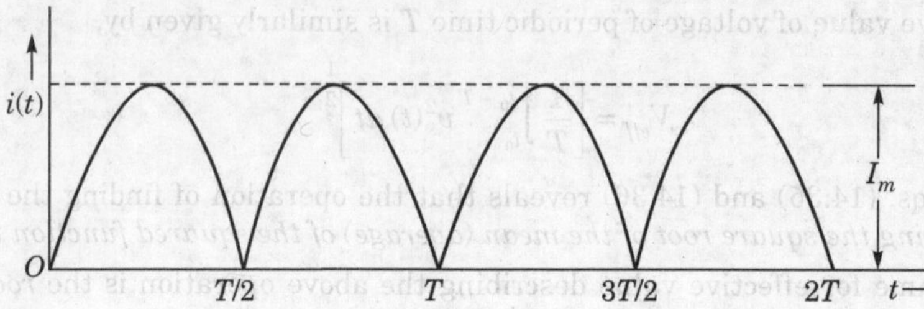

Solution.

$$I^2_{rms} = \left[\frac{2}{T}\int_0^{T/2} i^2(t)\,dt\right] \quad ...(1)$$

$$= \frac{2}{T}\int_0^{T/2} I_m{}^2 \sin^2 \omega t\,dt$$

$$= \frac{I_m{}^2}{2}$$

Hence $$I_{rms} = \frac{I_m}{\sqrt{2}}$$

Thus the r.m.s. value is the same as for the sinusoidal wave. In fact it is not necessary to use Eq. (1) for this computation because we see directly that the area of $i^2(t)$ over any period $\frac{T}{2}$ is the same as that of the regular sine wave. Hence the r.m.s. value must be the same as for sine wave.

Example 14.2. *Find the r.m.s. value of the non-sinusoidal periodic current i(t).*

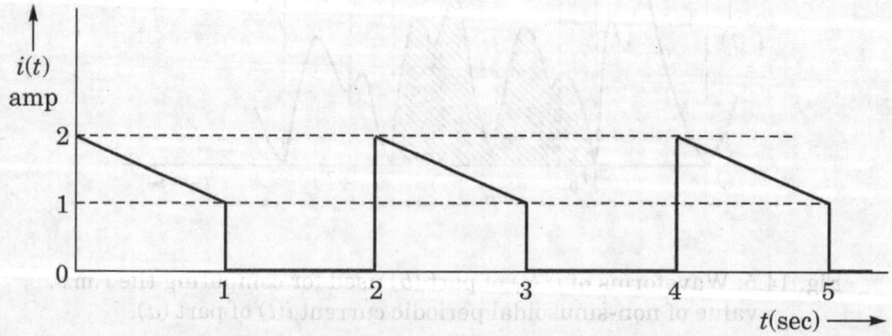

Solution. The waveform of current may be described over the period from 0 to 2 by,

$$i(t) = \begin{cases} (2-t), 0 < t < 1 \\ 0, 1 < t < 2 \end{cases} \quad ...(1)$$

Hence I_{rms} is given by,

$$I^2_{rms} = \left[\frac{1}{2}\left\{\int_0^1 (2-t)^2\, dt + \int_1^2 0\, dt\right\}\right]$$

$$= \frac{1}{2}\int_0^1 (t-2)^2\, dt$$

Hence $\quad I_{rms} = \sqrt{\frac{7}{6}}$ amp.

Example 14.3. *The figure below gives a train of cosine squared pulses derived by squaring the halfwave rectified waveform. Compute the effective value of voltage v (t).* **[Ans.** $3\sqrt{3}$ *volts***]**

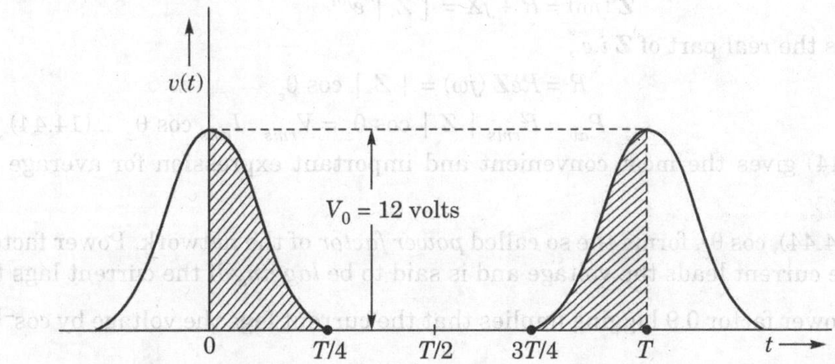

Solution. Since the areas under the shaded parts are same, we may put,

$$V_{eff} = \frac{1}{T}\left[2\int_0^{T/4} (V_0 \cos^2 \omega t)^2\, dt\right]$$

$$= \frac{1}{T}\left[2V_0^2 \int_0^{T/4} \left(\frac{\cos 2\omega t + 1}{2}\right)^2 dt\right]$$

$$= \frac{V_0^2}{2T}\left[\int_0^{T/4} (1 + 2\cos 2\omega t + \cos^2 2\omega t)\, dt\right]$$

$$= \frac{V_0^2}{2T}\left[t + \sin 2\omega t + \frac{1}{2}\left(t + \frac{1}{4}\sin 4\omega t\right)\right]_0^{T/4}$$

$$= \frac{3V_0^2}{16}$$

Hence $\quad V_{eff} = \frac{\sqrt{3}}{4} V_0 = \frac{\sqrt{3}}{4} \times 12 = 3\sqrt{3}$ volts.

14.4. Average Power and Complex Power

(*A*) *Resistive Load.* We have already seen that for a resistor, the average power is given by,

$$P_{av} = \frac{1}{2} I_m^2 R \text{ watts} \quad ...(14.39)$$

$$= \frac{1}{2} \cdot \frac{V_m^2}{K} \text{ watts.} \quad ...(14.40)$$

But $I_{rms} = \frac{I_m}{\sqrt{2}}$ and $V_{rms} = \frac{V_m}{\sqrt{2}}$. Hence average power may be put as,

$$P_{av} = I_{rms}^2 \cdot R = \frac{V_{rms}^2}{R} \text{ watts} \quad ...(14.41)$$

(*B*) *Complex Load.* Let the one port network contain no independent source and let it have driving point impedance given by,

$$\mathbf{Z}(j\omega) = R + jX = |Z| e^{j\theta z} \quad ...(14.42)$$

Then R is the real part of $\mathbf{Z}$ *i.e.,*

$$R = Re\mathbf{Z}(j\omega) = |Z| \cos \theta_z \quad ...(14.43)$$

Hence $$P_{av} = I_{rms}^2 |Z| \cos \theta_z = V_{rms} \cdot I_{rms} \cos \theta_z \quad ...(14.44)$$

Eq. (14.44) gives the most convenient and important expression for average power in a complex circuit.

In Eq. (14.44), $\cos \theta_z$, forms the so called *power factor* of the network. Power factor is said to be *leading* if the current leads the voltage and is said to be *lagging* if the current lags the voltage.

Thus a power factor 0.9 lagging implies that the current lags the voltage by $\cos^{-1} 0.9$ *i.e.* 25° 46′.

Phasor Notation in Complex Load

Let the current and voltage phasors be,

$$\mathbf{I} = Ie^{j\alpha} \quad ...(14.45)$$

$$\mathbf{V} = Ve^{j\beta} \quad ...(14.46)$$

Here I and V are r.m.s. values and equal the corresponding peak values divided by $\sqrt{2}$.

Then impedance $\mathbf{Z}$ is given by,

$$\mathbf{Z} = \frac{\mathbf{V}}{\mathbf{I}} = \frac{V}{I} e^{j(\beta - \alpha)} \quad ...(14.47)$$

Comparing Eqs. (14.42) and (14.47), we get

$$\theta_z = \beta - \alpha \quad ...(14.48)$$

Conjugate of current $\mathbf{I}$, indicated by $\mathbf{I}^*$ is given by

$$\mathbf{I}^* = I e^{-j\alpha} \quad ...(14.49)$$

Hence $$\mathbf{VI}^* = VI e^{j(\beta - \alpha)} \quad ...(14.50)$$

$$= VI e^{j\theta_z} \quad ...(14.51)$$

Hence in accordance with Eq. (14.44), the average power may be written as,

$$P_{au} = R_e \, \mathbf{VI^*} \text{ watts} \qquad ...(14.52)$$

The imaginary part of **VI*** may be indicated by Q.

Thus
$$Q = I_m \, \mathbf{VI^*} \qquad ...(14.53)$$

The phasor sum of the average power and Q power is given by,

$$\mathbf{S} = P_{av} + jQ = \mathbf{VI^*} \qquad ...(14.54)$$

Quantity S is called the *complex power* or the *phasor power*. Now Q is known as the *reactive power* and equals I_m **VI*** or I_m **S**. It may also be written in a form similar to Eq. (14.44). Thus we get,

$$Q = V_{rms} I_{rms} \sin \theta \text{ vars} \qquad ...(14.55)$$

The unit for reactive power is *volt-ampere reactive,* abbreviated by *var*. Further a positive sign is assigned to Q for reactive power for the inductor and a negative sign for the capacitor.

From Eqs. (14.52) and (14.53), the complex power **S** has its magnitude given by

$$|\,\mathbf{S}\,| = \sqrt{P_{av}^{\ 2} + Q^2} = V_{rms} I_{rms} \; va \qquad ...(14.56)$$

The unit of phasor power S is *volt ampere,* abbreviated as *va*. This is also sometimes called the *apparent power* since it is simply the product of voltmeter and ammeter readings.

Expressions for p_{av} and Q in terms of G and B. Current **I** is related to the admittance Y by the equation,

$$\mathbf{I} = \mathbf{YV} \qquad ...(14.57)$$

Hence
$$\mathbf{S} = \mathbf{VI^*} = \mathbf{VV^*Y^*} = |\,\mathbf{V}\,|^2\,\mathbf{Y^*} \qquad ...(14.58)$$

Now
$$\mathbf{Y} = G + jB \qquad ...(14.59)$$

Hence
$$\mathbf{Y^*} = G - jB \qquad ...(14.60)$$

But
$$\mathbf{S} = P_{av} + JQ$$

From Eq. (14.58) then we get,

$$P_{av} + jQ = |\,V\,|^2\,(G - jB) \qquad ...(14.61)$$

In Eq. (14.61), equating the real and the imaginary parts, we get,

$$P_{av} = V^2_{rms}\, G \text{ watts} \qquad ...(14.62)$$

and
$$Q = -\,V_{rms}\, B \text{ vars} \qquad ...(14.63)$$

Expressions for P_{av} and Q in terms of R and X

Since
$$\mathbf{V} = \mathbf{I.Z} \qquad ...(14.64)$$

we get,
$$\mathbf{S} = \mathbf{VI^*} = \mathbf{I\,I^*Z} = |\,\mathbf{I}\,|^2\,\mathbf{Z} \qquad ...(14.65)$$

But
$$\mathbf{Z} = R + jX \qquad ...(14.66)$$

Hence
$$P_{av} = I_{rms}^{\ 2}\, R \text{ watts} \qquad ...(14.67)$$

and
$$Q = I_{rms}^{\ 2}.\, X \text{ vars} \qquad ...(14.68)$$

Total Power in all the Elements. The average power I_{av} is a scalar quantity and is always positive. The total average power supplied by a source to any multi-element one-port network is, therefore, the sum of average power for each element in the network.

Thus we have,

$$\text{total } P_{av} = P_{av1} + P_{av2} + \ldots \qquad \ldots(14.69)$$

where P_{av1}, P_{av2} etc. are the average powers in element number, 1, 2 etc.

Similarly the total reactive power in any one-port network is the sum of the reactive power in each element in the network. Thus we have,

$$\text{total } Q = Q_1 + Q_2 + \ldots \qquad \ldots(14.70)$$

where Q_1, Q_2 etc. are the reactive powers in element number 1, 2, etc.

Addition of Eqs. (11.69) and (11.70) yields that the total complex power in any one-port network equals the sum of the complex power of each element in the network. Thus,

$$\text{total } S = S_1 + S_2 + \ldots \qquad \ldots(14.71)$$

Example 14.4. *A current source $i(t) = 10\sqrt{2}\ \sin t$ drives the network show. Under steady state, determine (i) the driving point impedance, (ii) average power in the network, (iii) the reactive power, (iv) the complex power, (v) the r.m.s. voltage across the network and (vi) the power factor.*

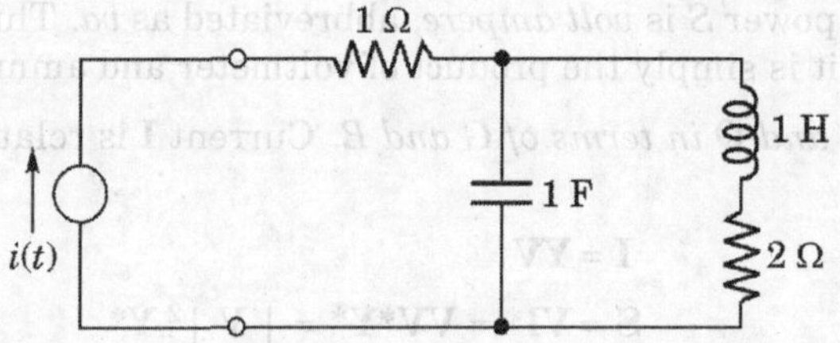

Solution. The equivalent transform network is as below :

Combining the two shunt arms, the network reduces to the form shown in Fig. (*b*).

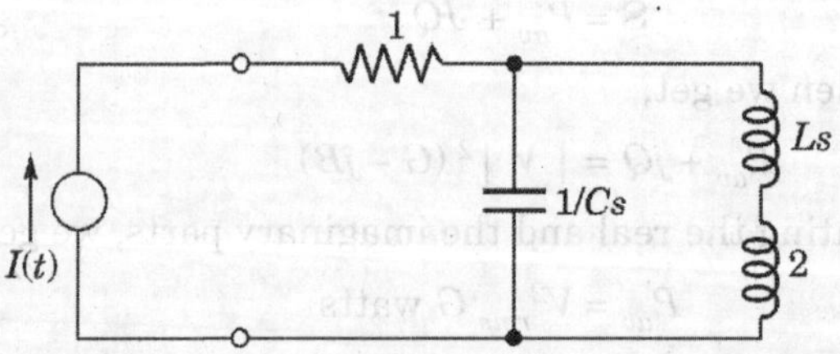

Fig. (*a*)

$$\text{Here } \frac{1}{Z_p} = Cs + \frac{1}{Ls+2} = \frac{s^2LC + 2Cs + 1}{Ls + 2}$$

$$\text{Hence} \qquad Z_p = \frac{Ls + 2}{s^2\ LC + 2Cs + 1}$$

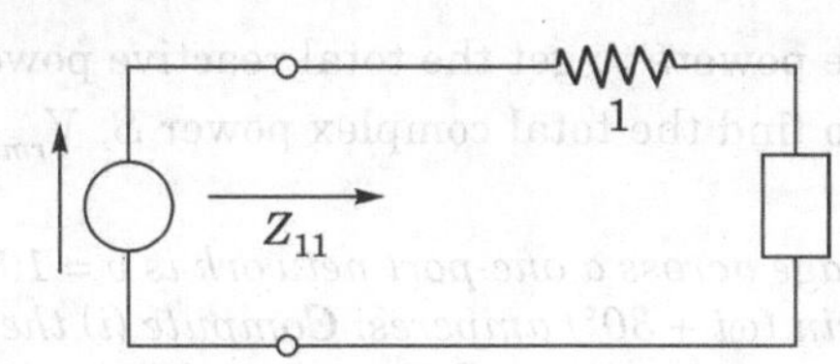

Hence $Z_{11} = Z_p + 1 = \dfrac{Ls}{s^2\, LC + 2Cs + 1} + 1.$

Under sinusoidal steady state,

$$Z_p = \frac{j\,\omega\,L + 2}{-\,\omega^2\,LC + 2\,(j\omega) + 1} = \frac{2 + j}{-1 + 2j + 1}$$

$$= \frac{1}{2} - j$$

Hence $Z_{11} = Z_p + 1 = \dfrac{3}{2} - j$

Average power $P_{av} = I_{rms}^{\;2} \,.\, R_e\, Z_{11} = (10)^2 \times \dfrac{3}{2} = 150$ watts

Reactive power $Q = I_{rms}^{\;2} \,.\, I_m\, Z_{11} = (10)^2 \times (-\,1) = -\,100$ vars.

Hence $S = P_{av} + jQ$

$= 150 + j\,(-\,100)$

$|\,S\,| = 50\,\sqrt{9 + 4} = 50\sqrt{13}\ va$

$$V_{rms} = \frac{50\sqrt{13}}{I_{rms}} = \frac{50\sqrt{13}}{10} = 5\sqrt{13} \text{ volts}$$

Power factor $pf = \cos\theta_z = \cos\,(\tan^{-1} - 2) = \cos\,(-\,63°\,26')$

$= .4473$ leading.

Note. The analysis may be completed alternatively by :

(*i*) finding currents in the capacitor branch and inductor branch separately ;

(*ii*) finding the average power in these branches and in the one ohm resistor ;

(*iii*) adding these average powers to get the total average P_{av} for the entire network ;

(*iv*) finding the reactive power in each branch ;

(*v*) adding these reactive powers to get the total reactive power ; and

(*vi*) proceeding further to find the total complex power S, V_{rms} and power factor as done in the above analysis.

Example 14.5. *The voltage across a one-port network is v = 100 cos (ωt – 30°) volts while the current in the network is i = 6 sin (ωt + 30°) amperes. Compute (i) the instantaneous power p(t), (ii) average power P_{av} in watts, (iii) reactive power Q in vars and (iv) complex power S in volt-amperes.*

Solution. (*i*) Instantaneous power $p(t)$ is given by,

$$p(t) = vi = 100 \cos(\omega t - 30°) \times 6 \sin(\omega t + 30°)$$
$$= 600 \sin(\omega t + 30°) \cos(\omega t - 30°)$$
$$= \frac{600}{2} [\sin(2\,\omega t) + \sin(30° + 30°)]$$
$$= 300 [\sin 2\,\omega t + 0.866]$$

(*ii*) $$v = 100 \cos(\omega t - 30°)$$
$$i = 6 \sin(\omega t + 30°) = 6 \cos(\omega t - 60°)$$

Hence current lags the voltage by 30°

Hence power factor is cos 30° lagging

Hence $$P_{av} = V_{rms} I_{rms} \cos 30° = \frac{100}{\sqrt{2}} \cdot \frac{6}{\sqrt{2}} \times 0.866 = 259.6 \text{ watts}$$

(*iii*) Reactive power $$Q = V_{rms} . I_{rms} \sin 30° = \frac{100}{\sqrt{2}} \times \frac{6}{\sqrt{2}} \times 0.866 = 150 \text{ vars.}$$

(*iv*) Complex power $$S = V_{rms} . I_{rms} = \frac{100}{\sqrt{2}} \times \frac{6}{\sqrt{2}} = 300 \text{ volt amperes.}$$

Example 14.6. *The network shown below operates in the sinusoidal steady state and v_1 = 10 cos 3t. Determine (a) effective current in each of the passive elements (b) complex power in each of the passive elements and (c) the average power, the reactive power and the complex power in the network.*

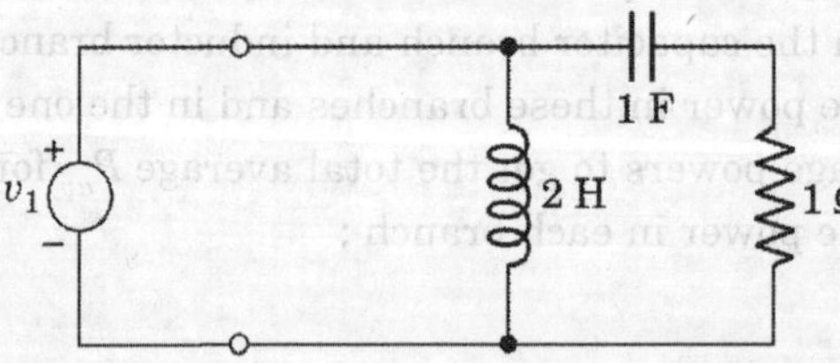

Solution. The equivalent network in the sinusoidal steady state is as shown in Fig. (*a*).

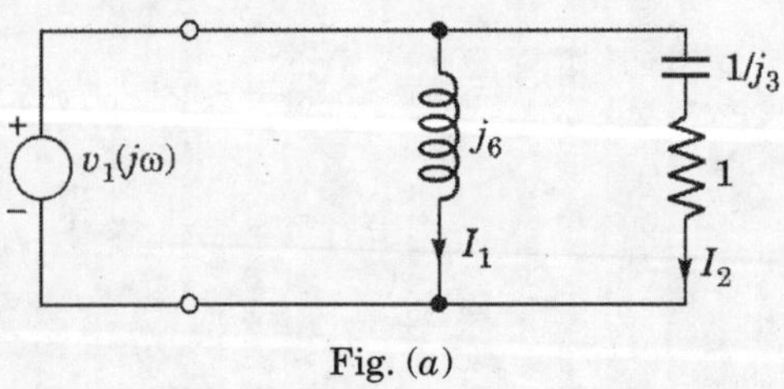

Fig. (*a*)

Effective current

$$\mathbf{I}_1 = \frac{\mathbf{V_1}}{j\,6} = \frac{10/\sqrt{2}}{j\,6} = -\,j\,\frac{5}{3\sqrt{2}} = -\,j\,1.179$$

$$|\ I_1\ | = 1.179 \text{ amperes}$$

$$\mathbf{I}_2 = \mathbf{V}_1 . \mathbf{Y}_2 = \mathbf{V}_1 . \frac{j\,3}{1 + j\,3} = \mathbf{V}_1 \frac{j\,3\,(1 - j3)}{10} = \mathbf{V}_1 . \frac{9 + j3}{10}$$

$$\text{Hence } |\ I_2\ | = \frac{10}{\sqrt{2}} . \frac{3}{10} \sqrt{9 + 1} = 3\sqrt{5} = 6.671 \text{ amps.}$$

Power in resistor

$$R = |\ I_2\ |^2 R = (6.671)^2 \times 1 = 45 \text{ watts}$$

Power in capacitor

$$= |\ I_2\ |^2 \frac{1}{j\omega C} = 45 \times \frac{1}{\sqrt{3}} = -\,15\,j = 15 \text{ vars capacitive}$$

Power in inductor

$$= |\ I_1\ |^2 . j\,\omega\,L = \left(\frac{25}{18}\right) \times j\,6 = j\,.\,\frac{25}{3} = \frac{25}{3} \text{ vars inductive}$$

Average power in the entire circuit

$$= \text{Power in the dissipative element } R = 45 \text{ watts}$$

$$\text{Reactive power in the entire circuit} = -\,15 + j\,\frac{25}{3} = -\,j\,\frac{20}{3} = \frac{20}{3} \text{ vars capacitive}$$

$$\text{Complex power } S \text{ in the entire circuit} = 45 - j\,\frac{20}{3}$$

Magnitude

$$|\ S\ | = \sqrt{(45)^2 + \left(\frac{20}{3}\right)^2} = 45.5\ va.$$

14.5. Power Transfer

Here we consider a two-port network to which a source is connected at the input port and a load, consisting of one or more elements, is connected at the output port as shown in Fig. 14.6 (*a*). At the load terminals 2.2′, we apply Thevenin's theorem to the network lying to the left, then the resulting Thevenin's equivalent network is as shown in Fig. 14.6 (*b*).

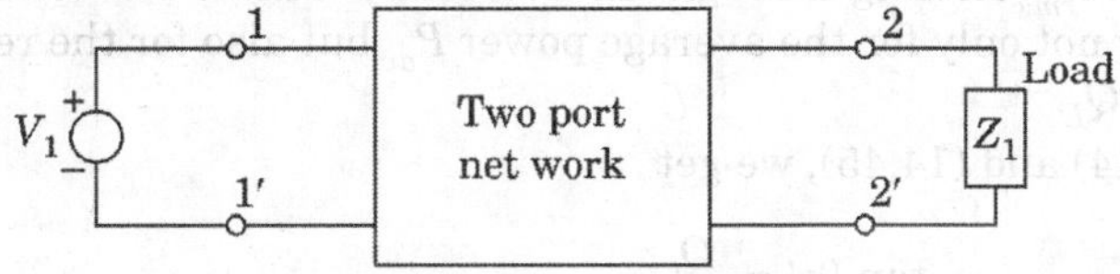

(*a*) Loaded 2-port network

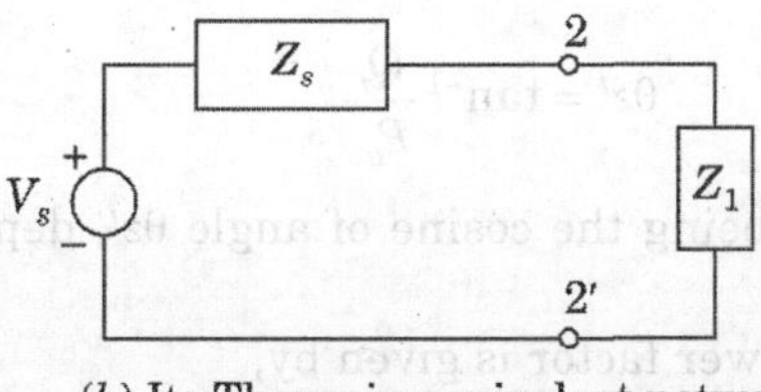

(*b*) Its Thevenin equivalent network

Fig. 14.6. Two-port network and its Thevenin equivalent network.

Here we take up the consideration of optimising power transfer and some of the problems arising in the process.

14.5.1. Power Factor Correction

We assume the load to be of fixed value. Let the complex power in the load be $P_{av} + j\,Q$. The industrial load, in general, is inductive, making reactive Q_L positive. Larger the magnitude of reactive power Q_L, smaller is the power factor *i.e.* smaller is the ratio of P_{av} to the complex power S. We need, therefore, increase the power factor by reducing the magnitude of reactive power Q_L. This may be accomplished by introducing negative reactive power Q_C into the network to cancel a part or all of Q_L. To do so, we connect a capacitor in parallel with the load as shown in Fig. 14.7 (*a*) without altering the terminal voltage at the load.

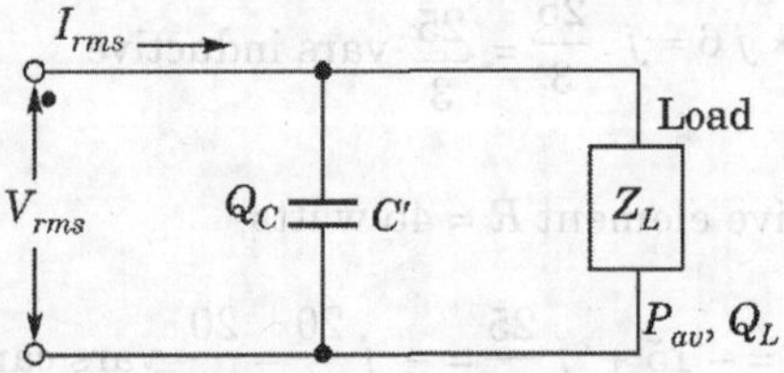

(*a*) Load with a capacitor for power factor correction

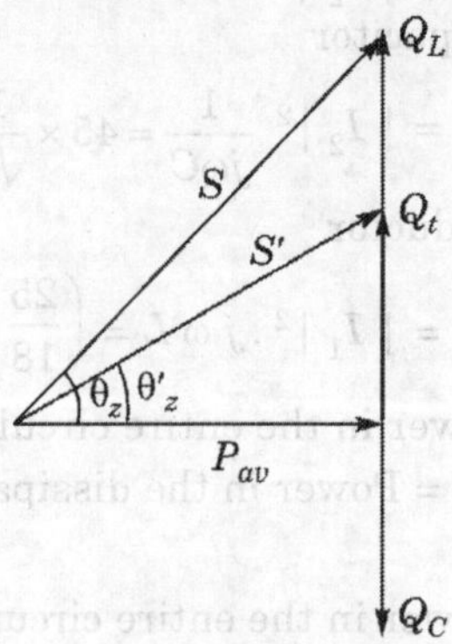

(*b*) Phasor diagram

Fig. 14.7. Power factor correction by capacitor.

Now the complex power S is given by,

$$S = \sqrt{P_{av}^{\,2} + Q_t^{\,2}} = V_{rms}.I_{rms}\ va \qquad ...(14.72)$$

where Q_t is the total reactive power and is given by,

$$Q_t = Q_L - Q_C \qquad ...(14.73)$$

By introducing Q_C, total reactive power reduces from its original value Q_L to new value Q_t equal to $(Q_L - Q_C)$. Hence the product $V_{rms}.I_{rms}$ reduces. Hence for a fixed voltage V_{rms} across the load terminals, current I_{rms} flowing through the new load reduces. The consumer has to pay to the power supply company not only for the average power P_{av} but also for the reactive power. Hence it is beneficial to reduce Q_L.

From Eqs. (14.44) and (14.45), we get

$$\tan \theta z' = \frac{Q_t}{P_{av}}$$

or

$$\theta z' = \tan^{-1} \frac{Q_t}{P_{av}} \qquad ...(14.74)$$

Thus the power factor, being the cosine of angle $\theta z'$, depends on and is a measure of the relative size of Q_t and P_{av}.

From Eq. (14.44), the power factor is given by,

$$pf = \cos \theta z' = \frac{P_{av}}{V_{rms} I_{rms}} = \frac{P_{av}}{\sqrt{P_{av}^2 + Q_t^2}} \quad ...(14.75)$$

Thus in order to maximise the power factor *i.e.* to make it approach unity, we must make $| Q_t | << P_{av}$. On the other hand, power factor approaching zero implies $P_{av} << Q_t$.

Fig. 14.7 (*b*) gives the phasor diagram showing the complex power S present in a circuit before power factor correction. By introducing capacitive power Q_C, the net reactive power reduces from Q_L to Q_t and new complex power is S'. The phase angle reduces from original value θz to $\theta z'$ and the power factor increases accordingly.

In a given circuit, with known values of Q_L and P_{av}, it may be necessary to determine the value of C needed to produce the desired power factor. The following steps are involved in the process :

(*i*) For given P_{av} and for desired value of θz, determine the requisite total reactive power Q_t.

(*ii*) Knowing the given Q_L, find the value of capacitive power Q_C needed using the following equation,

$$Q_C = Q_t - Q_L \quad ...(14.76)$$

or

$$| Q_C | = Q_L - Q_t \quad ...(14.76\ a)$$

(*iii*) Determine the value of capacitor C, using the relation,

$$C = \frac{Q_C}{- V_{rms}^2\ \omega} \quad ...(14.77)$$

Eq. (14.77) follows from the relation,

$$Q_C = V_{rms}^2 \cdot B_c = - V_{rms}^2 \cdot \omega C \quad ...(14.78)$$

Example 14.7. *A given load operating at 200 volts r.m.s., 50 cycle / sec. has average power* P_{av} *= 400 watts and reactive power Q = 500 vars lagging. Find the value of capacitor C which must be connected in shunt with the load in order to improve the power factor to 0.9 lagging.*

Solution. Let Q_t be the total reactive power in the corrected condition. Then phase angle $\theta z'$ under corrected condition is given by,

$$\tan \theta z' = \frac{Q_t}{P_{av}}$$

Hence $$Q_t = P_{av} \tan \theta z' = 400 \tan (\cos^{-1} 0.9) = 193.08 \text{ vars.}$$

Let Q_C be the power in capacitor C.

Then $$Q_C = Q_t - Q_l = - (500 - 193.08) = - 306.92 \text{ vars.}$$

Hence $$C = \frac{Q_C}{- V_{rms}^2 \omega} = \frac{- 306.92}{- (200)^2 \times 2\pi \times 50} \text{ farad} = 24.43\ \mu\text{F.}$$

14.5.2. Maximum Power Transfer by Impedance Matching

Fig. 14.6 (6) gives the Thevenin's equivalent for the general loaded 2-port network. The load impedance Z_L is a complex impedance and may be put in the form,

$$Z_L = R_L + jX_L \quad ...(14.79)$$

Similarly Z_s, the impedance of the Thevenin's equivalent voltage source, is a complex impedance and may be put as,

$$Z_s = R_s + jX_s \qquad ...(14.80)$$

Fig. 14.8 shows the same network in the revised form. Here V_s and Z_s are the voltage and impedance respectively of the Thevenin's equivalent voltage generators. However, the same may represent any general voltage source.

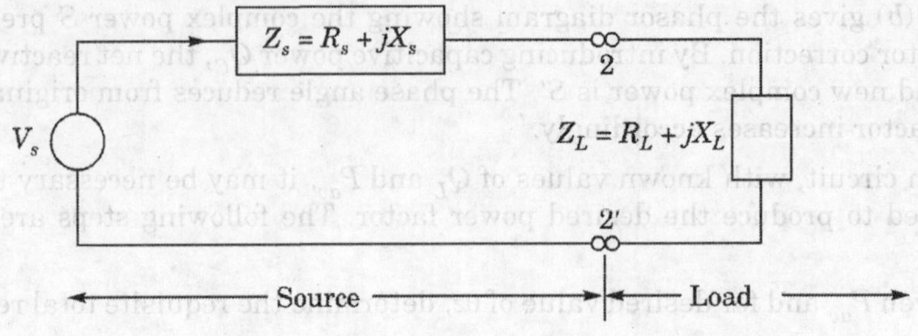

Fig. 14.8. A general voltage source with complex load impedance.

We assume here that it is possible to vary individually both the resistive part R_L and the reactive part X_L of the load impedance. We now determine the values of R_L, and X_L in relation to R_S and X_S for maximum transfer of power from the source to the load.

The phasor current is given by,

$$\mathbf{I_L} = \frac{\mathbf{V}_S}{\mathbf{Z}_S + \mathbf{Z}_L} \qquad ...(14.81)$$

$$= \frac{\mathbf{V}_S}{(R_S + R_L) + j(X_S + X_L)} \qquad ...(14.82)$$

The power in the load is then given by,

$$P_L = |I_L|^2 R_L = \frac{V_S^2 R_L}{(R_S + R_L)^2 + (X_S + X_L)^2} \qquad ...(14.83)$$

Let us first assume R_L to be constant and assume X_L, alone to be variable. Then the value of X_L which maximises P_L, the average power in the load, is obtained by differentiating P_L with respect to X_L and equating this derivative to zero. Thus,

$$\frac{dP_L}{dX_L} = V_S^2 R_L \left[\frac{-2(X_S + X_L)}{\{(R_S + R_L)^2 + (X_S + X_L)^2\}}\right] \qquad ...(14.84)$$

Equatmg $\frac{dP_L}{dX_L}$ to zero, we get

$$X_L = -X_s \qquad ...(14.85)$$

This, therefore, forms a condition for maximum transfer of power.

Substituting $(X_L + X_S) = 0$ in Eq. (14.83), we get

$$P_L' = \frac{V_S^2 R_L}{(R_S + R_L)^2} \qquad ...(14.86)$$

Now the condition under which this P_L', as given by equation (14.86), will be maximum may be obtained by differentiating P_L' with respect to R_L and equating this derivative to zero. This yields.

$$R_L = R_S,\ R_L \text{ and } R_S \text{ positive} \quad ...(14.87)$$

Thus the maximum power transfer takes place when the reactive components of $\mathbf{Z}_L$ and $\mathbf{Z}_S$ cancel and when the real components of $\mathbf{Z}_L$ and $\mathbf{Z}_S$ are equal *i.e.* when $\mathbf{Z}_L$ is complex conjugate of $\mathbf{Z}_S$. The condition for maximum transfer of power from the source to load may be put as,

$$\mathbf{Z}_S = \mathbf{Z}_L^* \quad ...(14.88)$$

14.5.3. Maximum Power Transfer by Transformer Adjustment

In the network of Fig. 14.8, power is being fed directly from the source V_S to the load impedance Z_L,. Instead of this, power may be fed to the load through a transformer as shown in Fig. 14.9. This transformer is assumed to be ideal, *i.e.* we assume that the magnetising and the leakage inductances and the internal losses are negligible. Let V_L and I_L be the voltage and current respectively in the output winding of the transformer. Then,

$$V_S \cdot I_S = -V_L \cdot I_L \quad ...(14.89)$$

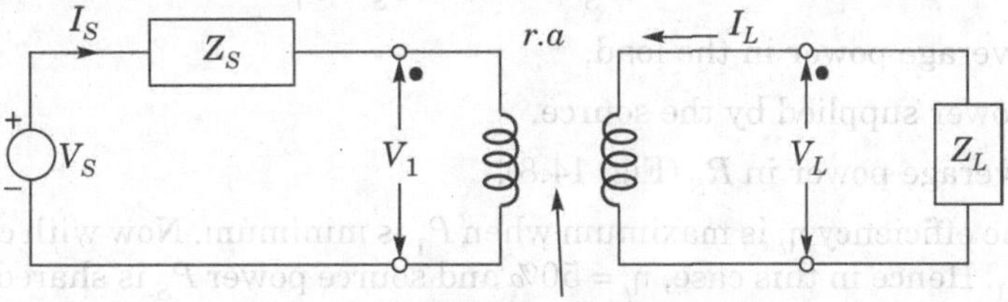

Fig. 14.9. Transformer adjustment for maximising power transfer.

Then the power transfer to the load may be maximised by adjustment of the transformation ratio of the transformer.

Let a be the ratio of secondary voltage, to the primary voltage. Then

$$V_L = a \cdot V_1 \quad ...(14.90)$$

Then the driving point impedance at the primary of the transformer with the secondary terminated in Z_L is given by,

$$Z_1 = \frac{Z_L}{a^2} \quad ...(14.91)$$

Now Z_1 may be written as below :

$$Z_1 = |Z_1| e^{j\theta} = |Z_1| \cos\theta + j|Z_1| \sin\theta \quad ...(14.92)$$

Then the average power in Z_1 may be written as,

$$P_1 = I_1^2 |Z_1| \cos\theta$$

$$= \frac{V_S^2 |Z_1| \cos\theta}{(R_S + |Z_1|\cos\theta)^2 + (X_S + |Z_1|\sin\theta)^2} \quad ...(14.93)$$

By altering a, only the magnitude $|Z_1|$ may be adjusted. The value of a for which power P_L is maximum may be obtained by equating to zero, the derivative $\frac{dP_L}{d|Z_1|}$. By doing so and on simplification, we get

$$|Z_1| = \sqrt{R_S^2 + X_S^2} = |Z_S| \quad ...(14.94)$$

Hence Eq. (14.91) yields,

$$\frac{1}{a^2}|Z_L| = |Z_S| \quad ...(14.95)$$

or

$$a = \sqrt{\left|\frac{Z_1}{Z_S}\right|} \quad ...(14.96)$$

Eq. (14.96) gives the value of a for maximum transfer of power. However, this method of feeding through a transformer and adjustment of ratio a yields a maximum power P_L, to load somewhat less than that obtained by adjusting the load Z_L to be conjugate of Z_S.

14.5.4. Efficiency of Power Transfer

Efficiency of power transfer is given by the following relation :

$$\eta_t = \frac{P_L}{P_S} \times 100\% = \frac{P_L}{P_S + P_1} \times 100\% \quad ...(14.97)$$

where P_L is the average power in the load,

P_S is the power supplied by the source,

and P_1 is the average power in R_S (Fig. 14.8).

Evidently the efficiency η_t is maximum when P_1 is minimum. Now with conjugate match, $R_S = R_L$ so that $P_L = P_1$. Hence in this case, $\eta_t = 50\%$ and source power P_S is shared equally by the two resisters R_L and R_S. This low efficiency of power transfer is permissible in communication systems involving two powers but is not permissible in power systems which involve large powers. In power systems, R_L is made large compared to R_S so that $P_1 << P_L$, thus making the power transfer efficiency η_t high.

14.6. Insertion Loss

We have already considered the topic of transfer of power from a source to a load and have studied the conditions under which either the power transfer is maximum or transfer efficiency is maximum. Now we take up the study of effect of inserting any circuit in between the source and the load, on the power transfer. In general there results as loss in power transfer. This loss caused by insertion of a circuit is called the *insertion loss.*

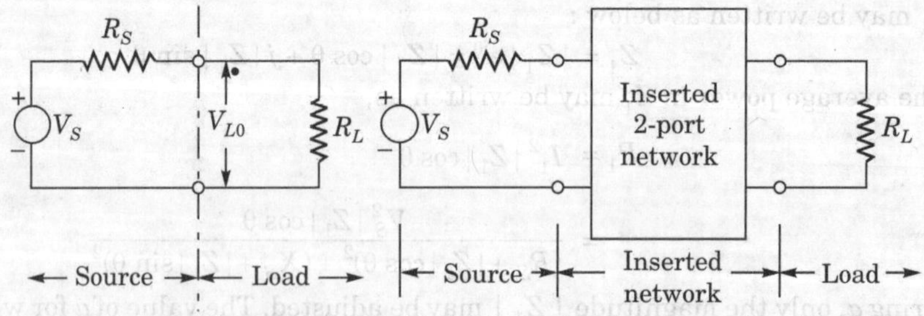

(*a*) No inserted network. (*b*) With inserted network.

Fig. 14.10. Networks with and without insertion loss.

Let us consider the circuit of Fig. 14.10 (*a*) in which a resistive load R_L is fed from a source V_S with resistance R_S. In this simple case under consideration, impedances have been assumed to be resistive. Then, the power transfer is maximum when $R_L = R_S$. Let this maximum power be denoted by I_{avl}. This power constitutes the *available power* from the source since this is the power under the best condition. Under no circumstances, can the output exceed this value. Available power is then given by,

$$P_{avl} = \left(\frac{V_S}{2R_S}\right)^2 R_s = \frac{V_S^2}{2R_S} \quad ...(14.98)$$

If $R_L \neq R_S$, the power in the load is,

$$P_{L_0} = \frac{V_S^2 R_L}{(R_L + R_S)^2} \quad ...(14.99)$$

This is the power in R_L without any inserted network, *i.e.* without any insertion loss.

Next let a two-port network N be inserted between the source and the load. Let the voltage at the load be V_L. Then the power in the load is,

$$P_L = \frac{V_L^2}{R_L} \quad ...(14.100)$$

This power P_L in the load is less than the power PL_0. Thus there is a loss in power caused by the insertion of network N. We may consider here that because of insertion of network N and because of R_0 not being equal to R_S, a part of the power going to R_L has been *reflected*. Then this reflected average power is,

$$P_R = P_{avl} - P_L \quad ...(14.101)$$

Reflection Coefficient Squared. The ratio of reflected power P_R to the available power P_{avl} may be called the *reflection coefficient squared.* Thus, we get the following expression for the reflection coefficient squared,

$$|\rho|^2 = \frac{P_R}{P_{avl}} = \frac{P_{avl} - P_L}{P_{avl}} = 1 - \frac{P_L}{P_{avl}} \quad ...(14.102)$$

where $|\rho|^2$ is always positive.

Further $\rho(j\omega) \times \rho(-j\omega) = |\rho(j\omega)|^2$ ...(14.103)

where $\rho(j\omega)$ is the reflection coefficient of sinusoidal excitation of frequency ω.

Substituting the values of P_L and P_{avl} from Eqs. (14.100) and (14.98) into Eq. (14.102), we get

$$|\rho|^2 = 1 - \frac{V_L^2}{R_L} \cdot \frac{4R_S}{V_S^2}$$

$$= 1 - \frac{4R_S}{R_L}\left(\frac{V_L}{V_S}\right)^2 \quad ...(14.104)$$

where V_L and V_S are the r.m.s. values of $\mathbf{V}_L$ and $\mathbf{V}s$.

The Transmission Coefficient Squared. The ratio of power P_L to available power P_{avl} is called the *transmission coefficient squared* and may be denoted by $|t(j\omega)|^2$, where $t(j\omega)$ is the transmission coefficient at frequency ω.

Then $$|t(j\omega)|^2 = \frac{P_L}{P_{avl}} \quad ...(14.105)$$

$$= \frac{4R_S}{R_L}\left(\frac{V_L}{V_S}\right)^2 \quad ...(14.106)$$

Combining Eqs. (14.104) and (14.105), we get

$$|\rho(j\omega)|^2 + |t(j\omega)|^2 = 1 \quad ...(14.107)$$

Thus $\dfrac{\text{Reflected Power + Transmitted Power}}{\text{Available Power}} = 1$ ...(14.108)

Insertion Loss in nepers. The power in the load resistor R_L ($R_L \neq R_S$) without any inserted network as shown in Fig. 14.10 (*a*) is P_{L_0}, given by Eq. (14.99). The power in the load resistor R_L with network N inserted as shown in Fig. 14.10 (*b*) is P_L, given by Eq. (14.100). The effect of insertion of network N thus results in loss of power in R_L from P_{L_0} to P_L and may be described by the *insertion power ratio* given by the following equation :

$$\text{Insertion power ratio} = \frac{P_{L_0}}{P_L} = e^{2\alpha} \quad \text{...(14.109)}$$

where α is the *insertion loss in nepers.*

Now from Eqs. (14.99) and (14.100), we get

$$\frac{P_{L_0}}{P_L} = \frac{V_S^2 R_L^2}{(R_L + R_S)^2 V_L^2}$$

$$= \left(\frac{R_L}{R_L + R_S}\right)^2 \left[\frac{Vs(j\omega)}{V_L(j\omega)}\right]^2 \quad \text{...(14.110)}$$

$$= \frac{4R_L R_S}{(R_L + R_S)^2} \cdot \frac{1}{|t(j\omega)|^2} \quad \text{...(14.111)}$$

The insertion loss is more commonly expressed in decibels. Thus

$$\alpha = 10 \log \frac{P_{L_0}}{P_L} \text{ dB} \quad \text{...(14.112)}$$

$$= 20 \log \left(\frac{R_L}{R_L + R_S}\right)\left(\frac{V_S}{V_L}\right) \text{dB} \quad \text{...(14.113)}$$

Sometimes a gain in power may result due to insertion of a network. This may then be regarded as a negative insertion loss.

Problem 14.8. *The given figure shows a voltage source 10 sin t with resistance 2 Ω feeding a load of 1 Ω resistive. A network as shown is then inserted in between the source and the load. Find the insertion loss in dB.*

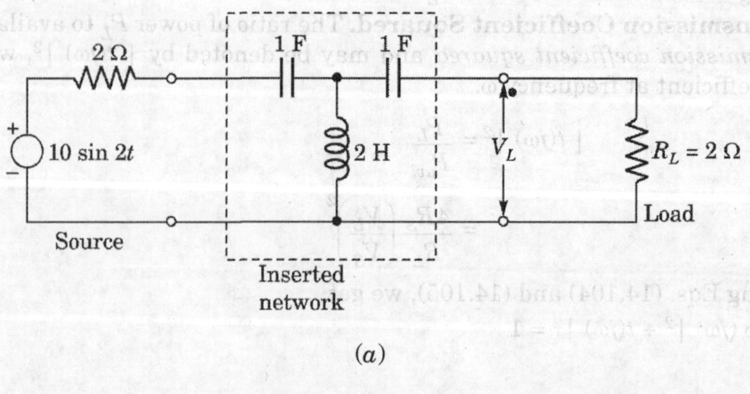

(*a*)

Solution. Fig. (*a*) shows the corresponding transform network.

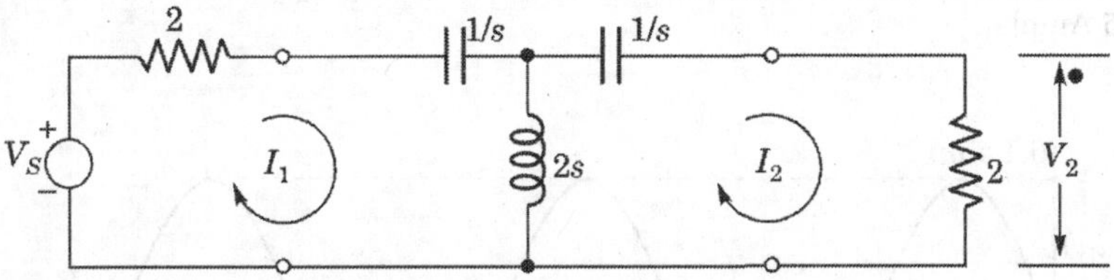

(*b*)

Then application of Kirchhoff's voltage law to the two loops yields

$$V_S = I_1\left(2 + \frac{1}{s} + 2s\right) - I_2(2s) \quad ...(1)$$

$$0 = -I_1(2s) + I_2\left(2 + \frac{1}{s} + 2s\right) \quad ...(2)$$

From Eq. (2),
$$\frac{I_1}{I_2} = \frac{2 + \frac{1}{s} + 2s}{2s} = \frac{2s^2 + 2s + 1}{2s^2} \quad ...(3)$$

Hence from Eq. (1),
$$\frac{V_S}{I_3} = \frac{2s^2 + 2s + 1}{2s^2} \times \frac{2s + 2s + 1}{s} - 2s$$

$$= \frac{(4s^2 + 2s + 1)(2s + 1)}{2s^3} \quad ...(4)$$

But
$$\frac{V_L}{I_2} = 2 \quad ...(5)$$

Hence from Eqs. (4) and (5), we get

$$\frac{V_S}{V_L} = \frac{(4s^2 + 2s + 1)(2s + 1)}{4s^2} \quad ...(6)$$

But
$$\frac{P_{L_0}}{V_L} = \left(\frac{R_L}{R_L + R}\right)^2 \cdot \left(\frac{V_S}{V_L}\right) \quad ...(7)$$

and
$$R_L = R_S = 2.$$

Hence
$$\frac{P_{L_0}}{P_L} = \frac{1}{4} \cdot \left[\frac{(-4\omega^2 + j2\omega - 1)(j2\omega + 1)}{4(j\omega)^3}\right]^2$$

$$= \frac{[(1 - 8\omega^2) + j(4\omega - 8\omega^3)]^2}{-64\omega^6}$$

Hence
$$\left|\frac{P_{L_0}}{P_L}\right| = \frac{6\omega^6 + 1}{+64\omega^2}$$

But
$$\omega = 1$$

Hence
$$\left|\frac{P_{L_0}}{P_L}\right| = \frac{65}{64}$$

Hence
$$\alpha = 10 \log^{\left|\frac{P_{L_0}}{P_L}\right|} = 10 \log^{\frac{65}{64}} = 0.103 \text{ dB}.$$

EXERCISES

14.1. Determine the r.m.s. value of current shown in the following figure produced by a halfwave rectifier. [**Ans.** 0.05 Amp]

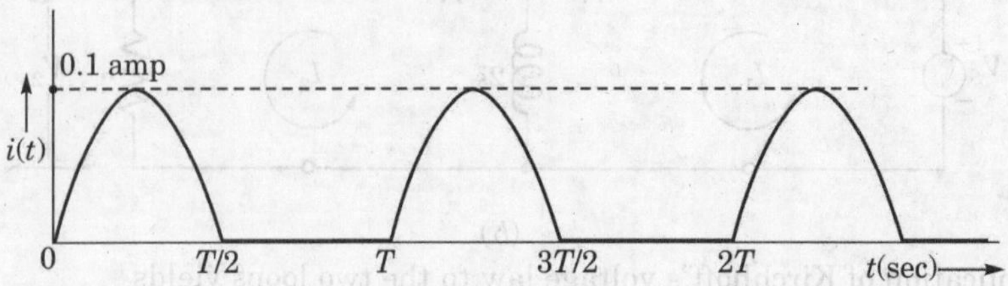

14.2. Voltage v shown in Fig. (*a*) is applied to a one-port network with reference direction as shown in Fig. 14.1. For current $i(t)$ as shown in Fig. (*b*), plot the waveform of power $p(t)$, energy $\omega(t)$ and determine the energy received by the network per cycle. Repeat the exercise for current waveforms of Figs. (*c*) and (*d*).

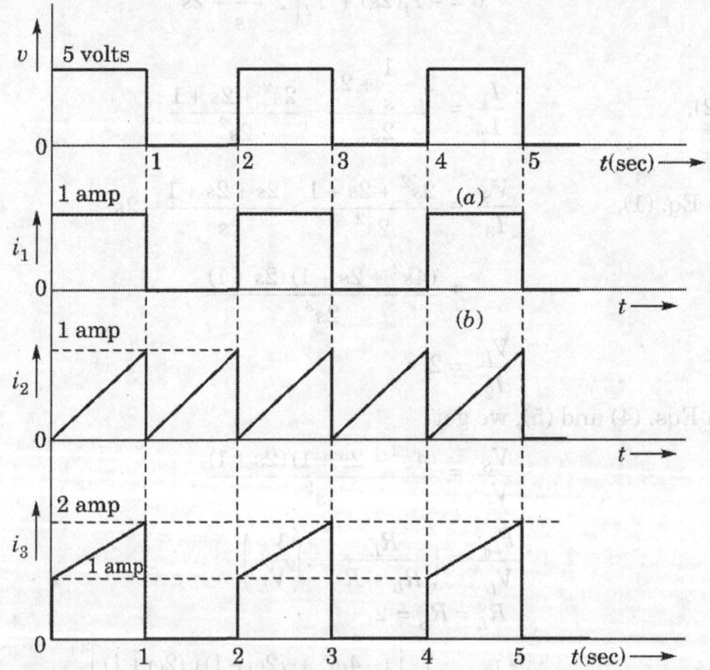

[**Ans.** 5 joules ; 2.5 joules ; 7.5 joules]

14.3. Current $i(t)$ as shown in the figure is applied to resistor $R = 5\ \Omega$. Sketch from $t = 0$ to $t = 3T$, the following quantities : (*i*) power $P_R(t)$ and (*ii*) energy $\omega_R(t)$. Calculate the energy absorbed per cycle as function of T.

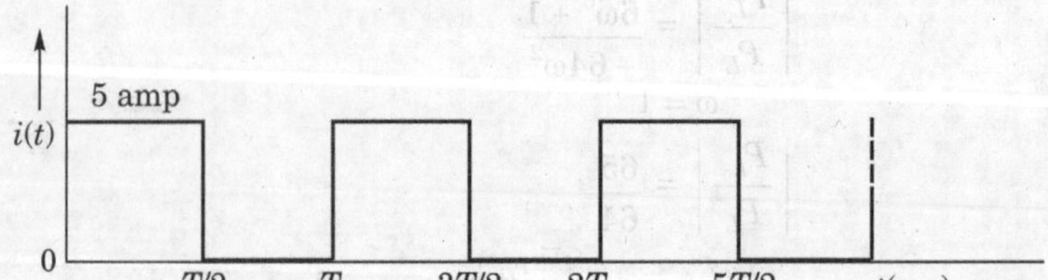

[**Ans.** 112.5 T joules]

14.4. Repeat the Exercise 14.3 if the current $i(t)$ is applied to a capacitor of 4 μF instead of resistor. Assume $v_c(0) = 0$.

$$\left[\textbf{Ans.}\ \frac{25T^2}{32 \times 10^{-6}} \text{ joules}\right]$$

14.5. Determine the r.m.s. value of $v(t)$ for the sawtooth voltage waveform shown below.

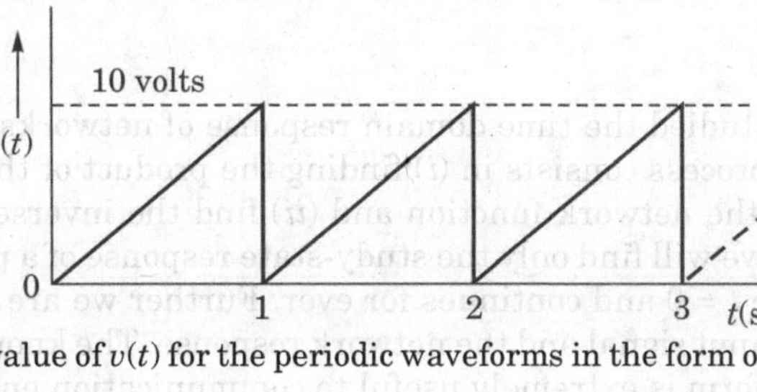

$$\left[\textbf{Ans.}\ \frac{10}{\sqrt{3}} \text{ volts}\right]$$

14.6. Determine the r.m.s. value of $v(t)$ for the periodic waveforms in the form of isosceles triangle as shown in the figure.

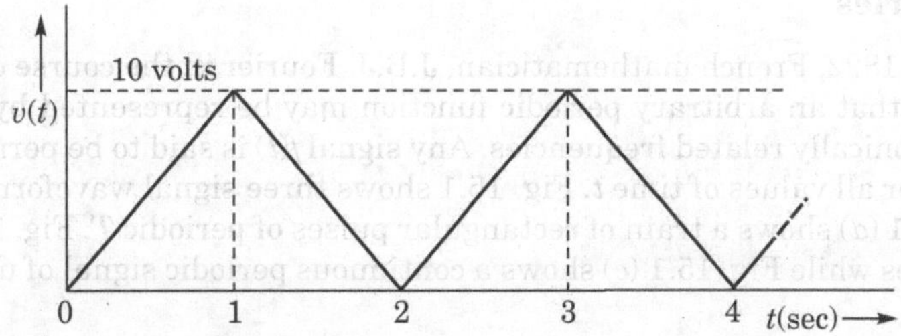

$$\left[\textbf{Ans.}\ \frac{10}{\sqrt{3}} \text{ volts}\right]$$

14.7. Determine the r.m.s. value of voltage for the periodic waveform in the form of a triangle shown below.

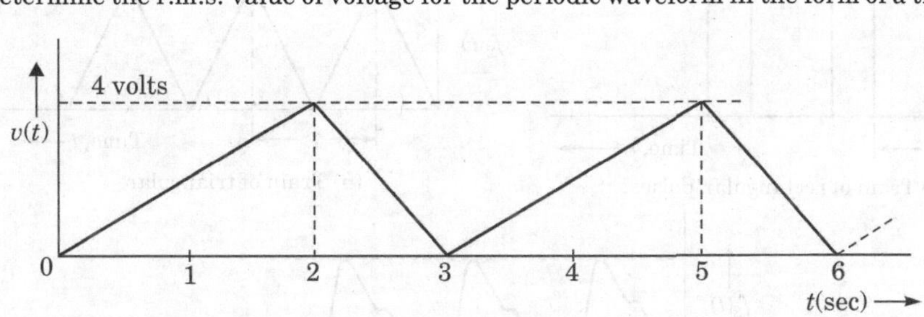

$$\left[\textbf{Ans.}\ \frac{4}{\sqrt{3}} \text{ volts}\right]$$

14.8. The voltage across a one-port network is $v = 100 \cos \omega(t)$ volts while the current in the network is $i = 4 \cos(\omega t + 45°)$ amperes. Compute, (*i*) the instantaneous power $p(t)$, (*ii*) average power p_{av} in watts, (*iii*) reactive power in vars and (*iv*) complex power S in va.

$$\left[\textbf{Ans.}\ (i)\ 200\left\{\frac{1}{\sqrt{2}} + 2 + (\cos \omega t + 45°)\right\};\ (ii)\ 141.42 \text{ watts}\right.$$

$$\left.(iii)\ 141.42 \text{ vars and } (iv)\ 200 \text{ va}\right]$$

14.9. A given load operating at 220 volts r.m.s., 50 cycles/sec. has average power p_{av} = 300 watts and reactive power Q_L = 150 vars lagging. Compute the value of capacitor C which should be connected in shunt with the load in order to improve the power factor to 0.95 lagging.

[**Ans.** 3.38 μF]

15

Fourier Series and Signal Spectrum

15.1. Introduction

We have already studied the time domain response of networks with periodic inputs using Laplace transform. The process consists in (*i*) finding the product of the Laplace transform of the input signal and that of the network function and (*ii*) find the inverse Laplace transform of this product. In this chapter, we will find only the study-state response of a periodic input which, in and ideal case, begins at time $t = 0$ and continues for ever. Further we are here interested only in the *frequency content of* the input signal and the network response. The knowledge of frequency content of a periodic signal waveform is extremely useful to communication engineers.

15.2. Fourier Series

In the year 1822, French mathematician, J.B.J. Fourier in the course of study of problem of heat flow showed that an arbitrary periodic function may be represented by an infinite series of sinusoids of harmonically related frequencies. Any signal $f(t)$ is said to be periodic with time period T if $f(t) = f(t + T)$ for all values of time t. Fig. 15.1 shows three signal waveforms which are periodic in nature. Fig. 15.1 (*a*) shows a train of rectangular pulses of periodic T. Fig. 15.1 (*b*) shows a train of triangular pulses while Fig. 15.1 (*c*) shows a continuous periodic signal of unrecognizable shape.

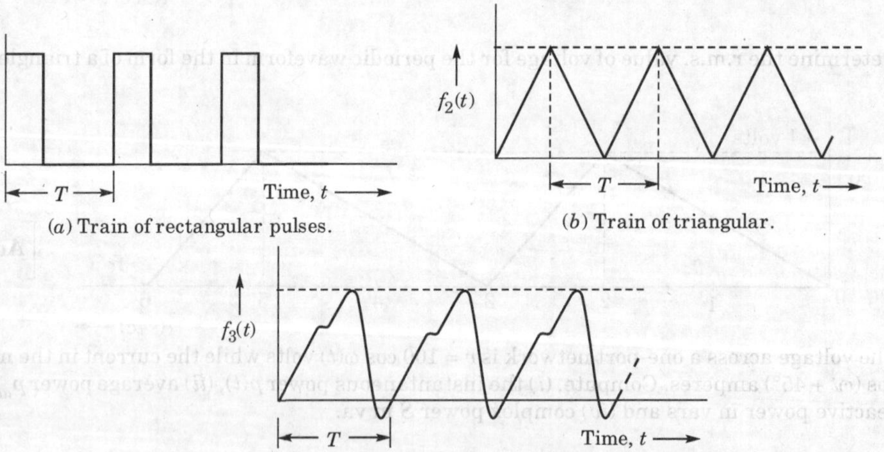

(*a*) Train of rectangular pulses. (*b*) Train of triangular. (*c*) Continuous periodic signal of unrecognisable shape.

Fig. 15.1 Three periodic wave forms each of periodic time T.

Any periodic function $f(t)$ may be described by the following Fourier series :

$$f(t) = a_0 + a_1 \cos \omega t + a_2 \cos 2\omega t + \ldots\ldots + a_n \cos n\omega t + \ldots\ldots$$
$$+ b_1 \sin \omega t + b_2 \sin 2\omega t + \ldots\ldots + b_n \sin n\omega t + \ldots\ldots \quad \ldots(15.1)$$

where ω_0 is the fundamental frequency in radians/second and is given by,

$$\omega_0 = 2\pi f_0 = \frac{2\pi}{T} \quad \ldots(15.2)$$

where f_0 is the fundamental frequency in cycles/sec. and equals $1/T$.

The frequency $n\omega_0$ is referred to as the nth harmonic of the fundamental frequency ω_0. Putting $n = 0, 1, 2, 3$ etc., we may state that any periodic function may be described in terms of components of frequency f_0, its second harmonic, third harmonic etc. Coefficients a_1, a_2 and b_1, b_2 ...... are called the Fourier coefficients.

It may be readily seen that summation of any two terms of the Fourier series yields a periodic function.

Fourier Analysis. Fourier analysis consists in the following steps :

(*i*) determination of the values of Fourier coefficients $a_0, a_1, a_2, ..., b_1, b_2, ...$

and (*ii*) deciding sum numbers of terms in the Fourier series to be included in what may be called *truncated Fourier series*, such that this truncated Fourier series still represents the function with adequate accuracy.

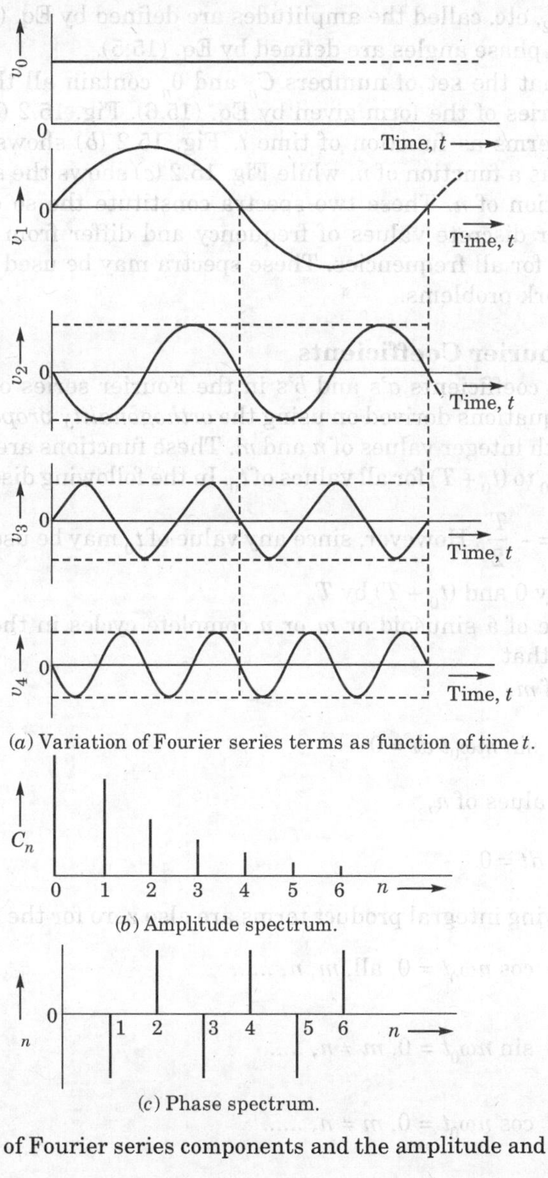

(*a*) Variation of Fourier series terms as function of time t.

(*b*) Amplitude spectrum.

(*c*) Phase spectrum.

Fig. 15.2. Plots of Fourier series components and the amplitude and phase spectra.

In case, the series converges rapidly, we need include only a few terms.

Alternative Form of Fourier Series. We now proceed to rewrite the Fourier series as given by Eq. (15.1) in an alternative form. To do so, let us consider the summation ($a_n \cos n\omega_0 t + b_n \sin n\omega_0 t$).

Let $\quad (a_n \cos n\omega_0 t + b_n \sin n\omega_0 t) = C_n \cos (n\omega_0 t + \theta_n)$ ...(15.3)

Obviously then, $$C_n = \sqrt{a_n^2 + b_n^2} \quad ...(15.4)$$

and $$\theta_n = -\tan^{-1} \frac{b_n}{a_n} \quad ...(15.5)$$

Then combining pairs of terms in Eq. (15.1) we may rewrite Eq. (15.1) in the following form :

$$f(t) = C_0 + C_1 \cos (\omega_0 + \theta_1) + C_2 \cos (2\omega_0 t + \theta_2) + \ldots\ldots + C_n \cos (n\omega_0 t + \theta_n) + \ldots \quad ...(15.6)$$

where $\quad C_0 = a_0$.

Coefficients C_1, C_2, etc. called the amplitudes are defined by Eq. (15.4) and θ_1, θ_2, etc. called the phase angles are defined by Eq. (15.5).

It may be seen that the set of numbers C_n and θ_n contain all the information needed to construct the Fourier series of the form given by Eq. (15.6). Fig. 15.2 (*a*) shows the variation of various Fourier series terms as function of time *t*. Fig. 15.2 (*b*) shows the so-called amplitude spectrum, *i.e.* plot of C_n as a function of *n,* while Fig. 15.2 (*c*) shows the so-called phase spectrum, *i.e.* plot of θ_n, as a function of *n*. These two spectra constitute the so called the line spectra of discrete spectra valid for discrete values of frequency and differ from the so called continuous spectra which is defined for all frequencies. These spectra may be used for signal representation and for solution of network problems.

15.3. Evaluation of Fourier Coefficients

Evaluation of the coefficients *a*'s and *b*'s in the Fourier series of Eq. (15.1) may be done making use of integral equations derived on using the *orthogonality property* of the set of functions $\cos n\omega_0 t$ and $\sin m\omega_0 t$ with integer values of *n* and *m*. These functions are orthogonal over the time interval extending from t_0 to $(t_0 + T)$ for all values of t_0. In the following discussion we will frequently use the value $t_0 = 0$ or $t_0 = -\dfrac{T}{2}$. However, since any value of t_0 may be used, we may for the sake of convenience, replace t_0 by 0 and $(t_0 + T)$ by T.

The average value of a sinusoid or *m* or *n* complete cycles in the periodic time *T* is zero. Hence we may conclude that

(*i*) for all values of *m*,

$$\int_0^T \sin m\omega_0 t \, dt = 0 \quad ...(15.7)$$

and (*ii*) for all non-zero values of *n*,

$$\int_0^T \cos n\omega_0 t \, dt = 0 \quad ...(15.8)$$

Further the following integral product terms are also zero for the stated values of *m* and *n* :

$$\int_0^T \sin m\omega_0 t \; \cos n\omega_0 t = 0, \text{ all, } m, n, \ldots\ldots \quad ...(15.9)$$

$$\int_0^T \sin m\omega_0 t \; \sin n\omega_0 t = 0, \; m \neq n, \ldots\ldots \quad ...(15.10)$$

$$\int_0^T \cos m\omega_0 t \; \cos n\omega_0 t = 0, \; m \neq n, \ldots\ldots \quad ...(15.11)$$

However, in Eqs. (15.10) and (15.11), with $m = n$, the integrals assume non-zero values. Thus we have

$$\int_0^T \sin^2 m\omega_0 t\, dt = \frac{T}{2}, \text{ all } m, \text{......} \qquad \text{...(15.12)}$$

and

$$\int_0^T \cos^2 n\omega_0 t\, dt = \frac{T}{2}, \text{ all } n, \text{......} \qquad \text{...(15.13)}$$

The following three steps are involved in the procedure for evaluation of coefficients a's and b's.

(*i*) Multiplying both LHS and RHS of Eq. (15.1) by a suitable factor,

(*ii*) Integrating the resulting expression term by term over the time interval from 0 to T and

(*iii*) Using Eqs. (15.7) to (15.13) to evaluate the integrals. Most of these integrals are zero. Thus may we evaluate all the coefficients a's and b's.

Evaluation of a_0. Following the above procedure, let the multiplying factor be 1. Then the integral equation is,

$$\int_0^T f(t)\, dt = a_0 \int_0^T dt + \int_0^T f_1(t) dt \text{ ......} \qquad \text{...(15.14)}$$

where function $f_1(t)$ represents the summation of the remaining terms on the RHS of Eq. (15.1).

Thus

$$f(t) = \sum_{n=1}^{\infty} (a_n \cos n\omega_0 t + b_n \sin n\omega_0 t) \qquad \text{...(15.15)}$$

Now every term in the infinite summation of $f_1(t)$ on being integrated from 0 to T has zero values as per Eqs. (15.7) and (15.8). Also the first term on the right hand side of Eq. (15.14) equals $a_0 T$. Then Eq. (15.14) yields,

$$a_0 = \frac{1}{T} \int_0^T f(t)\, dt \qquad \text{...(15.16)}$$

Eq. (15.16) indicates that a_0 is nothing but the average value of $f(t)$ over a period.

Evaluation of a_n. Let the multiplying factor be cos $n\omega t$. Then Eq. (15.1) yields,

$$\int_0^T f(t) \cos n\omega_0 t\, dt = \int_0^T a_0 \cos n\omega_0 t\, dt + \int_0^T f_1(t) \cos n\omega_0 t\, dt \text{ ......} \qquad \text{...(15.17)}$$

All the terms in the right hand side of Eq. (15.17) become zero except the term of the form of Eq. (15.13), having the value $T/2$.

Hence we get the following expression for the coefficient a_n,

$$a_n = \frac{2}{T} \int_0^T f(t) \cos n\omega_0 t\, dt \qquad \text{...(15.18)}$$

Evaluation of Coefficient b_n. Let the multiplying factor be sin $n\omega_0 t$. Then Eq. (15.1) yields,

$$\int_0^T f(t) \sin \omega_0 t\, dt = \int_0^T a_0 \sin n\omega_0 t\, dt + \int_0^T f_1(t) \sin n\omega_0 t\, dt \qquad \text{...(15.19)}$$

Here again all the terms in the right hand side of Eq. (15.19) become zero except the one of the form of Eq. (15.12), having value $T/2$. Accordingly we get the following expression for the coefficient b_n,

$$b_n = \frac{2}{T}\int_0^T f(t)\sin n\omega_0 t\, dt \qquad ...(15.20)$$

Use of Eqs. (15.16), (15.18) and (15.20) enables us to evaluate all the Fourier coefficients.

Example 15.1. *Fig. Ex. 15.1 shows a square voltage signal having the following values :*

$$v(t) = \begin{cases} -V, & 0 < t < \dfrac{T}{4} \\ V, & \dfrac{T}{4} < t < \dfrac{3T}{4} \\ -V, & \dfrac{3T}{4} < t < T \end{cases}$$

Find the Fourier series for this waveform.

Solution. By inspection we see that the average value over one period is zero. Hence $a_0 = 0$. [It is not necessary to use Eq. (15.16) to evaluate a_0].

The value of coefficient a_1 may be obtained from Eq. (15.18) on putting $n = 1$. Thus, we get

$$a_1 = \frac{2}{T}\left[-V\int_0^{T/4}\cos\omega_0 t\, dt + V\int_{T/4}^{3T/4}\cos\omega_0 t\, dt - V\int_{3T/4}^{T}\cos\omega_0 t\, dt\right] \qquad ...(i)$$

$$= \frac{2V}{\omega_0 T}\left[-\sin\frac{\omega_0 T}{T} + \left(\sin\frac{3\omega_0 T}{4} - \sin\frac{\omega_0 T}{4}\right) - \left(\sin\omega_0 T - \sin\frac{2\omega_0 T}{4}\right)\right] \qquad ...(ii)$$

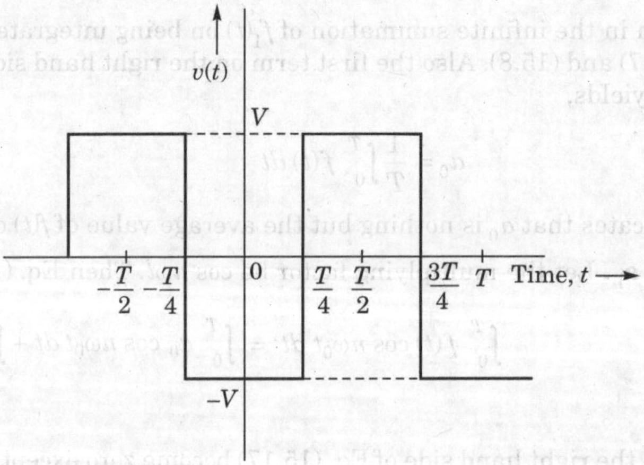

Fig. (Ex. 15.1). A square wave or rectangular wave of amplitude $2V$ and period $T = \dfrac{2\pi}{\omega_0}$.

But $\omega_0 T = 2\pi$. Hence Eq. (*ii*) yields,

$$a_1 = \frac{V}{\pi}[-1-2-1] = \frac{-4V}{\pi} \qquad ...(iii)$$

Applying this procedure for all values of n, we get

$$a_n = \begin{cases} \dfrac{-4V}{n\pi}, & n = 1, 5, 9 \\ \dfrac{4V}{n\pi}, & n = 3, 7, 11 \\ 0, & n = \text{even integers} \end{cases} \qquad ...(iv)$$

Similarly making use of Eq. (15.20), we find that

$$b_n = 0, \text{ all } n \qquad ...(v)$$

Hence the Fourier series is,

$$v(t) = -\frac{4V}{\pi}\left[\cot \omega_0 t - \frac{1}{3}\cos 3\omega_0 t + \frac{1}{5}\cos 5\omega_0 t - \frac{1}{7}\cos 7\omega_0 t + ...\right] \qquad ...(vi)$$

From Eq. (*iv*) we find that Fourier coefficients a_2, a_4, a_6, etc., are all zero. From Eq. (*v*) we observe that all b coefficients are also zero. Thus we find that for the given periodic square wave, most of the Fourier coefficients are zero. This results, as we will see later on, from certain symmetries in the signal waveform. Figs. (*b*) and (*c*) show the spectrum respectively for the given square waveform.

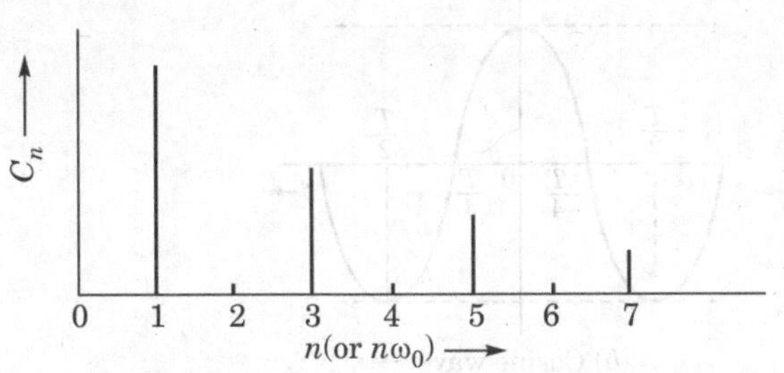

Fig. (*b*) (Ex. 15.1). Amplitude spectrum.

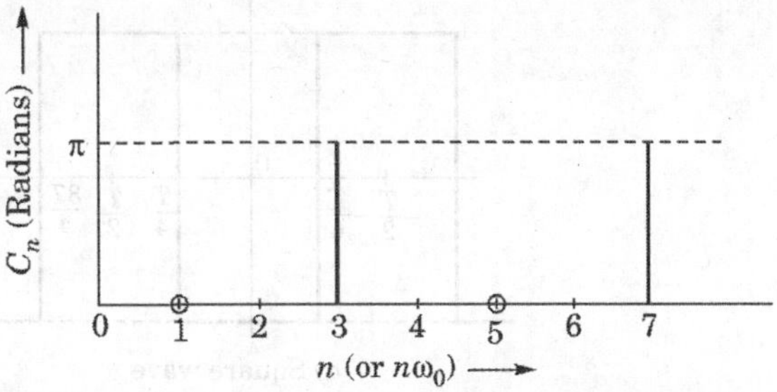

Fig. (*c*) (Ex. 15.1). Frequency spectrum.

15.4. Use of Fourier Series in Network Analysis

Any periodic signal may be expressed in the form of a Fourier series. Hence the response of a given network to the given periodic signal is the same as the summation of responses to the Fourier series components of the signals. Thus consider the periodic signal of Example 15.1. Fig. 15.3 (*a*) shows this square wave periodic signal applied to a network. Fig. 15.3 (*b*) shows n sinusoidal voltage sources in series, each having amplitude given by Fourier coefficients and each of frequency $n\omega_0$, where n is an integer. These sinusoidal sources may replace the square wave signal source of Fig. 15.3 (*a*). The total response of the given network to these n sinusoidal sources may be determined by superposition.

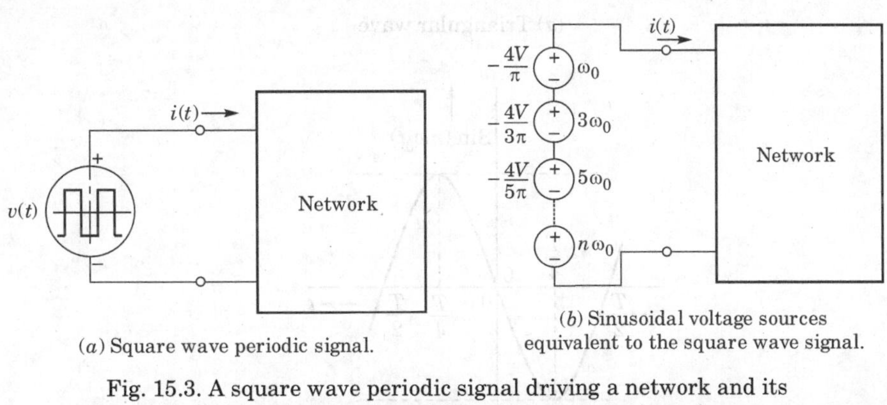

(*a*) Square wave periodic signal.

(*b*) Sinusoidal voltage sources equivalent to the square wave signal.

Fig. 15.3. A square wave periodic signal driving a network and its Fourier equivalent sinusoidal voltage sources in series.

15.5. Waveform Symmetries as related to Fourier Coefficients

Ordinarily all the Fourier coefficients of a periodic wave have to be evaluated making use of Eqs. (15.16), (15.18) and (15.20). However, in most cases, it becomes possible to adopt certain short cuts and thereby simplify evaluation of Fourier coefficients.

Even Functions. Let there be a function $f(t)$ such that,

$$f(t) = f(-t) \qquad \text{...(15.21)}$$

A function satisfying Eq. (15.21) is said to be an *even function.* Evident in Fourier series, constant a_0 and functions $\cos n\omega_0 t$ constitute even functions. Other examples of even functions are $|\sin t|$, t^n for even values of n, square wave of Fig. 15.4 (*a*).

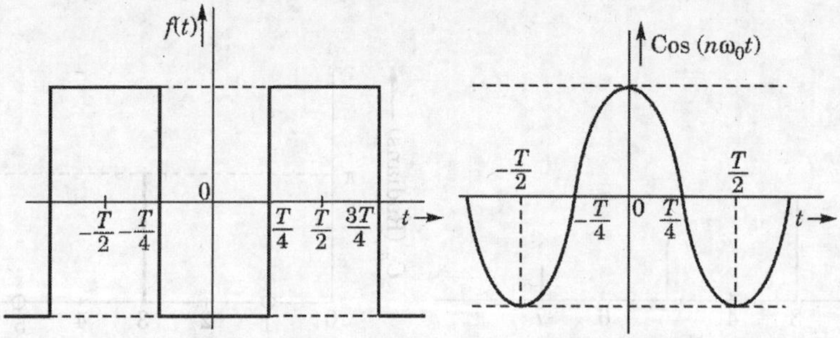

(*a*) Square wave (*b*) Cosine wave

Fig. 15.4. Examples of even functions.

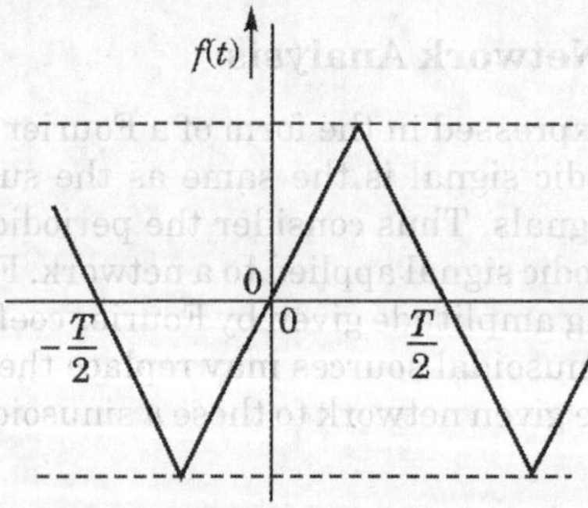

(*a*) Triangular wave

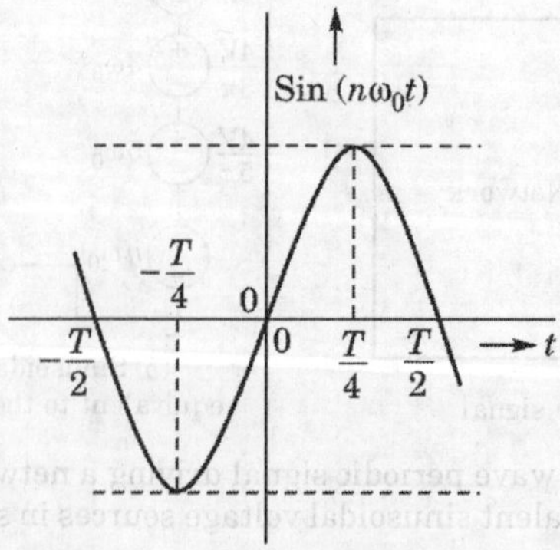

(*b*) Sine wave

Fig. 15.5. Examples of odd functions.

Odd Functions. Let there be a function $f(t)$ such that,

$$f(t) = -f(-t) \qquad ...(15.22)$$

A function satisfying Eq. (15.22) is said to be an *odd function*. Typical examples of odd functions are $\sin n\omega_0 t$, t^n for n odd. Fig. 15.5 shows two odd functions.

Summation of Even and Odd Functions. The sum of a number of even functions is even and likewise the sum of a number of odd functions is odd. Thus, we write

Sum of even functions = even function ...(15.23)

Sum of odd functions = odd function ...(15.24)

Next if an odd function is added to an even function, the resultant is neither fully even nor fully odd and may be said to contain an even function component and an odd function component.

Thus the sum of even functions and odd functions may be expressed as,

$$f(t) = f_e(t) + f_0(t) \qquad ...(15.25)$$

where

$$f_e(t) = Ev\ f(t) \qquad ...(15.26)$$

and

$$f_0(t) = Od\ f(t) \qquad ...(15.27)$$

From Eq. (15.25),

$$f(-t) = f_e(-t) + f_0(-t) \qquad ...(15.28)$$

$$= f_e(t) - f_0(t) \qquad ...(15.29)$$

Adding Eq. (15.29) to Eq. (15.25), we get

$$f_e(t) = \frac{1}{2}\,[f(t) + f(-t)] \qquad ...(15.30)$$

Subtracting Eq. (15.29) from Eq. (15.25), we get

$$f_0(t) = \frac{1}{2}\,[f(t) - f(-t)] \qquad ...(15.31)$$

We have so far, in this article, obtained several useful results which we now apply to the equations giving the Fourier coefficients. We are here basically interested in comparing $f(t)$ and $f(-t)$. Hence, we choose the interval of integration as extending from $-T/2$ to $+T/2$ corresponding to $t_0 = -T/2$. Accordingly Eq. (15.18) giving the Fourier coefficient a_n may be written as,

$$a_n = \frac{2}{T}\left[\int_{-T/2}^{+T/2} f_e \cos n\omega_0 t\,dt + \int_{-T/2}^{+T/2} f_0 \cos n\omega_0 t\,dt\right] \qquad ...(15.32)$$

Similarly Eq. (15.32) giving the Fourier coefficient b_n may be written as,

$$b_n = \frac{2}{T}\left[\int_{-T/2}^{T/2} f_e \sin n\omega_0 t\,dt + \int_{-T/2}^{T/2} f_0 \sin n\omega_0 t\,dt\right] \qquad ...(15.33)$$

Eqs. (15.32) and (15.33) involve function product. It becomes necessary, therefore, to study and use the following relations :

Odd function × Odd function = Even function ...(15.34)

Even function × Even function = Even function ...(15.35)

Even function × Odd function = Odd function ...(15.36)

Further for any even function f_0,

$$\int_{-t_0}^{t_0} f_e(t)\,dt = 2\int_0^{t_0} f_0(t)\,dt \quad ...(15.37)$$

and for any odd function f_0,

$$\int_{-t_0}^{t_0} f_0(t)\,dt = 0 \quad ...(15.38)$$

where t_0 may have any value.

In the light of the above results, we now study various important symmetries possible in periodic functions.

(I) Even Functions f(t). For any even function $f(t)$, the odd part f_0 is zero. Hence the second term in the right hand side of Eq. (15.33) becomes zero. Further as per Eq. (15.36), the integrand in the first term in the right hand side of Eq. (15.33) is an odd function. Hence as per Eq. (15.38), this first term also becomes zero. Thus $b_n = 0$.

Similarly in Eq. (15.32), the second term on the right hand side becomes zero. Hence Eq. (15.32) yields,

$$a_n = \frac{2}{T}\int_{-T/2}^{T/2} f(t)\cos n\omega_0 t\,dt \quad ...(15.39)$$

The product $f(t)\cos n\omega_0 t$ is even function as per Eq. (15.35). Hence as per Eq. (15.37),

$$a_n = \frac{4}{T}\int_0^{T/2} f(t)\cos n\omega_0 t\,dt \quad ...(15.40)$$

Similarly, $$a_0 = \frac{2}{T}\int_0^{T/2} f(t)\,dt \quad ...(15.41)$$

From the above discussion, we conclude that the *Fourier series expansion of an even periodic function contains only cosine terms and a constant.*

(II) Odd Function f(t). For an odd function $f(t)$, $f_e = 0$. Hence the first term in RHS of Eq. (15.32) becomes zero. Also the product $f_0 \cos n\omega_0 t$ forms an odd function, so that as per Eq. (15.38), the second term in the RHS of Eq. (15.32) also becomes zero. Hence $a_n = 0$. Similarly $a_n = 0$.

Finally in Eq. (15.33), the first term on the RHS becomes zero. Hence Eq. (15.33) yields,

$$b_n = \frac{2}{T}\int_{-T/2}^{T/2} f(t)\sin n\omega_0 t\,dt \quad ...(15.42)$$

The integrand $f(t)\sin n\omega_0 t$, being the product of two odd functions, forms an even function. Hence as per Eq. (15.37),

$$b_n = \frac{4}{T}\int_0^{T/2} f(t)\sin n\omega_0 t\,dt \quad ...(15.43)$$

Hence we conclude that the *Fourier series expansion of an odd periodic functions contains only sine terms.*

(III) Halfwave Symmetry. A function having halfwave symmetry is given by,

$$f(t) = -f\left(t \pm \frac{T}{2}\right) \quad ...(15.44)$$

Fig. 15.6 shows that functions possessing halfwave symmetry. In each case, the waveform extending for time interval from say $-\frac{T}{2}$ to 0 is negative of the waveform extending from 0 to $\frac{T}{2}$. Obviously this

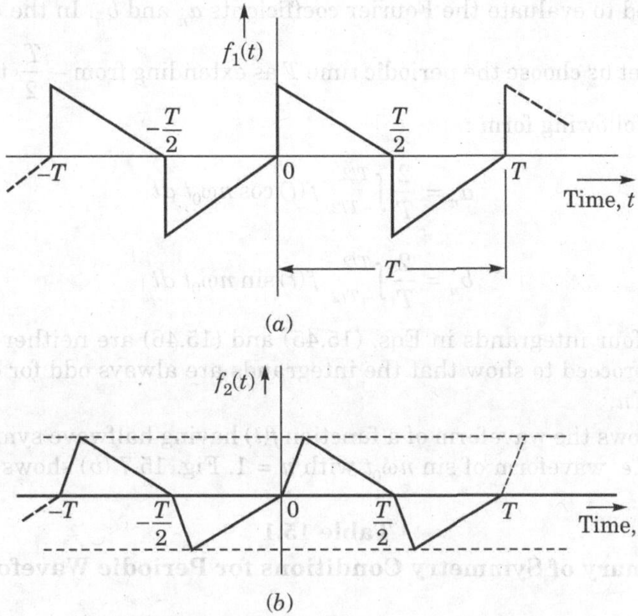

Fig. 15.6. Examples of halfwave symmetry functions.

function is neither even nor odd and thus is formed by an even function and an odd function.

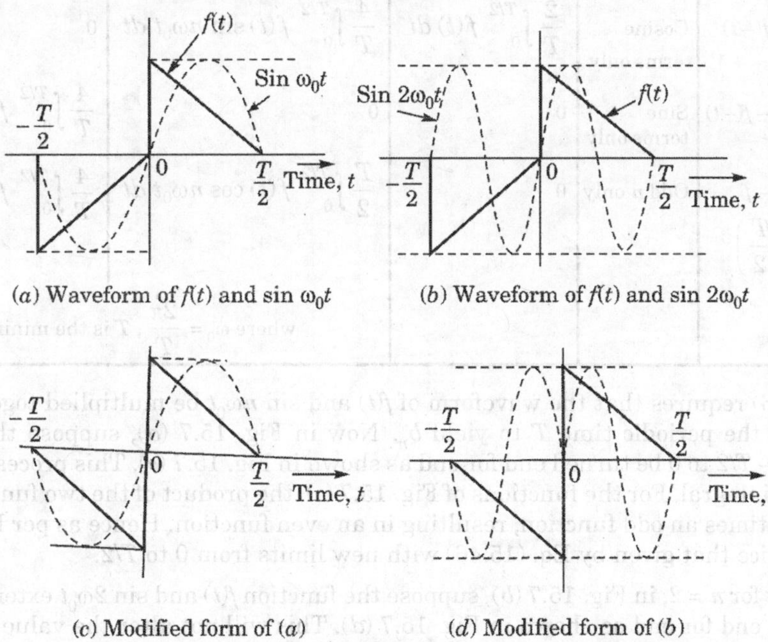

Fig. 15.7. Graphical proof of the conclusion that a periodic function with halfwave symmetry contains only odd harmonics.

Now we proceed to evaluate the Fourier coefficients a_n and b_n. In the case of function with halfwave symmetry, let us choose the periodic time T as extending from $-\dfrac{T}{2}$ to $+\dfrac{T}{2}$. Hence a_n and b_n may be put in the following form :

$$a_n = \frac{2}{T}\int_{-T/2}^{T/2} f(t)\cos n\omega_0 t\,dt \qquad \text{...(15.45)}$$

$$b_n = \frac{2}{T}\int_{-T/2}^{T/2} f(t)\sin n\omega_0 t\,dt \qquad \text{...(15.46)}$$

Evidently the four integrands in Eqs. (15.45) and (15.46) are neither odd nor even for all values of n. We now proceed to show that the integrands are always odd for even values of n and even for odd values of n.

Fig. 15.7 (a) shows the waveform of a function $f(t)$ having halfwave symmetry. It also shows waveform of sin $\omega_0 t$, *i.e.* waveform of sin $n\omega_0 t$ with $n = 1$. Fig. 15.7 (b) shows the waveform of sin $n\omega_0 t$ with

Table 15.1

Summary of Symmetry Conditions for Periodic Waveforms

Nature of Symmetry	*Condition*	*Property*	a_0	$a_n (n \neq 0)$	b_n
Even	$f(t) = f(-t)$	Cosine terms only	$\frac{2}{T}\int_0^{T/2} f(t)\,dt$	$\frac{4}{T}\int_0^{T/2} f(t)\sin n\omega_0 t\,dt$	0
Odd	$f(t) = -f(-t)$	Sine terms only	0	0	$\frac{4}{T}\int_0^{T/2} f(t)\sin n\omega_0 t\,dt$
Halfwave Symmetry	$f(t) = -f\left(t = \frac{T}{2}\right)$	Odd n only	0	$\frac{T}{2}\int_0^{T/2} f(t)\cos n\omega_0 t\,dt$	$\frac{4}{T}\int_0^{T/2} f(t)\sin n\omega_0 t\,dt$

where $\omega_0 = \dfrac{2\pi}{T}$, T is the minimum period.

$n = 2$. Eq. (15.46) requires that the waveform of $f(t)$ and sin $n\omega_0 t$ be multiplied together and then integrated over the periodic time T to yield b_n. Now in Fig. 15.7 (a), suppose the function $f(t)$ extending from $-T/2$ to 0 be turned end for end as shown in Fig. 15.7 (c). This process will not alter the value of the integral. For the functions of Fig. 15.7 (c), the product of the two functions signifies an odd function times an odd function, resulting in an even function. Hence as per Eq. (15.37), the value of b_1 is twice that given by Eq. (15.46) with new limits from 0 to $T/2$.

Similarly for $n = 2$, in Fig. 15.7 (b), suppose the function $f(t)$ and sin $2\omega_0 t$ extending from $-T/2$ to 0 be turned end for end as shown in Fig. 15.7 (d). This will not alter the value of the integral given by Eq. (15.46). For the two functions shown in Fig. 15.7 (d) the product of these two functions signifies an even function times an odd function, resulting in an odd function. Hence as per Eq. (15.38), the value of this integral is zero.

This method may be repeated for all higher values of n and also to Eq. (15.45), giving the following results :

$$a_0 = 1,\ a_n = 0,\ b_n = 0, \ldots n \text{ even} \qquad \ldots(15.47)$$

$$a_n = \frac{4}{T}\int_0^{T/2} f(t)\cos n\omega_0 t\, dt \ldots n \text{ odd} \qquad \ldots(15.48)$$

$$b_n = \frac{4}{T}\int_0^{T/2} f(t)\sin n\omega_0 t\, dt \ldots n \text{ odd} \qquad \ldots(15.49)$$

We may thus summarize that the *Fourier series expansion of a periodic function with halfwave symmetry contains only odd harmonics.*

Table 15.1 summarizes the symmetry conditions for periodic waveforms.

Example 15.2. *Obtain Fourier series expansion of the periodic triangular waveform shown in Fig. Ex. 15.2.*

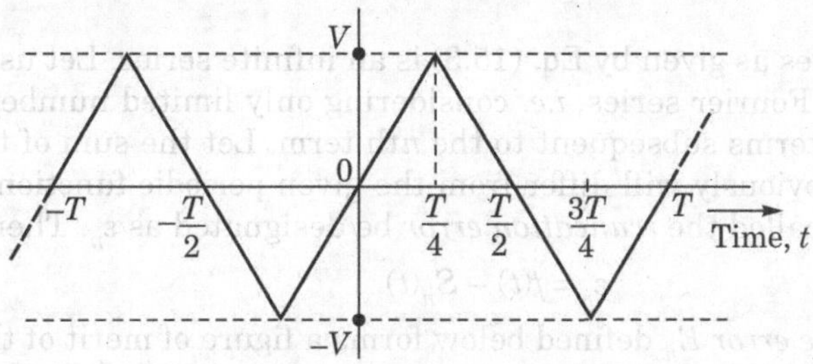

Fig. Example 15.2.

Solution. Obviously this waveform is an odd function so that the symmetry conditions require that $a_0 = 0$ and $a_n = 0$. The b coefficients have to be evaluated. The function may be expressed as below :

$$v(t) = \begin{cases} \dfrac{4VT}{T}, & 0 < t < \dfrac{T}{4} \\ 2V - \dfrac{4VT}{T}, & \dfrac{T}{4} < t < \dfrac{3T}{4} \end{cases}$$

Hence as per Eq. (15.43), $\quad b_n = \dfrac{4}{T}\displaystyle\int_0^{T/2} f(t)\sin \omega_0 t\, dt$

For $n = 1$,

$$b_1 = \frac{4}{T}\left[\int_0^{T/2} \frac{4VT}{T}\sin \omega_0 t\, dt + \int_{T/4}^{T/2}\left(2V - \frac{4Vt}{T}\right)\sin \omega_0 t\, dt\right]$$

On integration, we get $\quad b_1 = \dfrac{8V}{\pi^2}$

Similarly by putting $n = 3, 5$, etc., we get

$$b_3 = \frac{8V}{\pi^2 3^2},\ b_5 = \frac{8V}{\pi^2 5^2} \text{ etc.}$$

Hence the Fourier series expansion is,

$$v(t) = \frac{8V}{\pi^2}\left(\sin \omega_0 t + \frac{1}{3^2}\sin 3\omega_0 t + \frac{1}{5^2}\sin 5\omega_0 t + \ldots\ldots\right)$$

15.6. Convergence in Truncated Series

We have assumed earlier that the Fourier series given by Eq. (15.3) represents a periodic function. However, it is possible to write this Fourier series for a periodic function provided that certain conditions, called the *Dirichlet conditions* are satisfied. Mathematician Dirichlet was the first to establish these conditions and hence the name.

Dirichlet conditions require that in each period (*i*) the function should have a finite number of discontinuities (*ii*) the function should possess a finite number of maxima and minima and (*iii*) the function should be absolutely convergent, *i.e.*

$$\int_0^T |f(t)|\, dt < \infty \qquad \text{...(15.50)}$$

In the following discussion, we (*i*) assume a strong form of the Dirichlet conditions (*ii*) exclude impulse functions and derivatives of impulse functions and (*iii*) also exclude such functions as sin (1/*t*), t^2, sin (1/*t*) etc.

The Fourier series as given by Eq. (15.3) is an infinite series. Let us first study the effect of *truncating* the infinite Fourier series, *i.e.* considering only limited number of terms upto say the *n*th term and drop all terms subsequent to the *n*th term. Let the sum of this truncated series be $S_n(t)$. This sum $S_n(t)$ obviously will differ from the given periodic function $f(t)$. Let the difference between $f(t)$ and $S_n(t)$, called the *truncation error* be designated as ε_n. Then we may write,

$$\varepsilon_n = f(t) - S_n(t) \qquad \text{...(15.51)}$$

The *mean-square error* E_n defined below forms a figure of merit of the series

$$E_n = \frac{1}{T}\int_0^T [\varepsilon_n(t)]^2\, dt \qquad \text{...(15.52)}$$

The Least Square Property. The least square property of Fourier series states that the truncated Fourier series S_n minimizes the value of E_n as found from Eq. (15.52), *i.e.* no smaller mean square error E_n can be found for another series with the same number of terms. To appreciate this point, let us refer to the series of Example 15.1 as given by Eq. (*iv*). To simplify the study, let us choose $V = \pi/4$. Consider the truncated series consisting of only the first term. This is then given by,

$$S_1 = \cos \omega_0 t \qquad \text{...(15.53)}$$

Similarly the truncated series consisting of first two and the first three terms are given by

$$S_1 = \cos \omega_0 t - \frac{1}{3}\cos 3\omega_0 t \qquad \text{...(15.54)}$$

$$S_3 = \cos \omega_0 t - \frac{1}{3}\cos 3\omega_0 t + \frac{1}{5}\cos 5\omega_0 t \qquad \text{...(15.55)}$$

Let us compare this series S_3 with another series P_3 given below,

$$P_3 = c_1 \cos \omega_0 t + c_3 \cos 3\omega_o t + c_5 \cos 5\omega_0 t \qquad \text{...(15.56)}$$

Then as per least square property, we may state that there exist no values of c_1, c_3, c_5 which minimize the error better than the values given in Eq. (15.55). The same is true for series p_3 with $c_5 = 0$ when compared to S_2 or series p_2 with $c_5 = c_3 = 0$ when compared to S_1.

Thus the error, no doubt, will be minimized by using truncated Fourier series but we have no specific means of ensuring that this error becomes less than some prescribed value. We may only use trial and error method consisting in including more and more terms of the Fourier series until the desired specification regarding error is reached.

Having studied the consequence of truncating a Fourier series, we now revert to the Dirichlet conditions. These Dirichlet conditions permit a periodic function to possess a finite number of discontinuities in each time period. These discontinuities may be in the form of jumps in $f(t)$ as shown in Fig. 15.8. This is significant in network analysis since we often come across this type of function, a typical example being the square wave. Now the question arises as to what value will the complete Fourier series $f(t)$ or the truncated series $S_n(t)$ assume at the discontinuity. Let the function $f(t)$ be discontinuous at time t_1 and let the limits to the left and to the right of t_1 be $f(t-)$ and $f(t_1+)$. Then the value at $t = t_1$ is given by,

$$f(t_1) = \frac{f(t_1+) + f(t_1-)}{2} \qquad ...(15.57)$$

Eq. (15.57) may be put as,

$$f(t_1) - f(t_1-) = f(t_1+) - f(t_1) \qquad ...(15.58)$$

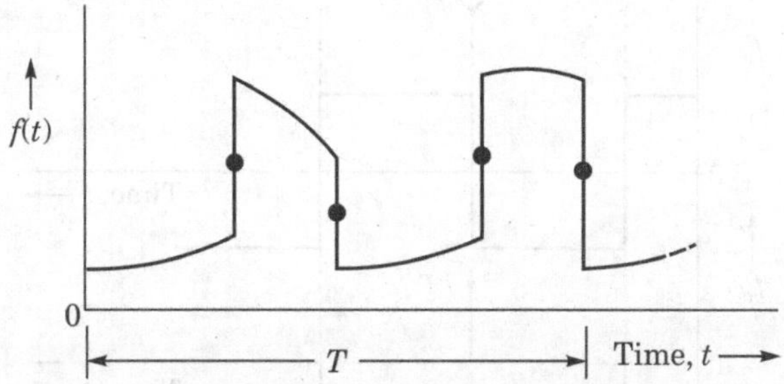

Fig. 15.8. Discontinuities *in* $f(t)$. The dots indicate the values assumed by the truncated series at the discontinuities.

Thus the series assumes a value midway between the two limiting values of the function. In Fig. 15.8 these values at the discontinuities are shown by dots.

Taking the case of truncated series, since only a limited number of terms have been included, it is natural to expect that this function $S_n(t)$ will not pass through all the three points $f(t_1-)$, $f(t_1)$ and $f(t_1+)$, a condition requiring infinite slope. Hence there results considerable error near the discontinuity. This phenomenon was first investigated by Willard Gibbs and is accordingly known as the Gibbs phenomenon.

Fig. 15.9 shows the overshoot and damped oscillatory decay characterizing Gibbs phenomenon. The overshoot is 9% of the total jump of discontinuity with $n \to \infty$, *i.e.* full Fourier series.

As *n*, the number of terms included in the truncated series increases, the frequency of oscillation increases while the decay time decreases.

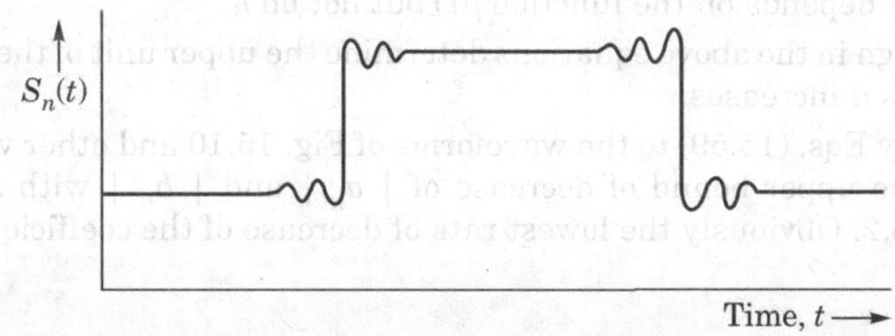

Fig. 15.9. Overshoot and oscillatory decay characterizing Gibbs phenomenon.

Let us next consider the waveforms shown in Fig. 15.10. Here function f_b is derivative of function f_a, f_c is derivative of f_b and f_d is derivative of f_c. We here study the frequency content of three of these waveforms namely f_a, f_b and f_c. By inspection we may guess that more terms in truncated Fourier series will be needed to represent function f_b than f_a and similarly function f_c than f_b. This results because of the decreasing smoothness of waveform of function f_a, f_b and f_c.

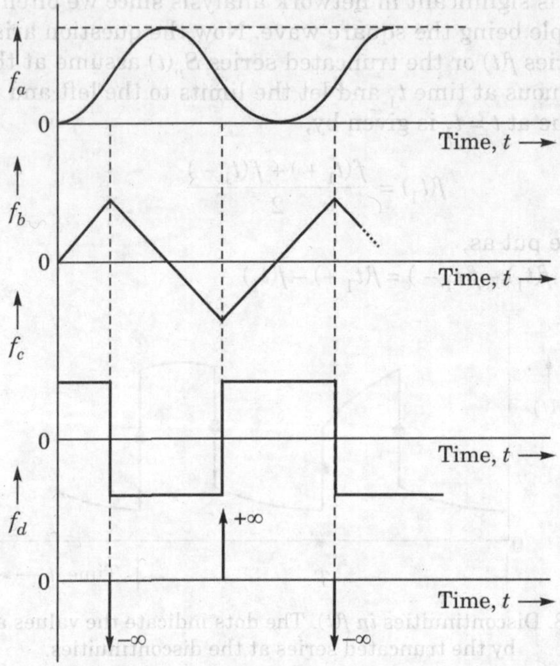

Fig. 15.10. Four waveforms obtained on progressive differentiation in going from the top to the bottom.

The manner in which the Fourier coefficients diminish with increasing n may be expressed in terms of the number of times the function may be differentiated to produce a jump discontinuity. Let the derivative so required be kth derivative. Then the following inequalities apply for Fourier coefficients a_n and b_n :

$$|a_n| \leq \frac{M}{n^{k+1}} \quad \text{...(15.59 a)}$$

$$|b_n| \leq \frac{M}{n^{k+1}} \quad \text{...(15.59 b)}$$

where the constant M depends on the function $f(t)$ but not on n.

The equality sign in the above equations determine the upper unit of the values of decreasing Fourier coefficients as n increases.

If we now apply Eqs. (15.59) to the waveforms of Fig. 15.10 and other waveforms, we arrive at laws describing the upper bound of decrease of $| a_n |$ and $| b_n |$ with n. These results are tabulated in Table 15.2. Obviously the lowest rate of decrease of the coefficients in $1/n$.

Table 15.2

Function	*Condition*		*Low describing upper bound of decrease of* $\mid a_n \mid$ *and* $\mid b_n \mid$ *with n*
	Jump in	*Impulse in*	
Square Wave	$f(t)$	$f'(t)$	$\frac{1}{n}$
Triangular	$f'(t)$	$f''(t)$	$\frac{1}{n^2}$
Parabolic Wave	$f''(t)$	$f'''(t)$	$\frac{1}{n^3}$
—	$f^{k-1}(t)$	$f^k(t)$	$\frac{1}{n^k}$

Alternatively the rate of decrease of the Fourier coefficients with n may be expressed in dB/octave by plotting $\mid a_n \mid$ or $\mid b_n \mid$ in dB against n (or $n\omega_0$) on a logarithmic scale as in Fig. 15.11. The upper bound for the slopes in the cases of square wave, triangular wave and parabolic wave of Table 15.2 are seen to be – 6, – 12 and – 18 dB/octave. Thus we may conclude that this upper bound decreases at the rate of $6(k + 1)$ dB/octave, where k is the number of times the function has to be differentiated to produce a jump discontinuity.

The above study permits us to form an idea about the magnitude spectrum for a given time domain waveform and in the reverse order, to anticipate the time domain waveform from a given magnitude spectrum. This is extremely useful to an engineer. Thus any waveform $f(t)$ containing jumps implies that its magnitude spectrum contains lines diminishing as $1/n$. Similarly a waveform in which the slope changes abruptly at one or more points in a period and with no jumps indicates that the magnitude spectrum follows at the most $\frac{1}{n^2}$ law.

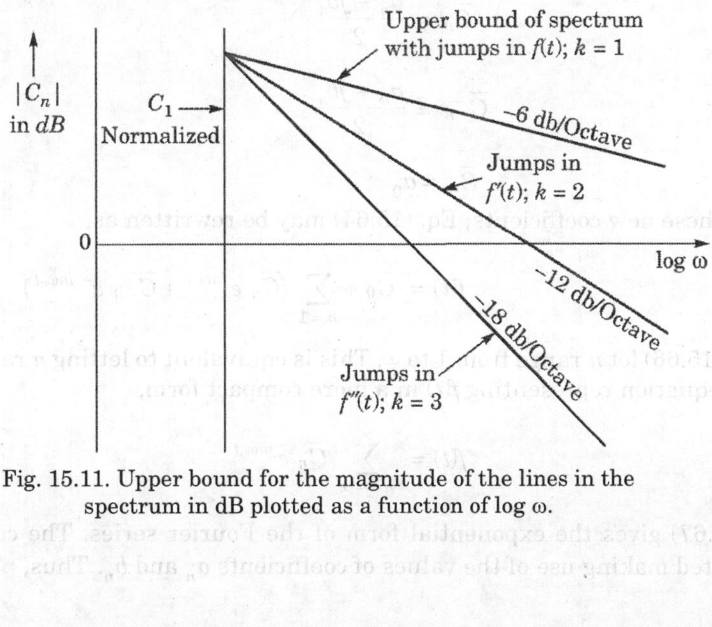

Fig. 15.11. Upper bound for the magnitude of the lines in the spectrum in dB plotted as a function of log ω.

Similarly a function with parabolic wiggles will have a magnitude spectrum following at the most $1/n^3$ law. However, as the wiggles reduced progressively, the waveform becomes more and more smooth reaching the ultimate in smoothness namely, the sinusoid itself.

15.7. Exponential Form of Fourier Series

We may express a Fourier series in the form of an exponential series. To do so we make use of the following relations :

$$\cos n\omega_0 t = \frac{1}{2}(e^{jn\omega_0 t} + e^{-jn\omega_0 t}) \quad ...(15.60)$$

$$\sin n\omega_0 t = \frac{1}{2j}(e^{jn\omega_0 t} - e^{-jn\omega_0 t}) \quad ...(15.61)$$

Let us next put the Fourier series as given by Eq. (15.1) in the following form on grouping together the sine and cosine terms,

$$f(t) = a_0 + \sum_{n=1}^{\infty} (a_n \cos n\omega_0 t + b_n \sin n\omega_0 t) \quad ...(15.62)$$

On substituting the values of $\cos n\omega_0 t$ and $\sin n\omega_0 t$ from Eq. (15.60) and (15.61) into Eq. (15.62), we get

$$f(t) = a_0 + \sum_{n=1}^{\infty} \left(a_n \frac{e^{jn\omega_0 t} + e^{-jn\omega_0 t}}{2} + b_n \frac{e^{jn\omega_0 t} - e^{-jn\omega_0 t}}{2j} \right) \quad ...(15.63)$$

On rearranging, we get $$f(t) = a_0 + \sum_{n=1}^{\infty} \left[\left(\frac{a_n - jb_n}{2} \right) e^{jn\omega_0 t} + \left(\frac{a_n + jb_n}{2} \right) e^{-jn\omega_0 t} \right] \quad ...(15.64)$$

For simplifying Eq. (15.64) we introduce the following new coefficients,

$$\overline{C}_n = \frac{a_n - jb_n}{2} \quad ...(15.65\ a)$$

$$\overline{C}_{-n} = \frac{a_n + jb_n}{2} \quad ...(15.65\ b)$$

$$\overline{C}_n = a_0 \quad ...(15.65\ c)$$

Using these new coefficients, Eq. (15.64) may be rewritten as,

$$f(t) = \overline{C}_0 + \sum_{n=1}^{\infty} (\overline{C}_n e^{jn\omega_0 t} + \overline{C}_{-n} e^{-jn\omega_0 t}) \quad ...(15.66)$$

In Eq. (15.66) let n range from 1 to ∞. This is equivalent to letting n range from $-\infty$ to $+\infty$ in the following equation representing $f(t)$ in a more compact form,

$$f(t) = \sum_{n=-\infty}^{\infty} \overline{C}_n e^{jn\omega_0 t} \quad ...(15.67)$$

Eq. (15.67) gives the exponential form of the Fourier series. The coefficient $\overline{C}_n$ may be readily evaluated making use of the values of coefficients a_n and b_n. Thus,

$$\overline{C}_n = \frac{1}{2}[a_n - jb_n] = \frac{1}{T}\int_0^T f(t)\cos n\omega_0 t\, dt$$

$$- \frac{j}{T}\int_0^T f(t)\sin n\omega_0 t\, dt \qquad ...(15.68)$$

$$= \frac{1}{T}\int_0^T f(t)(\cos n\omega_0 t - j\sin n\omega_0 t)\, dt \qquad ...(15.69)$$

$$= \frac{1}{T}\int_0^T f(t)\, e^{-jn\omega_0 t}\, dt \qquad ...(15.70)$$

Eqs. (15.68) to (15.70) apply whether n is positive, negative or zero.

In denoting these new C-coefficients, we have used tilde to distinguish between this complex $\overline{C}_n$ and the real C_n. Thus let us put,

$$\overline{C}_n = |\overline{C}_n|\, e^{j\phi n} \qquad ...[15.71\ (a)]$$

$$\overline{C}_{-n} = \overline{C}_n^{\,*} = |\overline{C}|\, e^{-j\phi n} \qquad ...[15.71\ (b)]$$

Then
$$|\overline{C}_n| = \frac{1}{2}\sqrt{a_n^2 + b_n^2} = \frac{1}{2}\, C_n \qquad ...(15.72)$$

and
$$\phi_n = \tan^{-1}\frac{b_n}{a_n} \qquad ...(15.73)$$

The above equations hold good for all values of n except $n = 0$, when

$$\overline{C}_n = a_0 \qquad ...(15.74)$$

$\overline{C}_0$ is real and forms the average or the d.c. value of $f(t)$.

We thus find that $\overline{C}_n$ differ from C_n and this accounts for the difference in the ordinary spectrum and the spectrum for the exponential form. However, the difference is simply a scale factor of 1/2 for all values of n except $n = 0$.

15.8. Steady State Response to Periodic Signals

Having expressed a periodic signal in the form of a Fourier series, we are now in position to take up the study of steady state response of a given network to a periodic signal input. The problem may be tackled by the following two methods :

(*i*) Direct Phasor Method

(*ii*) Spectrum Product Method

(*i*) **Direct Phasor Method.** We have already studied earlier the sinusoidal steady state analysis. The same method is used here, using the superposition principle.

For any given system, the phasor representing the response equals the product of the network function and the phasor representing the excitation. Thus for a given network, the response **I** is related to the excitation **V** by the following relation :

$$\mathbf{I} = Y\mathbf{V} \qquad ...(15.75)$$

This **V** may consist of a number of phasors $\mathbf{V}_1$, $\mathbf{V}_2$ etc. such that

$$\mathbf{V} = \mathbf{V}_1 + \mathbf{V}_2 + \ldots\ldots + \mathbf{V}_n \qquad ...(15.76)$$

Then the response **I** is given by,

$$\mathbf{I} = Y\mathbf{V}_1 + Y\mathbf{V}_2 + \ldots\ldots + Y\mathbf{V}_n \qquad ...(15.77)$$

The kth term of this sum may be written as,

$$\mathbf{I}_k = Y(k\omega_0)\mathbf{V}_k \qquad ...(15.78)$$

where $Y(k\omega_0)$ is the admittance at the frequency of the phasor $\mathbf{V}_k$ which is $k\omega_0$.

On transformation from the frequency domain to the time domain, we get the following expression for current i_k at time t,

$$i_k(t) = | I_k | \cos | (k\omega_0 t + \theta_k) | \quad ...(15.79)$$

The total response to the excitation **V** is the summation of the term like $i_k(t)$ given by Eq. (15.79) for all values of k. This summation gives the steady state response only. This method, in fact, consists in replacing one excitation, such as $\mathbf{V}_k$ by an infinite number of sources and then applying the principle of superposition to obtain the steady state response.

(*ii*) **Spectrum Product Method.** This method utilises the amplitude and phase spectra of the excitation, together with these spectra of the given network.

Thus we may write,

Amplitude spectrum of response = (Magnitude of network function)
× (Amplitude spectrum of excitation) ...(15.80)

and Phase spectrum of response = (Phase of network function)
× (Phase spectrum of excitation) ...(15.81)

On letting $\overline{C}_n = \mathbf{V}_n$ in Eq. (15.67), the excitation may be written as,

$$v(t) = \sum_{n=-\infty}^{\infty} \mathbf{V}_n \, e^{jn\omega_0 t} \quad ...(15.82)$$

On multiplying each $\mathbf{V}_n$ by the corresponding admittance as in Eq. (15.78), we get the following expression for the steady state response,

$$i(t) = \sum_{n=-\infty}^{\infty} Y(n\omega_0)\, \mathbf{V}_n \, e^{jn\omega_0 t} \quad ...(15.83)$$

The RHS of Eq. (15.83) may be simplified to the form of Eq. (15.79). Eq. (15.83) may be put in an alternative equivalent form in terms of the R_e (real) or I_m (imaginary) parts with n extending from 0 to ∞.

EXERCISES 15

15.1. Find the Fourier series for the function shown below and plot its frequency spectrum.

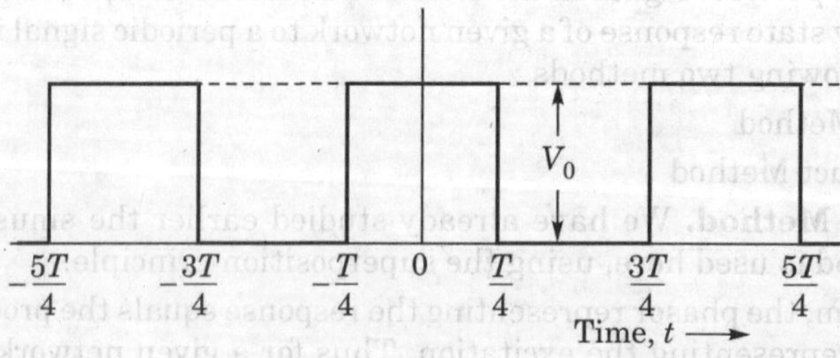

$$\left[\textbf{Ans.} \;\; v(t) = \frac{V_0}{2} + \frac{2V_0}{\pi}\left(\cos \omega_0 t - \frac{1}{3}\cos 3\omega_0 t + \frac{1}{5}\cos 5\omega_0 t \,...... \right) \right]$$

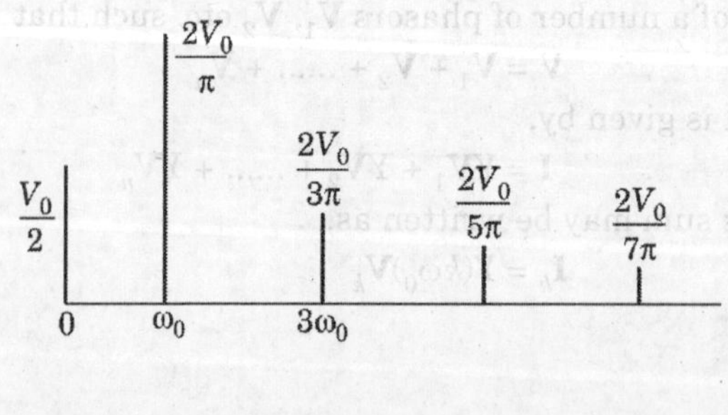

15.2. Find the Fourier series of the function shown below.

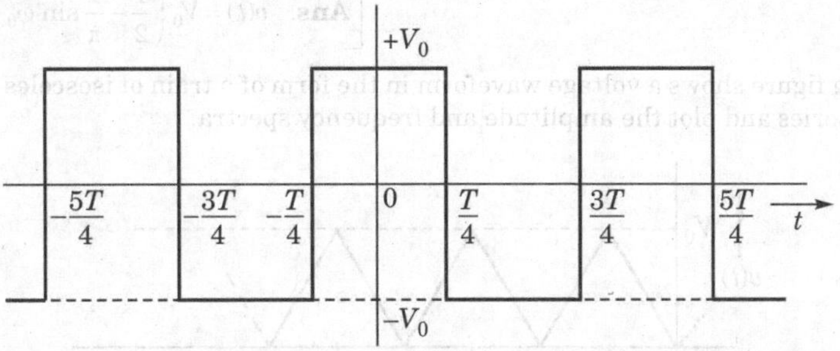

$$\left[\textbf{Ans. } v(t) = \frac{4V_0}{\pi}\left(\cos\omega_0 t - \frac{1}{3}\cos 3\omega_0 t + \frac{1}{5}\cos 5\omega_0 t - \frac{1}{7}\cos 7\omega_0 t + \ldots\ldots\right)\right]$$

15.3. Find the Fourier series for the voltage obtained at the output of a halfwave rectifier shown in the following figure. Plot the discrete spectrum of the waveform.

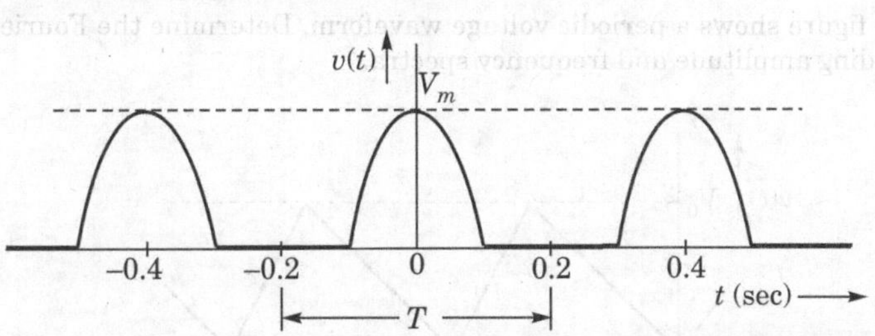

$$\left[\textbf{Ans. } v(t) = \frac{V_m}{\pi} + \frac{v_m}{\pi}\cos\omega_0 t + \frac{2V_m}{\pi}\frac{\cos n\pi t}{(1-n^2)}\cos n\omega_0 t\right.$$

where $\omega_0 = 5\pi$ radians/sec.
and n is an even integer.]

15.4. Find the Fourier series for the voltage obtained at the output of fullwave rectifier shown in the following figure :

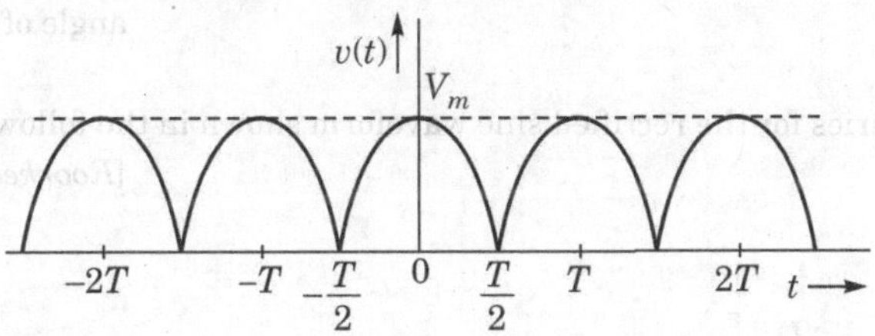

$$\left[\textbf{Ans. } v(t) = \frac{4V_m}{\pi}\left(\frac{1}{2} + \frac{1}{3}\cos\omega_0 t - \frac{1}{15}\cos 2\omega_0 t + \frac{1}{35}\cos 3\omega_0 t + \ldots\ldots\right)\right]$$

15.5. Find the Fourier coefficients and plot the amplitude and phase spectra for the voltage shown below.

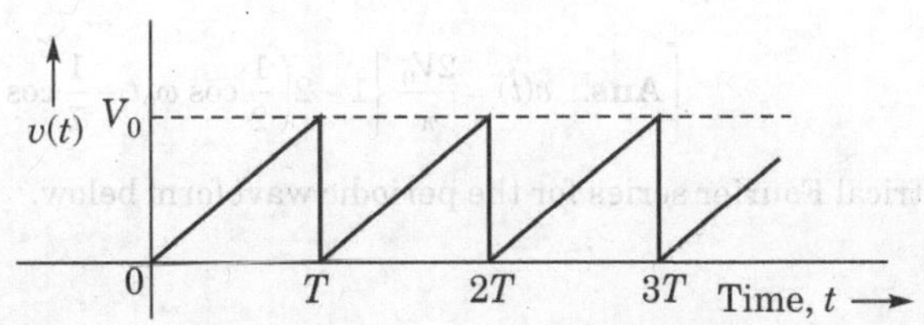

$$\left[\textbf{Ans.} \quad v(t) = V_0\left(\frac{1}{2} - \frac{1}{\pi}\sin \omega_0 + \frac{1}{2\pi}\sin 2\omega_0 t + \ldots\ldots\right)\right]$$

15.6. The following figure shows a voltage waveform in the form of a train of isosceles triangles. Determine the Fourier series and plot the amplitude and frequency spectra.

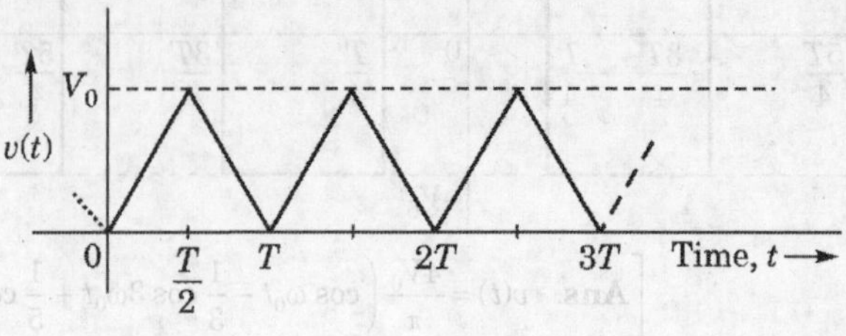

$$\left[\textbf{Ans.} \quad v(t) = \frac{V_0}{2} - \frac{4V_0}{\pi^2 n^2}\cos n\omega_0 t, n \text{ odd}\right]$$

15.7. The following figure shows a periodic voltage waveform. Determine the Fourier coefficients and plot the corresponding amplitude and frequency spectra.

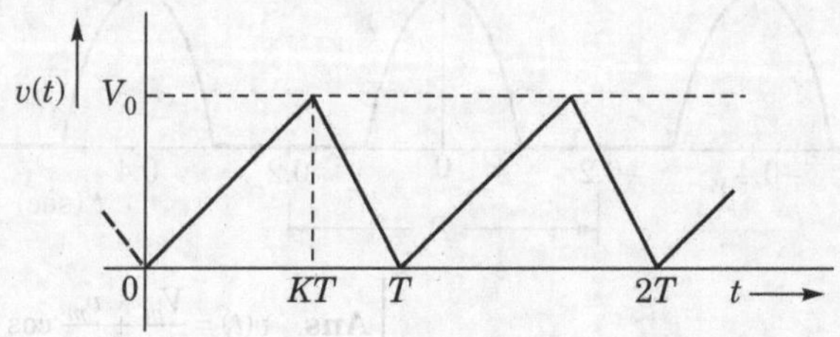

$$\left[\textbf{Ans.} \quad v(t) = |C_n| = \left\{\frac{V_e\sqrt{(1-\cos 2\pi\, nk)}}{\sqrt{2\pi^2\, n^2 k(1-k)}}\right\}\right.$$

$$\left.\text{angle of } C_n = \tan^{-1}\left\{\frac{-\sin 2\pi nk}{\cos 2\pi nk - 1}\right\}\right]$$

15.8. Find the Fourier series for the rectified sine waveform shown in the following figure.

[Roorkee BE (E and TCe) 1971, 72]

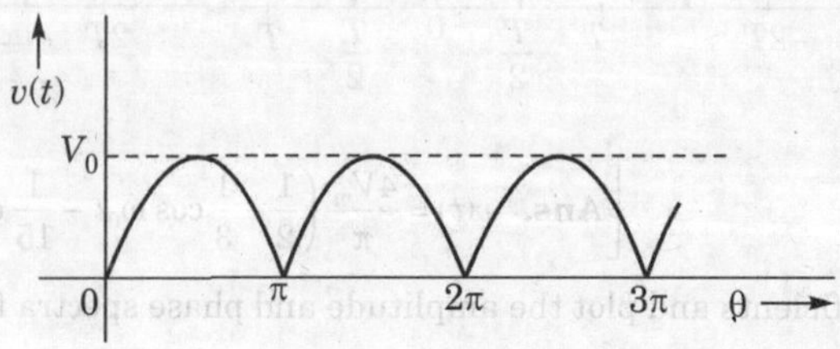

$$\left[\textbf{Ans.} \quad v(t) = \frac{2V_0}{\pi}\left\{1 - 2\left(\frac{1}{2}\cos\omega_0 t + \frac{1}{7}\cos 2\omega_0 t + \frac{1}{35}\cos 3\omega_0 t + \ldots\ldots\right)\right\}\right]$$

15.9. Find the trigonometrical Fourier series for the periodic waveform below.

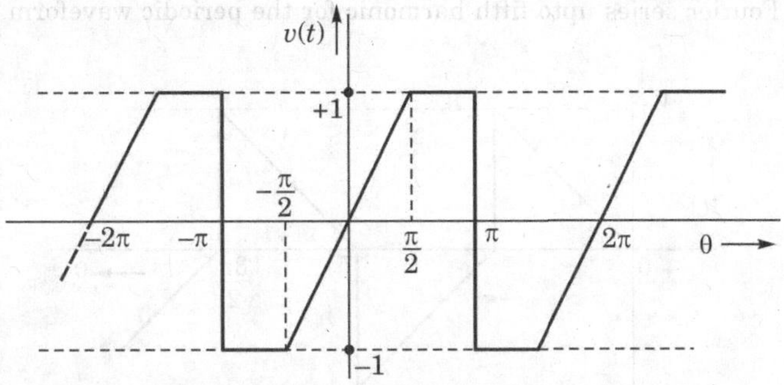

15.10. Obtain the exponential form of Fourier series for a periodic function.

(Roorkee BE 1971, 72)

15.11. Find the Fourier series for the waveform shown below.

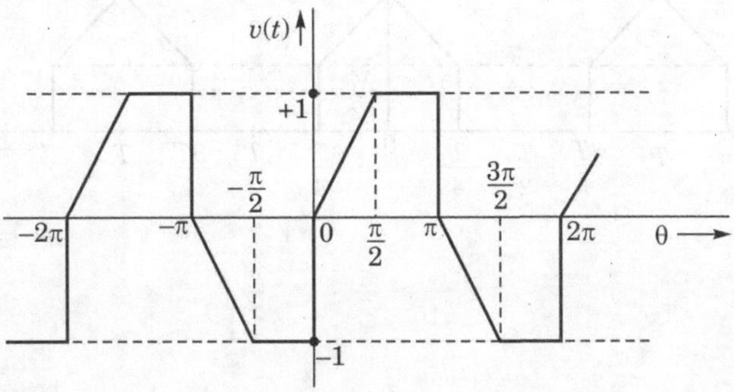

15.12. Obtain the Fourier series for the periodic triangular waveform shown below.

(U.P.S.C. Engg. Services 1975)

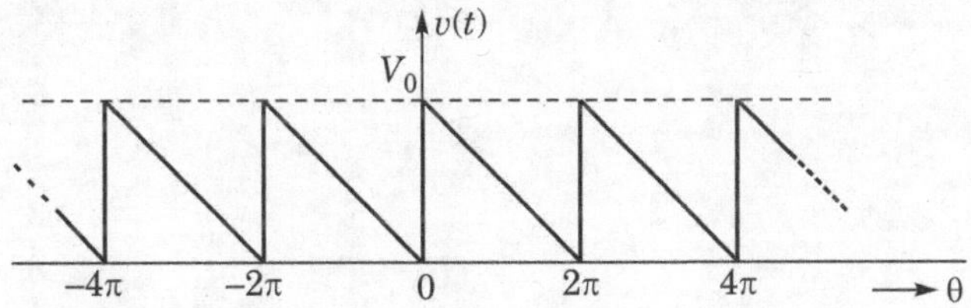

15.13. Determine the Fourier series for the following periodic waveform.

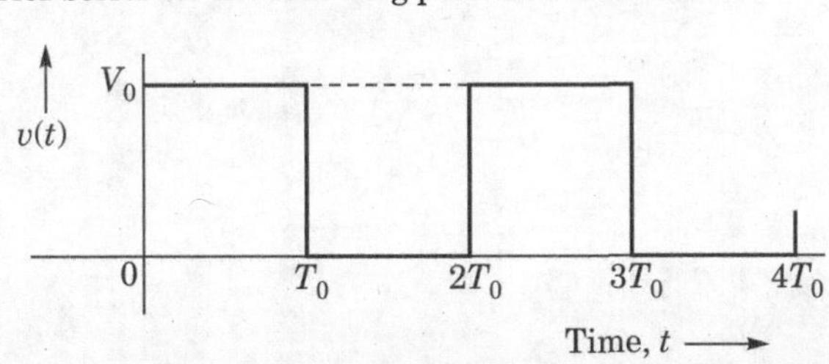

(U.P.S.C. Engg. Exam., 1975)

15.14. Determine the Fourier series upto fifth harmonic for the periodic waveform shown in the following figure.

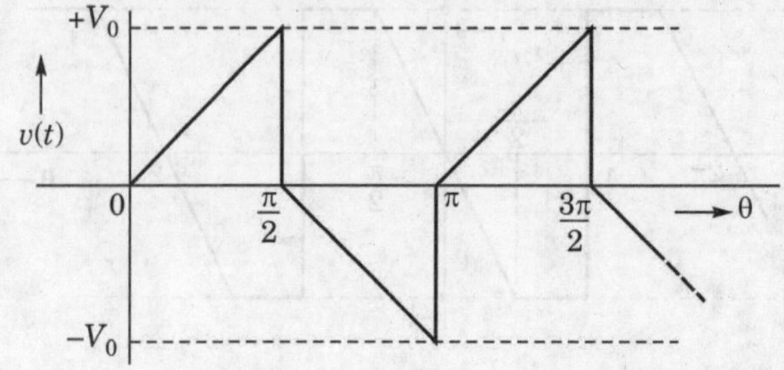

15.15. Determine the complex Fourier coefficients for the periodic function shown below.

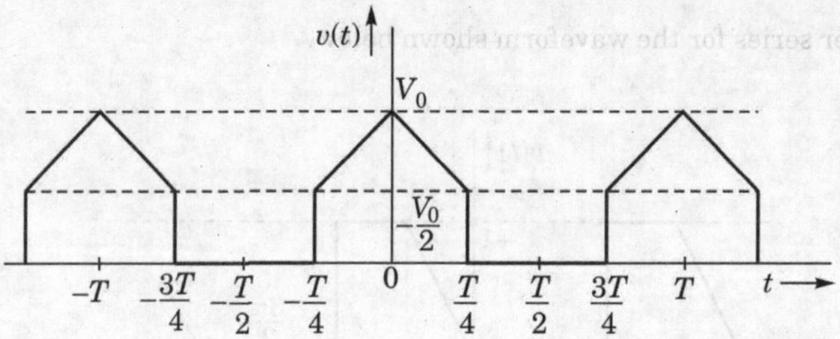

16

Fourier Integral and Continuous Spectra

16.1. Spectrum Envelope for a Recurring Pulse

In the last chapter, we had applied Fourier method to obtain a Fourier series equivalent to a periodic signal. In this chapter, we apply the Fourier method to an a periodic signal, *i.e.* a signal which occurs only once in some finite time interval and is never repeated. The resulting *Fourier integral* is obtained by letting the period T becomes infinite in the Fourier series. The line spectrum so obtained is a *continuous spectrum*.

Consider the waveform of a periodic rectangular pulse of magnitude V_0, duration a and time period T, as shown in Fig. 16.1. For the co-ordinates selected in Fig. 16.1, the function $f(t)$ may be expressed as

$$f(t) = \begin{cases} V_0, & -\frac{a}{2} < t < \frac{a}{2} \\ 0, & -\frac{T}{2} < t < -\frac{a}{2}, \quad \frac{a}{2} < t < \frac{T}{2} \end{cases} \qquad \text{...(16.1)}$$

Such periodic signals are used in radar systems. A quantity of considerable significance is the ratio a/T, referred to as the *duty cycle*, *duty ratio* or *duty factors* δ. In the present chapter, we are interested in the spectrum of $f(t)$ as the duty ratio becomes smaller and smaller and ultimately approaches zero.

The corresponding Fourier coefficients for $f(t)$ may then be obtained from Eq. (15.69) for all values of n. Thus, we get

$$\overline{C}_n = \frac{1}{T}\int_{-a/2}^{a/2} V_0 \, e^{-jn\omega_0 t} \, dt \qquad \text{...(16.2)}$$

$$= \frac{V_0}{T} \frac{1}{-jn\omega_0}\left[e^{-jn\omega_0 \frac{a}{2}} - e^{nj\omega_0 \frac{a}{2}}\right]$$

But $\qquad T = \dfrac{1}{f_0} = \dfrac{2\pi}{\omega_0}.$

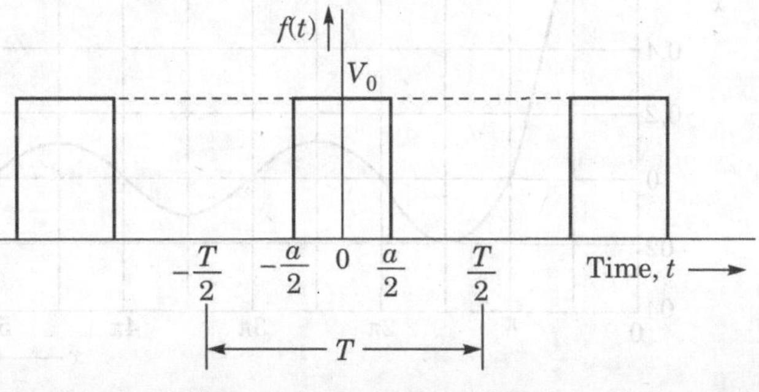

Fig. 16.1. A periodic rectangular pulse of amplitude V_0, duration a and time period T.

Hence
$$\overline{C}_n = \frac{V_0}{n\pi}\left[\frac{e^{jn\omega_0 \frac{a}{2}} - e^{-jn\omega_0 \frac{a}{2}}}{2j}\right]$$

$$= V_0 \frac{\omega_0 a}{2\pi}\left[\frac{\sin\left(n\omega_0 \frac{n}{2}\right)}{\left(n\omega_0 \frac{a}{2}\right)}\right] \qquad ...(16.3)$$

But $T = \dfrac{2\pi}{\omega_0}$. Hence Eq. (16.3) may be written as,

$$\overline{C}_n = V_0 . \frac{a}{T} . \frac{\sin\left(n\omega_0 \frac{a}{2}\right)}{\left(n\omega_0 \frac{a}{2}\right)} \qquad ...(16.4)$$

Let
$$x = n\omega_0 \frac{a}{2} \qquad ...(16.5)$$

Then Eq. (16.4) may be put as,

$$\overline{C}_n = V_0 . \frac{a}{T} \frac{\sin x}{x} \qquad ...(16.6)$$

Thus the Fourier coefficient $\overline{C}_n$ equals the product of the pulse amplitude V_0, duty ratio $\dfrac{a}{T}$ and the mathematical function $\dfrac{\sin x}{x}$. This last quantity $\dfrac{\sin x}{x}$ is a familiar mathematical function and Fig. 16.2 shows a plot of this function $\dfrac{\sin x}{x}$ against x. A study of the curve of Fig. 16.2 reveals that the function has value 1 when $x = 0$ corresponding to $n = 0$ in Eq. (16.4). It may also be seen that the function $\dfrac{\sin x}{x}$ and the coefficient $\overline{C}_n$ have both positive and negative values, corresponding to phase ϕ_n of either 0° or 180°.

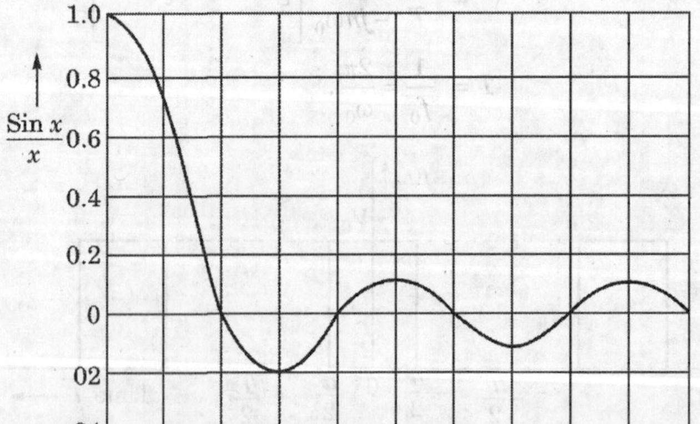

Fig. 16.2. Function $\dfrac{\sin x}{x}$ plotted against x.

Eq. (16.4) gives the values of coefficient $\overline{C}_n$ only for discrete frequencies $n\omega_0$, *i.e.* values of frequency at which there occur lines in the spectrum for $\overline{C}_n$. However, if we replace $n\omega_0$ by ω, the envelope of $\overline{C}_n$ so obtained is a *continuous function*. Thus we may write

$$\text{Envelope of} \qquad \overline{C}_n = V_0 \frac{a}{T} \frac{\sin\left(\omega \frac{a}{2}\right)}{\left(\omega \frac{a}{2}\right)} \qquad \text{...(16.7)}$$

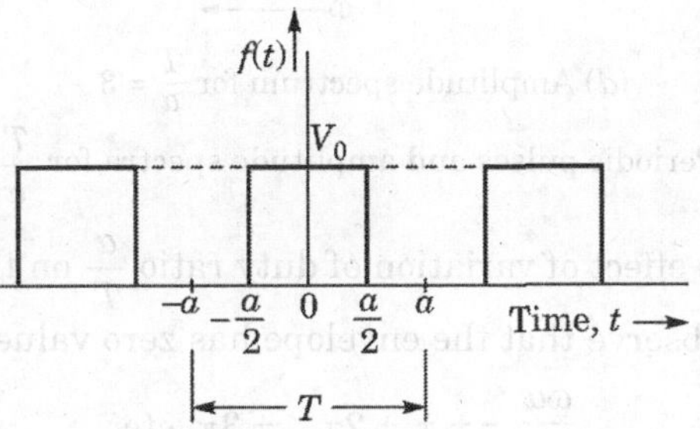

(*a*) Periodic pulses for $\frac{T}{a} = 2$

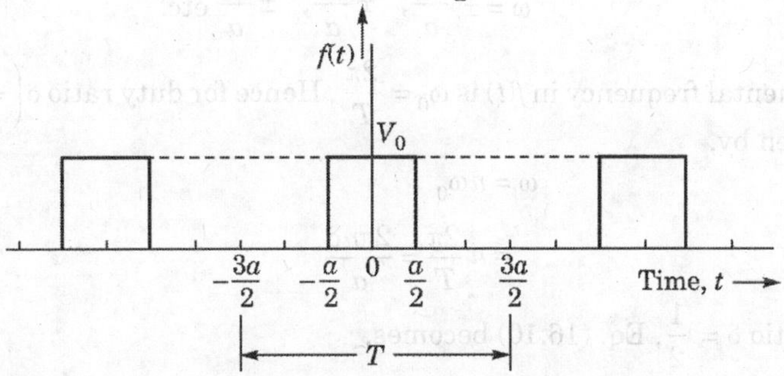

(*b*) Periodic pulses for $\frac{T}{a} = 3$

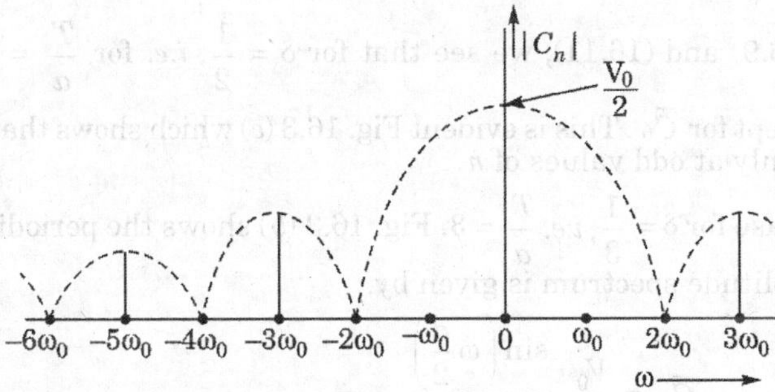

(*c*) Amplitude spectrum for $\frac{T}{a} = 2$

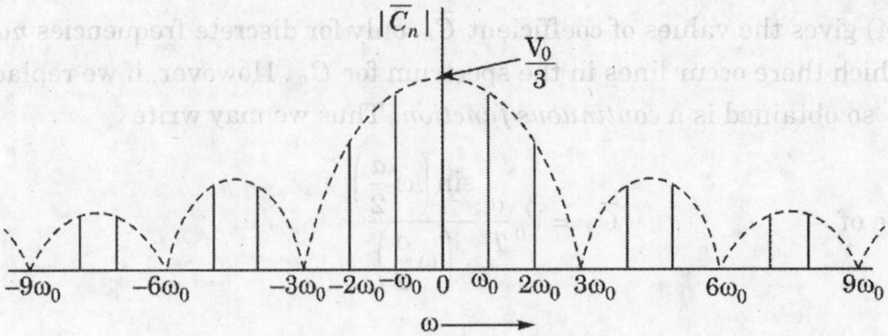

(*d*) Amplitude spectrum for $\frac{T}{a} = 3$

Fig. 16.3. Periodic pulses and amplitude spectra for $\frac{T}{a} = 2$ and $\frac{T}{a} = 3$.

Next we consider the effect of variation of duty ratio $\frac{a}{T}$ on the coefficient $\overline{C}_n$.

From Eq. (16.7) we observe that the envelope has zero value when,

$$\frac{\omega a}{2} = \pm\,\pi,\ \pm\,2\pi,\quad \pm\,3\pi, \text{ etc.} \qquad ...(16.8)$$

i.e. when

$$\omega = \pm\frac{2\pi}{a},\quad \pm\frac{4\pi}{a},\quad \pm\frac{6\pi}{a} \text{ etc.} \qquad ...(16.9)$$

The fundamental frequency in *f*(*t*) is $\omega_0 = \frac{2\pi}{T}$. Hence for duty ratio $\delta\left(=\frac{a}{T}\right)$, $\overline{C}_n$ has values at frequency ω is given by,

$$\omega = n\omega_0$$

$$= n\frac{2\pi}{T} = \frac{2\pi n\delta}{a} \qquad ...(16.10)$$

For duty ratio $\delta = \frac{1}{2}$, Eq. (16.10) becomes,

$$\omega = \frac{n\pi}{a} \qquad ...(16.11)$$

On comparing Eqs. (16.9) and (16.11), we see that for $\delta = \frac{1}{2}$, *i.e.* for $\frac{T}{a} = 2$, even valued harmonics have zero value except for $\overline{C}_0$. This is evident Fig. 16.3 (*c*) which shows that the amplitude spectrum has lines at $\pm\, n\omega_0$ only at odd values of *n*.

Next we consider the case for $\delta = \frac{1}{3}$, *i.e.* $\frac{T}{a} = 3$. Fig. 16.3 (*b*) shows the periodic pulses for $\frac{T}{a} = 3$. The envelope for the amplitude spectrum is given by,

Envelope for

$$\overline{C}_n = \frac{V_0}{3}\cdot\frac{\sin\left(\omega\frac{a}{2}\right)}{\left(\frac{\omega a}{2}\right)} \qquad ...(16.12)$$

Spectral lines will be present in the amplitude and phase spectra at,

$$\omega = n\omega_0 = \frac{2n\pi}{3a} \qquad ...(16.13)$$

On comparing Eq. (16.9) with Eq. (16.13), we find that the lines at $\pm\,3\omega_0$, $\pm\,6\omega_0$, etc. will have zero amplitude. Fig. 16.3 (*d*) shows the amplitude spectrum.

In a general case with $T/a = N$, the spacing between the lines is given by,

$$\Delta\omega = (n+1)\,\omega_0 - n\omega_0 = \omega_0 \quad ...(16.14)$$

and the amplitude of the line is given by,

$$|\overline{C}_n| = \frac{V_0}{N}\left|\frac{\sin\left(\frac{n\omega_0 a}{2}\right)}{\left(\frac{n\omega_0 a}{2}\right)}\right| \quad ...(16.15)$$

where $$\omega_0 = \frac{2\pi}{Na} \quad ...(16.16)$$

As N is increased to say 10,000 or more, the number of lines in a given frequency interval becomes very large so that the separation of lines becomes extremely small. Further the amplitude of the lines, as given by Eq. (16.15) also becomes very small. Thus more frequency components are required to make up the shorter pulse but the amplitudes of the frequency components so required are smaller.

With this background, now we are in a position to consider the case when in the limit N tends to infinity.

16.2. Fourier Integral and Fourier Transform

Now with reference to the periodic pulse of the last article, let N be increased tending to infinity in the limit. But since $\frac{a}{T} = \frac{1}{N}$, the limit $N \to \infty$ is the same as the limit for the period $T \to \infty$. Thus with reference to pulse of Fig. 16.1, let the pulse width remain fixed at a as $T \to \infty$. In effect, it amounts to a single pulse or non-recurring pulse of width a.

Let us first consider the product of T and $\overline{C}_n$. Thus,

$$\overline{C}_n\, T = \int_{-T/2}^{T/2} f(t)e^{-jn\omega_0 t}\, dt \quad ...(16.17)$$

But $\overline{C}_n$ is a complex quantity in general. Hence the product $C_n\,T$ be denoted by symbol $F(jn\omega_0)$.

Then $$F(jn\omega_0) = \overline{C}_n T = \frac{2\pi}{\omega_0}\overline{C}_n \quad ...(16.18)$$

But from Eq. (16.14), $\Delta\omega = \omega_0$. Hence Eq. (16.18) may be put as,

$$F(jn\omega_0) = 2\pi\frac{\overline{C}_n}{\Delta\omega} \quad ...(16.19)$$

Hence $$\overline{C}_n = \frac{F(jn\omega_0)\Delta\omega}{2\pi} \quad ...(16.20)$$

Reverting again to the case of recurring pulses of last article, let us divide Eq. (16.7) by Eq. (16.14) to get

Envelope of $$\frac{\overline{C}_n}{\Delta\omega} = a\frac{V_0}{2\pi}\cdot\frac{\sin\left(\frac{\omega a}{2}\right)}{\left(\frac{\omega a}{2}\right)} \quad ...(16.21)$$

The quantity on the R.H.S. of Eq. (16.21) is independent of N and hence also of T. Hence the envelope of $\frac{\overline{C}_n}{\delta\omega}$ does not change as $T \to \infty$. This important property does, in fact, hold good not only for the rectangular pulse but for all $f(t)$ which are non-recurring.

From Eq. (16.10),

$$\frac{\overline{C}_n}{\Delta\omega} = \frac{F(jn\omega_0)}{2\pi} \qquad ...(16.22)$$

Hence the conclusion reached for Eq. (16.21) will also apply for $F(jn\omega_0)$.

On substituting the value of $\overline{C}_n$ as given by Eq. (16.20) into Eq. (15.67), we get the following expression for $f(t)$,

$$f(t) = \lim_{T \to \infty} \sum_{n=-\infty}^{\infty} \frac{F(jn\omega_0)}{2\pi} e^{jn\omega_0 t} \, \Delta\omega \qquad ...(16.23)$$

Now as $T \to \infty$, $\Delta\omega \to d\omega$. Also the product $n\omega_n = n\Delta\omega_0 \to \omega$. Accordingly we may put the R.H.S. of Eq. (16.23) as an integral and rewrite Eq. (16.23) as

$$f(t) = \frac{1}{2\pi} \int_{-\infty}^{\infty} F(j\omega) e^{j\omega t} \, d\omega \qquad ...(16.24)$$

$F(j\omega)$ may be obtained from Eq. (16.17) on substituting ω for $n\omega_0$. Thus, we get

$$F(j\omega) = \int_{-\infty}^{\infty} f(t) \, e^{-j\omega t} \, dt \qquad ...(16.25)$$

subject to the following sufficient but not necessary condition,

$$\int_{-\infty}^{\infty} |f(t)| \, dt < \infty \qquad ...(16.26)$$

$F(j\omega)$ is the *Fourier integral* of function $f(t)$. Thus Eq. (16.25) enables us to obtain the Fourier integral of any function $f(t)$.

Fourier transform. Function $F(j\omega_0)$ is also called the *Fourier transform* of function $f(t)$. Thus Fourier transform is nothing but the Fourier integral. We may write,

$$F(j\omega) = \mathfrak{J} \, f(t) \qquad ...(16.27)$$

The symbol $\mathfrak{J}$ signifies 'Fourier transform of' Eq. (16.25) enables us to obtain $F(j\omega)$ for a given $f(t)$. The quantity $f(t)$ is in time domain whereas the quantity $f(j\omega)$ is in frequency domain. Thus Eq. (16.25) enables us to convert a quantity $f(t)$ in the time domain to the corresponding quantity in the frequency domain.

In the reciprocal direction, Eq. (16.24) enables us to compute time domain function $f(t)$ for a given frequency domain function $f(j\omega)$.

Function $f(t)$ constitutes the *Inverse Fourier transform of* function $f(j\omega)$ and we may write,

$$f(t) = \mathfrak{J}^{-1} \, F(j\omega) \qquad ...(16.28)$$

Symbol $\mathfrak{J}$ signifies 'Inverse Fourier transform of'.

Eqs. (16.24) and (16.25) constitute the *Fourier transform pair equations.*

Functions $F(j\omega)$ and $f(t)$ form the *Fourier transform pair* in the same sense that $F(s)$ and $f(t)$ form the Laplace transform pair.

Continuous spectra. Function $F(j\omega)$ may be expressed in an alternative fashion. Let $f(t)$ be a pulse of arbitrary shape and duration
$a < T$. Then Eq. (16.25) giving $F(j\omega)$ and Eq. (15.69) giving $\overline{C}_n$, may be put as below,

$$F(j\omega) = \int_{-a/2}^{-a/2} f(t)e^{-j\omega t}\, dt \qquad ...(16.29)$$

and
$$\overline{C}_n = \int_{a/2}^{-a/2} f(t)e^{-j_n\omega_0 t}\, dt \qquad ...(16.30)$$

The limits of integration for the integrals in the above two equations are the same.

On comparing the above equations we find that the expressions for $F(j\omega)$ and C_n are similar except for the difference that $F(j\omega)$ is a continuous function whereas $\overline{C}_n$ is defined only for discrete values of frequency.

$F(j\omega)$ being a complex quantity, may be put as,

$$F(j\omega) = | F(j\omega) | e^{j\phi(\omega)} \qquad ...(16.31)$$

Then we are quite justified in calling the quantity $| F(j\omega) |$ as the *continuous amplitude spectrum* and the quantity $\phi(\omega)$ as the *continuous phase spectrum* for the aperiodic function $f(t)$.

We may distinguish between the two types of spectra, namely the *discrete (or line) spectra* and the *continuous spectra*.

The following properties of continuous spectra are worth noting.

(*i*) The shape of the continuous amplitude and phase spectra for an aperiodic (ncn-recurring) function $f(t)$ is identical with the envelope of the discrete amplitude and phase spectra for the same pulse recurring.

(*ii*) All frequencies are present in the continuous amplitude spectrum since $F(j\omega)$ is defined for all $\omega(-\infty < \omega < \infty)$. However, the amplitude of any frequency component is vanishingly small, being equal to $\dfrac{F(j\omega)\,.\,d\omega}{3\pi}$ in accordance with Eq. (16.20).

16.3. A Few Typical Fourier Transforms

In the last article, mention was made that a sufficient but not necessary condition for a Fourier transform to exist is that it satisfies the Dirichlet conditions. The most important among the Dirichlet conditions is the requirement that

$$\int_{-\infty}^{\infty} | f(t) |\, dt < \infty \qquad ...(16.32)$$

Most of the familiar waveshapes such as step function, the ramp functions sine wave etc., however, do not meet this requirement. It will be shown in this article that if the impulse function is allowed to exist in the Fourier transform, this limitation given by inequality Eq. (16.32) may be removed.

Impulse Function. Consider the unit impulse function. This constitutes one of the simplest Fourier transforms. Then as per basic definition,

$$\Im[\delta(t)] = F(j\omega)$$

$$= \int_{-\infty}^{\infty} \delta(t)e^{-j\omega t}\, dt \qquad ...(16.33)$$

We may easily evaluate this integral making use of the following scanning function studied earlier,

$$\int_{-\infty}^{\infty} f(t)\delta(t - t_0)dt - f(t_0) \qquad ...(16.34)$$

Accordingly the integral of Eq. (16.33) has the following value,

$$\Im[\delta(t)] = 1 \qquad ...(16.35)$$

Then from the uniqueness property of Fourier transform, we may write,

$$\Im^{-1}[1] = \delta(t). \qquad ...(16.36)$$

Thus the Fourier transform of an impulse, such as shown in Fig. 16.4 (*a*) is a simple constant as shown in Fig. 16.4 (*b*).

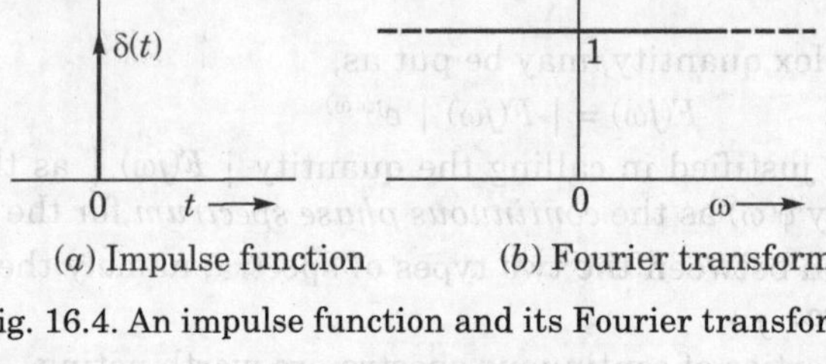

(*a*) Impulse function (*b*) Fourier transform

Fig. 16.4. An impulse function and its Fourier transform.

Exponential Function $e^{-a|t|}$. Next consider an exponential function defined for both positive and negative values of time t, as shown in Fig. 16.5 (*a*).

This function may be put as,

$$f(t) = e^{-a|t|}, \text{ all } t \qquad ...(16.37)$$

Then the corresponding Fourier transform is,

$$F(j\omega) = \int_{-\infty}^{0} e^{at}\, e^{-j\omega t}\, dt + \int_{0}^{\infty} e^{-at}\, e^{-j\omega t}\, dt \qquad ...(16.38)$$

$$= \frac{1}{a - j\omega} + \frac{1}{a + j\omega} = \frac{2a}{\omega^2 + a^2} \qquad ...(16.39)$$

The Fourier transform function as described by Eq. (16.39) is a real function, with zero phase contribution for all values of ω and is plotted Fig. 16.5 (*b*).

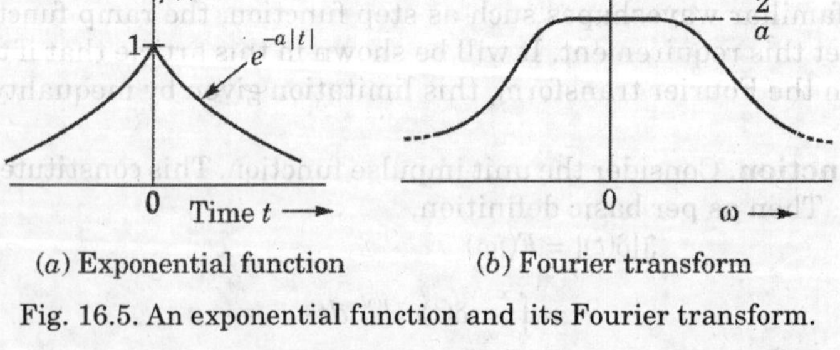

(*a*) Exponential function (*b*) Fourier transform

Fig. 16.5. An exponential function and its Fourier transform.

Function f(t) = 1. To obtain the Fourier transform of this function, we make use of function $f(t)$ as given Eq. by (16.37) and take the limit as a approaches zero. Under this condition $f(t)$ becomes 1. Thus we may write,

$$\Im[1] = \lim_{a \to 0} \int_{-\infty}^{\infty} e^{-a|t|}\, e^{-j\omega t}\, dt \qquad ...(16.40)$$

$$= \lim_{a \to 0} \frac{2}{\omega^2 + a^2} \qquad \text{...(16.41)}$$

The RHS of Eq. (16.41) equals zero for all values of a except when $\omega = 0$. For $\omega = 0$, in order to evaluate the quantity, we make use of l' Hospital's rule. Thus we differentiate both the numerator and the denominator and then let a approach zero.

Thus, we get

$$\lim_{a \to 0} \frac{2}{2a} = \infty \qquad \text{...(16.42)}$$

This indicates that $\mathfrak{J}[1]$ forms an impulse function at $\omega = 0$. The magnitude of the impulse function may be found by integrating $F(j\omega)$ for all values of ω to give the area under the function. Thus, we have

$$\int_{-\infty}^{\infty} \frac{2a}{\omega^2 + a^2} d\omega = 2\pi \qquad \text{...(16.43)}$$

Hence the Fourier transform of constant 1 is an impulse of magnitude 2π.

or $$\mathfrak{J}[1] = 2\pi\delta(\omega) \qquad \text{...(16.44)}$$

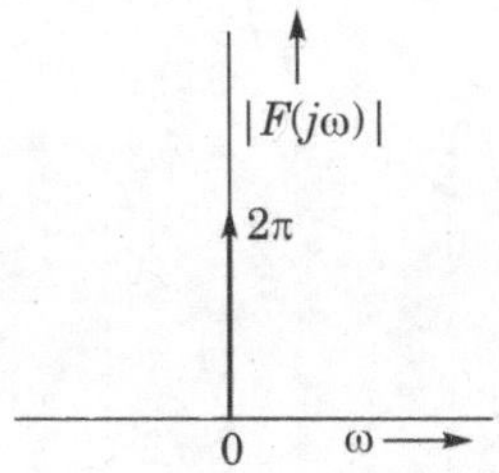

Fig. 16.6. Magnitude spectrum of the constant 1.

Fig. 16.6 shows the magnitude spectrum of constant 1.

Exponential Function $e^{j\omega_0 t}$. We now find the Fourier transform of $e^{j\omega_0 t}$, where ω_0 is a constant. For finding the transform, we make use of the result derived above. We have seen above that,

$$\int_{-\infty}^{\infty} 1.e^{-j\omega t}\, dt = 2\pi\delta(\omega) \qquad \text{...(16.45)}$$

Hence $$\mathfrak{J}[e^{j\omega_0 t}] = \int_{-\infty}^{\infty} 1.e^{(j\omega_0 - j\omega)t}\, dt = 2\pi\delta(\omega - \omega_0) \qquad \text{...(16.46)}$$

Cosine and Sine Functions. The cosine and sine functions may be expressed in terms of corresponding exponential functions as below,

$$\cos \omega_0 t = \frac{e^{j\omega_0 t} + e^{-j\omega_0 t}}{2} \qquad \text{...(16.47)}$$

and $$\sin \omega_0 t = \frac{e^{j\omega_0 t} - e^{-j\omega_0 t}}{2j} \qquad \text{...(16.48)}$$

We now make use of Eq. (16.46) to write the following Fourier transforms of $\cos \omega_0 t$ and $\sin \omega_0 t$,

$$\mathfrak{J}[\cos \omega_0 t] = \pi[\delta(\omega - \omega_0) + \delta(\omega + \omega_0)] \qquad \text{...(16.49)}$$

and $$\mathfrak{J}[\sin \omega_0 t] = -j\pi[\delta(\omega - \omega_0) - \delta(\omega + \omega_0)] \qquad \text{...(16.50)}$$

From Eqs. (16.49) and (16.50) we find that Fourier transform of both cosine and sine functions are expressed in terms of two impulse functions, each of magnitude π as shown in Fig. 16.7. The magnitude spectra for the cosine and sine functions are the same but the phase angles associated with the two functions differ.

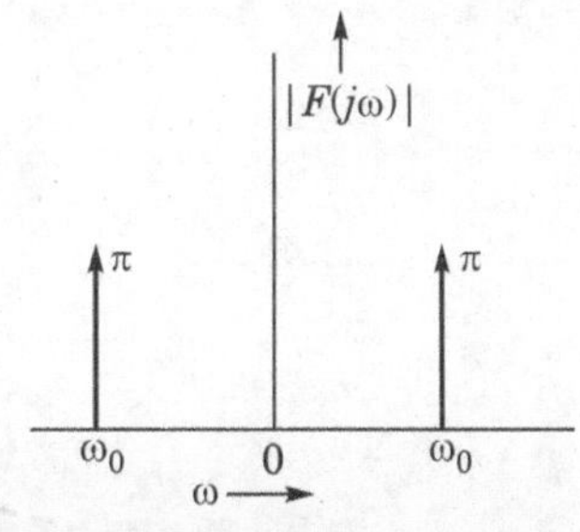

Fig. 16.7. Magnitude spectrum of cosine and sine functions of time.

The Signum Function Sgn (t). Fig. 16.8 shows the Signum function defined as below :

$$\text{Sgn}(t) = \begin{cases} +1, & t > 0 \\ 0, & t = 0 \\ -1 & t < 0 \end{cases} \qquad \text{...(16.51)}$$

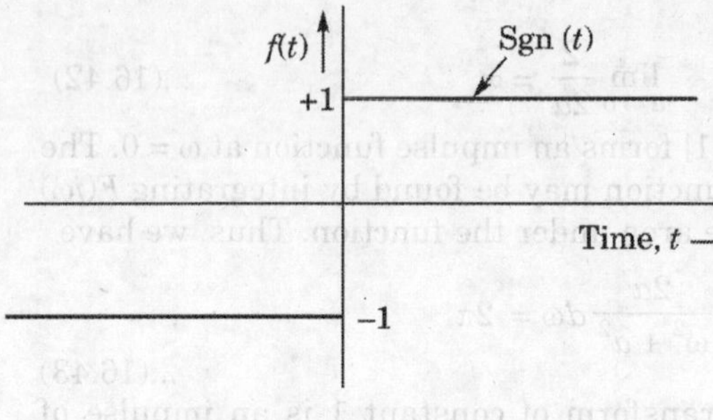

Fig. 16.8. The Signum function Sgn (t).

It is difficulty to obtain the Fourier transform of this function directly since the integral on the LHS of inequality (16.32) diverges and inequality (16.32) is not satisfied. Accordingly we follow an indirect method. First we express the function as a limiting case of other functions and then the Fourier transform is computed. Thus we express Sgn (t) as below,

$$\text{Sgn}(t) = \lim_{a \to 0} e^{-a|t|} \cdot \text{Sgn}(t) \qquad \text{...(16.52)}$$

Hence
$$\mathfrak{I}[\text{Sgn}(t)] = \lim_{a \to 0} \int_{-\infty}^{0} e^{-a|t|}\, \text{Sgn}(t)\, e^{j\omega t}\, dt \qquad \text{...(16.53)}$$

$$= \lim_{a \to 0} \left[\int_{-\infty}^{0} -e^{(a - j\omega)t}\, dt + \int_{0}^{\infty} e^{-(a + j\omega)t}\, dt \right] \qquad \text{...(16.54)}$$

$$= \lim_{a \to 0} \left[\frac{-1}{a - j\omega} + \frac{1}{a + j\omega} \right] \qquad \text{...(16.55)}$$

$$= \frac{2}{j\omega}$$

Fig. 16.9 shows the magnitude spectrum for the signum function and it is a plot of $2/\omega$ against frequency ω. Evidently it has infinite value at $\omega = 0$. The corresponding phase function $\phi(j\omega)$ is a constant equal to $-\pi/2$ for $\omega > 0$ and $+\pi/2$ for $\omega < 0$.

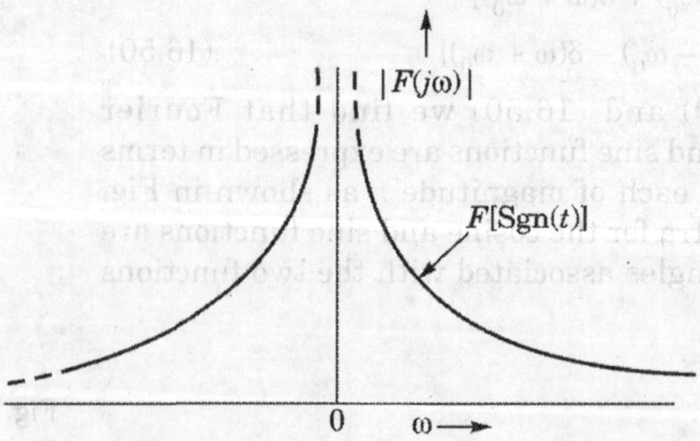

Fig. 16.9. Magnitude spectrum of the Signum function.

The unit step function. The unit step function is another function which does not satisfy inequality (16.32). However, we may utilize the Signum function to find the Fourier transform of the unit step function. This unit step function may be put as,

$$u(t) = \frac{1}{2}[1 + \text{Sgn}(t)] \qquad \text{...(16.56 } a)$$

But we known the Fourier transform of both the quantities within the bracket in the R.H.S. of Eq. (16.55). Thus, we get

$$\mathfrak{J}[u(t)] = \pi\delta(\omega) + \frac{1}{j\omega} \qquad \text{...(16.56 } b)$$

Fig. 16.10 shows the magnitude spectrum of a unit step function $u(t)$. This is a summation of (*i*) a rectangular hyperbola and (*ii*) the impulse function of strength π at $\omega = 0$.

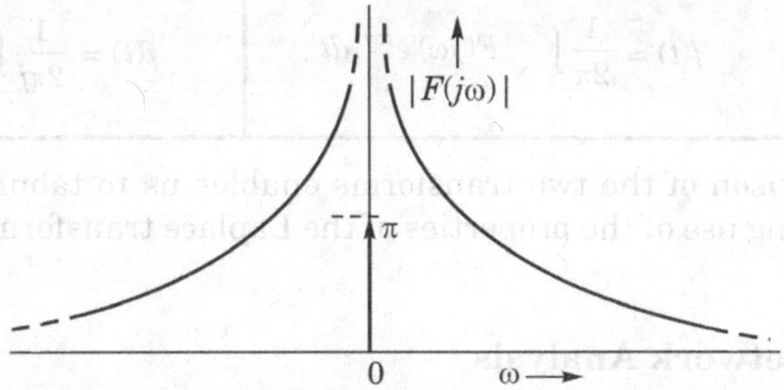

Fig. 16.10. Magnitude spectrum of a unit step function $u(t)$.

A generalised periodic function. Any periodic function fails to satisfy the inequality (16.32) and we may, therefore, expect the result to contain impulse functions. We use the following expression for the Fourier series for $f(t)$ as given by Eq. (15.67),

$$f(t) = \sum_{n=-\infty}^{\infty} \bar{C}_n \, e^{jn\omega_0 t} \qquad \text{...(16.57)}$$

The Fourier transform of $f(t)$ is,

$$\mathfrak{J}[f(t)] = F(j\omega) = \mathfrak{J}\left[\sum_{n=-\infty}^{\infty} \bar{C}_n \, e^{jn\omega_0 t}\right]$$

$$= \sum_{n=-0}^{\infty} \bar{C}_n \, \mathfrak{J}[e^{jn\omega_0 t}] \qquad \text{...(16.58)}$$

Eq. (16.46) gives the Fourier transform of an exponential function. Making use of this equation, we may write the following expression for the Fourier transform of given periodic function,

$$\mathfrak{J}[f(t)] = 2\pi \sum_{n=-\infty}^{\infty} \bar{C}_n \, \delta(\omega - n\omega_0) \qquad \text{...(16.59)}$$

16.3 (a) The Relationship of Fourier and Laplace Transforms

We have already noticed that there is exists a definite relationship between the Laplace and Fourier transforms. Table 16.1 gives the defining equations for the two transform pairs. However, the following differences have to be noticed carefully.

(*i*) The $j\omega$ in the Fourier transform occupies the same position as in the Laplace transform.

(*ii*) The limits of integration in the direct transform are different. The limits are one-sided in Laplace transform but are two-sided in Fourier transform.

(*iii*) The contour of integration in the inverse transform equation is also different, being along the imaginary axis in the inverse Fourier transform and being displaced by σ, in the inverse Laplace transform.

(*iv*) The Laplace transform of any function $f(t)$ equals the Fourier transform of $f(t)$ multiplied by a convergence factor $e^{-\sigma t}$ if $f(t) = 0$ for $t < 0$. Thus, we have

$$\mathcal{L}f(t) = \mathfrak{J}[f(t)^{-\sigma t}] \qquad ...(16.60)$$

Table 16.1. Comparison of Fourier and Laplace Transforms

	Fourier	Laplace
Direct transform	$f(j\omega) = \int_{-\infty}^{\infty} f(t)\, e^{-j\omega t}\, dt$	$F(s) = \int_{0}^{\infty} f(t)\, e^{-st}\, dt$
Inverse* transform	$f(t) = \dfrac{1}{2\pi}\int_{-\infty}^{\infty} F(j\omega)\, e^{j\omega t}\, dt$	$f(t) = \dfrac{1}{2\pi j}\int_{\sigma_1 - j\infty}^{\sigma_1 + j\omega} F(s) e^{st}\, dt$

The above comparison of the two transforms enables us to tabulate the properties of the Fourier transforms making use of the properties of the Laplace transform by simply substituting s by $j\omega$.

16.4. Application in Network Analysis

Fourier transforms may be used in network analysis in the same general way as the Laplace transforms. To illustrate the principle of application of Fourier transforms in network analysis, let us consider the exponential waveform given by the following equation,

$$i_1(t) = I_0 e^{-kt},\ t \geq 0 \qquad ...(16.61)$$

Function $i_1(t)$ has zero value for negative t and satisfies the condition :

$$\int_{-\infty}^{\infty} |f(t)|\, dt < \infty$$

provided that $k > 0$. Fig. 16.11 shows the waveform of $i_1(t)$. Then the Fourier transform of $i_1(t)$ is given by

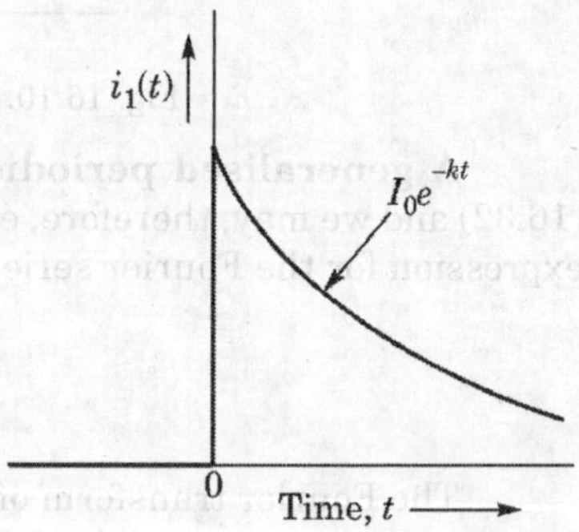

Fig. 16.11. Exponetial waveform.

$$I_1(j\omega) = I_0 \int_{-\infty}^{\infty} e^{-kt}\, u(t) e^{-j\omega t}$$

$$= \left.\frac{I_0\, e^{(-k + j\omega)t}}{-(k + j\omega)}\right|_0^{\infty} \qquad ...(16.62)$$

$$= \frac{I_0}{k + j\omega} \qquad ...(16.63)$$

Hence $\qquad I_1(j\omega) = \mathfrak{J}[i_1(t)] = \dfrac{I_0}{k + j\omega} \qquad ...(16.64)$

Magnitude

$$|\, I_1(j\omega)\, | = \frac{I_0}{\sqrt{\omega^2 + k^2}} \qquad ...(16.65)$$

Phase angle $\qquad \phi(j\omega) = -\tan^{-1}\left(\dfrac{\omega}{k}\right) \qquad ...(16.66)$

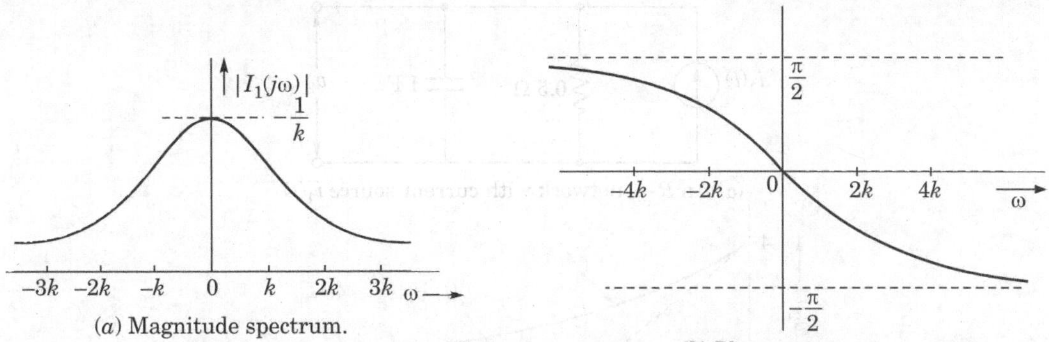

(*a*) Magnitude spectrum.

(*b*) Phase spectrum

Fig. 16.12. Magnitude and phase spectrum for the exponential waveform of Eq. (16.61).

Fig.16.12 shows plot of Eqs. (16.65) and (16.66) and these plots depict the continuous spectra for the exponential function given by Eq. (16.61).

But Fourier transform possesses the uniqueness property. Hence we may write the following inverse Fourier transform equation,

$$\mathfrak{J}^{-1}\frac{I_0}{j\omega + k} = I_0 e^{-kt}\, u(t) \qquad ...(16.67)$$

To proceed with the illustration of the use of Fourier transform in network analysis, we first obtain the Fourier transform of the first derivative of a time function $f(t)$. Thus from Eq. (16.24), we get

$$\frac{d}{dt} f(t) = \frac{1}{2\pi}\int_{-\infty}^{\infty} j\omega F(j\omega) e^{j\omega t}\, d\omega \qquad ...(16.68)$$

On comparing Eq. (16.68) with Eq. (16.24), we find that $j\omega\ F(j\omega)$ has replaced $F(j\omega)$. Hence we may write,

$$\mathfrak{J}\left[\frac{df(t)}{dt}\right] = j\omega\ F(j\omega) \qquad ...(16.69)$$

Now we are equipped to apply the Fourier transform in network analysis. For the purpose of this illustration let us choose a simple *RC* network shown in Fig. 16.13 (*a*). Let the current source be described as below

$$i_1(t) = 4e^{-1}\, u(t) \qquad ...(16.70)$$

Then for the element values shown in Fig. 16.13 (*a*), the following equation applies,

$$j\omega V_2\,(j\omega) + 2V_2(j\omega) = I_0(j\omega) = \frac{4}{j\omega + 1} \qquad ...(16.71)$$

Eq. (16.71) may be put as,

$$v_2(j\omega) = \frac{4}{(j\omega + 1)\,(j\omega + 2)} \qquad ...(16.72)$$

On expanding the RHS of Eq. (16.72) by use of partial fractions, we get

$$v_2(j\omega) = \frac{4}{j\omega + 1} - \frac{4}{j\omega + 2} \qquad ...(16.73)$$

On inverse Fourier transformation, Eq. (16.73) yields,

$$v_2(t) = 4e^{-t} - 4e^{-2t},\ t \geq 0 \qquad ...(16.74)$$

and $v_2(t)$ has zero value for $t < 0$.

The result is plotted in Fig. 16.13 (*b*).

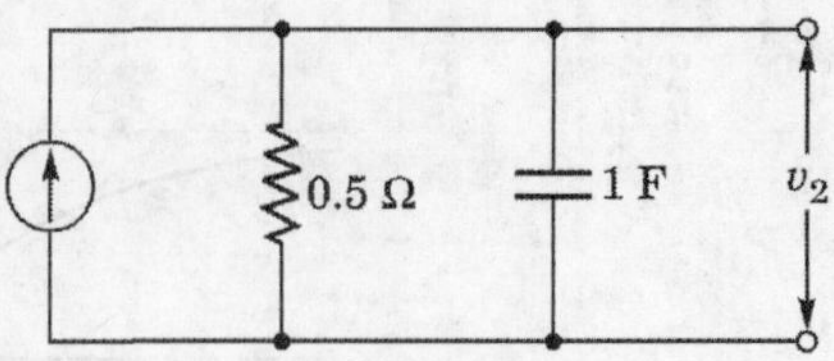

(a) An R–C network with current source $i_1(t)$

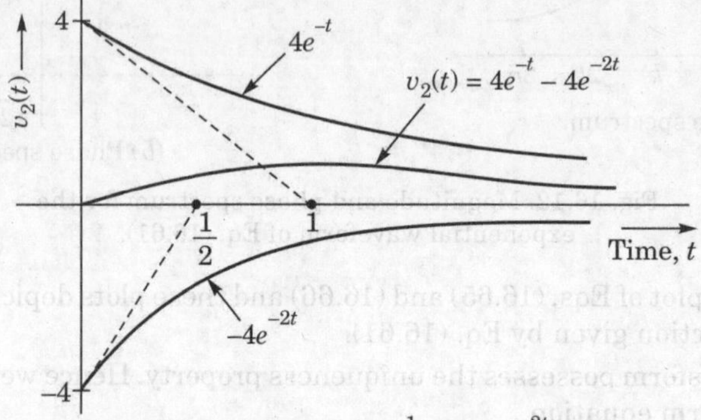

(b) Plot of two constant parts $4e^{-1}$ and $-4e^{-2t}$ of $v_2(t)$

Fig. 16.13. An R-C network and its response $v_2(t)$.

16.5. Bandwidth and Pulse Duration

By an *ideal or distortionless* transmission system is meant the one in which the output waveform is the same as the input waveform

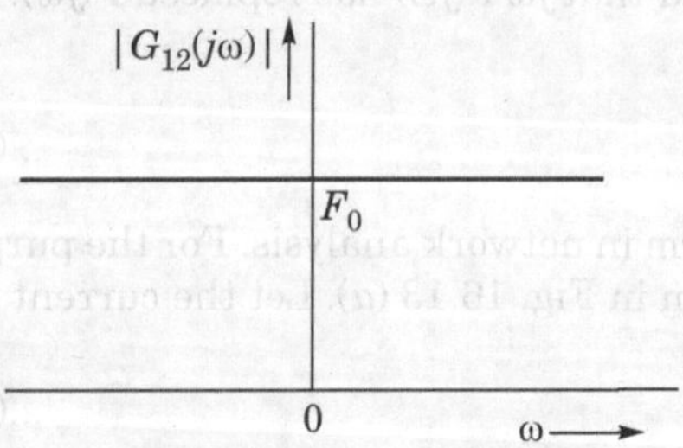

(a) Magnitude characteristic

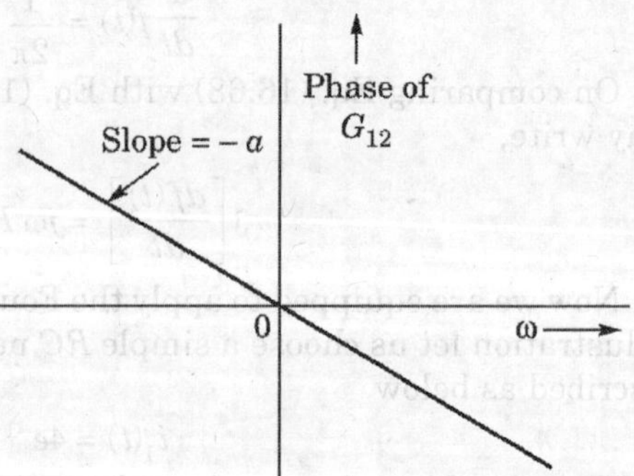

(b) Phase characteristic

Fig. 16.14. Magnitude and phase characteristics of an ideal transmission system.

except that (*i*) the magnitude of the output is scaled by a factor F_0 and (*ii*) the waveform is delayed a seconds. Thus for input $v_1(t)$, the output $v_2(t)$ in a distortionless system may be put as,

$$v_2(t) = F_0 v_1(t - a) \qquad ...(16.75)$$

If $F_0 > 1$, the transmission system is said to offer a gain. However if $F_0 < 1$, the system is said to offer a loss. Using Laplace transmission, Eq. (16.75) yields,

$$V_2(s) = F_0 v_1(s) e^{-sa} \qquad ...(16.76)$$

Hence in the sinusoidal steady state, Eq. (16.76) yields,

$$\frac{V_2}{V_1} = G_{12}(j\omega) = F_0 e^{-j\omega a} \qquad ...(16.77)$$

Thus in an ideal system,

$$| G_{12} | = F_0 \qquad ...(16.78)$$

where F_0 is a constant.

Now since F_0 is a constant, the magnitude characteristic for an ideal transmission system is as shown in Fig. 16.14 (*a*). The phase angle, on the other hand, decreases linearly with ω, as shown in Fig. 16.14 (*b*).

Physical transmission systems such as telephone lines or two-port networks fail to be ideal in the following two respects : (*i*) the magnitude of G_{12} (*j*ω) decreases with ω and (*ii*) the phase angle is noT a linear function of ω. Fig. 16.15 shows the typical nature of magnitude and phase characteristics of a physical (non-ideal) transmission system.

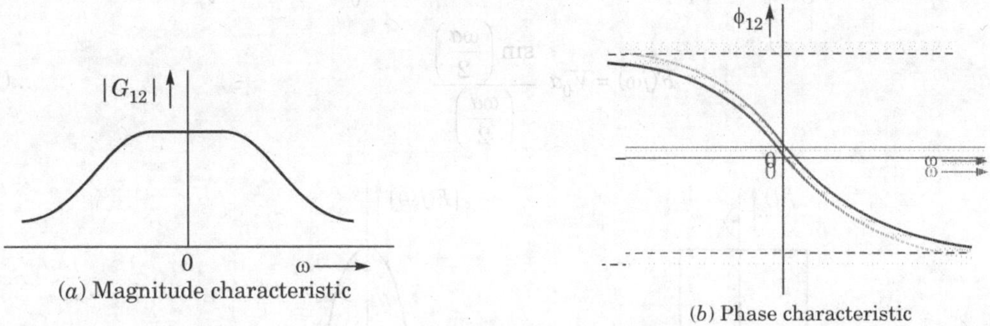

(*a*) Magnitude characteristic (*b*) Phase characteristic

Fig. 16.15. Magnitude and phase characteristics of a typical physical transmission system.

For a physical transmission system, the performance is described in terms of the so-called *band limited characteristic* or *ideal low-pass filter characteristic* shown in Fig. 16.16. This ideal low pass filter does not, however, exist physically but may be approximated by say a telephone transmission system.

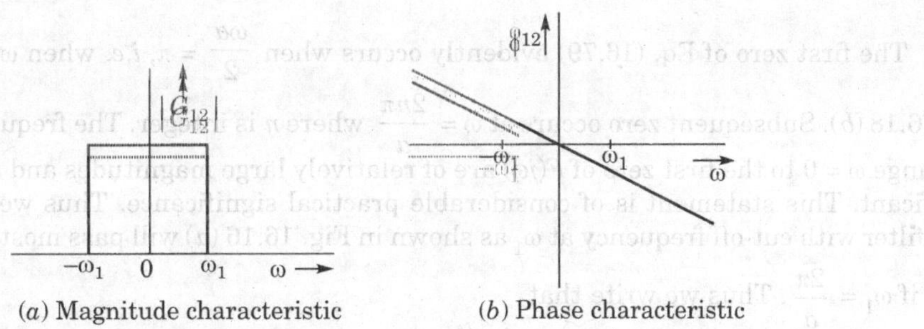

(*a*) Magnitude characteristic (*b*) Phase characteristic

Fig. 16.16. Magnitude and phase characeristics of a band-limited system.

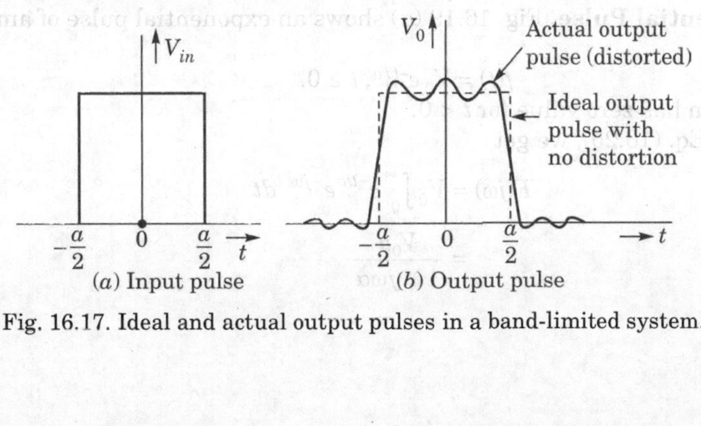

(*a*) Input pulse (*b*) Output pulse

Fig. 16.17. Ideal and actual output pulses in a band-limited system.

Pulses on passing through a band-limited system get distorted as shown in Fig. 16.17. The order of distortion depends on both the bandwidth of the system and the pulse width of the signal.

16.6. Different Pulses and their Amplitude Spectra

We now take up the study of several so called *time-limited* signal waveforms, *i.e.* waveforms which satisfy Eq. (16.26). Accordingly, we exclude the ramp function or the step function and consider waveforms which may be in a generic sense called pulses. We here under consider several different types of pulses and determine their amplitude spectra.

(*A*) **Rectangular Pulse.** Fig. 16.18 (*a*) shows a rectangular pulse of magnitude V_0 and width a. Then making use of Eqs. (16.4) and (16.19) with $n\omega_0 = \omega$, we may write

$$F(j\omega) = V_0 a \, \frac{\sin\left(\frac{\omega a}{2}\right)}{\left(\frac{\omega a}{2}\right)} \qquad \text{...(16.79)}$$

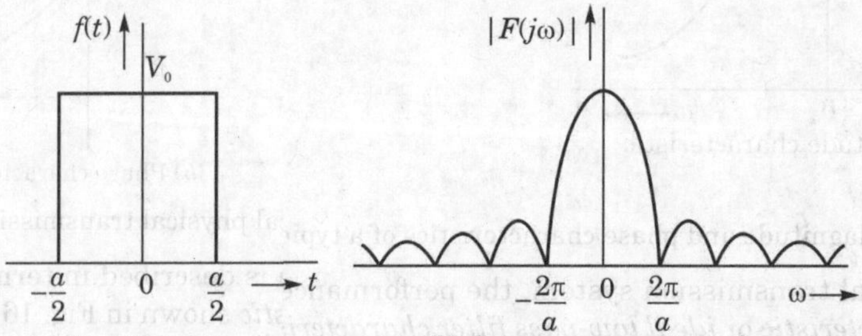

(*a*) Rectangular pulse (*b*) Continuous magnitude spectrum

Fig. 16.18. A rectangular pulse and its continuous magnitude spectrum.

The first zero of Eq. (16.79) evidently occurs when $\frac{\omega a}{2} = \pi$, *i.e.* when $\omega = \frac{2\pi}{2}$, as shown in Fig. 16.18 (*b*). Subsequent zero occurs at $\omega = \frac{2n\pi}{a}$ where n is integer. The frequency components in the range $\omega = 0$ to the first zero of $F(j\omega)$ are of relatively large magnitudes and are, therefore, most significant. This statement is of considerable practical significance. Thus we may state that an ideal filter with cut-off frequency at ω_1 as shown in Fig. 16.16 (*a*) will pass most of the energy of the pulse if $\omega_1 = \frac{2\pi}{a}$. Thus we write that

$$\omega_1 a = 2\pi \qquad \text{...(16.80)}$$

Thus the product of bandwidth ω_1 and the pulse width a is constant.

(*B*) **Exponential Pulse.** Fig. 16.19 (*a*) shows an exponential pulse of amplitude V_0 defined as below :

$$f(t) = V_0 e^{-t/a}, \; t \geq 0. \qquad \text{...(16.81)}$$

The function has zero value for $t < 0$.

Then from Eq. (16.25), we get

$$F(j\omega) = V_0 \int_0^{\infty} e^{-t/a} e^{-j\omega t} \, dt$$

$$= \frac{V_0 a}{1 + j\omega\alpha} \qquad \text{...(16.82)}$$

For the exponential function under consideration, neither the function $f(t)$ nor $F(j\omega)$ vanishes and hence the *width* of the pulse cannot

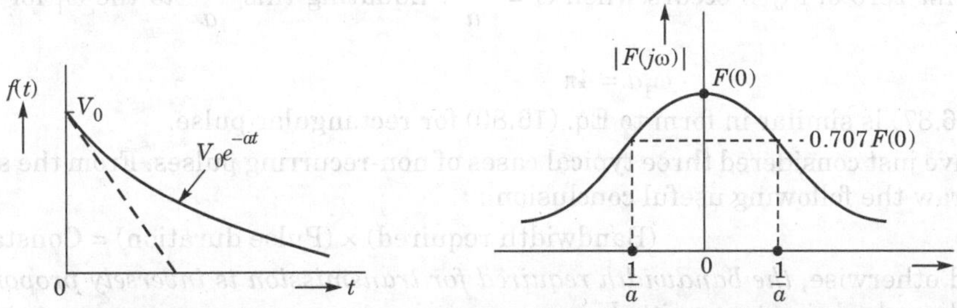

(*a*) Exponential signal (*b*) Continuous amplitude spectrum

Fig. 16.19. Exponential signal and its continuous amplitude spectrum.

be specified in the usual manner. However, in this case, the constant a of the exponential pulse constitutes a measure of time width of the pulse $f(t)$. A line, tangent to $f(t)$ at time $t = 0$ intersects the axis at time $t = a$.

The half power frequency is the frequency at which $|F(\omega)|$ equals 0.707 $F(0)$ as shown in Fig. 16.19 (*b*). This half power frequency may be found by equating the real and imaginary parts of the denominator in the RHS of Eq. (16.82). This yields the result $\omega = \frac{1}{a}$. This half power frequency may be equated to the cut-off frequency of the ideal filter. Thus, we have

$$\omega_1 a = 1 \qquad ...(16.83)$$

(*C*) **Triangular Pulse.** Fig. 16.20 (*a*) shows a triangular pulse of amplitude V_0 and duration a.

This may be expressed as,

$$f(t) = V_0 \left[1 - \frac{2}{a}|t|\right] \qquad ...(16.84)$$

Hence

$$F(j\omega) = V_0 \int_{-a/2}^{a/2} \left(1 - \frac{2}{a}|t|\right) e^{-j\omega t}\, dt \qquad ...(16.85)$$

$$= \frac{V_0\, a}{2} \cdot \frac{\sin\left(\frac{\omega a}{4}\right)}{\left(\frac{\omega a}{4}\right)} \qquad ...(16.86)$$

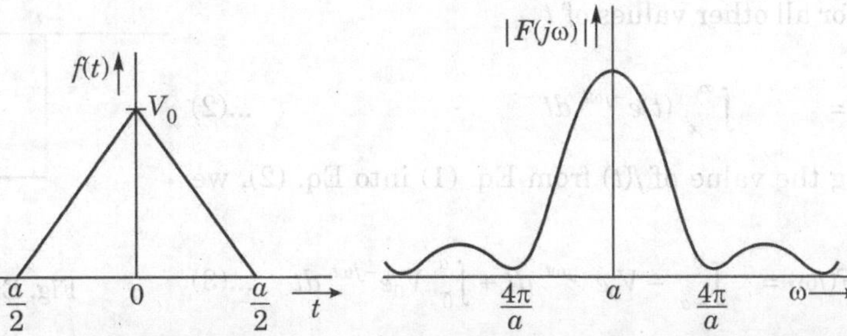

(*a*) Triangular pulse (*b*) Continuous amplitude spectrum

Fig. 16.20. Triangular signal and its continuous amplitude spectrum.

Fig. 16.20 (*b*) shows a plot of Eq. (16.86), *i.e.* it gives the continuous amplitude spectrum.

The first zero of $F(j\omega)$ occurs when $\omega = \dfrac{4\pi}{a}$. Equating this $\dfrac{4\pi}{a}$ to the ω_1 for the low pass filter, we get

$$\omega_1 a = 4\pi \qquad \text{...(16.87)}$$

Eq. (16.87) is similar in form to Eq. (16.80) for rectangular pulse.

We have just considered three typical cases of non-recurring pulses. From the study of these pulses, we draw the following useful conclusion :

$$\text{(Bandwidth required)} \times \text{(Pulse duration)} = \text{Constant} \qquad \text{...(16.88)}$$

Stated otherwise, *the bandwidth required for transmission is inversely proportional to the duration of the pulse being transmitted.*

Eq. (16.88) is applicable to all pulses, although we have considered here only three cases. Thus we may readily verify that it is true for an impulse function. An impulse function has zero width and it thus forms a limiting case of a pulse.

From Eq. (16.35), for a unit impulse, we get

$$f(j\omega) = \int_{-\infty}^{\infty} \delta(t)e^{-j\omega t}\, dt = 1 \qquad \text{...(16.89)}$$

Fig. 16.21 shows the continuous amplitude spectrum of this unit impulse. It is evident that for this unit impulse function, $F(j\omega)$ is constant and equals unity. This implies that the amplitude spectrum contains all frequencies with equal amplitude and has infinite bandwidth. Thus an infinite bandwidth is required to transmit a pulse of zero width. Thus Eq. (16.88) is satisfied in this case also.

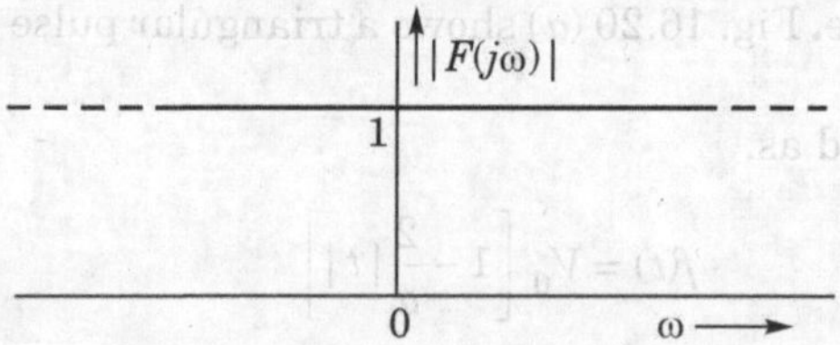

Fig. 16.21. Continuous amplitude spectrum for a unit impulse.

Example 16.1. *Find the continuous magnitude and phase spectra of a single pulse shown is Fig. 16.1.*

Solution. The given pulse may be expressed by,

$$f(t) = \begin{cases} -V_0, & -a < t < a \\ V_0, & 0 < t < a \\ 0, & \text{for all other values of } t \end{cases} \qquad \text{...(1)}$$

Then $F(j\omega) = \displaystyle\int_{-\infty}^{\infty} (t)e^{-j\omega t}\, dt$ ...(2)

Substituting the value of $f(t)$ from Eq. (1) into Eq. (2), we get

$$F(j\omega) = \int_{-a}^{0} -V_0 e^{-j\omega t}\, dt + \int_{0}^{a} V_0 e^{-j\omega t}\, dt \qquad \text{...(3)}$$

$$= \frac{V_0}{j\omega}\left[1 - e^{j\omega a}\right] - \frac{V_0}{j\omega}\left[e^{-j\omega a} - 1\right] = \frac{V_0}{j\omega}[2 - 2\cos\omega a]$$

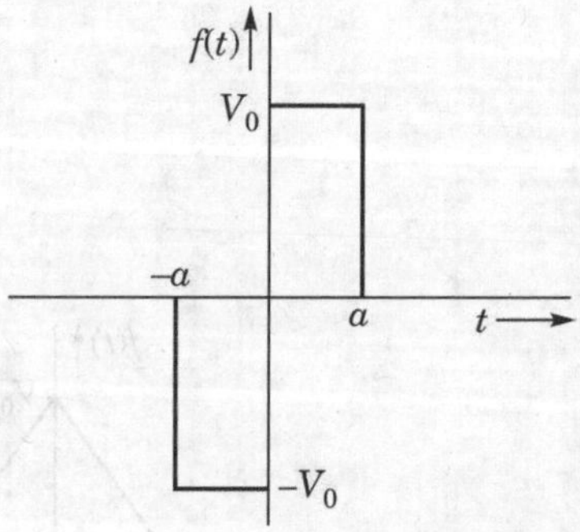

Fig. Example 16.1.

or $$F(j\omega) = \frac{2V_0}{j\omega}[1 - \cos \omega a]$$

The magnitude of $F(j\omega)$ becomes zero,

when $$1 - \cos \omega a = 0$$

i.e. when $$\cos \omega a = 1$$

or when $$\omega a = 2n\pi,$$

when n is an integer. Thus the frequency of zero amplitude is given by,

$$\omega = \frac{2n\pi}{a} = n\omega_0$$

where $$\omega_0 = \frac{2\pi}{a}$$

Fig. (*a*) shows the amplitude spectrum.

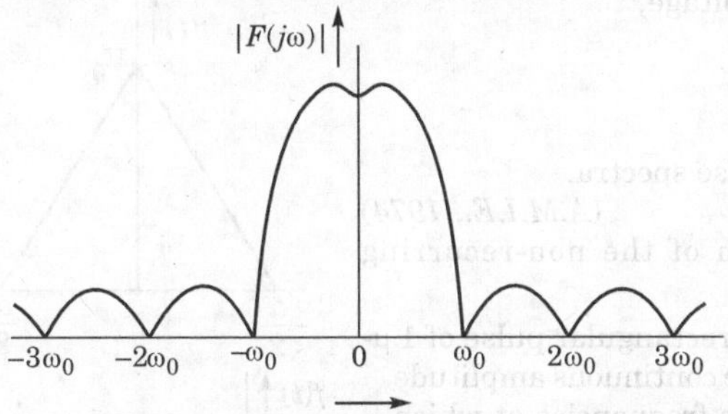

(*a*) Amplitude spectrum

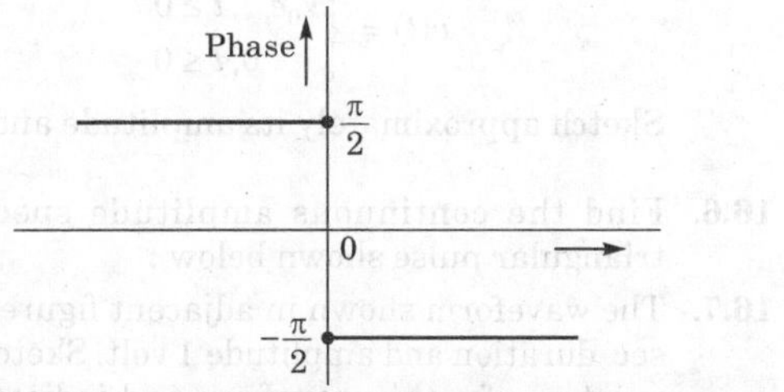

(*b*) Phase spectrum

The phase of the Fourier transform $F(j\omega)$ is given by,

$$\phi = \tan^{-1} \frac{\text{Imaginary part of } F(j\omega)}{\text{Real part of } F(j\omega)} = \tan^{-1} \frac{-2\dfrac{V_0}{\omega}(1 - \cos \omega a)}{0}$$

Thus $$\phi = \begin{cases} -\dfrac{\pi}{2} & \text{when } \omega \text{ is positive} \\ \dfrac{\pi}{2} & \text{when } \omega \text{ is negative.} \end{cases}$$

Fig. (*b*) shows the phase spectrum.

EXERCISES

16.1. Mention the test which should be applied before proceeding to find out the Fourier integral of a function. Is the test satisfactory for the function $f(t) = u(t)$? What modification is necessary to evaluate the Fourier integral of $v(t)$? Evaluate the Fourier integral of this function. (*A.M.I.E., 1975*)

$$\left[\textbf{Ans.}\ F(j\omega) = \pi\delta(\omega) + \frac{1}{j\omega}\right]$$

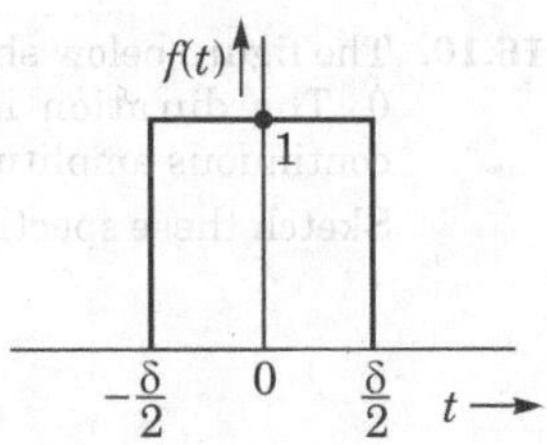

16.2. For the pulse shown below, prove that the Fourier transform is given by,

$$F(j\omega) = \delta \frac{\sin \dfrac{\omega\delta}{2}}{\dfrac{\omega\delta}{2}}$$

16.3. Find the Fourier transform of the following functions :

(*i*) unit impulse function $\delta(t)$; (*ii*) $f(t) = e^{-a/t}$, for all t ; (*iii*) $f(t) = 1$.

Draw their amplitude spectra.

16.4. Obtain the Fourier transform for the Signum function shown below. Draw its amplitude and phase spectra.

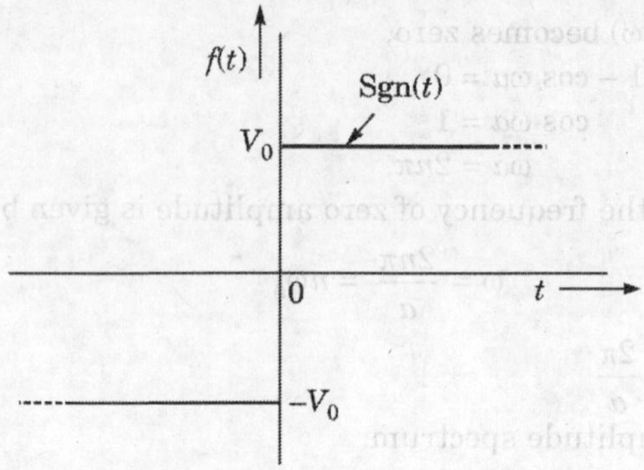

16.5. Find the Fourier transform of the exciting voltage,

$$v(t) = \begin{cases} V_0 e^{-t}, t \geq 0 \\ 0, t \leq 0 \end{cases}$$

Sketch approximately its amplitude and phase spectra.

(A.M.I.E., 1974)

16.6. Find the continuous amplitude spectrum of the non-recurring triangular pulse shown below :

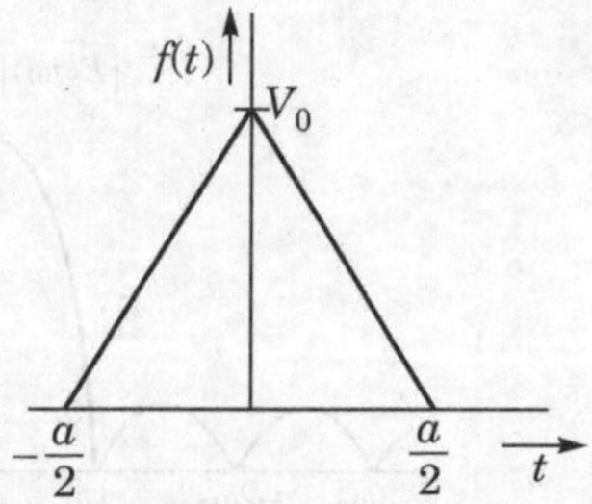

16.7. The waveform shown in adjacent figure is a rectangular pulse of 1 μ-sec. duration and amplitude 1 volt. Sketch the continuous amplitude spectrum for this waveform and indicate the frequencies at which the envelope of the amplitude has zero values.

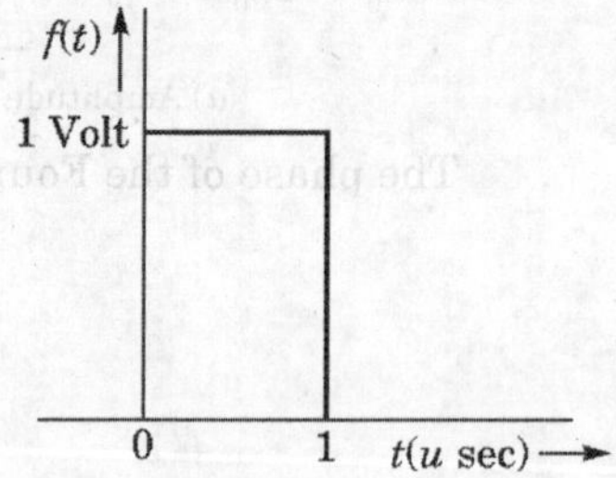

16.8. Determine the Fourier transform for the functions shown in adjacent figure. Sketch the continuous amplitude and phase spectra for this function.

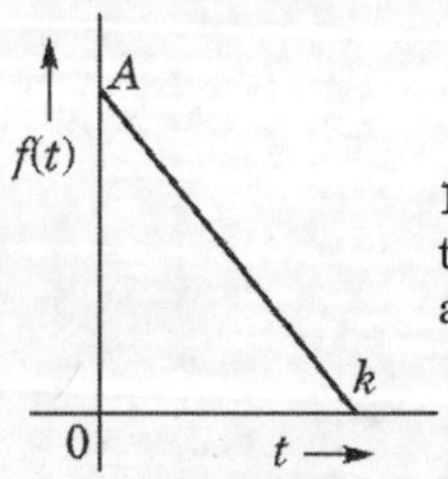

$$\left[\textbf{Ans. } F(j\omega) = AK\left\{\frac{(1-\cos\omega k)}{\omega^2 k^2} + j\frac{\sin\omega k - \omega k}{w^2 k^2}\right\}\right]$$

16.9. For the non-recurring cosine pulse $v = V_0 \cos t$ shown in adjacent figure determine the Fourier transform. Sketch the continuous amplitude and phase spectra for this function.

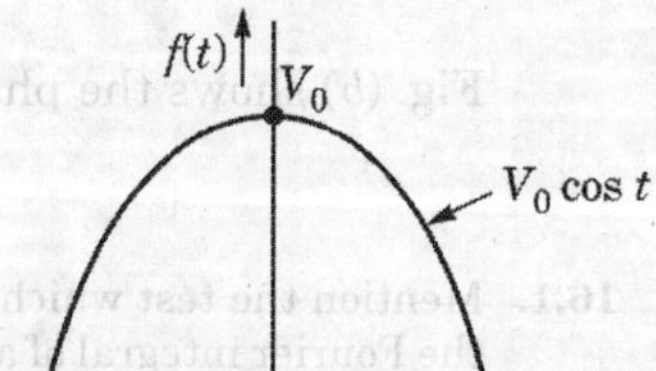

$$\left[\textbf{Ans. } \frac{2V_0}{1-\omega^2}\cos\frac{\omega\pi}{2}\right]$$

16.10. The figure below shows a stepped pulse symmetrical about $t = 0$. The duration is T. For this waveform, determine the continuous amplitude and phase spectra.

Sketch these spectra.

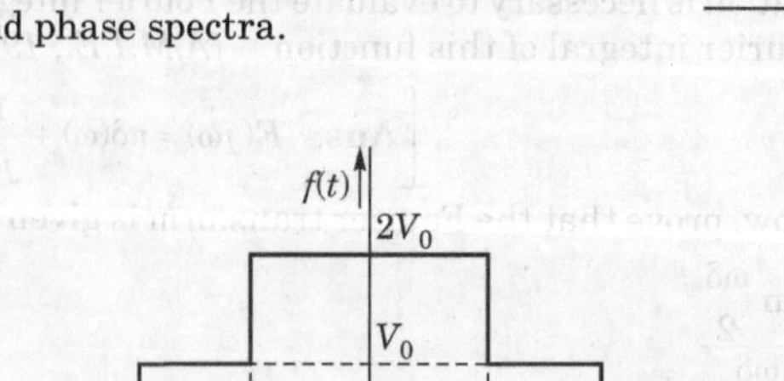

17

The Transmission Lines

17.1. Introduction

The term *transmission lines* in a general sense signifies any physical system for transmission of certain physical quantities. Thus the railway track even may be considered to form a transmission line for transmission of railway carriages. In the present context, however, the transmission line signifies a set of wires made of good electrical conductors such as aluminium or copper, used for transmission of an electrical energy. Excellent electrical insulation between the conductors is of vital importance. The nature of transmission line and its performance depend upon

(*i*) the amount of power to be transmitted and

(*ii*) the frequencies involved. From these considerations, the transmission lines may be put into following two categories :

(*a*) *Power lines* used for transmission of large quantities of power over a fixed frequency and

(*b*) *Communication lines* used for transmission of small quantities of power at band of frequencies.

In communication lines, at the sending end, some electrical quantity is altered in accordance with the information to be transmitted and at the receiving end, this electrical signal is received and converted to yield the original information. Thus in d.c. telegraphy, the d.c. voltage at the sending end of the transmission line is modulated in accordance with the telegraph signal. This modulated voltage must travel to the receiving end without distortion. Thus a communication line is required to be a more faithful medium of signal transmission as compared to a power line. On the other hand, a power line must transmit power with high efficiency since the power involved is high. In communication lines, power efficiency is not so important.

Fig. 17.1 shows a two-wire line fed at its sending end by a variable frequency voltage generator and terminated at its receiving end by a load impedance Z_R. Let the voltage and current at the sending end be E_S and I_S respectively. Similarly the voltage and current at the receiving end be E_R and I_R respectively. It may be noted that in transmission line theory current I_R at the receiving end is assumed to flow away from the line into the load whereas in general two-port network analysis, currents at either end is assumed to enter the network.

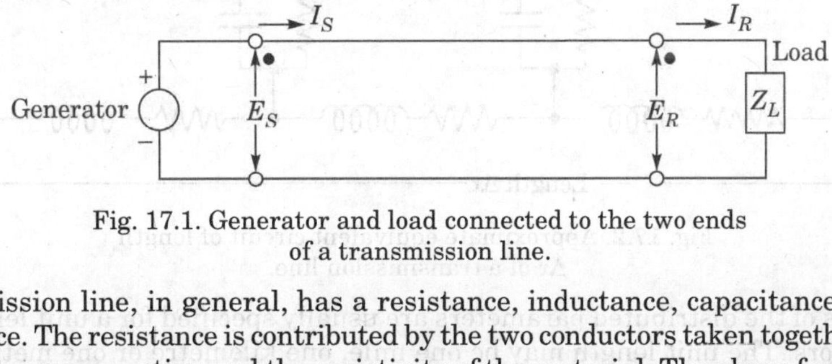

Fig. 17.1. Generator and load connected to the two ends of a transmission line.

A transmission line, in general, has a resistance, inductance, capacitance and leakance or shunt conductance. The resistance is contributed by the two conductors taken together and it depends upon the conductor cross-section and the resistivity of the material. The above four quantities form the primary parameters of a transmission line and these are denoted by R, L, C and G respectively. The values of these four parameters for a transmission line depend upon the type and construction of the line. The types of communication lines for use at frequencies extending from voice frequencies to high frequencies are : (*i*) open wire line (*ii*) paired cables and (*iii*) coaxial cables.

An open wire line is formed by running two wires of sufficient cross-sectional area on insulators firmly and rigidly supported by cross arms put at a certain height from ground by means of galvanised iron poles or any other structure. The conductors run parallel to each other with air as dielectric between them. A cable may consist of a large number of pairs of wires. Each pair consists of two wires which are insulated from each other by oil impregnated insulating paper wrapped around each and which are then twisted. A communication cable may contain hundreds of such pairs whereas a power cable may contain only two or three heavy conductors, insulated and protected heavily from each other.

A coaxial is formed, as the name indicates, by placing one solid conductor of smaller diameter axially inside another hollow conductor of larger diameter and of a certain thickness. The inner conductor is supported by solid discs of a certain dielectric material (usually polythene), the remaining space containing air. Alternatively the complete cable may be filled up by a solid dielectric material.

17.2. Distributed Parameters and Primary Constants

A uniform transmission line offers uniformly distributed series resistance, series inductance, shunt capacitance and shunt admittance. The series resistance is contributed by the conductors themselves and depends upon their resistivity and diameter. The inductance is contributed by the magnetic field of each of the conductor carrying a current. Further this inductance is considered in series with the distributed resistance since the effect of inductance is to oppose the flow of current. Finally there exists shunt admittance between the two wires of the transmission line, even though there is no physical connection between the two. This shunt admittance consists of two components namely the shunt conductance and the shunt capacitance. The shunt capacitance is contributed by the two conductors, placed parallel or twisted and separated by a dielectric. This dielectric, in between the wires is not perfect. Hence a small conduction current or leakage current flows in between the wires. This results in the shunt conductance. All the four parameters mentioned above are uniformly distributed along the line.

Because of the distributed nature of the parameters, it is not possible to represent the entire transmission line by an accurate equivalent circuit. However, if we take up a very small length Δx of a transmission line, this may be represented by the equivalent circuit of Fig. 17.2 using lumped parameters rather than the distributed parameters.

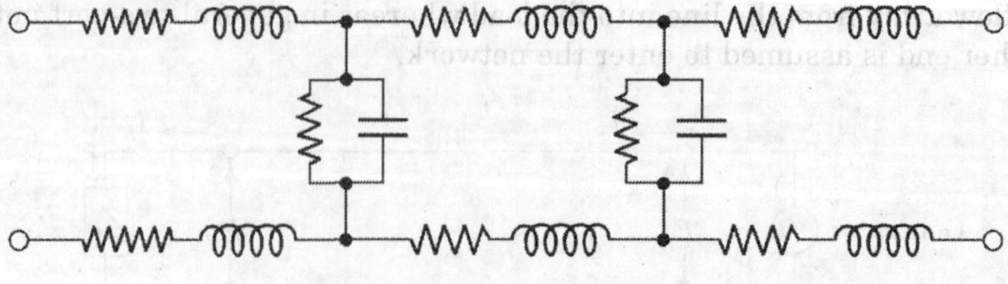

Fig. 17.2. Approximate equivalent circuit of length Δx of a transmission line.

The values of the distributed parameters are usually specified for a unit length, considering both the conductors. The unit length may be one mile, one kilometre or one metre. Thus the four parameter are defined as below :

R = Loop resistance per unit length
L = Loop inductance per unit length
C = Shunt capacitance per unit length
G = Shunt conductance per unit length.

Loop resistance R is the sum of the resistances of both the wires of unit length and may be expressed in ohms/metre, ohms/kilometre or ohms/mile. Similarly, the loop conductance L is the inductance of both the wires of unit length and may be expressed in mH/metre, mH/kilometre or mH/mile.

The capacitance C and the conductance G occur between the *two wires* and hence *loop* is not necessary.

The parameters, R, L, C and G are normally constant for a particular transmission line and are known as the *Primary constants* of the transmission line.

The values of these primary constants of a line depend on the construction of the line but may change appreciably for large signal frequency.

17.3. Loop Inductance

The loop inductance per unit length depends upon the nature of transmission line and its dimensions. Here we consider the three namely open wire line, two-wire cable and coaxial cable.

(A) Open wire line. Consider an open wire line having two circular conductors parallel to each other. Let the radius of each conductor be a and let them be separated by a distance d as shown in Fig. 17.3.

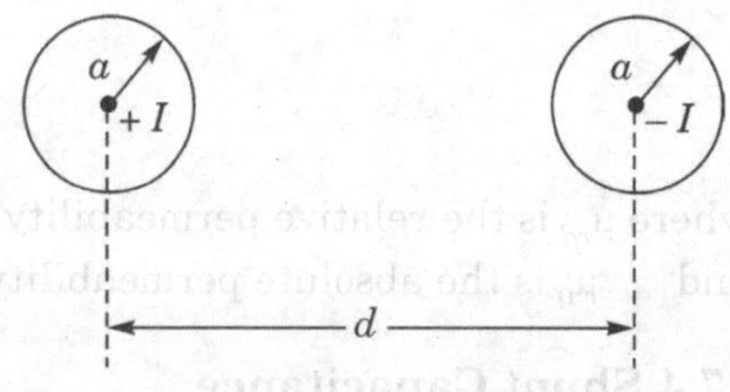

Fig. 17.3. Cross-section of a parallel wire line.

Then the self-inductance of the two-wires together is given by the equation,

$$L = \left(\mu_r + 9.21 \log \frac{d}{a}\right) 10^{-7} \text{ henrys/loop metre} \quad ...(17.1)$$

where μ_r is the relative magnetic permeability of the conductor material and is unity for non-magnetic material.

This expression can be derived from fundamental electromagnetic field theory.

The first term on the right hand side of Eq. (17.1) is called the *internal inductance* of the line and is due to the internal flux linkages in the conductors. The second term is known as the *external inductance* and is due to flux linkages with the flux external to the wires. Eq. (17.1) holds good only when the current distribution over the conductors is uniform. This is true only when $d >> a$ which is true for most of the parallel wire lines. At high frequencies the current tends to flow over the surface with a very small radial depth inside the conductor. This causes the internal inductance to become practically zero.

(B) Cables. In a cable, the two wires are very close to each other and are twisted so that there is hardly any flux linkage. Hence the inductance or a paired cable is very small and is practically negligible in comparison with its resistance and capacitance.

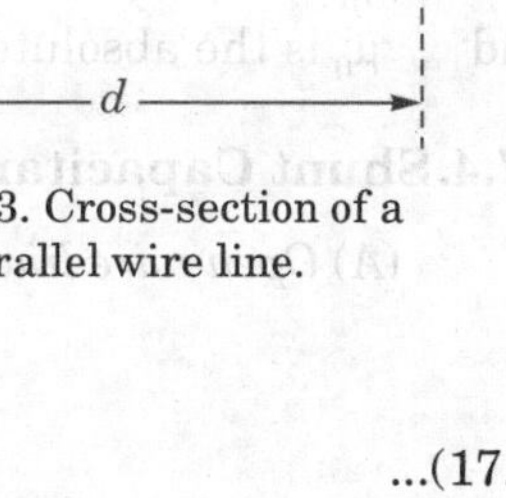

Fig. 17.4. Cross-section of a coaxial cable.

(C) Coaxial cable. Fig. 17.4 shows the cross-section of a coaxial cable which consists of an inner solid conductor of radius say a and an outer hollow tubular conductor of inner surface radius say b. Let c be the outer surface radius. The outer conductor forms a conducting sheath.

The self-inductance of this coaxial cable is given by the following equation :

$$L = \frac{\mu_d}{2\pi} \ln \frac{b}{a} + \frac{\mu_c}{8\pi}\left[\frac{4C^4}{(c^2-b^2)^2} \ln \frac{b}{c} - \frac{2c^2}{(c^2-b^2)}\right] \text{ henry/loop metre} \quad ...(17.2)$$

where μ_d is the permeability of the dielectric material
and μ_c is the permeability of the conductors.

The first terms on the right hand side of Eq. (17.2) is due to the flux linkages between the conductors while the second term is due to flux linkages within the conductors.

At high frequencies, the flux linkages inside the conductors become zero since the entire current tends to flow through the outer surface of the inner conductor and through the inner surface of the outer conductor. Hence at high frequencies, the self-inductance of a coaxial cable is given by,

$$L = \frac{\mu_d}{2\pi} \ln \frac{b}{a} \text{ henrys/loop metre} \quad ...(17.3)$$

$$= \frac{\mu_{rd}\mu_0}{2\pi} \times 2.3 \log_{10} \frac{b}{a} \text{ henrys/loop metre} \quad ...(17.4)$$

$$= (4.6 \times 10^{-7})\, \mu_{rd} \log_{10} \frac{b}{a} \text{ henrys/loop metre} \quad ...(17.5)$$

where μ_{rd} is the relative permeability of the dielectrical material
and μ_0 is the absolute permeability of the free space.

17.4. Shunt Capacitance

(*A*) *Open wire line*. The capacitance of the parallel wire line is given by the equation,

$$C = \frac{\pi\varepsilon_d}{\ln \frac{d}{a}} \text{ farads/metre for } d >> 5a \quad ...(17.6)$$

$$= \frac{12.07\, \varepsilon_r}{\log_{10} \frac{d}{a}} \; \mu\,\mu \text{ F/metre} \quad ...(17.7)$$

where ε_d is the dielectric constant of the dielectric material,
and ε_r is the relative dielectric constant of the dielectric material.

(*B*) *Coaxial Cable*. The capacitance of the coaxial cable is given by the following equation :

$$C = \frac{2\pi\varepsilon_d}{\ln \frac{b}{a}} \text{ farads/metre} \quad ...(17.8)$$

$$= \frac{24.14\, \varepsilon_r}{\log_{10} \frac{b}{a}} \; \mu\mu \text{ F/metre} \quad ...(17.9)$$

17.5. Loop Resistance

(*A*) *Open wire line*. The loop resistance of the open wire line is given by the following equations:

$$R_{dc} = \frac{2}{\pi a^2 \sigma} \text{ ohms/loop metre} \quad ...(17.10)$$

$$R_{ac} = \frac{R_{dc}}{2} a\sqrt{\pi f \mu_c \sigma} \text{ ohms/loop metre} \quad ...(17.11)$$

where R_{dc} is the d.c. loop resistance
R_{ac} is the a.c. loop resistance
σ is the conductivity of the conductors
f is the frequency in Hertz.

(*C*) *Coaxial Cable*. The loop resistance of coaxial cable is given by the following equations :

$$R_{dc} = \frac{1}{\pi\sigma}\left(\frac{1}{a^2} + \frac{1}{c^2 - b^2}\right) \text{ ohms/loop metre} \quad ...(17.12)$$

$$R_{ac} = \sqrt{\frac{f\mu_c}{4\pi\sigma}}\left(\frac{1}{a} + \frac{1}{b}\right) \text{ ohms/loop metre} \quad ...(17.13)$$

All the four parameters of any transmission line change somewhat with changes in weather conditions.

Example 17.1. *A parallel wire line is made up of two copper conductors each of radius I mm, separated by a distance of 30 cm in air. Conductivity of copper is 5.75 × 10⁷ mho / metre. Calculate the resistance, inductance and capacitance per kilometre of the line. Also calculate the a.c. resistance of the line at frequency of 30 kHz.*

Solution. $L = \left(\mu_r + 9.21 \log_{10}\frac{d}{a}\right) 10^{-7}$ henrys/loop metre.

Relative permeability μ_r for copper is unity.

Hence $$L = \left(1 + 9.21 \log \frac{30}{0.1}\right) \times 10^{-7} \text{ henrys/loop metre}$$

$$= 23.81 \times 10^{-7} \text{ henrys/loop metre}$$

$$= 2.381 \times 10^{-3} \text{ henrys/loop kilometre}$$

$$= 2.381 \text{ mH/loop kilometre}$$

$$C = \frac{12.07\,\varepsilon_r}{\log\frac{d}{a}}\ \mu\,\mu\text{ F/metre} = \frac{12.07}{\log\frac{30}{0.1}}\ \mu\,\mu\text{ F/metre}$$

$$= 24.86\ \mu\,\mu\text{ F/metre} = 0.02486\ \mu\text{F/kilometre}$$

$$R_{dc} = \frac{2}{\pi a^2 \sigma}\ \Omega\text{/loop metre} = \frac{2 \times 10^3}{\pi \times 10^{-6} \times 5.75 \times 10^7}\ \Omega\text{/loop km}$$

$$= 11.33\ \Omega\text{/loop kilometre}$$

$$R_{ac} = \frac{R_{dc}}{2} \cdot a\sqrt{\pi f \mu_c \sigma} = \frac{2}{\pi a^2 \sigma} \cdot \frac{a}{2}\sqrt{\pi f \mu_c \sigma} = \frac{1}{\pi a \sigma}\sqrt{\pi f \mu_c \sigma}$$

$$= \frac{1}{a}\sqrt{\frac{f\mu_c}{\pi\sigma}} = \frac{1}{10^{-3}} \times \sqrt{\frac{30 \times 10^3 \times 4\pi \times 10^{-7}}{\pi \times 5.75 \times 10^{-7}}}\ \Omega\text{/loop metre}$$

since $$\mu_c = \mu_0 = 4\pi \times 10^{-7} \text{ MKS units.}$$

On simplification, we get

$$R_{ac} = 0.01442\ \Omega\text{/loop kilometre}$$

$$= 14.42\ \Omega\text{/loop kilometre.}$$

Example 17.2. *A coaxial cable has inner conductor of diameter 0.2 cm. Inner diameter of outer conductor is 0.8 cm and the outer diameter of the outer conductor is 1.0 cm. The conductors are made of copper and the cable is filled with a material of relative dielectric constant 2.5. Calculate per loop kilometre, the low frequency and the high frequency inductance, capacitance, d.c. resistance and the a.c. resistance at frequency of 100 kHz. Assume conductivity of copper to be 5.75 × 10⁻⁷ S/ metre.*

Solution. The low frequency inductance of a coaxial cable is given by,

$$L_{lf} = \frac{\mu_{rd}\,\mu_0}{2\pi}\ln\frac{8}{2} + \frac{\mu_{rc}\,\mu_0}{8\pi} \times \left[\frac{4c^4}{(c^2-b^2)^2}\ln\frac{d}{c} - \frac{2c^2}{(c^2-b^2)}\right] \text{ henry/loop metre.}$$

Substituting the value, we get

$$L_{lf} = \frac{4\pi\times10^{-7}}{2\pi}\ln 4 + \frac{4\pi\times10^{-7}}{8\pi} \times \left[\frac{4(1)^4}{(1-0.64)}\ln\frac{10}{8} - \frac{2(1)^2}{(1-0.64)}\right] \text{ henry/loop metre}$$

$$= [2.7726 + 0.665]\ 10^{-7} \text{ henry/loop metre}$$

$$= 0.3488 \text{ m-henry/loop kilometre}$$

$$L_{hf} = \frac{\mu_{rd}\,\mu_0}{2\pi}\ln\frac{8}{2} \text{ henry/loop metre}$$

$$= 2.7726\times10^{-7} \text{ henry/loop metre}$$

$$= 0.277 \text{ m-henry/loop kilometre}$$

$$C = \frac{2\pi\,\varepsilon_{rd}\,\varepsilon_0}{\ln\dfrac{a}{b}} = \frac{2\pi\times2.5\times10^{-9}}{36\pi\times\ln 4} \text{ farad/metre} = 0.1002\ \mu\text{F/km}$$

$$R_{dc} = \frac{1}{\pi\sigma}\left[\frac{1}{a^2} - \frac{1}{c^2-b^2}\right] \text{ ohm/loop metre}$$

$$= \frac{1}{\pi\times5.75\times10^{7}}\left[\frac{1}{(0.2\times10^{-2})^2} - \frac{1}{(10^{-2})^2-(0.8\times10^{-2})^2}\right] \Omega\text{/loop metre}$$

$$= 1.538 \text{ ohms/loop kilometre}$$

$$R_{ac} = \sqrt{\frac{f\,\mu_{rc}\,\mu_0}{4\pi\sigma}}\left(\frac{1}{a}+\frac{1}{b}\right) \Omega\text{/loop metre}$$

$$= \sqrt{\frac{10^5\times4\pi\times10^{-7}}{4\pi\times5.75\times10^{7}}}\left[\frac{1}{0.2\times10^{-2}} + \frac{1}{0.8\times10^{-2}}\right] \Omega\text{/loop metre}$$

$$= 8.24 \text{ ohms/loop kilometre.}$$

17.6. Equivalent Circuit in Terms of Primary Constants

The equivalent circuit of a transmission line may now be drawn in terms of its primary constants for a specified length Δx and arranged in the form of T or π configurations as shown in Figs. 17.5 and 17.6.

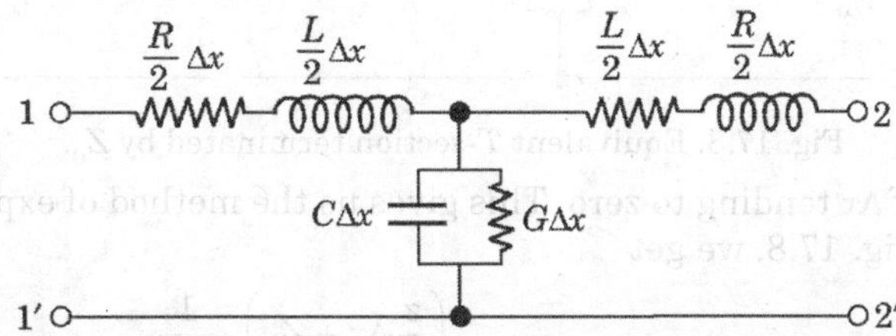

Fig. 17.5. Equivalent T-section of a line of length Δ.

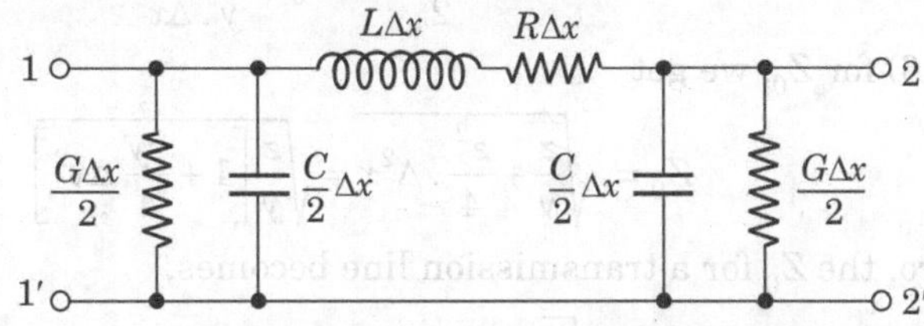

Fig. 17.6. Equivalent π-section of a line of length Δx.

If the length Δx is very small and infinitely large number of such sections are connected in cascade, the circuit behaves exactly as the transmission line of infinite length.

In order to study the behaviour of a transmission line, the series resistance R and series inductance L may be combined to form an impedance Z while the shunt capacitance C and the shunt conductance G may be combined to form an admittance y at a specified radian frequency ω. Thus the circuit of Fig. 17.5 may be represented in terms of z and y as shown in Fig. 17.7, where

$$z = (R + j\omega L) \text{ ohms} \quad ...(17.14)$$

and

$$y = (G + j\omega C) \text{ mhos} \quad ...(17.15)$$

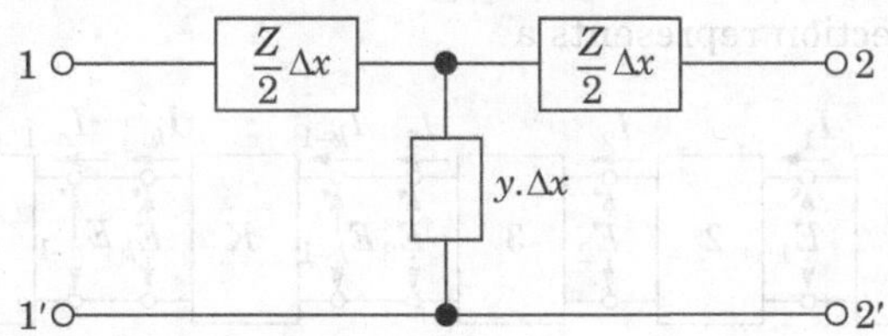

Fig. 17.7. Equivalent T-network in terms of z and y.

17.7. Secondary Constants of a Line

Consider a transmission line of infinite length. The input impedance of such a line is called its *characteristic impedance* and is denoted by Z_0. Now from this line of infinite length, a certain portion is cut away, the remaining portion will still remain infinite having input impedance equal to Z_0. Now if the cut-away portion is terminated at the receiving end by Z_0, it will behave as a line of infinite length. Thus if the equivalent T-network of a line of length Δx is terminated by its characteristic impedance as shown in Fig. 17.8, the input impedance will also be equal to the characteristic impedance Z_0 under

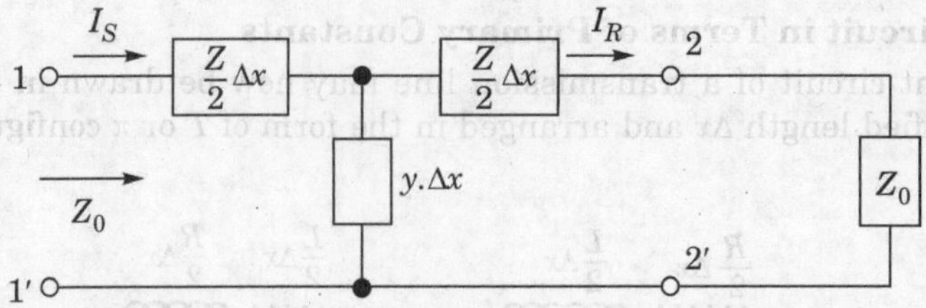

Fig. 17.8. Equivalent T-section terminated by Z_0.

the limiting condition of Δx tending to zero. This gives us the method of expressing the Z_0 in terms of z and y. Thus, from Fig. 17.8, we get

$$Z_0 = \frac{z}{2}\Delta x + \frac{\left(\frac{z}{2}\Delta x + Z_0\right)\frac{1}{y\,.\,\Delta x}}{\frac{z}{2}\Delta x + Z_0 + \frac{1}{y\,.\,\Delta x}} \qquad \text{...(17.16)}$$

Solving Eq. (17.16) for Z_0, we get

$$Z_0 = \sqrt{\frac{z}{y} + \frac{z^2}{4}\,.\,\Delta^2 x} = \sqrt{\frac{z}{y}\left[1 + \frac{zy}{4}\Delta x^2\right]} \qquad \text{...(17.17)}$$

when Δx approaches zero, the Z_0 for a transmission line becomes,

$$Z_0 = \sqrt{\frac{z}{y}} \qquad \text{...(17.18)}$$

Substituting the primary constants, we get

$$Z_0 = \sqrt{\frac{z}{y}} = \sqrt{\frac{R + j\omega L}{G + j\omega C}} \text{ ohms} \qquad \text{...(17.19)}$$

The current at the sending end is generally indicated by I_s while that at the receiving end is indicated by I_R as shown in Fig. 17.8. As the propagation of signal takes place from sending end to the receiving end, the current through the line reduces in magnitude and its phase angle changes.

Let a transmission line be constituted by n identical T-sections connected in cascade as shown in Fig. 17.9. Each section represents a

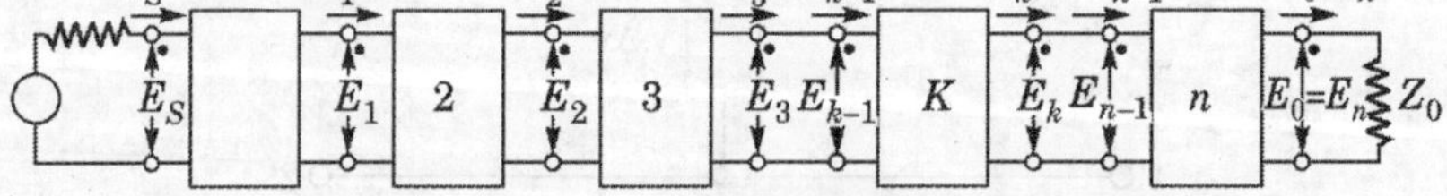

Fig. 17.9. Cascaded n-identical sections constituting a line.

specified length of line. The last section is terminated in Z_0, the characteristic impedance of the line. Hence each section is terminated in Z_0 and the behaviour of every section is the same under a set of conditions. Hence the ratio of input voltage to the input current of any section will be the same and equals Z_0. Thus we have

$$\frac{E_S}{I_S} = \frac{E_1}{I_1} = \frac{E_2}{I_2} = \text{......} = \frac{E_{k-1}}{I_{k-1}} = \frac{E_k}{I_k} = \text{......} \frac{E_0}{I_0} = Z_0 \qquad \text{...(17.20)}$$

Now consider the kth section representing the transmission line of unit length. Let this section be represented by its equivalent T-section as shown in Fig. 17.10.

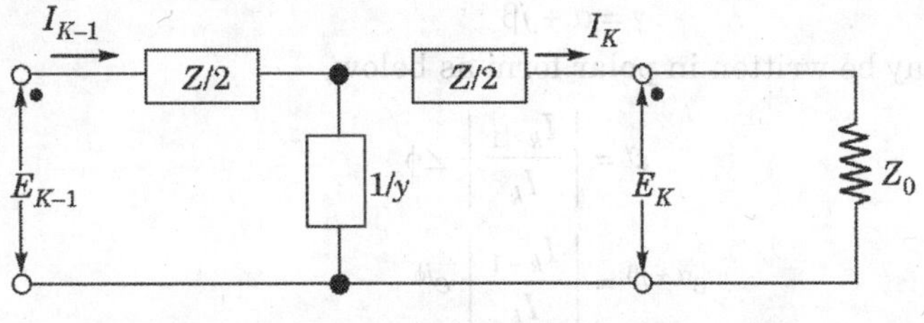

Fig. 17.10. A general unit-length kth section of line.

The output current I_k may then be obtained in terms of the input current I_{k-1} by considering the division of current through the two parallel branches.

Thus, we get

$$I_k = \frac{I_{k-1} \cdot \dfrac{1}{y}}{\dfrac{1}{y} + \dfrac{z}{2} + Z_0}$$

or

$$\frac{I_{k-1}}{I_k} = \frac{\dfrac{1}{y} + \dfrac{z}{2} + Z_0}{\dfrac{1}{y}} \qquad \text{...(17.21)}$$

But from Eq. (17.20),

$$\frac{E_{k-1}}{E_k} = \frac{I_{k-1}}{I_k} \qquad \text{...(17.22)}$$

Combining Eqs. (17.20) to (17.22) we get the following relation for any n-section equivalent circuit of transmission line,

$$\frac{E_S}{E_1} = \frac{E_1}{E_2} = \frac{E_2}{E_3} = \ldots\ldots = \frac{E_{k-1}}{E_k} = \ldots\ldots = \frac{E_{n-1}}{E_0} = \frac{I_S}{I_1} = \frac{I_1}{I_2} = \frac{I_2}{I_3} = \ldots\ldots = \frac{I_{k-1}}{I_k} = \ldots\ldots = \frac{I_{n-1}}{I_0}$$

$$= \frac{\dfrac{1}{y} + \dfrac{z}{2} + Z_0}{\dfrac{1}{y}} \qquad \text{...(17.23)}$$

From Eq. (17.23) we conclude that the ratio of input current to output current for any section is the same and is also equal to the ratio of input voltage to the output voltage.

The ratio $\dfrac{\dfrac{1}{y} + \dfrac{z}{2} + Z_0}{\dfrac{1}{y}}$ consists of complex quantities. Hence the ratios of currents and the ratio of voltages will also be, in general, complex. A complex quantity may be more conveniently expressed in logarithmic terms. Thus the voltage ratio or the current ratio may be expressed as below :

$$\frac{E_{k-1}}{E_k} = \frac{I_{k-1}}{I_k} = \frac{\dfrac{1}{y} + \dfrac{z}{2} + Z_0}{\dfrac{1}{y}} = \varepsilon^{\gamma} \qquad \text{...(17.24)}$$

where ε is the base of natural logarithm and γ (gamma) is known as the *propagation constant*. The constant γ is a complex quantity and may, therefore, be put as,

$$\gamma = \alpha + j\beta \qquad ...(17.25)$$

Eq. (17.25) may be written in polar form as below,

$$\varepsilon^{\gamma} = \left|\frac{I_{k-1}}{I_k}\right| \angle\phi \qquad ...(17.26)$$

or

$$\varepsilon^{\alpha + j\beta} = \left|\frac{I_{k-1}}{I_k}\right| e^{j\phi} \qquad ...(17.27)$$

Taking natural logarithm, Eq. (17.27) yields,

$$\alpha + j\beta = \ln\left|\frac{I_{k-1}}{I_k}\right| + j\phi \qquad ...(17.28)$$

Equating the real and imaginary parts in Eq. (17.28), we get,

$$\alpha = \ln\left|\frac{I_{k-1}}{I_k}\right| = \ln\left|\frac{\frac{1}{y} + \frac{z}{2} + Z_0}{\frac{1}{y}}\right| \text{ nepers/unit length} \qquad ...(17.29)$$

$$\beta = \phi = \arg\left[\frac{\frac{1}{y} + \frac{z}{2} + Z_0}{\frac{1}{y}}\right] \text{ radians/unit length} \qquad ...(17.30)$$

where 'arg' stands for *argument* of and signifies the *phase angle* of the function.

Eq. (17.29) shows that the real part α of the propagation constant γ is a measure of the *change in magnitude* of the current or voltage in each *T*-section. This quantity α is called the *attenuation constant* of the transmission line. Eq (17.30) shows that β equals the difference in phase angle between the input current and the output current or the corresponding voltages. This quantity β is called the *phase-shift constant* or the *delay constant* or the *wavelength constant* of the line. The quantities Z_0, γ, α and β are called the *secondary* constants of a line. It may be seen that β is negative when the output current leads the input current and is positive when it lags.

When *n* sections are connected in cascade for a particular length of a transmission line as shown in Fig. 17.9, the ratio of input to output currents for each section may be multiplied together to yield the ratio of input current I_S to the output current I_0 of the entire line. Thus,

$$\frac{I_s}{I_1} \times \frac{I_1}{I_2} \times \frac{I_2}{I_3} \times \ldots\ldots - \frac{I_{n-1}}{I_0} = \frac{I_s}{I_0} \qquad ...(17.31)$$

This yields $\dfrac{I_s}{I_0} = \varepsilon^{n\gamma}$ ...(17.32)

When the transmission line is of length *l*, then the ratio of input current to output current is given as,

$$\frac{I_s}{I_0} = \varepsilon^{\gamma l} \qquad ...(17.33)$$

For a transmission line of length Δx, Eq. (17.24) may be written as,

$$\varepsilon^{\gamma\Delta x} = 1 + \frac{zy}{2}\,\Delta^2 x + Z_0 y\,\Delta x \qquad ...(17.34)$$

On substituting the value of Z_0 from Eq. (17.17) into Eq. (17.34), we get,

$$\varepsilon^{\gamma\Delta x} = 1 + \frac{zy}{2}\Delta^2 x + \sqrt{zy}\,\Delta x\,\sqrt{1+\frac{zx}{4}\Delta^2 x} \quad ...(17.35)$$

Term $\sqrt{1+\frac{zx}{4}\Delta^2 x}$ may be expanded as below :

$$\left[1+\frac{zy}{4}\Delta^2 x\right]^{1/2} = 1 + \frac{zy}{8}\Delta^2 x - \frac{z^2y^2}{128}\Delta^4 x + ... \quad ...(17.36)$$

Similarly the exponential term $\varepsilon^{\gamma\Delta x}$ may be expanded as a power series as below :

$$\varepsilon^{\gamma\Delta x} = 1 + \gamma\,\Delta x + \frac{\gamma^2\Delta^2 x}{2} + \frac{\gamma^3\Delta^3 x}{6} \quad ...(17.37)$$

Hence Eq. (17.35) may be written as below :

$$1 + \gamma\,\Delta x + \frac{\gamma^2\Delta^2 x}{2} + \frac{\gamma^3\Delta^3 x}{6} + ... = 1 + \sqrt{zy}\,\Delta x + \frac{(\sqrt{zy})^2}{2}\Delta^2 x + \frac{(\sqrt{zy})^3\,\Delta^3 x}{8} \quad ...(17.38)$$

In Eq. (17.38), cancelling 1 from both the sides and dividing by Δx, we get

$$\gamma + \frac{\gamma^2\Delta x}{2} + \frac{\gamma^3\Delta^2 x}{6} + ... = \sqrt{zy} + \frac{(\sqrt{zy})^2}{2}\Delta x + \frac{\sqrt{(zy)^3}\,\Delta^{2x}}{8} \quad ...(17.39)$$

Eq. (17.39) applies to a transmission line if the length Δx is made to approach zero. Thus for transmission line, we get

$$\gamma = \sqrt{zy} = \sqrt{(R + j\omega L)(G + j\omega C)} \quad ...(17.40)$$

Eq. (17.40) is an important relation since it enables us to calculate the propagation constant γ, attenuation constant α and the phase-shift constant β provided that the primary constant R, L, G and C are given.

The phase shift constant or the wavelength constant β indicates the amount by which the phase of an input current changes in a unit distance. In a distance equal to one wavelength λ, the phase shift is 2π radians. Hence

$$\lambda = \frac{2\pi}{\beta} \quad ...(17.41)$$

The phase velocity of propagation is then given by,

$$v_p = f\lambda = \frac{\omega}{2\pi}\cdot\frac{2\pi}{\beta}$$

$$= \frac{\omega}{\beta} \quad ...(17.42)$$

Example 17.3. *The values of primary constants of an open wire line per loop kilometre are : $R = 10\ \Omega$, $L = 3.5$ mH, $C = 0.008\ \mu F$ and $G = 0.7\ \mu S$. For signal frequency of 1000 Hz, calculate the characteristic impedance Z_0, phase constant γ, attenuation constant α, phase shift constant β, wavelength λ and phase velocity v_p.*

Solution.

$$z = R + j\omega L = 10 + j2\pi \times 1000 \times 3.5 \times 10^{-3} = 10 + j21.99$$

$$= 24.15\ \underline{/65.55^\circ}$$

$$y = G + j\omega C = 0.7 \times 10^{-6} + j\pi \times 10^3 \times 0.008 \times 10^{-6}$$

$$= (0.7 + j\,16\pi)\,10^{-6} = 50.45 \times 10^{-6}\ \underline{/89.2^\circ}$$

$$Z_0 = \sqrt{\frac{z}{y}} = \sqrt{\frac{24.15\ \angle 65.55^\circ}{50.45 \times 10^{-6}\ \angle 89.2^\circ}} = 692\ \angle -11.82^\circ = 677 - j\,142$$

$$\gamma = \sqrt{zy} = \sqrt{24.15\ \angle 65.55^\circ \times 50.45 \times 10^{-6}\ \angle 8.92^\circ}$$

$$= \sqrt{24.15 \times 150.45 \times 10^{-6}}\ \angle \frac{66.55 + 89.2}{2}$$

$$= 0.03485\ \angle 77.37^\circ = 0.0077 + j\,0.03395$$

Hence $\alpha = 0.0077$ neper/kilometre

and $\beta = 0.03395$ radian/kilometre

$$\lambda = \frac{2\pi}{\beta} = \frac{2\pi}{0.03395} = 185 \text{ kilometres}$$

Phase velocity $v_p = \dfrac{\omega}{\beta} = \dfrac{2\pi \times 10^3}{0.03395} = 185{,}000$ kilometres/sec.

Example 17.4. *An underground cable has the following constants per loop kilometre : R = 53 Ω, L = 0.6 mH, C = 0.04 μF and G = 1 μS. The frequency of operation is 1000 Hz. Calculate Z_0, γ, α, β, λ and v_p for the cable.*

Solution. $z = R + j\,\omega L = 53 + j2\pi \times 10^3 \times 0.6 \times 10^{-3} = 53 + j3.77$

$$= 53.1\ \angle 4.10^\circ$$

$$y = G + j\,\omega C = 20^{-6} + j2\pi \times 10^3 \times 0.04 \times 10^{-6} = (1 + j80\pi)\ 10^{-6}$$

$$= 251 \times 10^{-6}\ \angle 89.76^\circ$$

$$Z_0 = \sqrt{\frac{z}{y}} = \sqrt{\frac{53.1\ \angle 4.10^\circ}{251 \times 10^{-4}\ \angle 89.76^\circ}} = 460\ \angle \frac{4.10^\circ - 89.76^\circ}{2}$$

$$= 460\ \angle -42.83^\circ = 371 - j313$$

$$\gamma = \sqrt{zy} = \sqrt{53.1\ \angle 4.10^\circ \times 251 \times 10^{-6}\ \angle 89.76^\circ}$$

$$= 0.1153\ \angle \frac{4.10^\circ + 89.76^\circ}{2} = 0.1153\ \angle 46.93^\circ$$

$$= 0.0788 + j0.0842$$

Hence $\alpha = 0.0788$ neper/kilometre

$\beta = 0.0842$ radian/kilometre

Wavelength $\lambda = \dfrac{2\pi}{\beta} = \dfrac{2\pi}{0.0842} = 74.6$ km.

Phase velocity $v_p = \dfrac{\omega}{\beta} = f\lambda = 74{,}600$ km/sec.

17.8. Line attenuation and Power Levels

If a transmission line is terminated in its characteristic impedance Z_0, then its input impedance will also be equal to Z_0. Let Z_0 be represented by its magnitude and phase angle by the following relation :

$$Z_0 = | Z_0 | \angle \theta \quad ...(17.43)$$

Then the input power at the sending end is,

$$P_S = E_s I_s$$
$$= | I_s^2 | \; | Z_0 | \cos \theta \quad ...(17.44)$$

The power at the receiving end is,

$$P_R = | I_R^2 | \; Z_0 | \cos \theta \quad ...(17.45)$$

Generally a transmission line is required to run for a long distance. In such a case, the attenuation of the sending end power becomes sufficiently large and the received power may becomes so small that it may not be of any practical use. One way to overcome this difficulty is to increase the input signal power to such a large value that the received power at the receiving end is at the desired high level. This proposition is not feasible since tremendous amount of signal power is then required at the sending end if the line is long, say a few thousand kilometres long. Further, the attenuation constant α introduces distortions since it differs as the signal frequency changes. This difficulty is overcome by using amplifiers, known as the *repeaters*, installed along the line at suitable intervals.

The ratio of power transmitted to the power received in a transmission line may be put as,

$$\frac{P_S}{P_R} = \left(\frac{I_S}{I_R}\right)^2 \quad ...(17.46)$$

From Eq. (17.46) we see that the transmission of power is related to the line attenuation.

Example 17.5. *A line is required to transmit power of 50 μ-watts and receive power of 100 μ-watts at the receiving end by using one repeater station having a gain of 60 dB. If the line attenuation is 0.1 neper per kilometre, determine (i) the maximum permissible length of the line and (ii) the maximum distance from the sending end to the repeater in order that the power input to the repeater does not fall below 5 μ-watts.*

Solution.

(*i*) Power gain $\frac{P_o}{P_i}$ of repeater is given by,

$$60 = 10 \log_{10} \frac{P_o}{P_i}$$

Hence $$\frac{P_o}{P_i} = 10^6.$$

The sending end power gets amplified by 10^6. Thus the effective sending end power equals $50 \times 10^{-6} \times 10^6 = 50$ watts. The receiving end power is required to be 10^{-4}.

Thus $$\frac{P_S}{P_R} = \frac{50}{10^{-4}} = 50 \times 10^4$$

This must equal $\left(\frac{I_S}{I_R}\right)^2$

Hence $$\frac{I_S}{I_R} = \sqrt{50 \times 10^4} = 707$$

Let l be the maximum length of the line.

Then $$\alpha l = \ln \left| \frac{I_S}{I_R} \right| = \ln \mid 707 \mid = 6.561$$

Hence $$l = \frac{6.561}{\alpha} = \frac{6.561}{0.1} = 65.61 \text{ kilometres.}$$

Thus the maximum length of line = 65.61 km.

(*ii*) In the second case, let the maximum distance of the repeater from the sending end be l_1.

Then for this position of repeater, the power ratio $\frac{P_S}{P_R}$ equals

$$\frac{50\ \mu \text{ watts}}{5\ \mu \text{ watts}}, \quad i.e. \quad 10$$

Hence $$\frac{I_S}{I_R} = \sqrt{10}$$

Hence $$\alpha l_1 = \ln \sqrt{10} = 1.1512$$

Hence $$l_1 = \frac{1.1512}{\alpha} = \frac{1.1512}{0.1} = 11.512 \text{ kilometres.}$$

Example 17.6. *A coaxial cable has characteristic impedance of 50 ∠0° and attenuation constant α of 1.2 dB / kilometre. A 20 kilometre length of this cable is terminated in its characteristic impedance and the input power to the line is 0.5 watt. Find (a) the output power and (b) output current.*

Solution. (*a*) Total attenuation = αl = 1.2 × 20 × 0.115 nepers = 2.76 nepers

Hence $$\ln \left| \frac{I_S}{I_R} \right| = 2.76.$$

Hence $$\frac{I_S}{I_R} = \varepsilon^{2.76} = 15.48.$$

Power ratio $$\frac{P_S}{P_R} = \left(\frac{I_S}{I_R}\right)^2 = (15.78)^2 = 249.$$

But $$P_S = 0.5 \text{ watt.}$$

Hence $$P_R = \frac{0.5}{249} \times 1000 \text{ mW} = 201 \text{ mW.}$$

(*b*) Input impedance of the line at the receiving end is

$$Z_0 = 50 \angle 0°$$

Hence $$P_S = |\, I_S \,|^2 \,|\, Z_0 \,|$$

or $$I_S^2 = \frac{P_S}{|\, Z_0 \,|} = \frac{0.5 \text{ watt}}{50 \text{ ohms}} = 0.01$$

Hence $$I_S = \sqrt{0.01} = 0.1 \text{ amp.}$$

Hence $$I_S = \frac{I_S}{15.78} = \frac{0.1 \text{ amp}}{15.78} = 6.35 \text{ mA.}$$

18

General Theory of Transmission Line

18.1. General Equation of a Transmission Line

The treatment afforded so far has been based on equivalent *T*-sections cascaded together with the distributed parameters considered as lumped ones. The equations are obtained under the limiting conditions and these equations are true for a transmission line having distributed parameters. The same result can be obtained alternatively by considering an incremental length of a transmission line and using the method of calculus. This method of analysis is more general and gives the desired results even when the line is not terminated in its characteristic impedance. Further, this method gives rise to certain equations which may be used for calculating the voltage and current at any distance from the sending end of the line.

Consider an incremental length Δx of a transmission line as shown in Fig. 18.1. The line is of length l. Terminals 1-1′ form the sending end while the terminals 2-2′ form the receiving end. At the sending end, the line has been terminated in an impedance Z_R, E_S and I_S are the voltage and current respectively at the sending end. Similarly E_R and I_R are the voltage and current respectively at the receiving end. The incremental length Δx is taken at a distance x from the sending end and at a distance y from the receiving end. Thus the

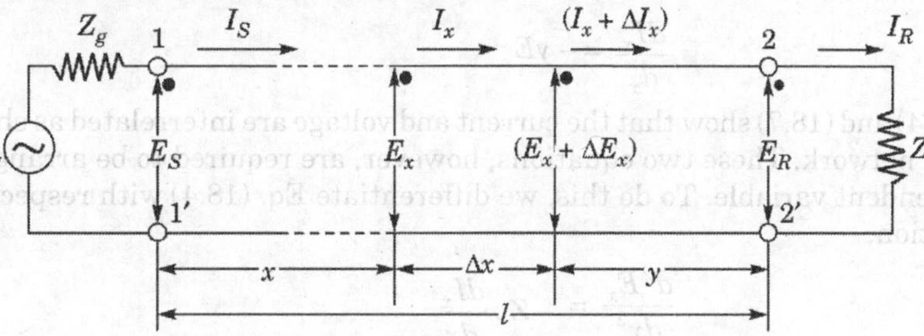

Fig. 18.1. A line with an incremental length Δx.

total length of the line l equals $(x + y)$ under the limiting condition when Δx approaches zero.

The average current through the element is $\left(I_x + \dfrac{\Delta I_x}{2}\right)$. Hence applying Kirchhoff's voltage law to the element gives us,

$$E_x - (E_x + E\Delta_x) = Z\Delta x\left(I_x + \frac{\Delta I_x}{2}\right) \qquad ...(18.1)$$

where Z is the series impedance per unit length.

Eq. (18.1) may be written as,

$$-\Delta E_x = Z\Delta x\left(I_x + \frac{\Delta I_x}{2}\right) \qquad ...(18.2)$$

Dividing by Δx, we get

$$\frac{\Delta E_x}{\Delta x} = -ZI_x - Z\,.\,\frac{\Delta I_x}{2} \qquad ...(18.3)$$

In the limit when $\Delta x \to 0$, the ratio of increments namely $\frac{\Delta E_x}{\Delta x}$ may be written as the derivative $\frac{dE_x}{dx}$.

Hence Eq. (18.3) becomes,

$$\frac{dE_x}{dx} = -ZI_x \quad \text{...(18.4)}$$

since ΔI_x becomes zero.

The average voltage along the element is $E_x + \frac{\Delta E_x}{2}$. Applying Kirchhoff's current law to the element, we get

$$I_x - (I_x + \Delta I_x) = y\Delta x\left(E_x + \frac{\Delta E_x}{2}\right) \quad \text{...(18.5)}$$

where y is the shunt admittance per unit length.

Eq. (18.5) may be written as,

$$\frac{\Delta I_x}{\Delta x} = -yE_x - y \cdot \frac{\Delta E_x}{2} \quad \text{...(18.6)}$$

Again in the limit when $\Delta x \to 0$, the ratio of increments namely $\frac{\Delta I_x}{\Delta x}$ may be replaced by derivative $\frac{\Delta I_x}{\Delta x}$ and quantity $y \cdot \frac{\Delta E_x}{2}$ becomes zero. Hence Eq. (18.6) yields,

$$\frac{dI_x}{d_x} = -yE_x \quad \text{...(18.7)}$$

Eqs. (18.4) and (18.7) show that the current and voltage are interrelated as should be expected in any physical network. These two equations, however, are required to be arranged so as to have only one independent variable. To do this, we differentiate Eq. (18.4) with respect to x to give the following equation,

$$\frac{d^2E_x}{dx^2} = -Z \cdot \frac{dI_x}{dx} \quad \text{...(18.8)}$$

Substituting the value of $\frac{dI_x}{dx}$ from Eq. (18.7) into Eq. (18.8), we get

$$\frac{d^2E_x}{dx^2} = zyE_x \quad \text{...(18.9)}$$

Similarly differentiating (18.7), we get

$$\frac{d^2I_x}{dx^2} = -y\frac{dE_x}{dx} \quad \text{...(18.10)}$$

Substituting the value of $\frac{dE_x}{dx}$ from Eq. (18.4) into Eq. (18.10), we get

$$\frac{d^2I_x}{dx^2} = zyI_x \quad \text{...(18.11)}$$

Eqs. (18.9) and (18.11) are the linear differential equations and form the fundamental equations describing the transmission line with distributed constants.

Now if

$$E_x = |E_x|\, \varepsilon^{j\omega t} \quad \text{...(18.12)}$$

and $$I_x = | I_x | \varepsilon^{j\omega t} \quad \text{...(18.13)}$$

then Eq. (18.9) and (18.11) are evidently of such a form that they represent wave motion.

Solutions of Eqs. (18.9) and (18.11) are

$$E_x = A_1 \varepsilon^{\sqrt{zy}\,x} = A_2 \varepsilon^{-\sqrt{zy}\,x} \quad \text{...(18.14)}$$

$$I_x = B_1 \varepsilon^{\sqrt{zy}\,x} + B_2 \varepsilon^{-\sqrt{zy}\,x} \quad \text{...(18.15)}$$

where A_1 and A_2 are constants having dimensions of voltage and B_1, B_2 are constants having dimensions of current. Obviously the constants A_1, A_2 are interrelated with constants B_1, B_2. In order to obtain relationship between these constants, we substitute values of E_x and I_x from Eqs. (18.14) and (18.15) into Eq. (18.4). Then, we get

$$\sqrt{zy}\, A_1 \varepsilon^{\sqrt{zy}\,x} - \sqrt{zy}\, A_2 \varepsilon^{-\sqrt{zy}\,x} = -zB_1 \varepsilon^{\sqrt{zy}\,x} - zB_2 \varepsilon^{-\sqrt{zy}\,x} \quad \text{...(18.16)}$$

In Eq. (18.16), equating the coefficients of like power of ε, we get

$$\sqrt{zy}\, A_1 = -ZB_1 \quad \text{...(18.17)}$$

and $$\sqrt{zy}\, A_2 = ZB_2 \quad \text{...(18.18)}$$

Eqs. (18.17) and (18.18) may be put as,

$$B_1 = -\sqrt{\frac{y}{z}}\, A_1 \quad \text{...(18.19)}$$

$$B_2 = \sqrt{\frac{y}{z}}\, A_2 \quad \text{...(18.20)}$$

Hence Eq. (18.15) for the current I_x may be put as,

$$I_x = -\sqrt{\frac{y}{z}}\, A_1 \,.\, \varepsilon^{\sqrt{zy}\,x} + \sqrt{\frac{y}{z}}\, A_2 \,.\, \varepsilon^{\sqrt{zy}\,x} \quad \text{... (18.21)}$$

Eqs. (18.14) and (18.21) are the most general equations in the sense that no condition has been put regarding the termination of the line at the receiving end. The constants A_1 and A_2 can, therefore, be evaluated under proper boundary conditions.

Line of Infinite length. In this case for $x = \infty$, voltage E_x becomes zero. Hence from Eq. (18.14), $A_1 = 0$. Also at $x = 0$, $E_x = E_s$ so that from Eq. (18.14), $A_2 = E_s$. Hence Eq. (18.14) gives,

$$E_x = E_x \varepsilon^{-\sqrt{zy}\,x} \quad \text{...(18.22)}$$

Also Eq. (18.12) yields

$$I_x = \sqrt{\frac{y}{z}}\, E_s \varepsilon^{-\sqrt{zy}\,x} \quad \text{...(18.23)}$$

Further at $x = 0$, $I_x = I_s$ so that Eq. (18.23) yields,

$$I_s = \sqrt{\frac{z}{y}}\, E_s \quad \text{...(18.24)}$$

Combining Eqs. (18.23) and (18.24), we get

$$I_x = I_S\, \varepsilon^{-\sqrt{zy}\,x} \quad \text{...(18.25)}$$

But characteristic impedance Z_0 is defined as the input impedance of an infinite line. Hence from Eq. (18.24), we get

$$Z_0 = \frac{E_S}{I_S} = \sqrt{\frac{z}{y}} \quad \text{... (18.26)}$$

For a unit distance from the sending end, *i.e.*, for $x = 1$, Eq. (18.25) yields

$$\sqrt{zy} = \ln\frac{I_S}{I_x} \qquad ...(18.27)$$

Quantity $\sqrt{zy}$ thus represents the variation in current as the energy propagates along the line and is as usual called the propagation constant. Then Eqs. (18.14) and (18.21) giving the voltage and current at a distance x from the sending end may be put as,

$$E_x = A_1\, \varepsilon^{\gamma x} + A_2\, \varepsilon^{-\gamma x} \qquad ...(18.28)$$

$$I_x = -\frac{A_1}{Z_0}\varepsilon^{\gamma x} + \frac{A_2}{Z_0}\varepsilon^{-\gamma x} \qquad ...(18.29)$$

Example 18.1. *An open wire transmission line has characteristic impedance* $Z_0 = 692\,\underline{/-11.82^\circ}$ *ohms and propagation constant* $\gamma = 0.03485\,\underline{/77.37^\circ}$. *The line is 300 kilometers long and is supplied power by a generator having internal resistance of 600 ohms. If the generator voltage is 3 volts at the sending end, calculate the voltage current and power at the receiving end when the line is terminated by* Z_0

Solution. Since the line has been terminated by Z_0, the input impedance at the sending will end also be Z_0

$$Z_0 = 692\,\underline{/-11.82^\circ} = 667 - j\,142$$

Hence the sending end current is,

$$I_S = \frac{3}{600 + 677 - j\,142} = \frac{3}{1277 - j\,142} = \frac{3}{1284\,\underline{/-6.35^\circ}}$$

or $\quad I_S = 0.002335\,\underline{/6.35^\circ}$ Amp. $= 2.335\,\underline{/6.35^\circ}$ mA

Then the current at the receiving end is given by

$$I_R = I_s\,\varepsilon^{-\gamma l} = I_s\,\varepsilon^{-\alpha l}\,.\,\varepsilon^{-j\beta l}$$

$$\gamma = 0.03485\,\underline{/77.37^\circ} = 0.0077 + j\,0.03395$$

Hence $\varepsilon^{-\alpha l} = \varepsilon^{-0.0077 \times 300} = \varepsilon^{-2.31} = 0.10$

and $\quad \varepsilon^{-j\beta l} = \varepsilon^{-j\,0.03395 \times 300} = \varepsilon^{-j\,10.185}$

Hence $\quad \varepsilon^{-\gamma l} = 0.1\,\underline{/-10.185}$ radians

$$= 0.1\,\underline{/-583.558^\circ}$$

Hence the current at the receiving end is

$$I_R = 2.335\,\underline{/6.35^\circ} \times 0.1\,\underline{/-583.56^\circ} \text{ mA}$$

$$= 0.2335\,\underline{/577.21^\circ} \text{ mA.}$$

The current at the receiving end thus lags behind the input current by more than one cycle and is one-tenth in magnitude. The voltage E_R at the receiving end is given by

$$E_R = I_R Z_0$$

$$= 0.2335 \times 10^{-3}\,\underline{/-577.21^\circ} \times 692\,\underline{/-11.82^\circ}$$

$$= 0.1617\,\underline{/-589.03^\circ} \text{ volts.}$$

The phase angle between E_R and I_R is the angle of the load impedance and hence the power at the receiving end is,

$$P_R = |\,E_R\,|\,.\,|\,I_R\,| \cos\theta = 0.1617 \times 0.2335 \cos 11.82^\circ \text{ watt}$$

$$= 36.93 \times 10^{-6} \text{ watt.}$$

18.2. Line Terminated in an Impedance other than Z_0

Fig. 18.1 shows a line terminated in an impedance Z_R which may be different from Z_0. Eqs. (18.28) and (18.29) are most general in nature and have no restriction regarding the terminating impedance at the receiving end. These equations are rewritten here for convenience:

$$E_x = A_1\, \varepsilon^{\gamma x} + A_2\, \varepsilon^{-\gamma x} \quad ...(18.30)$$

$$I_x = -\frac{A_1}{Z_0}\varepsilon^{\gamma x} + \frac{A_2}{Z_0}\varepsilon^{-\gamma x} \quad ...(18.31)$$

In these equations, x is the distance measured from the sending end of the line. Constants A_1 and A_2 are determined from the boundary conditions. Thus at $x = 0$,

$$E_x = E_S = E_g - I_S \cdot Z_g$$

and $\quad I_x = I_S.$

Similarly at $\quad x = l$

$$E_x = E_R = I_R \cdot Z_R$$

and $\quad I_x = I_R$

Using these boundary conditions, for $x = 0$, we get Eqs. (18.30) and (18.31),

$$E_g - I_S \cdot Z_g = A_1 + A_2 \quad ...(18.32)$$

and
$$I_S = -\frac{A_1}{Z_0} + \frac{A_2}{Z_0} \quad ...(18.33)$$

From Eqs. (18.32) and (18.33) eliminating I_S, we get

$$E_g - \frac{(A_2 - A_1)}{Z_0} Z_g = A_1 + A_2 \quad ...(18.34)$$

or
$$\left(1 - \frac{Z_g}{z_0}\right)A_1 + \left(1 + \frac{Z_g}{Z_0}\right)A_2 = E_g$$

or
$$(Z_0 - Z_g)A_1 + (Z_0 + Z_2)A_2 = E_g \cdot Z_0 \quad ...(18.35)$$

Again using the boundary condition for $x = l$, we get from Eqs. (18.30) and (18.31),

$$I_R Z_R = A_1 \cdot \varepsilon^{\gamma l} + A_2 \cdot \varepsilon^{\gamma l} \quad ...(18.36)$$

and
$$I_R = -\frac{A_1}{Z_0} \cdot \varepsilon^{\gamma l} + \frac{A_2}{Z_0}\varepsilon^{-\gamma l} \quad ...(18.37)$$

From Eqs. (18.36) and (18.37), we get

$$A_1 \cdot \varepsilon^{\gamma l} + A_2 \cdot \varepsilon^{-\gamma l} = Z_R\left[-\frac{A_1}{Z_0}\varepsilon^{\gamma l} + \frac{A_2}{Z_0}\varepsilon^{-\gamma l}\right] \quad ...(18.38)$$

On rearrangement Eq. (18.38) yields,

$$(Z_0 + Z_R)\, e^{\gamma l} A_1 + (Z_0 - Z_R)\, \varepsilon^{-\gamma l} A_2 = 0 \quad ...(18.39)$$

Solving Eqs. (18.35) and (18.39), we get the following expression for constants A_1 and A_2:

$$A_1 = \frac{E_g Z_0 (Z_0 - E_R)\, \varepsilon^{-\gamma l}}{D} \quad ...(18.40)$$

$$A_2 = \frac{-E_g E_0 (Z_0 + E_R)\,\varepsilon^{\gamma l}}{D} \quad \ldots (18.41)$$

where D is given by,

$$D = (Z_0 - Z_g)(Z_0 - Z_R)\,\varepsilon^{-\gamma l} - (Z_0 + Z_g)(Z_0 + Z_R)\,\varepsilon^{\gamma l} \quad \ldots (18.42)$$

Substituting values of A_1 and A_2 as given by Eqs. (18.40) and (18.41) into Eqs. (18.28) and (18.29), we get

$$E_x = \frac{E_g Z_0}{D}\,[(Z_0 - Z_R)\,\varepsilon^{-\gamma(l-x)} - (Z_0 + Z_R)\,\varepsilon^{\gamma(l-x)}] \quad \ldots (18.43)$$

$$I_x = \frac{E_g}{D}\,[-(Z_0 - Z_R)\,\varepsilon^{\gamma(l-x)} - (Z_0 + Z_R)\,\varepsilon^{\gamma(l-x)}] \quad \ldots (18.44)$$

where D is given by Eq. (18.42).

Eqs. (18.43) and (18.44) form the most general solution for a transmission line terminated in any impedance Z_R at the receiving end.

The distance $(l - x)$ appearing in Eqs. (18.43) and (18.44) can be considered as y measured from the receiving end. Usually the generator impedance Z_g is considered to be zero so that the sending end voltage E_S is equal to the generator voltage E_g. Then Eqs. (18.43) and (18.44) may be written in simpler and more useful form as below:

$$E_x = E_S \frac{(Z_0 + Z_R)\varepsilon^{\gamma y} - (Z_0 - Z_R)\varepsilon^{-\gamma y}}{(Z_0 + Z_R)\varepsilon^{\gamma l} - (Z_0 - Z_R)\varepsilon^{-\gamma l}} \quad \ldots (18.46)$$

and

$$I_x = \frac{E_S}{Z_0} \frac{(Z_0 + Z_R)\varepsilon^{\gamma y} + (Z_0 - Z_R)\varepsilon^{-\gamma y}}{(Z_0 + Z_R)\varepsilon^{\gamma l} - (Z_0 - Z_R)\varepsilon^{-\gamma l}} \quad \ldots (18.46)$$

Sometimes it is useful to represent the voltage and current in terms of quantities measured at the receiving end. This can be obtained by letting $y = 0$ when $E_x = E_R$ and then eliminating E_S from Eqs. (18.45) and (18.46). Thus, we get

$$E_R = E_S \frac{2Z_R}{(Z_0 + Z_R)\varepsilon^{\gamma l} - (Z_0 - Z_R)\varepsilon^{-\gamma l}}$$

or

$$E_S = \frac{E_R}{2Z_R}\,[(Z_0 + Z_R)\,\varepsilon^{\gamma l} - (Z_0 - Z_R)\,\varepsilon^{-\gamma l}] \quad \ldots (18.47)$$

Substituting this value of Es from Eq. (18.47) into Eqs. (18.45) and (18.46) and letting

$$I_R = \frac{E_R}{Z_R},$$ we get

$$E_x = \frac{I_R}{2}[(Z_0 + Z_R)\varepsilon^{\gamma y} - (Z_0 - Z_R)\varepsilon^{-\gamma y}] \quad \ldots (18.48)$$

and

$$I_x = \frac{I_R}{2Z_0}[(Z_0 + Z_R)\,\varepsilon^{\gamma y} + (Z_0 - Z_R)\,\varepsilon^{-\gamma y}] \quad \ldots (18.49)$$

These equations may be written in terms of hyperbolic functions which are readily available in form of tables for computation purposes. Thus collecting together terms of Z_0 and similarly terms of Z_R, we get

$$E_R = \frac{I_R}{2}[(\varepsilon^{\gamma y} - \varepsilon^{-\gamma y}) Z_0 + (\varepsilon^{\gamma x} + \varepsilon^{-\gamma y}) Z_R]$$

or $$E_x = E_R \cosh \gamma y + I_R Z_0 \sinh \gamma y \qquad ...(18.50)$$

Similarly $$I_x = I_R \cosh \gamma y + \frac{E_R}{Z_0} \sinh \gamma y \qquad ...(18.51)$$

The input impedance and transfer impedance of a four terminal network characterise the network completely. A transmission line is a four terminal network. Its input impedance and transfer impedance for any general terminating impedance Z_R may be obtained from Eqs. (18.48) and (18.49) by letting $y = l$, $E_x = E_S$ and $I_x = I_S$. Thus Eqs. (18.48) and (18.49) yield

$$Z_{in} = \frac{E_S}{I_S} = Z_0 \frac{(Z_0 + Z_R)\varepsilon^{\gamma l} - (Z_0 - Z_R)\varepsilon^{-\gamma l}}{(Z_0 + Z_R)\varepsilon^{\gamma l} + (Z_0 - Z_R)\varepsilon^{-\gamma l}} \qquad ...(18.52)$$

or $$Z_{in} = \frac{1 - \dfrac{Z_0 - Z_R}{Z_0 - Z_R}\varepsilon^{-2\gamma l}}{1 + \dfrac{Z_0 - Z_R}{Z_0 + Z_R}\varepsilon^{-2\gamma l}} \qquad ...(18.53)$$

and $$Z_t = \frac{E_S}{I_R} = \frac{1}{2}[(Z_0 + Z_R)\,\varepsilon^{\gamma l} - (Z_0 - Z_R)\,\varepsilon^{-\gamma l}] \qquad ...(18.54)$$

In hyperbolic forms these quantities are given as,

$$Z_{in} = Z_0 \frac{Z_R \cosh \gamma l + z_0 \sinh \gamma l}{Z_0 \cosh \gamma l + Z_R \sinh \gamma l} \qquad ...(18.55)$$

$$Z_i = Z_R \cosh \gamma l + Z_0 \sinh \gamma l \qquad ...(18.56)$$

Example 18.2. *A transmission line has $Z_0 = 650 \angle -12°$ ohms. $\alpha = 0.0075$ neper/km, $\beta = 0.034$ radian/km. It is 100 km in length. A generator having open circuit voltage of 3 volts and internal resistance of 600 ohms, supplies power at the ending end of the line. If the line is terminated in an impedance of 400 $\angle 45°$ ohms, calculate the receiving end voltage and the power in the terminating impedance.*

Solution. Using Eq. (18.43), for $x = l$,

$$E_R = \frac{2E_g Z_0 Z_R}{(Z_0 + Z_g)(Z_0 + Z_R)\,\varepsilon^{\gamma l} - (Z_0 - Z_g)(Z - Z_R)\,\varepsilon^{\gamma l}} \qquad ...(1)$$

Now $$Z_0 + Z_g = 650 \angle -12° + 600 = 650 \times 0.9781 - j650 \times 0.2097 + 600$$

$$= 636 + j135 + 600 = 1235 + j135 = 1243 \angle 6.233°$$

$$Z_R = 400 \angle 45° = 282.8 - j282.8$$

$$Z_0 + Z_R = 636 - j135 - 282.8 - j282.8 = 918.8 + j147.8 = 930 \angle 9.15°$$

$$\varepsilon^{\gamma l} = \varepsilon^{\alpha l} \angle \beta l = \varepsilon^{0.67} \angle -\frac{3.4 \times 180°}{2\pi} = 2.117 \angle 195°$$

Hence $$(Z_0 + Z_g)(Z_0 + Z_R)\,\varepsilon^{\gamma l} = 1243 \angle -6.233° \times 930 \angle 9.15 \times 2.117 \angle 195°$$

$$= 2.445 \times 10^6 \angle 197.917° = (-2.327 - j\,0.752)\,10^6$$

$$(Z_0 - Z_g) = 36 - j\,135 = 139.7 \angle -75.05°$$

$$(Z_0 - Z_R) = 636 - j135 - 282.8 - j282.8$$

$$= 353.2 - j417.8 = 546 \underline{/-49.77°}$$

$$\varepsilon^{-\gamma l} = 0.4724 \underline{/-195°}$$

Hence $(Z_0 - Z_g)(Z_0 - I_R)\,\varepsilon^{-\gamma l} = 139.7 \underline{/-75.05°} \times 546 \underline{/-49.77°} \times 0.4724 \underline{/-195°}$

$$= 3.6 \times 19° \underline{/319.82°}$$

$$= (2.57 + j2.325) \times 10^4$$

Hence $(Z_0 + Z_g)(Z_0 + Z_R)\,\varepsilon^{\gamma l} - (Z_0 - Z_g)(Z_0 - Z_R)\,\varepsilon^{-\gamma l}$

$$= (-2.327 - j0.752)\,10^6 - (2.75 + j2.325)\,10^6$$

$$= (-2.3545 - j0.7752)\,10^6 = 2.48 \times 10^6 \underline{/18.25°}$$

Hence $$E_R = \frac{2 \times 3 \times 650 \underline{/-12°} - 400 \underline{/45°}}{2.48 \times 10^6 \underline{/18.25°}} = 0.629 \underline{/14.75°} \text{ volts.}$$

Power developed in the load impedance Z_R is,

$$P_R = \frac{|E_R|^2}{|Z_R|} \cos\theta = \frac{(0.629)^2}{400} \times 0.707 \text{ watt} = 0.7 \text{ mW.}$$

Example 18.3. *In Example 18.2, if the generator impedance is zero and the sending end voltage is 3 volts, calculate using hyperbolic functions, the voltage and power at the receiving end.*

Solution. Using Eq. (18.50) for $x = 0$, we have

$$E_R = E_R \cos \gamma l + \frac{E_R}{Z_R} Z_0 \sinh \gamma l \qquad ...(1)$$

or
$$E_R = \frac{E_S Z_R}{Z_R \cosh \gamma l + Z_0 \sinh \gamma l} \qquad ...(2)$$

Now
$$\sinh \gamma l = \sinh(\alpha + j\beta)l = \sinh \alpha l \cos \beta l + j \cosh \alpha l \sin \beta l$$

$$= \sinh 0.75 \times \cos 195° + j \cos 0.75 \sin 195°$$

$$= [0.8223 \times (-0.9659) + j[1.2947 \times (-0.2588)]$$

$$= -0.795 - j0.335 = -0.863 \underline{/22.83}$$

$$\cosh \gamma l = \cosh(\alpha + j\beta)l = \cosh \alpha l \cos \beta l + \sinh \alpha l \times \sin \beta l$$

$$= 1.2947 \times (-0.9659) + j0.8223 \times (-0.2588)$$

$$= -1.25 - j0.213 = -1.268 \underline{/9.683°}$$

Hence
$$E_R = \frac{-3 \times 400 \underline{/45°}}{400 \underline{/45°} \times 1.268 \underline{/9.683°} + 650 \underline{/-12°} \times 0.863 \underline{/22.83°}}$$

$$= \frac{-1200 \underline{/45°}}{507.2 \underline{/54.683°} + 561 \underline{/10.83°}}$$

$$= \frac{-1200 \underline{/45°}}{294.5 + j414 + 551 + j105.5} = \frac{-1200 \underline{/45°}}{845.5 + j519.5}$$

$$= \frac{-1200 \underline{/45°}}{992 \underline{/31.58°}} = -1.21 \underline{/13.42°} \text{ volts}$$

$$P_R = \frac{|E_R|^2}{|Z_R|}\cos\theta = \frac{(1.21)^2}{400}\cos 45°$$

$$= \frac{1.465 \times 0.7071}{400} \text{ watt} = 2.59 \text{ mW.}$$

Example 18.4. *A transmission line has characteristic impedance $Z_0 = 650 \angle -12°$ ohms, attenuation constant $\alpha = 0.0075$ neper/km, and phase-shift constant $\beta = 0.034$ radian/km. The line is 100 kilometres long and is terminated in 200 ohms-resistance. If the sending end voltage is 1 volt, calculate the input impedance of the line and the current at the sending end.*

Solution. The input impedance of a line terminated in impedance Z_R is given by,

$$Z_{in} = Z_0 \frac{1 + \dfrac{Z_R - Z_0}{Z_R + Z_0}\varepsilon^{-2\gamma l}}{1 - \dfrac{Z_R - Z_0}{Z_R + Z_0}\varepsilon^{-2\gamma l}} \qquad ...(1)$$

Now $\quad Z_0 = 650 \angle -12° = 936 - j135$

$$Z_R - Z_0 = 200 - 636 + j135 = -436 + j135 = 456 \angle 162.8°$$

$$Z_R + Z_0 = 200 + 636 - j135 = 836 - j135 = 847 \angle -9.2°$$

$$\frac{Z_R - Z_0}{Z_R + Z_0} = \frac{456 \angle 162.8°}{847 \angle -9.2°} = 0.538 \angle 172°$$

$$\varepsilon^{-2\gamma l} = \varepsilon^{-2\alpha l}\,\varepsilon^{-j2\beta l} = e^{-1.5} \angle -6.8 \times \frac{180°}{\pi} = 0.223 \angle 389.5°$$

Hence $\quad Z_{in} = 650 \angle -12° \cdot \dfrac{(1 + 0.538 \angle 172° \times 0.223 \angle -389.5°)}{(1 - 0.538 \angle 172° \times 0.223 \angle -389.5°)}$

$$= 650 \angle -12° \cdot \frac{(1 + 0.12 \angle -217.5°)}{(1 - 0.12 \angle -217.5°)} = 650 \angle -12° \cdot \left(\frac{0.909 \angle 4.6°}{1.12 \angle -3.8°}\right)$$

$$= 527 \angle -3.6°$$

The input current is

$$I_S = \frac{Es}{Z_{in}} = \frac{2}{527 \angle -3.6°} = 1.897 \times 10^{-3} \angle 3.6° = 1.897 \angle 3.6° \text{ mA.}$$

Example 18.5. *Continue example 18.4 to calculate the values of receiving end current I_R receiving end voltage E_R, power P_R in the terminating impedance, sending end power P_R and the efficiency of transmission.*

Solution. Using Eq. (18.49) and putting $\gamma = l$, we get the following expression for I_S in terms of I_R etc.

$$I_S = \frac{I_R(Z_0 + Z_R)}{2Z_0}\left[\varepsilon^{\gamma l} - \frac{Z_R - Z_0}{Z_R + Z_0}\varepsilon^{-\gamma l}\right]$$

Now $\quad \varepsilon^{\gamma l} = \varepsilon^{\alpha l}\,\varepsilon^{j\beta l} = \varepsilon^{0.75} \angle \dfrac{3.4 \times 180°}{\pi} = 2.117 \angle 195°$

$$\varepsilon^{-\gamma l} = \varepsilon^{-\alpha l}\,\varepsilon^{-j\beta l} = \varepsilon^{0.75}\ \underline{/-195^\circ} = 0.4724\ \underline{/-195^\circ}$$

I_S has been calculated and found

$$= 0.001897\ \underline{/3.6^\circ}$$

Hence from Eq. (1),

$$0.001897\ \underline{/3.6^\circ} = \frac{I_R \times 847\ \underline{/-92^\circ}}{2 \times 650\ \underline{/-12^\circ}} [2.117\ \underline{/195^\circ} - 0.538\ \underline{/172^\circ} \times 0.4724\ \underline{/-195^\circ}]$$

$$= I_R \times 0.652\ \underline{/2.8^\circ}\ [-2.277 - j0.4477]$$

$$= I_R \times 0.652\ \underline{/2.8^\circ} \times 2.32\ \underline{/191.1^\circ}$$

Hence $$I_R = \frac{0.001897\ \underline{/3.6^\circ}}{0.652\ \underline{/2.8^\circ} \times 2.32\ \underline{/191.1^\circ}} = 1.25 \times 10^{-3}\ \underline{/-190.3^\circ}$$

$$= 1.25\ \underline{/-190.3^\circ}\ \text{mA} = 1.25\ \underline{/169.7^\circ}\ \text{mA}$$

$$E_R = I_R Z_R = 0.00125\ \underline{/169.7^\circ} \times 200 = 0.25\ \underline{/169.7^\circ}\ \text{volts}$$

$P_R = |E_R| \cdot |I_R| \cos\theta = 0.25 \times 1.25 \times 10^{-4}$ watt $= 0.3125$ mW

$P_S = |E_S| \cdot |I_S| \cos\theta = 1.897 \times 10^{-3} \cos(3.6^\circ)$ watt $= 1.892$ mW

Efficience of transmission is

$$\mu = \frac{0.3125\ \text{mW}}{1.892\ \text{mW}} \times 100 = 16.5\%.$$

18.3. Distortions in a Transmission Line

The propagation constant for a transmission line in terms of its primary constant is given by,

$$\gamma = \sqrt{(R + j\omega L)(G + j\omega C)} \quad \text{...(18.57)}$$

From this equation we may now obtain expressions for α and β. Thus

$$\alpha + j\beta = \sqrt{(R + j\omega L)(G + j\omega C)}$$

$$= \sqrt{(RG - \omega^2 LC) + j\omega(RC + LG)}. \quad \text{...(18.58)}$$

Squaring both sides of Eq. (18.58), we get

$$\alpha^2 - \beta^2 + j2\alpha\beta = (RG - \omega^2 LC) + j\omega(RC + LG) \quad \text{...(18.59)}$$

Equating real parts in Eq. (18.59), we get

$$\alpha^2 - \beta^2 = RG - \omega^2 LC$$

or $$\beta^2 = \alpha^2 - RG + \omega^2 LC \quad \text{...(18.60)}$$

In Eq. (18.59), equating the imaginary parts and squaring, we get

$$4\alpha^2\beta^2 = \omega^3(RC + LG^2) \quad \text{...(18.61)}$$

Substituting for β^2 from Eq. (18.60) into Eq. (18.61), we get

$$4\alpha^4 - 4\alpha^2(RG - \omega^2 LC) - \omega^2(RC + LG)^2 = 0 \quad \text{...(18.62)}$$

Eq. (18.62) yields,

$$\alpha = \sqrt{\frac{1}{2}[(RG - \omega^2 LC) + \sqrt{(RG - \omega^2 LC)^2 + \omega^2 (RC + LG)^2}]} \qquad ...(18.63)$$

neglecting the negative values of α.

From Eqs. (18.60) and (18.63), we get the following expression for β,

$$\beta = \sqrt{\frac{1}{2}[(\omega^2 LC - RG) + \sqrt{RG - \omega^2 LC)^2 + \omega^2 (RC + LG)^2}]} \qquad ...(18.64)$$

These expressions show that attenuation constant and the phase shift constant are functions of frequency. A transmission line is usually used to transmit signals of a large range of frequencies. Hence different frequencies are attenuated by different amounts. This constitutes the *frequency distortion.* Similarly different frequency components of a complex voltage wave will experience different amounts of phase shifts.

But phase velocity $v_p = \frac{\omega}{\beta}$ and β is not directly proportional to frequency *f*. Hence the phase velocity v_p will also be a function of frequency. Thus some frequencies will be delayed more than others. The phase relationship of the received frequencies will not be the same as relationship at the sending end. This is known as the *delay distortion* or the *phase distortion*.

In a high quality transmission line, the frequency distortion is reduced by use of network known as *equalizer* which has attenuation versus frequency characteristic just opposite to that of the line. The total attenuation then becomes constant in a particular frequency band. The increase in attenuation can be overcome by using larger gain in amplifiers.

Delay distortion is not very serious for voice and music transmission but becomes very important for picture-signal transmission. Delay equalizers are also available and can be used to eliminate the delay distortion. The attenuation constant of a line tends to become nearly independent of frequency in the high frequency range. The effect is more pronounced in cables and coaxial cables. Also the phase constant β becomes directly proportional to frequency so that the phase velocity v_p is substantially independent of frequency and no distortion occurs.

The characteristic impedance Z_0 of a line is also a function of frequency. Hence a line which is properly terminated by a certain value of Z_0 at one particular frequency, will not behave similarly terminated at other frequencies. This will cause the input impedance of the line to differ from Z_0 at different frequencies and this causes the input current to be different at different frequencies. Also at the receiving end terminals, reflections may occur at frequencies for which terminating impedance differs considerably from Z_0.

18.4. Distortionless Line

A transmission line may not produce any distortion provided that the line parameters have values which obey certain specific relationships.

In order to eliminate frequency distortion, the attenuation constant must be made independent of frequency. Now let us consider the expression for attenuation constant α given by Eq. (18.63) reproduced below:

$$\alpha = s\sqrt{\frac{1}{2}[RG - \omega^2 LC + \sqrt{RC - \omega^2 LC)^2 + \omega^2 (RC + LG)^2}]} \qquad ...(18.65)$$

Study of this equation shows that α can be made independent of frequency if the quantity under the inner radical sign gives only one frequency dependent term with positive sign namely the term $\omega^2 LC$. Thus the desired condition can be written as,

$$\sqrt{(RG - \omega^2 LC)^2 + \omega^2 (RC + LG)^2} = \omega^2 LC + K \qquad ...(18.66)$$

where K is constant.

Alternatively, we make $R = L = 0$ and thus make $\alpha = 0$. However, this method of making α independent of frequency is not feasible in physical transmission lines.

Now we solve Eq. (18.66) to obtain the value of K.

Eq. (18.66) may be written as,

$$(RG - \omega^2 LC)^2 + \omega^2 (RC + LG)^2 = \omega^4 L^2 C^2 + 2\omega^2 LCK + K^2$$

or $$R^2 G^2 + \omega^4 L^2 C^2 - 2\omega^2 LCRG + \omega^2 R^2 C^2 + \omega^2 L^2 G^2 + 2\omega^2 RCLG = \omega^4 L^2 C^2 + 2\omega^2 LCK + K^2 \qquad ...(18.67)$$

or $$R^2 G^2 + \omega^2 (R^2 C^2 + L^2 G^2) = K^2 + 2\omega^2 LCK \qquad ...(18.68)$$

For this identity to be true, the coefficients of like power of ω must be equal. Thus, we get

$$K = RG \qquad ...(18.69)$$

and $$2LCK = R^2 C^2 + L^2 G^2$$

or $$R^2 C^2 - 2LCRG + L^2 G^2 = 0$$

or $$(RC - LG)^2 = 0 \qquad ...(18.70)$$

or $$LG = RC \qquad ...(18.71)$$

or $$\frac{L}{R} = \frac{C}{G} \qquad ...(18.72)$$

Eq. (18.71) or Eq. (18.72) gives the desired condition for zero frequency distortion.

Substituting this condition in Eq. (18.66), we get

$$\alpha = \sqrt{RG} \qquad ...(18.73)$$

Eq. (18.73) shows that α is independent of frequency.

For no delay distortion, the phase velocity v_p, must be the same for all the frequencies. But $v_p = \frac{\omega}{\beta}$. Hence β must be directly proportional to frequency. Now let us consider the expression for β as given by Eq. (18.64) reproduced below:

$$\beta = \sqrt{\frac{1}{2}[(\omega^2 LC - RG) + \sqrt{(RG - \omega^2 LC)^2 + \omega^2 (RC + LG)^2}]} \qquad ...(18.74)$$

Let $\beta = \omega K$, where K is a constant to be evaluated.

In Eq. (18.74), squaring both the sides and rearranging, we get

$$\omega^2 (2K^2 - LC) + RG = \sqrt{(RG - \omega^2 LC)^2 + \omega^2 (RC + LG)^2} \qquad ...(18.75)$$

Again squaring both the sides and expanding the terms,

$$\omega^2 (2K^2 - LC^2) + R^2 G^2 + 2\omega^2 RG(2K^2 - LC) = R^2 G^2 + \omega^4 L^2 C^2 - 2\omega^2 LCRG + \omega^2 (R^2 C^2 + L^2 G^2 + 2LCRG)$$

or $$\omega^4 (2K^2 - RC)^2 + 2\omega^2 RG(2K^2 - LC) = \omega^4 L^2 C^2 + \omega^2 (R^2 C^2 + L^2 G^2) \qquad ...(18.76)$$

This identity will be true only when coefficients of like powers of ω are the same separately.

Hence $$(2K^2 - LC)^2 = L^2 C^2$$

or $$K = \sqrt{LC} \qquad ...(18.77)$$

Also $$2RG(2K^2LC) = R^2C^2 + L^2G^2 \quad ...(18.78)$$

Substituting the value of R from Eq. (18.77) into Eq. (18.73), we get

$$(RC - LG)^2 = 0$$

or $$RC = LG \quad ...(18.79)$$

Eq. (18.79) gives the condition for zero phase-delay distortion. This condition is the same as one obtained for zero frequency distortion.

Now if the condition $RC = LG$ is satisfied, the characteristic impedance Z_0 is given by,

$$Z_0 = \sqrt{\frac{R + j\omega L}{G + \omega C}} = \sqrt{\frac{\frac{LG}{C} + j\omega L}{G + j\omega C}} = \sqrt{\frac{L}{C}}$$

Thus $$Z_0 = \sqrt{\frac{L}{C}} = \sqrt{\frac{R}{G}} \quad ..(18.80)$$

Eq. (18.80) gives the value of Z_0 under condition of distortion-less transmission. It may be seen that under this condition, Z_0 becomes constant .and independent of frequency. Thus condition $LG = CR$ is necessary and also sufficient for distortionless transmission. However, such a perfect distortionless transmission is not possible in actual practice. A well-constructed and maintained transmission line has very small value of shunt conductance G. This will, therefore, require very large value of L in order to make LG equal RC. If G is increased, α and consequent total attenuation is increased resulting in poor efficiency of line. R cannot be reduced very much because this will require extremely large diameter conductor making the cost prohibitive. Thus, increasing the value of L is the only solution.

In actual practice, however, the condition for distortionless transmission namely $LG = CR$ cannot be satisfied throughout the period of operation of line since the parameters of the line undergo changes due to variations in temperature, wind and other seasonal changes. At high carrier frequencies, skin effect increases the value of R. Thus even a hypothetically distortionless line will have a small amount of distortion under actual operating conditions.

18.5. Line of Low Distortion

A transmission line may have low distortion under certain conditions even though the parameters may be such that they differ by large amounts from those desired for distortion transmission. Consider the operating frequency to be sufficiently large so that at the lowest frequency of operation, ωL is much larger than R and ωC is much larger than G. But $z = R + j\omega L$ and $y = G + j\omega C$. Hence both z and y will have angles nearly to equal $\pi/2$ radians whereas the magnitudes will be nearly equal to ωL and ωG respectively.

Now for small value of angle θ, we know that

$$\theta \approx \sin\theta \approx \tan\theta \quad ...(18.81)$$

If θ is nearly equal to $\frac{\pi}{2}$, $$\cos\theta \approx \cot\theta \approx \left(\frac{\pi}{2} - \theta\right) \quad ...(18.82)$$

or $$\theta \approx \frac{\pi}{2} - \cot\theta \quad ...(18.83)$$

Using the relation given by Eq. (18.83), z and y may be written in polar form as below:

$$z = \omega L \angle \frac{\pi}{2} - \frac{R}{\omega L} \quad ...(18.84)$$

$$y = \omega C \angle \frac{\pi}{2} - \frac{G}{\omega C} \quad ...(18.85)$$

Hence $$\gamma = \sqrt{zy} = \omega\sqrt{LC}\ \angle\left[\frac{\pi}{2} - \frac{1}{2}\left(\frac{R}{\omega L} + \frac{G}{\omega C}\right)\right] \quad ...(18.86)$$

The phase angle of γ is nearly equal to $\frac{\pi}{2}$ and, hence, using Eq. (18.82), we get

$$\theta = \frac{\pi}{2} - \cos\theta \quad ...(18.87)$$

Hence $$\cos\theta = \frac{1}{2}\left(\frac{R}{\omega L} + \frac{G}{\omega C}\right) \quad ...(18.88)$$

Now γ is written in terms of its real and imaginary parts as below,

$$\gamma = \alpha + j\beta = |\gamma| \cos\theta + j|\gamma| \sin\theta \quad ...(18.89)$$

Using Eq. (18.86) and (18.88), we get

$$\gamma = \alpha + j\beta = \frac{1}{2}\left(\frac{R}{\omega L} + \frac{G}{\omega C}\right)\omega\sqrt{LC} + j\omega\sqrt{LC} \quad ...(18.90)$$

since sin θ is nearly equal to unity.

Equating real and imaginary parts in Eq. (18.90), we get

$$\alpha = \frac{R}{2}\sqrt{\frac{C}{L}} + \frac{G}{2}\sqrt{\frac{L}{C}} \quad ...(18.91)$$

and $$\beta = \omega\sqrt{LC} \quad ...(18.92)$$

Also phase velocity $$v_p = \frac{\omega}{\beta} = \frac{1}{\sqrt{LC}} \quad ...(18.93)$$

Also from Eqs. (18.84) and (18.85), we get

$$Z_0 = \sqrt{\frac{z}{y}} = \sqrt{\frac{L}{C}}\ \angle\frac{1}{2}\left(\frac{G}{\omega C} + \frac{R}{\omega L}\right) \text{ radians} \quad ...(18.94)$$

Eqs. (18.91) and (18.93) show that α and v_p are independent of frequency and hence the frequency and phase-delay distortions are zero.

Eq. (18.94) shows that the magnitude of Z_0 is also independent of frequency. However, the phase angle of Z_0 is very small and becomes negligible at higher frequencies making Z_0 nearly a pure resistance.

18.6. Paired Telephone Cables

A telephone cable is formed by two wires insulated from each other by a layer of oil-impregnated paper and then twisted in pairs. A large number of such pairs may form one underground cable. Such transmission lines are called *telephone cable* because these are primarily designed to transmit low voltages. Such a construction leads to negligible inductance and shunt conductance at audio frequencies. Hence series impedance z and shunt admittance y may be written as,

$$z = R \quad \text{and} \quad y = j\omega C \quad ...(18.95)$$

Hence $$\gamma = \sqrt{zy} = \sqrt{\omega CR} = \sqrt{\omega CR}\ \angle 45^\circ \quad ...(18.96)$$

Hence $$\alpha + j\beta = (1 + j1)\sqrt{\frac{\omega CR}{2}} \quad ...(18.97)$$

In Eq. (18.97), equating the real and imaginary parts, we get

$$\alpha = \sqrt{\frac{\omega CR}{2}} \quad \text{...(18.98)}$$

$$\beta = \sqrt{\frac{\omega CR}{2}} \quad \text{...(18.99)}$$

and
$$v_p = \sqrt{\frac{2\omega}{CR}} \quad \text{...(18.100)}$$

These equations show that the frequency and delay distortion are directly proportional to the square root of frequency. Hence large distortion occurs at higher frequencies in a telephone cable.

Also
$$Z_0 = \sqrt{\frac{z}{y}} = \sqrt{\frac{R}{j\omega C}} = \sqrt{\frac{R}{j\omega C}} \angle -45° \quad \text{...(18.101)}$$

18.7. Loading of Lines

A well constructed and maintained lines has very small value of shunt conductance G. Hence the ratio $\frac{R}{L}$ is much larger than $\frac{G}{C}$. In order to approach the condition of distortionless transmission namely $\frac{R}{L} = \frac{G}{C}$, the four alternatives that suggest himselves are: (*i*) reduce R (*ii*) reduce C, (*iii*) Increase G and (*iv*) increase L. Out of these four, the first three are not practicable. R can be reduced only by excessively increasing the thickness of the conductors. This proves too costly. In order to reduce C, we are required to increase the spacing between the conductors. But the spacing maximum is restricted from physical considerations such as the size of line and also from the consideration of cost. Increased conductance G increases α and reduces the transmission efficiency. The only method practicable is to increase the inductance L. Inductance L may be conveniently increased without changing the physical construction of the line. This helps in reducing α and increasing Z_0 somewhat. Hence this is the best method for ensuring distortionless transmission.

Increasing the inductance of a line to reduce distortion, is known as *loading* and was first suggested by Oliver Heaviside. Inductance of a line may be increased in two ways : (*i*) By introducing lumped inductances in series with the line at suitable intervals. This is called *lumped loading* ; (*ii*) By increasing the distributed inductance throughout the length of a line. This is known as the *continuous loading.*

The continuous loading is used usually for submarine cables where it is difficult to provide lumped inductances. Continuous loading is provided by winding a tape of high permeability magnetic material such as steel throughout the length of the cable. This provide uniform loading as well as certain mechanical strength to the cable.

The lumped loading is usually provided in open-wire lines and telephone cables. An open-wire line has smaller R, larger L and smaller C as compared to a telephone cable. Hence an open-wire line has smaller distortion compared to a telephone cable. For an open-wire line typical values of $\frac{R}{L}$ and $\frac{G}{C}$ are 3000 and 90 respectively whereas for a telephone cable typical values are 9×10^4 and 25 respectively. Thus we see that the parameters of an open-wire line are nearer to the distortionless condition as compared to the parameters of a telephone cable. Accordingly lumped loading is mostly provided in underground telephone cables.

Unfortunately it is not possible to increase the inductance of a line without increasing its resistance because the wire used in forming a coil of certain inductance will have a certain resistance associated with it. Thus larger the value of added inductance, larger will be the increase in resistance. Hence increasing the inductance to approach the distortionless condition does not produce the desired effect efficiently. Further the a.c. resistance of the loading coil varies with frequency due to hysteresis and eddy current losses. A transmission line is, therefore, never free of distortions.

Loading also causes the line to act as low pass filter. Thus the attenuation of low frequency signals upto a certain frequency called the cut-off frequency, is very small and constant whereas the attenuation for all higher frequencies increases at a fast rate. Hence cables using carrier frequency operation are usually not loaded.

Consider a uniformly loaded cable whose inductance has been sufficiently increased so that $\omega L >> R$ and whose $G = 0$ or negligible.

Then $z = R + j\omega L$ and $y = j\omega C$. In polar form, z may be written as,

$$z = \sqrt{R^2 + \omega^2 L^2} \angle \frac{\pi}{2} - \frac{R}{\omega L} \qquad ...(18.102)$$

when the angle is nearly $\frac{\pi}{2}$.

Then propagation constant is given by,

$$\gamma = \sqrt{zy}$$

$$= \sqrt{\sqrt{R^2 + \omega^2 L^2} \angle \frac{\pi}{2} - \frac{R}{\omega L} . \omega C \angle \frac{\pi}{2}}$$

$$= \omega\sqrt{LC}\left(1 + \frac{R^2}{\omega^2 L^2}\right)^{1/4} \angle \frac{\pi}{2} - \frac{R}{\omega L} \qquad ...(18.103)$$

Since $wL >> R$, term $\frac{R^2}{\omega^2 L^2}$ may be neglected. Writing the expression of γ in rectangular co-ordinates now yields,

$$\gamma = \alpha + j\beta = \omega\sqrt{LC}\,\frac{R}{2\omega L} + j\omega\sqrt{LC} \qquad ...(18.104)$$

Equating the real and imaginary parts in Eq. (18.104), we get

$$\alpha = \frac{R}{2}\sqrt{\frac{C}{L}} \qquad ...(18.105)$$

$$\beta = \omega\sqrt{LC} \qquad ...(18.106)$$

and
$$v_p = \frac{1}{\sqrt{LC}} \qquad ...(18.107)$$

Example 18.4. *An underground cable having R = 53 Ω/loop km ; L = 0.6 m Henry/l. km; C = 0.04 μF/km and C = 1 mΩ/km, is loaded by loading coils of inductances 246 mH and resistance 7.3 ohms each at standard intervals of 7.88 miles. Calculate the values of Z_0, α, β and v_p for the loaded cable and show that the values are nearly the same as for a line of low distortions. Assume operating frequency of 1000 Hz.*

Solution.
$$z = R + j\omega L = 53 + j2\pi \times 1000 \times 0.6 \times 10^{-3} + \frac{7.3 + j2\pi \times 246}{7.88 \times 1.6}$$

$$= 53.58 + j126.4 = 137.3 \angle 67.15°$$

$$y = G + j\omega C = 10^{-6} + j2\pi \times 1000 \times 0.04 \times 10^{-6}$$

$$= 251 \times 10^{-6} \angle 89.76°$$

Hence
$$Z_0 = \sqrt{\frac{z}{y}} = \sqrt{\frac{137.3\,\angle 67.15^\circ}{251 \times 10^{-6}\,\angle 89.76^\circ}} = \sqrt{54.7 \times 10^4\,\angle -22.61^\circ}$$
$$= 740\,\angle -11.3^\circ$$
$$\gamma = \sqrt{zy} = \sqrt{137.3\,\angle 67.15^\circ \times 251 \times 10\,\angle 89.76^\circ}$$
$$= 0.1855\,\angle 78.45^\circ = 0.0371 + j\,0.1818$$
$$\alpha = 0.0371 \text{ neper/kilometre}$$
$$\beta = 0.1818 \text{ radian/kilimetre}$$
$$v_p = \frac{\omega}{\beta} = \frac{2\pi \times 1000}{0.1818} = 34550 \text{ km/sec.}$$

Using the formula for low distortion line

$$Z_0 = \sqrt{\frac{L}{C}}\,\angle \frac{1}{2}\left(\frac{G}{\omega C} - \frac{R}{\omega L}\right)$$

where L and R are the new values obtained by considering the loading coil inductance and resistance as uniformly distributed along the length of the line.

Hence total inductance of the cable is,

$$L' = 0.6 \times 10^{-3} + \frac{246 \times 10^{-3}}{7.88 \times 1.6} = 20.1 \times 10^{-3} \text{ H}$$

and
$$R' = 53 + \frac{7.3}{7.88 \times 1.6} = 53.58\ \Omega$$

Hence
$$Z_0 = \sqrt{\frac{20.1 \times 10^{-3}}{0.04 \times 10^{-6}}}\;\angle \frac{1}{2}\left(\frac{10^{-6}}{2\pi \times 1000 \times 0.04 \times 10^{-6}} - \frac{53.58}{2\pi \times 1000 \times 20.1 \times 10^{-3}}\right) \text{ rad.}$$
$$= 710\,\angle -0.21 \text{ rad.} = 710\,\angle -12^\circ$$
$$\alpha = \frac{R}{2}\sqrt{\frac{C}{L}} + \frac{G}{2}\sqrt{\frac{L}{C}}$$
$$= \frac{53.58}{2}\sqrt{\frac{0.04 \times 10^{-6}}{20.1 \times 10^{-3}}} + \frac{10^{-6}}{2}\sqrt{\frac{20.1 \times 10^{-3}}{0.04 \times 10^{-6}}}$$
$$= 0.03815 \text{ neper/km.}$$
$$\beta = \omega\sqrt{LC} = 2\pi \times 1000\sqrt{20.1 \times 10^{-3} \times 0.04 \times 10^{-6}}$$
$$= 0.1783 \text{ radian/km.}$$
$$v_p = \frac{1}{\sqrt{LC}} = 35200 \text{ km/sec.}$$

18.8. Campbell's Formula for Loaded Line

Usually lumped loading is used for open wire lines and underground cables. Coils having calculated values of inductance are inserted in series with the lines at fixed regular intervals. Analysis of lumped loaded lines can be made considering an equivalent asymmetrical *T*-section where half of the loading-coil inductance is considered in each series arm. Such a network is shown in Fig. 18.2,

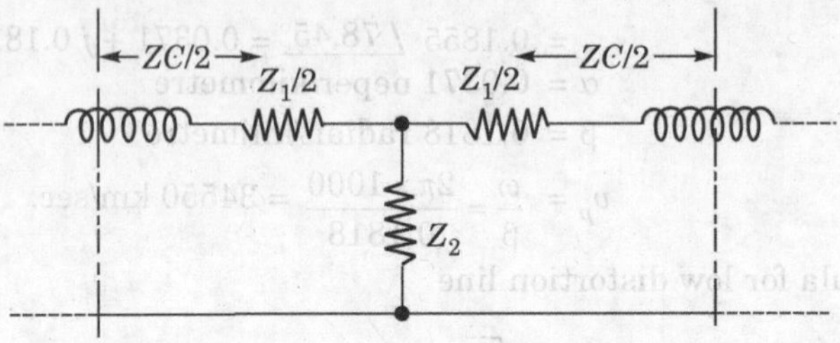

Fig. 18.2. Equivalent *T*-section of a line between two lumped loading coils of impedance Z_c.

where Z_c is the impedance of the loading coil. Series arm impedances are $\frac{Z_1}{2}$ each while the shunt arm impedance is Z_2. The characteristic impedance of this network is the input impedance when the network is terminated at the receiving end by the characteristic impedance.

Thus
$$Z_0 = \frac{Z_1}{2} + \frac{\left(\frac{Z_1}{2} + Z_0\right) Z_2}{\frac{Z_1}{2} + Z_2 + Z_0} \qquad \text{...(18.108)}$$

This yields,
$$Z_0 = \sqrt{Z_1 Z_2 + \frac{Z_1^2}{4}} \qquad \text{...(18.109)}$$

If the terminating impedance is made infinite or the terminals are open circuited, the input impedance is given by,

$$Z_{oc} = \frac{Z_1}{2} + Z_0 \qquad \text{...(18.110)}$$

On the other hand, if the terminating impedance is made zero, *i.e.* terminals are short circuited, the input impedance of the network is given by,

$$Z_{sc} = \frac{Z_1}{2} + \frac{\frac{Z_1 Z_2}{2}}{\frac{Z_1}{2} + Z_2} \qquad \text{...(18.111)}$$

In Eqs. (18.110) and (18.111) are multiplied, then from Eq. (18.109), we get

$$Z_0 = \sqrt{Z_{oc} \cdot Z_{sc}} \qquad \text{...(18.112)}$$

This result is very valuable in the sense that the characteristic impedance of a symmetrical network can be calculated by measuring its open-circuit and short circuit input impedances and using Eq. (18.112). At the same time, the series and shunt admittances can be determined in terms of Z_{oc} and Z_{sc}. Thus from Eq. (18.110), the series arm impedance is given as,

$$\frac{Z_1}{2} = Z_{oc} - Z_2 \qquad ...(18.113)$$

Eliminating Z_1 from Eqs. (18.113) and (18.111), we get

$$Z_2 = \sqrt{Z_{oc}(Z_{oc} - Z_{sc})} \qquad ...(18.114)$$

Let the loading coils be placed at regular intervals of d units of length. Then Eq. (18.55) gives the open circuit and short circuit input impedances of an equivalent T-section. Thus, we get

$$Z_{oc} = Z_0 \left. \frac{\cosh \gamma d + \dfrac{Z_0}{Z_R} \sinh \gamma d}{\dfrac{Z_0}{Z_R} \cos \gamma d + \sinh \gamma d} \right|_{Z_R \to \infty}$$

$$= Z_0 \cosh \gamma d \qquad ...(18.115)$$

and

$$Z_{sc} = Z_0 \left. \frac{Z_R \cosh \gamma d + Z_0 \sinh \gamma d}{Z_0 \cosh \gamma d + Z_R \sinh \gamma d} \right|_{Z_R \to \infty}$$

$$= Z_0 \tanh \gamma d \qquad ...(18.116)$$

Substituting the values of Z_{oc} and Z_{sc} from Eqs. (18.115) and (18.116) into Eq. (18.114), we get on simplification,

$$Z_2 = \frac{Z_0}{\sinh \gamma d} \qquad ...(18.117)$$

Also from Eq. (18.113), we get

$$\frac{Z_1}{2} = Z_0 \frac{\cosh \gamma d - I}{\sinh \gamma d} = Z_0 \tanh \frac{\gamma d}{2} \qquad ...(18.118)$$

Now including the half impedance of the loading coil in the series arm of the equivalent T-section of the line as shown in Fig. 18.2 gives the following expression for the total impedance of the half of the series arm:

$$\frac{Z_1'}{2} + \frac{Z_c}{2} = Z_0 \tanh \frac{\gamma d}{2} \qquad ...(18.119)$$

Now

$$\varepsilon^{\gamma d} = \frac{\dfrac{Z_1}{2} + Z_2 + Z_0}{Z_2} \qquad ...(18.120)$$

Substituting the value of Z_0 from Eq. (18.120) into Eq. (18.109) yields,

$$\sqrt{Z_1 Z_2 + \frac{Z_1^2}{4}} = Z_2(\varepsilon^{\gamma d} - 1) - \frac{Z_1}{2} \qquad ...(18.121)$$

Squaring both the sides of Eq. (18.121) yields,

$$Z_1 Z_2 + \frac{Z_1^2}{4} = Z_2^2(\varepsilon^{\gamma d} - 1)^2 + \frac{Z_1^2}{4} - Z_1 Z_2(\varepsilon^{\gamma d} - 1)$$

or

$$Z_2(\varepsilon^{\gamma d} - 1)^2 - Z_1 \varepsilon^{\gamma d} = 0$$

or $$\varepsilon^{2\gamma d} - 2\varepsilon^{\gamma d} + 1 = \frac{Z_1}{Z_2}\varepsilon^{\gamma d}$$

or $$\frac{\varepsilon^{\gamma d} + \varepsilon^{-\gamma d}}{2} = 1 + \frac{Z_1}{2Z_2} = \cosh \gamma d \qquad ...(18.122)$$

If the propagation constant of the equivalent T-section using the loading coils is γ', then substituting the new value $\frac{Z_1'}{2}$ from Eq. (18.119) and the value of Z_2 from Eq. (18.117) into Eq. (18.122), we get

$$\cosh \gamma' d = 1 + \frac{\left(\frac{Z_c}{2} + Z_0 \tanh \frac{\gamma d}{2}\right)}{Z_0 / \sinh \gamma d} \qquad ...(18.123)$$

Making use of Eq. (18.118), Eq. (18.123) yields,

$$\cosh \gamma' d = 1 + \frac{\frac{Z_c}{2} + Z_0 \frac{\cosh \gamma d - 1}{\sinh \gamma d}}{Z_0 / \sinh \gamma d} \qquad ...(18.124)$$

This is simplified to give,

$$\cosh \gamma' d = \frac{Z_2}{2Z_0} \sinh \gamma d + \cosh \gamma d \qquad ...(18.125)$$

Eq. (18.125) is known as the *Campbell's Formula* for loaded lines. This equation expresses the new propagation constant of the loaded line of length d in terms of (*i*) propagation constant of the unloaded line (*ii*) characteristic impedance of the unloaded line and (*iii*) impedance Z_c of the loading coil. It then becomes possible to calculate the values of new attenuation constant α' and new phase constant β'. From these constants we may then calculate the effect of loading on attenuation and distortions on lines.

In actual transmission lines, the shunt impedance Z_2 is that of the distributed capacitance and leakance at the operating frequency. The equivalent T-network for a transmission line loaded by inductance coils, therefore, consists of inductance in series arm and capacitance in the shunt arm. Such a network constitutes a *low pass filter* which transmits with zero attenuation signals of frequencies upto a definite value called the *cut-off frequency* of the filter and greatly attenuates all higher frequencies. Beyond the cut-off frequency, attenuation rises very rapidly as the frequency increases. Thus a loaded line cannot be used for transmission of a large range of signal frequencies. For this reason, a line used for carrier current operation cannot be loaded.

The cut-off frequency of the loaded line of length d is given by,

$$f_c = \frac{1}{\pi\sqrt{(L_c + L_d)\, Cd}} \qquad ...(18.126)$$

where L_c is the loading coil inductance.

Thus cut-off frequency is the maximum frequency which may be transmitted over loaded lines such as cables. The cut-off frequency may be increased by decreasing the loading coil inductance which in turn increases the attenuation and distortion. The cut-off frequency can also be increased by reducing d, the spacing of the loading coils. This requires larger number of relatively small size loading coils in a given length of the line, thereby increasing the cost. The overall cost of loading increases rapidly as the number of coils increases. Accordingly the most economical spacing and the best value of loading inductance L_c have to be most carefully calculated in designing the loaded line.

Example 18.5. *A underground cable having R = 55 Ω/l. km, L = 0.6 mH/l. km., C = 0.04 μF/km and G = 1 μS/km is loaded by coils having inductance of 0.1 henry and resistance of 8 ohms* *placed at regular interval of 2.5 km. Assuming an operating frequency of 800 Hz, calculate the new value of attenuation constant and the phase constants of the line using Campbell's formula. Also calculate the cut-off frequency of the cable.*

Solution. The various quantities involved in Campbell's formula are calculated below:

$$z = R + j\omega L = 55 + j2\pi \times 800 \times 0.6 \times 10^{-3} = 55 + j0.96\pi \approx 55 \angle 3.1^\circ$$

$$y = G + j\omega L = 10^{-6}(1 + j2\pi \times 800 \times 0.04) = 10^{-6}(1 + j64\pi) \approx 64\pi \times 10^{-6} \angle 89.71^\circ$$

$$Z_0 = \sqrt{\frac{z}{y}} = \sqrt{\frac{55}{64\pi \times 10^{-6}} \angle -88.61^\circ} = 523 \angle -43.3^\circ$$

$$\gamma = \sqrt{zy} = \sqrt{55 \times 64\pi \times 10^{-6} \angle -92.81^\circ} = 0.1052 \angle 46.4^\circ = 0.0726 + j0.0764$$

$$Z_c = 8 + j2\pi \times 800 \times 0.1 = 8 + j160\pi \approx 160\pi \angle 89.1^\circ$$

$$\sinh \gamma d = \sinh(\alpha + j\beta)d = \sinh \alpha d \cos \beta d + j \cosh \alpha d \sin \beta d$$

where d is the coil spacing in kilometres since α and β are per kilometre of length.

Hence $\sinh \gamma d = \sinh 0.1815 \cos 0.191 + j \cosh 0.1815 \sin 0.191$

$$= 0.171 + j0.1927 = 0.262 \angle 47.2^\circ$$

$$\cosh \gamma d = \cosh \alpha d \cos \beta d + j \sin \alpha d \sinh \beta d$$

$$= \cosh 0.1815 \cos 0.191 + j \sinh 0.1815 \sin 0.191$$

$$= 0.997 + j0.0344$$

Substituting these values in Campbell's formula, we get

$$\cos \gamma_d = \frac{160\pi \angle 89.1^\circ \times 0.262 \angle 47.2^\circ}{2 \times 523 \angle -43.3^\circ} + 0.997 + j0.0344$$

$$= 0.126 \angle 179.6^\circ + 0.997 + j0.344$$

$$= 0.126 + j0.0009 + 0.997 + 0.0344 = 0.871 + j0.0353$$

Let $\cosh(\alpha' + j\beta')d = A + jB$

Then $A = \cosh \alpha'd \cos \beta'd$

and $B = \sinh \alpha'd \sin \beta'd$

Then $A^2 + B^2 = \cosh^2 \alpha'd \cos^2 \beta'd + \sinh^2 \alpha'd \sin^2 \beta'd$

$$= \cosh^2 \alpha'd (1 - \cos^2 \beta'd) + \sinh^2 \alpha'd \sin^2 \beta'd$$

$$= \cosh^2 \alpha'd - \sin^2 \beta'd \quad ...(3)$$

since $\cosh^2 \alpha'd - \sinh^2 \alpha'd = 1$

In Eq. (3) adding 1 on both sides, we get

$$1 + A^2 + B^2 = \cosh^2 \alpha'd + \cos^2 \beta'd \quad ...(4)$$

In Eq. (4) completing the square by adding $2A$ on both the sides, we get

$$1 + 2A + A^2 + B^2 = \cosh^2 \alpha'd + \cos^2 \beta'd + 2\cosh \alpha'd \cos \beta'd = (\cosh \alpha'd + \cos \beta'd)^2$$

Hence $\cosh \alpha'd + \cos \beta'd = \sqrt{(1 + A^2) + B^2}$ ...(5)

Again in Eq. (4) completing the square by subtracting $2A$ from both the sides, we get

$$1 - 2A + A^2 + B^2 = \cosh^2 \alpha'd - \cos^2 \beta'd - \cosh \alpha'd \cos \beta'd = (\cosh \alpha'd - \cos \beta'd)^2$$

Hence $\cosh \alpha'd - \cos \beta'd = \sqrt{(1 - A^2) + B^2}$ ...(6)

Substituting the value of A and B in Eqs. (5) and (6), we get

$$\cosh \alpha' d + \cos \beta' d = \sqrt{(1.871) + (0.0353)^2} \approx 1.872 \quad ...(7)$$

$$\cosh \alpha' d - \cos \beta' d = \sqrt{(0.129)^2 + (0.0355)^2} = 0.1338 \quad ...(8)$$

From Eqs. (7) and (8),

$$\cosh \alpha' d = \frac{1.872 + 0.1338}{2} = 1.0029 \quad ...(9)$$

and

$$\cos \beta' d = \frac{1.872 - 0.1338}{2} = 0.8691 \quad ...(10)$$

From Eq. (9), $\alpha' d = 0.075$

From Eq. (10), $\beta' d = 29.65°$

Hence $\alpha' = \dfrac{0.075}{2.5} = 0.03$ neper/km

and $\beta' = \dfrac{29.56 \times 2\pi}{18 \times 2.5} = 0.207$ radian/km.

The cut-off frequency is given by,

$$f_c = \frac{1}{\pi\sqrt{(L_c + Ld)cd}} = \frac{1}{\pi\sqrt{(0.1 + 0.6 \times 2.5 \times 10^{-3}) \times 4 \times 10^{-8} \times 25}}$$

$$= 3160 \text{ Hz.}$$

18.9. Effect of Loading

The effect of loading is to increase the value of Z_0. If a line is terminated in Z_0, the input impedance of the line is $Z_0 = \dfrac{V_S}{I_S}$, where V_S and I_S are the sending end voltage and current respectively. If Z_0 is resistive, the sending end power W_S equals $\dfrac{V_S^2}{Z_0}$. Hence for the same power at the sending end, the sending voltage V_S increases with the increase in Z_0 caused by loading. Thus transmission of power takes place at higher voltage and at nearly unity power factor. This constitutes the most efficient method of power transmission.

The primary constants of a line which are responsible for loss of power are the loop resistance R and the shunt conductance G. The loop resistance R causes loss of power equal to I^2R whereas the shunt conductance G causes loss of power equal to V^2G. In a cable operating at audio frequencies, the I^2R loss usually predominates. However, the current I at any point in a transmission line equals $\dfrac{V}{Z_0}$ if the line is terminated by Z_0. Hence if Z_0 can be increased without increasing R, the current flow through the line gets reduced and the I^2R loss and the attenuation constant get reduced. However, V also increases simultaneously and the V^2G loss, consequently increases. But usually G is very small as compared to R. Hence there results definite reduction in attenuation constant by loading. Theoretically α will go on reducing until Z_0 reaches such a high value that V^2G loss equals I^2R loss. But other factors such as the a.c. resistance of the loading coil etc. do not allow this limiting condition to be reached.

19

Reflection in Transmission Lines

19.1. Wave Propagation on Line

Consider a line of infinite length or a line terminated in the characteristic impedance Z_0. For such a line, the voltage E and the current I at any distance x from the sending end are given by,

$$E = E_S \, \varepsilon^{-\gamma x} \quad \text{...(19.1)}$$

$$I = I_S \, \varepsilon^{-\gamma x} \quad \text{...(19-2)}$$

where E_S is the sending end voltage
and I_S is the sending end current.

Let us assume that both E_s and I_s are time variant and are given by,

$$E_S = E_{s_0} \, \varepsilon^{j\omega t} \quad \text{...(19.3)}$$

and

$$I_s = I_{s_0} \, \varepsilon^{j\omega t} \quad \text{...(l9.4)}$$

Then Eq. (19.1) may be written as,

$$E = E_S \, \varepsilon^{j\omega t} \, . \, \varepsilon^{-\alpha x} \, \varepsilon^{-j\beta x}$$

$$= E_{S_0} \, \varepsilon^{-\alpha x} \, \varepsilon^{-j(\beta x - \omega t)} \quad \text{...(19.5)}$$

Similarly Eq. (19.2) may be written as,

$$I = I_{S_0} \, \varepsilon^{j\omega t} \, \varepsilon^{-\alpha x}, \, \varepsilon^{-j\beta x}$$

$$= I_{S_0} \, \varepsilon^{-\alpha x} \, \varepsilon^{-j(\beta x - \omega t)} \quad \text{...(19.6)}$$

Here E_{S_0} and I_{S_0} are the peak values and E and I are phasors which are functions of both distance and time. Such equations arise in the solution of wave equations and represent the propagation of a wave in the x-direction through the medium which in this case in the physical line. The propagation of a wave is thus characterised by variation of voltage or current magnitude and phase angle with respect to time and distance as compared to their magnitudes and phase angles at the input or the sending end. Eqs. (19.5) and (19.6) show that the magnitude of phasors go on reducing as x increases due to the factor $\varepsilon^{-\alpha x}$. Hence the name *attenuation constant* (indicated by α) is justified. Also the phasors lag progressively more and more as x increases due to the factor $\varepsilon^{-\beta x} = \angle -\beta x^0$.

This can be made more clear by study of voltage phasors at a particular time t_1 as shown in Fig. 19.1. Points are-selected at equal distances x_0 starting from the sending end of the transmission line. Thus let this equal distance be one-eighth wavelength, *i.e.* $\frac{\lambda p}{8}$ Then this interval x_0 is given by,

$$x_0 = \frac{\lambda p}{8} = \frac{2\pi}{8\beta} \quad \text{..(19.7)}$$

Fig. 19.1 shows the voltage phasors OE_1, OE_2, etc. lagging behind E_s by phase angles βx_0, $2\beta x_0$ etc. respectively. Each of these phasors may be considered as representing maximum instantaneous voltage values which are seen to reduce in magnitude as distance x increases because of the factor $\varepsilon^{-\alpha x}$.

Now it may be assumed that all these phasors are rotating in anti-clockwise direction with an angular velocity of ω radians per second since input signal is a sinusoid of frequency ω radians/second.

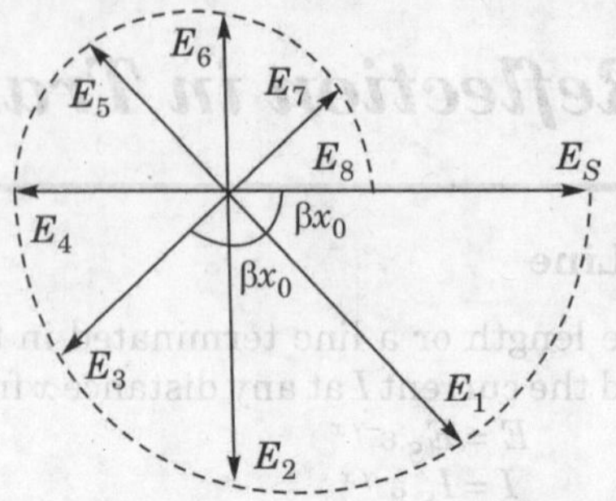

Fig. 19.1. Voltage phasors one-eighth wavelenght spacing along a line at a particular instant of time.

This may be considered as rotation of a wheel having spokes OE_s OE_1, OE_2 etc. of different sizes. This condition prevails at time t_1. Now if we plot the instantaneous values of these phasors at time t_1 against distance

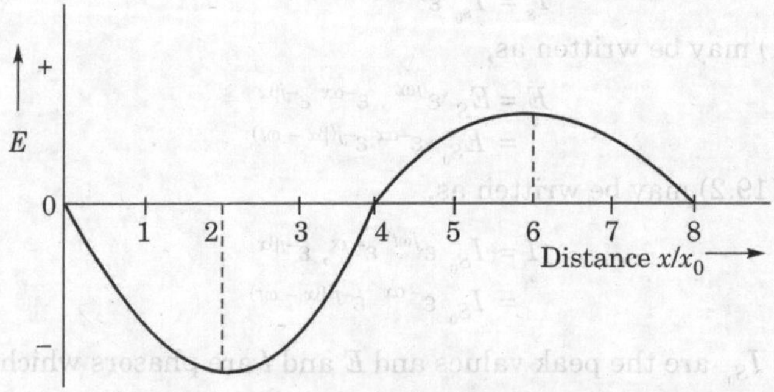

Fig. 19.2. Plot of phasor E against distance $\frac{x}{x_0}$ at time t_1.

x, we get a curve of the form shown in Fig. 19.2. This is an oscillating waveform whose amplitude reduces progressively with the increase of distance. Ultimately the amplitude becomes zero at x equal to infinity.

Next consider the situation at instant of time t_2 which lags behind the instant t_1 by one-eighth periodic time of the sinusoidal variation. At this instant t_2, all the phasors have undergone anti-clockwise rotation through 45°, *i.e.* one-eighth the periodic time and have taken up positions as shown in Fig. 19.3.

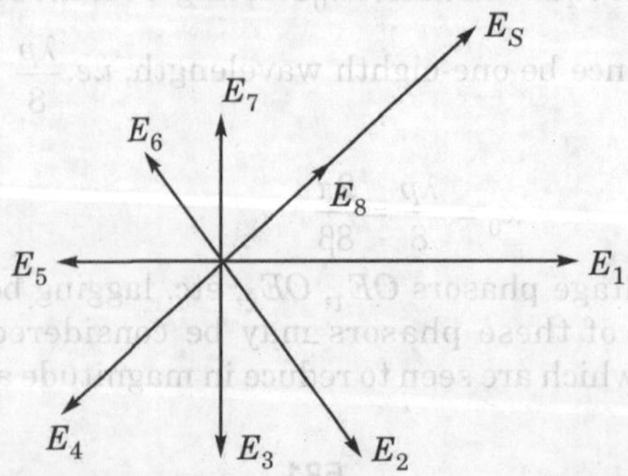

Fig. 19.3. Voltage phasors at one-eighth cycle later than those in Fig. 19.1.

Now if we plot the instantaneous values of these phasors at time t_2 against distance x, we again get an oscillating waveform shown in Fig. 19.4. This waveform is similar to that of Fig. 19.2 except that it

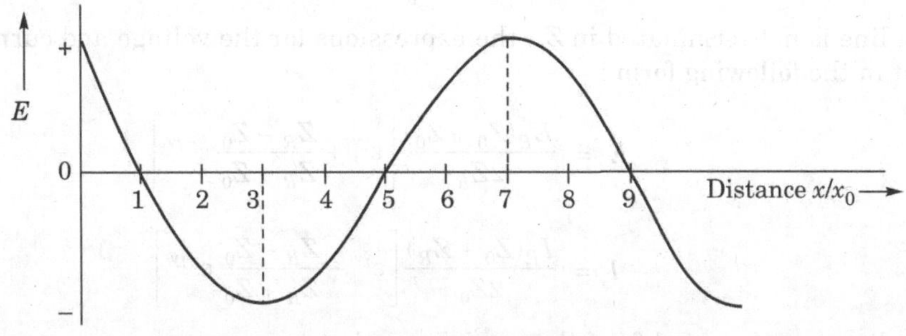

Fig. 19.4. Plot of phasor E against distance $\frac{x}{x_0}$ at time t_2.

has shifted by one-eighth wavelength towards the right, *i.e.* away from the sending end of the line. Thus we find that the voltage wave travels down the line from the sending end to the receiving end. This propagation is characterised by the amplitude of voltage or current constantly reducing with distance x on account of the factor $\varepsilon^{-\alpha x}$. Also the phase angle constantly changes along the line due to the factor $\varepsilon^{-j\beta x}$.

It may be seen that the wave motion exists due to the phase angles of the voltage phasors changing continuously. Thus the phase angles corresponding to the plot of Fig. 19.2 are propagated with a certain velocity known as the *phase velocity of propagation* denoted by v_p. This phase velocity v_p depends upon two quantities namely : (*i*) the wavelength λ which depends upon the value of β (*ii*) the angular velocity ω with which the phasors rotate and equals the rate of change of phase angle of the phasor. Thus the phase velocity of propagation is given by $v_p = \frac{\omega}{\beta}$.

If the instruments reading r.m.s. value are connected along the line, they will not record the phase angles but read only the r.m.s. values. These r.m.s. values vary with distance x from the sending end in accordance with the relations,

$$E_{rms} = E_S \varepsilon^{-\alpha x} \quad \text{...(19.8)}$$

and

$$I_{rms} = I_S \varepsilon^{-\alpha x} \quad \text{...(19.9)}$$

Fig. 19.5 shows the nature of variation of the r.m.s. value. E_{rms} with distance x.

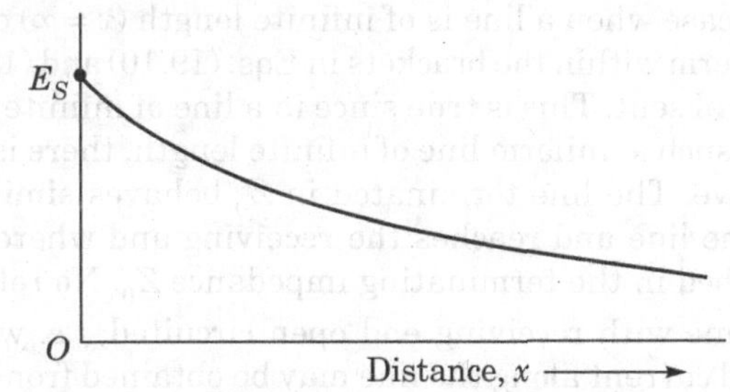

Fig. 19.5. Variation E_{rms} with distance x.

The above discussion regarding the propagation of wave along a transmission line consider the voltage and current because they are the quantities which can be readily measured. However actually the energy is being propagated along the line. This energy is contained in the electric and magnetic fields which are set up due to voltage difference and a current flowing through the line and lies in the region surrounding two wires of the line.

19.2. Propagation on a Line Terminated in Z_R

When a line is not terminated in Z_0, the expressions for the voltage and current along the line can be put in the following form :

$$E_x = \frac{E_R(Z_0 + Z_0)}{2Z_R}\left[\varepsilon^{\gamma y} + \frac{Z_R - Z_0}{Z_R + Z_0}\,\varepsilon^{-\gamma y}\right] \quad ...(19.10)$$

$$I_x = \frac{I_R(Z_0 + Z_R)}{2Z_0}\left[\varepsilon^{\gamma y} - \frac{Z_R - Z_0}{Z_R + Z_0}\,\varepsilon^{-\gamma y}\right] \quad ...(19.11)$$

where y is the distance measured from the receiving end.

We have already seen that the wave travels from the sending end to the receiving end with continuously decreasing magnitude. The expressions for voltage and current of such a travelling wave is given by Eqs. (19.3) and (19.4), where distance x is measured from the sending end and the expressions contain the factor $\varepsilon^{-\gamma x}$. If one travels backward from the receiving end towards the sending end, the magnitudes of voltage and current increase continuously as the distance from the receiving end increases. This is true for the wave coming from the sending end of the line. Hence for an observer at the receiving end, the wave contains the factor $\varepsilon^{\gamma y}$. This wave travelling from the sending end to the receiving end constitutes the *incident wave*.

The expressions for voltage E_x and current I_x as given by Eqs. (19.10) and (19.11) contain the factor $\varepsilon^{-\gamma y}$ also. This factor causes the amplitudes of voltage and current to decrease as the distance from the receiving end increases. Hence this part of the expression may be considered to represent a wave travelling from the receiving end to the sending end. Such a wave may be termed as the *reflected wave*.

Thus when a line is not terminated in Z_0, the above two waves always exist along the line and the voltage phasor or current phasor at any point on the line is the sum of the two waves. The amplitude and the phase angle of the reflected wave relative to the incident wave depend upon $\mathbf{Z}_0$ and $\mathbf{Z}_R$ and are given by the factor $(\mathbf{Z}_R - \mathbf{Z}_0)/(\mathbf{Z}_R + \mathbf{Z}_0)$. Thus greater the difference between $\mathbf{Z}_0$ and $\mathbf{Z}_R$, larger will by the amplitudes of the reflected wave. The difference between $\mathbf{Z}_0$ and $\mathbf{Z}_R$ forms the mismatch.

19.3. Reflection in an Open-circuited Line

Consider first the case when a line is of infinite length ($x = \infty$) or is terminated in Z_0 so that $Z_R = Z_0$. Then the second term within the brackets in Eqs. (19.10) and (19.11) becomes zero indicating that the reflected wave is absent. This is true since in a line of infinite length, the energy travels in one direction only. Along such a uniform line of infinite length, there is no discontinuity which may send back a reflected wave. The line terminated in Z_0 behaves similarly. In this case, the wave travels smoothly down the line and reaches the receiving and where the energy of the incoming wave is completely absorbed in the terminating impedance Z_0. No reflected wave is thus set up.

In this case of a line with receiving end open circuited, *i.e.* with Z_R equal to infinity, the expression for voltage and current along the line may be obtained from Eqs. (19.10) and (19.11) and are given by

$$E_x = \frac{E_R}{2}\,[\varepsilon^{\gamma y} + \varepsilon^{-\gamma y}] \quad ...(19.12)$$

$$I_x = \frac{E_R}{2Z_0}[\varepsilon^{\gamma y} - \varepsilon^{-\gamma y}] \quad ...(19.13)$$

The rotating phasors and the correspond waveforms for Eq. (19.12) as functions of distance y/y_0 from the receiving end are drawn in Fig. 19.6 for two instants of times : one at time $t = 0$ and the other at $t = 1/4f$, f being the frequency in Hertz. The distance y_0 in the figure is taken as $\lambda p/8$.

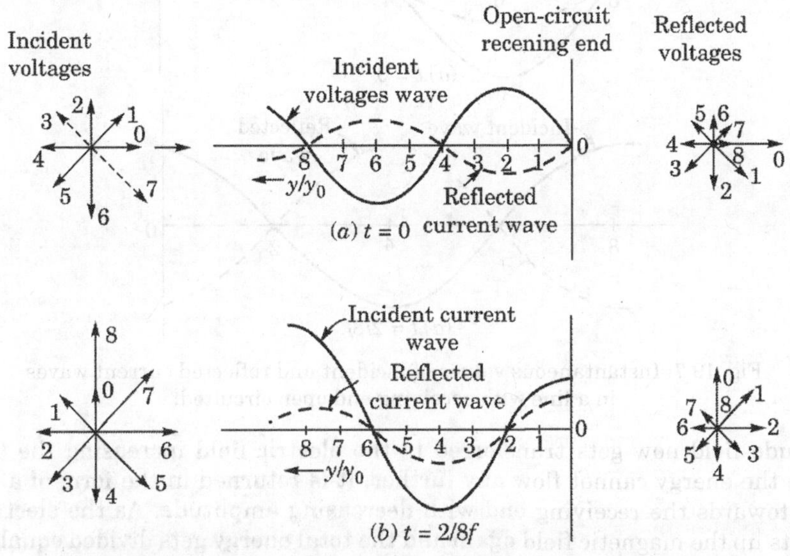

Fig. 19.6. Rotating voltage phasors for incident and reflected waves and their instantaneous values for the open circuited load.

The incident voltage wave varying as $\varepsilon^{\gamma y}$ is shown by solid curves while the reflected wave varying as $\varepsilon^{\gamma y}$ is shown by dashed line. The reflected wave is seen to have the same amplitude as the incident wave at the receiving end, *i.e.* at $y = 0$. Eqs. (19.12) and (19.13) show that the incident and the reflected voltage waves at the receiving end are in the same phase. The reflected wave has the same waveform as that of the incident wave had the line been of infinite length. The total voltage across the line at any point is then vector sum of the incident and reflected voltage waves.

Fig. 19.7 shows the waveforms of the incident and reflected current waves plotted against the distance y/y_0 from the receiving end for the same two instants of time as shown in Fig. 19.6. It may be seen that the reflected current wave at the receiving end is 180° out of phase with the incident current wave but has the same magnitude as the incident current wave. This condition is true and also necessary in order that the total current at the receiving end is zero for the open circuit condition at all instants of time.

Thus the magnetic field associated with the current abruptly becomes zero at the open circuited receiving end. However, this change in the magnitude field causes a voltage to be induced. The energy stored

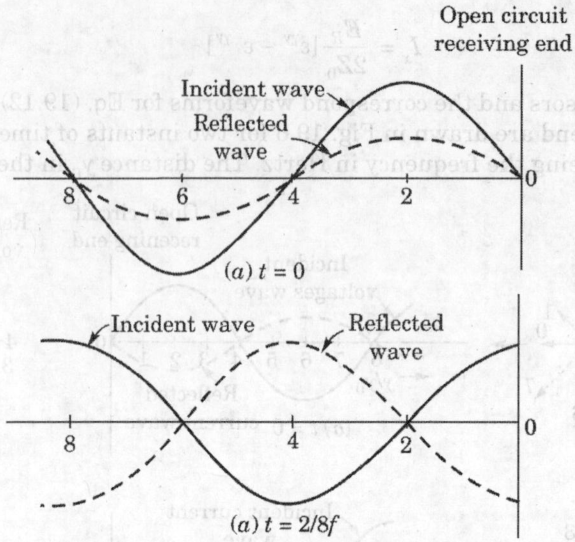

Fig. 19.7. Instantaneous values of incident and reflected current waves in a line with receiving end open circuited.

in the magnitude field now gets transferred to the electric field increasing the energy already existing. Since the energy cannot flow any further, it is returned in the form of a reflected wave which travels towards the receiving end with decreasing amplitude. As the electric field moves backward it sets up the magnetic field again and the total energy gets divided equally between the two fields. Since the open circuit presents zero load, energy is not absorbed and the reflected wave has the same amplitude as the incident wave at the receiving end. Thus the electric fields gets doubled at the instant of reflection. Hence the reflected voltage wave starts back in the some phase as the incident wave whereas the magnetic field becomes zero at the instant of reflection. Hence the total current at the point of reflection must be zero which requires that the incident and the reflected current waves are opposite in phase having equal magnitude at the point of reflection. These same conditions are shown by Eqs. (19.12) and (19.13).

Now let I_R' be the component of the current at the receiving end as caused by the incident wave and let I_R'' be the component of current at the receiving end due to the reflected wave. Similarly let E_R' and E_R'' be the components of the voltage at the receiving end due to the incident and reflected waves respectively. The Eqs. (19.12) and (19.13) for open circuited line for $y = 0$ give,

$$E_R' = \frac{E_R}{2}, E_R'' = \frac{E_R}{2} \quad ...(19.14)$$

$$I_R' = \frac{E_R}{2Z_0}, I_R'' = -\frac{E_R}{2Z_0} \quad ...(19.15)$$

Hence $$\frac{E_R''}{E_R'} = 1\underline{/0^\circ} \text{ and } \frac{I_R''}{I_R'} = -1 = 1\underline{/180^\circ} \quad ...(19.16)$$

Eq. (19.16) shows that the voltage components of incident and reflected waves are in phase while the corresponding current components are out of phased but have equal magnitudes.

Then Eqs. (19.12) and (19.13) may be written in terms of E_R' E_R'', I_R and I'' as below :

$$E_x = E_R' \varepsilon^{\gamma y} + E_R'' \varepsilon^{-\gamma y} \quad ...(19.17)$$

$$I_x = I_R' \varepsilon^{\gamma y} + I_R'' \varepsilon^{-\gamma y} \quad ...(19.18)$$

In a simliar manner, we may write E_x and I_x in terms of E_s', I_s', E_s'' and I_s'' where E_s' and I_s' are the components of sending end voltage and current due to initial or the incident wave while E_s'' and I_s'' are the components due to reflected wave.

Thus, we get

$$E_x = E_S' \varepsilon^{-\gamma x} + E_S'' \varepsilon^{\gamma x} \quad ...(19.19)$$

$$I_x = I_S' \varepsilon^{-\gamma x} + I_S'' \varepsilon^{\gamma x} \quad ...(19.20)$$

where $E_S' = A_2,\ E_S'' = A_1,\ I_S' = \dfrac{A_2}{Z_0}$ and $I_S'' = -\dfrac{A_1}{Z_0}$

Combining these values with those given by Eqs. (19.14) and (19.15), we get

$$\frac{E_S'}{I_S'} = -\frac{E_S''}{I_S'} = \frac{E_R'}{I_R'} = -\frac{E_R''}{R_R'} = Z_0 \quad ...(19.21)$$

The voltage and current at the sending end may then be obtained from Eqs. (19.17) and (19.18) by substituting $x = 0$. Thus, we get

$$E_S = E_S' + E_S'' \quad ...(19.22)$$

$$I_S = I_S' + I_S'' \quad ...(19.23)$$

Similarly the voltage and the current at the receiving end are obtained from Eqs. (19.17) and (19.18) by substituting $x = 0$. Thus, we get

$$E_S = E_S' + E_S'' \quad ...(19.24)$$

$$I_R = I_R' + I_R'' \quad ...(19.25)$$

In Eqs. (19.22) to (19.25), the summation must necessarily be done vectorially.

19.4. Reflection in a Short Circuited Line

In the terminating impedance Z_R is made zero the receiving end is said to be short circuited. The voltage and current at any point along the line are then obtained from Eqs. (19.10) and (19.11) by putting $Z_R = 0$. Thus, we get

$$E_x = \frac{I_R Z_0}{2} [\varepsilon^{\gamma y} - \varepsilon^{-\gamma y}] \quad ...(19.26)$$

$$I_x = \frac{I_R}{2} [\varepsilon^{\gamma y} - \varepsilon^{-\gamma y}] \quad ...(19.27)$$

Short circuit makes the terminal voltage E_R zero which forces the electric field to become zero. The energy contained in the electric field cannot vanish but gets transferred to the magnetic field. This energy in the magnetic field accordingly gets doubled and hence sends a reflected wave. At the receiving end, therefore, the incident and the reflected components of current must be in the same phase and equal in magnitude while the incident and the reflected components of voltage must be opposite in phase and equal in magnitude. These conditions are given by Eqs. (19.26) and (19.27) which shows that the two current components are added while the two voltage components oppose each other.

The waveform of instantaneous values of current phasors for short circuited line will, therefore, be the same as the instantaneous values of voltage phasors for an open circuited line shown in Fig. 19.6. Similarly the plot of instantaneous values of voltage phasors for short circuited line are the same as that for instantaneous values of current phasors for an open circuited line shown in Fig. 19.7.

19.5. Reflection in a Line Terminated in Impedance other than Z_0

Eqs. (19.10) and (19.11) give the voltage and current phasors along a transmission line in terms of voltage and current actually available for measured at the receiving end and in terms of Z_R and Z_0. The earlier two cases form the special cases or the extreme cases with $Z_R = \infty$, $Z_R = 0$. Now we take up the cases of a general value Z_R. It may be seen from Eqs. (19.10) and (19.11) that the amplitude and phase of the reflected component depend upon the values of Z_R and Z_0. If $Z_R = Z_0$, the reflected components becomes zero. If $Z_R \neq Z_0$, *i.e.* if the line is not properly terminated, reflection, in general, will occur at the receiving end.

Any discontinuity in the line parameters such as a junction of an open wire line with a cable of different Z_0, causes a redistribution of energy between the electric and magnetic fields and sets up a reflected wave. In an infinitely long line or in a line terminated in Z_0, the impedance of the line is Z_0 at all in points which then determine the distribution of energy in the fields. The ratio of voltage to current at all points along the line and at the load end is then the same and no interchange of energy between the electric and magnetic fields takes place. Hence there is no opportunity for reflection to occur.

Reflection, in general, is undesirable, primarily because it causes reduction in transmission efficiency. Further if the generator impedance at the sending end is not equal to Z_0, then the reflected wave received back at the sending end of the line is again reflected causing a new incident wave. The energy thus oscillates back and forth on the line until it gets dissipated in the line. This trouble becomes more pronounced in long lines having small attenuation. However, in long lines, amplifiers or repeaters are used to reduce the overall attenuation in both directions of transmission. Hence the reflected wave has an amplitude nearly equal to that of the incident wave.

If the overall attenuation of line is not large, the reflected wave received at the sending end appears as an echo of the transmitted signal. This type of distortion is very annoying to both the subscribers in telephone communication and should, therefore, be reduced to a low value by using impedance matching transformers or networks wherever necessary. However, in a practical system, it may not be possible to provide perfect termination at all frequencies of interest. Hence, in general, a certain amount of reflection will be present in a transmission line.

19.6. Reflection Coefficient

The ratio of amplitudes of reflected to incident voltage com-ponents at the receiving end of a line is called the *reflection coefficient* and is usually denoted by k.

From Eqs. (19.10),

$$E_R'' = \frac{E_R(Z_R - Z_0)}{2Z_R} \qquad \text{...(19.28)}$$

and

$$E_R' = \frac{E_R(Z_R + Z_0)}{2Z_R} \qquad \text{...(19.29)}$$

Hence reflection coefficient k

$$= \frac{\text{Reflected voltage at the load}}{\text{Incident voltage at the load}}$$

$$= \frac{E_R''}{E_R'}$$

$$= \frac{Z_R - Z_0}{Z_R + Z_0} \qquad \text{...(19.30)}$$

Thus reflection coefficient will be, in general, a complex quantity having a magnitude and a phase angle. The polarity of the reflected wave and hence the sign of k depends upon the magnitudes and angles of Z_R and Z_0. Smaller the magnitude of reflection coefficients k, better is the line. When $Z_R = Z_0$, $k = 0$. Eqs. (19.10) and (19.11) may now be rewritten using term k as below,

$$E_x = \frac{E_R(Z_R + Z_0)}{2Z_R}\,(\varepsilon^{\gamma y} - k\,\varepsilon^{-\gamma y}) \qquad \text{...(19.31)}$$

$$I_x = \frac{I_R(Z_R + Z_0)}{2Z_0} (\varepsilon^{\gamma y} - k\,\varepsilon^{-\gamma y}) \qquad ...(19.32)$$

The input impedance and the transfer impedance of a line can now be written in terms of reflection coefficient k as below :

$$Z_{in} = Z_0 \left[\frac{e^{\gamma l} + k\,\varepsilon^{-\gamma l}}{\varepsilon^{\gamma l} - k\,\varepsilon^{-\gamma l}}\right] \qquad ...(19.33)$$

and
$$Z_t = \frac{E_S}{I_R} = \frac{(Z_R + Z_0)}{2} (\varepsilon^{\gamma l} + k\,\varepsilon^{-\gamma l}) \qquad ...(19.34)$$

Example 19.1. *An underground cable has $Z_0 = 400 \angle -40°$, $\alpha = 0.079$ neper/km and $\beta = 0.084$ radian 1 km. If the receiving end current $I_R = 0.005 \angle -190°$ and the line is terminated by an impedance $Z_R = 600 \angle -20°$, calculate the reflection coefficient and voltage and current in the line at a distant of 10 km from the receiving end.*

Solution. Reflection coefficient is given by,

$$k = \frac{Z_R - Z_0}{Z_R + Z_0}$$

Now
$$Z_0 = 400 \angle -40° = 306.4 - j\,257.1$$
$$Z_R = 600 \angle -20° = 563.8 - j\,205.2$$

Hence
$$k = \frac{(563.8 - j\,205.2) - (306.4 - j\,257.1)}{(563.8 - j\,205.2) + (306.4 - j\,257.1)} = \frac{257.4 + j\,51.9}{870.2 - j\,462.0}$$

$$= \frac{262.6 \angle 11.4°}{986 \angle -28°} = 2.67 \angle 39.4°$$

$$\varepsilon^{\gamma y} = \varepsilon^{\alpha y}\,\varepsilon^{j\beta y} = \varepsilon^{-0.76} \angle \frac{0.84 \times 180}{\pi} = 2.2034 \angle -48.1°$$

$$\varepsilon^{-\gamma y} = \varepsilon^{-\alpha y}\,\varepsilon^{-j\beta y} = \varepsilon^{-0.79} \angle \frac{0.84 \times 180}{\pi} = 0.4538 \angle -48.1°$$

Hence
$$E_x = \frac{E_R(Z_R + Z_0)}{2Z_R} (\varepsilon^{\gamma y} + k\,\varepsilon^{-\gamma y}) = \frac{0.005 \angle 190° \times 985 \angle -28°}{2}$$

$$[2.2034 \angle 48.1° + 0.267 \angle 39.4° \times 0.4538 \angle -48.1°]$$

$$= 2.462 \angle -218° [1.47 + j1.64 + 0.1194 - j0.0183]$$

$$= 2.462 \angle -218° \times 2.27 \angle 45.6° = 5.6 \angle 172.4° \text{ volts}$$

$$I_x = \frac{IR\,(Z_R + Z_0)}{2Z_0} (\varepsilon^{\gamma y} + k.\varepsilon^{-\gamma y}) = \frac{0.005 \angle -190° \times 985 \angle -28°}{2 \times 400 \angle -40°}$$

$$[2.2034 \angle 48.1° - 2.67 \angle 39.4° \times 0.4538 \angle -48.1°]$$

$$= 0.00616 \angle -178° [1.3506 - j1.6583]$$

$$= 0.00616 \angle -178° \times 2.14 \angle 50.9° = 0.0132 \angle -127.1° \text{ Amp.}$$

19.7. Reflection Factor and Reflection Loss

We have seen that whenever reflection occurs due to improper termination at the receiving end, the incident energy is not completely absorbed by the load. This concept may be extended and applied to the junction of any two impedances. Thus in Fig. 19.8 a source of voltage E and impedance Z_1 is connected to a load of impedance Z_2. Since Z_2 differs from Z_1, reflection of energy takes place resulting in a change in the ratio of voltage to current and alteration in the distribution of energy between the electric and magnetic field. The energy transferred to Z_2 is less than that with impedance matching. A *reflection loss* is said to have occurred.

The magnitude of the reflection loss may be determined by the ratio of the current actually flowing through the load impedance to that under matched condition. Image matching between the impedances Z_1 and Z_2 with an ideal source of voltage E as shown in Fig. 19.8 can be obtained by use of an ideal transformer and a phase shifting network inserted between Z_1 and Z_2 The turns ratio of the transformer will then have to be such that,

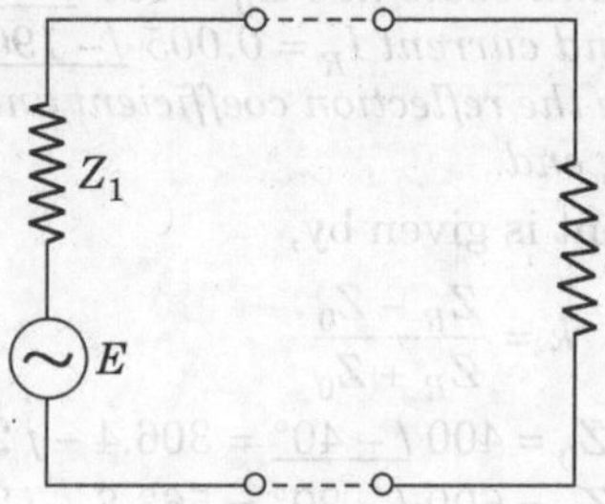

Fig. 19.8. Generator with impedances Z_1 and Z_2 to determine the reflection loss.

$$\frac{I_1}{I_2} = \sqrt{\frac{Z_2}{Z_1}} \qquad \text{...(19.35)}$$

where I_1 and I_2 are currents in the primary and the secondary sides of the transformer and Z_1 is the impedance offered by the primary winding when Z_2 is connected in the secondary. Thus Z_2 can be image matched to the source impedance Z_1 by selecting proper turn-ratio of the transformer while the phase angle can be adjusted by the phase-shifting network. Thus when Z_2 is image matched to the source impedance Z_1, the current flowing through the generator and through the primary of the transformer is given as,

$$I_1 = \frac{E}{2Z_1} \qquad \text{...(19.36)}$$

If the current in the secondary winding of the transformer and in the load impedance Z_2 under image matched condition is designated as I_2', then

$$I_2' = I_1\sqrt{\frac{Z_1}{Z_2}} = \frac{E}{2Z_1}\sqrt{\frac{Z_1}{Z_2}} = \frac{E}{\sqrt{Z_1 Z_2}} \qquad \text{...(19.37)}$$

On the other hand, the current in the load impedance Z_1 without image matching is given by,

$$I_2 = \frac{|E|}{|Z_1 + Z_2|} \qquad \text{...(19.38)}$$

Thus the ratio of current actually flowing through the load impedance to that which would flow under the image matched condition is given by the ratio of Eq. (19.38) to Eq. (19.37). Thus, we get

$$\frac{I_2}{I_2'} = \frac{\dfrac{|E|}{|Z_1 + Z_2|}}{\dfrac{E}{|2\sqrt{Z_1 Z_2}|}} = \frac{|2\sqrt{Z_1 Z_2}|}{|Z_1 + Z_2|} \qquad \text{...(19.39)}$$

The expression given by Eq. (19.39) indicates the change in current in the load due to reflection at the mismatched junction and is called *reflection factor* and is indicated by the symbol k. Thus,

$$k = \frac{|2\sqrt{Z_1 Z_2}|}{|Z_1 + Z_2|} \qquad ...(19.40)$$

where Z_1 and Z_2 are the impedances seen looking both ways at a junction. This treatment assumes that the junction between impedances Z_1 and Z_2 may be considered as junction of any two impedances in a transmission line system. The question of reflection comes up only when there is a wave propagation. In case of lumped networks, the terms *mismatch loss* and *mismatch* factor will be more appropriate.

The reflection loss or mismatch loss is defined as the number of nepers or decibels by which the current in the load under image matched condition would exceed the current actually flowing in the load. Hence Reflection loss in nepers $= \ln \left|\frac{I_2'}{I_2}\right| = \ln \left|\frac{1}{k}\right| = \ln \left|\frac{Z_1 + Z_2}{2\sqrt{Z_1 Z_2}}\right|$ ...(19.41)

$$\text{Reflection loss in dB} = 20 \log_{10} \left|\frac{Z_1 + Z_2}{2\sqrt{Z_1 Z_2}}\right| \qquad ...(19.42)$$

where the number of decibels refers only to current ratio and has nothing to do with voltage or power ratios.

In some cases, the quantity $\ln \left|\frac{1}{k}\right|$ may become negative which signifies *reflection gain* instead of reflection loss. From Eq. (19.41) or Eq. (19.42) we see that the reflection loss depends upon the angles of the impedances Z_1 and Z_2 since the magnitude of $(Z_1 + Z_2)$ depends upon their angles.

Eq. (19.41) may also be written as,

$$\text{Reflection loss in nepers} = \ln \left|\frac{1}{4}\sqrt{\frac{Z_1}{Z_2}} + \frac{1}{4}\sqrt{\frac{Z_2}{Z_1}}\right| \qquad ...(19.43)$$

Eq. (19.43) shows that the reflection loss is a function of magnitude as well as the angle of $\frac{Z_1}{Z_2}$ or $\frac{Z_2}{Z_1}$. If the angle of $\frac{Z_1}{Z_2}$ is zero then the reflection loss is positive for all values of $\frac{Z_1}{Z_2}$. As the angle becomes larger, the reflection loss becomes negative giving reflection gain for large range of values of $\frac{Z_1}{Z_2}$ on both sides of $\frac{Z_1}{Z_2} = 1$.

19.8. Insertion Loss in a Transmission Line

The insertion loss in a four terminal network has already been discussed earlier. When a line or a four-terminal network is inserted between a source and a load, it may either improve or deteriorate the impedance match between the source and the load. At the same time it may have resistive elements. Hence the overall effect of insertion may be to increase or decrease the power delivered to the load. This thus causes either *negative or positive insertion loss.*

The *insertion loss* caused by a line or a network is the number of nepers or decibels by which the current in the load is reduced by insertion. A negative insertion loss represents an insertion gain and may be caused by an impedance matching network.

It may be readily seen that the insertion loss is the resultant of several individual losses. Thus consider the network of Fig. 19.9 which

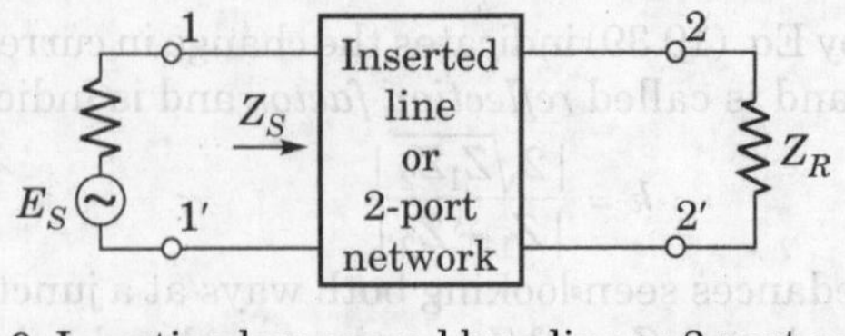

Fig. 19.9. Insertion loss caused by a line or 2-port network.

shows a line or a 2-port network inserted between a source and a load. Let Z_i be the input impedance of the inserted line or network. If Z_i is not equal to Z_s, then a reflection loss takes place at the junction 1-1′. The line or the 2-port network, so inserted, itself causes certain attenuation loss. Again if Z_R is not matched with the output impedance Z_0 of the inserted network, another reflection loss takes places at terminal pair 2-2′. The insertion loss caused by a line or a network may be calculated knowing (*i*) load caused I_R' with load connected directly to the source and (*ii*) load current I_R with line or network inserted.

The current I_R with line inserted may be obtained from the general expression for the current at the receiving end of the line by substituting $x = l$. Thus, we get

$$I_R = \frac{2Z_0E_S}{(Z_0+Z_S)(Z_0+Z_R)\,\varepsilon^{\gamma l}+(Z_0-Z_S)(Z_R-Z_0)\,\varepsilon^{-\gamma l}} \quad ...(19.44)$$

The current I_R' that flows in the load without the line or network inserted, is given by

$$I_R' = \frac{E_S}{Z_S+Z_R} \quad ...(19.45)$$

Hence

$$\frac{I_R'}{I_R} = \frac{(Z_0+Z_S)(Z_0+Z_R)\,\varepsilon^{\gamma l}+(Z_0-Z_S)(Z_R-Z_0)\,\varepsilon^{-\gamma l}}{2Z_0(Z_S+Z_R)} \quad ...(19.46)$$

An approximation can be made in Eq. (19.44) by considering a long line or a line whose α is large so that the second term in the numerator of Eq. (19.46) may be neglected in comparison with the first. Then Eq. (19.46) becomes,

$$\frac{I_R'}{I_R} = \frac{(Z_0+Z_S)(Z_0+Z_R)\,\varepsilon^{\alpha l}\,\varepsilon^{j\beta l}}{2Z_0(Z_S+Z_R)} \quad ...(19.47)$$

Multiplying both the numerator and the denominator by $2\sqrt{Z_SZ_R}$, Eq. (19.47) becomes,

$$\frac{I_R'}{I_R} = \frac{2\sqrt{Z_SZ_R}\,(Z_0+Z_S)(Z_0+Z_R)\,\varepsilon^{\alpha l}\,\varepsilon^{j\beta l}}{(Z_S+Z_R)\,2Z_0\times 2\sqrt{Z_SZ_R}} \quad ...(19.48)$$

In the calculation of the insertion loss, in nepers or decibels, only magnitudes of the quantities are of interest. Hence taking only the absolute values and rearranging the terms in Eq. (19.48), we get

$$\left|\frac{I_R'}{I_R}\right| = \left|\frac{Z_S+Z_0}{2\sqrt{Z_SZ_0}}\right|\left|\frac{Z_R+Z_0}{2\sqrt{Z_RZ_0}}\right|\left|\frac{2\sqrt{Z_SZ_R}}{Z_S+Z_R}\right|\varepsilon^{\alpha l} \quad ...(19.49)$$

Now the first term on the right hand side of Eq. (19.40) is nothing but $\dfrac{1}{k_S}$.

where k_S is the reflection factor at terminals 1-1′ caused by mismatch between the source impedance Z_S and the input impedance of the line. Since the line has been assumed to be very long, its impedance may be approximated to Z_0. Thus, we have

$$\left|\frac{Z_R + Z_S}{2\sqrt{Z_S Z_0}}\right| = \frac{1}{k_S} \qquad \text{...(19.50)}$$

Similarly, we get

$$\left|\frac{Z_R + Z_0}{2\sqrt{Z_S Z_0}}\right| = \frac{1}{k_R} \qquad \text{...(19.51)}$$

where k_R is the reflection factor at the terminals 2-2′ due to mismatch between the load impedance Z_R and the output impedance of the line which approximates Z_0.

Considering the third term, we get

$$\left|\frac{2\sqrt{Z_S Z_R}}{Z_S + Z_R}\right| = k_{SR} \qquad \text{...(19.52)}$$

where k_{SR} may be considered to be the reflection factor due to mismatch between the source impedance Z_S and the load impedance Z_R.

Finally the term $\varepsilon^{\alpha l}$ gives the attenuation loss in the line itself. Hence Eq. (19.47) may be written as,

$$\left|\frac{I_R'}{I_R}\right| = \frac{k_{SR}}{k_S\, k_R} \cdot e^{\alpha l} \qquad \text{...(19.53)}$$

The insertion loss in nepers

$$= \ln\left|\frac{1}{k_S}\right| + \ln\left|\frac{1}{k_R}\right| - \ln\left|\frac{1}{k_{SR}}\right| + e^{\alpha l} \qquad \text{...(19.54)}$$

Insertion loss in decibles

$$= 20\left[\log\frac{1}{k_S} + \log\frac{1}{k_R} - \log\frac{1}{k_{SR}} + 0.4343\alpha l\right] \qquad \text{...(19.55)}$$

In Eqs. (19.52) and (19.53), the logarithmic term in $1/k_{SR}$ or log $1/k_{SR}$ has a negative sign. This term equals the reflection loss with load directly connected. Hence this loss is subtracted from the rest of the expressions in order to give the expression for the insertion loss.

If the line is not long or if α is small, the approximation used in Eq. (19.47) does not apply and the insertion loss must be calculated from Eq. (19.46). Eqs. (19.54) and (19.55) may also be applied to any four terminal network by using $l = 1$ and taking α as the attenuation of the network.

Example 19.2. *An open-wire transmission lines having $Z_0 = 650 \underline{/-12°}$ omhs is terminated in Z_0 at the receiving end. If this line is supplied from a source of internal resistance 300 Ω, calculate line reflection factor and the reflection loss at the sending end terminal.*

Solution. Reflection factor : $\left|\frac{2\sqrt{Z_1 Z_2}}{Z_1 + Z_2}\right|$

$$Z_1 = 300\ \Omega \text{ and } Z_2 = Z_0 = 560 \underline{/-12°} = 636 - j135$$

Hence inflection factor, $\lambda = \frac{2\sqrt{300 \times 650}}{(300 + 636) - j135} = \frac{884}{936 - j145} = \frac{884}{946} = 0.935$

Reflection loss = $\ln\left|\frac{1}{k}\right|$ = ln 1.07 = 0.0677 neper

or reflection loss in decibels = $20 \log_{10}\frac{1}{k}$ = $20 \log_{10} 1.07$ = 0.588.

Example 19.3. *An open wire transmission line having $Z_0 = 750 \underline{/-13°}$, $\alpha = 0.007$ neper/kilometre and $\beta = 0.025$ radians/km is terminated in load resistance of 400 omhs. If the length of the* *line is 300 kilometres, and the line is supplied power from a source of internal impedance 200 $\underline{/0°}$, calculate the approximate value of insertion loss when this line is inserted between the generator and the load. Compare the result with the exact value of insertion loss.*

Solution. The approximate value of insertion loss is given by,

$$\text{Insertion loss is nepers} = \ln\left|\frac{1}{k_S}\right| + \ln\left|\frac{1}{k_R}\right| - \ln\left|\frac{1}{k_{SR}}\right| + \alpha l$$

$$k_S = \frac{2\sqrt{Z_S Z_0}}{|Z_S + Z_0|} = \frac{2\sqrt{200\times 750}}{|200 + 730 - j168.7|} = 0.82$$

$$k_R = \frac{2\sqrt{Z_R Z_0}}{|Z_R + Z_0|} = \frac{2\sqrt{400\times 750}}{|400 + 730 - j168.7|} = 0.958$$

$$k_{SR} = \frac{2\sqrt{Z_R Z_R}}{|Z_S + Z_R|} = \frac{2\sqrt{200\times 400}}{|200 + 400|} = 0.943$$

$$\text{Hence insertion loss} = \ln\frac{1}{0.82} + \ln\frac{1}{0.958} - \ln\frac{1}{0.943}$$

$$= 0.1989 + 0.0421 - 0.0583 + (0.007 \times 300)$$

$$= 2.2827 \text{ nepers} = 19.8 \text{ dB.}$$

This exact value of current ratio for calculatnig the insertion loss is given by,

$$\frac{I_R''}{I_R} = \frac{(Z_0 + Z_S)(Z_0 + Z_R)\,\varepsilon^{\gamma l} + (Z_0 - Z_S)(Z_R - Z_0)\,\varepsilon^{-\gamma l}}{2Z_0(Z_S + Z_R)}$$

$$\varepsilon^{\gamma l} = \varepsilon^{\alpha l}\,\varepsilon^{j\beta l} = \varepsilon^{2.1} \Big/ \frac{7.5\times 180}{\pi} = 8.1662\,\underline{/430°}$$

$$\varepsilon^{-\gamma l} = \varepsilon^{-\alpha l}\,\varepsilon^{-j\beta l} = \varepsilon^{-2.1}\,\underline{/-430°} = 0.1225\,\underline{/-430°}$$

$$\text{Hence } \frac{I_R'}{I_R} = -\frac{(930 - j168.7)(1130 - j2168.7)\,8.1162\,\underline{/430°} + (530 - j168.7)(-330 + j168.7)0.1225\,\underline{/-430°}}{2\times 750\,\underline{/-13°}\times 600}$$

$$= \frac{945\,\underline{/-10.3°}\times 1143\,\underline{/-8.1°}\times 8.1162\,\underline{/430°} + 556\,\underline{/-17.6°}\times 370\,\underline{/152.9°}\times 0.1225\,\underline{/-430°}}{9\times 10^4\,\underline{/-13°}}$$

$$\text{or} \quad \frac{I_R'}{I_R} = \frac{8.82\times 10^6\,\underline{/411.6°} + 2.52\times 10^4\,\underline{/-294.7°}}{9\times 10^5\,\underline{/-13°}}$$

$$= \frac{549 + j693.3}{90\,\underline{/-13°}} = 9.82\,\underline{/64.6°}$$

$$\text{Hence insertion loss} = \ln\left|\frac{I_R'}{I_R}\right| = \ln 9.82 = 2.2844 \text{ nepers} = 19.842 \text{ dB.}$$

This shows that the approximate value of insertion loss is only slightly less than the exact value.

19.9. Distance to a Line Fault

A transmission line may become faulty due to following reasons :

(*i*) *Open circuit*. In this case, one of the conductors gets broken.

(*ii*) *Short circuit*. In this case, the insulation between the conductors breaks down.

(*iii*) *Leakage*. A heavy leakage current may flow resulting in termination of the line in a certain value of resistance.

In all these cases, reflection of energy takes place from the point of fault. The input impedance of such a line is given by,

$$Z_i = Z_0 \frac{\varepsilon^{\gamma l} + k \cdot \varepsilon^{-\gamma l}}{\varepsilon^{\gamma l} - k \cdot \varepsilon^{-\gamma l}}$$

$$= Z_0 \frac{\varepsilon^{\alpha l}\, \varepsilon^{j\beta l} + k \cdot \varepsilon^{-\alpha l}\, \varepsilon^{-j\beta l}}{\varepsilon^{\alpha l}\, \varepsilon^{j\beta l} - k \cdot \varepsilon^{-\alpha l}\, \varepsilon^{-j\beta l}} \qquad ...(19.56)$$

Now $e^{j\beta l}$ and $e^{-j\beta l}$ may be written in terms of sine and cosine of angle βl. Thus, Eq. (19.36) becomes,

$$Z_{in} = Z_0 \left[\frac{\varepsilon^{\alpha l} (\cos \beta l + j \sin \beta l) + k\varepsilon^{-\alpha l} (\cos \beta l - j \sin \beta l)}{\varepsilon^{\alpha l} (\cos \beta l + j \sin \beta l) - k \cdot \varepsilon^{-\alpha l} (\cos \beta l - j \sin \beta l)} \right]$$

$$= Z_0 \left[\frac{(\varepsilon^{\alpha l} + k\varepsilon^{-\alpha l}) \cos \beta l + j(\varepsilon^{\alpha l} - k\varepsilon^{-\alpha l}) \sin \beta l}{(\varepsilon^{\alpha l}\ k\varepsilon^{-\alpha l}) \cos \beta l + j(\varepsilon^{\alpha l} + k\varepsilon^{-\alpha l}) \sin \beta l} \right]$$

$$= Z_0 \left[\frac{(\varepsilon^{\alpha l}\ k\varepsilon^{-\alpha l}) + j(\varepsilon^{\alpha l} - k\varepsilon^{-\alpha l}) \tan \beta l}{(\varepsilon^{\alpha l} - k\varepsilon^{-\alpha l}) + j(\varepsilon^{\beta l} + k\varepsilon^{-\alpha l}) \tan \beta l} \right] \qquad ...(19.57)$$

Eq. (19.57) shows that the input impedance is a function of the electrical angle βl which varies (*i*) with the length of the line and (*ii*) with the frequency of the input signal which varies the value of β. The magnitude of tangent of an angle varies between the limits zero and infinity according to the value of the angle. Hence the input impedance oscillates between the minimum and the maximum values as tan βl varies between zero and infinity. Thus Z_{in} is maximum for $\beta l = \frac{n\pi}{2}$, where n is an even integer and is minimum for $\beta l = \frac{m\pi}{2}$, where m is an odd integer. The magnitude of the input impedance thus varies with the length of line or with the frequency as shown in Fig. 19.10. The magnitude $|Z_{in}|$ is also affected by the value of α of line which depends upon the frequency and the reflected wave is affected by increasing the length of the line.

It may be seen that the difference between a maximum and a successive minimum impedance point represents a change in βl equal to $\pi/2$ radians or one-fourth of a wavelength. Thus the difference between two consecutive maximum impedance points such as *A* and *B*

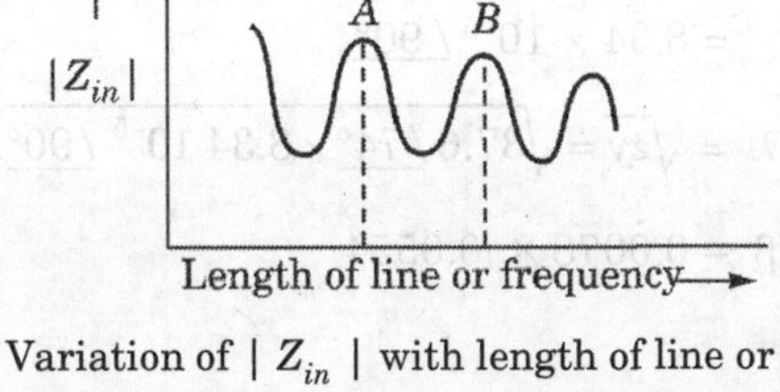

Fig. 19.10. Variation of $|Z_{in}|$ with length of line or frequencies.

shown in Fig. 19.10 will represents a change in electrical length of one-half wavelength. If the distance of reflection points is s, then it may be expressed in terms of wavelength λ, corresponding to frequency f_1 as below,

$$s = p\lambda_1 \qquad ...(19.58)$$

where p is the constant of proportionality.

At point B, the frequency may be considered to be f_2 and wavelength λ_2 but the point of reflections at the same distance. However, electrically the length of line is one-half wavelength longer, thus,

$$s = (p + \tfrac{1}{2})\lambda_2 \qquad ...(19.59)$$

Substituting the value of p from Eq. (19.58) into Eq. (19.59) and using the relation $v = f\lambda$, we get

$$s = \left(\frac{s}{\lambda_1} + \frac{1}{2}\right)\lambda_2$$

or

$$s = \frac{\lambda_1\lambda_2}{2(\lambda_1 - \lambda_2)} \qquad ...(19.60)$$

$$= \frac{v_1v_2}{2(v_1f_2 - v_2f_1)} \qquad ...(19.61)$$

The velocities v_1 and v_2 may be determined from the relation $v = \omega/\beta$, where ω_1 and ω_2 are known from the measurement and β_1 and β_2 can be determined from the line parameters. Then Eq. (19.61) may be used to give the distance to a line fault or the point of reflection by measurement carried out at one end of the line. However it is necessary to determine with accuracy frequencies f_1 and f_2 which make $| Z_{in} |$ maximum. This may be done by actually plotting the curve of Fig. 19.10 for the faulty line plotting $| Z_{in} |$ against frequency. Alternatively the maximum impedance points may be used in place of maximum impedance points.

In many cases, the phase velocity of propagation for the frequency range f_1 to f_2 may not change appreciable so that $v_1 = v_2 = v$. This approximation reduces Eq. (19.61) to the following,

$$s = \frac{v}{2(f_2 - f_1)} \qquad ...(19.62)$$

Example 19.4. *A transmission line has the following primary constants per loop kilometre : R = 10.4 Ω, L = 0.0036 henery, C = 0.0083 μF and G = 0. An open circuit fault has developed at an unknown distance from the sending end. The measurement of input impedance shows that the maximum values occur at frequencies of 1420 and 1860 Hz. Calculate the exact and approximate values of the distance to the fault.*

Solution. In the approximate calculation, the velocity may be calculated as the average of the two frequencies at which impedance maxima occur.

Thus selecting the average frequency at 1600 Hz, we get

$$z = R + j\omega L = 10.4 + j2\pi \times 1600 \times 0.0036 = 10.4 + j36.2 = 37.9 \underline{/74^\circ}$$

$$y = G + j\omega C = j2\pi \times 1600 \times 0.0083 \times 10^{-6} = j8.34 \times 10^{-5}$$

$$= 8.34 \times 10^{-5} \underline{/90^\circ}$$

Hence

$$\lambda = \sqrt{zy} = \sqrt{37.6 \underline{/74^\circ} \times 8.34\, 10^{-5} \underline{/90^\circ}} = 0.056 \underline{/82^\circ}$$

$$\alpha + j\beta = 0.0078 \times j0.0554$$

$$v = \frac{\omega}{\beta} = \frac{2\pi \times 1600}{0.0554} = 1.814 \times 10^5 \text{ km/sec.}$$

Hence the approximate distance to the fault is given as,

$$s = \frac{1.814 \times 10^5}{2(1860 - 1420)} = 206.1 \text{ km.}$$

Exact solution

At $\quad f_1 = 1420$ Hz,

$$z_1 = R_1 + j\omega 1L = 10.4 + j^2\pi \times 1420 \times 0.0036 = 10.4 + j32.1 = 33.73 \underline{/\ 72°}$$

$$y_1 = j\omega_1 C = j2\pi \times 1420 \times 0.0083 \times 10^{-6} = 7.5 \times 10^{-5} \underline{/\ 90°}$$

Hence $\quad \gamma = \sqrt{33.73\ \underline{/72°} \times 7.4 \times 10^5 \underline{/90°}} = 0.0499 \underline{/\ 81°} = 0.0078 + j0.0493$

$$v_1 = \frac{\omega_1}{\beta_1} = \frac{2\pi \times 1420}{0.0493} = 1.81 \times 10^5 \text{ km/sec.}$$

At $\quad f_2 = 1860$ Hz.

$$z_2 = R + j\omega^2 L = 10.4 + j^2\omega \times 1860 \times 0.0036 = 10.4 + j42.1 = 43.3 \ \underline{/\ 76.1°}$$

$$y_2 = j\omega_2 C = j2\pi \times 1860 \times 0.0083 \times 10^{-6} = 9.5 \times 10^{-5} \underline{/\ 90°}$$

Hence $\quad \gamma_2 = \sqrt{43.3\ \underline{/67.1°} \times 9.7 \times 10^5 \underline{/90°}} = 0.0648 \underline{/\ 82.05°} = 0.00784 + j0.0643$

$$v_2 = \frac{\omega_2}{\beta_2} = \frac{2\pi \times 1860}{0.0643} = 1.82 \times 10^5 \text{ km/sec.}$$

The exact distance to the fault is given by,

$$s = \frac{v_1 v_2}{2(v_1 f_2 - v_2 f_1)} = \frac{1.81 \times 10^6 \times 1.82 \times 10^5}{2(1.81 \times 1860 - 1.82 \times 142)\ 10^5}$$

$$= \mathbf{209.8 \text{ km.}}$$

20

Transmission Lines at Radio Frequencies

20.1. Introduction

A transmission line may be required to carry signals in VHF range such as in television or radar systems. Such a line has behaviour entirely different from that in the normal telephone communication. Conventional telephone cable has very high attenuation loss at high frequencies and are unsuitable for use at these high frequencies. Open-wire lines and coaxial cables, however, are popularly used. Open-wire line is extensively used as feeder for feeding the output power of a radio transmitter to the transmitting aerial. Coaxial cable, on the other hand, is popularly used as feeder in television systems.

A transmission line used at radio frequencies permits several simplifying approximations. Hence the performance of the line may be analysed in a simpler way. The following are the salient features of a radio frequency line :

(*i*) The line has considerable skin effect so that almost the entire current may be assumed to flow through the outer surface of the conductor. Thus the internal inductance of the wires may be considered to be zero.

(*ii*) At these high frequencies, reactance ωL is much larger than resistance R. This results because the a.c. resistance of the wires increases proportional to square root of frequency f because of the skin effect while the inductive reactance increases directly as the frequency f.

(*iii*) The lines are so well constructed that shunt conductance G may be considered to be zero at all frequencies.

The study of the transmission lines at radio frequencies may be made under the following two categories :

(*a*) *Low dissipation lines*—in which case R is small in comparison with ωL, and (*b*) *Zero dissipation lines or Lossless lines*—in which case R is negligible in comparison with ωL.

20.2 Parameter of Open-wire at Radio Frequencies

At high frequencies, the current can be assumed to be flowing through the surface of skin of the conductor. The *skin depth* is the depth upto which current flows. The skin effect reduces the effective cross-section area of the conductor through which the current flows. This increases the resistance. At the same time, the internal inductance gets reduced to zero almost since no current flows through the inner part of the conductor cross section. Accordingly Eq. (20.1) for parallel-wire line becomes,

$$L = 9.21 \times 10^{-7} \log_{10} \frac{d}{a} \text{ henry/loop metre} \qquad ...(20.1)$$

where d is the spacing between the conductors, and a is the radius of each conductor, both in metres.

The capacitance of open wire line is not effected by skin effect or the frequency of signal. Hence the expression for capacitance remains unaltered. Thus with air ($\varepsilon_r = 1$) as the dielectric, the capacitance of open wire line at high frequencies is given by the following expression :

$$C = \frac{12.07}{\log_{10} \frac{d}{a}} \text{ pF/metre} \qquad ...(20.2)$$

The a.c. resistance of a wire at high frequencies depends upon the thickness of the surface layer through which the current flows. This thickness, called the *equivalent depth of penetration,* may be found by use of electromagnetic field theory and is given by,

$$\delta = \sqrt{\frac{2}{\omega\mu\sigma}} \text{ metres} \qquad ...(20.3)$$

where δ is the depth of penetration along the radius of the conductor cross section,

μ is the permeability of the materials and

σ is the conductivity, all in M.K.S. units.

Copper, being a non-magnetic material, has permeability same as, that of space and equals $\mu = \mu_0 = 4\pi \times 10^{-7}$ M.K.S. units while the conductivity s of copper at 20°C is about 5.75×10^{-7} Seimen/metre. Substitution of these values of μ and σ in Eq. (20.3) yields the following expression for the depth of penetration in copper,

$$\delta = \frac{0.0664}{\sqrt{f}} \text{ metre} \qquad ...(20.4)$$

The d.c. resistance of round conductor of radius *a* metre is given by,

$$R_{dc} = \frac{1}{\pi a^2 \sigma} \text{ ohms/metre} \qquad ...(20.5)$$

If δ is small, the effective cross-sectional area of the conductor through which a.c. current flows becomes $2\pi a\delta$ approximately. Hence the a.c. resistance of the conductor is given by,

$$R_{ac} = \frac{1}{2\pi a\delta\sigma} \text{ ohms/metre} \qquad ...(20.6)$$

Substituting the value of δ from Eq. (20.3) into Eq. (20.6) and taking the ratio of a.c. resistance to the d.c. resistance, we get

$$\frac{R_{ac}}{R_{dc}} = \frac{a}{2\delta} = \frac{a}{2}\sqrt{\pi f \mu\sigma} \qquad ...(20.7)$$

On substituting the values of μ and σ for copper, we get

$$\left.\frac{R_{ac}}{R_{dc}}\right|_{copper} = 7.53a\sqrt{f} \qquad ...(20.8)$$

where *a* is in metres frequency *f* is in Hertz.

Eq. (20.8) shows that the ratio of a.c. resistance to d.c. resistance of a conductor increases directly with the radius and directly with the square root of frequency.

The a.c. resistance of an open wire line at any frequency *f* may be obtained by combining Eqs. (20.5) and (20.8). Thus for an open wire line with copper conductor, we have

$$R_{ac} = \frac{7.53 \times 2\sqrt{f}}{5.75 \times 10^{-7} \times \pi a}$$

$$= \frac{8.34 \times 10^{-8} \sqrt{f}}{a} \text{ ohms/loop metre} \quad ...(20.9)$$

This equation is true only when the separation between the wire is greater than 20 a, otherwise the proximity of the two conductors results in crowding of currents on the sides of the conductors. This further increases the resistance.

20.3. Parameters of Coaxial Lines at Radio Frequencies

At high frequencies, the flow of current is confined within the depth of penetration in both inner and outer conductors. Thus the outer conductor actually works as an electrostatic shield to external interferences. Hence coaxial line forms an excellent transmission line for high frequency signals. Neglecting the internal inductance, the inductance of a coaxial line at high frequencies is given by Eq. (17.5), where μ_r may be taken as unity for air as the dielectric. Thus, we get the following expression for the inductance of a coaxial line

$$L = 4.6 \times 10^{-7} \log_{10} \frac{b}{a} \text{ henrys/loop metre} \quad ...(20.10)$$

where b is the inner radius of the outer conductor and a is the outer radius of the inner conductor.

The capacitance does not change with frequency except for the dielectric constant of spacers used to maintain the position of the central conductor. Hence the capacitance of coaxial line at high frequencies is given by,

$$C = \frac{24.14\, \varepsilon_r}{\log_{10} \dfrac{b}{a}} \pi\text{F/metre} \quad ...(20.11)$$

The spacers are usually made of polyethylene or of polystyrene which have relative dielectric constant of 2.26 and 2.56 respectively. These spaces have the effect of increasing the average value of dielectric constant above that of space. The effective value of dielectric constant of the coaxial cable is then given by,

$$\varepsilon_r' = 1 + (\varepsilon_r - 1)\frac{t}{s} \quad ...(20.12)$$

where ε_r is the relative dielectric constant of the spacers,

t is the thickness of the spacers and

s is the centre-to centre distance between the spacers.

Eq. (20.12) is true only when s is small compared with the wavelength of signal being transmitted.

The d.c. resistance of a coaxial line is given by Eq. (20.12) from which, we get the following expression for the a.c. resistance of a coaxial line.

$$R_{ac} = \frac{1}{2\pi\delta a}\left(\frac{1}{a} + \frac{1}{b}\right) \text{ ohms/loop metre}$$

$$= \frac{\sqrt{\pi f \mu\sigma}}{2\mu\alpha}\left(\frac{1}{a} + \frac{1}{b}\right) \text{ ohms/loop metre}$$

or

$$R_{ac} = \sqrt{\frac{f\,\mu}{4\pi\alpha}}\left(\frac{1}{a} + \frac{1}{b}\right) \text{ ohms/loop metre} \quad ...(20.13)$$

This equation is the same as Eq. (20.13) assuming that the depth of penetration is very small as compared to radii of conductors. Substituting the values of μ and σ for copper, Eq. (20.13) becomes,

$$R_{ac} = 4.17 \times 10^{-8} \sqrt{f}\left(\frac{1}{a}+\frac{1}{b}\right) \text{ ohms/loop metre} \qquad ...(20.14)$$

Comparing this equation with Eq. (20.9), it may be seen that for the same value of a in both the cases, the a.c. resistance of a coaxial line is smaller than that of an open wire line because radius b exceeds radius a.

A coaxial line contains dielectric spacers at regular intervals along the length. Hence depending on the quality of the material, certain dielectric loss takes place. This loss can be considered as the shunt conductance loss in parallel with the shunt capacitance, specially at high frequencies. The quantity of the insulating material is usually expressed in terms of its power factors when the material is used as dielectric in a capacitor C. The shunt susceptance is given as,

$$y = G + j\omega C \qquad ...(20.15)$$

and the *power factor* is expressed as the *cosine* of the angle between the vector y and G as shown in Fig. 20.1. Thus the power factor of a dielectric material may be expressed as,

$$pf = \cos\theta = \frac{G}{\sqrt{G^2+\omega^2C^2}} \qquad ...(20.16)$$

Usually the conductance of a good dielectric material is small so that the denominator of Eq. (20.16) can be approximated by neglecting G^2 in comparison with ω^2C^2. This approximation is more valid at high frequencies and gives larger value of power factor. Hence it will give the worse condition of transmission for designing system. With this approximation.

$$pf = \frac{G}{\omega C}$$

or $$G = \omega C \times pf \qquad ...(20.17)$$

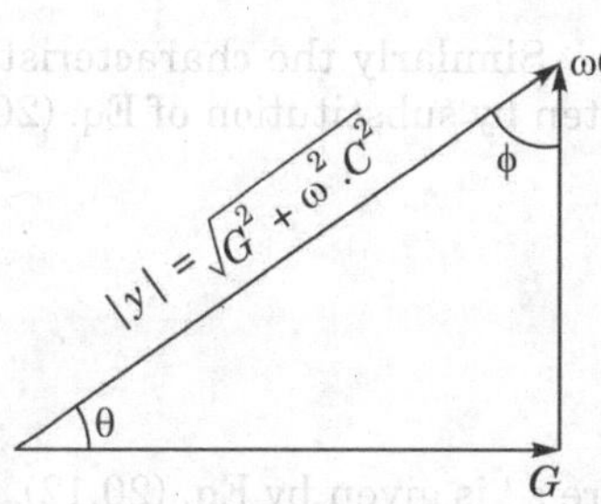

Fig. 20.1. Loss triangle or susceptance triangle for dielectrics.

Sometimes the quality of dielectric is expressed in terms of the *dissipation factor* which is defined as the ratio of energy dissipated to the energy stored in the dielectric per cycle and is proportional to the tangent of the angle ϕ as shown in Fig 20.1. Thus,

$$\tan\phi = \frac{G}{\omega C}$$

Under the assumption that $G << \omega C$, the power factor and the dissipation factor become equal. Polystyrene at 1 MHz has power factor of only 0.00007. Accordingly even at 6 MHz, the frequency upto which coaxial lines are used for transmission of signals, the conductance may be neglected. A well designed and maintained open-wire line does not have any conductance.

20.4. Secondary Constant of a Dissipationless Line

A line may be used for transmission of signals at very high frequencies in which case the physical length of the line may be quite small say a few centimetres but electrically the line may be several wavelengths long. In such case, the resistance of the line may be very small compared to its reactance. Hence such high frequency lines may be considered as lossless with $\alpha = 0$ and $G = 0$. Such an assumption simplifies the analysis and performance of the line. Actually such an ideal and perfect line may not be available physically at all. Also in certain cases, assumption of lossless line may lead to absurd results in which case R may have to be considered giving *lowloss lines* or *small dissipation* lines.

The secondary constants of a lossless line can be determined by considering that

$$z = j\omega L$$

and

$$y = j\omega C$$

so that the characteristic impedance Z_0 is given as,

$$Z_0 = \sqrt{\frac{z}{y}} = \sqrt{\frac{L}{C}} \text{ ohms} \quad ...(20.18)$$

Eq. (20.18) shows that the characteristic impedance of a dissipationless line is purely resistive and may called *characteristic resistance,* indicated by R_0. Substituting the values of L and C for an *open wire line* at high frequencies from Eq. (20.1) and (20.2) into Eq. (20.18), R_0 may be written in terms of the dimensions of the line. Thus for open wire line,

$$R_0 = \sqrt{\frac{9.2 \times 10^{-7}}{12.07 \times 10^{-12}}} \log_{10} \frac{d}{a} \text{ ohms.}$$

or

$$R_0 = 276 \log_{10} \frac{d}{a}$$

$$= 120 \ln \frac{d}{a} \text{ ohms} \quad ...(20.19)$$

Similarly the characteristic impedance of a coaxial line in terms of its dimensions can be written by substitution of Eq. (20.10) and (20.11) into Eq. (20.18) giving,

$$R_0 = \sqrt{\frac{4.6 \times 10^{-7}}{24.14 \times 10^{-12}\, \varepsilon_r'}} \log_{10} \frac{b}{a} \text{ ohms} = \frac{138}{\sqrt{\varepsilon_r'}} \log_{10} \frac{b}{a} \text{ ohms}$$

$$= \frac{60}{\sqrt{\varepsilon_r'}} \ln \frac{b}{a} \text{ ohms} \quad ...(20.20)$$

where ε_r' is given by Eq. (20.12).

Thus it is possible to design a transmission line to have any desired value of characteristic resistance by suitably changing the dimensions. However the design value of R_0 may not exactly be obtained in practice, due to some difficulties in erection or construction of a line. Hence certain tolerance should always be provided in obtaining more practical values of dimensions of a line. The practical values of R_0 within which an open wire line may be designed varies from about 280 to 800 ohms for d/a from 10 to about 800 whereas for a coaxial line, R_0 may vary from 40 to 100 ohms for b/a ratio from about 2 to 5.

The propagation constant is given by

$$\gamma = \sqrt{zy} = \alpha + j\beta = \sqrt{-\omega^2 LC} = j\omega\sqrt{LC} \quad ...(20.21)$$

Hence

$$\alpha = 0 \text{ and } \beta = \omega\sqrt{LC} \text{ radians/metre} \quad ...(20.22)$$

where the values of L and C are for one metre length of line.

Substituting the values of L and C for open wire line as well as for coaxial line, it is found that β is the same for both the lines and is directly proportional to frequency. The phase velocity of propagation is

$$v_p = \frac{\omega}{\beta} = \frac{1}{\sqrt{LC}} \text{ metres/second} \quad ...(20.23)$$

For open-wire line this becomes,

$$v_p = 3 \times 10^8 \text{ metres/second.}$$

Thus we see that the phase velocity of propagation in an air-spaced lossless open-wire line is equal to the velocity of light in free space.

For coaxial line, $v_p = \dfrac{3 \times 10^8}{\sqrt{\varepsilon_r'}}$ metres/second ...(20.24)

This equation shows that the effect of dielectric other than air, is to reduce the phase velocity of propagation in a dissipationless line.

20.5. Voltage and Currents in a Lossless Line

The voltage at any distance y from the receiving end of a line terminated in impedance Z_R, is given by,

$$\mathbf{E}_x = \frac{\mathbf{E}_R(\mathbf{Z}_R + \mathbf{Z}_0)}{2Z_R}(\varepsilon^{\gamma y} + K\,\varepsilon^{-\gamma y})$$

where E_R is the voltage at the receiving end and **K** is the reflection coefficient.

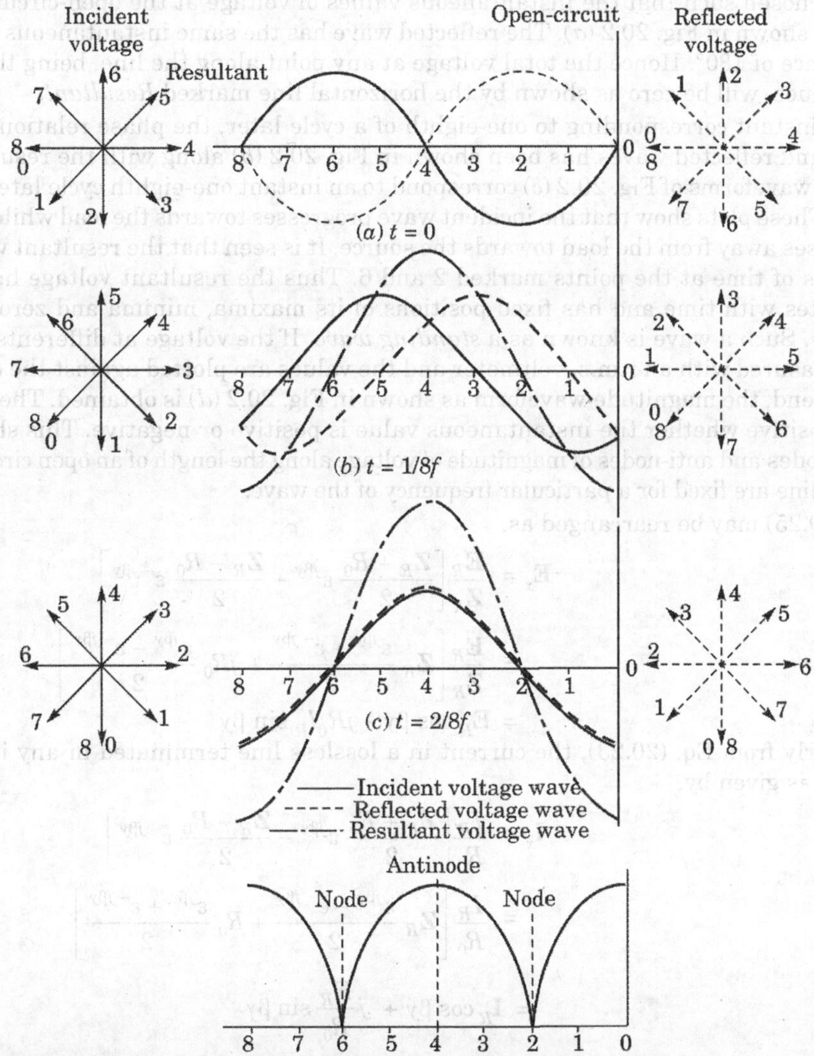

Fig. 20.2. Rotating phasors and their instantaneous values for open circuit load in a lossless line (*a*) at $t = 0$, (*b*) at $t = 1/8\,f$, (*c*) at $t = 2/8\,f$, (*d*) r.m.s. values of voltage along the line.

For lossless line α is zero and $\mathbf{Z}_0 = R_0$ so that

$$\mathbf{E}_x = \frac{\mathbf{E}_R(\mathbf{Z}_R + R_0)}{2\mathbf{Z}_R}(\varepsilon^{j\beta y} + K\,\varepsilon^{-j\beta y}) \qquad ...(20.25)$$

In Eq. (20.25), the term varying with $\varepsilon^{-\beta y}$ gives the incident wave while the term varying with $\varepsilon^{-\beta y}$ gives the reflected wave. The magnitude of the reflected wave moving back toward the source is dependent on the value of the reflection coefficient *K*. The magnitudes of rotating vectors corresponding to the sinusoidal signal input remain constant along the entire length of the line. Also the magnitude of
reflected wave remains constant at all the points along the line. For an open circuited line, the instantaneous values of phasors for different instants of time for one wavelength long line from the receiving end terminals are shown in Fig. 20.2.

For an open-circuit load, the reflection coefficient **K** is unity and hence the magnitude of the reflected wave is exactly the same as that of the incident wave at every point along the line. The time $t = 0$ is chosen such that the instantaneous values of voltage at the open-circuited receiving end is zero as shown in Fig. 20.2 (*a*). The reflected wave has the same instantaneous values with a phase difference of 180°. Hence the total voltage at any point along the line, being the vector sum of the two values, will be zero as shown by the horizontal line marked *Resultant*.

At an instant corresponding to one-eighth of a cycle later, the phase relationship between the incident and reflected waves has been shown in Fig. 20.2 (*b*) along with the resultant voltage. Similarly the waveforms of Fig. 20.2 (*c*) correspond to an instant one-eighth cycle later than that of Fig. 20.2 (*b*). These plots show that the incident wave progresses towards the load while the reflected wave progresses away from the load towards the source. It is seen that the resultant voltage is zero at all instants of time at the points marked 2 and 6. Thus the resultant voltage has magnitude which oscillates with time and has fixed positions of its maxima, minima and zero value points along the line. Such a wave is known as a *standing wave.* If the voltage at differents points along the line is measured with an r.m.s. voltmeter and the values are plotted against the distance from the receiving end, the magnitude waveform as shown in Fig. 20.2 (*d*) is obtained. The r.m.s. values are always positive whether the instantaneous value is positive or negative. This shows that the positions of nodes and anti-nodes of magnitude of voltage along the length of an open circuited lossless transmission line are fixed for a particular frequency of the wave.

Eq. (20.25) may be rearranged as,

$$\mathbf{E}_x = \frac{\mathbf{E}_R}{\mathbf{Z}_R}\left[\frac{\mathbf{Z}_R + R_0}{2}\,\varepsilon^{j\beta y} + \frac{\mathbf{Z}_R - R_0}{2}\,\varepsilon^{-j\beta y}\right]$$

$$= \frac{\mathbf{E}_R}{\mathbf{Z}_R}\left[\mathbf{Z}_R\,\frac{\varepsilon^{j\beta y} + \varepsilon^{-j\beta y}}{2} + jR_0\,\frac{\varepsilon^{j\beta y} - \varepsilon^{-j\beta y}}{2j}\right]$$

$$= \mathbf{E}_R \cos \beta y + jR_0 I_R \sin \beta y \qquad ...(20.26)$$

Similarly from Eq. (20.23), the current in a lossless line terminated in any impedance $\mathbf{Z}_R$ other than $\mathbf{Z}_0$ is given by,

$$\mathbf{I}_x = \frac{I_R}{R_0}\left[\frac{\mathbf{Z}_R + R_0}{2}\,\varepsilon^{j\beta y} - \frac{\mathbf{Z}_R - R_0}{2}\,\varepsilon^{-j\beta y}\right]$$

$$= \frac{I_R}{R_0}\left[\mathbf{Z}_R\,\frac{\varepsilon^{j\beta y} - e^{-j\beta y}}{2} + R_0\,\frac{\varepsilon^{j\beta \gamma} + \varepsilon^{-j\beta y}}{2}\right]$$

$$= \mathbf{I}_R \cos \beta y + j\frac{\mathbf{E}_R}{R_0}\sin \beta\gamma \qquad ...(20.27)$$

Since $$\beta = \frac{2\pi}{\lambda}$$

Eqs. (20.26) and (20.27) can be written as,

$$\mathbf{E}_x = \mathbf{E}_R \cos\left(\frac{2\pi}{\lambda}y\right) + j\mathbf{I}_R R_0 \sin\left(\frac{2\pi}{\lambda}y\right) \quad ...(20.28)$$

$$\mathbf{I}_x = \mathbf{I}_R \cos\left(\frac{2\pi}{\lambda}y\right) + j\frac{\mathbf{E}_R}{R_0} \sin\left(\frac{2\pi}{\lambda}y\right) \quad ...(20.29)$$

Now if the line is open circuited at the receiving end, $\mathbf{I}_R$ becomes zero giving,

$$\mathbf{E}_{oc} = \mathbf{E}_R \cos \frac{2\pi}{\lambda} y \quad ...(20.30)$$

$$\mathbf{I}_{oc} = j\frac{\mathbf{E}_R}{R_0} \sin \frac{2\pi}{\lambda} \lambda \quad ...(20.31)$$

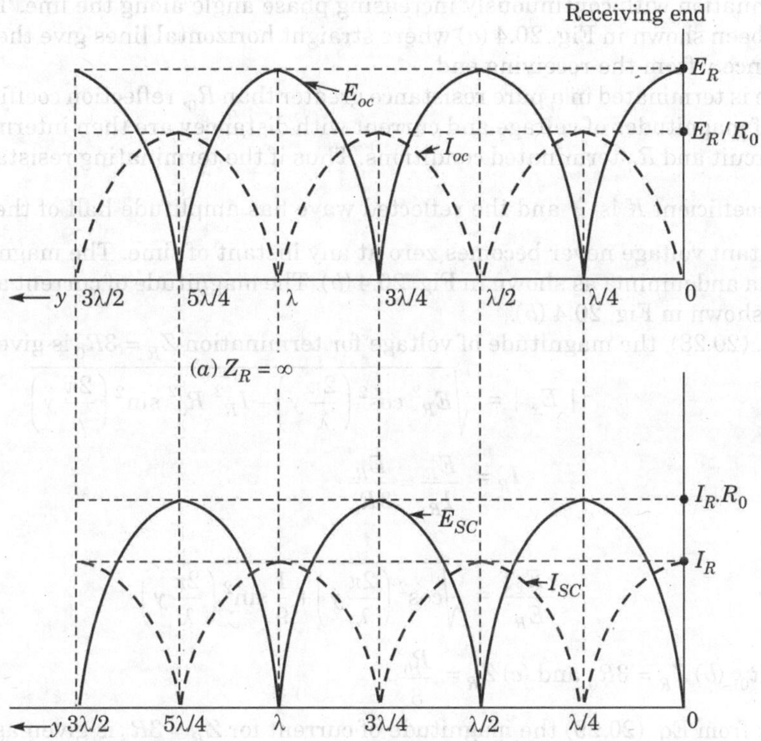

Fig. 20.3. Magnitude of voltage and current in a lossless line plotted against distance y from the receiving end under open circuit and short circuit conditions.

The magnitudes of voltage and current given by Eqs. (20.30) and (20.31) can be plotted for different values of y and have been shown in Fig. 20.3 (*a*), where the negative sign arising out of the cosine function has been neglected since the measuring instrument does not distinguish between positive and negative signs. Similarly with the receiving end short circuited, $\mathbf{E}_R$ becomes zero and Eqs. (20.28) and (20.29) can be written as,

$$\mathbf{E}_{sc} = jI_R \mathbf{R}_0 \sin \frac{2\pi}{\lambda} y \quad ...(20.32)$$

$$\mathbf{I}_{sc} = I_R \cos \frac{2\pi}{\lambda} y \qquad ...(20.33)$$

These magnitudes have been plotted against distance y in Fig. 20.3 (*b*). It may be seen that in both these cases, the voltage and current are always in phase quadrature along the entire length of the line. Hence no power gets transmitted by the line under the open circuit or the short condition at the receiving end.

In actual practice, even the best designed and constructed line will have certain losses. Hence the voltage and current nodal points along the entire length of line will not exhibit zero values but will have small minima.

If the line is terminated in R_0 so that $\mathbf{Z}_R = R_0$, the reflection coefficient K becomes zero and Eq. (20.25) becomes,

$$\mathbf{E}_x = \mathbf{E}_R\, \varepsilon^{j\beta y} \qquad ...(20.34)$$

Similarly

$$\mathbf{I}_x = \mathbf{I}_R\, \varepsilon^{j\beta y} \qquad ...(20.35)$$

Eqs. (20.34) and (20.35) show that the voltage and current magnitudes remain constant and there is no attenuation with continuously increasing phase angle along the line. This condition of magnitude has been shown in Fig. 20.4 (*a*) where straight horizontal lines give the plots of $\mathbf{E}_R$ and $\mathbf{I}_R$ against distance y from the receiving end.

If the line is terminated in a pure resistance greater than R_0, reflection coefficient $\mathbf{K}$ becomes positive. Plots of magnitudes of voltage and current with distancey are then intermediate between those of open circuit and R_0-terminated conditions. Thus if the terminating resistance equals $3R_0$, the reflections coefficient K is $\frac{1}{2}$ and the reflected wave has amplitude half of the incident wave. Hence the resultant voltage never becomes zero at any instant of time. The magnitude of voltage then has maxima and minima as shown in Fig. 20.4 (*b*). The magnitude of current also has maxima and minima as shown in Fig. 20.4 (*b*).

From Eq. (20.28), the magnitude of voltage for termination $Z_R = 3R_0$ is given by

$$| E_x | = \sqrt{E_R^{\,2} \cos^2\left(\frac{2\pi}{\lambda} y\right) + I_R^{\,2} R_0^{\,2} \sin^2\left(\frac{2\pi}{\lambda} y\right)}$$

But

$$I_R = \frac{E_R}{I_R} = \frac{E_R}{3R_0}$$

Hence

$$\frac{| E_x |}{E_R} = \sqrt{\cos^2\left(\frac{2\pi}{\lambda} y\right) + \frac{1}{9} \sin^2\left(\frac{2\pi}{\lambda} y\right)} \qquad ...(20.36)$$

(*a*) $Z_R = R_0$, (*b*) $Z_R = 3R_0$ and (*c*) $Z_R = \dfrac{R_0}{3}$.

Similarly from Eq. (20.29) the magnitude of current for $Z_R = 3R_6$ is given as,

$$\frac{| I_x |}{I_R} = \sqrt{\cos^2\left(\frac{2\pi}{\lambda} y\right) + 9 \sin^2\left(\frac{2\pi}{\lambda} y\right)} \qquad ...(20.37)$$

The voltage maxima occur at integral multiples of $\frac{\lambda}{2}$ or at every $\frac{n\lambda}{2}$ from the receiving end and the first voltage maximum occurs at the receiving end, where $n = 0$. This is true since termination by a resistance much greater than R_0 tends to the condition of $Z_R \to \infty$ or towards the open circuit condition. Similarly the current minimum occurs at receiving end and successive minima occur at every $\frac{n\lambda}{2}$ point for the receiving end.

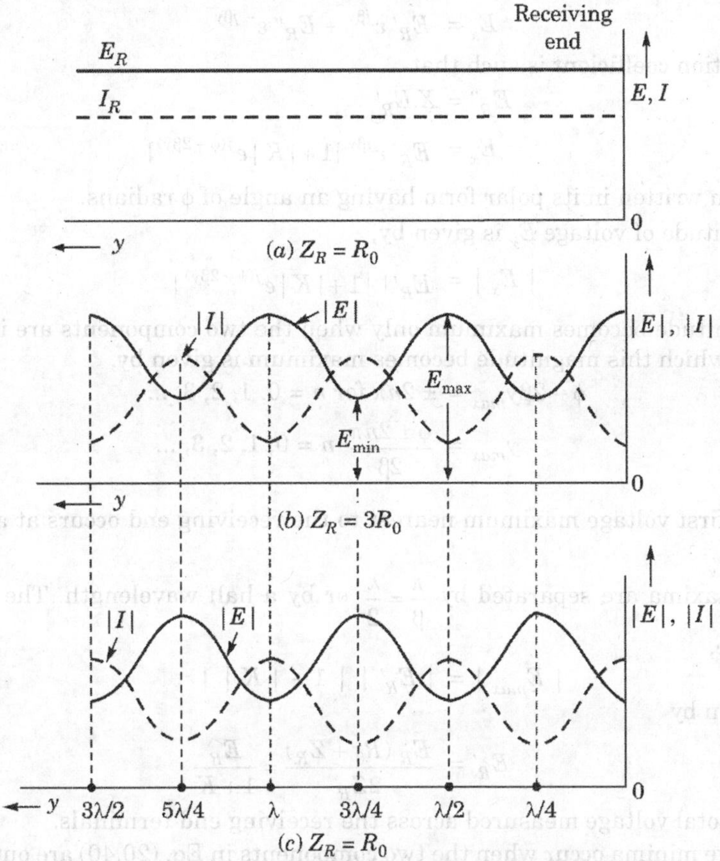

Fig. 20.4. Magnitude of voltage and current in a lossless line plotted against distace y from the receiving end.

For $Z_R = \frac{R_0}{3}$ the value of reflection coefficient if is $-\frac{1}{2}$. Hence the phase of the reflected wave is reversed in relation to that for $Z_R = 3R_0$. The variation of magnitude of voltage is now given by Eq. (20.37) while the variation of magnitude of current is given by Eq. (20.36). Thus the maxima and minima points get interchanged between voltage and current as compared to the case of $Z_R = 3R_0$. Fig. 20.4 (c) shows the variation of magnitude of voltage and current in this case. As the terminating resistance is reduced, the condition approaches the short circuit condition and the magnitude of current increases while that of voltage decreases.

In both the cases with finite terminating resistance, voltage and current at the receiving terminals are finite. Hence certain amount of power is transmitted by the line and transferred to the load resistance.

The above considerations show that standing wave will always be present as long as $Z_R \neq R_0$. However, the amplitude of the standing wave depends upon the mismatch at the load ; larger the mismatch larger is the amplitude of the standing wave.

If a lossless line is terminated in a complex impedance Z_R, reflection coefficient **K** is also complex and the reflected wave is neither in phase nor out of phase with the incident wave. Hence the points of maximum or minimum voltage will not fall at the receiving end but get shifted. This shift can be calculated by considering Eq. (20.10) for a dissipationless line reproduced below,

$$E_x = E_R' \varepsilon^{j\beta y} + E_R'' \varepsilon^{-j\beta y}$$

The reflection coefficient is such that

$$E_R'' = X.E_R' \quad \text{...(20.38)}$$

Hence
$$E_x = E_R' \varepsilon^{j\beta y} [1 + |K| e^{j(\phi - 2\beta y)}] \quad \text{...(20.39)}$$

where K has been written in its polar form having an angle of ϕ radians.

The magnitude of voltage E_x is given by,

$$|E_x| = E_R'|\,|1 + |K| e^{j(\phi - 2\beta y)}| \quad \text{...(20.40)}$$

This magnitude becomes maximum only when the two components are in phase. Thus the distance y_{max} at which this magnitude becomes maximum is given by,

$$\phi - 2\beta y_{max} = \pm 2n\pi \text{ for } n = 0, 1, 2, 3, \ldots$$

or
$$y_{max} = \frac{\phi \pm 2n\pi}{2\beta} \quad n = 0, 1, 2, 3, \ldots \quad \text{...(20.41)}$$

Thus the first voltage maximum nearest to the receiving end occurs at a distance $\frac{\phi}{2\beta}$ and the successive maxima are separated by $\frac{\pi}{\beta} = \frac{\lambda}{2}$ or by a half wavelength. The magnitude of the maximum will be,

$$|E_{max}| = |E_R'|\,|1 + |K|\,| \quad \text{...(20.42)}$$

where E_R' is given by

$$E_R' = \frac{E_R (R_0 + Z_R)}{2Z_R} = \frac{E_R}{1 + K} \quad \text{...(20.43)}$$

where E_R is the total voltage measured across the receiving end terminals.

The voltage minima occur when the two components in Eq. (20.40) are out of phase by 180°. The distance y_{min} at which a minimum occurs, is then given by,

$$\phi - 2\beta y_{min} = \pm (2n + 1)\pi, \quad n = 0, 1, 2, \ldots$$

Hence
$$y_{min} = \frac{\phi \pm (2n + 1)\pi}{2\beta}, \quad n = 0, 1, 2, 3, \ldots \quad \text{...(20.44)}$$

The magnitude of voltage minima is given by,

$$|E_{min}| = |E_R'|\,(1 - |K|) \quad \text{...(20.45)}$$

The voltage minimum points are separated from voltage maximum points by a distance of $\frac{\pi}{2\beta}$ or $\frac{\lambda}{4}$.

The current maxima and minimum can be determined by use of Eq. (19.23) which may be written as,

$$I_x = I_R' (\varepsilon^{j\beta y} - K \varepsilon^{-j\beta y}) \quad \text{...(20.46)}$$

where
$$I_{R'} = \frac{I_R (Z_R + R_0)}{2R_0} = \frac{E_R'}{R_0} \quad \text{...(20.47)}$$

Eq. (20.46) shows that current maxima occur at points where voltage minima occur as given by Eq. (20.44). Similarly current minima occur at location of voltage maxima. The magnitudes of current maxima and minima may similarly be determined. Thus,

$$|I_{max}| = |I_R'|\,(1 + |K|) \quad \text{...(20.48)}$$

$$|I_{min}| = |I_R'|\,(1 - |K|) \quad \text{...(20.49)}$$

The expressions are general and can be used for any type of terminations starting from open circuit to short circuit conditions.

20.6. Standing Wave Ratio

An important quantity in the study of lossless lines is the *standing wave ratio.* Figs. 20.3 and 20.4 show the variation of magnitude of voltage and current along the length of a lossless transmission line under various conditions of terminating impedance. These magnitude plots do not change with time and are known *as standing waves.* A lossless line when not properly terminated in its characteristic impedance or resistance is said to possess standing waves. The points of minimum voltage are called voltage *antinodes* while points of maximum voltage are called voltage *nodes.* Similarly *current antinodes* and *current nodes* are the points of current maximum and current minimum respectively. Obviously then voltage nodes coincide with current antinodes and voltage antinodes coincide with current nodes.

The standing wave ratio is defined as the ratio of the magnitude of a standing wave at an antinode to the magnitude at a node. It is represented by the symbol S. Thus,

Standing Wave Ratio,

$$S = \frac{|E_{max}|}{|E_{min}|} \qquad ...(20.50)$$

Since the standing wave is present only when there is reflection, it can be expected that the standing wave ratio is related in some manner with the reflection coefficient. This relation is easily obtained by substituting the values of $|E_{max}|$ and $|E_{min}|$ from Eqs. (20.42) and (20.45) into Eq. (20.50). Thus, we get

$$S = \frac{1+|K|}{1-|K|} \qquad ...(20.51)$$

The magnitude of reflection coefficient can be determined in terms of standing wave ratio from Eq. (20.51) giving,

$$|K| = \frac{S-1}{S+1} = \frac{|E_{max}|-|E_{min}|}{|E_{max}|+|E_{min}|} \qquad ...(20.52)$$

It may be seen that the standing wave ratio is always real having a *minimum* value of unity.

Standing wave ratio can be easily determined by measurement on actual line. A voltmeter moved along the length of the line measures the maximum and the minimum values of voltage. The distance between two consecutive maxima or two consecutive minima corresponds to one half wavelength. Thus the wavelength may be determined.

If the lossless line is terminated by a pure resistance R_r, the reflection coefficient is given by,

$$K = \frac{R_r - R_0}{R_r + R_0} = \frac{\frac{R_r}{R_0} - 1}{\frac{R_r}{R_0} + 1} \angle 0° \quad \text{if} \quad R_r > R_0$$

$$= \frac{1 - \frac{R_r}{R_0}}{1 + \frac{R_r}{R_0}} \angle 180° \quad \text{if} \quad R_r < R_0$$

Substituting these values of K in Eq. (20.51) gives us,

$$S = \frac{1 + \dfrac{\dfrac{R_r}{R_0} - 1}{\dfrac{R_r}{R_0} + 1}}{1 - \dfrac{\dfrac{R_r}{R_0} - 1}{\dfrac{R_r}{R_0} + 1}} = \frac{R_r}{R_0} \text{ when } R_r > R_0 \qquad \text{...(20.53)}$$

and

$$S = \frac{1 + \dfrac{1 - \dfrac{R_r}{R_0}}{1 + \dfrac{R_r}{R_0}}}{1 - \dfrac{1 - \dfrac{R_r}{R_0}}{1 + \dfrac{R_r}{R_0}}} = \frac{R_0}{R_r} \text{ when } R_r < R_0 \qquad \text{...(20.54)}$$

If the value of R_0 of the line is known, the terminating resistance value R_r can be calculated by measurement of standing wave ratio on the line.

Example 20.1. *An open wire line is made of copper conductors of cross-sectional radius 1.0 mm, separated 30.5 cm apart. If conductivity of copper is 5.75 × 10⁷ mho/metre and the signal frequency is 1 MHz, calculate the depth of penetration δ, a.c. resistance of the line per loop kilometre and the primary constants L and C. Assume G = 0. Hence calculate R_0, β, λ_p and v_p.*

Solution. Depth of penetration δ is,

$$\delta = \frac{0.0664}{\sqrt{f}} = \frac{0.0664}{\sqrt{10^6}} = 0.0664 \times 10^{-3} \text{ metre}$$

A.C. resistance is,
$$R_{ac} = \frac{1}{2\pi a\delta\sigma} \text{ ohms/metre}$$

$$= \frac{1}{2\pi \times 10^{-3} \times 0.0664 \times 10^{-3} \times 5.75 \times 10^{7}} \text{ ohms/metre}$$

$$= \frac{2000}{23.97} \text{ ohms/loop kilometre}$$

$$= 83.4 \text{ ohms/loop kilometre.}$$

Inductance L is given by,

$$L = 9.21 \times 10^{-7} \log_{10} \frac{d}{a} \text{ henry/loop metre}$$

$$= 9.21 \times 10^{-7} \log_{10} \frac{30.5}{0.1} \text{ H/l.m.} = 2.29 \times 10^{-3} \text{ H/l. km.}$$

Capacitance C is given by,
$$C = \frac{12.07}{\log_{10} \dfrac{d}{a}} 10^{-12} \text{ F/m}$$

$$= \frac{12.07 \times 10^{-12}}{\log_{10} \dfrac{30.5}{0.1}} \text{ F/m} = 4.85 \times 10^{-2} \text{ μF/l. km.}$$

$$Z = R = j\omega L = 83.4 + j2\pi \times 10^6 \times 2.29 \times 10^{-3}$$
$$= 83.4 + j14.4 \times 10^3$$

Thus R is negligible as compared to ωL.

Hence
$$R_0 = \sqrt{\frac{L}{C}} = \sqrt{\frac{4.29 \times 10^{-3}}{4.85 \times 10^{-9}}} = 686 \text{ ohms}$$

$$\beta = \omega\sqrt{LC} = 2\pi \times 10^6 \sqrt{2.29 \times 10^{-3} \times 4.85 \times 10^{-9}}$$
$$= 20.93 \text{ radians/km.}$$

$$\lambda_p = \frac{2\pi}{\beta} = \frac{2\pi \times 1000}{20.93} = 300 \text{ metre}$$

$$v_p = \frac{\omega}{\beta} = \frac{1}{\sqrt{LC}} = \frac{1}{\sqrt{2.29 \times 10^{-6} \times 4.85 \times 10^{-12}}}$$
$$= 3 \times 10^8 \text{ metres/sec.}$$

Example 20.2. *A coaxial line is formed of an inner copper conductor of diameter 2 mm and the outer conductor of inner diameter 10 mm. Spacers of thickness 4 mm are placed 1 metre apart along the length. The relative dielectric constant of the spacer material is 2.5 with power factor of 0.00007. The signal frequency is 2 MHz. Calculate the primary constants per kilometre.*

Solution. The inductance of the coaxial line is

$$L = 4.6 \times 10^{-7} \log_{10} \frac{b}{a} = 4.6 \times 10^{-7} \log_{10} \frac{10}{2} \text{ H/metre}$$
$$= 3.22 \times 10^{-7} \text{ H/metre} = 0.322 \times 10^{-3} \text{ H/metre.}$$

The effective value of dielectric constant as modified by the spacers is,

$$\varepsilon_r' = 1 + (\varepsilon_r - 1)\frac{t}{s} = 1 + (2.5 - 1)\frac{0.4}{100} = 1.006$$

Hence the capacitance parameter is,

$$C = \frac{24.14\,\varepsilon_r'}{\log_{10}\frac{b}{a}} \text{ pF/metre} = \frac{24.14 \times 1.006}{\log_{10}\frac{10}{2}} \text{ pF/metre}$$

$$= \frac{24.14 \times 1.006 \times 10^{-3} \times 10^6}{\log_{10} 5} \text{ pF/km} = 0.03475 \text{ mF/km.}$$

The a.c. resistance is given by,

$$R_{ac} = \sqrt{\frac{f\mu}{4\pi\sigma}}\left(\frac{1}{a} + \frac{1}{b}\right) \text{ ohms/metre}$$

$$= 4.17 \times 10^{-8}\sqrt{2 \times 10^6}\left(\frac{1}{10^{-3}} + \frac{1}{5 \times 10^{-3}}\right) \times 10^3 \text{ ohms/km}$$

$$= 70.8 \text{ ohms/kilometre.}$$

The conductance parameter is,

$$G = \omega C \times \text{Power factor}$$
$$= 2\pi \times 2 \times 10^6 \times 0.03475 \times 10^{-6} \times 7 \times 10^{-5}$$
$$= 2.967 \times 10^{-5} \text{ mho/km}$$

Example 20.3. *A lossless transmission line operated at frequency of 1 MHz has $R_0 = 686$ and $\beta = 20.92$ radians per kilometre. The line is terminated in a pure resistance of 364 ohms and the voltage across the load is 2 volts. Calculate the magnitude and phase of voltage and current at a distance of a 500 metres from the load. Also determine the values of $|E_{max}|$, $|E_{min}|$, $|I_{max}|$, $|I_{min}|$ and the standing wave ratio.*

Solution. $E_x = E_R \cos \beta y + jR_0 I_R \sin by$

Since β is given in radians/kilometre y is also required to be expressed in kilometres. Substituting the values,

$$E_x = 2\cos\left(\frac{20.92 \times \frac{1}{2} \times 180}{\pi}\right) + j\frac{686 \times 6}{364}\sin\left(\frac{20.92 \times \frac{1}{4} \times 180}{\pi}\right)$$

$$= -2\cos 59° - j3.773 \sin 59° = -1.03 - j3.235$$

$$= 3.39 \underline{/252.33°} \text{ volts}$$

$$I_x = I_R \cos \beta y + j\frac{E_R}{R_0}\sin \beta y = -5.5 \times 10^{-3}\cos 59° - j\frac{2}{686}\sin 59°$$

$$= -2.833 \times 10^{-3} - j2.5 \times 10^{-3} = 3.78 \times 10^{-3} \underline{/221.5°} \text{ Amp.}$$

Determination of maximum and minimum values the value of reflection coefficient **K** and the values of $\mathbf{E}_R'$ and $\mathbf{I}_R'$..

Hence
$$K = \frac{P_R - R_0}{R_R + R_0} = \frac{364 - 686}{364 + 686} = 0.3067 \underline{/108°}$$

From Eqs. (20.43) and (20.47),

$$E_R' = \frac{E_R(R_0 + R_R)}{2R_R} = \frac{2(686 + 364)}{2 \times 364} = 2.883 \text{ volts}$$

$$I_R' = \frac{I_R(R_R + R_0)}{2R_0} = \frac{2 \times 1050}{364 \times 2 \times 686} = 4.21 \times 10^{-3} \text{ Amp.}$$

Using Eqs. (20.42), (20.45), (20.48) and (20.49), we get

$$|E_{max}| = |I_R'|(1 + |K|) = 2.883 \times 1.3067 = 3.765 \text{ V}$$

$$|E_{min}| = |E_R'|(1 - |K|) = 2.883 \times 0.6933 = 1.997 \text{ V}$$

$$|I_{max}| = |I_R'|(1 + |K|) = 4.21 \times 10^{-8} \times 1.3067 = 5.5 \times 10^{-3} \text{ Amp.}$$

$$|I_{min}| = 4.21 \times 10^{-3} \times 0.6933 = 2.918 \times 10^{-3} \text{ Amp.}$$

$$S = \frac{|E_{max}|}{|E_{min}|} = \frac{3.765}{1.997} = 1.887 = \frac{R_0}{R_r} \; (R_r < R_0)$$

It will be observed from Eq. (20.41) that the first voltage maximum corresponding to $n = 0$ occurs at a distance of $\lambda/4$ from the load since the angle ϕ of K is 180° or π radians whereas the first voltage minimum and the first current maximum given by Eq. (20.44) occur at $y_{min} = 0$ or at the load by taking $n = 0$ with negative sign.

Example 20.4. *A lossless line carrrying a signal of wavelength 10 metres has $R_0 = 300 \angle 0°$ ohms. Load impedance is $Z_R = 100 - j60$ and the voltage measured across the load impedance is $E_R = 10 \angle 0°$ volts. Calculate maximum and minimum values of voltage and current and also the distances of first maximum and first minimum from the load end terminals. Also determine the value of standing wave ratio.*

Solution. Reflection coefficient

$$K = \frac{Z_R - R_0}{R_R + R_0} = \frac{100 - j60 - 300}{100 - j60 + 300} = 0.516 \angle 205.2°$$

$$= -0.467 - j0.22$$

$$\mathbf{E}_R' = \frac{\mathbf{E}_R}{1 + K} = \frac{10\angle 0°}{1 - 0.467 - j0.22} = 17.37 \angle 22.5° \text{ volts.}$$

$$\mathbf{I}_R' = \frac{\mathbf{E}_R'}{R_0} = \frac{17.37 \angle 22.5°}{300 \angle 0°} = 0.0579° \angle 22.5° \text{ amp.}$$

The first voltage maximum occurs at,

$$y_{max} = \frac{\phi}{2\beta} = \frac{\phi \times \lambda}{2 \times 2\pi} = \frac{205.2° \times 10}{2 \times 360°} = 2.85 \text{ metres.}$$

Successive voltage maxima occur at intervals of a half wavelength from y_{max} point. These voltage maximum points also correspond to current minimum points.

The first voltage minimum is spaced $\lambda/4$ from the first voltage maximum point. Hence its distance from the receiving end is given by,

$$y_{min} = y_{max} + \frac{\lambda}{4} = 2.85 - 2.5 = 0.35 \text{ metre}$$

$$| E_{max} | = | E_R' | (1 + | K |) = 17.37 \times 1.516 = 26.3 \text{ volts.}$$

$$| E_{min} | = | E_R' | (1 - | K |) = 17.37 \times 0.484 = 8.4 \text{ volts.}$$

$$| I_{max} | = | I_R' | (1 + | K |) = 0.0579 \times 1.516 = 0.0877 \text{ Amp.}$$

$$| I_{min} | = | I_R' | (1 - | K |) = 0.0579 \times 0.484 = 0.028 \text{ Amp.}$$

$$S = \frac{|E_{max}|}{|E_{min}|} = \frac{26.3}{8.4} = 3.13.$$

Example 20.5. *A 40 MHz open wire line is required to be constructed of copper conductor of diameter 3.264 mm. Characteristic impedance is required to be 400 ohms. Calculate (i) the spacing d between wires and (ii) the total value of L and C for 5 metres of the lines.*

Solution. $Z_0 = 276 \log_{10} \dfrac{d}{a}$

Hence $400 = 276 \log_{10} \dfrac{2d}{0.3264}$

where d is in cm.

Then $\log_{10} \left(\dfrac{2d}{0.3264}\right) = \dfrac{400}{276} = 1.45$

Hence $d = 4.6$ cm.

For lossless radio frequency line, inductance parameter is given by,

$$L = 9.21 \times 10^{-7} \log_{10} \frac{d}{a} \text{ H/l.m.}$$

Substituting the values, $L = 9.21 \times 10^{-7} \times 1.45 = 1.335 \times 10^{-7}$ H/loop metre.

Hence for 5 metre length inductance = 5 × 1.335 = 6.675 μH.

Capacitance parameter for the lossless radio frequency line is given by,

$$C = \frac{12.07}{\log_{10} \dfrac{d}{a}} \text{ pF/metre}$$

Substituting the values, $C = \dfrac{12.07}{1.45} = 8.32$ pF/metre

Hence for 5 metre length, capacitance is 8.22 × 5 = 4.16 pF.

Example 20.6. *An airfilled coaxial line has C equal to 20 pF / metre and the inner conductor has diameter of 1 mm. Calculate (i) the inductance of the line per metre (ii) the inner radius of the outer conductor (iii) Ro (iv) β and λ at a frequency of 25 MHz. Neglect losses.*

Solution. Capacitance parameter of coaxial line is given by

$$C = \frac{24.14}{\log_{10} \dfrac{b}{a}} \text{ pF/metre}$$

Hence $20 = \dfrac{24.14}{\log_{10} \dfrac{b}{a}}$

Hence $\log_{10} \dfrac{b}{a} = \dfrac{24.14}{20} = 1.207$

But $L = 4.6 \times 10^{-7} \log_{10} \dfrac{b}{a}$ H/metre

Substituting the value of $\log_{10} \dfrac{b}{a}$, we get

$$L = 4.6 \times 10^{-7} \times 1.207 = 5.55 \times 10^{-7} \text{ H/metre}$$

Now $\dfrac{b}{a} = \text{antilog } 1.207 = 16.11$

Hence the radius of outer conductor is

$$b = 16.11 \times a = \frac{16.11 \times 0.1}{2} = 0.805 \text{ cm}$$

$$R_0 = 138 \log_{10} \frac{b}{a} = 138 \times 1.207 = 166.5 \text{ ohms.}$$

$$\beta = \omega\sqrt{LC} = 2\pi \times 25 \times 10^6 \sqrt{20 \times 10^{-12} \times 5.55 \times 10^{-7}}$$

$$= 0.524 \text{ radians/metres.}$$

$$\lambda = \frac{2\pi}{\beta} = \frac{2\pi}{0.524} = 12 \text{ metre.}$$

Example 20.7. *A transmission line is terminated by an impedance Z_R. Measurements taken on the line show that the standing wave minima are 105 cm apart and the first minimum is 30 cm from the load end of the line. The standing wave ratio S is 2.3 and R_0 is 300 ohms. Find Z_R in terms of its resistive and reactive components.*

Solution. Standing wave minima points correspond to voltage minima points. Hence two consecutive E_{min} points are separated 105 cm.

Hence $$\frac{\lambda}{2} = 105 \text{ cm}$$

or $$\lambda = 2.1 \text{ metres}$$

The first voltage minimum is given by

$$y_{min} = \frac{\phi + \pi}{2\beta} = \left(\frac{\phi + \pi}{4\pi}\right)\lambda = \frac{\phi + \pi}{4\pi} \times 2.1$$

Hence $$\phi + \pi = \frac{y_{min} \times 4\pi}{2.1} = \frac{0.3 \times 4\pi}{2.1} = \frac{4\pi}{7}$$

Hence $$\phi = \frac{4\pi}{7} - \pi = \frac{-3\pi}{7} = -77.14°.$$

To determine Z_R, it is necessary to determine the magnitude and the angle of reflection coefficient K.

Since $$\mathbf{K} = \frac{\mathbf{Z}_R - R_0}{\mathbf{Z}_R + R_0}, \quad \mathbf{Z}_R = R_0 \cdot \frac{1 + \mathbf{K}}{1 - \mathbf{K}}$$

The magnitude of **K** is determined from the value of S.

Thus $$|K| = \frac{S-1}{S+1} = \frac{2.3-1}{2.3+1} = \frac{1.3}{3.3} = 0.394$$

Hence $$K = 0.394 \angle -77.14° = 0.0882 = j0.384$$

Hence $$\mathbf{Z}_R = 300 \frac{1.0882 - j0.384}{0.9118 + j\,0.384} = 300 \frac{1.153 \angle -19.9°}{0.989 \angle 22.8°}$$

or $$\mathbf{Z}_R = 350 \angle -42.7° = 257 - j237.5.$$

Assuming $v_p = 3 \times 10^6$ metres/second, we get the signal frequency

$$f = \frac{3 \times 10^8}{2.1} = 143 \times 10^6 \text{ Hz.}$$

20.7. Input Impedance of the Lossless Line

Consider a lossless line of length l units. The input impedance of this line is the impedance seen by the generator at sending end. This can be obtained by the use of Eqs. (20.26) and (20.27) by putting $x = l$. Thus, we have

$$\mathbf{E}_S = \mathbf{E}_R \cos \beta l + jR_0\mathbf{I}_R \sin \beta l$$

and
$$\mathbf{I}_S = \mathbf{I}_R \cos \beta l + \frac{\mathbf{E}_R}{R_0} \sin \beta l$$

Taking the ratio, we get

$$Z_S = \frac{\mathbf{E}_S}{R_S} \frac{\mathbf{E}_R \cos \beta l + jR_0\mathbf{I}_R \sin \beta l}{\mathbf{I}_S \cos \beta l + j\dfrac{\mathbf{E}_R}{R_0} \sin \beta l}$$

Substitution $\mathbf{E}_R = \mathbf{I}_R.Z_R$ and cancelling $\mathbf{I}_R$ from both numerator and denominator, we get

$$\mathbf{Z}_R = R_0\left[\frac{\mathbf{Z}_R \cos \beta l + jR_0 \sin \beta l}{R_0 \cos \beta l + j\mathbf{Z}_R \sin \beta l}\right] = R_0\left[\frac{\mathbf{Z}_R + jR_0 \tan \beta l}{R_0 + j\mathbf{Z}_R \tan \beta l}\right] \quad ...(20.55)$$

The sending end impedance or the input impedance is, in general, a complex quantity even when Z_R is resistance. Further the variation of Z_S with βl is periodic. The period in which Z_S changes from maximum value to minimum value corresponds to π radians, *i.e.* for $l = \lambda/2$.

Another useful expression of the input impedance may be obtained from Eqs. (19.22) and (19.23). Thus, we have

$$Z_S = \frac{\mathbf{E}_S}{\mathbf{I}_S} = \frac{\dfrac{\mathbf{E}_R(\mathbf{Z}_R + R_0)}{2\mathbf{Z}_R}(\varepsilon^{j\beta l} + K\varepsilon^{-j\beta l})}{\dfrac{\mathbf{I}_R(\mathbf{Z}_R + R_0)}{2R_0}(\varepsilon^{j\beta l} - K\varepsilon^{-j\beta l})}$$

$$= R_0\left(\frac{1\angle \beta l + |K| \angle \phi - \beta l}{1\angle \beta l - |K| \angle \phi - \beta l}\right) \quad ...(20.56)$$

where ϕ is the angle of reflection coefficient K for any terminating impedance $\mathbf{Z}_R$.

Eq. (20.56) may be simplified further by dividing numerator and denominator both by $1\angle \beta l$. Thus, we get

$$Z_S = R_0\left(\frac{1 + |K| \angle \phi - 2\beta l}{1 - |K| \angle \phi - 2\beta l}\right) \quad ...(20.57)$$

The variation of Z_S with the length of line can be better studied by a phasor diagram representing Eq. (20.57) where the numerator is

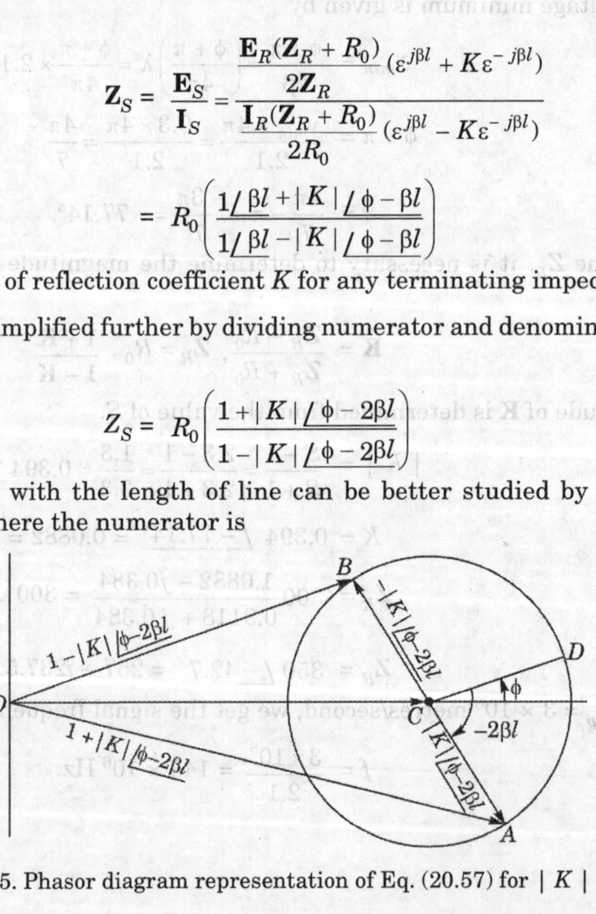

Fig. 20.5. Phasor diagram representation of Eq. (20.57) for $|K| = 1/3$.

considered as one phasor and the denominator as another. Such a diagram can drawn for a given magnitude of K having an arbitrary angle ϕ. For example, the phasor diagram shown in Fig. 20.5 has been drawn for $|K| = 1/3$ giving $S = 2$. For each value of K, a separate circle will be required to be drawn. The line OC represents unit value and the circle is drawn with a radius equal to one-third of OC and with centre at C so that any point on this circle represents the constant magnitude of K. A line CD is drawn at an angle ϕ, which is the phase angle of K. The line CA drawn at an angle $-2\beta l$ measured from the line CD now represents the phasor $|K| \angle \phi - 2\beta l$. The vector sum of OC and CA is then OA which represents the numerator of Eq. (20.57). The phasor $|K| \angle \phi - 2\beta l$ is represented by a line drawn at an angle of 180° with the phasor $|K| \angle \phi - 2\beta l$. This is represented by line CB and OB being the phasor sum of OC and OB represents the denominator of Eq. (20.57).

It may be seen from this phasor diagram that as the length l is increased or β is increased by increasing the frequency, the phasors CA and CB will rotate in clockwise direction. A condition is reached when phasors OA and OB are in phase giving rise to purely resistive input impedance. This happens when $(\phi - 2\beta l)$ is an integral multiple of p including zero, *i.e.*

$$(\phi - 2\beta l) = \pm n\pi, \qquad n = 0, 1, 2, 3, ...$$

or

$$2\beta l = \phi \pm n\pi$$

or

$$l = \frac{\phi}{2\beta} \pm n\frac{\lambda}{4}, \qquad n = 0, 1, 2, 3, ... \qquad ...(20.58)$$

For these lengths of line, the input impedance of the line is purely resistive and has either the maximum value or the minimum value. These maximum and minimum values alternate every quarter wavelength change in the length l of the line. This is true since half a revolution of the vector R corresponds to $\lambda/4$ in terms of wavelength. The input resistance is maximum when $(\phi - 2\beta l)$ is either zero or an even multiple of π so that the vector OA corresponding to the numerator of Eq. (20.57) is maximum and the vector OB corresponding to the denominator of Eq. (20.57) is minimum, both being in the same phase.

The maximum value of input impedance (resistive) is,

$$R_{in(max)} = R_0\left(\frac{1+|K|}{1-|K|}\right)$$

$$= R_0 S \qquad ...(20.59)$$

The minimum input impedance (resistive) occurs when $(\phi - 2\beta l)$ equals π radians or an odd multiple of π radians so that AO has minimum value and vector OB has maximum value, both being in the same phase. This minimum value is given by,

$$R_{in\ (min)} = R_0\left(\frac{1-|K|}{1+|K|}\right) = \frac{R_0}{S} \qquad ...(20.60)$$

It may be seen that the conditions of impedance maximum and minimum are the same as the conditions for voltage maximum and minimum as given by Eqs. (20.41) and (20.44). Hence it can be said that impedance maxima occur at voltage maxima while the impedance minima occur at voltage minima, both values being purely resistive.

20.8. Input Impedance of Open and Short Circuited Loss-less lines

The input impedance of a lossless line terminated in any impedance $\mathbf{Z}_R$ is given by Eq. (20.55).

For short circuited dissipationless lines, $\mathbf{Z}_R = 0$ so that,

$$\mathbf{Z}_{SC} = jR_0\,\beta l$$

$$= jR_0 \tan \frac{2\pi l}{\lambda} \qquad \text{...(20.61)}$$

This equation shows that the input impedance of short circuited lossless line is a pure reactance.

The input impedance of a lossless line as given by Eq. (20.55) may alternatively by put as,

$$Z_S = R_0 \frac{1 + j\dfrac{R_0}{\mathbf{Z}_R}\tan\beta l}{\dfrac{R_0}{\mathbf{Z}_R} + j\tan\beta l}$$

For open circuited dissipationless line, $Z_R = \infty$ so that the imput impedance is,

$$\mathbf{Z}_{oc} = -j\frac{R_0}{\tan\beta l} = -jR_0\cot\frac{2\pi l}{\lambda} \qquad \text{...(20.62)}$$

Thus the input impedance of an open-circuited lossless line is also a pure reactance. The magnitude of the reactance can be normalised with respect to R_0 and the variation of $\mathbf{Z}_{sc}/R_0$ or $\mathbf{Z}_{oc}/R_0$ may be considered as a function of the length l of the line in terms of wavelength. These variations are repetitive functions of length with a period of $l = \lambda/2$ because of the tangent function involved in Eqs. (20.61) and (20.62). The reactance varies from $-\infty$ to $+\infty$. Fig. 20.6 shows the variation of X/R_0 for a short circuited dissipationless line as a function of length. Similarly Fig. 20.7 shows the variation of $\mathbf{Z}_{oc}/R_0$ for an open circuited lossless line as a function of length l.

It may be seen from the curves in Figs. 20.6 and 20.7 that a short circuited line of length less than $\lambda/4$ behaves as an inductance whereas an open circuited line of lengths less than $\lambda/4$ behaves as a capacitance. Further the signs of input reactance reverse every quarter wavelength as shown in Figs. 20.6 and 20.7.

It is obvious also that short circuited and open circuited lines have performance similar to a resonant circuit. Such lines may, therefore, be used as reactive circuit elements. The input impedance

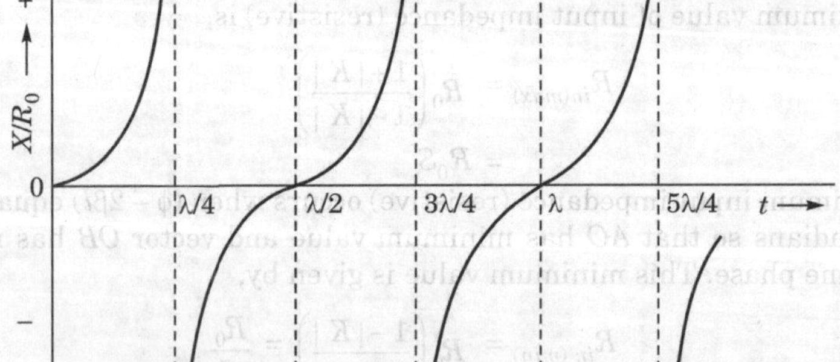

Fig. 20.6. Variation of input impedance of a short circuited lossless line as a function of length l.

of a quarter wave short-circuited line varies with frequency in a manner similar to its variation with length l. This variation is similar to the impedance *versus* frequency variation of a parallel-tuned circuit. Similarly, the impedance *versus* frequency variation of an open-circuited $\lambda/4$ line is similar to the impedance *versus* frequency variation of a series resonant circuit upto frequencies which make the length l equal to $\lambda/2$. Accordingly short-circuited and open circuited $\lambda/4$ lossless lines may be conveniently used as tuned circuits.

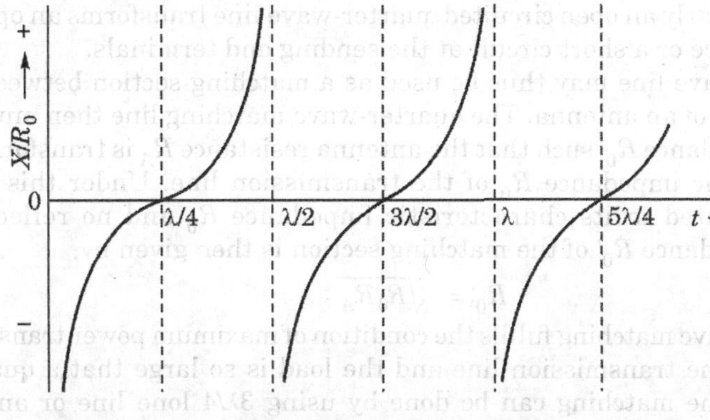

Fig. 20.7. Variation of input impedance of an open circuited lossless line as a function of length l.

The input impedance of a λ/4 short-circuited line is an infinite reactance, *i.e.* the line behaves as an open circuit. On the other hand, the input impedance of a λ/4 open-circuited line is a zero reactance, *i.e.* the line behaves as a short circuit.

The curves shown in Figs. 20.6 and 20.7 pertain to ideal lossless line. In practice, however, a line always has a small resistance giving rise to a real part of a resistive component in the input impedance. This shows that a certain amount of power loss always takes place. Also the zero and infinite impedance conditions are never attained. Instead of these, minimum and maximum values are obtained.

20.9. Quarter-wave Line as an Impedance Transformer

The input impedance of a lossless line given by Eq. (20.55) may be rearranged below,

$$\mathbf{Z}_s = \mathbf{Z}_i = R_0 \left[\frac{\dfrac{\mathbf{Z}_R}{\tan\left(\dfrac{2\pi l}{\lambda}\right)} + jR_0}{\dfrac{R_0}{\tan\left(\dfrac{2\pi l}{\lambda}\right)} + j\mathbf{Z}_R} \right]$$

When the line is made λ/4 long, the input impedance becomes

$$Z_{i(\lambda/4)} = \frac{R_0^{\,2}}{\mathbf{Z}_R} \qquad \text{...(20.63)}$$

Eq. (20.63) is true for any value of terminating impedance. Thus a quarter wave line can be considered as a transformer to match a load impedance $\mathbf{Z}_R$ to a source impedance $\mathbf{Z}_s$ by proper selection of the value of R_0 so as to satisfy Eq. (20.63).

The matching section of line should be properly designed so that its characteristic resistance R_0 satisfies (20.63), *i.e.* R_0 is given by

$$R_0 = |\sqrt{Z_s\, Z_R}\,| \qquad \text{...(20.64)}$$

Such line sections are often referred to as the *quarter wave transformer.* However it may be seen that Eq. (20.63) is satisfied for only one frequency or for a narrow band of frequencies.

A quarter wave line may be considered as *impedance invertor* since it can transform a low impedance at the load side into a high impedance at the generator side or *vice versa.* This can be explained by referring to λ/4 short circuited or open-circuited line. Thus a quarter-wave line having zero impedance or short circuit at one end transforms it into infinite impedance or open circuit at the other end. Similarly an open circuited quarter-wave line transforms an open circuit termination into a low impedance or a short circuit at the sending end terminals.

A quarter-wave line may thus be used as a matching section between a transmission line and a resistive load of an antenna. The quarter-wave matching line then must be designed to have characteristic impedance R_0' such that the antenna resistance R_A is transformed into a value equal to the characteristic impedance R_0 of the transmission line. Under this condition this line is effectively terminated in its characteristic impedance R_0 and no reflection take place. The characteristic impedance R_0' of the matching section is then given by,

$$R_0' = \sqrt{R_0 R_A} \quad ...(20.65)$$

Such a resistive matching fulfils the condition of maximum power transfer also. If the physical distance between the transmission line and the load is so large that a quarter wave line is not sufficient, then same matching can be done by using $3\lambda/4$ lone line or any line odd number of quarter waves long. However, longer matching sections reduce the efficiency of transmission because of increase in losses such as resistance etc.

When matching sections are used, it is desirable to keep the same spacing between wires in the case of open wire lines and the same inner radius of the outer conductor in coaxial lines for constructional facilities. Hence the range of values of $\mathbf{Z}_S$ and Z_R which can be matched by a quarter-wave line, is limited. The value may be about 10 times the minimum value.

A quarter wave transformer may also be used when the load impedance is not a pure resistance. In such a case, matching section should be connected at a voltage-minimum point where the transmission line has a resistive input impedance given by R_0/S. Then the matching section should have characteristic resistance given by

$$R_0' = \sqrt{R_0 \cdot \frac{R_0}{S}} = R_0\sqrt{\frac{1}{S}} \quad ...(20.66)$$

Thus the matching section may be connected at a certain distance from the load, the distance being formed by the original transmission line.

A short circuited quarter-wave line can also be used as an insulator to support an open wire line as shown in Fig. 20.8. This is possible since the input impedance of the quarter wave line as seen by the main transmission line is infinite or very high at the frequency which makes the line of length $\lambda/4$. At other frequencies, a small amount of loss may take place. However, the configuration may be conveniently used for a single frequency or for a narrow band of frequencies. Such $\lambda/4$ lines are called *copper* insulators.

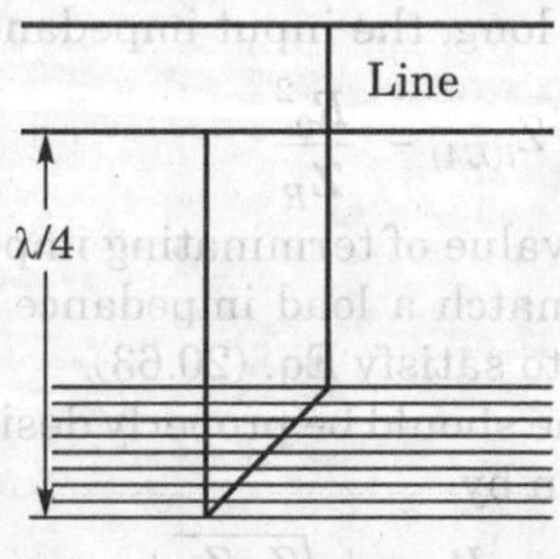

Fig. 20.8. Quarter-wave line as insulator.

20.10. The Half-wave Line

When the length of a transmission line is equivalent to $\lambda/2$, the input impedance becomes,

$$\mathbf{Z}_3 = \mathbf{Z}_{in} = R_0\left[\frac{\mathbf{Z}_R + jR_0 \tan\left(\frac{2\pi}{\lambda}.\frac{\lambda}{2}\right)}{R_0 + j\mathbf{Z}_R \tan\left(\frac{2\pi}{\lambda}.\frac{\lambda}{2}\right)}\right]$$

or
$$Z_S\left(\frac{\lambda}{2}\right) = Z_R \qquad ...(20.67)$$

Thus the input impedance of a half-wave line is equal to the terminating impedance. A half-wave line, therefore, may be considered as one-to-one transformer. Such a line may be used in cases where the source and the load are not adjacent. The length of the line can be made any integral multiple of $\lambda/2$. Thus a group of capacitors can be placed in parallel with respect to the source by connecting each capacitor at a distance of $\lambda/2$ from each other across the line if the line is divided into n sections each of $\lambda/2$ length. Therefore, an open-wire line should not have its insulators spaced at half wave intervals because then the effect will be cumulative, lowering the insulation resistance of the line and hence increasing the value of G at the high frequencies for which the line has been designed to be lossless.

20.11. The One-eighth Wavelength Line

Another interesting condition of a transmission line in terms of its length in wavelengths occurs when the line is one-eighth wave long. The input impedance of such a line with $l = \lambda/8$ given by,

$$\mathbf{Z}_S\left(\frac{\lambda}{8}\right) = R_0\left[\frac{\mathbf{Z}_R + jR_0 \tan\frac{\pi}{4}}{R_0 + j\mathbf{Z}_R \tan\frac{\pi}{4}}\right]$$

$$= R_0\left[\frac{\mathbf{Z}_R + jR_0}{R_0 + j\mathbf{Z}_R}\right] \qquad ...(20.68)$$

If the terminating impedance is resistive so that

$$\mathbf{Z}_R = R_R, \text{ then}$$

$$\mathbf{Z}_S\left(\frac{\lambda}{8}\right) = R_0\frac{R_R + jR_0}{R_0 + jR_R}$$

Then the numerator and the denominator have identical magnitudes. Hence the magnitude of the input impedance is given by

$$\left|\mathbf{Z}_S\left(\frac{\pi}{8}\right)\right| = R_0 \qquad ...(20.69)$$

Thus a $\lambda/8$ line may be used to transform any load impedance to the value of the characteristic resistance of the line or it may be used to provide a magnitude match between a load resistance and a source of internal resistance R_0.

Example 20.8. *A $9/16\lambda$ long lossless line has $Z_S/R_0 = 1.5 + j0.9$, where $\mathbf{Z}_S$ is the impedance and R_0 is the characteristic resistance. Find the load impedance normalised to R_0 and also the standing wave ratio.*

Solution. Load impedance may be calculated making use of the following relation :

$$\frac{\mathbf{Z}_S}{R_0} = \frac{\mathbf{Z}_R + jR_0 \tan\beta l}{R_0 + j\mathbf{Z}_R \tan\beta l}$$

$$= \frac{\dfrac{\mathbf{Z}_R}{R_0} + j\tan\beta l}{1 + j\dfrac{\mathbf{Z}_R}{R_0}\tan\beta l}$$

Substituting the values,

$$1.5 + j0.9 = \frac{\dfrac{\mathbf{Z}_R}{R_0} + j\tan\left(\dfrac{2\pi}{\lambda}\cdot\dfrac{9\lambda}{16}\right)}{1 + j\dfrac{\mathbf{Z}_R}{R_0}\tan\left(\dfrac{2\pi}{\lambda}\cdot\dfrac{9\lambda}{16}\right)}$$

or $$(1.5 + j0.9)\left[1 + j\frac{\mathbf{R}_R}{R_0}\tan\frac{\pi}{8}\right] = \frac{\mathbf{Z}_R}{R_0} + j\tan\frac{\pi}{8}$$

or $$\frac{\mathbf{Z}_R}{R_0}[1 - j1.4142(1.5 + j0.9)] = 1.5 + j6.4858$$

or $$\frac{\mathbf{Z}_R}{R_0} = \frac{1.5 + j0.4858}{1.3728 + j0.6213} = \frac{1.574\,\angle 17.95^\circ}{1.508\,\angle -24.4^\circ} = 0.772 + j0.702$$

Reflection coefficient $$\mathbf{K} = \frac{\mathbf{Z}_R - R_0}{\mathbf{Z}_R + R_0} = \frac{(\mathbf{Z}_R/R_0) - 1}{(\mathbf{Z}_R/R_0) + 1} = \frac{-0.228 + j0.702}{1.772 + j0.702}$$

Hence $$|K| = \frac{\sqrt{(0.228)^2 + (0.702)^2}}{\sqrt{(1.772)^2 + (0.702)^2}} = \frac{0.738}{1.908} = 0.3865$$

Hence standing wave ratio $$S = \frac{1 - |K|}{1 + |K|} = \frac{1.3865}{0.6135} = 2.26.$$

Example 20.9. *If a lossless line has $R_0 = 200$ ohms, what length of the line will be required to obtain at the input an inductance of 8 μH at frequency of 70 MHz with far end short circuited ? Repeat the calculations for open circuited receiving end.*

Solution. The input impedance of a short circuited line is a pure reactance given by,

$$\mathbf{Z}_{SC} = jR_0\tan\left(\frac{2\pi l}{\lambda}\right)$$

Substituting the values,

$$j2\pi \times 70 \times 10^6 \times 8 \times 10^{-6} = j200\tan\left(\frac{2\pi l}{\lambda}\right)$$

or $$\tan\left(\frac{2\pi l}{\lambda}\right) = \frac{15\pi \times 70}{200}$$

or $$\frac{2\pi l}{\lambda} = \tan^{-1} 17.6 = \frac{86.75 \times \pi}{180} \text{ radians}$$

Hence $$\frac{l}{\lambda} = \frac{86.75 \times \pi}{180 \times 2\pi} = \frac{1}{4.15}$$

Hence $$l = \frac{\lambda}{4.15}.$$

The input impedance of an open circuited line is given by

$$\mathbf{Z}_{OC} = -jR_0 \cot\left(\frac{2\pi l}{\lambda}\right)$$

Substituting the values,

$$j2\pi \times 70 \times 10^{-6} \times 8 \times 10^{-6} = -j200 \cot\left(\frac{2\pi l}{\lambda}\right)$$

Hence $$\cot \frac{2\pi l}{\lambda} = -\frac{2\pi \times 560}{200} = -17.6$$

or $$\cot\left(\pi - \frac{2\pi l}{\lambda}\right) = 17.6$$

Hence $$\pi - \frac{2\pi l}{\lambda} = \cot^{-1} 17.6 = \frac{3.25 \times \pi}{180} \text{ radians}$$

Hence $$\frac{2l}{\lambda} = 1 - \frac{3.25}{180}$$

Hence $$l = 0.981\ \frac{\lambda}{2}.$$

20.12. Powers and Impedance Measurement of Line

The voltage and current phasors for a lossless line can be written as,

$$\mathbf{E}_x = \frac{\mathbf{I}_R(\mathbf{Z}_R + R_0)}{2}\,[\varepsilon^{j\beta y} + \mathbf{K}\varepsilon^{-j\beta y}] \qquad ...(20.70)$$

and $$\mathbf{I}_x = \frac{\mathbf{I}_R(\mathbf{Z}_R - R_0)}{2R_0}\,[\varepsilon^{j\beta y} - \mathbf{K}\varepsilon^{-j\beta y}] \qquad ...(20.71)$$

These may be modified and written as,

$$\mathbf{E}_x = \frac{I_R(\mathbf{Z}_R - R_0)}{2}\,[1 + |\,K\,|\,\angle \phi - 2\beta y\,] \qquad ...(20.72)$$

$$\mathbf{I}_x = \frac{\mathbf{I}_R(\mathbf{Z}_R + R_0)}{2R_0}\,[1 - |\,K\,|\,\angle \phi - 2\beta y\,] \qquad ...(20.73)$$

These phasors may be drawn giving a phasor diagram similar to Fig. 20.5 and is shown in Fig. 20.9. Hence phasors OA and OB represent $\mathbf{E}_x$ and $\mathbf{I}_x.R_0$ respectively. We have already seen

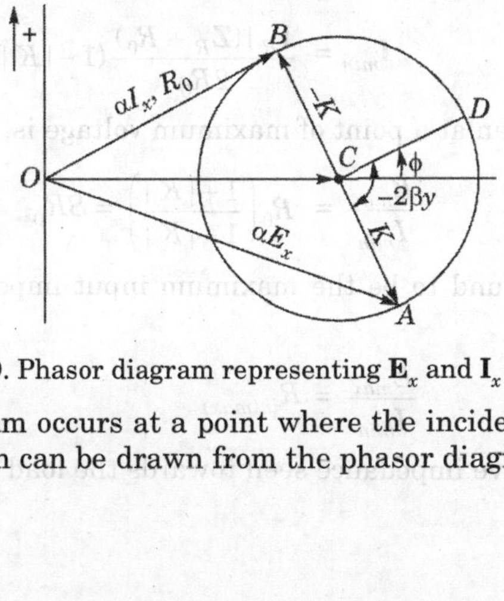

Fig. 20.9. Phasor diagram representing $\mathbf{E}_x$ and $\mathbf{I}_x$ phasors.

that a voltage or current maximum occurs at a point where the incident and the reflected waves are in phase. The same conclusion can be drawn from the phasor diagram of Fig. 20.9. Hence OC

represents the phasor $1\angle 0$ being the incident wave while $|K|\angle\phi - 2\beta y$ being proportional to the reflected wave is represented by *CA*. Similarly $-|K|\angle\phi - 2\beta y$ has been represented by *CB*. Thus when *CA* is in phase with *OC*, then *OA* has maximum value. This maximum value is given by Eq. (20.72) putting $(\phi - 2\beta y) = 0$. Thus,

$$\mathbf{E}_{max} = \frac{I_R\,|(\mathbf{Z}_R + R_0)|}{2}(1 + |K|) \qquad ...(20.74)$$

Similarly current maximum occurs when incident and reflected current waves are in phase, *i.e.* when *CB* is in phase with *OC*. The magnitude of current maximum is then obtained from Eq. (20.73). Thus, we get

$$\mathbf{I}_{max} = \frac{\mathbf{I}_R\,|(\mathbf{Z}_R + R_0)|}{2R_0}(1 + |K|) \qquad ...(20.75)$$

From Eqs. (20.74) and (20.75) it may be seen that,

$$\frac{E_{max}}{I_{max}} = R_0 \qquad ...(20.76)$$

Thus R_0 for a line may be found by measuring E_{max} and I_{max}. Further E_{min} and I_{min} are obtained when the incident and the reflected waves are out of phase with each other. A change in the sign of $|K|$ from positive to negative alters the E_{max} to E_{min} and I_{max} to I_{min}. Here again the ratio of E_{min} to I_{min} equals R_0. Thus,

$$\frac{E_{min}}{I_{min}} = R_0 \qquad ...(20.77)$$

The minimum points are sharper than the maximum points. Hence R_0 as determined from Eq. (20.77) is more accurate in comparison with that determined from Eq. (20.76).

It may be seen from Eqs. (20.72) and (20.73) and also from Fig. 20.9 that when voltage phasor *OA* is maximum, the current phasor *OB* is minimum and *vice-versa.* Thus a voltage maximum occurs at the same point of the line as a current minimum. That has already been observed during the study of standing wave ratio.

Fig. 20.9 shows that maximum voltage and minimum current values occur when the two phasors *OA* and *OB* are in phase. Similarly minimum voltage and maximum current values occur when the two phasors *OA* and *OB* are in phase. This means that the impedance seen towards the load at the point of E_{max} or I_{min} will be resistive, whatever be the terminating impedance. Writing the value of I_{min} from Eq. (20.73) as

$$\mathbf{I}_{min} = \frac{\mathbf{I}_R\,|(\mathbf{Z}_R + R_0)}{2R_0}(1 - |K|) \qquad ...(20.78)$$

the resistive impedance seen at a point of maximum voltage is,

$$\frac{E_{max}}{I_{min}} = R_0\left(\frac{1 + |K|}{1 - |K|}\right) = SR_0 \qquad ...(20.79)$$

But this value is found to be the maximum input impedance (resistive) as given by Eq. (20.59). Hence

$$\frac{E_{max}}{I_{min}} = R_{in(max)} \qquad ...(20.80)$$

Similarly the resistive impedance seen towards the load at a point of minimum voltage is,

$$\frac{E_{min}}{I_{max}} = R_0\left(\frac{1-|K|}{1+|K|}\right) = \frac{R_0}{S} = R_{in(max)} \qquad ...(20.81)$$

The power flowing through the line at the point of voltage maximum or at the point of voltage minimum is the real power flowing into a resistance *of* R_{max} or R_{min} value.

$$\text{Power } p = \frac{E_{max}^{\ 2}}{R_{in(max)}} \qquad ...(20.82)$$

The same power should flow through the line at the point of voltage minimum since the line is lossless.

Hence
$$P = \frac{E_{min}^{\ 2}}{R_{in(min)}} \qquad ...(20.83)$$

Multiplying together Eqs. (20.82) and (20.83), we get

$$P^2 = \frac{E_{max}^{\ 2}\, E_{min}^{\ 2}}{R_{in(max)} \cdot R_{in(min)}}$$

Substituting $R_{in(max)} = SR_0$ and $R_{in(min)} = \frac{R_0}{S}$, the power flow through the line becomes,

$$P = \frac{|E_{max}| \cdot |E_{min}|}{R_0} \qquad ...(20.84)$$

Multiplying together Eqs. (20.79) and (20.81), we get

$$E_{max} \cdot E_{min} = R_0^{\ 2} I_{max}\, I_{min} \qquad ...(20.85)$$

Combining Eqs. (20.84) and (20.85), we get another expression for power flow through a transmission line as

$$P = |I_{max}| \cdot |I_{min}| \cdot R_0 \qquad ...(20.86)$$

From this consideration it will seem proper to increase the magnitude of voltage for transmission of larger amount of power. However a transmission line has a certain insulation resistance between the two wires due to dielectric material which may be air as in the case of open-wire lines and coaxial lines. Hence a transmission line has a *breakdown voltage* at which the insulation resistance breaks down and a discharge takes place across the dielectric material between the two wires. This places a short circuit across the line and no transmission takes place. Such a breakdown is more serious in coaxial lines because the separation between the conductors is very small as compared to that in open wire lines. Smaller breakdown voltage is thus needed in coaxial lines. This limits the value E_{max} and hence limits the maximum power that can be transmitted. Eq. (20.84) shows that for a given value of E_{max} the power flow is maximum when $|E_{max}|$ equals $|E_{min}|$, *i.e.* when no reflection takes place.

By making certain measurements on the line, it is possible to determine the complex value of terminating impedance Z_R. This has been demonstrated in example 20.7, where calculations have been done according to the principle of reflections on lines terminated in complex load impedances. However, these calculations can be simplified by incorporating the principles in the form of an equation.

The load impedance $\mathbf{Z}_R$ may be determined by measurement of standing wave ratio S and wavelenth λ on a line. Thus an open-wire line or a slotted coaxial line may be used as a *very high frequency bridge* for measurement of an unknown impedance. For such a use of lossless line, it is necessary to determine the value of R_0 of the line either by measurements or by calculations. Then two measurements are needed, one of the standing wave ratio and the other of the distance y' from the load to the nearest or the first point of *voltage minimum*. The wavelength λ may be determined from frequency and velocity or by measuring the distance between successive minima.

At a voltage minimum point, the input impedance of the line is purely resistive and is given by,

$$Z_{in} = R_{in(min)} = \frac{R_0}{S}$$

The input impedance at any point distant y from the receiving end is given by,

$$\mathbf{Z}_{in} = R_0 \left[\frac{\mathbf{Z}_R + jR_0 \tan\left(\frac{2\pi y}{\lambda}\right)}{R_0 + j\mathbf{Z}_R \tan\left(\frac{2\pi y}{\lambda}\right)} \right]$$

where $\mathbf{Z}_R$ is the terminating impedance.

At the point of first voltage minimum at a distance y' from the load end, the input impedance becomes,

$$\frac{R_0}{S} = R_0 \left[\frac{\mathbf{Z}_R + jR_0 \tan\left(\frac{2y}{\lambda}y'\right)}{R_0 + j\mathbf{Z}_R \tan\left(\frac{2y}{\lambda}y'\right)} \right] \quad ...(20.87)$$

Solving Eq. (20.87) for $\mathbf{Z}_R$, we get

$$\mathbf{Z}_R = R_0 \left[\frac{1 - jS \tan\left(\frac{2\pi}{\lambda}\right)y'}{S - j \tan\left(\frac{2\pi}{\lambda}\right)y'} \right] \quad ...(20.88)$$

Knowing the value of R_0, S and y', $\mathbf{Z}_R$ may be calculated easily.

When a line is not matched and reflection occurs, it is possible to relate the transmitted power to the standing wave ratio S. Let the magnitude of the incident wave be E_i and that of the reflected wave be E_r. Then in a lossless line, the magnitude of the voltage maximum as given by Eq. (20.74) is given by,

$$|E_{max}| = |E_i| + |E_r| = \frac{I_R |(\mathbf{Z}_R + R_0)|}{2}(1 + |K|)$$

The magnitude of voltage minimum is given by,

$$|E_{min}| = |E_i| - |E_r| = \frac{|I_R|(\mathbf{Z}_R + R_0)|}{2}(1 - |K|)$$

The standing wave ratio is given as,

$$S = \frac{|E_{max}|}{|E_{min}|} = \frac{|E_i| + |E_r|}{|E_i| - |E_r|} = \frac{1 + |K|}{1 - |K|} \quad ...(20.89)$$

The power flow through the line is given by Eq. (20.84) as

$$P = \frac{|E_{max}| . |E_{min}|}{R_0}$$

Substituting the values of E_{max} and E_{min}, we get

$$P = \frac{(|E_i| + |E_r|)(|E_i| - |E_r|)}{R_0} = \frac{|E_i|^2 - |E_r|^2}{R_0} \qquad ...(20.90)$$

Eq. (20.90) gives total power transmitted through the line and delivered to the load in terms of two power terms : (*i*) P_i, the power transmitted in the incident wave and (*ii*) P_r, the power travelling back in the reflected wave. The incident power P_i, can be considered as the maximum power that can be delivered to the load under matched conditions of termination. Hence considering the ratio of power P delivered to the load to the power transmitted by the incident wave gives,

$$\frac{P}{P_i} = \frac{|E_i|^2 - |E_r|^2}{|E_i|^2} = 1 - \frac{|E_i|^2}{|E_i|^2} = 1 - |K|^2$$

or

$$\frac{P}{P_i} = 1 - \left(\frac{S-1}{S+1}\right)^2 = \frac{4S}{(S+1)^2} \qquad ...(20.91)$$

When $S = 1$, *i.e.* with no reflections, $P = P_i$ or the power delivered to the load equals the power contained in the incident wave. As the value of S increases, the power delivered to the load reduces rapidly and becomes only a very small percentage of the matched power available to the load. This shows the desirability of operating a line under matched condition of load so as to obtain the maximum advantage of a line and also to eliminate reflections giving rise to other troubles.

In many cases, however, it is not possible to obtain impedance matched conditions either through change of load impedance or through selection of proper line. In such cases, impedance matching networks or transmission lines may be used in the form *of matching stubs,* specially at higher frequencies where loss of power is more significant. Use of a quarter wave line as an impedance transformer has already been considered. A quarter wave line is widely used for impedance matching at v.h.f, u.h.f., and microwave frequencies. However, impedance matching by the quarter-wave line or any other fixed-length line is valid only for a single frequency for which it is designed. Accordingly such a system can be used either for a single frequency or a narrow band of frequencies.

Example 20.10. *A transmission line has R_0 = 150 ohms and is found to have a standing wave ratio of 3.5. The first voltage minimum is 30 volts and occurs at a distance of 80 cm from the load. If the line is lossless and operated at 30 MHz, compute the complex load impedance and the power delivered to the load.*

Solution. Since the line is dissipationless, the velocity of propagation will be equal to that of the light. Hence

$$\lambda = \frac{4 \times 10^8}{30 \times 10^6} = 10 \text{ metres}$$

Also we have,

$S = 3.5$, $R_0 = 150\ \Omega$, $y' = 0.8$ metre and $E_{min} = 30$ volts.

Hence

$$\mathbf{Z}_B = \mathbf{R}_0 \left[\frac{1 - jS\tan\left(\frac{2\pi y'}{\lambda}\right)}{S - j\tan\left(\frac{2\pi y'}{\lambda}\right)}\right] = 150\left[\frac{1 - j3.5\tan\left(\frac{2\pi \times 0.8}{10}\right)}{3.5 - j\tan\left(\frac{2\pi \times 0.8}{10}\right)}\right]$$

$$= 150\,\frac{(1 - j\,1.923)}{(3.5 - j\,0.5498)} = 150\,\frac{2.168\,\angle -62.5^\circ}{3.54\,\angle -8.9^\circ}$$

$$= 91.9\,\angle -53.6^\circ = 54.4 = j73.9$$

Power delivered to the load is given by,

$$P = \frac{E_{min}^{2}}{R_{in(min)}}$$

Now $\quad E_{min} = 30 \text{ volts} \quad \text{and} \quad R_{in(min)} = \frac{R_0}{S} = \frac{150}{3.5}$

Hence $\quad P = \frac{(32)^2 \times 3.5}{150} = 15 \text{ watts.}$

20.13. Single Stub Impedance Matching on Lines

We have seen in Art. 20.8 that the input impedance of an open circuited or short circuited lossless line is purely reactive. Such a section is usually connected across the line at a convenient point and cancels the reactive part of impedance at this point seen looking towards the load. Such a section is called *impedance matching stub*. Since the stub is connected in shunt across the main transmission line, it becomes possible to use the stub of desired length and construction without any restriction imposed by the main line.

Usually the length of matching stub is kept within quarter wavelength so that the stub remains practically lossless at all high frequencies. A short circuited stub of length less than $\lambda/4$ offers inductive reactance at the input while an open circuited stub of lengthless than $\lambda/4$ offers capacitive reactance at the input. Thus depending upon the requirement, either the short circuited stub or the open circuited stub may be used. Both types of stubs are widely used.

Since the matching stubs are connected in parallel with the main transmission line, it is easier to consider the analysis in terms of admittances rather than impedances.

The method of connecting a stub is shown in Fig. 20.10 where a short circuited stub has been connected at a distance y_1 from the receiving end. When a line is terminated in an impedance Z_R, reflections take place. The input conductance of the line seen towards the load at a point of voltage maximum will be $\frac{1}{SR_0}$ and at a point of voltage minimum will be $\frac{S}{R_0}$, where S is the standing wave ratio and R_0 is the characteristic resistance of the lossless line. Hence at some point intermediate between a voltage maximum and a voltage minimum, the input conductance of the line can be expected to be equal to $1/R_0$. Let this point be AA' at a distance y_1 from the receiving end. The conductance is maximum at a voltage minimum. Hence the distance y_1 of terminals AA' from the receiving end will be less than the distance y_2 of a voltage minimum before insertion of the stub as shown in Fig. 20.10. The input admittance of the line at AA' before insertion of the stub can be written as,

$$Y_a = \frac{1}{R_0} \pm jB \qquad \text{...(20.92)}$$

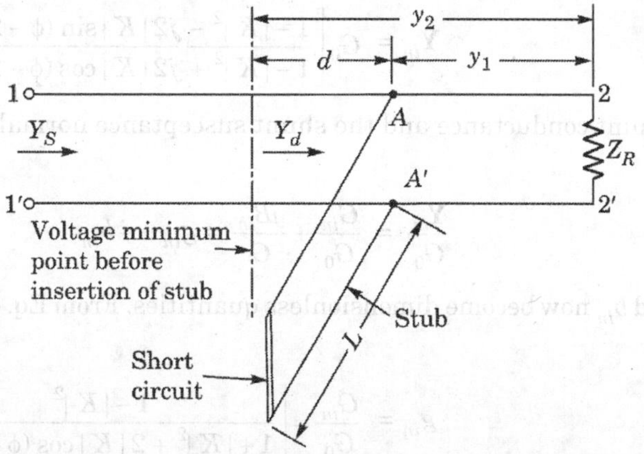

Fig. 20.10. Short circuited stub for impedance matching.

The value of susceptance B may be positive or negative depending upon the terminating impedance $\mathbf{Z}_R$. This susceptance B is required to be eliminated in order to provide impedance matching and thus making the line smooth. Now if a stub having input susceptance $\mp B$ is connected across the points A-A' on the main transmission line, then the total input admittance $\mathbf{Y}_d$ at the points A-A' becomes,

$$\mathbf{Y}_d = \frac{1}{R_0} \pm jB \mp jB = \frac{1}{R_0} \qquad ...(20.93)$$

Thus the transmission line has at points A-A' input impedance of R_0 when looking towards the load. Hence it may be said that line has been terminated at A-A' by an impedance equal to R_0 and the rest of the line towards the sending end becomes smooth. However, reflections and standing waves are present on the section of the line of length y_1 extending from A-A' to the receiving end. But this is not very serious because the length y_1 can be made very small by selecting the first voltage minimum from the load end.

In the above method, it is necessary to determine y_1 and the length L of the stub. Hence two measurements must be made on the original line with the given load. The quantities which can be easily measured on a line are standing wave ratio S and the position of voltage minimum from the load end. Now the location of the stub can be fixed with reference to this original voltage minimum by placing the stub at a distance d as shown in Fig. 20.10 and the actual value of load impedance $\mathbf{Z}_R$ is not needed.

The input admittance $\mathbf{Y}_{in}$ at any point of the line at a distance y from the load end can be written by use of Eq. (20.57) as follows,

$$\mathbf{Y}_{in} = \frac{1}{R_0}\left[\frac{1-|K|\angle\phi-2\beta y}{1+|K|\angle\phi-2\beta y}\right] \qquad ...(20.94)$$

The expression has been selected here since it does not involve $\mathbf{Z}_R$. Expressing $1/R_0$ as conductance G_0 and changing the polar form of Eq. (20.49) into rectangular co-ordinates form, we get

$$\mathbf{Y}_{in} = G_0\left[\frac{1-|K|\cos(\phi-2\beta y)-j|K|\sin(\phi-2\beta y)}{1+|K|\cos(\phi-2\beta y)+j|K|\sin(\phi-2\beta y)}\right]$$

on rationalisation, we get

$$\mathbf{Y}_{in} = G_0 \left[\frac{1 - |K|^2 - j2|K|\sin(\phi - 2\beta y)}{1 - |K|^2 + j2|K|\cos(\phi - 2\beta y)} \right] \quad ...(20.95)$$

The input shunt conductance and the shunt susceptance normalized with respect to G_0 can be written as,

$$\frac{\mathbf{Y}_{in}}{G_0} = \frac{G_{in}}{G_0} + \frac{jB_{in}}{G} = g_{in} + j\,b_{in}$$

where g_{in} and b_{in} now become dimensionless quantities. From Eq. (20.95) these can be written as,

$$g_{in} = \frac{G_{in}}{G_0} = \left[\frac{1 - |K|^2}{1 + |K|^2 + 2|K|\cos(\phi - 2\beta y)} \right] \quad ...(20.96)$$

$$b_{in} = \frac{B_{in}}{G_0} = \left[\frac{|K|\sin(\phi - 2\beta y)}{1 - |K|^2 + 2|K|\cos(\phi - 2\beta y)} \right] \quad ...(20.97)$$

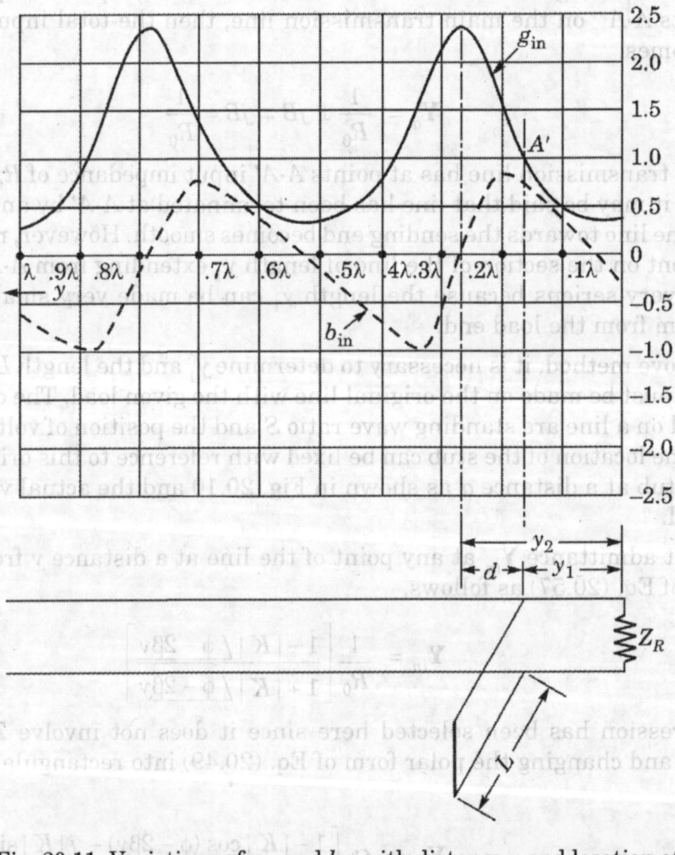

Fig. 20.11. Variations of g_{in} and b_{in} with distance y and location of a short circuited stub for $|K| = 0.4$ and $\phi = 0°$.

For a given value of $\mathbf{Z}_R$, the magnitude of $\mathbf{K}$ is fixed. Hence g_{in} and b_{in} vary with distance y as shown in Fig. 20.11 for arbitrary values of $|K|$ equal to 0.4 and $\phi = 20°$. It may be seen from these curves that the curves repeat themselves every half wavelength. On changing the value of terminating impedance $\mathbf{Z}_R$, the magnitude $|K|$ and angle ϕ of reflection coefficient $\mathbf{K}$ change. Accordingly the maximum and minimum values of g_{in} and b_{in} change and so also the position of their occurrences. However, the nature of the curves giving variation of g_{in} and b_{in} with distance y remain essentially unaltered.

The value of g_{in} in seen to have a maximum whose magnitude and position can be calculated from Eq. (20.96). The g_{in} will be maximum when the denominator becomes minimum, *i.e.*, when the cosine function becomes – 1.

Hence $$\phi - 2\beta y_2 = -\pi$$

or $$\frac{4\pi}{\lambda} y_2 = \phi + \pi$$

or $$y_2 = \left(\frac{\phi + \pi}{4\pi}\right)\lambda \qquad \text{...(20.98)}$$

Using this value of y_2 in Eq. (20.96), we get

$$g_{in(max)} = \frac{G_{in(max)}}{G_0} = \frac{1 - |K|^2}{1 + |K|^2 - 2|K|}$$

$$= \frac{1 + |K|}{1 - |K|} = S \qquad \text{...(20.99)}$$

But $$G_{in(max)} = \frac{1}{R_{in(min)}}$$

Hence Eq. (20.99) shows that

$$R_{in(min)} = \frac{R_0}{S}$$

and hence the point of $g_{in(max)}$ is a voltage minimum point at a distance y_2 from the load end.

Eq. (20.97) shows that b_{in} will be zero at the point of $g_{in(max)}$ which means that the input impedance at the point of voltage minimum is purely resistive. But this is not of great significance here. The voltage minimum point has the importance that the position of matching stub is usually determined with respect to this point. Since the purpose of stub is to eliminate the reactance of the line impedance by resonance, the stub should be placed at a point where the input impedance of the line has its real part equal to R_0 of the line. This location of the stub is obtained by the intersection of the g_{in} curves with a horizontal line drawn from unity as shown in Fig. 20.11. Hence at the point A, $g_{in} = 1$ or $G_{in} = G_0$ and the stub should be connected across the line at this point at a distance y_1 from the load end as shown in Fig. 20.11.

Puttingg$_{in}$ = 1 in Eq. (20.96), we get

$$1 = \frac{1 - |K|^2}{1 + |K|^2 + 2|K|\cos(\phi - 2\beta y_1)}$$

From this equation, we get

$$\cos\left(\phi - \frac{4\pi}{\lambda} y_1\right) = |K| \qquad \text{...(20.100)}$$

or $$\phi - \frac{4\pi}{\lambda} y_1 = -\pi + \cos^{-1}(|K|)$$

Hence $$y_1 = \left(\frac{\phi + \pi - \cos^{-1}|K|}{\pi} \right) \frac{\lambda}{4} \quad ...(20.101)$$

Form Eqs. (20.98) and (20.100), the distance d from the voltage minimum point is given as,

$$d = y_2 - y_1 = \frac{\cos^{-1}|K|}{\pi} \frac{\lambda}{4} = \frac{\cos^{-1}\left(\frac{S-1}{S+1}\right)}{\pi} \cdot \frac{\lambda}{4} \quad ...(20.102)$$

The value of d can be calculated from this.

In Fig. 20.11, there is another point B distant d from first voltage minimum and at this point also the matching stub may alternatively be connected. But ordinarily the stub is placed on the load side of the voltage minimum since the length of the line containing standing waves is then small.

Next it is required to determine the length L of the stub which will provide matching stub connected at point A. This can be obtained by calculating the input susceptance of the line at point A using Eqs. (20.97) and (20.100).

From Eq. (20.100),

$$\cos(\phi - 2\beta y_1) = -|K| \quad \text{or} \quad \cos\theta = -|K|$$

where $$\theta = (\phi - 2\beta y_1)$$

Then $$\cos(\pi + \theta) = |K|$$

and $$\sin(\pi + \theta) = -\sin\theta = \sqrt{1 - |K|^2}$$

or $$\sin(\phi + 2\beta y_1) = -\sqrt{1 - |K|^2}$$

Substituting these values in Eq. (20.97), we get

$$b_{in} = \frac{B_{in}}{G_0} \left[\frac{2|K|\sqrt{1-|K|^2}}{1-|K|^2} \right]$$

or $$B_{in} = G_0 \left(\frac{2|K|}{\sqrt{1-|K|^2}} \right) \quad ...(20.103)$$

Thus value of B_n is positive as shown in Fig. 20.11. A similar value of B_{in} with negative sign is obtained at point B by considering $\cos(\pi - \theta) = |K| = \cos(\pi - \phi + 2\beta y)$. To neutralize the positive susceptance of the line, a negative susceptance is required. This is provided by a short circuited stub.

Thus $$\frac{1}{\mathbf{Z}_{sc}} = \frac{1}{jR_0 \tan\beta L}$$

or $$\mathbf{Y}_{sc} = -JG_0 \cot\beta L$$

or $$B_{sc} = -C_0 \cot\beta L \quad ...(10.104)$$

Such a stub should have the same value of R_0 and β as the main line. This can be obtained easily by having construction of the stub similar to the main line. The magnitudes of susceptances given by Eqs. (20.103) and (20.104) must be the same. Thus

$$\cot\beta L = \frac{2|K|}{\sqrt{1-|K|^2}}$$

or
$$\tan\left(\frac{2\pi}{\lambda}l\right) = \frac{\sqrt{1-|K|^2}}{2|K|}$$

or
$$L = \frac{\lambda}{2\pi}\tan^{-1}\left(\frac{\sqrt{1-|K|^2}}{2|K|}\right) \quad ...(20.105)$$

But
$$|K| = \frac{S-1}{S+1} \text{ so that } 1-|K|^2 = \frac{4S}{(S+1)^2}$$

Hence
$$L = \frac{\lambda}{2\pi}\tan\left(\frac{\sqrt{S}}{S-1}\right) \quad ...(20.106)$$

With this length of the short-circuited stub connected across the line at a distance d towards the load measured from the first voltage minimum point existing before insertion of the stub, the susceptance of the main line at A gets cancelled and the line appears to be terminated in R_0 at this point. The section of the line extending from the generator to point A then becomes smooth.

If the stub is connected at point B, the susceptance of the line is negative. Hence an open circuited stub is required. Alternatively a short circuited stub of length L' is required, where L' is given by,

$$L' = \frac{\lambda}{2} - L \quad ...(20.107)$$

Since cot $(\pi - \theta) = -\cot\theta$, Eq. (20.104) gives,

$$B_{sc} = -G_0\cot\beta L' = -G_0\cot\beta\left(\frac{\lambda}{2}-L\right) = -G_0\cot(\pi-\beta L)$$
$$= G_0\cot\beta L \quad ...(20.108)$$

Eq. (20.108) shows that magnitude of susceptance of the short circuited stub of length $\left(\frac{\lambda}{2}-L\right)$ is the same as that of a short circuited stub of length L. However, the two susceptances have opposite signs. This is necessary in order that this susceptance B_{sc} may cancel the susceptance of the main line at point B.

Usually a short circuited stub is preferred to an open circuited stub for the following reasons :

(*i*) It is easy to provide short circuit or zero resistance across any pair of terminals by simply connecting a large plate of conducting material, whereas it is difficult to keep perfect open circuit condition requiring very high insulation resistance across the stub terminals. This becomes more difficult at high frequencies involved in stub matching.

(*ii*) The short circuited stub has lower loss of energy due to radian because a large metal plate can always be used at the shorted end disallowing any radiation of energy. This is particularly true for a coaxial line which can be completely sealed for all radiations by the short circuiting plate.

(*iii*) The same stub can be used for matching at different frequencies or for different loads by varying the length of stub by means of a sliding short-circuiting bar.

Example 20.11. *A transmission line of length 2λ/9 is terminated as shown in the following figure. If the line has R_0 = 100 ohms calculate the length L of the open-circuited stub required to make the input impedance at points A-A′ purely resistive.*

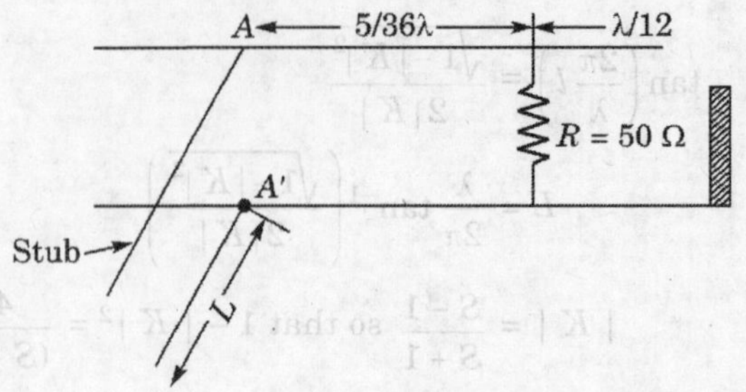

Solution. The section of the line having electrical length equal to $\frac{\lambda}{12} \times \frac{360°}{\lambda} = 30°$ is short circuited at the far end. Hence this section will offer a pure reactance across the resistance R. This reactance is given by,

$$\mathbf{Z}_{sc} = jR_0 \tan \beta l = j100 \tan 30° = j57.74$$

Susceptance $\quad B_{sc} = -\frac{1}{57.74} = -0.0173$

Admittance $\quad G_R = \frac{1}{50} = 0.02 \text{ S}$

The parallel combination of R and $\mathbf{Z}_{sc}$ may be considered as the terminated load impedance Z_R. Then

$$\frac{1}{\mathbf{Z}_R} = \mathbf{Y}_R = 0.02 - j0.0173$$

Hence the input impedance is

$$\mathbf{Z}_{in} = R_0 \left[\frac{1 + j\frac{R_0}{\mathbf{Z}_R} \tan \beta l}{\frac{R_0}{\mathbf{Z}_R} + j \tan \beta l} \right] = 100 \left[\frac{1 + j(2 - j1.73) \tan 50°}{2 - j1.73 + j \tan 50°} \right]$$

$$= 100 \left[\frac{3.065 + j2.3826}{2 - j0.5382} \right] = 187.8 \angle 22.8° = 173 + j72.7$$

Hence $\quad \mathbf{Y}_{in} = \frac{1}{187.8 \angle 22.8°} = 5.33 \times 10^{-3} \angle 22.8°$

$$= 4.91 \times 10^{-3} - j2.063 \times 10^{-3}$$

The susceptance -2.063×10^3 is required to be neutralised by the positive susceptance of an open circuited stub of length say θ electrical degrees. Then this neutralizing susceptance is given by,

$$B_{oc} = \frac{1}{-jR_0 \cot \theta} = j\frac{1}{R_0} \tan \theta$$

Hence $\quad 2.06 \times 10^{-3} = \frac{\tan \theta}{100}$

Hence $\quad \tan \theta = 0.2063$

or $\quad \theta = 11.9°$

This gives the electrical length of the stub.

Example 20.12. *A lossless line having R_0 = 300 ohms is terminated by a load resistance of 78 W. The frequency of operations is 40 MHz. What type of single stub will be required to provide an impedance when placed nearest to the load ? Calculate its length and find its location.*

Solution. The reflection coefficient is given by,

$$\mathbf{K} = \frac{\mathbf{Z}_R - R_0}{\mathbf{Z}_R - R_0} = \frac{78 - 300}{78 + 300} = -0.587$$

Hence $\quad | K | = 0.587$ and ϕ = it radians.

The first voltage minimum occurs at $y_2 = \lambda/2$ where

$$\lambda = \frac{300}{40} = 7.5 \text{ metres.}$$

The location of the stub nearest to the load is given by,

$$d = \frac{\cos^{-1} | K |}{\pi} \cdot \frac{\lambda}{4} = \frac{\cos^{-1}(0.587)}{\pi} \times \frac{7.5}{4} = 0.563 \text{ metre.}$$

Hence the stub is located at a distance y_1 = 3.75 – 0.563 = 3.187 metres from the load.

The susceptance of the line at the location of the stub will be positive. Hence a short circuited stub will be needed to provide the impedance match.

The length of this short-circuited stub is given by,

$$L = \frac{\lambda}{2\pi} \tan^{-1}\left(\frac{\sqrt{1 - | K |^2}}{2 | K |}\right) = \frac{7.5}{2\pi} \tan^{-1}\left(\frac{\sqrt{1 - [0.587]}}{2 \times 0.587}\right)$$

$$= \frac{7.5}{2\pi} = \tan^{-1} 0.689 = 0.72 \text{ metre.}$$

20.14. The Circle Diagram for Lossless Line

The phasor diagram shown in Fig. 20.5 is important since it gives variation in the input impedance of a line with its length for a given value of **K**. Similar circle diagrams can be drawn for different values of **K** and then the impedance may be calculated. These calculations can be simplified if the circle diagram is made more general. Consider the equation for the input impedance of a lossless line, normalised with respect to R_0 of the line as,

$$\frac{\mathbf{Z}_{in}}{R_0} = \frac{1 + | K | \underline{/\phi - 2\beta y}}{1 - | K | \underline{/\phi - 2\beta y}} = r_{in} + jx_{in} \qquad \text{...(20.109)}$$

This equation is applicable to all lossless lines regardless of their characteristic impedance values. Since the input impedance is in general, complex, it may be shown having a real part r_{in} and an imaginary part x_{in}, both being normalised.

Eq. (20.109) may be written in terms of standing wave ratio as,

$$r_{in} - 1 + jx_{in} = (r_{in} + 1 + jx_{in}) \left(\frac{S - 1}{S + 1}\right) \underline{/\phi - 2\beta y} \qquad \text{...(20.110)}$$

Finding square of the quantities in Eq. (20.110), we get

$$(r_{in} - 1)^2 + x_{in}{}^2 = [(r_{in} + 1)^2 + (x_{in})^2] \left(\frac{S - 1}{S + 1}\right)^2$$

This equation on being rearranged yields,

$$r_{in}{}^2 - r_{in}\frac{S^2+1}{S} + x_{in}{}^2 = -1$$

By adding the quantity $\left(\frac{S^2+1}{2S}\right)^2$ on both sides and completing the squares, we get

$$r_{in}{}^2 - 2r_{in}\left(\frac{S^2+1}{2S}\right) + \left(\frac{S^2+1}{2S}\right)^2 + x_{in}{}^2 = \left(\frac{S^2+1}{2S}\right)^2 - 1$$

or

$$\left(r_{in} - \frac{S^2+1}{2S}\right) + x_{in}{}^2 = \left(\frac{S^2-1}{2S}\right)^2 \qquad ...(20.111)$$

Eq. (20.111) is of the form,

$$(x-c)^2 + y = r^2$$

which represents a circle of radius r and with its centre displaced from origin along the positive x-axis by c. Thus Eq. (20.111) represents a family of circle each circle for a different value of standing wave ratio S and with radius of circles given by,

$$r = \frac{S^2-1}{2S} = \frac{S - \frac{1}{S}}{2} \qquad ...(20.112)$$

The centre of the circle is shifted along the positive real axes by an amount,

$$c = \frac{S^2+1}{2S} = \frac{S + \frac{1}{S}}{2} \qquad ...(20.113)$$

The family of the circles for different values of S is drawn in Fig. 20.12 plotting r_{in} along the x-axis and x_{in} along the y-axis. With $S = 1$, the circle is of radius zero and with $c = 1$, *i.e.* with centre at (1, 0). Hence Eq. (20.111) when solved for $S = 1$ given $x_{in} = 0$ and $r_{in} = 1$ showing that the line is properly terminated in R_0 and is, therefore, a smooth line. As the value of S increases, the radius of the constant S circle also increases and simultaneously the centre of the circle moves away more and more along the x-axis or r_{in}-axis as shown in Fig. 20.12.

The limiting or maximum value of S is infinity corresponding to an open circuit or short circuit termination. When $S = \infty$, Eqs. (20.112) and (20.113) show that the constant-S circle has infinite radius with its centre situated at infinity. Hence the y-axis corresponding to x_{in} be-comes the constant-S circle for $S = \infty$, showing that the input impedance of an open or short circuited line is purely reactive. Thus a given constant-S circle represents all values of r_{in} and x_{in} for a given value of $\frac{\mathbf{Z_R}}{R_0}$. A line drawn from the origin to a given point on the circle of given value of S represents $\frac{\mathbf{Z}_{in}}{R_0}$ in magnitude and phase angle. The resistive and the reactive components are then given by the projection of $\frac{\mathbf{Z}_{in}}{R_0}$ vector on x and y-axis giving the values of r_{in} and x_{in} components.

When $\mathbf{Z}_{in}/R_0$ vector lies on the r_{in} axis with magnitude S, the line input impedance has maximum value given as,

$$\frac{\mathbf{Z}_{in}}{R_0} = S = \frac{1+|K|}{1-|K|} \qquad ...(20.114)$$

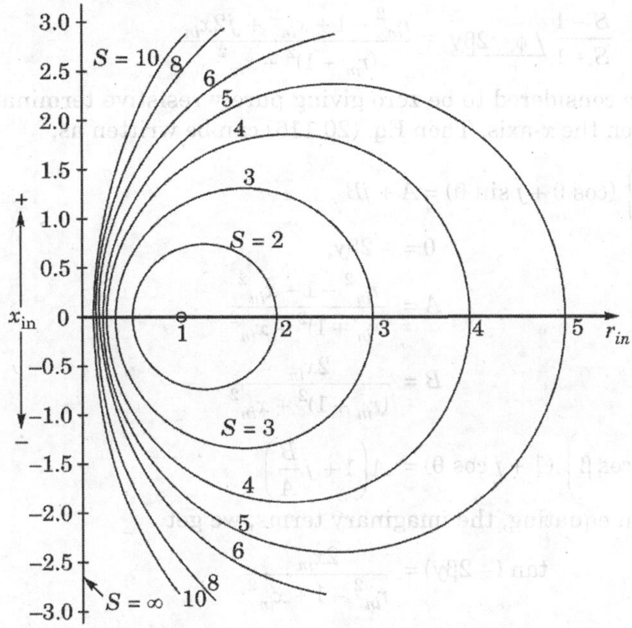

Fig. 20.12. Family of contant-S circles.

Comparing Eq. (20.114) with Eq. (20.109) we find that Eq. (20.114) is true only when,

$$\phi - 2\beta y = 0.$$

Hence the point corresponding to $r_{in} = S$, $x_{in} = 0$ on the family of circles, represents maximum input resistance at a point of voltage maximum on the line. By convention this point is chosen as the starting point with $\beta y = 0$.

When $\mathbf{Z}_{in}/R_0$ vector lies on the r_{in}-axis with magnitude $1/S$, the line input impedance has minimum value given by,

$$\frac{\mathbf{Z}_{in}}{R_0} = \frac{1}{S} = \frac{1-|K|}{1+|K|} \qquad ...(20.115)$$

Eq. (20.115) can be obtained from Eq. (20.109) by making

$$\phi - \beta y = +\pi.$$

If terminating impedance is considered purely resistive (*i.e.* f = 0), the condition for minimum resistive impedance of the line becomes,

$$\beta y = -\frac{\pi}{2}.$$

Thus travelling back along the line through a $\pi/2$ electrical radians (or $\lambda/4$ distance), the impedance vector rotates through an angle of $-\pi$ radians on the circle diagram. Thus a βy scale is also required to be placed on the circle diagram in order that the input impedance of the line at any point may be obtained. The βy scale *increases clockwise* in order to make βy a negative angle. The βy scale can be obtained by considering Eq. (20.110) once again. Thus,

$$\frac{S-1}{S+1} \underline{/\phi - 2\beta y} = \frac{r_{in} - 1 + jx_{in}}{r_{in} + 1 + jx_{in}}$$

On rationalizing the right hand side of this equation, we get

$$\frac{S-1}{S+1}\,\underline{/\,\phi - 2\beta y} = \frac{r_{in}^{\,2} - 1 + x_{in}^{\,2} + j2x_{in}}{(r_{in}+1)^2 + x_{in}^{\,2}} \qquad ...(20.116)$$

Angle ϕ may be considered to be zero giving purely resistive termination of line so that βy scale may start at 0° on the x-axis. Then Eq. (20.116) can be written as,

$$\left(\frac{S-1}{S+1}\right)(\cos\theta + j\sin\theta) = A + jB$$

where

$$\theta = -\,2\beta y,$$

$$A = \frac{r_{in}^{\,2} - 1 + x_{in}^{\,2}}{(r_{in}+1)^2 + x_{in}^{\,2}}$$

$$B = \frac{2x_{in}}{(r_{in}+1)^2 + x_{in}^{\,2}}$$

or

$$\left(\frac{S-1}{S+1}\cos\beta\right)(1 + j\cos\theta) = A\left(1 + j\frac{B}{A}\right)$$

In this equation equating, the imaginary terms, we get

$$\tan(-\,2\beta y) = \frac{2x_{in}}{r_{in}^{\,2} - 1 + x_{in}^{\,2}} \qquad ...(20.117)$$

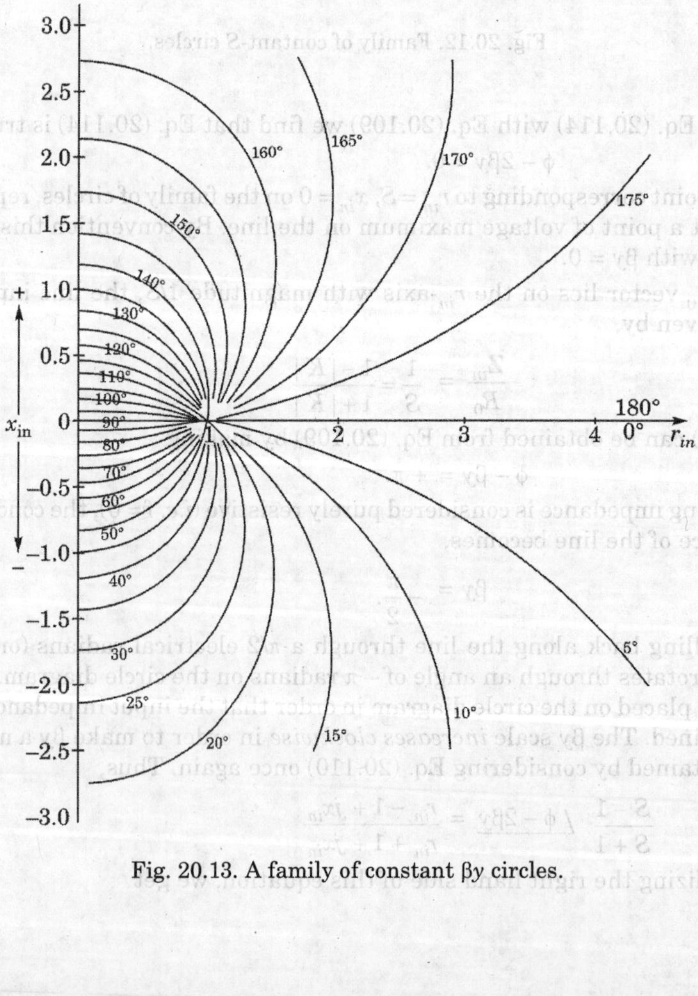

Fig. 20.13. A family of constant βy circles.

or $$r_{in}^2 - 1 + x_{in}^2 = \frac{-2x_{in}}{\tan(2\beta y)}$$

or $$r_{in}^2 - 1 + x_{in}^2 = \frac{2x_{in}}{\tan(2\beta y)} = 0$$

Completing the square by adding and subtracting $\frac{1}{\tan^2(2\beta y)}$ gives,

$$r_{in}^2 + \left[x_{in} + \frac{1}{\tan(2\beta y)}\right]^2 = 1 + \frac{1}{\tan^2(2\beta y)}$$

$$= \frac{1}{\sin^2(2\beta y)} \qquad \text{...(20.118)}$$

The curve represented by Eq. (20.118) for constant value of βy is a circle of radius,

$$r = \frac{1}{\sin(2\beta y)}$$

Its centre is displaced along the x_{in} axis (*i.e.* along the *y*-axis) by an amount,

$$c = \frac{-1}{\tan 2\beta y} \qquad \text{...(20.120)}$$

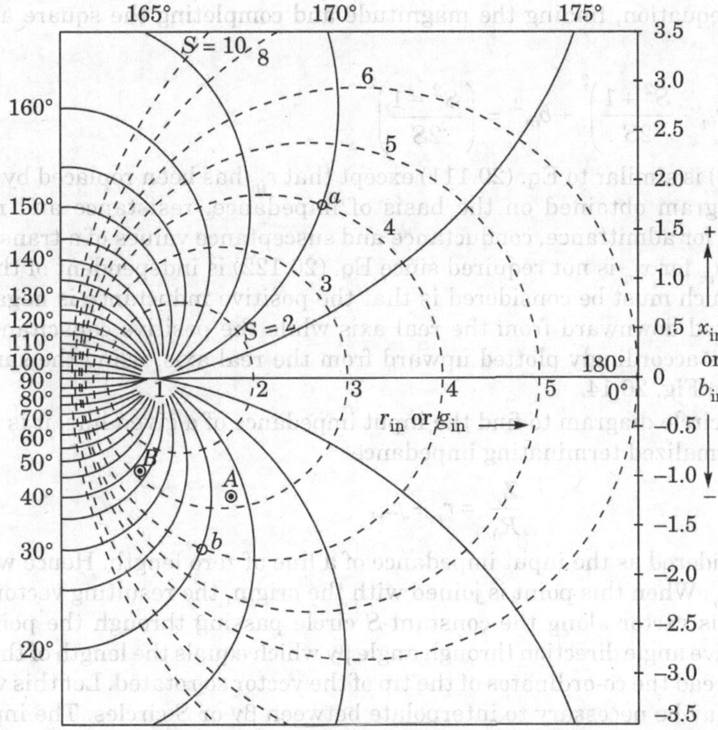

Fig. 20.14. Transmission line impedance/admittance circle diagram.

The family of curves represented by Eq. (20.118) are drawn in Fig. 20.13. It may be seen that all the circles for constant βy values pass through the point $r_{in} = 1$, $x_{in} = 0$. To complete the transmission line diagram, the diagrams of Figs. 20.12 and 20.13 are superimposed on each other using the same scale for each. Such a diagram is shown in Fig. 20.14.

Consider the input admittance of a line normalised to its R_O value written as,

$$\frac{\mathbf{Y}_{in}}{G_0} = \frac{1}{r_{in} + jx_{in}} = \frac{r_{in}}{r_{in}^2 + x_{in}^2} - j\frac{x_{in}}{r_{in}^2 + x_{in}^2} \quad ...(20.121)$$

$$= g_{in} - jb_{in}$$

Comparing Eq. (20.121) with Eq. (20.109), it may be seen that r_{in} can be replaced by g_{in} and x_{in} by $-b_{in}$ and the two equations become the same if $+ \mid K \mid$ is also replaced by $- \mid K \mid$.

$$\therefore \quad g_{in} - jb_{in} = \frac{1 - |K| \angle \phi - 2\beta y}{1 + |K| \angle \phi - 2\beta y} = \frac{1 - \left(\frac{S-1}{S+1}\right) \angle \phi - 2\beta y}{1 + \left(\frac{S-1}{S+1}\right) \angle \phi - 2\beta y}$$

or $$g_{in} - jb_{in}\left[1 + \left(\frac{S-1}{S+1}\right) \angle \phi - 2\beta y\right] = 1 - \left(\frac{S-1}{S+1}\right) \angle \phi - 2\beta y$$

or $$(g_{in} - 1 - jb_{in}) = (g_{in} + 1 - jb_{in})\left(\frac{S-1}{S+1}\right) \angle \phi - 2\beta y$$

From this equation, finding the magnitude and completing the square as in the previous case, we get

$$\left(g_{in} - \frac{S^2+1}{2S}\right)^2 + b_{in}^2 = \left(\frac{S^2-1}{2S}\right)^2 \quad ...(20.122)$$

Eq. (20.122) is similar to Eq. (20.111) except that r_{in} has been replaced by g_{in} and x_{in} by b_{in}. Thus a circle diagram obtained on the basis of impedance, resistance and reactance can be conveniently used for admittance, conductance and susceptance values of a transmission line. The substitution of $-b_{in}$ for x_{in} is not required since Eq. (20.122) is independent of the sign of b_{in}. The only difference which must be considered is that the positive inductance is negative susceptance and hence is plotted downward from the real axis while the positive capacitance forms positive susceptance and is accordingly plotted upward from the real axis, using the same scale for both values as shown in Fig. 20.14.

To use the circle diagram to find the input impedance of a given line, it is first necessary to determine the normalized terminating impedance

$$\frac{\mathbf{Z}_r}{R_0} = r_r + jx_r,$$

which can be considered as the input impedance of a line of zero length. Hence we enter the chart at the point $r_r + jx_r$. When this point is joined with the origin, the resulting vector indicates $\mathbf{Z}_R/R_0$. Now we rotate this vector along the constant-S circle passing through the point $r_r + jx_r$ in the clockwise or negative angle direction through angle βy which equals the length of the line in electrical degrees. We then read the co-ordinates of the tip of the vector so rotated. Let this vector be $r_m + jx_m$. In doing this, it may be necessary to interpolate between βy or S circles. The input impedance of the line terminated in $\mathbf{Z}_R$ is then,

$$\mathbf{Z}_{in} = R_0(r_m + jx_m) \quad ...(20.123)$$

The input admittance of a line may be similarly obtained by considering the load admittance.

An open circuited line has $S = 0$ and the corresponding S-circle is the y-axis. Hence the input impedance is always a pure reactance. This input impedance may be determined by the intersection of the y-axis with the βy circle corresponding to the length of line.

A short circuited line also has the y-axis as its S-circle. But now the intersection of βy circle with the y-axis gives the susceptance.

Example 20.13. *A transmission line has R_0 = 100 ohms and is 5.55 metres long. If λ = 10 metres and the terminating impedance $\mathbf{Z}_R$ = 175 – j118 ohms, obtain by use of circle-diagram, the input impedance at the sending end of the line, the standing wave ratio and the magnitude and angle of the reflection coefficient.*

Solution. The normalized load impedance is,

$$\frac{\mathbf{Z}_R}{R_0} = \frac{175 - j118}{100} = 1.75 - j1.18.$$

The length of the line in electrical degrees is

$$\beta y = \frac{360 y}{\lambda} = \frac{360}{10} \times 5.55 = 200°$$

Since βy circles are periodic at intervals of 180°, the length of the line may be considered to be only 200 – 180 = 20°.

We now enter the chart of Fig. 20.14 at the point A corresponding to

$$\frac{\mathbf{Z}_R}{R_0} = 1.75 - j1.18.$$

By interpolation between the circles of $S = 2$ and $S = 3$ at this point A, the value of S is found to be 2.8.

At point A, actually $\beta y = 0$ but in the chart it represents some value say $(\beta y)_r$. This can be used to determine the angle ϕ, the angle of the reflection coefficient **K**. Consider the first voltage maximum which according to Eq. (20.41) occurs at,

$$y_{max} = \frac{\phi}{2\beta}$$

so that

$$\phi = 2\beta y_{max}.$$

A voltage maximum corresponds to an impedance resistive. Hence indicated βy value is zero whereas actually it should be βy_{max}. The difference between the actual and the indicated values of βy in the two cases must be the same. Hence,

$$\beta y_{max} - 0 = 0 - (\beta y)_r$$

or

$$\phi = -2(\beta y)_y \qquad ...(1)$$

In the given problem,

$$(\beta y)_r = 17.5°$$

Hence using Eq. (1),

$$\phi = -2(\beta y)_r = -35°.$$

In order to obtain the input impedance, we travel along the $S = 2.8$ circle in the clockwise direction starting from point A upto the intersection with βy circle of value 37.5° and mark the point B as shown in Fig. 20.14. The point B may be obtained alternatively by drawing the circle for $S = 2.8$ and using Eqs. (20.112) and (20.113).

The input impedance is then,

$$\mathbf{Z}_{in} = 100(0.80 - j0.92)$$
$$= (80 - j92) \text{ ohms}.$$

The magnitude of reflection coefficient K cannot be determined from the circle diagram but can be easily calculated from the known value of S. Thus

$$K = \frac{S-1}{S+1} = \frac{2.8-1}{2.8+1} = 0.74.$$

Hence $\mathbf{K} = 0.474 \underline{/-35°}$

Example 20.14. *A transmission line has been terminated in a normalized admittance y_r = 2.75 + j1.77 which corresponds to a capaci-tive load.. If the line is of length corresponding to 30 electrical degrees, determine the normalized input admittance of the line.*

Solution. We enter the circle diagram of Fig. 20.14, at point a corresponds to

$$\mathbf{y}_r = 2.75 + j1.77.$$

The βy value at this point is 170° while the standing wave ratio $S = 4$.

Now we travel along the $S = 4$ circle in the clockwise direction starting from point a through an angle of 30 degrees and arrive at point b which is the point of intersection of $S = 4$ circle and βy = 20° curve. The normalized input admittance is then given by

$$\mathbf{y}_{in} = 1.46 - j1.75$$

This offers an inductive reactance.

Example 20.15. *The standing wave ratio on a lossless line is 2 with the first voltage minimum occurring at a distance of 70 electrical degrees from the load end. Find the normalized-value of the terminating impedance.*

Solution. The first voltage minimum corresponds to an im-pedance minimum (resistive) which must be on the real axis of the circle diagram between values 0 and 1. Hence we enter the circle diagram at the intersection of the real axis with the circle for $S = 2$. The indicated βy value here is 90°. Motion towards the load is required which is obtained by rotating or moving in anticlockwise direction through 70° to locate the intersection of $S = 2$ circle with $\beta y = 20°$ circle. This gives

$$\frac{\mathbf{Z}_r}{R_0} = 1.5 - j0.7.$$

20.15. The Smith Chart

The circle diagram discussed in Article 20.14 is also known sometimes as "bicircular impedance chart". Although it is quite useful in calculating impedances and admittances in transmission line problems, it has many disadvantages For example, the constant S and βy circles are not concentric making interpolation difficult and only a limited range of impedance values can be enclosed in a chart or reasonable size. Hence a modified chart was developed by P.H. Smith. This chart is known as *Smith Circle Diagram* or simply *Smith Chart*.

It has several advantages over the simple circle diagram and has accordingly superseded the circle diagram for use in transmission line problems.

The Smith Polar Chart is obtained by using Eq. (20.116) reproduced below,

$$\left(\frac{S-1}{S+1}\right) \underline{/\phi - 2\beta y} = |K| \underline{/\phi - 2\beta y} = \frac{r_{in}^2 - 1 + x_{in}^2 + j2x_{in}}{(r_{in}+1)^2 + x_{in}^2}$$

or $\quad |K| \underline{/\phi + 2\beta y} = U + jV \qquad$ ...(20.124)

where $$U = \frac{r_{in}^2 - 1 + x_{in}^2}{(r_{in}+1)^2 + x_{in}^2} \qquad \text{...(20.125)}$$

and $$V = \frac{2x_{in}}{(r_{in}+1)^2 + x_{in}^2} \qquad \text{...(20.126)}$$

From Eqs. (20.125) and (20.126) we eliminate x_{in} to get an equation is U, V and r_{in}. To do so, we first rearrange Eq. (20.125) to get,

$$U[(r_{in}+1)^2 + x_{in}^2] = r_{in}^2 - 1 + x_{in}^2$$

or
$$x_{in}^2 = \frac{U(r_{in}+1)^2 - r_{in}^2 + 1}{1-U} \qquad \text{...(20.127)}$$

Substituting the value of x_{in} as given by Eq. (20.127) into Eq. (20.126), we get

$$V = \frac{2\sqrt{\dfrac{U(r_{in}+1)^2 - r_{in}^2 + 1}{1-U}}}{(r_{in}+1)^2 + \dfrac{U(r_{in}+1)^2 - r_{in}^2 + 1}{1-U}}$$

or
$$V\left(\frac{r_{in}+1}{1-U}\right) = \sqrt{\frac{U(r_{in}+1)^2 - r_{in}^2 + 1}{1-U}}$$

Squaring both sides gives,

$$V^2\left(\frac{r_{in}+1}{1-U}\right) = \frac{U(r_{in}+1)^2}{1-U} - \frac{r_{in}^2 - 1}{1-U}$$

Multiplying throughout by $\left(\dfrac{1-U}{r_{in}+1}\right)^2$ gives,

$$U(1-U) - \frac{(r_{in}^2 - 1)(1-U)}{(r_{in}+1)^2} = V^2$$

or
$$U^2 - U - \frac{U(r_{in}^2 - 1)}{(r_{in}+1)^2} + \frac{r_{in}^2 - 1}{(r_{in}+1)^2} + V^2 = 0$$

or
$$U^2 - U\left[1 + \frac{r_{in}^2 - 1}{(r_{in}+1)^2}\right] + \frac{r_{in}^2}{(r_{in}+1)^2} + V^2 = \frac{1}{(r_{in}+1)^2}$$

or
$$U^2 - 2U\frac{r_{in}}{(r_{in}+1)^2} + \frac{r_{in}^2}{(r_{in}+1)^2} + V^2 = \frac{1}{(r_{in}+1)^2}$$

or
$$\left[U - \left(\frac{r_{in}}{r_{in}+1}\right)\right]^2 + V^2 = \frac{1}{(r_{in}+1)^2} \qquad \text{...(20.128)}$$

Next we eliminate r_{in} from Eqs. (20.125) and (20.126) to obtain an equation relating U, V and x_{in}. To do this, we first divide Eq. (20.125) by Eq. (20.16), to get

$$\frac{U}{V} = \frac{r_{in}^2 - 1 + x_{in}^2}{2x_{in}}$$

Hence
$$r_{in} = \frac{2U}{V}x_{in} - x_{in}^2 + 1 \qquad \text{...(20.129)}$$

Now we substitute this value of r_{in} in Eq. (20.126), to get

$$V = \frac{2x_{in}}{\dfrac{2U}{V}x_{in} - x_{in}^2 + 1 + 2\sqrt{\dfrac{2U}{V}x_{in} - x_{in}^2 + 1} + 1\, x_{in}^2}$$

or $$V\left[\frac{2U}{V}x_{in}+2+2\sqrt{\frac{2U}{V}x_{in}-x_{in}^2+1}\right]=2x_{in}$$

or $$\sqrt{\frac{2U}{V}x_{in}-x_{in}^2+1}=\frac{x_{in}}{V}-\frac{U}{V}x_{in}-1$$

Squaring both the sides gives,

$$\frac{2U}{V}x_{in}-x_{in}^2+1=\frac{x_{in}^2}{V^2}+\frac{U^2}{V^2}x_{in}^2+1-\frac{2U}{V^2}x_{in}^2-\frac{2x_{in}}{V}+\frac{2U}{V}x_{in}$$

Multiplying throughout by $\frac{V^2}{x_{in}^2}$, we get

$$U^2-2U+1+V^2-\frac{2V}{x_{in}}=0$$

or $$(U-1)^2+\left(V-\frac{1}{x_{in}}\right)^2=\frac{1}{x_{in}^2} \qquad ...(20.130)$$

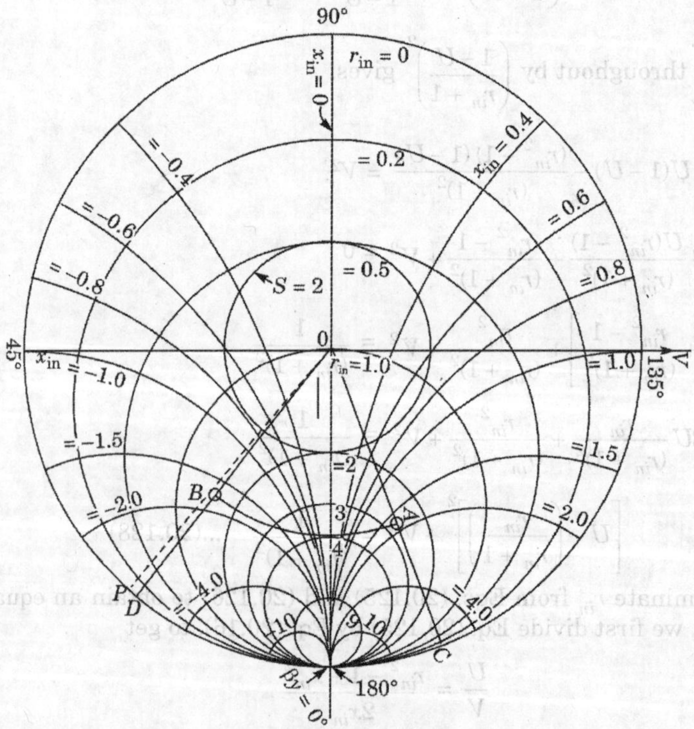

Fig. 20.15. Smith Chart.

Eq. (20.128) represents as set of circles each for a constant value of r_{in} with their centres on the U-axis at a point $\frac{r_{in}}{(r_{in}+1)}$ and with radii equal to $\frac{r_{in}}{(r_{in}+1)}$. Eq. (20.130) represents a set of constant r_{in} circles with their centres at $\left(1, \frac{1}{x_{in}}\right)$ and radii equal to $\frac{1}{x_{in}}$. These two families of circles have been drawn in Fig. 20.15. In this diagram, the new variables U and V are related with the reflection coefficient by,

$$|K| \underline{/\phi - 2\beta y} = U + jV \qquad ...(20.131)$$

The value of $|K|$ can never exceed unit. Hence maximum magnitudes of U, V and impedances are limited to unity. *All possible values of impedances are contained within this outer circle of unity radius.* Accordingly the input impedance of a lossless line for any value of terminating impedance varying from 0 to infinity can be readily obtained by use of the chart. The angle of the polar co-ordinates given by Eq. (20.131) has been shown with $\beta y = 0$ on the U-axis and increasing in the clockwise direction as in the case in the impedance circle diagram of Fig. 20.14. The angle βy then corresponds to the length of line in electrical degrees. In commercially available Smith Chart, the βy angles are also indicated in terms of wavelength, the complete unit circle representing $\lambda/2$ length of line and divided into as many parts as possible. The line length increases in clockwise direction for motion towards the generator and in anti-clockwise direction for motion towards the load.

At the centre of the unit circle represented by 0 in Fig. 20.15, the value of resistance component is unity indicating termination of line by R_0, the value at extreme left of U-axis is zero indicating a short circuit and the value at the extreme right is infinity indicating an open circuit at the load end. Any distance measured radially from the centre 0 ($r_{in} = 1$, $x_{in} = 0$) is proportional to the magnitude of K or S so that constant-S circle can be drawn on the chart at the time of calculations without complicating the chart itself, the centre 0 representing $S = 1$ circle while the outer unit circle representing $S = \infty$. The impedance of a line may be read at any point on the constant-S circle.

This Smith Chart may also be used for admittances by simply changing r_{in} and x_{in} axes by g_{in} and b_{in} with the usual consideration that capacitive susceptance is positive and hence placed above the U-axis or the x-axis while inductive susceptance is negative and hence placed below the U-axis. The point on the extreme left of g_{in}-axis then represents zero conductance or an open circuit and the point on the extreme right of g_{in}-axis represents infinite conductance or a short circuit. Commercially available Smith Chart contains a very large number of circles so that values may be obtained very accurately. However still the accuracy of calculations is limited because of interpolation which may be required in many cases. The amount of accuracy obtainable from Smith Chart is sufficient for design and analysis purposes.

20.16. Solution of Problems by Smith Chart

Example 20.14 may be solved by Smith Chart, the procedure being similarly to that used in impedance circle diagram. The load admittance is given as $\mathbf{y}_r = 2.75 + j1.77$. To enter the chart at this point, a constant conductance circle corresponding to the value 2.75 is re-quired to be drawn. Alternatively the value of 2.75 may be interpolated between the circle of 2.7 and 2.8 values. The intersection of this circle with that of constant susceptance circle for 1.77 obtained by interpolation is the point representing y_r and is shown as point A in Fig. 20.15.

We then draw the line OA joining the origin O with point A and extend it to the unit circle at point C. With O as centre and radius equal to OA, we draw a constant-S circle. The intersection of this circle with the real axis gives the value of standing wave ratio which in this case is recorded as 4.

We now move along the unit circle from point C in clockwise direction, (representing movement towards the generator) by an amount equal to 30 electrical degrees which is equivalent to 60° in space and arrive at point D. We then join point D to the centre O intersecting the constant S-circle at point B. Co-ordinates of point B namely $1.5 - j1.7$ give the input admittance.

Example 20.15 can also be solved by Smith Chart. We first draw a circle for $S = 2$. At a voltage minimum, the line has minimum resistive impedance. This point, therefore, is on the left hand side of the origin on the real axis. Hence on the unit circle we rotate from the real axis in anticlockwise direction (*i.e.* towards load) by an amount equal to electrical degrees and mark the point D on the unit circle. Intersection of line OD with the circle of $S = 2$ gives normalized terminating impedance as $Z_r = 1.5 - j0.7$. Having determined $\mathbf{Z}_r$, we may find the input impedance for any length of line. For example, if the line is 115° electrical degrees long, *i.e.* 0.3195 λ long, the input impedance is obtained by rotating in clockwise direction from point D to the point marked 135°. Intersection of this axis with the circle of $S = 2$ gives the input impedance of the line as

$$Z_{in} = 0.8 + j\,0.59.$$

The magnitude of K is calculated from the relation

$$|\,K\,| = \frac{S-1}{S+1}.$$

Thus for $S = 2$, $|\,K\,| = 1/3$. The angle of K is twice the angle of point D. Then $\phi = -40°$. Hence the unit circle is divided in actual angles starting from $\beta y = 0$ point to $-180°$ in clockwise direction and from $\beta y = 0$ to 180° in anti-clockwise direction. Thus ϕ may read directly.

An open circuited line has $\mathbf{K} = 1\underline{/0°}$ or $S = \infty$ which corresponds to the unit circle of the chart representing $r_{in} = 0$ for all lengths of line. Thus the input impedance of an open circuited line is purely reactive, the value of reactance depending on the length of the line.

A short circuited line also has $S = \infty$ which corresponding to the unit circle of the Smith Chart. The short circuited line may, therefore, be considered in terms of admittance. The input conductance $g_{in} = 0$ for all lengths of line while the value of input susceptance may be determined by the length of the line, *i.e.* βy angle around the chart.

20.17. Single Stub Matching by Smith Chart

The problem on impedance matching by short circuited or open circuited stubs can also be solved by using Smith Chart. Since the matching stubs are usually connected in parallel with the main transmission line at selected points, the problem will be solved by considering admittances.

Considering Example 20.12 in which the normalized load admittance is given as 3.85, we draw the constant-S circle with C as the centre and radius equal to 3.85 as shown in Fig. 20.16. The $S = 3.85$ circle intersects the maximum conductance so that $Y/G° = S$. Hence the same point gives the voltage minimum point. The terminating impedance being resistive, the receiving end point is also on the real axis. Hence the first voltage minimum occurs at λ/2 from the load end.

Now we draw the circle representing $g_{in} = 1$ and hence passing through the centre C. The stub has to be connected at a point where the conductance of the line is unity. Hence we follow $S =$ 3.85 circle from the real axis (voltage minimum point) towards load in anticlockwise direction upto the point B, the point of intersection of $S = 3.85$ and $g_{in} = 1$ circle. We then extend the CB upto the unit circle which gives the distance of stub from the voltage minimum point as 0.075λ. Hence the stub should be connected at a distance of (0.5 – 0.075)λ = 0.425 × 7.5 metre = 3.187 metres from the load end since λ = 7.5 metres.

At the point B, susceptance of the line is + 1.45 which should be cancelled by a susceptance of $b_{in} = -1.45$ offered by the short-circuited stub.

A short circuited line has $S = \infty$. Hence the intersection of $b_{in} = -1.45$ curve with the outermost unit circle gives the length of the stub represented by the angle measured in counter-clockwise direction (towards the load) from this point of intersection to the right end of the real axis, *i.e.* infinite admittance point. This is 70°. Hence the length of the short circuited stub is

$$\frac{35}{360}\lambda = 0.096\lambda = 0.096 \times 7.5 = 0.72 \text{ metre}$$

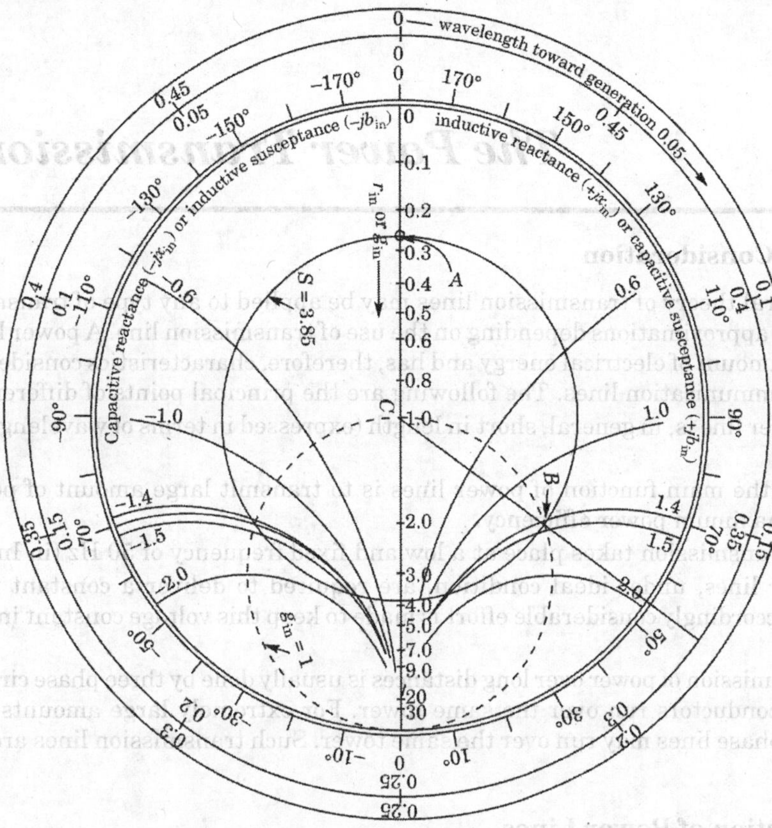

Fig. 20.16. Stub matching using Smith Chart.

An open circuited stub can also be used in which case the length should be measured from the left end of the real axis in anticlockwise direction giving the required length as 0.154λ.

21

The Power Transmission Lines

21.1. General Consideration

The general theory of transmission lines may be applied to any type of transmission line on making suitable approximations depending on the use of transmission line. A power line is required to carry a large amount of electrical energy and has, therefore, characteristics considerably different from those of communication lines. The following are the principal points of difference :

(*i*) A power line is, in general, short in length (expressed in terms of wavelength), not exceed $\lambda/10$ typically.

(*ii*) Since the main function of power lines is to transmit large amount of power, they are designed for a maximum power efficiency.

(*iii*) The transmission takes place at a low and fixed frequency of 50 Hz (in India).

(*iv*) Power lines, under ideal condition, are required to deliver a constant voltage at the receiving end. Accordingly considerable effort is made to keep this voltage constant inspite of widely varying loads.

The transmission of power over long distances is usually done by three phase circuits requiring three separate conductors run over the same tower. For extremely large amounts of power, two separate three-phase lines may run over the same tower. Such transmission lines are called *double circuit lines.*

21.2. Construction of Power Lines

Power distribution lines are usually single phase two-wire lines in which the expressions developed for general transmission line will apply. In three-phase lines, on the other hand, a fourth conductor known as the neutral is used for return path of current. Under normal balanced condition of transmission, the current in the neutral wire is zero. Hence the line parameters namely *R, L, C* and *G* are based on single wire values. For example, the loop resistance of the line will be the resistance of a single wire of the three-phase line, the shunt conductance of the loop is the conductance of one wire to neutral and the capacitance will also be that between one wire of the circuit and the neutral.

A power line conductor is required to be of large cross-sectional area in order to carry the desired high power without getting excessively heated. For providing flexibility, each conductor is made of a number of strands of wire. Fig. 21.1 (*a*) shows the section of a three strand conductor while Fig 21.1 (*b*) shows the cross-section of a seven strand conductor with one central strand surrounded by six strands. The entire cable is twisted along its length in order to provide good mechanical strength. For still greater cross-sectional area of the cable of Fig. 21.1 (*b*), another oppositely spiraled layer of 12 strands may be used. This forms a 19-strand cable. Next layer requires strands to fill the angular space. Each successive layer requires strands increasing in number by six. Thus we may have cables of 3, 7, 19, 37, 61, 91, etc. strands.

The calculation of parameters of such cables is done with the help of an equivalent radius known as *Geometric Mean Radius* (GMR) which depends upon the number of strands and the physical radius of the cable. The value of GMR is 1.6 *r* for 3-strand cable and 2.18 *r* for 7-strand cable, where *r* is the radius of each strand. Standard tables provide values of GMR for various stranded cables.

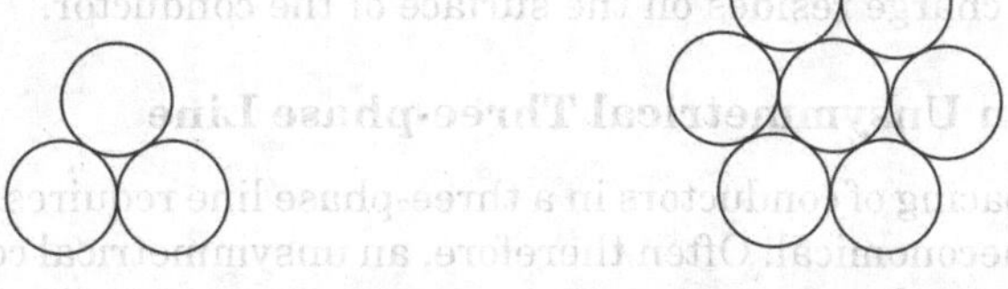

(*a*) Three strands, each of radius *r*. (*b*) Seven strands, each of radius *r*.

Fig. 21.1. Three and seven strand conductors.

Often the central strand of the cable is made of steel for providing mechanical strength. Sometimes first layer strands or even second layer strands are made of steel. The remaining layer strands are made of aluminium instead of copper, from the consideration of cost and good electrical conductivity at low frequencies. Such cables are known as *Aluminium Cable Steel Reinforced* (ACSR). In ACSR cable, almost the complete current flows through the aluminium strands since the electrical conductivity of steel is very poor as compared to aluminium. The GMR value may then be calculated by considering the aluminium strands only and neglecting the steel strands. However, accurate values of GMR, considering the steel strands also, are provided by the manufacturers.

21.3. Parameters of Symmetrical Three-Phase Line

The simplest form of a three-phase power line is one in which the three conductors are placed at the apex of an equilateral triangle with centre-to-centre spacing of d, as shown in Fig. 21.2. Let the currents through the conductors a, b and c be I_a, I_b and I_c respectively. Then $I_b + I_c = -I_a$, in a balanced three-phase system. Thus the current through conductor a may be considered as the return current for conductors b and c.

The inductance of conductor a per unit length is then given by

$$L_a = 2 \times 10^{-7} \ln \frac{b}{r_m} \text{ Henry/m} \qquad ...(21.1)$$

where r_m is the GMR value of the conductor a.

The reactance $\omega l L_a$ of line of length l metres on being multiplied with the current I_c through the conductor a gives the series voltage drop in the conductor. This voltage drop on being subtracted from phase-to-neutral voltage at the sending end yields the phase-to-neutral voltage at the receiving end. The other two cables have the same value of L_a provided that they are similarly built.

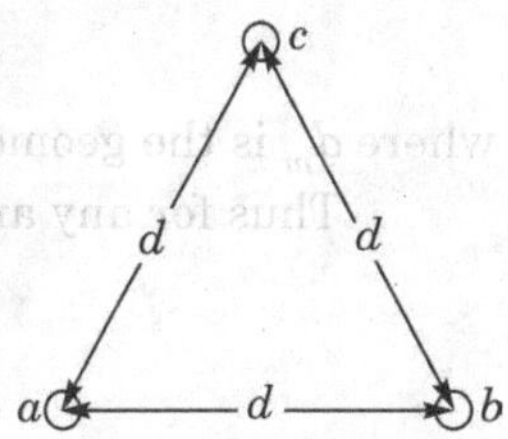

Fig. 21.2. Equilaterally spaced three-phase line.

The capacitance C_{aN} of wire a to neutral may be found by first considering wires b and c as one plate of a capacitor with wire a as the other plate. This assumption is true since under normal working condition of a three-phase line, the total charge on conductors b and c taken together is equal and opposite to that on conductor a. Let this capacitance be C_{abc}. Then C_{aN} is twice of C_{abc}, *i.e.* twice the capacitance of a parallel wire line with separation d and radius of wire same as that of conductor a. Accordingly C_{aN} is given by,

$$C_{aN} = \frac{2\pi\varepsilon}{\ln \dfrac{d}{r_c}} \text{ Farad/metre} \qquad ...(21.2)$$

where r_c is the physical radius of the conductors.

Substituting the value of ε for free space in Eq. (21.2), we get

$$C_{aN} = \frac{1}{18 \times 10^9 \ln \dfrac{d}{r_e}} \text{ Farad/metre} \qquad ...(21.3)$$

It may be noted that the physical radius r_c rather than GMR r_m is used in Eqs. (21.2) and (21.3) since electrostatic charge resides on the surface of the conductor.

21.4. Parameters of an Unsymmetrical Three-phase Line

The equilateral spacing of conductors in a three-phase line requires careful design of towers. This at times becomes uneconomical. Often therefore, an unsymmetrical conductor arrangement is used. Fig. 21.3 shows two such arrangements.

The inductance of any phase wire is obtained by considering the *geometric mean distance* (GMD) among the three conductors. This GMD in this case equals $(d_{ab} \cdot d_{bc} \cdot d_{ac})^{1/3}$. The inductance of wire a is then given by,

$$L_a = 2 \times 10^{-7} \ln \frac{\sqrt[3]{d_{ab} \cdot d_{bc} \cdot d_{ac}}}{r_m} \text{ Henry/metre} \quad ...(21.4)$$

where r_m is the GMR value of the conductor.

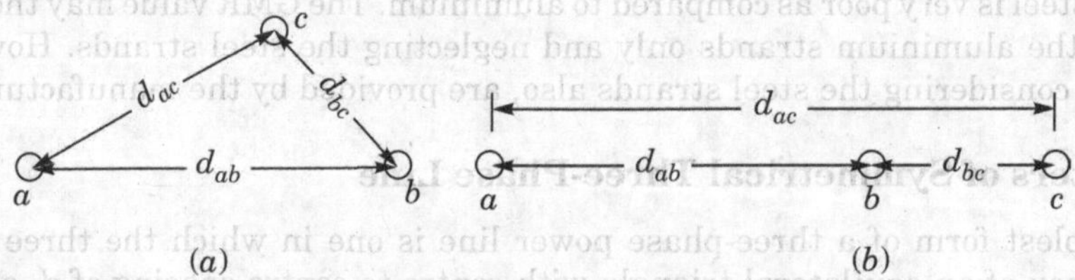

Fig. 21.3. Unsymmetrical three-phase lines.

The capacitance between phase wire a and neutral is given by,

$$C_{aN} = \frac{2\pi\varepsilon}{\ln \frac{\sqrt[3]{d_{ab} \cdot d_{bc} \cdot d_{ac}}}{r_c}} \text{ Farad/metre}$$

$$= \frac{2\pi\varepsilon}{\ln \frac{d_m}{r_c}} \text{ Farad/metre} \quad ...(21.5)$$

where d_m is the geometric mean distance among the conductors and r_c is the radius of the cable.

Thus for any arrangement of conductors in space ($\varepsilon = \varepsilon_0$), the capacitance C_{aN} becomes,

$$C_{aN} = \frac{1}{18 \times 10^9 \ln \frac{d_m}{r_c}} \quad ...(21.6)$$

The series resistance R depends on the diameter and number of strands in the cable and the conductivity of the strand material.

The power transmission lines are required to stand very high voltages. Hence excellent insulation is provided so that under normal working conditions, leakance G may be neglected.

Earth, being a good conductor of electricity, influences the capacitance of each wire to neutral depending on their distances from ground. However, this effect is usually negligibly small.

Example 21.1. *A horizontally spaced three-phase line has conductor spacing of 6 metres each conductor being 37 strands, 500,000 cir, mil copper cable. Calculate the inductance and capacitance of wires per kilometre length.*

Solution. From standard wire tables, the GMR value for the given copper cable is found to be 0.793 cm and the overall diameter of the cable is 2.07 cm.

Then inductance of each cable is

$$L_a = 2 \times 10^{-7} \ln \frac{(6 \times 6 \times 12)^{1/3}}{0.793 \times 10^{-2}} \text{ H/metre} = 1.37 \text{ mH/kilometre.}$$

The capacitance of a conductor to neutral is,

$$C_{aN} = \frac{1}{18 \times 10^9 \ln \dfrac{d_m}{r_c}} = \frac{1}{18 \times 10^9 \ln \dfrac{(6 \times 6 \times 12)^{1/3}}{1.035 \times 10^{-2}}} \text{ F/metre}$$

$$= 0.00844 \text{ μF/kilometre.}$$

The resistance of such a cable is found from tables to be 0.0742 ohm per kilometre at 50 Hz and at normal temperature of 25°C. This shows that the loss due to resistance and hence that attenuation constant of such a line is very small.

Example 21.2. *Three-phase line of Example 21.1 is operated at 220 kV for a length of 100 kilometres, transmitting power of 150,000 kV A. If equal line currents flow through the cables, calculate the resistive and reactive voltage drop per kilometre of line.*

Solution. Power transmitted per phase

$= 50,000$ kVA

Current per phase $= \dfrac{50,000}{220} = 227.5$ A

Resistive drop per km $= 227.5 \times 0.0742 = 16.87$ volts

Series reactance/km $= 2\pi \times 50 \times 1.37 \times 10^{-3} = 0.431\ \Omega$

Hence reactive drop/km $= 0.431 \times 227.5 = 97.8$ volts.

21.5. Equivalent Circuit of a Power Line

The equivalent circuit for a general transmission line may be used for a power line also and we may then calculate the line current, phase-to-neutral voltages and per phase loads. However, it is more usual to employ an equivalent circuit for long lines derived from the line equations. The equivalent circuit for a short line may be represented by lumped elements equal to the total series parameters of the line and half the shunt susceptance at each end to form a π-section.

Fig 21.4 shows the *T* and π equivalents circuits derived from the line equations for a long line. These circuits, however, apply for one particular frequency, which is the case in power transmission.

The series impedance *z* per unit length of line equals $(R + j\omega L)$ ohms while the shunt admittance *y* per unit length equals $j\omega C$ mhos, neglecting the leakage conductance.

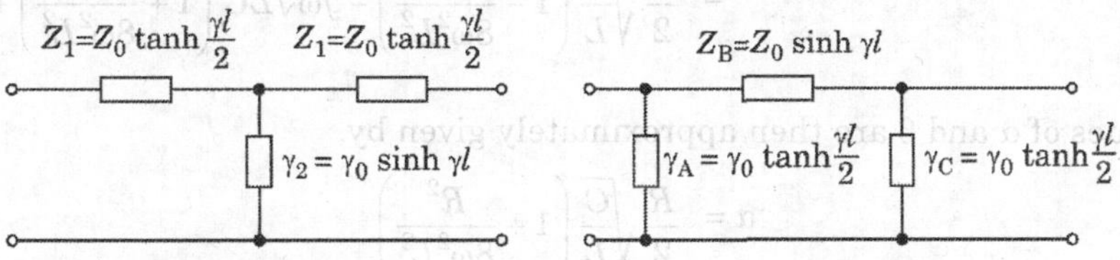

(*a*) *T*-section. (*b*) π-section.

Fig. 21.4. *T* and π equivalent circuits of a transmission line.

Hence $$\gamma = \sqrt{zy} = \sqrt{(R + j\omega L)(j\omega C)}$$

$$= \sqrt{-\omega^2 LC + j\omega CR} \qquad \text{...(21.7)}$$

$$Z_0 = \sqrt{\frac{z}{y}} = \sqrt{\frac{(R + j\omega L)}{j\omega C}}$$

$$= \sqrt{\frac{L}{C} - j\frac{R}{\omega C}} \quad ...(21.8)$$

But R being very small, Eq. (21.8) may be written as,

$$Z_0 = \sqrt{\frac{L}{C}\left(1 - j\frac{R}{\omega L}\right)} \quad ...(21.8\ a)$$

But R being very small, Eq. (21.8 *a*) may be written as,

$$Z_0 \approx \sqrt{\frac{L}{C}}\left(1 - j\frac{R}{2\omega L}\right) \quad ...(21.9)$$

Eq. (21.9) shows that the impedance Z_0 has angle θ given by,

$$\theta = \tan^{-1}\left(-\frac{R}{2\omega L}\right) \approx \frac{-R}{2\omega L} \quad ...(21.10)$$

Since $\frac{R}{2\omega L}$ is very small compared to unity, Z_0 may be further approximated to,

$$Z_0 \approx \sqrt{\frac{L}{C}} \quad ...(21.11)$$

Thus Z_0 becomes purely resistive and may be denoted by R_0.

Similarly the propagation constant as given by Eq. (21.7) may be expanded by binomial theorem as follows :

$$\gamma = (-\omega^2 LC + j\omega CR)^{1/2}$$

$$= (-\omega^2 LC)^{1/2} + \frac{1}{2}(-\omega^2 LC)^{-1/2}(j\omega CR)$$

$$+ \frac{1}{8}(-\omega^2 LC)^{-3/2}(\omega^2 C^2 R^2) - \text{H.F.}\,(-\omega^2 LC)^{-5/2} \times (j\omega^3 C^3 R^3) +$$

$$= j\omega\sqrt{LC} + \frac{R}{2}\sqrt{\frac{C}{L}} + j\frac{R^2}{8\omega L}\sqrt{\frac{C}{L}} - \frac{1}{16}\frac{R^3}{\omega^2 L^2}\sqrt{\frac{C}{L}} + \ldots\ldots$$

$$= \frac{R}{2}\sqrt{\frac{C}{L}}\left(1 - \frac{R^2}{8\omega^2 L^2}\right) - j\omega\sqrt{LC}\left(1 + \frac{R^2}{8\omega^2 L^2}\right) + \ldots$$

...(21.12)

The values of α and β are then approximately given by,

$$\alpha = \frac{R}{2}\sqrt{\frac{C}{L}}\left(1 + \frac{R^2}{8\omega^2 L^2}\right) \quad ...(21.13)$$

$$\beta = \omega\sqrt{LC}\left(1 + \frac{R^2}{8\omega^2 L^2}\right) \quad ...(21.14)$$

Usually the quantity $\frac{R}{\omega C}$ for power lines is so small that its square value can be neglected in comparison to unity and α, β can be further approximated to the values :

$$\alpha \approx \frac{R}{2}\sqrt{\frac{C}{L}} = \frac{R}{2R_0}$$

$$\beta \approx \omega\sqrt{LC} \qquad ...(21.16)$$

The velocity of propagation may be obtained by use of Eq. (21.14). Thus velocity of propagation

$$v = \frac{\omega}{\beta} = \frac{1}{\sqrt{LC}\left(1+\dfrac{R^2}{8\omega^2 L^2}\right)} \qquad ...(21.17)$$

If the line is lossless and the conductors are in free space, the velocity of propagation is given by $v = 1/\sqrt{LC}$ and this equals the velocity of light. Eq. (21.17) shows that the velocity of propagation is reduced from theoretical maximum due to the presence of resistance R in the line. In fact the line resistance, internal inductance and line insulation with value of ε_r other than unity, all contribute to the reduction of velocity of propagation below that of light in free space. However, since the value of $R/\omega L$ is quite small, the reduction in velocity of propagation is very small.

Because of single frequency operation of power line, the complete length of line may be represented by a single equivalent π-section. Thus the total parameters for a line of l units can be considered as $zl = Z$ and $yl = Y$ for the series and the shunt arms of the equivalent circuit. Then for the π circuit of Fig. 21.4 (*b*), the design equations may be written as,

$$Z_B = Z_0 \sinh \gamma l = \sqrt{\frac{Z}{Y}}\,.\sinh\sqrt{ZY}$$

or

$$Z_B = Z\frac{\sinh\sqrt{ZY}}{\sqrt{ZY}} \qquad ...(21.18)$$

The shunt element can be written as

$$Y_A = Y_C = Y_0 \tanh\frac{Y}{Z} = \sqrt{\frac{Y}{Z}}\tanh\frac{\sqrt{ZY}}{2}$$

or

$$Y_A = Y_C = \frac{Y}{2}\cdot\frac{\tanh\dfrac{\sqrt{ZY}}{2}}{\dfrac{\sqrt{ZY}}{2}} \qquad ...(21.19)$$

The hyperbolic functions for complex numbers are difficult to calculate. Hence hyperbolic functions are expressed as power series. Thus, we have

$$\frac{\sinh\sqrt{ZY}}{\sqrt{ZY}} = 1 + \frac{ZY}{\underline{/3}} + \frac{(ZY)^2}{\underline{/5}} + ... \qquad ...(21.20)$$

$$\frac{\tanh(\sqrt{ZY/2})}{\sqrt{ZY/2}} = 1 - \frac{ZY}{12} + \frac{(ZY)^2}{120} - ... \qquad ...(21.21)$$

Now since the electrical length of a power line expressed in terms of wavelength is small, we may neglect second order and higher order terms in Eqs. (21.20) and (21.21).

Hence Eqs. (21.18) and (21.21) may be written as,

$$Z_B = Z\left(1+\frac{ZY}{6}\right) \qquad ...(21.22)$$

$$Y_A = Y_C = \frac{Y}{2}\left(1-\frac{ZY}{12}\right) \qquad ...(21.23)$$

Similarly the elements of T-network of Fig. 21.4 may be expressed by the following approximate equations :

$$Z_1 = \frac{Z}{2}\left(1 - \frac{ZY}{12}\right) \qquad ...(21.24)$$

$$Y_2 = Y\left(1 + \frac{YZ}{6}\right) \qquad ...(21.25)$$

Any of these two networks may be solved for given conditions of the line.

21.6. Chain Parameters or ABCD Parameters

In general, the power transmission network may contain a large number of lines having different parameters and connected either in cascade or in parallel. In such case, solution by T or π networks becomes very complicated and time-consuming. We then prefer to use the *chain parameters,* also called *ABCD parameters* or *General Circuit Constants.* These have already been defined earlier. Thus if E_S and I_S are the voltage and current respectively at the sending end and E_R and I_R are the voltage and current at the receiving end, then E_S and I_S may be expressed as,

$$E_S = A.E_R + B.I_R \qquad ...(21.26)$$

$$I_S = C.E_R + D.I_R \qquad ...(21.27)$$

Using matrix notation, Eqs. (21.26) and (21.27) may be written as,

$$\begin{bmatrix} E_S \\ I_S \end{bmatrix} = \begin{bmatrix} A & B \\ C & D \end{bmatrix} \begin{bmatrix} E_R \\ I_R \end{bmatrix} \qquad ...(21.28)$$

The general transmission line equations in hyperbolic form may be written for power lines as follows :

$$E_S = E_R \cosh \sqrt{ZY} + I_R Z_0 \sinh \sqrt{ZY}$$

$$I_S = I_R \cosh \sqrt{ZY} + \frac{E_R}{Z_0} \sinh \sqrt{ZY}$$

The above Eqs. may be written in matrix form as :

$$\begin{bmatrix} E_S \\ I_S \end{bmatrix} = \begin{bmatrix} \cosh \sqrt{ZY} & Z_0 \sinh \sqrt{ZY} \\ \frac{1}{Z_0} \sinh \sqrt{ZY} & \cosh \sqrt{ZY} \end{bmatrix} \begin{bmatrix} E_R \\ I_R \end{bmatrix} \qquad ...(21.29)$$

Comparing Eqs. (21.28) and (21.29), we get

$$\left.\begin{aligned} a &= \cosh \sqrt{ZY} \\ B &= Z_0 \sinh \sqrt{ZY} \\ C &= \frac{1}{Z_0} \sinh \sqrt{ZY} \\ D &= \cosh \sqrt{ZY} \end{aligned}\right\} \qquad ...(21.29a)$$

It may be seen that $A = D$. This is true for a symmetrical network. Thus a transmission line forms a symmetrical network. Let Δ be the determinant of the matrix of Eq. (21.28) or Eq. (21.29).

Then $$\Delta = AD - BC = 1 \qquad ...(21.30)$$

This is true for any linear, passive, bilateral symmetrical or unsymmetrical network.

Eq. (21.28) may be solved for output quantities E_R and I_R in terms of input quantities E_S and I_S. Thus, we get

$$E_R = DE_S - BI_S \qquad ...(21.31)$$

$$I_R = -CE_S + AI_S \qquad ...(21.32)$$

These equations may be put in the matrix form as below :

$$\begin{bmatrix} E_R \\ -I_R \end{bmatrix} = \begin{bmatrix} D & B \\ C & A \end{bmatrix} \begin{bmatrix} E_S \\ -I_S \end{bmatrix} \qquad \text{...(21.33)}$$

Eq. (21.33) gives the relation which is inverse of that given by Eq. (21.28). In Eq. (21.33), the negative sign is associated with I_R and I_S because the directions of flow of both I_R and I_S are opposite to the conventional directions assumed in calculations of chain parameters.

The values of chain parameters in terms of hyperbolic functions as given by Eq.(21.29 *a*) may be replaced by approximate expressions in terms of line parameters obtained by series expansion of the hyperbolic sine and cosine functions. Neglecting all higher order terms excepting the first order terms, we then get

$$\left.\begin{aligned} A &= 1 + \frac{ZY}{2} \\ B &= Z\left(1 + \frac{ZY}{6}\right) \\ C &= Y\left(1 + \frac{ZY}{6}\right) \\ D &= A \end{aligned}\right\} \qquad \text{...(21.34)}$$

It is possible to relate the elements of a π-network to the chain parameters by utilizing the relation between *y*-parameters and the chain parameters (*ABCD* parameters). The desired relations are :

$$\left.\begin{aligned} A &= -\frac{y_{22}}{y_{21}} \\ B &= -\frac{1}{y_{21}} \\ C &= -\frac{\Delta y}{y_{11}} \\ D &= -\frac{y_{11}}{y_{21}} \end{aligned}\right\} \qquad \text{...(21.35)}$$

where Δy is the determinant of the *y*-parameter mixture. The element of a symmetrical π-network are shown in Fig. 21.5 in terms of admittances. From this it is easy to write the following relations :

$$y_{11} = Y_A + Y_B \qquad \text{...(21.36)}$$

$$-y_{12} = -y_{21} = Y_B \qquad \text{...(21.37)}$$

$$y_{22} = Y_A + Y_B \qquad \text{...(21.38)}$$

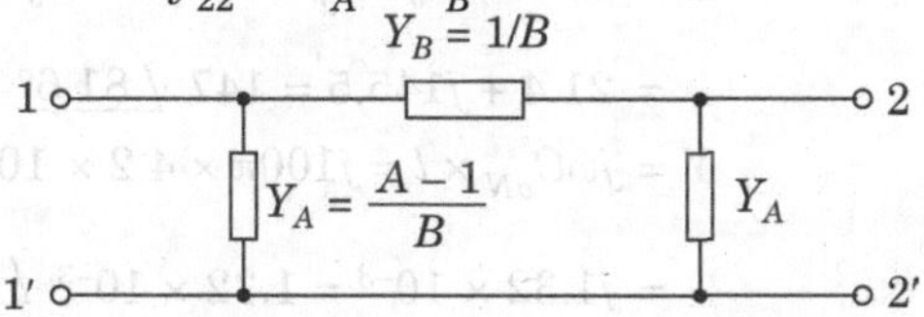

Fig. 21.5. Elements of π-network in terms of *ABCD* parameters.

Combining Eqs. (21.35) to (21.38), the elements of the π-network are given as

$$\left.\begin{aligned} Y_A &= \frac{A-1}{B} \\ Y_B &= \frac{1}{B} \end{aligned}\right\} \qquad \text{...(21.39)}$$

In a similar manner it is possible to obtain the elements of a symmetrical T-network in terms of $ABCD$ parameters. The result is shown in Fig. 21.6.

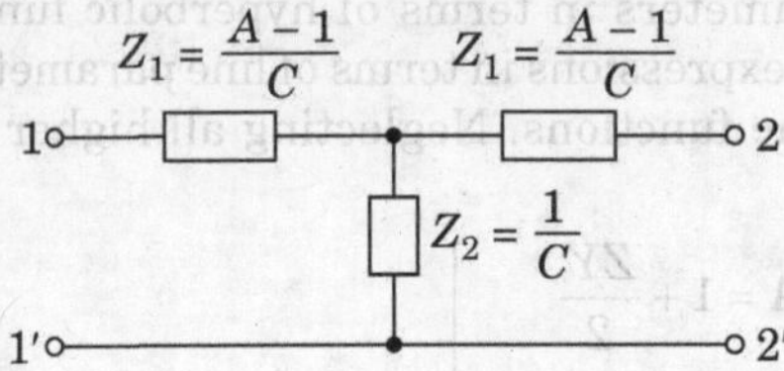

Fig. 21.6. Elements of a T-network in terms of $ABCD$ parameters.

Example 21.3. *A 50 Hz ; three-phase power line is 500 km long. The conductors are 90,000 cir. mil 37 strand, copper cables having an outside diameter of 1.092 inches and GMR = 0.0349 foot. The resistance of each conductor at 50 Hz is 0.0428 ohm / kilometre. If the conductors are equilaterally spaced at 36 feet, calculate the approximately equivalent (π-network and the ABCD parameters. If the receiving voltage E_R = 100 kV line-to-neutral and the power received is 50 MW at 0.86 power factor lagging, calculate the voltage E_S at the sending end of the line.*

Solution. Line resistance

$$= R \times l = 0.0428 \times 500 = 21.4\ \Omega$$

Line inductance, $$L_a = 2 \times 10^{-7} \ln \frac{d}{r_m} = 2 \times 10^{-7} \ln \frac{36}{0.0349} \text{ Henry/metre}$$

Total line inductance $$= L_a \times l$$

$$= 500 \times 10^3 \times 2 \times 10^{-7} \ln \frac{36}{0.0349} \text{ Henry} = 0.463 \text{ H.}$$

Total line-to-neutral capacitance

$$= l \times C_{aN}$$

$$= \frac{500 \times 10^3}{18 \times 10^9 \ln \dfrac{36 \times 2 \times 12}{1.092}} \text{ F} = 4.2\ \mu\text{F}$$

$$Z = (R \times l) + j\omega L_a \times l = 21.4 + j100\pi + 0.463$$

$$= 21.4 + j145.5 = 147 \underline{/81.6^\circ}$$

$$Y = j\omega C_{aN} \times l = j100\pi \times 4.2 \times 10^{-6}$$

$$= j1.32 \times 10^{-3} = 1.32 \times 10^{-3} \underline{/90^\circ}$$

$$ZY = 147 \underline{/81.6^\circ} \times 1.32 \times 10^{-3} \underline{/90^\circ} = 0.194 \underline{/171.0^\circ}$$
$$= -0.192 + j0.02835$$

$$Z_B = Z\left(1 + \frac{ZY}{6}\right) = 147 \underline{/81.6^\circ} (1 - 0.032 + j0.004725)$$

$$= 147 \angle 81.6^\circ \times 0.968 \angle 0.28^\circ = 142 \angle 81.88^\circ = 19.9 + j141$$

$$Y_A = \frac{Y}{2}\left(1 - \frac{ZY}{12}\right) = 0.66 \times 10^{-3} \angle 90^\circ \; [1 + 0.016 - j0.00236]$$

$$= 0.67 \times 10^{-3} \angle 89.97^\circ = 2.01 \times 10^{-3} + j0.67 \times 10^{-3}.$$

This determines the elements of an equivalent π network. The $ABCD$ parameters are calculated as below :

$$A = 1 + \frac{ZY}{2} = 1 - 0.096 + j0.01417 = 0.904 \angle 0.9^\circ$$

$$B = Z\left(1 + \frac{ZY}{6}\right) = 142 \angle 81.88^\circ$$

$$C = Y\left(1 + \frac{ZY}{6}\right) = 1.32 \times 10^{-3} \angle 90^\circ \times 0.968 \angle 0.28^\circ$$

$$= 1.278 \times 10^{-3} \angle 90.28^\circ$$

$$D = A = 0.904 \angle 0.9^\circ.$$

The current I_R at the receiving end per phase is,

$$I_R = \frac{W}{3E_R \times \text{p.f.}} = \frac{50 \times 10^6}{3 \times 10^5 \times 0.86} = 194 \text{ Amp.}$$

The angle of current I_R is $\cos^{-1}(0.86)$ or 30.71° lagging behind E_R. The voltage E_S at the sending end is given by,

$$E_S = AE_R + BI_R.$$

Substituting the values, we get

$$E_S = 0.904 \angle 0.9^\circ \times 10^5 + 142 \angle 81.88^\circ \times 194 \angle -36.71^\circ$$

$$= (9.04 \times 10^4 + j1.42 \times 10^3) + (1.73 \times 10^4 + j2.143 \times 10^4)$$

$$= 10.77 \times 10^4 + j2.285 \times 10^4 = 110 \times 10^3 / \angle 12^\circ \text{ volts.}$$

21.7. Real and Reactive Powers

As the receiving end, certain quantity of power expressed in *watts, kilowatts* or *megawatts,* is said to have been consumed. This power constitutes the *real power* or the *active power* and this is the power which has come over the transmission line from the generating station or the source and has flown to a load or energy sink. Another component of power is the *reactive power* which is present due to transfer or circulation of energy stored in electric and magnetic fields present along a line or in the equipment connected at the receiving end. The reactive power is expressed in terms of voltamperes (reactive) abbreviated as *vars,* or larger units such as *kilovars* or *megavars.* The reactive power is the product of voltage and quadrature current component. This energy is actually neither generated nor consumed but simply circulates in the system. Hence a concept of *positive* or *negative* vars may be developed indicating the direction of flow of energy which depends upon whether the load is capacitive or inductive. Generally vars are considered as *flowing from or generated in* devices predominantly capacitive in nature or *flowing to or absorbed in* devices which are predominantly inductive.

The load volt-ampere may be expressed as

$$\mathbf{VI^*} = VI(\cos\theta + j\sin\theta)$$

$$= P + jQ \quad ...(21.40)$$

where **I*** represents the conjugate of **I** and **VI*** is called the *vector power.* The quantity θ is positive when positive vars are supplied to a capacitive load or to the capacitive susceptance of the transmission line. Negative vars are assumed as absorbed in the inductive reactance of a line or in an inductive load. Thus a transmission line takes positive vars in its capacitance and negative vars in its inductive reactance. The amount of positive vars taken is dependent on the line voltage while the negative vars absorption is dependent on line current. When the line is terminated in Z_0, the energy stored in the line capacitance is equal to that stored in the line inductance. Hence positive vars taken by the line capacitance equals the negative vars absorbed by the line inductance. Hence no external vars need be supplied.

With high line voltages, the load impedance is much higher than Z_0. Hence load absorbs large negative or inductive vars. Hence the line is required to *generate* more positive vars than the negative vars taken by its inductance in order to equalise the total positive and negative vars of the system. With low line voltages, the load impedance may become much smaller than Z_0 causing heavy currents to flow in the line. This gives rise to more negative vars in the line inductance than the positive vars in the system. The additional positive vars required must be introduced in the line by operation of additional generators at a leading angle or by use of synchronous capacitors on the line.

Flow of current, both in-phase and quadrature components, produces power loss in the line resistance and hence the supply of vars to a line requires additional equipment. Hence it is desirable that a power line be operated at high voltages and low currents so that the line is not heavily loaded. This requires load impedance to be higher than Z_0 so that the line may actually contribute the reactive voltampere to the usual inductive loads. However such an ideal operation is not always possible due to heavy costs of erection of a line and such lines carry heavier loads than permitted.

21.8. Receiving-end Power Circle Diagram

A power circle diagram is graphical method of solving for active power and reactive volt-ampere conditions on a line. In such cases, it is assumed that E_g and E_R are constant, an assumption justified in most causes.

Consider Eq. (21.26) rewritten below :

$$E_S = AE_R + BI_R$$

Multiplying this equation by $\frac{E_R}{B}$ yields,

$$\frac{E_S E_R}{B} = \frac{A}{B} E_R^{\ 2} + E_R \,.\, I_R$$

or

$$E_R I_R = P_R + jQ_R = \frac{E_R E_R}{B} - \frac{A}{B} E_R^{\ 2} \quad ...(21.41)$$

If the receiving-end voltage E_R is in kilo-volts line to neutral and the line current I_R is in amperes, then the per phase quantities of Eq. (21.41) will be in megawatts and mega vars.

If ϕ is the phase angle of E_S with respect to E_R, then

$$P_R + jQ_R = \frac{|E_S \cdot E_R| \angle \phi}{B} - \frac{A}{B} E_R^{\ 2} \quad ...(21.42)$$

Since E_S and E_R are assumed to be fixed, the second term on the right hand side of Eq. (21.42) represents a vector from origin whose angle depends upon the angles of A and B. The magnitude of first term on the right of Eq. (21.42) is constant for a given line but the angle is variable. The locus of the right side of this equation is then a circle whose radius is determined by the first term and centre is given by the second term on the right side. This circle is now the locus $P_R + JQ_R$ for fixed E_S and E_R, and with ϕ variable. A scale of angles representing ϕ can be marked on this circle starting from the point for which $\phi = 0$.

The dimensions for plotting the graph may be obtained by putting

$$A = |A| \angle\alpha$$

and
$$B = |B| \angle\beta$$

Then Eq. (21.42) may be written as,

$$P_R + jQ_R + \frac{|A|}{|B|} E_R[\cos(\beta - \alpha) - j\sin(\beta - \alpha)] = \frac{|E_S \cdot E_R|}{L} \angle\phi$$

where the angle of A/B has been written as $(\beta - \alpha)$ because usually β is much larger than α, thus avoiding unnecessary calculation. Taking the squared magnitude of the above equation, we get

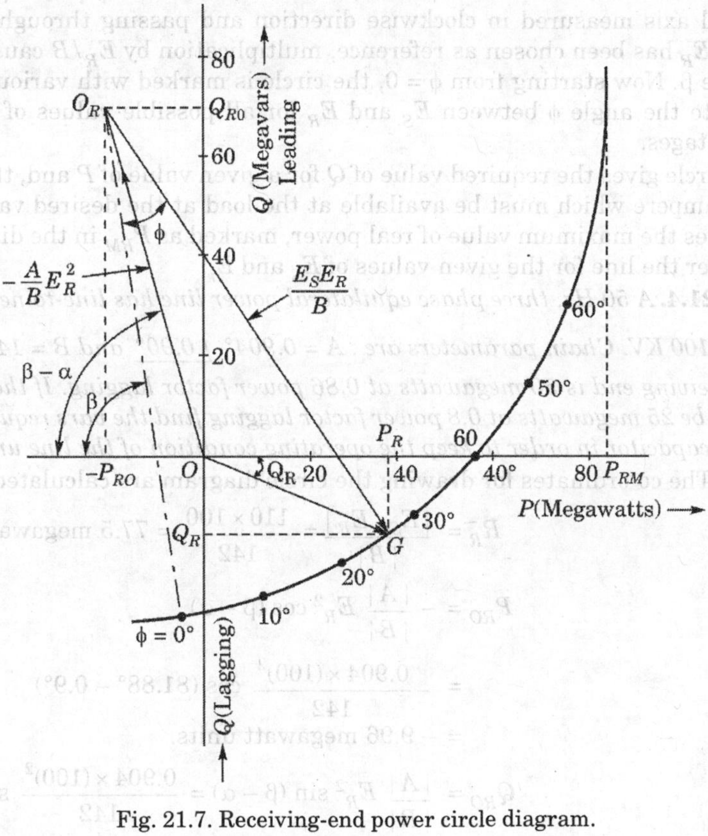

Fig. 21.7. Receiving-end power circle diagram.

$$\left[P_R + \frac{|A|}{|B|} E_R^2 \cos(\beta - \alpha)\right]^2 + \left[Q_R - \frac{|A|}{|B|} E_R^2 \sin(\beta - \alpha)\right]^2 = \frac{E_S^2 E_R^2}{B^2} \quad ...(21.43)$$

Since E_S, E_R and B are constants, Eq. (21.43) represents a circle. The radius of the circle is then

$$E_R = \frac{|E_S E_R|}{B} \text{ megawatt units} \quad ...(21.44)$$

where the scale of the graph is such that the actual length R_R is measured in megawatt units. The co-ordinates of the centre of circle are,

$$P_{RO} = -\frac{|A|}{|B|} E_R^2 \cos(\beta - \alpha) \text{ megawatts} \qquad ...(21.45)$$

and

$$Q_{RO} = \frac{|A|}{|B|} E_R^2 \sin(\beta - \alpha) \text{ megawatts} \qquad ...(21.46)$$

These co-ordinates are measured along equal scales of megawatts and megavars plotted along the abscissa and ordinate as shown in Fig. 21.7. The line OO_R represents $-(A/B)\,E_R^2$, so that O_R is the centre of the circle whose radius is represented as O_RG which is proportional to $| E_S . E_R | /B$. The line OG is the vector sum of OO_R and O_RG and represents $P_R + jQ_R$ whose value changes as $| E_S.E_R | /B$ changes with angle f along the circle. The radius vector has an angle $(\phi - \beta)$, where β is the angle of B. The reference line for $\phi = 0$ is, therefore, obtained by plotting a line at an angle of β from the real axis measured in clockwise direction and passing through the centre O_R as shown. Although E_R has been chosen as reference, multiplication by E_R/B causes the diagram to rotate by an angle β. Now starting from $\phi = 0$, the circle is marked with various values of angles which will indicate the angle ϕ between E_S and E_R for all possible values of P_R and Q_R at the assumed fixed voltages.

Thus the circle gives the required value of Q for a given value of P and, therefore, indicates the relative volt-ampere which must be available at the load at the desired values of E_S and E_R. The circle also gives the maximum value of real power, marked as P_{RM} in the diagram, which may be transmitted over the line for the given values of E_S and E_R.

Example 21.4. *A 50 Hz, three phase equilateral power line has line-to-neutralvoltages* E_S = *110 KV and* E_R = *100 KV. Chain parameters are : A = 0.904°* $\angle 0.90°$ *and B = 142* $\angle 81.88°$. *Power received at the receiving end is 50 megawatts at 0.86 power factor lagging. If the real power at the receiving end is to be 25 megawatts at 0.8 power factor lagging find the vars required to be supplied by a synchronous capacitor in order to keep the operating condition of the line unaltered.*

Solution. The co-ordinates for drawing the circle diagram are calculated as below :

$$R_R = \frac{|E_S . E_R|}{|B|} = \frac{110 \times 100}{142} = 77.5 \text{ megawatt units.}$$

$$P_{RO} = -\frac{|A|}{|B|} E_R^2 \cos(\beta - \alpha)$$

$$= -\frac{0.904 \times (100)^2}{142} \cos(81.88° - 0.9°)$$

$$= -9.96 \text{ megawatt units.}$$

$$Q_{RO} = \frac{|A|}{|B|} E_R^2 \sin(\beta - \alpha) = \frac{0.904 \times (100)^2}{142} \sin(81.88° - 0.9°)$$

$$= 62.85 \text{ megavar units}$$

Since the voltages are line-to-neutral, all power values are per phase values. The receiving end power circle diagram is shown in the figure, by using the same scale *for x* and *y* axes. The power drawn at the receiving end is 50 megawatts at 0.86 power factor lagging.

Hence

$$P_R = \frac{50}{3} = 16.67 \text{ megawatts per phase}$$

$$Q_R = \frac{50}{3} \cdot \frac{\sin(-30.71)}{0.86} = -9.9 \text{ megavars.}$$

These values are located on the circle diagram at the point C which gives angle $\phi = 11°$. The angle is nearly the same as calculated previously.

The load changes to 25 megawatts at 0.8 power factor lagging, the voltage conditions remaining unaltered. Hence we draw a load line *OM* from the origin corresponding to 0.8 p.f., *i.e.* at an angle of 36.87° from the *x*-axis. This line is then the locus of all values of P_R and Q_R which have the same power factor of 0.8 lagging. The circle diagram then shows that a load of 14.3 megawatts and 10.7 megavars lagging will be carried by the line at $\phi = 8.7°$.

It is required that the line should carry 25 megawatts at 0.8 power factor lagging. This condition is satisfied by point *M* on the 0.8 p.f. line as shown in the figure. Point *M* shows that the line is required to carry 18.5 megavars lagging. Thus the co-ordinates of point *M* are $P_M + jQ_M = 25 - j18.5$. However, the given line under the given operating conditions and 0.8 power factor lagging will carry a load as indicated by the point *N* on the circle diagram obtained by the vertical projection of the point *M*. The co-ordinates of point *N* are $P_N + jQ_N = 25 - j6.5$.

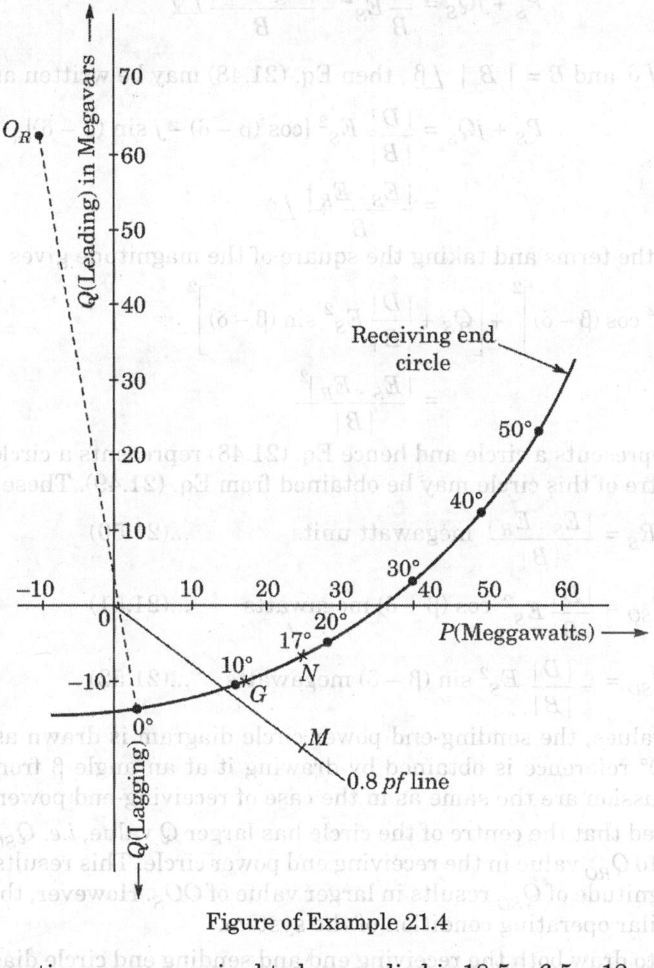

Figure of Example 21.4

Hence extra reactive power required to be supplied is 18.5 – 6.5 = 12 megavars at a leading angle. Hence a synchronous capacitor able to deliver 12 megavars should be connected across the line. Then the specified load can be carried at the specified voltages with $\phi = 17°$ by the system.

21.9. Sending End Power Circle Diagram

In case, we take the sending end voltage and current as independent, then Eq. (21.31) relating E_R with E_S and I_S may be taken as the starting point. Thus the equation

$$E_R = D.E_S - B.I_S$$

may be used for drawing the circle diagram giving the sending end or input conditions for fixed given values of E_S and E_R.

Multiplying the above equation by $\frac{E_S}{B}$ and rearranging the terms, we get

$$\frac{D}{B}E_S^2 - \frac{E_S \cdot E_R}{B} = E_S \cdot I_S = P_S + jQ_S \quad ...(21.47)$$

Let the voltages be expressed in kilo-volts phase-to-neutral. Then the terms in Eq. (21.47) will be in megawatts and megavars per phase with the line current expressed in amperes.

Let ϕ be the angle of E_R with respect to E_S. Then Eq. (21.47) may be written as

$$P_S + jQ_S = \frac{D}{B}E_S^2 - \frac{|E_S . E_R|}{B} \angle\phi \quad ...(21.48)$$

If $D = |D| \angle\delta$ and $B = |B| \angle\beta$, then Eq. (21.48) may be written as,

$$P_S + jQ_S = \frac{|D|}{|B|} E_S^2 [\cos(\beta - \delta) - j\sin(\beta - \delta)]$$

$$= \frac{|E_S . E_R|}{B} \angle\phi$$

Rearranging the terms and taking the square of the magnitude gives

$$\left[P_S = \frac{|D|}{|B|} E_S^2 \cos(\beta - \delta)\right]^2 + \left[Q_S + \frac{|D|}{|B|} E_S^2 \sin(\beta - \delta)\right]^2$$

$$= \frac{|E_S . E_R|^2}{|B|} \quad ...(21.49)$$

Eq. (21.49) represents a circle and hence Eq. (21.48) represents a circle. The radius and co-ordinates of the centre of this circle may be obtained from Eq. (21.49). These are

Radius $\quad R_S = \frac{|E_S . E_R|}{|B|}$ megawatt units ...(21.50)

$$P_{SO} = \frac{|D|}{|B|} E_S^2 \cos(\beta - \delta) \text{ megawatts} \quad ...(21.51)$$

$$Q_{SO} = -\frac{|D|}{|B|} E_S^2 \sin(\beta - \delta) \text{ megawatts} \quad ...(21.52)$$

From these values, the sending-end power circle diagram is drawn as shown in Fig. 21.8. The radius for $\phi = 0°$ reference is obtained by drawing it at an angle β from the reference axis. Other points of discussion are the same as in the case of receiving-end power circle diagram.

It may be noted that the centre of the circle has larger Q value, *i.e.* Q_{SO} has larger negative values as compared to Q_{RO} value in the receiving end power circle. This results because E_S is larger than E_R. Larger magnitude of Q_{SO} results in larger value of OO_S. However, the radius O_SG remain the same under similar operating condition of the system.

It is possible to draw both the receiving end and sending end circle diagrams on the same P and Q axes and thus combine the two diagrams into a single power circle diagram for a given line and given operating conditions. Such a power circle diagram is much more useful and gives additional information. This combined power circle diagram for the line of Example 21.3 has been drawn in Fig. 21.9. Use of Eqs. (21.50) to (21.52) for the sending end circle diagram yields,

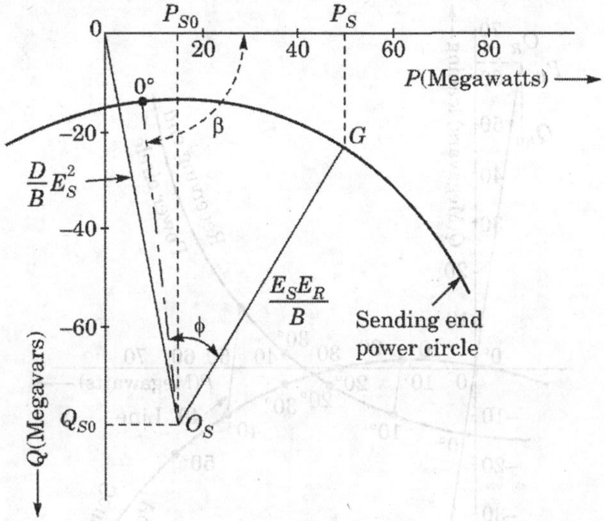

Fig. 21.8. Sending-end power-circle diagram.

$$R_S = 77.5 \text{ megawatt units}$$

$$P_{SO} = \frac{0.904 \times 1.21 \times 10^4}{142} \cos 80.98°$$

$$= 12.05 \text{ megawatts.}$$

$$Q_{SO} = -\ 76 \text{ megavars.}$$

The additional utility of this combined power circle diagram may be made evident by drawing say 11° line as shown in Fig. 21.9. This is easily done by obtaining 11° point on the receiving end circle diagram from the previous values of P_R = 16.67 MW and Q_R = – 9.9 megavars. The 11° point on the sending end circle is then obtained by measurement of angle. This point *is* $P_R = 14.3 + j1.7$. Thus it is seen that the line itself takes (9.9 + 1.7), *i.e.* 11.6 megavars of leading reactive power so that it delivers 9.9 megavars of lagging load reactive power and forms the case of lightly loaded line, where $Z_l >> Z_0$. This forms the ideal case.

The main drawback of the circle diagrams is that the values cannot be accurately plotted or read from the diagrams except when very large size circle diagrams are used.

Lastly let us consider the case when this line is loaded very heavily corresponding to $\phi = 40°$. This gives $P_R + jQ_R = 48.7 + j12.4$ and $P_S + jQ_S = 51.5. - j9.2$ approximately as read from the combined circle diagram of Fig. 21.9. This shows that 2.8 megawatts of real power is lost in the line resistance. The load actually takes 12.4 megavars of leading reactive power but because the line is heavily loaded, the line inductance causes the input to be 9.2 magavars of lagging reactive power to the line.

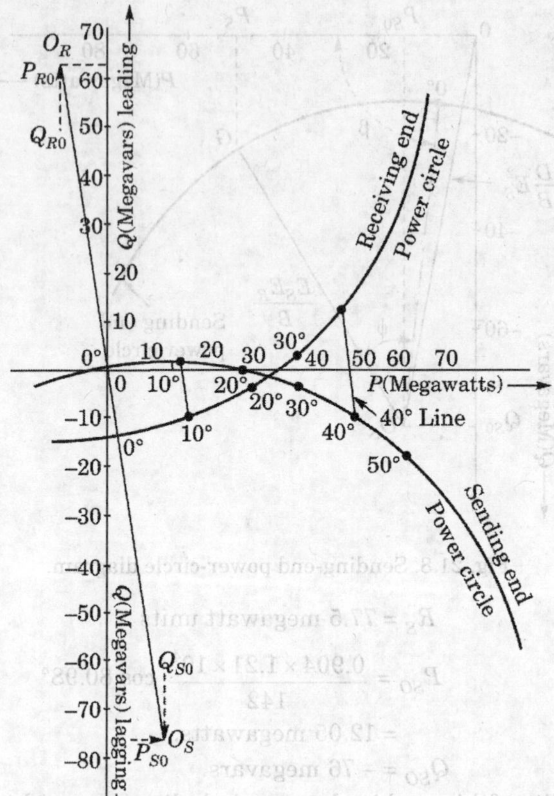

Fig. 21.9. Receiving and sending power-circle diagram combined for the line of Example 21.3.

22

Resonance and Selectivity

22.1. Introduction

A two terminal network, in general, offers a complex impedance consisting of resistive and reactive components. If a sinusoidal voltage is applied to such a network, the current is then out of phase with the applied voltage. Under special circumstances, however, the impedance offered by the network is purely resistive. The phenomenon is called *resonance* and the frequency of applied signal at which resonance is called the *frequency of resonance*. The nature of resonance depends upon whether the inductance and the capacitance are in series or in parallel. Accordingly, we classify the resonant circuits into the following two categories :

(*i*) Series resonant circuit,

(*ii*) Parallel resonant circuit.

22.2. Series Resonance

Fig. 22.1 shows a series *RLC* circuit. A sinusoidal voltage **V** sends a current **I** through the circuit. The circuit is said to be resonant when the resultant reactance is zero, *i.e.* the circuit is purely resistive.

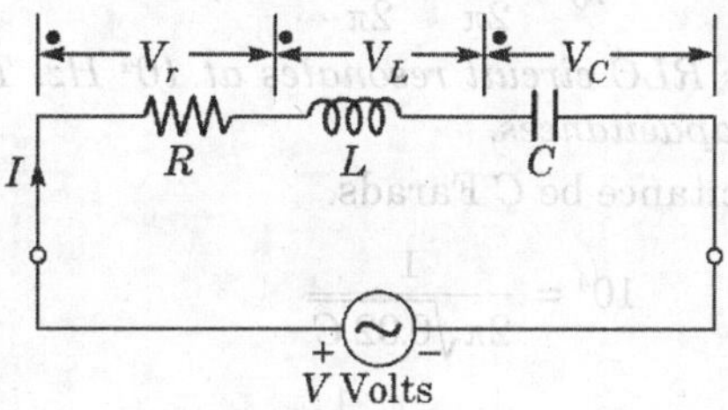

Fig. 22.1. Series *RLC* circuit connected to a voltage source *V*.

The impedance **Z** of the circuit is given by,

$$\mathbf{Z} = R + j\omega L + \frac{1}{j\omega C} \qquad ...(22.1)$$

where **Z** and *R* in ohms

L is in Henrys

C is in Farads

and ω is the angular frequency of applied voltage in radians/sec.

Current $$\mathbf{I} = \frac{\mathbf{V}}{\mathbf{Z}} = \frac{V}{R + j\left(\omega L - \dfrac{1}{\omega C}\right)} \qquad ...(22.2)$$

At resonance the impedance **Z** becomes purely resistive. Thus at resonance,

$$\omega_0 L = \frac{1}{\omega_0 C} \qquad ...(22.3)$$

where ω_0 is the frequency of resonance in radians/second.

From Eq. (22.3), we get

$$\omega_0 = \frac{1}{\sqrt{LC}} \quad \text{...(22.4)}$$

or

$$f_0 = \frac{1}{2\pi\sqrt{LC}} \quad \text{...(22.5)}$$

where f_0 is the frequency of resonance in Hertz.

At resonance, putting

$$\omega L = \frac{1}{\omega C} \text{ in Eq. (22.2), we get } I = \frac{V}{R}.$$

The condition is called *series resonance*.

Series resonance at any desired frequency f_0 may be obtained by varying either L, or C or both. For fixed values of L and C series resonance may be achieved by varying the frequency of applied signal.

Example 22.1. *A series RLC circuit consists of a resistance 10 Ω, an inductance of 0.1 Henry and a capacitance of 0.001 μF. Calculate the frequency of resonance in Hertz and in radians / second.*

Solution. Frequency of resonance

$$\omega_0 = \frac{1}{\sqrt{LC}} = \frac{1}{\sqrt{0.1 \times 0.001 \times 10^{-6}}} = 10^5 \text{ radians/sec.}$$

$$f_0 = \frac{\omega_0}{2\pi} = \frac{10^5}{2\pi} = 15{,}920 \text{ Hertz.}$$

Example 22.2. *A series RLC circuit resonates at 10^4 Hz. The value of inductance is 0.02 Henry. Calculate the value of capacitances.*

Solution. Let the capacitance be C Farads.

Then

$$10^4 = \frac{1}{2\pi\sqrt{0.02\,C}}$$

Hence

$$C = \frac{1}{(2\pi \times 10^4)^2 \times 0.02} = 1.268 \times 10^{-8} \text{ Farad.}$$

22.3. Phasor Diagram of Series RLC Circuit

The nature of the phasor diagram of a series *RLC* circuit depends upon the frequency f of applied signal in relation to the frequency of resonance f_0. Three different cases may be considered : (*i*) $f = f_0$, (*ii*) $f < f_0$ and (*iii*) $f > f_0$.

With $f = f_0$, the reactance X_l of inductor L equals the reactance $X_c \left(= \frac{1}{\omega C}\right)$ of capacitor C. The circuit is then purely resistive and the voltage **V** across the circuit is in phase with the current I. The phasor diagram for the series *RLC* circuit of Fig. 22.1 for the series resonance condition is shown in Fig. 22.2 (*a*).

With $f < f_0$, negative reactance X_c of capacitor C exceeds the positive reactance X_l of inductor L. Hence the overall reactance is capacitive. Current I leads the applied voltage V. Voltage V_l leads the current by 90° while the voltage V_c lags behind current I by 90°. The phasor diagram is shown in Fig. 22.2 (*b*).

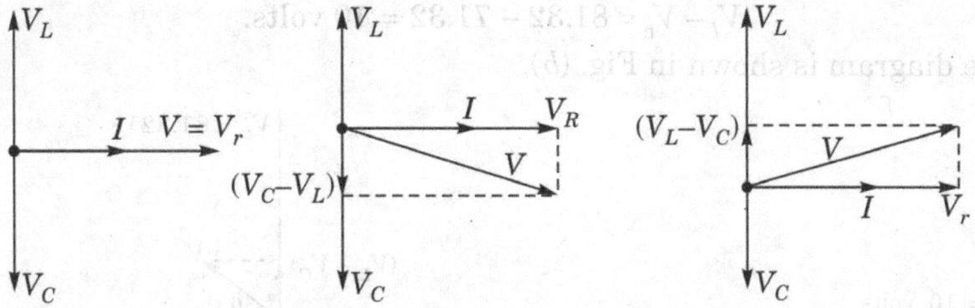

(a) $f = f_0$ (b) $f < f_0$ (c) $f > f_0$

Fig. 22.2. Phasor diagram of the series *RLC* circuit.

With $f > f_0$, reactance X_l exceeds the reactance X_c. The overall reactance is inductive. Current I lags behind the applied voltage V. The phasor diagram is shown in Fig. 22.2 (*c*).

Example 22.3. *A series RLC circuit consists of a resistance R = 10 Ω, inductance L = 0.2 H and capacitance C = 0.2 μF. Calculate the frequency of resonance. A 10 volts sinusoidal voltage at the frequency of resonance is applied across the circuit. Draw the phasor diagram showing the value of each phasor. Also calculate values of* (i) *current and* (ii) *voltage across R, C and L and draw the phasor diagram when 10 volt 850 Hz voltage is applied to the circuit.*

Solution. Frequency of resonance

$$f_0 = \frac{1}{2\pi\sqrt{LC}} = \frac{1}{2\pi\sqrt{0.2 \times 0.2 \times 10^{-6}}} = 796 \text{ Hz.}$$

At f = f₀

$$I = \frac{V}{R} = \frac{10 \text{ volts}}{10 \text{ ohms}} = 1 \text{ amp.}$$

$$V_r = I \times R = 1 \times 10 = 10 \text{ volts}$$

$$V_l = I \times \omega L = 1 \times 2\pi \times 796 \times 0.2 = 10^3 \text{ volts}$$

$$V_c = V_l = 10^3 \text{ volts.}$$

Hence phasor diagram is as shown in Fig. (*a*).

At f = 850 Hz

$$\omega L = 2\pi \times 850 \times 0.2 = 1068\ \Omega$$

$$\frac{1}{\omega C} = \frac{1}{2\pi\ 850 \times 0.2 \times 10^{-6}} = 936.5\ \Omega$$

$$\mathbf{I} = \frac{V}{R + j\left(\omega L - \dfrac{1}{\omega C}\right)} = \frac{10}{10 = j\,(1068 - 936.5)} = \frac{10}{10 = j131}$$

Magnitude
$$I = \frac{10}{\sqrt{10^2 + (131)^2}} = 76.15 \times 10^{-3} \text{ amp.}$$

Let θ be the phase angle of current I relative to voltage V.

Then
$$\theta = -\tan^{-1}\frac{131}{10} = -85.6^\circ$$

$$V_r = IR = 76.15 \times 10^{-3} \times 10 = 76.15 \times 10^{-2} \text{ volt.}$$

$$V_c = \frac{1}{\omega C} = 76.15 \times 10^{-3} \times 936.5 = 71.32 \text{ volts.}$$

$$V_l = I \times \omega L$$

$$= 76.15 \times 10^{-3} \times 1068 = 81.32 \text{ volts.}$$

$$V_l - V_c = 81.32 - 71.32 = 10 \text{ volts.}$$

The phase diagram is shown in Fig. (*b*).

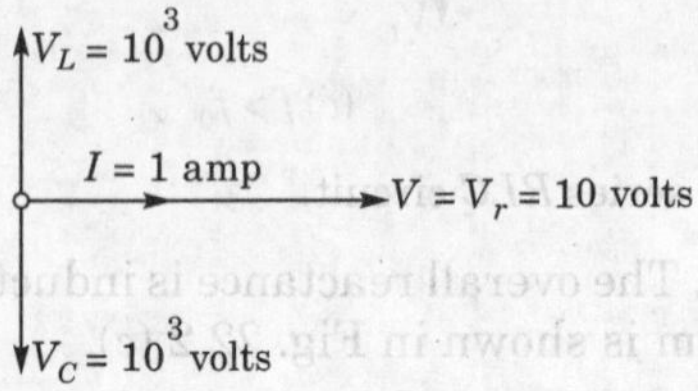

Fig. (*a*)

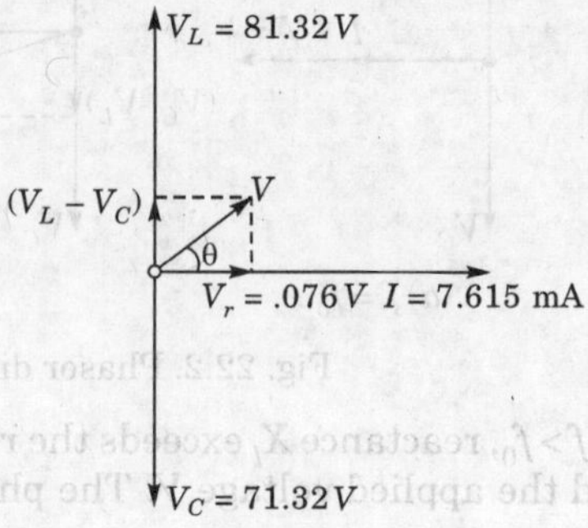

Fig. (*b*)

22.4. Reactance and Impedance Curves of a Series RLC Circuit

The reactance of inductor $L = X_l = \omega L$ and its impedance $Z_l = 0 + j\omega L = 0 + jX_l$. Thus the impedance of an inductor is always imaginary, leading the resistor R by 90°. Curve (*a*) in Fig. 22.3 shows the variation of X_l (= ωL) with frequency. This is a straight line. The reactance of capacitor C is

$$X_c = \frac{1}{\omega C} = \frac{1}{2\pi f_c}$$

and its impedance, $Z_c = 0 + \dfrac{1}{j\omega C} = 0 - j\,\dfrac{1}{\omega C} = 0 - jX_c$.

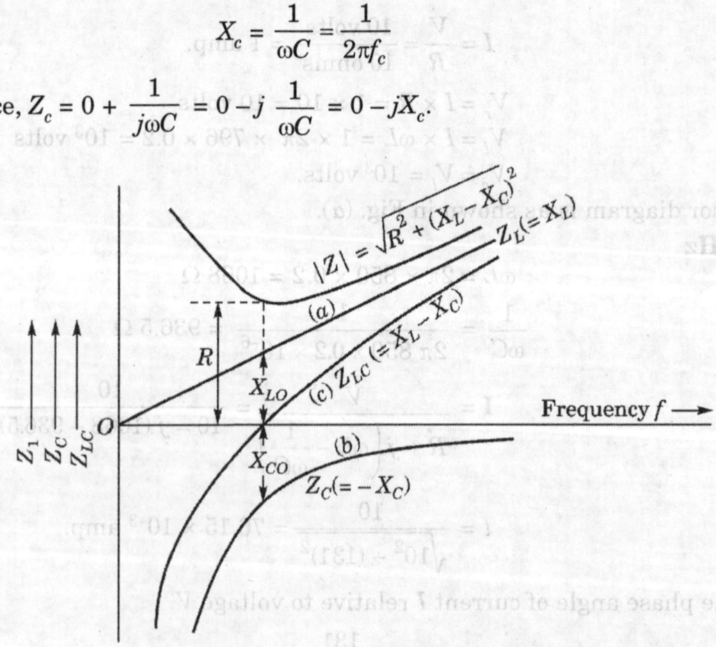

Fig. 22.3. Variation of impedances of inductor L, capacitor C, L and C jointly and total series circuit.

Thus the impedance of a capacitor is always imaginary and lags behind the resistor by 90°.

Curve (*b*) in Fig. 22.3 shows the variation of $Z_c \left(= -\dfrac{1}{\omega C}\right)$ with frequency. This is a hyperbolic curve.

The impedance of L and C in series is given by

$$Z_{lc} = 0 + j\omega L + \frac{1}{j\omega C} = 0 + j(X_l \times X_c).$$

The variation of (X_l and X_c) is shown by curve C in Fig. 22.3. This curve has both positive and negative values depending upon whether X_l is greater than or less than X_c. Also this curve crosses the X-axis at frequency f_0 which is the frequency of series resonance. At this frequency $X_c = X_l$. At frequency greater than f_0, $X_l > X_0$, *i.e.* $(X_l - X_c)$ is positive and the circuit is inductive in nature. On the other hand, at frequencies less than f_0, $X_l < X_c$, *i.e.* $(X_l - X_c)$ is negative and the circuit is capacitive in nature.

The impedance of the entire RLC circuit is given by,

$$Z = R + j\left(\omega L - \frac{1}{\omega C}\right) \quad ...(22.6)$$

$$= R + j(X_l - X_c) \quad ...(22.7)$$

Hence $$|Z| = \sqrt{R^2 + (X_l - X_c)^2} \quad ...(22.8)$$

Curve (d) in Fig. 22.3 shows the nature of variation of Z with frequency. *At* $f = f_0$, $Z = R$ since $X_l = X_c$. This is the minimum value of Z.

22.5. Variation of Current and Voltages with Frequency in a Series RLC Circuit

In a series RLC circuit, impedance **Z** is given by,

$$\mathbf{Z} = R + j\left(\omega L \frac{1}{\omega C}\right).$$

Hence current **I** in the series circuit is given by,

$$\mathbf{I} = \frac{\mathbf{V}}{\mathbf{Z}} = \frac{\mathbf{V}}{R + j\left(\omega L - \dfrac{1}{\omega C}\right)}$$

Magnitude $$|I| = \frac{V}{\sqrt{R^2 + \left(\omega L - \dfrac{1}{\omega C}\right)^2}} \quad ...(22.9)$$

At resonance, $\omega L = \dfrac{1}{\omega C}$ and $\mathbf{Z} = R$ and this is the minimum value of **Z.**

Hence from Eq. (22.9), at resonance

$$I = \frac{V}{R}.$$

Hence the current is maximum at resonance.

At frequencies either below or above the resonance frequency, Z is greater than R so that I is smaller than $\dfrac{V}{R}$. Curve maked I in Fig. 22.4 shows the nature of variation of current I with frequency.

The voltage across the capacitor C is given by,

$$\mathbf{V}_c = \mathbf{I}\frac{1}{j\omega C} = \frac{1}{j\omega C} \cdot \frac{\mathbf{V}}{R + j\left(\omega C - \dfrac{1}{\omega C}\right)} \quad ...(22.10)$$

Hence magnitude

$$V_c = \frac{V}{\omega C \sqrt{R^2 + \left(\omega L - \frac{1}{\omega C}\right)^2}} \qquad \text{...(22.11)}$$

Curve marked V_c in Fig. 22.4 gives the variation of voltage V_c with frequency.

The frequency f_c at which V_c is maximum may be obtained by equating $\frac{dV}{d\omega}$ to zero. This results in,

$$f_c = \frac{1}{\omega C}\sqrt{\frac{1}{LC} - \frac{R^2}{2L^2}} \qquad \text{...(22.12)}$$

Obviously $f_c < f_0$

The voltage across the inductor L is given by,

$$\mathbf{V}_l = \mathbf{I}\, j\omega L = \frac{\mathbf{V} j\omega L}{R + j\left[\omega L - \left(\frac{1}{\omega C}\right)\right]} \qquad \text{...(22.13)}$$

Magnitude,

$$|V_l| = \frac{\mathbf{V} j\omega L}{\sqrt{R^2 + \left(\omega L - \frac{1}{\omega C}\right)^2}} \qquad \text{...(22.14)}$$

Curve marked V_l in Fig. 22.4 gives the variation of V_l with frequency. The frequency f_1 at which V_l is maximum may be obtained by equating $\frac{dV_l^2}{d\omega}$ to zero. Thus, we get

$$f_l = \frac{1}{2\pi\sqrt{LC - \frac{C^2R^2}{2}}} \qquad \text{...(22.15)}$$

Obviously $f_1 > f_0$.

It may be seen from Eq. (22.15) that $f_l > f_0$.

Voltage V_c and V_l have equal values and opposite phases at the frequency of resonance f_0 as shown by their point of intersection P.

If R is extremely small, both f_l and f_c tend to equal f_0.

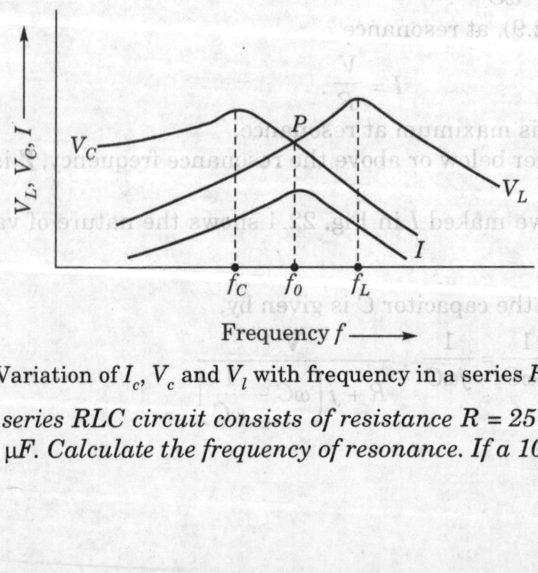

Fig. 22.4. Variation of I_c, V_c and V_l with frequency in a series *RLC* circuit.

Example 22.4. *A series RLC circuit consists of resistance R = 25 Ω, inductance L = 0.01 H and capacitance C = 0.04 μF. Calculate the frequency of resonance. If a 10 volts voltage of frequency* *equal to the frequency of resonance is applied to this circuit, calculate the values of voltages V_c and V_l across C and L respectively. Find the frequencies at which these voltages V_c and V_l are maximum.*

Solution. $$f_0 = \frac{1}{2\pi\sqrt{LC}} = \frac{1}{2\pi\sqrt{0.01 \times 0.04 \times 10^{-6}}} = 7960 \text{ Hz.}$$

At $f = f_0$,

$$I = \frac{V}{R} = \frac{10 \text{ volts}}{25 \text{ volts}} = 0.4 \text{ amp.}$$

Hence $$V_l = I.\omega_0 L = 0.4 \times 2\pi \times 7960 \times 0.01 = 200 \text{ volts.}$$

$$V_0 = I.\frac{1}{\omega_0 C} = \frac{0.4}{2\pi \times 7960 \times 0.04 \times 10^{-6}} = 200 \text{ volts.}$$

The freqency at which V_c is maximum, is given by

$$f_c = \frac{1}{2\pi}\sqrt{\frac{1}{LC} - \frac{R^2}{2L^2}} = \frac{1}{2\pi}\sqrt{\frac{1}{0.01 \times 0.04 \times 10^{-6}} - \frac{(25^2)}{2(0.01)^2}}$$

$$= 7958 \text{ Hz.}$$

The frequency at which V_l is maximum is given by,

$$f_1 = \frac{1}{2\pi\sqrt{LC - \frac{C^2R^2}{2}}}$$

$$= \frac{1}{2\pi\sqrt{(0.01 + 0.04 \times 10^{-6}) - \frac{(0.04 \times 10^{-6} \times 25^2)}{2}}} = 7968 \text{ Hz.}$$

22.6. Selectivity and Bandwidth

A series *RLC* circuit gives unequal response to voltages of different frequencies. At the frequency of resonance the impedance is minimum and the current is maximum. As the frequency of the applied voltage is either reduced or increased from this resonance frequency, the impedance increases and the current fall. Fig. 22.5 shows the variation of current *I* with frequency. Thus a series *RLC* circuit possesses frequency selectivity.

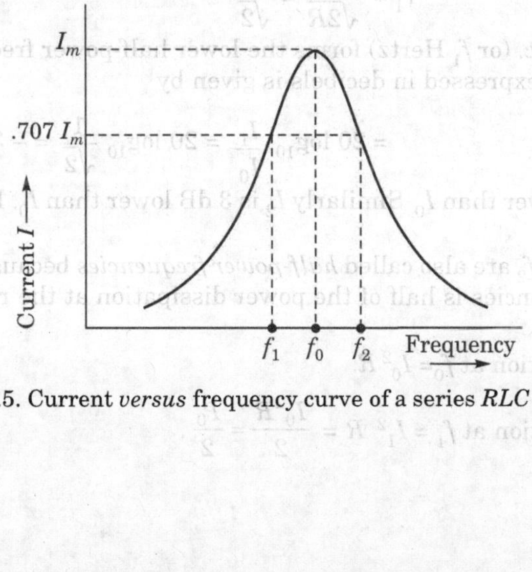

Fig. 22.5. Current *versus* frequency curve of a series *RLC* circuit.

Fig. 22.5 shows current *versus* frequency curves of a series *RLC* circuit for small value of *R*. The frequencies f_1 and f_2 at which current *I* falls to $\frac{1}{\sqrt{2}}$ (or 0.707) of its maximum value $I_0 \left(= \frac{V}{R}\right)$ are called *half-power frequencies* or *3 dB frequencies.* The bandwidth $(f_2 - f_1)$ is called the *half-power bandwidth* or *3 dB bandwidth* or simply the *bandwidth* of the circuit.

Selectivity of a resonant circuit is defined as the ratio of resonant frequency f_0 to the 3-dB bandwidth. Thus selectivity

$$= \frac{\text{Resonance frequency}}{\text{3 dB bandwidth}} = \frac{f_0}{(f_2 - f_1)} \quad \text{...(22.16)}$$

The current in the series *RLC* circuit is given by,

$$\mathbf{I} = \frac{\mathbf{V}}{R + j\left(\omega L - \frac{1}{\omega C}\right)}$$

Let ω_2 be such a frequency that

$$\omega_2 L - \frac{1}{\omega_2 C} = R \quad \text{...(22.17)}$$

Then at frequency ω_2

$$\mathbf{I}_2 = \frac{\mathbf{V}}{R + jR}$$

Magnitude $$I_2 = \frac{V}{\sqrt{2}R} = \frac{I_0}{\sqrt{2}}.$$

Thus ω_2 radians/sec. (or f_2 Hertz) gives the upper half-power frequency.

Similarly, let ω_1 be such a frequency that,

$$\omega_1 L - \frac{1}{\omega_1 C} = -R$$

Then the current at frequency ω_1 is given by,

$$I_2 = \frac{\mathbf{V}}{R - jR}$$

Magnitude $$I_1 = \frac{V}{\sqrt{2}R} = \frac{I_0}{\sqrt{2}}$$

Thus ω_1 radians/sec. (or f_1 Hertz) forms the lower half-power frequency.

This current ratio expressed in decibels is given by

Ratio in decibels $$= 20 \log_{10} \frac{I_1}{I_0} = 20 \log_{10} \frac{1}{\sqrt{2}} = -3.$$

Thus *I*1 is 3 dB lower than I_0. Similarly I_2 is 3 dB lower than I_0. Hence f_1 and f_2 are called 3 dB frequencies.

Frequencies f_1 and f_2 are also called *half-power frequencies* because the power dissipation in the circuit at these frequencies is half of the power dissipation at the resonant frequency f_0. This may be seen as below :

P_0 = Power dissipation at $f_0 = I_0^2 R$.

P_1 = Power dissipation at $f_1 = I_1^2 R = \frac{I_0^2 R}{2} = \frac{P_0}{2}$.

$$P_2 = \text{Power dissipation at } f_2 = I_2^2\, R = \frac{I_0^2 R}{2} = \frac{P_0}{2}$$

22.7. Quality Factor or Q Factor

(A) **Q of a Coil.** Every inductor possesses a small resistance in addition to its inductance. Lower the value of this resistance *R*, better is the quality of the coil. The quality factor or the *Q*-factor of an inductor at the operating frequency ω is defined as the ratio of reactance of the coil to its resistance.

Thus for a coil, $$Q = \frac{\omega L}{R} \qquad ...(22.18)$$

where *L* is the effective inductance of the coil in Henrys
and *R* is the effective resistance of the coil in Ohms.

Obviously *Q* is a dimensionless ratio.

The *Q*-factor may be defined in an alternate and more basic way as below :

$$Q = 2\pi \frac{\text{Maximum energy stored per cycle}}{\text{Energy dissipated per cycle}} \qquad ...(22.19)$$

Thus consider a sinusoidal voltage *V* of frequency ω radians/second applied to an inductor *L* of effective internal resistance *R* as shown in Fig. 22.6 *(a)*. Let the resulting peak current through the coil be I_m.

Then the maximum energy stored in the inductor $= \frac{1}{2} L.I_m^2$.

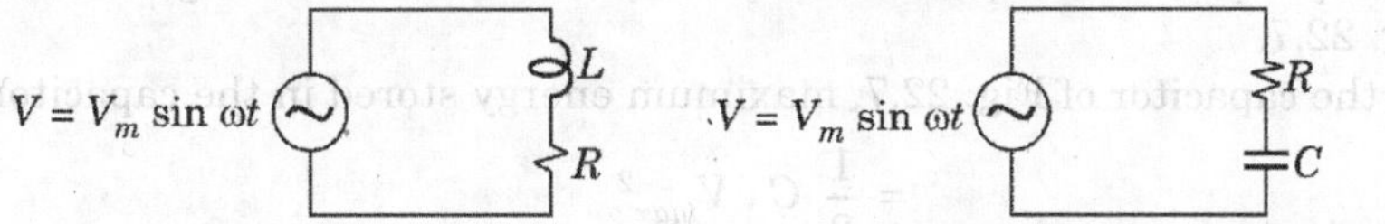

(a) Coil *L* with effective internal resistance *R*.

(b) Condenser *C* with effective series resistance *R*.

Fig. 22.6. *R-L* and *R-C* circuits connected to a sinusoidal voltage sources.

The average power dissipated in the inductor per cycle

$$= \left(\frac{I_m}{\sqrt{2}}\right)^2 R.$$

Hence the energy dissipated in the inductor per cycle

= Power × Periodic time for one cycle

$$= \left(\frac{I_m}{\sqrt{2}}\right)^2 R.T = \frac{I_m^2}{2}.R.\frac{1}{f}$$

Hence $$Q = 2\pi . \frac{\frac{1}{2} L I_m^2}{\frac{I_m^2}{2} . \frac{R}{f}} = \frac{2\pi f L}{R} = \frac{\omega L}{R}.$$

(A) **Q of a capacitor.** Fig. 22.6 *(b)* shows a capacitor *C* with small series resistance *R* associated with it. The *Q* factor or the quality factor of a capacitor at the operating frequency is defined as the ratio of the reactance of the capacitor to its series resistance.

Thus, $$Q = \frac{1}{\omega C R} \qquad ...(22.20)$$

In this case also, the Q is a dimensionless quantity. Eq. (22.19) giving the alternative definition of Q holds good in this case also. Thus for the circuit of Fig. 22.6 (*b*), on application of a sinusoidal voltage of value V volts and frequency ω, the maximum energy stored in the capacitor

$$= \frac{1}{2} CV_{max}^2$$

where V_{max} is the maximum value of voltage across the capacitance C.

But if $\quad R << \omega C$

then $\quad V_{max} = \dfrac{I_m}{\omega C}$

where I_m is the maximum value of current through C and R.

Hence the maximum energy stored in capacitor C is

$$\frac{1}{2} \cdot \frac{I_m^2}{\omega^2 C^2}$$

$$\text{Energy dissipated per cycle} = \frac{I_m^2 R}{2f}$$

Hence
$$Q = 2\pi \frac{\frac{1}{2} \frac{I_m^2}{\omega^2 C}}{\frac{I_m^2 L}{2f}} = \frac{2\pi . f}{\omega^2 CR} = \frac{1}{\omega CR}.$$

Often a lossy capacitor is represented by a capacitance C with a high resistance R_p in shunt as shown in Fig. 22.7.

Then for the capacitor of Fig. 22.7, maximum energy stored in the capacitor

$$= \frac{1}{2} C . V_{max}^2$$

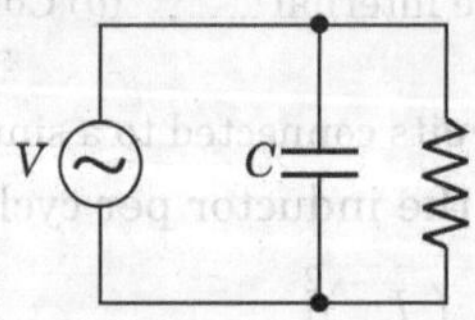

Fig. 22.7. Alternative method of representing a lossy capacitor.

$$= \frac{1}{2} CV_m^2 \qquad \text{...(22.21)}$$

where V_m is the maximum value of the applied voltage. Average power dissipated in resistance R_p

$$= \frac{\left(\frac{V_m}{\sqrt{2}}\right)^2}{R_p} = \frac{V_m^2}{2R_p}.$$

$$\text{Energy dissipated per cycle} = \frac{V_m^2}{2R_p} \cdot \frac{1}{f} \qquad \text{...(22.22)}$$

Hence $$Q = 2\pi \cdot \frac{\frac{1}{2}CV_m^2}{\frac{V_m^2}{2R_p f}} = \omega C R_p \quad ...(22.23)$$

Circuit magnification factor. Referring to the series *RLC* circuit of Fig. 22.1, at resonance the current I_0 through the series circuit equal to $\frac{V}{R}$. The voltage across the inductor at resonance is given by,

$$V_l = I_0 X_l = \frac{V}{R} \cdot (\omega_0 L) = Q_0 V \quad ...(22.24)$$

Similarly the voltage across the capacitor *C* is given by,

$$V_c = I_0 \cdot X_c$$

$$= \frac{V}{R} \cdot \frac{1}{\omega_0 C} = Q_0 V \quad ...(22.25)$$

From Eqs. (22.24) and (22.25) we find that at resonance, the voltages across *L* and *C* are each equal to *Q* times the applied voltage *V*. This *Q* may be considerably greater than the unity. Thus the voltage across *L* (or *C*) may be made greater than applied voltage. Because of this, the *Q*-factor is also sometimes referred to as the *circuit magnifica-tion factor* or simply the *magnification factor*.

22.8. Series Resonance and Selectivity of Series RLC Circuit with Frequency Variable

The impedance of a series *RLC* circuit is given by,

$$\mathbf{Z} = R + j\left(\omega L - \frac{1}{\omega C}\right) \quad ...(22.26)$$

where ω is any frequency.

For ω close to the resonant frequency ω_o, Eq. (22.26) does not yield very accurate results.

It is desirable in such a case to use a special relation valid only for frequencies close to the resonant frequency. Thus Eq. (22.26) may be put as,

$$\mathbf{Z} = R\left[1 + j\left(\frac{\omega L}{R} - \frac{1}{\omega CR}\right)\right]$$

$$= R\left[1 + j\left(\frac{\omega_0 L}{R} \cdot \frac{\omega}{\omega_0} - \frac{1}{\omega_0 CR} \cdot \frac{\omega_0}{\omega}\right)\right] \quad ...(22.27)$$

At resonance, $\omega_0 L = \frac{1}{\omega_0 C}$

Hence $$\frac{\omega_0 L}{R} = \frac{1}{\omega_0 CR} = Q_0 \quad ...(22.28)$$

where Q_0 is the value of *Q* at resonance.

Hence Eq. (22.27) may be put as,

$$\mathbf{Z} = R\left[1 + jQ_0\left(\frac{\omega}{\omega_0} - \frac{\omega}{\omega_0}\right)\right] \quad ...(22.29)$$

Fractional frequency variation is given by,

$$\delta = \frac{\omega - \omega_0}{\omega_0} \qquad ...(22.30)$$

Hence $\frac{\omega}{\omega_0} = 1 + \delta$

Hence Eq. (22.29) may be put as,

$$\mathbf{Z} = R\left[1 + jQ_0\left(1 + \delta - \frac{1}{1+\delta}\right)\right] = R\left[1 + jQ_0\delta\left(\frac{2+\delta}{1+\delta}\right)\right] \qquad ...(22.31)$$

If ω is close to ω_0, then $\delta << 1$.

Hence $2 + \delta \approx 2$

and $1 + \delta \approx 1$.

Hence Eq. (22.31) reduces to,

$$\mathbf{Z} = R[1 + 2j2Q_0\delta] \qquad ...(22.32)$$

Hence current $\mathbf{I} = \frac{\mathbf{V}}{\mathbf{Z}} = \frac{\mathbf{V}}{R[1 + jQ_0\delta]}$ ...(22.33)

Fig. 22.8 shows the variation of current I with frequency as obtained from Eq. (22.32).

At resonance, $\delta = 0$. Hence from Eq. (22.32),

$$\mathbf{Z} = R \text{ and } I = \frac{V}{R} = I_0.$$

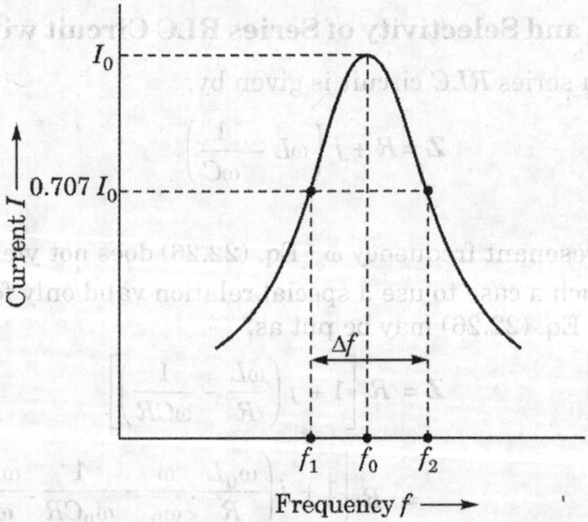

Fig. 22.8. Variation of current with frequency in a series *RLC* current.

At half-power frequencies f_1 and f_2, the magnitude of reactive component of impedance equals the resistance, *i.e.*,

$$\left(\omega L - \frac{1}{\omega C}\right) = \pm R$$

so that $\mathbf{Z} = \pm jR$.

At these half-power frequencies f_1 and f_2, current

$$\mathbf{I} = \frac{I_0}{2} = 0.707\ I_0.$$

From Eq. (22.32), at half-power frequencies,

$$2Q_0\delta = \pm 1 \quad ...(22.34)$$

In Eq. (22.34), the positive sign applies for the upper half-power frequency f_2 while the negative sign applies for lower half power frequency f_2.

For upper half-power frequency f_2, from Eq. (22.34),

$$2Q_o\left(\frac{f_2 - f_0}{f_0}\right) = \pm 1$$

Hence $$\frac{f_2 - f_0}{f_0} = \frac{1}{2Q_0} \quad ...(22.35)$$

Similarly, $$\left(\frac{f_0 - f_1}{f_0}\right) = \frac{1}{2Q_0} \quad ...(22.36)$$

From Eqs. (22.35) and (22.36) we see that $(f_2 - f_0) = (f_0 - f_1)$, *i.e.* the half-power frequencies f_2 and f_1 are symmetrically disposed with respect to the resonant frequency f_0. Also the response curve, *i.e.* current *versus* frequency curve is symmetrical about the resonant frequency f_0.

But Eqs. (22.35) and (22.36) are true only when $\delta << 1$. This condition is satisfied only when the circuit is highly selective *i.e.* when Q_0 is large. For low Q circuit, *i.e.* when R is large, the half-power frequencies f_1 and f_2 are away from the resonant frequency f_0. The impedance **Z** is then given by the Eq. (22.31) instead of Eq. (22.32). Half-power frequencies must then be calculated from Eq. (22.31), *i.e.* from the following equation.

$$Q_0\delta\left(\frac{2+\delta}{1-\delta}\right) = \pm 1 \quad ...(22.37)$$

Thus for low selectivity circuit, $(f_2 - f_0) \neq (f_0 - f_1)$, *i.e.* the response curve is not symmetrical about the resonant frequency.

Referring back to Eqs. (22.35) and (22.36) for high Q circuit, by addition of the equations, we get

$$\frac{f_2 - f_1}{f_0} = \frac{1}{Q_0} \quad ...(22.38)$$

Let half-power bandwidth $(f_2 - f_1)$ be indicated by Δf (or B Hertz). Then selectivity

$$= \frac{f_0}{\Delta f} = Q_0 \quad ...(22.39)$$

From Eq. (22.39) we find for a given value of f, the bandwidth Δf varies inversely with Q_0. Larger the value of Q_0, lesser is the bandwidth and more selective is the circuit.

$\omega_1\omega_1 = \omega_2^2$ – At half-power frequencies, $Z = R \pm jR$. Hence from Eq. (22.26), at lower half-power frequency ω_1,

$$\omega_1 L - \frac{1}{\omega_1 C} = +R \quad ...(22.40)$$

Similarly, at upper half-power frequency ω_2,

$$\omega_2 L - \frac{1}{\omega_2 C} = -R \quad ...(22.41)$$

Adding Eqs. (22.40) and (22.41), we get

$$(\omega_1 + \omega_2)L - \left(\frac{1}{\omega_1} + \frac{1}{\omega_2}\right)\frac{1}{C} = 0$$

or $$(\omega_1 + \omega_2)L = \frac{1}{C}\left(\frac{\omega_1 + \omega_2}{\omega_1\omega_2}\right)$$

Hence $$\omega_1 + \omega_2 = \frac{1}{LC} \quad ...(22.42)$$

But $$\omega_2^2 = \frac{1}{LC}$$

Hence $$\omega_1\omega_2 = \omega_2^2 = \frac{1}{LC} \quad ...(22.43)$$

22.9. Selectivity of Series RLC Circuit with Capacitance Variable

In certain cases, we feed to a series RLC circuit a fixed frequency signal and it is required to vary the capacitance C to obtain the condition of resonance. In such a case, as C is varied, the response current in the circuit varies as shown in Fig. 22.9. The maximum response is reached when the value of C is such that the circuit resonates at the frequency of the applied signal.

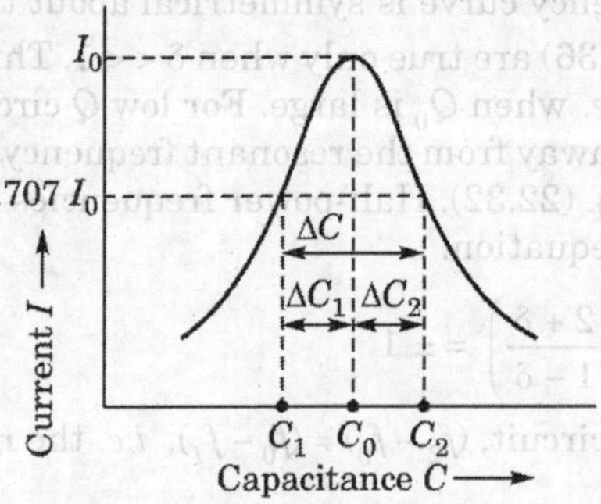

Fig. 22.9. Response of a series RLC circuit with C variable.

Let C_0 be the value of C at resonance and let C_1 and C_2 be the values of capacitance C at which the magnitude of reactance $\left(\omega L - \frac{1}{\omega C}\right)$ equals the resistance R.

Then $$\omega L - \frac{1}{\omega C_1} = -R \quad ...(22.44)$$

and $$\omega L - \frac{1}{\omega C_2} = R \quad ...(22.45)$$

At resonance $$\omega L = \frac{1}{\omega C_0} \quad ...(22.46)$$

From Eqs. (22.44) and (22.45), we get

$$\frac{1}{\omega C_1} - \frac{1}{\omega C_2} = 2R \quad ...(22.47)$$

However, if the circuit is highly selective, then

$$\Delta C_1 << C_0 \quad \text{and} \quad \Delta C_2 << C_0$$

Hence $$C_2 = C_0 + \Delta C_2 \approx C_0$$

and $$C_1 = C_0 - \Delta C_1 \approx C_0.$$

For highly selective circuit, ΔC_1 and ΔC_2 are small and almost equal.

Then $$C_1 + C_2 \approx 2C_0 \quad ...(22.48)$$

$$C_1C_2 \approx C_0^2 \quad \text{...(22.49)}$$

Substituting the value of C_1C_2 from Eq. (22.49) into Eq. (22.47), we get

$$\frac{C_2 - C_1}{\omega C_0^2} = 2R \quad \text{...(22.50)}$$

Combining Eqs. (22.50) and (22.46), we get

$$\frac{C_2 - C_1}{C_0} . \omega L = 2R$$

or
$$\frac{C_2 - C_1}{C_0} = \frac{2R}{\omega L} = \frac{2}{Q_0} \quad \text{...(22.51)}$$

$(C_2 - C_1)$ gives the total variation in C in moving from one half-power condition to the other. The quantity $\frac{C_0}{C_1 - C_2}$ thus gives the selectivity of the series tuned circuit with C variables and this equals $\frac{Q_0}{2}$, as may be seen from Eq. (22.51).

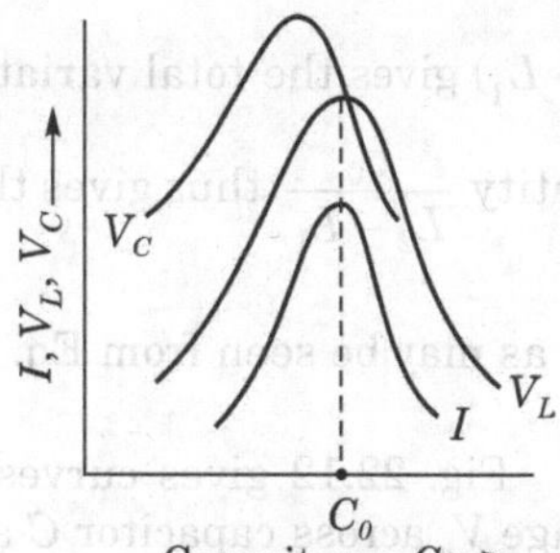

Fig. 22.10. Variation of current I and voltages V_l and V_c with variation of C.

Fig. 22.10 gives curves showing variation of current I, voltage V_l across inductor L and voltage V_c across capacitor C as C is varied. Voltage V_l (= $\omega L.I$) varies in the same manner as current I and becomes maximum at resonance, *i.e.* when $C = C_0$.

At resonance $V_l = V_c$, *i.e.* $I\omega L = \frac{1}{\omega C_0}$ so that $\omega L = \frac{1}{\omega L_0}$.

22.10. Selectivity of Series RLC Circuit with L Variable

In certain cases, we feed to a series *RLC* circuit, a fixed frequency signal and it is required to vary the inductance L to obtain the condition of resonance. In such a case, as L is varied, the current varies as shown in Fig. 22.11. The maximum response is obtained when the value of L is such that the circuit resonates at the frequency of the applied signal.

Let L_0 be the value of L at resonance and let L_1 and L_2 be the values of L at which the magnitude of reactance $\left(\omega L - \frac{1}{\omega C}\right)$ equal the resistance R.

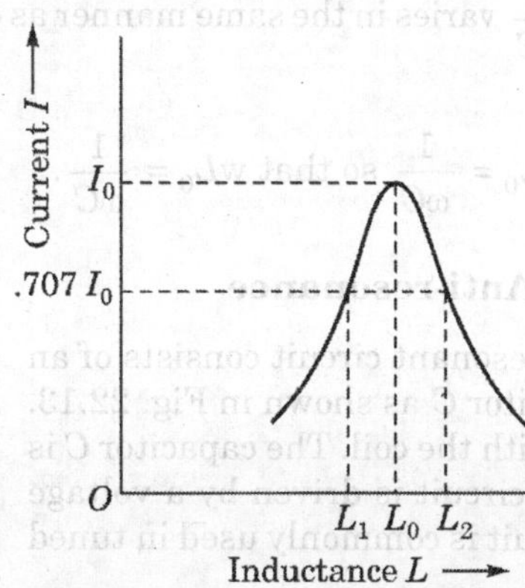

Fig. 22.11. Response of a series *RLC* circuit with L variable.

Then $$\omega L_1 - \frac{1}{\omega C} = -R \quad ...(22.52)$$

and $$\omega L_2 - \frac{1}{\omega C} = R \quad ...(22.53)$$

At resonance $$\omega L_0 = \frac{1}{\omega C} \quad ...(22.54)$$

Subtracting Eq. (22.52) from Eq. (22.53), we get

$$\omega L_2 - \omega L_1 = 2R$$

or $$\frac{L_2 - L_1}{L_0} = \frac{2R}{\omega L_0} = \frac{2}{Q_0} \quad ...(22.55)$$

$(L_2 - L_1)$ gives the total variation in L in moving from one-half power condition to the other. The quantity $\frac{L_0}{L_2 - L_1}$ thus gives the selectivity of the series *RLC* circuit with L variable and this equal $\frac{Q_0}{2}$, as may be seen from Eq. (22.55).

Fig. 22.12 gives curves showing variation of current I, voltage V_l across inductor L and voltage V_c across capacitor C as L is varied.

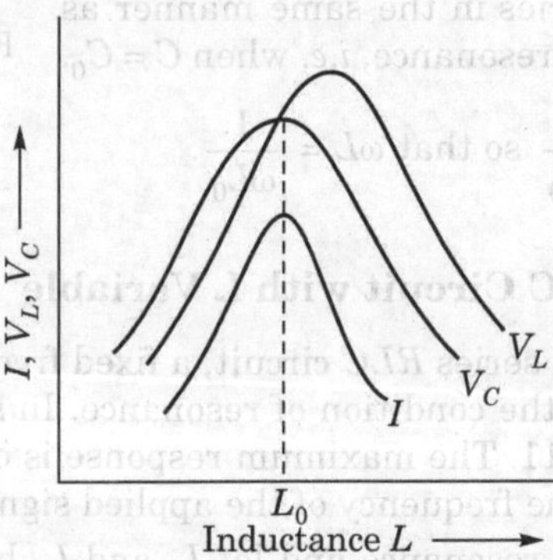

Fig. 22.12. Variation of current I and voltages V_c and V_l with variation of L.

Voltage V_C, being equal to $\frac{1}{\omega C}$ varies in the same manner as current I and becomes maximum at resonance, *i.e.* when $L = L_0$.

At resonance $V_l = V_c$, *i.e.* $I\omega L_0 = \frac{1}{\omega C}$ so that $wL_0 = \frac{1}{\omega C}$.

22.11. Parallel Resonance or Anti-resonance

A parallel resonant or anti-resonant circuit consists of an induc-tor L in parallel with a capacitor C as shown in Fig. 22.13. R is a small resistance associated with the coil. The capacitor C is assumed to be lossless. The tuned circuit is driven by a voltage source V. Such a parallel tuned circuit is commonly used in tuned amplifiers, oscillators etc.

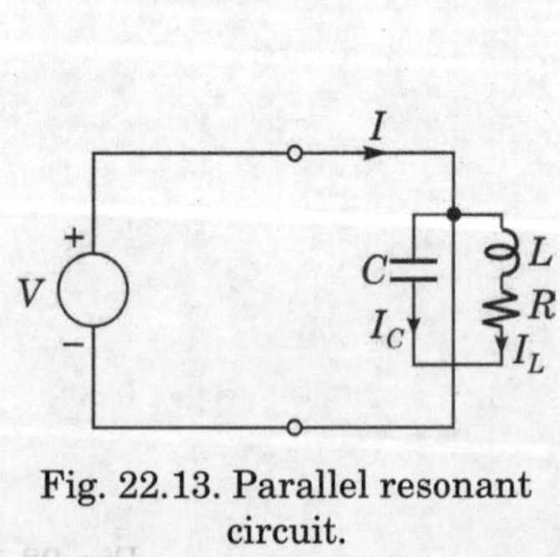

Fig. 22.13. Parallel resonant circuit.

Analysis of parallel tuned circuit may be done more conveniently in terms of admittances instead of impedances. Thus admittance of the inductive branch is given by

$$Y_1 = \frac{1}{R+j\omega L} = \frac{R - j\omega L}{R^2 + \omega^2 L^2} \qquad \text{...(22.56)}$$

Admittance of capacitor C is given by

$$Y_c = j\omega C \qquad \text{...(22.57)}$$

Total admittance

$$Y = Y_l + Y_c$$

$$= \frac{R}{R^2 + \omega^2 L^2} - j\left[\frac{\omega L}{R^2 + \omega^2 L^2} - \omega C\right] \qquad \text{...(22.58)}$$

At resonance,

$$\frac{\omega_0 L}{R_0^2 + \omega^2 L^2} - \omega_0 C = 0$$

or

$$R^2 + \omega_2{}^2 L^2 = \frac{L}{C} \qquad \text{...(22.59)}$$

Hence

$$\omega_0 = \sqrt{\frac{1}{LC} - \frac{R^2}{L^2}} \qquad \text{...(22.60)}$$

or

$$f_0 = \frac{1}{2\pi}\sqrt{\frac{1}{LC} - \frac{R^2}{L^2}} \qquad \text{...(22.61)}$$

Eq. (22.61) may also be put as,

$$f_0 = \frac{1}{2\pi}\sqrt{\frac{1}{LC}} \cdot \sqrt{1 - \frac{CR^2}{L}} \qquad \text{...(22.62)}$$

Considering the three elements, L, C and R in series, the Q_0 is given by $\frac{\omega_s L}{R}$ or $\frac{1}{\omega_s CR}$, where ω_s is the series resonant frequency in radians/sec.

Then

$$Q_0{}^2 = \frac{\omega_s L}{R} \cdot \frac{1}{\omega_s CR} = \frac{L}{CR^2} \qquad \text{...(22.63)}$$

Substituting $Q_0{}^2$ for $\frac{L}{CR^2}$, Eq. (22.63) yields,

$$f_0 = \frac{1}{2\pi}\sqrt{\frac{1}{LC}} \cdot \sqrt{1 - \frac{1}{Q_0^2}} \qquad \text{...(22.64)}$$

But the frequency of series resonance is given by,

$$f_s = \frac{1}{2\pi}\sqrt{\frac{1}{LC}} \qquad \text{...(22.65)}$$

Hence

$$f_0 = f_s\sqrt{1 - \frac{1}{Q_0^2}} \qquad \text{...(22.66)}$$

From Eq. (22.66) we find that the frequency of parallel resonance f_0 differs from the frequency of series resonance f_s. However, if Q_0 exceeds 10, then the factor $\sqrt{1 - \frac{1}{Q_0^2}} \approx 1$ and $f_0 = f_s$.

22.12. Impedance of Parallel Tuned Circuit

(A) At resonance. From Eq. (22.58), the admittance of the parallel tuned circuit at resonance is given by,

$$Y_a = \frac{R}{R^2 + \omega_0^2 L^2} \quad ..(22.67)$$

But from Eq. (22.59), $R^2 + \omega_0{}^2 L^2 = \frac{L}{C}$.

Hence $$Y_a = \frac{R}{\frac{L}{C}} = \frac{1}{\frac{L}{CR}} \quad ...(22.68)$$

Hence impedance at resonance is given by,

$$Z_a = R_a = \frac{L}{CR} \quad ..(22.69)$$

This is a pure resistance and is often called the *dynamic resistance* of the parallel tuned circuit.

From Eq. (22.69) we see that lower the resistance R of the coil, higher is the value of the resistance R_a at resonance.

The current drawn from supply source at resonance is called the *make up current* and equals $\frac{V}{L/CR} = \frac{VCR}{L}$. The current in the capacitor branch or inductor branch is called *forced oscillatory current* and equal $V\omega_0 C$.

Hence $$\frac{\text{Oscillatory current}}{\text{Make up current for supply}} = \frac{V\omega_0 C}{\frac{VCR}{L}}$$

$$= \frac{L\omega_0}{R} = Q_0 \quad ...(22.70)$$

Thus the parallel tuned circuit at resonance exhibits current magnification of $Q_0 \left(= \frac{\omega_0 L}{R} \right)$ while the series resonant circuit exhibits voltage magnification of the same value Q_0.

The dynamic resistance R_a of the parallel tuned circuit may also be expressed in terms of Q_0. Thus

$$R_a = \frac{L}{CR} = \frac{L\omega_0}{R} \cdot \frac{1}{\omega_0 L}$$

$$= \frac{1}{\omega_0 C} Q_0 \quad ...(22.71)$$

Also $$R_a = \frac{L}{CR} = L\omega_0 \frac{1}{\omega_0 CR} = \omega_0 L Q_0 \quad ...(22.72)$$

(B) Impedance at a frequency Close to Resonant Frequency

The impedance of parallel tuned circuit of Fig. 22.13 at any frequency ω is given by,

$$Z = \frac{(R + j\omega L)\left(\frac{1}{\omega C}\right)}{R + j\left(\omega L - \frac{1}{\omega C}\right)} \qquad \text{...(22.73)}$$

$$= \frac{2\left(1 + j\frac{\omega L}{R}\right)\left(\frac{1}{j\omega C}\right)}{R\left[1 + j\frac{\omega L}{R}\left(1 - \frac{1}{\omega^2 LC}\right)\right]}$$

$$= \frac{\frac{L}{CR} + \frac{1}{j\omega C}}{1 + j\frac{\omega L}{R}\left(1 - \frac{1}{\omega^2 LC}\right)} \qquad \text{...(22.74)}$$

Eq. (22.74) gives the general expression for impedance of a parallel circuit at any frequency ω. In most cases, however, we are concerned with frequencies close to the resonant frequency of the parallel tuned circuit. For such frequencies, let δ give the *fractional frequency deviation* or the *fractional detuning* defined as below,

$$\delta = \frac{\omega - \omega_0}{\omega_0} \qquad \text{..(22.75)}$$

Then
$$\frac{\omega}{\omega_0} = 1 + \delta \qquad \text{...(22.76)}$$

Hence
$$\frac{\omega L}{R} = \frac{\omega_0 L}{R} \cdot \frac{\omega}{\omega_0} = Q_0(1 + \delta) \qquad \text{...(22.77)}$$

Also
$$\frac{1}{\omega_0 LC} = \frac{\omega_0^2}{\omega^2} \cdot \frac{1}{\omega_0^2 LC} \qquad \text{...(22.78)}$$

For
$$Q > 10,\ \omega_0 \approx \frac{1}{\sqrt{LC}}$$

Hence
$$\frac{1}{\omega^2 LC} = \frac{\omega_0^2}{\omega^2} \qquad \text{...(22.79)}$$

Hence Eq. (22.74) yields,

$$Z = \frac{\frac{L}{CR}\left(1 - j\frac{R}{\omega L}\right)}{1 + j\,Q_0(1 + \delta)\left(1 - \frac{\omega_0^2}{\omega^2}\right)} \qquad \text{...(22.80)}$$

$$= \frac{L}{CR} \cdot \frac{\left[1 - j\frac{1}{Q_0(1 + \delta)}\right]}{1 + jQ_0\,(1 + \delta)\left[1 - j\frac{1}{(1 + \delta)^2}\right]}$$

$$= \frac{L}{CR} \cdot \frac{1 - j\frac{1}{Q_0(1 + \delta)}}{1 + jQ_0\left[(1 + \delta) - \frac{1}{(1 + \delta)}\right]}$$

$$= \frac{L}{CR}, \frac{1 - j\dfrac{1}{Q_0(1+\delta)}}{1 + Q_0\delta\left(\dfrac{2+\delta}{1+\delta}\right)} \qquad ...(22.81)$$

At parallel resonance, $\omega = \omega_0$ and $\delta = 0$.
Hence at resonance, the impedance of the parallel circuit is,

$$Z_0 = \frac{L}{CR}\left(1 - j\frac{1}{Q_0}\right) \qquad ...(22.82)$$

For $Q_0 >> 10$, $\dfrac{1}{Q_0}$ is small in comparison with unity and may, therefore, be neglected.

Hence $$Z_0 \approx \frac{L}{CR} \qquad ...(22.83)$$

This impedance at resonance is a pure resistance and may be denoted by R_t.

Eq. (22.81) gives the impedance of the parallel circuit for any value of δ. However, if the signal frequency is close to resonance, *i.e.* $\delta << 1$, then neglecting δ in comparison with unity, Eq. (22.81) may be written as,

$$Z = \frac{L}{RC} \cdot \frac{1 - j\dfrac{1}{Q_0}}{1 + f2\delta Q_0} \qquad ...(22.84)$$

Further if $Q_0 > 10$, $\dfrac{1}{Q_0} << 1$. Then Eq. (22.84) reduces to,

$$Z = \frac{L}{CR} \cdot \frac{1}{1 + j2\delta Q_0} \qquad ...(22.85)$$

$$= \frac{R_t}{1 + j2\delta Q_0} \qquad ...(22.86)$$

or $$\frac{Z}{R_t} = \frac{1}{1 + j2Q_0} \qquad ...(22.87)$$

Fig. 22.14 gives the nature of variation of relative impedance $\dfrac{Z}{R_t}$ of the parallel tuned circuit with frequency f. The impedance is

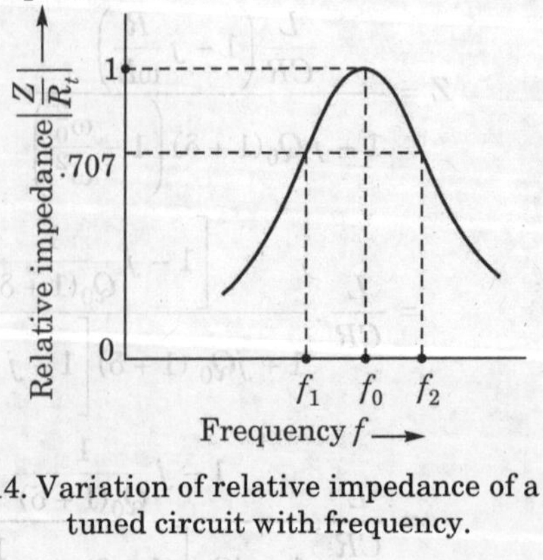

Fig. 22.14. Variation of relative impedance of a parallel tuned circuit with frequency.

maximum at resonance and falls off supply for frequencies either below or above this. The frequencies f_1 and f_2 at which the impedance falls to $\frac{R_t}{\sqrt{2}}$ (or 0.707 R_t) constitute the half-power frequencies or the 3 dB frequencies.

22.13. Selectivity and Bandwidth of Parallel Tuned Circuit

Fig. 22.15 (*a*) shows a voltage source V of the impedance R_g driving the parallel tuned. Fig. 22.15 (*b*) shows an equivalent circuit in which the voltage generator has been replaced by equivalent current generator making use of Norton's theorem.

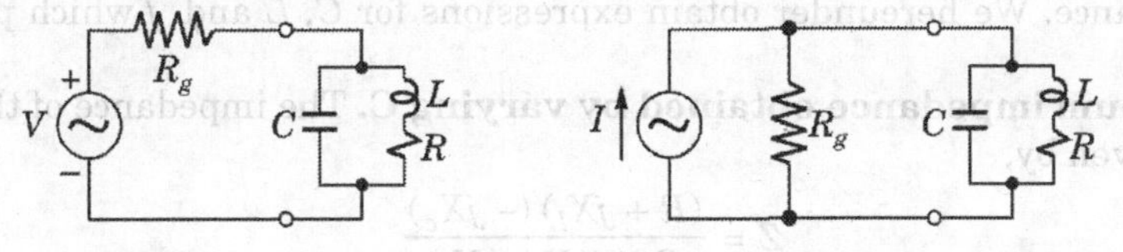

(*a*) Parallel tuned circuit driven by a voltage source. (*b*) Equivalent circuit using the equivalent current generator.

Fig. 22.15. A parallel tuned circuit driven from a voltage source and its equivalent circuit.

We proceed to find the selectivity and bandwidth of the parallel circuit neglecting the source resistance R_g. Under this condition, a constant current I flows through the parallel circuit and the output voltage across the parallel circuit is given by,

$$V_0 = IZ \quad \text{...(22.88)}$$

Current I being constant, the output voltage V_0 varies exactly in the same fashion as the impedance Z of the parallel circuit. The response of the parallel circuit, *i.e.* the output voltage V_0 is maximum at resonance and falls off on either side in accordance with the curve of Fig. 22.14.

At the half-power frequencies f_1 and f_2, the impedance Z falls to a value $\frac{Z_t}{\sqrt{2}}$. Hence from Eq. (22.87),

$$|1 + j2\delta Q_0| = \sqrt{2}$$

or $$2\delta Q_0 = \pm 1$$

or $$\delta = \pm \frac{1}{2Q_0} \quad \text{...(22.89)}$$

At upper half-power frequency f_2,

$$\frac{f_2 - f_0}{f_0} = \frac{1}{2Q_0}$$

At lower half-power frequency f_1,

$$\frac{f_1 - f_0}{f_0} = \frac{1}{2Q_0}.$$

Hence $$(f_2 - f_1) = \frac{f_0}{Q_0} \quad \text{...(22.90)}$$

or $$Q_0 = \frac{f_0}{(f_2 - f_1)} = \frac{f_0}{B} \quad \text{...(22.91)}$$

This Q_0 is a measure of the selectivity of the parallel resonant circuit.

Higher the value of Q_0, more selective is the circuit and smaller is the 3 dB bandwidth ($f_2 - f_1$) of B. Q_0 may also be put as,

$$Q_0 = \frac{\omega_0 L}{R} = \frac{1}{\omega_0 CR} = \frac{1}{R}\sqrt{\frac{L}{C}} \qquad ...(22.91\ a)$$

22.14. Maximum Impedance Conditions with C, L and f Variable

Ed. (22.60) gives the frequency of resonance of a parallel circuit in terms of L, C and R. This condition of resonance can be achieved by varying any of the following three quantities : *(a)* capacitance C, *(b)* inductance L or *(c)* frequency f. At resonance the impedance offered by the circuit is maximum. Hence in practice, we very one of the three quantities namely C, L or f so as to obtain maximum impedance. We hereunder obtain expressions for C, L and f which provide maximum impedance.

(A) **Maximum impedance obtained by varying C.** The impedance of the parallel circuit of Fig. 22.15 is given by,

$$Z = \frac{(R + jX_l)(-jX_c)}{R + j(X_l - X_c)} \qquad ...(22.92)$$

where $\qquad X_l = \omega L$ and $X_c = \dfrac{1}{\omega C}$.

Magnitude $\qquad |Z| = \dfrac{\sqrt{R^2 + X_l^2}\ .X_c}{\sqrt{R^2 + (X_l - X_c)^2}}$. $\qquad$ ...(22.93)

Hence $\qquad |Z|^2 = \dfrac{(R^2 + X_l^2).X_c^2}{R^2 + (X_l - X_c)^2}$ $\qquad$ ...(22.94)

The value of X_c which makes Z maximum will also make $|Z|^2$ maximum. The value X_c may be obtained by differentiating $|Z|^2$ (or $|Z|$) with respect to X_c and equating $\dfrac{d|Z|^2}{dX_c}$ to zero.

Hence, we get

$$[R^2 + (X_l - X_c)^2].\ 2X_c\,(R^2 + Xl^2) + 2\,(R^2 + Xl^2)\,X_c^2\,(X_l - X_c) = 0 \qquad ...(22.95)$$

or $\qquad 2X_c\,(R^2 + Xl^2)\,[R^2 + (X_l - X_c)^2 + X_c\,(X_l - X_c)] = 0$ $\qquad$ ...(22.96)

X_c, being equal to $\dfrac{1}{\omega C}$, cannot be zero since this will require C to be infinite. Also $(R^2 + X_l^2)$ cannot be zero since it is the sum of squares of two real quantities. Hence $[R^2 + (X_l - X_c)^2 + X_c\,(X_l - X_c)]$ must become zero.

Thus $\qquad R^2 + X_l^2 - X_c\,.\,X_l = 0$ $\qquad$ ...(22.97)

Hence $\qquad X_c = \dfrac{R^2 + R_l^2}{X_l}$ $\qquad$ ...(22.98)

or $\qquad X_c = X_l\left[1 + \left(\dfrac{R^2}{X_l}\right)\right]$ or $X_c = X_l\left(1 + \dfrac{1}{Q_0^2}\right)$ $\qquad$ ...(22.99)

Eqs. (22.98) and (22.99) give the value of reactance X_c for maximum impedance.

Eq. (22.97) may be written as,

$$R_2 + \omega^2 L^2 = \frac{L}{C} \qquad ..(22.100)$$

or $$\omega^2 L^2 C^2 = L - CR^2$$

or $$\omega = \sqrt{\frac{1}{LC} - \frac{R^2}{L^2}} \quad ...(22.101)$$

Comparing Eq. (22.101) with Eq. (22.60), we find that $\omega = \omega_0$, the frequency of parallel resonance or the frequency of unity power factor or zero net reactance. We thus find that when capacitor C is adjusted for maximum impedance, the condition of unity power factor automatically gets satisfied. This capacitance variation method of tuning is, therefore, preferred in electronic experiments.

(*B*) **Maximum impedance obtained by varying inductance, L.** Eq. (22.94) gives $|Z|^2$, where $|Z|$ is the magnitude of the impedance of the parallel circuit of Fig. 22.15. The value of X_l which makes $|Z|$ maximum will also make $|Z|^2$ maximum. This value of X_l may be obtained by differentiating $|Z|^2$ with respect to X_l and equating $\frac{d|Z|^2}{dX_l}$ to zero. Thus, we get

$$\frac{d|Z|^2}{dX_l} = \frac{2[R^2 + (X_l - X_c)^2]X_l X_c^2 - 2(R^2 + X_l^2)X_c^2(X_l - X_c)}{[R^2 + (X_l - X_c)^2]^2} \quad ...(22.102)$$

Equating $\frac{d|Z|^2}{dX_l}$ to zero, we get

$$R^2 . X_l + (X_l - X_c)^2 . X_l - (X_l - X_c)(R^2 + X_l^2) = 0$$

or $$X_c[X_l . X_c - X_l^2 + R^2] = 0 \quad ...(22.103)$$

Now X_c cannot be zero.

Hence $$X_l^2 - X_c . X_l - R^2 = 0 \quad ...(22.104)$$

Hence $$X_l = \frac{X_c}{2} + \sqrt{\left(\frac{X_c}{2}\right)^2 + R^2} \quad ...(22.105)$$

Eq. (22.105) gives the value of reactance X_l for maximum impedance.

Eq. (22.104) may be written as,

$$\omega_{0l}^2 L^2 - \frac{L}{C} - R^2 = 0$$

or $$\omega_{0l}^2 = \frac{1}{LC} + \frac{R^2}{L^2} \quad ...(22.106)$$

Hence $$\omega_{0l} = \sqrt{\frac{1}{LC} + \frac{R^2}{L^2}} \quad ...(22.107)$$

Comparing Eq. (22.107) with Eq. (22.60), we find that with L adjusted for maximum impedance, $\omega_0 \neq \omega_{0l}$ where ω_0 is the frequency of parallel resonance, *i.e.*, the frequency of unity power factor or zero net resistance. Thus in a practical circuit if inductance L is adjusted for maximum impedance, the power factor is not unity and net reactance of the parallel circuit is not zero.

(*C*) **Maximum impedance obtained by varying the frequency.** The value of frequency ω which makes $|Z|^2$ maximum may be obtained by equating to zero the derivative $\frac{d|Z|^2}{d\omega}$. On so doing, we arrive at the following expression for frequency which makes $|Z|$ maximum,

$$\omega_{0f} = \left[\frac{1}{LC}\sqrt{1 + \frac{2R^2C}{L} - \frac{R^2}{L^2}}\right]^{1/2} \quad ...(22.108)$$

Obviously this frequency ω_{0f} is not equal to ω_0, the frequency of unity power factor resonance.

Maximum impedance conditions for high Q circuit. The frequencies ω_0, ω_{0l} and ω_{0f} as obtained above for the three cases of C variable, L variable and frequency f variable respectively, differ somewhat. The difference is significant only in low Q circuit. Radio circuits, usually employ parallel circuits having high Q values. In such cases, $L >> R$ so that we may neglect terms involving R/L. Hence in high Q circuit, all the three frequency ω_0, ω_{0l} and ω_{0f} reduce to the same value. Thus

$$\omega_0 = \omega_{0l} = \omega_{0l} = \frac{1}{\sqrt{LC}} \qquad ...(22.109)$$

22.15. Effect of Source Impedance on Sharpness of Resonance Curve

Let R_g be the internal impedance of the source driving the parallel circuit as shown in Fig. 22.15. Then from Fig. 22.15 (*a*) the current through the parallel circuit is given by,

$$I = \frac{V}{R_0 + Z} \qquad ...(22.110)$$

The voltage across the parallel circuit is,

$$V_c = \frac{V.Z}{R_g + Z} \qquad ...(22.111)$$

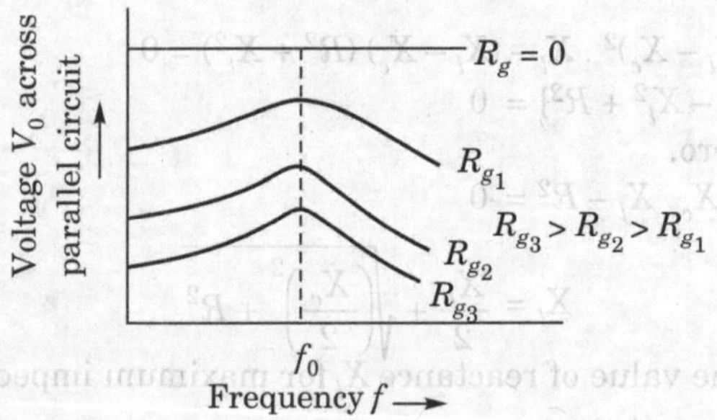

Fig. 22.16. Effect of generator impedance on output voltage curve.

It is apparent that :

(*i*) with $R_g = 0$, the output voltage V_0 across the tuned circuit is independent of frequency as shown by the horizontal line for $R_g = 0$, in Fig. 22.16.

(*ii*) with non-zero value of R_g, as the frequency departs from the resonant value, the parallel circuit impedance decreases and for fixed value of R_2, progressively smaller fraction of the source voltage V becomes available across the parallel circuit. The V_0 *versus* frequency curve thus becomes peaky at resonant frequency f_0. Higher the value of source resistance R_g, more peaky is the V_0 *versus* frequency curve as shown in Fig. 22.16.

22.16. Design of Parallel Tuned Circuit

The admittance of the parallel circuit as shown in Fig. 22.14 is given by Eq. (22.58) reproduced below :

$$Y = \frac{R}{R^2 + \omega^2 L^2} - j\left(\frac{\omega L}{R^2 + \omega^2 L^2} - \omega C\right) \qquad ...(22.112)$$

At unity power factor resonance, the susceptance part of admittance must become zero.

Thus at unity power factor resonance, admittance and impedance of the parallel circuit are real quantities and are given by,

$$Y_0 = \frac{R}{R^2 + \omega_0^2 L^2} \quad ...(22.113)$$

and
$$Z_0 = R_0 = \frac{R^2 + \omega_0^2 L^2}{R} \quad ...(22.114)$$

Hence
$$\omega_0 L = X_1 = \sqrt{R(R_0 - R)} \quad ...(22.115)$$

From Eq. (22.114),

$$Q_0 = \frac{\omega_0 L}{R} = \sqrt{\frac{R_0 - R}{R}} \quad ...(22.116)$$

Further from Eq. (22.112) for unity power factor resonance,

$$\frac{\omega_0 L}{R^2 + \omega_0^2 L^2} = \omega_0 C \quad ...(22.117)$$

Hence
$$\frac{L}{C} = R^2 + \omega_0{}^2 L^2 \quad ...(22.118)$$

Combining Eqs. (22.114) and (22.118), we get

$$\frac{\omega_0 L}{\omega_0 C} = R.R_0 \quad ...(22.119)$$

Hence
$$\frac{1}{\omega_0 C} = X_C = \frac{RR_0}{\omega_0 L} = R_0 \sqrt{\frac{R}{\sqrt{R_0 - R}}} \quad ...(22.120)$$

or
$$\frac{1}{\omega_0 C} = \frac{R_0}{Q_0} \quad ...(22.121)$$

Eqs. (22.115), (22.116) and (22.121) may be used in designing an anti-resonant circuit.

Parallel tuned circuits are employed as tuned load in tuned amplifiers used for amplifying either a single radio frequency or a narrow band of frequencies. Use of tuned circuit has the added advantage that the tuned circuit transforms small value branch resistance $\left(\frac{1}{\omega_0 C} \text{ or } \omega_0 L\right)$ into large value R_0 necessary for appropriate impedance match.

Example 22.5. *Design an anti-resonance circuit which may transform branch resistance of 10 ohms into effective resistance of 8,000 ohms at the anti-resonant frequency of 10^7 radians / second*

Solution. Branch resistance

$$\omega_0 L = 80\ \Omega$$
$$\omega_0 = 10^7 \text{ radians/sec}$$

Hence
$$L = \frac{80}{10^7} = 80 \times 10^{-7} \text{ Henry} = 8\ \mu\text{H}.$$

Effective resistance R_0 of the tuned circuit

$$= Q_0 \omega_0 L.$$

Hence
$$Q_0 = \frac{R_0}{\omega_0 L} = \frac{8000}{80} = 100.$$

But
$$Q_0 = \frac{\omega_0 L}{R}.$$

Hence
$$R = \frac{\omega_0 L}{Q_0} = \frac{80}{100} = 0.8\ \Omega.$$

Also $$Q_0 = \frac{1}{\omega_0 CR}$$

Hence $$C = \frac{1}{\omega_0 Q_0 R} = \frac{1}{10^7 \times 100 \times 0.8} = 0.125 \times 10^{-8} \text{ Farad.}$$

Thus the required values of the components of the parallel circuit are :

$R = 0.8$; $L = 8\ \mu H$;
$C = 0.125 \times 10^{-8}$ Farad ; $Q_0 = 100$.

22.17. Coupled Circuits

Two circuit are said to be coupled when energy can be transferred from one to other. In most cases, coupling between two circuits is produced by having inductive coupling between two coils, one in each circuit. Thus current flowing in one coil results in magnetic flux which induces voltage in the other coil. This induced voltage result in current in the second coil. Thus transfer of energy takes place from one circuit (primary circuit) to the other circuit (secondary circuit).

The primary and the secondary circuits may be of the following three types :

(*a*) both primary and secondary circuits untuned

(*b*) primary circuit tuned and the secondary untuned and

(*c*) both primary and secondary tuned.

Instead of taking up a detailed analysis, we have take up only the band pass characteristics of coupled circuits and their important features.

Effective Impedance of Primary Circuit. For understanding the function of coupled circuits, we here take up the determination of effective impedance of primary in the presence of coupled secondary. We consider the case when both the primary and the secondary are tuned circuits.

Fig. 22.17 shows the inductively coupled circuits. Let. X_p and X_s be the reactances of the primary and the secondary circuits respectively.

Then $$X_p = \omega L_p - \frac{1}{\omega C_p} \qquad ...(22.122)$$

and $$X_s = \omega L_s - \frac{1}{\omega C_s} \qquad ...(22.123)$$

Current I_p in the primary is then given by,

$$I_p = -\frac{V - j\omega M I_s}{R_p + jX_p} \qquad ...(22.124)$$

Current I_s induced in the secondary circuit because of the flow of current I_p in the primary is given by,

$$I_s = \frac{jI_p \omega M}{(R_s + jX_s)} \qquad ...(22.125)$$

$$= -\frac{j\omega M I_p (R_s - jX_s)}{(R_s + jX_s)(R_s - jX_s)}$$

$$= \frac{-j\omega M I_p (R_s - jX_s)}{R_s^2 + X_s^2} \qquad ...(22.126)$$

Substituting the value of I_s from Eq. (22.126) into Eq. (22.124), we get

$$I_p(R_p + jX_p) = V - j\omega M\left[\frac{-j\omega M I_p(R_s - jX_s)}{R_s^2 + X_s^2}\right] \qquad ...(22.127)$$

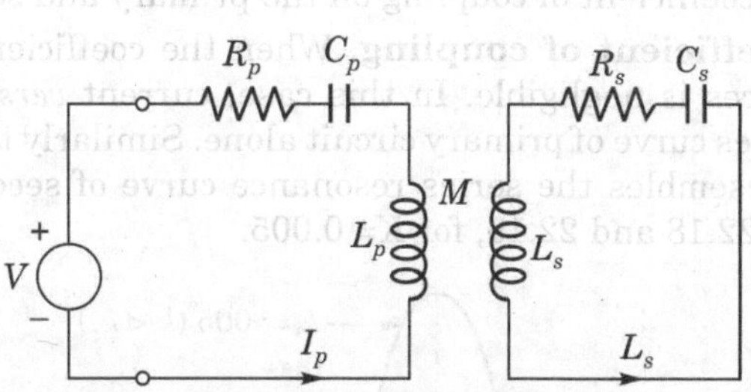

Fig. 22.17. Inductively coupled coils.

On rearranging Eq. (22.127) yields,

$$V = I_p\left[(R_p + jX_p) + \frac{\omega^2 M^2 (R_s + jX_s)}{R_s^2 + X_s^2}\right] \qquad ...(22.128)$$

$$= I_p\left[\left(R_p + \frac{\omega^2 M^2 R_s}{R_s^2 + X_s^2}\right) + j\left(X_p - \frac{\omega^2 M^2 X_s}{R_s^2 + X_s^2}\right)\right] \qquad ...(22.129)$$

Then the effective impedance of the primary is given by,

$$Z'_P = \frac{V}{I_p}\left(R_p + \frac{\omega^2 M^2 R_s}{R_s^2 + X_s^2}\right) + j\left(X_p - \frac{\omega^2 M^2 X_s}{R_s^2 + X_s^2}\right) \qquad ...(22.130)$$

Hence, effective primary resistance $R'_p = R_p + \dfrac{\omega^2 M^2 X_s}{R_s^2 + X_s^2}$ ...(22.131)

effective primary reactance $X'_p = X_p - \dfrac{\omega^2 M^2 X_s}{R_s^2 + X_s^2}$ ...(22.132)

From Eqs. (22.131) and (22.132) we find that (*i*) original primary resistance and reactance have been modified by components caused by secondary circuit impedance reflected to the primary.

Thus,

resistance component of reflected impedance $= \dfrac{\omega^2 M^2 R_s}{R_s^2 + X_s^2}$ ...(22.133)

reactive component of reflected impedance $= \dfrac{\omega^2 M^2 X_s}{R_s^2 + X_s^2}$ ...(22.134)

Similarly the primary impedance is reflected in the secondary circuit. The nature and magnitude of the impedance reflected from the secondary in the primary influences the primary current. Similarly the nature and magnitude of the impedance reflected from the primary into the secondary influences the secondary current. However, when the mutual inductance M is small, the coupled impedance are small. Then the influence of the coupled impedances on the primary and secondary circuit currents are small. On the other hand, if the coefficient of coupling K between coils is large, mutual inductance M is large, coupled impedances are large and the primary and secondary circuit currents are greatly influenced. Considerable transfer of power then takes place from the primary to the secondary circuit.

22.18. Effect of Coefficient of Coupling

When two *RLC* circuits, as shown in Fig. 22.17 tuned to the same frequency, are coupled together, the resulting behaviour of the two circuits depends upon the degree of coupling. We consider here the effect of coefficient of coupling on the primary and secondary currents.

(*A*) **With small coefficient of coupling.** When the coefficient of coupling is small, the effect of coupled impedances is negligible. In this case, current *versus* frequency curve for the primary resembles the series curve of primary circuit alone. Similarly the current *versus* frequency curve for the secondary resembles the series resonance curve of secondary circuit alone. These curves are shown in Figs. 22.18 and 22.19, for $K = 0.005$.

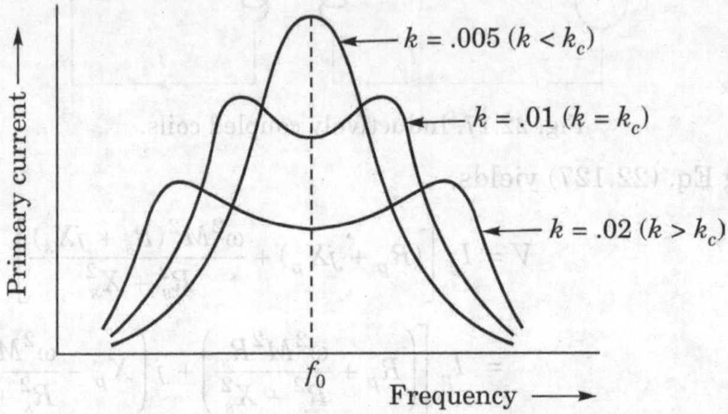

Fig. 22.18. Primary current *versus* frequency curves for different values of coefficient of coupling.

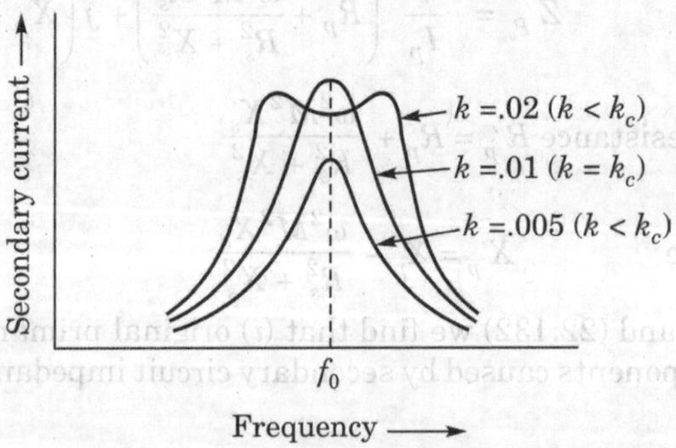

Fig. 22.19. Secondary current *versus* frequency curves for different values of coefficient of coupling.

(*B*) **Critical coefficient of coupling.** As the coefficient of coupling k increases, the primary current *versus* frequency curve broadens and at the same time the peak value of primary current reduces. Similarly with the increase of k, the secondary current *versus* frequency curve also broadens but the peak value of secondary current increases. As the coefficient of coupling progressively increases, a stage is reached when the secondary current becomes maximum. For this value of k, the secondary current curve is somewhat broader than the resonance curve of the secondary circuit considered alone and the curve has a relatively flat top. At the same time, for this value of d, the primary current curve has two peaks. These curves for primary and secondary currents are shown in Figs. 22.18 and 22.19 for $k = 0.01$. At this value of k, the resistance component of impedance reflected from the secondary into the primary equals the resistance of the primary. The coefficient of coupling is then said to have critical value. This *critical coefficient of coupling* is generally indicated by k_c. The critical coupling causes the secondary current to have maximum possible value.

Mathematically we may state that for $k = k_c$.

$$R_p = \frac{\omega_0^2 M^2 R_s}{R_s^2 + X_s^2} \quad ...(22.135)$$

But $X_s = 0$, since the secondary also is at resonance.

Hence $$R_p = \frac{\omega_0^2 M^2}{R_s} \quad ...(22.136)$$

But $$Q_p = \frac{\omega_0 L_p}{R_p} \quad ...(22.137)$$

and $$Q_s = \frac{\omega_0 L_s}{R_s} \quad ...(22.138)$$

where Q_p and Q_s are Q-factors of primary and secondary circuits respectively.

From Eqs. (22.137) and (22.138), we get

$$R_p R_s = \frac{\omega_0^2 L_p L_s}{Q_p Q_s} \quad ...(22.139)$$

Combining Eqs. (22.135) and (22.138), we get

$$\omega_2{}^2 M^2 = \frac{\omega_0^2 L_p L_s}{Q_p Q_s} \quad \text{or} \quad \frac{M^2}{L_p L_s} = \frac{1}{Q_p Q_s} \quad ...(22.140)$$

But $$\frac{M^2}{L_p L_s} = k_c{}^2.$$

Hence $$k_c{}^2 = \frac{1}{Q_p Q_s} \quad ...(22.141)$$

If $$Q_p = Q_s = Q,$$

then $$k_c = \frac{1}{Q} \quad ...(22.142)$$

(*C*) **Large coefficient of coupling.** If k exceeds the critical values k_c. (*i*) Both the primary and the secondary currents have lower and lower values at $\omega = \omega_0$.

(*ii*) both primary and secondary current curves have more and more prominent double humps and

(*iii*) the peak spread increases.

At resonance frequency, the primary current is small because of the large value of coupled resistance. At the humps or the current maxima of the primary current, the coupled reactance exactly neutralises the primary reactance.

Since the secondary current depends on the primary current, its tends to have maximum values at frequencies, where the primary current is maximum. Hence the secondary current curve has double humps for $k > k_c$. Figs. 22.18 and 22.19 show the double humped primary and secondary currents respectively for $k = 0.02$ *i.e.* $k > k_c$.

From Fig. 22.19 it is clear that the secondary current curve tends to have maximum flatness for k slightly exceeding the critical value.

22.19. Band Pass Characteristic of Coupled Circuit

We have already seen that the reactances reflected from the secondary into the primary circuit is given by,

$$X_r = \frac{\omega^2 M^2 X_s}{R_s^2 + X_s^2}$$

But in most of the circuits $R_p << \omega X_p$ and $R_z << \omega X_s$. Hence the equivalent reactance of the primary may be taken as,

$$X_{eq} = X_p - \frac{\omega^2 M}{X_s} \quad ...(22.143)$$

At resonant frequency f_0, X_{eq} becomes zero. Hence

$$X_p - \frac{\omega^2 M^2}{X_s} = 0$$

or
$$\omega^2 M^2 = X_p X_s = \left(\omega L_p - \frac{1}{\omega C_p}\right)\left(\omega L_s - \frac{1}{\omega C_s}\right)$$

$$= \omega^2 L_p L_s \left(1 - \frac{1}{\omega^2 L_p C_p}\right)\left(1 - \frac{1}{\omega^2 L_s C_s}\right)$$

Hence
$$M^2 = L_s L_p \left(1 - \frac{1}{\omega^2 L_p L_p}\right)\left(1 - \frac{1}{\omega^2 L_s C_s}\right) \quad ...(22.144)$$

But angular resonant frequency is given by

$$\omega_0{}^2 = \frac{1}{L_p C_p} = \frac{1}{L_s C_s} \quad ...(22.145)$$

Hence Eq. (22.144) may put as,

$$M^2 = L_p L_s \left(1 - \frac{\omega_0^2}{\omega^2}\right)\left(1 - \frac{\omega_0^2}{\omega^2}\right) \quad ...(22.146)$$

But
$$K^2 = \frac{M^2}{L_p L_s}.$$

Hence Eq. (22.146) may be written as,

$$k^2 = \left(1 - \frac{\omega_0^2}{\omega^2}\right)^2$$

Hence
$$\omega_0{}^2 = (1 \pm k)\omega^2 \quad ...(22.147)$$

or
$$f_0{}^2 = (1 \pm k) f^2 \quad ...(22.148)$$

Hence
$$f = \frac{f_0}{\sqrt{1 \pm k}} \quad ...(22.149)$$

$$\approx \frac{f_0}{1 \pm \dfrac{k}{2}} \quad ...(22.150)$$

Eq. (22.150) gives two values of frequency f at which reactance is zero and current I_p is maximum. Let these frequencies be f_1 and f_2.

Then $$f_1 = \frac{f_0}{1 + \frac{k}{2}} \qquad \text{...(22.151)}$$

and $$f_2 = \frac{f_0}{1 - \frac{k}{2}} \qquad \text{...(22.152)}$$

Frequency range $(f_2 - f_1)$ may be called the *width of passband.*

Thus $$\Delta f = (f_2 - f_1) = f_0\left(1 - \frac{k}{2}\right)^{-1} - f_0\left(1 + \frac{k}{2}\right)^{-1}$$

$$= f_0 k.$$

But $K = \frac{1}{Q_0}$ for critical coupling.

Hence $$\Delta f = f_0 k = \frac{f_1}{Q_0} \qquad \text{...(22.153)}$$

From Eq. (22.153) we find that the width of passband depends upon the coefficient of coupling k and varies inversely as the Q of the circuits.

22.20. Use of Double Tuned Circuits in Radio Receivers

A broadcast receiver in ideal condition is expected to have uniform response to amplitude modulated signal occupying a total bandwidth of 10 kHz centred about the carrier frequency. Single tuned circuit used as the load impedance in an amplifier fails to meet his requirement. Firstly, its response is not flat topped. Secondly its response falls very slowly with frequency at the edges of the 10 kHz band. Double tuned circuits with critical coupling are popularly used as load impedance in the I.F. (Intermediate frequency) amplifier stage in a superheterodyne receiver. The double tuned circuits meets the ideal condition regarding bandwidth to a very large extent. The critically double tuned circuit has an almost flat topped response with very small double humps. A flat topped response permits equal reproduction of all audio modulating frequencies, *i.e.* permits high fidelity. Further the response drops rapidly with frequency at the edges of the 10 kHz passband, *i.e.* the circuit has highly selectivity.

Fig. 22.20 shows response curves of an amplifier with single tuned and double tuned circuits with critical coupling. In the case of double tuned circuit, the passband with almost constant response may be taken as bandwidth between points P_1 and P_2 on the curve having

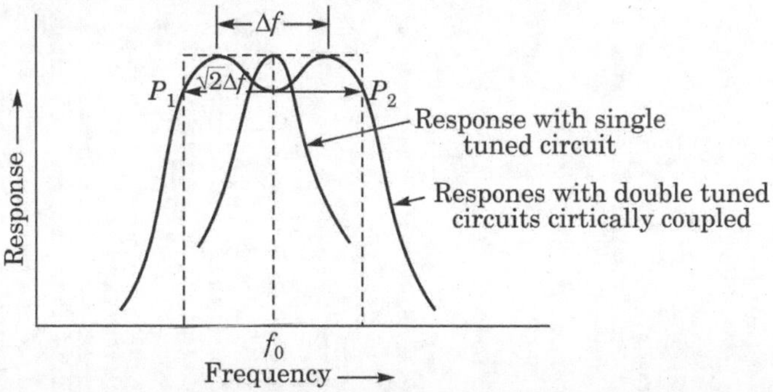

Fig. 22.20. Response curve of an amplifier with single tuned and double tuned circuit.

response equal to that at the centre frequency. It may be shown that this bandwidth equals $\sqrt{2}\,\Delta f$, where Δf is the bandwidth between current peaks.

The slope of the sides of the response curve depends on the *Q*-factor of the circuit. Higher the *Q*, steeper the curves. Hence high *Q* circuit should be used for better selectivity. But as is evident from Fig. 22.20, the sides of the response curves of single tuned circuit remain less steep. However large *Q* may be chosen. Double tuned circuits have to be used for good selectivity.

EXERCISES 22

22.1. A coil of inductance 0.2 Henry and resistance 5 Ω is connected in series with a capacitor of value 0.05 μF. Find the frequency of series resonance of this circuit in Hz. [**Ans.** 1592 Hz]

22.2. An *RLC* series circuit consists of capacitor of value 0.05 μF. It resonates at 5000 Hz. Calculate the value of inductance *L*. [**Ans.** 20.28 mH]

22.3. A series *RLC* circuit consists of resistance $R = 20\ \Omega$, inductance $L = 0.05$. H and capacitance $C = 0.05$ μF. Calculate the frequency of resonance. A sinusoidal voltage of r.m.s. value 20 volts and frequency equal to the frequency of resonance is applied to this series circuit. Calculate the value of (*i*) current (*ii*) voltages across *R*, *C* and *L* and (*iii*) phase angle of the current. Repeat the calculations for signal frequency of 3000 Hz.

[**Ans.** At $f_0 : I = 1$ Amp; $V_r = 0$, volts; $V_c = 10^3$ votls; $V_l = 10^3$ volts; At $f = 3000$ Hz; $I = 0.1644$ Amp ; $V_r = 3.88$ volts; $V_c = 174.6$ volts; $V_l = 155$ volts; $f = 80.6°$]

23

Filters

23.1. Introduction

An *electric wave filter* or simple *filter* is an electric network which *passes* or allows unattenuated transmission of electric signal within certain frequency range and *stops* or disallows transmission of electric signal outside this range.

Electric wave filters may be classified as below according to their use :

(*a*) **Low pass filters.** These filters reject all frequencies above a specified value.

(*b*) **High pass filters.** These filters reject all frequencies below a specified value.

(*c*) **Band pass filters.** A band pass filter passes or allows transmission of a band of frequencies and rejects all frequencies beyond this band.

(*d*) **Band elimination fitters.** A band elimination filter rejects or disallows transmission of a limited band of frequencies but allows transmission of all other frequencies.

The following three factors characterise a filter:

(*a*) **Characteristic impedance Z_0.** This should be so chosen that the filter may fit into a given line or between two pieces of equipment.

(*b*) **Pass band.** Filter should have very low (ideally zero) attenuation in the *pass band* and high attenuation in the *stop band* or attenuation band.

(*c*) **Cut-off frequency.** This frequency demarcates the pass band and the stop band.

An ideal filter offers zero attenuation in the pass band and infinite attentuation in the stop band. Practical filters fail to satisfy these ideals due to reflections resulting from terminal impedance inequalities and due to losses caused by imperfect conductors and dielectrics. A well designed filter, however, closely approximates the ideal one.

23.2. Decibel and Neper

Study of filters involves study of attenuation in the filter. The units of attenuation of a filter or any electric network are : (*i*) *decibel* (or *bel*) and (*ii*) *neper.*

Bel. Bel is fundamentally a unit of power ratio at the two ports of a network. Thus let P_i be the power input to a network at the sending end or input end and let P_0 be the power output of the network at the receiving end or the output end. Then the output power/input power ratio in Bels is given by,

Power transfer ratio or power gain in Bels

$$= \log_{10} \frac{P_0}{P_i} \qquad ...(23.1)$$

In the case of a filter or attenuation, $P_0 < P_i$ so that the power transfer ratio in Bels comes out to be negative, *i.e.* an attenuation takes place.

Hence power loss or attenuator in Bels

$$= -\log_{10} \frac{P_0}{P_i}$$

$$= \log_{10} \frac{P_i}{P_0} \qquad ...(23.2)$$

Bel is a large unit. Accordingly in practice, more convenient unit is decibel (abbreviated as dB) which is one-tenth of Bel.

Thus power gain in dB $= 10 \log_{10} (P_0/P_i)$ ...(23.3)

and power attenuation in dB

$$= 10 \log_{10} (Pi/P_0) \quad ...(23.4)$$

In case, the power P_i and P_0 are associated with equal impedan-ces, then the power ratio may be expressed as the square of voltage ratio or current ratio.

Thus with equal impedances,

$$\text{Power gain in dB} = 10 \log_{10} \left| \frac{V_0}{V_i} \right|^2$$

$$= 20 \log_{10} \left| \frac{V_0}{V_i} \right| \quad ...(23.5)$$

or

$$\text{Power gain in dB} = 10 \log_{10} \left| \frac{I_0}{I_i} \right|^2 = 20 \log_{10} \left| \frac{I_0}{I_i} \right| \quad ...(23.6)$$

Similarly power attenuation in dB

$$= 10 \log_{10} \left| \frac{V_0}{V_i} \right|^2 = 20 \log_{10} \left| \frac{V_0}{V_i} \right| \quad ...(23.7)$$

or power attenuation in dB

$$= 10 \log_{10} \left| \frac{I_i}{I_0} \right| = 20 \log_{10} \left| \frac{I_i}{I_0} \right| \quad ...(23.8)$$

Neper. Neper is fundamentally a unit of current ratio or voltage ratio. Let in a two-port network, the current entering at the input terminals be I_i and that leaving at the output terminals be I_0. Then the attenuation in Neper is expressed by the relation,

$$\text{Attenuation in Nepers} = 10 \log_e \left| \frac{I_i}{I_0} \right| \quad ...(23.9)$$

If the voltage at the input terminals is V_i and that at the output terminals is V_0, then

$$\text{Attenuation in nepers} = \log_e \left| \frac{V_i}{V_0} \right| \quad ...(23.10)$$

Relationship between neper and decibels. From Eq. (23.8),

$$\text{Attenuation in dB} = 20 \log_{10} \left| \frac{I_i}{I_0} \right| = 10 \log_e \left| \frac{I_i}{I_0} \right|$$

$$= 8.686 \log_e \left| \frac{I_i}{I_0} \right| \quad ...(23.11)$$

The attenuation in dB = 8.686 × Attenuation in nepers.

23.3. Basic Relation in a Filter

Filter networks in general, consist of one or more sections symmetrical T or π-networks or their half sections. Fig. 23.1 (*a*) shows a symmetrical T-section. Z_1 is the total impedance in the series arm while Z, is the impedance in the shunt arm. This T-section may be considered to be built up of two unsymmetrical half-sections as shown in Fig. 23.1 (*a*).

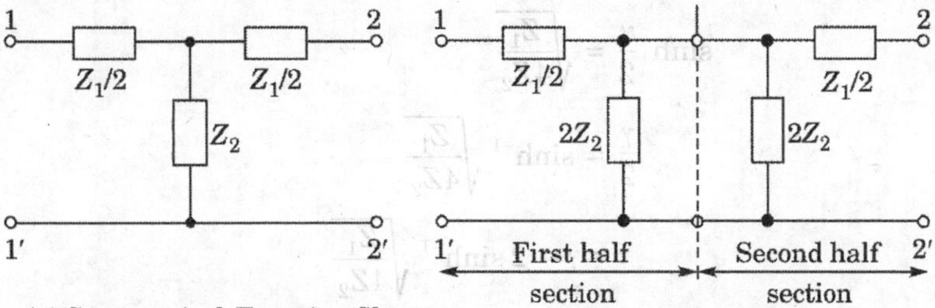

(a) Symmetrical T-section filter. (b) Two half-section.

Fig. 23.1. Symmetrical T-section filter and constituent two half sections.

Fig. 23.2 (a) shows a symmetrical π-section filter. Here also Z_1 is the total impedance in the series arm while Z_2 is the total impedance of the shunt arm. Thus π-section may be considered to be built up of two unsymmetrical half-sections as shown in Fig. 23.2 (b).

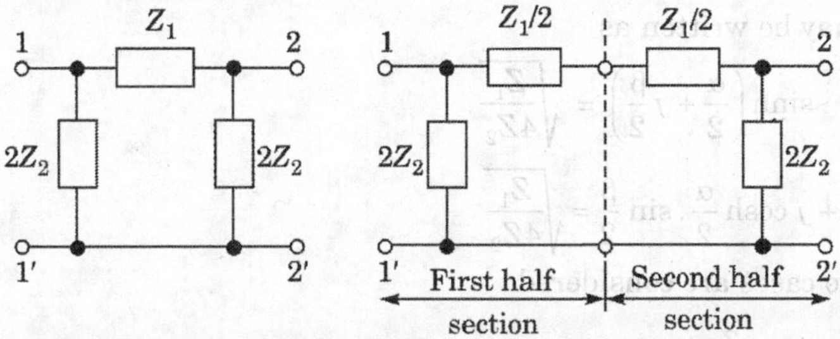

(a) Symmetrical π-section filter. (b) Two half-sections.

Fig. 23.2. Symmetrical π-section filter and its constituent two half sections.

The transfer constant θ of a two-port network in terms of *ABCD* parameters is given by the relation :

$$\theta = \cosh^{-1} \sqrt{AD} \qquad ...(23.12)$$

For a symmetrical network such as the *T*-section of Fig. 23.1 (*a*), the transfer constant θ becomes the propagation constant γ and is given by,

$$\theta = \gamma = \alpha + j\beta = \cosh^{-1} \sqrt{AD} \qquad ...(23.13)$$

But for the *T*-section of Fig. 23.1 (*a*),

$$A = \frac{z_{11}}{z_{21}} = 1 + \frac{Z_1}{2Z_2}$$

and

$$D = \frac{z_{22}}{z_{21}} = 1 + \frac{Z_1}{2Z_2}$$

or

$$A = D + 1 + \frac{Z_1}{2Z_2}$$

Hence

$$\gamma = \cosh^{-1} A$$

$$= \cosh^{-1} \left(1 + \frac{Z_1}{2Z_2}\right) \qquad ...(23.14)$$

or

$$1 + \frac{Z_1}{2Z_2} = \cosh \gamma = 1 + 2 \sinh^2 \frac{\gamma}{2}.$$

Hence $$\sinh \frac{\gamma}{2} = \sqrt{\frac{Z_1}{4Z_2}}$$

or $$\frac{\gamma}{2} = \sinh^{-1} \sqrt{\frac{Z_1}{4Z_2}} \qquad ...(23.15)$$

Hence $$\theta = \gamma = 2 \sinh^{-1} \sqrt{\frac{Z_1}{4Z_2}} \qquad ...(23.16)$$

Whenever γ (or θ) is purely imaginary, $\alpha = 0$ and $\gamma = j\beta$. Then the attenuation offered by the filter is zero. The transmission is then said to be free or unattenuated.

Z_1 and Z_2 are reactances and may, under ideal conditions be assumed to be pure. Then the ratio $\frac{Z_1}{4Z_2}$ will be real and either positive or negative depending upon whether Z_1 and Z_2 are of the same or different kinds.

Eq. (23.15) may be written as

$$\sinh\left(\frac{\alpha}{2} + j\frac{\beta}{2}\right) = \sqrt{\frac{Z_1}{4Z_2}}$$

or $$\sinh \frac{\alpha}{2} \cos \frac{\beta}{2} + j \cosh \frac{\alpha}{2} . \sin \frac{\beta}{2} = \sqrt{\frac{Z_1}{4Z_2}} \qquad ...(23.17)$$

Following two cases are considered :

(*A*) $\mathbf{\frac{Z_1}{Z_2} > 0}$. When $\frac{Z_2}{4Z_2}$ is positive, *i.e.*, impedances Z_1 and Z_2 have the same sign, then the right hand side of Eq. (23.17) yields a real number. Hence from Eq. (23.17),

$$\sinh \frac{\alpha}{2} . \cos \frac{\beta}{2} = \sqrt{\frac{Z_1}{4Z_2}} \qquad ...(23.18)$$

and $$\cosh \frac{\alpha}{2} \sin \frac{\beta}{2} = 0 \qquad ...(23.19)$$

From Eq. (23.19), $$\sin \frac{\beta}{2} = 0$$

so that $\frac{\beta}{2} = \pm n\pi$, where $n = 0, 1, 2$ etc.,

Also $$\cos \frac{\beta}{2} = 1.$$

Hence from Eq. (23.18),

$$\sinh \frac{\alpha}{2} = \sqrt{\frac{Z_1}{4Z_2}} \qquad ...(23.20)$$

or $$\alpha = 2 \sinh^{-1} \sqrt{\frac{Z_1}{4Z_2}} \qquad ...(23.20\ a)$$

Thus we conclude that when $\frac{Z_1}{4Z_2}$ is positive, α is real, *i.e.* attenuation takes place. Accordingly the frequency range over which $\frac{Z_1}{4Z_2} > 0$, constitutes the so-called *attenuation band* or the *stop band*.

(*B*) $\frac{Z_1}{4Z_2} < 0$. Next consider the condition when $\frac{Z_1}{4Z_2} < 0$. Then $\sqrt{\frac{Z_2}{4Z_2}}$ is imaginary. Hence from Eq. (23.17), we get

$$\sinh\frac{\alpha}{2}\cos\frac{\alpha}{2} = 0 \qquad ...(23.21)$$

Then either $$\sinh\frac{\alpha}{2} = 0 \qquad ...(23.22\ a)$$

or $$\cos\frac{\beta}{2} = 2$$

Taking $\sinh\frac{\alpha}{2} = 0$, $\alpha = 0$, *i.e.* attenuation is zero. The frequency range over which $\frac{Z_1}{4Z_2} < 0$ and $\alpha = 0$, constitutes the so-called *pass band* or *the transmission band.*

Further since $\sinh\frac{\alpha}{2} = 0$, $\cosh\frac{\alpha}{2} = 1$.

Hence from Eq. (23.17),

$$j\sin\frac{\beta}{2} = \sqrt{\frac{Z_1}{4Z_2}} \qquad ...(23.23)$$

or $$\beta = 2\sin^{-1}\sqrt{\frac{-Z_1}{4Z_2}} \qquad ...(23.24)$$

Within the pass band, Eq. (23.24) gives the value of phase constant β as a function of reactances Z_1 and Z_2, *i.e.* as a function of frequency.

Further when $\frac{Z_1}{4Z_2}$ is negative and $\left|\frac{Z_1}{4Z_2}\right| > 1$, Eq. (23.23) yields, $\sin\frac{\beta}{2} > 1$. This is absurd.

This signifies that for free transmission, $-1 < \frac{Z_1}{4Z_2}$.

Thus we conclude that for free transmission through a filter, $\frac{Z_1}{4Z_2}$ must be negative and numerically less than unity, *i.e.*

$$-1 < \frac{Z_1}{4Z_2} < 0 \qquad ...(23.25)$$

When $\frac{Z_1}{4Z_2} < -1$, then Eq. (23.22 *b*) applies, *i.e.* $\cos\frac{\beta}{2} = 0$. Hence $\sin\frac{\beta}{2} = \pm 1$.

Hence $\frac{\beta}{2} = (2n-1)\frac{\pi}{2}$, where $n = 1, 2, ...$ ...(23.26)

In this range, from Eq. (23.17) putting $\cos\frac{\beta}{2} = 0$,

$$j\cosh\frac{\alpha}{2} = \sqrt{\frac{Z_1}{4Z_2}} \quad \text{or} \quad \cosh\frac{\alpha}{2} = \sqrt{\left|\frac{Z_1}{4Z_2}\right|}$$

Hence $$\alpha = 2\cosh^{-1}\sqrt{\left|\frac{Z_1}{4Z_2}\right|} \qquad ...(23.27)$$

It may, however, be noted that the above discussion assumes elements to be pure reactance.

Cut-off frequencies. For a given network, as the frequency of the applied signal is altered, the frequencies at which conditions change from transmission to attenuation or *vice versa* are termed as *cut-off frequencies.*

Eq. (23.25) defines these cut-off frequencies. Thus these cut-off frequencies are given by the equations :

$$\frac{Z_1}{4Z_2} = 0 \qquad \text{...(23.28)}$$

and
$$\frac{Z_1}{4Z_2} = -1 \qquad \text{...(23.29)}$$

Eq. (23.28) yields, $Z_1 = 0$ ...(23.30)

Eq. (23.29) yields, $Z_1 + 4Z_2 = 0$ ...(23.31)

23.4. Characteristics Impedance of a Filter in Pass and Stop Bands

The characteristic impedance is given by,

$$Z_0 = \sqrt{\frac{B}{C}} \qquad \text{...(23.32)}$$

But
$$B = \frac{(z_{11}z_{22} - z_{12}z_{21})}{z_{21}} \quad \text{and} \quad C = \frac{1}{z_{21}}.$$

Hence
$$Z_0 = \sqrt{z_{11}z_{22} - z_{12}z_{21}} \qquad \text{...(23.33)}$$

For the *T*-section of Fig. 23.1 (*a*).

$$z_{22} = z_{11} = Z_2 + \frac{Z_1}{2}$$

and
$$z_{12} = z_{21} = Z_2$$

Hence
$$Z_{0T} = \sqrt{\left(Z_2 + \frac{Z_1}{2}\right)^2 - Z_2{}^2} = \sqrt{Z_1Z_2 + \frac{Z_1{}^2}{4}}$$

or
$$Z_{0T} = \sqrt{\mathbf{Z_1Z_2}\left(1 + \frac{Z_1}{4Z_2}\right)} \qquad \text{...(23.34)}$$

Let the filter network be constituted by pure reactances only and let Z_1 and Z_2 be reactances of opposite nature.

Let
$$Z_1 = jX_1 \quad \text{and} \quad Z_2 = jX_2$$

Then
$$Z_{0T} = \sqrt{-X_1X_2\left(1 + \frac{X_1}{4X_2}\right)} \qquad \text{...(23.35)}$$

In Pass Band. We have noted that in the pass band, Z_1 and Z_2 (and hence X_1 and X_2) are of opposite sign and further $-1 < \frac{X_1}{4X_2} < 0$. Hence in the pass band, both the quantities $-X_1X_2$ and $\left(1 + \frac{X_1}{4X_2}\right)$ are positive. Hence in Eq. (23.35), the entire quantity within the radical sign becomes positive. Hence Z_{0T} is real, *i.e.*, resistive and let it be indicated by R_0.

Accordingly when such a network is terminated in a resistive load equal to R_0, then the input impedance of the network is also R_0. The network then transmits power to the resistive load without attenuation. Further if the source driving the network has internal impedance equal to R_0, the entire system from source to load is matched and maximum power is delivered to the load.

In Stop Band with $\frac{X_1}{4X_2} > 0$. X_1 and X_2 are of the same sign and further $\frac{X_1}{4X_2} > 0$. Substitution of this condition in Eq. (23.35) yields a real negative quantity with the radical sign. Hence the characteristic impedance Z_0 is a pure resistance.

In Stop Band with X_1 and X_2 of opposite signs and $\frac{X_1}{4X_2} < -1$. In this case, X_1X_2 as well as $\left(1+\frac{X_1}{X_2}\right)$ are negative. Hence the entire quantity under the radical sign in Eq, (23.35) is negative. Hence the characteristic impedance Z_0 is a pure reactance.

Characteristic Impedance of π-Network. For π-section of Fig. 23.2 (*a*).

$$z_{11} = z_{22} = \frac{(2Z_2)(Z_1 + 2Z_2)}{Z_1 + 4Z_2}$$

$$= \frac{\frac{Z_1}{2} + Z_2}{1 + \frac{Z_1}{4Z_2}} \qquad ...(23.36)$$

$$z_{12} = z_{21} = \frac{Z_2}{1 - \frac{Z_1}{4Z_2}} \qquad ...(23.37)$$

Hence from Eq. (23.33),

$$Z_0\pi = \sqrt{\left[\frac{Z_2 + \frac{Z_1}{2}}{1 + \frac{Z_1}{4Z_2}}\right]^2 - \left[\frac{Z_2}{1 + \frac{Z_1}{4Z_2}}\right]^2} = \frac{1}{1 + \frac{Z_1}{4Z_2}}\sqrt{\left(Z_2 + \frac{Z_1}{2}\right)^2 - Z_2^{\,2}}$$

$$= \frac{\sqrt{\frac{Z_1^{\,2}}{4} + Z_1Z_2}}{1 + \frac{Z_1}{4Z_2}}$$

$$= \frac{Z_1Z_2}{\sqrt{1 + \frac{Z_1}{4Z_2}}} \qquad ...(23.38)$$

$$= \frac{Z_1Z_2}{\sqrt{Z_1Z_2\left(1 + \frac{Z_1}{Z_2}\right)}} \qquad ...(23.39)$$

Hence $$Z_0\pi = \frac{Z_1Z_2}{Z_0T} \qquad ...(23.40)$$

Assuming Z_1 and Z_2 to be pure reactances and substituting these in Eq. (23.38), we find that in the case of π-network also, in the pass band, the characteristic impedance is a pure resistance while in the stop band, the characteristic impedance is purely reactive.

23.5. Classification of Filters

Filters may be classified according to one of the following two ways :

(*A*) **According to their frequency characteristic.** According to this method, filters may be classified as :

(*i*) Low Pass Filters
(*ii*) High Pass Filters
(*iii*) Band Pass Filters and
(*iv*) Band Elimination Filters.

Fig. 23.3 gives the attenuation *versus* frequency characteristics of these different filters under ideal conditions. Thus in a low pass filter, the pass band extends from zero to cut-off frequency f_1 in which region attenuation is zero. The attenuation band extends from cut-off frequency f_1 to infinity and in this range attenuation is large.

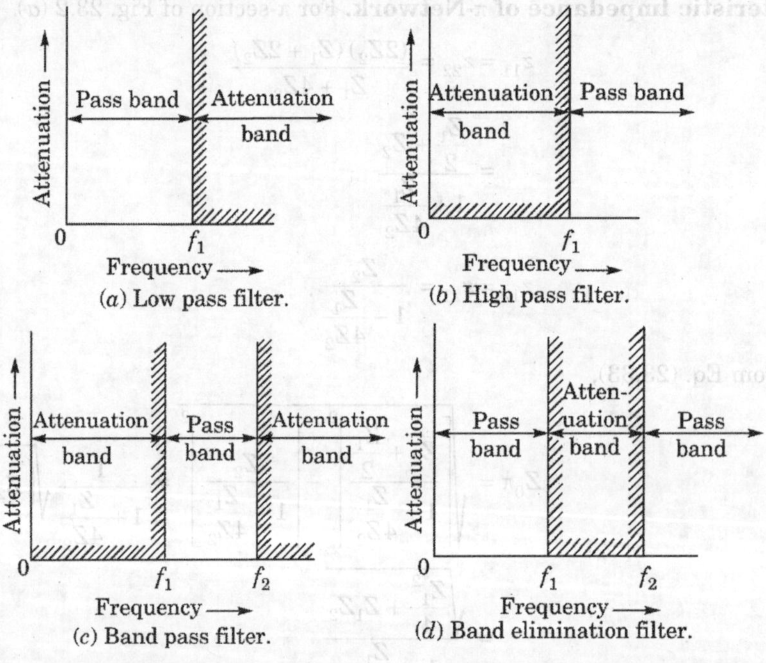

Fig. 23.3. Attenuation *versus* frequency characteristic of ideal filters.

In a high pass filter, the pass band extends from cut-off frequency to infinity and attenuation band lies below cut-off frequency as shown in Fig. 23.3 (*b*).

In a band pass filter, the pass band extends from cut-off frequency f_1 to cut-off frequency f_2 as shown in Fig. 23.3 (*c*). The attenuation band extends below frequency f_1 and beyond frequency f_2. A band pass filter may be obtained by cascading a low pass filter with a high pass filter, where cut-off frequency f_1 of high pass filter is less than the cut-off frequency f_2 of low pass filter.

In a band elimination filter, the pass band extends beyond cutoff frequency f_2 and below cut-off frequency f_1 as shown in Fig. 23.3 (*d*). The attenuation band extends from frequency f_1 to frequency f_2. A band elimination filter may be obtained by cascading a low pass filter with a high pass filter, where cut-off frequency f_2 of high pass filter is greater than the cut-off frequency f_1 of low pass filter.

(*B*) **Depending upon the relation between Z_1 and Z_2.** Thus filters may be classified as,

(*i*) constant-*k* filters or prototype filters and
(*ii*) *m*-derived filters.

In a constant-*k* filter, the series impedance Z_1 and the shunt impedance Z_2 are related by the relation,

$$Z_1 Z_2 = k^2 \quad \text{...(23.41)}$$

where *k* is a constant independent of frequency. In almost all cases, the product Z_1Z_2 is real and has the dimensions of resistance squared. Then,

$$Z_1 Z_2 = k^2 = R_0^2.$$

R_0 is called the "design impedance" of the filter section.

The constant-*k*, *T* or π-sections are also referred to as the *prototype filters*.

The *m-derived* filters, on the other hand, do not have the product $Z_1 Z_2$ equal to k^2 but have the same characteristic impedance as the corresponding constant-*k* sections but have much sharper attenuation characteristics.

23.6. Constant-k Low Pass Filters

Fig. 23.4 shows *T* and π-sections of a constant-*k* low pass filter.

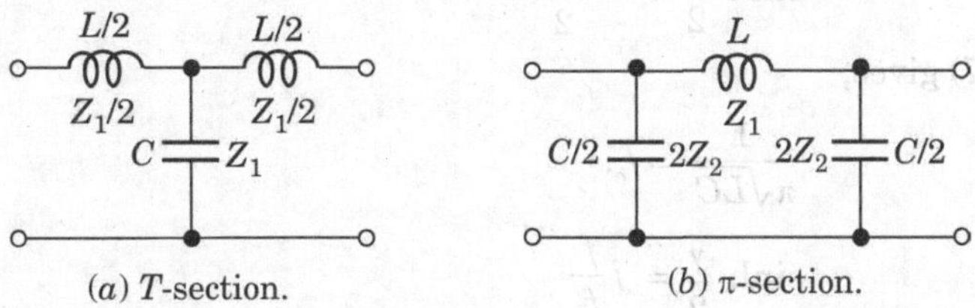

(*a*) *T*-section. (*b*) π-section.

Fig. 23.4. *T* and π-sections of constant-*k* low pass filter.

In both *T* and π-sections,

Total series impedance $= Z_1 = j\omega L$ ...(23.42)

Total shunt impedance $= Z_2 = Z_2 = \dfrac{1}{j\omega C}$ ...(23.43)

Hence $\quad Z_1 Z_2 = \dfrac{L}{C}$ ...(23.44)

Hence design resistance

$$R_0 = \sqrt{Z_1 Z_2} = \sqrt{\frac{L}{C}} \quad \text{...(23.45)}$$

Also $\quad \dfrac{Z_1}{4Z_2} = -\dfrac{\omega^2 LC}{4}$ ...(23.46)

Pass band is given by, $\quad -1 < \dfrac{Z_1}{4Z_2} < 0.$

Hence the two cut-off frequencies are given by the relations,

$$\frac{Z_1}{4Z_2} = 0 \quad \text{and} \quad \frac{Z_1}{4Z_2} = -1$$

The limit $\dfrac{Z_1}{4Z_2} = 0$ yields $Z_1 = j\omega L = 0$, *i.e.* $\omega = 0$ or $f = 0$. This gives the first cut-off frequency.

The limit $\quad \dfrac{Z_1}{4Z_2} = -1$ yields $-\dfrac{\omega^2 LC}{4} = -1.$

This gives, $$\omega_c = \frac{2}{\sqrt{LC}}$$

or $$f_c = \frac{1}{\pi\sqrt{LC}} \qquad ...(23.47)$$

Eq. (23.47) yields the second cut-off frequency.

Thus the pass band of this constant-k low pass filter extends from 0 to f_c, *i.e.*, from 0 to $\frac{1}{\pi\sqrt{LC}}$.

Variation of α and β with frequency. Propagation constant γ is given by,

$$\sinh\frac{\gamma}{2} = \sqrt{\frac{Z_1}{4Z_2}} = \sqrt{\frac{-\omega^2 LC}{4}}$$

or $$\sinh\frac{\gamma}{2} = \frac{j\omega\sqrt{LC}}{2} \qquad ...(23.48)$$

But Eq. (23.47) gives,

$$\frac{1}{\pi\sqrt{LC}} = f_c.$$

Hence $$\sinh\frac{\gamma}{2} = j\frac{f}{f_c} \qquad ...(23.49)$$

The pass band extends for frequency range as given by,

$$-1 < \frac{Z_1}{4Z_2} < 0$$

i.e. $$-1 < \frac{-\omega^2 LC}{4} < 0$$

or $$-1 < -\left(\frac{f}{f_c}\right)^2 < 0$$

or $$1 > \left(\frac{f}{f_c}\right)^2 > 0$$

or $$f_c > f > 0.$$

In this passband, attenuation is zero, *i.e.* the real part of γ is zero, *i.e.* $\gamma = j\beta$.

Hence Eq. (23.48) reduces to,

$$\sinh\left(j\frac{\beta}{2}\right) = \sqrt{\frac{Z_1}{4Z_2}} = \frac{j\omega\sqrt{LC}}{2}$$

or $$\sin\frac{\beta}{2} = \sqrt{\left|\frac{Z_1}{4Z_2}\right|} = \frac{\omega\sqrt{LC}}{2} = \frac{f}{f_c}.$$

Hence $$\beta = 2\sin^{-1}\sqrt{\left|\frac{Z_1}{4Z_2}\right|}$$

$$= 2\sin^{-1}\left(\frac{f}{f_c}\right) \qquad ...(23.50)$$

Thus in the pass band, $0 < f < f_c$,

$$\alpha = 0 \quad \text{and} \quad \beta = 2 \sin\, 2 \sin^{-1}\left(\frac{f}{f_c}\right) \qquad ...(23.51)$$

In the attenuation band

$$f > f_c \quad \text{or} \quad \frac{Z_1}{4Z_2} < -1.$$

Then in accordance with Eq. (23.26), $\beta = \pi$ radians and in accordance with Eq. (23.27).

$$\alpha = 2 \cosh^{-1} \sqrt{\left|\frac{Z_1}{4Z_2}\right|} \qquad ...(23.52)$$

or

$$\alpha = 2 \cosh^{-1}\left(\frac{f}{f_c}\right) \qquad ...(23.53)$$

Thus in the attenuation band,

$$f < f,\ \alpha = 2 \cosh^{-1}\left(\frac{f}{f_e}\right)$$

and

$$\beta = \pi \text{ radians} \qquad ...(23.54)$$

Fig. 23.5 gives curves showing the variations of attenuation constant α and phase constant β with frequency f in the pass band and the attenuation band,

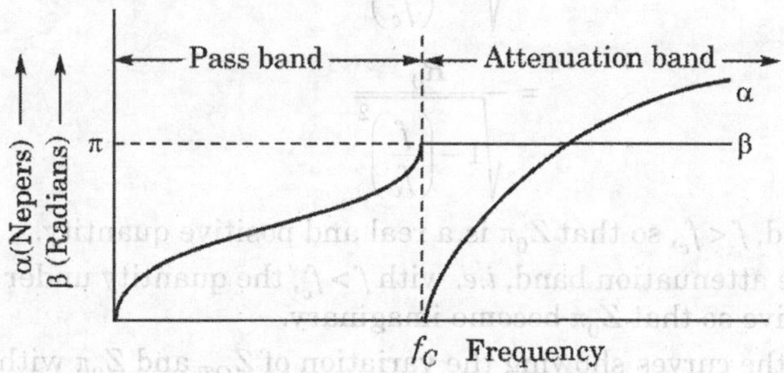

Fig. 23.5. Variation of α and β with frequency in a constant-k low pass filter.

Characteristic Impedance. The characteristic impedance of a T-section filter in accordance with Eq. (23.34) is given by,

$$Z_{OT} = \sqrt{Z_1 Z_2\left(1 + \frac{Z_1}{4Z_2}\right)}$$

For the low pass filter under consideration,

$$Z_{OT} = \sqrt{\frac{L}{C}\left(1 - \frac{\omega^2 LC}{4}\right)} \qquad ...(23.55)$$

or

$$Z_{OT} = \sqrt{\frac{L}{C}}\sqrt{1 - \left(\frac{f}{f_c}\right)^2} \qquad ...(23.56)$$

$$= R_0\sqrt{1-\left(\frac{f}{f_c}\right)^2} \quad \text{...(23.57)}$$

In the pass band, $f < f_c$, so that Z_{0T} is real.

In the attenuation band, *i.e.,* with $f > f_c$, the quantity under the radical sign in Eq. (23.57) becomes negative so that Z_{0T} becomes imaginary.

Similarly the characteristic impedance of a π-section filter, in accordance with Eq. (23.40) is given by,

$$Z_0\pi = \frac{Z_1 Z_2}{Z_0\pi}$$

$$= \sqrt{\frac{Z_1 Z_2}{\left(1+\frac{Z_1}{4Z_2}\right)}} \quad \text{...(23.58)}$$

For the low pass filter under consideration,

$$Z_{0T} = \frac{\sqrt{\frac{L}{C}}}{\sqrt{1-\left(\frac{f}{f_c}\right)^2}}$$

$$= \frac{R_0}{\sqrt{1-\left(\frac{f}{f_c}\right)^2}} \quad \text{...(23.59)}$$

In the pass band, $f < f_c$, so that $Z_0\pi$ is a real and positive quantity.

However, in the attenuation band, *i.e.* with $f > f_c$, the quantity under the radical sign in Eq. (23.59) becomes negative so that $Z_0\pi$ become imaginary.

Fig. 23.6 gives the curves showing the variation of Z_{OT} and $Z_0\pi$ with frequency in the pass band for a constant-*k* low pass filter. It may be seen from these curves that Z_0 of a constant-*k* low pass filter varies over a wide range even within pass band. This is an undesirable property since with a variable Z_0, it is impossible to match the filter with a fixed resistance load over the entire pass band.

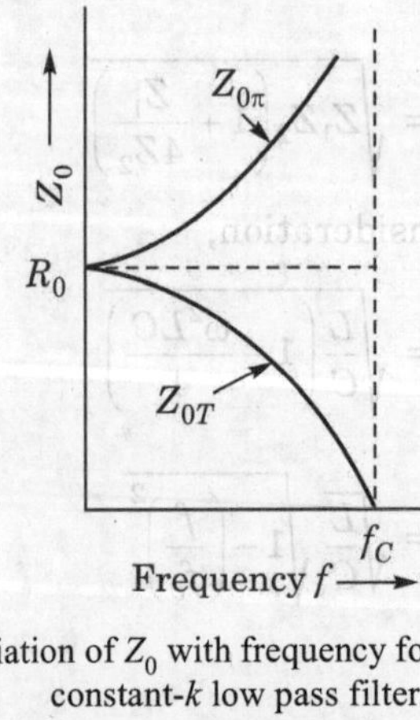

Fig. 23.6. Variation of Z_0 with frequency for *T* and π-sections constant-*k* low pass filter.

23.7. Constant-k High Pass Filters

Fig. 23.7 shows T and π-sections of a constant-k high pass filter.

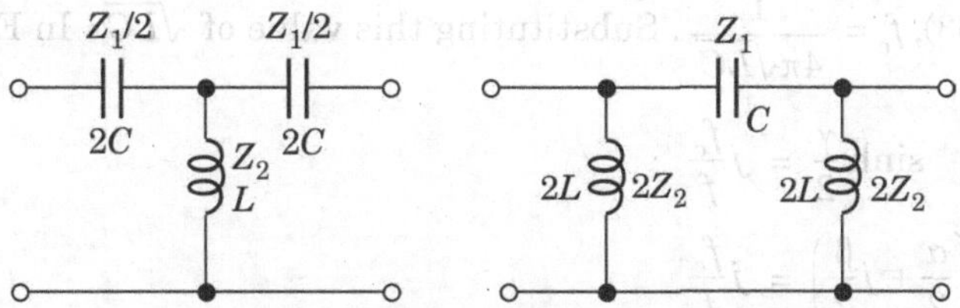

Fig. 23.7. T and π-sections of a constant-k high pass filter.

Nominal Impedance or Design Impedance. In both T and π-sections,

Total series impedance $= Z_1 = \dfrac{1}{j\omega C}$

and total shunt impedance $= Z_2 = j\omega L.$

Hence $$Z_1 Z_2 = \frac{L}{C} \qquad \text{...(23.60)}$$

Thus in the case of high pass filter as well, design resistance

$$R_0 = \sqrt{Z_1 Z_2} = \sqrt{\frac{L}{C}} \qquad \text{...(23.61)}$$

Cut-off Frequency. Pass band is given by,

$$-1 < \frac{Z_1}{4Z_2} < 0.$$

Hence the two cut-off frequencies are given by the relations,

$$\frac{Z_1}{4Z_2} = 0 \quad \text{and} \quad \frac{Z_1}{4Z_2} = -1.$$

The limit $\dfrac{Z_1}{4Z_2} = 0$ yields $Z_1 = \dfrac{1}{j\omega C} = 0$, *i.e.*, $\omega = \infty$

The limit $\dfrac{Z_1}{4Z_2} = -$ yields $-\dfrac{12}{\omega_c^2 4LC} = -1$, where ω_c is the cut-off frequency.

or $$\omega_c = \frac{1}{2\sqrt{LC}} \qquad \text{...(23.62)}$$

or $$f_c = \frac{1}{4\pi\sqrt{LC}} \qquad \text{...(23.63)}$$

Eq. (23.63) yields the lower cut-off frequency. Thus the pass band of constant-k high pass filter extends from f_c to ∞, *i.e.* from $\dfrac{1}{4\pi\sqrt{LC}}$ to ∞.

α and β. The propagation constant γ is given by,

$$\sinh\frac{\gamma}{2} = \sqrt{\frac{Z_1}{4Z_2}}\sqrt{\frac{-1}{4\omega^2 LC}}$$

or $$\sinh\frac{\gamma}{2} = \frac{j}{4\omega\sqrt{LC}} \quad ...(23.64)$$

From Eq. (23.63), $f_c = \dfrac{1}{4\pi\sqrt{LC}}$. Substituting this value of $\sqrt{LC}$. In Eq. (23.64), we get

$$\sinh\frac{\gamma}{2} = j\frac{f_c}{f} \quad ...(23.65)$$

or $$\sinh\left(\frac{\alpha}{2} + j\frac{\beta}{2}\right) = j\frac{f_c}{f} \quad ...(23.66)$$

The pass band extends for the frequency range as given by,

$$-1 < \frac{Z_1}{4Z_2} < 0$$

or $$-1 < \frac{-1}{4\omega^2 LC} < 0$$

or $$-1 < -\left(\frac{f_c}{f}\right)^2 < 0$$

or $$1 > \frac{f_c}{f} > 0$$

or $$f_c < f < \infty.$$

In this pass band, attenuation is zero, *i.e.*, the real part of propagation constant γ is zero.

i.e., $$\gamma = 0 + j\beta.$$

Hence Eq. (23.64) reduces to the following :

$$\sinh\left(j\frac{\beta}{2}\right) = \sqrt{\frac{Z_1}{4Z_2}} = \pm\frac{j}{2\omega\sqrt{LC}} = \pm j\frac{f_c}{f} \quad ...(23.67)$$

or $$\sinh\frac{\beta}{2} = \sqrt{\left|\frac{Z_1}{4Z_2}\right|} = \pm\frac{j}{2\omega\sqrt{LC}} = \pm\frac{f_c}{f} \quad ...(23.68)$$

Hence $$\beta = 2\sin^{-1}\sqrt{\frac{Z_1}{4Z_2}} = 2\sin^{-1}\sqrt{\left(\frac{f_c}{f}\right)^2} \quad ...(23.69)$$

or $$\beta = \pm 2\sin^{-1}\left(\frac{f_c}{f}\right) \quad ...(23.70)$$

Thus in the passband extending from f_c to ∞,

$$\alpha = 0 \text{ and } \beta = \pm 2\sin^{-1}\left(\frac{f_c}{f}\right) \quad ...(23.71)$$

At $f = f_c$, $\beta = \pm 2\sin^{-1}(1) = \pm\pi$

while at $f = \infty$, $\beta = \pm 2\sin^{-1}(0) = 0$.

In the attenuation extending from 0 to f_c

$$\frac{Z_1}{4Z_2} < -1$$

Hence in accordance with Eq. (23.26),

$$\frac{\beta}{2} = (2n-1)\frac{\pi}{2}$$

or $$\beta = \pi \text{ radians.}$$

Also in accordance with Eq. (23.27),

$$\alpha = 2\cosh^{-1}\sqrt{\left|\frac{Z_1}{4Z_2}\right|} = 2\cosh^{-1}\sqrt{\left(\frac{f_c}{f}\right)^2}$$

or $$\alpha = 2\cosh^{-1}\left(\frac{f_c}{f}\right) \text{ nepers} \quad ...(23.72)$$

Thus in the attenuation band, $0 < f < f_c$,

$$\alpha = 2\cosh^{-1}\left(\frac{f_0}{f}\right) \text{ nepers, } \beta = \pi \text{ radians} \quad ...(23.73)$$

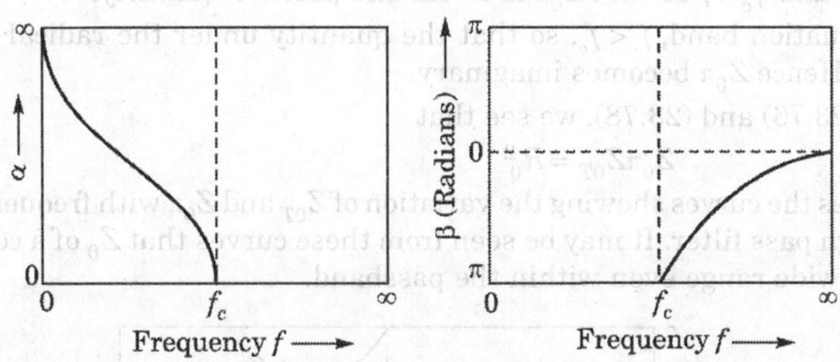

(*a*) Attenuation constant α. (*b*) Phase constant β.

Fig. 23.8. Variation of α and β with frequency for a constant-*k* high pass filter.

Fig. 23.8 shows the variation of attenuation constant α and phase constant β with frequency in the case of a constant-*k* high pass filter.

Characteristic Impedance Z_0. The characteristic impedance of a *T*-section filter in accordance with Eq. (23.34) is given by,

$$Z_{0T} = \sqrt{Z_1 Z_2\left(1 + \frac{Z_1}{4Z_2}\right)}$$

For the high pass filter under consideration

$$Z_{0T} = \sqrt{\frac{L}{C}\left(1 - \frac{1}{4\omega^2 LC}\right)} \quad ...(23.74)$$

or $$Z_{0T} = \sqrt{\frac{L}{C}}\sqrt{1 - \left(\frac{f_c}{f}\right)^2} \quad ...(23.75)$$

$$= R_0\sqrt{1 - \left(\frac{f_c}{f}\right)^2} \quad ...(23.76)$$

In the pass band $f_c < f$ so that Z_{0T} is real.

In the attenuation band, $f < f_c$ so that the quantity under the radical sign in Eq. (23.76) becomes negative and hence Z_{0T} becomes imaginary.

The characteristic impedance of a π-section filter in accordance with Eq. (23.40) is given by,

$$Z_{0\pi} = \frac{Z_1 Z_2}{Z_{0T}} = \sqrt{\frac{Z_1 Z_2}{\left(1 + \frac{Z_1}{4Z_2}\right)}} \qquad \text{...(23.77)}$$

For the high pass filter under consideration,

$$Z_{0\pi} = \frac{\sqrt{\frac{L}{C}}}{\sqrt{1 + \frac{1}{4\omega^2 LC}}} = \frac{\sqrt{\frac{L}{C}}}{\sqrt{1 - \left(\frac{f_0}{f}\right)^2}}$$

$$= \frac{R_0}{\sqrt{1 - \left(\frac{f_c}{f}\right)}} \qquad \text{...(23.78)}$$

In the pass band, $f_c < f$ so that $Z_0\pi$ is a real and positive quantity.

In the attenuation band, $f < f_c$, so that the quantity under the radical sign in Eq. (23.78) becomes negative. Hence $Z_0\pi$ becomes imaginary.

From Eqs. (23.76) and (23.78), we see that

$$Z_0\pi Z_{0T} = R_0^2 \qquad \text{...(23.79)}$$

Fig. 23.9 gives the curves showing the variation of Z_{0T} and $Z_0\pi$ with frequency in the passband for a constant-*k* high pass filter. It may be seen from these curves that Z_0 of a constant-*k* high pass filter varies over a wide range even within the passband.

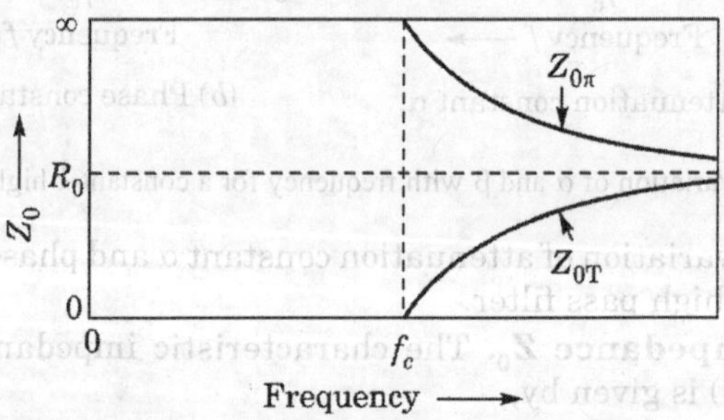

Fig. 23.9. Variation of Z_0 with frequency for *T* and π-sections constant-*k* high pass filter.

23.8. Design of Constant-*k* Low Pass and High Pass Filters

Often it is required to design a constant-*k* filter for a given cut-off frequency and for feeding a given load resistance. So far as the cut-off frequency is concerned, we may obtain any cut-off frequency by suitable choice of elements forming the filter. However, no choice of elements yields a Z_0 which may remain the same over the pass band. A perfect impedance match between the filter and the load may be achieved at only one frequency. In practice the load resistance is made to equal the Z_0 of the filter at zero frequency in case of low pass filter and at infinite frequency in case of high pass filter, *i.e.* the load resistance is made equal to the design resistance (or the nominal resistance) R_0 of the filter.

(A) Low Pass Filter

$$R_0 = \sqrt{\frac{L}{C}} \qquad \text{...(23.80)}$$

and cut-off frequency $$f_c = \frac{1}{\pi\sqrt{LC}} \qquad \text{...(23.81)}$$

Combining Eqs. (23.80) and (23.81), we get

$$L = \frac{R_0}{\pi f_c} \qquad \text{...(23.82)}$$

and $$C = \frac{1}{\pi f_c R_0} \qquad \text{...(23.80)}$$

Eqs. (23.82) and (23.83) give the values of elements L and C in terms of cut-off frequency f_c and design resistance R_0.

(B) High Pass Filter

$$R_0 = \sqrt{\frac{L}{C}} \qquad \text{...(23.84)}$$

and $$f_c = \frac{1}{4\pi\sqrt{LC}} \qquad \text{...(23.85)}$$

Combining Eqs. (23.84) and (23.85), we get

$$L = \frac{R_0}{4\pi f_c} \qquad \text{...(23.86)}$$

and $$C = \frac{1}{4\pi f_c R_0} \qquad \text{...(23.87)}$$

For constant-*k* high pass filters, Eqs. (23.86) and (23.87) give the values of elements L and C in terms of cut-off frequency f_c and nominal characteristic impedance R_0.

Example 23.3. *For the given T-section low pass filter, determine the cut-off frequency and nominal characteristic impedance* R_0.

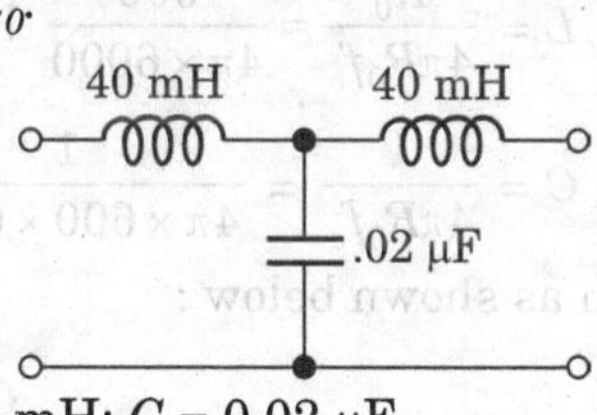

Solution. $L = 80$ mH; $C = 0.02$ μF

Cut-off frequency $$f_c = \frac{1}{\pi\sqrt{LC}} = \frac{1}{\pi\sqrt{(80 \times 10^{-3})(0.02 \times 10^{-6})}} \text{ Hz} = 7.962 \times 10^3 \text{ Hz}$$

$$R_0 = \sqrt{\frac{L}{C}} = \sqrt{\frac{80 \times 10^{-3}}{0.02 \times 10^{-6}}} \text{ ohms} = 2 \times 10^3 \text{ ohms.}$$

Example 23.4. *Design constant-k low pass T and π-sections filters having cut-off frequency = 3000 Hz and nominal characteristic impedance* $R_0 = 600\ \Omega$.

Solution. $$L = \frac{R_0}{\pi f_c} = \frac{600}{\pi \times 3000} \text{ H} = 63.68 \text{ mH}$$

$$C = \frac{1}{\pi R_0 f_c} = \frac{1}{\pi \times 600 \times 3000} \text{ Farad} = 0.1753\ \mu\text{F}.$$

Hence the required T and π-section filters are as shown below :

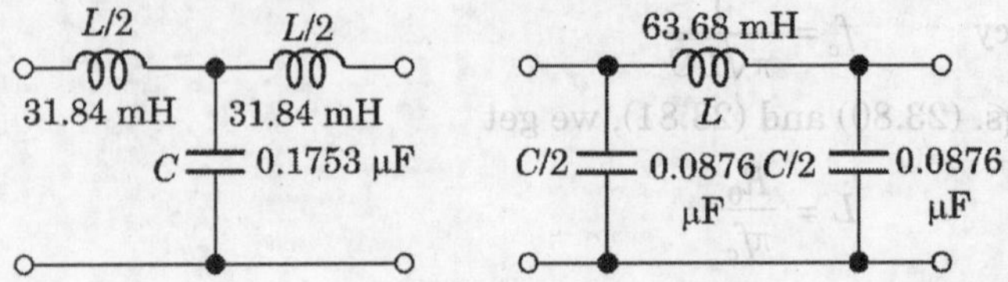

Example 23.5. *Design a constant-k low pass filter having cut-off frequency = 2000 Hz and nominal characteristic impedance R_0 = 600 Ω. Also find the frequency at which this filter offers attenuation of 19.1 dB.*

Solution.
$$L = \frac{R_0}{\pi f_c} = \frac{600}{\pi \times 2000} \text{ H} = 95.54 \text{ mH}$$

$$C = \frac{1}{\pi R_0 f_c} = \frac{1}{\pi \times 600 \times 2000} \text{ F} = 0.263\ \mu\text{F}$$

Attenuation of 19.1 dB expressed in nepers equals

$$\frac{19.1}{8.686} = 2.2 \text{ nepers.}$$

$$\alpha = 2 \cosh^{-1} (f/f_c)$$

Hence
$$\frac{f}{f_c} = \cosh \frac{\alpha}{2} = \cosh \frac{2.2}{2} = 1.6685.$$

Hence
$$f = 1.6685 \times f_c = 1.6685 \times 2000 = 3337 \text{ Hz}.$$

Example 23.6. *Design constant-k high pass T and π-section filter having cut-off frequency of 6 kHz and nominal characteristic resistance R_0 = 600 Ω.*

Solution.
$$L = \frac{R_0}{4\pi R_0 f_c} = \frac{600}{4\pi \times 6000} \text{ H} = 7.962 \text{ mH}$$

$$C = \frac{1}{4\pi R_0 f_c} = \frac{1}{4\pi \times 600 \times 6000} \text{ F} = 0.02212\ \mu\text{F}.$$

The T and π-sections are then as shown below :

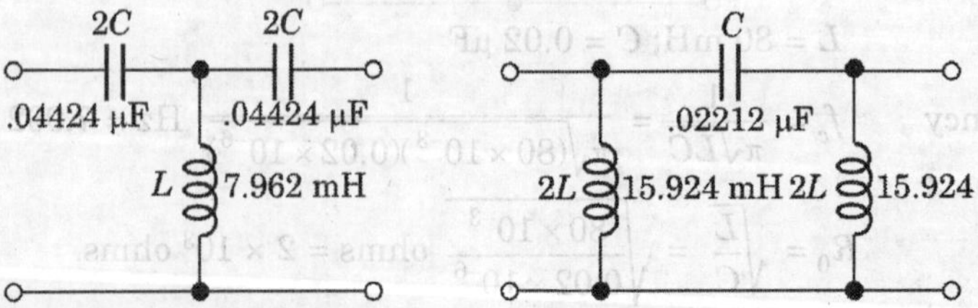

Example 23.7. *Design a T-section constant-k high pass filter having cut-off frequency of 10 kHz and nominal characteristic resistance R_0 = 600 Ω. Also find : (i) its characteristic impedance and phase constant at 25 kHz and (ii) attenuation at 5 kHz.*

Solution.
$$L = \frac{R_0}{4\pi f_c}$$

$$= \frac{600}{4\pi \times 10^4} \text{ H} = 4.777 \text{ mH}.$$

$$C = \frac{1}{4\pi R_0 f_c} = \frac{1}{4\pi \times 600 \times 10^4} \text{ Farad} = 0.01326 \text{ μF}.$$

Accordingly each capacitor in the series arm of *T*-section is $2C$ *i.e.* 0.02652 μF while the inductor in the shunt arm is L, *i.e.* 4.777 mH.

At $$f = 25 \text{ kHz}$$

$$Z_{0T} = R_0\sqrt{1-\left(\frac{f_c}{f}\right)^2} = 600\sqrt{1-\left(\frac{10}{25}\right)^2} = 545\ \Omega$$

or $$\beta = 2\sin^{-1}\left(\frac{f_c}{f}\right) = 2\sin^{-1}\left(\frac{10}{25}\right) = 47.2°.$$

In the attenuation band, α is given by,

$$\alpha = 2\cosh^{-1}\left(\frac{f_c}{f}\right) \text{ nepers}$$

$$= 2\cosh^{-1}\left(\frac{10}{5}\right) \text{ nepers} = 2.6 \text{ nepers}$$

23.9. Band Pass Filters

A band pass filter, under ideal circumstances, allows transmission with zero attenuation frequencies in the pass band and offers in infinite attenuation to frequencies outside this band. There are two common methods of obtaining the band pass characteristics: (*i*) conventional *L-C* filter and (*ii*) use of two coupled parallel tuned circuits. The first type of band pass filter is considered here. It may in its simplest form be obtained by connecting a high pass filter and a low pass filter in tandem. The low pass filter has cut-off frequency higher than that of the high pass filter. The overlapping region of the pass bands of the two constituent filters constitutes the pass band of the band pass filter. Such a combination filter is uneconomical. Hence its practice, low pass filter action and high pass filter action are combined into a single filter action. Fig. 23.10 shows a simple band pass filter. It is a conventional *T*-section filter in which the series impedance Z_1 is a series resonant circuit (L_1 and C_1 in series) while the shunt impedance Z_2 is a parallel tuned circuit (L_2 and C_2 in parallel). Components L_1, C_1, L_2 and C_2 are so chosen that the series resonance frequency of series arm equals the parallel resonance frequency of the shunt arms. Let this frequency be ω_0 radians/second.

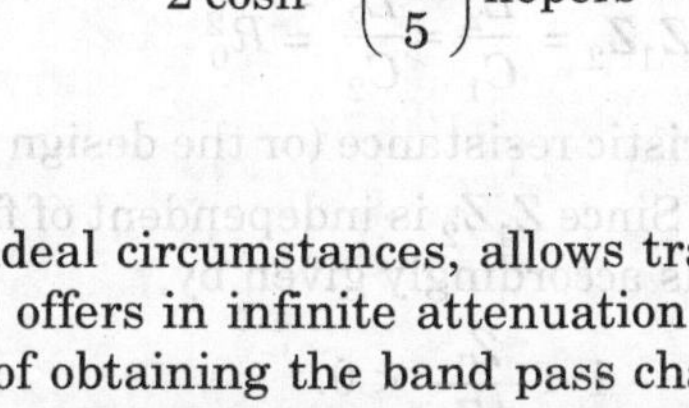

Fig. 23.10. Band pass filter.

Then for series arm, $$\omega_0^2 L_1 C_1 = 1 \qquad ...(23.88)$$

and for shunt arm, $\omega_0^2 L_2C_2 = 1$ ...(23.89)

Hence $$L_1C_1 = L_2C_2 = \frac{1}{\omega_0^2} \quad ...(23.90)$$

(A) Nominal Characteristic Resistance R_0. For the circuits of Fig. 23.10.

$$Z_1 = j\omega L_1 + \frac{1}{j\omega C_1} = j\left(\frac{\omega^2 L_1C_1 - 1}{\omega C_1}\right) \quad ...(23.91)$$

$$Z_2 = \frac{j\omega L_2\left(\frac{1}{j\omega C_2}\right)}{j\omega L_2 + \frac{1}{j\omega C_2}}$$

$$= j\frac{\omega L_2}{(1-\omega^2 L_2C_2)} \quad ...(23.92)$$

Hence $$Z_1Z_2 = \frac{L_2(\omega^2L_1C_1 - 1)}{C_1(\omega^2L_2C_2 - 1)} \quad ...(23.93)$$

But $L_1C_1 = L_2C_2$.

Hence Eq. (23.93) reduces to

$$Z_1Z_2 = \frac{L_2}{C_1} = \frac{L_2}{C_2} = R_0^2 \quad ...(23.94)$$

where R_0 is the nominal characteristic resistance (or the design resistance) of the band pass filter.

(B) Cut-off Frequencies. Since Z_1Z_2 is independent of frequency, the filter is a constant-k filter. The pass band of the filter is accordingly given by,

$$-1 < \frac{Z_1}{4Z_2} < 0.$$

The cut-off frequency is given by,

$$-1 = \frac{Z_1}{4Z_2} \quad \text{or} \quad Z_1 = -4Z_2 \quad ...(23.95)$$

or $$Z_1^2 = 4Z_1Z_2 = -4R_0^2$$

Hence $$Z_1 = \pm j_2R_0 \quad ...(23.96)$$

Eq. (23.96) defines two cut-off frequencies. At cut-off frequency f_1, Z_1 equals $-j2R_0$ while at cut-off frequency f_2, Z_1 equals $+j2R_0$. Accordingly the impedance Z_1 of series arm at frequency f_1 is negative of the impedance Z_1 at frequency f_2.

Thus $$\left(\omega_1 L_1 - \frac{1}{\omega_1 C_1}\right) = -\left(\omega_2 L_1 - \frac{1}{\omega_2 C_2}\right)$$

or $$1 - \omega_1^2 L_1C_1 = \frac{\omega_1}{\omega_2}(\omega_2^2 L_1C_1 - 1) \quad ...(23.97)$$

But $$L_1C_1 = \frac{1}{\omega_0^2}$$

Hence Eq. (23.97) yields,

$$1 - \left(\frac{f_1}{f_0}\right)^2 = \frac{f_1}{f_2}\left(\frac{f_2^2}{f_0^2} - 1\right)$$

or $$f_0^2 - f_1^2 = \frac{f_1}{f_2}(f_2^2 - f_0^2)$$

or $$f_0^2(f_1 + f_2) = f_1 f_2(f_1 + f_2)$$

Hence $$f_0^2 = f_1 f_2 \quad ...(23.98)$$

or $$f_0 = \sqrt{f_1 f_2} \quad ...(23.99)$$

Thus f_0, *i.e.* the resonant frequency of shunt arm or series arm is geometric mean of the cut-off frequencies.

Fig. 23.11 shows the nature of variation of attenuation, phase shift and the characteristic impedance Z_0 with frequency for a prototype bandpass filter.

It may be seen from Fig. 23.11 (*a*) that the attenuation, in the attenuation band increases rather slowly with frequency. This is the limitation of constant-*k* filters.

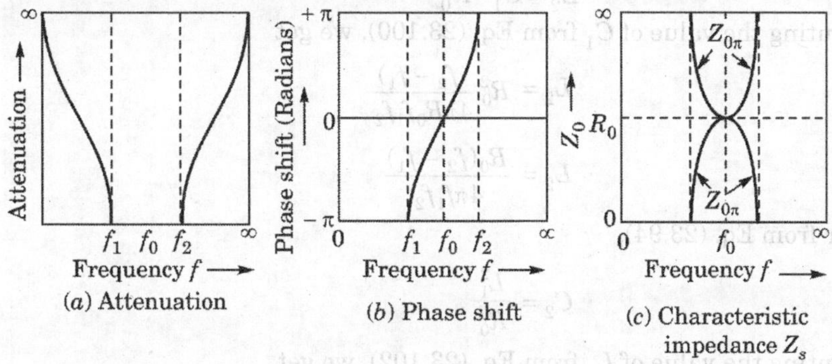

Fig. 23.11. Variation of attenuation, phase shift and characteristics impedance in constant-*k* band pass filter.

It may be seen from Fig. 23.11 (*c*) that the characteristic impedance Z_0 varies appreciably with frequency in the passband. Hence impedance match is not possible.

23.10. Design of constant-k Band Pass Filter

Design of bandpass filter consists in finding the values of its circuit elements for desired values of nominal characteristic impedance R_0 and cut-off frequencies f_1 and f_2.

Thus at lower cut-off frequency f_1.

$$Z_1 = -j2R_0$$

or $$\frac{1}{\omega_1 C_1} - \omega L_1 = 2R_0 \quad \text{or} \quad 1 - \omega_1^2 L_1 C_1 = 2R_0 \omega_1 C_1$$

or $$1 - \frac{f_1^2}{f_0^2} = 4\pi f_1 R_0 C_1 \quad \text{or} \quad 1 - \frac{f_1^2}{f_1 f_2^2} = 4\pi R_0 f_1 C_1$$

or $$f_2 - f_1 = 4\pi R_0 f_1 f_2 C_1$$

Hence $$C_1 = \frac{(f_2 - f_1)}{4\pi R_0 f_1 f_2} \quad ...(23.100)$$

But from Eq. (23.88),

$$L_1 = \frac{1}{\omega_0^2 C_1}$$

or $$L_1 = \frac{1}{4\pi^2 f_0^2 C_1}$$

$$= \frac{1}{4\pi^2 f_1 f_2 C_1} \quad ...(23.101)$$

Substituting the value of C_1 from Eq. (23.100) into Eq. (23.101), we get

$$L_1 = \frac{R_0}{\pi(f_2 - f_1)} \quad ...(23.102)$$

From Eq. (23.94),

$$L_2 = C_1 \cdot R_0^2$$

Substituting the value of C_1 from Eq. (23.100), we get

$$L_2 = R_0^2 \frac{(f_2 - f_1)}{4\pi R_0 f_1 f_2}$$

or $$L_2 = \frac{R_0(f_2 - f_1)}{4\pi f_1 f_2} \quad ...(23.103)$$

Further from Eq. (23.94),

$$C_2 = \frac{L_1^2}{R_0^2}$$

Substituting the value of L_1 from Eq. (23.102), we get

$$C_2 = \frac{1}{R_0^2} \cdot \frac{R_0}{\pi(f_2 - f_1)}$$

or $$C_2 = \frac{1}{\pi R_0 (f_2 - f_1)} \quad ...(23.104)$$

Example 23.8. *Design a prototype band pass filter section having cut-off frequencies of 2000 Hz and 500 Hz and nominal characteristic impedance of 600 ohms.*

Solution. $$L_2 = \frac{R_0}{\pi(f_2 - f_1)} = \frac{600}{\pi(5000 - 2000)} \text{ H} = 63.68 \text{ mH.}$$

$$\frac{L_1}{2} = 31.84 \text{ mH.}$$

$$C_1 = \frac{(f_2 - f_1)}{4\pi R_0 f_1 f_2} = \frac{(5000 - 2000)}{4\pi \times 600 \times 5000 \times 2000} \text{ F} = 0.0381 \text{ μF}$$

$$2C_1 = 0.0872 \text{ μF}$$

$$L_2 = \frac{R_0(f_2 - f_1)}{4\pi f_1 f_2} = \frac{600(5000 - 2000)}{4\pi \times 5000 \times 2000} \text{ H} = 14.33 \text{ mH.}$$

$$C_2 = \frac{1}{\pi R_0 (f_2 - f_1)} = \frac{1}{\pi \times 600(5000 - 2000)} \text{ F} = 0.1769 \text{ μF.}$$

Hence the bandpass filter is as shown below:

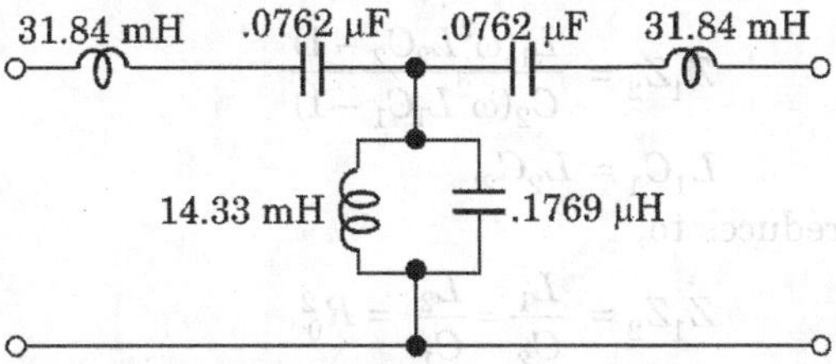

23.11. Band Stop Filter or Band Elimination Filter

In certain devices it is necessary to eliminate or disallow a band of frequencies say from f_1 and f_2 and to allow transmission of frequencies on the lower and higher sides. A band stop filter may be used in such cases.

A band stop filter may in its simplest form be obtained by connecting in tandem a low pass filter with high pass filter such that the cut-off frequency f_1 of high pass filter is higher than the cut-off frequency f_1 of low pass filter. The overlapping attenuation bands of the two filters then constitutes the stop band of the band stop filter. Such a combination is uneconomical. Hence in practice, low pass filter action and the high pass filter action are combined into a single filter section. Fig. 23.12 shows a constant-k band stop filter. It is a conventional T-section filter in which the series arm impedance Z_1 is a parallel tuned circuit (L_1 and C_1 in shunt) while the shunt arm impedance Z_2 is a series tuned circuit (L_2 and C_2 in series). The components L_1, C_1, L_2 and C_2 are so chosen that the shunt resonance frequency of series arm equals the series resonance frequency of shunt arm. Let this frequency be ω_0 radians/second or f_0 Hertz.

Then for the series arm,

$$\omega_0^2 L_1 C_1 = 1 \qquad \text{...(23.105)}$$

and for the shunt arm,

$$\omega_0^2 L^2 C_2 = 1 \qquad \text{...(23.106)}$$

Hence

$$L_1 C_1 = L_2 C_2 = \frac{1}{\omega_0^2} \qquad \text{...(23.107)}$$

(A) Nominal characteristic impedance R_0. For the circuit of Fig. 23.12,

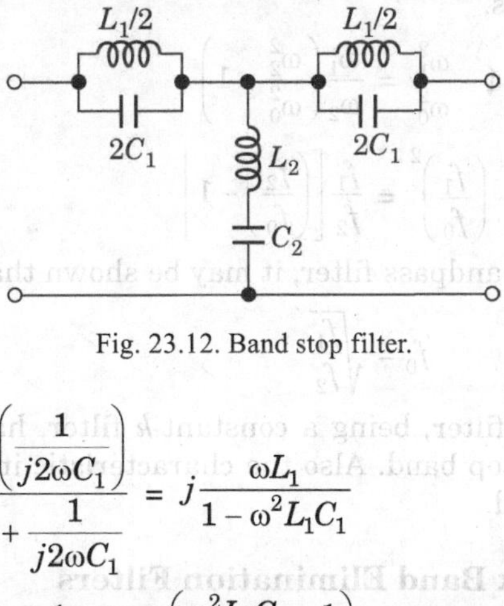

Fig. 23.12. Band stop filter.

$$Z_1 = \frac{\dfrac{j\omega L_1}{2}\left(\dfrac{1}{j2\omega C_1}\right)}{\dfrac{j\omega L_1}{2} + \dfrac{1}{j2\omega C_1}} = j\frac{\omega L_1}{1 - \omega^2 L_1 C_1} \qquad \text{...(23.108)}$$

$$Z_2 = j\omega L_2 + \frac{1}{j\omega C_2} = j\left(\frac{\omega^2 L_2 C_2 - 1}{\omega C_2}\right) \qquad \text{...(23.109)}$$

Hence $$Z_1Z_2 = \frac{L_1(\omega^2 L_2C_2 - 1)}{C_2(\omega^2 L_1C_1 - 1)} \qquad \text{...(23.110)}$$

But $$L_1C_1 = L_2C_2.$$

Hence Eq. (23.110) reduces to,

$$Z_1Z_2 = \frac{L_1}{C_2} = \frac{L_2}{C_1} = R_0^2 \qquad \text{...(23.111)}$$

where R_0 is the design resistance or the nominal characteristic impedance of the band stop filter.

(B) Cut-off frequencies. Since Z_1Z_2 is independent of frequency, the filter is a constant-k filter. The pass band of the filter is accordingly given by,

$$-1 < \frac{Z_1}{4Z_2} < 0.$$

The cut-off frequency is given by,

$$-1 = \frac{Z_1}{4Z_2}$$

or $$Z_1 = -4Z_2$$

or $$Z_1^2 = -4Z_1Z_2 = -4R_0^2$$

Hence $$Z_1 = \pm j2R_0 \qquad \text{...(23.112)}$$

Eq. (23.112) defines the two cut-off frequencies. At cut-off frequency f_1, Z_1 equals $+j2R_0$ while at cut-off frequency f_2, Z_1 equals $-j2R_0$. Accordingly the impedance Z_1 of series arm at frequency f_1 is negative of the impedance Z_1 at frequency f_2.

Thus $$\frac{\omega_1 L_1}{1 - \omega_1^2 L_1C_1} = \frac{\omega_2 L_1}{1 - \omega_2^2 L_1C_1}$$

or $$1 - \omega_1^2 L_1C_1 = \frac{\omega_1}{\omega_2}(\omega_2^2 L_1C_1 - 1) \qquad \text{...(23.113)}$$

But $$L_1C_1 = \frac{1}{\omega_0^2}$$

Hence Eq. (23.113) yields,

$$1 - \frac{\omega_1^2}{\omega_0^2} = \frac{\omega_1}{\omega_2}\left(\frac{\omega_2^2}{\omega_0^2} - 1\right)$$

or $$1 - \left(\frac{f_1}{f_0}\right)^2 = \frac{f_1}{f_2}\left[\left(\frac{f_2}{f_0}\right) - 1\right]$$

Hence as in the case of bandpass filter, it may be shown that,

$$f_0 = \sqrt{\frac{f_1}{f_2}} \qquad \text{...(23.114)}$$

Further this band stop filter, being a constant-k filter, has attenuation which increases slowly with frequency in the stop band. Also the characteristic impedance Z_0 varies appreciably with frequency in the pass band.

23.12. Design of Constant-k Band Elimination Filters

For a given value of design resistance R_0 and for desired cut-off frequencies f_1 and f_2, it is possible to determine the values of circuit components of constant-k band stop filter.

Thus at lower cut-off frequency f_1,

$$Z_1 = +j2R_0$$

or $$j\frac{\omega_1 L_1}{1-\omega_1^2 L_1 C_1} = +j2R_0$$

or $$1-\omega_1^2 L_1 C_1 = \frac{\omega_1 L_1}{2R_0}$$

or $$1-\frac{f_1^2}{f_0^2} = \frac{\pi f_1 L_1}{R_0}$$

or $$1-\frac{f_1^2}{f_1 f_2} = \frac{\pi f_1 L_1}{R_0}$$

or $$f_2 - f_1 = \frac{\pi f_1 f_2 L_1}{R_0}$$

Hence $$L_1 = \frac{R(f_2-f_1)}{\pi f_1 f_2} \quad ...(23.115)$$

But $$\omega_0^2 L_1 C_1 = 1$$

Hence $$C_1 = \frac{1}{\omega_0^2 L_1} = \frac{1}{4\pi^2 f_0^2 L_1}$$

or $$C_2 = \frac{\pi f_1 f_2}{R_0(f_2-f_1)\,4\pi^2 f_1 f_2}$$

Hence $$C_1 = \frac{1}{4\pi R_0(f_2-f_1)} \quad ...(23.116)$$

Further from Eq. (23.111),

$$L_2 = C_1 \cdot R_0^2 = \frac{R_0}{4\pi(f_2-f_1)} \quad ...(23.117)$$

or $$C_2 = \frac{L_1}{R_0^2} = \frac{(f_2-f_1)}{\pi R_0 f_1 f_2} \quad ...(23.118)$$

23.13. m-derived Filters

Study of attenuation and characteristic impedance curves of constant-*k* filters reveals that these filters have two obvious draw-backs :

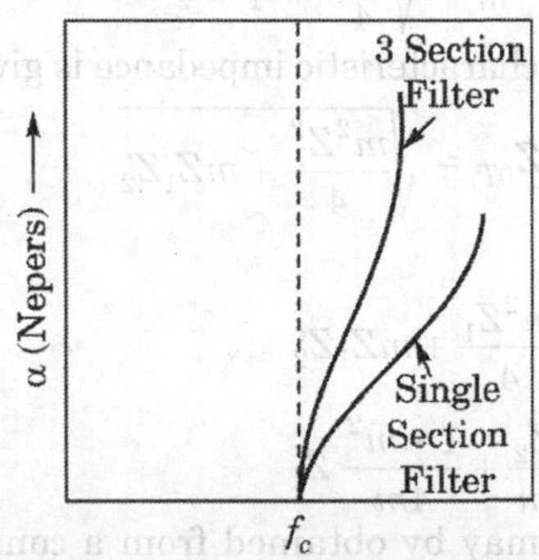

Fig. 23.13. Attenuation characteristic for single section and three-section constant-*k* low-pass filters.

(*i*) in the attenuation band, the attenuation does not increase rapidly with frequency beyond the cut-off frequency and

(*ii*) in the passband, the characteristic impedance Z does not remain constant but varies widely from the nominal value R_0.

Hence when the filter is terminated in a fixed resistive load, mismatch and associated reflections occur at different frequencies.

Regarding attenuation characteristic, some improvement in attenuation band beyond cut-off may be achieved by connecting two or more similar constant-*k* sections in tendem.

Thus by connecting three identical constant-*k* low-pass filter sections, attenuation in the attenuation band beyond the cut-off frequency gets tripled as shown in Fig. 23.13. Thus a more sharp cut-off is achieved.

Use of several identical constant-*k* sections improves the attenuation characteristic in the attenuation band. However this expendient fails to improve the Z_0 characteristic in the passband.

By use of *m*-derived filter sections, it become possible to get very rapid attenuation rise in the attenuation band just beyond cut-off. However, it fails to provide constant Z_0 over the entire pass band. This constant Z_0 may be achieved by use of terminating half sections in conjunction with the *m*-derived sections.

Elements of m-derived Filter Section. Here we take up the derivation of *m*-derived *L* and π-sections starting from a constant-*k* section.

(A) m-derived T-section. Fig. 23.14 (*a*) shows a general constant-*k* section of *T*-type while Fig. 23.14 (*b*) gives the corresponding *m*-derived filter having the same characteristic impendance. The series arm of the *m* derived section has been obtained by multiplying the series arm element of constant-*k* section by a constant *m*. The shunt arm element Z_2 is also modified in such a way that the modifying filter has the same characteristic impedance.

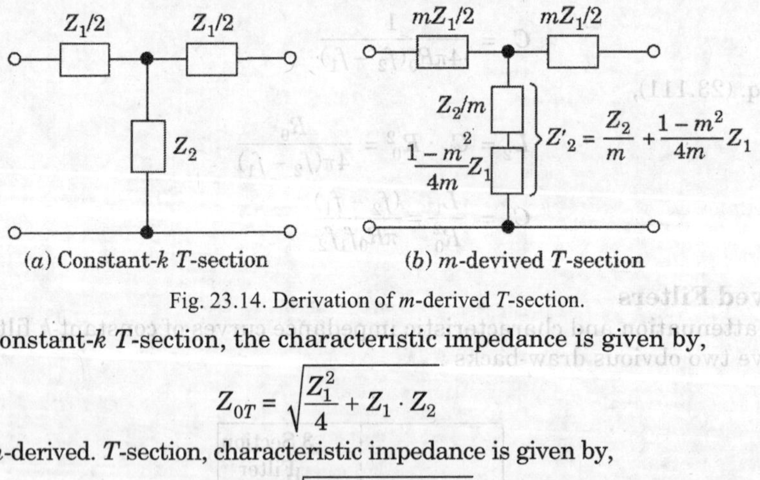

(*a*) Constant-*k* *T*-section (*b*) *m*-devived *T*-section

Fig. 23.14. Derivation of *m*-derived *T*-section.

For the constant-*k* *T*-section, the characteristic impedance is given by,

$$Z_{0T} = \sqrt{\frac{Z_1^2}{4} + Z_1 \cdot Z_2}$$

For the *m*-derived. *T*-section, characteristic impedance is given by,

$$Z_{0T'} = \sqrt{\frac{m^2 Z_1^2}{4} + mZ_1 Z_2'} \quad \text{...(23.119)}$$

But $Z_{0T'}$ must equal Z_{0T}.

Hence $$\frac{Z_1^2}{4} + Z_1 Z_2 = \frac{m^2 Z_1}{4} + mZ_1 Z_2'$$

Hence $$Z_2' = \frac{Z_2}{m} + \frac{1-m^2}{4m} Z_1 \quad \text{...(23.120)}$$

Thus an *m*-derived section may by obtained from a constant-*k*-section by multiplying the series arm impedance by *m* and altering the shunt arm impedance as given by Eq. (23.120). Of course, m must have a value between 0 and 1. *i.e.* $0 < m < 1$. If m exceeds unity, factor $\frac{1-m^2}{4m}$ in the expression for Z_2' may make Z_2' a negative quantity.

(B) m-derived π-section Filter. Next consider the constant-*k* π-section of Fig. 21.15 (*a*). The corresponding *m*-drived section is shown in Fig. 23.15 (*b*). Both these filters must have the same characteristic impedance.

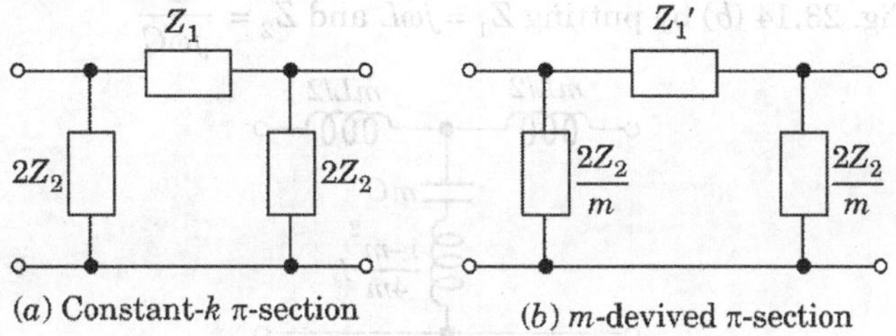

Fig. 23.15. Derivation of *m*-derived *n*-section.

The shunt are elements of the *m*-derived section are obtained by multiplying the shunt arm elements of the constant-*k* section by the factor $\frac{1}{m}$. The series, arm element Z'_1 of the *m*-derived π-section must also be modified such that the modified section has the same characteristic impedance.

For constant-*k* π-section, characteristic impedance is given by,

$$Z_0\pi' = \sqrt{\frac{Z_1 Z_2}{1+\frac{Z_1}{4Z_2}}}$$

For *m* derived section of Fig. 23.15 (*b*) the characteristic impedance is given by,

$$Z_0\pi' = \sqrt{\frac{Z_1'\frac{Z_2}{m}}{1+\frac{Z_1'}{(4Z_2/m)}}} \qquad ...(23.121)$$

Equating $Z_0\pi$ to $Z_0\pi'$, we get

$$Z_1' = \frac{mZ_1\left(\frac{4m}{1-m^2}\right)Z_2}{mZ_1+\left(\frac{4m}{1-m^2}\right)Z_2} \qquad ...(23.122)$$

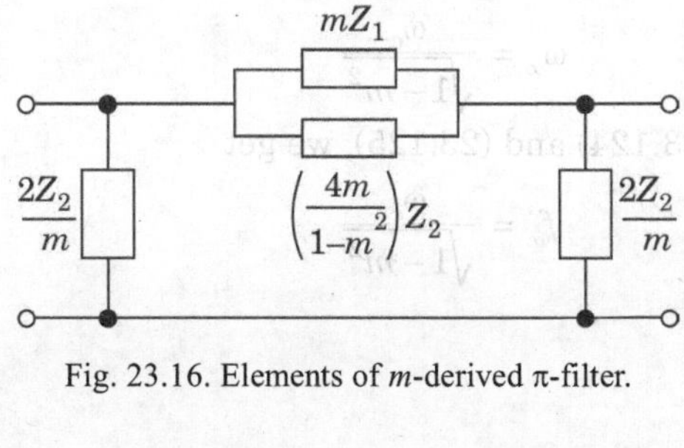

Fig. 23.16. Elements of *m*-derived π-filter.

Eq. (23.122) shows that Z_1' is formed by a parallel combination of mZ_1 and $\left(\dfrac{4m}{1-m^2}\right)Z_2$. Accordingly the m-derived π-section of Fig. 23.15 (b) may be redrawn as shown in Fig. 23.16.

23.14. m-derived Low Pass Filters

(A) T-section. Fig. 23.17 shows the m-derived low pass T-section filter. This is obtained from that shown in Fig. 23.14 (b) by putting $Z_1 = j\omega L$ and $Z_2 = \dfrac{1}{j\omega C}$.

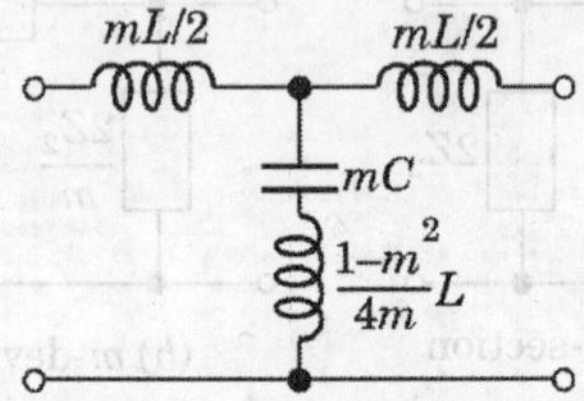

Fig. 23.17. m-derived low pass T-section filter.

The impedance of the shunt arm is $\dfrac{Z_2}{m} + \dfrac{1-m^2}{4Z}Z_1$. Since Z_1 is $j\omega L$ and $Z_2 = \dfrac{1}{j\omega C}$, the shunt arm is constituted by a series combination of capacitance mC and inductance $\dfrac{1-m^2}{4m}L$.

It may be readily seen that the shunt arm is a series LC circuit which offers almost zero impedance at the frequency of its series resonance. At this resonant frequency, the transmission through the filter is zero, *i.e.* the attenuation is infinite. Let this frequency of infinite attenuation be denoted by f_∞. At this frequency, reactance mC equals the reactance of $\dfrac{1-m^2}{4m}L$.

Hence $\dfrac{1}{\omega_\infty mC} = \left(\dfrac{1-m^2}{4m}\right)\omega_\infty L$ or $\omega_\infty = \dfrac{2}{\sqrt{1-m^2}\sqrt{LC}}$ ...(23.123)

or
$$f_\infty = \frac{1}{\pi\sqrt{LC}\sqrt{1-m^2}} \text{ Hz} \quad ...(23.124)$$

The cut-off frequencies f_c in Hertz and ω_c in radians-second are given by,

$$f_c = \frac{1}{\pi\sqrt{LC}} \quad ...(23.125)$$

and
$$\omega_c = \frac{2}{\sqrt{LC}} \quad ...(23.126)$$

From Eqs. (23.123) and (23.126), we get

$$\omega_\infty = \frac{\omega_c}{\sqrt{1-m^2}} \quad ...(23.127)$$

Similarly from Eqs. (23.124) and (23.125), we get

$$f_\infty = \frac{\omega_c}{\sqrt{1-m^2}} \quad ...(23.128)$$

From Eq. (23.128),

$$1 - m = \left(\frac{f}{f_\infty}\right)^2$$

Hence $$m = \sqrt{1 - \left(\frac{f_c}{f_\infty}\right)^2} = \sqrt{1 - \left(\frac{\omega_c}{\omega_\infty}\right)^2} \quad ...(23.129)$$

For desired value of cut off frequency f_c and frequency f_∞ for infinite attenuation, the value of m may be calculated from Eq. (23.129). Knowing f_c, R_0 and m, the values of components of m derived low pass filter may be calculated.

(B) π-section. Fig. 23.18 shows the m-derived low pass π-section filter. This is obtained from Fig. 23.15 (*b*) by putting $Z_1 = j\omega L$ and $Z_2 = \frac{1}{j\omega C}$. The series arm consists of parallel combination of impedance $mj\omega L$ and $\frac{4m}{1-m^2}\cdot\frac{1}{j\omega C}$. Hence it is constituted by inductance mL in shunt which capacitance $\frac{1-m^2}{4m}C$.

The series arm is parallel LC circuit which offers infinite impedance and hence zero transmission through it at the frequency of its parallel resonance. At this frequency of zero transmission or infinite attenuation, the reactance of capacitance $\frac{1-m^2}{4m}C$ equals the reactance of inductance mL.

Thus $$\omega_\infty mL = \frac{1}{\omega_\infty L\left(\frac{1-m^2}{4m}\right)} \quad \text{or} \quad \omega_\infty^2 = \frac{4}{LC(1-m^2)}$$

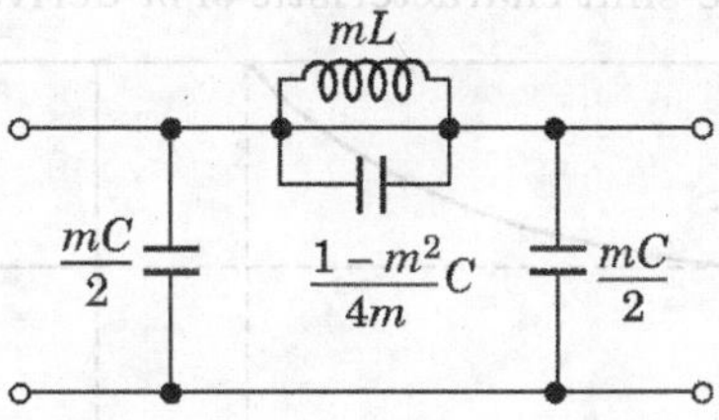

Fig. 23.18. *M*-derived low pass π-section filter.

Hence $$\omega_\infty = \frac{2}{\sqrt{LC}}\cdot\frac{1}{\sqrt{1-m^2}} \quad ...(23.130)$$

or $$f_\infty = \frac{1}{\pi\sqrt{LC}}\cdot\frac{1}{\sqrt{1-m^2}} \quad ...(23.131)$$

But cut-off frequency ω_c equals $\frac{2}{\sqrt{LC}}$

Hence $$\omega_\infty = \frac{\omega_c}{\sqrt{1-m^2}} \quad ...(23.132)$$

and $$f_\infty = \frac{f_c}{\sqrt{1-m^2}} \quad ...(23.133)$$

Thus in both T and π-section m-derived filters, same equations relate f_∞ and f_c. Similarly Eq. (21.129) giving m in terms of f_c and f_∞ holds good in this case of π-section as well.

23.15. Attenuation Phase Shift and Z_0 *Characteristic* of m derived Low Pass Filter

Solid curved in Fig. 23.19 gives the attenuation characteristic of a m derived low pass filter. The chain dotted curve gives the attenuation characteristic of corresponding constant k filter. In m derived filter, the attenuation remains zero upto cut-off frequency f_c and then increases rapidly to become infinite at frequency f_∞. Thus in m derived filter, a relatively sharp cut-off is obtained. This sharpness of cut-off may be increased by (*i*) reducing the value of m and (*ii*) by placing several m-derived sections in tandem.

It may, however, be seen from Fig. 23.19 that the attenuation of m-derived low pass filter decreases rapidly with increase of frequency beyond f_∞. This tendency may be counteracted by connecting a constant k-section in tandem with the m-derived section.

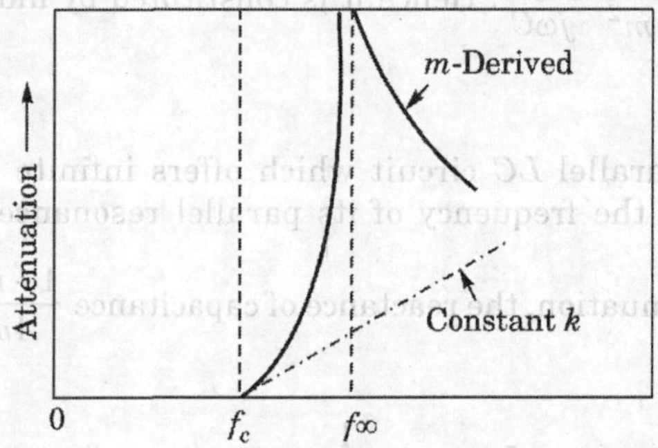

Fig. 23.19. Attenuation *versus* frequency curves of m-derived and constant k filters.

Fig. 23.20 shows the phase-shift characteristic of m-derived low pass filter section.

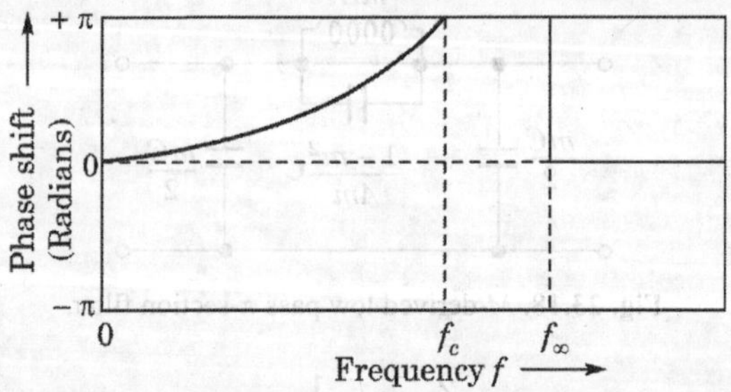

Fig. 23.20. Phases shift characteristic of m-derived low pass filter.

Fig. 23.21 gives the Z_0 characteristic of m-derived low pass T and π-section filters. These characteristics are the same as those for constant k-section.

The constant m in m-derived filter may have any value between 0 and 1. The attenuation characteristic of the m-derived section will vary widely with change of m. Fig. 23.22 gives the attenuation *versus* frequency curves of m-derived low pass filters for values of m = 0.4,0.6 and 1.0. As the value of m reduces, the sharpness of attenuation curve increases. For m = 1, the m-derived filter reduces to simple constant-k filter.

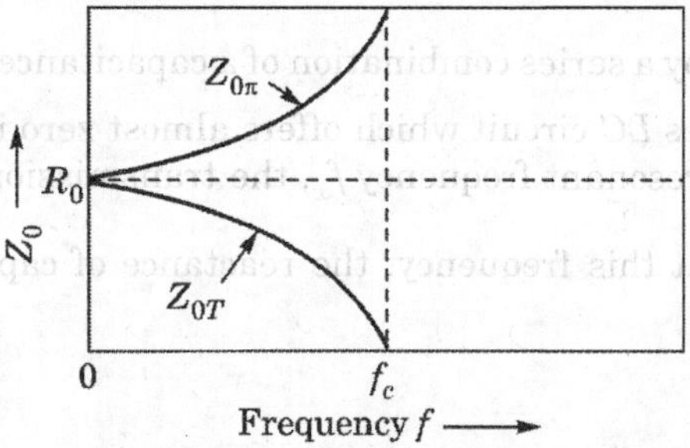

Fig. 23.21. Z_0 characteristic of m-derived low pass filter sections.

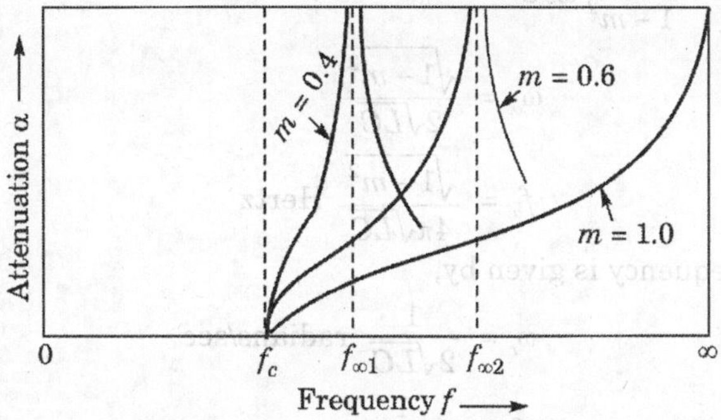

Fig. 23.22. Attenuation *versus* frequency curves of m-derived low pass filter for different values of m.

23.16. m-derived High Pass Filters

(*A*) **T-section.** Fig. 23.23 (*a*) shows a constant-*k* high pass *T*-section filter while Fig. 23.23 (*b*) shows the corresponding *m*-derived filter. This is obtained from that shown in Fig. 23.14 (*b*) by putting

$$Z_1 = \frac{1}{j\omega C}$$

and $$Z_2 = j\omega L.$$

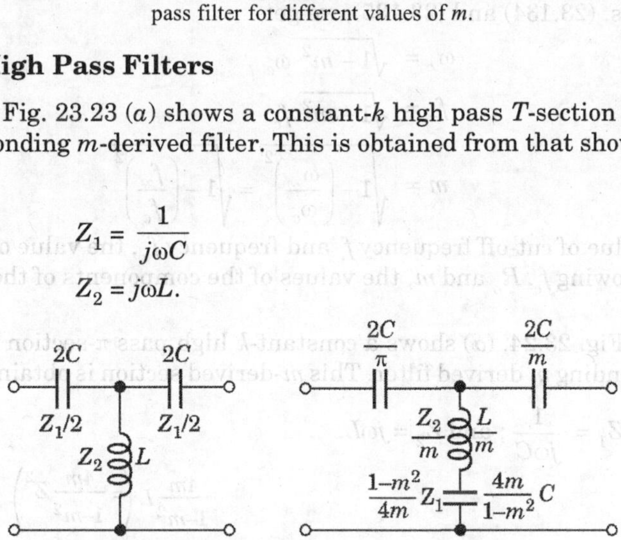

Fig. 23.23. High pass constant-k and m-derived T-section filter.

The impedance of shunt arms is $\dfrac{Z_2}{m} + \dfrac{1-m^2}{4m} Z_1$. Since

$$Z_1 = \frac{1}{j\omega C} \quad \text{and} \quad Z_2 = j\omega L,$$

the shunt arm is constituted by a series combination of a capacitance $\frac{4m}{1-m^2}C$ and inductance $\frac{L}{m}$. Thus the shunt arm is a series LC circuit which offers almost zero impedance at the frequency of its series resonance. At this resonant frequency f_∞, the transmission though the filter is zero, *i.e.* the attenuation is infinite. At this frequency, the reactance of capacitance $\frac{4}{1-m^2}C$ equals the reactance of inductance $\frac{L}{m}$.

Hence
$$\frac{1}{\frac{4m}{1-m^2}\omega_\infty C} = \frac{\omega_\infty L}{m} \quad \text{or} \quad \omega_\infty^2 = \frac{1-m^2}{4LC}$$

Hence
$$\omega_\infty = \frac{\sqrt{1-m^2}}{2\sqrt{LC}} \qquad ...(23.134)$$

or
$$f_\infty = \frac{\sqrt{1-m^2}}{4\pi\sqrt{LC}} \text{ Hertz} \qquad ...(23.135)$$

But the cut-off frequency is given by,
$$\omega_c = \frac{1}{2\sqrt{LC}} \text{ radians/sec} \qquad ...(23.136)$$

and
$$f_c = \frac{1}{4\pi\sqrt{LC}} \qquad ...(23.137)$$

Hence from Eqs. (23.134) and (23.135), we get
$$\omega_\infty = \sqrt{1-m^2}\,\omega_c \qquad ...(23.138)$$

Similarly,
$$f_\infty = \sqrt{1-m^2}\,f_c \qquad ...(23.139)$$

Hence
$$m = \sqrt{1-\left(\frac{\omega_\infty}{\omega_c}\right)^2} = \sqrt{1-\left(\frac{f_\infty}{f_c}\right)^2} \qquad ...(23.140)$$

For desired value of cut-off frequency f_c and frequency f_∞, the value of m may be calculated from Eq. (23.140). Knowing f_c, R_o and m, the values of the components of the m derived filter may be calculated.

(*B*) **π-section.** Fig. 23.24. (*a*) shows a constant-*k* high pass π-section filter while Fig. 23.24 (*b*) shows the corresponding *m* derived filter. This *m*-derived section is obtained from that shown in Fig. 23.16 by putting $Z_1 = \frac{1}{j\omega C}$; and $Z_2 = j\omega L$.

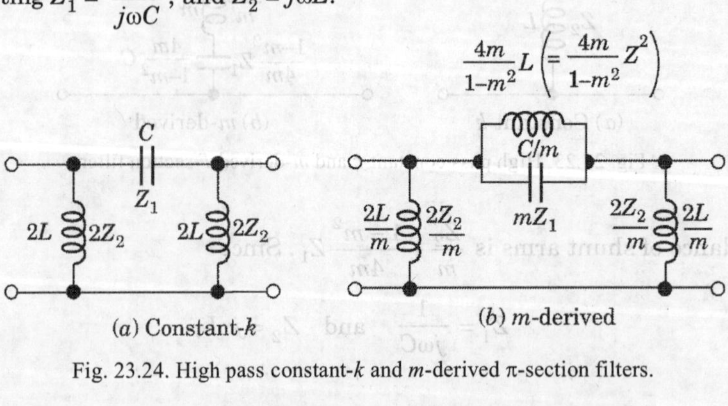

Fig. 23.24. High pass constant-*k* and *m*-derived π-section filters.

It may be readily seen that the series arm is a parallel tuned circuit which offers infinitely large impedance at the frequency of its parallel resonance. At this frequency, the transmission through the filter is zero, *i.e.* the attenuation is infinite. At this frequency f_∞, the reactance of capacitance C/m equals the reactance of inductance $\frac{4m}{1-m^2}L$.

$$\text{Thus} \quad \omega_\infty \frac{4m}{1-m^2}L = \frac{1}{\frac{\omega_\infty C}{m}} \quad \text{or} \quad \omega_\infty = \frac{\sqrt{1-m^2}}{2\sqrt{LC}} \quad \text{...(23.141)}$$

$$\text{and} \quad f_\infty = \frac{\sqrt{1-m^2}}{4\pi\sqrt{LC}} \quad \text{...(23.142)}$$

Eq. (23.141) giving the value of ω_∞ for π-section is the same as Eq. (23.134) for T-section. Hence Eqs. (23.138), (23.139) and (23.140) giving values of ω_∞, f_∞ and m apply for π-section m-derived high pass filter as well.

23.17. Attenuation Phase Shift and Z_0 Characteristic of m-derived High Pass Filter

The solid curve in Fig. 23.25 gives the attenuation *versus* frequency curve of a m-derived high pass filter. The chain dotted curve gives the attenuation *versus* frequency curve for the corresponding constant-k filter. The attenuation remains zero in the frequency range extending from cut-off frequency f_c to infinity and becomes infinite at a frequency f_∞ slightly lower than the cut-off frequency f_c. In constant-k filter, the attenuation becomes infinity at zero frequency.

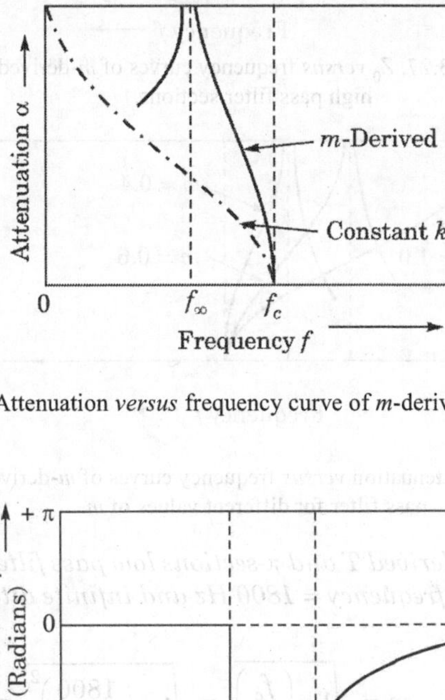

Fig. 23.25. Attenuation *versus* frequency curve of m-derived high pass filter.

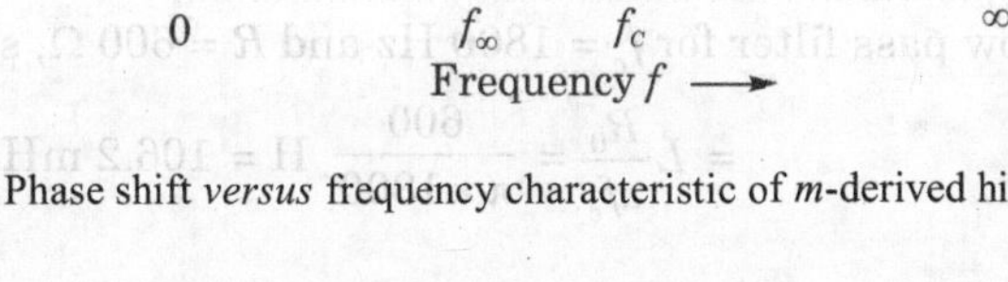

Fig. 23.26. Phase shift *versus* frequency characteristic of m-derived high pass filter.

A relatively sharp cut-off may thus be achieved in the case of m-derived filter. The sharpness of cut-off may be increased by reducing the value of m. The sharpness of attenuation curve may also be increased by placing several m-derived sections in tandem.

In the case of m-derived high pass filter, the attenuation decreases rapidly with decrease of frequency below f_∞. This tendency may be counteracted by connecting a prototype section in tandem with the m-derived section. Fig. 23.26 shows the phase shift *versus* frequency curve for the m-derived high pass filter section.

Fig. 23.27 gives the Z_0 *versus* frequency curves of m-derived high pass filter sections of T-type and π-type. These characteristics are the same as those of constant-k section.

The constant m in m-derived high pass filter determines the sharpness of attenuation characteristic in the attenuation band. Fig. 23.28 gives the attenuation *versus* frequency characteristics of m-derived high pass filter for values of m equal to 0.4, 0.6 and 1.0. It may be seen from these curves that as the value of m reduces, the sharpness of attenuation curve increases. For $m = 1.0$, the m-derived section reduces to simple constant k-section.

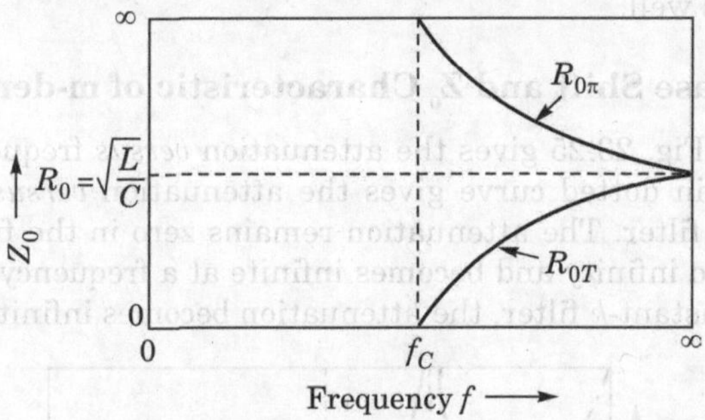

Fig. 23.27. Z_0 *versus* frequency curves of m-derived high pass filter sections.

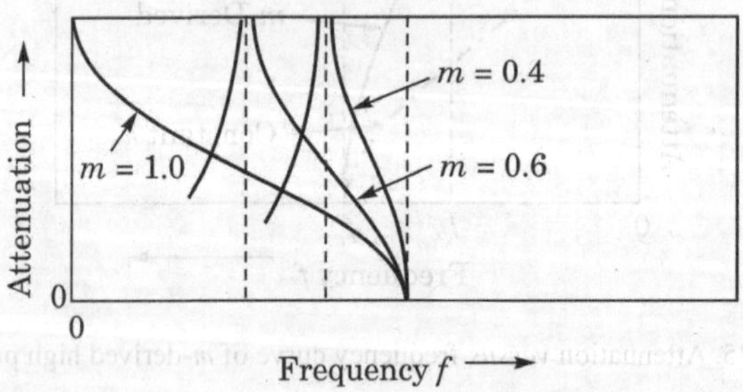

Fig. 23.28. Attenuation *versus* frequency curves of m-derived high pass filter for different values of m.

Example 23.7. *Design m-derived T and π-sections low pass filters for nominal characteristic impedance $R_0 = 600$ ohms, cut-off frequency = 1800 Hz and infinite attenuation frequency $f_\infty = 2000$ Hz.*

Solution.
$$m = \sqrt{1 - \left(\frac{f_c}{f_\infty}\right)} = \sqrt{1 - \left(\frac{1800}{2000}\right)^2} = 0.436$$

For the prototype low pass filter for $f_c = 1800$ Hz and $R = 600\ \Omega$, series arm inductance

$$= L\frac{R_0}{\pi f_c} = \frac{600}{\pi \times 1800} \text{ H} = 106.2 \text{ mH}$$

Shunt arm capacitance

$$= L\frac{1}{\pi R_0 f_c} = \frac{1}{\omega \times 600 \times 1800} \text{ F} = 0.2948 \ \mu\text{F}.$$

The *T*-section of *m*-derived filter is shown in Fig. 23.17. The values of the elements are :

$$\frac{mL}{2} = \frac{0.436 \times 106.2}{2} \text{ mH} = 23.15 \text{ mH}.$$

$$C = 0.436 \times 0.2948 \ \mu\text{F} = 0.1285 \ \mu\text{F}$$

$$\frac{1-m^2}{4m}L = \frac{1-(0.436)^2}{4 \times 0.436} \times 106.2 \text{ mH} = 49.32 \text{ mH}.$$

The π-section of *m*-derived filter is shown in Fig. 23.18.

The values of the elements are :

$$\frac{mC}{2} = \frac{0.436 \times 0.2948}{2} \ \mu\text{F} = 0.0642 \ \mu\text{F}$$

$$mL = 0.436 \times 106.2 \text{ mH} = 46.3 \text{ mH}.$$

$$\frac{1-m^2}{4m}L = \frac{1-(0.436)^2}{4 \times 0.436} \times 0.2948 \ \mu\text{F} = 0.1369 \ \mu\text{F}.$$

Example 23.8. *Design T and π-sections of m-derived high pass filter having nominal characteristic impedance (nominal impedance) of 600 ohms, cut-off frequency = 4 kHz and infinite attenuation at 3.6 kHz.*

Solution.

$$m = \sqrt{1-\left(\frac{f_\infty}{f_c}\right)^2} = \sqrt{1-\left(\frac{3.6}{4}\right)^2} = 0.436.$$

For the prototype high pass filter having f_c = 4 kHz and R_0 = 600 ohms.

Series arm capacitance

$$C = \frac{1}{4\pi f_c R_0} = \frac{1}{4\pi \times 4000 \times 600} \text{ F} = 0.08323 \ \mu\text{F}$$

Shunt arm inductance,

$$L = \frac{R_0}{4\pi f_c} = \frac{600}{4\pi \times 4000} \text{ H} = 11.95 \text{ mH}.$$

T-section of *m*-derived filter shown in Fig. 23.23 (*b*). The values of the circuit elements are:

$$\frac{2C}{m} = \frac{2 \times 0.08323}{0.436} \ \mu\text{F} = 0.3822 \ \mu\text{F}$$

$$\frac{L}{m} = \frac{11.95}{0.436} \text{ mH} = 27.46 \text{ mH}$$

$$\frac{4m}{1-m^2}C = \frac{4 \times 0.436}{1-(0.436)^2} \times 0.08323 \ \mu\text{F} = 0.1795 \ \mu\text{F}$$

The π-section of *m*-derived filter is shown in Fig. 23.24 (*b*).

The values of the circuit elements are :

$$\frac{2L}{m} = \frac{2 \times 11.95}{0.436} \text{ mH} = 54.92 \text{ mH}.$$

$$\frac{C}{m} = \frac{0.08323}{0.436}\ \mu F = 0.1911\ \mu F.$$

$$\frac{4m}{1-m^2}L = \frac{4 \times 0.436}{1-(0.436)^2} \times 11.95\ mH = 25.72\ mH.$$

23.18. Composite Filters

In constant k-filter, the attenuation in the attenuation band increases slowly being zero at a remote frequency. In m-derived filter on the other hand, attenuation reaches a very high value at a frequency f_∞ very close to the cut-off frequency but the attenuation decreases for frequencies beyond f_∞.

In order to get the best results, composite filters are used. A composite filter contains :

(*i*) One or more constant-k section to produce cut-off, *i.e.* transition from pass band to the stop band at a specified frequency f_c.

(*ii*) One or more m-derived sections to give infinite attenuation at frequency close to f_c.

(*iii*) Two termination half sections, with m-06 to provide almost constant input and output impedances.

Fig. 23.29 gives block schematic arrangement of a typical composite filter using two constant-k sections, two m-derived sections and a termination half section at each end. The various sections are connected in tandem. This composite filter may be designed to have any desired attenuation *versus* frequency characteristic.

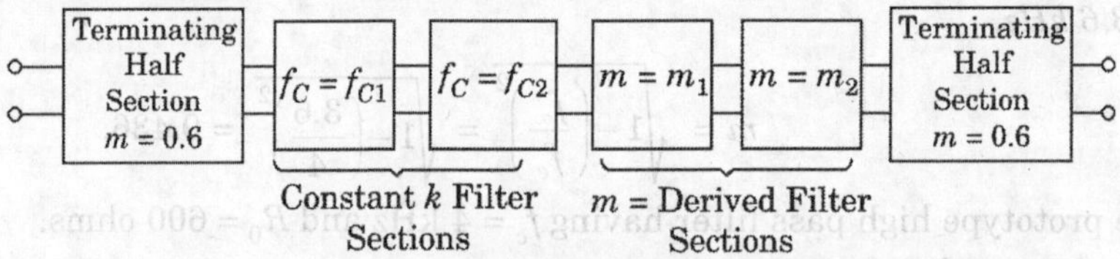

Fig. 23.29. Block schematic diagram of a typical composite filter.

Fig. 23.30 shows the attenuation *versus* frequency characteristics of low pass (*i*) constant-k filter section, (*ii*) m-derived section, and (*iii*) composite filter forming a combination of the two section. Both constant-k and m derived filters fail to have desirable attenuation *versus* frequency characteristic. In constant-k filter the attenuation rises slowly with frequency in the attenuation band. In m-derived filter, the attenuation falls rapidly with frequency in the frequency range beyond the frequency of infinite attenuation. By combining a constant-k section with an m-derived section to form a composite filter, the attenuation *versus* frequency curve is far superior to that of either of the constituent filter sections. Thus, as is evident from Fig. 23.30, in the frequency range from the f_c to f_∞, the attenuation rises very rapidly with frequency and beyond frequency f_∞, the attenuation falls only nominally with frequency.

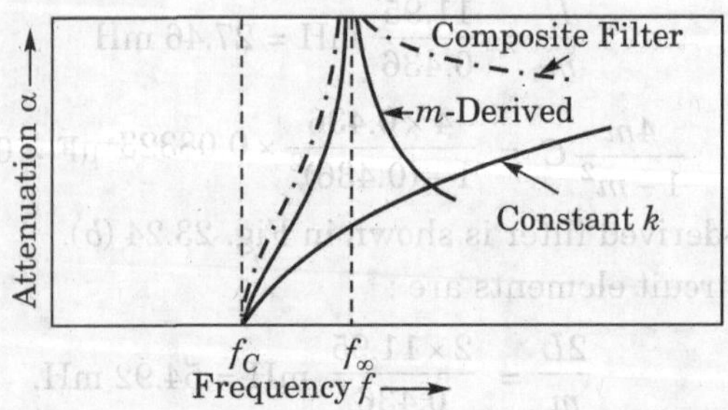

Fig. 23.30. Attenuation *versus* frequency curve of a composite filter.

23.19. Terminating Half-sections

A major defect of a constant-k filter section is that its impedance in the passband, although resistive, varies with frequency. This causes mismatch and reflection. Hence it becomes difficult to terminate properly a constant-k filter. Hence we often use a half section or L-section as the impedance transforming device at each end of a composite filter.

Fig. 23.31 (a) shows an m-derived T-section. The impedance offered by this section at each end is Z_{0T}. Now the elements of this T-section are rearranged as shown in Fig. 23.31 (b) to yield the corresponding π-section. Let $Z_0\pi'$ be the characteristic impedance of this π-section. Next this π-section is split up into two halves. One such half-section is shown in Fig 23.31 (c). Then the image impedance of this half section seen from the two ends are Z_{0T} and $Z_0\pi'$ as shown in Fig. 23.31 (c).

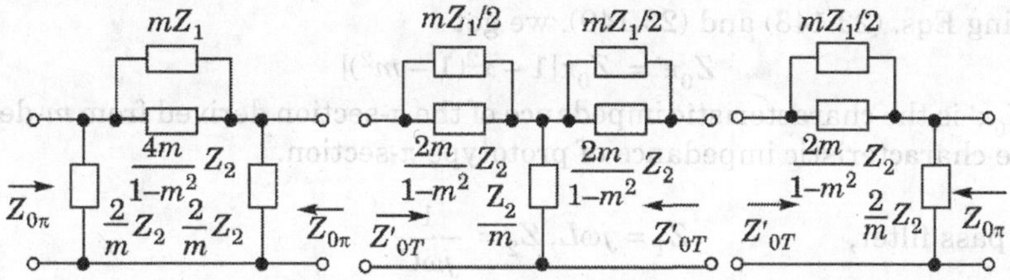

(a) m-derived π-section (b) Corresponding π-section (c) Corresponding half section

Fig. 23.31. Derivation of half π-section from m-derived T-section.

Then $$Z_0\pi' = \frac{Z_1' Z_2'}{Z_{0T}} \qquad \text{...(23.143)}$$

But $$Z_1' = mZ_1 \quad \text{and} \quad Z'_2 = \frac{Z_2}{m} + \frac{1-m^2}{4m} Z_1 .$$

Also $$Z_{0T} = \sqrt{\frac{Z_1^2}{4} + Z_1 Z_2} \qquad \text{...(23.144)}$$

Hence $$Z_0\pi' = \frac{mZ_1\left[\dfrac{Z_2}{m} + \dfrac{1-m^2}{4m} Z_1\right]}{\sqrt{Z_1 Z_2}\sqrt{1+\dfrac{Z_1}{4Z_2}}}$$

$$= \frac{Z_1 Z_2\left[1+(1-m^2)\dfrac{Z_1}{4Z_2}\right]}{\sqrt{Z_1 Z_2}\sqrt{1+\dfrac{Z_1}{4Z_2}}} \qquad \text{...(23.145)}$$

But design impedance,

$$R_0 = \sqrt{Z_1 Z_2}$$

Also let $$\frac{-Z_1}{4Z_2} = +x^2 \qquad \text{...(23.146)}$$

Then Eq. (23.145) may be put as,

$$Z_0\pi' = \frac{R_0^2[1-(1-m^2)x^2]}{R_0\sqrt{1-x^2}} = \frac{R_0[1-x^2(1-m^2)]}{\sqrt{1-x^2}} \qquad \text{...(23.147)}$$

or $$\frac{Z_0\pi'}{R_0} = \frac{1 - x^2(1 - m^2)}{\sqrt{1 - x^2}} \qquad \text{...(23.148)}$$

But $$Z_0\pi = \frac{Z_1 Z_2}{Z_{0T}} = \frac{R_0^2}{\sqrt{\frac{Z_1^2}{4} + Z_1 Z_2}}$$

$$= \frac{R_0^2}{\sqrt{Z_1 Z_2}\sqrt{1 + \frac{Z_1}{4Z_2}}} = \frac{R_0}{\sqrt{1 - x^2}} \qquad \text{...(23.149)}$$

Combining Eqs. (23.148) and (23.149), we get

$$Z_0\pi' = Z_0\pi[1 - x^2(1 - m^2)] \qquad \text{...(23.150)}$$

Hence $Z_0\pi'$ is the characteristic impedance of the π-section derived from m-derived T-section while $Z_0\pi$ is the characteristic impedance of prototype π-section.

For low pass filter, $$Z_1 = j\omega L,\ Z_2 = \frac{1}{j\omega C}$$

Hence $$\frac{Z_1}{4Z_1} = \frac{-\omega^2}{\omega_c^2} \quad \text{or} \quad x = \frac{\omega^2}{\omega_c^2}$$

Hence Eq. (23.147) yields, $$Z_0\pi' = \frac{R_0\left[1 - (1 - m^2)\frac{f^2}{f_c^2}\right]}{\sqrt{1 - \frac{f^2}{f_c^2}}} \qquad \text{...(23.151)}$$

For high pass filters, $$Z_1 = \frac{1}{j\omega C},\ Z_2 = j\omega L$$

$$\frac{Z_1}{4Z_2} = \frac{1}{j\omega C \times j\omega L} = \frac{-1}{\omega^2 LC} = \frac{-f_c^2}{f^2}.$$

Hence Eq. (23.147) yields, $$Z_0\pi' = \frac{R_0\left[1 + (1 - m^2)\frac{f^2}{f_c^2}\right]}{\sqrt{1 - \frac{f^2}{f_c^2}}} \qquad \text{...(23.152)}$$

Thus obviously, $$x = \sqrt{x^2} = \sqrt{\frac{Z_1}{4Z_2}} = \frac{f}{f_c} \text{ for Low Pass Filter}$$

$$= \frac{f_c}{f} \text{ for High Pass Fitter.}$$

Fig. 23.32 shows curves giving $\frac{Z_0\pi'}{R}$ against relative frequency x (*i.e* f/f_c for low pass filter and f_c/f for high pass filter) for various values of m. We find that for $m = 0.6$, $Z_0\pi'$ remains practically constant at the value $R_0 = \left(\sqrt{\dfrac{L}{C}}\right)$ for all values of relative frequency x upto 0.85, *i.e.* upto $f = 0.85f_c$ in low pass filter and $\dfrac{f_c}{0.85} = 1.18f_c$ in high pass filter.

Beyond this frequency, $Z_0\pi'$ rapidly approaches infinity. Thus in order to obtain almost constant characteristic impedance, such π-section using $m = 0.6$ are suitable for connecting into lines of constant impedance. These m derived half sections or L-sections having $m = 0.6$ are called terminating half sections. Any T-section, whether prototype or m-derived, may be joined to a terminating half section with $m = 0.6$ and thus avoid mismatch. It is necessary then that T-section has characteristic impedance equal to the nominal characteristic impedance $R_0 = \left(\sqrt{\dfrac{L}{C}}\right)$ of the L-section.

Fig. 23.33 shows an m-derived T-section terminated on each side by one-half of the above mentioned π-section. On the right, a load $Z_r = Z_0\pi' = \sqrt{\dfrac{L}{C}}$ is connected. The m used for the T-section is not necessarily the same as the m used for the terminating half-sections. The Z_{0T} between points B and C will be unaffected by a change in the value of m for the T-section. It may then be proved that the network impedances are matched at all points and if $m = 0.6$, the impedance found looking into the filter through the terminating half section is essentially constant over the pass band.

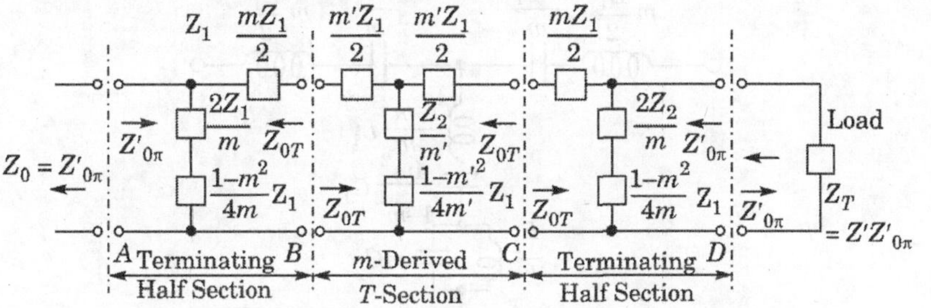

Fig. 23.33. Matching by means of terminating half-sections.

The design procedure for a composite filter may then be but as follows :

(*i*) A constant-k T-section filter is designed for required cut-off frequency and characteristic impedance.

(*ii*) The m-derived sections are then designed on the basis of the T-section, values of m being chosen for desired values of frequencies of infinite attenuation.

(*iii*) All the m-derived T-sections are connected in tandem and are terminated at each end by half- section derived with $m = 0.6$. Then the entire filter have a practically constant $Z_0 = (\sqrt{L/C}$ of the prototype) and also have the desired f_c and frequencies of infinite attenuation.

Such a filter when connected between transmission lines or between pieces of apparatus will have an impedance which is essentially a constant pure resistance.

Fig. 23.34 (*a*) shows an m-derived π-section filter. The elements of this π-section are rearranged as shown in Fig. 23.34 (*b*) to yield the corresponding T-section. Let $Z_0\pi'$ be the characteristic impedance of this T-section. Next this T-section is split into two halves. One such half section is shown in Fig. 23.34 (*c*). Then the image impedances of this half-section seen from the two ends are $Z_0\pi$ and Z_{0T} as shown in Fig. 23.34 (*c*).

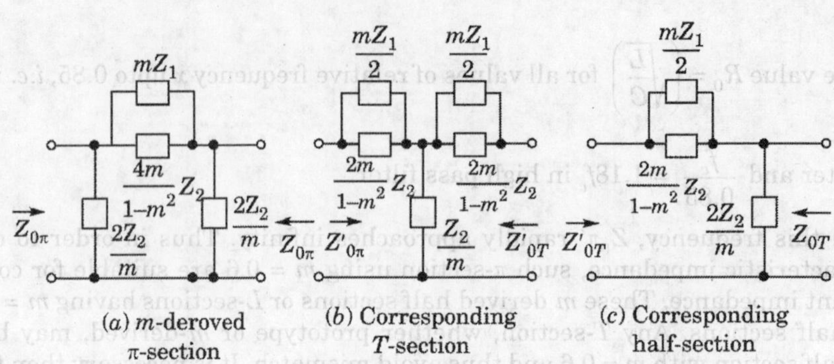

Fig. 23.34. Derivation of T-section from m-derived π-section.

The expression for image impedance Z_{0T}, may be obtained by a procedure similar to that followed in the case of terminating half-section of Fig. 23.31. It may also be shown that image impedance Z_{0T} with $m = 0.6$ remains almost constant at the value $R_0 = (\sqrt{L/C})$ over almost the complete pass band.

23.20. The m-derived Band Pass Filter

Fig. 23.10 gives the T-section constant-k band pass filter. Corresponding m-derived T-type band pass filter may be obtained by the usual procedure namely (*i*) treating the entire series arm impedance as Z_1 and the shunt arm impedance as Z_2 and (*ii*) substituting these values of Z_1 and Z_2 in the m-derived T-section of Fig. 23.14 (*b*). This results in the m-derived T-section band pass filter of Fig. 23.35.

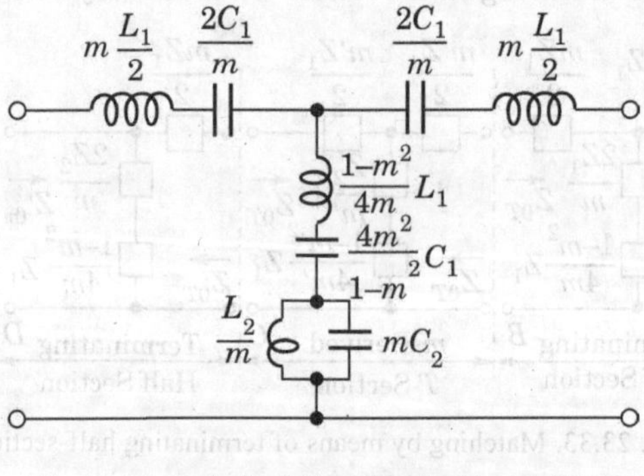

Fig. 23.35. m-derived T-section band pass filter.

Infinite attenuation results when the shunt arm impedance is zero, *i.e.* when

$$\frac{Z_2}{m} + \frac{1-m^2}{3m} Z_1 = 0 \quad \text{...(23.153)}$$

Substituting the values of Z_1 and Z_2 from the prototype T-section band pass filter of Fig. 23.10, we get

$$\frac{1}{m}\left(\frac{j\omega_\infty L_2}{1-\omega_\infty L_2 C_2}\right) + j\frac{1-m^2}{4m}\left(\frac{\omega_\infty^2 L_1 C_1 - 1}{\omega_\infty C_1}\right) = 0 \quad \text{...(23.154)}$$

or $$\frac{\omega_\infty^2 L_2 C_1}{\omega_\infty^2 L_2 C_2 - 1} = \frac{1-m^2}{4}(\omega_\infty^2 L_1 C_1 - 1) \quad \text{...(23.155)}$$

Solution of this equation yields the expression for frequencies of infinite attenuation in terms of the circuit elements.

But $$L_1C_1 = L_2C_2 = \frac{1}{\omega_c^2} \qquad ..(23.156)$$

Combining Eqs. (23.155) and (23.156), we get

$$\frac{1-m^2}{4}\left(\frac{f_\infty^2}{f_0^2}-1\right)^2 = \pi^2 f_\infty^{\ 2} L_1 C_1 \qquad ...(23.157)$$

But from Eq. (23.100), $$C_1 = \frac{f_2 - f_1}{4\pi R_0 f_1 f_2}$$

Also from Eq. (23.103), $$L_2 = \frac{R_0(f_2 - f_1)}{4\pi f_1 f_2}$$

On substituting these values of L_2 and C_1 in Eq. (23.157), we get

$$\frac{1-m^2}{4}\left(\frac{f_\infty^2}{f_0^2}-1\right)^2 = 4\pi^2 f_\infty^2 \cdot \frac{R_0(f_2-f_1)(f_2-f_1)}{4\pi f_1 f_2\, 4\pi R_0 f_1 f_2} \qquad ...(23.158)$$

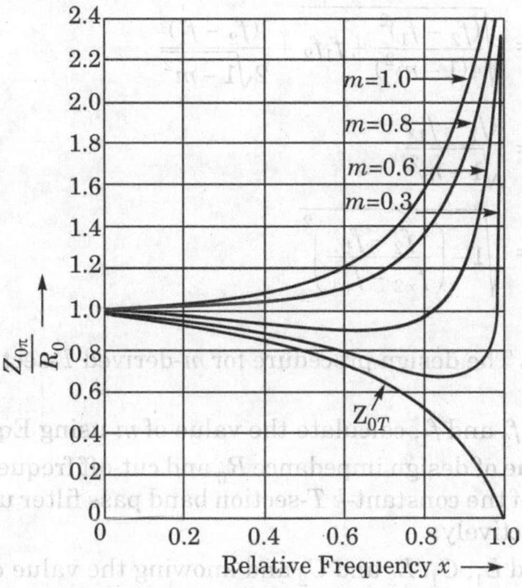

Fig. 23.32. Variation of Z_0/R with frequency for different values of m.

But $f_1 f_2 = f_0^{\,2}$. Hence Eq. (23.158) may be put as,

$$\frac{1-m^2}{4}\left(\frac{f_\infty^2}{f_0^2}-1\right)^2 = \frac{f_\infty^2}{4f_0^4}(f_2 - f_1)^2$$

or $$(1-m^2)\,(f_\infty^2 - f_1 f_2)^2 = f_\infty^2\,(f_2 - f_1)^2$$

$$\sqrt{1-m^2}\,(f_\infty^2 - f_1 f_2) = f_\infty (f_2 - f_1) \qquad ...(23.160)$$

On putting $\sqrt{1-m^2} = x$ and rearranging Eq. (23.159), we get

$$x f_\infty^2 - f_\infty (f_2 - f_1) - x f_1 f_2 = 0 \qquad ...(23.161)$$

Hence $$f_\infty = \frac{+(f_2 - f_1) \pm \sqrt{(f_2 - f_1)^2 + 4x^2 f_1 f_2}}{2x}$$

or $$f_\infty = \frac{(f_2 - f_1)}{2\sqrt{1 - m^2}} \pm \sqrt{\frac{(f_2 - f_1)}{4(1 - m^2)} + f_1 f_2} \quad ...(23.162)$$

From Eq. (23.161) it is evident that the term under the radical sign is larger that the term $\frac{(f_2 - f_1)}{2\sqrt{1 - m^2}}$ and Eq. (23.161) will yield one value of f_∞ as a negative frequency having no physical significance. Hence ± sign is prefixed to the quantity $\frac{(f_2 - f_1)}{2\sqrt{1 - m^2}}$ rather than to the quantity under the radical sign. Accordingly, we get the following two values of f_∞.

$$f_{\infty 1} = \sqrt{\frac{(f_2 - f_1)^2}{4(1 - m^2)} + f_1 f_2} - \frac{(f_2 - f_1)}{2\sqrt{1 - m^2}} \quad ...(23.162)$$

$$f_{\infty 2} = \sqrt{\frac{(f_2 - f_1)^2}{4(1 - m^2)} + f_1 f_2} + \frac{(f_2 - f_1)}{2\sqrt{1 - m^2}} \quad ...(23.163)$$

Hence $$(f_{\infty 2} - f_{\infty 1}) = \frac{(f_2 - f_1)}{\sqrt{1 - m^2}} \quad ...(23.164)$$

Hence $$m = \sqrt{1 - \left(\frac{f_2 - f_1}{f_{\infty 2} - f_{\infty 1}}\right)^2} \quad ...(24.165)$$

Design Procedure. The design procedure for m-derived T-section band pass filter consists of the following steps :

(*i*) Knowing $f_{\infty 2}$, $f_{\infty 1}$, f_2 and f_1, calculate the value of m using Eq. (23.165).

(*ii*) Knowing the value of design impedance R_0 and cut-off frequencies f_1 and f_2, calculate the elements C_1, L_1, L_2 and C_2 of the constant-k T-section band pass filter using Eqs. (23.100), (23.101), (23.102) and (23.103) respectively.

(*iii*) Having calculated L_1, C_1, L_2 and C_2 and knowing the value of m, calculate the values of elements of the m-derived T-section bandpass filter using Fig. 23.35.

Attenuation, Phase Shift and Z_0 Curves. Fig. 23.36 (*a*) gives the variation of attenuation with frequency for m-derived bandpass filter. The attenuation increases sharply beyond the passband and reaches infinity at frequencies $f_{\infty 1}$ and $f_{\infty 2}$. As frequency reduces below $f_{\infty 1}$ or increases beyond $f_{\infty 2}$, the attenuation again decreases as shown in Fig. 23.36 (*a*).

Fig. 23.36 (*b*) shows the variation of phase shift β with frequency for the m derived bandpass filter.

Fig. 23.36 (*c*) gives the variation of characteristic impedance Z_0 with frequency for the T-section m-derived bandpass filter.

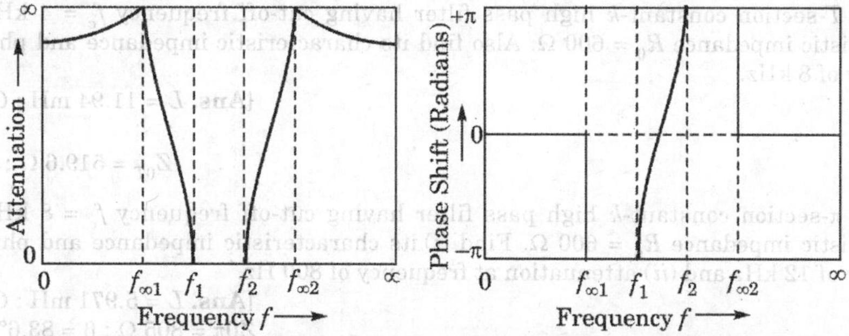

(*a*) Attenuation *versus* frequency curve. (*b*) Pass shift *versus* frequency curve.

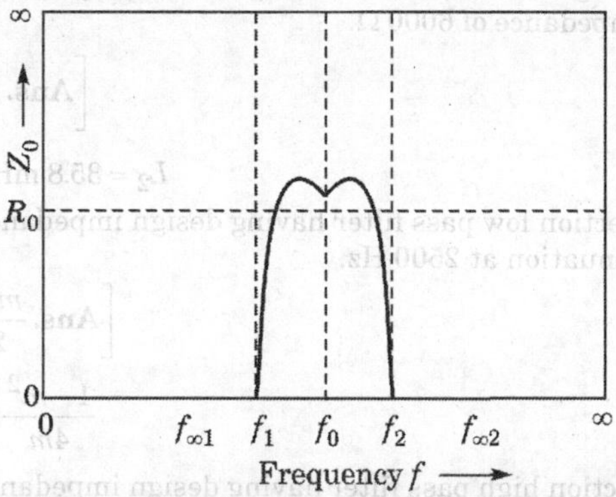

(*c*) Z_0 *versus* frequency curve for *T*-section.

Fig. 23.36. Attenuation, Phase shift and Z_0 curves for *m*-derived *T*-section bandpass filter.

EXERCISES 23

23.1. For the given π-section low pass filter, find the cut-off frequency and the design resistance R_0.

[**Ans.** f_c = 1592 Hz ; R_0 = 500 Ω]

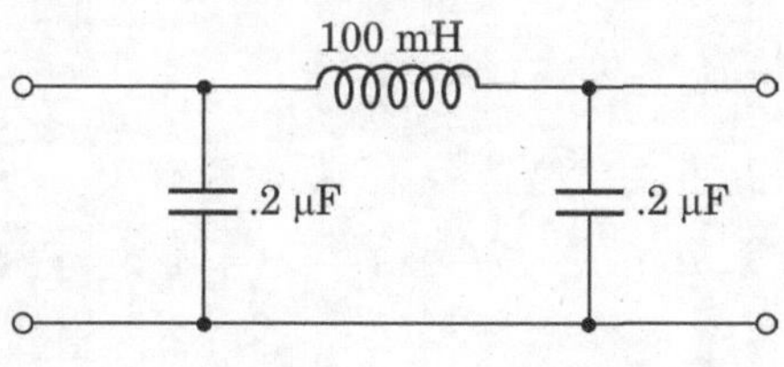

23.2. Design a constant-*k* low pass filter having cut-off frequency of 7.5 kHz and nominal characteristic impedance R_0 of 600 ohms.

[**Ans.** Series inductance L = 25.48 mH,
Shunt capacitance C = 0.0707 μF]

23.3. Design a constant-*k* low pass filter having cut-off frequency of 500 Hz and nominal characteristic impedance R_0 = 500 Ω. Also find the frequency at which this filter produces attenuation of 38.2 dB.

[**Ans.** Series arm inductance L = 31.84 mH
Shunt arm capacitance C = 3.1275 μF
f = 22.84 kHz]

23.4. Design a T-section constant-k high pass filter having cut-off frequency f_c = 4 kHz and nominal characteristic impedance R_0 = 600 Ω. Also find its characteristic impedance and phase constant at frequency of 8 kHz.

[**Ans.** L = 11.94 mH ; C = 0.03317 μF ;

Z_{0T} = 519.6 Ω ; $\beta = \frac{\pi}{3}$ radians]

23.5. Design a π-section constant-k high pass filter having cut-off frequency f_c = 8 kHz and nominal characteristic impedance R_0 = 600 Ω. Find (*i*) its characteristic impedance and phase constant at frequency of 12 kHz and (*ii*) attenuation at frequency of 800 Hz.

[**Ans.** L = 5.971 mH ; C = 0.01659 μF ;
$Z0\pi$ = 805 Ω ; β = 83.6° ; α = 6 Nepers]

23.6. Design a constant-k bandages filter section having cut-off frequencies of 1000 Hz and 4000 Hz and nominal characteristic impedance of 6000 Ω.

[**Ans.** $\frac{L_1}{2}$ = 31.84 mH ; $2C_1$ = 0.199 μF ;

L_2 = 35.8 mH ; C_2 = 0.177 μF (see Fig. 23.10)]

23.7. Design an m-derived T-section low pass filter having design impedance of 600 Ω, cut-off frequency of 2400 Hz and infinite attenuation at 2500 Hz.

[**Ans.** $\frac{mL}{2}$ = 11.1 mH ; mC = 0.06172 μF ;

$\frac{1-m^2}{4m}L$ = 0.6575 mH (see Fig. 23.17)]

23.8. Design an m-derived I-section high pass filter having design impedance of 600 Ω, cut-off frequency of kHz and infinite attenuation at 4.8 kHz.

[**Ans.** $\frac{2C}{m}$ = 0.738 μF ; $\frac{L}{m}$ = 132.7 mH ;

$\frac{4m}{1-m^2}C$ = 1.475 μF (see Fig. 23.36)]

24

Attenuators

24.1. Introduction

Attenuators are typically 4-terminal resistive networks used for reducing the signal level by given amount, *i.e.* for producing desired and known amounts of loss. Since the resistance of a resistor is independent of frequency an attenuator using resistive elements produces loss which is independent of frequency. Attenuators may be symmetrical or asymmetrical in form. An asymmetrical attenuator may also be used for matching two unequal impedances when the insertion loss can be tolerated. Such an impedance matching attenuator has the advantage over an impedance matching transformer that it avoids distortion.

A resistive attenuator does not introduce any phase shift. Thus phase shift $\beta = 0$. Hence the propagation constant γ is simply equal to the attenuator constant α.

An attenuator may be either of fixed attenuation type or variable attenuator type. A fixed attenuation type attenuator is often called an *attenuating pad* or simply *pad*. Variable attenuator type attenuators are used as volume controls or faders in radio broadcasting stations. Attenuators are used also in laboratories for obtaining small value voltage or current for test purpose.

24.2. Symmetrical Attenuators

Symmetrical attenuators are placed between two equal impedances of value equal to the characteristic impedances of the attenuators. Using resistive elements alone in an attenuator, its characteristic impedance Z_0 is also resistive.

$$\text{Attenuation in } dB = 10 \log_{10} \frac{P_1}{P_2} \quad \text{...(24.1.)}$$

where P_1 is the input power
and P_2 is the output power.

In the case of a symmetrical attenuator, both terminal pairs are matched to the same resistance, namely the characteristic resistance R_0 of the attenuator.

Then
$$\frac{P_1}{P_2} = \frac{R_0 I_S^2}{R_0 I_R^2} \quad \text{...(24.2)}$$

$$= \frac{I_S^2}{I_R^2} \quad \text{...(24.3)}$$

where I_S is the input current
and I_R is the output current.

Let $\sqrt{\dfrac{P_1}{P_2}}$ be denoted by N,

$$\frac{P_1}{P_2} = N^2 = \left(\frac{I_S}{I_R}\right)^2 \quad \text{...(24.4)}$$

Then $$D = 10 \log_{10} \left(\frac{I_S}{I_R}\right)^2 \quad ...(24.5)$$

$$= 20 \log_{10} \frac{I_S}{I_R} \quad ...(24.6)$$

$$= 20 \log_{10} N \quad ...(24.7)$$

Hence $$N = \text{antilog } \frac{D}{20} \quad ...(24.7a)$$

Symmetrical attenuators may be put into four categories :
(*a*) Symmetrical T-attenuators,
(*b*) Symmetrical *n*-attenuators,
(*c*) Symmetrical Bridged T-attenuators and
(*d*) Symmetrical Lattice attenuators.

24.3. Symmetrical T-Attenuators

Fig. 24.1 shows the symmetrical *T*-attenuator. It is driven at the input port by a voltage source *V* of internal resistance R_0 and it feeds a resistor R_0 at the output port.

An attenuator is designed for desired values of R_0 and attenuation. The elements R_1 and R_2 (Fig. 24.1) are then chosen such that these desired values of R_0 and attenuation are obtained.

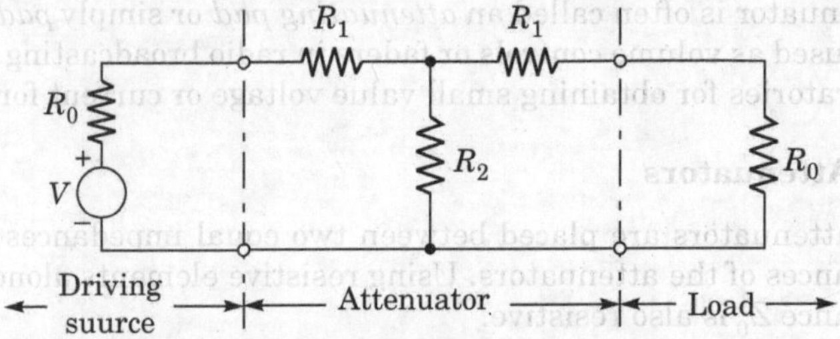

Fig. 24.1. Symmetrical *T*-attenuator.

The *T*-attenuator of Fig. 24.1 is a symmetrical *T*-network using resistances only. Hence $Z_0 = R_0$ and $\gamma = \alpha$. The elements R_1 and R_2 are then given by,

$$R_1 = R_0 \tanh \frac{\alpha}{2} \quad ...(24.8)$$

and $$R_2 = R_0 / \sinh \frac{\alpha}{2} \quad ...(24.9)$$

But by definition of propagation constant γ,

$$e^{\gamma} = \frac{I_S}{I_R}$$

and $\gamma = \alpha$ for resistance attenuator.

Hence $$e^{\alpha} = \frac{I_S}{I_R} = N \quad ...(24.10)$$

Combining Eqs. (24.8) and (24.10), we get

$$R_1 = R_0 \cdot \tanh \frac{\alpha}{2} = R_0 \frac{e^{\alpha/2} - e^{-\alpha/2}}{e^{\alpha/2} + e^{-\alpha/2}} = R_0 \frac{e^{\alpha} - 1}{e^{\alpha} + 1}$$

or $$R_1 = R_0 \frac{N-1}{N+1} \quad ...(24.11)$$

Similarly, $$R_2 = \frac{R_0}{\sinh \alpha} = \frac{2R_0}{(e^{\alpha} - e^{-\alpha})} = \frac{2R_0}{N - \frac{1}{N}}$$

or $$R_2 = R_0 \cdot \frac{2N}{N^2 - 1} \qquad \text{...(24.12)}$$

Eqs. (24.11) and (24.12) constitute the design equations for the symmetrical T-attenuator.

Alternative Derivation of Design Equations. The design equations (24.11) and (24.12) may be obtained directly from Fig. 24.1 without using the equations (24.8) and (24.9).

On applying Kirchhoff's voltage law to the mesh BCD, we get

$$R_2(I_S - I_R) = I_R(R_1 + R_0)$$

or $$I_S R_2 = I_R(R_1 + R_2 + R_0)$$

Hence $$N = \frac{I_S}{I_R} = \frac{R_1 + R_2 + R_0}{R_2} \qquad \text{...(24.13)}$$

The attenuator is terminated by load resistance R_0. Hence on looking from the load terminal CE into the attenuators, impedance obtained must be R_0. Thus,

$$R_0 = R_1 + R_2 \parallel (R_1 + R_0) = R_1 + \frac{R_2(R_1 + R_0)}{(R_1 + R_2 + R_0)}$$

$$= R_1 + \frac{R_1 + R_0}{N} \qquad \text{...(24.14)}$$

or $$NR_0 = NR_1 + R_1 + R_0$$

Hence $$R_1 = R_0 \frac{N - 1}{N + 1} \qquad \text{...(24.15)}$$

Eq. (24.15) is the same as the design equation (24.11).

From Eq. (24.13),

$$NR_2 = R_1 + R_2 + R_0$$

or $$(N - 1)R_2 = R_1 + R_0 \qquad \text{...(24.16)}$$

Substituting the value of R_1 from Eq. (24.15) into Eq. (24.16), we get,

$$(N - 1)R_2 = R_0 \frac{N - 1}{N + 2} + R_0 = R_0 \frac{2N}{N + 1}$$

Hence $$R_2 = R_0 \frac{2N}{N^2 - 1} \qquad \text{...(24.17)}$$

Eq. (24.17) is the same as the design equation (24.12).

Example 24.1. *Design a symmetrical T-attenuator to give attenuation of 40 dB and to work into a line of 600 Ω impedance.*

Solution. In symmetrical T-attenuator, the current ratio $N(= I_S/I_R)$ is given by,

$N (= IS/I_R)$ is given by

$$N = \text{antilog } D/20$$

Hence $$N = \text{antilog} \frac{40}{20} = 100$$

$$R_0 = 600\ \Omega.$$

Then each of the series arm resistors (Fig. 24.1) is given by,

$$R_1 = \frac{N-1}{N+1} R_0 = \frac{100-1}{100+1} \times 600 = 588.1\ \Omega$$

The shunt arm resistor R_2 is given by,

$$R_2 = R_0 \frac{2N}{N^2-1} = \frac{600 \times 2 \times 100}{(100)^2 - 1} = 12\ \Omega$$

Example 24.2. *Design a symmetrical T-attenuator to provide attenuation of 60 dB and to work into a load of 400 Ω impedance.*

Solution. For symmetrical T-attenuator, current ratio $N(= I_S/I_R)$ is given by

$$N = \text{antilog}\ \frac{D}{20} = \text{antilog}\ \frac{60}{20} = 1000$$

$$R_0 = 400\ \Omega$$

The each of the series arm resistors (Fig. 24.1) is given by,

$$R_1 = R_0 \frac{N-1}{N+1} = \frac{400\,(1000-1)}{(1000+1)} = 399\ \Omega$$

The shunt arm resistor R_2 is given by,

$$R_2 = R_0 \frac{2N}{N^2-1} = \frac{400 \times 2 \times 1000}{(1000)^2 - 1} = 0.8\ \Omega$$

Example 24.3. *Design a symmetrical T-attenuator to give 20 dB attenuation and to have characteristic impedance of 300 Ω.*

(Grade I.T.E., May 1964)

Solution. $D = 20$ dB

Hence for symmetrical T-attenuator, the current ratio

$N(= I_S/I_R)$ is given by,

$$N = \text{antilog}\ \frac{D}{20} = \text{antilog}\ \frac{20}{20} = 10$$

Then each of the series arm resistors (Fig. 24.1) is given by,

$$R_1 = \left(\frac{N-1}{N+1}\right) 300 = \frac{300\,(10-1)}{(10+1)} = 245.44$$

The shunt arm resistor R_2 is given by,

$$R_2 = \frac{2N}{N^2-1} \times R_0 = \frac{300 \times 2 \times 10}{(100-1)} = 60.6\ \Omega$$

Example 24.4. *An attenuator is composed of symmetrical T-section having series arm each of 200 Ω and shunt arm of 400 Ω. Derive expression for and calculate (a) the characteristic impedance of this net work and (b) attenuation per section.*

Solution. $R_1 = 200\ \Omega,\ R_2 = 300\ \Omega$

$$R_1 = R_0 \frac{N-1}{N+1} = 200 \qquad \text{...(1)}$$

$$R_2 = R_0 \frac{2N}{N^2 - 1} = 400 \quad ...(2)$$

Dividing Eq. (1) by Eq. (2), we get

$$\frac{(N-1)^2}{2N} = \frac{1}{2}$$

or $(2N^2 - 2N + 1) = 2N$

or $N^2 - 3N + 1 = 0$

Hence $N = 2.618$ or 0.382.

Value of N equal to 0.382 is inadmissible since it provides gain rather than attenuator.

Thus $N = 2.618$

Hence $D = 20 \log_{10} N = 20 \log_{10} {}^{2.618} = 8.36$ dB

But $R_1 = R_0 \dfrac{N-1}{N+1}$

or $200 = R_0 \dfrac{2.618 - 1}{2.618 + 1}$

Hence $R_0 = 447\ \Omega$.

Example 24.5. *An attenuator is composed of symmetrical T-section having series arm each of 100 Ω and shunt arm of 300 Ω. Derive expression for and calculate (a) the characteristic impedance of this network and (b) attenuation per section.*

Solution. $R_1 = 100\ \Omega,\ R_2 = 300\ \Omega$

$$R_1 = R_0 \frac{N-1}{N+1} = 100 \quad ...(1)$$

$$R_2 = R_0 \frac{2N}{N^2 - 1} = 300 \quad ...(2)$$

Dividing Eq. (1) by Eq. (2), we get,

$$\frac{(N-1)^2}{2N} = \frac{1}{3}$$

or $3N^2 - 8N + 3 = 0$

Hence $N = 2.215$ or 0.451.

Value $N = 0.451$ is inadmissible since it provides gain rather than attenuation.

Hence $N = 2.215$

$D = 20 \log N = 20 \log 2.215 = 6.908$ dB

But $R_1 = R_0 \dfrac{2.215 - 1}{2.215 + 1}$

or $100 = R_0 \dfrac{2.215 - 1}{2.215 + 1}$

Hence $R_1 = 264.6\ \Omega$.

24.4. Symmetrical π-attenuator

Fig. 24.2 shows symmetrical π-attenuator. It is driven by a voltage source V of internal resistance R and it feeds a resistor R_0 at the output port. R_0 is the characteristic resistance of the symmetrical π-attenuator using resistors only.

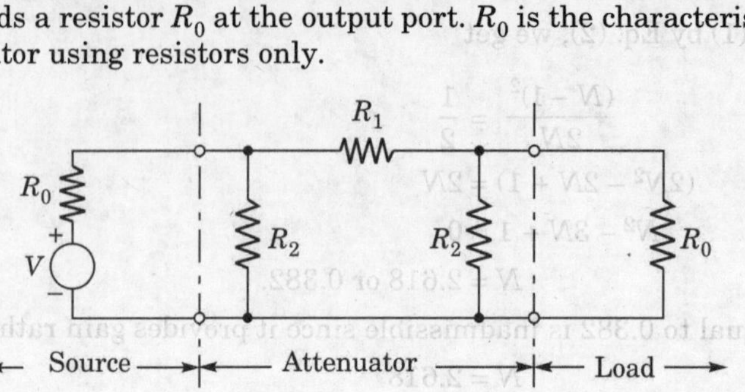

Fig. 24.2. Symmetrical π-attenuator.

The design of the attenuator consists in finding the value of R_1 and R_2 (Fig. 24.2), given the values of R_1 and propagation constant γ.

In this case also, since the attenuator is formed by resistors only, $Z_0 = R_0$ and $\gamma = a$.

Also $$e^{\gamma} = \frac{I_S}{I_R}$$

But $$\gamma = a$$

Hence $$e^{\alpha} = \frac{I_S}{I_R}$$

Hence from Eq. (24.4),

$$e^{\alpha} = \sqrt{\frac{P_1}{P_2}} = N \qquad ...(24.18)$$

Now the series and the shunt arm resistors of symmetrical π-network can be specified in terms of Z_0 (or R_0) and γ or α in the case by the following equations :

$$R_1 = R_0 \sinh \alpha \qquad ...(24.19)$$

$$R_1 = R_0 \coth \alpha/2 \qquad ...(24.20)$$

From Eq. (24.19), $$R_1 = R_0 \frac{e^{\alpha} - e^{-\alpha}}{2} = R_0 \frac{N - \frac{1}{N}}{2}$$

$$= R_0 \frac{N^2 - 1}{2N} \qquad ...(24.21)$$

From Eq. (24.20),

$$R_2 = R_0 \frac{\cosh \alpha/2}{\sinh \alpha/2} = R_0 \frac{e^{\alpha/2} + e^{-\alpha/2}}{e^{\alpha/2} - e^{-\alpha/2}} = R_0 \frac{e^{\alpha} + 1}{e^{\alpha} - 1}$$

$$= R_0 \frac{N-1}{N+1} \qquad ...(24.22)$$

Eqs. (24.21) and (24.22) constitute the design equations for the symmetrical π-attenuator of Fig. 24.2.

Example 24.6. *Design a symmetrical π-attenuator to provide attenuation of 40 dB and to work into a line of 600 Ω characteristic impedance.*

Solution. For the symmetrical π-attenuator, the current ratio $N(= I_S/I_R)$ is given by,

$$N = \text{antilog}\ \frac{D}{20} = \text{antilog}\ \frac{40}{20} = 100$$

$$R_0 = 600\ \Omega$$

Then series arm resistor R_1 (Fig. 24.2) is given by,

$$R_1 = R_0 \frac{N^2 - 1}{2N} = \frac{600\,(100^2 - 1)}{200} = 29{,}997\ \Omega$$

Each of the shunt arm resistor is given by,

$$R_2 = R_0 \frac{N+1}{N-1} = \frac{600\,(100+1)}{(100-1)} = 612\ \Omega.$$

Example 24.7. *Design a symmetrical π-attenuator to provide attenuation of 20 dB and design impedance of400 Ω.*

Solution. For the symmetrical π-attenuator, the current ratio $N(= I_S/I_R)$ is given by

$$N = \text{antilog}\ \frac{D}{20} = \text{antilog} = \frac{20}{20} = 100$$

$$R_0 = 400\ \Omega.$$

Then series arm resistor R_1 (Fig. 24.2) is given by,

$$R_1 = R_0 \frac{N^2 - 1}{2N} = \frac{400\,(100-1)}{20} = 1980\ \Omega$$

Each of the shunt arm resistors is given by,

$$R_2 = \frac{R_0(N+1)}{(N-1)} = \frac{400\,(10+1)}{(10-1)} = 489\ \Omega.$$

Example 24.8. *An attenuator is composed of symmetrical π-section having series arm of 200 Ω and shunt arm each of 400 Ω. Derive expression for and calculate (a) the characteristic impedance of this network and (b) attenuation per section.*

Solution. $R_1 = 200\ \Omega\ ;\ R_2 = 400\ \Omega$

$$R_2 = R_2 \frac{N^2 - 1}{2N} = 200 \qquad \text{...(1)}$$

$$R_2 = R_0 \frac{N+1}{N+1} = 400 \qquad \text{...(2)}$$

Dividing Eq. (1) by Eq. (2), we get

$$\frac{(N-1)^2}{2N} = \frac{1}{2}$$

or $$N^2 - 3N + 1 = 0$$

Hence $$N = 2.618 \text{ or } 0.382.$$

Value of $N = 0.382$ is inadmissible since it gives gain rather than attenuation.

Hence $$N = 2.618$$

$$D = 20 \log_{10} N = 20 \log_{10}{}^{2.618} = 8.36 \text{ dB}$$

$$R_2 = R_0 \frac{N+1}{N-1}$$

or $$400 = R_0 \frac{2.618+1}{2.618-1} = R_0 \frac{3.618}{1.618}$$

Hence $$R_0 = \frac{400 \times 1.618}{3.618} = 179\ \Omega.$$

Example 24.9. *An attenuator is composed of symmetrical π-section having series arm of 100 Ω and shunt arm each of 300 Ω. Derive expression for and calculate (a) the characteristic impedance of this network and (b) attenuation per section.*

Solution. $R_1 = 100\ \Omega$; $R_2 = 300\ \Omega$

$$R_1 = R_0 \frac{N^2-1}{2N} = 100 \qquad ...(1)$$

$$R_2 = R_0 \frac{N+1}{N-1} = 300 \qquad ...(2)$$

Dividing Eq. (1) by Eq. (2), we get

$$\frac{(N-1)^2}{2N} = \frac{1}{3} \quad \text{or} \quad 3N^2 - 8N + 3 = 0$$

Hence $N = 2.215$ or 0.451

Value of $N = 0.451$ is inadmissible since it provides gain rather than attenuation.

Hence, we take $N = 2.215$

Hence $D = 20 \log_{10}{}^{2.215} = 6.908$ dB

$$R_2 = R_0 \frac{N+1}{N-1}$$

or $$300 = R_0 \frac{2.215+1}{2.215-1} = R_0 \frac{3.215}{1.215}$$

Hence $$R_0 = \frac{300 \times 1.215}{3.215} = 113.4\ \Omega.$$

24.5. Symmetrical Bridged T-Attenuator

Fig. 24.3 gives this attenuator driven by a voltage source V of internal resistance R_0 and feeding a resistor R_0 at the output port. R_0 is the characteristic resistance of the attenuator.

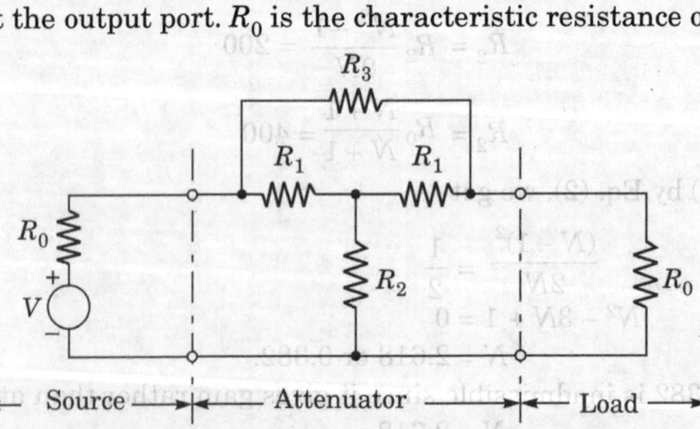

Fig. 24.3. Symmetrical bridged-T attenuator.

In this case also, since the attenuator is formed by resistors only, $Z_0 = R_0$ and $\gamma = \alpha$.

Hence $$e^{\gamma} = e^{\alpha} = \frac{I_S}{I_R}$$

Hence from Eq. (24.4), $$e^{\alpha} = \sqrt{\left(\frac{P_1}{P_2}\right)} = N.$$

The bridged-*T* network may be designed to have any characteristic resistance R_0 and desired attenuation by making,

$$R_3R_2 = R_1^2 = R_0^2 \quad \text{...(24.23)}$$

With $R_1 = R_0$, the propagation constant γ (= α in this case) can be expressed as,

$$\gamma = \log_e\left(1 + \frac{R_3}{R_0}\right) \quad \text{...(24.24)}$$

or

$$\gamma = \log_e\left(1 + \frac{R_0}{R_2}\right) \quad \text{...(24.25)}$$

Hence

$$e^{\gamma} = 1 + \frac{R_3}{R_0} \quad \text{...(24.26)}$$

$$= 1 + \frac{R_0}{R_2} \quad \text{...(24.27)}$$

Now for this resistive attenuator, $\gamma = \alpha$ so that $e^{\gamma} = e^{\alpha} = N$.

Hence

$$N = 1 + \frac{R_3}{R_0} \quad \text{...(24.28)}$$

$$= 1 + \frac{R_0}{R_2} \quad \text{...(24.29)}$$

Hence

$$R_3 = R_0(N-1) \quad \text{...(24.30)}$$

$$R_2 = \frac{R_0}{(N-1)} \quad \text{...(24.31)}$$

$$R_1 = R_0 \quad \text{...(24.32)}$$

Eqs. (24.30), (24.31) and (24.32) form the design equations for the symmetrical Bridged *T*-attenuator.

It may be noted that :

(*i*) in symmetrical bridged *T*-attenuator, in order to vary the attenuation *N*, without altering R_0, only two resistors namely R_2 and R_3 have to be varied.

(*ii*) in symmetrical *T*-attenuator or in symmetrical π-attenuator, in order to vary the attenuator *N*, without altering R_0, three resistors have to be varied.

Thus it is economical and convenient to use bridged *T*-attenuator wherever variable attenuation is required.

Example 24.10. *Design a symmetrical bridged T-attenuator with attenuation of 20 dB and design impedance of 600 Ω.*

Solution. $D = 20$ dB ; $R_0 = 600\ \Omega$.

Current ratio $N(= I_S/I_R)$ is given by,

N = antilog $D/20$ = antilog 20/20 = 10

Then the elements of bridged *T*-attenuator (Fig. 24.3) are calculated using design equations as given below :

$$R_3 = R_0(N-1) = 600\ (10-1) = 5400\ \Omega$$

$$R_2 = R_0/(N-1) = \frac{600}{10-1} = 66.68\ \Omega$$

$$R_1 = R_0 = 600\ \Omega.$$

Example 24.11. *Design a symmetrical bridged T-attenuator with design impedance of 300 Ω and attenuation of (a) 20 dB (b) 40 dB (c) 60 dB.*

Solution. (*a*) $D = 20$ dB ; $R_0 = 300\ \Omega$

Current ratio $N = \text{antilog } D/20 = \text{antilog } 20/20 = 10.$

Then the elements of bridged *T*-attenuator (Fig. 24.3) are calculated using the design equations as given below :

$$R_3 = R_0(N-1) = 300(10-1) = 2700\ \Omega$$

$$R_2 = R_0/(N-1) = 300/(10-1) = 33.33\ \Omega$$

$$R_1 = R_0 = 300\ \Omega$$

(*a*) $D = 400$ dB; $R_0 = 300\ \Omega$

$$N = \text{antilog } 40/20 = 100$$

$$R_3 = R_0(N-1) = 300\ (100-1) = 29{,}700\ \Omega$$

$$R_2 = R_0/(N-1) = 300/(100-1) = 3.03\ \Omega$$

$$R_1 = R_0 = 300\ \Omega$$

(*b*) $D = 60$ dB, $R_0 = 300\ \Omega$

$$N = \text{antilog } 60/20 = 1000$$

$$R_3 = R_0(N-1) = 300\ (1000-1) = 299{,}700\ \Omega$$

$$R_2 = R_0/(N-1) = 300/(1000-1) = 0.3\ \Omega$$

$$R_1 = R_0 = 200\ \Omega.$$

24.6. Symmetrical Lattice Attenuator

Fig. 24.4 gives this attenuator with characteristic resistance R_0. This attenuator, being a symmetrical network, is placed between load resistances R_0 and is driven by source V of internal resistance R_0.

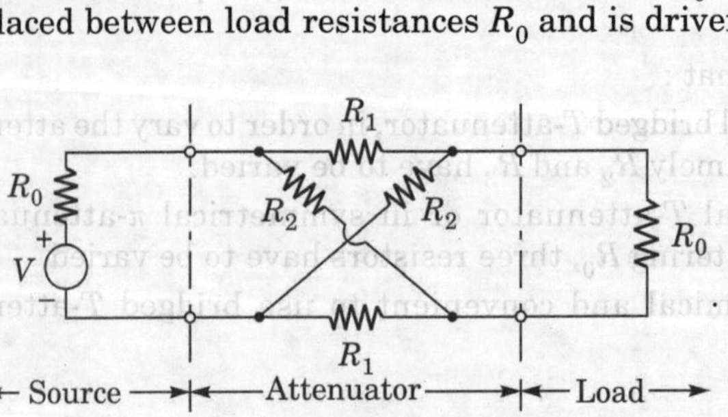

Fig. 24.4. Symmetrical lattice attenuator.

Since the attenuator is formed by resistors, $Z_0 = R_0$ and $\gamma = \alpha$.

Hence $$e^{\gamma} = e^{\alpha} = \frac{I_S}{I_R}$$

Hence from Eq. (24.4),

$$e^{\alpha} = \sqrt{\frac{P_1}{P_2}} = N.$$

The series and the diagonal arm resistors of this lattice attenuator may be specified in terms of R_0 and γ (= α in this case).

Thus $$R_1 = R_0 \tanh \alpha/2 \quad ...(24.33)$$

$$R_2 = R_0 \coth \alpha/2 \quad ...(24.34)$$

Eq. (24.33) yields, $$R_1 = R_0 \frac{e^{\alpha/2} - e^{-\alpha/2}}{e^{\alpha/2} + e^{-\alpha/2}} = R_0 \frac{e^{\alpha} - 1}{e^{\alpha} + 1}$$

or $$R_1 = R_0 \frac{N-1}{N+1} \quad ...(24.35)$$

Similarly Eq. (24.34) yields, $$R_2 = \frac{R_0}{\tanh \alpha/2} = R_0 \frac{N+1}{N-1} \quad ...(24.36)$$

Eqs. (24.35) and (24.36) form the design equations for the symmetrical lattice attenuator.

Example 24.12. *Design a symmetrical lattice attenuator to have characteristic impedance of 600 Ω and attenuation of 20 dB.*

Solution. $R_0 = 600\ \Omega$; $D = 200$ dB

Then $N (= I_S/I_R)$ is given by

Then $$N = \text{antilog } \frac{D}{20} = \text{antilog } \frac{20}{20} = 10.$$

Series arm resistors R_1 and diagonal arm resistors R_2 are then calculated from the design equations as below :

$$R_1 = R_0 \frac{N-1}{N+1} = 600 \times \frac{10-1}{10+1} = 490.9\ \Omega$$

$$R_2 = R_0 \frac{N+1}{N-1} = 600 \times \frac{10+1}{10-1} = 733.3\ \Omega.$$

Example 24.13. *Design a symmetrical lattice attenuator to have characteristic impedance of 300 Ω and attenuation of (a) 20 dB (b) 40 dB.*

Solution. (*a*) $R_0 = 300\ \Omega$; $D = 20$ dB

Current ratio $N (= I_S/I_R)$ is given by,

$$N = \text{antilog } D/20 = \text{antilog } 20/20 = 10$$

The series arm resistors R_1 (Fig. 24.4) and diagonal are resistors, are then calculated from the design equations as below :

$$R_1 = R_0 \frac{N-1}{N+1} = \frac{300\,(10-1)}{(10+1)} = 245.45\ \Omega$$

$$R_2 = R_0 \frac{N+1}{N-1} = \frac{300\,(10+1)}{(10-1)} = 366.6\ \Omega$$

(*b*) $$R_0 = 300\ \Omega\ ;\ D = 40 \text{ dB}$$

$$N = \text{antilog } 40/20 = 100$$

$$R_1 = R_0 \frac{N-1}{N+1} = \frac{300\,(100-1)}{(100+1)} = 249\ \Omega$$

$$R_2 = R_0 \frac{N+1}{N-1} = \frac{300\,(100+1)}{(100-1)} = 306.6\ \Omega.$$

24.7. Asymmetrical Attenuators

Asymmetrical attenuators are used when the attenuator is required to work between two unequal impedances. The asymmetrical attenuator is then so designed that these two unequal impedances form image impedances.

The values of the constituent elements may then be calculated knowing the values of the image impedances and the loss in the attenuator. Let N_α be the attenuation.

Then
$$N_\alpha = \sqrt{\frac{P_1}{P_2}} = \sqrt{\frac{I_S^2}{I_R^2} \cdot \frac{R_{i_1}}{R_{i_2}}} = \frac{I_S}{I_R}\sqrt{\frac{R_{i_1}}{R_{i_2}}} \quad \text{...(24.37)}$$

where R_{i_1} and R_{i_2} are the image impedances of the symmetrical attenuator.

The asymmetrical attenuator may be of 3 main types :

(*a*) Asymmetrical *T*-attenuator.

(*b*) Asymmetrical *L*-attenuator.

(*c*) Asymmetrical π-attenuator.

24.8. Asymmetrical T-attenuator

This attenuator is very widely used in communication circuits. Fig. 24.5 gives the attenuator terminated in its image resistances R_{i_1} and R_{i_2}.

The image transfer constant θ_i of this attenuation is given by,

$$e^{\theta_i} = \sqrt{\frac{V_S \cdot I_R}{V_R \cdot I_R}} \quad \text{...(24.38)}$$

$$\theta_i = A_i + jB_i \quad \text{...(24.39)}$$

where A_i is the attenuation and B_i is the phase angle.

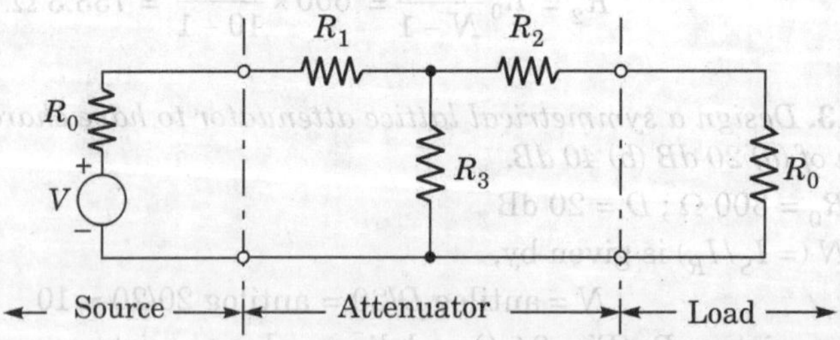

Fig. 24.5. Asymmetrical *T*-attenuator.

Now since attenuator is formed of resistors only, V_S and V_R are in phase with I_S and I_R. Hence $B_i = 0$ and $\theta_i = A_i$ Nepers.

The elements of an asymmetrical *T*-network are given by the following equations :

$$R_1 = \frac{R_{i_1}}{\tanh\theta_i} - \frac{\sqrt{R_{i_1} \cdot R_{i_2}}}{\sinh\theta_i} \quad \text{...(24.40)}$$

$$R_2 = \frac{R_{i_2}}{\tanh\theta_i} - \frac{\sqrt{R_{i_1} \cdot R_{i_2}}}{\sinh\theta_i} \quad \text{...(24.41)}$$

$$R_3 = \frac{\sqrt{R_{i_1} \cdot R_{i_2}}}{\sinh \theta_i} \qquad ...(24.42)$$

In the above equations, $\theta_i = A_i$ Nepers.

Eqs. (24.40) to (24.42) form the design equations for the asymmetrical *T*-attenuator and permit calculations of elements R_1, R_2 and R_3 for desired values of image resistances R_{i_1} and R_{i_2} and for desired value of loss A_t Nepers.

Example 24.14. *Design an asymmetrical T-attenuator with 40 dB loss to work between a source impedance of 100 Ω and load impedance of 600 Ω.*

Solution. $R_{i_1} = 100\ \Omega$; $R_{i_2} = 600\ \Omega$; $D = 40$ dB.

Converting decibel to neper,

$$A_i = 40 \times 0.115 = 4.6 \text{ Nepers.}$$

Then the elements of asymmetrical *T*-attenuator are

$$R_3 = \frac{\sqrt{R_{i_1} \cdot R_{i_2}}}{\sinh A_i} = \frac{\sqrt{100 \times 600}}{\sinh 4.6} = \frac{\sqrt{100 \times 600}}{49.74} = 4.923$$

$$R_2 = \frac{R_{i_2}}{\tanh A_i} - R_3 = \frac{600}{\tanh 4.6} - 4.923 = \frac{600}{0.9998} - 4.923$$

$$= 600.2 - 4.923 = 5923.28\ \Omega.$$

$$R_1 = \frac{R_{i_1}}{\tanh A_i} - R_3 = \frac{100}{0.9998} - 4.92 = 95.1\ \Omega.$$

Example 14.15. *Design an asymmetrical T-attenuator to produce attenuation of 20 dB and to work between source impedance of 200 Ω and load impedance of 800 Ω.*

Solution. $R_{i_1} = 200\ \Omega$; $R_{i_2} = 800\ \Omega$; $D = 20$ dB

Converting decibles to nepers,

$$A_i = 20 \times 0.115 = 2.3 \text{ nepers.}$$

Then elements of asymmetrical *T*-attenuator (Fig. 24.5) are :

$$R_3 = \frac{\sqrt{R_{i_1} \cdot R_{i_2}}}{\sinh A_i} = \frac{\sqrt{200 \times 800}}{\sinh 2.3} = \frac{400}{4.937} = 81.02\ \Omega$$

$$R_2 = \frac{R_{i_2}}{\tanh A_i} - R_{i_3} = \frac{800}{0.98} - 81.02\ \Omega$$

$$= 816.32 - 81.02\ \Omega = 735.30\ \Omega$$

$$R_1 = \frac{R_{i_1}}{\tanh A_i} - R_3 = \frac{200}{0.98} - 81.02$$

$$= 204.08 - 81.02 = 123.06\ \Omega.$$

24.9. Asymmetrical L-Attenuator

This is the simplest type of attenuator using only two resistors. Further since it offers low attenuation, it may be used as impedance matching circuit between two unequal impedances equal to the image impedances of the attenuators. Fig. 24.6 gives this attenuator terminated in its image resistances R_{i_1} and R_{i_2}.

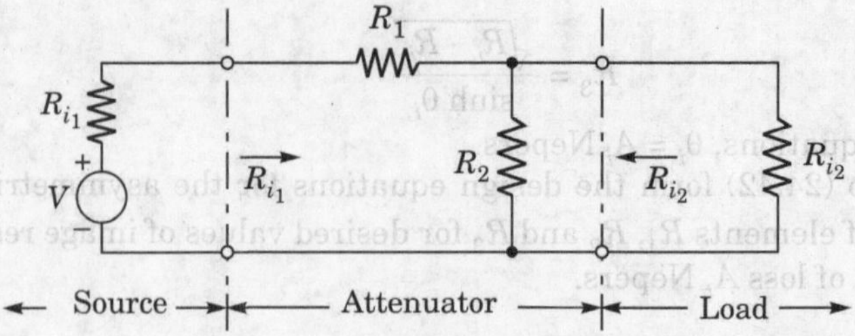

Fig. 24.6. Asymmetrical *L*-attenuator.

From Fig. (24.6), we get

$$R_{i_1} = R_1 + \frac{R_{i_2} \cdot R_2}{R_{i_2} + R_2} \quad \text{...(23.43)}$$

and

$$R_{i_2} = \frac{R_2(R_1 + R_{i_1})}{R_2 + R_1 + R_{i_1}} \quad \text{...(24.44)}$$

Eqs. (24.43) and (24.44) may be written as,

$$R_{i_1} \cdot R_2 + R_{i_1} \cdot R_{i_2} = R_1 R_2 + R_{i_2} \cdot R_1 + R_{i_2} \cdot R_2 \quad \text{...(24.45)}$$

and

$$R_{i_2} \cdot R_2 + R_{i_2} \cdot R_1 + R_{i_1} \cdot R_{i_2} = R_1 \cdot R_2 + R_{i_1} \cdot R_2 \quad \text{...(24.46)}$$

Adding Eqs. (24.45) and (24.46), we get

$$2R_{i_1} \cdot R_{i_2} = 2R_1 R_2$$

Hence

$$R_1 = \frac{R_{i_1} \cdot R_{i_2}}{R_2} \quad \text{...(24.47)}$$

Substituting the value of R_1 as given by Eq. (24.47) into Eq. (24.45) and rearranging, we get

$$R_2 = \frac{\sqrt{R_{i_1} \cdot R_{i_2}{}^2}}{(R_{i_1} - R_{i_2})} \quad \text{...(24.48)}$$

Substituting the value of R_2 as given by Eq. (24.48) into Eq. (24.45), we get

$$R_1 = \frac{R_{i_1} \cdot R_{i_2} \sqrt{R_{i_1} \cdot R_{i_2}}}{\sqrt{(R_{i_1} \cdot R_{i_2}{}^2)}}$$

or

$$R_1 = \sqrt{R_{i_1}(R_{i_1} - R_{i_2})} \quad \text{...(24.49)}$$

Eqs. (24.48) and (24.49) form the design equations for the symmetrical *L*-attenuator for given values of image resistances R_{i_1} and R_{i_2}. It is, of course, necessary that the resistor R_1 be placed on the side facing the higher of the two impedances (forming the image resistances).

Example 24.16. *Design an asymmetrical L-attenuator to work with image impedances of 600 Ω and 400 Ω.*

Solution.

$$R_1 = \sqrt{R_{i_1}(R_{i_1} - R_{i_2})} = \sqrt{600\,(600 - 400)} = 346.4\ \Omega$$

$$R_2 = \sqrt{\frac{R_{i_1} \cdot R_{i_2}{}^2}{(R_{i_1} - R_{i_2})}} = \sqrt{\frac{600 \times 400 \times 400}{(600 - 400)}} = 400\sqrt{\frac{600}{200}} = 692.8.$$

24.10. Asymmetrical L-attenuator working between two equal impedances with a given loss

Fig. 24.7 gives the circuit.

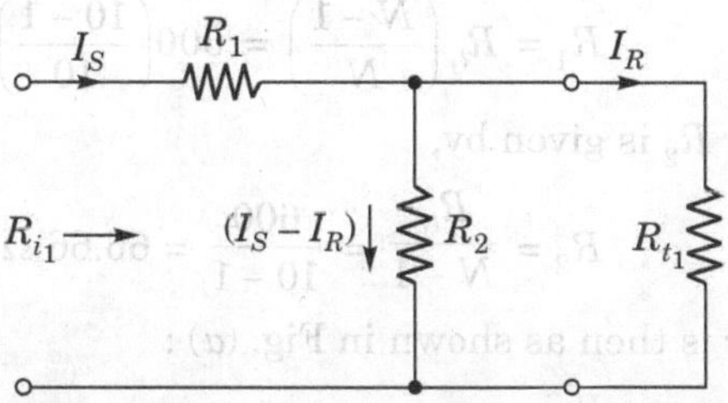

Fig. 24.7. Alternative form of asymmetrical L-attenuator.

Application of kVL to the closed mesh yields,

$$R_3(I_S - I_R) = I_R \cdot R_{t_1} \quad ...(24.50)$$

where R_{t_1} is the iterative impedance of the L-network. Eq. (24.50) yields,

$$R_2 I_5 = I_R (R_{t_1} + R_2)$$

Hence $$N = \frac{I_S}{I_R} = \frac{R_{t_1} + R_2}{R_2} \quad ...(23.51)$$

From Eq. (24.51) on solving for R_2, we get

$$R_2 = \frac{R_{t_1}}{N-1} \quad ...(24.52)$$

But iterative impedance of the asymmetrical L-network of Fig. 24.7 is given by,

$$R_{t_1} = \frac{R_1}{2} + \sqrt{\frac{R_1^2}{4} + R_1 R_2} \quad ...(24.53)$$

Hence $$\left(R_{t_1} - \frac{R_1}{2}\right) = \sqrt{\frac{R_1^2}{4} + R_1 R_2} \quad ...(24.54)$$

On substituting the value of R_2 from Eq. (24.52) into Eq. (24.54), we get

$$\left(R_{t_1} - \frac{R_1}{2}\right)^2 = \frac{R_1^2}{4} + R_1 \frac{R_{t_1}}{N-1} \quad ...(24.55)$$

On rearranging, Eq. (24.55) yields,

$$R_{t_1} = R_1 \frac{N}{N-1} \quad ...(24.56)$$

Hence $$R_1 = R_{t_1}\left(\frac{N-1}{N}\right) \quad ...(24.57)$$

Eqs. (24.52) and (24.57) form the design equations of the L-type asymmetrical attenuator when the attenuation and the equal resistances between which it has to work, have been specified.

Example 24.17. *Design an asymmetrical L-attenuator to operate into a resistance of 600 Ω and provide attenuation of 20 dB.*

Solution. $$R_{t_1} = 600\ \Omega$$

$$N = \text{antilog } \frac{D}{2} = \text{antilog } \frac{20}{2} = 10$$

The series arm resistor R_1 is given by,

$$R_1 = R_{t_1}\left(\frac{N-1}{N}\right) = 600\left(\frac{10-1}{10}\right) = 540\ \Omega$$

The shunt arm resistor R_2 is given by,

$$R_2 = \frac{R_{t_1}}{N-1} = \frac{600}{10-1} = 66.66\ \Omega$$

The desired attenuator is then as shown in Fig. (*a*) :

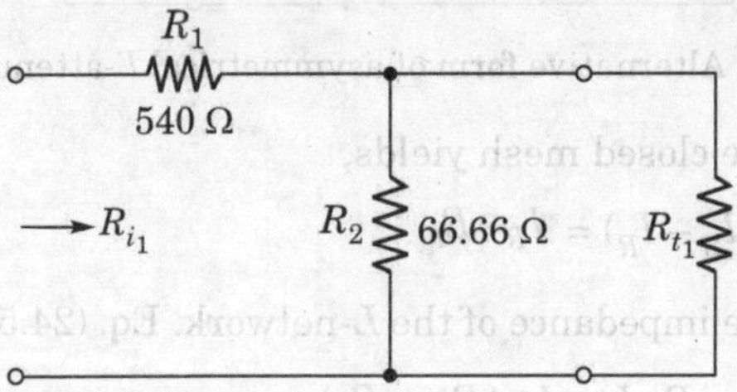

Fig. (*a*)

Example 24.18. *Design an asymmetrical L-attenuator to operate into a resistance of 400 Ω and provide attenuation of (a) 15 dB and (b) 20 dB.*

Solution $R_{t_1} = 400\ \Omega$

(*a*) $N = \text{antilog } D/20 = \text{antilog } 15/20 = 5.623$

$$R_1 = R_{t_1} \cdot \frac{N-1}{N} = \frac{400(4.623)}{5.623} = 328.8\ \Omega$$

$$R_2 = R_{t_1}(N-1) = \frac{400}{4.623} = 86.52\ \Omega$$

(*b*) $N = \text{antilog } 40/20 = 100$

$$R_1 = R_{t_1} \frac{N-1}{N} = \frac{400 \times 99}{100} = 396\ \Omega$$

$$R_2 = \frac{R_{t_1}}{(N-1)} = \frac{400}{99} = 4.04\ \Omega$$

24.11. Asymmetrical π-Attenuator

Fig. 24.8 gives the circuit of asymmetrical π-attenuator terminated in its image impedances R_{i_1} and R_{i_2}. The admittances, Y_1, Y_2 and Y_3 are given by

$$Y_3 = \frac{\sqrt{Y_s \cdot Y_l}}{\sinh \theta_i} \quad \text{...(24.58)}$$

$$Y_1 = \frac{Y_s}{\tanh \theta_i} - Y_3 \quad \text{...(24.59)}$$

$$Y_2 = \frac{Y_l}{\tanh \theta_i} - Y_3 \quad \text{...(24.60)}$$

and Y_s where Y_i are the admittance of the source and the load respectively and θ_i is the image transfer constant.

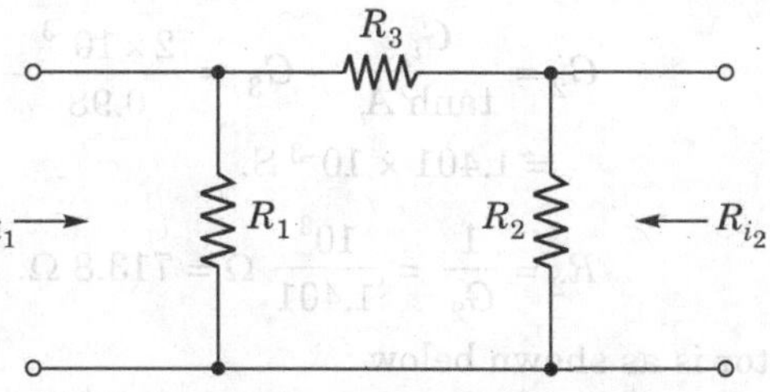

Fig. 24.8. Asymmetrical π-attenuator.

For attenuator of Fig. 24.8 using pure resistances. $Y_1 = G_1$, $Y_2 = G_2$, $Y_3 = G_3$, $Y_s = G_{i_1}$, $Y_l = G_{i_2}$ and $\theta_i = A_i$ in nepers. Then Eqs. (24.58) to (24.60) may be put as

$$G_3 = \frac{\sqrt{G_{i_2} \cdot G_{i_1}}}{\sinh A_i} \quad \text{...(24.61)}$$

$$G_1 = \frac{G_{i_1}}{\tanh A_i} - G_3 \quad \text{...(24.62)}$$

$$G_2 = \frac{G_{i_2}}{\tanh A_i} - G_3 \quad \text{...(214.63)}$$

Conductances G_1, G_2 and G_3 are reciprocal of resistance R_1, R_2 and R_3 respectively. Eqs. (24.61) to (24.63) may be used to calculate the resistances R_1, R_2 and R_3 if the image impedances R_{i_1} and R_{i_2} and the loss D are given. Thus Eqs. (24.61) to (24.63) form the design equations for this network.

Example 24.19. *Design an unbalanced asymmetrical π-attenuator with loss of 20 dB to operate between 200 Ω line and 500 Ω line* (*Grad I.T.E. May 1963*)

Solution. It is given that

$$R_{i_1} = 200\ \Omega,\ R_{i_2} = 500\ \Omega \text{ and } D = 20 \text{ dB}$$

Hence
$$G_{i_1} = \frac{1}{200}\ \text{S} = 50\ \text{mS}$$

$$G_{i_2} = \frac{1}{500}\ \text{S} = 2\ \text{mS}$$

On converting decibles into nepers,

$$A_i = 20 \times 0.115 = 2.3 \text{ nepers}$$

Hence
$$G_3 = \frac{\sqrt{G_{i_1} G_{i_2}}}{\sinh A_i} = \frac{\sqrt{5 \times 10^{-3} \times 2 \times 10^{-3}}}{\sinh 2.3} = \frac{\sqrt{10} \times 10^{-3}}{4.94}\ \Omega$$

Hence
$$R_3 = \frac{1}{G_3} = \frac{4.94}{\sqrt{10} \times 10^{-3}} \text{ mho} = 1563\ \Omega$$

$$G_1 = \frac{G_{i_1}}{\tanh A_i} - G_3 = \frac{5 \times 10^{-3}}{0.98} - \frac{1}{1563} = 10^{-3}\ [5.102 - 0.640]$$

$$= 4.462 \times 10^{-3} \text{ S.}$$

Hence $$R_1 = \frac{1}{G_1} = \frac{10^3}{4.462}\ \Omega = 2241.\ \Omega$$

$$G_2 = \frac{G_{i_2}}{\tanh A_i} - G_3 = \frac{2 \times 10^{-3}}{0.98} - \frac{1}{1563} = 10^{-3}\ [2.041 - 0.640]$$

$$= 1.401 \times 10^{-3}\ \text{S}.$$

Hence $$R_2 = \frac{1}{G_2} = \frac{10^3}{1.401}\ \Omega = 713.8\ \Omega.$$

The desired attenuator is as shown below :

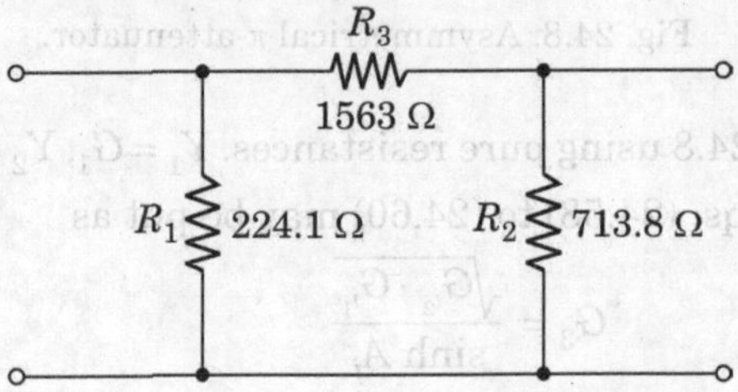

Example 24.20. *Design an unbalanced asymmetrical π-attenuator with loss of 40 dB to operate between 200 Ω line and 800 Ω line.*

Solution. $R_{i_1} = 200\ \Omega$; $R_{i_2} = 800\ \Omega$; $D = 40$ dB.

Hence $$G_{i_1} = \frac{1}{200}\ \text{S} = 5\ \text{mS}$$

$$G_{i_2} = \frac{1}{800}\ \text{S} = 1.25\ \text{mS}$$

On converting decibels into nepers

$$A_i = 40 \times 0.115 = 4.6\ \text{Nepers}$$

Hence $$G_3 = \frac{\sqrt{G_{i_1} \times G_{i_2}}}{\sinh A_i} = \frac{\sqrt{5 \times 10^{-3} \times 1.25 \times 10^{-3}}}{\sinh 4.6}$$

$$= \frac{2.5 \times 10^{-3}}{49.74}\ \text{S} = 0.05\ \text{mS}$$

$$R_3 = \frac{1}{G_3} = 20\ \text{k}\Omega$$

$$G_1 = \frac{G_{i_1}}{\tanh a_i} - G_S = \frac{5 \times 10^{-3}}{0.9998} - 0.05 \times 10^{-3}\ \text{S} = 4.951 \times 10^{-3}\ \text{S}$$

$$R_1 = \frac{1}{G_1} = \frac{10^3}{4.951}\ \Omega = 202\ \Omega$$

$$G_2 = \frac{G_{i_2}}{\tanh A_i} - G_3 = \frac{1.25 \times 10^{-3}}{0.9998} - 0.05 \times 10^{-3} = 1.2002 \times 10^{-3}\ \text{S}$$

Hence $$R_2 = \frac{1}{G_2} = \frac{10^3}{1.2002}\ \Omega = 833.2\ \Omega$$

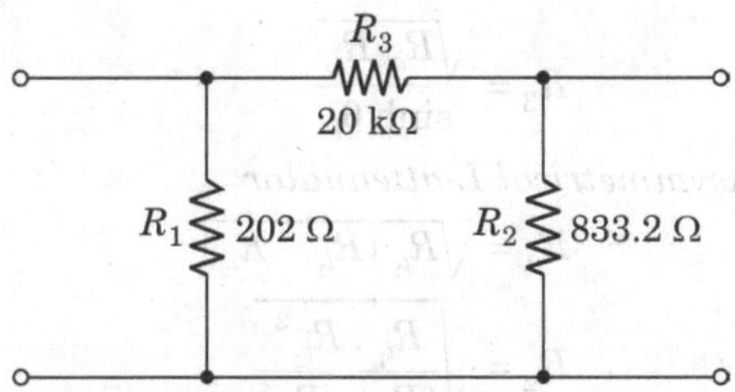

SUMMARY

Symmetrical Attenuator is placed between two equal impedances of value equal to the characteristic impedance of the attenuation.

Asymmetrical Attenuator is placed between two unequal impedances of values equal to the image impedances of the attenuator. It may thus be used for matching two unequal impedances.

Attenuation in dB equals

$$10 \log_1 \frac{p_1}{p_2} = 10 \log_{10} \left(\frac{I_S}{I_R}\right)^2 = 20 \log_{10} \frac{I_S}{I_R}$$

Types of symmetrical Attenuators

(*i*) Symmetrical *T*-attenuator
(*ii*) Symmetrical π-attenuator
(*iii*) Symmetrical Bridged *T*-attenuator
(*iv*) Symmetrical Lattice attenuator

Design Equations for Symmetrical T-attenuator

$$R_1 = R_0 \frac{N-1}{N+1}\,;\; R_2 = R_0 \frac{2N}{N^2-1}$$

Design Equations for Symmetrical π-attenuator

$$R_1 = R_0 \frac{N^2-1}{2N}\,;\; R_2 = R_0 \frac{N+1}{N-1}$$

Design Equations for symmetrical Bridged T-attenuator

$$R_3 = R_0(N-1)\,;\; R_2 = \frac{R_0}{N-1}\,;\; R_1 = R_0$$

Design Equations for Symmetrical Lattice Attenuator

$$R_1 = R_0 \frac{N-1}{N+1}\,;\; R_2 = R_0 \frac{N+1}{N-1}$$

Types of Asymmetrical Attenuators

(*i*) Asymmetrical *T*-attenuator
(*ii*) Asymmetrical *L*-attenuator
(*iii*) Asymmetrical π-attenuator

Design Equations of Asymmetrical T-attenuator

$$R_1 = \frac{R_{i_1}}{\tanh \theta_i} - \frac{\sqrt{R_{i_1} R_{i_2}}}{\sinh \theta_i}$$

$$R_2 = \frac{R_{i_2}}{\tanh \theta_i} - \frac{\sqrt{R_{i_1} R_{i_2}}}{\sinh \theta_i}$$

$$R_3 = \frac{\sqrt{R_{i_1} R_{i_2}}}{\sinh \theta_i}$$

Design Equations for Asymmetrical L-attenuator

Series arm resistor $R_1 = \sqrt{R_{i_1} (R_{i_1} - R_{i_2})}$

Shunt arm resistor $R_2 = \sqrt{\frac{R_{i_1} . R_{i_2}{}^2}{(R_{i_1} - R_{i_2})}}$

Design Equations for Asymmetrical L-attenuator working between two equal impedances

Shunt arm resistor $R_2 = \frac{R_{t_1}}{N-1}$

Series arm resistor $R_1 = R_{t_1}\left(\frac{N-1}{N}\right)$

Design Equations for Asymmetrical π-attenuator

Series arm resistor $G_3 = \frac{\sqrt{G_{i_1} G_{i_2}}}{\sinh A_i}$

Shut arm resistors $G_1 = \frac{G_{i_1} G_{i_2}}{\sinh A_i}$

$$G_2 = \frac{G_{i_2}}{\tanh A_i} - G_3 .$$

REVIEW QUESTIONS

24.1. Draw the circuit of symmetrical T-attenuator. Derive the design equations giving the series and shunt arm resistors in terms of (*i*) the characteristic impedance R_0 and (*ii*) the current ratio $N(= I_S/I_R)$.

24.2. Draw circuit of symmetrical π-attenuator. Derive the design equations giving the series and shunt arm resistors in terms of (*i*) the characteristic impedance R_0 and (*ii*) the current ratio $N(= I_S/I_R)$.

24.3. Draw the circuits of symmetrical lattice attenuator. Derive the design equations for the circuit resistances in terms of (*i*) the characteristic impedance R_0 and (*ii*) the current ratio N.

24.4. Draw the circuit of asymmetrical T-attenuator. Write the design equations for the circuit resistances in terms of (*i*) the images resistances and (*ii*) the image transfer constant θ.

24.5. Draw the circuit of asymmetrical L-attenuator. Derive the design equations for the circuit elements in terms of the image resistances R_{i_1} and R_{i_1}.

24.6. Draw the circuit of asymmetrical L-attenuator working between two equal impedances with a given loss. Derive the design equations for the circuit elements in terms of (*i*) the iterative resistance R_{i_1} and (*ii*) the current ratio N.

24.7. Draw the circuit of asymmetrical π-attenuator. Write design equations for the current elements in terms of (*i*) image conductances G_{i_1} and G_{i_2} and (*ii*) image transfer constant θ_i.

NUMERICAL QUESTIONS

24.1. Design symmetrical T-attenuator for attenuation of 20 dB and to work in a line of 600 ohms impedance.
(AM.I.E., May, 1966)
[Ans. R_1 = 490.9 Ω ; R_2 = 121.2 Ω**]**

24.2. Design symmetrical T-attenuator to give 20 dB attenuation and to have characteristic impedance of 75 ohms.
(Grade I.T.E. May, 1964)
[Ans. R_1 = 61.35 Ω ; R_2 = 15.15 Ω**]**

24.3. An attenuator is composed is symmetrical T-section having series arm each of 175 ohms and shunt arm of 350 ohms. Derive expression for and calculate the characteristic impedance of this network and attenuation per section. *(A.M.I.E., May 1972)*

[**Ans.** R_0 = 391.3 Ω ; 8.36 dB]

24.4. An attenuator is composed of symmetrical T-section having series arm each of 200 Ω and shunt arm of 300 Ω. Derive expression for and calculate the characteristic impedance of this network and attenuation per section. [**Ans.** R_0 = 400 Ω ; 9.542 dB]

24.5. Design symmetrical-π attenuator to provide attenuator of 20 dB and to work into a line of 600 Ω characteristic impedance. [**Ans.** R_1 = 2970 Ω ; R_2 = 733 Ω]

24.6. Design symmetrical-π attenuator to provide attenuation of 60 dB and to work into a line of 600 Ω characteristic impedance. [**Ans.** R_1 = 300 kΩ ; R_2 = 601 Ω]

24.7. An attenuator is composed of symmetrical-π section having series arm of 175 Ω and shunt arm each of 350 Ω. Derive expression for and calculate
(*i*) the characteristic impedance of the network and
(*ii*) attenuation per section. [**Ans.** R_0 = 156 Ω ; 8.36 dB]

24.8. An attenuator is composed of symmetrical-π section having series arm of 200 Ω and shunt arm each of 300 Ω. Derive expression for and calculate
(*i*) the characteristic impedance of the network and
(*ii*) attenuation per section. [**Ans.** R_0 = 150 Ω ; 9.542 dB]

24.9. Design symmetrical bridged-T attenuator with attenuation of 40 dB and design impedance of 600 Ω. *(Grade I.T.E.I. May, 1970)*

[**Ans.** R_1 = 600 Ω ; R_2 = 6.06 Ω ; R_2 = 59.4 kΩ]

24.10. Design symmetrical bridged-T attenuator with design impedance of 400 Ω and attenuation of (*a*) 23 dB and (*b*) 40 dB. [**Ans.** (*a*) R_1 = 400 Ω ; R_2 = 44.4 Ω ; R_3 = 3600 Ω
(*b*) R_1 = 400 Ω ; R_2 = 4.04 Ω ; R_3 = 39600 Ω]

24.11. Design a symmetrical lattice attenuator to have attenuation of 20 dB and characteristic impedance of 500 ohms. What will be its equivalent T-structure ? *(A.M.I.E. Nov., 1964)*

[**Ans.** R_1 = 409.09 Ω, R_2 = 611.11 Ω. Equivalent T-section has R_1 = 409.9 Ω and R_2 = 101.01 Ω]

24.12. Design a symmetrical lattice attenuator to have characteristic impedance of 400 Ω and attenuation of (*a*) 20 dB and (*b*) 30 dB. [**Ans.** (*a*) R_1 = 327 Ω ; R_2 = 489 Ω
(*b*) R_1 = 375 Ω ; R_2 = 426 Ω]

24.13. Design a T-type attenuator pad to have attenuator of 40 dB and to work between source impedance of 70 ohms and load impedance of 600 ohms. *(AM.I.E. May, 1972)*

[**Ans.** R_1 = 64.89 Ω, R_2 = 596.08 Ω ; R_0 = 4.12 Ω]

24.14. Design an a symmetrical T-attenuator to produce attenuation of 20 dB and to work between source impedance of 400 Ω and load impedance of 900 Ω.[**Ans.** R_2 = 286.63 Ω ; R_1 = 796.83 Ω ; R_3 = 121.53 Ω]

24.15. Design an asymmetrical L-attenuator to work into image impedances of 400 Ω and 300 Ω.

[**Ans.** Series arm resistor R_1 = 200 Ω, S hunt arm resistor R_2 = 600 Ω]

24.16. Design an L-attenuator to operate into a resistance of 500 Ω and to provide attenuation of 15 dB. *(A.M.I.E. May, 1976)*

[**Ans.** R_1 = 411 Ω ; R_3 = 108 Ω]

24.17. Design an asymmetrical L-attenuator to operate into a resistance of 300 Ω and to provide attenuation of (*a*) 20 dB (*b*) 30 dB. [**Ans.** (*a*) R_1 = 270 Ω ; R_2 = 33.3 Ω,
(*b*) R_1 = 290.5 Ω ; R_2 = 9.8 Ω]

24.18. Design an asymmetrical π-attenuator with loss of 20 dB to operate between 200 Ω line and 800 Ω line.

[**Ans.** Series arm resistor R_3 = 1976 Ω,
Shunt arm resistors R_1 = 217.6 Ω ; R_2 = 1300 Ω]

24.19. Design an unbalanced asymmetrical π-attenuator with loss of 15 dB to operate between 400 Ω line and 625 Ω line.

[**Ans.** Series arm resistor R_1 = 1360 Ω
Shunt arm resistor R_1 = 517 Ω ; R_2 = 1028 Ω]

25
Equalizers

25.1. Introduction

In general, any electrical circuit has non-uniform attenuation *versus* frequency and phase delay *versus* frequency characteristics. This leads to distortion. Ideally a circuit should have the same attenuation and the same phase delay over the entire operating frequency range. This is achieved by adding equalizers to the given circuit.

Equilizers are networks designed to have attenuation *versus* frequency and phase delay *versus* frequency characteristics inverse to those of the circuit to be equalized resulting in overall uniform response of entire operating frequency range.

Classification of Equalizers. Equalizers may be put into two categories: (*a*) Attenuation or amplitude equalizers and (*b*) Phase or Delay equalizers:

(A) **Attenuation or Amplitude Equalizer.** It is a network designed to have attenuation *versus* frequency characteristic inverse to that of the circuit to be equalized.

Attenuation equalizers are used (*i*) in carries telephone system at medium to high frequencies. For lower frequencies, equalization is achieved by loading the cable. This simultaneously results in reduced attenuation (*ii*) in transmission, recording and reproduction of speech and must compensate for the frequency characteristics of various transducers, transmission lines, amplifiers etc. (*iii*) in feedback control systems or servomechanisms.

(B) **Phase or Delay Equalizer.** It is a network designed to have phase delay *versus* frequency characteristic inverse to that of the circuit to be equilized. Delay equalizer may be constructed using reactive elements exclusively.

Delay equalizers are used in such cases where it is important to preserve the waveform of the input signal such as in fascimile and TV signal transmission over lines.

25.2. Equalizer Configuration

Equalizer may be of the following two types: (*a*) two terminal equalizers and (*b*) four terminal equilizers. Two terminal equalizers may further be of two types: (*i*) series type (*ii*) shunt type. Four terminal equalizers may assume one of the following configuration: *L*, *T*, π, bridge-*T* and lattice.

Series Equalizer. Two terminal equalizers form the simplest equalizer networks. The series equalizer (of the two terminal type) is connected in series with the sending or receiving end of the network to be corrected. Fig. 25.1 shows a series equalizer placed in series with the load.

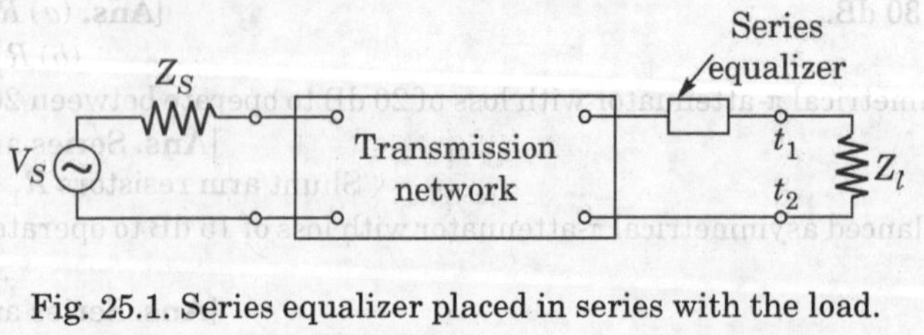

Fig. 25.1. Series equalizer placed in series with the load.

Let the equalizer be needed to work into load impedance R_o and let the desired ratio of input to output power be M (equal to attenuation of D decibels).

Then $$D = \log_{10} M$$

or $$M = \text{antilog } D/10 \qquad ...(25.1)$$

Fig. 25.2 shows the equivalent circuit for the series equalizer of Fig. 25.1. The circuit to the left of the load terminals $t_1 - t_2$ including the equalizer is represented by its Thevenin's equivalent comprising of voltage V, resistance R_o and reactance $2X_1$.

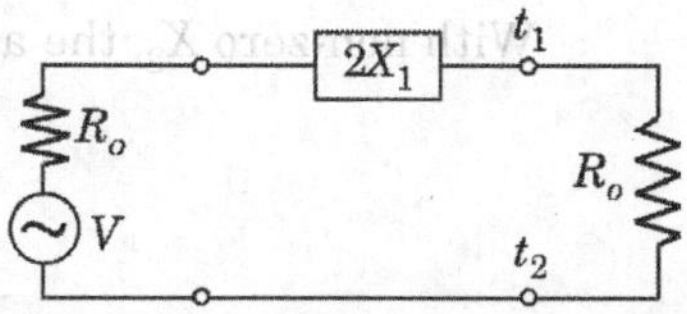

Fig 25 2 Circuit equivalent to that of Fig. 25.1.

Then from Fig. 25.2, maximum power output P_{max} results when $X_1 = 0$. Then input power P_i equals P_{max}. We then get,

$$P_i = P_{max} = \left(\frac{V}{2R_o}\right)^2 R_o = \frac{V^2}{4R_o} \qquad ...(25.2)$$

With non-zero P_1, actual output power is given by

$$P_i = \frac{V^2 R_o}{4R_o^2 + 2X_1^3} \qquad ...(25.3)$$

Hence $$M = \frac{P_i}{P_o}$$

$$= \frac{4R_o^2 + 4X_1^2}{4R_o^2} = 1 + \frac{X_1^2}{R_o^2} \qquad ...(25.4)$$

Thus knowing M and R_0, we may calculate X_1. Eqs. (25.1) and (25.4) form the *design equations* of the series equalizer.

(*b*) **Shunt Equalizer.** The shunt equalizer (of the two terminal type) is connected in shunt with the sending or receiving end of the network to be equalized. Fig. 25.3 shows a shunt equalizer placed in shunt with the load impedance.

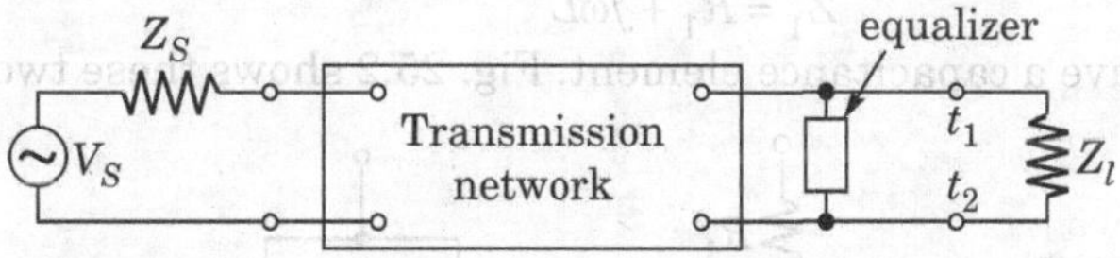

Fig. 25.3. Two terminal shunt equalizer placed in shunt with the load impedance.

Fig. 25.4 shows a circuit equivalent to the circuit of Fig. 25.3. The circuit to the left of the load terminals $t_1 - t_2$ including the equalizer represents the Norton's equivalent comprising the current generator I, shunt resistance R_o and shunt reactance $\frac{X_2}{2}$.

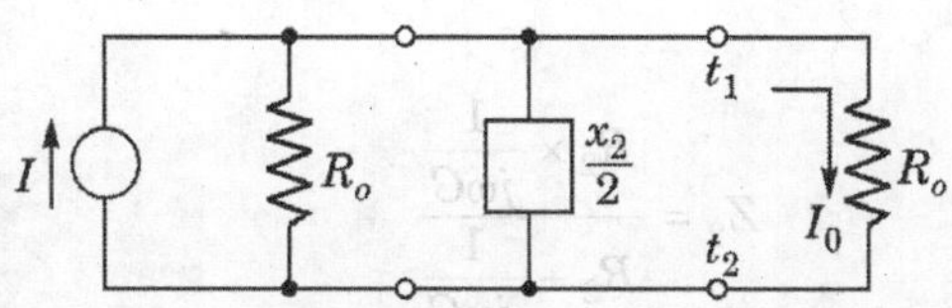

Fig. 25.4. Circuit equivalent to that of Fig. 25.3.

From the circuit of Fig. 25.4 we conclude that for maximum output power P_{max}, X_2 must be zero. Thus $P_i = P_{max}$. Thus, we get

$$P_i = P_{\max} = \left(\frac{I}{2}\right)^2 R_0 = \frac{I^2 R_0}{4} \qquad \text{...(25.5)}$$

With non-zero X_2, the actual output power is given by,

$$P_0 = I_0{}^2 R_0 = R_0 \left[\frac{I \dfrac{1}{R_0}}{\dfrac{1}{R_0} + \dfrac{1}{R_0} + \dfrac{1}{jX_0/2}} \right]$$

or

$$P_o = R_0 \frac{I^2}{\left[2 + \dfrac{2R_0}{X_2}\right]^2}$$

$$= \frac{I^2 R_0 X_2^2}{4(R_0 + X_2^2)} \qquad \text{...(25.6)}$$

Hence

$$M = \frac{P_i}{P_0}$$

$$= \frac{X_2^2 + R_0^2}{X_2^2} = 1 + \frac{R_0^2}{X_2^2} \qquad \text{...(25.7)}$$

Thus knowing M and R_0, we may calculate X_2. Then Eqs. (25.1) and (25.7) form the design equations for the two terminal shunt equalizer.

25.3. Inverse Impedance

Two impedances Z_1 and Z_2 are said to be inverse when their geometric mean is a real number. Thus,

$$Z_1 Z_2 = R^2 \qquad \text{...(25.8)}$$

where R is a resistance.

Let $$Z_1 = R_1 + j\omega L \qquad \text{...(25.9)}$$

Then Z_2 must have a capacitance element. Fig. 25.2 shows these two impedances Z_1 and Z_2.

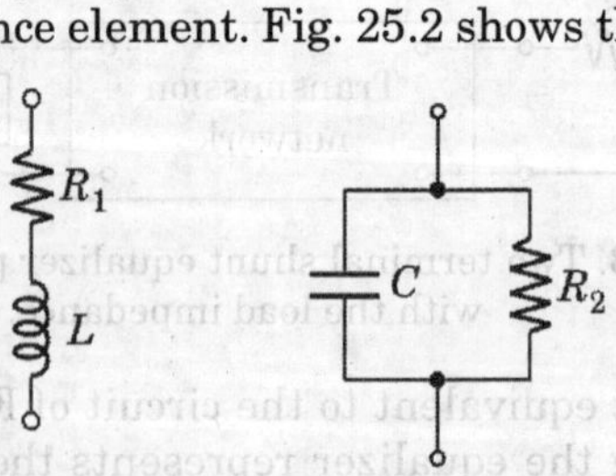

(a) Impedance Z_1 (b) Impedance Z_2

Fig. 25.5. Inverse impedances.

From Fig. 25.5 (6),

$$Z_2 = \frac{R_2 \times \dfrac{1}{j\omega C}}{R_2 + \dfrac{1}{j\omega C}}$$

$$= \frac{-j\dfrac{R_2}{\omega C}}{R_2 - j\dfrac{1}{\omega C}}$$

or
$$Z_2 = \frac{-jR_2}{\omega CR_2 - j} \cdot \frac{\omega CR_2 + j}{\omega CR_2 + j}$$

$$= \frac{R_2 - j\omega CR_2^2}{1 + \omega^2 C^2 R_2^2} \qquad \text{...(25.10)}$$

Substituting these values of Z_1 and Z_2 as given by Eqs. (25.9) and (25.10) into Eq. (25.8), we get

$$R_2^2 = (R_1 + j\omega L)\left(\frac{R_2 - j\omega CR_2^2}{1 + \omega^2 C^2 R_2^2}\right)$$

$$= \frac{R_1R_2 + \omega^2 LCR_2^2 + j(\omega LR_2 - \omega CR_2^2 R_1)}{1 + \omega^2 C^2 R_2^2} \qquad \text{...(25.11)}$$

Evidently then the reactive part on the R.H.S. in Eq. (25.11) has to be zero.

Thus, we get $\omega LR_2 = \omega CR_2^2 R_1$

or
$$\frac{L}{C} = R_1R_2 = R_0^2 \qquad \text{...(25.12)}$$

Eq. (25.12) gives the necessary condition for impedances Z_1 and Z_2 to be inverse.

Typical Inverse Impedances. We have already considered one pair of inverse network shown in Fig. 25.5. A few other typical inverse impedances are shown in Fig. 25.6.

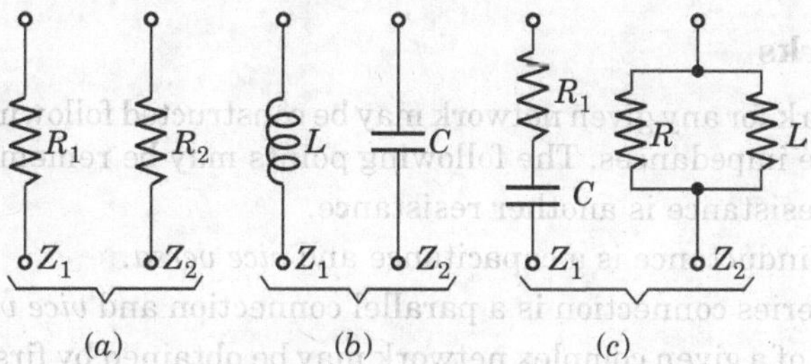

Fig. 25.6. Typical inverse impedances.

Let us consider these cases and verify the condition

$$Z_1Z_2 = R^2$$

Case (*a*) $Z_1 = R_1$ and $Z_2 = R_2$.

Hence $Z_1Z_2 = R_1R_2 = R_2$. Thus product Z_1Z_2 is a real number. Hence the two impedances of Fig. 25.6 (*a*) are inverse impedances.

Case (*b*) In this case,

$$Z_1 = jwL$$

and
$$Z_2 = \frac{1}{j\omega C}$$

Hence
$$Z_1Z_2 = \frac{j\omega L}{j\omega C} = \frac{L}{C}.$$

Thus the product Z_1Z_2 is a real number. Hence the two impedances of Fig. 25.6 (*b*) are inverse impedances.

Case (*c*)
$$Z_1 = R_1 - \frac{j}{\omega C} = \frac{R_1\omega C - j}{\omega C}$$

and
$$Z_2 = \frac{R_2 + \times\, j\omega L}{R_2 + j\omega L}$$
$$= \frac{j\omega L R_2(R_2 - j\omega L)}{(R_2 + j\omega L)(R_2 - j\omega L)}$$
$$= \frac{\omega^2 L^2 R^2 + j\omega L R_2^2}{R_2^2 + \omega^2 L^2}$$

Hence
$$Z_1 Z_2 = \frac{(R_1\omega C - j)(\omega^2 L^2 R_2 + j\omega L C R_2^2)}{\omega C(R_2^2 + \omega^2 L^2)}$$
$$= \frac{(R_1\omega^2 C L^2 R_2 + \omega C R_2^2) + j(\omega^2 L C R_1 R_2^2 - \omega^2 L^2 R_2)}{\omega C(R_2^2 + \omega^2 L^2)} \qquad \ldots(25.13)$$

In Eq. (25.13) equating the imaginary part on the R.H.S. to zero, we get
$$\omega^2 L C R_1 R_2{}^2 = \omega^2 L^2 R^2$$

or
$$\frac{L}{C} = R_1 R_2 \qquad \ldots(25.14)$$

Condition given by Eq. (25.14) for the impedances of Fig. 25.6 (*c*) to be inverse is the same as Eq. (25.12) for the impedances of Fig. 25.5.

25.4. Inverse Networks

An inverse network for any given network may be constructed following the procedure adopted above for simple inverse impedances. The following points may be remembered:

(*i*) inverse of a resistance is another resistance.

(*ii*) inverse of an inductance is a capacitance and *vice versa*.

(*iii*) inverse of a series connection is a parallel connection and *vice versa*.

Thus the inverse of a given complex network may be obtained by first splitting it into simple units, finding the inverse of each unit and then building up the total inverse network.

Example 25.1. *Obtain the inverse network configuration for the network shown in Fig. (a) below and obtain expressions for this inverse network elements in terms of the elements of the given network.*

Solution. Let the resistance R_0 be the design impedance of the system. The inverse network may then be drawn by

(*i*) converting each series branch circuit into parallel one and *vice versa*.

(*ii*) converting each resistance element R into corresponding resistance element R_0^2/R.

(*iii*) converting each inductance L into capacitance $C' = L/R_0^2$.

(*iv*) converting each capacitance C into inductance $L' = CR_0^2$.

This yields the inverse network of Fig. (*b*).

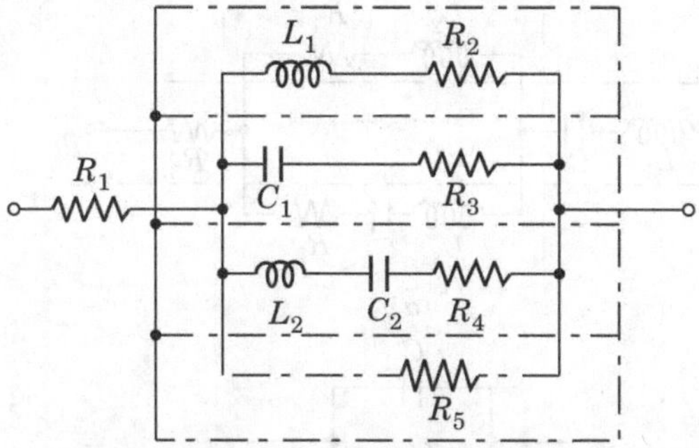

(a)

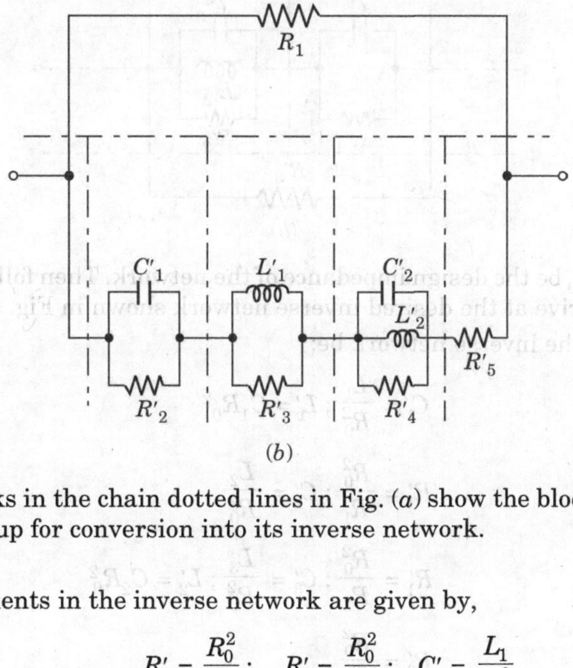

(b)

The various blocks in the chain dotted lines in Fig. (*a*) show the blocks into which the given network has been split up for conversion into its inverse network.

The various elements in the inverse network are given by,

$$R_1' = \frac{R_0^2}{R_1}; \quad R_2' = \frac{R_0^2}{R_2}; \quad C_1' = \frac{L_1}{R_0^2}$$

$$L_1' = C_1 R_0^2; \quad R_3' = \frac{R_0^2}{R_3}$$

$$C_2' = \frac{L_2}{R_0^2};$$

$$L_2' = C_2 R_0^2; R_4' = \frac{R_0^2}{R_4}; R_5' = \frac{R_0^2}{R_5}$$

Example 25.2. *Draw the inverse network of the network shown in Fig. (a) and write expressions for the elements of the inverse network in terms of the elements of the given network.*

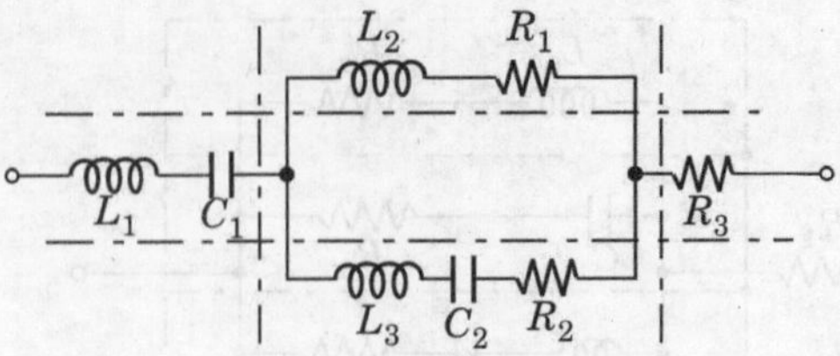

(a)

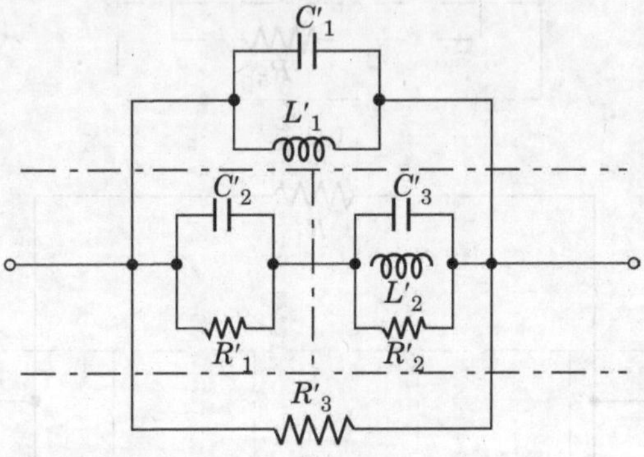

(b)

Solution. The R_0 be the design impedance of the network. Then following the rules outlined in Example 25.1, we arrive at the desired inverse network shown in Fig. (*b*).

Let elements of the inverse network be:

$$C_1' = \frac{L_1}{R_0^2}\ ;\ L_1' = C_1R_0{}^2$$

$$R_1' = \frac{R_0^2}{R_1}\ ;\ C_2' = \frac{L_2}{R_0^2}$$

$$R_1' = \frac{R_0^2}{R_2}\ ;\ C_3' = \frac{L_3}{R_0^2}\ ;\ L_2' = C_2R_0^2$$

$$R_3' = \frac{R_0^2}{R_3}\ .$$

25.5. Constant Resistance Equalizer

A two terminal equalizer of either the shunt type or the series type, suffers from the drawback that its impedance varies with frequency causing impedance mismatch and consequent reflection losses. Accordingly it is preferred to use a four terminal equalizer which offers a constant impedance (usually resistive) and hence avoids reflection loss when terminated in its design impedance.

A constant resistance equalizer is a four-terminal equalizer using series and shunt arm impedances which are inverse of each other with respect to a constant resistance usually the design resistance of the equalizer. Such an equalizer always presents a constant input and output resistance at all frequencies.

Fig. 25.7 (*a*) shows a simple-four terminal constant resistance equalizer. The series impedance Z_1 is inverse of the shunt impedance Z_2 *i.e.* $Z_1Z_2 = R^2$.

Let Z; be the input impedance at terminals 1—1′.

Then
$$Z_i = \frac{Z_1 R}{Z_1 + R} + \frac{Z_2 R}{Z_2 + R} = \frac{2RZ_1Z_2 + R^2(Z_1 + Z_2)}{(Z_1 + R)(Z_2 + R)}$$

$$= \frac{2R_1Z_1Z_2 + R^2(Z_1 + Z_2)}{Z_1Z_2 + R(Z_1 + Z_2) + R^2} \quad ...(25.15)$$

But $Z_1Z_2 = R^2$

Hence Eq. (25.15) may be put as,

$$Z_i = \frac{2R^3 + R^2(Z_1 + Z_2)}{R^2 + R(Z_1 + Z_2) + R^2}$$

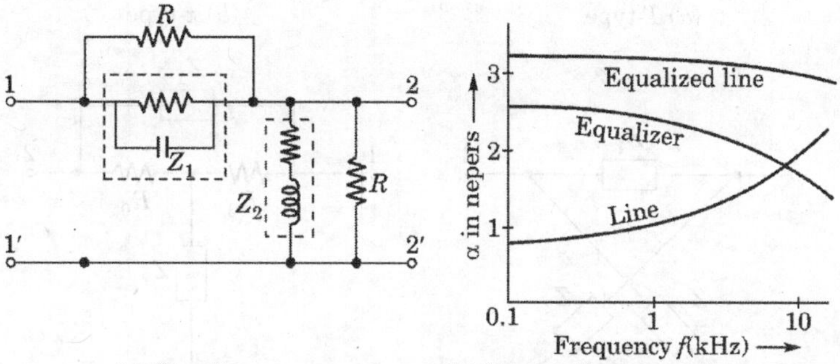

(a) Circuit (b) Attenuation *versus* frequency characteristic

Fig. 25.7. A simple four-terminal constant resistance equalizer.

$$= R\left[\frac{2R^2 + R(Z_1 + Z_2)}{2R^2 + R(Z_1 + Z_2)}\right] = R \quad ...(25.16)$$

Let this R be made equal to the characteristic impedance of the line to be equalized. Then with the line terminated in such an equalizer, the attenuation *versus* frequency characteristic of such an equalized line is almost horizontal as shown in Fig. 25.7 (*b*). Thus there will be almost no reflection loss. A more complex equalizer is needed, whenever a large range of attenuation is required to be equalized.

A constant resistance equalizer is terminated in its iterative impedance R_0. Hence its attenuation α equals its insertion loss. This simplifies the design.

Types of Constant Resistance Equalizers. Fig. 25.8 shows four typical constant resistant equalizer configurations. In each case, the condition $Z_1Z_2 = R_0^2$ is satisfied.

The T and π types use 7 elements each while the lattice and the bridged-T types use 4 elements each. Hence from the consideration of economy of elements, the lattice and the bridged-T types are preferred. Further these two types have characteristic impedance satisfying the relation $Z_1Z_2 = R_0^2$. The lattice type is used with unbalanced line such as open wire line while the bridged-T type is used with the balanced line such as coaxial line.

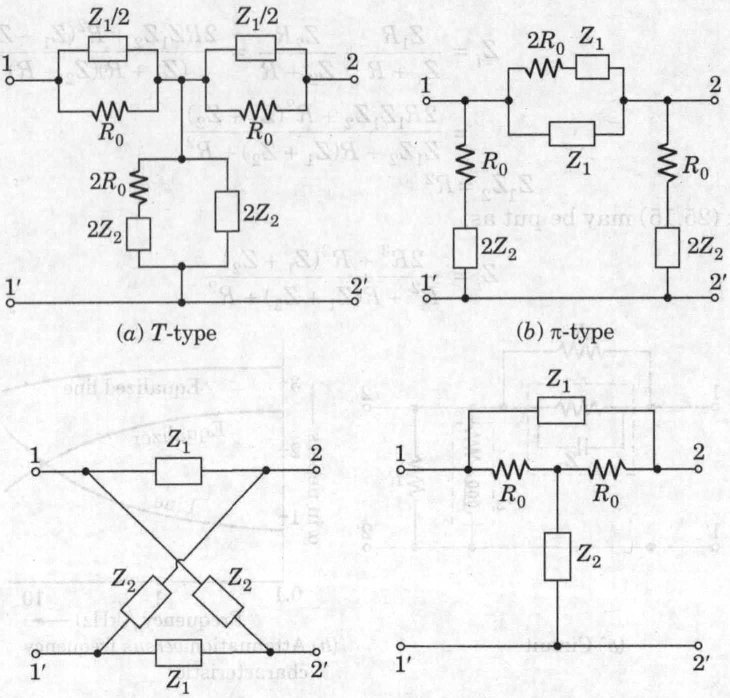

(c) Lattice type (d) Bridged-T type

Fig. 28.8. Constant resistance equalizer configuration.

25.6. Simple Four Terminal Equalizers

The following are the four popularly used four-terminal equalizers:

(a) Full series equalizer (b) Full shunt equalizer

(c) Bridged-T equalizer (d) Lattice equalizer.

The reactive components Z_1 and Z_2 fulfil the reaction $Z_1Z_2 = R_0^2$ resulting in constant characteristic impedance throughout the operating frequency range. Hence knowing one reactance say Z_1 it is possible to compute the other namely Z_2.

25.7. Full Series Equalizer

Fig. 25.9 gives the configuration of full series equalizer.

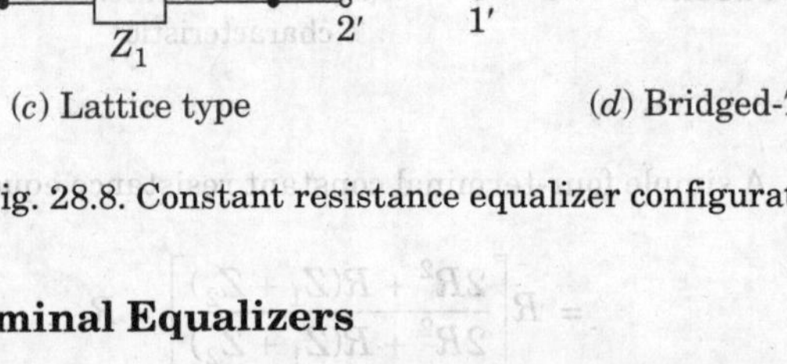

Fig. 25.9. Configuration of full series equalizer.

From Fig. 25.9, the input impedance Z_i is given by,

$$Z_i = \frac{R_0 Z_1}{R_0 + Z_1} + \frac{R_0 Z_2}{R_0 + Z_2} \qquad \text{...(25.17)}$$

$$= \frac{R_0[Z_1(R_0 + Z_2) + Z_2(R_0 + Z_1)]}{(R_0 + Z_1)(R_0 + Z_2)}$$

$$= \frac{R_0[2Z_1Z_2 + R_0(Z_1 + Z_2)]}{R_0^2 + R_0(Z_1 + Z_2) + Z_1Z_2} \qquad \text{...(25.18)}$$

But $Z_1Z_2 = R_0^2$. Hence Eq. (25.18) yields,

$$Z_i = R_0 \qquad \text{...(25.19)}$$

Hence $$|V_S| = I_1 Z_i = I_1 \cdot R_0 \qquad \text{...(25.20)}$$

But $$|V_R| = I_1 \cdot Z_R \qquad \text{...(25.21)}$$

$$= I_1 \cdot \frac{R_0 Z_2}{Z_0 + Z_2} \qquad \text{...(25.22)}$$

Hence $$M = \frac{\text{Input Power}}{\text{Output Power}} = \left|\frac{V_S}{V_R}\right|^2 = \left|\frac{R_0 + Z_2}{Z_2}\right|^2$$

$$= 1 + \frac{R_0^2}{X_2^2} = 1 + \frac{X_1^2}{R_0^2} \qquad \text{...(25.23)}$$

Since Z_1 and Z_2 are pure reactances and are equal to X_1 and X_2 and $X_1X_2 = R_0^2$.

Eq. (25.23) forms the design equation for the series equalizer. Then if the loss M is given and R_0 is known, X_1 and X_2 maybe computed from Eq. (25.23).

The following two specific cases are considered.

(I) $X_i = \omega L_1$

But $$X_1X_2 = R_0^2$$

Hence $$\omega L_1 \frac{1}{\omega C_2} = R_0^2 \quad \text{or} \quad \frac{L_1}{C_2} = R_0^2 \qquad \text{...(25.24)}$$

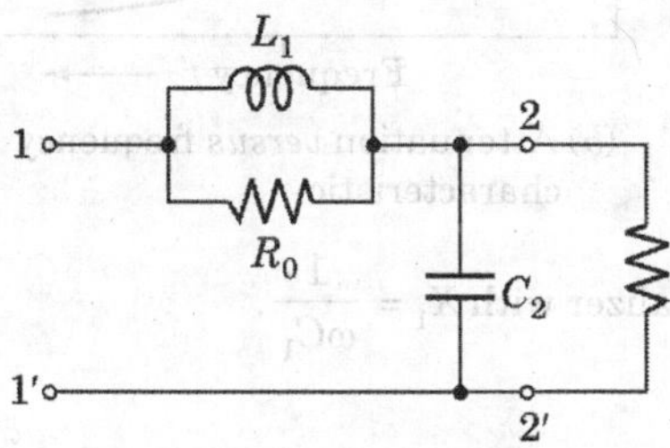

(*a*) Circuit diagram

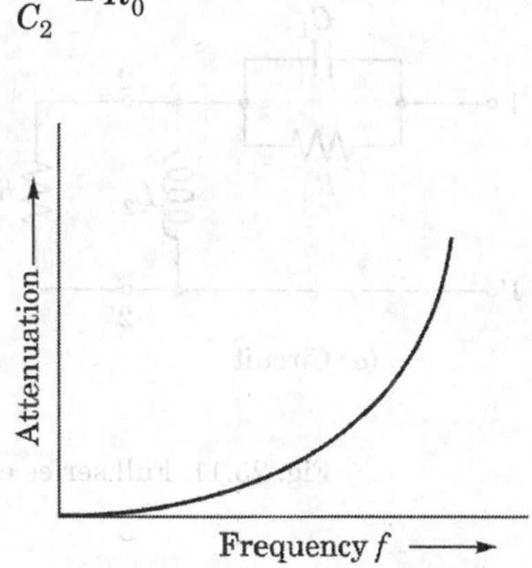

(*b*) Attenuation *versus* frequency characteristic

Fig. 25.10. Full series equalizer with $X_1 = \omega L_1$.

Then from Eq. (25.23),

$$M = 1 + \frac{(\omega L_1)}{R_0^2} \text{ or } L_1 = \frac{R_0\sqrt{M-1}}{\omega} \qquad \text{...(25.25)}$$

Eq. (25.25) enables us to compute L_1 knowing M, R_0 and ω. Having found L_1, Eq. (25.24) may be used to compute C_2.

Fig. 25.10 (*a*) gives the circuit of this full series equalizer, while Fig. 25.10 (*b*) shows the attenuation *versus* frequency characteristic.

It may be seen from Fig. 25.10 (*b*) that the attenuation is zero $f = 0$ and is infinity for $f = \infty$.

(II) $X_1 = \dfrac{1}{\omega C_1}$.

Again $\qquad X_1X_2 = R_0^2$

Hence $\qquad \dfrac{1}{\omega C_1} \cdot \omega L_2 = R_0^2$ or $\dfrac{L_2}{C_1} = R_0^2 \qquad$ ...(25.26)

Then from Eq. (25.23),

$$M = 1 + \frac{R_0^2}{X_2^2} = 1 + \frac{R_0^2}{\omega^2 L_2^2} \qquad \text{...(25.27)}$$

or

$$L_2 = \frac{R_0}{\omega\sqrt{M-1}} \qquad \text{...(25.28)}$$

Eq. (25.28) permits us to compute L_2 knowing M, R_0 and ω. Having found L_2, Eq. (25.26) may be used to compute C_1.

Fig. 25.11 (*a*) gives the circuit of full series equalizer with $X_1 = \dfrac{1}{\omega C_1}$ while Fig. 25.11 (*b*) gives the attenuation *versus* frequency characteristic. It may be seen form Fig. 25.11 (*b*) that the attenuation is infinite at $f = 0$ and is zero at ∞.

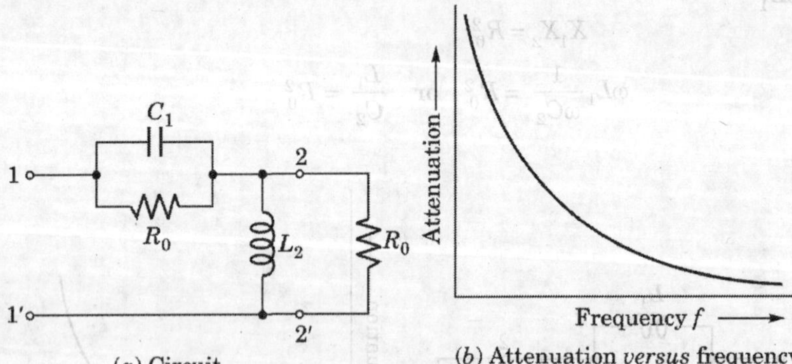

(*a*) Circuit

(*b*) Attenuation *versus* frequency characteristic

Fig. 25.11. Full series equalizer with $X_1 = \dfrac{1}{\omega C_1}$.

25.8. Full Shunt Equalizer

Fig. 25.12 gives the configuration of full shunt equalizer.

From Fig. 25.12, the input impedance Z_i is given by,

$$Z_i = \frac{(R_0 + Z_2)(R_0 + Z_1)}{R_0 + Z_2 + R_0 + Z_1}$$

$$= \frac{Z_1 R_2 + R_0^2 + R_0(Z_1 + Z_2)}{2R_0 + (Z_1 + Z_2)} \quad ...(25.29)$$

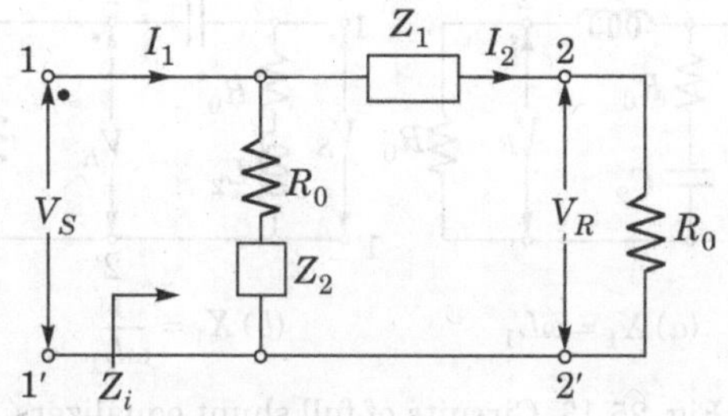

Fig. 25.12. Configuration of full shunt equalizer.

But $Z_1Z_2 = R_0^2$. Hence Eq. (25.29) yields,

$$Z_i = \frac{2R_0^2 + R_0(Z_1 + Z_2)}{2R_0 + (Z_1 + Z_2)}$$

$$= R_0\left[\frac{2R_0 + Z_1 + Z_2}{2R_0 + Z_1 + Z_2}\right] = R_0 \quad ...(25.30)$$

Hence $\quad V_S = I_1 \cdot Z_i = I_1 \cdot R_0$

Also $\quad V_R = I_2 \cdot R_0$

Hence $$\frac{V_S}{V_R} = \frac{I_1 R_0}{I_2 R_0} = \frac{I_1}{I_2} \quad ...(25.31)$$

But $$\frac{I_2}{I_1} = \frac{R_0 + Z_2}{2R_0 + Z_1 + Z_2} = \frac{R_0 Z_1 + Z_1 Z_2}{2R_0 Z_1 + Z_1^2 + Z_1 Z_2}$$

or $$\frac{I_2}{I_1} = \frac{R_0 Z_1 R + R_0^2}{2R_0 Z_1 + Z_1^2 + R_0^2} = \frac{R_0(R_0 + Z_1)}{(R_0 + Z_1)^2} = \frac{R_0}{R_0 + Z_1}$$

...(25.32)

Hence $$M = \frac{\text{Input Power}}{\text{Output Power}} = \left|\frac{V_S}{V_R}\right|^2 = \left|\frac{I_1}{I_2}\right|^2$$

$$= \left|\frac{R_0 + Z_1}{R_0}\right|^2 \quad ...(25.33$$

or $$M = 1 + \frac{X_1^2}{R_0^2} = + \frac{R_0^2}{X_2^2} \quad ...(25.34)$$

since X_1 and X_2 are pure reactances and $X_1X_2 = R_0^2$.

Eq. (25.34) forms the design equation for the full shunt equalizer. Then if attenuation M and R_0 are known, X_1 and X_2 may be calculated from Eq. (25.34).

Here again following two cases present themselves:

Case (I): $X_1 = \omega L_1$ and Class (II): $X_1 = \dfrac{1}{\omega C_1}$.

These two cases and their design equations are indentical with those of corresponding cases of full series equalizer. The resulting circuits are given in Fig. 25.13.

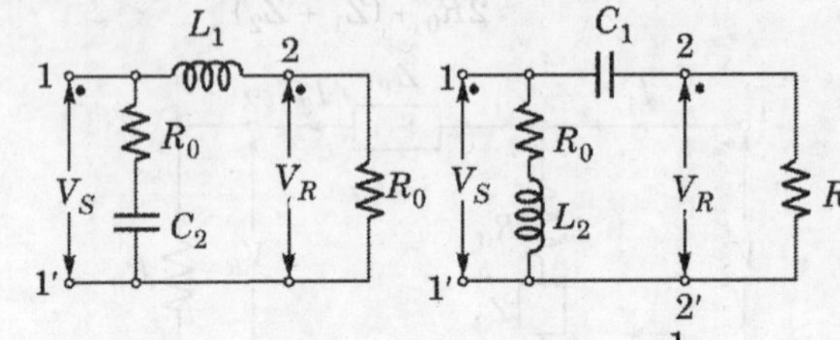

(a) $X_1 = \omega L_1$ (b) $X_1 = \dfrac{1}{\omega L_1}$

Fig. 25.13. Circuits of full shunt equalizers.

The attenuation *versus* frequency curves for the circuits of Fig. 25.13 (*a*) and (*b*) are indentical with the curves of full series equalizers shown respectively in Fig. 25.10 (*a*) and Fig. 25.10 (*b*).

25.9. Bridged-T Equalizer

Bridged-*T* equalizers may be used as attenuation equalizers and as phase or delay equalizers. However, they are used more commonly as phase equalizers because of simplicity of design.

Bridged-*T* equalizers of both the types are constant resistance type so that insertion of such an equalizer in the circuit does not upset impedance relationships.

An attenuation equalizer has resistance as well as reactance components. Phase or delay equalizer, on the other hand, has reactance components only.

(A) **Bridged-*T* Attenuation Equalizer.** Fig. 25.8 (*b*) shows the configuration of bridged-*T* attenuation equalizer. For functioning as an attenuation equalizer, Z_1 has resistive and reactive components. Let Z_1 be a parallel combination of resistor R_1 and inductance L_1 as shown in Fig. 25.14. Then for constant resistance operation of the equalizer Z_2 must be a combination of a resistor say R_2 and a capacitor say C_1 as shown in Fig. 25.14. Let R_0 be the design resistance. Then $Z_1Z_2 = R_0^2$.

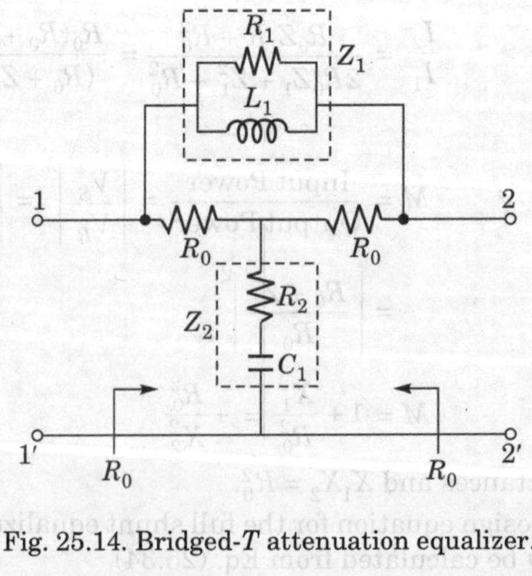

Fig. 25.14. Bridged-*T* attenuation equalizer.

Then for Z_1 and Z_2 to be inverse impedances Eq. (15.12) gives,

$$R_1R_2 = \frac{L_1}{C_1} = R_0^2. \qquad \text{...(25.35)}$$

The characteristic impedance Z_0 of the bridge-T network of Fig. 25.14 is given by,

$$Z_0 = \sqrt{Z_1 Z_2}$$

But from Fig. 25.14, $Z_0 = R_0$

Thus
$$R_0^2 = Z_1 Z_2 \qquad ...(25.36)$$

Eq. (25.36) is the desired condition for constant resistance equalizer. Thus for bridged-T equalizer, characteristic impedance equals the design resistance R_0, a property which makes bridged-T network superior to other networks.

We now proceed to find the attenuation loss α which also forms the insertion loss since the equalizer is terminated in R_0.

The propagation constant P of a bridged-T network of Fig. 25.14 is given by,

$$P = \ln\left[1 + \frac{Z_1}{Z_0}\right] \qquad ...(25.37)$$

But
$$Z_0 = R_0$$

Hence
$$P = \ln\left[1 + \frac{Z_1}{Z_0}\right] \qquad ...(25.38)$$

But
$$Z_1 = \frac{R_1 \times j\omega L_1}{R_2 + j\omega L_1} \qquad ...(25.39)$$

Substituting the value of Z_1 from Eq. (25.39) into Eq. (25.38), we

$$P = \ln\left[1 + \frac{jR_1\omega L_1}{R_0(R_1 + j\omega L_1)}\right]$$

or
$$\alpha + j\beta = \ln\left[\frac{R_0R_1 + j\omega L_1(R_0 + R_1)}{R_0R_1 + j\omega L_1 R_0}\right] \qquad ...(25.40)$$

Equating the real parts in Eq. (25.40), we get

$$\alpha = \ln\left[\frac{R_0^2R_1^2 + \omega^2L_1^2(R_0 + R_1^2)}{R_0^2R_1^2 + \omega^2L_1^2R_0^2}\right]$$

$$= \frac{1}{2}\ln\left[\frac{R_0^2R_1^2 + \omega^2L_1^2R_0^2 + \omega^2L_1^2 + 2\omega^2L_1^2R_0R_1}{R_0^2R_1^2 + \omega^2L_1^2R_0^2}\right]$$

or
$$\alpha = \frac{1}{2}\ln\left[1 + \frac{\omega^2L_1^2R_1(R_1 + 2R_0)}{R_0^2R_1^2 + \omega^2L_1^2R_0^2}\right] \qquad ...(25.41)$$

Eqs. (25.35) and (25.41) form the design equations of the bridged-T attenuation equalizer. If the attenuation loss α, design impedance R_0 and frequency $f\left[= \frac{\omega}{2\pi}\right]$ are given, the elements of the bridged-T attenuation equalizer of Fig. 25.14 may be calculated from these design equations.

(B) **Bridged-T Phase or Delay Equalizer.** It uses a bridged-T network with all elements as pure reactances. Fig. 25.15 (*a*) shows the circuit configuration.

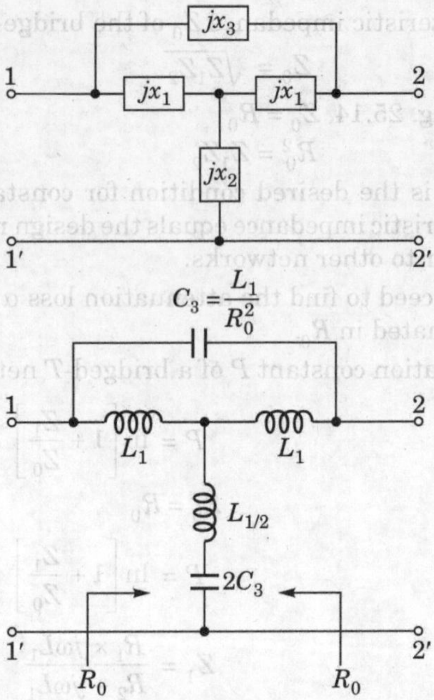

(a) Circuit configuration

(b) Typical circuit

Fig. 25.15. Bridged-*T* phase equahzer.

A properly designed bridged-*T* phase equalizer has zero attenuation at all frequencies *i.e.* the equalizer forms an all pass equalizer.

The characteristic impedance of a bridged-*T* network is given by,

$$Z_0^2 = \frac{Z_3 Z_1(Z_1 + 4Z_2)}{4(Z_1 + Z_2)} \qquad \text{...(25.42)}$$

In Fig. 25.15 (*a*), $Z_3 = jX_3$, $\frac{Z_1}{2} = jX_2$, $Z_2 = jX_2$ and $Z_0 = R_0$.

Hence $$R_0^2 = \frac{jX_3 \cdot 2jX_1(2jX_1 + 4jX_2)}{4(2jX_1 + jX_3)}$$

$$= \frac{-X_1 X_3(X_1 + 2X_2)}{(2X_1 + X_2)} \qquad \text{...(25.43)}$$

Let X_1 and X_3 be the inverse impedences.

Then $$jX_1 \cdot jX_3 = R_0{}^2 \quad \text{or} \quad -X_1X_3 = R_0^2 \qquad \text{...(25.44)}$$

Then Eq. (25.43) yields,

$$R_0^2 = \frac{R_0^2(X_1 + 2X_2)}{(2X_1 + X_3)} \quad \text{or} \quad 1 = \frac{X_1 + 2X_2}{2X_1 + X_3}$$

Hence $$X_2 = \frac{X_1 + X_3}{2} \qquad \text{...(25.45)}$$

Phase shift. We now proceed to compute the phase shift β.

The propagation constant *P* of a bridged-*T* network is given by,

$$e^P = \frac{Z_0(Z_1+Z_3)+\dfrac{Z_1Z_3}{2}}{Z_0(Z_1+Z_3)-\dfrac{Z_1Z_3}{2}} \qquad ...(25.46)$$

or
$$\frac{e^P-1}{e^P+1} = \frac{\dfrac{2Z_1Z_3}{2}}{2Z_0(Z_1+Z_3)}$$

or
$$\frac{e^{P/2}-e^{-P/2}}{e^{P/2}+e^{-P/2}} = \frac{Z_1Z_3}{2Z_0(Z_1+Z_3)} \qquad ...(25.47)$$

or
$$\tanh P/2 = \frac{2jX_1 \cdot jX_3}{2R_0(2jX_1+X_3)} = \frac{-X_1X_3}{jR_0(2X_1+X_3)}$$

$$= \frac{-jR_0^2}{R_0(2X_1+X_3)} \text{ since } -X_1X_3 = R_0^2$$

$$= \frac{-jR_0}{2X_1-(R_0^2/X_1)} \text{ since } X_3 = \frac{-R_0^2}{X_1}$$

$$= \frac{+jR_0}{R_0^2-2X_1^2} \qquad ...(25.48)$$

Hence
$$\frac{P}{2} = \tanh^{-1}\frac{jR_0X_1}{(R_0^2-2X_1^2)} \qquad ...(25.49)$$

or
$$P = \alpha + j\beta = 2j\tan^{-1}\frac{R_0X_1}{R_0^2-2X_1^2} \qquad ...(25.50)$$

Equating the real and the imaginary parts, we get

$$\alpha = 0 \quad \text{and} \quad \beta = 2\tan^{-1}\frac{R_0X_1}{(R_0^2-2X_1^2)} \qquad ...(25.51)$$

The relation $\alpha = 0$ implies that the equalizer will pass signals of all the frequencies. Accordingly this equalizer is called the all-pass equalizer.

Eqs. (25.44), (25.45) and (25.51) constitute the design equations for the bridged-*T* phase equalizer. Knowing the phase shift β and design impedance R_0, we may compute X_1 making use of Eq. (25.51). Knowing X_1, we may compute X_3 from Eq. (25.44). Finally having computed X_1 and X_3, we may compute X_2 from Eq. (25.45).

25.10. Lattice Equalizer

This is the one most popularly used in the communication systems, Lattice equalizer may be used either as attenuation equalizer or as phase equalizer. Further it is of the constant resistance type so that its insertion in any system does not upset impedance relationships.

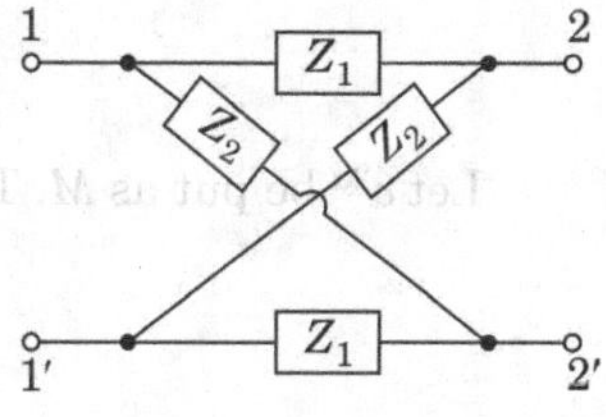

Fig. 25.16. Configuration of lattice network.

Fig. 25.16 shows the circuit configuration. For constant-resistance property, the relation to be satisfied is $Z_1Z_2 = R_0^2$.

The characteristic impedance Z_0 of this lattice network is given by,

$$Z_0 = \sqrt{Z_1Z_2} \qquad ...(25.52)$$

But
$$Z_1Z_2 = R_0^2$$

Hence $$Z_0 = \sqrt{R_0^2} = R_0 \qquad ...(25.53)$$

The characteristic impedance of the constant resistance lattice equalizer equals the constant resistance R_0. The propagation constant P of this lattice network is given by,

$$P = \ln \frac{Z_0 + Z_1}{Z_0 - Z_1} \qquad ...(25.54)$$

or $$e^P = \frac{1 + Z_1 / Z_0}{1 - Z_1 Z_0} \qquad ...(25.55)$$

But $$Z_0 = \sqrt{Z_1 Z_2}$$

Hence $$e^P = \frac{1 + \sqrt{Z_1 / Z_2}}{1 - \sqrt{Z_1 / Z_2}} \text{ or } e^{(\alpha + j\beta)} = \frac{1 + x}{1 - x} \qquad ...(25.56)$$

where $$x = \sqrt{Z_1 / Z_2}$$

It may be noted that if Z_1 and Z_2 are interchanged then x becomes $\frac{1}{x}$ and $\frac{1-x}{1+x}$ becomes $-\left(\frac{1-x}{1+x}\right)$. Thus the modulus of $\frac{1+x}{1-x}$ remains unchanged and hence the attenuation α remains unchanged. On the other hand, the argument of $\frac{1+x}{1-x}$ changes sign and hence β changes to $(\beta + \pi)$.

If the characteristic impedance Z_0 is a pure resistance R_0, Eq. (22.55) becomes,

$$e^P = \frac{1 + Z_1 / R_0}{1 - Z_1 / R_0} \qquad ...(25.57)$$

Putting $Z_1 = R_1 + jX_1$ and $P = \alpha + j\beta$ Eq. (25.57) yields,

$$e^{(\alpha + j\beta)} = \frac{1 + \dfrac{R_1 + jX_1}{R_0}}{1 - \dfrac{R_1 + jX_1}{R_0}} = \frac{\left(1 + \dfrac{R_1}{R_0}\right) + j\dfrac{X_1}{R_0}}{\left(1 - \dfrac{R_1}{R_0}\right) - j\dfrac{X_1}{R_0}} \qquad ...(25.58)$$

Squaring both the sides of Eq. (25.58) and taking only the real parts of each side, we get

$$e^{2\alpha} = \frac{\left(1 + \dfrac{R_1}{R_0}\right)^2 + \left(\dfrac{X_1}{R_0}\right)^2}{\left(1 - \dfrac{R_1}{R_0}\right)^2 - \left(\dfrac{X_1}{R_0}\right)^2} \qquad ...(25.59)$$

Let $e^{2\alpha}$ be put as M. Then Eq. (22.59) may be put as,

$$M = \frac{\left(1 + \dfrac{R_1}{R_0}\right)^2 + \left(\dfrac{X_1}{R_0}\right)^2}{\left(1 - \dfrac{R_1}{R_0}\right)^2 - \left(\dfrac{X_1}{R_0}\right)^2} \qquad ...(25.60)$$

But as per basic definition of propagation constant,

$$e^{\alpha} = \frac{I_1}{I_2}$$

Hence $$M = e^{2\alpha} = \frac{I_1^2}{I_2^2} = \frac{I_1^2 R_0}{I_2^2 R_0} = \frac{P_1}{P_2} \qquad \text{...(25.61)}$$

since the input impedance and output impedance each equals R_0.

Also as per basic definition, attenuation is given by,

$$D = 10 \log \frac{P_1}{P_2}$$

or $$\frac{D}{10} = \log \frac{P_1}{P_2}$$

or $$\frac{P_1}{P_2} = \text{antilog } \frac{D}{10}$$

Hence $$M = \text{antilog}\left(\frac{D}{10}\right) \qquad \text{...(25.62)}$$

Eq. (25.62) may be used in the design of lattice equalizer when attenuation at two different frequencies is known.

We have considered two cases: (*i*) X_1 is inductance *i.e.* Z_1 is a series combination of a resistance R_1 and inductance L_1, (*ii*) Z_1 is a capacitor in shunt with a resistor *i.e.* it may be put in the form of a resistor in series with a capacitance C_1.

Thus $$Z_1 = R_1 - j\frac{1}{\omega L_1}.$$

Case (i): X = ωL₁.

Then $Z_1 = R_1 + j\omega L_1$.

Eq. (25.60) may then be written as,

$$M = \frac{\left(\frac{R_0 + R_1}{R_0}\right)^2 + \left(\frac{\omega L_1}{R_0}\right)^2}{\left(\frac{R_0 - R_1}{R_0}\right)^2 + \left(\frac{\omega L_1}{R_0}\right)^2} = \frac{(R_0 + R_1)^2 + (2\pi f L_1)^2}{(R_0 - R_1)^2 + (2\pi f L_1)^2}$$

$$= \frac{\left(\frac{R_0 + R_1}{2\pi L_1}\right)^2 + f^2}{\left(\frac{R_0 - R_1}{2\pi L_1}\right)^2 + f^2} \qquad \text{...(25.63)}$$

or $$M = \frac{A^2 + f^2}{B^2 + f^2} \qquad \text{...(25.64)}$$

where $$A = \frac{R_0 + R_1}{2\pi L_1} \qquad \text{...(25.65)}$$

and $$B = \frac{R_0 - R_1}{2\pi L_1} \qquad \text{...(25.66)}$$

If attenuation D at two different frequencies is known, then A and B may be computed from Eq. (25.64). Knowing A, B and R_0, Eqs. (25.65) and (25.66) may be used to compute R_1 and L_1.

The impedance Z_2 of each of the shunt arms is simply the inverse of Z_1 and may be computed from the relationship $Z_1 Z_2 = R_0^2$.

Case (*ii*): X = $\mathbf{\dfrac{1}{\omega C_1}}$

In this case,

$$Z_1 = R_1 - j\frac{1}{\omega C_1}.$$

Then Eq. (25.60) may be written as,

$$M = \frac{(R_0 + R_1)^2 + \left(\dfrac{1}{\omega C_1}\right)^2}{(R_6 - R_1)^2 + \left(\dfrac{1}{\omega C_1}\right)^2} = \frac{(R_0 + R_1)^2 + \left(\dfrac{1}{2\pi f C_1}\right)^2}{(R_6 - R_1)^2 + \left(\dfrac{1}{2\pi f C_1}\right)^2}$$

or $$M = \frac{[(R_0 + R_1)2\pi C_1]^2 f^2 + 1}{[(R_0 - R_1)2\pi C_1]^2 f^2 + 1} \qquad ...(25.67)$$

or $$M = \frac{Pf^2 + 1}{Qf + 1} \qquad ...(25.68)$$

where $$P = 2\pi C_1(R_0 + R_1) \qquad ...(25.69)$$

and $$Q = 2\pi C_1(R_0 - R_1) \qquad ...(25.70)$$

If attenuation D at two frequencies is known, then P and Q may by computed from Eq.(25.68). Knowing P, Q and R_0. Eqs. (25.69) and (25.70) may be used to compute R_1 and C_1. The impedance Z_2 of each of the shunt arms is simply the inverse of the impedance Z_1 and may be computed from the relation $Z_1Z_2 = R_0^2$.

Lattice Attenuation Equalizer. In lattice attenuation equalizer, impedances Z_1 and Z_2 have resistive as well as reactive components. Further in order to be a constant resistance equalizer, impedance Z_1 must be inverse of Z_2 with reference to the design resistance R_0. Thus if $Z_1 = R_1 + j\omega L_1$, then Z_2 must be a parallel combination of resistance R_2 and capacitance C_2. Fig. 25.17 shows a constant resistance lattice attenuation equalizer in which Z_1 is a series combination of an inductor and a resistor.

Since impedance Z_1 is inverse of Z_2, we get

$$R_1R_2 = \frac{L}{C} = R_0^2 \qquad ...(25.71)$$

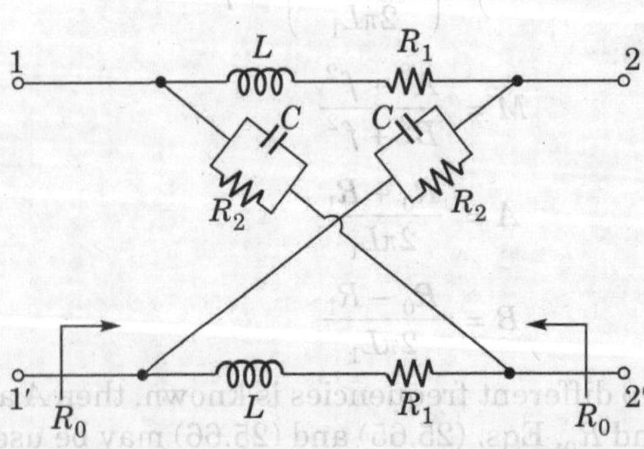

Fig. 25.17. Atypical constant resistance lattice attenuation equalizer.

We now proceed to evaluate the attenuation or the insertion loss. The attenuation α forms the real part of the propagation constant P given by

$$P = \ln \frac{1 + \dfrac{Z_1}{R_0}}{1 - \dfrac{Z_1}{R_0}} \qquad \text{...(25.72)}$$

But $\qquad Z_1 = R_1 + j\omega L.$

Hence Eq. (25.72) may be put as,

$$P = \ln \frac{1 + \dfrac{R_1 + j\omega L}{R_0}}{1 - \dfrac{R_1 + j\omega L}{R_0}}$$

or

$$\alpha + j\beta = \ln \frac{(R_0 + R_1) + j\omega L}{(R_0 - R_1) - j\omega L} \qquad \text{...(25.73)}$$

In Eq. (25.73), equating the real parts on both the sides, we get

$$\alpha = \ln \left[\frac{(R_0 + R_1)^2 + \omega^2 L^2}{(R_0 - R_1)^2 - \omega^2 L^2} \right]^{1/2}$$

$$= \frac{1}{2} \ln \left[\frac{(R_0 - R_1)^2 + 4R_0 R_1 + \omega^2 L^2}{(R_0 - R_1)^2 + \omega^2 L^2} \right]$$

$$= \frac{1}{2} \ln \left[1 + \frac{4R_0 R_1}{(R_0 - R_1)^2 + \omega^2 L^2} \right] \qquad \text{...(25.74)}$$

In most cases, R_1 is chosen to equal R_0. Then Eq. (25.74) yields,

$$\alpha = \frac{1}{2} \ln \left[1 + \frac{4R_0^2}{\omega^2 L^2} \right] \qquad \text{...(25.75)}$$

Eqs. (25.71), (25.74) and (25.75) from the design equations for the lattice attenuation equalizer.

Fig. 25.18 shows the nature of variation of attenuation α with frequency $f\left(=\dfrac{\omega}{2\pi}\right)$.

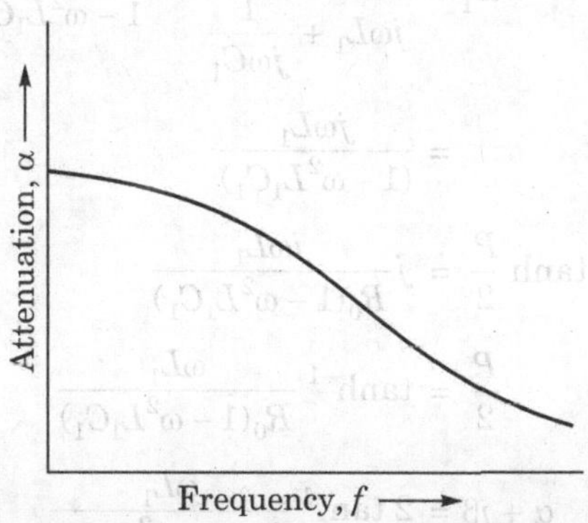

Fig. 25.18. Attenuation *versus* frequency curve of a lattice attenuation equalizer.

Lattice phase or delay equalizer. A phase equalizer uses only reactive components. Accordingly Fig. 25.19 (*a*) shows the configuration of lattice phase equalizer while Fig. 25.19 (*b*) shows the circuit diagram of a typical such equalizer. Further lattice phase equalizer is also a constant resistance equalizer.

Since the equalizer is a constant resistance type,

$$Z_1Z_2 = jX_1(jX_2) = R_0^{\,2} \qquad \text{...(25.76)}$$

or

$$R_0^2 = -X_1X_2 \qquad \text{...(26.77)}$$

Each shunt arm is inverse of the series arm with respect to R_0.

Hence

$$\frac{L_1}{C_2} = \frac{L_2}{C_1} = R_0^2 \qquad \text{...(25.78)}$$

We now proceed to calculate the phase shift β of the equalizer.

The propagation constant P is given by,

$$\tanh\frac{P}{2} = \sqrt{\frac{Z_1}{Z_2}} = \frac{Z_1}{\sqrt{Z_1Z_2}} \qquad \text{...(25.79)}$$

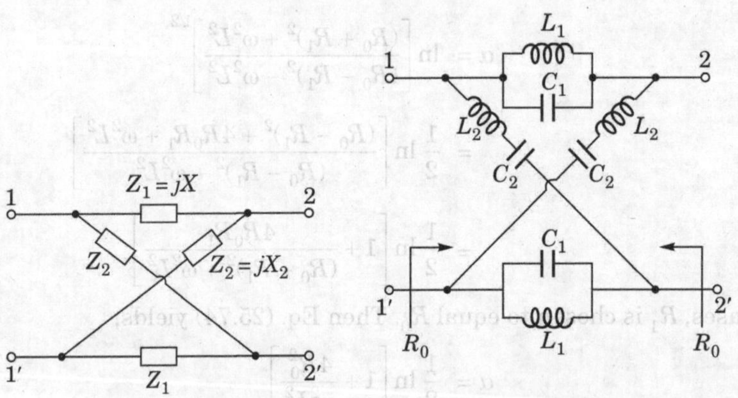

(*a*) Circuit configuration (*b*) Typical circuit

Fig. 25.19. Constant resistance lattice phase equalizer.

But

$$Z_1 = \frac{j\omega L_1 \dfrac{1}{j\omega C_1}}{j\omega L_1 + \dfrac{1}{j\omega C_1}} = \frac{\dfrac{L_1}{C_1}\cdot j\omega C_1}{1-\omega^2L_1C_1}$$

$$= \frac{j\omega L_1}{(1-\omega^2L_1C_1)} \qquad \text{...(25.80)}$$

Hence

$$\tanh\frac{P}{2} = j\frac{j\omega L_1}{R_0(1-\omega^2L_1C_1)}$$

or

$$\frac{P}{2} = \tanh^{-1}\frac{\omega L_1}{R_0(1-\omega^2L_1C_1)}$$

or

$$\alpha + j\beta = 2\tan^{-1}\frac{\omega L_1}{R_0(1-\omega^2L_1C_1)} \qquad \text{...(25.81)}$$

In Eq. (25.81), equating the real part, we get

$$\alpha = 0 \qquad \ldots(25.82)$$

Similarly equating the imaginary parts, we get

$$\beta = 2 \tan^{-1} \frac{\omega L_1}{R_0(1 - \omega^2 L_1 C_1)} \qquad \ldots(25.83)$$

Since $\alpha = 0$, the equalizer forms an all-pass equalizer. Eq. (25.78) and (25.83) form the design equations for the constant resistance lattice phase equalizer.

Fig. 25.20 shows the phase shift *versus* frequency characteristic of a typical constant resistance lattice phase equalizer. It may be seen from this curve that at some frequency f_a, called the critical frequency, β equals π. This frequency f_a is nothing but the anti-resonant frequency of the series arm of the equalizer of Fig. 25.19 (*b*). This becomes evident from Eq. (25.83) wherein term $(1 - \omega^2 LC)$ becomes zero. This critical frequency f_a is given by,

$$f_a = \frac{1}{2\pi\sqrt{L_1 C_1}}$$

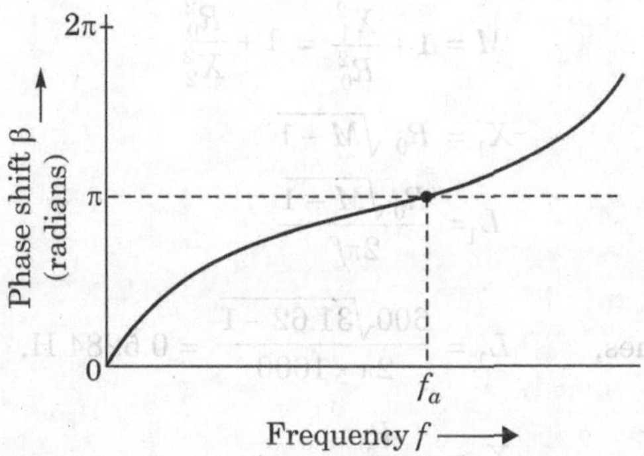

Fig. 25.20. Phase shift *versus* frequency characteristic of a typical constant resistance lattice phase equahzer.

At this frequency, Eq. (25.83) yields,

$$\beta = 2 \tan^{-1}, \alpha = 2\frac{\pi}{2} = \pi. \qquad \ldots(25.84)$$

Example 25.3. *For full series equalizer of Fig. 25.10 (a), it is given that attenuation M at 1000 Hz is 13 dB. Design resistance R_0 is 600 Ω. Compute the values of L_1 and C_2.*

Solution. $13 = 10 \log_{10} M$

Hence $M = 20$

Hence $$L = \frac{R_0\sqrt{M-1}}{\omega} = \frac{600\sqrt{20-1}}{2\pi \times 1000} = 0.416 \text{ henry}$$

$$C_2 = \frac{L_1}{R_0^2} = \frac{0.216}{(600)^2} \text{ F} = 1.155 \ \mu\text{F}.$$

Example 25.4. *Design the full series equalizer of Fig. 25.11 (a) for design resistance $R_0 = 600$ Ω and attenuation of 18 dB at 2000 Hz. Calculate the attenuation M at 4000 Hz.*

Solution. $18 = 10 \log_{10} M$

Hence $M = \text{antilog } 1.8 = 63.09$

$$L_2 = \frac{R_0}{\omega\sqrt{M-1}} = \frac{600}{2\pi \times 2000\sqrt{63.09-1}} \text{ H} = 6.06 \text{ mH}$$

Hence $$C_1 = \frac{L_2}{R_0^2} = \frac{6.06 \times 10^{-3}}{360,000} \text{ F} = 0.1683 \ \mu\text{F}.$$

$$M \text{ at } 4000 \text{ Hz} = 1 + \frac{R_0^2}{\omega^2 L^2}$$

$$= 1 + \frac{(600)^2}{(2\pi \times 4000 \times 6.06 \times 10^{-3})^2} = 16.52.$$

Example 25.5. *Design the full shunt equalizer of Fig. 25.13 (a) for design resistance $R_0 = 600$ Ω and attenuation of 15 dB at 1000 Hz. Calculate the attenuation at frequencies of 2000 and 3000 Hz.*

Solution. $15 = 10 \log M.$

Hence $M = \text{antilog } 1.5 = 31.62$

But $$M = 1 + \frac{X_1^2}{R_0^2} = 1 + \frac{R_0^2}{X_2^2}$$

Hence $$X_1 = R_0 \sqrt{M-1}$$

or $$L_1 = \frac{R_0\sqrt{M-1}}{2\pi f}$$

Substituting the values, $$L_1 = \frac{600\sqrt{31.62-1}}{2\pi \times 1000} = 0.5284 \text{ H}.$$

Also $$X_2 = \frac{R_0}{\sqrt{M-1}}.$$

Hence $$C_2 = \frac{\sqrt{M-1}}{2\pi f R_0} = \frac{\sqrt{31.62-1}}{2\pi \times 1000 \times 600} \text{ F} = 1.4676 \ \mu\text{F}.$$

At $f = 2000$ Hz,

$$M = 1 + \frac{X_1^2}{R_0^2} = 1 + \left(\frac{2\pi \times 2000 \times 0.5284}{600}\right)^2 = 123.47$$

At $f = 300$ Hz,

$$M = 1 + \left(\frac{2\pi \times 3000 \times 0.5284}{600}\right)^2 = 276.$$

Example 25.6. *Design the full shunt equalizer of Fig. 25.31 (b) for design resistance $R_0 = 600$ Ω. and attenuation of 16 dB at 400 Hz. Calculate the attenuation at frequencies of 600 Hz and. 1200 Hz.*

Solution. $16 = 10 \log M.$

Hence $M = \text{antilog } 1.6 = 39.81$

But $$M = 1 + \frac{X_1^2}{R_0^2} = 1 + \frac{R_0^2}{X_2^2}$$

Hence $$X_1 = R_0\sqrt{M-1}$$

or $$\frac{1}{2\pi f C_1} = R_0\sqrt{M-1}$$

or $$C_1 = \frac{1}{2\pi f R_0\sqrt{M-1}} = \frac{1}{2\pi \times 400 \times 600\sqrt{39.8-1}}\ \text{F} = 0.1064\ \mu\text{F}.$$

Also $$\sqrt{M-1} = \frac{R_0}{R_2}$$

or $$X_2 = \frac{R_0}{\sqrt{m-1}}$$

or $$2\pi f L_2 = \frac{R_0}{\sqrt{M-1}}$$

or $$L_2 = \frac{R_0}{2\pi f\sqrt{M-1}} = \frac{600}{2\pi \times 400\sqrt{39.81-1}} = 0.038\ \text{H}.$$

At $$f = 600\ \text{Hz},$$

$$M = 1 + \frac{R_0^2}{X_2^2} = 1 + \left(\frac{600}{2\pi \times 600 \times 0.038}\right)^2 = 18.54.$$

At $$f = 1200\ \text{Hz},$$

$$M = 1 + \frac{R_0^2}{X_2^2} = 1 + \left(\frac{600}{2\pi \times 600 \times 0.038}\right)^2 = 5.835.$$

Example 25.7. *The series arm of a lattice equalizer used in conjunction with a telephone line of characteristic impedance $Z_0 = 600\ \Omega$ consists of a resistor of 400 Ω in series with an inductor of 40 mH. Find the shunt arm of the lattice.* (Grad. I.T.E., Nov., 1964)

Solution. The lattice equalizer used with telephone line will be constant resistance attenuation equalizer (as shown in Fig. 25.16).

It is given that the design resistance

$$R_0 = 600\ \Omega,$$

$$R_1 = 400\ \Omega$$

and $$L_1 = 40\ \text{mH}$$

But $$R_1 R_2 = \frac{L}{C} = R_0^2$$

Hence $$R_2 = \frac{R_0^2}{R_1} = \frac{(600)^2}{400} = 900\ \Omega.$$

Also $$C = \frac{L}{R_0^2} = \frac{0.04}{(600)^2} = \frac{0.04}{360{,}000}\ \text{F} = 0.111\ \mu\text{F}.$$

Example 25.8. *A constant resistance lattice attenuation equalizer has series arm containing a. resistor $R_1 = 1\ k\Omega$ in series with an inductor $L_1 = 50$ mH. If the resistance of the shunt arm is 250 Ω, compute the characteristic impedance and the capacitance of the shunt arm.*

Solution. The circuit is as shown in Fig. 25.17. It is given that $R_1 = 1000\ \Omega$. $L_1 = 0.05$ H

and $$R_2 = 250\ \Omega.$$

But $$R_1 R_2 = \frac{L_1}{C_1} = R_0^2$$

Hence $R_0^2 = 1000 \times 250$

Hence $R_0 = 500\ \Omega$

Also $C_2 = \dfrac{L_1}{R_0^2} = \dfrac{0.05}{250{,}000}\ \text{F} = 0.2\ \mu\text{F}.$

Example 25.9. *In a constant resistance lattice attenuation equalizer, having characteristic impedance of 1 Ω, the diagonal arm consists of resistance L_2 = 1 Ω in series with a capacitor C_2 = 0.05 F. Find the series arm.* (Grad. I.E.T.E., Nov., 1975)

Solution. The equalizer being a constant resistance equalizer, the series arm has to be inverse of the diagonal arm. Hence the circuit is as shown below.

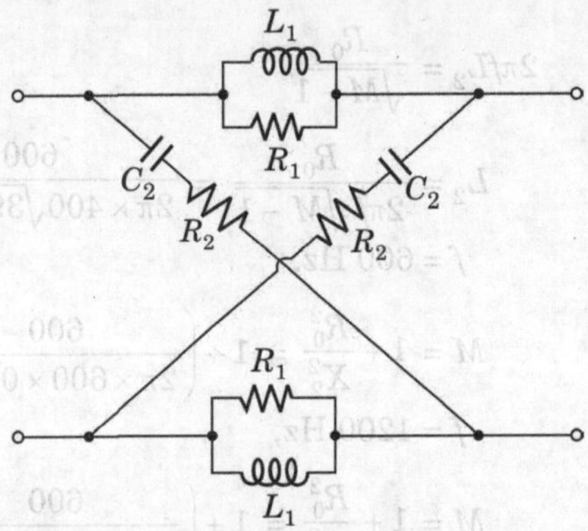

It is given that $R_2 = 1\ \Omega$, $C_2 = 0.05$ F and $R_0 = 1\ \Omega$.

But for a constant resistance equalizer,

$$R_1R_2 = \frac{L_1}{C_2}R_0^2$$

Hence $R_1 = \dfrac{R_0^2}{R_2} = \dfrac{(1)^2}{1} = 1\ \Omega.$

Also $L_1 = C_2R_0^2 = (0.05)\,(1)^2\ \text{H} = 0.05\ \text{H}.$

Example 25.10. *In a constant resistance lattice attenuation equalizer having characteristic impedance R_0 of 600 Ω, the series arm consists of a resistance $R_1 = R_0$ in series with an inductor L_1. If the insertion loss is 3 dB at 1000 Hz, calculate the values of elements of the equalizer.*

Solution. The circuit is the same as that of Fig. 25.17. Since the equalizer is a constant resistance equalizer,

$$R_1R_2 = R_0^2 = \frac{L_1}{C}$$

But $R_1 = R_0 = 600.$

Hence $R_2 = 600\ \Omega.$

At 1000 Hz, $D = 3$ dB.

$M = \text{antilog}\ 3/10 = 2$

But $e^{2\alpha} = M$

and $\alpha = \dfrac{1}{2}\ln\left[\dfrac{4R_0^2}{\omega^2L_1}\right]$

Hence $$M = 1 + \frac{4R_0^2}{\omega^2 L_1^2}$$

or $$2 = 1 + \frac{4R_0^2}{\omega^2 l_1^2}$$

or $$\omega^2 L_0{}^2 = 4R_0^2$$

Hence $$L_1 = \frac{2R_0}{2\pi f} = \frac{2 \times 600}{2\pi \times 100} = 0.19 \text{ H.}$$

Hence $$C_2 = \frac{L_1}{R_0^2} = \frac{0.19}{360{,}000} \text{ F} = 0.528\ \mu\text{F.}$$

Example 25.11. *Design a constant resistance lattice attenuation equalizer to produce attenuation of 20 dB at 50 Hz and 3 dB at 3000 Hz. Calculate its loss at 500 Hz. The equalizer is working between two impedances of 500 Ω each.*

Solution. At $f = 50$ Hz, $D = 20$.

Hence $M = \text{antilog } 2 = 100$

At $f = 3000$ Hz, $D = 3$.

Hence $M = \text{antilog } 3/10 = 2$

But $$M = \frac{A^2 + f^2}{B^2 + f^2}$$

At $$f = 50 \text{ Hz}, \; 100 = \frac{A^2 + (50)^2}{B^2 + (50)^2}$$

or $$A^2 - 100B^2 = (50)^2 [100 - 1] = 99 \times 2500$$

or $$A^2 - 100\, B^2 = 0.2475 \times 10^6 \qquad \text{...}(i)$$

Similarly at $f = 3000$ Hz,

$$2 = \frac{A^2 + (3000)^2}{B^2 + (3000)^2}$$

or $$A^2 - 2B^2 = (3000)^2$$

or $$A^2 - 2B^2 = 9 \times 10^6 \qquad \text{...}(ii)$$

Solving Eqs. (*i*) and (*ii*) for A^2 and B^2, we get

$$98B^2 = 10^6(9 - 0.2475) = 10^6(8.7525)$$

Hence $$B = \pm 10^3 \sqrt{\frac{8.7525}{98}} = \pm\, 0.2988 \times 10^3$$

Hence $$A^2 = (10^6 \times 9) + 2B^2 = 10^3\,[9 + 1.093]$$

Hence $$A = \pm\, 3.177 \times 10^3$$

But $$A = \frac{R_0 + R_1}{2\pi L_1}$$

Substituting the values, we get

$$\pm\, 3.177 \times 10^3 = \frac{500 + R_1}{2\pi L_1} \qquad \text{...}(iii)$$

But $$B = \frac{R_0 - R_1}{R\pi L_1}$$

Substituting the values,

$$\pm 0.2988 \times 10^3 = \frac{500 - R_1}{2\pi L_1} \quad \text{...}(iv)$$

Adding Eqs, (*iii*) and (*iv*), we get

$$\frac{500}{\pi L_1} = 10^3\,[\pm 3.177 \pm 0.2988]$$

$$= 10^3\,[3.746 \text{ or } 2.898]$$

The other two values are not physically realizable.

Hence $$L_1 = \frac{500}{\pi \times 3.746} \text{ or } \frac{500}{\pi \times 2.898} \text{ mH} = 42.48 \text{ or } 54.92 \text{ mH}$$

Next subtracting Eq. (*iv*) from Eq. (*iii*), we get

$$\frac{R_1}{\pi L_1} = 10^3\,[\pm 3.177 \mp 0.2288] = 10^3\,(2.898 \text{ or } 3.746)$$

or $$R_1 = \pi \times 10^3\,[(2.898 \times 42.98) \text{ or } (3.746 \times 54.92)]$$

$$= 386.7 \text{ or } 646.3\ \Omega$$

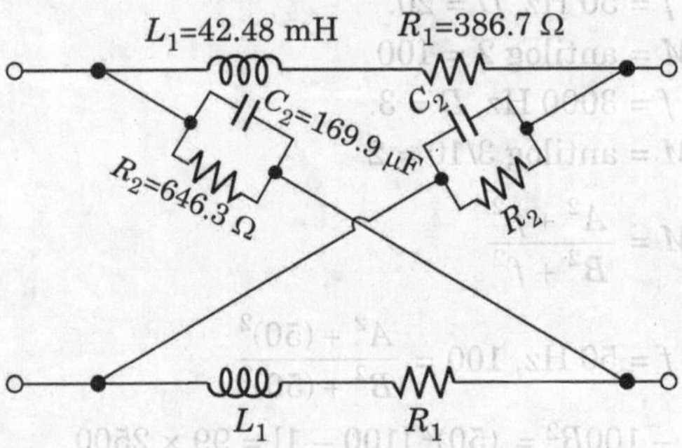

(*a*)

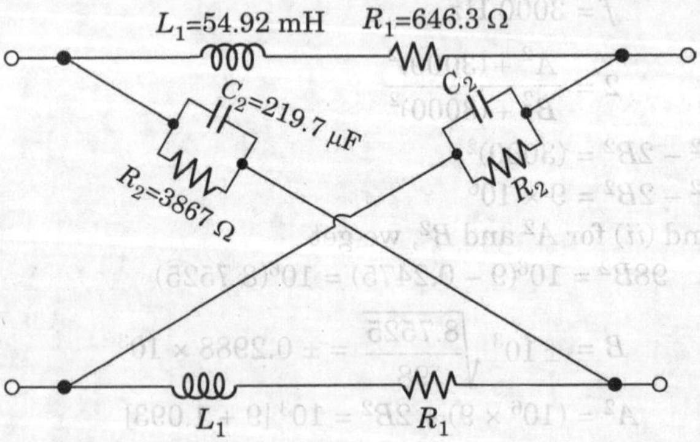

(*b*)

But $$R_1 R_2 = R_0^2$$

Hence $$R_2 = \frac{R_0^2}{R_1} = \frac{250{,}000}{386.7 \text{ or } 646.3} = 646.3 \text{ or } 386.7\ \Omega.$$

Further $$\frac{L_1}{C_2} = R_0^2$$

Hence $$C_2 = \frac{L_1}{R_0^2} = \frac{L_1}{(500)^2} = \frac{42.48 \text{ or } 54.92}{250{,}000} \text{ F}$$

$= 169.9\ \mu F$ or $219.7\ \mu F$.

Thus the equalizer has the configuration and values shown below:

M at 500 Hz is given by,

$$M = \frac{A^2 + (500)^2}{B^2 + (500)^2} = \frac{(10.093 \times 10^6) + (25 \times 10^4)}{(0.2988 \times 10^3) + (25 \times 10^4)}$$

$$= 34.48$$

$$\text{Loss in dB} = 10 \log 30.38 = 14.48 \text{ dB}.$$

REVIEW QUESTIONS

25.1. (*a*) What is meant by an equalizer?
(*b*) What is the difference between amplitude equalizer and phase equalizer?
(*c*) Describe typical types of attenuation and phase equalizers. Discuss their applications in line communication. (*Grad. I.T.E., May, 1968*)

25.2. (*a*) What is an equalizer?
(*b*) How does it differ from a filter or an attenuator?
(*c*) Describe some of its applications.
(*d*) Explain the working pf any one type of equahzer.
(*Grad. I.T.E., May, 1973*)

25.3. (*a*) Enumerate the various two terminal and four terminal equalizers.
(*b*) What are the principal applications of equalizers?

25.4. Describe the working of one type of equalizer used in transmission lines. What is the purpose of using equalizers?
(*Grad. I.T.E., May, 1972*)

25.5. Explain what is meant by "inverse network". Illustrate by giving simple example. (*Grad. I.T.E. May 1960, May, 1966*)

25.6. (*a*) What is meant by the term "inverse impedance"?
(*b*) Derive a network configuration which is inverse of (*i*) a series *R–L* circuit (*ii*) series *R–C* circuit.

25.7. Draw the network configuration which is inverse of the network shown in Fig. (*a*) and obtain expressions for the elements of the inverse network in terms of the elements of the given network.

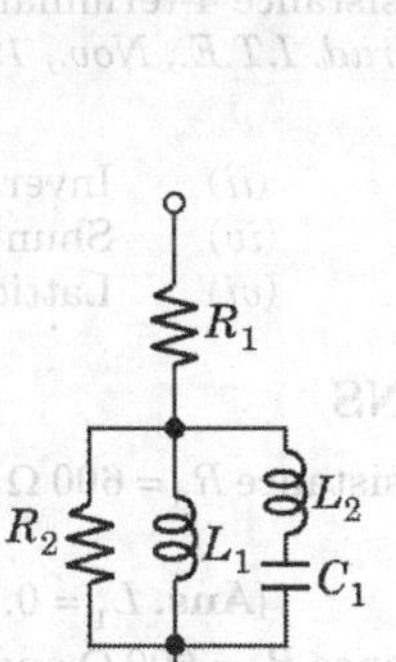

Fig. (*a*)

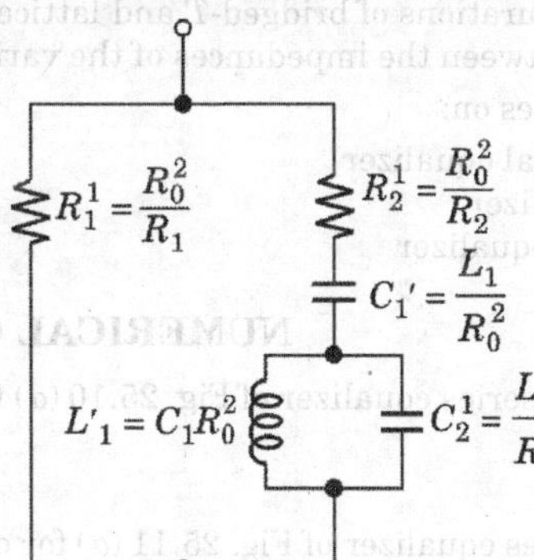

Fig. (*b*)

[**Ans.** Fig. (*b*) shows the inverse network along with the expression for its elements]

25.8. Which are the four types of constant resistance equalizers used in practice? Illustrate your answer with sketches. Explain their use in communication system.(*Grad. I.T.E., May, 1962, 63, 64*)

26.9. Derive an expression for the loss curve of a constant resistance equahzer. (*Grad. I.T.E., May, 1961, 63, 64, 66, Nov., 1967*)

27.10. Explain in detail with the help of diagrams, the working of a constant resistance equalizer. Explain why this equalizer is called constant resistance equahzer.(*Grad. I.T.E., Nov., 1968, May, 1969*)

28.11. Design constant resistance equahzer having 10 dB loss as the maxi-mum at frequency 8.5 kHz and to match 600–600 ohms.

25.12. Derive the design equations for the 2-terminal series and shunt equalizers. Why are the four-terminal equalizers preferred over 2-terminal equahzers?

25.13. Explain the need of attenuation equalizer network in telephone communication. Give configurations of any four-terminal attenuation equalizer working between two equal resistances. (*Grad., I.T.E., 1961*)

25.14. Derive the design equations for the equalizer for use with the unloaded telephone cable. (*AM.I.E., May, 1965*)

25.15. Give the circuit configuration of full series equalizer and develop its design equations for the following two cases: (*i*) $X_1 = \omega L_1$ and (*ii*) $X_1 = \dfrac{1}{\omega L_1}$. Draw the attenuation *versus* frequency characteristics for the two cases.

25.16 Give the circuit configuration of full shunt equalizer and develope its design equations for the following two cases: (*i*) $X_1 = \omega L_1$ and (*ii*) $X_1 = \dfrac{1}{\omega L_1}$. Draw the attenuation *versus* frequency characteristics for the above two cases.

25.17. Derive the design equations for the bridged-*T* delay equalizer.

(*A.M.I.E., May, 1971*)

25.18. Draw the circuit diagrams of two bridged-*T* networks out of which one is meant for tone control in audio frequency reproduction system while the other is meant for equalizing delay in facimile and signal transmission over lines. Give brief explanatory description of the working of these two networks. (*A.M.I.E., May, 1971*)

25.19. Derive expressions for the characteristic impedance Z_0 and propagation constant P of a constant resistance lattice equalizer. Prove that α remains unaffected when the positions of Z_1 and Z_2 in the lattice are interchanged. What is the effect on β?

(*Grad. I.T.E., May, 1963, Nov., 1965; A.M.I.E., Nov., 1970*)

25.20. Give the configurations of bridged-*T* and lattice constant resistance 4-terminal equalizers. Show the relationship between the impedances of the various arms.(*Grad. I.T.E., Nov., 1964*)

25.21. Write short notes on:

(*i*) Two terminal equalizer (*ii*) Inverse impedance

(*iii*) Delay equalizer (*iv*) Shunt equalizer

(*v*) Bridged-*T* equalizer (*vi*) Lattice equalizer.

NUMERICAL QUESTIONS

25.1. Design the full series equalizer of Fig. 25.10 (*a*) for design resistance $R_0 = 600\ \Omega$ and attenuation of 16 dB at 800 Hz.

[**Ans.** $L_1 = 0.7437$ H; $C_2 = 2.06\ \mu$F]

25.2. Design the series equalizer of Fig. 25.11 (*a*) for design resistance $R_0 = 600\ \Omega$ and attenuation of 20 dB at 400 Hz. Calculate the attenuation M at 1000 Hz.[**Ans.** $L_2 = 24$ mH, $C_1 = 0.66\ \mu$F, $M = 16.84$]

25.3. Design the full shunt equalizer of Fig. 25.13 (*a*) for design resistance $R_0 = 600\ \Omega$ and attenuation of 8 dB at 800 Hz. Calculate the attenuation at frequencies of 1200 Hz and 1800 Hz.

[**Ans.** $L_1 = 0.272$ H; $C_2 = 0.756\ \mu$F; $M_1 = 12.68$; $M_2 = 27.281$]

25.4. Design the full shunt equahzer of Fig. 25.13 (*b*) for design resistance $R_0 = 600\ \Omega$ and attenuation of 10 dB at 600 Hz. Calculate the attenuation at 1500 Hz and 3000 Hz.

[**Ans.** $C_1 = 0.1474\ \mu$F; $L_2 = 0.053$ H; $M_1 = 2.44$; $M_2 = 1.36$]

25.5. The shunt arm qf a constant resistance lattice attenuation equalizer used with a line of characteristic impedance $Z_0 = 600\ \Omega$ consists of a resistor 1000 Ω in parallel with a capacitor of 0.2 μF. Find the series arm. **[Ans.** R_1 = 360 Ω; L_2 = 72 mH]

25.6. A constant resistance lattice attenuation equahzer has series arm consisting of a resistor R_1 = 1100 Ω and capacitor C_1 = 0.02 μF. The resistance of the shunt arm is 250 Ω. Compute the characteristic impedance and the inductance of the shunt arm.

[Ans. R_0 = 500 Ω; L_2 = 5 mH]

25.7. In a constant resistance lattice attenuation equahzer having characteristic resistance of 10 Ω, the diagonal arm consists of a resistance R_2 of 50 Ω in series with an inductor L_2 = 1 mH. Find the series arm. **[Ans.** R_1 = Ω, **C**$_1$ = 10 μF; R_1 and C_2 are in parallel]

25.8. In a constant resistance lattice attenuation equahzer having characteristic impedance of R_0 = 600 Ω, the series arm consists of a resistor R_1 = R_0 in the series with an inductor L_1. If the insertion loss is 6 dB at 1200 Hz, calculate the values of the elements of the equalizer. **[Ans.** R_2 = 600 Ω; L_1 = 0.092 H; C_2 = 0.255 μF; R_2 and C_2 are in parallel]

26

Artificial Lines

26.1. Introduction

In laboratory testing of equipments like telegraph relays, telephone repeaters etc. we often need transmission lines several kilometres long with the two ends terminating in the laboratory. The need of physical line of such a length may be avoided by use of an artificial line formed by placing a lumped network to simulate the actual transmission line. Of course, such an equivalence is usually valid for a single frequency. Exact simulation over a band of frequencies is rather difficult. Further phase shift error gets introduced. Correction factor is then needed for each network element. Formation of entire artificial line consists in determining the elements in a section and the number of such sections.

Any desired length of line may be built on adding proper number of networks in cascade. With artificial line designed for equivalence at a certain frequency f_1, the equivalence will be valid also for any lower frequency.

26.2. Design of Artificial Lines

Fig. 26.1 shows two forms of lumped circuit equivalents of a transmission line. In both T and π type equivalent circuit representations of a transmission line,

$$\text{Series arm impedance} = Zl \quad \text{...(26.1)}$$

$$\text{Shunt arm admittance} = yl \quad \text{...(26.2)}$$

where Z is the series arm impedance per unit length, y is the shunt arm admittance per unit length of transmission line and l is the length of the line.

But the total series arm impedance of the equivalent T circuit of Fig. 26.1 (a) is given by,

$$Z_1 = 2Z_0 \tanh \frac{\gamma l}{2} \quad \text{...(26.3)}$$

where Z_0 is the characteristic impedance and γ is the propagation constant.

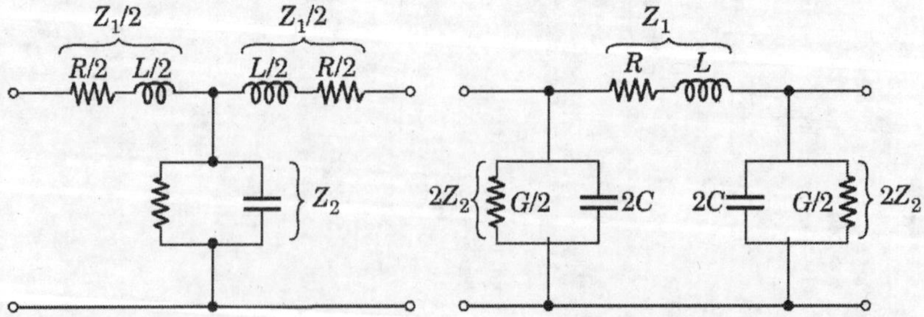

(a) T-equivalent circuit (b) π-equivalent circuit

Fig. 26.1. T and π-equivalent circuits of a transmission line.

The shunt arm impedance of the equivalent circuits is given by,

$$Z_2 = \frac{Z_0}{\sinh \gamma l} \quad \text{...(26.4)}$$

Eqs. (26.3) and (26.4) may be rewritten as,

$$\frac{Z_1}{2} = Z_0 \frac{\gamma l}{2}\left[\frac{\tanh \gamma l}{\gamma l/2}\right] \quad \text{...(26.5)}$$

$$= \frac{\gamma l}{2}\left[\frac{\tanh \gamma l}{\gamma l/2}\right] \quad \text{...(26.6)}$$

and

$$y_2 = \frac{1}{Z_2} = \frac{\gamma l}{Z_0}\left[\frac{\sinh \gamma l}{\gamma l}\right] \quad \text{...(26.7)}$$

$$= \gamma l\left[\frac{\sinh \gamma l}{\gamma l}\right] \quad \text{...(26.8)}$$

Eqs. (26.6) and (26.8) make use of the relations.

$$Z_0 = \sqrt{\frac{Z}{y}} \text{ and } \gamma = \sqrt{Zy}.$$

On comparing Eqs. (26.6) and (26.8) with Eqs. (26.1) and (26.2) we find that the original series impedance Z_1 and the shunt admittance Y_2 need to be modified to get the exact equivalent circuit. Thus in order to get an exact equivalence, the impedances of the series arms have to be multiplied by a factor tanh $(\gamma l/2)/(\gamma l/2)$ while the admittance of the shunt arm has to be multiplied by sinh $(\gamma l/2)/\gamma l$. These factors are called the *correction factors*.

Proceeding in the above manner, we may obtain expressions for the correction factors needed in π-type equivalent circuit. Thus for π-type equivalent circuit, the correction factor for series arm impedance is sinh $\gamma l/\gamma l$ while the correction factor for shunt arm admittance is tanh $(\gamma l/2)/(\gamma l/2)$.

26.3. Applications of Physical and Artificial Lines

Physical and artificial transmission lines are put to a variety of uses such as :

(*i*) In laboratories to simulate a long physical transmission line.

(*ii*) In network analyzer for analyzing power system.

(*iii*) As pulse generator and time delay circuit in radar and television systems.

(*iv*) As balancing network for circuits using hybrid coils.

(*v*) As filter section at high frequencies.

(*vi*) As variable attenuator for comparison in attenuation and in measurement of transmission losses.

(*vii*) For display of varying attenuation and phase over a wide range of frequencies.

26.4. Line a Filter Section

At very high frequencies, it is difficult to fabricate lumped circuit elements such as coils and capacitors since the values required are very low while the interconnecting wires have large capacitance.

Line as a Band-pass Filter. A small section of a high frequency lossless line is equivalent to either a capacitor or an inductor when the far end of the line is either open circuited or short circuited. The impedance of such an inductor or capacitor may assume any value from zero to infinity. Thus any high quality line such as coaxial line may be made to present at its input terminal any desired low or high value of inductance or capacitance. Such an arrangement using a transmission line as L or C at very high frequencies permits us to obtain such high value of circuit Q as are not obtainable through use of conventional lumped L or C.

(*a*) **Stub Band Pass Filter.** A stub of suitably arranged coaxial line may be used as a filter section. Fig. 26.2 (*a*) shows cross-section of a stub of coaxial line. Such a device acts as a band-pass filter with multiple pass bands. The pass band so obtained is wide compared to that obtainable with conventional filters. Accordingly such a stub filter is referred to as *multiple wideband filter*. Fig. 26.2 (*b*) shows the electrical equivalent circuit, where Z_1, Z_2 and Z_3 are the impedances of sections a_1, a_2 and a_3 of the stub.

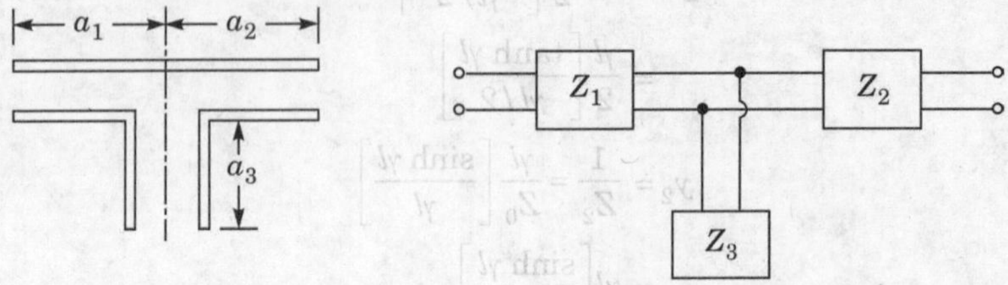

(*a*) Cross section (*b*) Electrical equivalent circuit

Fig. 26.2. Coaxial stub band pass filter and its equivalent circuit.

(*b*) **Line as Low pass Filter using radial metallic disc.** Fig. 26.3 *(a)* shows a piece of coaxial line with a metallic disc placed radially. The disc is connected with the central wire and insulated from the outer conductor by an insulating sleeve. Fig. 26.3 (*b*) shows the electrical equivalent circuit. The two sections a_1 and a_2 of the coaxial line on either side of the disc form inductances indicated by impedances Z_1 and Z_2 and a capacitance C as shown in Fig. 26.3 (*b*). This constitutes a low pass filter.

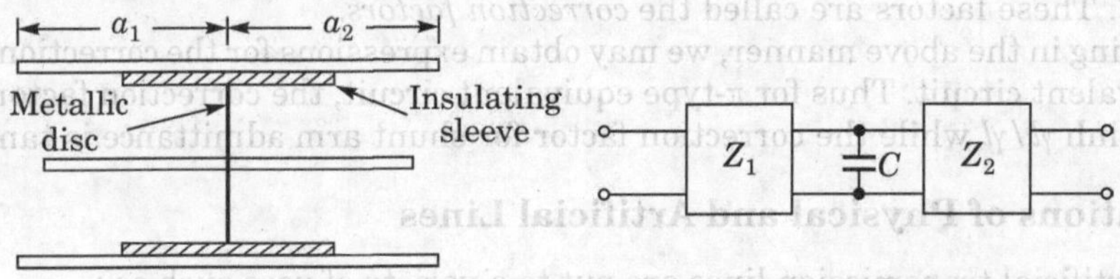

(*a*) Cross-section (*b*) Electrical equivalent circuit

Fig. 26.3. Coaxial line as low pass filter using radial metallic disc.

(*c*) **Coaxial line as low pass filter using four discs.** Fig. 26.4 (*a*) gives the cross-sectional view of a section of coaxial line with 4 metallic discs arranged as shown. Fig. 26.4 (*b*) gives its electrical equipment circuit. The equivalent circuit provides a band pass filter action.

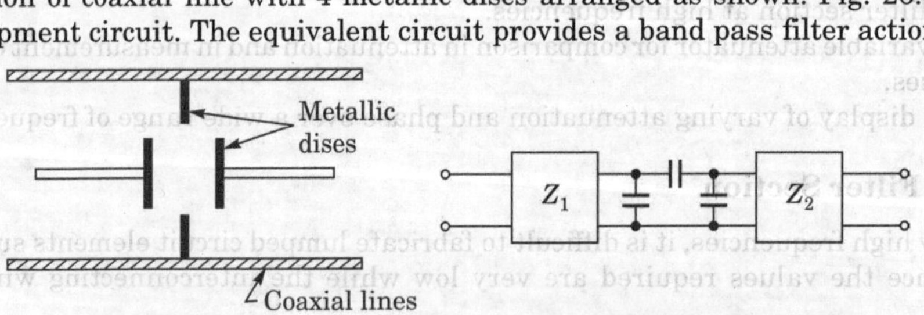

(*a*) Cross-section (*b*) Electrical equivalent circuit

Fig. 26.4. Coaxial line band pass filter using four discs.

26.5. Transmission Line as a Pulse Generator

There are various types of periodic pulses such as rectangular, saw tooth, triangular, trapezoidal etc. Out of these, the rectangular pulse is the most fundamental and all other pulses may be obtained from it through operations such as differentiation, integration etc.

Fig. 26.5 shows a true rectangular voltage pulse of total magnitude say V_0 volts extending from zero to + V_0. In an ideal rectangular pulse, the rise and decay times are zero. Hence an ideal rectangular pulse may be considered as the summation or subtraction of two step voltages.

Thus if a positive step voltage of $+V_0$ volts at time $t = t_1$ is added to a negative step voltage $-V_0$ at time $t = t_2$ as shown in Fig. 26.5 (*b*), the resulting signal is the rectangular pulse of Fig. 26.5 (*a*).

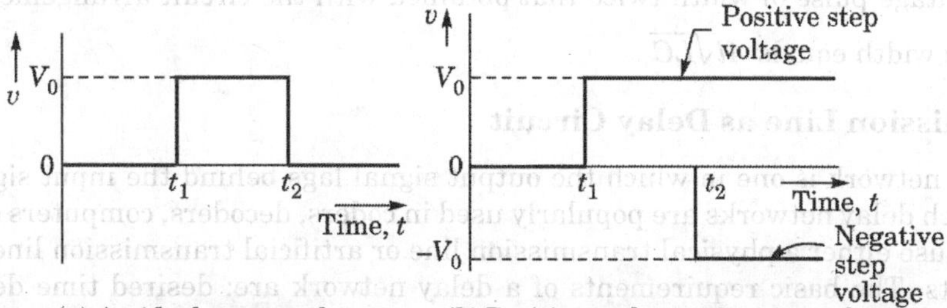

(*a*) An ideal rectangular voltage pulse (*b*) Positive and negative step voltages added to yield a pulse

Fig. 26.5. Formation of an ideal rectangular voltage pulse.

Thus if after the application of a positive step voltage V_0 at time t_1, the same is subtracted at time t_2, the resulting net voltage is a rectangular pulse. The application of a step voltage is a kind of transient which quickly adjusts itself to a steady state.

Such transient conditions when established in a lossless transmission line result in formation of rectangular pulse. In a transmission line of length l, inductance L per unit length and capacitance C per unit length, the length of the rectangular pulse so formed will be $2l\sqrt{LC}$. The magnitude of the rectangular pulse will be V_0 where V_0 is the initial voltage distribution. It is assumed, however, that the primary constants R and G of the line are zero. Thus in a lossless transmission line, the pulse width depends on the length of the line while the pulse magnitude V_0 depends on the voltage applied to the line.

Fig. 26.6 (*a*) shows a transmission line used as a pulse forming network. If switch S_1 is closed and S_2 is opened, the line charges to say voltage V_0. Let at time $t = t_1$, switch S_1 be suddenly opened and S_2 be closed. This results in a rectangular voltage pulse across the resistor R_0 connected across the output terminals. The duration of the pulse is $2l\sqrt{LC}$.

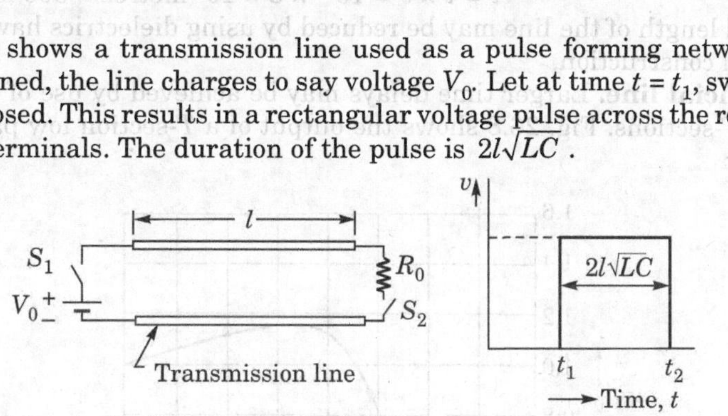

(*a*) Circuit rectangular (*b*) Resulting output voltage pulse

Fig. 26.6. Transmission line as pulse forming network.

Usual coaxial line needed for such a purpose would be very large since we need a length of about 300 metres for 1 μs pulse width. In order to reduce the requirement of length of line, the inner conductor of the coaxial line is made in the form of a helix wound on an insulated core running along the axis of the cable. Such an inner conductor has high inductance. Hence such a coaxial line is usually referred to as a *high impedance coaxial line.* Only about one metre length of such a line is needed to produce a pulse of 1 μs width. The switches S_1 and S_2 may be mechanical, electronic or even an artificial line.

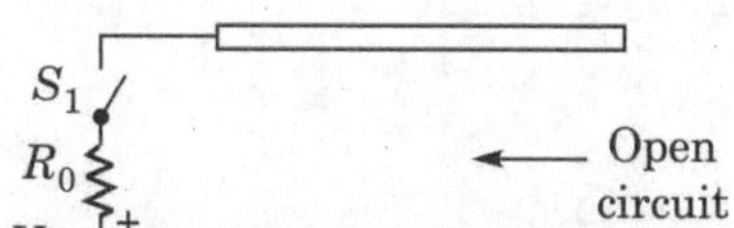

Fig. 26.7. Alternative arrangement of transient line functioning as pulse forming network.

Fig. 26.7 shows an alternative arrangement. Here the load impedance R_0 is placed across the sending end of the line and the far end is open circuited. Hence the transient formed on closing the switch S_1 travels to the open circuited far end, gets reflected to reach the sending end and reduces to zero. This result in a rectangular voltage pulse of width twice that obtained with the circuit arrangement of Fig. 26.6. Thus the pulse width equals $4l\sqrt{LC}$.

26.6. Transmission Line as Delay Circuit

A delay network is one in which the output signal lags behind the input signal by a finite time delay. Such delay networks are popularly used in coders, decoders, computers etc. Such delay networks may use either a physical transmission line or artificial transmission line using lumped circuit elements. The basic requirements of a delay network are: desired time delay, minimum distortion, stability, size and cost.

In a lossless line, the velocity of propagation of electromagnetic waves is given by,

$$v = \frac{3 \times 10^8}{\sqrt{\mu_r \cdot \varepsilon_r}} \text{ m/s} \qquad ...(26.9)$$

where μ_r is the relative permeability

and θ_r is the relative dielectric constant.

With air as the dielectric,

$$\mu_r = 1 \quad \text{and} \quad \varepsilon_r = 1.$$

Hence as per Eq. (26.9), the velocity of propagation is,

$$v = 3 \times 10^8 \text{ m/s.}$$

Hence for 1 μs time delay, the length of the line required is,

$$l = t \times v = 10^{-6} \times 3 \times 10^8 \text{ metres} = 300 \text{ metres.}$$

The required length of the line may be reduced by using dielectrics having higher μ_r and ε_r and by using helical construction.

Use of artificial line. Larger time delays may be achieved by use of lumped parameters and using several T-sections. Fig. 26.8 shows the output of a T-section low pass filter using unit step input signal. It

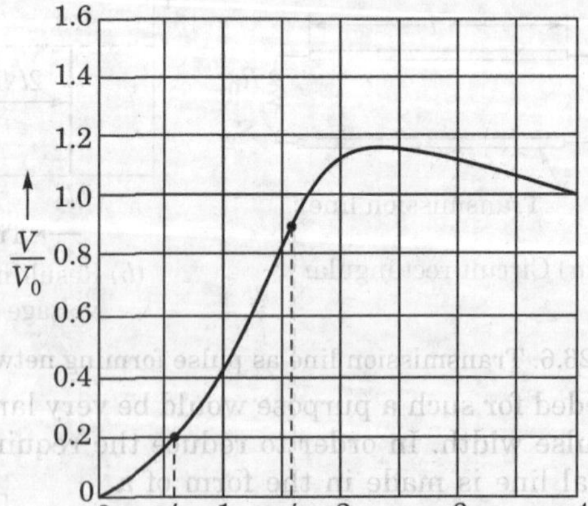

Fig. 26.8. Response of a T-section low pass filter using unit step input signal

may be seen that the output voltage rises at first slowly and then rapidly, reaches a maximum and then decreases gradually to finally reach the steady state value V_0. The rise time t_r is defined as the time taken by the output to rise from 10% to 90% of the steady state value V_0. For the curve of

Fig. 26.8 for a single T-section low pass filter, this rise time is given by,

$$ut_r = 1.65 - 0.52 = 1.13$$

where $$u = \frac{1}{\sqrt{LC}}.$$

Hence rise time $$t_r = 1.13\sqrt{LC} \qquad ...(26.10)$$

The delay time t_d is defined as the time taken by the output voltage to rise to 50% of its steady state value. From Fig. 26.8, for a single T-section low pass filter, for unit step input, the delay time is,

$$ut_d = 1.07$$

Hence $$t_d = 1.07\sqrt{LC} \qquad ...(26.11)$$

Design of lumped parameter delay line. The design parameters are: characteristic impedance R_0, total delay time t_d, and effective rise time t_r. With n similar lumped parameter networks connected in cascade, the total delay time is given by,

$$T_d = nt_d \qquad ...(26.12)$$

It is assumed that the rise time varies approximately as the cube root of n, the number of sections.

Hence $$T_d = t_r \cdot n^{1/3} \qquad ...(26.13)$$

Combining Eqs. (26.12) and (26.13), we get,

$$\frac{T_d}{T_r} = n^{2/3}\left(\frac{t_d}{t_r}\right)$$

Hence $$n\left(\frac{T_d}{T_r}\right)^{3/2}\left(\frac{t_r}{t_d}\right)^{3/2} \qquad ...(26.14)$$

But from Eqs. (26.10) and (26.11), we get

$$\frac{t_r}{t_d} = \frac{1.13}{1.07} = 1.06 \qquad ...(26.15)$$

Combining Eqs. (26.14) and (26.15), we get

$$n = \left(\frac{T_d}{T_r}\right)^{3/2}(1.06)^{3/2} = 1.1\left(\frac{T_d}{T_r}\right)^{3/2} \qquad ...(26.16)$$

Eq. (26.16) gives the required number of similar lumped sections to be used for specified delay time t_d and rise time t_r.

For a lossless line,

$$R_0 = \sqrt{\frac{L}{C}} \qquad ...(26.17)$$

Hence $$L = CR_0^2$$

Substituting this value of L in Eq. (26.11), we get

$$t_d = 1.07\sqrt{CR_0^2C} = 1.07CR_0$$

But $$t_d = \frac{T_d}{n}.$$

Hence $$\frac{T_d}{n} = 1.07CR_0.$$

Hence $$C = \frac{T_d}{1.07nR_0} \qquad ...(26.20)$$

Substituting this value of C in Eq. (26.18), we get

$$\frac{L}{R_0^2} = \frac{T_d}{1.07nR_0}$$

Hence $$L = \frac{R_0 T_d}{1.07n} \qquad ...(26.21)$$

Equations (26.16), (26.20) and (26.21) form the design equations for the multisection lumped parameter delay line.

Example 26.1. *Design an artificial line to simulate an actual transmission line whose distributed constants are :*

$$R = 10\ \Omega/\text{loop km};\ L = 3.8\ \text{mH}/\text{loop km}$$
$$C = 0.007\ \mu\text{F}/\text{km};\ G = 1\ \mu\text{S}/\text{km}.$$

Frequency range of operation extends from 300 Hz to 6 kHz. Overall phase shift should be within 0.1 radian.

Solution. The attenuation constant α and phase constant β both vary with frequency. Hence the artificial line should be designed for the highest frequency of operation namely 6 kHz, where α and β will have the largest values. This permits determination of length l of line to meet the condition that αl and βl are small. Hence γl is also small and Eqs. (26.1) and (26.2) may be used to design the artificial line.

The propagation constant γ is given by

$$v = \sqrt{(R + j\omega L)(G + j\omega C)}$$

Thus $$\omega = 2\pi f = 2\pi \times 6 \times 10^3 = 37.7 \times 10^3$$

Substituting the values of R, L, C and G, we get

$$\gamma = \sqrt{(10 + j37.7 \times 10^3 \times 3.8 \times 10^{-3})(1 + j37.7 \times 10^3 \times 0.007) \times 10^{-6}}$$

$$= \sqrt{(10 + j143.26)(1 + j263.9) \times 10^{-6}}$$

or $$\gamma = \sqrt{143.6\underline{/86^\circ} \times 264\ \underline{/90^\circ} \times 10^{-6}} = 194.7\ \underline{/88^\circ} \times 10^{-3}$$

or $$\alpha + j\beta = (6.795 + j194.58) \times 10^{-3}$$
$$= (0.0068 + j0.195)/\text{km}$$

Hence $$\beta = 0.195\ \text{radian/km}.$$

But the overall shift *i.e.* βl has to be less than 0.1.

Thus $$\beta l < 0.1$$

or $$l < \frac{0.1}{0.195} = 0.5128\ \text{km}.$$

For convenience of design we may take $l = 0.5$ km. Then in the equivalent T-network, the series impedance in each arm is,

$$\frac{Z_1}{2} = \frac{Zl}{2} = \frac{(R + j\omega L)}{2} \times \frac{1}{2} = \frac{R}{4} + j\omega\frac{L}{4}$$

and shunt element is $$Z_2 = \frac{1}{YL} = \frac{1}{(G + j\omega C)^{1/2}} = \frac{1}{0.5G + j0.5\omega C}$$

The section of the desired artificial line is then as shown.

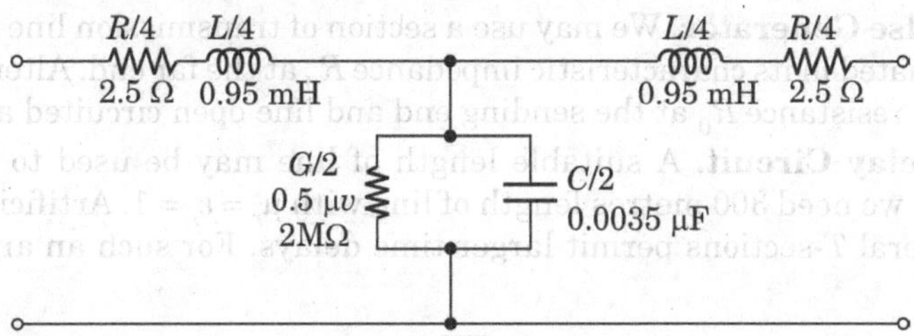

Example 26.2. *Design a delay line using T-sections with characteristic impedance R_0 = 600 Ω, total delay time of 1.5 µs and rise time of 0.4 µs.*

Solution. $R_0 = 600\ \Omega$; $T_d = 1.2 \times 10^{-6}$ sec

$$T_r = 0.4 \times 10^{-6} \text{ sec.}$$

Let n be the number of T-sections used.

Then $$n = 1.1\left(\frac{T_d}{T_r}\right)^{1.5} = 1.1\left(\frac{1.2\times10^{-6}}{0.4\times10^{-6}}\right)^{1.6} = 5.716$$

Hence the number of sections to be used may be taken as 6.

Hence $$C = \frac{T_d}{1.07nR_0}$$

$$= \frac{1.2\times10^{-6}}{1.07\times6\times600} \text{ F} = 0.00031\ \mu\text{F}$$

and $$L = \frac{R_0T_d}{1.07n}$$

$$= \frac{600\times1.2\times10^{-6}}{1.07\times6}\quad L = 0.112 \text{ mF}$$

$$\frac{L}{2} = 0.056 \text{ mH.}$$

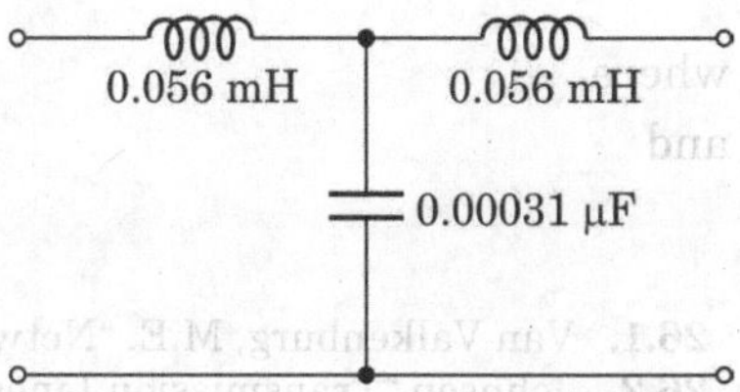

Hence each of the desired 6 T-sections connected in cascade is as shown.

SUMMARY

Applications of Physical and Artificial Lines

(*i*) in laboratories to simulate a long physical transmission line
(*ii*) in network analyzer
(*iii*) as pulse generator
(*iv*) as time delay circuit
(*v*) as balancing network in circuits using hybrid coils
(*vi*) as filter section at high frequencies
(*vii*) as variable attenuator
(*viii*) for display of varying attenuation and phase over wide frequency range.

Line as a Bandpass Filter. A coaxial line may be used as a bandpass filter. Alternatively a coaxial line with four discs may be used.

Line as a Low Pass Filter. A coaxial line with radial metallic disc may be used as a low pass filter.

Line as a Pulse Generator. We may use a section of transmission line with source V_o at the input end and terminated in its characteristic impedance R_0 at the far end. Alternatively we may use a section of line with resistance R_0 at the sending end and line open circuited at the far end.

Line as a Delay Circuit. A suitable length of line may be used to produce the desired delay. For 1 μs delay we need 300 metres length of line with $\mu_r = \varepsilon_r = 1$. Artificial line using lumped parameters and several T-sections permit larger time delays. For such an artificial line, for each section

$$\text{rise time } t_r = 1.13\sqrt{LC}$$

$$\text{delay time } t_d = 1.07\sqrt{LC}$$

Design equations are:

$$n = 1.1\left(\frac{T_d}{T_r}\right)^{1.5}$$

$$C = \frac{T_d}{1.07nR_0}$$

$$L = \frac{R_0 T_d}{1.07n}$$

where $T_d = nt_d$

and $t_r = t_r n^{1/3}$

REFERENCES

26.1. Van Valkenburg, M.E. "Network Analysis", Prentice Hall of India Pvt. Ltd., New Delhi, 1974.
26.2. Johnson "Transmission Lines and Networks", McGraw Hill Kogakusha Ltd., Tokyo.
26.3. Hancock "An Introduction to the Principles of Communication Theory", McGraw Hill Book Company.

REVIEW QUESTIONS

26.1. Comment on the need of artificial lines in communication systems.
26.2. What are the principal applications of physical and artificial lines in communication systems?
26.3. Describe the use of a transmission line as a bandpass filter.
26.4. Describe the use of a transmission line as a low pass filter.
26.5. Describe the use of a transmission line as a pulse generator.
26.6. (*a*) Describe how a transmission line may be used as a delay circuit.
(*b*) Describe the use of artificial line for producing large time delays.
26.7. Establish the design equations for lumped parameter delay line.

NUMERICAL QUESTIONS

26.1. Design an artificial line to simulate an actual transmission line whose distributed constants are:

R = 12 Ω/loop km ; L = 4.2 mH/loop km
C = 0.01 μF/km ; G = 1.2 μS/km.

Frequency range of operation extends from 300 Hz to 5.4 kHz. Overall phase shift should be within 0.12 radian.

[**Ans.** In the T network; Each series arm has resistor = 3.24 Ω and inductor = 1.134 mH. The shunt arm has resistor 1.5432 Ω in parallel with C = 0.0054 μF]

26.2. Design a delay line having T-sections with characteristic impedance R_0 = 400 Ω, total delay time of 1.5 μs and rise time of 0.6 μs.

[**Ans.** Each series arm inductance L = 0.07 mH, Shunt arm capacitance C = 0.000876 μF]

27

Synthesis of One-Port L-C Networks

27.1. Introduction

So far we have dealt with the analysis of a given network *i.e.* finding the response $R(s)$ *i.e.* output of a given network to excitation $E(s)$ at the input terminals. Now we take up briefly the subject of network synthesis which concerns itself with the evaluation of elements of a network from the knowledge of excitation $E(s)$ and the response $R(s)$. Instead of excitation and response, usually the driving point immittance (*i.e.* impedance or admittance) is given and the network elements are determined from the knowledge of this immittance. Such a synthesis is called *driving point synthesis.*

The basic principle of driving point synthesis is to break up the driving point immittance $I(s)$ into a sum of simpler positive real functions and then synthesize these individual functions as elements of overall network characterized by driving point immittance $I(s)$.

Three types of passive elements are resistor R, inductor L and capacitor C. Accordingly we may take up synthesis of these *R-L*, *R-C* or *L-C* networks. In this chapter we take the study of properties of one-port *L-C* networks and take up the synthesis of such networks.

27.2. Reactive Networks

Since an *L-C* one-port network contains no resistive elements, it is said to be *dissipationless.* The driving point immittance (either impedance or admittance) may be found by combining impedance or admittance expression for the elements in the network. Thus an inductor L has impedance of Ls and admittance $\frac{1}{Ls}$. A capacitor C has impedance of $\frac{1}{Cs}$ admittance of Cs.

Any given network, how so ever complicated, may be split up into either series or parallel combination of *L-C* elements.

Let the entire network be found by series combination of a number of L and C, elements as shown in Fig. 27.1 (*a*). Then the total impedance of this combination is given by,

$$Z_1(s) = Z_1(s) + Z_2(s) + \dots + Z_n(s) \qquad \dots(27.1)$$

or

$$Z_t(s) = (L_1 + L_2 + \dots)s + \left(\frac{1}{C_1} + \frac{1}{C_2} + \dots\right)\frac{1}{s} \qquad \dots(27.2)$$

$$= L_{eq}s + \frac{1}{C_{eq}s} \qquad \dots(27.3)$$

where L_{eq} is the equivalent inductance of the series system and C_{eq} is the equivalent capacitance of the series system. Hence the series combination of L and C may be represented by L_{eq} in series with C_{eq} as shown in Fig. 27.1 (*a*).

Eq. (27.3) may be written as,

$$Z_t(s) = L_{eq} \cdot \frac{s^2 + \dfrac{1}{L_{eq}C_{eq}}}{s} \qquad \text{...(27.4)}$$

Next consider the entire network to be formed by parallel combination of L and C elements as shown in Fig. 27.1 (*b*).

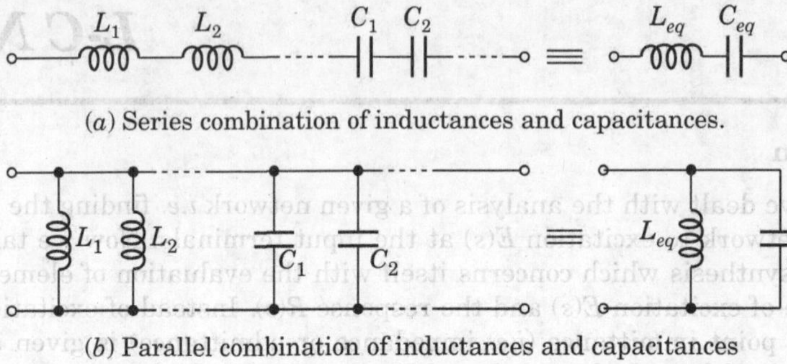

(*a*) Series combination of inductances and capacitances.

(*b*) Parallel combination of inductances and capacitances

Fig. 27.1. Equivalent impedance and admittance function representations.

Then the total admittance of this parallel combination is given by,

$$Y_t(s) = Y_1(s) + Y_2(s) + \ldots + Y_n(s) \qquad \text{...(27.5)}$$

or

$$Y_t(s) = (C_1 + C_2 + \ldots)s + \left(\frac{1}{L_1} + \frac{1}{L_2} + \ldots\right)\frac{1}{s} \qquad \text{...(27.6)}$$

$$= C_{eq}s + \frac{1}{L_{eq}s} \qquad \text{...(27.7)}$$

where C_{eq} is the equivalent capacitance of the parallel combination of elements and L_{eq} is the equivalent inductance of the parallel combination of elements.

Eq. (27.7) may be rewritten as,

$$Y_t(s) = C_{eq} \frac{s^2 + \dfrac{1}{L_{eq}C_{eq}}}{s} \qquad \text{...(27.8)}$$

Hence the parallel combination of L and C may be represented by L_{eq} in shunt with C_{eq} as shown in Fig. 27.1 (*b*).

Eq. (27.4) for $Z_t(s)$ and Eq. (27.8) for $Y_t(s)$ are similar in form, the only difference being in the multiplying constant.

From the above we conclude that (*a*) the driving point impedance for a complex network consisting of series elements may be got on adding the impedances and reciprocals of admittances, (*b*) the driving point admittance of a complex network consisting of parallel elements may be got on adding the admittances and the reciprocals of impedances.

Any given network may be arbitrarily divided into a number of series and parallel networks. Hence the expressions for driving point immittance is a combination of terms of the form of Eqs. (27.4) and (27.8) and their reciprocals.

Example 27.1. *Obtain the driving point impedance Laplace function for the given network.*

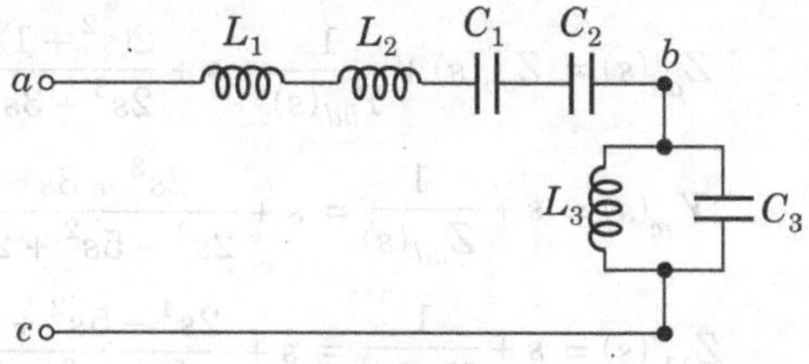

Fig. Ex. 27.1

Solution. The driving point impedance is given as,

$$Z_{ac} = Z_{ab} + \frac{1}{Y_{bc}} = (L_1 + L_2)s + \left(\frac{1}{C_1} + \frac{1}{C_2}\right)\frac{1}{s} + \frac{1}{C_3 s + \frac{1}{L_3 s}}$$

$$= L_{12}s + \frac{1}{C_{12}s} + \frac{1}{C_3 s + \frac{1}{L_3 s}}$$

where $$L_{12} = L_1 + L_2$$

and $$\frac{1}{C_{12}} = \frac{1}{C_1} + \frac{1}{C_2}$$

or $$Z_{ac} = L_{12}\frac{s^2 + \frac{1}{L_{12}C_{12}}}{s} + \frac{s}{C_3\left(s^2 + \frac{1}{L_3C_3}\right)}$$

$$= L_{12}\frac{s^4 + \left(\frac{1}{L_{12}C_{12}} + \frac{1}{L_3C_3} + \frac{1}{L_{12}C_3}\right)s^2 + \frac{1}{L_{12}L_3C_{12}C_3}}{s^3 + \frac{1}{L_3C_3}}$$

Example 27.2. *Obtain the driving point admittance Laplace function for the given network.*

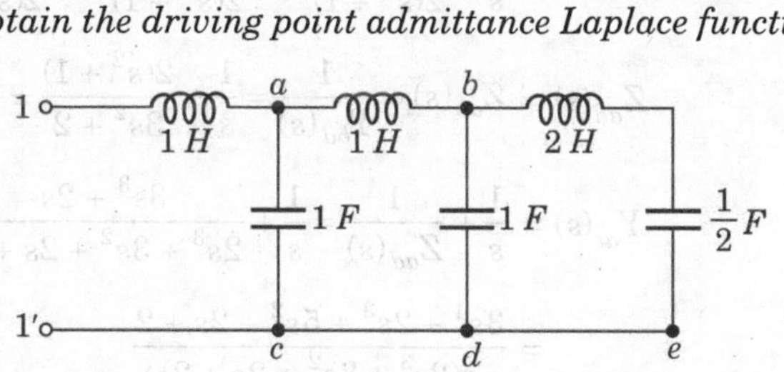

Fig. Ex. 27.2

Solution. The driving point admittance for this network may be found by placing the network elements into several series and parallel groups.

This impedance from node b to node e is given by,

$$Z_{be}(s) = 2s + \frac{2}{s} = \frac{2(s^2 + 1)}{s} \quad \text{...(1)}$$

Admittance between nodes b and d is,

$$Y_{bd}(s) = s + \frac{s}{2(s^2 + 1)} = \frac{2s^3 + 3s}{2(s^2 + 1)} \quad \text{...(2)}$$

$$Z_{ad}(s) = Z_{ab}(s) + \frac{1}{Y_{bd}(s)} = s + \frac{2(s^2+1)}{2s^3+3s} = \frac{2s^4+5s^2+2}{2s^3+3s}$$

$$Y_{ac}(s) = s + \frac{1}{Z_{ad}(s)} = s + \frac{2s^3+3s}{2s^4+5s^2+2} = \frac{2s^5+7s+5s}{2s^4+5s^2+2}$$

$$Z_{11}'(s) = s + \frac{1}{Y_{ac}(s)} = s + \frac{2s^4+5s^2+2}{2s^5+7s^3+5s} = \frac{2s^6+9s^4+10s^2+2}{2s^5+7s^3+5s}$$

$$Y_{11}'(s) = \frac{1}{Z_{11}'(s)} = \frac{2s^5+7s^3+5s}{2s^6+9s^4+10s^2+2}.$$

Example 27.3. *Obtain the driving point impedance function as a quotient of polynomials for the given network.*

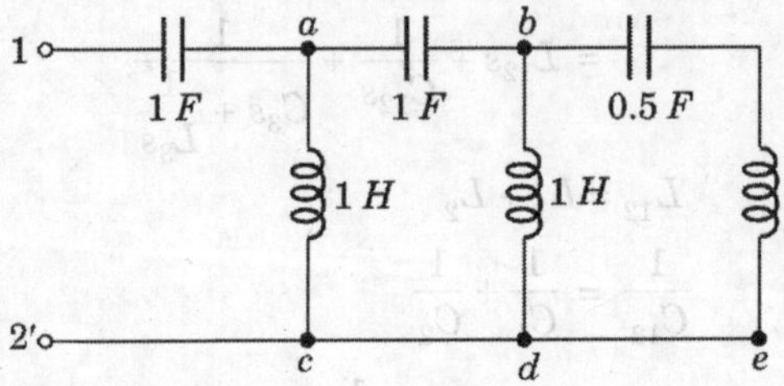

Fig. Ex. 27.3

Solution. The impedance between nodes b and e is given by,

$$Z_{be}(s) = \frac{2}{s} + 2s = \frac{2(s^2+1)}{s}$$

Admittance between nodes b and d is,

$$Y_{bd}(s) = \frac{1}{s} + \frac{s}{2(s^2+1)} = \frac{2s^2+2+s^2}{2(s^2+1)} = \frac{3s^2+2}{2(s^2+1)}$$

$$Z_{ad}(s) = Z_{ab}(s) + \frac{1}{Y_{bd}(s)} = \frac{1}{s} + \frac{2(s^2+1)}{3s^2+2} = \frac{3s^2+2+2s^3+2s}{(3s^2+2)s}$$

$$Y_{ac}(s) = \frac{1}{s} + \frac{1}{Z_{ad}(s)} = \frac{1}{s} + \frac{3s^3+2s}{2s^3+3s^2+2s+2}$$

$$= \frac{3s^4+2s^3+5s^2+2s+2}{s(2s^3+3s^2+2s+2)}$$

$$Z_{12}(s) = \frac{1}{s} + \frac{1}{Y_{ac}(s)} = \frac{1}{s} + \frac{2s^4+3s^3+2s^2+2s}{3s^4+2s^3+5s^2+2s+2}$$

$$= \frac{2s^5+6s^4+4s^3+7s^2+2s+2}{3s^5+2s^4+5s^3+2s^2+2s}.$$

Example 27.4. *Obtain the driving point admittance function as a quotient of polynomials for the given network.*

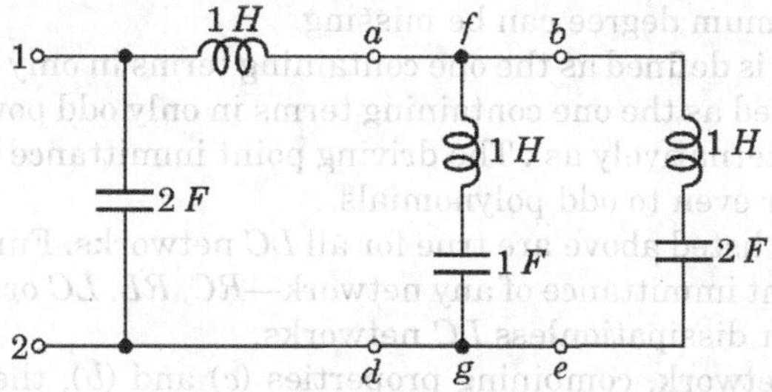

Fig. Ex. 27.4

Solution. Impedance between nodes *b* and *e* is,

$$Z_{be}(s) = s + \frac{1}{2s} = \frac{2s^2+1}{2s}$$

Admittance $$Y_{be}(s) = \frac{2s}{2s^2+1}$$

Impedance of 1*H* and 1 *F* in the shunt arm between nodes *f* and *g* is,

$$Z_{fg}(s) = s + \frac{1}{s} = \frac{s^2+1}{s}$$

Hence $$Y_{fg}(g) = \frac{s}{s^2+1}$$

Admittance between nodes *a* and *d* is,

$$Y_{ad}(s) = \frac{s}{s^2+1} + \frac{2s}{2s^2+1} = \frac{2s^3+s+2s^3+2s}{(s^2+1)(2s^2+1)} = \frac{4s^3+3s}{2s^4+3s^2+1}$$

$$Z_{ad}(s) = \frac{2s^4+3s^2+1}{4s^3+3s}$$

Impedance $$Z_{1d}(s) = s + Z_{ad}(s) = s + \frac{2s^4+3s^2+1}{4s^3+3s} = \frac{6s^4+6s^2+1}{4s^3+3s}$$

Admittance $$Y_{1d}(s) = \frac{4s^3+3s}{6s^4+6s^2+1}$$

Admittance $$Y_{12}(s) = \frac{1}{2s} + Y_{1d}(s) = \frac{1}{2s} + \frac{4s^3+3s}{6s^4+6s^2+1} = \frac{14s^4+12s^2+1}{12s^5+12s^3+2s}.$$

27.3. Common Features of Expressions for Driving Point Immittance

Study of various expressions for the driving point immittances physical *L–C* networks reveals the following properties :

(*a*) All expressions for driving point immittance, as well as the intermediate expressions, are quotients of polynomials in *s* with a constant multiplier.

(*b*) The orders of the numerator and denominator polynomials never differ by more than one.

(*c*) All terms in any polynomial are consistently either even power of *s* or odd powers of *s*. In addition, if the numerator polynomial contains terms in only even powers of *s*, then the denominator polynomial must contain terms in only even powers of *s* and *vice-versa.*

(*d*) In any polynomial with terms in even powers of *s*, no term of degree less than the maximum degree can be missing. Similarly in any polynomial with terms in odd powers of *s*, no terms of degree less than the maximum degree can be missing.

An *even polynomial* is defined as the one containing terms in only even powers of s. Similarly an *odd polynomial* is defined as the one containing terms in only odd powers of s. Hence statement (*c*) above may be stated alternatively as : The driving point immittance function quotient of either odd to even polynomials or even to odd polynomials.

The four properties listed above are true for all *LC* networks. Further properties (*a*) and (*b*) are true for all driving point immittance of any network—*RC, RL, LC* or *RLC*. However, properties (*c*) and (*d*) are true only for dissipationless *LC* networks.

Thus for an *L–C* network, combining properties (*c*) and (*b*), the driving point impedance function (so also driving point admittance function) may be written as a ratio of quotient of an even to odd polynomial as below :

$$Z(s) = \frac{a_{2n}s^{2n} + a_{2n-2}s^{2n-2} + \ldots + a_2 s^2 + a_0}{b_{2n-1}s^{2n-1} + b_{2n-3}s^{2n-3} + \ldots + b_1 s} \quad \ldots(27.9)$$

However with $a_0 = 0$, s may be factored out of both numerator and denominator so that the driving point function becomes a quotient of odd to even polynomials.

The numerator polynomial of Eq. (27.9) is an expression in s^2 and may be factored into its n roots. In the denominator polynomial, s is factored out and the rest of the polynomial may be factored into $(n — 1)$ roots in s^2. Hence Eq. (27.9) may be put as,

$$Z(s) = H\frac{(s^2 + s_1^2)(s^2 + s_3^2)\ldots(s^2 + s_{2n-1}^2)}{s(s^2 + s_2^2)(s^2 + s_4^2)\ldots(s^2 + s_{2n-2}^2)} \quad \ldots(27.10)$$

where H is a constant and is given by

$$H = \frac{a_{2n}}{b_{2n-1}} \quad \ldots(27.11)$$

Now consider the factor $(s^2 + s_1^2)$. This factor has two roots given by,

$$s^2 = -s_1^2$$

or

$$s = \pm js_1 \quad \ldots(27.12)$$

These roots are purely imaginary and indicate the radian frequency ω. Thus Eq. (27.12) may be put as,

$$s = \pm j\omega_1 \quad \ldots(27.13)$$

Every factor in the numerator and denominator of Eq. (27.10) yields two such imaginary roots.

On replacing s_n by ω_n, Eq. (27.10) may be put as,

$$Z(s) = \frac{H}{s}\cdot\frac{(s^2 + \omega_1^2)(s^2 + \omega_3^2)\ldots}{(s^2 + \omega_2^2)(s^2 + \omega_4^2)\ldots} \quad \ldots(27.14)$$

However, if $a_0 = 0$ in Eq. (27.9), the driving point impedance may be put as,

$$Z(s) = Hs\frac{(s^2 + \omega_2^2)(s^2 + \omega_4^2)\ldots}{(s^2 + \omega_1^2)(s^2 + \omega_3^2)\ldots} \quad \ldots(27.15)$$

Restricting our study only to the sinusoidal steady state, we may put $s = j\omega$ so that $s^2 = -\omega^2$. Hence Eq. (27.14) may be put as,

$$Z(j\omega) = \pm\frac{H}{j\omega}\cdot\frac{(\omega^2 - \omega_1^2)(\omega^2 - \omega_3^2)\ldots}{(\omega^2 - \omega_2^2)(\omega^2 - \omega_4^2)\ldots} \quad \ldots(27.16)$$

Similarly Eq. (26.15) may be put as,

$$Z(j\omega) = \pm j\omega H\cdot\frac{(\omega^2 - \omega_2^2)(\omega^2 - \omega_4^2)\ldots}{(\omega^2 - \omega_1^2)(\omega^2 - \omega_3^2)\ldots} \quad \ldots(27.17)$$

In Eqs. (27.16) and (27.17) the ± sign is introduced since more (– 1) factors may have been removed from the numerator than the denominator or *vice-versa.*

In sinusoidal steady state, the driving point immittance functions for a general *R-L-C* network are complex and are of the form,

$$Z(j\omega) = R(\omega) + jX(\omega) \qquad ...(27.18)$$

and

$$Y(j\omega) = G(\omega) + jB(\omega) \qquad ...(27.19)$$

However, for an *LC* network, $Z(j\omega)$ and $Y(j\omega)$ as given by Eqs. (27.16) and (27.17) are purely imaginary since $(\omega^2 - \omega_n^2)$ terms are always real and constant *H* is always real and positive. Thus for *L–C* networks,

$$Z(j\omega) = jX(\omega) \qquad ...(27.20)$$

and

$$Y(j\omega) = jB(\omega) \qquad ...(27.21)$$

The impedance function $Z(j\omega)$ being purely reactive, the *LC* networks are called *reactive networks.*

27.4. Separation Property of Reactive networks

An *L–C* network offers a purely reactive impedance $X(\omega)$. It may be shown that the derivative $\frac{dX}{d\omega}$ is always positive, *i.e.*

$$\frac{dX}{d\omega} > 0 \qquad ...(27.22)$$

Thus on plotting *X* against ω, the slope of the curve is always positive, *i.e. X* always increases with the increase of ω. Thus as we increase the frequency from a value ω_1, the impedance *X* increases from X_1 reaching infinity at a certain higher value as shown in Fig. 27.2. At this frequency of infinite reactance, the sign of *X* changes, *i.e.* $X(\omega)$ becomes $-\infty$. For higher values of ω, reactance *X* increases becoming less and less negative. Thus the slope is again positive as given by curve *CD* in Fig. 27.2. At some frequency, *X* becomes zero and then beyond this frequency, *X* again becomes positive and ultimately reaches infinity at a higher frequency. Beyond this frequency, the cycle repeats. Frequencies at which *X* becomes zero are called *zeros* while frequencies at which *X* becomes infinite in magnitude are called *poles.* The zero frequencies are also called *resonant frequencies* while pole frequencies are called *antiresonant frequencies.*

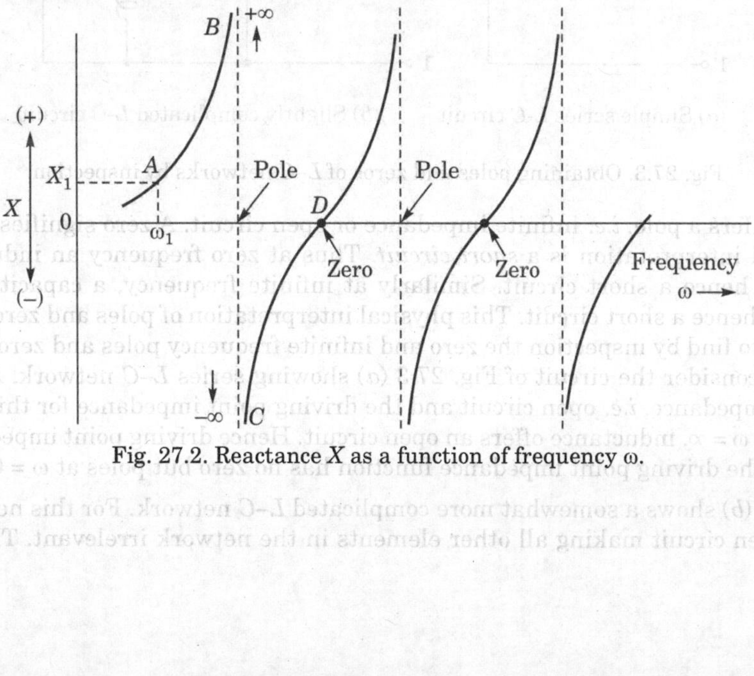

Fig. 27.2. Reactance *X* as a function of frequency ω.

Now in a reactive network since $\frac{dX}{d\omega}$ is always positive, the poles and zeros must *alternate*, *i.e.* zero must lie in between two poles and similarly a pole must lie in between two zeros. This property of a reactive network is referred to as the *separation property*.

Location of Poles and Zeros by Inspection of the Network. A factor $(\omega^2 - \omega_n^2)$ in the numerator of $X(\omega)$ locates two zeros, one at $\omega = +\omega_n$ and the other at $\omega = -\omega_n$. Similarly a factor $(\omega^2 - \omega_m^2)$ in the denominator of $X(\omega)$ locates two poles, one at $\omega = +\omega_m$ and the other at $\omega = -\omega_m$. However, there remains the location of poles and zeros at zero frequency and at infinite frequency. To do this let us consider an inductance L. Its reactance is given by,

$$X_L = \omega L \qquad \text{...(27.23)}$$

Then X_L has a zero at $\omega = 0$ and a pole at $\omega = \infty$. A capacitance C has reactance given by,

$$X_c = \frac{-1}{\omega C} \qquad \text{...(27.24)}$$

X_c is infinite at $\omega = 0$ and is zero at $\omega = \infty$. Thus X_c has a zero at $\omega = \infty$ and a pole at $\omega = \infty$. These properties are summarized in Table 26.1.

Table 27.1

Pole and Zero Properties of X_c and X_L

ω	X_c	X_L
0	Pole	Zero
∞	Zero	Pole

For an LC network, a physical significance can be attributed to the terms zero and pole. Thus a pole signifies infinite impedance and its physical interpretation is an *open circuit*. Thus at $\omega = 0$, a capacitor C offers a pole, *i.e.* infinite impedance or open circuit. Similarly at $\omega = \infty$,

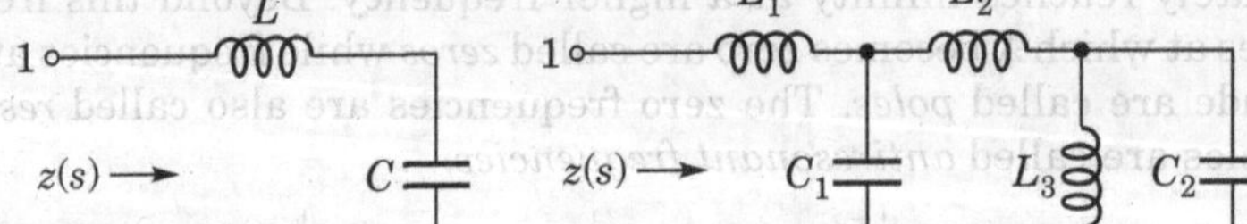

(*a*) Simple series *L-C* circuit (*b*) Slightly complicated *L-C* circuit

Fig. 27.3. Obtaining poles and zeros of *L–C* networks by inspection.

an inductor L offers a pole, *i.e.* infinite impedance or open circuit. A zero signifies zero impedance and its physical interpretation is a *short circuit.* Thus at zero frequency an inductor offers zero impedance and hence a short circuit. Similarly at infinite frequency, a capacitance offers zero impedance and hence a short circuit. This physical interpretation of poles and zeros at $\omega = 0$ and $\omega = \infty$ permits us to find by inspection the zero and infinite frequency poles and zeros of a given L–C network. Thus consider the circuit of Fig. 27.3 (*a*) showing series L–C network. At $\omega = 0$ (d.c), C offers infinite impedance, *i.e.* open circuit and the driving point impedance for this network has a pole at $\omega = 0$. At $\omega = \infty$, inductance offers an open circuit. Hence driving point impedance has a pole at $\omega = \infty$. Thus the driving point impedance function has no zero but poles at $\omega = 0$ and $\omega = \infty$.

Fig. 27.3 (*b*) shows a somewhat more complicated L–C network. For this network, at $\omega = \infty$, L acts as an open circuit making all other elements in the network irrelevant. The driving point impedance $Z(s)$ has therefore a pole at $\omega = \infty$. At $\omega = 0$, inductances L_1, L_2 and L_3 behave as short circuits while capacitances C_1 and C_2 behave as open circuits. Thus there is a zero impedance path from terminal 1 to terminal 1′ through inductances L_1—L_2—L_3. The driving point impedance $Z(s)$ thus has a zero at $\omega = 0$. We thus conclude that the driving point impedance $Z(s)$ of the network of Fig. 27.3 (*b*) has a pole at $\omega = \infty$ and a zero at $\omega = 0$.

Location of Poles and Zeros from Inspection of Reactance Function. The driving point impedance as given by Eq. (27.9) may be rewritten as below,

$$Z(s) = \frac{a_n s^n + a_{n-2} s^{n-2} + \ldots + a_0}{b_m s^m + b_{m-2} s^{m-2} + \ldots + b_1 s} \qquad \ldots(27.25)$$

where n is an even integer and m is an odd integer.

Consider the situation when $s = j\omega$ approaches infinity. Then only the highest ordered term of the numerator and the denominator need be considered. Then Eq. (27.25) may be written as,

$$\lim_{s \to \infty} Z(s) = \lim_{s \to \infty} \frac{a_n s^n}{b_m s^m} \qquad \ldots(27.26)$$

But integers n and m are never equal and can differ by at the most unity. Hence as $s \to \infty$, $Z(s)$ approaches zero if $m > n$ and approaches infinity if $m < n$. Further since n and m can differ by only unity, the pole or zero at $\omega = \infty$ will be *simple* and not multiple.

We thus conclude as below : In the driving point impedance function of an LC network, if the order of the numerator polynomial is greater than the order of the denominator polynomial ($n > m$), then there is a simple pole at infinity. If, however, the converse is true ($m > n$), then there is a simple zero at infinity.

As $s = j\omega$ becomes very small, only the lowest ordered terms in the polynomials of the impedance function need be considered. Then Eq. (26.25) may be written as,

$$Z(s) = \frac{\ldots + a_2 s^2 + a_0}{\ldots + b_3 s^3 + b_1 s} \qquad \ldots(27.27)$$

The following two possibilities are being considered :

(*a*) $a_0 \neq 0$ (*b*) $a_0 = 0$.

With $a_0 \neq 0$,

$$\lim_{s \to 0} Z(s) = \lim_{s \to 0} \frac{H}{s} = +\infty \qquad \ldots(27.28)$$

Thus there is a pole at zero frequency.

With $a_0 = 0$,

$$\lim_{s \to 0} Z(s) = \lim_{s \to 0} Hs = 0 \qquad \ldots(27.29)$$

Thus there is a zero at zero frequency.

We thus conclude as follows for the driving point impedance function of an L–C network : (*i*) If the lowest ordered term of the numerator polynomial is of higher order than the lowest ordered term of the denominator, then there is a simple zero at zero frequency, (*ii*) If the converse is true, then there is a simple pole at zero.

We thus find that for L–C networks, in all cases, zero and infinity frequencies are either poles or zeros and there poles and zeros are simple.

Example 27.5. *The driving point impedance of an L–C network is given by,*

$$Z(s) = 3\frac{(s^2+1)(s^2+16)}{s(s^2+9)}$$

Obtain the locations of poles and zeros by inspection. Plot the pole-zero configuration and also the reactance X(ω) as a function of frequency ω.

Solution. The order of the numerator polynomial is 4 and that of the denominator polynomial is 3. Since the order of the numerator polynomial is greater than that of the denominator polynomial, there is a simple pole at $\omega = \infty$.

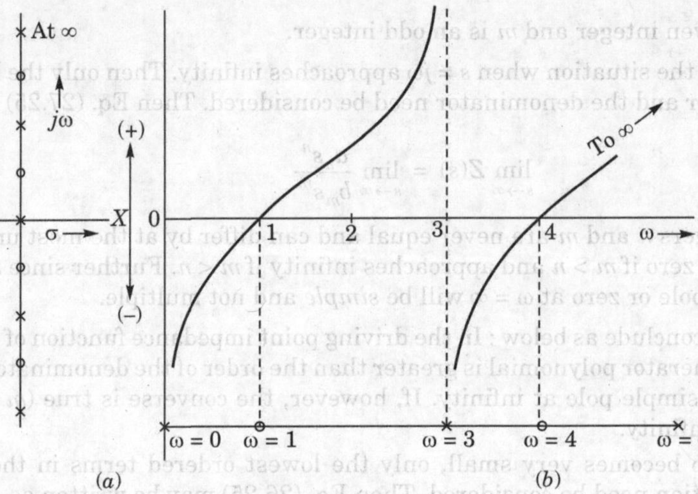

Fig. Ex. 27.5

For small values of s, $Z(s)$ approaches $\frac{H}{s}$. Hence there is a zero at zero frequency. Further by inspection of the numerator polynomial, there are finite zeros at $\omega = \pm 1$ and $\omega = -4$. Similarly by inspection of the denominator polynomial, there is a finite pole at $\omega = \pm 3$. The pole zero configuration is shown in Fig. (*a*) while a plot of the reactance function is shown in Fig. (*b*).

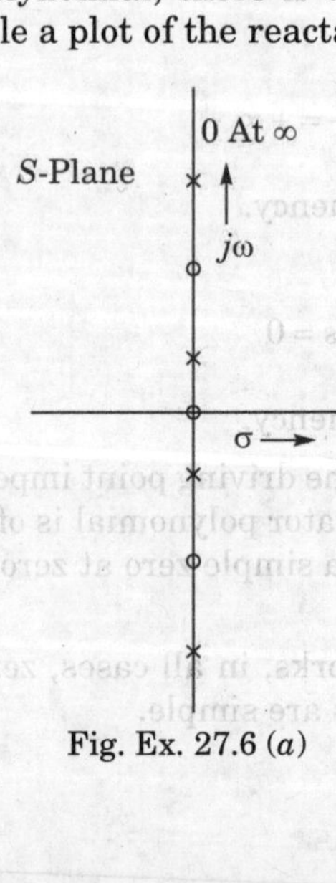

Fig. Ex. 27.6 (*a*)

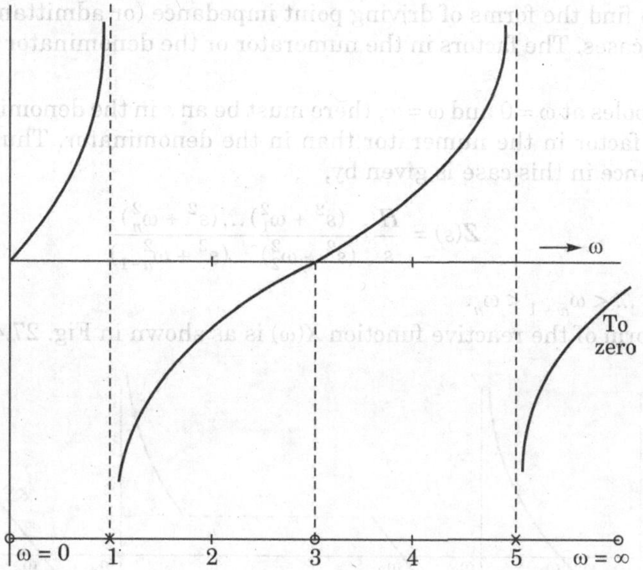

Fig. Ex. 27.6 (*b*)

The reactance function $X(\omega)$ is obtained from given expression for $Z(s)$. Different values of ω are substituted in this equation to get $X(\omega)$ which is then plotted.

Example 27.6. *Driving point impedance function of an L–C network is given by,*

$$Z(s) = 2\frac{s(s^2+9)}{(s^2+1)(s^2+25)}$$

Obtain the locations of poles and zeros by inspection. Plot the pole-zero configuration and also the reactance $X(\omega)$ as a function of frequency ω.

Solution. The order of the numerator polynomial is 3 while that of the denominator polynomial is 4. Hence there is a simple zero at infinite frequency.

Further for small values of s, $Z(s)$ approaches Hs. Hence there is a simple zero at zero frequency.

Further inspection of the numerator and denominator polynomials indicates finite zero at $\omega = \pm 3$ and finite poles at $\omega = \pm 1$ and $\omega = \pm 5$. Hence Fig. (*a*) gives the *s*-plane representation while Fig. (*b*) gives the reactance function plot.

27.5. The Four Forms of Reactance Function of *L–C* Networks

We have seen earlier that for *L–C* networks, zero and infinite frequencies are always either zero or poles. Hence there are four possible combinations of these conditions. These are tabulated in Table 27.2.

Table 27.2.
Four Possible Combinations of Pole-Zero Conditions

Case	$\omega = 0$	$\omega = \infty$
I	Pole	Pole
II	Zero	Zero
III	Pole	Zero
IV	Zero	Pole

We proceed to find the forms of driving point impedance (or admittance) which correspond to each of these four cases. The factors in the numerator or the denominator may be of two forms : s and $(s^2 + \omega_n^2)$.

Case I. With poles at $\omega = 0$ and $\omega = \infty$, there must be an s in the denominator polynomial and one excess $(s^2 + \omega_n^2)$ factor in the numerator than in the denominator. Thus the general form of driving point impedance in this case is given by,

$$Z(s) = \frac{H}{s} \cdot \frac{(s^2 + \omega_1^2) \ldots (s^2 + \omega_n^2)}{(s^2 + \omega_2^2) \ldots (s^2 + \omega_{n-1}^2)} \quad \ldots(27.30)$$

where $\omega_1 < \omega_2 < \omega_3 < \ldots < \omega_{n-1} < \omega_n$.

The general form of the reactive function $X(\omega)$ is as shown in Fig. 27.4.

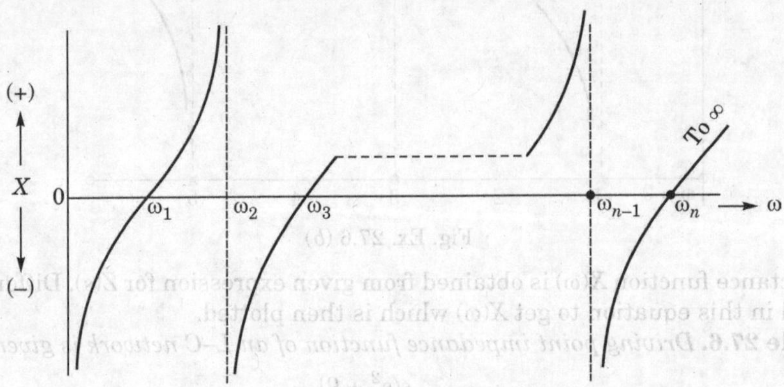

Fig. 27.4. Reactance plot for case I : Poles at $\omega = 0$ and $\omega = \infty$.

Case II. With zeros at $\omega = 0$ and $\omega = \infty$, there must be an s term in the numerator polynomial and an excess $(s^2 + \omega_n^2)$ term in the denominator polynomial. Thus the general form of driving point impedance in this case is given by,

$$Z(s) = Hs \frac{(s^2 + \omega_2^2) \ldots (s^2 + \omega_{n-1}^2)}{(s^2 + \omega_1^2) \ldots (s^2 + \omega_n^2)} \quad \ldots(27.31)$$

where $\omega_1 < \omega_2 < \omega_3 < \ldots < \omega_{n-1} < \omega_n$.

The general form of the reactance function $X(m)$ is as shown in Fig. 27.5.

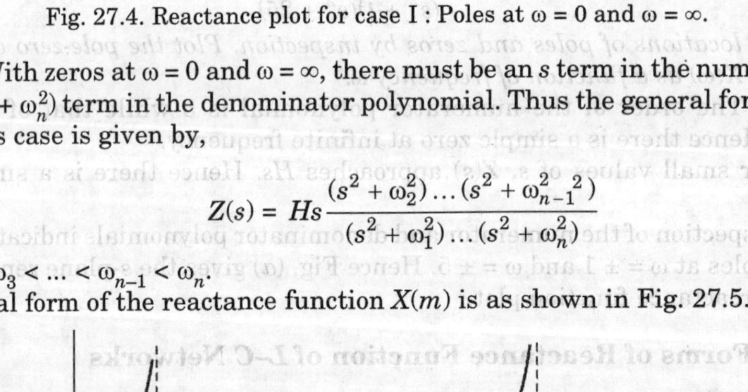

Fig. 27.5. Reactance plot for case II : Zeros at $\omega = 0$ and $\omega = \infty$.

Case III. A pole at $\omega = 0$ requires a term H/s in the impedance function. A zero at $\omega = \infty$ requires that the order of the denominator polynomial be greater than the order of the numerator polynomial. But there already exists a factor s in the denominator. Hence there must be equal number of $(s^2 + \omega_n^2)$ type terms in the numerator and the denominator. Hence the driving point impedance for this case is of the following general form :

$$Z(s) = \frac{H}{s} \cdot \frac{(s^2 + \omega_1^2) \dots (s^2 + \omega_{n-1}^2)}{(s^2 + \omega_2^2) \dots (s^2 + \omega_n^2)} \qquad \dots(27.32)$$

The general form of reactance function $X(\omega)$ for this case is shown in Fig. 27.6.

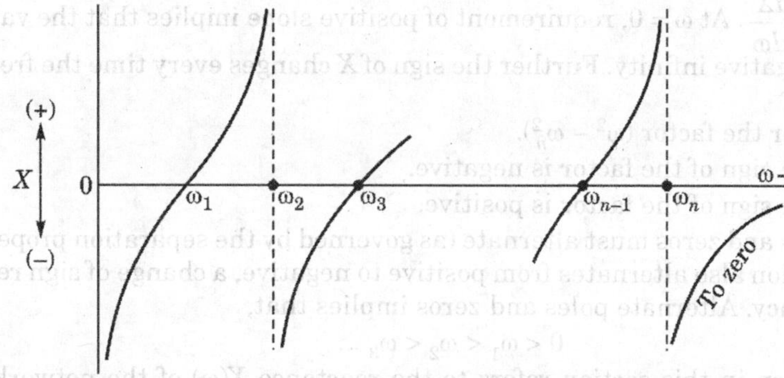

Fig. 27.6. Reactance plot for case III : Pole at $\omega = 0$; zero at $\omega = \infty$.

Case IV. A zero at $\omega = 0$ requires a term Hs in the numerator. A pole at $\omega = \infty$ requires that the order of the numerator polynomial be greater than the order of the denominator polynomial. But there already exists a term s in the numerator. Hence there must be equal number of $(s^2 + \omega_n^2)$ type terms in the numerator and the denominator. Hence the driving point impedance for this case is of the following general form :

$$Z(s) = Hs \frac{(s^2 + \omega_2^2) \dots (s^2 + \omega_n^2)}{(s^2 + \omega_1^2) \dots (s^2 + \omega_{n-1}^2)} \qquad \dots(27.33)$$

The general form of reactance function $X(\omega)$ for this case is shown in Fig. 27.7.

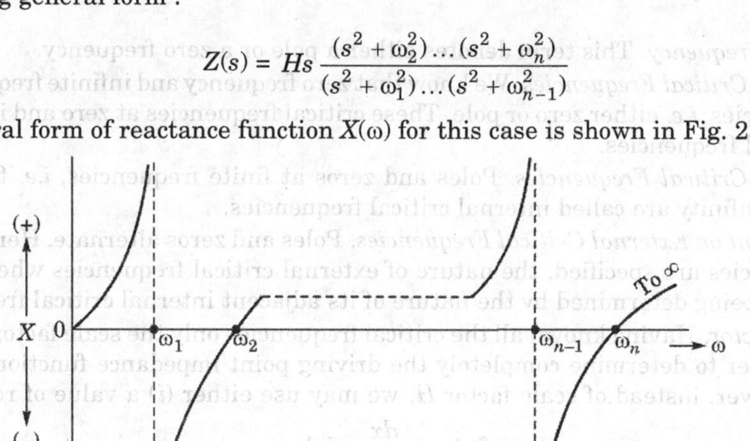

Fig. 27.7. Reactive plot for case IV : Zero at $\omega = 0$; Pole at $\omega = \infty$.

The above four cases may be put into two groups. Thus case I and case III form one group. For this group, in the sinusoidal steady state ($s = j\omega$), the reactance function may be put into the following general form :

$$X(\omega) = \pm \frac{H}{\omega} \cdot \frac{(\omega^2 - \omega_1^2)(\omega^2 - \omega_3^2)\ldots}{(\omega^2 - \omega_2^2)(\omega^2 - \omega_4^2)\ldots} \quad \ldots(27.34)$$

Case II and case IV form another group. For this group, in the sinusoidal steady state, the reactance function is of the following general form :

$$X(\omega) = \pm H\omega \frac{(\omega^2 - \omega_2^2)(\omega^2 - \omega_4^2)\ldots}{(\omega^2 - \omega_1^2)(\omega^2 - \omega_3^2)\ldots} \quad \ldots(27.35)$$

In Eqs. (27.34) and (27.35), the sign of the reactance function must be so selected as to give a positive slope to $\frac{dX}{d\omega}$. At $\omega = 0$, requirement of positive slope implies that the value of X at $\omega = 0$ be either zero or negative infinity. Further the sign of X changes every time the frequency passes a pole or a zero.

Next consider the factor $(\omega^2 - \omega_n^2)$.

If $\omega < \omega_n$, the sign of the factor is negative.

If $\omega > \omega_n$, the sign of the factor is positive.

But the poles and zeros must alternate (as governed by the separation property). The sign of the reactance function also alternates from positive to negative, a change of sign resulting at every pole or zero frequency. Alternate poles and zeros implies that,

$$0 < \omega_1 < \omega_2 < \omega_3 \ldots \quad \ldots(27.36)$$

The discussion in this section refers to the reactance $X(\omega)$ of the network. However it is equally true for the susceptance function $B(\omega)$ where admittance $Y(j\omega) = jB(\omega)$.

The function of factor H is to fix the scale of the reactance and hence it is referred as the *multiplying factor* or the *scale factor*.

27.6. Specifications of Reactance Functions

We now study the various quantities which completely specify the impedance function for an LC network.

Critical frequency. This term denotes either a pole or a zero frequency.

External Critical Frequencies. We know that zero frequency and infinite frequency are always critical frequencies, *i.e.* either zero or pole. These critical frequencies at zero and infinity are called external critical frequencies.

Internal Critical Frequencies. Poles and zeros at finite frequencies, *i.e.* frequencies other than zero and infinity are called internal critical frequencies.

Constraint on External Critical Frequencies. Poles and zeros alternate. Hence if the internal critical frequencies are specified, the nature of external critical frequencies whether pole or zero gets defined it being determined by the nature of its adjacent internal critical frequency.

Scale Factor. Having known all the critical frequencies only the scale factor H remains to be specified in order to determine completely the driving point impedance function for the reactive network. However, instead of scale factor H, we may use either (*i*) a value of reactance at some non-critical frequency or (*ii*) a value of slope $\frac{dx}{d\omega}$ of the reactance curve at some frequency other than a pole.

All these specifications for reactive network are summarized below :

Specifications for Reactive Network

I. Internal critical frequencies

II. Information about scale factor H in one of the following forms :

(*a*) Value of H

(*b*) Value of X at a non-critical frequency

(c) Value of $\frac{dx}{d\omega}$ at a non-pole frequency.

When the above two types of specifications are given, we may find $Z(s)$ on (i) using the value of H and (ii) substituting $\omega = s/j$ in the equations of the form of Eq. (27.34) or Eq. (27.35).

27.7. Synthesis of One-port L–C Networks using Foster's Reactance Theorem

We now take up the design of L–C networks meeting the $Z(s)$ specifications. The design procedure follows one given by R.M. Foster and goes after his name.

Let us first consider the case I mentioned in section 27.5. The driving point impedance function for case I given by Eq. (27.30) is reproduced below :

$$Z(s) = \frac{H}{s} \cdot \frac{(s^2+\omega_1^2)(s^2+\omega_3^2)(s^2+\omega_5^2)\ldots}{(s^2+\omega_2^2)(s^2+\omega_4^2)(s^2+\omega_6^2)\ldots} \quad \ldots(27.37)$$

where there is one excess factor of the form $(s^2 + \omega_n^2)$ in the numerator than in the denominator.

We now resort to partial fraction expansion of reactive function.

In such a partial fraction expansion, the term of the type $(s^2 + \omega_2^2)$ will expand as below,

$$\frac{N(s)}{(s^2+\omega_2^2)} = \frac{N(s)}{(s+j\omega_2)(s-j\omega_2)} = \frac{k_2}{(s+j\omega_2)} + \frac{k^*{}_2}{(s-j\omega_2)} \quad \ldots(27.38)$$

where k_2^* is complex conjugate of k_2.

It may, however, be shown that the k-coefficients in the partial fraction expansion of terms with imaginary roots are always real and positive. Hence k_2 and k_2^* are equal. Hence Eq. (27.38) may be put as

$$\frac{N(s)}{(s^2+\omega_2^2)} = \frac{k_2}{s+j\omega_2} + \frac{k_2}{s-j\omega_2} = \frac{2k_2 s}{s^2+\omega^2} \quad \ldots(27.39)$$

Similar form of expansion applies to $(s^2 + \omega_4^2)$ term etc. Hence Eq. (27.37) for case I may be put as,

$$Z(s) = \frac{k_0}{s} + \frac{2k_2 s}{s^2+\omega_2^2} + \frac{2k_4 s}{s^2+\omega_4^2} + \ldots + Hs \quad \ldots(27.40)$$

The first term in Eq. (27.40) gives a pole at $\omega = 0$, while the last term is needed to give a pole at $\omega = \infty$, the necessary conditions characterizing case I.

The H value of the coefficient maybe verified by 1' Hospital's rule or by direct division.

Let us assume the total impedance $Z(s)$ to be constituted by a series combination of impedances $Z_1(s)$, $Z_2(s)$ etc. Then we may write,

$$Z(s) = Z_1(s) + Z_2(s) + \ldots + Z_n(s) \quad \ldots(27.41)$$

Now each term in Eq. (27.41) is identified as the impedance of a simple network configuration. All these constituent networks on being combined in series must give a network having the required driving point impedance $Z(s)$.

Thus the impedance Z_1 in Eq. (27.41) is associated with the term $\frac{k_0}{s}$ in Eq. (27.40). Thus we may put,

$$Z_1(s) = \frac{k_0}{s} \quad \text{......(27.42)}$$

Evidently $Z_1(s)$ as given by Eq. (27.42) represents a capacitor C of value $1/k_0$.

Next the impedance $Z_n(s)$ in Eq. (27.41) is associated with the term Hs in Eq. (27.40). Thus we may write,

$$Z_n(s) = Hs \quad \text{...(27.43)}$$

Evidently $Z_n(s)$ as given by Eq. (27.43) represents an inductor of value H henrys.

The remaining intermediate terms have the same general form and each represents a parallel combination of an inductor and a capacitor. Consider an inductor L in shunt with a capacitor C. The impedance of such a parallel combination is given by,

$$Z(s) = \frac{1}{Cs + \dfrac{1}{Ls}} = \frac{(1/C)s}{s^2 + \dfrac{1}{LC}} \quad \text{...(27.44)}$$

On comparing Eq. (27.44) with Eq. (27.39), we get the following expressions for capacitor C_n and inductor L_n.

$$C_n = \frac{1}{2k_n} \quad \text{...(27.45)}$$

$$L_n = \frac{1}{\omega_n^2 C_n} = \frac{2k_n}{\omega_n^2} \quad \text{...(27.46)}$$

where n refers to the term $\dfrac{2k_n s}{s^2 + \omega_n^2}$ in Eq. (27.40).

These results are tabulated in Table 27.3.

Table 27.3.
Values of Elements in First Foster Form

Terms	*Network*	*Element values*
$\dfrac{k_0}{s}$	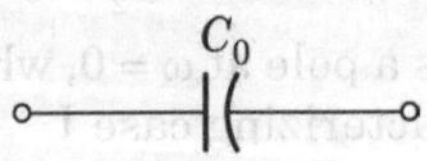	$C_0 = \dfrac{1}{k_0}$ Farad
Hs	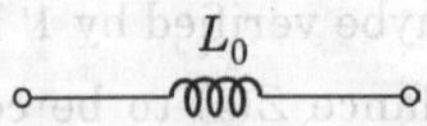	$L_0 = H$ Henry
$\dfrac{2k_n s}{s^2 + \omega_n^2}$	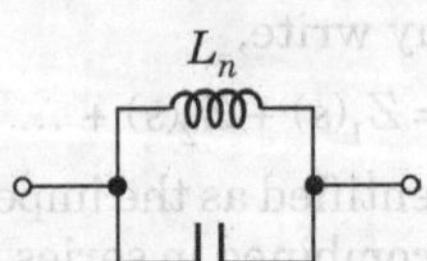	$L_n = \dfrac{2k_n}{\omega_n^2}$ Henry

Fig. 27.8 shows the network realized corresponding to the expanded expression of Eq. (27.40). The network realization is called the First *Foster Form* and corresponds to the case I.

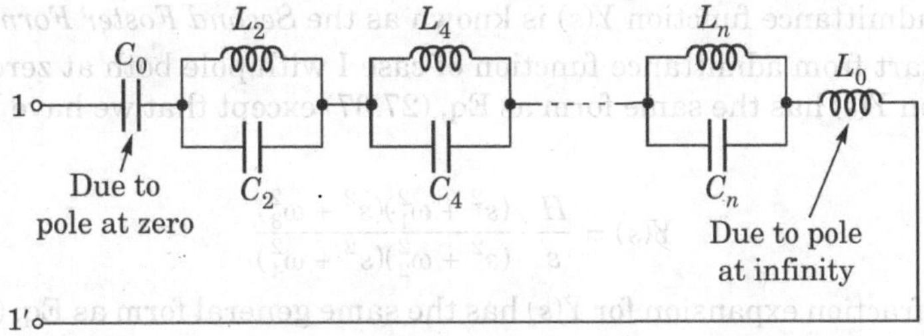

Fig. 27.8. Network of the first Foster form.

Role of Elements in the First Foster Form. We may now study the role of various elements in the network realization of first Foster form in terms of the pole-zero configuration.

(a) Capacitor C_0. This capacitor C_0 represents the term k_0/s which corresponds to a pole at the origin.

(b) Inductor L_0. It represents the term Hs which corresponds to a pole at infinity.

(c) Parallel L_n–C_n *Network.* This represents the term $(s^2 + \omega_n^2)$ in the denominator of $Z(s)$. The frequency ω_n represents a pole frequency. Thus parallel resonance of L_n and C_n results in a pole of $Z(s)$. Zeros of $Z(s)$ cannot be associated with any of these elements. Reactance of each parallel circuit changes sign as frequency increases through antiresonance. However at some frequency, the reactances of a certain group of these parallel circuits is equal and opposite to the reactance of all remaining parallel circuits. This results in a zero of $Z(s)$. These zeros may be thought of as being caused by series resonance of (*i*) first parallel network with the rest of the network (*ii*) first and second parallel network with the rest of the network and so on. Finally the last parallel network resonates with the preceding network taken together.

In case I considered above, these are poles both at $\omega = 0$ and $\omega = \infty$. The remaining 3 cases differ from case I in that there is no pole either at $\omega = 0$ or at $\omega = \infty$ or at both. Hence networks corresponding to these cases can be realized by leaving out either C_0 or L_0 or both. Thus consider the case when there is no s term in the denominator of $Z(s)$.

Then there will no $\frac{k_0}{s}$ term in the partial fraction expansion of $Z(s)$. C_0 is, therefore, absent, *i.e.* replaced by short circuit. Next consider the case when the order of the denominator polynomial exceeds the order of numerator polynomial. Then there will be no Hs factor in the partial fraction expansion of $Z(s)$ and hence there will be no inductor L_0 in the circuit, *i.e.* L_0 is replaced by a short circuit. Thus the difference in the four cases I to IV exists regarding the nature of these "end elements". This is summarized in Table 27.4 where a dash indicates absence of C_0 or L_0 element, *i.e.* a short circuit.

Table 27.4

Nature of End Elements in First Foster Form

Case	C_0	$\omega = \infty$	C_0	L_0
I	Pole	Pole	Present	Present
II	Zero	Zero	—	—
III	Pole	Zero	Present	—
IV	Zero	Pole	—	Present

Second Foster Form. Foster in 1924 proved that if the admittance function $Y(s)$ for a network is given, it is possible to realize a physical network from this function. This form of network realized from the admittance function $Y(s)$ is known as the *Second Foster Form.*

We again start from admittance function of case I with pole both at zero and infinity. This admittance function $Y(s)$ has the same form as Eq. (27.37) except that we have $Y(s)$ instead of $Z(s)$. Thus, we have

$$Y(s) = \frac{H}{s} \cdot \frac{(s^2 + \omega_1^2)(s^2 + \omega_3^2)}{(s^2 + \omega_2^2)(s^2 + \omega_4^2)} \qquad ...(27.47)$$

The partial fraction expansion for $Y(s)$ has the same general form as Eq. (27.40) and is given by,

$$Y(s) = \frac{k_0}{s} + \frac{2k_2 s}{s^2 + \omega_2^2} + \frac{2k_4 s}{s^2 + \omega_4^2} + \ldots + Hs \qquad ...(27.48)$$

In Eq. (27.48), the first term corresponds to a pole at $\omega = 0$ while the last term corresponds to a pole at $\omega = \infty$.

Let us assume the total admittance $Y(s)$ to be constituted by a parallel combination of admittance $Y_1(s)$, $Y_2(s)$ etc. Then we may write

$$Y(s) = Y_1(s) + Y_2(s) + \ldots + Y_n(s) \qquad ...(27.49)$$

Each term in Eq. (27.49) is identified as the admittance of a simple network configuration. All these constituent networks on being combined in parallel must give the network having the required driving point admittance $Y(s)$.

Thus the admittance $Y_1(s)$ in Eq. (27.49) is associated with the term $\frac{k_0}{s}$ in Eq. (27.48). We may thus put,

$$Y_1(s) = \frac{k_0}{s} \qquad ...(27.50)$$

Evidently $Y_1(s)$ as given by Eq. (27.50) represents an inductor of $L = \frac{1}{k_0}$. Similarly $Y_n(s)$ in Eq. (27.49) is associated with the term Hs in Eq. (27.48). Thus we may write,

$$Y_n(s) = Hs \qquad ...(27.51)$$

Obviously then $Y_1(s)$ as given by Eq. (27.51) represents a capacitor of value H farad.

The remaining intermediate terms have the same general form and each represents a series combination of an inductor and a capacitor. This is dual of the network found for the first Foster form. This admittance of a series combination of L and C is given by,

$$Y(s) = \frac{1}{Ls + \dfrac{1}{Cs}} = \frac{s/L}{s^2 + \dfrac{1}{LC}} \qquad ...(27.52)$$

On comparing Eq. (27.52) with Eq. (27.39), we get the following expression for the inductor L_n and capacitor C_n :

$$L_n = \frac{1}{2k_n} \qquad ...(27.53)$$

$$C_n = \frac{1}{L_n \omega_n^2} = \frac{2k_n}{\omega_n^2} \qquad ...(27.54)$$

where n refers to the term $\frac{2k_n s}{s^2 + \omega_n^2}$ in Eq. (27.48). These results are tabulated in Table 27.5.

Table 27.5
Values of Elements in Second Foster Form

Terms	*Network*	*Element values*
$\frac{k_0}{s}$	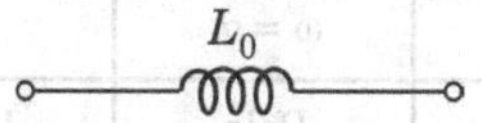	$C_0 = \frac{1}{k_s}$ Henry
Hs	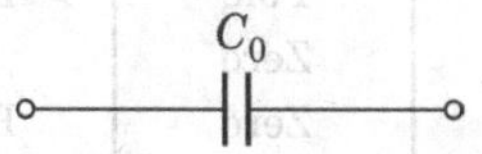	$C_0 = H$ Farad
$\frac{2k_n s}{s^2 + \omega_n^2}$	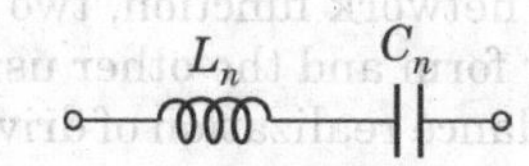	$L_n = \frac{1}{2k_n}$ Henry $C_n = \frac{2k_n}{\omega_n^2}$ Farad

Fig. 27.9 shows the network realized corresponding to the expanded expression of Eq. (27.48). The network realization is called the second Foster form and corresponds to the case I.

Role of Elements in the Second Foster Form.

(*a*) *Inductor* L_0. It represents the term k_0/s in the partial fraction expansion of $y(s)$ and corresponds to a pole at the origin.

(*b*) *Capacitor* C_0. It represents the term *Hs* which corresponds to a pole at infinity.

(*c*) *Series* L_n–C_n *Network*. This represents the term $(s^2 + \omega_n^2)$ in the denominator of $Y(s)$. The frequency ω_n represents a pole frequency which is associated with *series resonance* (in contrast with the parallel resonance in the case of first Forster form) of the *L–C* network. Thus every pole is associated directly with specific *LC* elements in the sense that series resonance within these *L–C* combination causes the network to have a pole of admittance. The zeros of $Y(s)$ cannot be identified. Every element, however, contributes towards zero of admittance. Susceptance of each series circuit changes sign as frequency increases, through resonance. However, at some frequency, the suspectance of a certain group of these series circuits is equal and opposite to the susceptance of the remaining series circuits. This results in a zero of $Y(s)$. These zeros may be thought of as being caused by parallel resonance of (*i*) first series networks with the rest of the networks, (*ii*) first and second series networks with the rest of the networks and so on. Finally the last series network resonates with the preceding networks taken together.

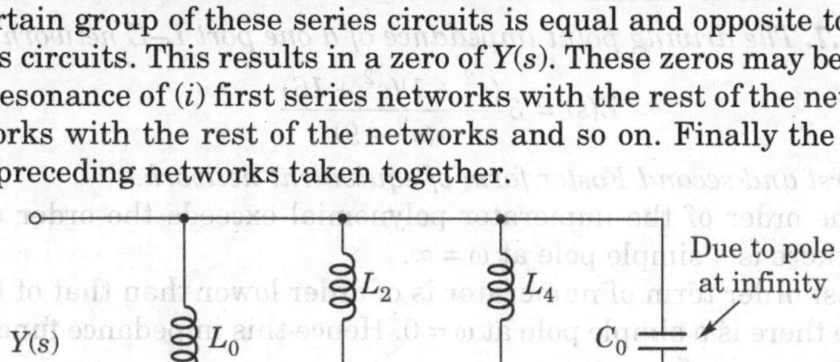

Fig. 27.9. Network of the second Foster form.

In case I considered above, there are poles of $Y(s)$ at both $\omega = 0$ and $\omega = \infty$. The remaining three cases differ from case I in that there is no pole either at $\omega = 0$ or at $\omega = \infty$ or at both. Hence networks corresponding to these cases can be realized by leaving out either C_0 or L_0 or both. The presence of a zero instead of a pole thus signifies the absence of the end elements. The end conditions for the four cases of the second Foster form of network are summarized in Table 27.6 for admittance function. A dash is used to indicate the absence of an element, *i.e.* an open circuit.

Table 27.6

Nature of End Elements in Second Foster Form

Case	$\omega = 0$	$\omega = \infty$	L_0	C_0
I	Pole	Pole	Present	Present
II	Zero	Zero	—	—
III	Pole	Zero	Present	—
IV	Zero	Pole	—	Present

We thus see that for any given network function, two completely equivalent networks can be designed, one using the first Foster form and the other using the second Foster form. The first Forster form of network is series impedance realization of driving point impedance $Z(s)$. The second Foster form of network is a parallel admittance realization of driving point admittance $Y(s)$. $Y(s)$ is obtained on inverting $Z(s)$. This process of inversion interchanges poles and zeros. Hence for a given set of specifications, $Z(s)$ and $Y(s)$ will never have the same case classification. The case classification gets changed as given in Table 27.7. The information given in this table may readily be verified.

Table 27.7

Change of Case Classification on Inversion

Z(s)	*Corresponding Y(s) = 1/Z(s)*
Case I	Case II
Case II	Case I
Case III	Case IV
Case IV	Case III

Example 27.7. *The driving point impedance of a one port L–C network is given by,*

$$Z(s) = 3\frac{(s^2+1)(s^2+16)}{s(s^2+9)}$$

Obtain the first and second Foster form of equivalent network.

Solution. The order of the numerator polynomial exceeds the order of the denominator polynomial. Hence there is a simple pole at $\omega = \infty$.

Further lowest order term of numerator is of order lower than that of lowest order term of denominator. Hence there is a simple pole at $\omega = 0$. Hence this impedance function is of class I and the partial fraction expansion is,

$$Z(s) = \frac{k_0}{s} + \frac{k_2}{s+j3} + \frac{k_{2^*}}{s-j3} + Hs \qquad \text{...(1)}$$

The constants of this equation may be evaluated by the Heaviside rule as follows :

$$k_0 = \frac{3\times 16}{9} = \frac{16}{3}$$

$$k_2 = \left.\frac{3(s^2+1)(s^2+16)}{s(s-j3)}\right|_{s=-j3} = \frac{28}{3}$$

By inspection, $H = 3$

$$C_0 = \frac{I}{k_0} = \frac{3}{16} \text{ Farad}$$

$$L_0 = H = 3 \text{ Henrys}$$

$$C_2 = \frac{1}{2k_2} = \frac{3}{2 \times 28} = \frac{3}{56} \text{ Farad}$$

$$L_2 = \frac{2k_2}{\omega_n^2} = \frac{2 \times \frac{28}{3}}{9} = \frac{56}{27} \text{ Henrys.}$$

Hence the element values in the first Foster form are as shown in Fig. Ex. 27.7 (*a*).

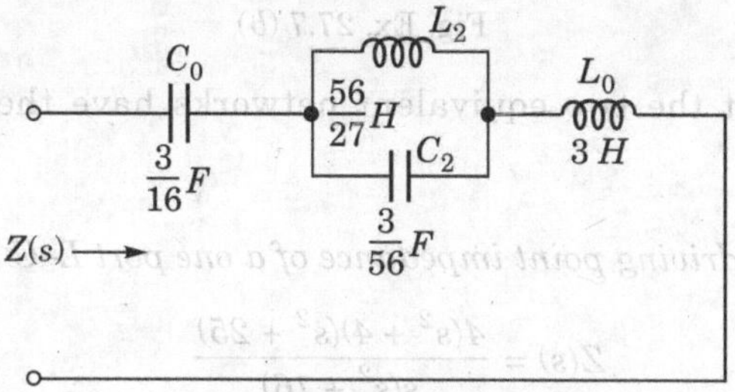

Fig. Ex. 27.7 (*a*)

To determine the second Foster form of network, we first find the admittance function.

Thus $$Y(s) = \frac{1}{Z(s)} = \frac{1}{3} \cdot \frac{s(s^2+9)}{(s^2+1)(s^2+16)}$$

Since $Z(s)$ belongs to case I, corresponding $Y(s)$ is of case II. Thus there are no admittance poles at $\omega = 0$ and to $= \infty$. This admittance function $Y(s)$ on partial fraction expansion yields,

$$Y(s) = \frac{2k_1 s}{s^2+1} + \frac{2k_3 s}{s^2+4^2} \qquad \ldots(2)$$

The two constants k_1 and k_3 may be found by the Heaviside method. Thus, we get

$$k_1 = \frac{1}{3} \cdot \frac{s(s^2+9)}{(s-j1)(s^2+16)}\bigg|_{s=-j1} = \frac{4}{45}$$

$$k_3 = \frac{1}{3} \cdot \frac{s(s^2+9)}{(s^2+1)(s-j4)}\bigg|_{s=-j4} = \frac{7}{90}$$

Hence $$Y(s) = \frac{2 \cdot \frac{4}{45} s}{s^2+1} = \frac{2 \times \frac{7}{90} \times s}{s^2+9}$$

$$L_1 = \frac{1}{2k_1} = \frac{45}{8} \text{ Henry}$$

$$C_1 = \frac{2k_1}{\omega_1^2} = \frac{8}{45 \times 1} = \frac{8}{45} \text{ Farad}$$

$$L_3 = \frac{1}{2k_3} = \frac{90}{2 \times 7} = \frac{45}{7} \text{ Henry}$$

$$C_3 = \frac{2k_3}{\omega_3^2} = \frac{7}{45 \times 16} = \frac{7}{720} \text{ Farad.}$$

Hence the element values in the second Foster form are as shown in Fig. Ex. 27.7 (*b*).

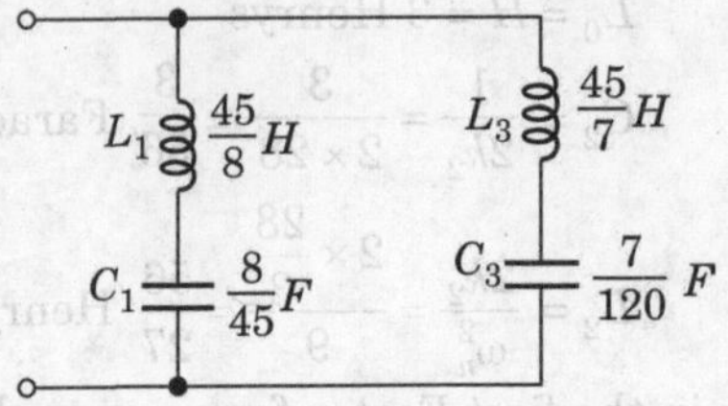

Fig. Ex. 27.7 (*b*)

It may be seen that the two equivalent networks have the same number of network elements.

Example 27.8. *The driving point impedance of a one port L–C network is given by,*

$$Z(s) = \frac{4(s^2 + 4)(s^2 + 25)}{s(s^2 + 16)}$$

Obtain the first and second Foster form of equivalent networks.

Solution. The order of the numerator polynomial exceeds the order of the denominator polynomial. Hence there is a simple pole at $\omega = \infty$.

Further lowest order term of numerator is of order lower than that of the lowest order term of denominator. Hence there is a simple pole at $\omega = 0$. Hence this impedance function is of class I and the partial fraction expansion is,

$$Z(s) = \frac{k_0}{s} + \frac{2k_2 s}{s^2 + 16} + Hs \qquad \text{...(1)}$$

The constants of this equation may be evaluated by the Heaviside rule as follows :

$$k_0 = \frac{4(4)(25)}{16} = 25$$

$$k_2 = \left. \frac{4(s^2 + 4)(s^2 + 25)}{s(s - j4)} \right|_{s=-j4} = \frac{27}{8}$$

By inspection $H = 4$.

$$C_0 = \frac{1}{k_0} = \frac{1}{25} \text{ Farad}$$

$$L_0 = H = 4 \text{ Henry}$$

$$C_2 = \frac{1}{2k_2} = \frac{8}{27 \times 2} = \frac{2}{27} \text{ Farad}$$

$$L_2 = \frac{2k_2}{\omega_2^2} = \frac{27/4}{16} = \frac{27}{64} \text{ henry.}$$

Hence the element values in the first Foster form are as shown in Fig. Ex. 27.8 (*a*).

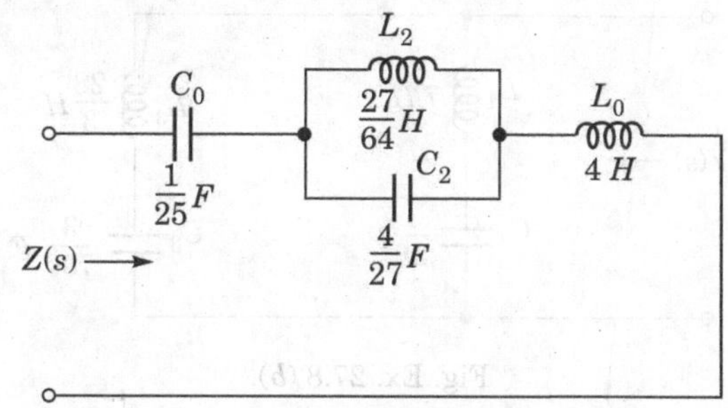

Fig. Ex. 27.8 (*a*)

To determine the second Foster form of the network we first find the admittance function.

Thus
$$Y(s) = \frac{1}{Z(s)} = \frac{s(s^2+16)}{4(s^4+4)(s^2+25)}$$

Since $Z(s)$ belongs to Case I, corresponding $Y(s)$ is of Case II. Thus there are no admittance poles at $\omega = 0$ and $\omega = \infty$. This admittance function $Y(s)$ on partial fraction expansion yields,

$$Y(s) = \frac{2k_1 s}{s^2+4} + \frac{2k_3 s}{s^2+25}$$

The two constants k_1 and k_3 may be found by the Heaviside method. Thus, we get

$$k_1 = \frac{1}{4}\cdot\frac{s(s^2+16)}{(s-j^2)(s^2+25)}\bigg|_{s=-j2} = \frac{1}{14}$$

$$k_3 = \frac{1}{4}\cdot\frac{s(s^2+16)}{(s^2+4)(s-j5)}\bigg|_{s=j5} = \frac{3}{56}$$

Hence
$$Y(s) = \frac{2\times\frac{1}{14}s}{s^2+14} + \frac{2\times\frac{3}{56}s}{s^2+25}$$

$$L_1 = \frac{1}{2k_1} = \frac{14}{2} = 7 \text{ Henry}$$

$$C_1 = \frac{2k_1}{\omega_1^2} = \frac{1}{7\times 4} = \frac{1}{28} \text{ Farad}$$

$$L_2 = \frac{1}{2k_3} = \frac{56}{2\times 3} = \frac{28}{3} \text{ Henry}$$

$$C_2 = \frac{2k_3}{\omega_3^2} = \frac{3/28}{25} = \frac{3}{700} \text{ Farad.}$$

Hence the elements in the second Foster form are as shown in Fig. Ex. 27.8 (*b*).

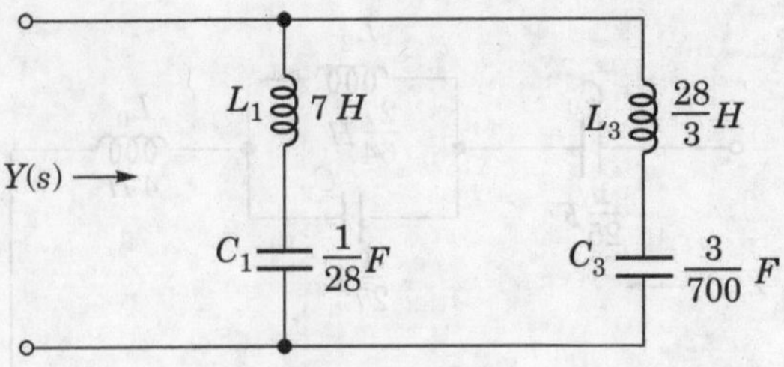

Fig. Ex. 27.8 (*b*).

27.8. Proof of the Separation Property

We have seen that an immittance function is composed of, at most, the following three types of terms :

$$\frac{k_0}{s}, \frac{2k_n s}{s^2 + \omega_n^2}, Hs$$

The reactance expressions for these terms are :

$$X_1 = -\frac{k_0}{\omega} \qquad \text{...(27.55)}$$

$$X_n = \frac{2k_n \omega}{-\omega^2 + \omega_n^2} \qquad \text{...(27.56)}$$

$$X_3 = \omega H \qquad \text{...(27.57)}$$

The susceptance expression have exactly the same form.

On differentiating X_1, X_n and X_3 with respect to ω, we get

$$\frac{dX_1}{d\omega} = +\frac{k_0}{\omega^2} \qquad \text{...(27.58)}$$

$$\frac{dX_n}{d\omega} = +\frac{2k_n\omega^2 + 2k_n\omega_n^2}{(\omega_n^2 - \omega^2)^2} \qquad \text{...(27.59)}$$

$$\frac{dX_3}{d\omega} = +H \qquad \text{...(27.60)}$$

Each of these three derivatives is positive for both positive and negative values of frequency ω.

The reactance function for the driving point terminals (the same is true for susceptance function) is the sum of the reactances.

Thus
$$X = \sum_{j=1}^{n} X_j \qquad \text{...(27.61)}$$

On differential term by term, we get

$$\frac{dX}{d\omega} = \sum_{j=1}^{n} \frac{dX_j}{d\omega} \qquad \text{...(27.62)}$$

But since each of the typical derivatives given by Eqs. (27.58) to (27.60) are positive for both positive and negative values of ω, $\frac{dX}{d\omega}$ must also be positive.

Thus $$\frac{dX}{d\omega} > 0 \qquad ...(27.63)$$

for both positive and negative values for frequency ω.

Since $\frac{dX}{d\omega}$ is always positive, the separation property follows.

Example 27.9. *The driving point impedance of a one port L-C network is given by,*

$$Z(s) = 2\frac{s(s^2+4)}{(s^2+1)(s^2+2s)}$$

Obtain the first and second Foster form of equivalent networks.

Solution. The order of the numerator is less than the order of the denominator. Hence there is a simple zero at infinity. Further the lowest ordered term in the numerator is of higher order than the lowest ordered term in the denominator. Hence there is a simple zero at zero. Hence the impedance function forms case II. Hence there will be no L_0 and C_0 elements in the first Foster form and no $\frac{k_0}{s}$ and Hs terms in the partial fraction expansion.

The partial fraction expansion of Z(*s*) is,

$$Z(s) = \frac{2k_1 s}{s^2+1^2} + \frac{2k_3 s}{s^2+5^2}$$

The constants k_1 and k_3 may be evaluated by Heaviside rule as follows :

$$k_1 = \left.\frac{2s(s^2+4)}{(s-j1)(s^2+25)}\right|_{s=-j1} = \frac{2(-j)(-1+4)}{(-2j)(-1+25)} = \frac{1}{8}$$

$$k_3 = \left.\frac{2s(s^2+4)}{(s^2+1)(s-j5)}\right|_{s=-j5} = \frac{2(-5j)(-25+4)}{(-25+1)(-10j)} = \frac{7}{8}$$

Hence $$Z(s) = \frac{2\times\frac{1}{8}s}{s^2+1} + \frac{2\times\frac{7}{8}s}{s^2+25} = \frac{5}{4(s^2+1)} + \frac{75}{4(s^2+25)}$$

$$C_1 = \frac{1}{2k_1} = \frac{1}{2\times\frac{1}{8}} = 4 \text{ Farad}$$

$$L_1 = \frac{2k_1}{\omega_1^2} = \frac{1}{4\times 1} = \frac{1}{4} \text{ Henry}$$

$$C_3 = \frac{1}{2k_3} = \frac{1}{2\times\frac{7}{8}} = \frac{4}{7} \text{ Farad}$$

$$L_3 = \frac{2k_3}{\omega_3^2} = \frac{7/4}{25} = \frac{7}{100} \text{ Henry.}$$

Hence the element values in the first Foster equivalent network are as shown in Fig. Ex. 27.9 (*a*).

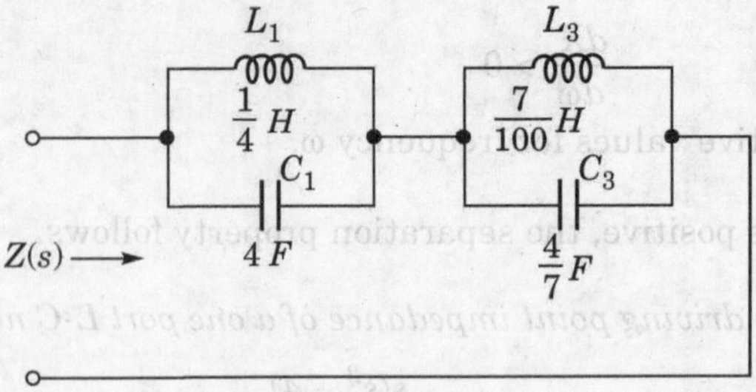

Fig. Ex. 27.9 (*a*)

To determine the second Foster form equivalent circuit, we first find the admittance function.

Thus $$Y(s) = \frac{1}{Z(s)} = \frac{(s^2+1)(s^3+25)}{2s(s^2+4)}$$

Since $Z(s)$ belongs to case II, $Y(s)$ belongs to case I. Hence partial fraction expansion of expression for $Y(s)$ is as below :

$$Y(s) = \frac{k_0}{s} + \frac{k^2}{s+j2} + \frac{k^2}{s-j2} + Hs$$

Constants k_0 and k_2 may be evaluated by using Heaviside rule. Thus,

$$k_0 = \left.\frac{(s^2+1)(s^2+25)}{2(s^2+4)}\right|_{s=0} = \frac{25}{8}$$

$$k_2 = \left.\frac{(s^2+1)(s^2+25)}{2s(s-j2)}\right|_{s=-j2} = \frac{(-4+1)(-4+25)}{2(-j2)(-j4)} = \frac{63}{16}$$

By inspection $$H = \frac{1}{2}$$

Hence $$Y(s) = \frac{25}{8s} + \frac{2\times\frac{63}{16}\times s}{s^2+4} + \frac{s}{2}$$

Elements of the second Foster form equivalent circuit are

$$L_0 = \frac{1}{k_0} = \frac{8}{25} \text{ Henry}$$

$$C_0 = H = \frac{1}{2} \text{ Farad}$$

$$L_2 = \frac{1}{2k_2} + \frac{16}{2\times 63} = \frac{8}{63} \text{ Henry}$$

$$C_2 = \frac{2k_2}{\omega_2^2} = \frac{2\times 63}{16\times 4} = \frac{63}{32} \text{ Farads.}$$

Hence the element values in the second Foster equivalent network are as shown in Fig. Ex. 27.9 (*b*).

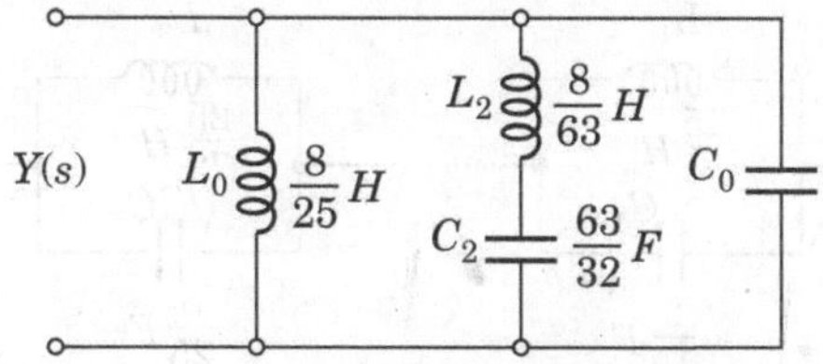

Fig. Ex. 27.9 (*b*)

Example 27.10. *The driving point impedance of a one port L–C network is given by,*

$$Z(s) = 5\frac{s(s^2 + 4)}{(s^2 + 1)(s^2 + 9)}$$

Obtain the first and second Foster form of equivalent network.

Solution. The order of the numerator polynomial is less than the order of the denominator polynomial. Hence there is a simple zero at infinity. Further the lowest ordered term in the numerator is of higher order than the lowest ordered term in the denominator. Hence there is a simple zero at zero frequency. Hence the impedance function forms case II. Hence there will be no L_0 and C_0 elements in the Foster form and no k_0/s and Hs terms in the partial fraction expansion.

The partial fraction expansion of $Z(s)$ is,

$$Z(s) = \frac{2k_1 s}{s^2 + 1} + \frac{2k_3 s}{s^2 + 9}$$

The constants k_1 and k_3 may be evaluated by Heaviside rule as follows :

Thus
$$k_1 = \left.\frac{5s(s^2 + 4)}{(s - j)(s^2 + 9)}\right|_{s=-j1} = \frac{15}{16}$$

$$k_3 = \left.\frac{5s(s^2 + 4)}{(s^2 + 1)(s - j3)}\right|_{s=-j3} = \frac{25}{16}$$

Hence
$$Z(s) = \frac{2 \times \frac{15}{16} s}{s^2 + 1} + \frac{2 \times \frac{25}{16} s}{s^2 + 9} = \frac{15s}{8(s^2 + 1)} + \frac{25s}{8(s^2 + 9)}$$

$$C_1 = \frac{1}{2k_1} = \frac{16}{2 \times 15} = \frac{8}{15} \text{ Farad}$$

$$L_1 = \frac{2k_1}{\omega_1^2} = \frac{15/8}{1} = \frac{15}{8} \text{ Henry}$$

$$C_3 = \frac{1}{2k_3} = \frac{16}{2 \times 25} = \frac{8}{25} \text{ Farad}$$

$$L_3 = \frac{2k_3}{\omega_3^2} = \frac{25/8}{9} = \frac{25}{72} \text{ Henry.}$$

Hence the elements in the first Foster equivalent network are shown in Fig. Ex. 27.10 (*a*).

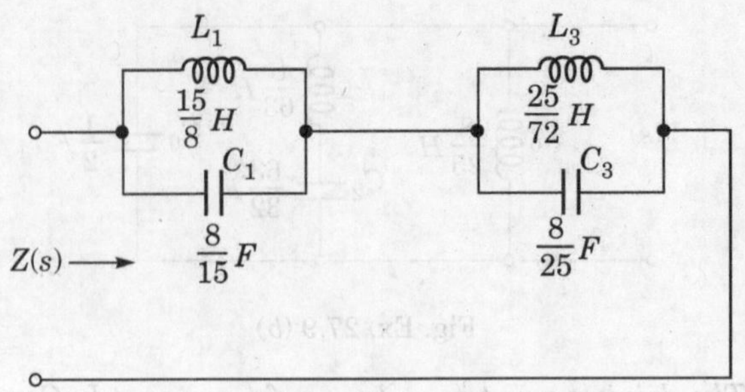

Fig. Ex. 27.10 (*a*).

To determine the second Foster form of network, we first find the corresponding admittance function.

Thus $$Y(s) = \frac{1}{Z(s)} = \frac{(s^2+1)(s^2+9)}{5s(s^2+4)}.$$

Since $Z(s)$ belongs to case II, $Y(s)$ belongs to case I. Hence partial fraction expansion of expression for $Y(s)$ is as below :

$$Y(s) = \frac{k_0}{s} + \frac{k_2}{s+j2} + \frac{k_2}{s-j2} + Hs$$

Constants k_0 and k_2 may be evaluated by using Heaviside rule.

Thus, $$k_0 = \left.\frac{(s^2+1)(s^2+9)}{5(s^2+4)}\right|_{s=0} = \frac{9}{20}$$

$$k_2 = \left.\frac{(s^2+1)(s^2+9)}{5s(s-j2)}\right|_{s=-j2} = \frac{3}{8}$$

By insecpection $$H = \frac{1}{5}$$

Hence $$Y(s) = \frac{9}{20s} + \frac{2\times\left(\frac{3}{8}\right)s}{s^2+4} + \frac{1}{5}s = \frac{9}{20s} + \frac{3s}{4(s^2+4)} + \frac{s}{5}$$

Elements of the second Foster form of equivalent circuit are :

$$L_0 = \frac{1}{k_0} = \frac{20}{9} \text{ Henry}$$

$$C_0 = H = \frac{1}{5} \text{ Farad}$$

$$L_2 = \frac{1}{2k_2} = \frac{8}{2\times 3} = \frac{4}{3} \text{ Henry}$$

$$C_2 = \frac{2k_2}{\omega_2^2} = \frac{3/4}{4} = \frac{3}{16} \text{ Farad.}$$

Hence the elements in the second Foster form of equivalent network are as shown in Fig. Ex. 27.10 (*b*).

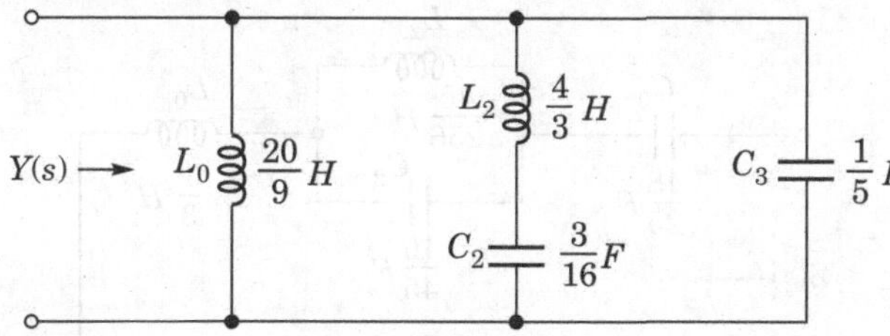

Fig. Ex. 27.10 (*b*)

Example 27.11. *The driving point admittance of a one-port L–C network is given by,*

$$Y(s) = \frac{3s^2(s^2+16)}{(s^2+1)(s^2+25)}$$

Obtain the first and second Foster form of equivalent networks.

Solution. $$Y(s) = \frac{1}{Y(s)} = \frac{(Y^2+1)(s^2+25)}{3s(s^2+16)} \qquad ...(1)$$

The order of the numerator polynomial in Eq. (1) exceeds the. order of the denominator polynomial. Hence there is simple polecat $\omega = \infty$.

Further lowest order term of numerator is of order lower than than of the lowest order term of denominator. Hence there is a simple pole at $\infty = 0$. Hence this impedance function is of class I and the partial fraction expansion is,

$$Z(s) = \frac{k_0}{s} + \frac{2k_2 s}{\omega^2+16} + Hs$$

The constants of this equation may be evaluated by Heaviside rule. Thus,

$$k_0 = \frac{1\times 25}{3\times 16} = \frac{25}{48}$$

$$k_2 = \left.\frac{(s^2+1)(s^2+25)}{3s(s-j4)}\right|_{s=-j4} = \frac{45}{32}$$

By inspection $H = \frac{1}{3}$

$$C_0 = \frac{1}{k_0} = \frac{48}{25} \text{ Farad}$$

$$L_0 = H = \frac{1}{3} \text{ Henry}$$

$$C_2 = \frac{1}{2k_2} = \frac{32}{3\times 45} = \frac{16}{45} \text{ Farad}$$

$$L_2 = \frac{2k_2}{\omega_2^2} = \frac{45/32}{16} = \frac{45}{256} \text{ Henry.}$$

Hence the elements in the first Foster form of equivalent network are as shown in Fig. Ex. 27.11 (*a*).

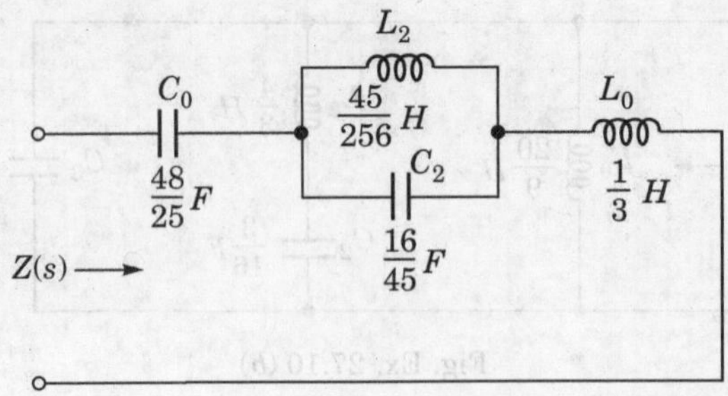

Fig. Ex. 27.11 (*a*)

Since $Z(s)$ belongs to case I, $Y(s)$ belongs to case II. Thus there are no admittance poles at $\omega_0 = 0$ and $\omega_0 = \infty$. This admittance function $Y(s)$ on partial fraction expansion yields,

$$Y(s) = \frac{2k_1 s}{s^2+1} + \frac{2k_3 s}{s_2+25} \quad \text{...(3)}$$

The two constants k_1 and k_3 may be found by Heaviside rule. Thus, we get

$$k_1 = \left.\frac{3s(s^2+16)}{(s-j1)(s^2+25)}\right|_{s=-j1} = \frac{15}{16}$$

$$k_3 = \left.\frac{3s(s^2+16)}{(s^2+1)(s-j5)}\right|_{s=-j5} = \frac{9}{16}$$

Hence $$Y(s) = \frac{2\times\frac{15}{16}s}{s^2+1} + \frac{2\times\frac{9}{16}s}{s^2+25}$$

$$= \frac{15s}{32(s^2+1)} + \frac{9s}{8(s^2+25)}$$

$$L_1 = \frac{1}{2k_1} = \frac{16}{2\times 15} = \frac{8}{15} \text{ Henry}$$

$$C_1 = \frac{2k_1}{\omega_1^2} = \frac{15/8}{1} = \frac{15}{8} \text{ Farad}$$

$$L_3 = \frac{1}{2k_3} = \frac{16}{2\times 9} = \frac{8}{9} \text{ Henry}$$

$$C_3 = \frac{2k_3}{\omega_3^2} = \frac{9/8}{25} = \frac{9}{200} \text{ Farad.}$$

Hence the element values in the second Foster form of equivalent network are as shown in Fig. Ex. 27.11 (*b*).

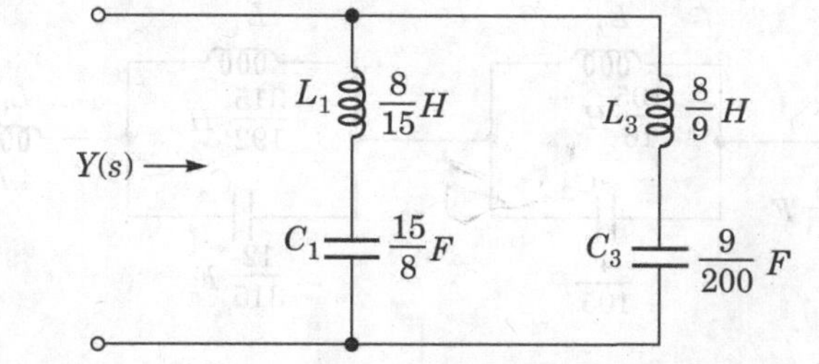

Fig. Ex. 27.11 (*b*)

Example 27.12. *The driving point impedance of a one port LC network is given by,*

$$Z(s) = \frac{4(s^2 + 1)(s^2 + 9)(s^2 + 25)}{s(s^2 + 4)(s^2 + 16)}$$

Obtain the first and second Foster forms of equivalent network.

Solution. The order of the numerator polynomial exceeds the order of the denominator polynomial. Hence there is a simple pole at $\omega = \infty$.

Further the order of the lowest order term in the numerator is lower than the order of the lowest order term in the denominator. Hence there is a simple pole at $\omega = 0$. Hence this impedance function is of Class I and the partial fraction expansion is,

$$Z(s) = \frac{k_0}{s} + \frac{2k_2 s}{s^2 + 4} + \frac{2k_4 s}{s^2 + 6} + Hs \quad \text{...(1)}$$

The constants of this equation may be evaluated by the Heaviside rule. Thus, we get

$$k_0 = \left.\frac{4(s^1 + 1)(s^2 + 9)(s^2 + 25)}{(s^4 + 4)(s^2 + 16)}\right|_{s=0} = \frac{4 \times 1 \times 9 \times 25}{4 \times 16} = \frac{225}{16}$$

$$k_2 = \left.\frac{4(s^2 + 1)(s^2 + 9)(s^2 + 25)}{s(s - j2)(s^2 + 16)}\right|_{s=-j2} = \frac{105}{8}$$

$$k_4 = \left.\frac{4(s^2 + 1)(s^2 + 9)(s^2 + 25)}{s(s^2 + 4)(s - j4)}\right|_{s=-j4} = \frac{315}{24}$$

By inspection $H = 4$

$$C_0 = \frac{1}{k_0} = \frac{16}{225} \text{ Farad}$$

$$L_0 = H = 4 \text{ Henry}$$

$$C_2 = \frac{1}{2k_2} = \frac{8}{2 \times 105} = \frac{4}{105} \text{ Farad}$$

$$L_2 = \frac{2k_2}{\omega_2^2} = \frac{105/4}{4} = \frac{105}{16} \text{ Henry}$$

$$C_4 = \frac{1}{2k_4} = \frac{24}{2 \times 315} = \frac{12}{315} \text{ Farad}$$

$$L_4 = \frac{2k_4}{\omega_4^2} = \frac{315/12}{16} = \frac{315}{192} \text{ Henry.}$$

Hence the elements in the first Foster form of equivalent network are as shown in Fig. Ex. 27.12 (*a*).

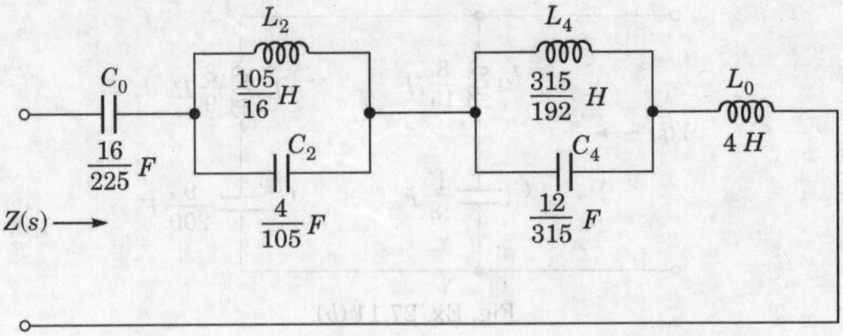

Fig. Ex. 27.12 (*a*)

$$Y(s) = \frac{1}{Z(s)} = \frac{s(s^2+4)(s^2+16)}{4(s^2+1)(s^2+9)(s^2+25)}$$

Since $Z(s)$ belongs to Case I, the corresponding $Y(s)$ is of Case II. Thus there are no admittance poles at $\omega = 0$ and $\omega = \infty$. This admittance function $Y(s)$ on partial fraction expansion yields,

$$Y(s) = \frac{2k_1 s}{(s^2+1)} + \frac{2k_3 s}{(s^2+9)} + \frac{2k_5 s}{s^2+25}$$

The constants k_1, k_3 and k_5 may be evaluated by the Heaviside rule. Thus,

$$k_1 = \left.\frac{s(s^2+4)(s^2+16)}{4(s-j1)(s^2+9)(s^2+25)}\right|_{s=-j1} = \frac{15}{512}$$

$$k_3 = \left.\frac{s(s^2+4)(s^2+16)}{s(s^2+1)(s-j3)(s^2+25)}\right|_{s=-j3} = \frac{105}{3072}$$

$$k_5 = \left.\frac{s(s^2+4)(s^2+16)}{4(s^2+1)(s^2+9)(s-j5)}\right|_{s=-j5} = \frac{63}{1024}$$

$$L_1 = \frac{1}{2k_1} = \frac{512}{2\times 15} = \frac{256}{15} \text{ Henry}$$

$$C_1 = \frac{2k_1}{\omega_1^2} = \frac{15/256}{1} = \frac{15}{256} \text{ Farad}$$

$$L_3 = \frac{1}{2k_3} = \frac{3072}{2\times 105} = \frac{1536}{105} \text{ Henry}$$

$$C_3 = \frac{2k_3}{\omega_3^2} = \frac{105/1536}{9} = \frac{105}{13824} \text{ Farad}$$

$$L_5 = \frac{1}{2k_5} = \frac{1024}{2\times 63} = \frac{512}{63} \text{ Henry}$$

$$C_5 = \frac{2k_5}{\omega_5^2} = \frac{6^3}{51^3 \times 25} = \frac{63}{12800} \text{ Farad.}$$

Hence the elements in the second Foster form are as shown in Fig. Ex. 27.12 (*b*).

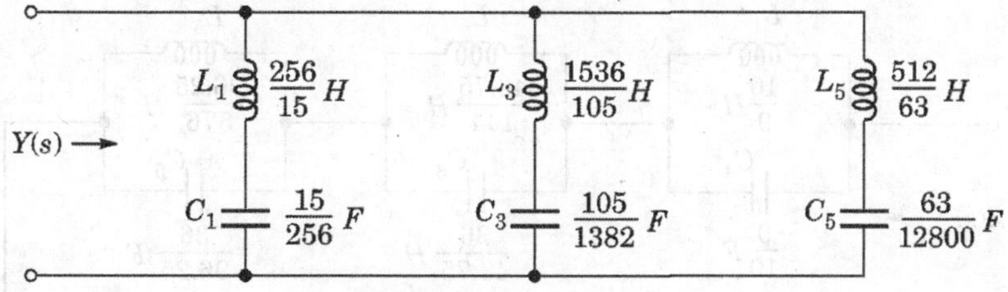

Fig. Ex. 27.12 (*b*)

Example 27.13. *The driving point impedance of a one port L–C network is given by,*

$$Z(s) = \frac{5s(s^2 + 2.25)(s^2 + 9)}{(s^2 + 1)(s^2 + 4)(s^2 + 16)}$$

Obtain the first and second Foster form of equivalent network.

Solution. The order of the numerator polynomial is less than the order of the denominator polynomial. Hence there is a simple zero at $\omega = \infty$. Further the lowest ordered term in the numerator is of higher order than the lowest ordered term in the denominator. Hence there is a simple zero at $\omega = 0$. Hence the impedance function forms case II. Hence there will be no L_0 and C_0 elements in the first Foster form and no k_0/s and Hs terms in the partial fraction expansion. The partial fraction expansion of $Z(s)$ is,

$$Z(s) = \frac{2k_1 s}{s^2 + 1} + \frac{2k_3 s}{s^2 + 4} + \frac{2k_5 s}{s^2 + 16}$$

The constants k_1, k_3 and k_5 may be evaluated by Heaviside rule. Thus, we get

$$k_1 = \left.\frac{5s(s^2 + 2.25)(s^2 + 9)}{(s - j1)(s^2 + 4)(s^2 + 16)}\right|_{s=-j1} = \frac{5}{9}$$

$$k_3 = \left.\frac{5s(s^2 + 2.25)(s^2 + 9)}{(s^2 + 1)(s - j2)(s^2 + 16)}\right|_{s=-j2} = \frac{43.75}{72}$$

$$k_5 = \left.\frac{5s(s^2 + 2.25)(s^2 + 9)}{(s^2 + 1)(s^2 + 4)(s - j4)}\right|_{s=-j4} = \frac{96.25}{72}$$

$$C_1 = \frac{1}{2k_1} = \frac{9}{2 \times 5} = \frac{9}{10} \text{ Farad}$$

$$L_1 = \frac{2k_1}{\omega_1^2} = \frac{10/9}{1} = \frac{10}{9} \text{ Henry}$$

$$C_3 = \frac{1}{2k_3} = \frac{72}{2 \times 43.75} = \frac{36}{43.75} \text{ Farad}$$

$$L_3 = \frac{2k_3}{\omega_3^2} = \frac{43.75/36}{4} = \frac{43.75}{144} \text{ Henry}$$

$$C_5 = \frac{1}{2k_5} = \frac{72}{2 \times 96.25} = \frac{36}{96.25} \text{ Henry}$$

$$L_5 = \frac{2k_5}{\omega_5^2} = \frac{96.25/36}{16} = \frac{96.25}{576} \text{ Henry.}$$

Hence the element values in the first Foster form of equivalent network are as shown in Fig. Ex. 27.13 (*a*).

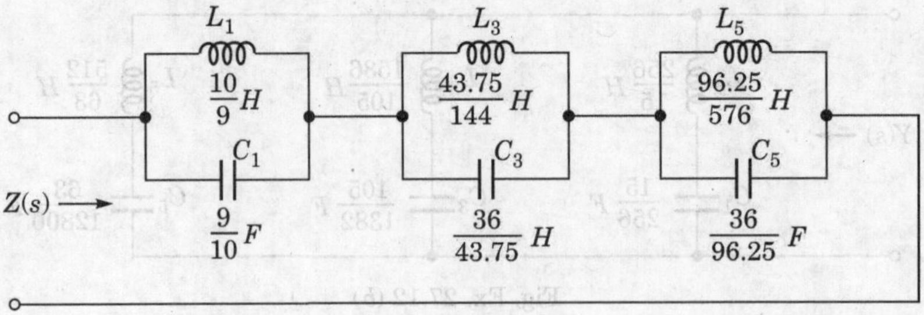

Fig. Ex. 27.13 (*a*)

To determine the second Foster form of equivalent circuit, we first obtain the admittance function

Thus $$Y(s) = \frac{1}{Z(s)} = \frac{(s^2+1)(s^2+4)(s^2+16)}{5s(s^2+2.25)(s^2+9)}$$

Since $Z(s)$ belongs to case II $Y(s)$ belongs to case I. Hence partial fraction expansion for $Y(s)$ is as below :

$$Y(s) = \frac{k_0}{s} + \frac{2k_2 s}{s^2+2.25} + \frac{2k_4 s}{s^2+9} + Hs$$

Constants k_0, k_2 and k_4 may be evaluated by using Heaviside rule.

Thus $$k_0 = \left.\frac{(s^2+1)(s^2+4)(s^2+16)}{5(s^2+2.25)(s^2+9)}\right|_{s=0} = 0 = \frac{64}{10125} = 6.32 \times 10^{-3}$$

$$k_2 = \left.\frac{(s^2+1)(s^2+4)(s^2+16)}{5s(s-1.5j)(s^2+9)}\right|_{s=-j1.5} = 0.198$$

$$k_4 = \left.\frac{(s^2+1)(s^2+4)(s^2+16)}{5s(s^2+2.25)(s-j3)}\right|_{s=-j3} = 0.46$$

By inspection $H = \frac{1}{5}$

Elements of the second Foster form of equivalent circuit are :

$$L_0 = \frac{1}{k_0} = \frac{10^3}{6.32} = 158 \text{ Henry}$$

$$C_0 = H = \frac{1}{5} = 0.2 \text{ Farad}$$

$$L_2 = \frac{2}{2k_2} = \frac{1}{2\times 0.198} = 2.52 \text{ Henry}$$

$$C_2 = \frac{2k_2}{\omega_2^2} = \frac{2\times 0.198}{2.25} = 0.1765 \text{ Farad}$$

$$L_4 = \frac{1}{2k_4} = \frac{1}{2\times 0.46} = 1.087 \text{ Henry}$$

$$C_4 = \frac{2k_4}{\omega_4^2} = \frac{0.92}{9} = 0.102 \text{ Farad.}$$

Hence the element values in the second Foster form of equivalent circuit are as shown in Fig. Ex. 27.13 (*b*).

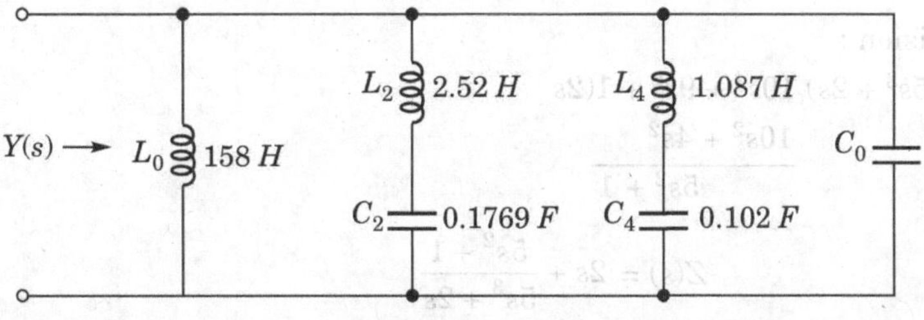

Fig. Ex. 27.13 (*b*).

27.9. Cauer Form of Reactive Networks

Foster reactance theorem was extended by Cauer in 1927. Cauer established that a reactance function may be represented by two different network configurations by a *continued fraction expansion* of the driving point impedance. The basic Cauer form of network realization is the *ladder network* shown in Fig. 27.10. From Fig. 27.10 the driving point impedance *Z*(*s*) of such a ladder network may be written in the form of a continued fraction as below,

$$Z(s) = Z_1 + \cfrac{1}{Y_2 + \cfrac{1}{Y_3 + \cfrac{1}{Y_4 + \cfrac{1}{Y_5 + \cfrac{1}{Y_6 + \dots}}}}} \qquad \dots(27.64)$$

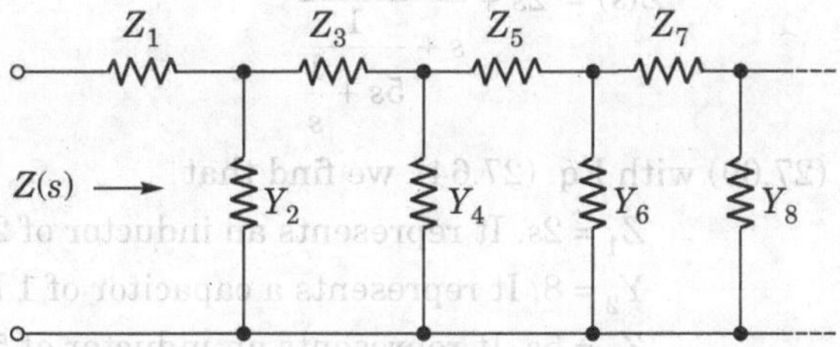

Fig. 27.10. Ladder network.

Let us consider a driving point impedance with a pole at infinity. Let this *Z*(*s*) be given by,

$$Z(s) = \frac{a_n s^n + a_{n-2} s^{n-2} + \dots}{b_m s^m + b_{m-2} s^{m-2} + \dots} \qquad \dots(27.65)$$

where $n > m$.

We now proceed to put *Z*(*s*) in the continued fraction form. The process is (*i*) to divide (*ii*) invert and divide (*iii*) repeat step (*iv*), until the expansion terminates.

Cauer networks are of two types designed as First Cauer network and second Cauer network. First Cauer network may again be of two types : (*a*) with pole at infinity and (*b*) with zero at infinity. We first consider the first Cauer network with pole at infinity. This is illustrated with the help of an example.

First Cauer Network with a pole at Infinity. Let us take the following example :

$$Z(s) = \frac{10s^4 + 9s^2 + 1}{5s^3 + 2s} \qquad ...(27.66)$$

On direct division :

$$\begin{array}{l} 5s^3 + 2s)\ 10s^4 + 9s^2 + 1(2s \\ \qquad\quad\ \underline{10s^2 + 4s^2} \\ \qquad\qquad\quad 5s^2 + 1 \end{array}$$

Hence $$Z(s) = 2s + \frac{5s^2 + 1}{5s^3 + 2s} \qquad ...(27.67)$$

On inverting the remainder term and dividing, we get

$$\begin{array}{l} 5s^2 + 1)\ 5s^3 + 2s\ (s \\ \qquad\quad\ \underline{5s^2 + s} \\ \qquad\qquad\quad s \end{array}$$

Hence $$Z(s) = 2s + \frac{1}{s + \frac{s}{5s^2 + 1}} \qquad ...(27.68)$$

On further inverting and dividing, we get

$$\begin{array}{l} 5)\ 5s^2 + 1\ (5s \\ \quad\ \underline{5s} \\ \qquad\quad 1 \end{array}$$

Hence $$Z(s) = 2s + \frac{1}{s + \frac{1}{5s + \frac{1}{s}}} \qquad ...(27.69)$$

On comparing Eq. (27.69) with Eq. (27.64), we find that

$Z_1 = 2s$. It represents an inductor of 2 Henrys

$Y_2 = 8$. It represents a capacitor of 1 Farad

$Z_3 = 5s$. It represents an inductor of 5 Henrys

$Y_4 = 8$. It represents a capacitor of 1 Farad.

The network representing $Z(s)$ in this problem is, therefore, as shown in Fig. 27.11.

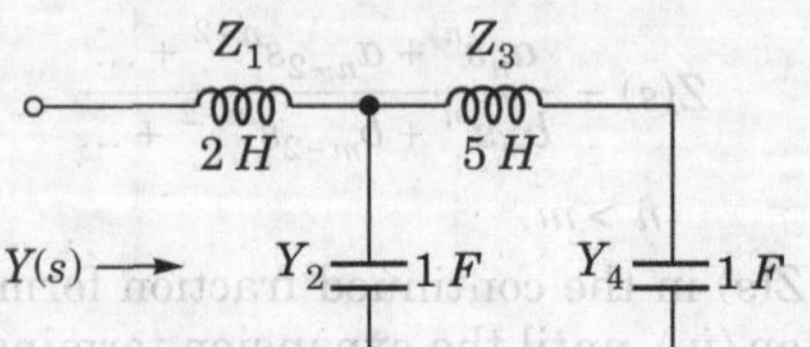

Fig. 27.11. First Cauer network for Eq. (27.26).

$Z(s)$ given by Eq. (27.66) has a pole at infinity. For $Z(s)$ with a pole at infinity, the first Cauer network is always of the form given in Fig. 27.12 consisting of series inductors and shunt capacitors extending to the extent needed for the continued fraction expansion.

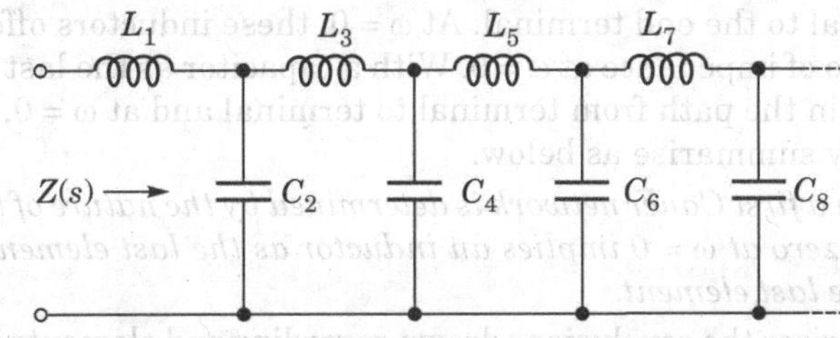

Fig. 27.12. General form of first Cauer network with a pole infinity.

First Cauer Network with Zero at Infinity. In this case, in the expression for $Z(s)$, $m > n$ by unity. Hence in this case, before the continued fraction expansion can be made, it is necessary to invert the polynomial. The form of expansion is,

$$Z(s) = \cfrac{1}{Y_2 + \cfrac{1}{Z_3 + \cfrac{1}{Y_4 + \cfrac{1}{Z_5 + \ldots}}}} \quad \ldots(27.70)$$

On comparing Eq. (27.70) with Eq. (27.64), we find that the only difference is that in Eq. (27.70), $Z_1 = 0$. Since $Z_1 = 0$, the first series inductor L_1 is absent from Fig. 27.12. Hence the general form of first Cauer network with zero at infinity is as shown in Fig. 27.13.

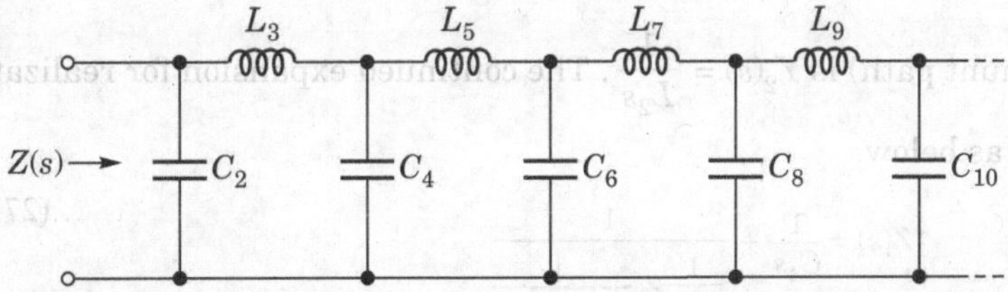

Fig, 27.13. General form of first Cauer network with zero at infinity.

First Element in the First Cauer Network. Thus in the general form of first Cauer network (*i*) a pole at infinity requires that the first element be a series inductor while (*ii*) a zero at infinity requires that the first element be a shunt capacitor.

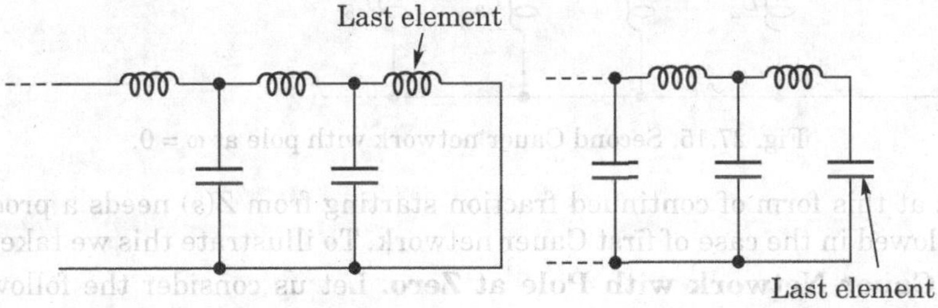

(a) With inductor as the last element

(*b*) With capacitor as the last element

Fig. 27.14. Last elements in first Cauer network.

Last Element in the First Cauer Network. A ladder network may end in one of the following two ways : (*i*) with an inductor as shown in Fig. 27.14 (*a*) and (*ii*) with a capacitor as shown in Fig. 27.14 (*b*). With inductor as the last element, there are, in general, several inductors in the series path from output terminal to the end terminal. At ω = 0, these inductors offer zero impedance and hence there results a zero of impedance at ω = 0. With a capacitor as the last element, there results a break or discontinuity in the path from terminal to terminal and at ω = 0, there results a pole of impedance. Thus we may summarise as below.

The last element in a first Cauer network is determined by the nature of the impedance function Z(s) at zero frequency. A zero at ω = 0 implies an inductor as the last element while a pole at ω = 0 implies a capacitor as the last element.

Table 27.8 summarises the conclusions drawn regarding end elements in first Cauer network.

Table 27.8

End Elements in First Cauer Network

Case	ω = 0	ω = ∞	*First element*	*Last element*
I	Pole	Pole	*L*	*C*
II	Zero	Zero	*C*	*L*
III	Pole	Zero	*C*	*C*
IV	Zero	Pole	*L*	*L*

Second Cauer Network with Pole at ω = 0. The second Cauer network is also a ladder network but it has capacitors in the series path and inductors in the shunt path as shown in Fig. 27.15. Then the impedance of the first element is $Z_1(s) = \dfrac{1}{C_1 s}$ while the admittance of the second element (in the shunt path) is $Y_2(s) = \dfrac{1}{L_2 s}$. The continued expansion for realization of this second Cauer network is as below.

$$Z(s) = \frac{1}{C_1 s} + \cfrac{1}{\cfrac{1}{L_2 s} + \cfrac{1}{\cfrac{1}{C_1 s} + \dots}} \qquad \dots(27.71)$$

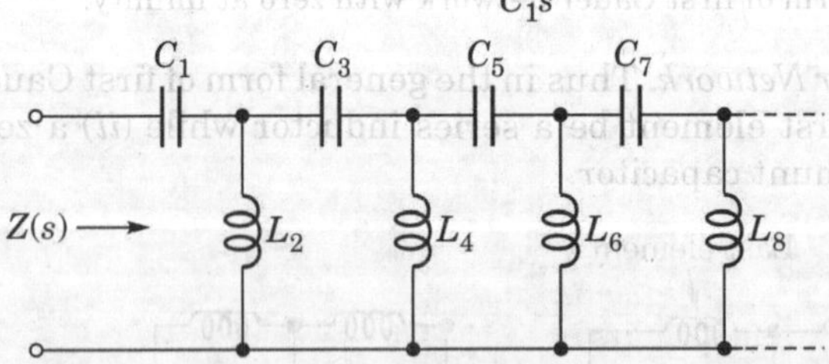

Fig. 27.15. Second Cauer network with pole at ω = 0.

In arrive at this form of continued fraction starting from *Z*(*s*) needs a procedure different from the one followed in the case of first Cauer network. To illustrate this we take up an example.

Second Cauer Network with Pole at Zero. Let us consider the following impedance function :

$$Z(s) = \frac{s^4 + 6s^2 + 4}{s^3 + 2s} \qquad \dots(27.72)$$

Before we expand this function, we turn it end for end to yield,

$$Z(s) = \frac{4 + 6s^2 + s^4}{2s + s^3} \quad \text{...(27.73)}$$

We now divide the denominator into the numerator,

$2s + s^3\,)\;\; 4 + 6s^2 + s^4\; (2/s$

$\qquad\qquad\;\; 4 + 2s^2$

$\qquad\qquad\;\; \overline{4s^2 + s^4}$

Thus $$Z(s) = \frac{2}{s} + \frac{4s^2 + s^4}{2s + s^3} \quad \text{...(27.74)}$$

We now repeatedly follow the invert and divide procedure until we arrive at zero remainder. On inverting, we get

$$Z(s) = \frac{2}{s} + \frac{1}{\dfrac{2s + s^3}{4s^2 + s^4}} \quad \text{...(27.75)}$$

We divide : $4s^2 + s^4)\;\; 2s + s^3\; (1/2s$

$\qquad\qquad 2s + \frac{s^3}{2}$

$\qquad\qquad \overline{\qquad \frac{s^3}{2}}$

Hence $$Z(s) = \frac{2}{s} + \frac{1}{\dfrac{1}{2s} + \dfrac{\frac{1}{2}s^3}{4s^2 + s^4}}$$

We invert and divide

$\frac{1}{2}s^3\,)\;\; 4s^2 + s^4\; (8/s$

$\qquad\quad 4s^2$

$\qquad\quad \overline{\quad s^4}$

Hence $$Z(s) = \frac{2}{s} + \frac{1}{\dfrac{1}{2s} + \dfrac{1}{\dfrac{8}{s} + \dfrac{s^4}{\frac{1}{2}s^3}}} \quad \text{...(27.76)}$$

Final invert-and-divide step gives,

$s^4)\;\; \frac{1}{2}s^3\; (\frac{1}{2}s$

$\qquad \frac{1}{2}s^3$

$\qquad \overline{\quad \times}$

Hence $$Z(s) = \frac{2}{s} + \cfrac{1}{\cfrac{1}{2s} + \cfrac{1}{\cfrac{8}{5} + \cfrac{1}{\cfrac{1}{2s}}}} \qquad ...(27.77)$$

On comparing Eq. (27.77) with Eqs. (27.64) and (27.71) we may identify the elements of this second Cauer network as below :

$Z(s) = \frac{2}{s}$ represents a capacitor of value $\frac{1}{2}$ Farad

$Y_2(s) = \frac{1}{2s}$ represents an inductor of value 2 Henrys

$Z_3(s) = \frac{8}{s}$ represents a capacitor of value 1/8 Farad

$Y_4(s) = \frac{1}{2s}$ represents an inductor of value 2 Henrys.

Hence the second Cauer network equipment to the impedance function $Z(s)$ given by Eq. (27.72) is as shown in Fig. 27.16.

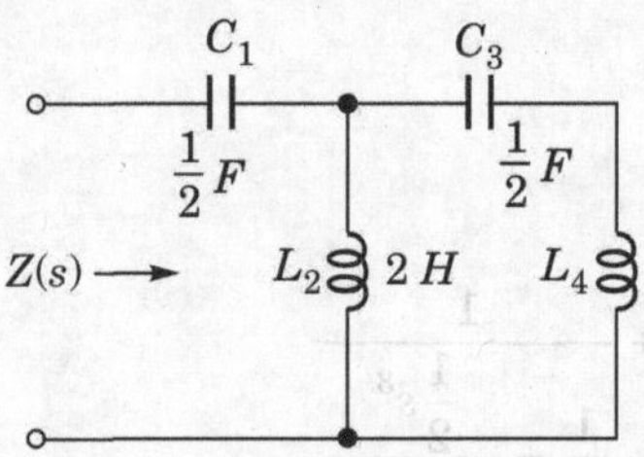

Fig. 27.16. Second Cauer network realization of $Z(s)$ of Eq. (27.72).

Impedance $Z(s)$ of Eq. (27.72) is quotient of even-to-odd polynomial. This implies that the function has a pole at zero. Next we consider a second Cauer network with zero at zero.

Second Cauer Network with zero at zero. In this case, it is necessary to first invert and then divide. Hence the continued fraction will be of the following form :

$$Z(s) = \cfrac{1}{\cfrac{1}{L_2 s} + \cfrac{1}{\cfrac{1}{C_3 s} + \cfrac{1}{\cfrac{1}{L_4 s + ...}}}} \qquad ...(27.78)$$

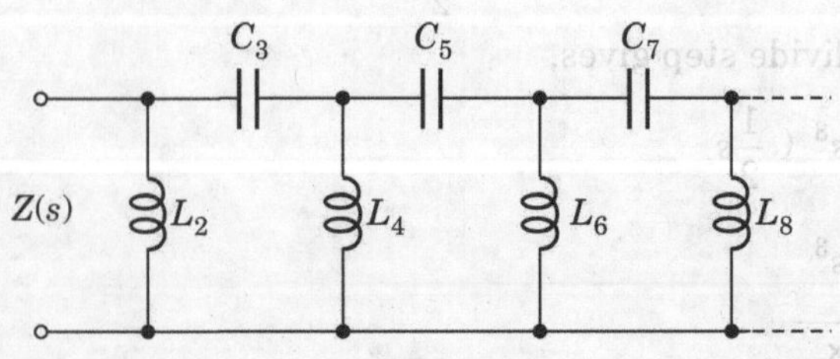

Fig. 27.17. Second Cauer network with zero at $\omega = 0$.

On comparing Eq. (27.78) with Eq. (27.71) we find that the only difference is that in Eq. (27.78), $\frac{1}{C_1 s}$ is absent. Since $C_1 = 0$, the first series capacitor is absent from Fig. 27.15. Hence the general form of second Cauer network with zero at zero is as shown in Fig. 27.17.

First element in the second Cauer network. In the general form of second Cauer network (*i*) a pole at zero requires, that the First element be a series capacitor while (*ii*) a zero at $\omega = 0$ required that the first element be a shunt inductor.

Last element in the second Cauer network. The second Cauer network may end in one of the following two ways : (*i*) with a capacitor as shown in Fig. 27.18 (*a*) or (*ii*) with an inductor as shown in Fig. 27.18 (*b*). With capacitor as the last element, there are several capacitors in the series path from input terminal to the end. At $\omega = \infty$, these capacitors offer zero impedance and hence there results a zero of impedance at $\omega = \infty$. With an inductor as the last element, there results a break or discontinuity in the path from terminal to terminal and at $\omega = \infty$, there results a pole of impedance. Thus we may summarize as below :

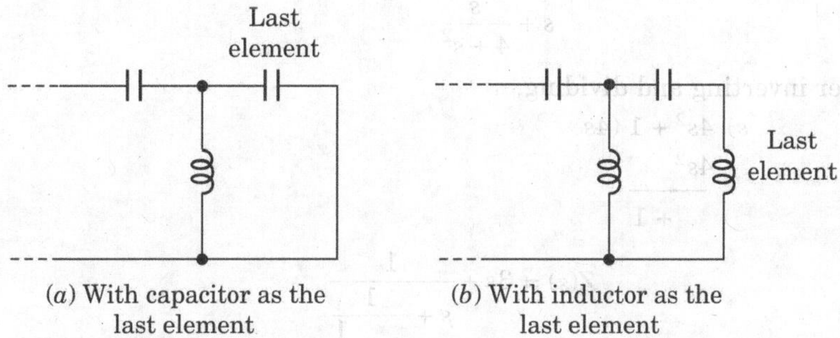

Fig. 27.18. Last elements in the second Cauer network,

The last element in second Cauer network is an inductor if the Z(s) has a pole at infinity and it is a capacitor if Z(s) has a zero at infinity.

Table 27.9 summarizes the conclusions drawn regarding the end elements in second Cauer network.

Table 27.9
End Elements in Second Cauer Network

Case	$\omega = 0$	$\omega = \infty$	*First element*	*Last element*
I	Pole	Pole	*C*	*L*
II	Zero	Zero	*L*	*C*
III	Pole	Zero	*C*	*C*
IV	Zero	Pole	*L*	*L*

Example 27.14. *The driving point impedance of an LC network is given by*

$$Z(s) = \frac{12s^4 + 10s^2 + 1}{4s^3 + 2s}$$

For this impedance function, (a) determine the first Cauer configuration and (b) determine the value of each element in the network.

Solution. On direct division,

$$4s^3 + 2s)\ 12s^4 + 10s^2 + 1\ (3s$$
$$\underline{12s^4 + 6s^2}$$
$$4s^2 + 1$$

Hence
$$Z(s) = 3s + \frac{4s^2 + 1}{4s^3 + 2s}$$

On inverting the remainder term and dividing, we get

$$4s^2 + 1)\ 4s^3 + 2s\ (s$$
$$\underline{4s^2 + s}$$
$$s$$

Hence
$$Z(s) = 3s + \cfrac{1}{s + \cfrac{s}{4 + s^2}}$$

On further inverting and dividing,

$$s)\ 4s^2 + 1\ (4s$$
$$\underline{4s^2}$$
$$+1$$

Hence
$$Z(s) = 3s + \cfrac{1}{s + \cfrac{1}{4s + \cfrac{1}{s}}}$$

$Z_1 = 3s$ represents an inductor of 3 Henrys

$Y_2 = s$ represents a capacitor of 1 Farad

$Z_3 = 4s$ represents an inductor of 4 Henrys

$Y_4 = s$ represents a capacitor of 1 Farad.

The first Cauer network is then as below :

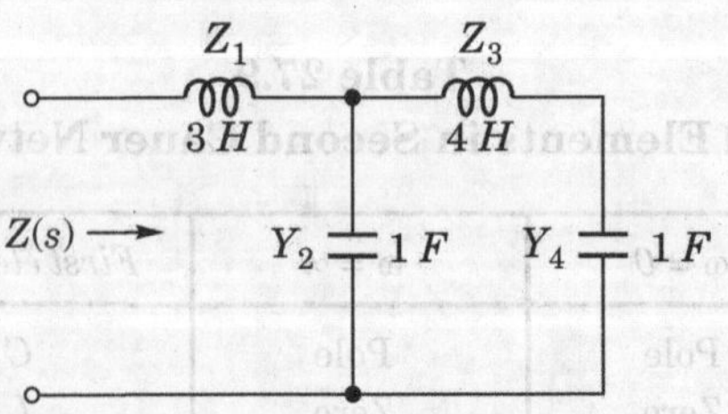

Fig. Ex. 27.14

Example 27.15. *The driving point impedance of an LC network is given by,*

$$Z(s) = \frac{s^4 + 6s^2 + s^4}{4s^3 + 2s}$$

For this impednce function (i) determine the second Cauer configuration and (ii) determine the value of each element in the network.

Solution. On turning the driving point impedance end for end, we get

$$Z(s) = \frac{4 + 6s^2 + s^4}{4s + 2s^3}$$

We now divide the denominator into the numerator,

$$4s + 2s^3)\ 4 + 6s^2 + s^4\ (1/s$$
$$\underline{4 + 2s^2}$$
$$4s^2 + s^4$$

Thus $$Z(s) = \frac{1}{s} + \frac{4s^2 + s^4}{4s + 2s^3}$$

On inverting,

$$Z(s) = \frac{1}{s} + \cfrac{1}{\cfrac{4s + 2s^3}{4s^2 + s^4}}$$

On dividing :

$$4s^2 + s^4)\ 4s + 2s^3\ (1/s$$
$$\underline{4s + s^3}$$
$$s^3$$

Hence $$Z(s) = \frac{1}{s} + \cfrac{1}{\cfrac{1}{s} + \cfrac{s^2}{4s^2 + s^4}}$$

On inverting and dividing,

$$s^3)\ 4s^2 + s^4\ (4/s$$
$$\underline{4s^2}$$
$$+s^4$$

Hence $$Z(s) = \frac{1}{s} + \cfrac{1}{\cfrac{1}{s} + \cfrac{1}{\cfrac{4}{s} + \cfrac{1}{\cfrac{1}{s}}}}$$

$Z_1(s) = \frac{1}{s}$ represents a capacitor of value 1 Farad

$Y_2(s) = \frac{1}{s}$ represents an inductor of value 1 Henry

$Z_3(s) = \frac{4}{s}$ represents a capacitor of value $\frac{1}{4}$ Farad

$Y_4(s) = \frac{1}{s}$ represents an inductor of value 1 Henry.

Hence the second Cauer network equivalent to the given impedance function is as shown in Fig. Ex. 27.15.

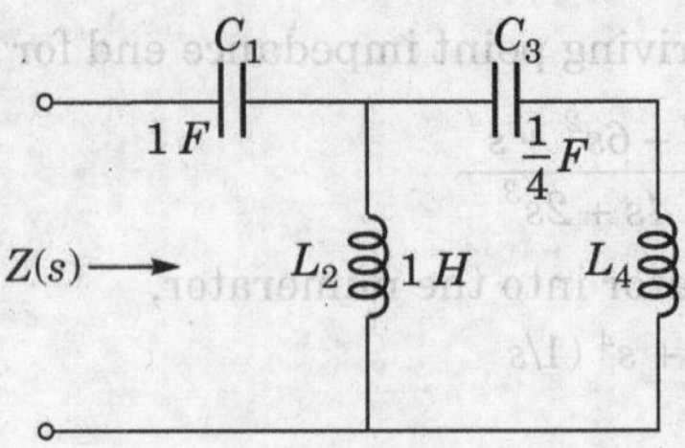

Fig. Ex. 27.15.

Example 27.16. *The driving point impedance of an LC network is given by,*

$$Z(s) = \frac{6s^3 + 2s}{12s^4 + 8s^2 + 1}$$

For this impedance function, find equivalent first Cauer network.

Solution. On inverting and dividing,

$$6s^3 + 2s)\; 12s^4 + 8s^2 + 1\; (2s$$
$$\frac{12s^4 + 4s^2}{4s^2 + 1}$$

Hence
$$Z(s) = \cfrac{1}{2s + \cfrac{4s^2 + 1}{6s^3 + 2s}}$$

On further inverting and dividing,

$$4s^2 + 1)\; 6s^3 + 2s\; (3s/2$$
$$\frac{6s^3 + \frac{3s}{2}}{+\frac{s}{2}}$$

Hence
$$Z(s) = \cfrac{1}{2s + \cfrac{1}{\cfrac{3s}{2} + \cfrac{s/2}{4s^2 + 1}}}$$

On further inverting and dividing,

$$s/2)\; 4s^2 + 1\; (8s$$
$$\frac{4s^2}{+1}$$

Hence
$$Z(s) = \cfrac{1}{2s + \cfrac{1}{\cfrac{3s}{2} + \cfrac{1}{8s + \cfrac{1}{\cfrac{s}{2}}}}}$$

$$Y_2(s) = 2s. \text{ Hence } C_2 = 2\text{ F}$$

$$Z_3(s) = \frac{3s}{2}. \text{ Hence } L_3 = \frac{3}{2}\text{ H}$$

$$Y_4(s) = 8s. \text{ Hence } C_4 = 8\text{ F}$$

$$Z_5(s) = \frac{s}{2}. \text{ Hence } L_4 = \frac{1}{2} \text{ H.}$$

Hence the first Cauer network equivalent to the given impedance function is as shown in Fig. Ex. 27.16.

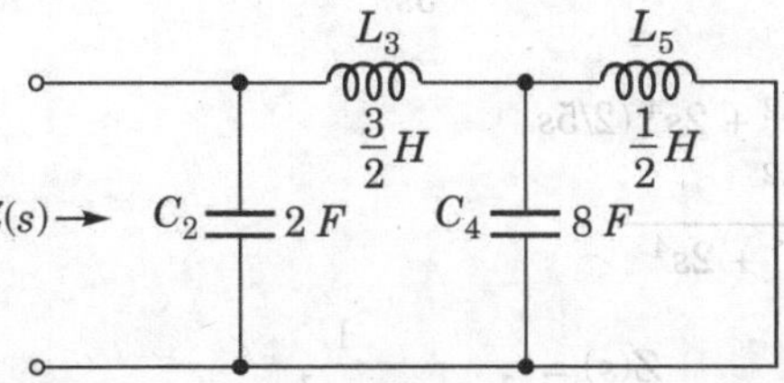

Fig. Ex. 27.16.

Example 27.17. *The impedance function of an LC network is given by,*

$$Z(s) = \frac{8s^3 + 3s}{2s^4 + 10s^2 + 3}$$

For this impedance function, find second network.

Solution. On turning $Z(s)$ function end for end, we get

$$Z(s) = \frac{3s + 8s^3}{3 + 10s^2 + 2s^4}$$

On inverting, we get

$$Z(s) = \frac{1}{\dfrac{3 + 10s^2 + 2s^4}{3s + 8s^3}}$$

On dividing :

$$3s + 8s^3)\ 3 + 10s^2 + 2s^4\ (1/s$$
$$\underline{3 + 8s^2}$$
$$2s^2 + 2s^4$$

Hence $$Z(s) = \frac{1}{\dfrac{1}{s} + \dfrac{2s^2 + 2s^4}{3s + 8s^3}}$$

On inverting $$Z(s) = \frac{1}{\dfrac{1}{s} + \dfrac{1}{\dfrac{3s + 8s^3}{2s^2 + 2s^4}}}$$

On dividing :

$$2s^2 + 2s^4)\ 3s + 8s^3\ (3/2s$$
$$\underline{3s + 3s^3}$$
$$+ 5s^3$$

Hence $$Z(s) = \cfrac{1}{\cfrac{1}{s} + \cfrac{1}{\cfrac{3}{2s} + \cfrac{1}{\cfrac{2s^2 + 2s^4}{5s^3}}}}$$

On dividing :

$$5s^3)\ 2s^2 + 2s^4\ (2/5s$$
$$\underline{2s^2}$$
$$+ 2s^4$$

Hence $$Z(s) = \cfrac{1}{\cfrac{1}{s} + \cfrac{1}{\cfrac{3}{2s} + \cfrac{1}{\cfrac{2}{5s} + \cfrac{1}{\cfrac{5}{2s}}}}}$$

$Y_2(s) = \dfrac{1}{s}$ represents an inductor of 1 Henry

$Z_3(s) = \dfrac{3}{2s}$ represents a capacitor of $\dfrac{2}{3}$ Farad

$y_4(s) = \dfrac{2}{5s}$ represents an inductor of $\dfrac{5}{2}$ Henrys

$Z_5(s) = \dfrac{5}{2s}$ represents a capacitor of $\dfrac{2}{5}$ Farad.

Hence the second Cauer network is as shown in Fig. Ex. 27.17.

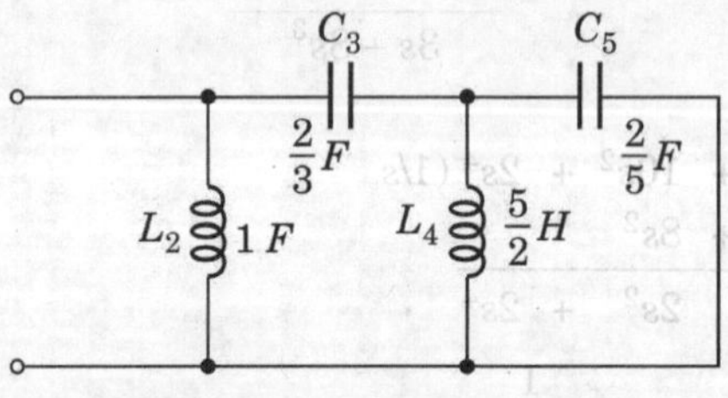

Fig. Ex. 27.17.

27.10. Choice of Network Realization

In section 27.6 we have studied the specifications which we must know in order to determine completely the driving point impedance function for reactive network. The following are these specifications :

(*i*) all internal critical frequencies

(*ii*) the scale factor H or an equivalent specification.

We have later seen that a network for a given $Z(s)$ may be realized in 4 basic forms namely (*i*) first Foster network (*ii*) second Foster network (*iii*) first Cauer network and (*iv*) second Cauer network. In any network, the number of unknowns equals the number of elements and these unknowns should be specified by $Z(s)$. In the solution of a set of equations, the number of specifications must equal the number of unknowns. However, for an LC network, we have seen that the number of specifications should be one more than the number of internal critical frequencies. Hence we conclude that the minimum number of elements in a network realization must be one more than the number of internal critical frequencies. Care must, however, be taken to count each pair of conjugate critical frequencies as one critical frequency.

Thus knowing the number of elements required to realize a network specification and ascertaining the nature of end elements from the behaviour (whether pole or zero) at zero and infinite frequencies, we are in a position to draw the four possible network configurations directly by inspection of the pole-zero configuration.

Example 27.18. *For the given pole-zero configuration, determine the four possible network configurations.*

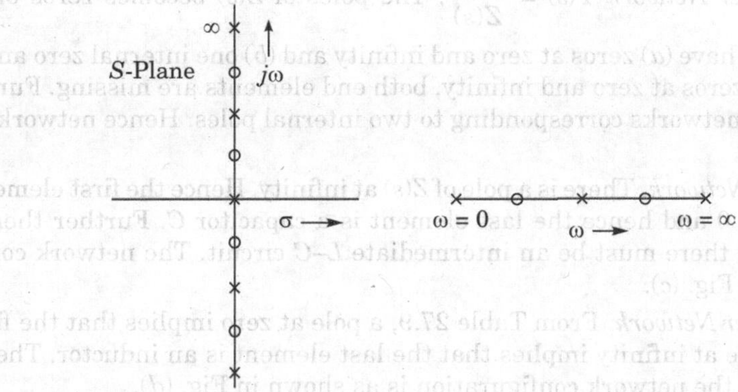

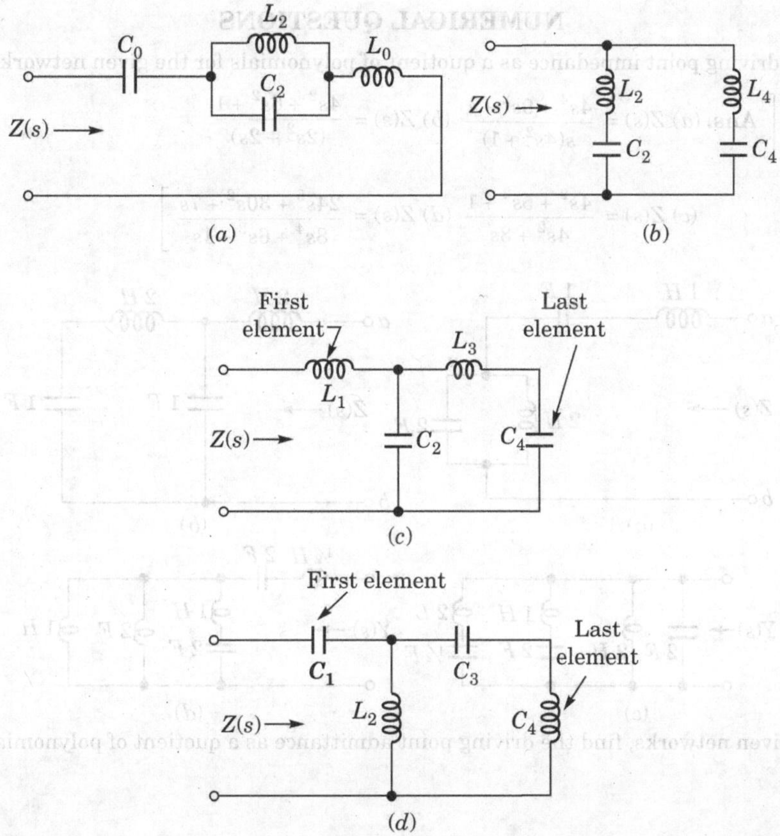

Fig. Ex. 27.18.

Solution. Internal critical frequencies consist of one pole and two zeros for $Z(s)$. The external critical frequencies are constrained by the separation property to be poles. Since there are in all three internal critical frequencies, the number of elements in network realization must be four. We now consider the four possible network realizations one by one.

(*i*) *First Foster Network.* Because zero and infinity are both poles, the end elements are present in the basic first Foster form of network given in Fig. 26.8. The network has one parallel tuned LC network to give one pole. The network is shown in Fig. (*a*).

(*ii*) *Second Foster Network* $Y(s) = \dfrac{1}{Z(s)}$. The poles of $Z(s)$ becomes zeros of $Y(s)$ and *vice versa*. Thus for $Y(s)$ we have (*a*) zeros at zero and infinity and (*b*) one internal zero and two internal poles. Since there are zeros at zero and infinity, both end elements are missing. Further there are present two series LC networks corresponding to two internal poles. Hence network configuration is as shown in Fig. (*b*).

(*iii*) *First Cauer Network.* There is a pole of $Z(s)$ at infinity. Hence the first element is inductor. There is a pole at $\omega = 0$ and hence the last element is a capacitor C. Further there should be 4 elements in all. Hence there must be an intermediate L–C circuit. The network configuration is, therefore, as shown in Fig. (*c*).

(*iv*) *Second Cauer Network.* From Table 27.9, a pole at zero implies that the first element is a capacitor while a pole at infinity implies that the last element is an inductor. There can be four elements in all. Hence the network configuration is as shown in Fig. (*d*).

NUMERICAL QUESTIONS

27.1. Find the driving point impedance as a quotient of polynomials for the given networks.

$$\left[\textbf{Ans.}\ (a)\ Z(s) = \frac{4s^4 + 9s^2 + 1}{s(4s^2 + 1)} \quad (b)\ Z(s) = \frac{4s^2 + 6s^2 + 1}{(2s^2 + 2s)}\right.$$

$$\left.(c)\ Z(s) = \frac{4s^2 + 5s^2 + 1}{4s^2 + 3s} \quad (d)\ Z(s) = \frac{24s^5 + 30s^2 + 7s}{8s^4 + 6s^2 + 1s}\right]$$

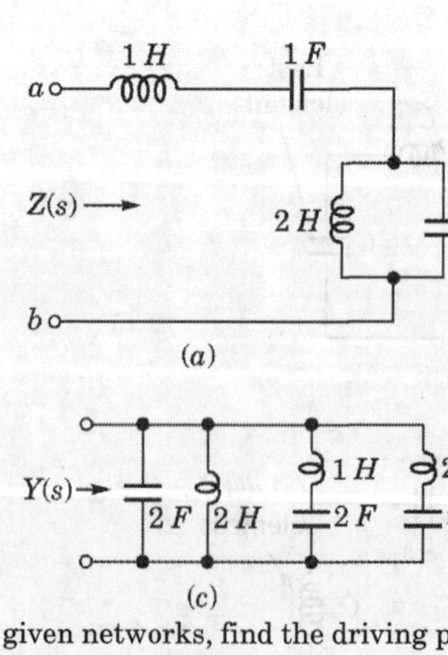

(*a*)

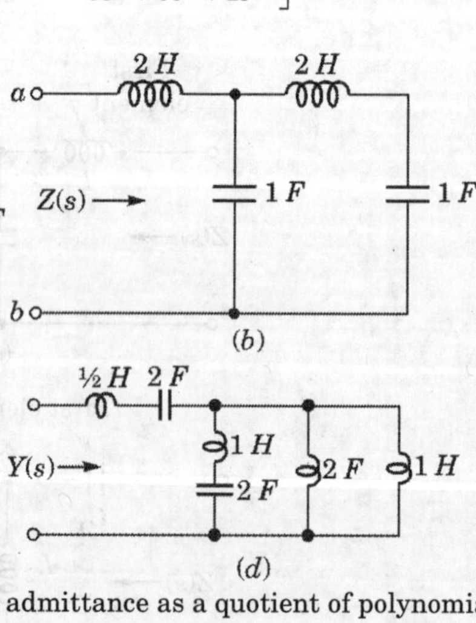

(*b*)

(c)

(*d*)

27.2. For the given networks, find the driving point admittance as a quotient of polynomials in *s*.

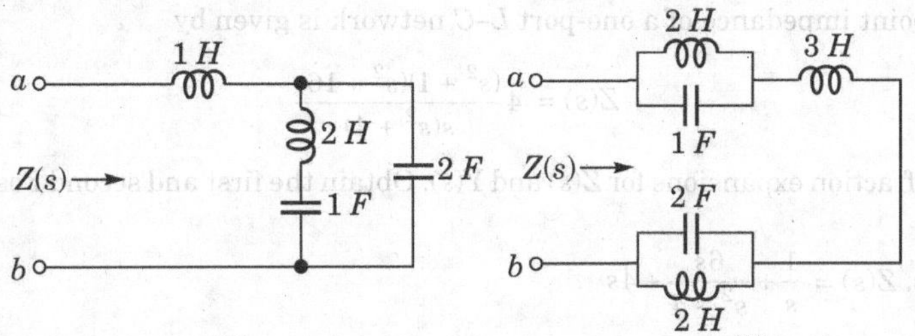

(a) (b)

[**Ans.** (a) $Y(s) = \dfrac{16s^6 + 30s^4 + 20s^2 + 2}{8s^4 + 12s^3 + 4s}$ (b) $Y(s) = \dfrac{20s^2 + 6s}{18s^4 + 17s^2 + 3}$]

27.3. For the network given below, obtain the driving point admittance as a quotient of polynomials in s.

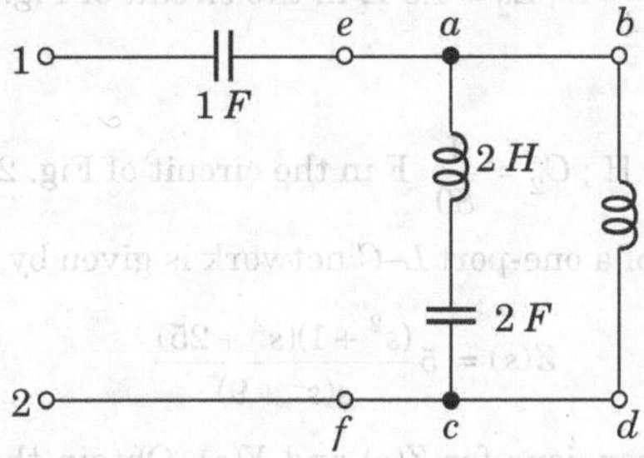

[**Ans.** (a) $Y_{12}(s) = \dfrac{8s^6 + 18s^4 + 9s^2 + 1}{16s^5 + 20s^3 + 3s}$]

27.4. The driving point impedance of an *L–C* network is given by

$$Z(s) = \frac{(s^2 + 4)(s^2 + 16)}{s(s^2 + 9)}$$

Obtain by inspection, the location of poles and zeros.

[**Ans.** Poles at ω = ± 3, ω = 0, ω = ∞
Zeros at ω = ±2, ω = ± 4]

27.5. The driving point impedance of an *L–C* network is given by,

$$Z(s) = \frac{2(s^2 + 1)(s^2 + 9)}{(s^2 + 4)}$$

Obtain by inspection, the locations of poles and zeros.

[**Ans.** Poles at ω = ± 2, ω = 0, ω = ∞
Zeros at ω = ± 1, ω = ± 3]

27.6. The driving point impedance of an L-C network is given by,

$$Z(s) = 3\frac{s(s^2 + 16)}{(s^2 + 4)(s^2 + 25)}$$

Obtain by inspection, the locations of zeros and poles.

[**Ans.** Zeros at ω = 0, ω = ± 4, ω = ∞
Poles at ω = ± 2, ω = ± 5]

27.7. The driving point impedance of an *L–C* network is given by,

$$Z(s) = 4\frac{s(s^2 + 25)}{(s^2 + 4)(s^2 + 36)}$$

Obtain by inspection, the locations of poles and zeros.

[**Ans.** Zeros at ω = 0, ω = ± 5, ω = ∞
Poles at ω = ± 2, ω = ± 6]

27.8. The driving point impedance of a one-port L–C network is given by

$$Z(s) = 4\frac{(s^2+1)(s^2+16)}{s(s^2+4)}$$

Write partial fraction expansions for $Z(s)$ and $Y(s)$. Obtain the first and second Foster form of equivalent networks

[**Ans.** $Z(s) = \frac{1}{s} + \frac{6s}{s^2+4} + 4s$

$Y(s) = \frac{s}{20(s^2+1)} + \frac{s}{5(s^2+16)}$

First Foster network :

C_0 = 1 Farad ; L_0 = 4 H ; $C_2 = \frac{1}{6}$ F ; L_2 = 1.5 H in the circuit of Fig. 26.8.

Second Foster network :

L_1 = 20 H ; $C_1 = \frac{1}{20}$ F ; L_2 = 5 H ; $C_2 = \frac{1}{80}$ F in the circuit of Fig. 27.9]

27.9. The driving point impedance of a one-port L–C network is given by,

$$Z(s) = 5\frac{(s^2+1)(s^2+25)}{s(s^2+9)}$$

Write the partial fraction expansions for $Z(s)$ and $Y(s)$. Obtain the first and second Foster form of equivalent networks.

[**Ans.** $Z(s) = \frac{125}{95} + \frac{640s}{9(s^2+9)} + 5s$

$Y(s) = \frac{s}{15(s^2+1)} + \frac{2}{15}\cdot\frac{s}{s^2+25}$

First Foster network :

$C_0 = \frac{9}{125}$ Farad ; L_0 = 9 Henry ; $C_2 = \frac{9}{640}$ F ;

$L_2 = \frac{640}{81}$ H in the circuit of Fig. 26.8

Second Foster network:

L_2 = 15 H ; $C_2 = \frac{1}{15}$ F ; $L_4 = \frac{15}{2}$ H ; $C_4 = \frac{2}{375}$ F

in the circuit shown below of Fig. 27.9]

2 7.10. The driving point impedance of a one-port L–C network is given by

$$Z(s) = 4\frac{s(s^2+9)}{(s^2+1)(s^2+16)}$$

Obtained the first and second Foster form of equivalent networks.

[**Ans.** First Foster Network :

$L_2 = \frac{32}{15}$ H ; $C_2 = \frac{15}{32}$ F ; $L_4 = \frac{7}{60}$ H ; $C_4 = \frac{15}{28}$ F in the circuit of Fig. 27.8.

Second Foster Networks :

$L_0 = \frac{9}{4}$ H ; $C_0 = \frac{1}{4}$ F ; $L_2 = \frac{9}{14}$ H ; $C_2 = \frac{14}{81}$ F in the circuit of Fig. 27.9]

27.11. The driving point impedance of a one-port L–C network is given by,

$$Z(s) = \frac{6s(s^2+9)}{(s^2+4)(s^2+25)}$$

Obtain the first and the second Foster form of equivalent networks.

[**Ans.** First Foster network :

$$L_2 = \frac{15}{4}\text{ H}; C_2 = \frac{7}{10}\text{ F}; L_4 = \frac{32}{175}\text{ H}; C_4 = \frac{7}{32}\text{ F}$$

in the circuit of Fig. 27.8. Second Foster network:

$$L_0 = \frac{27}{50}\text{ H}; C_0 = \frac{1}{6}\text{ F}; L_2 = \frac{27}{40}\text{ H}; C_2 = \frac{40}{243}\text{ F}$$

in the circuit of Fig. 27.9]

27.12. The driving point admittance of one-port L-C network is given by,

$$Y(s) = \frac{8(s^2+9)(s^2+36)}{s(s^2+25)}$$

Obtain the first and the second Foster form of equivalent networks.

[**Ans.** First Foster form of equivalent network :

$$L_2 = \frac{2}{243}\text{ H}; C_2 = \frac{27}{2}\text{ F}; L_4 = \frac{11}{7776}\text{ H};$$

$$C_4 = \frac{216}{11}\text{ F in the circuit of Fig. 27.8}$$

Second Foster form of equivalent network:

$$L_0 = \frac{25}{2592}\text{ H}; C_0 = 8\text{ F}; L_2 = \frac{25}{1408}\text{ H}; C_2 = \frac{1408}{625}\text{ F}$$

in the circuit of Fig. 27.9]

27.13. The driving point impedance of a one-port L–C network is given by,

$$Z(s) = \frac{2(s^2+4)(s^2+16)(s^2+36)}{s(s^2+9)(s^2+25)}$$

Obtain the first and second Foster forms of equivalent network.

[**Ans.** First Foster form of equivalent network :

$$C_0 = \frac{512}{25}\text{ F}; L_0 = 2\text{ H}; C_2 = \frac{8}{105}\text{ F}; L_2 = \frac{105}{72}\text{ H};$$

$$C_4 = \frac{200}{2079}\text{ F}; L_4 = \frac{2079}{5000}\text{ H in the circuit of Fig. 27.8.}$$

Second Foster form of equivalent network :

$$L_2 = \frac{256}{35}\text{ H}; C_2 = \frac{35}{1024}\text{ F}; L_4 = \frac{160}{21}\text{ H};$$

$$C_4 = \frac{21}{2560}\text{ F}; L_5 = \frac{1280}{297}\text{ H}; C_6 = \frac{297}{46080}\text{ F}\Big]$$

27.14. The driving point impedance of a one-port L–C network is given by,

$$Z(s) = \frac{2s(s^2+9)(s^2+25)}{(s^2+1)(s^2+16)(s^2+36)}$$

Obtain the first and the second Foster form of equivalent network.

[**Ans.** First Foster form of equivalent network :
$L_2 = 0.7314$ H ; $C_2 = 1.367$ F ; $L_4 = 0.026$ H ;
$C_4 = 2.381$ F ; $L_6 = 0.033$ H ; $C_6 = 0.842$ F
in the circuit of Fig. 27.8.
Second Foster form of equivalent network:
$L_0 = 0.781$ H ; $C_0 = 0.5$ F ; $L_2 = 0.19$ H ;
$C_2 = 0.5833$ F ; $L_4 = 0.3367$ H ; $C_4 = 0.1188$ F]

27.15. The driving point impedance of an L–C network is given by

$$Z(s) = \frac{10s^4 + 12s^2 + 1}{2s^3 + 2s}$$

For this impedance function (a) determine the first Cauer configuration and (b) determine the value of each element of the network.

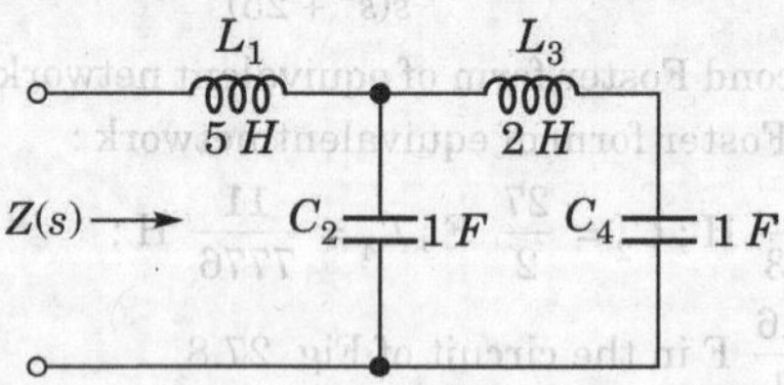

Ans.

27.16. Driving point impedance of an L–C network is given by

$$Z(s) = \frac{s^4 + 10s^2 + 2}{s^3 + 4s}$$

For this impedance function, determine the equivalent second Cauer network.

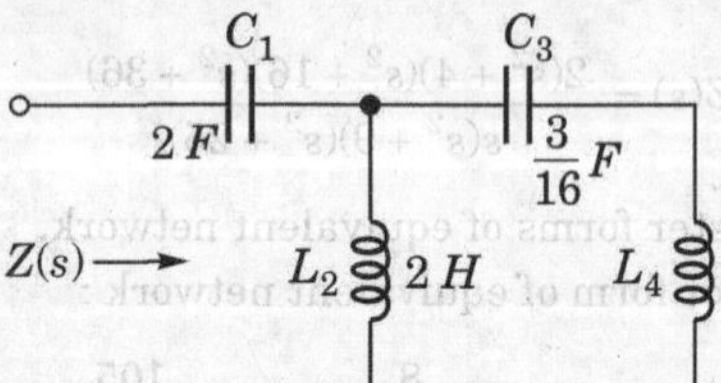

Ans.